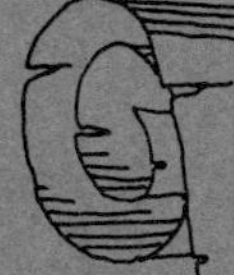

TO THE READER

§ Scientology is a religious philosophy containing spiritual counseling procedures intended to assist an individual to attain peace of mind and Spiritual Freedom. The mission of the Church of Scientology is a simple one: to help the individual attain full awareness of himself as a Spiritual Being, and of his relationship to the Supreme Being. The attainment of the benefits and goals of Scientology requires each individual's dedicated participation as only through his own efforts can he himself, as a Spiritual Being, achieve these.

§ This is part of the religious literature and works of the Founder of Scientology, L. Ron Hubbard. It is presented to the reader as part of the record of his personal research into Life, and should be construed only as a written report of such research and not as a statement of claims made by the Church or the author.

§ Scientology and its substudy, Dianetics, as practiced by the Church, address only the "Thetan" (Spirit). Although the Church, as are all churches, is free to engage in spiritual healing, it does not, as its primary goal is increased *spiritual awareness* for all. For this reason, the Church does not wish to accept individuals who desire treatment of physical or mental illness but prefers to refer these to qualified specialists of other organizations who deal in these matters.

§ The Hubbard Electrometer is a religious artifact used in the Church confessional. It in itself does nothing, and is used by Ministers only, to assist parishioners in locating areas of spiritual distress or travail.

We hope the reading of this book is only the first stage of a personal voyage of discovery into the new and vital world religion of Scientology.

This book belongs to John McKee

Date ____________________

THE BOARD OF DIRECTORS
CHURCH OF SCIENTOLOGY
OF CALIFORNIA

You can always write
to

Ron.

**All mail
addressed to me
shall be received by me.
I am always willing to help.
By my own creed,
a being is only as valuable
as he can serve others.**

**Any message
addressed to me
and sent to the address
of the nearest Scientology Church
listed in the back of this book,
will be forwarded to me
directly.**

MODERN MANAGEMENT TECHNOLOGY DEFINED

HUBBARD DICTIONARY OF ADMINISTRATION AND MANAGEMENT

by

L. Ron Hubbard

Published by
Church of Scientology of California
Publications Organization United States
2723 West Temple Street
Los Angeles, California 90026

The Church of Scientology of California is a non-profit organization.

Scientology is an applied religious philosophy.
Dianetics ® and Scientology ® are registered names.

First printing 1976
Copyright © 1949, 1950, 1951, 1952, 1953, 1954, 1955, 1956, 1957, 1958, 1959, 1960, 1961, 1962, 1963, 1964, 1965, 1966, 1967, 1968, 1969, 1970, 1971, 1972, 1973, 1974, 1975, 1976 by L. Ron Hubbard.
ALL RIGHTS RESERVED.

The E-meter is not intended or effective for the diagnosis, treatment or prevention of any disease.

A Dianetics Publication.
Dianetics is the trademark of L. Ron Hubbard in respect of his published works.

Compiled and edited by
The LRH Personal Secretary Office,
LRH Personal Compilations Bureau

LRH Personal Secretary: Alethiea C. Taylor
LRH Personal Compilations Bureau I/C: Pat Brice
Editor: Ernie Ryan
Compilers/Researchers: Cliff Von Shura, Barbara de Celle, Maggie Sibersky, Pat Broeker, Jim Dincalci
Manuscript Typist: Rae Chase
Design: Arthur Hubbard
Artists: André Clavel, Arthur Hubbard

ISBN 0-88404-040-2

Printed in the U.S.A. by Kingsport Press

Typeset by Freedmen's Organization, Los Angeles

Important Note

One of the biggest barriers to learning a new subject is its nomenclature, meaning the set of terms used to describe the things it deals with. A subject must have accurate labels which have exact meanings before it can be understood and communicated.

If I were to describe parts of the body as "thingamabobs" and "whatser-names," we would all be in a confusion, so the accurate naming of something is a very important part of any field.

A student comes along and starts to study something and has a terrible time of it. Why? Because he or she not only has a lot of new principles and methods to learn, but a whole new language as well. Unless the student understands this, unless he or she realizes that one has to "know the words before one can sing the tune," he or she is not going to get very far in any field of study or endeavor.

Now I am going to give you an important datum:

The only reason a person gives up a study or becomes confused or unable to learn is because he or she has gone past a word that was not understood.

The confusion or inability to grasp or learn comes AFTER a word that the person did not have defined and understood.

Have you ever had the experience of coming to the end of a page and realizing you didn't know what you had read? Well, somewhere earlier on that page you went past a word that you had no definition for.

Here's an example. "It was found that when the crepuscule arrived the children were quieter and when it was not present, they were much livelier." You see what happens. You think you don't understand the whole idea, but the inability to understand came entirely from the one word you could not define, *crepuscule* which means twilight or darkness.

This datum about not going past an undefined word is the most important fact in the whole subject of study. Every subject you have taken up and abandoned had its words which you failed to get defined.

Therefore, in studying Scientology be very, very certain you never go past a word you do not fully understand. If the material becomes confusing or you can't seem to grasp it, there will be a word just earlier that you have not understood. Don't go any further, but go back to BEFORE you got into trouble, find the misunderstood word and get it defined.

That is why we have a dictionary. It will not only be the new and unusual words that you will have to look up. Some commonly used words can be misdefined and so cause confusion. So don't depend on our dictionary alone. Use a general English language dictionary as well for any non-Scientology word you do not understand when you are reading or studying.

Scientology words and their definitions are the gateway to a new look and understanding of life. Understanding them will help you live better, and will assist you along the road of truth that is Scientology.

Note

While this dictionary has attempted to include all Scientology management and administration words and terms, there is a chance you might find some words not included.

If you discover any missing words, please write them to:

Dictionary Staff
LRH Personal Secretary
Saint Hill Manor
East Grinstead
Sussex, England

The Editor

Contents

Introduction

By Scientology study technology, understanding ceases on going past a misunderstood word or concept.

If a person reading a text comes to the word "Felix Domesticus" and doesn't know it simply means HOUSE CAT, the words which appear thereafter may become "meaningless," "uninteresting" and he may even become slightly unconscious, his awareness shutting down.

Example: "Wind the clock and put out the Felix Domesticus and then call Algernon and tell him to wake you at 10:00 am," read as an order by a person who didn't bother to find out that "Felix Domesticus" means "house cat" or "the variety of cat which has been domesticated" will not register that he is supposed to call Algernon, will feel dopey or annoyed and probably won't remember he's supposed to wake up at 10:00 am.

In other words, when the person hit a misunderstood word, he ceased to understand and did not fully grasp or become aware of what followed after.

All this applies to a sentence, a book, a post or a whole organization.

A crashing misunderstood will block off further ability to study or apply data. It will also block further understanding of an organization, its organizing board, an individual post or duties and such misunderstoods can effectively prevent knowledge of or action on a post.

ALL THIS IS THE MOST COMMON CAUSE OF AN UNACCEPTABLE POST PRODUCT, OR NO PRODUCT AT ALL.

The difficulties of an organization in functioning or producing stem from this fact.

The by no means complete list of words that have to be fully cleared and understood just to talk about organization as a subject, and to intelligently and happily work in an organization EVEN AS ITS LOWEST EMPLOYEE are:

A Company
A Board of Directors
Top Management
Policy
Management
Programmes
Targets
Orders

Technology
Know-How
Organizing Board
Post
Hat
Cope
Purposes
Organize
Duties
A Checksheet
A Checklist
A Communication Channel
A Command Channel
A Relay Point
A Stable Terminal
Double Hatted
A Product
Aberration
VIABILITY

This is key vocabulary. Out of a full understanding of what is implied by each, a brilliantly clean view is attained of the whole subject of organization, not as a fumble but as a crisp usable activity.

Unless one at least knows the basic words completely so that they can be used and applied they will not buffer off confusions that enter into the activity.

There is a lot to organization. It requires trained administrators who can forward the programs. But a "trained" administrator who does not grasp the principles of organization itself is only a clerk.

At this current writing Man has not had administrative training centers where actual organization was taught. It was learned by "experience" or by working in an organization that was already functioning. But as the principles were not the same company to company and nation to nation, the differences of background experiences of any set of administrators differed to such a degree that no new corps could be assembled as a team.

Thus it was said to require a quarter to a half a century to make a company. But the number of ineffective bureaucracies and national failures which existed stated clearly that there were too few skilled administrators and too few training activities.

Man's happiness and the longevity of companies and states apparently depend upon organizational know-how. Hiring specialized experts to get one out of trouble is a poor substitute for knowing what it is all about in the first place.

Organization is actually a simple subject, based on a few basic patterns which if applied produce success.

If one would dream and see his dreams an actuality, one must also be able to organize and to train organizational men who will make those dreams come true.

Guide to the Dictionary

This dictionary is uniquely comprehensive in that as well as containing the bulk of the words and abbreviations needed to study the powerful and fantastically successful management and administrative technology of Scientology, as developed by L. Ron Hubbard, it also contains a large number of conventional business management and administration terms.

Thus whether one is studying the management and administrative technology developed for the Church of Scientology or any other business management or administrative technology this book is a must.

The Scientology definitions are mainly extracts taken from the works of L. Ron Hubbard. Some are extracts taken from the works of L. Ron Hubbard's Aides and top executives in Scientology. The entry words for all Scientology definitions are in bold face type. In compiling these definitions the editorial staff have chosen to omit the conventional use of the ellipsis (. . .) which would indicate an intentional omission of words in the definition. This is so that each definition imparts a complete uninterrupted thought to the reader and allows him to form a concept of the word without distraction or the inclusion of data not contributory to the *definition.*

At the beginning of several definitions a word or phrase sometimes appears in parentheses such as (Flag) (Post), (Flag Ship Org), or (FOLO). These serve to designate specific areas of Scientology organizations, posts, organizing boards and subjects that the term or definition originates from or applies to only.

The purpose of the Scientology definitions is solely to aid a person in the study of Scientology management and administrative technology. Some of these definitions are taken from early Scientology policy letters and issues which have since been cancelled. These are included because the words defined are mentioned in later policy letters and issues that are in current use. Thus the purpose of these definitions is not to set Scientology policy but to aid in the study of Scientology management and administrative technology.

The conventional business management and administration definitions were researched and formulated by the editorial staff after extensive study in these subjects. A great deal of effort was made to ensure these are as clear and straightforward as possible to aid any person engaged in the study of business administration and management. The entry words for these are in light face type which differentiates these from the Scientology terms and definitions.

A section of organizing boards is included at the end of the dictionary to show the structure of various Scientology organizations as they evolved from 1961 to 1976. Any business organization in the world could be set up to run more successfully from the standard Scientology Seven Division Organizing Board released by L. Ron Hubbard.

A complete list of the references used for the Scientology definitions appears in the reference summary at the back of the dictionary.

Scientology is the fastest growing religion on the planet by actual surveys and statements by sociologists. The management and administrative technology of Scientology developed by L. Ron Hubbard is the source of this expansion.

Whether you are studying this or any conventional business management and administration technology this dictionary is the guide to modern business and management technology.

The Editor

MODERN MANAGEMENT TECHNOLOGY DEFINED

HUBBARD DICTIONARY OF ADMINISTRATION AND MANAGEMENT

ABBREVIATED BOOKKEEPING, the term **abbreviated bookkeeping** has been used to mean **bookkeeping** which by-passed and ignored the use of personal accounts. In other words, the double entry is effected by entries made directly between the organization's bank account and another impersonal account of the organization. (BPL 14 Nov 70 VI)

ABERRATED CONDITION, mental mass accumulates in a vast complexity solely because one would not confront something. To take apart a problem requires only to establish what one could not or would not confront. When no-confront enters, a chain may be set up which leads to total complexity and total unreality. This, in a very complex form, we call an **aberrated condition.** People like that can't solve even rudimentary problems and act in an aimless and confused way. To resolve their troubles requires more than education or discipline. It requires processing. Some people are so "complex" that their full **aberration** does fully not resolve until they attain a high level of OT. (HCO PL 18 Sept 67)

ABERRATION, 1. by definition "a crooked line." It is from the Latin *aberratio*, "a wandering from," and from the Latin *errare*, to wander or to err. A sane person thinks, looks and sees in straight lines. Black is black, white is white. The **aberrated** person looks toward black and wanders off in his gaze to something else and makes the error of saying it is "grey." You can consider **aberration** in a passive way (supinely, of no force or action). A person is sane or not sane. He thinks straight or crookedly. Now consider **aberration** in a forceful way. A person looks, then an opposing force to him pushes aside his gaze or distracts it. But the really sane, forceful person looks right on through and past the opposition and sees what is there anyway. (HCOB 19 Aug 67) **2.** the number of out-points the guy is carrying around in his skull is how **aberrated** he is. That has very little to do with his sanity. It has everything to do with his competence. (ESTO 10, 7203C05 SO II) **3. aberration** is just the basis of out-points. (ESTO 4, 7203C02 SO II) **4.** a chain of vias based on a primary non-confront. (HCO PL 18 Sept 67) **5. aberration** is non-straight line by definition. (HCOB 5 Dec 73)

Aberration (Def. 1)

AB FACTOR, we don't wholly guarantee you and your co-auditor that you will co-audit in the Level VI co-audit for one team member may be case type **A** and the other **B**. A case type **A** can run through anything. A case type **B** stops at a comma. Thus one gets too far out of pace with the other and it's just too hard on one member of the team who would be, of course, the type **B** and already in trouble. It would be selfish indeed of a type **A** to force a type **B** to run GPMs far beyond where he or she has had them run. We will try to put the team together in the Level VI co-audit and mostly do but this **AB factor** is a technical one and we can't do anything about it short of good auditing. (HCO PL 11 Jun 64) [See PC TYPE A, PC TYPE B in *Dianetics and Scientology Technical Dictionary*.]

ABILITY, **1.** the **ability** to complete a cycle of action, to handle the matter so it does not have to be handled again. (HCO PL 22 Feb 68) **2. ability** is measured not by opinion, but by the person's **ability** to raise statistics and produce the product of the particular post. (BPL 4 Jul 69R V)

ABILITY MAGAZINE, *Ability* **magazine** should be issued semi-monthly. Issues shall be used broadly as mailing pieces and are not to go just to the membership and be forgotten. The first *Ability* of the month shall be an *Ability* major issue, the second issue of the month shall be an *Ability* minor issue. *Ability* major: shall consist of informative technical material, advertisements and programs. *Ability* minor: shall be dedicated only to programs such as extension course, such as training, such as processing results. *Ability* major is mainly of interest to the membership and informed Scientologists. *Ability* minor shall be of interest to the broad public. (HCO PL 24 Oct 58, *Ability Magazine*) [*Ability* is published by the Church of Scientology Washington D.C.]

Able Bodied Seaman (Def. 1)

ABLE-BODIED SEAMAN, **1.** a Sea Org **AB** is a Sea Org member in good standing who has completed his **AB** checksheet. Gender or age are irrelevant. The vital datum is that an **AB** knows enough to make himself useful aboard a Sea Org ship. An **AB** knows the basic tech of the sea and he can survive on the sea. (FSO 156) **2.** a permanent rating as **able-bodied seaman** is required before any higher deck rating or appointment can be considered permanent. An **AB** rating requires the completion of checksheet and demonstration of competence on deck. (LRH Def. Notes, circa Aug 67) **3.** a trained **seaman** more highly skilled than an ordinary seaman. **Able** = having enough power, skill, etc., to do something; capable; worth of being. **Bodied** = having a body or substance, especially of a specific kind. **Seaman** = a sailor, mariner. (SO ED 214 INT) **4.** qualified sailor. (FO 196) *Abbr.* AB.

ABLE-BODIED SEAMAN CONFERENCE, instituted on a trial basis at Flag only. It is composed of all present **ABs** on the ship, as active members. Its purpose is to make and keep Sea Org ship tech known and applied. To back up command in all phases of ship operation, and to ensure optimum survival for its members including their rapid promotion as deserved. (FSO 156)

ABSENTEE MANAGEMENT, see MANAGEMENT, ABSENTEE.

AC-1A FORM, this form is filled in by the Treasury Secretary each Friday evening. The **form** provides additional data and verification for the AC-1/2 for financial management purposes. (BPL 4 Dec 72 IIRB)

AC-1 FORM, **1.** reports the gross income of the organization for the week, shows the calculation of the corrected gross income and the allocation of the corrected gross income. The corrected gross income is the income available for use and is calculated by deducting various items as detailed on the **form**. The **AC-1 form** does not apply to an AO, SH, FOLO, Estates Org or any non-service org. These orgs will use the AC-2 form. (BPL 4 Dec 72 IIRB) **2.** HCO WW **form AC-1** is the only proportionate breakdown acceptable to HCO WW Accounts. (HCO PL 19 Sep 62) [The above HCO PL was cancelled by BPL 10 Oct 75 IV.]

AC-2 FORM, the AC-1 form does not apply to an AO, SH, FOLO, Estates Org or any non-service org. These orgs will use the **AC-2 form**. The **AC-2 form** follows the AC-1 form exactly except that the management bills payment does not conform to the scale laid out for the AC-1 and the allocation of the proportionate amount is not per the percentages given. (BPL 4 Dec 72 IIRB)

ACADEMY, **1.** in Scn the **academy** is that department of the Technical Division in which courses and training are delivered; Department 11, Division 4. (BTB 12 Apr 72R) **2.** (**Academy** of Scn) headed by the Director of Training, the **academy** is responsible for the technical excellence of Scn practice tomorrow. Precise scheduling, crisp training and true, direct answers to the students' questions make an **academy**. A bad **academy** results in a bad HGC tomorrow as many graduates become staff auditors. A good **academy** is known by its snappy scheduling and the degree of basic data and action the student actually absorbs. (HCO PL 20 Dec 62) **3. Academy** of Scn purpose: to train the best auditors in the world. To coach outside and staff auditors for employment in the HGC. (HCO London, 9 Jan 58) *Abbr.* Acad.

Academy (Def. 1)

ACADEMY ADMINISTRATOR, purpose: to handle the comm lines and supplies of the **academy.** (HCO London 9 Jan 58)

ACADEMY COURSES, 1. academy training Level 0-IV. (HCO PL 4 Nov 71 II) **2.** an **academy course** then hereafter means 160 hours of class instruction to certificate for all levels zero to IV. (HCO PL 11 Dec 64)

ACADEMY INSTRUCTOR, duties of an **Academy Instructor:** (1) to train with accuracy and precision the students we have, (2) to leave administrative duties to the academy administrator, (3) to get coaches to do a better job of coaching, (4) to read TRs to the students. If they have a question on them to read again the TR and ask them what the TR said. If they still do not get it, repeat the above. (5) to get the students to execute the TRs with the same snap and precision as was expected of students in the 18th ACC, (6) to run a tight 8-C on the students. (SEC ED 37, 15 Jan 59)

ACADEMY SENIOR INSTRUCTOR, should handle the advanced class and do no administrative work. His job is making sure the student is an auditor at course end. (HCOB 9 May 58)

ACC ADMINISTRATOR, purpose: to ensure a smooth running **ACC** as regards material. Works under ACC Chief Instructor and ACC Conductor. Supervises ACC Clerk. (HCO PL 24 Feb 60) [The above HCO PL was cancelled by BPL 10 Oct 75 III.]

ACC CHIEF INSTRUCTOR, purpose: to turn out auditors who are responsible for clearing their pcs and who know and can use the best methods of doing so; makes an ACC the greatest real education on this planet. (HCO PL 24 Feb 60) [The above HCO PL was cancelled by BPL 10 Oct 75 III.]

ACC CLERK, purpose: to create an orderly **ACC** by performing efficiently the routine work of **ACC** Administration. The **ACC Clerk** works directly under the ACC Administrator, who is under the ACC Chief Instructor, who is under the ACC Conductor. It is an HCO post. (HCO PL 24 Feb 60) [The above HCO PL was cancelled by BPL 10 Oct 75 III.]

ACCEPTANCE, 1. a formal indication by a debtor of willingness to pay a bill of exchange, usually writing the word "accepted" and his signature across the face of the document. 2. the bill of exchange itself. 3. in law, the agreement by one party with the terms of an offer of another so that a contract becomes legally binding between them.

ACCEPTANCE SAMPLING, the concept of inspecting or testing a portion of a product in order to decide whether or not the whole amount is acceptable and/or meets the standards required.

ACCEPTANCE TEST, testing a program or project early in development to determine whether or not the completed final work will produce the expected result.

ACCEPTING AN ALMOST, *Example:* a messenger **accepting** the **almost** of *turning down* the heat. The order was to *turn it off.* An executive or communicator or messenger who **accepts** and forwards **an almost** is permitting dev-t. Orders given are to be executed and reported done, not to be nearly done or almost done. A communicator can often be tripped up by this form of dev-t. It is most easily spotted by insisting that the original order or orders be returned with the compliance so that any terminal on the line can tell at a glance what was ordered, and what was done. (BPL 30 Jan 69)

ACCIDENT PRONENESS, a manifestation of a tendency to succumb. (HCO PL 3 Nov 70 II)

ACC INSTRUCTOR HAT, purpose: to train the best auditors on earth. Works directly under

ACC Chief Instructor, who is under ACC Conductor. (HCO PL 24 Feb 60) [The above HCO PL was cancelled by BPL 10 Oct 75 III.]

ACCOMMODATION COUNSELORS, (Flag) room and food registrars are to be called **Accommodation Counselors**. They reg immediately after the training and service reges have completed. The training and processing reges sign-up the person for the services and then when the subject of room and food comes up, they direct the person to the **accommodation counselor**. (BFO 45) *Abbr.* AC.

ACCOUNT, simply a sheet of paper (or page of a book) headed at the top as to the category of inflow or outflow of the organization or else the name of the outside person with whom the organization deals. It is divided by a line down the middle to give a left-hand side and right-hand side. The left-hand side of an **account** is the receiving or inflow side and the right-hand side is the outflow side. (BPL 14 Nov 70 II)

ACCOUNTABILITY, 1. being charged with the responsibility for the results or effects of something. 2. the duty that a junior person has to a senior for reporting on the progress or performance of a job that they both share responsibility for completing.

ACCOUNTANCY, the practice of using the book-keeping records to analyze and report upon the financial transactions of a business for a particular period of time. In short it means the preparation of financial reports. (BPL 14 Nov 70 II)

ACCOUNTANT, purpose: to expedite, handle and police the financial items from the moment they enter the organizational comm lines to the moment they depart. (HCO London, 9 Jan 58)

ACCOUNT, CHARGE, a business arrangement between a company and an individual allowing the individual to obtain goods or services on credit, paying for them later within an agreed time period.

ACCOUNT, DESCRETIONARY, type of investment account wherein the investor leaves buying and selling, within limits or overall, to the discretion of his broker or an advisor.

ACCOUNT, DRAWING, a weekly or monthly record of cash payments made to an owner, director or executive to cover expenses or to a sales representative as advances against commissions due.

ACCOUNT EXECUTIVE, in advertising it is that person who manages a client's account by liaising and negotiating with the client. An account executive may manage several clients' accounts and ensures that they receive the services they are paying for. The term is also applied to stock brokers.

ACCOUNT, EXPENSE, 1. a special account out of which an employee of a firm is reimbursed for expenses incurred in the transaction of business affairs. 2. a record of business expenses paid for by an employee and submitted to his employer for approval and reimbursement.

ACCOUNTING, the game of **accounting** is just a game of assigning significances to figures. The man with the most imagination wins. But there must be correct figures and there must not be gross misassignment of debts as profits or the whole thing won't hang together. (HCO PL 25 Jun 67)

ACCOUNTING, the action of noting down, classifying, ensuring the accuracy of, evaluating and interpreting the financial facts and figures of an organization or business.

ACCOUNTING COST CONTROL, the use of accounting procedures to study the recorded transactions of a business in an effort to control costs. Accounting cost control can spot the inefficient use or misappropriation of funds and establish responsibility for such. Bills paid twice, overexpenditures, unauthorized expenditures etc., are all the subject of accounting cost control. See OPERATIONAL COST CONTROL.

ACCOUNT, LEDGER, a page or several pages in a ledger listing all the transactions with a specific firm. The page is divided in half with a record of transactions resulting in debts to that firm posted on the left-hand side of the page or debit side and a record of transactions resulting in credit with that firm posted on the right-hand or credit side of the account. By totalling each side of the account it can be seen if one owes money to that firm or has credit with that firm.

ACCOUNTS AND MATERIEL BUREAU, **1.** bureaux accounts will be handled under Supply and Materiel Bureau which will be renamed **Accounts and Materiel Bureau** and operate under the Coordination Bureau and LRH Comm authority. (CBO 27) **2.** supply and materiel becomes **Accounts and Materiel** and is the Division 3 of bureaux with Supply and Materiel as Branch 4. (CBO 28)

ACCOUNTS ASSISTANT TO THE ORGANIZATION SECRETARY, there will no longer be income and disbursement posts as separate personnel. Both these posts will be held by one person with the title **Accounts Assistant to the Organization Secretary**, effective at once. (HCO PL 18 Jun 64)

ACCOUNT, SAVINGS, a private account into which a depositor puts savings money that the bank pays interest on, with the right of withdrawing funds by presenting his passbook so that the bank teller may record the transaction or by giving required notice to the bank.

ACCOUNTS CLEARANCE, it does not mean "bills known" or "bills arranged to be paid." It means "all bills paid." (HCO PL 1 Aug 72) [The above HCO PL was cancelled by BPL 10 Oct 75 X.]

ACCOUNTS CLEARANCE SLIP, slip which says—John Jones has been **cleared** by **Accounts** for one HCA course, April 25, 1965, signature in full of cashier. (HCO PL 15 Mar 65 II) [The above HCO PL was cancelled by BPL 10 Oct 75 V.]

ACCOUNTS DEPARTMENT, there are two sections to the **Accounts Department**. One is the Income Section. The other is the Disbursement Section. (HCO PL 6 May 64)

ACCOUNTS DIVISIONS, these are: the Income Division and the Disbursement Division. They are in separate areas and are run by different persons. (HCO PL 23 Nov 61)

ACCOUNTS FILES ADMINISTRATOR, this staff member will help the accounts assistant with **files** and in other ways as contained in the administrative directive of the post. (HCO PL 18 Jun 64)

ACCOUNTS, MARGINAL, accounts of creditors or potential creditors who are questionable risks or have a poor credit rating.

ACCOUNTS PAYABLE, 1. accounts of sums payable to a company's creditors. 2. the amounts thus owed to a creditor.

ACCOUNTS POLICING, it is the specific duty of the Treasury Secretary in an org to pick up and trace the course of every particle of money through the entire organization, from the time it enters through the mail or with a customer, until it exits from the org as a disbursement or a reserve action. That is quite a job, and it is the most important job a Treasury Secretary has got. It sums up the purpose of the post. It is called **accounts policing**. To **police** something means "to control, regulate, keep in order, administer." The anatomy of **accounts policing** is: (1) **policing** income to ensure that the org is collecting the income from the services that it delivers, and that all org income is channelled into treasury and into the bank without delays. (2) **policing** disbursements to ensure that financial planning occurs and that only monies which are so designated and authorized are allocated out of the org **accounts.** (3) **policing** reserves to ensure that the org never spends more than it makes, and that it builds up substantial reserves through excellent control of its income-outgo flows. (BPL 1 Feb 72 I)

ACCOUNTS RECEIVABLE, accounts which show money owed by a customer to the company. Depending on the collectibility of these accounts receivable, they may be acceptable as collateral for a loan or sold outright to a commercial factor for a percentage of their value giving the commercial factor the authority to collect and retain the debts thus collected.

ACCOUNTS RECORDS, any and all items that may be considered to be **accounts records** meaning: bills, cancelled checks, invoices, receipts, chits, lists, record books, and any other item that may be considered by you to have to do with **accounts.** (HCO PL 25 Sept 59)

ACCOUNTS SYSTEM, a Scn **accounts system** is simple. It works. It consists of writing an invoice on a four-copy machine for everything received and a disbursement voucher on a four-copy disbursement machine for everything expended, even petty cash, with a completed statement of what Accounts knows of the expenditure. The **system** consists of four files—one with a file for every creditor, one with a file for every debtor, one with a complete file for every bank **account** and one with a file for every weekly breakdown envelope. A board with nails on it for pinning up invoices for every category on the breakdown sheet and a book to put income sheets in plus an adding machine and cabinets completes the entire **system.** (HCO PL 20 Dec 62)

ACCOUNTS UNIT FOR SAINT HILL, manages the **accounts.** Handles all financial records, income, disbursement and reports for the Org Sec and maintains all **accounts** files and the purchase order system. Purchases for **Saint Hill.** (HCO PL 18 Dec 64, *Saint Hill Org Board*)

ACCOUNT, SUSPENSE, a temporary account in which are entered credits and charges until they are assigned properly to their correct permanent accounts.

ACCRUAL, 1. the natural growth of a fund due to interest being paid into it. 2. the interest resulting from an investment.

ACCRUED EXPENSES, **expenses** for which the organization is liable, i.e. a liability account. (BPL 14 Nov 70 V)

ACCRUED INTEREST, interest accumulated by or accrued on a bond since the last interest payment so that the buyer pays the market price plus the accruement.

ACC SUPERVISOR, purpose: to ensure for HCO that the administration of an **Advanced Clinical Course** runs smoothly from beginning to end. That proper quarters are secured in accordance with HCO policy. That all required supplies and materials are acquired and on hand as scheduled. (HCO PL 24 Feb 60)

ACCUMULATING GRAPH, an **accumulating graph** merely means you keep adding one day's statistic to those of the day before. (BPL 8 Feb 72)

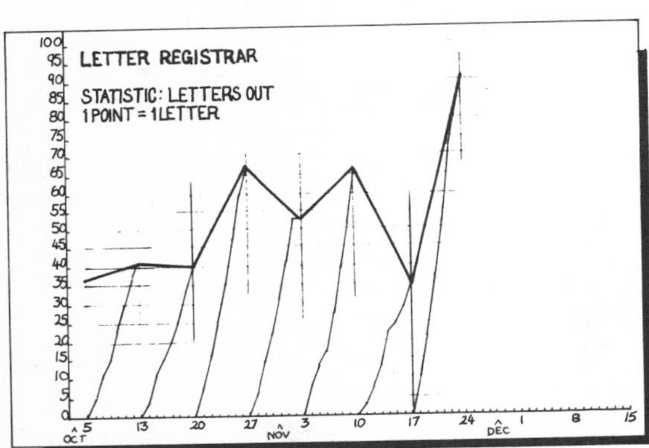

Accumulating Graph

ACE FIGHTER TEAMS, the Battle of Britain has two **Ace Fighter Teams. Ace Fighter Team** One is a Division 6 trouble shooter set of establishers on rotation building up and strengthening org Division 6s to pour new people into orgs. **Ace Fighter Team** Two is the second prong of the UK group operation. In this **Ace Fighter Team** Two, only seasoned veterans and star **fighters** will be assigned with CS-6 permission (touring to spread the word on Scn to every town and leaving behind new groups). (BO 37 UK)

ACID TEST RATIO, (or quick ratio or liquid ratio) the ratio of total cash, accounts receivable and the market value of saleable investments of a business to its current liabilities, the result acting as a guide to credit rating and establishing a company's ability to handle current obligations.

ACK, 1. a despatch thanking the person (for the report) with the report and date of it and some mention of what was in it so he isn't left in mystery as to which one or what it was. (CBO 348R) **2.** the first answer to a telex origination may add data which requires a third telex in the cycle. This would be sent by the originator to get done or find out whatever more is needed. This similarly requires a speedy answer. If the orginator is now satisfied and has gotten the needed information or compliance desired, he sends the **ack,** which ends the comm cycle. That **"ack"** indicates that the reply was received and thus ends the telex comm cycle. (This takes the place of the nod or smile at the end of the face-to-face comm cycle described in chapter ten of *Dianetics '55*.) (BPL 12 Jun 73R II) **3.** this word ends a comm cycle. It is the best way to end a telex comm cycle. It is the *final* telex on that cycle. (BPL 8 Apr 73 I) **4.** the **acknowledged** yellow copy of a communication. (*HTLTAE*, p. 117) *—v.* to **acknowledge.** To stamp **"ack"** and initial. (*HTLTAE*, p. 117)

Ack (Def. 2)

ACKNOWLEDGEMENT, something said or done to inform another that his statement or action has been noted, understood and received. "Very good," "okay," and other such phrases are intended to inform another who has spoken or acted that his statement or action has been accepted. An **acknowledgement** also tends to confirm that the statement has been made or the action has been done and so brings about a condition not only of communication but of reality between two or more people. Applause at a theater is an **acknowledgement** of the actor or act plus approval. **Acknowledgement** itself does not necessarily imply an approval or disapproval or any other thing beyond the knowledge that an action or statement has been observed and is received. In signaling with the morse code the receiver of a message transmits an R to the sender as a signal that the message has been received, which is to say **acknowledged**. There is such a thing as **over-acknowledgement** and there is such a thing as **under-acknowledgement**. A correct and exact **acknowledgement** communicates to someone who has spoken that what he has said has been heard. An **acknowledgement** tends to terminate or end the cycle of a communication, and when expertly used can sometimes stop a continued statement or continued action. An **acknowledgement** is also part of the communication formula and is one of its steps. The Scientologist, sometimes, in using Scientologese abbreviates this to **"ack"**; he **"acked"** the person. (LRH Def. Notes) *Abbr.* Ack.

ACKNOWLEDGEMENT OFFICER, you have an **Acknowledgement Officer** who is doing **acknowledgements** of standard reports coming in. He just plain **acks** them. (BPL 9 Apr 73 II)

ACKNOWLEDGEMENT REPORT, a staff member who does some action which is above the call of duty of his or her post hat may write an **acknowledgement report** on himself detailing what it was he did and how it benefited the org. This is sent to Division 1 for filing in his or her personnel file. In reviewing staff for promotion, such self **acknowledgements** are taken into account in assessing the staff member's responsibility level, along with other data and statistics. (HCO PL 11 Nov 66) [The above HCO PL has been cancelled by BPL 10 Oct 75 IV.]

ACQUIRE, to gain possession, ownership or power over something as an acquiring of funds or property.

ACQUISITION, 1. the act of gaining possession, ownership or power over something as an acquiring of funds or property. 2. the thing so gained or acquired.

ACTAD, 1. action addressee, the person to whom the communication goes for action. (*HTLTAE* p. 117) **2.** the **actad** message has four copies, each of which is under the eye of some individual and each of which is demanding that the message be acknowledged and completed. (*HTLTAE* p. 88)

ACTING, 1. a prefix to a title meaning appointed conditionally and if shows good statistics for a year will become of permanent title. (HCO PL 13 Mar 66) **2.** if it is appointed from Saint Hill why then that becomes an **acting**, which is the first rank, and for a while the post is held under an **acting** status and then is held in a full status. The **acting** is simply removed. (SH Spec 61, 6505C18) **3. acting** is prefixed to a title until checksheets are passed. (FO 79) **4.** where other posts are held without qualification above the rating of able bodied seaman or engineman first class the word **acting** will always be used in writing title and name and these may not be written or used without **acting** before them, or the letter **"A."** (LRH Def. Notes circa Aug 67)

ACTING ETHICS OFFICER, any Ethics Officer is to be known only as **Acting Ethics Officer** until he or she has covered the OEC section on ethics and has proven competent on post. (LRH ED 39 INT)

ACTING FLAG OFFICER, there is always an **Acting Flag Officer.** It may be the Commodore, which is signed simply "Commodore," or in his absence it may be one of his deputies. The title **Acting Flag Officer** means that for that time, he is head of the flotilla, the ships' senior officers and crews wherever they may be, and all connected organizations. (FO 3342)

ACTION, Action Bureau. (7012C04)

ACTION, 1. that motion which makes planning an actuality. 2. the carrying out of assigned tasks.

ACTION AFFLUENCE, the formula for **action affluence** is: (1) economize on needless or dispersed actions that did not contribute to the present condition. Economize financially by knocking off all waste. (2) make every action count and don't engage in any useless actions. Every new **action** to contribute and be of the same kind as *did* contribute. (3) consolidate all gains. Any place we have gotten a gain, we keep it; don't let things relax or go downhill or roller-coaster. Any advantage or gain we have, keep it, maintain it. (4) discover for yourself what caused the condition of **affluence** in your immediate area and strengthen it. (LRH Def. Notes)

ACTION BUREAU, 1. where an org is in trouble (stats down) the **Action Bureau** Flag takes it over. Based on searching and accurate evaluation, mission orders are written to correct the outpoints and get the stats up and the org viable. If it is a major situation in a major org the mission goes from Flag to the org. The mission is operated by

Flag **Action**. (FBDL 191R) **2.** evaluates the extreme condition and establishes the why or decides on special investigation, writes up appropriate mission orders for another liaison bureau to run or briefs and sends, via the Comm Bureau, missionaires, and keeps after the matter until the extreme condition up is understood and published for use or the extreme condition down is gotten back up. (CBO 7) **3.** is responsible for the speed and quality of the mission and for operating it while it is out. All missions, immediate, courier, emergency, garrison, go through **Action**. (FO 2756) **4.** the basic purpose of **Action** is planning and emergencies. When all else fails you have to sent it to the **Action Bureau**. Somebody isn't complying with your orders and so forth and your orders being valid orders would have to be implemented by a mission. That's how we force the thing home. (7012C04) **5.** Operations. Called the **Action Bureau** on Flag, they run missions into orgs to handle extreme conditions and to do special projects for clients. Any special service a client might need is handled by them expertly and flawlessly. They must have a pool of management experts to draw from who are fully trained in Flag mission tech. They operate strictly by Sea Org mission procedure. If need be, they can call on org staff who are qualified to go on missions. They have priority. Missions are sent by approved evals only. There is a complete and highly refined technology of mission operation in the Sea Org. (BPL 13 Feb 73R) **6.** FOLO **Action Bureau** selects missionaires from MU, prepares, briefs, fires Flag missions, sends preparations file via External Comm Bureau to Flag and gets missionaires trained and controls the missionaire unit. (CBO 192) **7.** the Sea Org **Action Bureau** is established in the Office of LRH Flag. It is headed by the Chief of Sea Org Operations. It consists of: Evaluation Branch, Action Orders Branch, Operations Branch. It is clearly the purpose of an Admin Unit to collect, file and compile, post and organize data. And it is clearly the function of the **Action Bureau** to find the situations in that data that urgently need handling, to demand action and obtain a proposal from the Action Orders Branch that can be passed at an aides or assistant aides conference and the Flag Org or continental commanding officer that can then be written up and launched as a mission. (FO 2474) **8.** consists of Evaluation Branch, Planning Branch, Mission Preparations Branch and Operations Branch. (CBO 18) **9.** **Action** has planning, briefing, operations. (FBDL 12)

ACTION FILES, it is possible, through a communications system, to organize files so that they are **action files,** so that they are the memory of a mind which thinks. A file should have three sections: (1) the **action file,** which holds a datum that calls for **action** at a certain time, and injects it back into the system at the proper moment, (2) working files, which hold the information that is valuable to the operation, (3) dead files, which could be junked without any loss of value to the operation. (*HTLTAE*, p. 64)

ACTION SKILL, the ability to take the right action to handle a situation.

ACTIVE, 1. engaging in Scn full or part time in an org, forming org, city office, franchise or individually in the field. (LRH ED 259 INT) **2.** a major issue of the continental magazine must be mailed out every other month to all **active** persons in the files. **Active** means members and **active** files. (HCO PL 23 Sept 64) **3.** (CF and address) the simple test for **active** is do they ever answer? (HCO PL 23 Sept 64)

ACTIVE FIELD STAFF MEMBER, one who is in constant communication with his selectees for the purpose of getting them onto the bridge and into the org for service. (BPL 15 Jun 73R I)

ACTIVE FILES, are simply "the **files** of those persons who are members and those persons who have been trained or processed and those persons who have expressed a desire to be trained or processed." (HCO PL 8 Apr 65)

ACTIVE MONEY, funds that are in active use being exchanged hand to hand within society or those funds being used in business dealings.

ACTIVITY LEARNING (OR TEACHING), a method of learning which requires that one get involved in or carry out the practical aspects of how to do something as opposed to learning straight theory in textbooks and lectures, with little practical application. This can take the form of workshops, field trips, projects, group discussions, etc.

ACTUALS, commodities or products traded on a market (i.e. spot market) that one can take delivery of immediately as opposed to futures markets where a commodity becomes available in the future.

ADDED INAPPLICABLE DATA, just plain added data does not necessarily constitute an out-point. It may be someone being thorough. But when the data is in no way applicable to the scene or situation and is **added** it is a definite out-point. In using this out-point be very sure you also understand the word *inapplicable* and see that it is only an out-point if the **data** itself does not apply to the subject at hand. (HCO PL 30 Sept 73 I)

ADDED TIME, in this out-point we have the reverse of dropped time. In **added time** we have, as the most common example, something taking longer than it possibly could. (HCO PL 30 Sept 73 I)

Added Time

ADDED VALUE, increase in value of an item by reason of production and distribution. *Example:* cloth to manufacture a shirt cost $1.00 per square yard. Production cost=50¢. Distribution cost=50¢. Added value per square yard of cloth=$1.00.

ADDENDUM, an addition to a report, book or motion at a formal meeting etc. An addendum does not change the original but adds to it.

ADDITIVES, 1. in the period up to 1966 we were plagued by an occasional obsessiveness to **add** to any process or policy. **Additives** made things unworkable. (HCO PL 30 May 70, *Important, Cutatives*) **2.** people **add** things that aren't there. If it isn't written into the line-up it isn't there. (HCO PL 16 Jan 61)

ADD-ON SALES, additional sales made to a customer after a prior purchase. Such sales can account for as much as 50% of a company's income.

ADDRESS, 1. the **address** files contain, ready for use in mailings, all the names in central files and ready reference designations about these persons. **Address** is the name-status index of central files. (HCO PL 23 Sept 64) **2.** keeps up-to-date the Scientologist **address** files, cuts plates and has charge of all **address** equipment and **address** area, furnishes **addresses** or **addressed** envelopes or tapes for all departments. Furnishes card files of names for departments. (HCO PL 18 Dec 64, *Saint Hill Org Board*) **3.** this means the location of the terminals outside the org that the org contacts. (HCO PL 7 Jul 71) **4.** the central files index as well as who gets the magazine. (HCO PL 18 Nov 69 I)

ADDRESS COORDINATOR, see WW ADDRESSO COORDINATOR.

ADDRESS FILES, see ADDRESS.

ADDRESS-IN-CHARGE, under **Address-In-Charge,** the up-to-date **addresses** of all persons in the live and inactive files of CF are kept readily useable on a proper **address** machine. All mailing and mail functions of the organization properly come under **Address-In-Charge.** This is external mailings. The internal dispatch system can also be included here if in use. All franking machinery also comes under **Address-In-Charge** as well as stamps and their safekeeping. (HCO PL 20 Dec 62)

ADDRESSOGRAPH, 1. the card file system of central files, and **addresso** plates are tabbed and reflect CF exactly without further card files. **Addresso** gives letter reg card files from the **addresso** plates. (HCO PL 12 Jan 62) **2. addresso** is the name-status index of central files. The **address** files contain, ready for use in mailings, all the names in central files and ready reference designations about these people. The **addresses** are normally stored in some sort of **addressing** equipment. **Addresso** plates are tabbed in such a way that they reflect CF exactly. As a person's grade or training level increases the tabbing is changed to reflect this. Copies of all invoices are routed via reception and **addresso** to CF so that **addresses** can be kept up to date and accurate. Copies of training and processing certificates are sent via **addresso** to CF so that the tabbing is updated. (BPL 17 May 69R) *Abbr.* Addresso.

ADDRESSOGRAPH MACHINE, a machine which prints addresses on mail. It uses little stencils, each of which has a desired address typed on it. It feeds these stencils and the mail through it so that each piece of mail gets neatly addressed with a different address.

ADDRESS SECTION, **section** in Department 2, Department of Communications. **Address section** handles all **address** actions and equipment, keeps **address** files. (HCO PL 17 Jan 66 II)

ADDRESS UNKNOWN, if a person's **address** is **unknown**, his plate should be removed from active addressograph files until a correct **address** is obtained, and his CF folder must be marked **address unknown.** (BPL 11 Nov 66R) *Abbr.* add unk.

ADEQUATE DATA, a plus-point. No sectors of omitted **data** that would influence the situation. (HCO PL 3 Oct 74)

ADJUSTMENT DIVISION, your next **division** after Technical Division is not really Qualifications but Correction. It would be called the Correction Division or the **Adjustment Division.** But Qualifications would also serve. (SH Spec 77, 6608C23)

ADMIN CHECKLIST, the head of an org or portion of an org is directly responsible for all **admin** functions and actions in that org or its portion. The head of an org (or the HCOES where there is no Commanding Officer) must have routinely (at least weekly) submitted to him a **checklist** of all **admin** functions in that org showing their state. This **checklist** is to contain every basic action of **admin** in that org such as finance summaries to ________ (date), payroll, bills files, tax summaries, CF files, OIC graphs, addresses, FSM commission files, FSM commissions etc. Anything **administrative** that has to be worked on and kept up must be on that **checklist.** (FO 2286)

ADMIN CYCLE, the correct sequence is: (1) have a normal information flow available, (2) observe, (3) when a bad indicator is seen become very alert, (4) do a data analysis, (5) do a situation analysis, (6) obtain more data by direct inspection of the area indicated by the situation analysis, (7) handle. (HCO PL 15 May 70 II, *Data Series No. 5, Information Collection*)

ADMIN CYCLE DRILL, (1) study and grasp the Data Series PLs. (2) study out the ideal scene for your post, section, department and division. (3) work a stat for post, section, department and division. (4) work out the ideal scene for your org or ship or activity and its stat. (5) work out the ideal scene for the whole SO. (6) work out the stat for the whole SO. (7) work out how your post ideal scene contributes to the whole SO. If not refine your own ideal scene. (8) work out how your stat expresses your own ideal scene. To do this requires a lot of data to be dug up. But when you finish it you really got it. (FO 2584)

ADMIN DUTIES, when one says **admin duties** one refers to the org functions. There is a great deal of Admin Org actions for a ship's officer—personnel, personnel control, conferences, FP, con or OOD in port, org boards, hats, checksheets and packs for division personnel—a lot of purely org duties that prevent a technical officer from doing his job. We put a Deputy Fourth Mate to take care of the org duties of Qual. This has worked out at least to permit the Fourth Mate to C/S and run the technical aspects of the product of the division. (FO 2660)

ADMINISTER, "to have charge of; direct: manage." It is taken from the Latin *administrare*, to be an aid to: *ad-*, to + *ministrare*, to serve. From minister, servant. (HCO PL 29 Oct 71 II)

ADMINISTRATION, **1.** (**admin**) A contraction or shortening of the word **administration, admin** is used as a noun to denote the actions involved in **administering** an organization. The clerical and executive decisions, actions and duties necessary to the running of an organization, such as originating and answering mail, typing, filing, dispatching, applying policy and all those actions, large and small, which make up an organization. You will also see the word **admin** in connection with the three musts of a well run organization. It is said that its ethics, tech and **admin** must be "in," which means they must be properly done, orderly and effective. The word derives from *minister*, which means to serve. **Administer** means to manage, govern, to apply or direct the application of laws, or discipline, to conduct or execute religious offices, dispense rights. It comes from the Latin, *administrare*, to manage, carry out, accomplish, to attend, wait, serve. In modern English, when they use **administration** they mean management or running a government or the group that is in charge of the organization or the state. (LRH Def. Notes) **2.** contains the establishment of the communication lines, and the flow lines and the information lines and so on, so that you can get team operation. (FEBC 1, 7011C17 SO) **3.** the subject of how to organize or establish or correct the spaces, terminals, flows, line duties, equipment, materiel and so forth of a production group so as to establish optimum volume, quality and viability. (HCO PL 4 Jun 71) **4.** the principles, practices and rationalized techniques employed in achieving the objectives or aims of an organization. We commonly call this **"admin"** as a shortening of it and to designate the work of doing it. (HCO PL 9 Nov 68) **5.** a form of communication. Adequate **administration** consists of keeping certain communication terminals in place and making sure that the proper particles go to and through the proper terminals. (PAB 78) **6.** consists of the formation and handling of the lines and terminals involved in production. (HCOB 25 Aug 71) **7.** includes promotion, personnel, lines or anything, not ethics, mentioned in policy letters. (FO 495) *Abbr.* Admin.

ADMINISTRATION TRAINING OFFICER, it is the primary function of the Assistant Assoc Sec to act at this time as an **Administration Training Officer** to all departments to shape their administrative lines and actions and also "to get people to get the work done." (HCO PL 12 May 59)

ADMINISTRATIVE ABILITY, the ability of an individual to formulate policy or procedure which will result in the safe, efficient and profitable running of an organization or business. The ability to interpret and apply already laid down policy to the same results.

ADMINISTRATIVE ASSISTANT TO THE BOARD, executive of the Founding Church of Scientology, Washington, D.C., supplanting the post of Org Sec. (FCPL 9 Oct 58)

ADMINISTRATIVE COUNCIL, the Administrative Division shall no longer be governed by a Director of Administration but shall be governed by an **Administrative Council** which shall be composed of the Director of Procurement, the Director of Material and the Director of Business. (FCPL 9 Oct 58)

ADMINISTRATIVE DIVISION, 1. there are two divisions in a Central Organization. One is technical, the senior division; the other is **administration.** The **Administrative Division** consists of three departments: Promotion and Registration, Material and Accounts. These care for the three basic functions of contacting and signing up people, taking care of quarters and supplies, and handling all matters of finance. (HCO PL 20 Dec 62) **2.** purpose: to ensure good and accurate communication inside organization. To handle business and **administration** affairs. To ensure good working quarters and conditions for and good work from organizational personnel. (HCO PL 12 Oct 62) **3.** the three departments of the **Administrative Division** shall be the Department of Procurement, the Department of Material and the Department of Business. (FCPL 9 Oct 58)

ADMINISTRATIVE EXPENSE, research, general managerial and **administrative expenses.** (HCO PL 26 Jun 64)

ADMINISTRATIVE LETTERS, 1. normal general policy enforcement or advices by the Executive Director are carried in **administrative letters.** These are on yellow paper, are mimeographed and are usually designated general non-remimeo. The Executive Director's **administrative letters** are different from others in being headed above their subject title: Executive Director Directive. They remain in force unless cancelled. (HCO PL 22 Feb 65 III) **2.** pale salmon paper. HCO Divs—green ink, Org Divs—red ink, Public Divs—black ink. Purpose: normal general policy enforcement or advices. Usually designated general non-remimeo. Remain in force until cancelled. (HCO PL 13 Jun 69)

ADMINISTRATIVE MANAGEMENT, see MANAGEMENT, ADMINISTRATIVE.

ADMINISTRATIVE MATTERS, means personnel arrangements, supervision and duties of personnel in that office and execution of tasks assigned. (HCO PL 20 Jan 66 II)

ADMINISTRATIVE PERSONNEL, 1. an **administrative personnel** is there to keep the lines moving and the function of his post operating. **Administrative personnel** gets Scn to the public, keeps the public happy and the organization solvent. **Administrative personnel** are there to keep **administration** out of technical hands and let technical work. (HCO PL 29 May 61) **2.** the function of the **administrative personnel** in a Central Organization is to make technical quality possible and get it delivered to Scientologists and the public. (HCO PL 29 May 61)

ADMINISTRATIVE TRAINING DRILLS, 1. these **TRs** fall into six categories: (1) mest **TRs** 0-4 (2) people **TRs** 0-4 (3) mest bull-bait **TRs** 0-4 (4) people bull-bait **TRs** 0-4 (5) reach and withdraw mest (6) reach and withdraw people. The dynamics they cover are 3 (groups) and 6 (physical universe). The purpose of these **TRs** is to **train** the student to get compliance with, and complete a cycle of action on **administrative** actions and orders, in spite of the randomities, confusions, justifications, excuses, traps and insanities of the third and sixth dynamics, and to confront such comfortably while doing so. (BTB 7 Feb 71) **2.** the purpose of the **admin TRs** was to drill and train FEBC students to get through the noise created by staff members and to get the job done. (FO 2982)

ADMINISTRATOR, 1. one who can make things happen at the other end of a communication line which result in discovered data or handled situations. A very good **administrator** can get things handled over a very long distance. A mediumly skilled **administrator** has a shorter reach. As this scale declines we get people who can make things happen only at arm's length. A skilled **administrator** therefore can be defined as one who can establish and maintain communication lines and can thereby discover, handle and improve situations and conditions at a distance. (HCO PL 15 Oct 73) **2.** an auditor on the third dynamic, only he audits lots of people at the same time. (FO 3005) **3.** the terms **Administrator** and Director of **Administration** are interchangeable. (HCO PL 5 Dec 62) **4.** (post) oversaw all **administrative** actions. (HCO PL 30 Jan 62)

ADMINISTRATOR, a person who is named by a court to manage or dispose of the estate left by a deceased person or one who is legally incompetent.

ADMIN SCALE, I have developed a **scale** for use which gives a sequence (and relative seniority) of subjects relating to organization:

goals
purposes
policy
plans
programs
projects
orders
ideal scenes
stats
valuable final products.

This **scale** is worked up and worked down until it is (each item) in full agreement with the remaining items. In short, for success all these items in the **scale** must agree with all other items in the **scale** on the same subject. (HCO PL 6 Dec 70) See SCALE OF IMPORTANCE.

ADMIN TRAINING CORPS, 1. purpose: to build strong teams of **administrative** executives for the Sea Org to take it to new heights of production. (FO 3324R-5) **2.** the **Admin Training Corps** modelled on the already successful Tech Training Corps (TTC) is established in each AO/SH, FOLO and CC, and EULO, as **training corps** for the orgs themselves. (FO 3324) *Abbr.* ATC.

ADMIN UNIT, 1. the **Admin Unit** and CIC are now the Data Bureau. (OODs 15 Aug 70) **2.** it is clearly the purpose of an **Admin Unit** to collect, file and compile, post and organize data. (FO 2474) **3.** the "office" or **Admin Unit** heretofore placed under CS-7 (then CS-9) is now an autonomous **unit** under the Staff Captain called the Flag Executive Office Unit and the person in charge is the Flag Executive Office Manager. (FO 2381) **4.** a person assigned to the Office Manager is an expeditor. The Officer Manager plus expeditors plus Flag Org internal actions makes up the **Admin Unit.** Every duty in the **Admin Unit** is assigned by functions, not hats. These functions are written up as to how they are done. They are such things as address, posting graphs, briefing, debriefing, mission files, CIC traffic boards, etc. (FO 2379) **5.** composed of all clerical and operational personnel. CIC is kept up by the **Admin Unit.** (FO 2439)

ADMIN UNIT SPECIALIST, a person entering the **Admin Unit** automatically becomes an expeditor and will remain so until trained up on the following functions: stats, posting and pinning, mail logging in and out, CIC filing, excerpting, handling of requests from LRH and aides. When the above training is completed the expeditor is qualified as an **Admin Unit specialist.** (FO 2493)

ADVANCE, 1. the payment of money before it is due. The payment may be for service or goods still to be delivered. 2. to supply money or goods on credit.

ADVANCE CLO ISSUES, issues sent in Flag mail packs for CLO remimeo and distribution: FBDLs, CBOs, Project Orders and Program Orders. (FO 3124)

ADVANCED COURSE REVIEW CONSULTANT, the duty of a solo **review consultant** is to personally handle pre-OT solo jams rapidly with metered two-way communication. (OODs 16 May 72)

ADVANCED ORG ADDRESSO, includes the names and **addresses** of those persons who have bought something from the **AO** and those persons who are eligible or may come to the **AO.** (BPL 19 May 72R)

ADVANCED ORGANIZATION, 1. the **advanced** courses were at first separate in the Office of LRH at Saint Hill and then became the Advanced Orgs (AOs) under the Sea Org. (HCOB 8 Oct 71 II) **2.** that **organization** which runs the **advanced** courses. Its production then is OTs. (FO

508) **3. organization** whose function is to run the Clearing and OT Courses. (FO 1151) **4. Advanced Organizations** deal in the upper levels of OT. They are staffed with Sea Org members. They have direct lines to Flag. (FO 1604) *Abbr.* AO.

ADVANCE ENROLLMENT REGISTRATION, deals in future business, and is a function of the Advance Scheduling Registrar. The game with future business is to: (1) get the advance scheduling book evenly filled up, and (2) then more full, and (3) to concentrate on persons advance scheduled, keeping them hot, encouraging advance payments, helping them overcome stops, etc., and driving them into the org for service, (4) then keeping Tech advised of what's in the book from week to week and what its future is, (5) and rescheduling those persons who don't arrive on their scheduled date. (HCO PL 28 Nov 71R I)

ADVANCE! MAGAZINE, 1. the **magazine** of the **Advanced** Organization. Its purpose is to sell **advanced** courses, solo training, books, tapes and meters, and monitor the line of information and reality to those following the route to OT. (FO 688RA) **2. magazine** mailed by an **advanced** org each month to all persons in their CF. (BPL 20 May 72R)

Advance! Magazine (Def. 1)

ADVANCE MIMEO PACKS, packs sent by Flag to assist the org in quickly duplicating Flag issues applicable for general use or for information in **advance** of receipt of bulk issues for distribution. The **packs** contain: HCO PLs, HCOBs, EDs INT and EDs CONT (including LRH EDs, SO, SO/WW, etc.), FDDs, tally sheets, HCO Info Letters, Advice Letters, Admin Letters, any other issue for all orgs or all continental orgs such as FCOs, FPJOs, FPMGOs, Finance Directives, etc. (FO 3124)

ADVANCE PAYMENT, 1. payment well in **advance**—not for service to be taken "tomorrow" or "in a few days." (HCO PL 29 May 70) [The above HCO PL was replaced by BPL 29 May 70.] **2.** prepayments replaces the term **advance payments.** (HCO PL 15 Jan 72RA) *Abbr.* AP.

ADVANCE PAYMENT RECEIVED, payment received by an AO (or OTL or ship) from a student in **advance** of the time when he will use the service. Any **payment** which results in the student having unused credit in his account can be considered an **advance payment**, whether the student qualifies for a 5% discount or not. For the 5% discount to apply, the student makes his **payment** well in **advance** of using the service, usually prior to his arrival at the org. (FO 1828)

ADVANCE PAYMENT REPORT, the Income Department (Director of Income) must fill in the **advance payment report** each week. This report is compiled by taking the total amount of APs unused, adding the APs received this week and minusing the amount of the APs used this week. This will show you the total amount of APs you have unused each week. (HCO PL 26 Nov 65R)

ADVANCE PAYMENT USED, 1. the statistic of the Advance Scheduling Registrar is: total amount of **advance payments used** for the week. The definition of **advance payment used** is the total of the week's debit (**APU**) invoices written against previous **advance payments.** (Refunds on AP do not count as **APUs** for stat purposes.) (HCO PL 15 Sept 71 I) **2.** any use of services or items (such as bookstore) against existing credit, i.e., for which the student has paid previously. The exact value of that individual service, based on what the student paid for it, is the **advance payment used.** As an example, a student having paid for OT 1-8 as a package, now begins OT 1. The cashier writes a debit invoice for the value of OT 1, at a prorated price consistent with the package price paid by the student. This (debit invoice) amount then becomes an **advance payment used** and is marked as such on the debit invoice. Where and when the student's previous **payment** was made is not important—except that the payment must have been received eventually by the Sea Org at one of its AOs, bases or ships before the **payment** can be considered received or **used.** (FO 1828) **3. APU**—this is written on the invoice when the student starts a service for which he has already paid the advanced payment. (FO 2988) *Abbr.* APU. See PREPAYMENT.

ADVANCE PAYMENT USED FCCI, (Flag) the amount of money used that week from past **FCCI payments** on account for future processing. This is part of the delivery sum. (FSO 667RC)

ADVANCE PAYMENT USED PUBLIC STUDENT, (Flag) the value of **AP used by public students** whose training is being paid for by themselves and is validly part of delivery sum only on a completion. Org future promises then paid off by orgs do not count as this is a form of student freeloaderism. (FSO 667RC)

ADVANCE REGISTRATION PACK, each org has an **advance registration pack.** Combined AO-SH orgs have a **reg pack** for AO services and a separate **reg pack** for SH services. **Advanced registration packs** are mailed out to persons in CF who have expressed a want to be trained and/or processed. The **packs** even include filled out sign-up forms for the person's signature and give the person the opportunity to pay for his service in **advance** or at least make a reservation payment. (BPL 20 May 72R)

ADVANCE RESERVATION BOOK, this **book** (also called the **book** of letter scheduling) is a date-order reference of what people are due to arrive when. (HCO PL 18 Feb 73 I)

ADVANCE RESERVATIONS RECORDS I/C, mainly concentrates on those people who have made a decision i.e., to come to Saint Hill. Her function is giving information and encouraging the person in all possible ways to get here fast fast fast. Not to be found by their schedule date, as this gives a stuck point in time which is a lie. We want them here now. This terminal pushes, pressures, shoves and gets them here. At this stage the whole concentration is on getting them to enroll. It is also to be understood that this unit totally concentrates on the upstat person. This differs from the Letter Registrar who is weeding out the able from the less able. When an individual has said he is coming, and is eligible for SH, he is then entirely in the hands of the **Advance Reservations Records I/C.** The **Advance Reservations Records I/C** mainly concentrates on those people who are coming within six weeks to four months ahead. **Advance Reservations Records I/C** continues writing to people and calling them in, even after they have enrolled. (HCO PL 29 Nov 68)

ADVANCE SCHEDULING REGISTRAR, the prime purpose of the **Advance Scheduling Registrar** is: to help LRH **schedule** and secure individuals by mail in **advance** for technical services and ensure the future prosperity of the organization. The **Advance Scheduling Registrar** keeps two large heavy books. One is for students; one for preclears. It is laid out one page per week two years in **advance.** He receives letters from the letter registrar that are hot prospects and schedules the person promptly and informs him asking for any correction of date. As individuals are scheduled their names and addresses are entered in the book for the week they are arriving. This **registrar** uses also prepared registration packets which even include sign-up forms and give the opportunity to pay for the service in **advance,** or at least, make a reservation payment in **advance.** (HCO PL 21 Sept 65 VI)

ADVANCE SO ISSUES, issues sent in Flag mail packs to provide **SO** Orgs, ships and units with fast information from Flag in advance of bulk issues from their CLO or OTL or mimeo distribution point. They contain: FOs, Base Orders, FCOs. (FO 3124)

ADVERTISEMENT, BLIND, advertisement done with no reference to the company. An example would be a help-wanted advertisement in which a position is described but the company's name is not given.

ADVERTISING, an action done to call public attention to a product or service by presenting it to the public via mass media. The object is to inform public enough to create interest, demand or favorable opinion for the thing advertised which then increases sales or usage.

ADVERTISING BUDGET, the sum of money set aside to advertise, promote or otherwise increase the sales of a product or line of products; a promotional allowance.

ADVERTISING, COOPERATIVE, a type of promotion activity wherein the manufacturer and local distributor or retail source share the cost of advertising a certain product or line of goods.

ADVERTISING, CORRECTIVE, advertising done to correct misleading or incorrect claims made by earlier advertising. In the United States the Federal Trade Commission has the power to require this of a company or business.

ADVERTISING, COUPON, a type of advertisement that includes in its format a reply form or coupon for the reader to fill in and mail to the advertiser, either ordering an item or service or requesting additional information.

ADVERTISING, NATIONAL, advertising of products or services on a national basis or with coverage in the majority of selected locations in the country, easily identifiable due to a popular product name or well-known manufacturer.

ADVERTISING PORTFOLIO, a sales representative's portfolio of proofs of past, current and future advertisements for the products he sells and other related promotional material.

ADVICE, anything you can do off-the-cuff that he will accept and do that is more beneficial to him than what he is doing. (SH Spec 30, 6407C15)

ADVICE LETTERS, pale salmon paper. HCO Divs—green ink, Org Divs—red ink, Public Divs —black ink. Purpose: normal general policy enforcement or **advices**. Usually designated general non-remimeo. Remain in force until cancelled. (HCO PL 13 Jun 69) [The above HCO PL was cancelled by BPL 10 Oct 75 VII.]

ADVISOR, the executive secretaries have one **Advisor** for each of his or her divisions who operate as liaison officers. An **Advisor** has the rank of officer. The **Advisor** advises the executive secretary *not* the division he is in liaison with and issues no orders with his own authority and uses only the authority of the executive secretary even in conversation or letters. He must be given express orders to issue by the executive secretary even though he in fact writes them. An **Advisor** is really an aide to the executive secretary for the division he is appointed to **advise** upon. The **Advisor** is there to lighten the executive secretary's burden in all possible ways as they relate to the area of responsibility for which the **Advisor** is named. The executive secretary usually seeks the **advice** of an **Advisor** before handling a situation in that **Advisor's** type of division but is in no way bound to take it, whereas the **Advisor** is bound to issue and get executed any orders expressly given by the executive secretary. (HCO PL 20 Jan 66 II)

ADVISORY, the title **advisory** where used as a helper to an executive secretary is changed to "(HCO or Org) Exec Sec Communicator for (division represented)." (HCO PL 21 Jan 66)

ADVISORY COMMITTEE, 1. an **Advisory Committee**, as the **advisory** group of a division, meets every Friday about 5:30 pm and conducts its meeting on the statistics of the division for the week ending Thursday 2:00 pm (the day before). The **Ad Comm** assigns conditions for its departments, sections and persons for the division in accordance with statistics and confirms any personnel appointments or transfers or dismissals. (HCO PL 11 Jan 66) **2.** an **Advisory Committee** exists for each division in the org (seven) and is **advisory** to the Ad Council and is appointed by the Ad Council of the org and consists of the secretary of the division and the three directors (heads of departments) or in an Executive Division, the three office coordinators of the three executive division offices, who are the same as directors but have a different title. (HCO PL 13 Mar 66) **3.** there will be one **Adcomm** for each division except Division 7. It will be composed of the three directors of the division or their representatives, and chairmanned by the secretary of the division or his or her representative. The Divisional **Adcomm** has ready the statistics of the division and takes these up in an effort to improve them. The entire purpose of the **Adcomm** is to arrange to improve statistics for its departments, sections and units. The period taken up is the week closed on Thursday. (HCO PL 12 Aug 65) **4.** Advisory Councils are senior to **Advisory Committees.** An Adcouncil runs the whole org, an **Adcomm** runs only one of its divisions. (HCO PL 13 Mar 66) **5. Adcomms** establish and assign statistics for their departments and sections or units and individuals. (HCO PL 12 Oct 65) **6.** the basic purpose of an **Adcomm** is to **advise** the Assoc/Org Sec on promotional matters relating to the various departments. (HCO PL 9 Sept 64, *Purpose of Adcomm*) **7.** purpose: to **advise** the executives of the organization as to the needed changes and policies. To act as a meeting ground of department heads. To assemble and report the statistics of finance and action to the Association Secretary. To advance ideas for promotion and improvement. (HCO London, 9 Jan 58) **8.** composed only of the following persons: the Technical Director, the Director of Administration, the Director of Training, the Director of Processing, the Registrar, and HCO Secretary. (HCO PL 8 Apr 57) *Abbr.* Adcomm.

ADVISORY CONFERENCE, a group meeting at which new or altered policy or plans of action are suggested or advised for use but which does not necessarily formulate definite recommendations.

ADVISORY COUNCIL, 1. the income of the org and its delivery is the primary business of an **Advisory Council.** When it has accomplished its business in this it may then consider the limitation of expenditures. The **Advisory Council** planning is expressed in an executive directive drawn up for executive council approval. This usually covers the coming week but may also take up longer range planning. **Advisory Council** collects up all divisional FP submissions, sees to it that those things necessary to execute its planning have been FPed for, sees that at least 15% of the allocation is allotted to promotion and that there are adequate promo items to utilize this 15% without waste. This is the extent of **Advisory Council** in financial planning. The divisional FP submissions and the completed checklist with **Advisory Council** proposals and all work papers are then forwarded to executive council for approval. (HCO PL 23 Jun 75) **2.** does income and delivery planning. (HCO PL 23 Jun 75) **3.** the **Advisory Council** of an organization shall be composed of the heads of divisions and various representatives, duly elected, of field auditors, students, preclears and public bodies and representatives of subordinate organizations and a representative of the senior organization or, in case of the highest **Advisory Council**, a representative of the senior officer of Scn and the Board. Executive secretaries may not be members of the **Advisory Council.** All representatives of an **Advisory Council** must be elected to it by a majority vote of the **Advisory Council** and the appointment confirmed by the two executive secretaries, on submission of the results of election by the Secretary of the **Advisory Council.** Exception: heads of divisions are automatically appointed to the **Advisory Council.** The **Advisory Council** purpose is: to **advise** the executive secretaries or executive council as to required directives and policies and to implement directives and policy for approval and to examine statistics and conditions and implement remedies or intensification for approval and to originate and recommend for approval promotion ideas. (HCO PL 21 Dec 66 I) **4. Advisory Councils** are senior to Advisory Committees. An **Adcouncil** runs the whole org, an Adcomm runs only one of its divisions. **Advisory Councils** are **advisory** to the Board of Directors or the Executive Director or the Guardian and have no other powers. They cannot open or close bank accounts or change corporate status. They are appointed by a senior **Adcouncil** or the Executive Director or the Guardian. An **Adcouncil** consists of the two executive secretaries of an organization and the Executive Director. (HCO PL 13 Mar 66) **5.** it is composed of the HCO Executive Secretary and the Organization Executive Secretary and is understood to include LRH. Receiving all Adcomm statistics, the **Advisory Council** determines the states of conditions of the organization, each division or separate departments, and publishes the states assigned as from the Office of LRH. The **Advisory Council** does all minor planning and adjustments necessary as an executive admin letter, local. Should large changes be envisioned, the change must be authorized by LRH also and is issued as a SEC ED from Saint Hill. (HCO PL 12 Aug 65) **6.** at WW, the prime concern of the **Advisory Council** is the competence of executive secretaries of other organizations in keeping their divisions going well. In Area Orgs the concern of the **Advisory Council** is the competence of divisional secretaries, in keeping their divisions going well. All actions are taken only on statistics. (HCO PL 21 Jan 66) **7.** handles the gross divisional statistics, looking for steep ups (to assign affluence) or steep downs (to assign emergency). (HCO PL 30 Sept 65) **8.** we will call the **Advisory Council** the **AdCouncil**, never *AdCoun*, to avoid any errors in confusing it with Adcomm. (HCO PL 30 Sept 65) **9.** is composed of bureaux deputies who head internal bureaux functions on Flag, formerly division heads. (ED 1 Flag) **10.** that body of executives in immediate charge of an organization subject to supervision by a further governing authority. (HCO PL 1 Nov 66 II) **11.** purpose: to **advise** the executives of the organization as to needed changes and policies. To act as a meeting ground for department heads. To assemble and report the statistics of finance and action to the Executive Director. To advance ideas for promotion and improvement. (HCO PL 27 Nov 59) *Abbr.* Ad council.

ADVISORY COUNCIL CHECKLIST, an **Ad Council** must know every corner of the org's marketing, promotion, pricing, sales and delivery. This means surveys, pricing and things to sell. Things to promote. How to promote and who can one reach (CF, address, new publics). How to sell. How to deliver. How to get in repeat business. These actions have been assembled into an **Advisory Council checklist,** BPL 22 June 1975. Use of this **checklist** now becomes mandatory for **Ad Council** who may not touch expenditure matters until it has reviewed all points of the **checklist** and formulated an income planning which forces in promotion, delivery, and sales, and which remedies the weak points and removes the barriers to achieving these. The **checklist** serves as a guide to direct **Ad Council's** attention to vital areas, but may not be taken to supplant policy. (HCO PL 23 Jun 75)

ADVISORY COUNCIL WW, the **Advisory Council World Wide** meets every Wednesday afternoon. Its procedure is as follows: it takes up the Adcouncil SH minutes and passes or alters them and sends them on to the Executive Director for OK as a SEC ED. The **Adcouncil** then takes up the statistics of the International Division itself. It issues any orders as a SEC ED and forwards it to the Executive Director for approval and issue. It then takes up international statistics org by org and draws up general SEC EDs WW or individual SEC EDs for orgs and sends them to the Executive Director for approval and issue. (HCO PL 11 Jan 66)

AFFILIATION, the establishment of a close relationship with; a joining or connecting up so that the parts or branches so connected come under common control.

AFFLUENCE, sudden peaks of income (SH Spec 62, 6505C25)

Affluence

AFFLUENCE ATTAINMENT, consists of: (1) hard work, (2) in ethics, (3) standard tech, (4) doing the things that won, not new things untried as yet, (5) applying the formula of the condition one is in. (HCO PL 13 Nov 72)

AFFLUENCE FORMULA, (1) economize. Now the first thing you must do in **affluence** is economize and then make very very sure that you don't buy anything that has any future commitment to it, don't buy with any future commitments —nothing. That is all part of that economy, clamp it down. (2) pay every bill. Get every bill that you can possibly scrape up from any place, every penny you owe anywhere under the sun, moon and stars and pay them. (3) invest the remainder in service facilities, make it more possible to deliver. (4) discover what caused the condition of **affluence** and strengthen it. (HCO PL 23 Sept 67)

AFTER SERVICE INTERVIEW, an individual completing a major **service** is routed from Success to the registrar *via* the Promotion Department for an **"after service" interview.** Every single person has a story to tell of a major win or interesting occurrence from applying Scn technology, but the results being obtained and the wins in tech are unknown to promotion people. To remedy this situation, a line is established in order that promo people: (a) get data for current and future promotion of Scn and org **services,** and (b) are well informed of the wins and successes through the application of Scn technology. (BPL 22 Dec 71 III)

AGAINST ORGANIZATION, **"against organization** or posts and protesting at org behavior or existence." (HCOB 19 Aug 63)

AGAINST SCIENTOLOGY, attention off **Scn** and protesting **Scn** behavior or connections. (HCOB 19 Aug 63)

AGENDA, that which is placed before a committee, meaning a table of actions. (7201C02 SO)

AGENT, one who has the power or authority to act for or represent another as in the acquisition or disposal of goods, property, services, funds, etc.

AGENT FOR GREAT BRITAIN, [HASI was a foreign corporation doing business in UK. As such it had to have a designated **agent** responsible in law for the activities of the corporation in the UK. This is because without a legally assigned representative (called **agent**) the corporation would have no legal identity in the foreign country.]

AGFA GEVAFAX, photocopier machine. (FO 2152) [**Agfa Gevafax** is a brand name of a photocopier machine.]

AIDA, attention, interest, desire and action. These four things have been isolated as necessary ingredients to successful sales. A number of sales training courses are built around AIDA.

AIDE, **1.** an **aide** in a bureau (Flag, CLOs, OTLs, Org Liaison Office) is defined as the bureaux specialist and leading officer for that division, internal and external, in all its functions. **Aide** is the title of a Flag Staff Officer on Flag. "Assistant **aide**" is the title in a CLO. The org equivalent in duties and hat is a divisional secretary. In the case of an **aide** it is understood that the person **aided** is the Commodore. In the case of an assistant **aide,** the person **aided** is the Flag **aide.** (CBO 52) **2.** an

aide has a certain exact part of the functions of the org board to handle and keep going in all Scn, SO and Scn orgs. They could be considered the head of a division or function of a planet-wide org board. When that part of the planet-wide org board declines or is in trouble, it is the **aide** who is held responsible. Similarly, when the area is upstat it is the **aide** who is commended. (FO 2945) **3.** an **aide**, by definition, has to be an expert on the Data Series and how to conduct investigations. Otherwise an **aide** will consistently operate on "whys" derived from a dispatch line. The bulk of an **aide's** duties should consist of discovering, tracing, finding the data about and the real whys of situations and then getting ideas to handle them and programming and handling them. The remaining time at the disposal of an **aide** should be spent in implementing programs that have already been released to handle things and getting them in fully and completely. (FO 3064) **4.** the duties of an **aide** and an assistant **aide** could be broken down roughly into the following categories: (1) assistance to the Commodore, (2) assistance to their FB and CLO seniors, (3) administrative duties (including dispatches), (4) evaluations, (5) programming, (6) implementation of existing programs including logging compliances, (7) conference duties, (8) executive responsibility to juniors, (9) inspections and assistance in the nearby service org on those functions which apply to their post so as to maintain and continue familiarity with the existing scene. (FO 3064) **5.** an **aide** in the Flag Bureaux is required to do the following evaluations each week using the data available in the Data Bureau and applying the technology of the Data Series: (a) each branch of their own bureau at Flag based on the international stat of Scn organizations (plus franchise for CS-6), (b) each branch of their own bureau at Flag for Sea Org organizations based on the international Sea Org stat, (c) each assistant **aide** in CLOs covering their division or activity, (d) their divisional continental stat for each continental area. (FO 3064) **6.** it is clearly the function of **aides** and assistant **aides** to manage their opposite numbered divisions over the world. (FO 2474) **7.** there are now six **aides** to the Commodore. These are: CS-1, CS-2, CS-3, CS-4, CS-5, CS-6. (FO 795) **8.** the primary purpose of a Commodore's Staff **Aide** is to forward the actions and targets established by the Commodore and to assist him in accomplishing these. The next important purpose is to assist the Commodore in the planning and establishment of actions and targets. (CS Order 71) **9. Aide** is the title of a Flag Staff Officer on Flag who **aids** LRH with respect to a particular division, bureau, or zone of activity. (BTB 12 Apr 72R) **10.** International Secretary. (HCO PL 7 Mar 72)

AIDE'S COMMUNICATOR, all **communications** to any aide from any terminals other than staff must be routed via that **aide's communicator.** The **Aide's Communicator** sorts out all dev-t and handles as per dev-t policy. All out-going comms from aides to terminals other than staff go via the **Aide's Communicator** for logging orders. (FO 1548)

AIDES CONFERENCE, (DOC and **Aides Conference**) these fail by misuse. They are bodies to approve or modify prepared CSW of members for passing by higher authority. They are not planning bodies which originate. It can approve, reject or modify. Its individual members prepare CSW for the committee before its meeting. Authority senior to the committee is then assisted. The whole upset with committees is they are used wrongly. They are not there to plan. They are there as individuals to be informed and have a say in modifying or approving or rejecting material drawn up before. This is also true of the **Aides Conference,** FOs and PLs sent direct to me, for instance, is a committee or **conference** by-pass. These deny information and a say to all the other **aides.** Also I often have to submit them back to other individual **aides** to see if it is all right—a function of the **Aides Conference.** (FO 2653)

AIDES COUNCIL, 1. it is a coordinating body for an evaluation. It is a coordinating body so that somebody isn't trying to do something that somebody else is doing. They should be doing an evaluation of what should be evaluated, so that nothing gets away from it. (7205C18SO) **2.** the **aides** and the pure bureau functions are all devoted to a body called the **Aides Council,** which is engaged in management of external orgs. (ESTO 2, 7203C01 SO II) **3.** an **Aides Council** or A/**Aides** (or International Secretary or Assistant International Secretary) **Council** is held as (1) a product conference or (2) a program conference or (3) an establishment conference, but never two or three of these at the same time. (HCO PL 7 Mar 72) **4.** the **aide** or assistant **aide** in the CLO is a member of the **Aides Council.** Such a **council** is used for briefing and for recommending. A **council** handles situations by spotting them and requiring evaluations, plans and programs. The **council** reviews old programs and progress on them. (CBO 52) *Abbr.* AC.

AIDES LEVEL, the business you're in (**aides**) is putting up the stats of orgs. The action in which you're engaged, is find an org that has been responsible for income in the past and evaluate it, and that's at **aides level,** and that's what's known as Staff. Evaluations and MOs would be at **aides level**, Staff Aides. (7205C18SO)

AIDES ORDER, **1.** covers external matters having to do with FOLOs and outer orgs. Usually contains evaluations by myself or Flag management personnel. The program of an evaluation is sometimes issued as an FPGMO issued to senior executives on Flag and personnel concerned. They are numbered by area to which they apply. (HCO PL 24 Sept 70R) **2.** the basic order form of Flag is the **Aides Order.** This is an evaluation done by a Flag evaluator. It contains targets. (HCO PL 7 Aug 73 I) **3.** all programs and projects come from evaluations. They are the handling part of the evaluation in the program or project. These evaluations are issued as **Aides Orders.** (CBO 218RB) **4. Aides Orders** cover external matters having to do with CLOs and outer orgs, or whenever orders refer to both internal and external. **Aides Orders** are not exported: they go only to bureaux personnel and those on Flag who might be concerned in the order. (ED 1 Flag) *Abbr.* AO.

AIMS, the organizational goals and intentions. These are usually expressed in the policies of the organization.

ALERT COUNCIL WW, these eight posts work in close liaison and must meet weekly as the **Alert Council WW:** International Communications Officer, International Ethics Officer, International Admin Officer, International Special Programs Execution Officer, International Promotion Officer, International Technical Officer, International Declarations Officer and the International Treasurer WW. This **council** has advisory powers and is to draw up weekly for the LRH Comm WW, the Guardian WW and the HCO and Org Exec Secs WW an alert bulletin org by org giving a prediction of good expansion or trouble or contraction based on their respective fields of comm, ethics, admin pattern, tech, programs execution, public expansion and money with recommendations for any action in each org or generally. They are then to execute the action as individual officers when it is approved or as modified unanimously by the executives to whom it is sent. (HCO PL 21 Sept 67 *International Officers at WW, Alert Council*)

ALERT OFFICER, **1.** the major stats of an org are plotted in big stat books. The gross divisional stats are plotted in folders. These are gone through carefully each week by an **Alert Officer.** He is looking for dangerous stat situations or extremely good ones. All this information is written up in a published weekly Data Bureau stat report. (FBDL 192R) **2. officer** trained up to spot orgs in trouble or orgs shooting the moon and to make sure situations do get handled. (OODs 4 Jun 72) **3.** the **Alert Officer's** main duty is to find the things that need to be handled. The first thing he looks for is down stats. The second thing he looks for is unanswered comm—he ensures that Program Chiefs take care of the correspondence in the Data Bureau folders. He would also find high stats that need to be reinforced. He ensures the relevant terminals are informed of all these situations and maintains the necessary administrative procedures to see they are located, called to attention and handled. A routine duty of the **Alert Officer** is the weekly stat summary. (CBO 204)

ALL AUDITORS ACTION, whenever an org has a Tech or Qual backlog it is usual to call an **all auditor action.** Any admin personnel assist with scheduling and getting pcs in to the **auditors** without making pcs wait or wasting an **auditor's** time. All tech trained personnel in the org devote a certain number of hours in the day to delivering **auditing** for Tech or Qual and spend a certain amount of time on their regular posts until the backlog is gone. Too many of these **"all auditors"** can cut an org to bits. They are only done so long as there is a backlog. (LRH ED 49 INT)

ALL HANDS, an action requiring a huge burst of activity is called an **all hands** action. Thus a mailing to be stuffed in envelopes and mailed, a huge doorbell ringing campaign to get individual purposes, a big drive to persuade civic groups by individual calls—all these are **all hands** actions. (HCO PL 3 Dec 68)

ALLOCATION, how much one can pay or is going to pay (ED 459-28-1 Flag)

ALLOCATION, 1. a sum of money or a quantity set aside or allotted for a specific purpose. 2. the calculation of the correct amount of personnel, materials, machines or finances needed to obtain the planned results.

ALLOCATION BOARD, in Department 1, an **allocation board** is kept which shows vacancies. This **board** is a piece of cardboard which shows all divisions and departments of the org board aligned such as the org board. It is kept by personnel procurement and when a request for a staff member comes in, the personnel procurement officer writes on a small strip of paper the post that is vacant and who requested the personnel on the reverse side of the paper. A pin is then stuck through the end of the paper and it is stuck in the department where the vacancy is. At the top of each division and department is the maximum quota of personnel authorized for that department or division by the Ad Council and the current number of persons in the department concerned and the division. (HCO PL 14 Jan 66 II)

ALLOCATION PRODUCTION RATIO, the FBO has as a statistic the **allocation production ratio** of the org. If his **allocation** buys VFPs, he can expect a rising **allocation production ratio** statistic. Normally, this is assured by the use of an **allocation** system which **allocates** against VFPs. (BPL 4 Sept 71R)

ALLOCATION SUM, **1.** calculated by subtracting from gross income any bounced checks or refunds, book moneys, and "reimbursement" type receipts (payments for phone calls, postage, etc., by students or crew). **Allocation** percentages are then calculated from this figure. (FO 1980) **2.** that figure from which percentage **allocations** are derived. The **allocation sum** is gross income after adjustments have been made (per FO 1681) for bounced checks, refunds, advance payments received, advance payments used, and book monies. Also called "net income" or "corrected gross income." (FO 1828) **3.** the **allocation sum** for AOs (also called "corrected gross income" or "net income") is defined as: gross income *less* advance payments received, *plus* advance payments used. There are also adjustments for refunds or returned checks on services *used*, and a deduction for book income. The final result is the **allocation sum**, from which the allocation percentages are then derived. (FO 1681) **4.** the gross income less the congress, books and tapes sum. (HASI PL 19 Apr 57 *Proportionate Pay Plan*)

ALTERED COMPLIANCE, a type of dev-t where something was introduced or changed in the orders which made them non-optimum. This sometimes wastes and repeats all earlier traffic. (HCO PL 27 Jan 69)

ALTERED IMPORTANCE, an **importance** shifted from its actual relative **importance**, up or down. An out-point. (HCO PL 19 Sept 70 III)

ALTERED SEQUENCE, any things, events, objects, sizes in a wrong **sequence** is an out-point. The number series 3, 7, 1, 2, 4, 6, 5, is an **altered sequence**, or an incorrect **sequence**. Doing step two of a **sequence** of actions before doing step one can be counted on to tangle any **sequence** of actions. (HCO PL 19 Sept 70 III)

Altered Sequence

ALTER-IS, **1.** a composite word meaning the action of **altering** or changing the reality of something. Is-ness means the way it is. When someone sees it differently he is doing an **alter-is**; in other words, is **altering** the way it **is.** (LRH Def. Notes) **2.** alteration of orders and tech is worse than non-compliance. **Alter-is** is a covert avoidance of an order. Although it is apparently often brought about by non-comprehension, the non-comprehension itself and failure to mention it, is an avoidance of orders. (HCOB 22 Mar 67) **3.** uncertainty comes totally from lack of understanding. Understanding is barred out by the misunderstood word. All **alter-is** comes after the misunderstood word. (LRH ED 154 INT)

Alter-is (Def. 1)

ALTER-IS REPORT, staff member **report** of the **alteration** of design, policy, technology or errors being made in construction. (HCO PL 1 May 65)

ALTERNATIVE COSTS, see COSTS, ALTERNATIVE.

AMENDMENT, an addition, deletion, modification or revision made to a law, bill, constitution or motion, etc. If it is solely an addition being made the amendment may be called an addendum.

AMENDS PROJECT, an individual may clean his own file by approaching ethics and offering to make **amends.** Any **amends project** must benefit the org and be beyond the routine duties. It may not only benefit the individual. Offers to "get audited at own expense in Review" are acceptable as auditing will benefit everyone. No work one would normally do himself on post is acceptable **amends.** Doing what one should do anyway is not **amends,** it is the expected. No org funds may be employed in an **amends project.** (HCO PL 1 May 65)

AMERICAN COLLEGE OF PERSONNEL EFFICIENCY, DUBLIN, this establishment and its personnel cease to be in any way connected with the admin or information lines of HASI London, Founding Church D.C., or HCOs. This entire establishment reverts to status of Field Auditor. (HCOB 3 Nov 58) [This college, located in Dublin, Ireland, gave PE lectures and functioned to introduce people to Scn.]

AMERICAN PERSONALITY ANALYSIS, see OXFORD CAPACITY ANALYSIS.

AMERICAN SOCIETY OF CIVILIAN DEFENSE, see HUBBARD DIANETIC RESEARCH FOUNDATION.

AMNESTY, a general pardon for past offenses; the granting of such a pardon; a forgetting or intentional overlooking; the rendering of punishment null and void for offenses earlier than the **amnesty** date, known or unknown; forgiveness of past criminal or antisocial actions. (HCO PL 6 Mar 65)

AMORTIZATION, 1. the act of extinguishing a debt by installment payments or some agreed means such as the use of a sinking fund. 2. the money used to accomplish this.

ANALOGUE MODELS, training aids and techniques used to simulate actual situations in a business or activity. These are drills, wargames, etc. Analogue models can also be a set of established factors and relationships which, if accurately constructed, may be applied to current statistics to project the state of economy.

ANALYSIS, the breakdown of anything into clearly definable and understandable parts and the study of the relationship of the parts to the integrated whole. This can take the form of examining personnel performance, product quantity and quality, financial and production statistics, etc., in order to create or improve a beneficial condition or wipe out a bad one.

ANALYSIS, CATEGORY, market research method for determining whether market conditions are favorable to the introduction and development of a product.

ANALYSIS, CLUSTER, the analysis of a broad field of information on people or products, breaking it down into categories or clusters that share common characteristics.

ANALYSIS, CONCENTRATION, focusing of attention and action on those areas of a business which are of greatest importance, such as leading customers, major products, adequate stock levels, etc.

ANALYSIS, CONSEQUENCES, the examination and evaluation of a series of posed management alternatives to ascertain how the organization in each instance would be influenced in its operation, and if any of these plans were to fall short or fail, what would be the overall effect caused.

ANALYSIS, COST-BENEFIT, the evaluation of the worth of company benefits against costs so as to make choices that will give maximum benefits at minimum cost.

ANALYSIS, COVERAGE, a mathematical procedure to discover and establish the optimum stock levels to be carried by an organization in order to minimize stock costs while still meeting a standard level of production.

ANALYSIS, CRITICAL PATH, sophisticated evaluation technique wherein a complete plan is made for a project as to sequence of tasks involved, provisions for labor, material and overhead costs, tight time schedules and regular checks to be done at various stages along the way. Once in operation, reports on progress and results are made so that corrections of any variance or bottlenecks may be done at once. *Abbr.* CPA.

ANALYSIS, DEMAND, a study of the conditions in an economic scene that maintain increase or decrease demand or sales of a specific product or service.

ANALYSIS, ESTIMATE, cost accounting system for estimating direct costs as materials and equipment as well as indirect costs or overhead, including profit and selling price of the product or service involved.

ANALYSIS, FACTOR, analysis of a large or complex body of data to establish those factors or common denominator which lead to being able to understand the data and arrive at correlations and conclusions about it.

ANALYSIS, INPUT-OUTPUT, market research method, often presented in table or graph form, for finding out the costs and sales of various industries with a view to identifying markets to be pushed by discovering changes in technology, consumer demands and trading variables.

ANALYSIS, JOB, the determining of what duties, functions and responsibilities belong to specific jobs and what qualifications and salary are appropriate for the job.

ANALYSIS, MANPOWER, a technique used in manpower planning in which an analysis is made of all the employees in an organization or department according to job title and general work classification, age, sex, tenure and turnover experience, over a given period.

ANALYSIS, MARKET, that part of market research which establishes the characteristics and size of a market for a particular product or service such as the identification of potential buyers and sellers and the price they are willing to pay. Also called market intelligence.

ANALYSIS, MEANS-ENDS, the analysis of decisions to ensure that the means proposed will best accomplish the ends envisioned.

ANALYSIS, MEDIA, evaluation of the efficacy of various advertising media for promoting specific products and services and for reaching particular segments of the consumers market.

ANALYSIS, OCCUPATIONAL, defining the jobs in an organization and classifying them as to the principal tasks they hold in common sufficiently to be able to group them under broader occupational titles such as sales, service, clerical, etc.

ANALYSIS OF FAULTS, in repair or conversion of a ship, never repair a thing to fail the same way again. Do not be afraid of solving. If gauges break, don't just replace them. Find out why they broke. Be sure you have the real answer. Fix that; then replace the gauges. Don't keep leaving the same error in. It is a very expensive practice. It means continual repair bills doing the same repair over and over. Find and correct why it has to be repaired! If something is broken find out why it broke. Don't just put it back to be broken again. Eradicate the **fault**! (*Ship's Org Bk.*)

ANALYSIS, PRODUCT, market research study of products that finds out which product features are most valued by consumers, develops new products and improves old ones so they are suited to new uses.

ANALYSIS, REGRESSION, market research analysis founded on the idea that studying and knowing one trend can result in being able to relate and accurately forecast other trends, such as a general decline in the standard of living may be expected to curtail savings deposits, buying power in the luxury markets, etc.

ANALYSIS, TECHNICAL, in investments, the researching of the stock market and individual securities based on supply and demand with attention to volume, price movements, trends and patterns to assess the current market situation and its possible effect on the future not only of individual stocks but of market performance overall. Also called technical research.

ANALYST, a person who can break something down to its component parts, study them and establish the relationship of each of the parts to the others and to the integrated whole. He would then be capable of recommending desirable changes or improvements to increase productivity or efficiency, reduce cost or errors in personnel or equipment, etc.

ANALYTIC METHOD OF SELECTION, see SELECTION, ANALYTIC METHOD OF.

ANALYTIC RATING, see RATING, ANALYTIC.

ANATOMY OF THE HUMAN MIND COURSE, this **course** teaches about observation and understanding of the fundamentals of the **human mind.** End result is an ability to observe and understand the basic mechanisms and aberrations of the **human mind.** (CG&AC 75)

ANNOTATED DIAGRAM, an explanatory diagram such as a flow chart or organization chart.

ANNOYANCE REPORT, staff member **report** of anything about which one is **annoyed,** giving the person or portion of the org one is **annoyed** with. (HCO PL 1 May 65)

ANNUAL REPORT, a formal financial statement prepared annually by a corporation or business showing assets, liabilities, profits, etc. It shows the company's financial standing at the close of the business year, how well it did profit-wise for the year and any other data shareholders would be interested to know.

ANSWERING COPY, the message system we use is based on three copies of every telex. If you do not receive three you must instantly make three. Every phone, cable or telex message needs three copies. The first **copy** is the **answering copy.** It is called this because it is the **copy** which one reads and writes his **answer** to. (FO 2528)

ANSWERING SENSIBLY, "an intelligible response dealing at least vaguely with the question." (HCO PL 20 Mar 61 II)

ANTI-KICKBACK LAW, a law prohibiting an employer from receiving any of an employee's pay back (kickback) as a condition of employment.

ANTI-PIRATING AGREEMENT, an agreement between employers (often in the same industry) not to procure already employed personnel from each other.

ANTISOCIAL PERSONALITY, 1. the **antisocial personality** has the following attributes: (1) he or she speaks only in very broad generalities. (2) such a person deals mainly in bad news, critical or hostile remarks, invalidation and general suppression. (3) the **antisocial personality** alters, to worsen communication when he or she relays a message or news. Good news is stopped and only bad news, often embellished, is passed along. (4) a characteristic, and one of the sad things about an **antisocial personality,** is that it does not respond to treatment or reform or psychotherapy. (5) surrounding such a personality we find cowed or ill associates or friends who, when not driven actually insane, are yet behaving in a crippled manner in life, failing, not succeeding. (6) the **antisocial personality** habitually selects the wrong target. (7) the **antisocial** cannot finish a cycle of action. (8) many **antisocial** persons will freely confess to the most alarming crimes when forced to do so, but will have no faintest sense of responsibility for them. (9) the **antisocial personality** supports only destructive groups and rages against and attacks any constructive or betterment group. (10) this type of **personality** approves only of destructive actions and fights against constructive or helpful actions or activities. (11) helping others is an activity which drives the **antisocial personality** nearly berserk. Activities, however, which destroy in the name of help are closely supported. (12) the **antisocial personality** has a bad sense of property and conceives that the idea that anyone owns anything is a pretense made up to fool people. Nothing is ever really owned. (HCOB 27 Sept 66) **2.** the suppressive person. You, in speaking of it, actually marry up with old technology because they have looked for this fellow called the **antisocial person** for a long time. Freud used the term. Psychologists use the term. They've used the term for a long time. They know there is such a person called the **antisocial personality** and this is the personality for which they have been groping. We're calling it a suppressive because it is more explicit. (SH Spec 78, 6608C25)

AO1 FORM, see FORM AO1.

AO2 FORM, see FORM AO2.

AO3 FORM, see QUALIFICATIONS FORM AO3.

AO ALICANTE, the *Royal Scotman* and **AO Alicante** were more or less the same **AO.** (ED 68 Flag) *Abbr.* AOA.

AO-AOSH, BASE AND OTL MISSIONS, a **mission** is so classified when the **mission** personnel are permanently assigned or transferred to an **AO, AOSH** base, or **OTL.** (FO 2132)

AO DOMESTIC ACCOUNT, AOUK will establish two bank accounts under the headings of AO reserve account and **AO domestic account.** The **domestic account** will be for withdrawals of a ship type nature, i.e., financial planning, FSM commissions, weekly allocation for OTL **AO,** capital expenditure, etc. The signatories for this **account** will be LRH singly and any two of the following persons: Commanding Officer, Chief Officer, Supercargo, Third Mate, Purser and Director Disbursements. (FO 1120)

AO INSIGNIA, the OT badge is now the **AO insignia.** (FO 331)

AO LIAISON, 1. an **AO liaison** sees to all promotional matters, traffic and programs, because she is responsible for getting compliance. Information is sent to the **AO liaison** RSM Flag by the **AO liaison** for the **AO.** This includes all divisional reports, **AO** OODs, new names and addresses, a list of those in the shop, names and addresses of new FSMs and all promotional data, and proposals of Division 6. An **AO liaison** is a promotional **liaison,** nothing else. He or she gets compliance on promotional matters. (FO 1314) **2.** an **AO liaison** is only a relay point of information and will ensure compliance on all promotional orders and traffic for Flag Division 6. The type of information wanted is a total coverage of what the **AO** has been doing. (FO 1330)

AO LIAISON FOR FLAG, 1. the Advanced Organization is a functioning unit for the public and to that degree it is under the operation of Division 6 Flag. Flag Division 6 is responsible for every concern, part and operation of the Advanced Organization. To operate such an organization from a distance requires good definite liaison work to and from Flag and AO. The person who is in charge of this is under Division 6 Flag. His title is **"AOLF" AO Liaison for Flag** and has two representatives under him (1) AOLS who is the Flag Representative at Scotland for AO. (2) AOLWW who is the Flag Representative at WW for AO. (FO 986) **2.** there are three AO Liaisons at this time; the senior AO Liaison is **AO Liaison for Flag.** AO Liaisons under him are AOLWW, AOLS, AOL-LA. **AOLF** is responsible for AO Liaisons under him, their compliance and orders. The welfare of AOs is his concern. (FO 1237)

AOL-LA, 1. Advanced Organization Liaison Los Angeles (FO 1364) **2.** there are three AO liaisons at this time. The Senior AO Liaison is; AO liaison for Flag, AO liaisons under him are: AOLWW, AOLS, **AOL-LA. AOL-LA** is responsible for all AOLA and that it is so well promoted that US and Canadian students will know that AOLA is the proper location to go to and not AOUK. (FO 1237)

AOLS, 1. Advanced Organization Liaison Scotland. (FO 1364) **2. AOLS** is responsible for all AOUK, its comm lines, promotion activities and product. **AOLS** carries the job at pushing compliance at Pubs Org because she is conveniently near Pubs Org. (FO 1237)

AOLWW, 1. Advanced Organization Liaison World Wide. (FO 1364) **2.** the senior AO liaison is AO Liaison for Flag. AO liaisons under him are; **AOLWW**, AOLS, AOL-LA. **AOLWW** expedites AO comm lines going via OTLWW and to outer orgs, and ensuring that AO mailings from WW are speedily handled. Also **AOLWW** is in charge of AO activities at WW, making them go right etc. furnishing anything an AO may need at WW, Adv Reg Pack; Info Pack Routine, keeping informed on the activities of outer Orgs and passing on information useful in AO planning to Div 6 Flag, and knowing the activities of both AOs. (FO 1237)

AO PC, by **AO PC,** or pre-OT, is meant a VA or above. (BPL 12 Sept 72R)

A/OPERATIONS AIDE, the head of Bureau IV Flag is entitled Operations Aide. His opposite number in a CLO is entitled **A/Operations Aide.** (CBO 81)

AO RESERVE ACCOUNT, AOUK will establish two bank accounts under the headings of **AO reserve account** and AO domestic account. The **reserve account** is for deposits of all hard cash—no checks. The signatories for this account will be LRH singly, and the Commanding Officer and Chief Officer jointly. (FO 1120)

AO REVIEW CASE SUPERVISOR, (AO Review C/S) C/S who **C/Ses** for fast **reviews** on advanced course students. (HCO PL 25 Sept 74)

Apollo

APOLLO, the yacht *Apollo* (3,278 gross tons) measures 328 feet long and is 50 feet at her beam (widest point). Her draft is about 13—16 feet. Her top speed is 18 knots, but for optimum stability, depending on seas and weather, she usually cruises between 8 and 15 knots. Her usual ship's complement is 150 to 200 people. (FO 2674)

APOLLO TROUPE, the purpose of the **Apollo Troupe** is the creation of safe ports and safe countries through improved image, musical comm line, and fame for the *Apollo.* (OODs 12 Aug 74) *Abbr.* ATO. [The **Apollo Troupe** was a large troupe of musicians and dancers comprising several different bands, each with different names and styles of music and entertainment. The **troupe** was put together and worked with by L. Ron Hubbard during the course of the extensive musical research he was doing in 1974 and 1975.]

APPEARANCES, comes under the Department of Ethnics, Division 6, Department 16, Ethnic Acceptable **Appearance** Section. The Public Exec Sec, therefore, is directly responsible for the **appearance** of the org, its staff, its literature and publications so far as **appearance** and acceptability go. **Appearances** never worked under Department 1. "Image" is actually a PRO function and it is of vital interest to the Public Exec Sec as otherwise his promotion may be dulled or rendered null. The image of an org and its staff and its literature and publications actually is a form of projection into the public. (HCO PL 11 Dec 69, *Appearances in Public Divisions*)

APPEARANCES SECTION, section in Department 1, Department of Routing, **Appearances** and Personnel. **Appearances Section** sees that organization staff looks good, sees that all entrances are of easy access and channelled by signs, handles all signs. (HCO PL 17 Jan 66 II)

APPLICABLE DATA, a plus-point. The **data** presented or available **applies** to the matter in hand and not something else. (HCO PL 3 Oct 74)

APPLICANT, someone who has **applied** for staff, personally or in response to a mailing. (BPL 28 Apr 73)

APPLICANT LETTER, that is the most important mail. The **applicant letter** is an exceedingly precise thing. It says "I am coming in." It broadly divides into "I am coming in on a certain date" and "I am coming in." (HCOB 6 Apr 57)

APPLIED SCHOLASTICS, Applied Scholastics has been operating in the US and England for four years now. This program was started by credentialed teachers in the US who had been trained in study techniques developed by me for use in Scn training. **Applied Scholastics** has had excellent results increasing the ability of students to read and understand materials. (LRH ED 256 INT)

APPRAISE, to establish the worth or value of something by estimation or through the use of a sequence of tests or physical examinations designed to show up the value or condition of something.

APPRAISER, a person authorized to set or estimate the value or cost of something as a property appraiser. Usually this is a professional person who has experience in the manufacturing, marketing, use or ownership of such things.

APPRECIATION, an increasing in the value or market price of something often due to increased demand, superior design, scarcity or inflation.

APPRENTICE, a person learning a craft or trade who enters into a legal agreement with an employer to work for the employer usually for little or no pay in exchange for instruction in the trade.

APPRENTICEABLE OCCUPATION, an occupation calling for usually a four-year apprenticeship, two years of which are spent by the qualified beginner in formal training.

APPRENTICEABLE TRADE, in terms of time, a period of more than two years or an equivalent of 4,000 hours is deemed as the training period necessary to develop a competently skilled trade worker.

APPRENTICESHIP, the time spent as an apprentice working under the supervision of persons skilled in a trade with the intention of learning that trade.

APPRENTICESHIP, INDENTURED, an apprenticeship whereby the apprentice signs an indenture or apprenticeship training agreement which stipulates the conditions of employment such as wages and length of time the apprentice must work for the employer.

APPRENTICESHIP RATIO, the ratio of apprentices to journeymen in an organization, a proportion which may be part of its employment policy or which may be stipulated in a collective bargaining agreement.

APPRENTICESHIP TRAINING AGREEMENT, a contract between an employer and apprentice which lays out the terms of the apprenticeship such as wage rate, hours of work, length of apprenticeship. In the case of a minor the agreement is between the employer and the parents or legal guardian of the apprentice.

APPRENTICE SYSTEM, consists of performing as an assistant to the post to be relieved long enough so the post is learned. It is not somebody standing around waiting to take over the post. (FSO 96)

APPRENTICE TRAINING, see TRAINING, APPRENTICE.

APPRENTICING, apprenticing is just that: an "in training" period taking weeks to a month or more before the person (a) has studied all the materials of the post he is in training for; (b) has studied and knows his post in relationship to the org, his post in relationship to all other orgs and the Scn network; his post in relationship to himself; (c) has worked on the post long enough to know the post, its functions, lines, terminals, what particles flow through the post, what changes he makes to all these, what products he is expected to achieve and can achieve; (d) and before he has become a valuable and full contributive member of the org. (HCO PL 21 July 71 II)

APPROPRIATION, the allocation or setting aside of funds for a specific use such as payment of bills or building up of reserves etc.

A PRIORI DECISIONS, decisions based on opinion or theory as opposed to those based on experience or practical knowledge. Also known as armchair decisions.

APTITUDE FOR WORK, the degree of simplicity with which a person is able to do all aspects of his job and his willingness to assume responsibility for it. This is not an inherent quality but is a result of careful training and apprenticeship and taking the time to learn how to do the job.

APTITUDE TEST, mainly tests the ability of the testee to duplicate. It is also designed to measure the accident proneness (a manifestation of the tendency to succumb) of the testee. (HCO PL 3 Nov 70 II)

APTITUDE TEST, test designed to show up a person's potential for acquiring the knowledge or skill necessary to do a job. Different jobs have different requirements and thus aptitude tests can be devised to test mechanical aptitude, spatial orientation, clerical aptitude, etc.

ARBITER, a presiding justiciary who must be a minister appointed to the Chaplain's Court Unit. The chaplain (or the permanent or part time assisting **arbiter**) presides over all court hearings and renders judgment. (HCO PL 5 Aug 66 II)

ARBITRAGE, the purchase of securities on one market for quick resale on another market in order to take advantage of an advantageous price difference; a method of buying at a lower price to sell at a higher price for immediate profit.

ARBITRARY, 1. probably just a wrong why held in by law. And if so held in, it will crash the place. (HCO PL 13 Oct 70 II) **2.** a false order or datum entered into a situation or group. (OODs 16 Apr 70) **3.** anything which interrupts your ability to do your job. (7004C09SO) **4.** an interjected law or rule or decision which does not fit or is unnecessary. An **arbitrary** can be said to be something which actually violates natural law and which becomes, when held in place, an enforced lie. This causes endless board or governing body trouble whenever it occurs. (HCO PL 20 Oct 66 II) *—adj.* (a) derived from mere opinion or preference; not based on the nature of things; hence, capricious, uncertain, varying. (b) unrestrained in the exercise of will; of uncontrolled power or authority, absolute; hence, despotic, tyrannical. Usual forms of **arbitrary** are: disagreement, counter-policy, cross-order, other-intentionedness, counter-intention, no reality. (BPL 10 Nov 73 II)

ARBITRATION, a procedure for settling a dispute whereby the disputing parties agree on an impartial third party (called an arbitrator) who decides on the matter after a thorough examination of the issues presented by the disputing parties. The decision of the arbitrator is final and binding on the disputing parties.

ARBITRATION AGREEMENT, an agreement that if the need arises, an arbitrator agreeable to the disputing parties may be called in to settle the matter.

ARBITRATION BOARD, board set up to hear any complaints on examination fairness on Flag and CLOs. (Formerly HCO Board of Review). (ED 8 Flag)

ARBITRATION, COMPULSORY, arbitration in which the parties concerned are ordered to have their dispute referred to an arbitrator. Compulsory arbitration may be ordered by a state or federal agency, or may be required by law.

ARBITRATION, LABOR, a means of handling a labor dispute whereby the matter is submitted for decision to arbitrators agreeable to the disputing parties. The decision of the arbitrators becomes final and must be adhered to by the parties involved.

ARBITRATION, TERMINAL, a mediation agreed to by employer and employees as the final stage in settling a labor dispute.

ARBITRATION, VOLUNTARY, a form of arbitration where the conflicting parties willingly agree to settling the dispute by submitting it to arbitration.

ARBITRATOR, a person selected to examine and settle the issues involved between disputing parties. The arbitrator then recommends a handling which is binding on all parties involved.

ARC, a word from the initial letters of **Affinity, Reality, Communication**, which together equate to understanding. It is pronounced by stating its letters, **A-R-C.** To Scientologists it has come to mean good feeling, love or friendliness, such as "He was in **ARC** with his friend." One does not, however, fall out of **ARC**, he has an **ARC** break. (LRH Def. Notes)

ARC BREAK, a sudden drop or cutting of one's affinity, reality or communication with someone or something. Upsets with people or things come about because of a lessening or sundering of affinity, reality or communication or understanding. It's called an **ARC break** instead of an upset, because, if one discovers which of the three points of understanding have been cut, one can bring about a rapid recovery in the person's state of mind. It is pronounced by its letters **A-R-C break.** When an **ARC break** is permitted to continue over too long a period of time and remains in restimulation, a person goes into a "sad effect" which is to say they become sad and mournful, usually without knowing what is causing it. This condition is handled by finding the earliest **ARC break** on the chain, finding whether it was a **break** in **affinity, reality, communication**, or understanding and indicating it to the person, always, of course, in session. (LRH Def. Notes)

ARC BREAK AUDITOR, see ARC BREAK PROGRAM.

ARC BREAK PROGRAM, I routinely order orgs to pick up and smooth out at any org expense every **ARC broken** pc they can find in their files or areas as a special **program.** They put in an **ARC break** registrar who liaisons with accounts and with review and with CF searching for **ARC broken** pcs and students. A special genned-in full time auditor is put in review and at no charge to pcs is kept busy on **ARC breaks** only with it being an ethics offense to use him or the **ARC Break** Registrar for any other student, pc or duty. And you clean up the whole field from years and years back. This **ARC break** auditor cures the ARC breaks with Level III tech and sends the person to the usual registrar when done. This is his stable datum: if your pc is not smiling and happy at the end of session you are not auditing. The **ARC Break** Registrar has a special dual stat—how many **ARC broken** pcs have been found, in files, etc., how many contacted. The **ARC Break** Auditor has a special dual stat—how many **ARC breaks** (not pcs) found, how many handled. (ED 473 WW, 842 SH)

ARC BREAK REGISTRAR, see ARC BREAK PROGRAM.

ARC BREAKS FOUND/HANDLED, the **ARC Break** Auditor has a special dual stat—how many **ARC breaks** (not pcs) **found,** how many **handled.** (ED 473 WW, 842 SH)

ARC BROKEN, upset. (HCO PL 13 Mar 65 II)

ARC BROKEN FIELD, a **"field" ARC breaks** when you don't take an interest in individuals. Failure to comm to people, failure to lead them upward, failure to handle their upsets or get flubs repaired all lead to **ARC broken field.** If you don't do the basic usual case and training actions, if you ignore those people, if you don't write to them and care what happens to them you will **ARC break** them. (LRH ED 145 INT)

ARCHEOLOGY, 1. the study of the past as interpreted by bits and pieces of pottery, beads, skulls, graves, ancient structures. From these the type of civilization and custom is figured out. Anybody with a past life can figure out a lot from "a bit of pottery." (OODs 21 Mar 69) **2.** my definition of it: **archeology** is the art of reconstructing the past by finding material bits of it and figuring out the rest from that small evidence. (OODs 22 Mar 69)

ARCHIVES, rare items or old original issues of historical value go into specially prepared files marked **"archives."** (HCO PL 7 Feb 73 III)

ARC TRIANGLE, 1. the **A-R-C triangle**—its points being **affinity, reality** and **communication.** These are the three elements which combined give understanding. (HCO PL 18 Feb 72) **2.** consists of **affinity, reality** and **communication.** Of these communication is the most vital. (HCO PL 24 Feb 66)

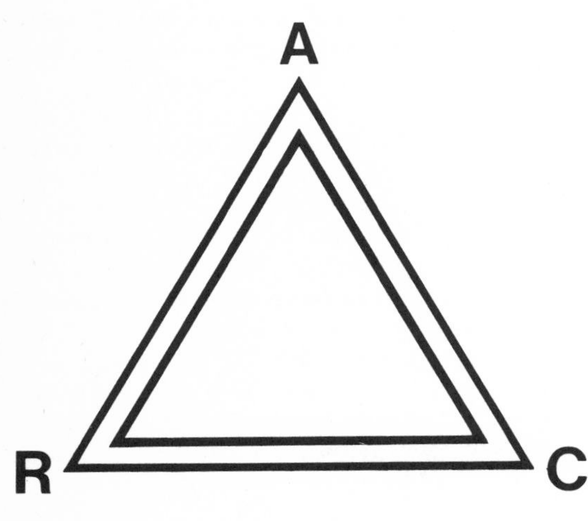

ARC Triangle

AREA, port and town and country (usage as in PRO **area** control). (FO 3094)

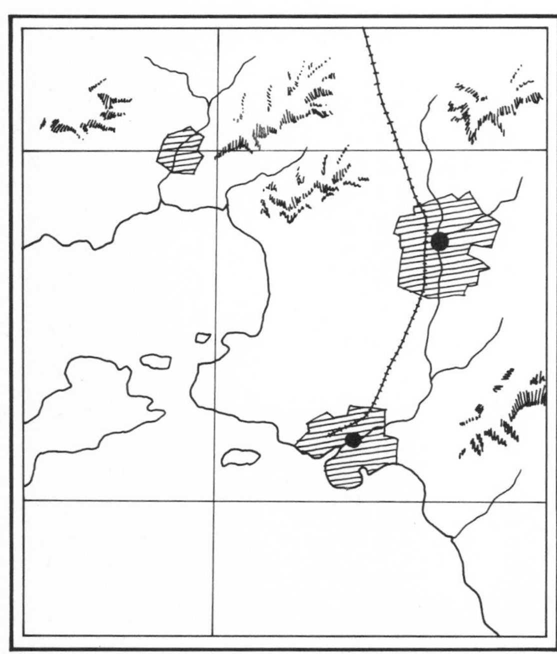

Area

AREA CASHIER AND COLLECTIONS SECTION, (in the Income Department) the **area cashier and collections** is total body traffic. It takes in all payments and **collections** in the **area**—meaning people who are on the premises. It must have its window, its own invoice machine, its own cash box and records, independent of the other sections. (HCO PL 18 Apr 69 II)

AREA CONCENTRATION, to saturate a specific geographical location with promotion or advertising.

AREA ESTATES ORG, the senior org over all **estates** functions for the whole of the new Flag Land Base. (ED 774R Flag)

AREA MAGAZINE, each and every org, but not franchise centers, may issue a magazine. Worldwide is to furnish two sets of copy monthly for such magazines. One set for the continental magazine, one set for a smaller **area magazine.** An **area magazine** should go to every person in the central files of an Area Org, unless restrained by an ethics order on that person cutting comm, regardless of the duplication of the continental org's mailings. (HCO PL 7 Dec 66, *Magazines Permitted All Orgs*)

AREA OBSERVATION, questions to provide Flag with a viewpoint of the area **observed.** (Flag Debriefer Org Area Observation Form 7 Aug 74) *Abbr.* Area Obs.

AREA OFFICE, now the **Area Office** services the area Central Organization, the central organization in that immediate area. And an **Area Office** means just this: it means "that HCO which does the work I have to do to keep that **Area Office** running." (5812C29)

AREA SEC, see HCO AREA SECRETARY.

ARIES, [The *Aries* was an ex air-sea rescue vessel. It was approximately 63 feet long and gas powered. She was used to train Sea Org members and was based in the Pacific area in 1970.]

ARMCHAIR DECISIONS, decisions that reflect a lack of experience or first hand knowledge of the area. Armchair decisions connote the idea of a person in authority making an arbitrary or opinionated decision on a matter when that person has virtually sat back in an armchair as a spectator and lacks experience to make the proper decision.

A ROUTING, goes directly across from own post to same org post in another org only. Do not go across to same post and then up or down. This is clearly marked at the top of all dispatches so routed **A Routing**, with no vias marked. (HCO PL 13 Mar 65 II)

ARRIVAL GI, total collected on arrival (of the person at the org) for the week. (BFO 119) [Only money collected after the person arrives at the org but before he starts any services may count on this stat.]

ART, **1.** (basic definition) **art** is a word which summarizes the quality of communication. (HCOB 30 Aug 65) **2.** **art** simply is an assistance to communication. The point where it communicates is the point where it's finished. (ESTO 9, 7203C05 SO I) **3.** it's an acceptable communication. (FEBC 1, 7011C17 SO)

ARTICLES OF ASSOCIATION, the associative contract between a company and its stockholders that stipulates the powers of the board of directors and the legal structure of the company.

ARTICLES OF INCORPORATION, the written document submitted by persons establishing a corporation and filed with state administrative authorities, requesting permission to operate a particular kind of business giving its corporate name, address, names of parties incorporating and amount of investment and stock to be issued.

ART OF PUBLIC RELATIONS, consists of how the truth is told and how the lie is disproven. (HCO PL 27 Oct 74)

ASIA, *Excalibur.* (FO 3192) [For a short time the ship *Excalibur* was called the *Asia.*]

AS IS, this refers to the condition something is presently in. Damaged or used goods are often sold as is at reduced prices under the condition that the buyer waives any claims against the seller after the transaction.

ASK OFF LGL, a person who says or writes in "to stop sending me information or letters" and who threatens **legal** action such as going to the police if mailings continue, is removed from the mailing list. His address plate is marked **ask off lgl** and is put into a separate drawer which is never activated until the person writes to "Put me back on" and also has clearance to be put back on the list from the A/G. (BPL 6 Dec 72)

ASK OFFS, persons who **ask off** mailing lists. (BPL 6 Dec 72)

ASR MASTER CARD FILE, a **file** which contains in alphabetical order one 5" x 8" card for each person that is **advance scheduled** and for when. The card is made out after a person has been **advance scheduled** and sent a **reg** pack. It is then filed in the **ASR master card file** for easy future reference and kept up-to-date. Having this card enables persons to be located easily and know if they are **advance scheduled** and for when without having to look all through the reservations book. (HCO PL 18 Feb 73 I)

ASSENT FORM, see PARENT OR GUARDIAN ASSENT FORMS.

ASSESSMENT, 1. a determination of the value of property, goods, etc., for taxation purposes. 2. the amount (of taxes, damages or a fine) calculated as owing.

ASSET, something of value owned by the organization at the end of the financial period concerned. (BPL 14 Nov 70 III)

ASSETS, CAPITAL, any assets of a long term or permanent nature such as land, buildings, machinery, etc., which may be subjected to continued use. Also called fixed assets.

ASSETS, CURRENT, a measure of what assets can be converted into cash readily or within a short period of time. Cash, short term investments, present inventory of stock or goods and accounts receivable usually make up current assets. Also called floating assets.

ASSETS, FIXED, 1. items used in current operations that have value and which would take a minimum of a year to convert into cash if they were sold for what it is worth. 2. land, buildings, machinery, industrial installations, tools, office equipment, etc., bought as a long term investment by a business and used in the manufacture of goods or delivery of services; capital assets.

ASSETS, FLOATING, see ASSETS, CURRENT.

ASSETS, HIDDEN, assets which are not immediately seen or especially one which is visible but its true value is not seen in an examination of the balance sheet. This applies especially to property which has had an incorrect figure of value assigned to it less than its current worth.

ASSETS, INTANGIBLE, such items as good will and patents which while they do not have tangible presence, are considered to be of value and thus appear as an asset on a company's balance sheet.

ASSETS, LIQUID, cash in banks or on hand as well as any securities which can be converted without delay into cash.

ASSETS, NET CURRENT, see CAPITAL, WORKING.

ASSETS, QUICK, cash, money in the bank, call loans, securities or other current assets that can be converted quickly into cash.

ASSETS, TANGIBLE, material assets that have physical existence and are appraisable.

ASSET STRIPPING, the purchase of a company by another in order to strip it of its assets and quickly dispose of them at a profit. No attempt is made to further develop the company. The sole view in mind is the liquidation of the purchased company's assets for financial gain.

ASSETS, WORKING, any other asset than a capital asset such as the raw materials, components, supplies, work-in-progress, completed products on hand and the sum represented by money owed to a company by its credit customers.

ASSIGN, to legally hand over a claim, right or property. The assignor is the person who is relieved of such while the assignee is the one who receives the claim, right or property.

ASSIGNING A COMPLEMENT, designating the post necessary to be held is what is meant by **assigning a complement.** (HCO PL 24 Jun 73)

ASSIGNMENT BOARD, a large cellulose or soft board at least three feet by five high exists in HGC Admin. Each auditor's name is printed on a card and each pc's name is put on a card. There is a column for each session period if there are more than one in the day. The auditors' names are in the column on the left on green cards and the pcs' are in the other columns on white cards. HGC Admin **assigns** and routes by moving cards on the **assignment board.** (HCO PL 4 Jul 65)

ASSIST, an **assist** in this definition means only auditing given after a physical injury or physical illness. Other auditing "to help case" or "to help perform duty" is not by this definition an **assist.** (FO 107)

ASSISTANT, a division and its personnel operating is the duty of the deputy. The valuable final product is the duty of the senior divisional officer. The deputy actually has products 1 and 3 (Org Series 10). The deputy system is not the apprentice system. In an apprentice system the deputy should be called an **assistant** to the actual post to keep the meaning straight. (FO 2660)

ASSISTANT, a person who helps or aids a superior and is learning the practical aspects of a job. Assistant is the term normally applied to white collar jobs, whereas apprentice is used similarly in the case of blue collar jobs.

ASSISTANT AIDE, 1. aide is the title of a Flag Staff Officer on Flag. **Assistant Aide** is the title in a CLO. The org equivalent in duties and hat is a divisional secretary. In the case of an aide it is understood that the person aided is the Commodore. In the case of an **assistant aide,** the person aided is the Flag Aide (CBO 52) **2.** (CLOs) each **assistant aide** of a bureau has the external to orgs and internal to the CLO functions of the bureau and its branches and sections. (FBDL 12)

ASSISTANT CAPTAIN FOR ESTATES, the **Assistant Captain for Estates** is there as back-up to the Captain, particularly when the Captain is double-hatted as the CO FSO. He is answerable to the Captain in ship matters and is responsible for a well functioning E/R, deck and galley. He sets stat quotas, coordinates, organizes and establishes the areas. Additionally, he gets compliance to the Captain's PGMs, which must be approved by LRH Comm FSO and network seniors. (FO 3576RA)

ASSISTANT CS-6, there will be an **Assistant CS-6** in each FOLO over Bureau 6 and under the CO FOLO for administrative purposes. The purpose of this post is to help the Commodore expand Scn on this planet by proper assistance to CS-6 in expanding, enhancing, safeguarding and strengthening the Division 6 Network. The products of this post are: (a) valid compliances to CS-6 orders, (b) upstat Division 6s. (CBO 332) *Abbr.* A/CS-6.

ASSISTANT ESTO MAA, 1. the one who helps handle the Estos and cross checks on them and helps them and acts as liaison between them and the Ethics Officer or HCO terminals of the org. (HCO PL 14 Mar 72 I) **2.** is responsible for Estos. (HCO PL 6 Apr 72)

ASSISTANT ETHICS OFFICER, the title **Assistant Ethics Officer** is used to indicate **ethics officers** who have an in-charge over them. (HCO PL 20 Jun 68)

ASSISTANT FLAG QUALITY CONTROL OFFICER, established in Department 21, Personal Officer of LRH US within the Office of LRH US. The post is an extension of the Flag AVU Quality Control Office. It is held as a part-time duty, but it is understood that at any time that the duties of the post require full-time duty, the post becomes single hatted. It is under the LRH Comm US for administrative purposes only. The command line for the **Assistant Flag Quality Control Officer** is Quality Control Officer Flag, AVU Officer, LRH Personal Communicator, Commodore for orders and other business of the post. The purpose of the post is to see that Flag quality specifications are met on all Flag literature printed in the US, that all such are of top top top quality and that no badly printed promo or other literature of a downgraded nature gets through. (FO 3572)

ASSISTANT GUARDIAN, **1.** an **Assistant Guardian** can exist in any org that is big enough. It may not be worn as an additional hat. It is appointed only by the Guardian. The **Assistant Guardian** does not act as Guardian in the Guardian's absence but only forwards direct orders from the Guardian and collects data for the Guardian. An **Assistant Guardian** has no power of his own not derived from the Guardian's authority directly and so may not act independently without exact instructions from the Guardian. (HCO PL 1 Mar 66) **2.** it is a primary duty of the Guardian and **Assistant Guardians** to get policy followed and in such a way as to expand the org and not stop flows. (HCO PL 26 Sept 67) *Abbr.* A/G.

ASSISTANT GUARDIAN FOR FINANCE, the post of **Assistant Guardian for Finance** is established to help Ron bring solvency and sanity to Scn orgs by ensuring more is never spent than made and substantial reserves are built up. (HCO PL 8 Dec 68) *Abbr.* A/GF.

ASSISTANT GUARDIAN POLICY KNOWLEDGE, the Office of LRH org board is revised and updated to incorporate the former GO Tech and Policy Knowledge Bureaux functions into the Office of LRH. The former titles of A/G Tech and **A/G Policy Knowledge** now become those of "Keeper of Tech" and "Keeper of Policy" respectively. (HCO PL 1 Oct 73)

ASSISTANT GUARDIAN TECH, see ASSISTANT GUARDIAN POLICY KNOWLEDGE.

ASSISTANT LITERATURE AIDES, D/CS-2 for Literature heads the Flag Literature Unit under CS-2. **Assistant literature aides** are posted in FOLO Department 19s, under the D/CO FOLO for *local* administrative purposes, and on a direct command line from D/CS-2 for Literature. Every FOLO must have an **Assistant Literature Aide** posted single-hatted. The function of **Assistant Literature Aide** FOLO is to provide assistance to D/CS-2 for Literature in the way of data collection, manufacturing expediting and supervising and literature distribution and utilization expediting. (FO 3557)

ASSISTANT PRODUCTION AIDE, (A/CS-4) is the coordination authority of Data, Action, External Comm and Org Management Bureaux. The product is organizations. (FBDL 12)

ASSISTANT REGISTRAR, **1.** hot files from central files get written to by registrar and ARC breaks with the organization get cared for by the **Assistant Registrar.** (SEC ED 1, 15 Dec 58) **2.** the **Assistant Registrar** is mainly concerned with the past, that is she handles ARC breaks. She is concerned with finding out why people are upset with us or why they have stopped communicating with us. She re-establishes communication with people. (SEC ED 66, 30 Jan 59)

ASSISTANT TO THE ORG SEC FOR ACCOUNTS, manages the **Accounts** Unit and is in full charge of its personnel. (HCO PL 18 Dec 64, *Saint Hill Org Board*)

ASSISTANT TO THE SUPERCARGO, to prevent the Supercargo from continually going into non-existence, due to having many duties ashore and ship duties becoming neglected a new post is created—named, **Assistant to the Supercargo.** This person handles ship duties for the Supercargo while she is ashore and is to ensure the smooth running of the post. The Supercargo and **Assistant to the Supercargo** may never be ashore at the same time. **Assistant to the Supercargo** also handles all the clerical work: typing, filing, etc., and can also be ashore on duties providing the Supercargo remains aboard. (FO 489)

ASSIST AUDITOR, he's just an **Assist Auditor.** He gives touch **assists** and runs out the last automobile accident and the delivery and something, something, something. That's all he does. It's usually one of the better word clearers. He's also assigned the double hat of **Assist Auditor.** (ESTO 11, 7203C06 SO I)

ASSOCIATED COMPANY, see COMPANY, ASSOCIATED.

ASSOCIATE MEMBER, **1.** (Gung-ho Group) one must sharply differentiate in giving out membership cards between the contributor of money or things and the action member, by always calling the money contributor an **"associate"** or "patron" and the time and effort contributor a "full member" or a "true group member" or an "active member" on the card. An active member should have a full credentials card with picture, thumb print and description. An **associate** just a name typed on a card. (HCO PL 3 Dec 68) **2.** giving money or things to a group are both a form of participation and contribution. But while this is an important matter, it does not involve actual action. Thus a contributor of money or objects to a group is yet withholding himself and his time. One should seek contribution of money and things. But the status granted for this is that of patron or associate, not of a true member of the group. (HCO PL 3 Dec 68) **3.** receives no discounts or services, pin and card only. (HCO PL 26 Oct 59) **4.** a member without time limit of Scn. An **associate member** does not receive publications but does receive a pin and a membership card. (PAB 74)

ASSOCIATION SECRETARY, **1.** in early days there was an HCO Secretary in charge of the functions of the first three divisions (Executive, HCO, Dissemination) and an **Association Secretary** in charge of the functions of the last four divisions. The org board evolved further and the HCO Executive Secretary became the person in charge of the functions of the first three divisions and the Organization Executive Secretary the last four. In the Sea Org these titles became Supercargo and Chief Officer but the functions were similar. (HCO PL 9 May 74) **2.** Organization Secretaries (US and Saint Hill) or **Association Secretaries** (Commonwealth and South Africa). (HCO PL 5 Mar 65 II) **3.** the **Association Secretary** runs the Central Organization. He is usually assisted by a secretary who expedites his communications, writes his letters and gets in his reports for the OIC and keeps it. (HCO PL 20 Dec 62) **4.** proper operation, willing performance of duty of its executives and personnel, its ample financial solvency and general high effectiveness of the technical and administrative functions of the Central Organization are all the responsibility of the **Association Secretary.** (HCO PL 20 Dec 62) **5.** the **Association Secretary** is looked upon to keep the organization in existence and functioning at a high level. HCO helps but the final responsibility of keeping an organization going is the **Association Secretary's.** (HCO PL 14 Feb 61, *The Pattern of a Central Organization*) **6.** the **Association Secretary** or Organization Secretary has full authority over his or her organization and personnel. It is his or her task to cope when policy does not exist, to hold the form of the organization, to keep it busy and prosperous and its morale high. (HCO PL 31 Jan 61, *Spheres of Influence*) **7.** procures persons, puts them bodily on post, puts the person's hands on the equipment or mest of the job, handles pay, supervises the actual conduct of the work (gets the work done), sees that the proper hours are kept, etc., and changes, transfers, or dismisses the personnel. (HCO PL 27 Feb 59) **8.** purpose: to execute policies and orders. To coordinate organizational activities. To care for legal and public concerns of the organization. (HCO London 9 Jan 58) *Abbr.* Assoc Sec, Assn Sec.

ASSURANCE, often used as a synonym of insurance. Assurance policies normally cover the occurrence of inevitable events which will occur at an unknown time. Life assurance is such an example. Insurance policies connote protection against random or chance mishaps occurring at any time. Fire or theft insurance is an example.

ATHENA, **1.** formerly the *Avon River.* (6903C27 SO) **2.** was phased over from a training vessel to a cramming vessel on 19 Jan 1972. The basic plan was to have a place where a rapid (one week) cramming action can take place for SO and EU Org staff members to gen them in on their posts and scene and on such things as translated tape use, tape recorder use, correct auditing comm cycle, and other short cycle matters and expertise they vitally need in their orgs. (FO 3132)

A to I Hat

A TO I HAT, **hat** content. A **hat** must contain: **(a)** a *purpose* of the post. **(b)** its relative position on the organizing board. **(c)** a write-up of the post (done usually by people who have held it before relief and when so done it has no further authority than advice). **(d)** a checksheet of all the policy letters, bulletins, advices, manuals, books and drills applicable to the post (as in a course checksheet). **(e)** a full pack of the written materials plus tapes of the checksheet plus manuals or equipment or books. (**f**) a copy of the organizing board of the portion of the org to which the post belongs. (**g**) a flow chart showing what particles are received by the post and what changes the post is expected to make in them and to where the post routes them. (**h**) the product of the post. (**i**) the statistic of the post, the statistic of the section, the statistic of the department and division to which the post belongs. (HCO PL 22 Sept 70)

A TO J, types of persons who have caused us considerable trouble. These persons can be grouped under "potential trouble sources." (HCO PL 27 Oct 64)

ATTESTATION, 1. to assert the validity of by oath or testimonial. 2. the signing of a written statement that asserts the validity, occurrence, genuineness, value, completion, etc., of something. 3. the signature itself.

ATTITUDE, the opinion one holds or the behavior one expresses toward some person, place, thing or symbol as a result of the concept he has of it. Attitudes can be changed through public relations, advertising, education, realization or the like.

ATTITUDE SURVEY, a survey designed to isolate the attitudes a person has to new or existing products, other people, the organization he works for, etc., etc.

ATTRITION, 1. a gradual breaking down due to friction or erosion. 2. a reduction in strength due to constant stress. 3. the reduction of staff in an organization due to unavoidable circumstances such as old age, retirement, death, etc. 4. a gradual decrease in salary levels paid due to hiring personnel at lower wages than their predecessors. This occurs because new staff do not qualify for the additional wages provided in an incremental payment system due to lack of seniority, proven value, etc.

AUDIO AID, any piece of equipment that records, reproduces, intensifies or carries sound over a distance which is used as an aid to education, work, research or the like. Tape recorders, microphones and PA systems are some examples.

AUDIO-VISUAL AID, any piece of equipment that records, reproduces, intensifies or carries both sound and visual images over a distance, which is used for education, work, research, etc. These can be used to instruct on how to do a job, inform one of company procedures or many other things. Television, motion pictures or slide films are examples.

AUDIT, 1. the process whereby an auditor inspects the accounts of a company to ensure they are correctly recorded, tallied and summarized and that profit, loss and expenditure figures have been honestly represented. A company may have an independent auditor audit its accounts as a check on the company's own financial and accounting systems. 2. any systematic study and evaluation of a problem or situation.

AUDIT BY ROTATION, procedure for auditing the accounts of a company in which the major parts of the accounts are examined in depth by rotation over a period of years as opposed to trying to audit all of a company's accounts regularly each year. Often auditors will take care not to establish a predictable pattern of handling any company's or group of companies' accounts.

AUDIT CYCLE, the period (usually about three years) during which an audit by rotation covers all the sections of the concern being audited.

AUDITED AT CAUSE, you have heard that a pc has to be **audited at cause.** This means he has to be **audited** in a way which puts him **at cause** over his bank and environment. Posts are the same way. (OODs 26 May 75)

AUDITING FLUBS, consist of corny things like running a rud but no F/N, failure to flatten a chain, bad TRs, auditing over out-ruds, chopping the pc before full end phenomena is attained. Evaluation or even chatter after the session can upset a pc that ended session on F/N VGIs. (HCO PL 8 Sept 70R)

AUDITING RUDIMENTS CHECKSHEET, used in straightening up HGC pcs or cancelling sessions on students. The **checksheet** should be used by Ds of P, supervisors and instructors seeking to establish whether or not the HGC or student auditor got the **rudiments** in during a session. (HCO PL 1 Jun 62)

AUDITING SECTION, **1.** that **section** of a training course where **auditing** occurs. It is not where auditing is taught. It is that **section** where **auditing** is experienced, as an auditor, as a preclear. Auditing is taught in theory and practical. It is only guided in the **auditing section.** (HCO PL 21 Oct 62) **2.** the student when he has passed minimal theory and practical for an auditing class, is then *also* assigned to the **auditing section.** While working in the **auditing section,** the student completes the requirements of the level he or she is auditing in. The **Auditing Section** is there to instill the fact that standard auditing gets results, that only results are acceptable and that extraordinary solutions get bad results. (HCO PL 14 May 62)

AUDITING SESSION, a precise period of time during which the auditor listens to the preclear's ideas about himself. (HCO PL 21 Aug 63)

AUDITING SUPERVISOR, 1. the post of **Auditing Supervisor** is abolished since all instructors are doing **auditing supervision** as a training measure. The missing action is that of Case Supervisor. (HCO PL 24 Jan 64, *Case Supervisor*) **2.** the **Auditing** Section is headed by the **Auditing Supervisor** (usually the Director of Training). The **Auditing Supervisor** does most of his or her inspection by studying auditing reports written by the auditor. In the event of no gain or worse, the **Auditing Supervisor** investigates the auditor's auditing in terms of gross auditing errors and finds and corrects these by close inspection of the next session. The **Auditing Supervisor** is not there to crack cases. The **Auditing Supervisor** is there only to get good auditing done. His or her attention is on the auditor, not the pc, an important fact which, if overlooked, will stagnate auditing results. (HCO PL 14 May 62) **3.** on the Saint Hill Special Briefing Course and in academies, supervision of the **Auditing** Section is done by the **Auditing Supervisor** and Auditing Instructor or instructors. The **Auditing Supervisor** and instructors are not there to audit cases. The **Auditing Supervisor** (or in some cases, the Course Supervisor as at Saint Hill) assigns all sessions and teams. There are three sources of observing auditing used by the **Auditing Supervisor** and instructors. These are: (a) direct observation of the session; (b) study of the auditor's report; (c) observation of the preclear. The **Auditing Supervisor** combines all three, giving the most time to (a) direct observation of the session. (HCO PL 21 Oct 62) **4.** ensures students can audit. (HCO PL 15 May 63)

AUDITING TIME, **time** spent in sessions and does not include doing the folder admin which is done at once after the session and sent to case supervisor. (FO 2151)

AUDIT, INTERNAL, a relatively independent investigation activity within an organization carried on by an internal audit executive or group as an aid to management, having the responsibility of verifying the reliability of records and reporting on the financial effectiveness of programs and operations.

AUDIT LEDGER, in this **ledger** one can see how much was banked, how much was drawn out of the bank, what the income was, what the money was spent on, and how much you have in the bank. In other words, you have all your money affairs condensed into eight sheets of paper instead of spread over thousands upon thousands of invoices, vouchers, checks and other pieces of paper of different types. (HCO PL 10 Oct 70 I)

AUDIT, MANAGEMENT, an analysis and recommendation by a qualified and impartial person, such as an outside management consultant, of the quality of management in a business. It looks at how efficiently the current management handles finances, personnel, personnel training, production, sales, planning, organization, etc. In analyzing this it usually gets around to looking at the management personnel as well. The resulting recommendation shows the current picture and recommends an appropriate handling to increase the efficiency of management.

AUDIT, MARKETING, in overall marketing planning, the review and appraisal of marketing strategy, current services, activities and accomplishments.

Auditor (Def. 1)

AUDITOR, 1. Scn processing is done on the principle of making an individual look at his own existence, and improve his ability to confront what he is and where he is. An **auditor** is the person trained in the technology and whose job it is to ask the person to look, and get him to do so. The word **auditor** is used because it means one who listens, and a Scn **auditor** does listen. (*Scn 0-8*, p. 14) **2.** an **auditor** (literally: one who listens) is a trained Scn minister or minister-in-training, who delivers Scn or Dn **auditing.** (BPL 24 Sept 73RA XIII)

AUDITOR, that person who inspects the accounts of a company to ensure they are correctly recorded, tallied and summarized and that profit and loss figures have been honestly represented as such.

AUDITOR CONFERENCE, normally follows directly after the departmental meeting. Keep **conference** brief. Ensure all **auditors** adequately set up with pcs for the day (scheduled by Director of Processing). Set production targets for each unit **auditor** daily. (Director of Processing sets overall **auditing** hours and completion targets for each unit.) (BPL 23 Nov 72)

AUDITOR CORRECTION LIST, HCO Bulletin 27 March 1972, *Auditor Correction List, Study Correction List 3.* This one **corrects auditors** who are having a rough time. (LRH ED 257 INT)

AUDITOR CORRESPONDENTS, correspondents needed in every org to provide ample materials for use in the *Auditor* so that the *Auditor* can show the world successful Scn and Scientologists and make them want more Scn. (LRH ED 159R-I)

AUDITOR ESTIMATION TEST, general **test** questions used directly or to make up **tests** for HGC auditor proficiency or for students or internes seeking to qualify as HGC **auditors.** It may be required of any HGC *en masse* at any time to rate the tech proficiency of that department. The **test** is verbal and accompanied by the **auditor** having to demonstrate with the examiner marking the form used in the **test.** (HCO PL 21 Sept 65 II)

AUDITOR-IN-CHARGE OF CO-AUDIT, those terminated from the SHSBC may join the **Co-audit** Unit, listing their goals to Clear. One of themselves is to be **in charge** of the unit and will be known as the **Auditor-In-Charge of Co-audit.** (HCO PL 20 Sept 62)

AUDITOR MAGAZINE, see AUDITOR, THE.

AUDITOR MAJOR ISSUE, it is the vital statistics motif of the original *Auditor,* containing proper ads and specializing in the names and faces of people, graduates from SH and academies, etc.; long lists, lots of lists of names, even in tiny type, as provided by correspondents in orgs and by SH. This **issue** is a fat *Auditor.* (HCO PL 25 Nov 68)

AUDITOR MINOR ISSUE, an *Auditor* **minor** is sent out to the entire list we have every two months. This is a thinner, more elementary, *Auditor.* (HCO PL 25 Nov 68)

AUDITOR NEWS OFFICER, the executive who handles and supervises all correspondents for the editor, responsible to see that the editors are supplied with more than enough on-policy materials for issues. (BPL 29 Nov 68R)

AUDITOR'S CLUB, club for **auditors** and for those who wish to be **auditors.** It has free membership. Those belonging to this **club** are entitled to (1) all mailings of the *Auditor* magazine, (2) **auditor's club** identification card for special admission to special functions, (3) Gradation Chart to show the next step as an auditor, (4) mailings of new HCOBs up to their training level, (5) complete information pack on training, (6) personal help of the **Auditor's Club** Reg in speeding their progress as a fully trained auditor. (SO ED 41 INT)

AUDITOR'S DAY, in recognation of all the auditors throughout the world, **Auditor's Day** is officially established. It is to be held each year on the second Sunday of September. This **day** is set aside for any **auditor,** anywhere, so he can receive the full acknowledgement of his or her valuable abilities and actions in the freeing of man. He can receive this validation in many different forms and ways. This is his day. (BPL 12 Jul 73R II)

AUDITORS DIVISION, the Enrollment Division is transferred from HCO (Saint Hill) Ltd. to HCO (WW) Ltd., and is renamed **Auditors Division.** The head of the **Auditors Division** is the Director of Auditors. The purpose of the **Auditors Division** is to make all **auditors** well trained and successful. Enrollment in academies, proper certification, enrollment at Saint Hill are all functions of the **Auditors Division.** Central files and address comes under the **Auditors Division.** *Saint Hill News* comes under the **Auditors Division.** Keeping the Saint Hill course fully enrolled is the responsibility of the **Auditors Division.** (HCO PL 11 Mar 64, *Departmental Changes Auditors Division*)

AUDITOR, THE, 1. the Journal of Scn. Journal means: a daily newspaper; a periodical dealing especially with matters of current interest. (HCO PL 27 Nov 68) **2.** a magazine issued at Saint Hill called the *Auditor,* the Saint Hill journal of the Auditors Division. (HCO PL 11 Mar 64, *Auditors Division New HCO WW Organization*) **3.** the *Auditor* magazine is the number one main income getter in the long run for SH Orgs. Aside from letters and advance registration and selectee advice packs planned in advance, on-policy, hard-sell *Auditors* that offer the services of Saint Hill with heavy impact and that are mailed all at once on schedule are the backbone of SHs. (LRH ED 159R-I INT) [*The Auditor* is published by the Saint Hill organizations.]

AUDITOR TRAINEE PROGRESS BOARD, a vertical **auditor trainee progress board** is kept by the Interne Supervisor. This has a space under each of the headings, left to right. Boxes along the top, left to right, serve to indicate the exact action the **trainee** is doing. The **trainee's** name is on a tab that is pinned to the space. The name tab is merely dated each time it is moved to the right. Thus the Interne Supervisor can chase up any faltering student. (HCOB 7 Jan 72)

AUDIT, PERSONNEL, a periodic evaluation of a company's personnel policies and practices in relationship to all its employees, to ascertain how closely they approximate reliable personnel administration and to what extent they are adhering to the organization's original tenets.

AUDIT, SALES, an accounting of sales by product, size of product, methods and locations of distribution, heaviest purchasing periods, replacement rate, etc.

AUTHORITARIAN, *—n.* a person who gives orders without reasons. A person who arbitrarily tries to think for others instead of letting them think for themselves. (*HTLTAE*, p. 118)

AUTHORITARIAN ACTIONS, arbitrary **actions.** (*DAB* Vol. II, 1951-52, p. 141)

AUTHORITARIANISM, is little more than a form of hypnotism. Learning is forced under threat of some form of punishment. A student is stuffed with data which has not been individually evaluated. (*DAB*, Vol. II, 1951-52, p. 9)

AUTHORITY, the degree of power or right to give orders, demand obedience or assume control that is vested in a specific job. Authority cannot function properly without responsibility.

AUTHORITY AND VERIFICATION UNIT, **1.** is going in at LRH Personal Communicator level so that **authorities and verifications** of correctness are done at that level instead of my own. (OODs 14 Apr 72) **2.** the **unit** at Flag that does exactly those functions. (HCO PL 28 Jul 73RA) **3.** orders may only be issued from Flag to orgs or areas or any part thereof whether by dispatch or telex, with proper and passed evaluation. An area will sag if: (1) the evaluation it is being handled on is not severely pure per Data Series, (2) it receives orders that are part of no evaluation at all. The second is by far the most serious. Only if the Data Series is in full and exact use will a consequent increase of SO and Scn strength and stats occur. This is the mission of **AVU. AVU** sees that: (a) needed evaluations are done, (b) evaluations are severely pure per Data Series and are on the exact scene, (c) that barriers to (a) and (b) are rapidly called to attention and are properly handled per (a) or (b). (FO 3149-1) **4.** the **Authorization and Verification Unit** is in Department 21 (Source). All actions must have the **unit's authorization** before they are taken. This is one of the keys to the workability of the multiple viewpoint management system. (BPL 13 Feb 73R) **5.** it is the point at which all Staff, FB and other evaluations and resulting plans, programs, projects and orders are **authorized and verified** for issue. The unit has the responsibility of catching and handling all errors in such traffic before they are issued. (CBO 301-2) *Abbr.* AVU.

AUTOCRATIC CONTROL, tight control exercised over a company or part of it by the person in charge. The person acts similarly to an autocrat who must have absolute control and maintains a domineering status over those below him.

AUTO-EVALUATION SLIPS, on the American Personality Analysis or the Oxford Capacity Analysis, there are the personality traits, lettered from A to J. For purposes of auto-evaluation, the total span of the top (+100) to the bottom (—100) for each trait has been divided into sections numbered 1, 2, 3 and 4. These sections are divided as follows: from +70 and above to +100 is section 1. From +20 and above to +69 is section 2. From —40 and above to +19 is section 3. From —100 and above to —39 is section 4. Each trait therefore has four possible **auto-evaluation** cards. The cards, say, for happy, trait B, are lettered B1, B2, B3 and B4. According to the score made by the person tested, a card is selected on the basis of that person's score. A person scoring +50 on active would have card E2 selected scoring +10 on appreciative would have card I3 selected, and so on. These **auto-evaluation slips** and the graph are part of the eight unit automatic evaluation packet for the PE foundation. (See HCO Policy Letter of March 2, 1961, *Automatic Evaluation Packet For PE Foundation*) (BPL 28 Apr 61R)

AUTO FINANCING, the concept that if a company establishes the right profit margin it can meet the costs of expenditure on capital assets without having to rely on financing.

AUTOMATED, **automatically** run by machinery, not people. (HCO PL 30 Aug 70)

Automated

AUTOMATIC EVALUATION PACKET, the following items are the current extent of the **evaluation packet.** It is intended that when a person is tested, his test is marked and **automatically evaluated**, and the **evaluation** (with the literature tentatively listed below) is sent to the **evaluator**. When the person tested comes in for his or her **evaluation** appointment, **evaluation** is done from the **automatic evaluation** strictly in accordance with the model **evaluation** script. The person is then given the whole **packet** and is directed to the registrar or whatever routing is arranged. The **packet** is his or her property. (1) graph, **evaluation** slips. (2) form letter giving IQ and future. (3, 4, 5, 6 and 7 are letterpress sheets.) (3) What is Scn? (4) the cheapest way—PE Co-audit. (5) the fastest way—individual processing. (6) the educational way—books, training. (7) the state of release. (8) two free tickets for a test they can give their friends. (HCO PL 2 Mar 61)

AUTOMATIC REGISTRAR, **automatic registrar** machines are used so enrollment in training and in individual processing can be effected at once by any visitor. An **automatic registrar** has all the information about training or processing and all the forms and routing displayed on a board with pigeonholes. It is prominently displayed. One is for training. One is for processing. Each is a full sales talk and has all forms. (HCO PL 23 Jan 61)

AUTOMATION, 1. the reduction of the need for human labor in an activity because of the introduction of self operating machinery to do the same functions. 2. the use of electronic devices and servomechanisms to perform physical or mental tasks which then obviate the need for people to do such. Modern security systems are an example with their use of electronic sensing devices to open or close doors, sound alarms or silently alert security personnel remote from the area.

AUTOMATIZATION, the use of machines to either replace or assist human control.

AUTONOMOUS, it operates independently of local control and is under the direct control of its own seniors. (BPL 10 Feb 72R I)

AUTONOMOUS ACTION, something dreamed up all by themselves, pushed forward all by themselves, not coordinated in any way with any other management anyplace. (7208C02 SO)

AUTONOMOUS UNIT, an **autonomous unit** is totally self-sufficient and operates with no higher orders. (FBDL 12)

AUTONOMOUS WORK GROUPS, see GROUPS, AUTONOMOUS WORK.

AUTONOMY, "self-government" and "independence." In other words areas or orgs operated independently on self-government. (FO 2534)

AVERAGE, 1. the figure that results from adding a quantity of figures and dividing the sum by the number of figures added together. The average of the numbers 1, 2, 3 and 4 is 2.5. 2. the general tendency, attitude or figure indicated by the total of related figures, statistics or data available.

AVERAGES, various formulas for measuring the trend of stock prices with built-in devices to compensate for stock splits and dividends.

AVOIDABLE COSTS, see COSTS, AVOIDABLE.

AVON, the (ship) *Avon River.* (BO 11, Circa 10 Jun 67)

AVON RIVER, **1.** yacht *Avon River.* (BO 14, 6 Jun 67) **2.** the *Avon River* remains the flagship and her company are Flag personnel. (FO 327) [The *Avon River*, later renamed the *Athena*, was a converted North Sea trawler approximately 145 feet long and steam driven.]

AVU AUTHORIZATION OFFICER, the purposes of **AVU Authorization Officer** are (1) to receive and **authorize** submissions which are on-origin and on-policy and which apply the relevant Dn and Scn technology to the subject of the submission. (2) to bring about corrections and improvements in submissions so as to increase effectiveness by increasing numbers of exact applications of technology. (CBO 230)

AVU VERIFICATION OFFICER, the purposes of **AVU Verification Officer** are (1) to **verify** in evaluations submitted that the data as stated does exist and has been taken fully into account according to existing PLs and FOs. (2) to **verify** that the statistics as stated in evaluations are correct and do exist and do require evaluation. (3) to **verify** that completed handlings have brought about the ideal scene and that opportunities for further expansion are taken. (4) to **verify** that no necessary evaluation has been omitted. (CBO 225)

AWARD OF MERIT, (The Franchise **Award of Merit**) the **Award of Merit** is an **award** given quarterly to those missions who have produced consistently high statistics. The award, introduced in 1965, has been successful in encouraging production in missions. One **award**=one voucher equal to ten currency units. We define a currency unit as the full cost of one auditing hour at the local per policy cost. (At this time for example this is $50 in the U.S.) Each voucher may be exchanged as credit for ten currency units against any training at any org, Saint Hill or AO. (BPL 10 Sept 65R)

AWARE, marked by realization, perception or knowledge. (OODs 27 Apr 72)

AWARENESS, is the ability to perceive the existence of. (OODs 27 Apr 72)

AXIOMS OF EDUCATION, the logics of Dn are the science of **education.** Those are the **axioms of education.** (OS 2, 5610C18)

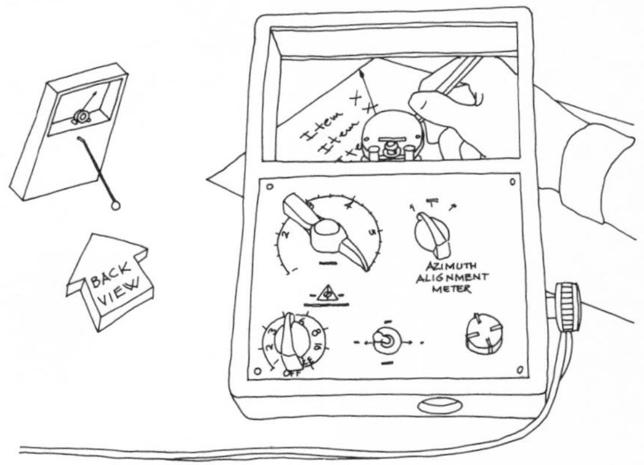

Azimuth Meter

AZIMUTH METER, a good auditor is expected to see his meter, pc and worksheet all at one time. No matter what he is doing he should always notice any **meter** movement if the meter needle moves. If he cannot do this he should use an **Azimuth meter** and not put paper over its glass but should do his worksheet looking through the glass at his pen and the paper—the original design purpose of the **Azimuth meter**. Then even while writing he sees the **meter** needle move as it is in his line of vision. (HCOB 28 Feb 71)

B

BABIES, **1.** anyone below six years old is to be called "little children" or **"babies."** (FO 1630) **2.** (**babies**—small children) people who are under six years of age who are not cadets. (FO 3167)

Babies

BACHELOR OF SCIENTOLOGY COURSE, **1.** the Academy also teaches an upper level course once or more a year known as the **B. Scn** (Hubbard Clearing Scientologist) course. (HCO PL 20 Dec 62) **2.** the tapes for **B. Scn** and HCS courses are now as follows: 5th London ACC tapes, 21st US supplementary tapes. These are the total data given in these units. (HCO PL 10 Mar 59) **3.** the standard **B. Scn**/HCS course is in actuality the 20th ACC. The tapes to be used are the 20th ACC tapes. The texts are *Scientology Clear Procedure, Issue One* and *ACC Clear Procedure* as published in booklet form. The **B. Scn**/HCS course is five weeks in length. If comm course and upper indocs have not been covered by the student, the course becomes seven weeks in length. (HCOB 26 Dec 58) **4. B. Scn** (UK) or Hubbard Clearing Scientologist (US). (HCO PL 12 Feb 61) *Abbr.* B. Scn.

BACKFLASH, an unnecessary response to an order. This can get fairly wicked. They are not acknowledgments, they are comments or refutals. Example: "sell the bricks" as an order, is replied to by "bricks are hard to sell" or "we should have sold them yesterday." This is a disease peculiar to only a few staff members. They cannot receive an order directly and are seeking to be part of the communication, not the recipient. This goes so far as senseless "wilco's" or "I'll take care of it" when the executive only wants to know "is it done?" (HCO PL 10 Apr 63)

Backlog (Def. 1)

BACKLOG, *n.* **1.** an increasing accumulation of tasks unperformed or materials not processed. (HCO PL 26 Jan 72 I) **2.** (AVU) the definition of a **backlog** is anything in AVU for more than an hour. (CBO 340R) **3.** a **backlog** is negative production.

(HCO PL 19 Mar 72 II) **4.** for Tech Services a **backlog** is any service paid in full but not delivered. The service isn't delivered until it is completed. (BPL 8 Dec 72R)—*v.* to accumulate as a **backlog.** (HCO PL 26 Jan 72 I)

BACKLOGGING, a type of dev-t where if traffic or bodies begin to be **backlogged,** one can stall completely just handling the queries about the **backlog** without getting anything really done. (HCO PL 27 Jan 69)

BACK ORDERS, orders received for items temporarily out of stock. This is different from backlog in that backlog applies to all unfilled orders. Backlog accumulates where orders arrive at a faster rate than staff and equipment can process them.

BACK PAY, wages or additional wages owed to an employee for past work due to errors in the calculation of wages, changes in legislation awarding retroactive wage payments, arbitration awards, etc. Also called retroactive pay.

BACK-SELLING, a form of promotion that skips certain progressive steps in the sales chain of a product (manufacturer to wholesaler to retailer to consumer) such as a manufacturing company that promotes its products either directly to consumers or directly to retailers so that they in turn will demand the product from wholesalers.

BAD ACTION, is really just an out-point. (OODs 11 Apr 72)

BAD COMMUNICATION LINE, a **bad communication line** would be too slow, one on which messages become altered or get delivered to, or seen by, the wrong people, or where the message arrived in incomprehensible form or not at all. It could also be one that was so expensive it could not be used freely. Here is an uncertain, balky or dangerous **comm line.** (FO 2528)

BAD CONTROL, we define **bad control** as not-**control,** or as an unknown attempt at **control** without actually effecting **control.** (*POW,* p. 44)

BAD DEBT, a debt which is known or believed to be uncollectible and is written off as a loss.

BAD EXECUTIVE, he simply tries to do several posts, thus leaving many posts unsupervised and leaving many details uncoordinated and depriving staff of necessary liaison and supervision amongst the various posts. He takes the juicy tidbits which require "command decision" away from the posts and leaves each post a naked drudgery of petty detail; in other words, he scoops off the cream and does, to a slight degree, each of the jobs around and thus brings about a state of irresponsibility on the various terminals. (HCO PL 30 Oct 62)

BAD INDICATOR, what is a **bad indicator** really? It is merely an out-point taken from the five primary out-points. It is not "bad news" or "entheta" or a rumor. The "bad news" could easily be a falsehood and is an out-point, because it is false bad news! "Good" news when it is a falsehood is an out-point! (HCO PL 15 May 70 II, *Data Series No. 5, Information Collection*) *Abbr.* BI.

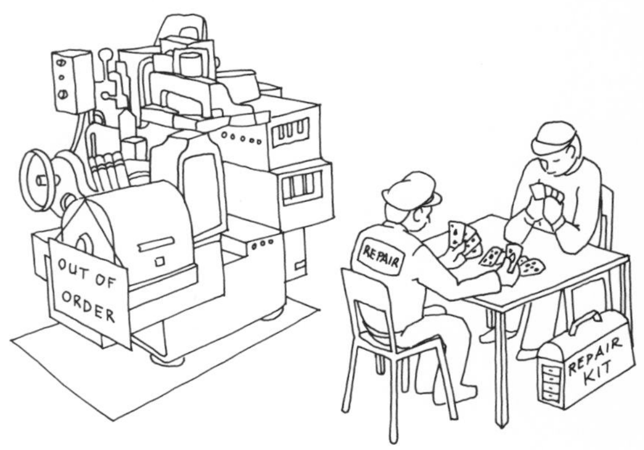

Bad Indicator

BAD INDICATORS, pc sour, mean, sad, etc. (HCO PL 10 Feb 66 II) *Abbr.* BIs.

BAD LEADERSHIP, bad leaders (1) issue no or weak orders (2) do not obtain or enforce compliance. **Bad leadership** isn't "grouchy" or "sadistic" or the many other things man advertises it to be. It is simply a **leadership** that gives no or weak orders and does not enforce compliance. (HCO PL 3 Nov 66)

BAD POLICY, ideas or procedures that were unsuccessful in assisting the basic purpose of an individual, species, organism, organization, become **bad policy.** (HCO PL 13 Mar 65, Division 1, 2, 3 *The Structure of Organization What is Policy?*)

BAD PROGRAM, a program is a **bad program** if it detracts from programs which are already moving successfully or distracts staff people or associates from work they are already doing (doing that is adding up to successful execution of other programs). (HCOB 12 Sept 59)

BAD SITUATION, 1. a situation is something that applies to survival and if you evaluate the word "situation" against survival, you've got it. A good situation is a high level of survival; a **bad situation** is a threatened survival and a no-situation is something that won't affect survival. (7201C02SO) **2.** a departure from the ideal scene. (HCO PL 17 Feb 72)

BAD WORKER, one who is unable to control the equipment he is supposed to control or the communication lines he is supposed to handle. (*POW,* p. 40)

Bad Worker

BAIT AND BADGER, a busy executive or division is not necessarily a producing executive or division. So if no products from him or staff for whatever reason, he's below danger. You don't have a head of div or org if you don't have products coming off and exchange occurring. Only *these,* not excuses or motions, tell the tale. You can get "PR" and glowing (but false) reports. You can get all sorts of things. But where are the products. So you **bait** (tease) **and badger** (nag) the head of div (or org) to impinge on him (draw his attention) until he snarls or cries or screams and spits out an out-point. You don't ask him like repetitive commands, "Why aren't you working?" You ask in many ways "Where are the products?" and he'll eventually tell you an out-point. Like "But I can't get out any products because they aren't products until they are back home telling people how good we are so how can I . . . ." Or "I just keep running around here and nothing happens." Or some other nonsense that *is* nonsense. That's his WHY. So you tell him, "Look, you don't get out products because you don't think you can!" or "You are just trying to look busy so you won't be thought idle." And if you're smart and on the ball, that will be it. The exec will cognite and go into smooth 2WC at once and you got him out of the Esto P/L Series 13 state into a confront. This is **"bait and badger"** to get him broken out of non-confronting. That's all that's wrong with him really. He doesn't look. (HCO PL 24 Apr 72)

BALANCE OF PAYMENTS, the balance between a nation's imports and exports (of products and services) and the attendant inflow and outflow of income over a given period of time, usually a fiscal year.

BALANCE SHEET, 1. is composed of all the accounts representing either assets or liabilities. These accounts are not terminatedly handled at the **balance sheet** date and so remain as **"balances."** Hence the term **"balance" sheet**—it is simply a sheet of paper listing down all those accounts not terminatedly handled and therefore still showing a **"balance."** (BPL 14 Nov 70 IV) **2.** simply a financial statement which lists down all the assets and liabilities of the organization at the end of the financial period concerned. (BPL 14 Nov 70 III)

BALANCE SHEET RATIOS, the ratios that are disclosed on balance sheets or financial accountings of a division, department, project or an entire company giving the breakdown of the relationship of specific assets to specific liabilities, investments to working capital, production costs to sales revenue, etc.

BALLOON MATURITY, the instance of completing the payment of a loan by making a final payment that is substantially larger than previous installments.

BANDA, a Methyl alcohol duplicator. (HCO PL 8 May 65 II)

Banda

BANK, an establishment which loans money and receives deposits for which interest is paid or safety is guaranteed. Various types of banks offer other financial services such as issuing or exchanging currency, cashing checks, safe deposit boxes, etc.

BANK-AGREEMENT, the common denominator of a group is the reactive **bank.** Thetans without **banks** have different responses. They only have their **banks** in common. They agree then only on **bank** principles. Person to person the **bank** is identical. So constructive ideas are individual and seldom get broad **agreement** in a human group. An individual must rise above an avid craving for **agreement** from a humanoid group to get anything decent done. The **bank-agreement** has been what has made earth a hell. (HCO PL 7 Feb 65)

BANK BALANCE, the amount of money that a depositor has in his bank account; the difference between deposits and withdrawals.

BANK, COMMERCIAL, a business organization authorized to receive and protect money and other valuables, lend money at interest, etc., as exemplified in customer checking and savings accounts, safe deposit vaults and loan and credit services.

BANK, CORRESPONDENT, a bank which regularly performs services for another bank in an area to which the other does not have direct access, such as foreign countries or far removed states.

BANK GROUP THINK, I differentiate between **bank group think** which occurs in the absence of leadership, and theta group agreement which is possible and a source of power when leadership exists. (FO 1844)

BANK HOLIDAY, a legal holiday or weekday when banks are not open for business.

BANK, INVESTMENT, a bank which sells stocks and bonds, sometimes in large blocks, and may buy outright from corporations new issues of securities.

BANK, NATIONAL, a commercial bank which is granted a charter by the federal government instead of by the state in which it is established.

BANK RECONCILIATION, the **bank reconciliation** is to show the name of each account, the balance per **bank** statement for each account, to which is added the outstanding deposits for each account (not credited by **bank**) less outstanding checks for each account (all checks expended which have not yet been debited to the account by **bank** statement). This will give you the **reconciled** balance for each account. A **bank reconciliation** basically shows the state of the account if all deposits and checks clear the **bank.** (BPL 4 Dec 72RA II) [The above BPL was cancelled and replaced by BPL 4 Dec 72 II RB.]

BANK RECONCILIATION SECTION, the **Bank Reconciliation Section** of the Department of Records, Assets and Material makes up the latest **bank** records of monies on deposit concurrent with the monthly bills summary. This **section** once each month (concurrent with the monthly bills summary) **reconciles** all **bank** statements, tapes all cancelled checks on their counterfoils and in short makes certain there ar no **bank** errors or omissions. (HCO PL 26 Nov 65R)

BANKRUPTCY, the state of an individual or company legally declared unable to pay its debts.

BANK, SAVINGS, a commercial bank which is authorized to receive and invest the savings money of private depositors and which pays interest on such deposits.

BANK, STATE, a commercial bank which is granted a charter by the state in which it is established.

BANK STATEMENT, a monthly statement prepared and sent out to a depositor by a bank. It lists such data as present balance, deposits and withdrawals for the month, service charges and interest.

BAR CHART, see CHART, BAR.

BARGAIN, 1. an agreement to do business made between a buyer and seller. 2. the terms of such an agreement. 3. a transaction seen as advantageous.

BARGAINING, the act of coming to terms with or settling a disagreement between parties as in the case of management and labor settling a wage dispute or establishing cooperative agreements.

BARGAINING, PLANT, collective bargaining restricted to the level of one manufacturing plant or factory but not occurring at all or many of the plants of a company, as in company bargaining.

BAROMETER, 1. a compilation of statistical data that predicts future market trends or business activity. 2. anything that serves to predict or indicate future action or change.

BARTER SYSTEM, basically money is "an idea backed by confidence." The idea is that the exchange of goods or services kind for kind is too clumsy. To carry your dozen eggs all over town until you find someone who has bread he will exchange for your eggs so you can have bread is too clumsy. That is called a **barter** (trading) **system** and is used in primitive tribes. To solve this, men get the idea of making metal or slips of paper to represent the eggs and the bread. Thus you don't need to look all over town. (HCO PL 27 Nov 71)

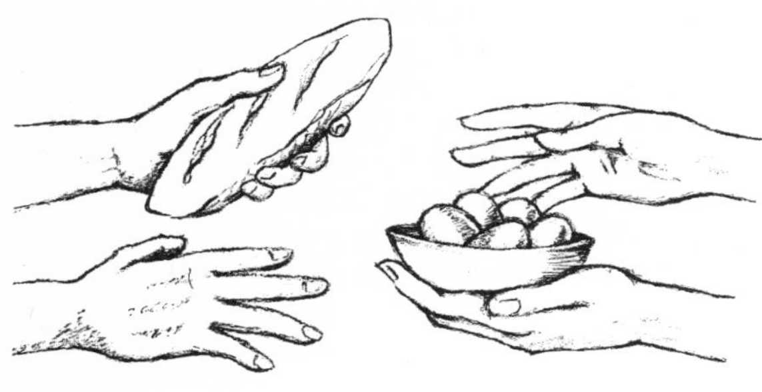

Barter System

BASE, the bottom of something considered its support. (HCO PL 9 Nov 68)

BASE FLAG ORDERS, all regulations and standing **orders** applying to **Flag's Base** which will remain in continuous force shall be issued as: **Base Flag Orders.** These issues may be approved only by myself. (BFO 1) *Abbr.* BFO.

BASE ORDER, **1.** has been used interchangeably for Flag Order. FOs started as **Base Orders.** Occasionally erroneously used at **bases.** Should be a CO (Continental Order) when locally issued. These are filed by area in consecutive number sequence in their own files. (HCO PL 24 Sept 70R) **2.** all **Base Orders** previously issued shall be considered to be in force as they apply and by this Flag Order are made into Flag Orders. (FO 1) *Abbr.* BO.

BASE ORGANIZATION, the sea project includes the Section III Base, ships, and allied activities. The controlling **organization** of the sea project is called The **Base Organization.** This is located ashore or at sea; according to accommodation. The **Base Organization** has seven divisions. These are: (7) the Executive Division which includes the Office of LRH, (1) HCO (Hubbard Communications Office), (2) the Dissemination and Preparation Division, (3) the Treasury Division, (4) the Production Division, (5) the Qualifications Division, (6) the Public Relations Division. These contain the usual policies and duties accorded generally to divisions of the same number in our organizations. Divisions 7, 1 and 2 are under the HCO Executive Secretary, Base. Divisions 3, 4, 5 and 6 are under the **Base Org** Executive Secretary, Base. The Divisions are under secretaries. Only those posts are filled which are active. Executives nearest empty posts fill the duties of those posts if required. All ships, executives, and personnel of the project come under the **base organization.** (LRH Def. Notes, circa May 1967)

BASE PAY, the basic wage received by an employee not including bonuses, overtime, profit sharing or the like.

BASIC ADMIN, Staff Status I, Staff Status II, Staff Member Hat, etc. (HCO PL 24 Sept 71)

BASIC COMPLEMENT, a **basic complement** would be the number required to fill the basic needs and handle the basic functions of something. (FO 3194RA-2)

BASIC COURSE COMPLETIONS, **basic course completions** cover those of the HAS **course,** HQS **course** and Anatomy of the Human Mind **course** where taught. (SO ED 191 INT)

BASIC COURSE INSTRUCTOR, **instructs** lower level courses. (HCO PL 18 Dec 64, *Saint Hill Org Board*)

BASIC COURSE POINTS, **basic course points** cover those of the HAS **course,** HQS **course** and Anatomy of the Human Mind **course** where taught. (SO ED 191 INT)

BASIC COURSES, HAS **course,** HQS **course** and Anatomy of the Human Mind **course** where taught. (SO ED 191 INT)

BASIC COURSE SUPERVISOR, handles all **courses** for the public or staff given at Saint Hill such as PE, HAS, HQS, and appoints and has control of their instructors. (HCO PL 18 Dec 64, *Saint Hill Org Board*)

BASICS, **basics** means **basic-s,** something that is **basic:** fundamental. (HCO PL 9 Nov 68)

BASIC SCIENTOLOGY LIBRARY, in the bookstore, a successful action has always been to sell packages. The most successful of these has been the **basic Scientology library** which consists of *Dianetics: The Modern Science of Mental Health, Science of Survival, Scientology: The Fundamentals of Thought, Advanced Procedure and Axioms, Scientology 8-8008, Creation of*

Human Ability, and *Dianetics 55!*. Wrap these up as a package and put up a sign saying: "The **Basic Scientology Library.** L. Ron Hubbard selected these seven books because they fully embrace all aspects of Scn data. Buy and read these books and you will acquire a much broader understanding of Scn." (FBDL 289)

Basic Scientology Library

BASIC SCN ORGANIZATION BOOK, all new hats and hat changes will appear as Secretarial to the Executive Director orders. When all hats of the organization have been completed as Secretarial to the Executive Director, they will be printed into a **basic Scn organization book** for general issue to staff. However, this **book** will only be a pattern and the hats themselves will be the authority of the post. (SEC ED 12, 16 Dec 58)

BASIC STAFF HAT, OEC Volume No. 0 available from Pubs Orgs. It tells how an org operates and gives the basic information necessary to a staff member to operate properly as one. (HCO PL 11 Aug 71 I)

BASIC STAFF PROFICIENCY CERTIFICATE, this consists of (a) a specified period on **staff** (variable from two weeks to three months depending on employment conditions at the time), (b) a demonstrated **proficiency** or outside training in his type of work, (c) a completed checksheet demonstrating prescribed study of specified materials (such as have been **staff** hat materials), (d) a completed checksheet of prescribed materials covering the character of the organization and its pattern and purpose, (e) a thorough knowledge of the org board and comm system used by org, (f) a clearance from the Ethics Section, (g) a final examination. (HCO PL 21 Apr 65)

BASIC STOCK, **1.** (PR&C paper and litho supplies) the **basic stock** consists of those standard items that have been used over and over for many, many months. (FSO 681) **2.** (PR&C paper and litho supplies quantitative definition) **basic stock** is that amount of stock needed to serve as an adequate supply resource to last through heavy use during a one month period. (FSO 681) **3.** (PR&C paper and litho supplies functional definition) **basic stock** is that paper or litho supply that is required to get out products. (FSO 681)

BASIC TECHNICAL CERTIFICATE, this **certificate** requires (a) a specified period on staff to be set from time to time, (b) a demonstrated proficiency in **technical** matters and a certificate from an Academy HQS or above, (c) a completed checksheet of basic org **technical** procedures for Estimations, the HGC, the Academy, Examinations, Review, Certification, Classification and Ethics, (d) a completed checksheet of prescribed materials covering the relationships of various **technical** posts and their policies and admin procedures, (e) the recommendation of a senior **technical** executive in the org, (f) a final examination. (HCO PL 21 Apr 65)

BASIC WHY, the **basic why** is always the major out-point which has all other out-points as a common denominator. And that's the real **why.** That explains everything. But what is this everything? All the other out-points. What is the major out-point that explains all other out-points that I've found in this area? And that could be the definition of a **why.** (ESTO 12, 7203C06 SO II)

BATCH PRODUCTION, see PRODUCTION, BATCH.

BATTERY OF TESTS, IQ, Leadership, Aptitude, OCA. (FO 3466R-1)

BATTING AVERAGE, stat of each Programs Chief which is computed as follows: up paid comps and up GI for the week divided by 2X the number of orgs they have. Example: a chief with 5 orgs has 3 up paid comps and 4 up GI for the week. His **batting average** is: $\frac{\text{3 up Pd comps \& 4 up GI}}{\text{2 x 5 orgs}} =$

$\frac{7}{10} =$ 0.70 **batting average.** (FSO 737)

BATTLE CONDITIONING, I developed the theory and practice of **Battle Conditioning** used in World War II. I did a paper on it for the Navy before the war and was sent over to the Army G2 with it and Army G2 got it in practice—training by crawling under machine-gun fire and all that. Must have saved a few hundred thousand lives. (OODs 24 Aug 70)

BATTLE OF BRITAIN, there was a gala event making the official opening (of the **Battle of Britain**) for all Scientologists in the UK. Every Scientologist had to choose their route in the **Battle of Britain.** They had five choices: (1) taking service directly, improving themselves, (2) joining mission or org staff, (3) joining the booksellers brigade which has battalions forming in various parts of the UK, (4) setting up a new mission in the UK, (5) signing up as an FSM individual. This event brought them together to make their choice. FBDL 381)

BATTLE PLAN, the **battle plan** was introduced on Flag in order to coordinate necessary actions and prepare strategy and tactics concerning management of AO/SHs and Class IV orgs. On stat night a meeting is held of the senior FB (Flag Bureau) execs and at this meeting a **Battle Plan** is drawn up to handle such things as what orgs will need evaluating, what orgs need program debugs, what orgs are doing fine etc., for the coming week based on stats. Duration of the meeting is usually no longer than one hour. **"Battle planning"** is a way of helping to win the "war." (BPL 1 Apr 73RA)

Battle Plan

BEANS, money. (HCO PL 13 Feb 71)

BEANSTALK, [Note: **beanstalk,** extending rack. **"Beanstalk"** is a trade name of Beanstalk Shelving Limited, Chichester, Sussex, England. These are used as basket systems in orgs and may be attached one on top of another resulting in a system of racks or baskets extending one above the other that look like a **beanstalk.**]

Beanstalk

BEAN THEORY, 1. finance is best understood as a commodity in terms of **beans.** So many **beans** issued to an activity and so many more **beans** back. **Beans** do not magically materialize into more **beans.** What brings back more **beans** for those issued is the production and industry of org staff and how wisely the **beans** are allocated. Even the interest one earns on a bank account is earned in fact by someone's production and ability to get more beans out of an activity than are put in. Where finance uses its **beans** to buy production and industry and projected income at a cost which requires the activity to be viable, it gets back more **beans** and a raised allocation-production ratio. The first rule of finance and any activity is *income greater than outgo.* Where finance can skillfully apply this to the divisions and personnel of an org as well as the org as a whole, the additional **beans** materialize because what is bought is production and the products which add up to the product of raised income and viability. (BPL 19 Mar 71) 2. buy more money made with allocations for expense (**bean theory**). A small sack of beans will produce a whole field of **beans.** Allocate only with that in mind and demand money be made. (HCO PL 9 Mar 72 I)

BEAR MARKET, see MARKET, BEAR.

BEEF UP A TA, send it **up** high (BPL 30 Jul 70R)

BEGINNING SCIENTOLOGIST COURSE, this is the first, lowest **course.** It is the old PE Course. It is not a level course. The **B.S. Course** is all evening PE, covering the *Problems of Work* and stressing how people need Scn, being in a mess, and their need for change. It has no auditing, just data. (HCO PL 31 May 65) *Abbr.* B.S. Course.

BEHAVIOR, 1. the way a person responds to stimuli in his immediate environment and the world around him. This is primarily determined by previous experience and education. 2. the manner in which a person achieves his own survival in carrying out his purposes and obtaining his goals.

BELOW SOURCE, doesn't recognize the causes of his problems. (HCO PL 23 Apr 65)

BENEFICIAL ACT, something that helps broadly. It can be a **beneficial act** to harm something that would be harmful to the greater number of dynamics. (HCO PL 1 Nov 70 III)

BENEFIT METHOD OF SELLING, see SELLING, BENEFIT METHOD OF.

BEST-WORST ISSUES, lists of **worst** to **best** orgs (for Sea Org and Scn international) issued weekly as the FB's stat briefing. (ED 31 FB)

BETRAY, to be disloyal or faithless to. (HCO PL 3 May 72)

BETTER DEAD CLUB, the "the world owes me a living" preclear (or student) is a candidate for the **Better Dead Club.** There were two branches of this **club,** by the way—**better dead** for their own sakes and **better dead** for the sake of others. Demands by individuals for free service on any pretext should be given a light, airy laugh. It doesn't do anybody any good, often not even the person who received it. (HCO PL 9 May 65, *Auditing Fees Preferential Treatment of Preclears Scale of Preference*)

BIG BOOK DISTRIBUTOR, by which is meant a wholesale bookseller to the trade. (HCO PL 19 Jul 65, *Discounts Central Orgs Books*)

BIG IDEA, a **big idea** is, usually, how to get more consumption of what you're producing. So all of your **big ideas,** the real **big ideas,** have to do with the increase of consumption. (FEBC 8, 7101C24 SO I)

BIG LEAGUE, the book, *Big League Sales Closing Techniques.* (BPL 1 Dec 72 R II)

"BIG LEAGUE" REGISTRATION SERIES, in order to make known all the salesmanship techniques and skills, research of the materials on the market has been done and as a result *Big League Sales Closing Techniques* written by Les Dane, an experienced US super-salesman, is highly recommended. The **"Big League" registration series** is written especially to align the techniques with the basic framework of Scn policy. (BPL 2 Nov 72RA) *Abbr.* BLRS.

BILGE BRIGADE, RPF's RPF. (FO 3434-27)

BILGES, the inside bottom of the vessel where water collects. (OODs 29 Sept 71)

BILLED AND DRILLED, by **billed** I mean you put up the guy's name and his duties and what the **drill** is, and then **drilling** it you go out and get him to do it. (6910C16 SO)

BILLING, 1. the action of sending out bills, statements, notices or otherwise informing a debtor of an amount owed. 2. a bill, statement or notice informing a debtor of an amount owed.

BILL OF EXCHANGE, an unconditional written order signed by one person directing another person to pay a specified amount of money to a third person, named in the document, on a particular date or on demand.

BILL OF LADING, a document made out by a transportation firm which acknowledges receipt of goods for shipping, states what was received and who it is being delivered to. Normally the shipper, transporter and receiver each get a copy of the bill of lading.

BILL OF PARTICULARS, a written and signed appointment of a Committee of Evidence naming (1) the chairman, secretary and members of the committee, (2) the interested party or parties, (3) the matter to be heard and a summary of data to hand. It is duly signed by the convening authority and a copy of it is furnished to each person whose name appears in it and to local legal files and a copy to the HCO WW Committee of Evidence via all upper committees. (HCO PL 7 Sept 63)

BILL OF SALE, a document showing the transfer of ownership of property from one person to another.

BILLS, all suppliers' **bills** due and other expenses committed to. (FSO 443)

BILLS OWING, a total accumulation of statements and purchases plus overdrafts and current payments due on mortgages, hire purchase (time payments) and loans and bond or share retirement but not the gross amount of mortgages, hire purchase (time payments) or loans or bonds. **Bills owing** *does not* include any inter-org bills owing. **Bills owing** includes outstanding purchase orders against which purchase has been activated but for which no bill has been received yet. (BPL 1 Jul 72R)

BILLS PAID, see GROSS BILLS PAID.

BILLS SUMMARY, see MONTHLY BILLS SUMMARY.

BILLY-(H)Ō, *n.* (colloquial, used in the intensive phrase) *like*~; *raining like*~(cats & dogs): *fighting like*~(fiercely). (*The Concise Oxford Dictionary of Current English*)

BIRD DOG, **1.** somebody sent in by an enemy to mess things up. (OODs 14 Dec 68)

BIRD DOG NAMES, (CF and address) people who are hostile such as a medico who wants our literature to eventually upset us. (HCO PL 23 Sept 64)

BIRTHDAY CONTRIBUTION FUND, sums sent in by orgs and FBOs to the Commodore as a **birthday** offering. The Commodore requested that they be placed in a separate **fund** to be used to make the ship and galley better for the crew. (ED 472 Flag) [Although the above definition appears on ED 472 Flag, the term **Birthday Contribution Fund** does not, but is in ED 473 Flag.] *Abbr.* BCF.

BLACKING, term expressing the action taken in a labor dispute wherein employees will not work with materials or parts about which there is something that is related to or violates a point under dispute.

BLACKLEG, a person who refuses to strike or takes the job of a striking worker; a scab or strikebreaker.

BLACKLIST, *n.* a list of persons considered undesirable for employment or dealings with. —*v.* to put a person's name on such a list.

BLACK PROPAGANDA, **1.** about the most involved employment of PR is its covert use in destroying the repute of individuals and groups. More correctly this is technically called **black propaganda.** (HCO PL 11 May 71 III) **2.** (**black**= bad or derogatory, **propaganda**=pushing out statements or ideas), the term used to destroy reputation or public belief in persons, companies or nations. It is a common tool of agencies who are seeking to destroy real or fancied enemies or seek dominance in some field. (HCO PL 21 Nov 72 I) **3.** the activity called **black propaganda** consists of spreading lies by hidden sources. It inevitably results in injustices being done by those who operate without verifying the truth. (OODs 17 May 71) **4.** when PR is used for the destruction of ideals or institutions or repute of persons, it is called, traditionally, **black PR.** This is usually covert and a distortion of truth or a whole cloth fabrication. (HCO PL 7 Aug 72) **5. black propaganda** is in its technical accuracy, a covert operation where unknown authors publicly effect a derogatory reaction and then remain unknown. (HCO PL 11 May 71 III) **6.** a covert attack on the reputation of a person, company or nation using slander and lies in order to weaken or destroy. (HCO PL 21 Nov 72 I) **7. black PR** also uses imagination in order to degrade or vilify or discredit an existing or fancied image. (HCO PL 7 Aug 72) *Abbr.* Black PR.

BLAMING MEST, I have noticed that, when personnel have been careless or incompetent to repair, they **blame** the **mest.** This is usually an effort to "get off the hook" and cover up lack of skill or industry. Given good equipment to begin with, beware of alarming tales on how it won't work. It will if competently handled. (FO 14)

BLANKET MARKET PENETRATION, the instance of reaching, covering and penetrating the consumers market over a wide scope or influencing a majority of potential buyers.

BLIND ADVERTISEMENT, see ADVERTISEMENT, BLIND.

BLINDNESS, the **blindness** of a person can stem from two sources, one of those is fixidity, he just never spans his attention and the other one is overts. An individual who has committed overts long enough and often enough on a certain area will not be able to perceive it anymore. He just doesn't see and by that we mean ocular. A person who commits overts often enough on another person will have that person disappear right in the physical universe before them. (ESTO 5, 7203C03 SO I)

BLOW, *v.* leave hurriedly. (HCO PL 25 Jun 72)

BLOW-OFFS, departures, sudden and relatively unexplained from sessions, posts, jobs, locations and areas. One can treat people so well that they grow ashamed of themselves, knowing they don't deserve it, that a **blow-off** is precipitated, and certainly one can treat people so badly that they have no choice but to leave, but these are extreme conditions and in between these we have the majority of departures: people leave because of their own overts and withholds. That is the factual fact and the hard bound rule. A man with a clean heart can't be hurt. The man or woman who must must must become a victim and depart is departing because of his or her own overts and withholds. It doesn't matter whether the person is departing from a town or a job or a session. The cause is the same. (HCOB 31 Dec 59)

BLOWS, *n.* desertions. (HCO PL 22 Sept 70) —*v.* recognizing the source of an aberration in processing **"blows"** it, makes it vanish. (HCO PL 18 Sept 67)

BLUE, 1. the color for ethics upstat folders per LRH Ethics Program No. 1 (FO 2366) **2.** the comcenter copy of a communication. (*HTLTAE*, p. 118)

BLUE CHIP, a stock market term referring to a highly successful firm with a history of paying good dividends and whose products and/or services are recognized for quality and wide usage.

BLUE-CHIP CREW LIST, crew list of those who are posted on basic complement posts and can be trusted to do the job. (ED 483 Flag)

BLUE CHIP INVESTMENT, see INVESTMENT, BLUE CHIP.

BLUE-CHIP POSTING, simply someone **posted** who can be trusted to do the job. It does not necessarily mean he can be trusted to do any job but refers to the specific **post.** (FO 3194RA-2)

BLUE COLLAR TRADE UNION, a union for persons employed in blue collar jobs as opposed to white collar and management trade unions.

BLUE COLLAR WORKER, a person who does manual labor and commonly wears rough clothes. Usually applied to persons in factory or assembly line jobs as opposed to white collar workers.

BLUE-EYED BOY, an employee who in the eyes of other employees is considered to be receiving preferential treatment by management.

BLUE FLAG, all Flag personnel wear a small **blue flag** no longer than three-quarters of an inch, which can be a blue bunting or felt rectangle, or a made-up Commodore's flag in metal on their right collar tab or right breast. (FO 1)

BLUE INVOICE, 1. blue debit and credit **invoices** are kept in the Department of Income for collection purposes. **Blue** not debit or credit invoices are routed to address and then CF. (Invoice routing for all orgs except Saint Hill.) (HCO PL 16 Feb 66) **2. invoice** copy distributed to the Department of Records, Assets and Materiel for record purposes (Saint Hill only). (HCO PL 13 Oct 66) **3.** (Saint Hill invoice routing) the additional set of **invoices** which are separated and used for income analysis by separating into income types is the **blue** set and are placed in the folder with the green invoices and bank deposit records at the end of each week. (BPL 18 Nov 67R)

BLUE LANYARD, Commodore's personal staff wear a **blue lanyard** with uniform B. With dress uniform they wear a blue and gold woven cord over the right shoulder. (FO 467)

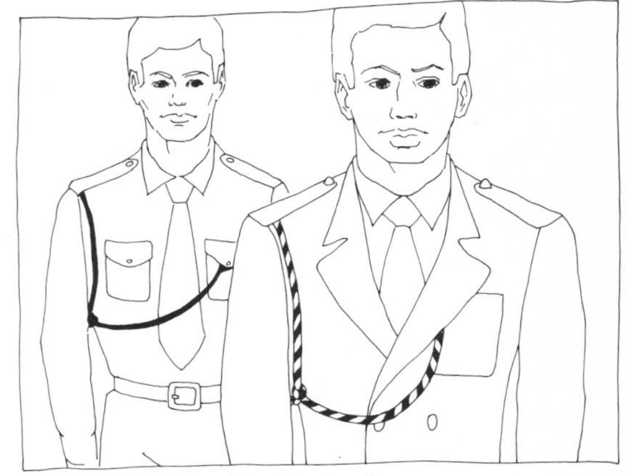

Blue Lanyard

BLUE SKY LAWS, the popular name for various state laws which have been passed to protect investors against securities frauds. Historically, the term is said to have originated when a judge remarked that a particular stock had about the same value as a patch of blue sky.

BLUE STAR, a Class II auditor who has his Staff Status II may assign his or her own ethics conditions when requested to do so. He or she may be given ethics hearings or removed from post pending an ordered Committee of Evidence for crimes or high crimes. (HCO PL 13 Feb 69)

BLUE TABBED LABEL, (or **blue** marked), tape color flash code for dictative tape, may be erased when transcribed and checked against copy. (HCO PL 7 Dec 65)

BOARD EXECUTIVE DIRECTIVE, color flash—dark blue ink on cream paper. These are the issues of the **Boards** of Directors of the Churches of Scientology and are separate and distinct from those executive directives written by LRH. Only LRH issues may be printed blue on white for EDs and only LRH issues may have the prefix HCO. (BPL 14 Jan 74R I) *Abbr.* BED

BOARD FINANCE OFFICER, one or two staff members in Treasury whose sole duty is handling the finance emergency, the creditors, the refunds and repayments. Put up a sign **"Board Finance Officer"** with another sign or two around pointing to that office—**"Board Finance Officer.** All **finance** matters." Give them a phone with a number. Give everyone else on staff that number as the **finance** number so they at once direct any callers to it. Instruct Dir Comm where to put all such mail—to the **Board Finance Officer.** And let the rest of staff get on with it. People put on the **finance** special post only handle the subjects of **finance** emergency. They do not handle all **finance** hats and lines in the org. (HCO PL 19 Nov 74)

BOARD ISSUES, BPLs (**Board** Policy Letters), **B**TBs (**Board** Technical Bulletins), **B**EDs (**Board** Executive Directives). These are similar in content to HCO PLs, HCOBs and LRH EDs respectively, but are written by someone other than LRH and issued on Flag by or for the **Boards** of Directors of the Churches of Scientology. **B**PLs and **B**TBs are valid until cancelled or revised. **B**EDs are valid for one year after which they expire unless cancelled before that. Distribution of **Board issues** is as indicated. They are printed on buff paper with green ink for **B**PLs, red for **B**TBs and dark blue for **B**EDs. (HCO PL 24 Sept 70R)

BOARD OF APPEAL, 1. the **Board's** duties consist of correcting any false reports, false accusations and third party activities which have been detrimental to the repute of the individual or harmful to his well being. The **Board** is to meet every Friday in the early afternoon each week. The **Board** will issue its findings on a weekly basis and these shall have the force of ethics orders. The membership of the board shall consist of a chairman of officer rank, a secretary and from one to three members. This membership shall be appointed by the Commanding Officer, the Captain or Deputy Captain of an AO, OTL, ship or SO unit. (FO 2024) **2.** This is separate from the OTL Last Court of Appeal which handles any Scientologist or Sea Org member. The **Board of Appeal** only handles cases within its own ship or SO unit. (FO 2350)

BOARD OF COMMENDATION, the Guardian can convene a **Board of Commendation** to look into affluences and find what caused them and publish the result and **commend** the responsible parties. (HCO PL 1 Mar 66)

BOARD OF DIRECTORS, the **Board of Directors** or owner of the vessel is responsible for the general overall control of the ship and its activities. A **Board of Directors,** however, is responsible only as a board. An individual member of a **board of directors** cannot issue orders which are not passed by the entire **board of directors.** At the top of an org board goes—**Board of Directors,** and under that—general planning, finance and ownership of the activity and its property, ships and its profits and final authority on all ships or fleet matters and their policy, conduct and operation. (FO 1109)

BOARD OF DIRECTORS, the shareholders of a corporation elect a Board of Directors. The number of votes cast by each shareholder is proportionate to the amount of shares he holds. The Board of Directors usually consists of at least three officers, a president, treasurer and secretary. The board acts as the representative of the corporation in managing the business. It formulates corporation policies, manages the day-to-day affairs of the business, declares dividends, issues stock, engages into contracts in the name of the corporation and exercises any additional powers granted it by the charter of the corporation.

BOARD OF INVESTIGATION, **1.** the purpose of a **Board of Investigation** is to help LRH discover the cause in any conflict, poor performance or down statistic. A **Board of Investigation** is composed of not less than three and not more than five members. A majority of the members must be senior to the persons being investigated except when this is impossible. The board may investigate by calling in a body on the persons concerned or by sitting and summoning witnesses or principals. A **Board of Investigation** is a much less serious affair than a Committee of Evidence. Persons appearing before it are not under duress or punishment. The whole purpose is to get at the facts. A **Board** may recommend a Committee of Evidence. (HCO PL 4 Jun 66) **2.** a **Board of Investigation** may (and should) be convened any time there is an unusual improvement in an org or its statistics. Such a **Board** must (a) isolate the reasons or changes which brought about the improvement. (b) draw up their findings in the form of policy or directives to pass them on to the convening authority and (c) recommend commending any person found responsible for the improvement (the **board** does not commend, it only recommends, the convening authority alone may issue the commendation). (HCO PL 31 Oct 66 II) *Abbr.* B of I.

BOARD OF ISSUES, a **Board of Issues** is established. The purpose, function and duties of this **Board** are to examine and approve policy letters, bulletins and EDs authorized by anyone other than LRH. These, when approved are designated as **Board Issues** and are valid for use by Scientology Churches and missions. The **Board of Issues** shall consist of the following: Chairman; D/CS-7 Flag, Secretary; Programs Bureau Aide Flag, member; External HCO Aide Flag, member; Flag Flag Representative. (BPL 14 Jan 74 II)

BOARD OF REVIEW, each OTL is constituted as a **Board of Review.** The **Board of Review** is headed by the Commanding Officer of the OTL and has two other members appointed by him. Member of the **board** must have completed the Org Exec Course. Occasionally, an administrative body issues a directive that: (a) cannot be executed (impractical), (b) results in lowered statistics, (c) causes contraction of an area. The **Board of Review** has no authority to write or issue new policy or issue new directives. It can only cancel a directive or new policy which is found to: (a) be impractical, (b) lower statistics, (c) cause contraction, (d) violate basic LRH policy. (HCO PL 20 Apr 69 I) [The above HCO PL was cancelled by BPL 10 Oct 75 VII.]

BOARD OF SCHEDULES, a **Board of Schedules** is instituted on the Flagship. Its purpose is to arrive at firm **schedules** of ship operation, thereby eliminating looseness of operation and unpredictability aboard and ashore.

BOARD OF TRUSTEES, the policies of this organization are established by the **Board of Trustees** and are formed by common agreement which then becomes reality by execution through its command lines. (SEC ED 41, 15 Jan 59)

BOARD POLICY LETTERS, color flash—green ink on cream paper. These are the issues of the **Boards** of Directors of the Churches of Scientology and are separate and distinct from those HCO Policy Letters written by LRH. Only LRH issues may be printed green on white for policy and only LRH issues may have the prefix HCO. (BPL 14 Jan 74R I) *Abbr.* BPL.

BOARD REPRESENTATIVE, that officer appointed by the local **board** of directors as their principal management officer for the org of that **board.** The **Board Representative** is the governing head of the org. He directs the org toward expansion from Flag and does everything necessary at Flag to assist the CO/ED and executives of the org to keep the org viable and rapidly expanding. The **Board Representative** constantly evaluates the org and provides properly evaluated effective Flag programs for his org and area. His programs, directions and orders are mandatory upon the org and must be complied with. The Flag Representative is the **Board Representative's** terminal for execution of his orders from Flag. The post of **Board Representative** supersedes the Flag Programs Chief post, which is discontinued when replaced by a **Board Representative.** (BPL 22 Jun 74)

BOARD RESOLUTION, orders or directions in Scn for anything relating to corporate status, starting or closing bank accounts and vital planning. (Black ink on white paper, signed by all board members.) (HCO PL 13 Mar 66)

BOARDS COPY, the message system we use is based on three copies of every telex. If you do not receive three you must instantly make three. Every phone, cable or telex message needs three copies. Your second **copy** is called the **boards copy.** Its purpose is to post on the traffic control board. The traffic board is a large cork board divided up into the different areas to which we communicate. Its purpose is to display message cycles clearly. (FO 2528)

BOARD TECHNICAL BULLETINS, color flash—red ink on cream paper. These are the issues of the **Boards** of Directors of the Churches of Scientology and are separate and distinct from those HCO Bulletins written by LRH. Only LRH issues may be printed red on white for technical bulletins and only LRH issues may have the prefix HCO. These board issues are valid as tech. The purpose of this distinction is to keep LRH's comm lines pure and to clearly distinguish between source material and other issues and so that any conflict and/or confusion on source can easily be resolved. (BPL 14 Jan 74R I) *Abbr.* BTB.

BOATS, the **boatswain (bosun)** is generally addressed as **"boats."** (FO 87)

BOATS AND TRANSPORT UNIT, see TRANSPORT UNIT.

BOATS IN-CHARGE, his responsibility is for the care, condition, and proper handling of **boats** and their motors—attached or detached. All ship's transport: cars, motorbikes, or other vehicles come under **boats in-charge.** All life saving equipment is under the **charge** of **boats in-charge.** (FO 2677)

BOATSWAIN, **bosun.** (*Ship's Org Bk.*)

BOATSWAIN OF THE WATCH, each watch the **boatswain of the watch** is ordered by the officer of the deck to thoroughly inspect the vessel from stem to stern—all decks, all quarters, and all holds. Anything found to be unseaman-like is corrected by him with the help of his deck force. (*SWPB*)

BODIES IN THE SHOP, 1. (Dissemination Division GDS) total number of pcs in the HGC, plus total number of students in the academy and HSDC, plus total number of pcs and students in Cramming and Review. (SO ED 43 INT) **2.** people who actually walk in to the registrar's office for an interview. (HCO PL 31 Oct 61 [The above HCO PL was cancelled by BPL 10 Oct 75 III.]

BODY, the news story has two parts, the lead which quickly tells what has happened, and the **body** which documents the lead. (BPL 10 Jan 73R)

BODY MIMICRY PROCESS, **process** where auditor and pc sit across from each other and the commands are hand signals which are answered by the same hand signal and the command is repeated by the auditor until it is duplicated by the pc. (HCO PL 31 May 65)

BODY OF KNOWLEDGE, (Logic 2)—a **body of knowledge** is a **body** of data, aligned or unaligned, or methods of gaining data. (*AP & A*, p. 64)

BODY Q AND A, some people **Q and A** with their **bodies.** The **body** is, after all, composed of mest. It follows the laws of mest. One of these laws is Newton's first law of motion: inertia. This is the tendency of a mest object to remain motionless until acted upon by an exterior force. Or to continue in a line of motion until acted upon by an exterior force. Well, the main force around that is continually acting on a human **body** is a thetan, the being himself. The **body** will remain at rest (since it is a mest object) until acted upon by the thetan that is supposed to be running it. If that being is an aberrated non-straight line being, the **body** reacts on him more than he reacts on the **body.** Thus he remains motionless or very slow. When the **body** is in unwanted motion; the being does not deter the motion as the **body** is acting upon him far more than he is reacting on the body. As a result, one of the manifestations is **Q and A.** He wants to pick up a piece of paper. The **body** inertia has to be overcome to do so. So he does not reach for the paper, he just leaves the hand where it is. This would be no action at all. If he then weakly forces the motion, he finds himself picking up something else like a paper clip, decides he wants that anyway and settles for it. Now he has to invent why he has a paper clip in his hand. His original intention never gets executed. Some people on medical lines are just there not because of actual illness but because they are just **Qing and Aing** with their **body.** The cure for this sort of thing (**Q and A** with a **body**) is objective processes. (HCOB 5 Dec 73)

BODY REGISTRAR, 1. (Sign-up **Registrar**) the prime purpose of the **Body Registrar** (**Body** Sign-up **Reg**) is: to help Ron sign up individuals for technical services who come into the organization and sign-up individuals again for further technical services and increase the activity and production of the org. The **Body Registrar** is then a sign-up **registrar** of individuals who come with their **bodies** into the org and then signs them up again for further services when they have completed the services they signed up for. This **registrar** signs up individuals for technical services and her concern is to move pcs and students further down the road to Clear by signing them up for technical services and then repeatedly signing them up for each next step. (HCO PL 21 Sept 65 VI) **2.** Dissem **body reg** functions: to enroll Scientologists in the org's CF for the major services of the org (hours of auditing, HSDC, HSDG, Academy training and Qual interneships). The CF is used to get the largest possible volume of business for the org. (LRH ED 112 INT)

BODY ROUTER, 1. there are two types of **body routers.** Type 1 is **body routers** operating outside the org bringing people into the org. Type 2 is **body routers** operating inside the org guiding and controlling the public once in the org so they make it to the Public Registrar. (BPL 1 Dec 72R IV) **2. body routers** route the public coming into the org so each person makes it to the registrar and gets signed up or at least buys a book. (LRH ED 159RA INT)

BODY ROUTING, a Division 6 action whereby expeditors, FSMs, volunteers and/or specially assigned Div 6 body routers in Dept 16 hand out tickets and bodily route new public into the org for introductory lectures and/or testing after which they see the Public Reg who signs them up and starts them on their first service in Div 4. (FBDL 469)

BODY SIGN-UP REG, **Body Reg.** (HCO PL 21 Sept 65 VI)

BOGEY, term used to describe limits imposed by employees on the amount of production occurring. In recession times when employees are afraid of being fired, they may impose such limits on production in the mistaken belief that it will make the smaller amount of work available, stretch further and thus make them appear essential in their jobs.

BOGGED-DOWN CASES, those **cases,** not psychotic, which cease to run well. A **bogged-down**

case does not find himself able to absorb information or acquire skill and certainly cannot be said to be running well. (HCO PL 2 Sept 70, *Instruction Protocol Official*)

BOGGED STUDENT, what is a **bogged student**? Is he stretched out on the floor snoring? No, he is groggy or puzzled or frowning or even emotionally upset by his misunderstood words. When not caught and handled he will go to sleep or just stare into space. (HCO PL 26 Jun 72)

BOLIVAR, **1.** see *GRINNEL*. **2.** Simon **Bolivar,** liberator of South America, 1783—1830. (HCO PL 12 Feb 67)

BOND, a legal paper evidencing a debt wherein the issuing company usually promises to pay the bondholder a stated amount of interest for a definite period of time and to repay the loan upon expiration. A bondholder, therefore, is a creditor of the company and not a part owner as is a stockholder.

BONUS, usually applies to money in excess of what is normally received, given in consideration of superior production. (OODs 28 Feb 75)

BONUS EARNINGS, earnings additional to the normal salary or hourly wage rate.

BONUS RANGE, what I am calling **bonus range** is when one week of collections take care of one month's operation. This permits expansion funds and gets some local **bonuses** being paid. (OODs 21 Aug 72)

BONUS SCHEME, a plan which establishes the amount of bonuses a person may earn and what conditions must be met to receive such. Usually a bonus scheme rewards staff on the basis of production which would be reflected by increased product output, increased sales, increased company income, etc.

BONUS SUM, (Flag) all monies remaining from the delivery **sum** up to a ceiling of $55,000 in any week once reserves and expenses have been covered and all debts to org payments or reserves have been paid and all Flag bills have been paid and Flag is in good operating condition, serve as FSO **bonuses** with 1/2 **bonus,** per quad **bonus** system, going to Commodore's Staff, Personal Office of LRH and Office of the Controller. With a new ship or shore installation afforded and income materially increased and paid for the $55,000 ceiling can be raised. (FSO 667RC)

BOOK ACCOUNT, see HCO BOOK ACCOUNT and HCO DIV ACCOUNT.

BOOK ADMINISTRATOR, purpose: to handle the printing of promotional and disseminating materials for the organization. To secure good prices and fast service on printed matters. (HCO PL 12 Feb 59) *Abbr.* B/A.

BOOK ADMINISTRATOR HCO WW, in charge of book and meter supply, sales and distribution. (HCO PL 5 Feb 62)

BOOK ADS AND DISTRIBUTION OFFICER, head of Div 2 of the Tours Org. The product of the **BA and D Officer** is sold and delivered **books.** He works on getting **book ads** placed in news media and on getting books placed in bookshops and sold by many different means. (BPL 15 Jun 73R)

BOOK AND BOTTLE, Op Pro by Dup. (ESTO 12, 7203C06 SO II)

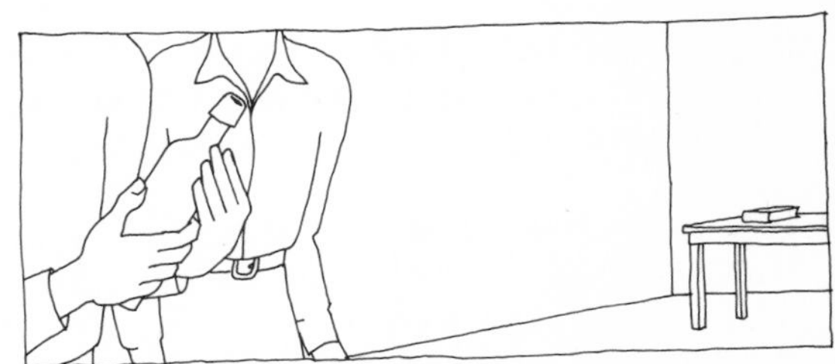

Book and Bottle

BOOK AUDITOR, **1. audits** preclears below classification levels without pay and operates study groups. (HCO PL 21 Oct 66 II) **2.** someone who has studied **books** on Scn and listens to other people to make them better. (HCO PL 21 Aug 63) See HUBBARD BOOK AUDITOR.

BOOK AWARD PROGRAM, see FSM AWARD PROGRAM.

BOOK DEPARTMENT OF HCO WW, the **Book Department of HCO WW** is regarded simply as a **book department**—its sole purpose being to supply **books** and other materials to individuals, bookstores and the HCOs throughout the world. It is not directly concerned with the dissemination of Scn, and it does not deal with any correspondence whatsoever apart from that entailed in the supply of **books,** etc. (HCO PL 14 Oct 60) [The above HCO PL was cancelled by BPL 10 Oct 72 III.]

BOOK DISTRIBUTION UNIT, belongs in the Public Promotion Department of the Public Planning Division (Div 6) in the Promotion and

Dissemination Section. This **unit** handles **book** advertising placement and **book** distribution. (HCO PL 24 Jul 69 II)

BOOK FLYER, 1. a printed promotion piece which advertises a **book.** (SO ED 45 INT) **2.** handbills (HCO PL 20 Nov 65R)

Book Flyer (Def. 1)

BOOKKEEPER, that person in a business who does the recording of all financial transactions.

BOOKKEEPING, a system of recording the transactions of a business. Specifically it means the recording, in monetary terms of the basic flows of a business. It records the business's sales and its purchases and it records the receipt of money in respect of sales and the disbursement of money in respect of purchases. And it would record any other flows such as the inflow of money by way of loans (or investments) received and the outflow of money by way of loans (or investments) made. (BPL 14 Nov 70 II)

BOOKLET, a small **book,** usually with paper covers. (FO 3275R)

BOOK OF IN PERSON SCHEDULING, registers people who **schedule** ahead **in person.** (HCO PL 6 Apr 65)

BOOK OF LETTER SCHEDULING, the **Letter** Reg actually registers. This is done by getting people to **schedule** courses and intensives. For example, on a questionaire, Bill says he someday wants to be trained, one intensifies this with when and gently coaxes Bill to say "next year" and then coaxes Bill in a next **letter** to say when next year. So Bill does and it becomes a fact and the **Letter** Registrar registers Bill on her **book of letter scheduling.** Such a **book** is best if heavy paper loose leaf, very heavy binding and snap ring for page removal and replacement. Thus such a **book** can have a page removed for a copy machine to copy, the page replaced and the copy sent on with no other work. One week can be one page or several pages if it goes to many students and pcs. One can keep the right side of the open double page for students and the left side for preclears and the week at the top of each page. Thus one can put a lot of pcs and students in it if it's big enough and can see week by week for months and even a year what is coming. (HCO PL 6 Apr 65)

BOOK OF PHONE SCHEDULING, registers people who **phone** in to **schedule.** (HCO PL 6 Apr 65)

BOOK ORDERERS, 1. (class of tabulation in central files) our first category is **book orders** and that is established by just this one fact: an invoice saying he bought something. We don't care what it was, Associate Membership, a **book,** anything. He bought something. That makes him a **book orderer.** (HCOB 6 Apr 57) **2.** persons who have **ordered books.** (HCO PL 7 Jan 64)

BOOK ORDERS, No. 1 of five classes of tabulation of central files. That is established by just this fact: an invoice saying he bought something, we don't care what it was, Associate Membership, a **book,** anything. He bought something—so your interest is, on that category, did this person buy something? That makes him a **book orderer.** (HCOB 6 Apr 57)

BOOK SECTION, stocks, inventories and keeps in supply all **books,** tapes, records, film, items and insignia and fills all orders rapidly. Notifies the director of all dwindling or over-stocked materials promptly. (HCO PL 18 Dec 64, *Saint Hill Org Board.*)

BOOKS-IN-CHARGE, manages the **Book** Section. Is accountable for all orders, stocks and shipments. (HCO PL 18 Dec 64, *Saint Hill Org Board.*)

BOOKS MAKE BOOMS BROCHURE, what is the **BMB**? It is a magnificent, full color **brochure** with over 40 photos, each one shot by Ron himself. As the name implies, this **brochure** gives you the full cycle on booming your org or mission and area showing the various methods of getting **books** sold right through the cycle of follow up, to sign up, to in the org for service. (FBDL 591) *Abbr.* BMB.

BOOK, TAPE, RECORD ADMINISTRATOR, sees that **books, tapes** and **records** are in supply adequate to meet the demand. He gets OKs to reprint **books,** to print **books,** to cut **records, tapes,** etc. He does not let his supply become exhausted, ever. If a publication (or **tape** or **record**) is going out of print, and not to be reprinted, he sees that this fact is published in the Scn magazine—that Dissemination Secretary is advised—that HCO WW Book Administrator is advised. If a **book** is to be continued in supply, he sees that the **book** is reprinted, getting proper OKs to do so, that the preparation of the MSS is done, and that Printing Hat follows through on it from there. (HCO PL 15 Mar 60) [The above HCO PL was cancelled by BPL 10 Oct 75 III.]

BOOK VALUE, book value of a stock is determined from a company's records, by adding all assets (generally excluding such intangibles as good will), then deducting all debts and other liabilities, plus the liquidation price of any preferred issues. The sum arrived at is divided by the number of common shares outstanding and the result is book value per common share. Book value of the assets of a company or a security may have little or no significant relationship to market value.

BOOM, a time of rapid expansion and growth of a business shown by rising statistics and increased production, sales, prices or values. The continuance of a boom depends on isolating and reinforcing the reasons for the boom.

BOOSTER RUNDOWN, (Flag only) where a student is not making his targets or is slow on lines and has been to word clearers and cramming we must assume that he has a case problem that is slowing his progress. The **Booster RD** is delivered by internes only of Class IV or above. The **rundown** is for Flag only. This **RD** consists of three or four separate lists done. Each list is taken to an F/Ning assessment. Done with flubless TRs, flubless metering and perfect auditor's code will give a real case **boost!** with increased reality on Scn or its organizations. (HCOB 20 Dec 75)

BOOSTER TRAINING, see TRAINING, BOOSTER,

BOOT, where an exchange involving two properties or items of unequal value is contemplated, a boot is the payment that makes up the difference. Example: X trades his new car in exchange for Y's older car plus $1,000.

BOOT CAMP, this is where one does his basic Sea Org training and only that. All new Sea Org recruits come here. It re-establishes the original successful formula for beginning SO members which was lots of physical work. (FO 2046)

BOOTS, all new recruits are referred to as **boots.** (FO 87)

BOSUN, **1.** the **bosun** and his deckhands is like a foreman and his gang. Traditionally, the First Mate and **Bosun** run the decks. The **Bosun** must be able to 8C like mad; he must be a leader and driver of men without being vicious. He should be an expert seaman, exceedingly well versed in ropes and their use. The **Bosun's** store is his domain. Here he keeps his ropes, tackle, shackles, blocks; he knows where the water measuring rods are, where the tools are, he sees they are returned at the end of each working day cleaned and in good condition. He sees to the landing and retrieving of boats, the handling of cargo, the condition of rigging and fenders—all the working rig of the decks. The **bosun** is the kind of man that when there is something tricky to be done, or some emergency, you immediately "send for the **Bosun.**" He is a seaman's seaman; a jack-of-all-trades and master of all of them. (*Ship's Org Bk.*) **2.** officer or seaman responsible for the supervision and maintenance of a ship's boats, ropes and decks. (FO 2674) **3. Boatswain.** (FO 87)

BOUGHT IN GOODS, completed components purchased by a firm for incorporation into its own products. Also called bought out goods.

BOUNCED CHECK, a **check** not honored by the bank and returned. (BPL 29 May 70R)

BOUNCED CHECK FLOAT, all income is banked into the Finance Office No. 1 Account and all counter checks and **bounced checks** are handled by this account. A **bounced check float** is kept in the FO No. 1 Account as a cushion against **bounced checks.** The **float** is accumulated from: (a) unused allocations returned by the org to the FBO, (b) any billings the FBO has collected from the org for overspending, (c) 1% of the CGI may be retained temporarily by the FBO for the **bounced check float** until the **float** reaches the equivalent of the average amount of one week's GI. (BPL 6 Jul 75 III)

BOUNDING MAIN, wide open seas. (OODs 17 Dec 71)

BOYCOTT, an organized action taken against a person, business or nation to prevent anyone from trading or doing business transactions with them. A boycott is usually instigated to remedy an abuse such as unfair labor dealings or disagreements with methods of operation.

BPI, 1. **broad public information** is a designation (**BPI**) that sometimes appears on an information letter. (HCO PL 2 Jul 64) **2. broad public interest.** (HCO PL 24 Feb 64, *Urgent Org Programming*) **3. broad public issue** (**BPI**) is a designation that sometimes appears on a policy letter or HCOB. This follows the same distribution procedure as for remimeo, with the exception that it may also be put in *The Auditor* and continental or Org magazines. (BPL 14 Apr 69R) **4.** designation on HCO Policy Letters and HCO Bulletins indicates dissemination and restriction as follows; **broad public issue**, give to HCOs of all types, all staff of central organizations, field auditors, put in magazines, do what you like with it. (HCO PL 22 May 59)

BRAINWASHING, 1. **brainwashing** is a very simple mechanism. One gets a person to agree that something *might* be a certain way and then drives him by introverting him and through self-criticism to the possibility that it is that way. Only then does a man believe that the erroneous fact was a truth. By gradient scale of hammering, pounding and torture, **brainwashers** are able to make people believe that these people saw and did things which they never did do. But its effectiveness is minor as Russia does not know enough about the mind, even though we recently taught nothing but German-Russian theory in our schools. (*AAR*, p. 84) **2.** is actually that technique by Pavlov which makes the dog believe that he can't tell the difference between a bell and a buzzer. Now I'll untangle that for you. They ring a bell and feed the dog, and they ring a bell and feed the dog, and they ring a bell and feed the dog. Now the dog is conditioned (psychological term) to be fed when the bell rings. Now, they buzz a buzzer and beat the dog, and buzz a buzzer and beat the dog, and they buzz a buzzer and beat the dog, and they buzz a buzzer and beat the dog. Now what they're really doing is adding up a bunch of engrams, they aren't conditioning him at all. And then they gradually reduce the sound of the bell to the sound of the buzzer, and reduce the sound of the buzzer to the sound of the bell till the dog can't tell the difference between the buzzer and the bell and at that moment he goes psychotic. He can't tell whether he's going to be beaten or fed. That is **brainwashing.** It is specific technology. (6804SM—) **3.** changing the values of things. (6804SM—) **4.** is subjection of a person to systematic indoctrination or mental pressure with a view to getting him to change his views or to confess to a crime. (HCO PL 20 Dec 69 VIII)

BRANCH, a new complete bureaux org board is posted and displayed on Flag and is being readied for export to CLOs. Instead of divisions, they are bureaux. Instead of depts they are **branches.** Section is retained. (FBDL 12)

BRANCH, 1. any part or extension of an organization or company that handles one aspect of the business such as the financial branch, personnel branch, sales branch, etc. 2. a local office of a company that has headquarters elsewhere; branch office. Example: a brewing company could have branches in several major cities. Each one would be capable of handling all aspects of production, sales and distribution that the company is overall engaged in.

BRANCH MANAGER, that person who manages a branch or branch office of an organization. The branch may be in the same location or remote from the organization's central offices or main location.

BRAND, the distinguishing symbol, mark or name associated with a particular product or service by which the consumer may readily identify it. A brand name is usually copyrighted by the owner.

BRAND LEADER, that brand of product in a field of similar products that is recognized as a leader due to any number of factors including superior quality, availability, amount of sales or public opinion.

BRAND NAME, the name given to a service or product by a manufacturer so that it may be distinguished easily from similar products on the market. The name is usually prominently displayed on the product. For example, in distinguishing manufacturers of denim garments the brand names often seen would be Levi's, Lee, Wrangler, etc.

BREAK-EVEN CHART, see CHART, BREAK-EVEN.

BREAK-EVEN POINT, that point where profits and losses balance. One has neither gained nor lost money at this point. A break-even point is often calculated before investing in something in order to determine at what point or after how much production or sales one will be making a profit.

BRIDGE, the raised platform with a clear view all around, from which the Captain controls the ship at sea. (FO 2674)

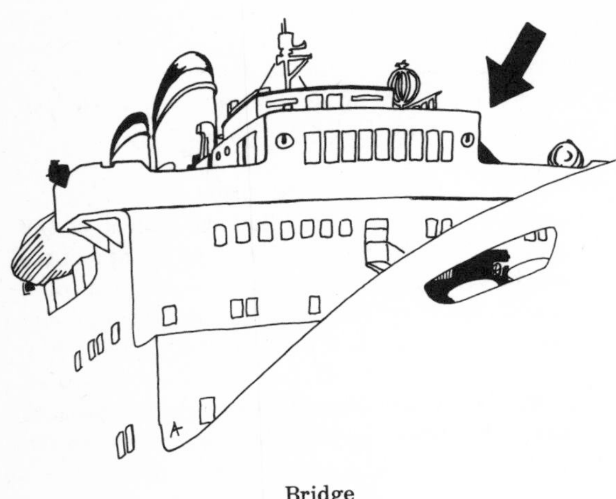

Bridge

BRIDGE, THE, the Classification, Gradation and Awareness Chart. This is the famous **bridge** mentioned at the end of *Dianetics: The Modern Science of Mental Health*. It is now complete and is functioning. The being enters it from somewhere in the minus regions as a beginning Scientologist and moves on up. By following this chart one can make release and then Clear. (HCO PL 5 May 65)

BRIEF, *v.* to give final instructions to; to coach thoroughly in advance; to give essential information to. (CBO 57-2)

BRIEFING, **1.** the Action Bureau is responsible for **briefing. Briefing** consists of all the data needed in the MOs and the MOs themselves. **Briefing** consists of genning the person in on all the data he will need to do his mission and also getting him to totally grasp his MOs. (FO 2756) **2. briefing** simply consists of the person **briefing** doing the following: (1) ensures that all mission information is available and is written. If it isn't written it isn't true. There is no verbal data given. There is no hidden data line. If something is missing then it is up to the person who is **briefing** to add it to the mission information but it must be in writing and approved. (2) ensures he has all the mission's orders. There are no verbal orders. All orders are in writing. (3) he gives the missionaires the mission information to study. (4) he gives the mission orders to the missionaires for study. (5) has the missionaires do clay demos of all mission orders, and any of the mission information as necessary to ensure a proper understanding. (6) he then checks the missionaires out on the data and the orders directly from the written materials. (7) when satisfied that the missionaires are **briefed** and can *do* a successful mission, he then sends them to be checked out by an examiner on the mission data and orders. (FO 1606)

BRIEFING OFFICER, see MISSION BRIEFING OFFICER.

BRIEFING PROGRESS BOARD, a **briefing progress board** makes it easy to keep track of several missionaires, missions and pending missions and the cycles which have to be done by the **Briefing** Officer to get the mission out. Each cycle as labelled on the board is necessary to be complete before the mission can fire. (CBO 187)

BRIEFING SHEET, to facilitate a mission **briefing,** the **Briefing** Officer prepares a **Briefing Sheet.** This is a checklist of what has to be done during a **briefing** by the missionaires. It is similar to a course checksheet in that it gives the exact steps necessary to complete a **briefing.** One copy is made for each missionaire. This is done in advance of the mission coming into **briefing.** The missionaire's name goes on it. As each item is done he ticks it off. (CBO 260)

BRIEFING TAPE, done to **brief** or **debrief** missionaires or to record a conference or to record special instructions to a person or group. It can then be used for reference or to settle any dispute. It can also be used to inform a staff or several staffs. A **briefing tape** is then a **tape** designed for a special and informed audience. (HCOB 10 Nov 71)

BRIGHT STUDENT, you will find that often you have very glib **students** you won't be able to find any fault in who yet won't be able to apply or use the data they are passing. This student is discussed as the **bright student.** (HCO PL 4 Oct 64)

BRINGING A BODY, we can tell in orgs who is making fresh individual decisions as that person has to **bring** each of his own dispatches in personally. (We call it, **bringing a body.**) He routes himself too! (HCO PL 16 Apr 65RA III)

BRINGING ORDER, putting in stable data and "stringing the lines" in spite of the confusion. (FEBC 10, 7101C24 SO III)

BRING ORDER, **1.** in times of stress, commotion, riot or threats to person, an HCO personnel may instantly deputize any other Scientologist merely by saying loudly, "HCO **bring order.**" Making it known in any way that the Scientologist or Scientologists present should intervene or act.

(HCO PL 17 Mar 65 II) **2.** also means bring justice. (*HCO MOJ*)

BROAD BANDED, we are being too **broad banded** meaning we offer too many things. The variety makes no solid punch. Thus the public can see no purpose. (ED 164 FAO)

BROAD HANDLINGS, see INT/CONT HANDLINGS.

BROAD PUBLIC ISSUE, see BPI in Abbreviations section.

BROADSHEET, THE, the broadsheet is so called because it is in the tradition of the 17th-18th century **broadsheet** which were news **sheets** or pamphlets which were given out or posted in public places to give news and views to the local population. **The broadsheet** was started in the UK as an action in the handling of attacks. This was at a time when we were being attacked in Parliament and in the press and on TV when no air time or newsprint time or newsprint was devoted to give our viewpoint or the true facts from our viewpoint. Thus we decided that if we could not get our viewpoints printed we would print and distribute them ourselves, giving them away if necessary. This was done throughout the British attack, the **broadsheets** were sought by far more individuals than we had previously envisaged. (BPL 31 Jan 69, *PRO Broadsheets*)

BROCHURE, a compact list and description of HASI services and books issued by a Central Org. Must contain only standard services. No dated material. Describes each activity crisply and shows how to obtain these services. (HCO PL 4 Feb 61)

BROKER, 1. an agent who buys or sells stock, goods, services, etc., at the request of another; stockbroker, insurance broker. 2. a middleman who, for a fee, obtains a buyer for a seller or vice versa.

BROKERAGE, a company or joint interest that functions as a broker for clients in transactions involving stocks, bonds, commodities, etc.

BROKERAGE FEE, the fee or commission charged to a client by a broker for making a purchase or sale on behalf of the client.

BROKERS' CONTRACT NOTES, a document sent by a broker to a client that confirms that a purchase or sale requested by the client has been made. Data such as what was bought or sold at what price and when is usually included on the note.

BROUGHT BY A BODY, A, B, C and D routings are not **brought by a body** ever, any more than routine org dispatches would be. By **brought by a body** is meant brought in person, not by HCO. (HCO PL 13 Mar 65 II)

B ROUTING, 1. goes up in one's own org and across and down again to the same post as own in the other org. Dispatches so routed are clearly marked at the top **B Routing** with a full list of vias, written on it by the sender. Each via initials and forwards or stops it, says exactly why and returns it to sender. (HCO PL 13 Mar 65 II) **2.** by channels. (HCO PL 1 May 65)

BUDDY, the purpose of the **buddy** is to help new arrivals become familiar with the environment and learn the lines of the ship. The **buddy** helps train up the new arrival as a specialist on his WQSB post and attests in Qual that this has been done. (FSO 72)

BUDDY SYSTEM, 1. a flagship service to newly arriving pcs, recruits and students called the **buddy system.** A well qualified and experienced crew member or officer will act as your **buddy** to help you do your orientation checksheet and familiarize you with your new surroundings. He will answer any queries you may have. He is there to help you feel at home. He is your stable terminal for any confusions you might have when first aboard. (FO 2674) **2.** a standard duty of the Chaplain, to assign an experienced crew member as buddy to any new arrival to the ship. It is then the responsibility of the experienced member to take the new arrival under wing—be a safe terminal, and help groove the newer member in on what is expected of him on the ship, and what different channels are available for his use. E.g. training, processing, SO No. 1 line, daily report line, divisional conference procedure, Qual Consultant, canteen, bookstore, etc., etc. The experienced member should take responsibility for handling any misunderstoods and confusions of the newer member. (FSO 39)

BUDGET, 1. a statement of the total amount of money or resources available to an activity within a stated period of time and a breakdown of how it will be spent or allocated. The amount allowed to a budget is normally a calculation of what the area needs to be functional or achieve its purpose. 2. an estimation of future costs.

BUDGET ALLOCATION, a financial plan of probable income and expenditures for a given period, assigning a certain amount of money for use in meeting expenses to each department, division and project within the organization.

BUDGETARY CONTROL, the execution of measures designed to contain expenditure or use within the limitations of a budget. This is largely done by ensuring that only those expenditures called for in a budget are made and that no more is spent on goods or services than was originally planned in the budget.

BUDGET DEPARTMENT, the department in an organization responsible for financial summaries of anticipated income and expenditures for a given period usually just ahead and often accompanied by a systematic plan for meeting expenses.

BUDGET DETERMINATION, the determination of how large or small a budget should be.

BUDGET, FIXED, a firm budget used to forecast future expenditures, sales results, etc., based on past and present trends and levels of activity; forecast budget.

BUDGET, FLEXIBLE, 1. a budget that takes into consideration variations in production or business activity and makes alternate provisions for these variations. A flexible budget is used when the amount of production, sales or activity is variable and can only be generally predicted or where costs vary to a large degree. 2. a budget which may have to change during the course of operations.

BUDGET MANUAL, see MANUAL, BUDGET.

BUDGET, MASTER, the final or overall budget of an organization representing the combined budgets of all other aspects of the organization.

BUDGET, PERSONNEL, a special graph showing the minimum to maximum salary range in the field for various positions compared to the salaries actually paid by a company for each employee in each of those positions.

BUDGET, SUMMARY, an overall budget which shows the various budgets of other departments or functions of a business. This allows an overall financial picture showing what each area has been allocated.

BUDGET, TIME, 1. an estimation of the time necessary to do a job or complete a contract. 2. an allocation of the amount of time available to be spent on a job or series of jobs in order to effectively comply with an obligation, complete a contract, fill an order, etc.

BUFFER STOCK, see STOCK, BUFFER.

BUG, any **bug** will be found to be a stop on obtaining the valuable final product. (OODs 28 Mar 71)

BUGGED, **1.** slang for snarled up or halted. (HCO PL 29 Feb 72 II) **2.** stalled (HCO PL 14 Dec 73)

BUGGED TARGETS, a type of dev-t where a **target** develops **bugs** in its forwarding which are not seen or reported. The target stalls. A furious traffic burst may eventually occur to redo it and catch it up. (HCO PL 27 Jan 69)

BUILDING FUND, **1.** the purpose of this account is to provide a cushion by which an organization which is becoming insolvent may be salvaged. The secondary purpose of the **building fund** is to purchase property, but when this is done, the purchase must be for cash or, if any mortgage is involved, all further payments than the initial payment must be made from the expense sum. **Building fund** monies, being under the control of only the International Board, may also be used for other board purposes without local consultation. These include research projects or experimental dissemination projects in the local area or research on an international basis. (HCO PL 18 Jan 65) **2.** 12 1/2 per cent of the allocation sum. (HASI PL 19 Apr 57, *Proportionate Pay Plan*)

BULK MAIL, letters in and out is defined as personal signed letters, not a form letter. This statistic does not include mailing pieces, leaflets or circulars. **Bulk mail** is defined as all particles—**mailing** pieces, magazines, letters, etc. (HCO PL 5 Feb 71 III) [The above HCO PL was cancelled by BPL 10 Oct 75 IX.]

BULL-BAIT DUMMY RUN, you take a whole bunch of questions which the public would be prone to ask and you'd be surprised how funny some of the questions are. "Well, I have a check here on the Farmers Bank of Des Moines and it is for $2,000 and I owe you $260, so if you could give me the change, why then I would be happy to buy . . . ." See what your cashier does. See what he says. See if he handles it at all. You find out the bulk of the cashiers sort of say, "Get out, get out—hah!" That's not the proper public response. And therefore, your **bull-bait dummy runs** pay off because the **bull-bait dummy run** tests the personnel. The plain dummy run just tests the lines. (FEBC 10, 7101C24 SO III)

BULL-BAITING, in coaching certain drills, the coach attempts to find certain actions, words, phrases, mannerisms or subjects that cause the student doing the drill to become distracted from the drill by reacting to the coach. As a **bullfighter** attempts to attract the **bull's** attention and control the **bull**, so does the coach attempt to attract and control the student's attention; however the coach flunks the student whenever he succeeds in distracting the student from the drill and then repeats the action until it no longer has any effect on the student. Taken from a Spanish and English sport of "**baiting**" which means to "set dogs upon a chained bull," but mainly "to attack or torment especially with persistent insult, criticism or ridicule." Also "to tease." (LRH Def. Notes)

BULLETIN, see HUBBARD COMMUNICATIONS OFFICE BULLETINS.

BULLETIN CHECKLIST, the **bulletin checklist** is issued one each month, before the 15th of the next month. It will be airmailed to all Scn orgs independently. No electronic stencil is cut for it. Two copies, one for the HES and one for the LRH Comm are sent by airmail to each Scn org independently. This cross-checks whether or not the mimeo distribution system is working. In listing all mimeos sent, the distribution designation of each is given on the **bulletin checklist.** (HCO PL 14 Apr 69) [The above HCO PL was replaced by BPL 14 Apr 69R which does not mention **bulletin checklist.**]

BULL MARKET, see MARKET, BULL.

BULLPEN, that, by the way, is technical nomenclature used in these big electronic brains. They have standard banks and **bullpens** and the **bullpen** is where the data waits to be answered. (SPR Lect 13, 5304C07)

BUMPING, a system whereby a person with seniority in a company can take the job of an employee with lesser seniority. Bumping would normally occur for reasons of higher wages, better conditions, increased status, etc.

BUREAU 1, **1.** (FB Org Board) External HCO. (FB CO 9-1) **2.** The Flag Bureaux Establishment **Bureau** has its opposite bureau in all FOLOs. At that level it is also called the Establishment **Bureau** but contains only the first and third branches—Internal and External HCO. The External HCO branch on Flag operates its opposite FOLO branches as a network. Through this it executes its functions at a continental level. FOLO **Bureau 1** also mans FOLO management on direction of Flag **Bureau 1.** (FO 3591)

BUREAU 1A, (FB Org Board) HCO FB. (FB CO 9-1)

BUREAU 2, (FB Org Board) Dissemination **Bureau.** (FB CO 9-1)

BUREAU 2A, (FB Org Board) Marketing **Bureau.** (ED 459-56 Flag)

BUREAU 3, (FB Org Board) Treasury **Bureau.** (FB CO 9-1)

BUREAU 4, **1.** (FB Org Board) Data **Bureau.** (FB CO 9-1) **2.** (CLO) **Bureau 4** is the production **bureau** and covers the functions of data collection, assembly, display and evaluation, mission activities, management activities and routing communications to and from orgs and Flag. (SO ED 96 INT)

BUREAU 4A, Management **Bureau.** (CBO 435R)

BUREAU 4B, Programs **Bureau.** (CBO 435R)

BUREAU 5, **1.** (FB Org Board) Action **Bureau.** (FB CO 9-1) **2.** (CLO) **Bureau 5** covers the standard functions done in Scn org Tech and Qual divisions. (SO ED 96 INT)

BUREAU 5A, **1.** (FB Org Board) Training and Services **Bureau.** (FB CO 9-1) **2.** there would be a Qual **Bureau**, or it's called a Correction **Bureau** in a CLO, and it's **Bureau 5A** because Training and Services is Bureau 5. It is released with its org board of HCO PL 14 August 1971. Revised 5 September 1971. The basic line design is the Qual in the org, the Qual **Bureau** (Correction **Bureau**) in the CLO, and then there is somebody in the Flag **Bureau** who is looking after that line. (7109C05 SO)

BUREAU 6, **1.** (Flag) the purpose of the Distribution **Bureau** (**Bureau 6**) is: to help LRH distribute Scn by putting Scn orgs in every spot of the globe such that every conceivable geographical area is totally covered. The valuable final product of **Bureau 6** is: new orgs. (FBDL 443) **2.** a **bureau** in the FB that manages FOLO Tours Orgs, groups, missions and creates new orgs as well as public surveys and campaigns. (BFO 122-6) **3.** (CLO) **Bureau 6** covers those functions done in Scn orgs, three Public Divisions. (SO ED 96 INT)

BUREAU 7, [Executive **Bureau.**]

BUREAU AIDES, **1.** the **Bureau Aides** are the heads of the **Bureau** Divisions and are at the same time responsible for opposite numbered divisions. (FBDL 3) **2.** Staff Aides' responsibilities are covered in various LRH CBOs. They are responsible for their opposite number divisions in all orgs.

They do divisional evaluations. FB **Bureaux Aides** run their **bureaux** and ensure all their **bureau** functions are carried out which add up to managed orgs. (CBO 435R)

BUREAU LIAISON OFFICER, 1. in Department 21 you have another post which is **liaison officer.** He's the **Bureau Liaison Officer.** Now, all of your communication to the **bureau** should go through a **Bureau Liaison Officer** and all the communication from a **bureau** should go to the **Bureau Liaison Officer.** (FEBC 12, 7102C03 SO II) **2.** the basic communication terminal through which the **bureau** communicates to the org. (FEBC 12, 7102C03 SO II) **3.** a **Bureaux Liaison Officer** will be established in orgs. At the moment he double-hats also as LRH Comm. The **Bureaux Liaison Officer** (in the LRH Comm Dept) is the one channel to CLOs which are the one channel of command for orgs. (LRH ED 135 INT) **4.** in each Scn org an officer in the department of the LRH Comm, who will be the single receipt and dispatch terminal for that org for its orders, reports, compliances, etc. (SO ED 96 INT) See FLAG REPRESENTATIVE.

BUREAU SYSTEM, 1. an *admin* **system** which extends authority and control as well as generates correction by admin checks and balances. Nowhere does it depend on current individual authority and individual authority can be considered as almost negligible in a well organized **bureau system.** (FO 2534) **2.** a **bureau system** is an extension of central authority and is itself an administrative generation of authority and orders. An autonomy succeeds only by a few stellar individuals being opportunely placed. A **bureau system** runs by admin and corrects itself by admin. (FO 2534)

BUREAUX, 1. a **bureaux** set up is defined as a team where each member works as a team member first and a trained specialist second, who contributes his specialty to the team effort. **Bureaux** exist to expand Dn and Scn by raising stats and delivery in existing activities and expanding the area by forming new activities whose stats and delivery are then raised. (CBO 51) **2.** a division is called a **bureau.** The plural (French) is *bureaux.* (CBO 52) **3.** the **bureau** is external. A **bureau** always has external products. The external management function and so on is the **bureau** function. **Bureau** is something that operates another org; it doesn't operate the org that's there. (ESTO 2, 7203C01 SO II) **4.** Flag Org, WW and Cont'l ECs go through **bureaux** which coordinates their orders, prevents conflict and makes a one channel communication line to orgs. (CBO 28) **5.** policy is the broad general outline originated by top management. Orders are the instructions issued by the next lower level of management to get things done that result in products. Here is where a **bureau** acts. It is a supervisor and orderer for top management. (FBDL 12) **6.** each CLO is patterned after the highly successful and standard 7 Division Org Board issued in HCO Policy Letters in 1967. Each division is called a **bureau.** (SO ED 96 INT) *Abbr.* BU.

BUREAUX ACTION, any stress or confusion in running the Flag **Bureaux** or a Continental Liaison **Bureaux** would *have* to be *made.* The flow is elementary. The data is gotten in=collected stats, reports, dispatches. It is condensed=plotted, assembled, filed, made available internally. A very high or very low stat is spotted by evaluations and all relevant data on it is found in the **bureaux** so as to locate and state the real why. The evaluation analysis is distributed. The action planning does a plan. Operations designates a branch office or the local unit to activate it. A missionaire goes or it is left to the **Bureaux** Liaison Office in the org. The plan is posted with the stat and when the stat recovers or we have the new data to publish on a high stat, the cycle is ended. This is actually all that is basically going on in **bureaux.** When you understand it as a simple, repeating cycle, you understand **bureaux action.** (CBO 50)

BUSH TELEGRAPH, the rumor factor. It is valueless in itself being fragmentary data. (HCO PL 13 Mar 65 II)

BUSINESS, remunerative activity. (7205C18 SO)

BUSINESS ADMINISTRATION, see ADMINISTRATION.

BUSINESS COMMUNICATIONS, the types of written or spoken communication that a business uses in the administration of its affairs, i.e., telex, dispatch, telephone, written directives and letters, verbal communications, etc.

BUSINESS CONDITIONS, the external conditions exerted by the environment which affect or modify business activities. These include prohibitive or inhibitive national or state legislation, availability of personnel, raw materials, fuel, current demand for goods or services, public opinion, scientific advancement, future trends, etc.

BUSINESS CONFERENCE, a group meeting on one or more business matters whose members are each qualified in their field to present data and valid viewpoints of the topics under discussion.

BUSINESS INDICATORS, see INDICATORS, BUSINESS.

BUSINESS ORGANIZATION, see ORGANIZATION.

BUSINESS PLANNING, see PLANNING, BUSINESS,

BUTLER, in general charge of domestic staff. Hires and dismisses domestic personnel. Looks after the security of the Manor, its doors, windows, locks. Has charge of all furnishing and decoration. Supervises all food preparation and serving. Serves as valet. Cares for all interior electrical supplies. Handles and sees to the repair of all domestic appliances and cooking fuel. Conserves heat and electricity. Has charge of all menus. (HCO PL 18 Dec 64, *Saint Hill Org Board*)

BUTTON, the primary thing you get from your survey is a **button.** This is the answer that was given the most number of times to your survey question. (BPL 13 Jul 72R)

BUYER, 1. a person who purchases goods or services for himself; customer, patron. 2. a person authorized or employed to purchase goods or services for another.

BUYER CREDIT, credit extended to someone solely for the purpose of buying goods or services. Such credit is not advanced for the purpose of manufacturing or investment in the marketing of goods or services.

BY DEP, the appearance of the **deputy** counts as attendance **by** the member but is noted in the minutes as "Smith **by deputy**" instead of "Smith." An Ad Council meeting is called to order by the Master at Arms who reads the roll call from a prepared list, marking absent with an X, present with a circle and **by dep** when **by deputy.** (HCO PL 2 Nov 66)

BYLAWS, a set of rules that a corporation adopts to handle its internal affairs and methods of operation. The bylaws are usually drawn up by the Board of Directors during the formative stages of a corporation.

BYPASS, 1. ignore the junior or juniors normally in charge of the activity and handle it personally. (HCO PL 16 Jan 66) **2.** jumping the proper terminal in a chain of command. (HCO PL 19 Jan 66 III)

C

CADET, any child who has passed his Staff Status II and AB or engine room checksheet and has a post which he is holding in the Sea Org and who has a good ethics record is hereafter to be referred to not in a generality of "children," but as a **cadet.** A **cadet** has rank equal to a deckhand or motorman. (FO 760)

Cadet

CADET ORG, it will be a Seven Division Org manned by children who have actual posts. Its org board must be planned out; must be standard. Any discipline goes through the **Cadet Org.** They must, every one of them, be hatted. Unless they are signed up SO members, the children are used in the galley or estates EPF only. There must be a nursery. There must be QMs on duty as reception. There must be stable personnel—and there only could be if this were to have the status of an org. You want quarters where you can have a baby care unit, dormitories, kitchens and moderate space for the **Cadet Org** desks, auditing and Qual functions. Why should they be miserable and knocked about when they can have their own **org** and be respected and demand respect from their elders as well, and feel proud of themselves. The real trick is to get them over to cause without their having to use naughtiness to be at covert cause. A **Cadet Org** could accomplish that. (ED 18 Area Estates)

CADET SCHOOL, the basic purpose of **Cadet School** is to: (a) have all **cadets** able to read quickly with a large vocabulary and compose well, (b) have all **cadets** able to write swiftly, legibly and elegantly, (c) have all **cadets** able to do arithmetic quickly, accurately and legibly, including addition, subtraction, multiplication and division, and including degrees, minutes and seconds. (FO 2013)

CAESAR MANAGEMENT, see MANAGEMENT, CAESAR.

CALCULATING MACHINE, basically an electronic or mechanical machine operated similar to a typewriter and having numbered keys which you press to feed in figures for addition, subtraction, multiplication and division. Pushing a final key will instantly give the answer to the mathematical figures fed in.

CALCULATOR see CALCULATING MACHINE.

CALLABLE, 1. a type of preferred stock which may be redeemed by the issuing company. 2. a bond issue, all or a portion of which may be redeemed by the issuing company under definite circumstances before maturity.

CALLER BOOK, the Personnel Chief must keep a **caller book** and note in it each person and time, with date and other particulars, a person comes to him asking for transfer. (FO 2127)

CALL-IN REGISTRATION, **calling in** paid-up persons, a function of the Advance Scheduling **Registrar.** An Advance Scheduling **Registrar** never never waits for tech to call in paid-up persons. The Advance Scheduling **Reg calls** these people **in!** (HCO PL 28 Nov 71R I)

CAMERA WORK, where plates are made and photos or art plates are made. This has a branch line, in color, which comes just before it of making color separation negatives. (FO 3574)

CAMOUFLAGED HOLE, **1.** a **hole** in the org line up that *appears* to be a post. Yet it isn't a held post because its duties are not being done. It is therefore a **hole** people and actions fall into without knowing it is there. It can literally drive an org mad to have a few of these around. **Camouflage** means "disguised" or made to appear something else. In this case a **hole** in the line up is **camouflaged** by the fact that somebody appears to be holding it who isn't. (HCO PL 10 Sept 70) **2.** means post not filled but only appears to be, thus leaving a **hole** in the line up. Such people always cause overwork by persons above or below them and are pretty dangerous to have around. (HCO PL 17 Nov 64). **3.** when a hat is not worn for any reason at all, one gets a breakdown at that point. We call this a **camouflaged hole.** Somebody has a title but doesn't do the duties or actions that go with it. (OODs 25 Apr 70) **4.** a **camouflaged hole** is one that looks like there is something there, but it is actually a **hole,** and of course that itself will generate dev-t. Now he's very obvious as a being and he may be carrying the title of Qual Sec but if he is not holding the actual post duties of Qual Sec he will generate just by that missingness, enormous dev-t, because the people all around him will have to wear the hat of Qual Sec. (ESTO 3, 7203C02 SO I) **5.** undetected neglect area. (HCO PL 19 Dec 69)

CAMPAIGN, basically a **campaign** is a series of connected activities to get something done; a planned course of action for some special purpose. (FBDL 325)

CAN'T BE DONE, in the matter of **can'ts,** an executive seldom orders the impossible and generally consults with people before issuing an order. A persistent **can't be done** means "I am unwilling." (HCO PL 10 Apr 63)

CAN'T BE SPARED PHENOMENON, this is where one staff member who produces well is considered so vital to the org's production that he **can't be spared** even for further training which will enhance his value to the org and its production. (FO 3367)

CANTEENS, **canteens** serve the purpose of providing crews and staffs with food, drinks, cigarettes and confections at those times when meals are not being served. (FO 2416)

Canteen

CAPACITY, 1. the measure of ability to pay a debt when due. 2. the ability to perform some task. 3. the degree of competency to deal with organizational situations, work and personnel.

CAPERS, PR events or actions. (HCO PL 27 Feb 74)

CAPITAL APPROPRIATION, funds set aside to spend on fixed assets.

CAPITAL ASSETS, see ASSETS, CAPITAL.

CAPITAL, FIXED, capital represented by land, buildings, plant equipment or other long lasting asset used over and over again over a long period of time.

CAPITAL GOODS, 1. goods of a permanent nature such as buildings and machinery necessary for the production of a company's commodities. 2. fixed assets.

CAPITALIZATION, total value of the securities issued by an organization which may be composed of bonds, debentures, preferred and common stock and surplus.

CAPITAL, LIQUID, currency, notes, securities, or other assets that will readily convert to cash. Also called current or quick capital.

CAPITAL, NOMINAL, total of the nominal or face value of a company's shares.

CAPITAL, RISK, term for capital used for long term loans or invested in businesses or ventures with an appreciable amount of risk. Also called venture capital.

CAPITAL, UNCALLED, company capital that is authorized for the issuance of more stock but about which stockholders have not yet been approached.

CAPITAL, VENTURE, see CAPITAL, RISK.

CAPITAL, WORKING, the current monies or net worth of an individual or company, after deducting current liabilities, that is available to be put to work in the operation. Also called net current assets.

CAPTAIN, 1. on Flag the **Captain** is double-hatted as the CO FSO and thus has an assistant **captain** though this is not necessarily the way it must be. Therefore, as CO FSO he is located in Dept. 19, wearing a separate hat from captain. The **Captain** runs his ship which includes the engine room, deck and galley, and carries out his post duties in accordance with his hat as established in FOs. He runs these areas via the Assistant **Captain,** Chief Engineer, 1st Mate and Chief Steward. He is the Senior Product Officer of the area, and wears the planning and programming hats. (FO 3576RA) **2.** the **Captain** in Department 21 is subject to owner or board; the highest authority aboard in all divisional and departmental matters, and subject to the owner's or board's and their Commodore, but the ship, its cargo, its crew and passengers, and all conduct of operations are subject to the **Captain.** This is regardless of his licenses or qualifications and he may be assisted by a yeoman, messenger, etc. (FO 1109) **3.** the Chief Product Officer for the ship. (ED 145 Flag) **4.** the senior officer in command of a ship, org, or area. (FO 2389) *Abbr.* Capt.

CAPTAIN'S MAST, the **Captain** of a ship is its judge and at sea **Captain's Mast** is held on Saturday morning. In a very large ship it is preceded by the Chief Officer's (or Executive Officer's) Mast wherein the Executive Officer passes on all offenders and sends the more reprehensible ones to the **Captain's Mast.** The **Captain** may, however, at any time sentence offenders. Up until only a century ago he had the authority to hang men until one hanged the son of the Secretary of the Navy of the US for mutiny, after which the custom lapsed. Modern practice limits the **Captain's Mast** punishment to ten days in the brig on bread and water. In merchant service the offender is logged and loses one or more day's pay as a result. In the Sea Organization the Commodore or the ship's **Captain** assigns conditions without the formality of a **mast** and these conditions and their rewards or penalties constitute in the main the bulk of Sea Organization justice. (FO 87)

CAPTAIN'S MESSENGER, the **Captain** of any major SO vessel has a **messenger.** The **messenger** carries the **Captain's Messages.** He helps the Captain's Yeoman keep the files and comm station. The **messenger** also serves as a guard. The **messenger** serves as Captain's Bowman in boats. The **messenger** carries packages or luggage for the Captain when ashore. The **messenger** may be sent on errands by the Captain's Yeoman. The **captain's messenger** on duty wears a tar hat and a petty officer cap badge on it and a duty belt which is white. (FO 1274)

CAPTAIN'S STEWARD, regardless of who is **captain,** there must be on major Sea Org vessels a **Captain's Steward.** The duties of a **Captain's Steward** are similar to those of a Commodore's Steward. The **Captain's Steward** keeps the quarters, clothes, laundry, equipment, dishes, silver, linen and supplies of the **Captain** up and cared for. The **Captain's Steward** serves the **Captain** at meals and prepares and serves snacks and coffee when the **Captain** is on long watches at sea. (FO 1274)

CAPTAIN'S YEOMAN, the **Captain** of Flag is entitled to a **yeoman.** The **Captain's Yeoman** handles the **Captain's** paper, letters, routings, arrangements and papers and helps the Captain keep his files. (FO 1274)

CARD VOTE, see VOTE, CARD.

CARE FOR IT, care for it is a broader concept than but similar to start, change or stop it. It includes guard it, help it, like it, be interested in it, etc. (HCO PL 17 Jan 62)

CARRIAGE, INSURANCE AND FREIGHT, **carriage, insurance and freight** means that the price quoted is inclusive of shipping costs, **insurance** and **freighting** charges to a specified address. (FO 2738) *Abbr.* CIF.

CARRIER, in an office, a carrier is one who carries written messages and various materials. In transportation and mail, the same definition applies. In insurance, the company that takes on the financial risk is known as a carrier.

CARRIER WAVE, a Public Relations Officer uses ideas to act as a **carrier wave** for his message. By **carrier wave** is meant the impulse to forward them along. (HCO PL 5 Feb 69 II)

CARTEL, a combine of several, usually large, companies that agree to fix prices, control regions, etc., in order to dominate the market for their products and/or services by escaping competition.

CASE ASSESSMENT FORM, the first action of an auditor with a pc new to him is to fill in the **Case Assessment Form.** This is done on the pc's auditing time. (See HCOB of November 18, 1960 for exact form.) (HCO PL 20 Mar 61 II) [HCOB 18 Nov 60, *Preclear Assessment Sheet* mentioned above is now issued as BTB 24 Apr 69R, *Preclear Assessment Sheet.*] See METER CASE ASSESSMENT FORM.

CASE FILE, it is vital that the HGC retain a **case file** for every **case** it ever processes. This specifically includes staff members. All auditor's reports, assessments and notes and recommendations concerning a **case,** including staff **cases,** must be part of this **file.** This **file** must be available to staff auditors processing the preclear. Anything an auditor knows about a **case,** as a general summary, should be put in the pc's **file** for future reference, especially at the end of an intensive. (HCO PL 30 Jan 61)

CASE SUPERVISOR, **1.** the **case supervisor** does the folders. The **case supervisor** does not interview cases but runs them by the book and folder. (HCO PL 1 Feb 66 III) **2. supervises** the **cases** of all students on the course. (HCO PL 18 Dec 64, *Saint Hill Org Board*) **3.** the **case supervisors** of an org are all located in Division 4, Department 12 in the HGC **case supervision** section headed by the Senior **CS.** This includes the Senior **CS,** the EX DN **CS,** the Grades **CS,** one or two DN **CSes,** the Academy or Student **CS** and the Staff **CS.** (HCO PL 26 Sept 74) *Abbr.* CS.

CASE SUPERVISOR CORRECTION LIST, HCO Bulletin 27 March 1972, Issue IV, *Case Supervisor Correction List, Study Correction List 4.* This one **corrects case supervisors,** gets them back on the rails. (LRH ED 257 INT)

CASH, any **cash** shown on a cash bills graph is **cash** salvaged from former allocations (org reserves) or current allocations. The **cash** expressed on the **cash** bills graph of the org must exist in actuality and must be real sums that can be expended. It may not be "credit coming to us from an FBO" nor collectible but not received sums. Even cheques delayed in clearing may not be part of this org **cash** figure. (HCO PL 29 Jan 71)

CASH, money or actual currency in hand or in the bank.

CASH/BILLS, **cash/bills** as reported by Div 3 includes sums actually *on hand* in the 3 org accounts (Main, Reserve, HCO Book) vs **bills** due and purchases newly ordered. (BPL 26 Apr 71RA)

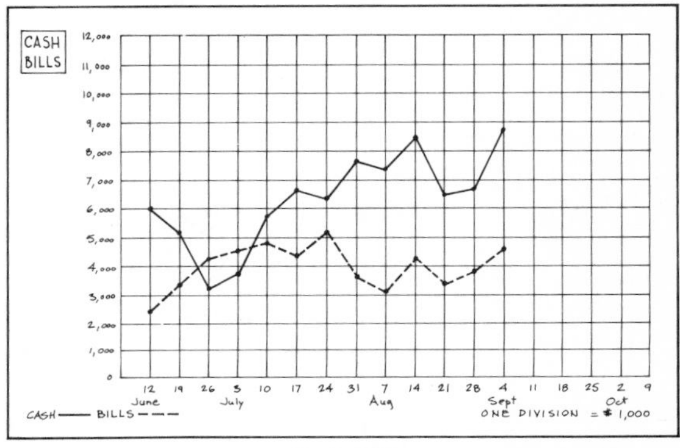

Cash/Bills

CASH BOOK, a record book of transactions listing the amounts of money spent (debits) and money received (credits), and whether the business was done in cash or via a bank.

CASH DIFFERENTIAL, this is a phrase used to describe the **difference** between what a department or organization receives in income and what it directly spends in costs. It does not include funds for research or the support of non-profit activities, gifts, royalties or other matters. It is a clean statement of so many pounds received due to a department's or an organization's activities less how many pounds that department or organization spent for salaries, materials, supplies, printing, advertising, maintenance and a general share of quarters, utilities, and general service. (HCO PL 26 Jun 64)

CASH FLOW, 1. the movement of cash in and out of an organization necessary to meet operating expenses on a daily, weekly, monthly or yearly basis. 2. record of the origin of all cash receipts, the items purchased with the cash, and the consequence of these transactions on an organization's ready cash supply.

CASHIER, a person who has charge of money in a bank or business. (HCO Admin Ltr 30 Jul 75)

Cashier

CASH ON HAND, cash on hand is from reconciled bank statements of org bank accounts. Any **cash** shown on a **cash**/bills graph is **cash** salvaged from former allocations (org reserves) or current allocations. The **cash** expressed on the **cash**/bills graph of the org must exist in actuality and must be real sums that can be expended. It may not be "credit coming to us from an FBO" nor collectible but not received sums. Even cheques delayed in clearing may not be part of this org cash figure (nor may any expenditures be committed against uncleared funds). The **cash on hand** figure may not include sums held in FBO No. 1 or No. 2 accounts, or in any Guardian Office accounts. (BPL 1 Jul 72R)

CASH RATIO, 1. in an organization, the cash ratio is the relative magnitude of liquid assets to its current liabilities. 2. in a bank, cash ratio is the relative magnitude of cash holdings to its deposit liabilities.

CASTING VOTE, see VOTE, CASTING.

CASUALTY CONTACT, a fruitful source of HAS Co-audit people is **casualty contact,** using his minister's card, an auditor need only barge into any non-sectarian hospital, get permission to visit the wards from the superintendent, mentioning nothing about processing but only about taking care of people's souls, to find himself wonderfully welcome. It's fabulous what one can get done in a hospital with a touch assist and locational processing. (HCOB 15 Sept 59)

CATASTROPHES, a type of dev-t. A **catastrophe** occurs by lack of prediction of a possible circumstance. Those things planned for do not become **catastrophes. Catastrophes** usually follow a period of excessive dev-t. (HCO PL 27 Nov 69)

CATEGORY ANALYSIS, see ANALYSIS, CATEGORY.

CAUSATION, self-determinism is entirely and solely the imposition of time and space upon energy flows. Imposing time and space upon objects, people, self, events, and individuals, is **causation.** (*Scn 8-80,* p. 44)

CAUSATIVE STATISTICS, in any set of statistics of several kinds or activities, you can always find one or more that are not "by luck" but can be directly caused by the org or a part of it. Amongst any set of statistics are those which can be pushed up regardless of the rest and if these aren't, then you know the worst—no management. (HCO PL 6 Nov 66 I)

CED PROJECT, when targets of a **Compliance Executive Directive** require a **project** to get it in, such a **project** shall be called **CED Project.** (BPL 24 Jul 73R III)

CEILING, is defined as the set figure on which an organization operates weekly, regardless of the income. (HCO PL 10 Dec 68)

CEILING PRICE, see PRICE, CEILING.

CELEBRITY, any person important in his field or an opinion leader or his entourage, business associates, family or friends with particular attention to the arts, sports and management and government. (HCO PL 23 May 76)

CELEBRITY CENTRE, 1. one of the major purposes of the **Celebrity Centre** and its staff is to expand the number of **celebrities** in Scn. It does this disseminating to and selecting **celebrities** to orgs. This is done by establishing itself as the stable datum for handling **celebrities.** If any **celebrity** wishes to know more about Scn, he is contacted by the **Celebrity Centre,** handled, disseminated to, and selected. (FO 2310) **2.** it is responsible for ensuring that **celebrities** expand in their area of power. This organization is also responsible for a **celebrity's** basic training in Scn. (FO 2361) *Abbr.* CC.

CELEBRITY DISSEMINATION DEPARTMENT, **Celebrity** Center Department 11A. Its product is **celebrity** broad **disseminations** of Scn. (BO 7 PAC, 17 Feb 74)

CELESTIAL NAVIGATION, simply the science of recognition of your position by the recognition of **celestial** (which means heavenly) objects (stars, moon, sun, planets, etc.) and estimating the angles between them and your horizon. (FO 3370)

CELLULAR ORGANIZATION, see ORGANIZATION, CELLULAR.

CENSUS SURVEY, a market research survey to obtain the total prospective buyers, or the market, for a product. When only a portion of prospective buyers or market is contacted, this is called a sample survey.

CENTRAL, (letter designations on HCOBs) HCO Area Offices only, no City Offices. These are issued only to HCO Area Offices. (HCOB 24 Feb 59)

CENTRAL BUREAUX ORDER, applies to SO **Bureaux.** It is distributed to **bureaux** personnel and SO org executives only. Usually noted under heading to what **bureau** it refers. Issued by the head of a **central bureau** at Flag. Black on white. Has no force on non-bureaux personnel. Similar to a Guardian's Order in content and effect. These regulate the organization and activity of SO **Bureaux** and their offices. **Bureaux** need master files for **bureaux** hats. (HCO PL 24 Sept 70R) *Abbr.* CBO.

CENTRAL COMMITTEE OF EVIDENCE, a **Central Committee of Evidence** is convened by the Association/Organization Secretary of any **Central** Organization or City Office. It has exactly the same powers and scope as the HCO Area Committee of Evidence, but would normally not handle cases involving field auditors, field technical practice or matters relating to disputes between public and the **Central** Organization or City Office as to fees, payments or service failures, which are all more properly the business of HCO. The **Central Committee of Evidence** is more properly concerned with all matters relating to the conduct and activities of organization members, administrative, technical and personal, fixing responsibility for various conditions or breakdowns within the organization and safeguarding the organization against personal conduct or security risks prejudicial to effectiveness and public repute. Threatened dismissals, requests for reinstatement, protests against transfers or injury to reputation as well as marital or second dynamic matters are all heard by the **Central Committee of Evidence.** (HCO PL 7 Sept 63)

CENTRAL FILES, **1.** a collection of **files,** one for every person who has *ever* bought something from an organization, gathered together in the one location in the organization. The name and address of every person in **central files** collectively make up the org mailing list. Conversely, every person on the org mailing list has a folder in **central files.** (BPL 17 May 69R I) **2.** receives and files all Scientologist and student correspondence for filing and files. Furnishes materials for departments and registrars. (HCO PL 18 Dec 64, *Saint Hill Org Board*) **3.** the purpose of **central files** is to collect and hold all names, addresses, pertinent data about and correspondence to anyone from anyone who has ever bought anything from the organization. (HCO PL 23 Sept 64) **4.** **central files** contains folders of persons who have bought something. Not idle lists. **CF** folders contain names of persons active in the last three years, persons who wrote to us or bought something. (HCO PL 16 Apr 62) **5.** the definition of the Div 2 **CF** is those who have bought something from the org. (FSO 360) **6.** these include a **file** folder for everyone who has ever bought anything from the Central Org. Everything about a person, except his financial statements, actual training record and test record is in **CF**, but data even on these, such as a profile sheet, can be included. For instance, a copy of an invoice, the profile of a new test taken, a notice of certification, all are forwarded to **CF** for filing. (HCO PL 14 Feb 61, *The Pattern of a Central Organization*) *Abbr.* CF.

CENTRAL FILES - ADDRESSO TASK FORCE, a **task force** is a specially trained, self-contained unit assigned to a specific mission or task, or any group assigned to a specific project. A **CF-addresso task force** is a specially trained, self-contained unit assigned to the specific project of handling backlogged and ill-matched **CFs** and **addressos** in SO and Area Orgs. (FO 3489)

CENTRAL FILES CLERK, you need a minimum of three people in CF: (1) CF Officer, (2) CF **Clerk,** (3) CF Liaison. The **CF Clerk** pulls and files folders for the org other than Dissem and files particles. Particles are filed in date order to save the registrars messing around with out of sequence folders. (HCO PL 18 Feb 73 IV)

CENTRAL FILES FOLDER, 1. the **CF folder** is the **folder** of a person who has bought something from an organization. In it is filed all the data concerning the person, any correspondence to or from the person to anyone in the organization. Everything about a person, except his financial statements, actual training record, and test record is in **CF**, but data even on these such as a notice of certification, can be included. (BPL 17 May 69R I) **2.** is the **folder** of a person who has bought something from an org. (HCO PL 8 Apr 65) **3. CF folders** contain names of persons active in the last three years, persons who wrote to us or bought something. (HCO PL 16 Apr 62) **4.** the **CF folder** is an interesting item all by itself because it is the body of the opposite number, the magic body of the person who is in the field. It's actually a magic body. It's a counterfeit body that the organization holds, so therefore a person is never in **CF** until he has originated himself to the organization. The definition of a **CF folder** is: it is that **folder** which contains all and everything (except for the testing records) that has been originated to an organization by an outside person. There should be a **folder** for every such person. (5812C16) **5.** these **folders** never decay unless the person dies or asks to be taken off the list. Everything relating to communication with this person and new invoices etc., including phone notes goes in his folder. (LRH ED 49 INT)

CENTRAL FILES IN-CHARGE, all files on Scientologists or applicants are under **Central Files In-Charge.** These include a **file** folder for every one who has bought anything from the Central Org. (HCO PL 20 Dec 62)

CENTRAL FILES INFORMATION SLIP, (**CF info slip**) with current invoice routing policy no copy of credit/debit invoices ever get to **CF.** The fact that a person has just made an AP or has just come into the org to start a service on AP used may not be known from the **CF** file. To remedy this situation and prevent further unusual solutions and complicated admin, the **CF information slip** is brought into use. The **CF info slip** is made out: (1) whenever an invoice is written for an AP received, whether in the mail or over the counter; (2) whenever an invoice is written for an AP used. The person who has written such an invoice fills in the **CF info slip** and routes it at once to **CF** via the ASR or org communication lines. (HCO PL 29 Apr 73 I)

CENTRAL FILES LIAISON, you need a minimum of three people in CF: (1) CF Officer, (2) CF Clerk, (3) **CF Liaison.** The **CF Liaison** only pulls, collects folders and files for *Dissem.* He never files particles, only **CF** folders and only for *Dissem.* (HCO PL 18 Feb 73 IV)

CENTRAL FILES OFFICER, you need a minimum of three people in CF: (1) **CF Officer,** (2) CF Clerk, (3) CF Liaison. The **Central Files Officer** is in charge of the section and sees to: (a) new folders being made up, (b) correction to addresses, (c) folders being pulled into the org (new business from Div 6), (d) folders filed, (e) the CF Clerk and CF Liaison producing, (f) sufficient file cabinets and adequate space for **CF** to expand into. (HCO PL 18 Feb 73 IV)

CENTRAL FILES/PROMOTION LIAISON, your post of **CF Liaison** is important to me. You have to select hot **files** from **CF** and get them written to by registrar and select ARC Breaks with the organization from **CF** and get them cared for by the Assistant Registrar. (SEC ED 1, 15 Dec 58)

CENTRAL FILES SECTION, (Dissemination Division) the prime purpose of the **Central Files Section** is: to help Ron collect and hold all names, addresses, pertinent data about and correspondence to anyone from anyone who has ever bought anything from the organization. (HCO PL 21 Sept 65 VI)

CENTRAL FILES UNIT, all **files** on Scientologists or applicants are under **Central Files** In-Charge. These include a **file** folder for everyone who has ever bought anything from the Central Org. The **files** are divided into live and inactive **files.** Magazines go out only to live **files.** But letters may be written to persons in live and inactive **files.** Everything about a person, except his financial statements, actual training record and test record is in **CF**, but data even on those, such as profile sheet, can be included. For instance a copy of an invoice, the profile of a new test taken, a notice of certification, all are forwarded to **CF** for **filing.** (HCO PL 20 Dec 62)

CENTRALIZATION, an organizing plan by which activities of the same type or similar in nature are brought together in an organization forming a central group, as in the establishment of one purchasing department for an entire company.

CENTRALIZED HIRING, see HIRING, CENTRALIZED.

CENTRALIZED MANAGEMENT, see MANAGEMENT, CENTRALIZED.

CENTRALIZED PURCHASING, see PURCHASING, CENTRALIZED.

CENTRAL OFFICE OF LRH ED, a new numbered series is established for the **Office of LRH** on Flag. Anyone in this **office** may use this series. The color of the paper is yellow or buff. The ink is blue. LRH Pers PRO Bureau, Compilations Unit and other **Central Office of LRH** activities have their orders and actions in these issues. (COLRHED 1R) *Abbr.* COLRHED.

CENTRAL ORGANIZATION, **1.** to clarify the functions and purposes of Scientology organizations, this was the original intention: Worldwide was to provide supreme control over Scientology and orgs over the world. Continental Orgs under the guidance of WW took full responsibility for their continental areas. **Central Orgs** under the guidance of Continental took full responsibility for their zones. Area Orgs took full responsibility for their own areas. WW founded new Continental Orgs. Continental Orgs founded **Central Orgs. Central Orgs** founded Area Orgs. Area Orgs founded Franchise Centres. This was the original pattern of intention. (LRH ED 1 INT) **2.** Class IV **Org.** (HCO PL 6 Feb 66) **3.** a **Central Org** promotes action in junior orgs and franchises and field and helps by training up their auditors and handling their tough pcs. An auditor in a lesser org or the field should know he can get training from the **Central Org** and should know that he can unload tough pcs on it. Services may be delivered to anyone in the continental area who wishes to take them in the **Central Org.** The **Central Org** promotes directly to the public in its own area, and helps the Area Orgs, franchises and groups to successfully carry out their functions so as to produce streams of customers from their areas to the **Central Org.** The **Central Org** has long been charged with holding the tech standard for its area. It must hold a standard, as a stable terminal, for all the flow lines of its continent. (LRH ED 34 INT) **4.** there are two divisions in a **Central Organization.** One is Technical, the senior division, the other is Administration. There are six departments. The Technical Division includes these three departments: the PE Foundation, the Academy of Scientology and the Hubbard Guidance Center. These carry out the three basic services of a **Central Organization**—public training and processing, individual training and individual processing. The Administrative Division consists of three departments: Promotion and Registration, Material and Accounts. These care for the three basic functions of contacting and signing up people, taking care of quarters and supplies, and handling all matters of finance. (HCO PL 14 Feb 61, *The Pattern of a Central Organization*) **5.** a **Central Organization** is basically a service **organization.** (5812C29)

CENTRAL PERSONNEL FILES SECTION, (**Central Personnel** Office) The purpose of the **Central Personnel Files Section** is to collect data relating to **personnel** from all orgs, coordinate it by continent and org, and by alphabetical order of the staff of that org, so that it can be used for postings, evaluations, and for monitoring the progress of each staff member wherever he may be. Therefore the purpose of the **files** is to furnish information on any staff member from any org in order in one folder. (BPL 12 May 73R II)

CENTRAL PERSONNEL OFFICE, **1.** The Flag **Central Personnel Office** exists on Flag headed by the **Central Personnel Officer,** with a command line into the Department One of every org. The purpose of the **Central Personnel Office** is: to help LRH accomplish internationally recruited **personnel** well trained before placing and all **personnel** well and properly posted. The purpose is achieved by ensuring that each individual org is recruiting and hiring, is training personnel before placement, and is posting **personnel** well and properly and continuing staff training in accordance with all **personnel** policy. (BPL 3 Apr 73R II) **2.** that **office** on Flag with branches in each continental area which supervises the recruitment, programming, training, posting and utilization of **personnel** in Sea Org and Scientology orgs in all continents. (CBO 214RA) *Abbr.* CPO.

CENTRAL PERSONNEL OFFICE FILES, **files** where records of every staff member of every org and operation past and present are kept. (BPL 13 Aug 73R II)

CENTRAL PERSONNEL OFFICER, the Flag **Central Personnel Office** exists on Flag headed by the **Central Personnel Officer.** (BPL 3 Apr 73R II) *Abbr.* CPO.

CENTRE MAGAZINE, the publication *Centre* **magazine** is authorized for issue by Franchise Office WW to field and missions. It is issued quarterly. The purpose of the **magazine** is to help Ron establish new missions and get existing ones active and expanded. It contains feature news photos of mission personnel in action, and of mission **centres.** Articles concern successful actions or good applications of tech in dissemination or administration and show how missions are changing their environments with Scn. (BPL 1 May 71R)

CERTAINTY, he walks over to the wall and pushes the button and the lights go on. He knows if he goes over to the wall and pushes that button the lights will go on, that's all. That's what's known as **certainty.** He doesn't hope the lights will go on, he knows they will. (ESTO 12, 7203C06 SO II)

CERTAINTY MAGAZINE, *Certainty* **magazine** should be issued semi-monthly. Issues shall be used broadly as mailing pieces and are not to go just to the membership and be forgotten. The first *Certainty* of the month shall be a *Certainty* major issue, the second issue of the month shall be a *Certainty* minor issue. *Certainty* major: shall consist of informative technical material, advertisements and programmes. *Certainty* minor: shall be dedicated only to programmes such as Extension Course, such as training, such as processing results.*Certainty* major is mainly of interest to the membership and informed Scientologists. *Certainty* minor shall be of interest to the broad public. (HCO PL 24 Oct 58, *Certainty* Magazine) [*Certainty Magazine* is published in the British Isles.]

CERTIFICATE COURSE, there are two courses to one class. First one does the **Certificate Course** (theory) and gets his **certificate.** Then one takes the Classification Course (practical) for that class and gets his Provisional Classification. (HCO PL 5 May 65)

CERTIFICATION BOARD, the **Certification Board** of a **Certified** Auditors' School has as its chief responsibility the **certifying** of students of the school. As such it is one of the most responsible and trustworthy posts of the Foundation and can be manned only by the most trustworthy personnel. The **Board** is headed by the Chief Examiner. He is the only full-time member of the **Board.** He may request, to aid him in check-running and examining students, auditors from the processing units or from the clearing service but he must not overstrain either organization. He is *not* to use, for check-runs, instructing auditors from the school. It is expected that the Chief Examiner deliver, himself, examinations to the students. And it is not expected that he **certify** anyone unless he himself has interviewed the person. The **board** has a dual purpose. First, it has in its charge the **certification** of students and second it has in its charge the awards given to instructing auditors and to auditors in the processing units. (Directive 12 Dec 50)

CERTIFICATION EXAM, this is a written test taken from the HCOBs, tapes, policy letters of the theory material the student studies. This test examines the student to ensure the student knows the data. (FO 1685)

CERTIFICATIONS AND CLASSIFICATION, (Saint Hill Org Board) handles **certifications and classifications** at Saint Hill and anything relating to them internationally. (HCO PL 18 Dec 64, *Saint Hill Org Board*)

CERTIFIED PUBLIC ACCOUNTANT, an accountant in the US who has passed his state's legal examination and holds a certificate authorizing him to practice his profession. *Abbr.* CPA.

CERTS AND AWARDS OFFICER, **1.** the **Certs and Awards Officer** maintains excellent hard cover log books which list (a) all personal attainments, including the name of the auditor for each grade, and (b) category list of all course completions. Prepares handsome **certificates** the org's publics will be proud to display, in advance and supplies these when attained for registrar presentation. Observes for any flubbed products and ensures these are corrected. Issues all the org's **certificates and awards** including membership cards. Keeps memberships up-to-date by calling for renewals. Issues preclears and students with data about their next step as a routine action. Calls in all provisional **certificates** within one year for interneships (inspection for admin courses) and permanent **certificate** validation. (BPL 7 Dec 71R I) **2.** (Gung-Ho Group) the **Certs and Awards Officer** gets made up and issued all **certificates,** memberships or otherwise, pins, etc., as well as conditions. (HCO PL 2 Dec 68)

CHAIN OF COMMAND, a structured line of management authority and communication in an organization used to pass down data and orders from seniors to juniors and information and compliances up from juniors to seniors. It may be used as well to send information laterally between persons of equal authority.

CHAIRMAN BOARD OF DIRECTORS OF HASI, INC., convenes and conducts **board** meetings. Signs on all bank accounts worldwide. Directs basic planning and promotion. Suggests policy to the **board.** Sees that corporate structures worldwide are properly composed and registered. (HCO PL 18 Dec 64, *Saint Hill Org Board*)

CHAIRMAN OF THE BOARD, the chief officer of a corporation's Board of Directors.

CHAIRMAN OF THE COMMITTEE, (**Committee** of Evidence) the **chairman** is appointed at the discretion of the Convening Authority appointing the **committee.** The appointment may be of a permanent nature but again at the discretion of the Convening Authority. The **chairman** may not appoint members to serve on the **committee.** The **chairman** presides over all meetings, conducts the largest part of the interrogation and sees that the **committee** properly executes its duties in all respects in a dignified and expeditious manner. The **chairman** may not interfere with the votes of the members and must include any divergences of opinion on the findings by dissenting members. The **chairman** sees to it that the findings are based on majority opinion. The **chairman** votes only in case of deadlock. The **chairman** may himself dissent from the majority opinion in the findings but if so, includes it as a separate opinion in the findings like any other member dissenting, and may not withhold findings from the Convening Authority for this reason. The **chairman** runs good S-C-S during all proceedings and gets evidence given rather than put in itsa lines. He gets the job done. (HCO PL 7 Sept 63)

CHANGE OF COMMAND CEREMONY, in the Sea Organization, when a new **commanding** officer takes **command** in a vessel or chapter or unit, relieving the former **commanding** officer of his duties, it is traditional to hold a formal **change of command ceremony.** It is a time for the crew of the vessel to pay their respects to the retiring **commanding** officer for the valuable leadership they received from him, and for the new **commanding** officer to be introduced to and welcomed by the crew over which he now assumes **command.** (FO 3348)

CHANGES LIST, includes all significant **changes** in method of operation, personnel or conditions in that organization that week. Included is any **change** which might affect gross income and gross divisional statistics. The **changes list** is compiled by I & R for the HCO Area Secretary or by the HCO Area Secretary and is presented at Divisional Officers Conference. (BO 44)

CHANNEL, one must remember to **channel** a basic purpose. A **channel** has two boundaries, one on either side of it. These must exist in an org. They consist of discipline of those who would distract or stray or wander or who help the opposition or suppress the basic purpose or sub-purposes or who cannot seem to learn or comply with policies or orders. Discipline must only be aimed at the above and where it is random or doesn't serve to **channel,** then it itself is a distraction or a barrier and will breed non-compliance. (HCO PL 13 Mar 65, *Division 1, 2, 3 The Structure of Organization What is Policy?*)

CHANNEL SKIPS, a type of dev-t where something is not forwarded in **channels** but **skips** vital points and if acted on confuses the area of the points **skipped.** (HCO PL 27 Jan 69)

CHANNELS OF DISTRIBUTION, the various distribution ways along which a product flows from producer to consumer.

CHAOS, 1. individual policy making on every post is the definition of **chaos.** (HCO PL 13 Mar 65, *Division 1, 2, 3 The Structure of Organization What is Policy?*) **2.** no line or particle control. (HCO PL 27 Feb 72) **3. chaos** and confusion are the result of an executive's (1) inability or unwillingness to simply supervise and do none of their work, and (2) inability to grant beingness or confront the good sense of other people. (HCO PL 4 Nov 70)

CHAOS MERCHANT, the suppressive person. (HCO PL 5 Apr 65)

CHAPLAIN, 1. the purpose of the **Chaplain** is to help Ron minister to others, to succor those who have been wronged and to comfort those whose burdens have been too great. It should be made well known to pcs and students that when they cannot elsewhere be heard, they always have recourse to the **Chaplain.** He is also the complaints department. The **Chaplain** holds services where required, regularly on Sunday, or marriages, christenings or funerals. The **Chaplain** takes over Ron's hat in all these things. (HCO PL 2 Aug 65 II) **2.** the **Chaplain's** primary duties are keeping people on the org board and the public in Scn. The **Chaplain's** main area of operation in preventing people from falling off the org board, is, auditors. He/she is concerned with the auditor's morale, and endeavors to see that their troubles and problems get seen to. The **Chaplain** also knows who is their next of kin and family. The reason for this area being chosen as **Chaplain's** priority is that auditors make others better, the able more able in using Scn tech and must not, above all be hindered by low morale, problems and troubles. (HCO PL 2 Sept 68, *Chaplain*) **3.** the **Chaplain** exists in the Qualifications Divisions to expedite and speed pcs/pre-OTs and students through their services. Refer to the **Chaplain** if you have any slow progress, stops, hindrances or if you are not progressing satisfactorily with your auditing. If there is any arbitrary or barrier preventing you from completing your auditing etc., see the **Chaplain.** (BPL 29 Jan 72R) **4.** (Correction Division) the **Chaplain** cares for those who have been neglected or fallen off lines, visits the sick, handles civil disputes and wrongs between individual Scientologists and Dianeticists and generally sees that justice is done. The **Chaplain** also advises the Dir Personnel Enhancement or the Cramming Officer of needed correction cycles on staff. (BPL 7 Dec 71R I)

Chaplain

CHAPLAIN'S COURT, the **Chaplain** (or the permanent or part time assisting arbiter) presides over all **Court** Hearings and renders judgement. The organization of this activity is similar to any civil proceedings and may, when conditions warrant have clerks and other personnel. The **Court,** may charge reasonable fees and has these as its statistic. Only civil matters may be heard or judged. All ethics matters must be referred to ethics. (HCO PL 5 Aug 66 II)

CHAPLAIN'S COURT UNIT, the purpose of the **Chaplain's Court Unit** is to resolve matters of dispute between individuals. Staff personnel, pcs, students and Scientologists may utilize this **Court Unit** to resolve their own disputes or legal affairs. (HCO PL 5 Aug 66 II)

CHARACTER, the term, when used in business, designates a debtor's willingness and ability to pay off debts he has incurred, as in noting affirmatively that a person is of "good character."

CHARACTER REFERENCE, a declaration in writing from previous employers, teachers or other appropriate contacts as to a person's character, abilities and reputation.

CHARGE ACCOUNT, see ACCOUNT, CHARGE.

CHARGE PLAN, the credit terms agreed to between a company and a customer which may include establishing credit limits, billing intervals and penalties for late or missed payments.

CHART, 1. a diagram drawn with lines, bars or curves that graphs the fluctuations of production statistics, prices, etc., and clearly shows trends, presenting an instant picture of what is happening in an area of an organization. 2. a sheet presenting in list, table or graphic form any kind of business or other information.

CHART, BAR, a type of chart on which parallel bars of relative lengths are drawn either vertically or horizontally to show statistical relationships in a body of data.

CHART, BREAK-EVEN, a chart or graph which shows at which point an organization has regained its expenditures but has made no profit.

CHART, COMPONENT BAR, a bar chart where each bar representing a quantity is made up of several factors or components. For example, a bar chart with bars representing the total population of a country could have each bar divided into components that show the percentage of people in that country under 21 years of age, between 21 and 65, and over 65. The various age groups or components in each bar could be shaded differently for emphasis.

CHARTER, a written grant by a national or state government to a colony, a group of citizens, a university, a commercial company, etc., bestowing the right of organization, with other privileges, and specifying the form of organization. (BPL 9 Mar 74)

CHART, FLOW, a graphic representation of the sequence of actions involved in accomplishing something. A typical flow chart might show pictures or drawings of the sequence of assembly of a certain product. A flow chart could be made to show the sequence of basic actions of a job, most efficient or economical manner of routing particles, handling goods, moving equipment, etc.

CHART, FLOW PROCESS, see CHART, PROCESS.

CHART, INPUT-OUTPUT, a type of flow chart which shows the origin and distribution of things. An example would be a chart showing the inflow of raw materials to a factory, how they are distributed within the factory and what happens to them until they exit from the factory as a product.

CHART, MULTIPLE BAR, a bar chart with bars of varying heights and containing different design patterns for further identification drawn to illustrate, for example, the comparative sales volume between diverse products produced by a company. Also called Compound Bar Chart.

CHART, ORGANIZATION, a chart or graphic representation of the structure of an organization showing all titles and their seniority, all divisions, departments or units of the organization and the functions and products of each; an organizing board.

CHART, PIE, a circular graph divided from the center to the circumference into pie-shaped parts in order to show the percentage relation between various parts as well as of a single part to the whole.

CHART, PROCESS, a type of flow chart showing the sequence and details of work involved in a process. The time and conditions required for each step are usually stated. Periodic analysis of process charts often leads to discoveries of how to increase efficiency of that process; also called flow process chart.

CHART, PROGRESS, horizontal bar chart showing by variously shaded, colored and patterned bars the stages of development and progress made on a project.

CHART, SCATTER, a diagram that has dots representing statistics, usually connected by a line to illustrate central tendencies, trends and performances.

CHARTS, FLIP, a sequence of charts gradiently arranged one underneath the other to show a sequence of actions, the logical development of some technique or principle, etc. They are usually set on a stand, flipped over in succession and viewed or discussed.

CHÂTEAU ELYSÉE, (Fifield Manor, Hollywood) the luxury 7-story French-*Normandie Château* located at 5930 Franklin Avenue, Hollywood, California. **Château:** a country house, especially one resembling a French castle. **Elysée:** (from Greek mythology) a place or heaven assigned to virtuous people. Any place or condition of ideal bliss or complete happiness. Paradise. (BO 23 US, 11 Jul 73)

Château Elysée

CHATTER, the only purpose of having a telex jargon is to keep telex **chatter** down to a bare minimum. **Chatter** is defined as hand transmission of comm between telex operators. **Chatter** should only be done in order to expedite the transmission of actual telex messages, which are always sent on tape. **Chatter** is sometimes valuable to unscramble line snarls—beyond that it should not be used at all. (BPL 5 Nov 72RA-1)

CHAUFFEUR, looks after the personal and company vehicles. Has charge of all automotive tools and repairs. Cleans and keeps in order the garage area and everything in it. (HCO PL 18 Dec 64, *Saint Hill Org Board*)

Chauffeur

CHECK, a **check** represents money which *is* there to be drawn and will be credited to the account of the org when deposited or when cleared by the bank. (BPL 28 May 71R)

Check

CHECK, a printed bank form representing money in the bank. The individual who has an account with the bank fills in the form designating to whom the money is to be paid, amount of the sum and signs the check authorizing the bank to withdraw the money from his account.

CHECK, DUSTBIN, market research method whereby the choice of products and volume consumed by an individual family is determined by having the household put all empty packages in a special dustbin, over a specific period of time, for checking by the research team.

CHECKLIST, 1. a **list** of actions or inspections to ready an activity or machinery or object for use or estimate the needful repairs or corrections. This is erroneously sometimes called a "checksheet" but that word is reserved for study steps. (HCOB 19 Jun 71 III) 2. a **list** of items, which when **checked** and inspected, ensures that the item or machine is fully operational. It points out those specific parts most likely to demand more frequent attention than given during its routine servicing. (FSO 78)

CHECKOUT, the action of verifying a student's knowledge of an item given on a checksheet. (HCOB 19 Jun 71 III)

CHECKOUT MINI COURSE, this course is a pre-requisite to all major Scn and Dn training courses. At Flag it was found that these policies were not being applied in the field in some cases, resulting in a loss of ability to apply Scn technology. The **course** should take about 2 hours. The end result of the **course** is the ability to do a standard starrate **checkout** and the knowledge of what happens when those policies are not applied. (HCO PL 5 Mar 71)

CHECK, PANTRY, a market research method in which householders are contacted to find out how many households have a particular product or products on hand.

CHECK-RUNNER, one who **checks** on the actual performance of a student or apprentice. He **runs** (meaning performs, observes, reports) **check** on the student or apprentice during the actual actions of the student or apprentice. Example: a student is supposed to be able to start and stop a steam engine. In his examination, the **check-runner** orders him to start and stop a steam engine and observes whether he does it correctly by the book or write-up the student studied. As a note, it would not be the opinion of the **check-runner** but an actual **checked** off list taken from the study materials of the student and each one would be passed or flunked. (LRH Def. Notes)

CHECK-RUNNING, see CHECK-RUNNER.

CHECKSHEET, a list of materials, often divided into sections, that give the theory and practical steps which, when completed, give one a study completion. The items are selected to add up to the required knowledge of the subject. They are arranged in the sequence necessary to a gradient of increasing knowledge on the subject. After each item there is a place for the initial of the student or the person **checking** the student out. When the **checksheet** is fully initialed, it is complete, meaning the student may now take an exam and be granted the award for completion. Some **checksheets** are required to be gone through twice before completion is granted. (HCOB 19 Jun 71 III)

CHECK SIGNING PROCEDURE, an executive with the authority to **sign checks** *must* for his own protection and that of the org, know and have the following before signing any check of any kind for anything: (1) amount of bills owed by the org, total and since when; (2) amount of cash in the bank *by bank statement* (not by adjustment of outstanding checks); (3) the adding machine tape of the **checks** being presented; (4) a disbursement voucher white clipped to each **check.** With these data one can see whether or not it is safe to **sign** a **check** or whether instead one must carefully plan one's way out of an impasse and preserve credit. (HCO PL 30 Jan 66 IV)

CHECK STUBS, counterfoils. (HCO PL 23 Jan 66)

CHECK TYPE ONE, pre-intensive interview and pre-goals assessment **check.** Before the preclear is audited in an intensive where SOP goals may be employed the checksheet is filled out by the D of P and passed by pc before a goals assessment is made. (HCO PL 25 Apr 61) [See HCO WW Form **CT1-CT8** for other D of P **checks.**]

CHIEF, 1. (Flag Bureaux) each of the branches is under a **chief.** (FO 3591) **2.** head of a branch in the Central Bureaux. SO______ (branch title) **Chief.** (FO 2544) **3.** the **Chief** Engineer is addressed as **"Chief."** (FO 87) *Abbr.* CH.

CHIEF ADMINISTRATOR, (post) in command of a base. (FO 196)

CHIEF ENGINEER, 1. in charge of ship's **engines, engineers,** motors, and all machinery, lines and pipes, fuel and water supply, tanks, valves, pumps, anodes, propellor, shaft and rudder and their maintenance, repair and operation, generators, electricity, services of the vessel, plumbing, etc. (FO 1109) **2.** in command of an **engine** room under the Captain. (FO 196) *Abbr.* C/E.

CHIEF ESTABLISHMENT OFFICER, a **Chief Establishment Officer + division** is an **Esto** who in a division has **Establishment Officers** under him due to the numerousness of the division. (HCO PL 7 Mar 72)

CHIEF ETHICS OFFICER, the title **Chief Ethics Officer** is used when he has three full time (or in Foundations, foundation time) **Ethics Officers.** (HCO PL 20 Jun 68)

CHIEF EXECUTIVE, see EXECUTIVE, CHIEF.

CHIEF INSTRUCTOR, one **Chief Instructor** is in charge of each unit (Saint Hill Special Briefing Course). He or she is responsible for the theory, practical and auditing supervision and folder marking and all other training and case and discipline matters relating to that student for the duration of his progress up through the levels covered by that unit. (HCO PL 27 Feb 65)

CHIEF MISSIONAIRE, 1. a **Chief Missionaire** exists as the senior **missionaire** of the unit (**Missionaire** Unit) as always. This is a matter of highest rank. The **Chief Missionaire** is nominally the product officer of the unit. He is deferred to for opinion by the Org Officer but is in fact holding a courtesy post and is expected to attend class full time. (FO 2725) **2.** all **missionaires** come under the **Chief Missionaire** who is appointed by the Flag Captain. (FO 1554) **3.** the **Chief Missionaire** is also the Operations Officer. (FO 1889)

Children (Def. 2)

CHIEF OFFICER, 1. in early days there was an HCO Sec in charge of the functions of the first three divisions (Exec, HCO, Dissem) and an Assoc Sec in charge of the functions of the last four divisions. The org board evolved further and the HCO Exec Sec became the person in charge of the functions of the first three divisions and the Org Exec Sec, the last four. In the Sea Org these titles became Supercargo and **Chief Officer** but the functions were similar. (HCO PL 9 May 74) **2.** (Org Exec Sec) Product Officer Divs 3, 4, 5, 6. (HCO PL 9 May 74) **3. Chief Officer,** Department 19, is the Captain's Representative for operations, finance, supply, material control, operations, maintenance, navigation, public (not official) relations and profitable current and future business, general control of Divisions 3, 4, 5 and 6 and their Departments 7 to 18. (FO 1109) **4.** second in command of a ship. (FO 196)

CHIEF OFFICER'S CONFERENCE, there is a **Chief Officer's Conference** consisting of the heads of Divisions 3, 4, 5 and 6 to advise them or ask for advices. It is headed by the **Chief Officer** and is called by him. It is in Div 7, Dept 19. (FO 1021)

CHIEF OFFICER'S MAST, see CAPTAIN'S MAST.

CHIEF OF SEA ORG OPERATIONS, the **Sea Org** Action Bureau is established in the Office of LRH Flag. It is headed by the **Chief of Sea Org operations.** (FO 2474)

CHIEF PETTY OFFICER, head of any department. (FO 196) See PETTY OFFICER.

CHIEF YEOMAN, **1.** the post of **Chief Yeoman** has been abolished. The head of Department One is the Recognitions Chief. (FO 1416) **2.** Department 1, which is in the charge of **Chief Yeoman,** has personnel, addresses, crews, recruiting, issuance of orders, record books, uniform of the day, complement of the ship, watch quarter and station bill, etc., assisted by various yeoman. (FO 1109)

CHILDREN, **1.** people who have not passed checksheets and have no paid posts in the Sea Org. (FO 760) **2.** a **child** is one who cannot handle an org or ship post. He or she is not on payroll. (FO 1630)

CHILDREN'S INSTRUCTOR, **instructs** Saint Hill **children** in Scientology. (HCO PL 18 Dec 64, *Saint Hill Org Board*)

CHINESE DRILL, see CHINESE SCHOOL.

Chinese School

CHINESE SCHOOL, **1.** as very few Westerners have ever seen a **Chinese** or Arab **school** in progress, it is very easy for them to miss the scene when one says **Chinese School.** The term has been used to designate an action where an instructor or officer, with a pointer, stands up before an assembled class and taps a chart or org board and says each part of it. A **Chinese** class sings out in unison (all together) in response to the teacher. They participate! **Chinese School,** then, is an action of class vocal participation. It is a very lively, loud affair. It sounds like chanting. It is essentially a system that establishes instant thought responses so that the student, given "2 x 2" thinks instantly "4." You could teach the laws of listing and nulling, The Auditor's Code, axioms and so on in this way. There are two steps in such teaching. (a) the instructor taps and says what it is, then asks the class what it is and they chant the answer; (b) when the class has learned by being told and repeating, the instructor now taps with the pointer and asks and the class chants the correct answer. Anything can be taught by **Chinese School** that is to be learned by rote; (HCO PL 13 May 72) **2.** staff or div staff all together in front of a big org board chanting together the hats, duties, and products of the org as visible on the org board. (HCO PL 9 Mar 72 III) **3.** an answering chorus of responses to a teacher's questions, the teacher standing by an org board or chart with a pointer. (HCO PL 14 May 70) —*v.* to teach staffs by repetition and demonstration. (LRH ED 53 INT)

CHIPS, the carpenter is generally addressed as **"Chips."** (FO 87)

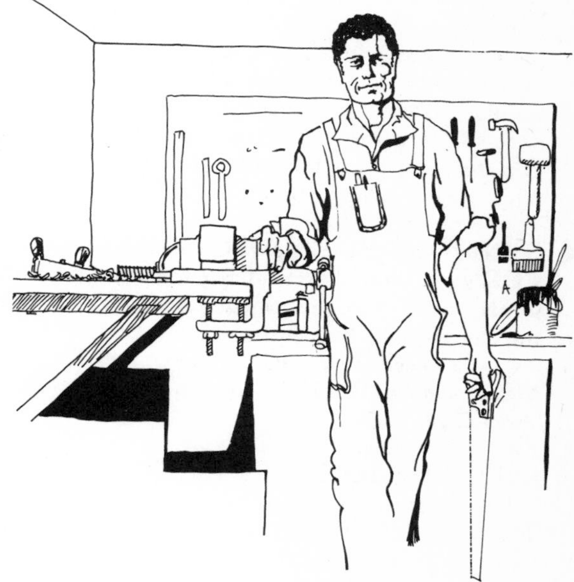
Chips

CHIT, ethics **chit.** (HCO PL 15 Dec 65)

CHRONICALLY SICK, violently PTS which is your **chronically sick.** (7205C11SO)

CHRONIC LOW TA CASE, a symptom of **chronic** apathy. He's not dangerous, just apathetic. It's somebody **chronically** below 2.0. (SH Spec 73, 6608C02)

CHURCH OF AMERICAN SCIENCE, there is a difference between the **Church of American Science** and the Church of Scientology. The **Church of American Science** is a Christian religion. It believes in the *Holy Bible,* Jesus is the Savior of man and everything that's necessary to be a Christian religion. People who belong to that church are expected to be Christians. These two churches fit together. We take somebody in as a **Church of American Science.** It doesn't disagree with his baptism or other things like that, and he could gradually slide over into some sort of better, wider activity such as the Church of Scientology and a little more wisdom and come a little more close to optimum. Then if he was good and one of the people that we would like to have around he would eventually slide into the HASI. So we have provided stepping stones to Scn with these organizations. (5410C04)

CHURCH OF SCIENTOLOGY MEMBERSHIP, today, with the great expansion of **Churches of Scientology** throughout the world, a new class of **church membership** is needed. It is additional to Lifetime, International and Associate Memberships. (1) It is called **Church of Scientology membership.** (2) It is free. (3) It does not have to be renewed annually. (4) It is terminated only by (a) announced departure of (b) expulsion from Scn. (5) It is open to anyone who is in agreement with the aims and creed of the religion **Scientology.** (BPL 24 Sept 73R XI)

CHURCH OF SCIENTOLOGY OF CALIFORNIA, the **Church of Scientology of California** has been the continental headquarters of the **church** since its incorporation in 1954, and is the senior ecclesiastic body in the United States. (*Scientology a World Religion Emerges in the Space Age*, p. 60)

CHURCH OF THE NEW FAITH, incorporated, Adelaide, South Australia, 18 August 1969, There is no significant difference between the **Church of the New Faith** and the Church of Scientology. A decision of the Court of Petty Sessions held at Perth, Western Australia, decided on 2nd December 1970 *Inter Alia* "The **Church of the New Faith** is a religion." (*The Scientology Religion*, pp. 93-95)

CHURCH REGISTER, a **register** for marriage, recognition and naming and funeral services to be kept in every **Church** of Scientology. (BPL 24 Apr 69R)

CINE, *—adj.* cinematographic; motion-picture: a cine camera, cine projector, cine film. [short for cinema] (*World Book Dictionary*)

CIPHER, a **cipher** is generally a substitution of letters or numbers for other letters or numbers. Scrambling their sequence is a common second step. Loosely, also means "code." (HCO PL 11 Sept 73)

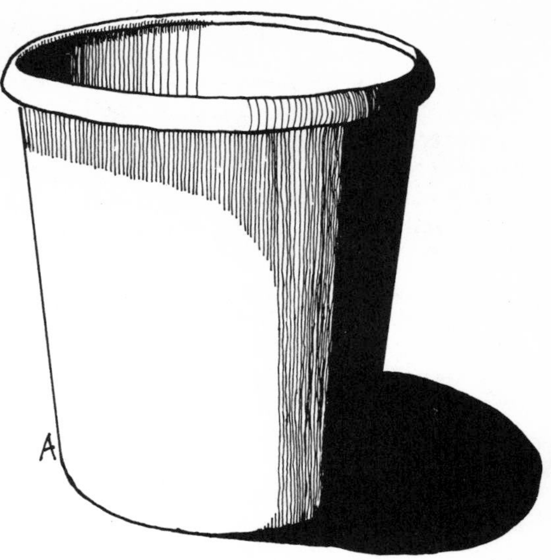

Circular File

CIRCULAR FILE, *Slang.* the waste basket. (HCO PL 9 May 65)

CITIZENS COMMISSION FOR HUMAN RIGHTS, the **Citizens Commission for Human Rights** works to secure the **rights** of mental patients and to guard against their abuse. It is a national organization composed of Scientologists and non-Scientologists who are concerned about psychiatric violations. (LRH ED 256 INT)

CITWASH, the public service unit for the **"City of Washington,"** abbreviated to **"Citwash."** Was a function performed by the Washington, D.C. Foundation. (LRH Def. Notes)

CITY CHURCHES, **city** offices. (HCO PL 6 Nov 64 II)

CITY OFFICE, **1.** has less than 35 staff members, has a Six Section System and org board. It gives training and processing as assigned by WW and its continental senior. It has Field Staff Members. Its Evening Foundation has the same type org board as the Day **City Office.** (HCO PL 21 Oct 66 II) **2.** Class I to III org. (HCO PL 6 Feb 66) **3.** any organization having less than ten persons is classed as a **City Office** or Forming Org. A **City**

THE ABOVE IS A CIPHER

Cipher

Office is organized to do PE and select persons to upper orgs to do co-audits and non-classed courses and incidental processing. A **City Office** may not have executive secretaries. It can have an HCO Area Sec and an Org Sec and an org board such as fits its actual functions. (HCO PL 30 Jan 66 II) **4.** a **City Office** evolves much as a large Central Organization did. A **City Office** is at its beginning characterized by the fact that everyone on staff wears all the hats. There is no individuation of departments. Later some semi-individuation can take place. This comes in as income grows. Even if all the titles are worn, the departments do not exist in fact and a condition can arise where people try to be department heads when they are really just sweeping floors. In a **City Office** at first one cannot afford to employ administrative staff who only administer. The first break-out of this is hiring a receptionist. A **City Office** is composed almost entirely of technical personnel who while working at technical activities (teaching, processing) somehow handle administration. A **City Office** invoices everything received, banks it all and pays all its salaries and bills by cheque. That is the lowest rung of an accounts department. Probably the Assn Sec in a **City Office** does this. The records are kept no further and someday get audited. The fundamental action of a **City Office** is technical service. A **City Office** which is well established may have seven or eight people on staff. A **City Office**, well-handled, can grow to become a Central Organization with a Six Department System. (HCO PL 21 Feb 61) *Abbr.* CITO.

CITY OFFICE DISCOUNT, **discount** of 40%. (HCO PL 19 Jul 65, *Discounts Central Orgs Books*)

CIVIL ACTIONS, by **civil** is meant disputes—marriages, separations, settlements, child care, money owed, that sort of thing. (HCO PL 2 Jun 65)

CIVIL COMMITTEE OF EVIDENCE, **1.** one person satisfactory to both contestants used in disputes between Scientologists or portions of Scn, the contestants abiding by the findings of the one person committee. (HCO PL 31 Mar 65) **2.** if a staff member wishes to sue a fellow staff member or right a wrong he or she may request a **Civil Committee of Evidence** of HCO. HCO usually appoints one senior staff member on which the two can agree. The senior staff member holds a session or sessions and both contenders must abide by his findings and award of any money or damages or return of property. There is no further appeal. A **Civil Committee of Evidence** follows the same procedure and has the same rights as any other Committee of Evidence. (HCO PL 17 Mar 65 II)

CIVIL HEARING, all **civil** matters in writing an ethics order are headed **Civil Hearing.** (HCO PL 2 Jun 65)

CLAIMS VERIFICATION BOARD, hereafter, no refund or repayment may be made by any org without its being passed by the **Claims Verification Board.** The **Board** is established under the Finance Bureau of the Guardian Office. The purpose of the **CVB** is to prevent the payment of false **claims** and to see to the validity and payment of **claims.** (BPL 14 Nov 74) *Abbr.* CVB.

CLASS, a technical certificate in Scn goes by **classes** on the Gradation Chart. The **class** of a Scientologist's certificate is noted in Roman numerals after his name on the org board. (HCO PL 13 Mar 66) *Abbr.* CL.

CLASS 0 AUDITOR, certificate is Hubbard Recognized Scientologist (HRS). The Academy Classification Course **Zero** teaches about communication. End result is an ability to **audit** others to Grade **Zero** Communications Release. (CG&AC 75)

CLASS 0 ORG, **1.** an academy that trains up to **class zero** and an HGC that processes up to **class zero.** An org board based on the six department system of summer 1964. Highest officers are an HCO Area Sec and an Org Sec. The rest are directors. (HCO PL 6 Feb 66) **2.** a Forming **Org,** unable yet to function fully, is a **Class Zero Org.** It is only at recognition and gives a **Class Zero** Course only and uses only Grade **Zero** processes. When it can give a Level I Course and use Grade I processes it is a Class I Org, and so on. (HCO PL 1 May 65 III)

CLASS Ia, it is expected that the student know the basics of Scn and be able to do duplicative processes. Theory section: Auditor's Code, *E-Meter Essentials,* basic scales, dynamics. Practical section: complete CCH section of HCO Policy Letter of May 3, 1962. TR 0, 1, 2, 3, 4. Model session. The complete E-meter check items on HCO Policy Letter of May 3, 1962. Auditing section: Op Pro by Dup, SCS and assists. (HCO PL 21 May 62)

CLASS I AUDITOR, **1.** certificate is Hubbard Trained Scientologist (HTS). The Academy Classification Course **I** teaches about problems. End result is an ability to **audit** others to Grade **I** Problems Release. (CG & AC 75) **2.** relatively unskilled. HCA/HPA graduate, field auditor called in part or full time or current staff auditor or HGC or academy personnel or executive. This auditor is asked what process he has had success with on pcs. What process he has confidence in. Whatever it is, as long as it's Scn, a **Class One auditor** is not permitted to use any other process on HGC pcs, regardless of their "case requirements." This is mandatory. (HCO PL 29 Sept 61)

CLASS Ib, it is expected that the student be able to do a good session with an E-meter and repetitive formal processes. Theory section: communication formula, E-meter tapes, tapes on the theory and attitudes of an auditor, Code of a Scientologist, basic materials of ARC and ARC straight wire. Havingness. Practical section: model session section of HCO Policy Letter of May 3, 1962. Auditing section: ARC straight wire done in model session. Havingness. Repetitive formal processes. (HCO PL 21 May 62)

CLASS I ORG, see CLASS 0 ORG.

CLASS IIa, 1. it is expected that a student be able to get good results with prepchecking and CCH's. Theory section: HCO Bulletins and tapes on prepchecking. Tapes on CCH's. Axioms. Practical section: handling pc part of HCO Policy Letter of May 3, 1962. Pertinent items of the practical processes section of HCO Policy Letter of May 3, 1962. Auditing section: prepchecking by HCO Policy Letter forms and HCO Bulletin of May 10, 1962 and CCH's. (The prepchecking is done in conjunction with CCH's, some of one, some of the other alternatively.) (HCO PL 21 May 62) **2.** the equivalent of HPA/HCA and results in the award of that certificate. The highest level of skill of an HPA/HCA is expected to be repetitive processes, assists, and the CCH's combined with prepchecking. (HCO PL 14 May 62 II)

CLASS II AUDITOR, 1. certificate is Hubbard Certified **Auditor** (HCA). The Academy **Classification** Course **II** teaches about relief, overt acts and withholds. End result is ability to **audit** others to Grade **II** Relief Release. (CG & AC 75) **2.** any auditor auditing on staff who has finally passed a perfect score on HCO quizzes on (1) *E-Meter Essentials,* (2) model session, (3) security checking HCO Bulletins, (4) Saint Hill Special Briefing Course tape of September 26, 1961. (These quizzes must embrace the most minute details of those items.) This auditor is thereafter permitted only to use security checks on HGC pcs, either standard checks or checks combined with specially devised checks. (HCO PL 29 Sept 61)

CLASS IIb, it is expected that the student have a complete command of the fundamentals of sessions and E-meters at an advanced level. Theory section: Auditor's Code, *E-Meter Essentials,* havingness, E-meter tapes. Practical section: TRs: TR 0, TR 1, TR 2, TR 3, TR 4. E-meter: trimming, on-off switch, sensitivity knob, tone arm handling, needle pattern reading, null needle, theta bops, rock slams, falls, rises, speeded rise, speeded fall, slowed rise, slowed fall, ticks, free needle, stuck needle. Body motion, tiny reads testing for a clean needle, finding Havingness process. Model session: script; beginning rudiments; end rudiments; rudiment doingness: room, auditor, W/H, PTP, untruth, etc., influence, commands, session W/Hs, auditor, room. And other drills as required. Auditing section: none. (HCO PL 21 May 62)

CLASS IIc, it is expected that the student have a theoretical and practical level command of processes for this lifetime and be able to audit a skilled model session with havingness and be able to keep all rudiments in. Theory section: basic HCO Bulletins and tapes on prepchecking and the CCH's, axioms, basic rudiment processes, tapes and bulletins. Practical section: CCH's: CCH 1, CCH 2, CCH 3, CCH 4. Two-way comm: drill. Handling pc: detecting missed W/Hs, ARC breaking PCs, getting off missed withholds, getting off invalidations, Q and Aing with pc. Practical processes: ARC Break action by goals, finding overts, forming "What" questions: when, all, appear, who system, finding bottom of chain, cleaning a needle reaction, cleaning a dirty needle. Auditing section: beginning ruds, locating havingness process and running it, and end rudiments (1 hour sessions only). Short sessioning. (HCO PL 21 May 62)

CLASS IId, it is expected that the student acquire a high level skill in handling the CCH's and prepchecking and administer these perfectly in an auditing session. Theory section: completion of CCH and prepchecking bulletins tapes. Practical section: getting pc into session, getting pc out of session, controlling pc's attention, holding up against pc's suggestions, creating R-factor, holding constant against adversity. And other drills as required. Auditing section: prepchecking and CCH's. Form 3 and Form 6A completed. (HCO PL 21 May 62)

CLASS IIIa, 1. it is expected of a student to have a theoretical and practical command of the basics of assessment. Theory section: basic bulletins and tapes on assessments. Problems intensive, advanced HCO Bulletins and tapes on rudiments. Practical section: Pre-Hav assessment, listing, testing completeness, nulling, checking, getting missed W/Hs off, getting item invalidations off, room. End rud, getting suppressions off, cleaning needle reaction, cleaning dirty needle, getting more goals or items, and other drills as required. Auditing section: none. (HCO PL 21 May 62) **2.** theory section: various tapes and bulletins on assessments. Problems intensive. Advanced HCO Bulletins and tapes on rudiments. Practical section: practical processes section of HCO Policy Letter of May 3, 1962 in full and any weakness remedied in any phase of practical. Auditing section: havingness. Getting rudiments in. Dynamic assessment, Pre-Hav assessment. Problems intensive. (HCO PL 14 May 62 II)

CLASS III AUDITOR, 1. certificate is Hubbard Professional **Auditor** (HPA). The Academy **Classification** Course **II** teaches about freedom, ARC and ARC Breaks. End result is ability to **audit** others to Grade **III** Freedom Release. (CG&AC 75) **2.** any staff auditor who has graduated up through class two skills and who is having excellent results with class two skills and who thereafter has been specially trained directly by a person who has attended and passed the Saint Hill Special Briefing Course and who has also passed a perfect examination by HCO on (1) all HCO Bulletins relating to Routine 3, (2) all Saint Hill tapes on Routine 3, (3) who has a good grasp of the technical side of auditing and can run a smooth session. This **Class Three auditor** may use Routine **3** on HGC pcs but may only utilize goals and terminals and levels that have been checked out and verified by a person graduated from the Saint Hill Special Briefing Course. He may not run engrams on HGC pcs. (4) who can find rudiments when out and get them in. (HCO PL 29 Sept 61)

CLASS IIIb, 1. it is expected of a student to have a high level command of the theory and practical aspects of the Class III skills and be able to audit by assessment. Theory section: further bulletins and tapes on assessments, basic Routine 3 process bulletins and tapes. Practical section: getting pc into session, getting pc out of session, controlling pc's attention, creating R-factor, holding up against pc's suggestion, holding constant against adversity. And other drills as required. Auditing section: dynamic assessment, Pre-Hav assessment, problems intensive. (HCO PL 21 May 62) **2.** theory section: Routine 3 processes, various HCO Bulletins and tapes on auditing and auditing attitudes. Practical: review of any weakness in practical. Auditing: current Routine 3 process. (HCO PL 14 May 62 II)

CLASS IIIc, it is expected of a student to have a high level command of routine 3 processes and to audit them with skill. Theory section: Routine 3 processes as given in tapes and bulletins. Auditing and auditing attitudes. Practical section: review of any weakness in practical and other drills as required. Auditing section: current Routine 3 processes. (HCO PL 21 May 62)

CLASS IV AUDITOR, 1. certificate is Hubbard Advanced **Auditor** (HAA). The Academy **Classification** Course **IV** teaches about abilities and service facsimiles. End result is ability to **audit** others to grade IV Ability Release. (CG&AC 75) **2.** any Class Three **auditor** who has achieved excellent results with Routine 3 and who has had his or her goal and terminal found and is a release and who has had engrams run on his or her own goals terminal chain and who has excellent subjective reality on engrams. This auditor may run Routine 3 and engrams on HGC pcs. (HCO PL 29 Sept 61)

CLASS IV C/S COURSE, teaches the basics of Scn 0-IV grade **C/Sing** and the set up for those grades. The status of a graduate at this level is actually that of a grades **C/S.** In order to become a fully qualified C/S one must do the SHSBC as one factually requires all the data of the hundreds of tapes and materials of the Saint Hill Special Briefing Course in order to fully understand the mind and development and full application of tech. The prerequisite for the **Class IV C/S Course** is academy 0-IV training. The **Class IV C/S Course** is available at any **Class IV** Org. (BPL 26 Apr 73R I)

CLASS IV ORG, Central Org. (HCO PL 6 Feb 66)

CLASS V AUDITOR, certificate is Hubbard Validated **Auditor** (HVA). The course, Saint Hill Special Briefing Course, teaches about chronological development of Scn with full theory and application. Processes taught are all Scn Grades 0 to IV processes, progress programs, assists, advance program processes. End result is ability to **audit** others to all Expanded Lower Grades Releases. (CG&AC 75)

CLASS VI AUDITOR, certificate is Hubbard Senior Scientologist (HSS). The course, Saint Hill Special Briefing Course, teaches about the full practical application of Scn grades, repair, set ups, assists and special cases tech up to Class VI.

Processes taught are Scn set up and repair processes and rundowns for special cases up to Class VI. End result is a superb auditor with full philosophic and technical command of materials to Level VI. (CG&AC 75)

CLASS VI C/S COURSE, this is the professional Scn **C/S Course.** On the **Class VI C/S Course** done after completion of the SHSBC, one learns to apply that great body of data to the resolution of any case by use of the fundamentals of the mind and of life taught only at this level. Available only at Saint Hill orgs. (BPL 26 Apr 73R I)

CLASS VII AUDITOR, certificate is Hubbard Graduate **Auditor** (HGA). Course is only available to Sea Org or 5-year contracted org staff. Teaches about power processing and review **auditing.** Processes taught are power and power plus processes. End result is ability to **audit** others to Grade V and VA Power Release. (CG&AC 75)

CLASS VII C/S COURSE, this is the level of the mighty power processes. It is a specialist **course** in power processing which contains specialized data beyond that of Class VI. It is a specialized case cracking level. Prerequisite is **Class VII** internship. Available only at Saint Hill Orgs. (BPL 26 Apr 73R I)

CLASS VIII AUDITOR, 1. certificate is Hubbard Standard Technical Specialist (HSTS). **Class VIII** Course teaches about exact handling of all cases to 100% result and specializes in OT processes and reviews. Processes taught are **Class VIII** procedures, all case set up actions, all processes and corrective actions, OT processes and reviews. End result is ability to handle all cases to 100% result. (CG&AC 75) **2.** an OT **auditor** trained in the special review technology used in all Quals for all levels and in particular the review technology of OT sections. (FO 497)

CLASS VIII CASE SUPERVISOR, certificate is Hubbard Specialist of Standard Tech (HSST). The **Class VIII C/S Course** teaches about **C/Sing** of 100% standard tech and OT **C/Sing.** Processes taught are Class VIII procedures, all case set up actions, all processes and corrective actions, OT processes and reviews. End result is flawless case supervision of all cases. (CG&AC 75)

CLASS VIII COURSE, 1. it is essentially a standard tech **course** that teaches the exact actions for every grade and section and correction and case supervision of all grades and sections. (FO 1268) **2. Class VIII** is sharp rapid standardization of auditing and case supervising with 100% gains. (FO 1746)

CLASS VIII COURSE DIRECTOR, in 1968 the full and part time **Class VIII Course** was under the general charge of the **Class VIII Course Director.** (FO 1450)

CLASS VIII C/S COURSE, (HSST) this is the 100% standard tech level of **case supervision** of Dn and grades. This level reviews earlier levels and concentrates on standard tech. The **Class VIII Course** is its prerequisite. It is available only at Saint Hill Orgs. (BPL 26 Apr 73R I)

CLASS IX AUDITOR, 1. certificate is Hubbard Advanced Technical Specialist (HATS). **Class IX** Course teaches about advanced developments. Processes taught are advanced procedures and developments since Class VIII. End result is ability to **audit** advanced procedures and special rundowns. (CG&AC 75) **2.** there's an auditor band which starts just before the exteriorization rundown and runs up to about the middle of 1970, which is a **IX.** (FEBC 10, 7101C24 SO III)

CLASS X AUDITOR, Class X Course is available only to Sea Org members. It teaches about L-**10**. Process taught is L-**10** OT, an upper level rundown whose basic tech comes from research into increasing OT powers. Obtained on Flag, the end result is ability to **audit** L-**10** OT. (CG&AC 75)

CLASS XI AUDITOR, Class XI Course is available only to Sea Org members. It teaches about L-**11** and L-**11** Expanded. Processes taught are L-**11** New Life Rundown and L-**11** Expanded New Life Expansion Rundown. Obtained on Flag, the end result is ability to **audit** L-**11** and L-**11** Expanded. (CG&AC 75)

CLASS XII AUDITOR, 1. **Class XII** Course is available only to Sea Org members. This level teaches about L-**12.** Process taught is L-**12** the Flag OT Executive Rundown. Obtained on Flag, the end result is ability to **audit** L-**12.** (CG&AC 75) **2.** the **XIIs** are flawless **auditors** and they take a case and finish it up. (OODs 23 Feb 71)

CLASS XII ORG, Flag. We are the only **Class XII org.** (OODs 31 Jan 76)

CLASS CHART, see CLASSIFICATION, GRADATION AND AWARENESS CHART.

CLASSED OFFICIAL ORG, there is no such thing as a **classed official org.** Any **official org** (not a franchise or gung-ho group) can perform and teach any **class** or grade up to **Class** IV. This includes Standard Dn HDC and HDG. Only an **official org** can teach academy courses and qualify students for Scn certificates. (HCO PL 15 Dec 69)

CLASSIFICATION, **1.** **classification** is in addition to certification and is by additional examination by HCO. **Classification** is sealed on any certificate by **"class"** and large Roman numerals and a Hubbard Communications Office ring, the Roman numerals denoting **class** to be huge and in the center of the seal. The object of **class** is that course completion alone may award a certificate. But course proficiency is denoted by a **class** seal. Auditors who have difficulty getting results should not be **classed. Classification** is not a matter of obligation to HCO. It is a special award and is not owed to anyone. (HCO PL 12 Aug 63) **2.** means that we require certain actions to have been done or conditions to have been attained before we say that individual is **classified** in that and let him go on up. (SH Spec 66, 6509C09)

CLASSIFICATION CHART ISSUE ONE, the general **classification chart issue one** is as follows:

Class	*Process Types*	*Certificate*
0	Listen Style,	HAS
I	Listen Style, Assists, R-1C Principles of ARC, Dynamics.	HAS **Classed**
II	Repetitive Processes, CCH's, Straight Wire, Tone 40 and Formal Auditing, Axioms, O/W.	HCA
III	Prepchecking, Metered Processes, Assessing, Old R2 and R2H.	HPA
IV	Service Facsimiles, ARC Break, Assessments, Programming, Missed W/Hs.	HCS
V	Implants, Engrams, Whole Track, Whole Track Case Analysis.	HAA
VI	OT Processes, Own GPMs, Old R3 and R4 Processes.	HSS
VII	Old Route One and other Drills.	HGA

(HCO PL 26 Nov 63)

CLASSIFICATION COURSE, **1.** the practical drills and student auditing portion of an auditor training course. After completion of the **classification course** the auditor is **classified** to that level and may audit pcs professionally on the processes of that level. (*PRD* Gloss) **2.** first one does the certificate course (theory) and gets his certificate. Then one takes the **classification course** (practical) for that class and gets his provisional **classification.** Every auditor must be **classified** now. (HCO PL 5 May 65)

CLASSIFICATION EXAM, **1.** this is a practical **exam.** The test consists of a checkout of TR-4, any of the meter drills of the level, and the auditing of a doll on the process or processes of that level with full TRs and admin. The examiner gives the student a mock C/S and the student audits the doll on that C/S. The student is required to pass this exam 100%. The student is flunked for out TRs, out meter drills, out admin, or out tech only. (FO 1685) **2.** this is just a good, comprehensive examination of the exact course he has completed earlier. It is in theory, practical and auditing. (HCO PL 3 Dec 64)

CLASSIFICATION, GRADATION AND AWARENESS CHART, the route to Clear, the bridge. On the right side of the **chart** there are various steps called the states of release. The left-hand side of the **chart** describes the very important steps of training on which one gains the knowledge and abilities necessary to deliver the grades of release to another. It is a guide for the individual from the point where he first becomes dimly aware of a Scientologist or Scn and shows him how and where he should move up in order to make it. Scn contains the entire map for getting the individual through all the various points on this **gradation scale** and for getting him across the bridge to a higher state of existence. (*AUD 107 ASHO*)

CLASS SEAL, **classification** is in addition to certification and is by additional examination by HCO. **Classification** is **sealed** on any certificate by **"class"** and large Roman numerals and a Hubbard Communications Office ring. The Roman numerals denoting **class** to be huge and in the center of the **seal.** The object of **class** is that course completion alone may award a certificate. But course proficiency is denoted by a **class seal.** (HCO PL 12 Aug 63)

CLAY PIGEON, any staff member who does not know ethics policy is a **clay pigeon. Clay pigeons** are used to throw up in the air and shoot at. (HCO PL 24 Feb 72)

CLEAN, *v.* get all the charge off. (*Clearing Course 1967 Instruction Booklet*)

CLEANERS, **1.** keeps domestic quarters, offices and outbuildings in good order. (HCO PL 18 Dec

64, *Saint Hill Org Board)* **2.** new recruits become swampers (deck), **cleaners** (Steward's Dept) and wipers (engine room). (FO 748)

Cleaners

CLEAN HANDS CLEARANCE CHECK, in order for an auditor who is regarded as a security risk to be considered to have **clean hands,** it is necessary for him to receive a **clean hands clearance check** from HCO. The **clean hands clearance check** consists of that auditor having the following rudiments put in very thoroughly by an HGC Class II staff auditor using prepclearing techniques. (1) auditor. "Are you willing to talk to me about your difficulties?" (2) withholds—last two pages of Joburg Form 3 or all of Form 3A; and all of an HCO WW Sec. Form 6A. Plus asking "Has a withhold been missed on you?" frequently as all such persons specialize in getting them missed. This will be checked out on completion by the HCO Area Secretary for any questions on Form 3 or 3A and Form 6A which may be still alive and for any missed or partial withholds. (HCO PL 27 Feb 62)

CLEANING CLEANS, doing something that is already done or ordering something to be done already done. (BPL 30 Jan 69)

CLEANING STATION, **1.** that particular area of a ship which one is responsible for to see that it is clean and nothing in its space gets damaged. (FO 315) **2.** a **cleaning station** is assigned to every staff member in the org, with a **cleaning stations** list drawn up to cover all areas of the org with all staff members participating. A staff member is usually assigned his own work area as a **cleaning station,** with the divisional officer I/C of the **cleaning stations** for his whole area. (HCO PL 16 Aug 74 IIR)

CLEAR, a **Clear** has risen from the analogy between the mind and the computing machine. Before a computer can be used to solve a problem, it must be **cleared** of old problems, of old data and conclusions. Otherwise, it will add all the old conclusions into the new one and produce an invalid answer. Processing **clears** more and more of these problems from the computer. The completely **cleared** individual would have all his self-determinism in present time and would be completely self-determined. (*Abil 114A*)

CLEAR AMERICA CRUSADE, **crusade** to boom USA (February 1974). Every Scientologist had to get in one new Scientologist by mid April. (AO 467-1)

Clear Bracelet

CLEAR BRACELET, **1.** Grade VII **Clear** is signified by a silver identification **bracelet** with the S and double triangle on it. (HCO PL 27 Oct 65) **2.** silver **Clear bracelets** are issued by HCO Secs at the expense of the HGC or the field pc to those who meet **Clear** requirements. (HCO PL 12 Aug 63)

CLEAR CHECKER, a **Clearing** Course student is not officially **Clear** before being pronounced so by a qualified **checker** and Qual and may not announce the fact as a fact until so **checked** by an authorized **Clear Checker** who has actually officially checked him out and until he/she has been

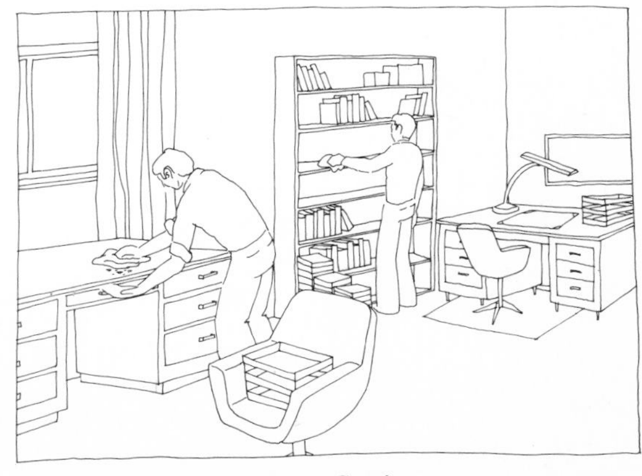

Cleaning Station

declared **Clear** by Qualifications Division SH. (HCO PL 16 Dec 66) See CONTINENTAL CLEAR CHECKER.

CLEAR CHECKOUT, 1. the **checkout** hereafter shall consist of (1) has run the materials of the Clearing Course to free needle. (2) is the person's TA between 2 and 3 with a loose or flowing needle? (3) Rehabbing all grades from Dn release up to Clear, making sure they have actually, each one, been run and attained. (4) a marked change in the person. (5) is the person cheerful and happy about being **Clear**? (HCO PL 13 Sept 67) 2. (Grade VI **Clear** Test) for a **clear checkout**, there must be no reaction on the needle. The needle must be completely free with the tone arm at **clear** read for the sex of the person being tested. The needle can be made to impulse with the body totally motionless, hands steady, and no tricks. Further the needle can also be shoved from one side of the dial to the other by the **Clear** looking at it. Records must be presented showing that all R6 materials have been run and no other characteristics or phenomena are required or demanded of the Grade VI **Clear.** (HCO PL 2 Apr 65, *Meter Checks*)

CLEAR ESTIMATE, [Called a case **estimate** now. Was an **estimate** of number of hours of auditing required to **clear** a person given to that person at his request.]

CLEARING, an operation whereby a badly cluttered communication channel may be swept clean. Sometimes an emergency exists which requires an enormous traffic volume and this has communicators slaving all up and down the lines. When a line or number of lines are to be **cleared** of an emergency situation which has ceased to exist, the Chief Communicator is informed by the deciding executive and all messages appertaining to the past situation are swept back to files whether they have been acknowledged or completed or not. (*HTLTAE,* p. 118)

CLEARING CONSULTANT, the title of "goal finder" is changed to a **Clearing Consultant.** (HCO PL 11 Apr 63, *Goals Finding and Goal Finders*)

CLEARING POST PURPOSE, is another way of saying "get the policy that establishes this **post** and its duties known and understood." (HCO PL 25 Nov 70)

CLEAR NEWS, news mailed twice monthly by Advanced Orgs to all persons who are **Clear** or above and persons who have expressed a reach for clear. (BPL 20 May 72R)

CLEAR PROFIT, income less *all* area expenses. (FO 2451)

CLEAR PROSPECTS CARD FILES, consist of "I Want to go **Clear** Club" members who have not yet signed up for the **Clearing** Course. (BO 47, 8 Aug 70)

CLEAR REGISTRAR, 1. the public **Reg** of an AO. (FO 3139) 2. a single hatted **registrar** on post in Div 6 AO/SH to do tour and event **regging.** She handles tour and event attendees for the duration they attend. At all other times these people come under Division 2. The name of this **registrar** in AOLA, AOSH UK, AOSH DK, is the **Clear Registrar.** (LRH ED 159R-1 INT) 3. the post of **Clear Registrar** is in Division 8, Dept 24. The **Clear Registrar** does not do any sign-ups in-the-org. She does sign-up people for **Clear** at *AO public events* and on *tours.* The **Clear Registrar** also handles the administration of the "I Want to go **Clear** Club." She is primarily responsible for the **Clear** Club cycle. (BO 47, 8 Aug 70)

CLEAR TEST, 1. the entirety of the **Clear test** is conducted with the **testee** on the E-meter. A **Clear test** form is used by the Director of Processing. The Director of Processing only conducts the E-meter **Clear test** and forwards all **tests** up to the HCO Board of Review. He cannot tell the person he is **Clear.** (SEC ED 150, 9 Mar 59) 2. for a release (formerly keyed-out **Clear**) check, the TA position may be anything from 2.0 to 3.0 with a floating needle. There is no other test of any kind for a release. Note that this is the old **"Clear Test."** It now is classified as a release. (HCO PL 2 Apr 65, *Meter Checks*)

CLERICAL WORK, the functions in an office of handling mail and inter-department communications, record keeping, filing, and typing.

CLINICAL, 1. at this point in Sea Org development, there are two categories of DPF members: new recruits and **clinical. Clinical** personnel include out-ethics cases, tiger types, persons who need extroverting from their environments, and the like. Not to put ethics in on these guys is very cruel indeed. Ethics is what is needed most; ethics and good 8-C. (FO 3126) 2. for review of actions, possible auditing, not to be included or used in crew in any way above SPF and DPF and then only temporary pending disposition. (OODS 27 Jan 72)

CLO COUNCIL WW, the **CLO Council WW** is established as a body composed of all properly appointed **CLOs** at **WW.** Its primary function is to serve as an examining body on complaints referred to it concerning orders and directions issued on or against Continental and/or Area Orgs. A complaint may be originated by a **CLO,** or the **CLO** may be ordered by his Continental Exec Council to raise it. The **Council** may only veto an order or directive already issued. It may not issue orders, plan or advise. It handles only after the fact of issue. No LRH order may ever be over-ridden by the **Council.** No Controller order may ever be over-ridden by the **Council.** No Guardian order may ever be over-ridden by the **Council.** (HCO PL 20 Apr 69 II) [The above HCO PL was cancelled by BPL 10 Oct 75 VII.]

CLO ETHICS OFFICER, the duties of an FB or **CLO Ethics Officer** in Bureau 1 are the general standard ethics actions external, making certain that ethics is standard and in throughout **CLOs** and orgs. A Bureau 1A FB or **CLO Ethics Officer** duties are internal in the FB or the **CLO.** (FO 3067)

CLO EXPENSE, a **CLO** is supported by funds from its nearest major org. This does not mean all funds above allocation for that org belong to a **CLO.** 10% of the CGI of the major org should be more than adequate to support a **CLO** since if the **CLO** is any good at management at all the income will be high in that major org. It is expected to send far more to SO reserves than it consumes. (HCO PL 9 Mar 72 I)

CLO LEVEL, Flag level—international whys applying to all orgs. **CLO level**—continental whys to remedy to get Flag programs and projects in. Org level—divisional and departmental and individual whys that prevent Flag programs and projects from going in. So that's the reason for a **CLO:** to observe and to send all data to Flag and to continentally find out why Flag projects and programs are not going "in" in an org and remedy that why and get the programs and projects in. That is a **CLO.** (HCO PL 22 Jul 71)

CLO-OTL RESERVES, any **reserves** that may be built up locally by book and pack sales, events, FSM commissions and booming the major org. It is expected to send far more to SO reserves than it consumes. (HCO PL 9 Mar 72 I)

CLOSED CORPORATION, see CORPORATION, CLOSED.

CLOSED SHOP, see SHOP, CLOSED.

CLOSE ORDER DRILLS, close=confined to specific persons or groups. **Order**=a command or direction. **Drills**=disciplined, repetitious exercise as a means of teaching and perfecting a skill or procedure. (ED 118 Flag)

CLOSE, THE, The final and most important stage of the sale. It begins when the salesman has successfully located and removed his prospect's key objections and arguments, and ends with the paperwork finalized and signed and payment received (*The Language of Salesmanship*)

CLOSE, THE, in investments, the term designates the end of a trading session or market day wherein all trades have been executed and closed or finalized.

CLOSURE, 1. at a meeting or conference, the ending of a discussion or debate at the chairman's suggestion or by taking a motion from the floor followed by a vote, in order to take up the next topic of business. 2. in British Government, closure enforces a time limit on a debate.

CLUSTER ANALYSIS, see ANALYSIS, CLUSTER.

COACH, a student who is standing in the role of "pc." (HCOTB 17 May 57)

Coach

COACHING THEORY, see THEORY COACHING.

COAT OF ARMS, in all ages and places, men have used symbols to communicate. From very early times, we find that people belonging to the same family or group or tribe wore similar clothing. Aside from being a matter of fashion, this also made it easy to identify one's group members even at a distance. In the Middle Ages, it became even more important to develop distinguishing symbols since a knight in full armor is not easy to identify. So the practice of designing distinguishing symbols and designs to be used by the knight, his retinue, his family and group became a very important art and science. Soon, every knight had his distinguishing marks which represented not only his symbolic prowess but also the heritage of his family and its connections. The **coat of arms** as a whole consists of several major parts: the crest, the mantling, the shield or escutcheon (a word coming from the Latin word, *scutum,* meaning shield) and the motto. If you inspect a **coat of arms** as a whole, knowing the relationship of the parts, you will see how it derives from a very simple representation of the basic armor of a knight, along with its distinguishing symbols, with the motto as the guiding principle on which he and his group operate, set just beneath it. The **coat of arms** became the rallying point and sign of recognition for any group of people. By it, they could identify themselves as a group with common purposes, common goals. (FO 3350)

Coat of Arms

CO-AUDIT, 1. a team of any two people who are helping each other reach a better life with Scn processing. (HCO PL 21 Aug 63) 2. we will call **co-audit** "Do it yourself therapy." Do it yourself therapy is the lowest cost therapy in the world. It is cheap because you give some when you get some. (HCO PL 23 Jan 61)

CO-AUDIT CASE SUPERVISOR, **(Co-Audit C/S) C/S** where a **co-audit** exists separate from the HGC lines. (HCO PL 25 Sept 74)

CO-AUDITOR ROUTE, preclear progresses as in the preclear route. Auditor progress, is by training for certificates only, not classification. There is a certificate for every level. (HCO PL 5 May 64)

CO COUNCIL, it is vital that **COs** of interdependent orgs in close proximity form amongst themselves a means of resolution of situations that require their coordinated attention and action. Each **CO** has exact problems. Each depends on the other orgs. The purpose of the **CO Council** is: to state and resolve their major current concerns and to form immediate and longer range actions to handle expansion. The chairman of the council is the **CO** of the Founding Org (Management Org) or its liaison office. The **council** meets no less than once a week and more frequently as needed. (FO 2810)

CODE, generally an arbitrary list of words that stand for words actually meant. (HCO PL 11 Sept 73)

CODE OF A PETTY OFFICER, (1) uphold command intention. (2) follow exactly the rules of the Sea Org. Let there be no out-ethics among **POs.** (3) always take command in a situation that needs urgent handling when there is no senior present. (4) wear your **Petty Officer** uniform every day. (5) insist on your rights as a senior rating. (6) back up your seniors. (7) take responsibility for your juniors. (8) never invalidate your status or let it be invalidated. Hard work and nothing else won you your title. Be proud of it. (9) increase your knowledge and skill in seamanship daily—a Petty Officer is an experienced sailor. (FO 1978)

CODE OF A SEA ORG MEMBER, the **code of a Sea Org member** has been distilled from the collected works of L. Ron Hubbard. These rules are not new; on the contrary they are the traditional ones with which the **Sea Org** was built. (FO 3281) [See the referenced FO for the full **code.**]

CODE OF REFORM, see REFORM CODE.

COFFEE SHOP AUDITING, **auditing** inevitably done casually out of **auditing** rooms by staff on staff or students on friends and students even when you try to prevent it. (HCO PL 20 Mar 61 II)

COGNITIONS, new concepts of life. (HCO PL 5 May 65)

COINS, 1. an organization has so many registrar minutes to invest. And the registrar minutes it has to invest determines the number of sign-ups which an organization has. Do you get how you figure out the **coins?** This is the internal economy of an organization and these are the real factors of economy. It's the HAS that makes them available to be spent. He's in charge of the personnel lines and spaces. So he also must be in charge of the potential **coins** the organization has to spend. Not dollars, they're worthless. He's in charge of how many auditing hours the HGC can furnish, how many instructor minutes can be furnished, how many typist minutes. (FEBC 10, 7101C24 SO III) **2.** the **coins** are the volume—potential volume of production per department for the final product of the department, not necessarily the final valuable product of the org. (FEBC 10, 7101C24 SO III)

COLD PROSPECTS, **prospects** who have not expressed a reach for training or processing. (SO ED 230 INT)

COLLATERAL, personal property pledged by the borrower to the lender to partially or fully cover the amount of a loan, and which is capable of being converted to cash.

COLLECTION, in business, the act of collecting cash, usually by a specified time, from customers who have made purchases on credit.

COLLECTION FOLDER, every person owing money has a **collection folder** into which copies of invoices of all payments made are filed, the **folder** to include copies of all contracts and notes. **Collection folders** are summarized monthly and statements are sent out monthly to debtors. (HCO PL 23 Jan 66)

COLLECTION PROCEDURE, contacting by phone, letter or in person credit customers who have not yet paid for their purchases.

COLLECTIONS LETTERS, **letters** encouraging payments. (BPL 13 Feb 68)

COLLECTIONS SECTION, (Income Dept) the **Collections Section** sends out all mailed statements to individuals and statements to orgs and acts and writes to **collect** any money owed the org from any source. It has its own statements books and files and receives whatever Area Cashier and Collections has uncollected when a person leaves the area. **Collections** should have a statement sheet for every person who owes the org money. (HCO PL 18 Apr 69 II)

COLLECTIVE OPINION, by the nature of the bank, **collective opinion** is always derogatory or bank, this being the one thing held in common by all. So the group ignores the good and embraces the bad. (HCO PL 21 Jan 65)

COLLECTIVE-THINK, **1.** is always closer to bank-think than individual reasoning. That's because the bank is the one constant people have in common. And it's crazy. So almost any individual alive can plan better than a group will execute and certainly better than a group can plan. Scn groups are far superior to human groups. But the rule still applies that **collective-think** is always less sane than the thinking of an individual. (HCO PL 18 Jan 65) **2.** every human has in common with every other human the same reactive bank. This is the most they have in common. The reactive bank—unconscious mind, whatever you care to call it—suppresses all decent impulses and enforces the bad ones. Therefore a Democracy is a **collective-think** of reactive banks. Popular opinion is bank-opinion. **Collective-think** is basically bank. (HCO PL 13 Feb 65)

COLLEGE OF SCIENTOLOGY, I am forming the **College of Scientology** with the headquarters at Saint Hill. It is part of HASI Arizona, Inc. Saint Hill will be the **College of Scientology** and the other orgs will have "Academies of Scientology." The **College of Scientology** will be the final recommending body for the issue of degrees, etc. (HCO PL 14 Oct 65, *College of Scientology*)

COLONEL WEBSPREAD, [**Colonel Webspread** is a comical cartoon character made up by L. Ron Hubbard. He is portrayed as an adventurous duck and rated as Chief of the Northern High Flying Duck Weather Warning Patrol in the OODs of 11 Oct 70]

COLOR FLASH SYSTEM, **color flash system** for dispatches and letters. (HCO PL 4 Jan 66 III) **BLUE, 1.** Division 7 (or white). (HCO PL 4 Jan 66 III) **2.** carbon copy of reports, messages, dispatches—intra-organizational (but not Advisory Committee or Board Minutes copy). (HCO PL 13 Dec 62) **3.** all hat write-ups, changes, notations. This is original, department head copy and copy in actual hat. (HCO PL 12 Sept 58) **BROWN,** Division 7—Public Activities. (HCO PL 23 May 69 IV) [The above HCO PL was cancelled by BPL 10 Oct 75 VII.] **BUFF,** Division 6 (or canary). (HCO PL 4 Jan 66 III) **GOLD,** HCO Division 1. (HCO PL 4 Jan 66 III) **GRAY, 1.** Division 5. (HCO PL 4 Jan 66 III) **2.** all internal dispatches between personnel of HCO (St. Hill) Ltd. (HCO PL 31 Mar 64, adds to HCO PL 13 Dec 62, *Re-Issue Series (7) Scn Organizations Communications System: Dispatches*) **GREEN, 1.** Division 4. (HCO PL 4 Jan 66 III) **2.** intra-organizational letters, memos, data sheets, reports, dispatches, field offices to Central Organizations and vice versa. (HCO PL 13 Dec 62) **3.** intra-organization letters, memos, data sheets, dispatches. All Scn organizations to all Scn organizations. Carbon copy of any green dispatch is green. (HCO PL 12 Sept 58) **ORANGE, 1.** Division 8—Distribution. (HCO PL 23 May 69 IV) [The above HCO PL was cancelled by BPL 10 Oct 75 VII.] **2.** used between HCO personnel only. (HCO PL 13 Dec 62) **3.** HCO Bulletins; HCO Policy Letters; dispatches between HCO personnel; all dispatches from HCO personnel to any and all organizations, departments and personnel. HCO carbon copies of dispatches are orange. Except HCO releases for hats which will be blue. (HCO PL 12 Sept 58) **PINK, 1.** financial reports—anything to do with cash inside all Scn orgs, also copies of Advisory Committee, Council and Board minutes; original of latter will be white, carbons pink. (HCO PL 13 Dec 62) **2.** all financial dispatches or reports amongst all organizations, departments or terminals. All purchase orders. All committee, council, staff meeting minutes including original (which should be on heavier paper than its carbons). (HCO PL 12 Sept 58) **PINK, DEEP,** Division 3. (HCO PL 4 Jan 66 III) **PINK, LIGHT,** (or violet) HCO Division 2. (HCO PL 4 Jan 66 III) **VIOLET, 1.** HCO Division 2 (or light pink). (HCO PL 4 Jan 66 III) **2.** all dispatches between personnel of Scientology Library and Research, Ltd., and all dispatches to other orgs' personnel from SLR, Ltd. (HCO PL 31 Mar 64, adds to HCO PL 13 Dec 62,*Re-Issue Series (7) Scn Organizations Communications System: Dispatches*) **WHITE, 1.** Division 7 (or blue). White paper is also used for letters to the field, business houses, board minutes, and for manuscripts and research notes. (HCO PL 4 Jan 66 III) **2.** letters to field, business houses, incoming and outgoing (white paper in files means original letters from "outside" organizations). White used for original only of Board and Advisory Committee minutes. Manuscript and research notes on white paper. (HCO PL 13 Dec 62) **3.** all board minute originals and carbons. Letters to field, business houses. Student reports. Testing. Case analysis. Forms for sign-ups. Releases. Contracts. MS and research notes, original and carbon. (White paper in file means original letters from outside people or organizations.) (HCO PL 12 Sept 58) **YELLOW,** Division 6—Public Planning. (HCO PL 23 May 69 IV) [The above HCO PL was cancelled by BPL 10 Oct 75 VII.] **YELLOW, CANARY, 1.** Division 6 (or buff). (HCO PL 4 Jan 66 III) **2.** carbon copy of business and field letters. (Means copy of letter we originated, *not* copy of dispatch.) (HCO PL 13 Dec 62) **YELLOW, PALE,** carbon copy of business and field letters outgoing. (HCO PL 12 Sept 58)

COLOR FLASH TABBED, the central files are divided up as follows: five classes of tabulation, **color** marked (**color flash tabbed**). They have little plastic tabs that go on top of them and a color is assigned to each class. That makes them easier than any file system you ever saw. (HCOB 6 Apr 57)

COLUMN, type of article other than straight news usually included in a newspaper. A **columnist** is entitled to use his byline as authority, he needs not name source. Does not necessarily express opinion or party line of paper, but can compliment or amplify it. A **column** should be public service journalism (to inform the public, expose rotten spots, act as an opinion leader, form a viewpoint for all). The **columnist** is solely responsible for the content of this **column** and can express his own viewpoint. (BPL 10 Jan 73R)

COMBAT INFORMATION CENTER, takes all the data from all known sources and areas and combines it in certain ways. (6806C01SO) See CONTROL INFORMATION CENTER.

COMBINATION, CORPORATE, the combining or association of corporations by an official agreement or unofficially, in order to pursue common goals.

COMBINATION, HORIZONTAL, a combining or association of companies offering the same or similar services or products.

COMBINATION, VERTICAL, a combining or association of companies engaged in different levels or phases of producing the same or directly related products. An example would be the combining of an electronic parts manufacturer with a radio and television manufacturer.

COMBINED STATISTIC, a **combined statistic** is of course where you take the same **statistics** from several functions and add them up to one line. A very large function added into a **combined** graph can therefore obscure bad situations. (HCO PL 6 Nov 66 I)

COMCENTER, Central Communications Office, of which there can be only one in any given communication system. (*HTLTAE,* p. 35)

COMMAND CHANNEL, 1. (communication routing) **command channels** go up through seniors over to a senior and down to a junior. Or they go up through all seniors. It is used upward for unusual permission or authorizations or information or important actions or compliances. Downward it is used for orders. (HCO PL 25 Oct 71 I) **2.** junior to senior to senior's senior or on down. (HCO PL 25 Jul 72)

COMMAND COMM CYCLE, essentially there is a **command comm cycle.** He who gives the order gets an answer! Compliance reports are never routed off the lines before they reach the originator of the order. To do so creates an atmosphere of non-compliance. A compliance report is not a **cycle** begun, it is not a **cycle** in progress. It is a **cycle** completed and reported back to the originator as done so that the **command comm cycle** is completed. (BPL 26 Jan 69RA)

COMMANDING OFFICER, **1.** the **Commanding Officer** of an organization is the Product Officer of that organization. He does nothing but think, eat, breathe—product. He knows the valuable final products of the organization; he demands them. When he doesn't get them he investigates by data analysis, finds the why, debugs it, writes a program. (ESTO 1, 7203C01 SO I) **2.** the org is commanded by the **Commanding Officer** (SO orgs) or the Executive Director (non-SO orgs). In the triangular system of the Flag Executive Briefing Course (FEBC) (Product-Org Officer System) the **CO** or ED coordinates the work of the Product Officer, Org Officer and Executive Esto. In most orgs the **CO** or ED is also the Product Officer of the org which is a double hat with **CO.** (HCO PL 7 Mar 72) **3.** the head of the org is the **Commanding Officer** or Executive Director. He is usually also the Product Officer. He is senior to the Exec Esto. (HCO PL 7 Mar 72) **4.** when the Captain leaves a ship even for a few hours or days, he always leaves someone in charge. This person is "the senior officer with the duty" and is in fact the **Commanding Officer** during the absence of the Captain. By virtue of that he is responsible for the ship and everyone aboard. (FO 3342) *Abbr.* CO.

COMMANDING OFFICER REPORTS, any and all **Commanding Officers** of ships, AOs, OTLs and special assignments shall write and send by fast airmail a daily **report** to the Commodore, Sea Organization. The **report** should include briefly any important occurrence and any decisions made during that day. (FO 1368)

COMMAND LINE, **1.** a **line** on which authority flows. It is vertical. (HCO PL 1 Apr 72) **2.** those on which orders and compliance travel from senior to junior and back as per the **command lines** on the org board. (FSO 137)

COMMANDO SALES TEAM, see SALES TEAM, COMMANDO.

COMMAND TEAM, there is an idea afoot to form **command teams** to send to existing orgs in populace areas to build them up. This would consist of at a guess a commanding officer, and HES (org officer), OES (product officer) and PES (Public Officer). These would all be Sea Org members. They would be in the area many months and would build a good, solid-going org. (OODs 13 Nov 71)

COMM BASKETS, three **baskets** constitute a **comm** station and consist of an "in," "pending," and "out." These **baskets** are for the use of the staff member to whom the station belongs and the communicator who distributes and picks up dispatches, messages and letters. (HCO PL 9 Feb 64)

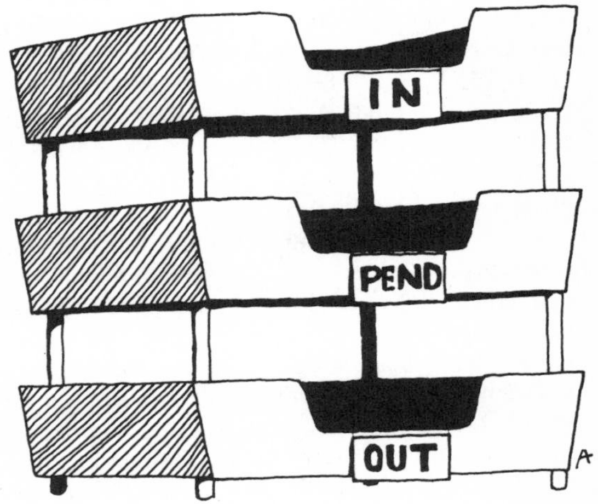

Comm Baskets

COMM CENTER BASKETS, the **comm center** contains a **basket** for each staff member. Each **basket** is tagged with the person's name, and underneath the name is their post or posts. Each person is responsible for delivering his own dispatches to the proper **baskets,** and for picking up daily his own dispatches (except in some larger orgs, where there is a communicator for this purpose). (HCO PL 13 Dec 62)

COMM CYCLE ADDITIVES, good auditing occurs when the comm cycle alone is used and is muzzled. Additives on the auditing comm cycle are any action, statement, question or expression given in addition to TRs 0-4. (HCO PL 1 Jul 65 II)

COMMENDABLE, we're going to introduce a new noun in Scientologese. It's a **commendable.** We need a word meaning a good action. There is no single word for it in English. Thus we coin the word a **commendable.** (FO 2610)

COMMERCE, the buying and selling of commodities and services between businesses, large industries, cities and nations.

COMMERCIAL APPRENTICE, a beginner or novice contracted to work for a business employer for a specified time usually in return for the job knowledge gained or related education.

COMMERCIAL BANK, see BANK, COMMERCIAL.

COMMERCIAL CREDIT, extent of credit allowed in transactions in business or industry such as the limit of credit a supplier extends to a manufacturer, manufacturer to wholesalers, or bank credit made available to a firm on which it may draw. Also called mercantile credit.

COMMERCIAL SURVEY, a market research technique based on doing investigative interviews that reveal such things as the popularity of and satisfaction consumers feel regarding existing competitve products as well as their acceptance level for new products.

COMM FILES SECTION, section in Department 2, Department of **Communication. Comm files section** handles all HCO files, handles telex files, handles personnel files, handles ethics files, handles LRH Communicator files, Xerox (office duplicator) machine. (HCO PL 17 Jan 66 II)

COMM FLOAT, used to cover the cost of telex traffic, postage and transport to and from any telex machine or post office. (FO 1400)

COMM FORMULA UNUSED, (a type of dev-t) all orders out answers in are on the **communication formula.** Failing to answer the question asked can triple traffic. (HCO PL 27 Jan 69)

COMM INSPECTION, to **inspect** in baskets for unanswered **communications.** The **Comm Inspector** goes through pending baskets weeding out dev-t and misrouted particles and putting them back on lines to the originator, and makes a complete report to the HCO Area Secretary. Goes through desk drawers, filing cabinets and any nook and cranny in the org searching for hidden letters, book or tape orders, requests for information, or any **communication** dead ended some place. The **Communication Inspector** has as his primary concern ferreting out jammed inflow lines and getting letters flowing. (HCO PL 25 Jan 66 II)

COMMISSION, a percentage of each sale or service fee, paid to a salesman, agent or broker and which may represent part or all of his income.

COMMITTEE, a group of persons headed by a chairman appointed to take up a special piece of business or proposal and present its findings to the executive level of an organization.

COMMITTEE OF EVIDENCE, 1. a **committee of evidence** is not a court. It is simply a fact-finding body with legal powers, convened to get at the facts and clean up the ARC breaks caused by rumor. When it has the truth of it, then a convening authority acts—but only in exact accordance with a justice code. (HCO PL 27 Mar 65) **2.** a fact-finding body composed of impartial persons properly convened by a convening authority which hears evidence from persons it calls before it, arrives at a finding and makes a full report and recommendation to its convening authority for his or her action. (HCO PL 7 Sept 63) **3.** a fact-finding group appointed and empowered to impartially investigate and recommend upon Scn matters of a fairly severe ethical nature. (*ISE,* p. 28) **4.** a **Committee of Evidence** is considered the most severe form of ethics action. A staff member may not be suspended or demoted or transferred illegally out of his division or dismissed without a **Committee of Evidence.** (HCO PL 29 Apr 65 III) **5.** a **Committee of Evidence** is convened by the Office of LRH through the HCO Secretary and is composed of staff members. Its purpose is entirely to obtain evidence and recommend action which the Office of LRH then modifies or orders. If a person is wrongly dismissed, demoted or transferred he or she may request a **Committee of Evidence** from the HCO Secretary and may have recourse. (HCO PL 10 Apr 65) *Abbr.* Comm Ev.

COMMITTEE OF EVIDENCE SECTION, HCO Division, Department 3, **Committee of Evidence Section** handles all matters regarding **Committees of Evidence.** (HCO PL 25 Jan 66)

COMMITTEE OF MESS PRESIDENTS, meets on matters of food quality and service and submits recommendations to the Chief Steward, Purser or Captain depending on the gravity of the situation. All complaints or suggestions about food go to the President of a mess who in turn takes it to the **committee.** In special cases such as a birthday or party where the action entails a cake or some small action, the President advises the Chief Steward by dispatch. (FO 2586)

COMMITTEE ORGANIZATION, see ORGANIZATION, COMMITTEE.

COMMITTEES, the whole upset with **committees** is they are used wrongly. They are not there to plan. They are there as individuals to be informed and have a say in modifying or approving or rejecting material drawn up before. (OODs 24 Jan 70)

COMM LINE, 1. (**communication line**) a **comm line** is the line on which particles flow, it is horizontal. A command line is a line on which authority flows. It is vertical. (HCO PL 1 Apr 72) **2.** these are the usual lines used aboard for handling dispatch and voice originations and replies, including commands and compliance, information, requests, etc. The comm basket system, messenger relay, intercom system, telephones, loud hailer, flags, radio, signals, sound powered phones, are all lines of communication. (FSO 137) **3.** (**comline**) a **communications line.** This does not refer to physical equipment but to the passage of ideas between two points. A flow of ideas, in two directions, on paper, establishes a **comline.** A verbal exchange of ideas can be considered a **comline** only when the discussion is summarized on paper and then sent over the line as a confirmation. (*HTLTAE,* p. 118)

COMM LOG, see LRH COMM LOG.

COMM MEMBER, the holder of the same post in another org is a **comm member.** (HCO PL 13 Mar 65, *Admin Technology, The Comm Member System*)

COMM MEMBER SYSTEM, 1. a direct **communications system** between the staff **member** of one org and only the exact staff post in another org without vias. It is governed by direct policies and regulations and its own technology of handling matters. It does not change or alter any existing internal or between-org policy or **communication** channels. (HCO PL 13 Mar 65 II) **2.** a **communications** and contact **system.** The staff **members** of organizations may **communicate** directly with the same post as their own at Saint Hill for information, guidance and orders. The holder of the same post in another org is a **comm member.** (HCO PL 13 Mar 65, *Admin Technology, The Comm Member System*)

COMMODITY, any transportable article of commerce which having value can be bought and sold.

COMMODORE, 1. head of the flotilla and related organizations as well as the immediate Flag organization above the level of Captains, which carry out and help him to carry out his duties. (FO 3342) **2.** a large amount of a **Commodore's** time, contrary to popular belief and tradition, is spent estimating the efficiency and standards of Captains and senior officers, inspecting the conditions of crews and seeing to their welfare, seeing that vessels and their equipment are in operational condition. This comes under the heading of inspection. But it is more than that; it is maintaining a visual information service which includes continuous awareness of the content of various communication lines; these include not only awareness of all types of reports but also the personal daily reports of individuals. This collection of information adds up to an awareness of the existing scene which changes daily. (FO 3342-2) **3.** the post of **Commodore** relates to Sea Org matters. (FO 766) **4.** a courtesy title for a Flag officer commanding several ships. (FO 2389) **5.** command of the flotilla and all ships, boats, bases and stations. (FO 196) *Abbr.* Cmdr, Cmdre.

COMMODORE QUEEN, the 150 (approximately) foot diesel vessel *Commodore Queen* purchased by UKLO. (FBDL 15 UK)

COMMODORE'S COXSWAIN, any and all ships or LRH personal vehicles including bikes and motorbikes are under the control of and are the responsibility of the **Commodore's Coxswain.** (FSO 17)

COMMODORE'S FLAG, 1. a ship, on which a **Flag** officer has his office and staff, flies, when he is aboard, a blue **flag** from the yardarm which is the **flag** signal that he is aboard. When he leaves or goes or is not aboard, the blue **flag** is lowered. In our case this is called the **Commodore's Flag.** We have such a flag. (FO 1) **2.** blue with white stars. (FO 38)

COMMODORE'S MESSENGERS, Commodore's Messengers are not in HCO; they are a unit under the **Commodore** for his use and orders. (FO 1872)

COMMODORE'S STAFF, 1. the lines of the **Commodore's Staff** are mainly concerned with external Sea Org actions, handling SO matters, Scn orgs, missions, etc. (FO 1490) **2.** the deputy of the Board of Directors is **Commodore** of the flotilla (who may be assisted by aides and other personnel known as **Commodore's Staff**). (FO 1109) **3.** the theory of appointment for the **Commodore's Staff** is based on: (1) a liaison officer for each of the seven divisions on each ship and (2) a communications service for the **Commodore** and (3) personal service for the **Commodore.** When the **Commodore** is afloat his **staff,** insofar as practical, is with him, performing their regular staff duties and any seamanship duties he may require in assisting him to handle ships or boats or operations in which they may be required to take an active part. Some of the **staff,** such as typist, may continue on in a shore office when the **Commodore** is afloat. Not all his **staff** always accompanies him but those who do may be expected to perform sea duties as well as **staff** duties. (FO 1) *Abbr.* CS. See AIDE.

COMMODORE'S STEWARD, 1. cares for the **Commodore's** quarters, clothes and meals afloat. (FO 1) **2.** is not called "Flag Steward" as she is not the steward of the Flag Section and should avoid other responsibilities as I would shortly have no steward but the Flag Section would have one. On the ship where I am Captain she is still the **Commodore's Steward.** (FO 87)

COMMODORE STAFF ORDERS, Commodore Staff Orders are created. Their designation is **CS Order.** These are **orders** necessary to **staff** and not concerning Flag. They will be typed and issued by our own yeoman. Where a **Staff Order** is necessary to be known to Flag it will also be issued as a Flag Order and handled by Division 1. (FO 795)

COMMODORE'S TRANSPORT I/C, Commodore's Transport I/C is responsible to the Second Deputy Commodore for the readiness and care of the **Commodore's transport** and boats and that of the Controller. (FO 3342)

COMMON ROOM, each house (or floor in a hotel) must have a **common room** for its members. This is a lounge which is used by all members for guests, or reading or relaxation during free time or liberties. Anyone who abuses the privilege of using the **common room** may be barred from it by the House Captain. The **common room** must have specific persons assigned to clean it every day as a cleaning station. (FO 3176R)

COMM STATION, three baskets constitute a **comm station** and consist of an "in," "pending," and "out." These baskets are for the use of the staff member to whom the station belongs and the communicator who distributes and picks up dispatches, messages and letters. Every administrative staff member, without exception, should have a **comm station.** (HCO PL 9 Feb 64)

COMM SYSTEM ESTABLISHMENTS SECTION, the **establishment** of internal org **communication systems** includes our **comm** centers, our **comm** stations. Director of **Communication** sees that every staff member has a basket in a **comm** center and a personal **comm** station near his area of work no matter who the staff member is—that includes the janitor! This is a **section** in the Department of **Communication,** the **Comm System Establishments Section.** It works out the **system,** puts up the baskets, establishes other needful **systems.** (HCO PL 25 Feb 66)

Communication (Def. 1)

COMMUNICATION, 1. the consideration and action of impelling an impulse or particle from source-point across a distance to receipt-point, with the intention of bringing into being at the receipt-point a duplication and understanding of that which emanated from the source-point. The formula of **communication** is: cause, distance, effect, with intention, attention and duplication with understanding. The component parts of **communication** are consideration, intention, attention, cause, source-point, distance, effect, receipt-point, duplication, understanding, the velocity of the impulse or particle, nothingness or somethingness. A **non-communication** consists of barriers. Barriers consist of space, interpositions (such as walls and screens of fast-moving particles), and time. A **communication** by definition does not need to be two-way. When a **communication** is returned, the formula is repeated, with the receipt-point now becoming a source-point and the former source-point now becoming a receipt-point. (HCO PL 4 Apr 72 III) **2. communication** consists of the flows of ideas or particles across space between solids. (*POW,* p. 81) **3.** simply a familiarization process based on reach and withdraw. When you speak you are reaching. When you cease to speak you are withdrawing. When he hears you, he's at that moment a bit withdrawn but then he reaches toward you with the answer. (HCOB 23 May 71R I) **4. communications** could be said to be the study and practice of interchanging ideas, individual to individual, individual to group, group to individual, and group to group. (*HTLTAE,* p. 1) *Abbr.* Comm.

COMMUNICATION BUREAU, **1.** the **communication bureau** has the cycle of receiving, logging and sending or distributing all comm, telexes, people, packages internal and external. The cycle is (1) in, (2) log, (3) send on the outflow to other points and (1) receive, (2) check, (3) distribute, on the inflow from other points. (CBO 7) **2.** consists of **Communication** Network Establishment Branch, Internal **Communication** Branch, External **Communication** Branch, and Transport Branch. (CBO 13R) **3.** the External **Communication Bureau.** (FEBC 1, 7011C17 SO)

Communication Center

COMMUNICATION CENTER, **1.** the **communication center** contains a basket for each staff member. Each basket is tagged with the person's name and underneath the name is their post or posts. Each person is responsible for delivering his own dispatches to the proper baskets and for picking up daily his own dispatches. In larger orgs a **comm center** and separate divisional **comm centers** may be instituted. The **comm center** would consist of one basket for each division plus a basket for L. Ron Hubbard and an outer org out-basket. Each divisional **comm center** is placed in the divisional working area with a basket for each staff member in that division plus a divisional in-basket and a divisional out-basket. An HCO dispatch courier would be responsible for delivering dispatches into the divisional in-baskets and from the divisional out-baskets into the **comm center** baskets. The Sec Sec is responsible for the distribution of dispatches from the divisional in-basket to staff members' baskets. (HCO PL 4 Jan 66 III) **2.** a **communication center** is useful only when it centers and channels all **communications** of specific kinds from the public to the organization and the organization to the organization. (An organism with more than one brain does not survive well. All **communication** channels must **center** in one room and area for all departments.) The types of **communication** to be handled thus are as follows: (1) callers in person, (2) callers by phone, (3) written dispatches within the organization to other parts of the organization, (4) personal letters to organization members, (5) posted orders and notices, (6) messages for staff from public to staff or staff to staff. (HASI PL 9 Apr 57)

COMMUNICATION COURSE, gives people a reality on Scn and teaches **communication** formula by dummy auditing. (HCO PL 12 Oct 62)

COMMUNICATION FORMULA, the **formula** of **communication** is: cause, distance, effect with intention, attention and duplication with understanding. (HCOB 5 Apr 73)

COMMUNICATION INSPECTION UNIT, (HCO Division, Department 2) this post is most active when letters out statistic has dropped. **Communication Inspection Unit** inspects all in-baskets and pending baskets for unanswered **communications** and reports to the HCO Area Secretary via Director of **Communication** what is found. If the statistic doesn't rise, may go around and empty pending baskets back onto lines routed back to sender, dev-t or misrouted particles, and reports what is found to HCO Area Secretary via Director of **Communication.** Inspects, when letters out still does not rise, drawers, file cabinets and other places unanswered **comm** may be stored, and reports what is found to HCO Area Secretary via Director of **Communication.** (HCO PL 25 Jan 66)

COMMUNICATION INSPECTOR, (HCO Division, Department 2) the purpose of the **Communication Inspector** is: to help Ron keep the organization there by assuring **communications** in to the organization are answered. The **Communication Inspector** has as his primary concern ferreting out jammed inflow lines and getting letters flowing. (HCO PL 25 Jan 66 II)

COMMUNICATION LINE, see COMM LINE.

COMMUNICATION MEDIA, word of mouth, newspaper, magazines, loudspeakers. (FEBC 2, 7101C18 SO I)

COMMUNICATION OFFICER, 1. what has formerly been called reception is redesignated **Communication Officer.** The post has outgrown what is commonly held to be reception responsibility. The **Communication Officer** is responsible for relaying anything or anyone that is received at or sent by Saint Hill. (HCO PL 18 Jun 64) **2.** the title **Communication Officer** is changed to HCO Area Secretary Saint Hill. The HCO Area Secretary Saint Hill is also a department head under, as such, the Organization Secretary. The duties of the HCO Area Secretary Saint Hill include heading the **Communications** Unit. (HCO PL 22 Feb 65 II) **3.** Promreg Department includes the HCO **Communicator,** who now becomes the **Communications Officer.** The department includes reception, all means of **communication,** the **comm** center, org board, central files and address, mail and mailing and any other purely promotional-**communication** function. (HCO PL 15 Mar 65 I)

COMMUNICATION ROUTING, there are three types of **communication routing.** They are: (1) horizontal fast flow, (2) command channels, (3) conference. (HCO PL 25 Oct 71 I)

COMMUNICATIONS AIDE, CS-1. (FO 1031)

COMMUNICATIONS DIVISION, this first **division** in actual fact is the **Communications Division.** It's called HCO with us but it's the **Communications Division.** This is analogous to getting things **communicating** as you would have to do in putting together any plant or factory. You'd first have to have something where people could get into **communication** with somebody about what you were doing otherwise nothing would happen thereafter. (SH Spec 77, 6608C23)

COMMUNICATIONS EXECUTIVE, in the Dianetic Counseling Group the **Communications Executive** has two divisions under his responsibility. Division 1 **Communications** Division headed by the **Communications** Secretary. Division 2 Dissemination Division headed by the Dissemination Secretary. (BPL 4 Jul 69R VI)

COMMUNICATIONS OFFICER COMMUNICATIONS UNIT, is in charge of the **Communications Unit,** its functions, its personnel, equipment and material. Handles all staff, transport and routing and all hired domestic transport. (HCO PL 18 Dec 64, *Saint Hill Org Board*)

COMMUNICATIONS SECRETARY, Division 1, **Communication** Division is headed by the **Communications Secretary** (in the Dianetic Counseling Group). (BPL 4 Jul 69R VI)

COMMUNICATIONS SYSTEM, 1. a **communications system** is not only the nervous **system** but also the brain of an organization—that is, it forms the medium, the mass of tissue through which the planning mind of the organization (all those individuals who originate plans, from the greatest to the smallest) operates. A mind cannot operate without memory. Whether that mind is running an organism or an organization, it must be able to **communicate** with its past. Memory is absolutely essential to the operation of an organization. (*HTLTAE,* p. 15) **2.** a **communications system** is a reason **system.** It produces reason on an organizational level, just as the individual minds of the personnel produce reason on an individual level. (*HTLTAE,* p. 64)

COMMUNICATIONS UNIT, 1. this contains all **comm** functions of the org, such as mimeograph, central files and address, mail and mailing, the **comm** center, the **comm** system, telephone, reception, telex, everyone's desk **comm** station or basket and the normal functions of hat checks, bulletin and policy checks, nominal supervision of the staff co-audit, the receipt and dispatch of all goods, the arrival, departure and absence of personnel, the keeping of the log book and any other record books and whatever other functions may be assigned to this unit and the HCO Area Secretary heading it. (HCO PL 22 Feb 65 II) **2.** handles all **communications** at Saint Hill. Does checkouts of technical and policy matters on staff. Acts as a watch during business hours. Has in its keeping all **communications** equipment and materials at Saint Hill and sees that it is properly used, clean and in good repair. (HCO PL 18 Dec 64, *Saint Hill Org Board*)

COMMUNICATION SYSTEM, the standard Scn **communication system** consists of a **comm** center, a basket as a **comm** station for every member of the crew near the place of work and an in-out-basket for every admin person. The **comm** center contains a basket for every crew member. There is also a **Comm Communicator.** (FO RS 16)

COMMUNICATOR, 1. one who keeps the lines (body, dispatch, letter, intercom, phone) moving or controlled for the executive. A **communicator's** title is always his or her executive's followed by "______**'s communicator."** To that, when there are more than one, may be added, "for . . ." being a function or division. The **Communicator** is to help the executive free his or her time for essential income earning actions, rest or recreation, and to prolong the term of appointment of the executive by safeguarding against overload. Policing compliance for a senior executive is a vital function of a **communicator.** (HCO PL 16 Nov 66) **2. Communicator,** Department 2, handles all ship's **communications,** comm center, messengers, telephones, intercom, bullhorns, whistles, ship's signals, siren, baggage, transport, vehicles, telexes, radios, walkie talkies, signals, flags, signaling and all forms of **communication,** pickup and delivery of ship's boats, their use and schedule, travel, travel arrangements, tickets, all **communication** logs and files. It is assisted by radio operators, signalmen, drivers, coxswain, typists, messengers, operators, etc. (FO 1109) **3.** purpose: to help LRH by maintaining fast, certain **communication** lines between all the terminals of the organization and between the organization and outside terminals, with proper routings. (FO 2528) **4.** (Gung-Ho Group) the **Communicator** handles all **communications** of whatever kind, in and out. (HCO PL 2 Dec 68) **5.** one who operates a post or comcenter. (*HTLTAE*, p. 119)

COMMUNITY, a number of people having common ties or interests living in the same place and subject to the same laws. (BPL 9 Mar 74)

COMMUNITY ACTION, the action of residents in a particular locality banding together to bring something about, as in achieving a particular goal or project or to correct an injustice.

COMPANY, **1.** a **company** has various actions. It is essentially a collection of small org boards combined to operate together as a large org board. (HCO PL 13 Sept 70 II) **2. company** in this policy letter is defined as the corporate entity of Flag. It does not mean the local org's corporation or the C of S. (HCO PL 10 Mar 71)

COMPANY, a corporation.

COMPANY, ASSOCIATED, 1. a company associated with another company in a subordinate relationship. 2. a company, fifty per cent of whose stock is held by another company.

COMPANY DIRECTOR, a member of an executive board or board of directors which has been appointed by the stockholders to govern the affairs of a corporation or institution.

COMPANY FILE, see FILE, COMPANY.

COMPANY (FLAG) LOGISTIC ITEMS SHIPPING COSTS, the **cost** of **shipping** to **Flag** items purchased as **company (Flag) logistic** purchases. Such items are **shipped** overland unless an OK to send by air freight has been received from one of: the Founder, the Controller or their Personal Communicators on their behalf, or the **Flag** Purser. (BPL 3 Nov 72RA)

COMPANY (FLAG) LOGISTIC PURCHASES, due to better local prices, quality or availability of certain items required by central management, these are ordered by **Flag** from FOLOs and occasionally from orgs. This would include such items as fuel and insurance bills of **Flag** but *not* such bills of stationships or orgs. It could include promotional items ordered for local printing, manufacturing or distribution, where these are specifically designated by **Flag** as **Flag** expense. All such **logistic purchases** must bear the authorization of one of the following terminals: the Founder, the Controller or their Personal Communicators on their behalf, or the **Flag** Purser. An external **purchase** order form or at times a telex authorizes the expense. (BPL 3 Nov 72RA)

COMPANY (FLAG) MISSIONAIRE EXPENSES PAID, funds given to **Flag** or FOLO missionaries on **Flag** mission orders to carry out their **mission** purpose or targets. Sometimes a **mission** stays longer than was intended or for other reasons requires additional funds. (BPL 3 Nov 72RA)

COMPANY, HOLDING, a company owning the stock or a majority of stock of another or other companies and usually having voting control; parent company.

COMPANY, JOINT STOCK, a group of individuals acting jointly to form and operate an organization, electing a board of directors and having a capital investment that is divided into transferable shares.

COMPANY LABOR POLICIES, see POLICIES, COMPANY LABOR.

COMPANY, MARKETING-ORIENTED, one that produces a product which fulfills a market or consumer demand as opposed to producing what is easy to produce.

COMPANY, NON-OPERATING, a company not engaged in actual production and marketing such as a holding or parent company or a travel agency not directly concerned with the operation of transportation means but working as travel arrangers in liaison with transportation organizations.

COMPANY, PARENT, see COMPANY, HOLDING.

COMPANY POLICIES, see POLICIES, COMPANY.

COMPANY, PRODUCTION-ORIENTED, a concern which relies on the manufacture of products that are technically easy for it to make in terms of labor and equipment rather than adjust to consumer demands.

COMPANY, PUBLIC, company that issues stock for sale to the public and the majority of whose stock is owned by persons other than its executives and employees.

COMPANY SCHOOL, a school set up by a business offering to its employees instruction and training in company procedures and individual jobs.

COMPANY, SHELL, 1. a company that does not actually operate but exists on paper only, sometimes formed to conceal illegal actions. 2. a company legally registered for the sole purpose of being sold to someone who has need of such a made-to-order company.

COMPANY STORE, a store owned and operated by a company that sells commodities to its employees.

COMPANY, TRUST, a bank or other organization that manages trusts and administers duties according to the stipulations therein which includes the authority to invest trust funds, oversee income, distribute earnings to beneficiaries, etc.

COMPENSATION, 1. money given or received as an exchange for work rendered, as in an employer-employee relationship. 2. money, aid, etc., given as a recompense for injury, loss or to settle a grievance or injustice.

COMPETENCE, **1.** the **competence** of a person is in direct ratio to his degree of consciousness and their awareness (now I'm talking about the eyeball) of their environment. **Competence** is directly proportional to those two things. So don't expect a half knocked out druggy to be very **competent.** He won't be. Now similarly the insane are all degrees of **competence.** There have been some of the most brilliant geniuses who are utterly screamingly insane. There have been some of the dumbest boobs that were utterly screamingly insane. It has nothing to do with it. It's not on the same scale. We're dealing now with the scale of aberration as the scale of **competence.** The number of out-points the guy is carrying around in his skull is how aberrated he is. It has very little to do with his sanity, it has everything to do with his **competence.** How conscious he is and his width of awareness (can he see?) is what demonstrates his **competence.** (ESTO 10, 7203C05 SO II) **2. competence** on any given subject is what a person is not unconscious on, and those things he can't see he is unconscious on and that determines his **competence.** (ESTO 10, 7203C05 SO II) **3.** when a person is **competent,** nothing can shake his pride. The world can yell, but it doesn't shake him. **Competence** is not a question of one being being more clever than another. It is one being being more able to do what he is doing than another is. (HCO PL 3 Apr 72) **4.** being **competent** means the ability to control and operate the things in the environment and the environment itself. When you see things broken down around the mechanic who is responsible for them, he is plainly exhibiting his **incompetence**—which means his inability to control those things in his environment and adjust the environment for which he is responsible—motors. When you see the mate's boats broken up you know he does not have control of his environment. Know-how, attention, and the desire to be effective are all part of the ability to control the environment. (HCO PL 30 Dec 70) **5.** the estimation of effort. (2ACC 31B, 5312C22)

COMPETITION, a striving with another or others in the same business field for leadership in sales, profit, position and exceptional recognition.

COMPETITOR, one in competition with or rivaling another in the same business market, striving to advance his product or service as superior or available at less cost.

COMPILATIONS SECTION, Department 21, Office of LRH. Formed in the first place with just exactly this purpose and no other purpose: to help LRH get out the magazine materials and the promotion materials that he gets out for Scn. (HCO PL 31 Jan 66)

COMPLEMENT, **1.** the officially allowed number of persons and the officially designated posts for an activity, whether an org or a ship. Without these basic **complements** orgs get misposted. A

complement is the full list of posts and where they belong on the org board, which must be held. (OODs 8 Nov 71) **2.** by name the list of men and officers of a ship. It's the number of officers and men allowed to a ship. But just because you are allowed those guys is no reason that those are the only guys you have. The word is very badly misunderstood. It is usually issued as something that we will try to adjust to. Now if we have got an overmanned area we will say maximum allowed **complement.** (ESTO 8, 7203C04 SO II) **3.** the maximum allowed personnel on permanent posts in an organization. (OODs 12 Nov 71) **4.** a **complement** lays down the allowed number of personnel per division/bureau and the total allowable number for the whole org. It is the basis for accurate postings to be done to gain maximum utilization. (FSO 518)

COMPLEMENT BOARD, now you've got the **complement board** and that is asking this question: who is double hatted and how many posts are held from above and how many posts are empty? You do that by workload. You, for the first time are in an optimum position to be able to adjust an org by workload. A function board doesn't have any posts on it. A post board has no names on it and a **complement** doesn't have post name or function on it. It says Dissem—four, or it says Department 4—three. (ESTO 8, 7203C04 SO II)

COMPLETED, (students and pcs **completed**) **completed** of course means only certified or classed or graded. (HCO PL 30 Sept 65)

COMPLETED STAFF WORK, **1.** an assembled package of information on any given situation, plan or emergency forwarded to me sufficiently **complete** to require from me only an "approved" or "disapproved." (HCO PL 21 Nov 62) **2.** an assembled dispatch or packet which (1) states the situation, (2) gives all the data necessary to its solution, (3) advises a solution, and (4) contains a line for approval or disapproval by myself with my signature. If documents or letters are to be signed as part of my action, they should be part of the package, all ready to sign, and each place they have to be signed is indicated with a pencil mark with a note in the recommendations saying signatures are needed. (HCO PL 21 Nov 62) **3.** means routed to the board, with all related policy letters clipped to the requested change and the new policy letter all written ready for issue. (HCO PL 17 Nov 64) **4.** if a problem is encountered it is forwarded only with a full recommendation for handling (**completed staff work** or **CSW**). (HCO PL 29 Feb 72) *Abbr.* CSW.

COMPLETE PLANNING, **1. complete planning** and programs are synonymous at this time and programs is the preferred word. (HCO PL 24 Jan 69) **2.** a plan would be the design of the thing itself. **Complete planning** would be all the targets plus the design. (HCO PL 18 Jan 69 II, *Planning and Targets*)

COMPLETION, **1.** the **completing** of a specific course or an auditing grade; meaning it has been started, worked through and has successfully ended with an award in Qual. (HCOB 19 Jun 71 III) **2.** a final valuable product. (ED 41 FAO) **3.** means a finished level or rundown. (HCO PL 29 Aug 71)

COMPLETION POINTS, see PAID COMPLETION POINTS.

COMPLEXITY, **1.** to the degree that a being cannot confront he enters substitutes which, accumulating, bring about a **complexity.** (HCO PL 18 Sept 67) **2.** I found that any **complexity** stemmed from an initial point of non-confront. This is why looking at or recognizing the source of an aberration in processing "blows" it, makes it vanish. (HCO PL 18 Sept 67)

COMPLIANCE, **1.** consists of: (1) agreement on the survival goals of the group and participation in working towards and accomplishing them by following the broad procedures laid down in policy and tech. (2) working towards specific goals for one's own post or area which contribute to the accomplishment of the whole group's goals, by following the procedures for that post or area as laid down in policy and/or tech. (3) carrying out the legal orders issued one that forward specific plans, programs and projects that implement specific policies in order to accomplish a goal or goals of the group, in an orderly fashion. (4) **compliance** is a series of actions, or a specific action, which duplicates what was intended to happen by the originator of the requirement or order. (BPL 20 Feb 73) **2.** the acting in accordance with, or the yielding to a desire, request, condition, direction, etc.; a consenting to act in conformity with, an acceding to; practical assent. (BPL 20 Feb 73)

COMPLIANCE EXECUTIVE DIRECTIVE, **1.** carries a program on how to get an LRH issue or issues implemented in an area that by evaluation has been found to need these issues implemented. May also carry a project to execute a target in the program. Drawn up by an area or continental LRH Comm and authorized by CS-7 on Flag for a local **CED.** International or continental **CEDs** are issued from Flag only and only with AVU authorization. Blue ink on blue paper. (HCO PL 24 Sept 70R) **2.** are for use by area LRH Comms and continental LRH Comms as well as Senior LRH Comms to, when necessary, compile a pack of LRH issues and to write a program on how to get these implemented in the area(s) that, by evaluation, have been found to need these issues implemented. Even getting in a single issue requires this handling. When such a program is drawn up and issued, it shall have the title of: **Compliance Executive Directive,** or **CED** for short. (BPL 24 Jul 73R III) *Abbr.* CED.

COMPLIANCE REPORT, 1. in practice a **compliance report** takes the following form: (1) it is in standard dispatch form routed through the usual channels. (2) it is headed at the top of the page in the middle **compliance report.** (3) it has a brief concise description of what was done. (4) it has clipped to it *all* the original orders so that the originator and communicators on the line can see at a glance what was ordered, and comparing this with what was done, see that it is in fact a **compliance,** a completed cycle. (5) any other relevant information is also clipped behind, such as a carbon of a letter written if that was what was ordered. (6) and it is addressed and goes to the person originating the order, via any communicator who logs it as a **compliance.** (7) it contains an attestation that what was done has been completed; such as "order attached completed." (BPL 26 Jan 69RA) **2.** a **compliance report** is exactly that. It is a **report** of **compliance,** a completed cycle reported to the originator done. It is not a cycle begun, it is not a cycle in progress. It is a cycle completed and reported back to the originator as done so that the command comm cycle is completed. (BPL 26 Jan 69RA) **3.** a **compliance report** is made out for each target as it's done, and the admin belonging to it is attached as evidence along with any other evidence of completion. (BPL 6 Mar 73)

COMPLY, 1. to merely commence a cycle is not to **comply.** To merely make some progress is not to **comply.** To drive it through to completion is. And to then report done to the originator is to put in a **compliance** report. (BPL 26 Jan 69RA) **2.** to act in accordance with, and fulfillment of, wishes, desires, requests, demands, conditions, or regulations; to fulfill the wishes or requirements of; to consent to. (BPL 20 Feb 73)

COMPONENT BAR CHART, see CHART, COMPONENT BAR.

COMPOUND BAR CHART, see CHART, MULTIPLE BAR.

COMPULSORY ARBITRATION, see ARBITRATION, COMPULSORY.

COMPUTER, an electronic machine which has built-in devices or can be programmed with the necessary instructions and data to solve complex mathematical problems, correlate, select or analyze data and rapidly print out the appropriate answers.

COMSTATION, 1. a **communications station.** A physical arrangement, in boxes, slots, wires, etc., of positions for **communications.** There is a **comstation** for every terman and terminal. (*HTLTAE,* p. 119) **2.** the **comstation** of any individual or section is merely eight boxes or slots or racks, which may be large or small, depending upon the volume expected. (*HTLTAE,* p. 36)

CONCENTRATION ANALYSIS, see ANALYSIS, CONCENTRATION.

CONCILIATION, the act of working out a business or labor dispute by bringing together the two or more interested parties to air their differences and reach a compromise agreeable to all concerned.

CONCILIATOR, in a business or labor dispute, one who acts as an intermediary between the parties involved to persuade them to adjust their differences and reach a compromise agreement satisfactory to all.

CONDITION, 1. a **condition** is an operating state. Organizationally, it's an operating state and oddly enough in the mest universe there are several formulas connected with these states. There are apparently certain formulas which have to be followed in this universe or you go appetite over tincup. (SH Spec 62, 6505C25) **2.** in Scn the term also means the ethics **conditions** (confusion,* treason, enemy, doubt, liability, non-existence, danger, emergency, normal, affluence, power change or power). The state or **condition** of any person, group or activity can be plotted on this scale of **conditions** which shows the degree of success or survival of that person, group or activity at any time. Data on the application of these **conditions** is contained in the ethics policies and tapes of Scn. (BTB 12 Apr 72R) [***The ethics condition** of confusion came later than the date of this BTB in HCO PL 9 Feb 74 and is added here by the editor in order that all the current ethics **conditions** are included.]

CONDITION I, **1. Condition I** is not the same as all hands. One can carelessly toss off "all hands to anchor stations" and even say **"Condition I** anchor stations" without sufficient reason. If it's a normal anchoring it usually is done in Condition II or even Condition III with a bosun and a hand at the anchor winch. **Condition I** means dangerous operation. You set **Condition I** when it's touch and go or may be. The best steersman, the best navigational team, the best radarman, the best QM, the best lookouts, the best conning officer, etc., make **Condition I, Condition I.** Things are dangerous. A dangerous approach to harbor, a dangerous pass crowded with ships, dangerous waters. A bad storm at its height. All these and more can demand **Condition I.** A damage control party, the Medical Officer set up, are all part of **Condition Is.** (FO 2464) **2.** by definition, **Condition I,** which means emergencies or periods which are risky, has the best specialists posted on the bridge and E/R. (OODs 30 Oct 71) **3.** a **Condition I** bill assigns the most competent person in each case to a key post to handle any emergency as a team. (OODs 7 Jun 70) **4. Condition I** isn't how you dispose of the crew around the ship. It's the expert in the right place, no excess people and ready to handle any goof-up. (OODs 7 Jun 70)

CONDITION II, **condition two** is an emergency situation or where an emergency may occur. Half the ship (Port or Starboard) is called up. If they are on 4 hours they are relieved by the other watch—4 on, 4 off. Continuing storms, bad seas, lots of ships about, docking, anchoring, a touchy but not really dangerous harbor approach or docking. Here again the best in that watch for a post is assigned in that watch. There is a damage control party. A **Condition II** usually comes alongside docks or leaves them. It is adequate to handle lines, anchor, all other actions including signals. (FO 2464)

CONDITION III, **1. Condition III** is considered normal. Smooth sea, no sweat, even a simple anchoring or heaving the anchor when done with no harbor or breakwater or traffic to contend with. It is usually 4 (hours) on, 8 off. Or there can be several watches if lots of officers and people are available. (FO 2464) **2. Condition III** = third of the ship on watch. (FO 80) **3.** under way with 3 watches. (BO 34, 16 Jun 67)

CONDITION VI, for normal **conditions** at sea, the ship's company is divided up into 6 watches, each watch controlling the ship at sea for two hours on a rotational basis. (FO 2674)

CONDITIONAL SYSTEM, the **conditional system** does not require completion of any auditing requirements to graduate. The certificate received is cross-stamped conditional. The student is required to interne on that level upon graduation, *before* going onto his next course in order to demonstrate his ability to apply his materials: e.g. a **conditional** HSDC would interne on Dn then do his Academy levels. A student on Academy levels would complete through IV then interne. (SO ED 401-1 INT)

CONDITIONAL TARGET, **1.** there is a type of **target** known as a **conditional target:** if I could just ______ then we could ______ and so accomplish ______. This is all right of course until it gets unreal. There is a whole class of **conditional targets** that have no if in them. These are legitimate **targets.** They have lots of will in them: "We will ______ and then ______." A valid **conditional target** would be "We will go there and see if the area is useful." All **conditional targets** are basically actions of gathering data first and if it is okay, then go into action on a vital target and operating target basis. (HCO PL 16 Jan 69) **2.** those which set up either/or to find out data or if a project can be done or where or to whom. (HCO PL 24 Jan 69) **3.** a survey of what's needed or feasible. Survey of what's wanted and needed. (HCO PL 18 Jan 69 II) *Abbr.* CT.

CONDITIONS BOARD, a fast flow **conditions board** posted near the Master at Arms' desk and visible to the public, giving areas for the various conditions. The name of a person is typed on a slip and moved with a thumbtack immediately the condition is assigned. (FO 411)

CONDITIONS CARD, when a whole ship is assigned a **condition** or a whole division or department, a **conditions card** as to that **condition** is made out and placed in the file of each personnel included. (FO 160)

CONDITIONS ORDER, any executive may assign any **condition** and improve any **condition** he assigns to any person immediately junior to him on his command channel or within his own office or area. To assign or improve a **condition** it is only necessary to write the **order** and send it to Mimeo or the Duplication Unit which duplicates it and sends the copies to Dir Comm for issue. An **order** so issued is called a **Conditions Order** and is published on the divisional flash paper not goldenrod. Where a mimeo or duplication line jams, an executive may post the order in his own handwriting on the staff notice board, filing two copies with the Ethics Officer, all on his division's color flash paper, using carbon paper and clip board. (HCO PL 5 Jan 68)

CONFER, to converse, talk together, now always on an important subject, or on some stated question; to hold **conference**, take counsel, consult. (FO 2645-2)

CONFERENCE, 1. the action of **conferring** or taking counsel, now always on an important or serious subject or affair. (FO 2645-2) **2. conferences** are called to advise and inform and to ask for advice and information. (FO 1021) **3.** (type of communication routing) this is a line usually from an executive to the chairman of a governing body such as Advisory Committee or Executive Committee or Aides Council or Commanding Officer Conference, etc. It is used for program clearance or policy requests. (HCO PL 25 Oct 71 I)

Conference (Def. 1)

CONFERENCE, a meeting between a group of persons to present a particular subject or area for examination calling for a free exchange of ideas, suggestions and proposals pertaining to the topic in hand.

CONFERENCE COMMUNICATOR, a **communicator** who sets up a temporary station for a given **conference,** so that the information which is developed in **conference** may get into the system. (*HTLTAE*, p. 81)

CONFERENCE LEADER, the person who is in charge of a conference and upon whom the responsibility is placed for successful leadership.

CONFESSIONAL CORPS, the function of the **corps** is to do modern **confessionals** on individual staff members or entire staffs of orgs in the continental area in which the **corps** is located as directed by Flag. The purpose of this **corps** is: to help Ron bring about, through the skillful application of the powerful tech of modern **confessionals,** honest, in-ethics and unafraid org staffs who enable increased production and high stats to occur. (FO 3276R)

CONFIDENCE, confidence is composed of knowing what other people do and know they are doing it or will do it. **Confidence** is confirmed by continuing survival. (FO 2471)

CONFIDENTIAL COURSES, Grades V, VI, Clearing Course, OT I, OT II, OT III, OT IV, OT V, OT VI, OT VII, OT VIII, Solo Course, Level VI SHSBC, Level VII Interneship, Class VIII, and all auditor classifications above VIII. (BPL 24 Sept 73RA XIII)

CONFIDENTIAL DATA, 1. such material so classified is contained in power processes, R6EW, Clearing Course, advanced courses and Solo C/S Course and above. (BPL 20 Sept 67R) 2. from power processing on up the **data** is **confidential.** Up to there, you can release Scn data as you always have—freely and to everyone. But this last bit is dangerous in unskilled or uneducated or unscrupulous hands and it is purely ours. It belongs to the Scientologists who keep the show on the road and must be available to them when they are ready. (HCO PL 11 Aug 71 V)

CONFIDENTIAL MATERIAL, 1. is data of which the illegal use would harm us. It is kept by the rule of controlled access. In this category is all of CIC, telex traffic and files, mission orders, debrief files, advance course data and ethics files. (FO 1669) 2. Grade V and above **materials** are classified as **confidential.** (BPL 10 Feb 71R)

CONFIRMATION COPY, (telex procedure) a **confirmation copy** is a repeat of the message, complete with its reference number, either a fourth **copy** of the transmission or an extra **copy** made up. It is marked clearly in writing or with a rubber stamp **confirmation copy** and routed on dispatch lines to the org or unit to which the telex was addressed (not to the relay points—to the org of final destination). If the message was sent to more than one org or unit, then each must get a **confirmation copy.** On receipt of **confirmation copies,** the communicator of the org or unit receiving them checks that the original message was received. This is checked against the telex master files. If receipt is verified, the **confirmation copy** is filed. (FO 2557)

CONFONE, a communication which is put through as a confirmation of a telephone conversation.

Without a confone, a telephone conversation cannot get into the system and must be considered never to have happened. (*HTLTAE,* p. 119)

CONFORMER, a worker who agrees to limit his output level to that level tacitly set by his fellow workers and contrary to management policy. The object is to hide the real output level of each worker to guarantee continued employment or so that work quotas are not increased, or where piecework rates are paid, to prevent the piecework rate from being lowered by management.

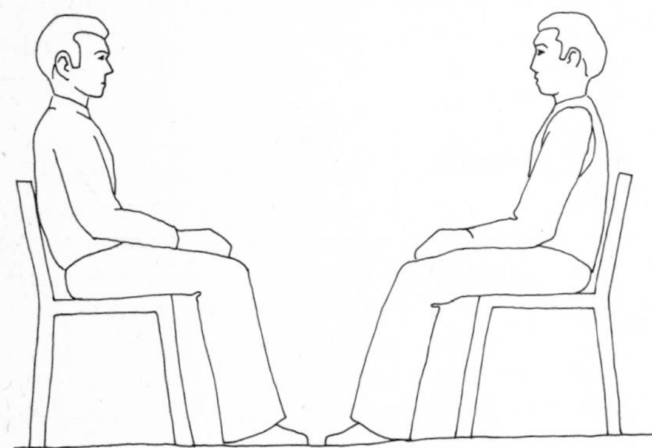

Confront (Def. 2)

CONFRONT, 1. to stand facing or opposing, especially in challenge, defiance or accusation. (OODs 27 Apr 72) **2.** to face without flinching or avoiding. (OODs 27 Apr 72) **3.** to be able to see what is or isn't before one. (CBO 190) **4.** direct observation. (HCO PL 18 Sept 67)

CONFRONTING, seeing. (HCO PL 18 Sept 67)

Confusion (Def. 1)

CONFUSION, 1. all a **confusion** is, is unpatterned flow. The particles collide, bounce off each other and stay in the area. Thus there is no product as to have a product something must flow out. (HCO PL 13 Sept 70 II) **2.** could be called an uncontrolled randomness. Only those who can exert some control over that randomness can handle **confusions.** Those who cannot exert control actually breed **confusions.** (*POW,* p. 26) **3.** any set of factors or circumstances which do not seem to have any immediate solution. More broadly, a **confusion** in this universe is random motion. (*POW,* p. 21) **4.** the definition of **confusion** is simply unstraight lines. (7201C02 SO) **5.** a **confusion** occurs whenever two or more things start creating against each other. (*POW,* p. 35) **6.** a **confusion** is only a **confusion** so long as all particles are in motion. A **confusion** is only a **confusion** so long as no factor is clearly defined or understood. **Confusion** is the basic cause of stupidity. (*POW,* p. 22)

CONFUSION AND THE STABLE DATUM, unless an executive or staff member fully grasps the basic principles of **confusion and** a **stable datum** then the org board is completely over his head, the reason for posts is not understood and dev-t becomes routine. A post on the org board is the **stable** point. If it is not held by someone it will generate **confusion.** If the person that is holding it isn't really holding it, the **confusion** inherent in that area on the org board zooms all over the place near and far. Any executive getting dev-t knows at once what posts are not held because dev-t is the **confusion** that should have been handled in that area by someone on post. With that **stable** terminal not **stable,** dev-t shoots about. (HCO PL 27 Oct 69)

CONFUSION FORMULA, there is a condition below treason. It is a condition of **confusion.** The **formula** of the condition is: find out where *you* are. The additional **formula** for the condition of **confusion** is: (1) locational on the area in which one is. (2) comparing where one is to other areas where one was. (3) repeat step (1). (HCO PL 9 Feb 74)

CONFUSION LEVEL, you can test promo by its **confusion level.** If the public has to read a whole long paragraph to find out what it's all about, they won't read it. So the delivery of your message has to be sharp, clear and fast. They have to get your message at once. Know what your message is and get it across with the least effort required by your reading public to grasp what you are saying instantly. (BPL 13 Jul 72R)

CONGLOMERATE, one large organization made up of many companies that frequently operate in widely diverse fields.

CONGRESS BOOKS AND TAPES SUM, the total receipts of **congresses, book and tape** sales before any expense deduction is made. (HASI PL 19 Apr 57, *Proportionate Pay Plan*) *Abbr.* CBT.

CONNING OFFICER, 1. the stand-by for the Captain while on watch. He receives appraised data from the OOW or from his or her own observation, evaluates it and changes course and speed when so required. Anything that would normally be appraised to the Captain is told to the **Conning Officer.** The **Conning Officer** is the one responsible for the ship if anything goes wrong. (FO RS 32) **2.** the **Conning Officer** is responsible for the ship and crew. Duties: (1) the **Conning Officer** single hands the ship while he trains the crew. (2) he safely puts the ship through its evolutions during all hands evolutions. (3) he controls the course and speed of the vessel. (4) in cruising a primary responsibility is external, other ships and storms and the motion of the vessel, while the OOD keeps the ship off rocks and shoals and fixed obstructions. (5) the **Conning Officer** sees that the ship makes good her distance toward destination, as safely and comfortably as possible, but within the time required by operational demands. (6) no pilot or bridge watch member or engine room errors relieve the **Conning Officer** of any of his responsibilities as above. **"Con"** stands for and is short for **"control."** (FO 2111) **3.** officer who is directing the ship's movements and is senior to the OOD. The **Conning Officer** is the one who chooses the courses and eases the ship. (FO 41) **4.** the **Conning Officer** is responsible for the competence of his watch members, the efficiency of the watch as a whole, and the safety of the ship while having the **con.** (FSO 546) **5.** the senior officer of a watch responsible for the vessel when his watch is on duty. (FO 2674) **6.** has **control** of the bridge. (6910C20 SO) **7.** a **con** ideally is an expert on S-C-S on an object. Only the object is a ship. (FO 3232) *Abbr.* Con.

CONSEQUENCES ANALYSIS, see ANALYSIS, CONSEQUENCES.

CONSERVATION, the cycle of action has at its exact center **conservation.** Start, increase, no change, decrease, stop. There is a complete maybe right in the middle of the cycle of action. That would be the null between increase and decrease. It would be the null point between growing and decaying. There is a plateau in there where something hits. It's an effort to maintain the state. The way you maintain the state is to have a maybe. You get an apparent stop which is what we call **conservation.** The maybe between growth and decay is **conservation.** (PDC 61)

CONSERVATIVE, when one is stuck on the time track it may seem pretty difficult to envision a future. In politics this is called "reactionary" or **"conservative."** These mean any resistance to change even when it is an improvement. The bad old days seem to be the good old days to such people. Yet the old days will not come again. One has to make the new days good. (HCO PL 11 Aug 74)

CONSIDERATION, enduring or continuing postulate, that's all a **consideration** is. It's a postulate that continues or endures. (5904C15)

CONSIDERATION, in the case of a contract it is something of value given or done by one party as an exchange or in consideration of something of value given or done by another party and without which the contract is not binding.

CONSIGNEE, a person who is entrusted with goods for custody or sale. If the goods are to be sold the consignee agrees to pay the sender or consignor after they are sold.

CONSIGNMENT, the delivery of goods, without transfer of title, from the owner or consignor to a consignee. After the consignee has sold the merchandise, he reimburses the consignor keeping a commission for his services.

CONSIGNOR, person who entrusts goods to another, called the consignee, on the agreement that he does not expect to be paid until after the articles have been sold by the consignee.

CONSISTENCY, when doing an evaluation, one can become far too fixated on out-points and miss the real reason one is doing an evaluation in the first place. To handle this, it is proper form to write up an evaluation so as to keep in view the reason one is doing one. This is accomplished by using this form:

SITUATION: ______
DATA: ________
STATS: __________
WHY: ___________
IDEAL SCENE: _____
HANDLING: ______

The whole of it should concern itself with the same general scene, the same subject matter. This is known as **consistency.** One does not have a situation about books, data about bicycles, stats of another person, a why about another area, a different subject for ideal scene and handling for another activity. The situation, whether good or bad, must be about a certain subject, person or area, the data must be about the same, the stats are of that same thing, the why relates to that same thing, the ideal scene is about the scene of that same thing and the handling handles that thing and especially is regulated by that why. A proper evaluation is all of a piece. (HCO PL 17 Feb 72)

CONSISTENT EVALUATION, all good **evaluations** are very **consistent**—all on same railroad track. Not pies, sea lions, space ships, but pies, apples, flour, sugar, stoves. (OODs 24 Feb 75)

CONSULTANT, **1.** an instructor who is on duty sporadically or from time to time but not routinely in any one place. (HCOTB 17 May 57) **2.** for public purposes all registrars may be called or sign themselves as **consultants.** (HCO PL 20 Dec 62) **3.** (Division 5, Department 15) uses two-way communication to establish what needs correcting. (HCO PL 8 Aug 70 III) [The above HCO PL was cancelled and replaced by BPL 7 Dec 71R I. The replacement issue does not have the post of **consultant** on it.]

CONSULTANT, an outside professional person well-qualified in a particular field or area who is called upon by businesses for expert advice. Examples include consultants on personnel management, economics, marketing, industrial planners, environmentalists, etc.

CONSULTANT AUDITOR, see CONSULTANT PLAN.

CONSULTANT MISSION, associated with the FLO (continental) is a **consultant mission.** This **mission** *is* a **mission.** It has all the privileges of a **mission.** It does however have added duties and responsibilities which are (a) to provide a location in which prospective Mission Directors and staffs can be trained and apprenticed on mission actions, and (b) to provide the FLO with advices as duly **consulted** and requested by the FLO. (CBO 144)

CONSULTANT PLAN, organizations have at one time or another nearly gone extinct because they employed outside auditors on an occasional or **"consultant"** basis. They keep several auditors "on call" and when they have a pc for them call them in. This measure is only an effort to preserve units. It is foolish as it eventually destroys units. At least three great evils result from "the **consultant** policy." (1) there is no way of setting up a staff training program or a staff auditing program that includes such people. (2) technical result suffers because the pc is not really given an HGC auditor but someone who is not under direct control of the Director of Processing. (3) HGC pcs often wander off from the HGC and turn up later in somebody's practice —even though the org investment in procuring that pc was great. So there will be no more of this **"consultant** auditor" idea. (HCO PL 21 Aug 64)

CONSULTANT POLICY, see CONSULTANT PLAN.

CONSULTATIVE SUPERVISION, see SUPERVISION, CONSULTATIVE.

CONSULTING MEMBERSHIP, two different memberships for franchised auditors will be available: (1) professional membership, (2) **consulting membership.** The **consulting member** will pay an annual subscription of 45 guineas sterling ($135.00), in return for which he receives a **consulting member** certificate, a weekly mailing of bulletins by air mail, the *Auditor* magazine monthly, and also participates in a two-way **consultation** service with Saint Hill. He will receive fast attention and advice from Saint Hill on his preclears and other activities, and Saint Hill will **consult** with him on how he achieves his results and success. (HCO PL 22 Apr 64)

CONSUMER, one who purchases goods and services.

CONSUMER ACCEPTANCE TEST, a market research technique whereby a product is let out to consumers in a limited quantity and monitored to see what the level of consumer acceptance is.

CONSUMER DISPOSABLE, a consumer product that is used once or only for a very short time before it must be disposed of.

CONSUMER DURABLE, a consumer product that endures, continuing to be usable for a relatively long time.

CONSUMER GOODS, goods bought and used by the public as opposed to goods, components or capital equipment used by industry to manufacture other goods.

CONSUMER, PROGRESSIVE, a consumer who would accept a price increase on an existing product or service if it were improved as opposed to a retrogressive consumer who is seeking to pay less for a product or service as it currently appears on the market.

CONSUMER PROMOTIONS, see PROMOTIONS, CONSUMER.

CONSUMER RESEARCH, see RESEARCH, CONSUMER.

CONSUMER, RETROGRESSIVE, see CONSUMER, PROGRESSIVE.

CONSUMPTION, in economics, the using up of consumer goods and services.

CONSUMPTION OFFICERS, there are **consumption officers** who get the products wanted outside and **consumed.** These are the Dissemination Secretary (Division 2) (old public) and the Distribution Secretary (Division 6) (new public). (FO 2794)

CONTACTS, people one knows who because of their knowledge in particular areas or positions in their companies might be of assistance.

CONTACT UNIT, formed in Division 1, Department 2 under the Third Mate. **Contact Unit** is responsible for operating communication, information, and facility lines between Flag and AO and may handle missions as necessary. (FO 558)

CONTEXT, the interrelated conditions in which something exists or occurs. (HCO PL 14 Dec 73)

CONTINENTAL CAPTAIN US, duties of the Office of the **Continental Captain US** are to ensure a steady continuing expansion of the US, South America, Canada and Asia, based on earlier successful actions. (CBO 115)

CONTINENTAL CHIEF, Continental Director. (HCO PL 1 Apr 64, *New Mimeo Line, HCO Executive Letter*)

CONTINENTAL CLEAR CHECKER, personnel appointed in certain **Continental** Orgs to perform the **checking** out of **Clears.** (HCO PL 7 Nov 66)

CONTINENTAL COMMITTEE, see CENTRAL COMMITTEE.

CONTINENTAL DIRECTOR, 1. the HCO Continental Secretary and the **Continental Director** of all areas shall be the senior HCO Area Secretary and the senior Association/Organization Secretary of the **continental** area. The offices of HCO Continental Secretary and **Continental Director** exist mainly to increase Scn activity and income in a **continental** area. (HCO PL 14 Jan 64) 2. **Continental Directors** oversee **continental** groups of organizations and act as designated board officers although not board members. (HCO PL 18 Dec 64, *Saint Hill Org Board*)

CONTINENTAL DIRECTOR DIRECTIVES, green ink on green paper; used for the issuance of board minutes and any broad area **directive** emanating from a **Director** of the International Board, or a **Continental Director.** A technical **directive** emanating from such a source shall be in red ink on green paper. (HCO PL 23 Feb 61)

CONTINENTAL DIVISION, Continental Executive **Division.** (HCO PL 1 Mar 66 II)

CONTINENTAL DIVISION 6 ESTABLISHMENT TEAM, (FOLO **Division 6**) team of at least four who rotate from org to org building up and recruiting up **Division 6s.** (BO 91, 23 Feb 74)

CONTINENTAL DIVISION 6 TOURS TEAM, (FOLO **Division 6**) team of at least three who lecture to and sell books to raw public in every town leaving behind new Scn groups. (BO 91, 23 Feb 74)

CONTINENTAL EVALUATOR, the function of the **Continental Evaluators** is to **evaluate** and provide competent **evaluations** and programs for all orgs and units in their zone of responsibility to the result of expanded orgs and raised stats. The motto of the **Continental Evaluators** is "No **continent,** org or unit left **unevaluated.**" (CBO 379)

CONTINENTAL EXECUTIVE DEPARTMENT, where a **Continental** Division has its home org as a Six **Department** Org, it is called a **Continental Executive Department.** (HCO PL 21 Oct 66)

CONTINENTAL EXECUTIVE DIVISION, there are eight divisions posted in every organization. There are two executive divisions, the International Executive Division and the Area Executive Division for every org. There are nine in a continental org, the International Executive Division, the **Continental Executive Division** and the normal seven divisions of the Area Org. There is *no* difference in the pattern of the WW or a **continental** or an area **executive division** except numbers of staff in it. All posts that appear in the International Executive Division will also eventually appear in the **Continental Executive Division** and an Area Executive Division as orgs grow and numbers of staff increase. When a **continental executive division** exists, then area orgs report by cable or telex to their Continental Org which then sends the data (OIC cable) by cable to WW. The Area Org where the **Continental** is located sends their data by dispatch to **Continental** which includes it in their cables to WW. (HCO PL 1 Mar 66 II)

CONTINENTAL FBO, 1. the **Continental Finance Office** is the **continental** management echelon of the **FBO** Network. It is headed by the **Continental FBO** who is responsible for successful operation of all **FBOs** under his command, and the expeditious handling of ever-increasing Sea Org reserve payments. (FO 3415R-1) **2.** the **FBO** Officer and the Office engaged in the financial management of a **continental** area under Sea Org control. (HCO PL 9 Mar 72 I)

CONTINENTAL FINANCE OFFICE, located, as an autonomous network, in Division 7, Branch 19, of the FOLO. The **Continental Finance Office** is the **continental** management echelon of the FBO Network. (FO 3415R-1)

CONTINENTAL FLAG REPRESENTATIVE, the immediate senior of a Flag Representative in any church organization is the **Continental Flag Representative** for that **continental** zone. The immediate senior of a **Continental Flag Representative** is the Flag Flag Representative. A **Continental Flag Representative** ranks with the CO of a Flag Operations Liaison Office but not above or below. (HCO PL 7 Aug 73 I)

CONTINENTAL FLAG REPRESENTATIVE OFFICE, the **Continental Flag Representative Office** in the Management Bureau at a FOLO ensures that **Flag** programs and legal orders do get done speedily and to a good result using any necessary nudging, debugging of management representatives and **FRs** per standard **Continental FR** procedures and verifying compliances as really done. Coordinates orders from the FOLO or other local network personnel (except GO) into orgs so that priorities are known and not cross ordered. Sees to it there is a trained and hatted **Flag Representative** Network on the **continent** that is able to carry out all its functions. Oversees management representatives' operation of org FRs. Sees to it that fully completed programs with all necessary evidence get back to **FR** Network on Flag. (CBO 375)

CONTINENTAL GROUPS OFFICER, (FOLO Division 6) **officer** to establish and run **groups.** (BO 91, 23 Feb 74)

CONTINENTAL HCO EXECUTIVE SECRETARIES, oversee **continental** groups of **HCO** offices. (HCO PL 18 Dec, 64, *Saint Hill Org Board*)

CONTINENTAL LIAISON OFFICE, 1. **Continental Liaison Offices** have become Flag Operations **Liaison Offices.** (FBDL 191R) **2.** the Sea Org office of a **continent** that manages that **continent.** (HCO PL 9 Mar 72 I) **3.** to relieve orgs from the burden of receiving orders from many different bosses (some say there are as many as 29 senior bodies) a new command channel pattern is set up. A central authority for each area has been established which channels all orders in one channel to the org. These are called **Continental Liaison Offices.** (LRH ED 130 INT) **4.** a **continental liaison office** is in charge of its **continental** areas. It has direct communication with orgs. Has or will have Finance Banking Officers and Bureaux Liaison Officers in each org. The first duty of a **continental liaison office** is to observe and get those observations into its own **continental** information center (CIC) and observations and reports and lists of its own activities to Flag. What are these activities? They are: (a) to observe, (b) to send observations by users, orgs and the publics to Flag, (c) to push in Flag programs and projects, (d) to find the why (reasons) that any *Flag* program or project is *not* going in in an org or franchise or public and remedy that why so the Flag program or project does go in, (e) keep itself set up and operating on the pattern planned for its establishment by Flag, (f) handle sudden emergencies. Those are the total duties of a **continental liaison office.** They are also the duties of an OTL in respect to its **CLO.** (HCO PL 22 Jul 71) **5.** the major purpose of a **CLO** or OTL is to make Flag planning become an actuality in orgs, franchises and thereby the various publics. (HCO PL 22 Jul 71) **6.** a command and communication and knowledge relay point of Flag. (CBO 134) **7.** Sea Org **Continental Liaison Offices (CLOs)** are the senior Sea Org offices in the **continents** where they exist. They are data **liaison offices** between Flag and SO orgs, stationships and OTLs, and get Flag orders carried out in their areas. They originate only by authority of Flag. (FO 2608) **8.** a **liaison office** is depended upon to see that data is supplied to Flag. Current contemporary data to Flag is a valuable final product of a **CLO.** (CBO 75) **9.** a **continental liaison office** implements, makes take place, makes known, makes occur Flag management policies and programs. It keeps Flag informed. A **CLO** acts to handle counter-policy situations. A **CLO** acts to keep stats up and the area cool and the orgs smooth. (FBDL 12) *Abbr.* CLO.

CONTINENTAL LIAISON OFFICER, **Continental Liaison Officers** are only in the business of getting stats up in each org and portion they represent and finding out for the executive secretaries WW why the stats aren't up. The authority of the **Continental Liaison Officer** at WW, for HCOs or the org portions is junior to the executive secretaries of any org. Only the HCO Executive Secretary WW and the Org Exec Sec WW are senior to the executive secretaries of orgs. The **Continental Liaison Officer** is not there to issue orders to orgs. He is at the service of orgs. HCO **Continental Liaison** is the WW communication point for the HCO Executive Secretaries in every org in the **continental** zone. The Org **Continental Liaison** is the WW communication point for the Org Executive Secretaries for every org in the **continental** zone. They are essentially representatives. They are there to get the stats of each org up by providing service from WW. (HCO PL 8 Sept 67 II)

CONTINENTAL MAGAZINES, **1. magazines** are a vital factor in solvency. Thus Area as well as **Continental** Orgs should issue **magazines.** Overlapping coverage does not matter. A **continental magazine** must go to every person in central files unless a person is on non-comm by reason of ethics orders or is dead filed. (HCO PL 7 Dec 66, *Magazines Permitted All Orgs*) **2.** (names) *Ability, Communication, Understanding, Reality, Affinity.* (HCO PL 16 Jul 65)

CONTINENTAL MAGAZINES MAJOR, **magazines** mailed by the Central Orgs every two months alternating with the minor to members and trained auditors and processed lists in their central files. (BPL 20 May 72R)

CONTINENTAL MAGAZINES MINOR, **magazines** mailed by the Central Orgs on in-between months to all orgs' central files lists in the overall area, less memberships. (BPL 20 May 72R)

CONTINENTAL MISSIONS OFFICER, (FOLO Division 6) **officer** to promote and establish new franchises. (BO 91, 23 Feb 74)

CONTINENTAL OFFICES, **Continental Offices** used to be called OTLs, called CLOs, will now be called something else. (7205C18 SO) [They are now called FOLOs.]

CONTINENTAL ORDER, issued by **Continental** Captain or the Commanding Officer of a FOLO. Distribution is all Sea Org personnel in the area. (HCO PL 24 Sept 70R) *Abbr.* CO.

CONTINENTAL ORGANIZATION, **1.** to clarify the functions and purpose of Scn organizations this was the original intention: Worldwide was to provide supreme control over Scn and orgs over the world. **Continental Orgs** under the guidance of WW took full responsibility for their **continental** areas. Central Organizations under the guidance of **Continental** took full responsibility for their zones. Area Organizations took full responsibility for their own areas. WW founded new **Continental Orgs. Continental Orgs** founded Central Orgs. Central Orgs founded Area Orgs. Area Orgs founded Franchise Centers. This was the original pattern of intention. (LRH ED 1 INT) **2.** the comparable order of a senior org cancels the order of or takes precedence over an org junior to it. The seniority is: Worldwide, **Continental,** Zone, Sub-zonal, Area, District Office. The Adcouncil WW can cancel or takes precedence over an Advisory Council **Continental.** An Advisory Council **Continental** takes precedence over that of an org junior to it. (HCO PL 13 Mar 66)

CONTINENTAL ORGANIZATION COMMITTEE OF EVIDENCE, the Convening Authority is the **Continental** Director. It handles matters relating to any Scn executive in a **continental** zone. It investigates any matter requested of it by the WW Committee of Evidence and reviews any lower organization Committee of Evidence matters or cases in its zone. (HCO PL 7 Sept 63)

CONTINENTAL RECRUITMENT CHIEF, **Continental Recruitment Chief** below FPPO **Continental** handles the planning and coordination of FPPO **Recruiters** and Sea Org org **Recruiters.** (FO 3475) [The above FO was cancelled by FO 3555.]

CONTINENTAL REPRESENTATIVE, the International Advisory Council would be made up of **representatives** of **continental** parts of the world and executives who represent types of divisions of organizations. It's about a fifteen-man Advisory Council. That Adcouncil is composed of **Continental Representatives.** Now these are **representatives** that **represent continental** areas. In other words they **represent** all the organizations and all the Scientologists on that **continent** in that **continental** area. They are specifically the **representatives** of the **Continental** Adcouncil but more importantly they **represent** all the other orgs and all those people too. (SH Spec 81, 6611C01)

CONTINGENCY PLANNING, see PLANNING, CONTINGENCY.

CONTINUOUS PROCESS PRODUCTION, see PRODUCTION, CONTINUOUS PROCESS.

CONTINUOUS SERVICE, consecutive **service** over a period of time in any Scn official organization i.e., City Office, Central Org (Day or Foundation) or Saint Hill. In other words, if a staff member transfers to another org, his service time in the previous org does count. In a foundation by **continuous service** is meant **continuous service** in the foundation only since the staff member working also in the day org is paid his **service** units for such in his day pay. (HCO PL 21 Jul 66)

CONTRACT, 1. the written, provable evidence of what the agreement actually is. (FO 2938) **2. contracts** are basically agreements in writing. (BPL 24 Jan 73 III)

CONTRACTED STAFF MEMBER, 1. one who has signed a two-and-a-half year or five year **contract.** (HCO PL 17 May 74R) **2.** those working on a **staff contract** for a social program, such a **contract** to be not less than two-and-a-half years. (BPL 12 Aug 74 II)

CONTRACT PURCHASING, see PURCHASING, CENTRALIZED.

CONTRARY FACTS, when two statements are made on one subject which are **contrary** to each other, we have **contrary facts.** Previously we classified this illogic as a falsehood, since one of them must be false. But in doing data analysis one cannot offhand distinguish which is the false fact. Thus it becomes a special out-point. (HCO PL 26 Nov 70)

CONTRIBUTION, I work on a theory of **contribution.** The way to **contribute** is to effectively and energetically wear one's hat, defend one's hat and not let anyone else do one's hat. I **contribute** to those who **contribute.** (FO 4)

CONTRIBUTISM, contributism is a philosophy in itself. You find it in the Factors. You also would apply it in economics. One **contributes,** one is **contributed** to. By others **contributing** to others who then **contribute** back, one is also benefited. (HCO PL 27 May 71)

CONTROL, the cycle of action of this universe is start, change and stop. This is also the anatomy of **control.** Almost the entire subject of **control** is summed up in the ability to start, change and stop one's activities, body and one's environment. (*POW,* p. 46)

CONTROL AREAS, areas within a fifty-mile radius of a Central Org. Any auditor within a fifty-mile radius of a Central Org must operate a District Office with finances completely under Central Org supervision and pay comparable to org staff. All franchises within these fifty-mile radius **control areas** are to be withdrawn by March 1st, 1963. (HCO PL 14 Feb 63)

CONTROL INFORMATION CENTER, 1. CIC contains all of Flag's security **information** (files, telexes, mission orders, etc.) and is not for everyone's access. **Control Information Center** does **control information** and maintains security for Sea Org operations. (FSO 615-1) **2.** the purpose of a **CIC** is to collect data related to management from all over, coordinate it by continent and org and month so that it can be evaluated and on need produce the whys for high or low stat situations. (CBO 189) **3.** the functional definition of **CIC** is: **CIC** is an administrative organization which assembles data from all points of observation in such a way as to indicate the inevitable solution. It is like a manual computer, with its program files, area boards and plotting table. (FO 2192) **4. CIC** is the program files, and statistic and alert **information** posted on the boards, and coordinated on the plotting table so that it gives the inevitable solution, plus some **information** to make life interesting for the crew. (FO 2192) **5.** the prime responsibility of **CIC** is the briefing and firing of missions including the coordination of all items and actions needed to get a mission off. (FO 1954) **6.** the whole essence of **CIC** is it takes separate channels of **information,** summates them for the channel and transfers the summation to the main board, which then indicates the action necessary. The main board then can predict, from the summation of the data and handle an area before it breaks down totally. **CIC** is a substitute for a captain. **CIC** should always know more about it than Command. (FO 898)

CONTROLLED DAYWORK, (or measured daywork) defines measuring the optimum amount of work that can be accomplished per day and thereby arriving at a daily production target.

CONTROLLED ECONOMY, a system of regulating a country's economy wherein decision-making government economists plan and control overall production, distribution, consumption, employment, wages and pricing. Also called planned economy.

CONTROLLED REPORT, a personnel-evaluating report in which a senior goes down an established checklist, checking off the qualities of performance and abilities evident to him in a junior's work.

CONTROLLER, Mary Sue Hubbard. (BPL 16 Aug 73) **2.** the post is just senior to the Guardian. The duties of the post consist of coordination of all Scn orgs and activities. There is just one **Controller** in all Scn, just as there is only one Guardian. The **Controller** is appointed by the Founder or in his absence by the Guardians and Board of Directors in single meeting. The term of the Office is for life as is that of the Guardian. (HCO PL 21 Jan 69)

CONTROLLER, (also comptroller) the executive in charge of financial operations for an organization under whose jurisdiction falls budgetary planning and control, accounting, internal auditing and statistical reports.

CONTROLLER COMM ORDER LOG, the **Controller Communicator** keeps a **Controller Comm order log.** Each incoming **order** by the **Controller** is entered into this **log.** (BPL 16 Aug 73)

CONTROLLER COMMUNICATOR, the purpose of the **Controller Communicator** is: to find and report situations to the **Controller** and to obtain compliance on orders issued by the **Controller.** All **Controller Communicators** operate under the authority of the **Controller.** The immediate senior of the **Controller Communicator** is the **Controller Communicator** Flag. The senior of the **Controller Communicator** Flag is the **Controller,** Mary Sue Hubbard. A Continental Guardian ranks with but not above or below a **Controller Communicator** for his Continental Guardian Office. (BPL 16 Aug 73)

CONTROLLING, the supervision of an activity against a laid down procedure, standard or policy and the correction of deviations from that procedure, standard or policy. Controlling is normally associated with management from the supervisory level up but can take the form of automated controlling as in the case of a machine that automatically rejects bottles not filled to the required level.

CONVENING AUTHORITY, that duly appointed official of Scn who appoints and **convenes** a Committee of Evidence to assist him in carrying out and justly exercising his or her **authority,** and who approves, mitigates or disapproves the findings and recommendations of the Committee of Evidence he or she appoints. The **Convening Authority** may not be a member of the committee and may not sit with it and may not interfere with its conduct of business or its evidence, but may disband a committee he or she convenes if it fails to be active in the prosecution of its business, and may **convene** another committee in its place. The **Convening Authority** may not increase penalties recommended by the committee he or she **convenes.** (HCO PL 7 Sept 63)

CONVERTIBLE, the right attached to certain preferred stocks, bonds or debentures whereby the holder may convert or exchange them for common stock or another security, usually of the same company.

COOK, 1. the **Cook** prepares and serves all meals and washes up. When the **Cook** is also the Purser, washing up may be assisted by other ship's company. The **Cook** also assists cleaning below decks. Safeguarding the use of fresh water is the **Cook's** responsibility at sea. Where there is an **assistant cook** but not a **cook,** the Purser closely supervises or prepares the actual preparation of meals, but stands helm watches. (*Ship's Org Bk.*) **2. cooks** for the family and living-in staff. Has charge of all equipment, dishes and the kitchen. Designates required supplies. (HCO PL 18 Dec 64, *Saint Hill Org Board*)

Cook (Def. 1)

COOK'S SICK CALL BOOK, any person treated by the **Cook** shall be noted in the **Cook's Sick Call Book** with name, date, hour and steps taken or medicine given and how much. Repeat doses are also noted. (FO 253)

COOPERATION, **cooperation** is senior to orders at all times, but **"co"** means *together.* There isn't any together where there is no understanding of what's occurring. So **cooperation** depends upon being able to see and grasp the scene. And the tech to make things go right. (OODs 5 May 74)

COOPERATIVE, an undertaking wherein a group of people form a business collectively owned and operated for their mutual benefit, distributing profits and losses equally to all its members.

COOPERATIVE ADVERTISING, see ADVERTISING, COOPERATIVE.

COORDINATE, to harmonize in a common action or effort. (FO 3404)

COORDINATING, the harmonious alignment of actions and people in an organization ensuring a smooth interacting performance overall.

COORDINATION, **1.** "combining in harmonious action" or "combination in suitable relation for the most effective or harmonious results." It does not mean "ordering along with." Before one orders into an org one should know what orders it is running on. (FBDL 152 Additional, FBDL 160 Additional) **2.** working in agreement together. (7208C02 SO)

COORDINATION AND PRIORITIES SETTING UNIT, **1.** (Management Bureau Flag) all orders are now channeled through a **Coordination and Priorities Setting Unit** in the Flag Rep Network and Execution Branch, where they get checked for accuracy against the current programs of your org, alignment with priorities, etc. (FBDL 488R) **2.** Branch 12A, the Flag Flag Rep Network and Execution Branch contains a **Coordination and Priorities Setting Unit.** All orders to an org must go through this **unit** for **coordination,** clearance for cross orders and **priorities setting.** In this branch boards are kept for each org that have on them the current program for the org, any LRH ED INT programs being worked on, telex and dispatch orders for the last month, current priorities and any other vital information pertaining to operating the org. (CBO 377)

COORDINATION BUREAU, **1.** the **Coordination Bureau** establishes, mans, oversees the training and processing and performance of duty of bureaux personnel and **coordinates** all internal bureaux functions. (CBO 7) **2.** the supervision of bureaux comes under the **Coordination Bureau.** (FSO 123) **3.** consists of **Coordinator** Branch, Bureau HCO Branch, Internal Bureau Supervision Branch, and External Bureau **Coordination** Branch. (CBO 23)

COORDINATION CONFERENCE, it is in the interest of network heads at the FOLO level to maintain full **coordination.** With the various reports that come up the network lines, each network head has a vast amount of data about each org. Pooling that data as a **coordination** council and using that to get LRH and Flag programs executed per policy and CBO on a concerted effort will greatly improve the effectiveness of FOLO management. The FOLO Networks hold regular **coordination conferences** at least three times per week. The CO FOLO and Management Rep are present. The **Coordination Conference** is chaired by the CO FOLO. Any network head may request a **coordination conference** at any time to the FR Continental. Minutes must be kept of each **conference** with a copy sent to Flag. (FBDL 488R)

COORDINATOR OF RESEARCH, in addition to other identities and titles there is that of LRH, Staff Member. As such I give staff lectures in the org where I am, assist where I can, crack cases and train students as **Coordinator of Research** (meaning application of **research**). (HCO PL 4 Jan 66 VI)

COORDINATORS, the three offices of the Executive Division are headed by **coordinators** rather than directors as in other divisions. They have the rank and privileges of directors of departments. **Coordinators** manage the activities and personnel of the office. The executive secretaries have first authority in their own offices of course. In chain of command the exec sec forwards all office administrative matters for his or her office through the **Coordinator.** Administrative matters means personnel arrangements, supervision and duties of personnel in that office and execution of tasks assigned. The executive secretaries do not forward HCO and org affairs through the **Coordinators** or the Division 7 Secretary but through Advisors. (HCO PL 20 Jan 66 II)

CO-OWNERSHIP, joint ownership of a business enterprise or property.

COPE, **1.** I've had an insight into what **cope** really is. It is the process of finding and correcting out-points without ever discovering a why and without organizing any return to the ideal scene. A **coper** goes, "Out-point found—correct it; out-point found—correct it; out-point found—correct it." This perpetual cycle never finds or corrects why these out-points. So it just gets worse and worse. (OODs 21 Sept 70) **2.** to handle whatever comes up. In the dictionary it means "to deal successfully with a difficult situation." We use it to mean "to handle any old way whatever comes up, to handle it successfully and somehow." (HCO PL 22 Sept 70) **3.** the right way to go about it is to have the tech of a job, plan it, get the materials, and then do it. This we call *organizing.* When this sequence is not followed, we have what we call **cope.** Too much **cope** will eventually break morale. One **copes** while he organizes. If he **copes** too long without organizing he will get a dwindling or no product. If he organizes only he will get no product. **Coping** while organizing will bit by bit get the line and action straighter and straighter and with less work you get more product. (OODs 15 May 71) **4.** doing the best one can with it. Single-handing goes with **cope.** (CBO 133)

COPE ORDER, the correction of an error, an omission or an out-point. (FEBC 1, 7011C17 SO)

Copy

COPY, 1. (graphic arts) the idea and words (brochures). (ED 459-49 Flag) **2.** the significances of the issue, what's in words. (BPL 29 Nov 68R) **3.** words to be used in the final product in any promotional piece. (ED 62 FAO)

CORPORATE, *adj.* belonging to a **corporation;** having to do with a **corporation.** (BPL 9 Mar 74)

CORPORATE COMBINATION, see COMBINATION, CORPORATE.

CORPORATE IDENTITY PROGRAM, the overall program of a company that creates its image and ensures its name, insignia and other distinguishing features are kept before the public. The promotional forms range from advertising and public relations to stationery and packaging design to lapel pins and vehicle identification.

CORPORATE IMAGE, the distinctive style a company presents operationally and visually within and without, to its own staff as well as to the public.

CORPORATE MANAGEMENT, see MANAGEMENT, CORPORATE.

CORPORATE PLANNING, see PLANNING, CORPORATE.

CORPORATE REGULARITY, by which is meant their **incorporation** must be passed upon and in accordance with policy. (HCO PL 31 Oct 64 II)

CORPORATE SOLE, 1. an individual may sell his franchise to another providing that other is going to operate it and be as a person in that area. The franchise may not be sold into any network for non-resident management. The proper US term for the type of company is **corporate sole;** meaning an individual in whom the property and funds of a social or religious group is invested. The **corporate sole** is a person who is a custodian of the funds and property of the group. This type of **"corporation"** is permissible in franchise. (HCO PL 10 Nov 69 II) **2.** the grantee may **incorporate** his mission as a **corporate sole** which means that the mission is permanent and continuous and can survive a change in personnel in charge of the mission. (BPL 20 Nov 69R)

CORPORATION, a group of persons who obtain a charter giving them as a group certain legal rights and privileges distinct from those of the individual members of the group. A **corporation** can buy and sell, own property, etc., as if its members were a single person. (BPL 9 Mar 74)

CORPORATION, a legal entity formed by a group of persons who have obtained a charter to engage in a profit or nonprofit business under a distinct corporate name. A corporation has legal rights and privileges separate and distinct from its owners. Primary among these is that a corporation's owners enjoy a limited liability to the corporation's creditors if a financial disaster occurs. Only the assets each owner has invested in a corporation are subject to a creditor's claims. An individual's personal assets are generally secure from the claims of a corporation's creditors because a corporation is an entity legally distinct from its owners as individuals.

CORPORATION, CLOSED, a corporation which does not sell its stock to the general public. The stock is held by a few shareholders who own and operate the corporation.

CORPORATION COORDINATOR, a newly created post, the function of which is concerned solely with the setting up and maintaining of new autonomous Scn **corporations** on a worldwide basis. It is a function of HCO Worldwide and comes under the aegis of the newly created HCO (WW) Ltd. (HCO PL 31 Jan 64)

CORPORATION, DOMESTIC, a corporation operating in the country or state in which its charter was granted.

CORPORATION, FOREIGN, 1. under Federal income tax law, a corporation formed under the laws of another country. 2. under state corporation laws, a corporation established under the laws of another state or country.

CORPORATION, MUNICIPAL, the organizational form through which a village, town, city, borough, county or other territory carries on its business affairs.

CORPORATION, NONPROFIT, a corporation which does not seek to make a profit for profit's sake and whose owners do not benefit from or share in any profits made. A nonprofit corporation would be one formed to benefit its patrons or serve society; such as a church, school, or charitable organization.

CORPORATION, NONSTOCK, a nonprofit entity which issues no stock; a nonprofit corporation.

CORPORATION, OPEN, a corporation which makes its stock available for sale to the general public, as opposed to a closed corporation, and whose stockholders receive at least an annual financial report.

CORPORATION, PRIVATE, a corporation formed to profit by engaging in commercial and industrial activities. It is owned and controlled by private individuals.

CORPORATION TAX, a tax imposed on the profits of a corporation by a Federal or state government.

CORRECT ACTION, the **correct action** is the **action** based on the right why that raised the stats, increased delivery and expanded the area. (CBO 51)

CORRECTED GROSS INCOME, 1. the AC-1 reports the gross income of the organization for the week, shows the calculation of the **corrected gross income** and the allocation of the **corrected gross income.** The **corrected gross income** is the **income** available for use and is calculated by deducting various items as detailed on the AC-1 form. (BPL 4 Dec 72 IIRB) **2.** in a Central Organization, all the money taken, whether in cash or checks, is banked in the Main Account at the Central Org's local bank. Ten per cent of this total taken during one week is remitted to HCO WW. This leaves 90% of the total take for that week in the Main Account. This balance is called the **corrected gross income.** (HCO PL 20 Feb 63) [The above HCO PL was cancelled by BPL 10 Oct 75 IV.] See ALLOCATION SUM.

CORRECT EXPANSION, **expansion** which when expanded can hold its territory without effort is proper and **correct expansion.** It is almost impossible to consolidate territory where one was not invited in in the first place and force had to be used in order to expand. (HCO PL 4 Dec 66)

CORRECTION ALERT FORM, **form** to ensure that quick reporting of persons or situations requiring correction can occur. A **correction alert form** is authorized for use by all Qual staff or any staff member in an org. These org **correction** reports could be filed in a divisional folder and used in evaluations on specific divisions and areas. (BPL 25 Oct 72R)

CORRECTION BUREAU, there would be a Qual Bureau in a CLO called a **Correction Bureau** and it's **Bureau** 5A. (7109C05 SO)

CORRECTION DIVISION, 1. your next division after Technical Division is not really Qualifications but **Correction.** It would be called the **Correction Division** or the Adjustment Division but Qualifications would also serve. (SH Spec 77, 6608C23) **2.** Division 5. (HCO PL 8 Nov 73RA) **3. Correction** unsnarls things, it finds out the why of things, why a job can't be done, why a target is stopped, why a mission failed, why a cycle cannot be completed, etc., etc. Once the why has been found, the cycle, target, etc., can usually now go ahead and be completed. Up to now it has been thought that once Qual or **Correction** stepped in to **correct** that it would also now step in, do all the work and complete the cycle. This is not right. Qual will handle it for you, to the point of finding why or how come it's jammed, then will hand it back to you to complete. (FO 1753) **4.** purpose of the **Correction Division:** to find and restore lost tech and safeguard knowledge; to ensure the technical honesty and results of Scn and Dn, **correct** them when needful and attest to them when attained. (BPL 7 Dec 71R I) **5.** (Qual) ensures org tech and admin staff cleared of misunderstoods and **corrected** in their tech and admin duties so that orgs that falter renew their purpose and deliver in quantity with quality without undue numbers of refunds and repayments and both public and org winning fully and we can get on with clearing the planet. (BPL 7 Dec 71R I)

CORRECTION FORMS, (used by the LRH Comm) a very vital tool in obtaining compliance is the **correction form.** It is very essential that a **correction form** may be started on any bugged or stalled compliance on the WHOs found by investigation to be not wearing their hats. The **correction form** handles the why behind non-compliance and results in overall improvement of the org. (BPL 19 Oct 73)

CORRECTIVE ADVERTISING, see ADVERTISING, CORRECTIVE.

CORRECT POLICY, the **correct policy** in operating bureaux is the **policy** that swiftly accomplishes the purpose of the bureaux. (CBO 51)

CORRECT RELATIVE IMPORTANCE, a plus-point. The **important** and **unimportant** are **correctly** sorted out. (HCO PL 3 Oct 74)

CORRECT SOURCE, a plus-point. Not wrong **source.** (HCO PL 3 Oct 74)

CORRECT TARGET, a plus-point. Not going in some direction that would be wrong for the situation. (HCO PL 3 Oct 74)

CORRECT TIME, correct time or the expected **time** period is a plus-point. (HCO PL 30 Sept 73 I)

CORRELATION, the degree of relationship that is shown to exist between one thing and another. Positive correlation is the increase or decrease occurring simultaneously between two random statistics. When both statistics simultaneously go up or down there is a possibility that they are both being affected by a common cause. Once the correlation between statistics has been noted, statistical management can isolate the factors affecting the statistical change. Negative correlation is when one stat goes up and another goes down simultaneously. In this situation there is also a possible common cause.

CORRESPONDENT BANK, see BANK, CORRESPONDENT.

COST, 1. the amount (usually money) that is demanded as an exchange for a product or service. 2. the amount expended to produce a profitable return or income.

COST ACCOUNTING, the recording, breaking down, summarizing and analyzing of operational cost data as an aid to management. Cost accounting informs management of current areas of cost and makes future predictions with advices on obtaining greater financial efficiency. It is the subject of how to produce as much or more at a smaller cost.

COST-BENEFIT ANALYSIS, see ANALYSIS, COST-BENEFIT.

COST-EFFECTIVENESS, the examination of an expense to see if its advantages could be obtained for less money or whether the expense could be allocated to better advantage or efficiency.

COSTING, 1. a precise art by which the total expenses of the organization administration and production must be adequately covered in the pricing allowing for all losses and errors in delivery and adequate to produce a reserve. (HCO PL 14 Dec 70) **2.** this is a detailed rundown of what the **costs** of the action will be—includes premises, pay of personnel, legal fee estimate, etc. Any and all **costs** are estimated and listed. (FO 2261)

COSTING, the action of determining the cost of various functions, products or services in a business; cost accounting.

COSTING FORMULA, the **costing formula** for pricing a book by the publishing agency (not the seller) is as follows: printing **cost** x 5 + 2x surface post to furthest org. This is the standard publisher **costing formula** and allows for discounts up to 50% for large distributors, overhead and royalties. To sell for less than this is to cause loss and prevent distribution. This also allows enough money for the distributor and the publisher both to advertise. This is a minimum price formula. (HCO PL 10 Feb 65)

COSTING, MARGINAL, the determination of what costs are marginal or variable. Those costs not fixed costs are usually termed marginal.

COSTING SYSTEM, a system designed to observe and control organizational costs and keep them within or below the specified limits. A costing system allows management a view of organizational operations and performance by monitoring production costs, labor costs, etc.

COST OF LIVING, the amount of money for food, clothing, shelter, medical attention, recreation, etc., that a person must pay at any given time to maintain a certain standard of living.

COST OF LIVING INDEX, 1. anything like a chart or graph that illustrates a comparison between the cost of living at various distinct time intervals. 2. a measurement of the cost of specific items or goods at different time intervals that serves as an indication of a fluctuation in the cost of living; consumer's price index.

COST PLUS PRICING, see PRICING, COST PLUS.

COST-PUSH INFLATION, see INFLATION, COST-PUSH.

COST REDUCTION PROGRAM, a program aimed at getting a maximum decrease in costs, relative to past costs or a standard cost.

COST REPORT, a report dealing with the costs of a corporation or business.

COSTS, ALTERNATIVE, the costs of various alternative courses of action a company's management has at its disposal. All costs of each alternative course of action, to the obtaining of an end product, would be taken into account when appraising opportunity cost.

COSTS, AVOIDABLE, those costs which, not being vitally essential, could be avoided. The launching of a research project to develop a new product would be an avoidable cost, while rent, basic equipment and labor costs are unavoidable costs.

COSTS, CRASH, the costs involved in implementing a crash program to complete a contract or obligation by the deadline set or within a revised deadline.

COSTS, DIRECT, the basic production costs of an article such as its materials, irrespective of manufacturing overhead costs. Together the direct cost plus overhead, or indirect cost, comprise the factory cost of an item. Also called prime costs.

COSTS, DIRECT LABOR, costs for labor directly involved in the manufacture of a product.

COSTS, DIRECT MATERIAL, those costs which are directly attributable to the material used to make a product.

COSTS, EMPLOYMENT, the cost to the employer of employee salaries, pensions, insurance, profit sharing, etc. Sometimes indirect costs are included such as the provision of facilities to better accommodate or convenience employees.

COSTS, FACTORY, the sum of the direct and indirect costs associated with the manufacture of a product; what it costs the factory to produce a product.

COSTS, FIXED, costs that do not vary with the amount of production or level of operation such as a fixed rental cost, taxation or depreciation.

COSTS, INDIRECT, a cost which cannot be directly attributed to the production of a specific product. In a factory producing a variety of products, rent, depreciation, utilities, and supervision would all function as indirect costs.

COSTS, INDIRECT LABOR, the cost of salaries for workers in production-associated services but not directly involved in the production of goods such as those in maintenance, equipment upkeep, supplies and guarding at night.

COSTS, INDIRECT MATERIAL, cost of plant material not being used directly in a product but found in materials used for cleaning and general maintenance.

COSTS, MIXED, costs that contain partially fixed and partially variable costs. When a company rents a car there may be a fixed cost for the car in addition to a cost that varies with how much use the car is put to.

COSTS, OPPORTUNITY, a company often has several courses of action it may pursue to make a profit. When it pursues a less profitable opportunity, the money lost or not made as income represents the opportunity cost.

COSTS, PRIME, see COSTS, DIRECT.

COSTS, REPLACEMENT, the costs at current market prices in a particular location of replacing items such as materials, components, goods, equipment, or a building.

COSTS, RUNNING, basic costs related to keeping a business in good running condition such as equipment maintenance, consumable supplies, wages, rent, taxes, daily services, etc.

COSTS, SELLING, expenses incurred in selling or marketing a product or service which includes salesmen's salaries, commissions, expense accounts, advertising, shipping, display boards, samples, etc.

COSTS, SEMI-VARIABLE, costs that vary in an indirect way with changes in the business activity level such as electric power, water, etc.

COSTS, STANDARD, a projection of the cost of producing something based upon the normal expenditures required to produce that product under current or expected economic conditions. The calculation of standard costs is important in discovering the source of overexpenditures or inefficiencies in the utilization of resources or manufacture of goods.

COSTS, START-UP, costs needed to launch or start a project or business, usually of a preparatory type that are separate to running costs to keep the business in operation.

COSTS, STEPPED, a fixed cost that steps up and fixes at a higher level. This could happen where increased productivity is planned requiring additional rental of space, vehicles, etc.

COST STUDY, a close study of the various costs incurred to produce a product or service.

COSTS, TURNOVER (PERSONNEL), the cost resulting from the replacement and hiring of personnel. This is not only what it costs to contact, interview and train personnel enough to get them on the job, but what it costs in decreased production or increased operating expense due to lack of needed personnel.

COSTS, UNIT, the cost calculated to be a standard for each unit of production such as cost of a particular service delivered or of a single product as well as dollar costs per labor hour, per bushel, ton or applicable measurement.

COSTS, VARIABLE, operating costs which vary directly with any variance of volume of production or sales or utilization, such as direct labor and power and materials consumed.

COUNCIL, a group of persons assembled to handle the administrative and legislative functions of an organization. (FSO 138)

COUNSELING, an effort to help others employing a wide range of techniques but generally recognized as that activity where a professional person or counselor causatively helps employees, students, etc., to resolve their problems and function better as a result.

COUNSELOR, 1. a professional person skilled in techniques that assist a person to resolve his problems. Counselors are often employed by companies as a service to employees and ideally help to create less troubled, more productive employees. 2. one who has knowledge in a specific area and can advise others of how a situation should be handled or what course of action to follow.

COUNTER CHECK, a **check** written by someone on a **check** form other than that supplied by his bank for his own account. **Counter checks** are just blank **check** forms obtainable in stationery stores, dime stores, etc. **Counter checks** are legal and valid in most states, providing they are properly made out and drawn on an account which *does* exist and which has an adequate balance to cover. A **counter check** is also a "postulate" **check** if the person either has no bank account or inadequate balance in his account to cover. (CO 1 US)

COUNTER-EFFORT, contrary action or **effort** to your action or **effort.** (HCO PL 1 Oct 70)

COUNTERFOILS, (stubs) example: checks when cleared and back from bank must be taped in to original check book into their stubs (**counterfoils**). (HCO PL 23 Jan 66)

COUNTER-INTENTION, (form of arbitrary) the receipt of a communication is an extremely important part of the sequence of actions that results in a compliance. Common reasons for the non-receipt of a communication is that arbitraries (or arbitrary factors) exist in the area. **Counter-intention** means a determination to follow a goal which is in direct conflict with that known to be the goal of the originator and the goals of the group (either a big goal or a little one). (BPL 10 Nov 73 II)

COUNTER-POLICY, 1. illegal **policy** set at unauthorized levels jams the actions of a group and are responsible for the inactivity, non-production or lack of team spirit. **Counter-policy** independently set jams the group together but inhibits its operation. (HCO PL 6 Dec 70) **2.** (form of arbitrary) the receipt of a communication is an extremely important part of the sequence of actions that result in a compliance. Common reasons for the non-receipt of a communication is that arbitraries (or arbitrary factors) exist in the area. **Counter-policy** means a local **policy** that demands a procedure or sequence of actions be followed that prohibits or inhibits the carrying out of the origination that is expected to be followed by a source which is senior to the originators of the **counter-policy.** (BPL 10 Nov 73 II) **3.** cancelling published orders or PLs or FOs or FSOs or OOD orders by rumor or inventing orders or policies that were never published and attributing them to Command. (OODs 20 Jan 71)

COUNTRY OF ORIGIN, the country from which something was exported but not necessarily produced. Goods produced in and exported from the same country are called domestic exports.

COUPON ADVERTISING, see ADVERTISING, COUPON.

COUPON BOND, a bond to which interest coupons are attached, to be clipped as they come due and presented by the owner in order to receive the interest payment.

COURIER, 1. there are five major types of Mission Orders. These types are (1) observation mission orders, (2) situation handling mission orders, (3) garrison mission orders, (4) project mission orders, (5) courier mission orders. The term "missionaire" is used for the personnel who conduct the first four types and **courier** is used for the last type. (FO 2936) **2.** the name **courier** implies outgoing mail. A **courier** is on the ship schedule and leaves with mail, etc., at routine times. (FO 2494) **3.** taking mail to and fro from org to org or from org to Flag would be done by a **courier.** (FO 2505)

COURIER LINES, courier lines carry mail. **Couriers** travel normally by air. (FO 2611R)

COURIER MISSION ORDERS, couriers escort or carry people or things to ensure safe arrival. All **couriers** go on **mission orders,** are briefed, debriefed. **Courier mission orders** are usually the same pattern but need rewriting when new routes are used. (FO 2936)

COURSE, in Scn a **course** consists of a checksheet with all the actions and material listed on it and *all* the materials on the checksheet available in the same order. A **course** must have a supervisor. He may or may not be a graduate and experienced practitioner of the **course** he is supervising but he must be a trained course supervisor. The final and essential part of a **course** is students. The final valuable product of any **course** is graduates who can apply successfully the material they studied and be successful in the subject. (HCO PL 16 Mar 71R)

COURSE ADMINISTRATOR, 1. the **course** staff member in charge of the **course** materials and records. (HCOB 19 Jun 71 III) **2.** a supervisor in a **course** of any size has a **course administrator** who has very exact duties in keeping up **course admin** and handing out and getting back materials and not losing any to damage or carelessness. The **Course Admin** is in charge of routing lines and proper send off and return of students to cramming or auditing or ethics. (HCO PL 16 Mar 71R) **3.** the **Course Administrator's** purpose is to help the **Course** Supervisor keep all bodies correctly arranged, placed or routed and to keep all **course** materials, folders, records, checksheets, invoices and dispatches handled, filled out and properly filed. (HCO PL 16 May 69) **4.** the supervisor is there to get the **course** materials fully understood and applied by the student. The **Course Administrator's** function of service to students is equally important. The **Course Administrator** must see that the **course** materials are available and in sufficient quantity and quality. (BPL 11 May 69R)

COURSE COMPLETION, a **course completion** is a checksheet not a condition or classification. (HCO PL 22 Mar 65, *Current Promotion and Org Program Summary Membership Rundown International Annual Membership*)

COURSE DEPARTMENT, 1. the **Course Department** procures, trains and graduates students of Scn. (HCO PL 18 Dec 64, *Saint Hill Org Board*) **2.** this, under the **Course** Supervisor, is responsible for about one third of the income received at Saint Hill. It consists of its technical and administrative staff, including the **Course** Secretary, Registrar and Letter Registrar. (HCO PL 28 May 64)

COURSE INSTRUCTOR, **Course** Supervisor. (HCO PL 17 May 65)

COURSE PROGRAMS DIRECTOR, arranges all TV **programs,** tape plays, live lectures and all social **programs.** (HCO PL 18 Dec 64, *Saint Hill Org Board)*

COURSE REGISTRAR, acts as **registrar** and Letter **Registrar** for the **Course.** Is responsible for procuring new students and the income level of the department. (HCO PL 18 Dec 64, *Saint Hill Org Board)*

COURSE SUPERVISOR, **1.** basically, someone who in addition to his other duties can refer the person to the exact bulletin to get his information and never tells him another thing. (6905C29) **2.** the **instructor** in charge of a **course** and its students. (HCOB 19 Jun 71 III) **3.** a **course** must have a **supervisor.** He may or may not be a graduate and experienced practitioner of the **course** he is **supervising** but he must be a trained **Course Supervisor.** He is not expected to teach. He is expected to get the students there, rolls called, checkouts properly done, misunderstoods handled, finding what the student doesn't dig and getting the student to dig it. The **supervisor** who tells students answers is a waste of time and a **course** destroyer as he enters out data into the scene even if trained and actually especially if trained in the subject. The **supervisor** is not an "instructor," that's why he's called a **supervisor.** A **supervisor's** skill is in spotting dope-off, glee and other manifestations of misunderstoods, and getting it cleaned up, not in knowing the data so he can tell the student. (HCO PL 16 Mar 71R) **4.** the **Course Supervisor** oversees all **Course** Department activities and is directly responsible for producing **course** income, the training of students and graduating auditors at a high level of technology and good will. (HCO PL 18 Dec 64, *Saint Hill Org Board)*

COURSE SUPERVISOR CORRECTION LIST, HCO Bulletin 27 March 1972R, Issue II, *Course Supervisor Correction List, Study Correction List 2R.* This is to get the **Course Supervisor** going well. (LRH ED 257 INT)

COURT MARTIAL, Committee of Evidence. (FO 236)

COURT OF APPEAL, see FOLO LAST COURT OF APPEAL.

COURT OF ETHICS, **1.** a **Court of Ethics** may be convened by any Ethics Officer. Any Scientologist of the status of officer or below may be summoned before a **Court of Ethics.** The summons is issued as an HCO Ethics Order. It must state when and where the person is to appear. (HCO PL 26 May 65 III) **2.** a **Court of Ethics** or Executive **Court of Ethics** is not a fact finding **court.** One is convened solely on statistics and known evidence. (HCO PL 26 May 65 III) **3.** a form of **ethics** hearings based on known data and convened on misdemeanors or crimes and authorized to direct discipline such as suspension from training or processing, payment of damages, restitution of wrongs, etc. (BTB 12 Apr 72R)

COVENANT, 1. a binding agreement made between two or more parties; legal contract. 2. a particular clause in such an agreement or contract.

COVERAGE ANALYSIS, see ANALYSIS, COVERAGE.

COVERING UP SITUATIONS, consists of actions to do just that, ranging from denial that a **situation** exists or data on it is not to hand, when it does exist and data on it is available—whether perceived or not, to ignoring **situations,** or failing to take actions to detect and locate **situations** in one's area. (FSO 788)

CPA, 1. Certified Public Accountant. 2. Critical Path Analysis.

CR, 1. credit. 2. creditor.

CRACKED CASE, **case** unmistakably improved and applicant is fully aware of it. (HCO PL 26 Jan 64)

CRAFT, a highly skilled and often artistic activity commonly employing only one or a small number of persons throughout the making of a product. A craft connotes the requirement of years of training in order to make or assemble precision parts to attain the product. Silversmithing and watchmaking are crafts.

CRAFTSMAN, 1. a highly skilled person who through substantial education and experience in a particular area is now accomplished in the range of activities covering all phases of producing the product of his trade. 2. a person who has attained technical perfection but has not yet attained artistic perfection in his trade.

CRAFT TRAINING, see TRAINING, CRAFT.

CRAMMING, there are two areas of **cramming:** (1) tech **cramming,** (2) admin **cramming.** There are two basic types of **cramming:** (a) to rapidly prepare a person for post or technical action, through intensive study, word clearing and drilling on *key* materials, (b) to rapidly correct a person after the fact of an error or flub, by finding the why, and handling that why with study and word clearing of the particular data involved and drilling the actions to a point of confidence and competence. This covers **cramming** orders sent to Qual or originated by the **Cramming** Officer or Qual Sec on out-points in the org. (BTB 8 Mar 75 II)

CRAMMING OFFICER, (Correction Division) purpose of the **Cramming Officer** is to help LRH to isolate and correct real causes for staff and student misapplication of technology or policy and see that the correct data is known, cleared of misunderstoods and drilled to confident certainty, thus ensuring the technical honesty of the organization. (BPL 7 Dec 71R I)

CRAMMING SECTION, a **section** of the Department of Review (Division 5, Department 14). The prime purpose of the Department of Review and all its sections and units is: to help Ron correct any non-optimum result of the organization and also to advise ways and means based on actual experience in the department to safeguard against any continued poor result from any technical personnel or the function of the organization. More specifically, the **Cramming Section** teaches students what they have missed. (HCO PL 10 Nov 65)

CRASH COSTS, see COSTS, CRASH.

CRAZY PEOPLE, **people** who explain how wrong it is all going and who have reasons why and who aren't putting it right are the real **crazy people** in the universe. The only ones **crazier** than they are, are the ones who are quite happy to have everything fail and go wrong with no protest from them. And the only ones even worse are those who work endlessly to make things go wrong and prevent anything from going right and oppose all efforts instinctively. (HCOB 19 Aug 67)

CREDIT, **1. credit** does not entirely deal with money. It has everything to do with confidence and reliability. (HCO PL 28 Jan 65) **2.** the word **credit** comes from the Latin *creditum* meaning something entrusted to another—a loan. In bookkeeping the word is used to mean any right-hand entry made to an account but the making of such right-hand entries does not necessarily mean the recording of a loan. In fact, when you make a right-hand entry to an impersonal account it means the recording of an outflow of a mest, service or money particle; it does not mean the recording of a loan. (BPL 14 Nov 70 III)

CREDIT ACCOUNT, the **credit account** is established as a service of Division 3. It is a savings **account** like a banking establishment delivers. Any member of the ship's company may use the service and are encouraged to do so as it is a safe place to save one's money. (FSO 621-1)

CREDIT BALANCE, a **credit balance** occurs when the sum of the **credit** entries exceeds the sums of the debit entries. (BPL 14 Nov 70 IV)

CREDIT CARD, usually a wallet size identification card that allows a person to buy items or obtain services on credit simply by showing a retailer the card and signing the bill. The card is backed by a credit card company which pays the bill and bills the credit card owner. Usually purchases made with a credit card are interest free for one month after which interest is payable.

CREDIT COLLECTED, **1. credit collected** includes **collection** for Qual services and any other services given on **credit,** freeloader **collections,** and any monies owed to the org for services or sales. (HCO PL 12 Mar 71 II) [The above HCO PL was cancelled by BPL 10 Oct 75 IX.] **2.** (Flag) this includes amounts collected for Flag on-board services or manufactured items, books, tapes, etc. (It does not include management fees even though these are on the same statement. They should be on a separate statement in the accounts file of the org.) (ED 103 FAO)

CREDIT CONTROL, any system of controlling the amount of credit extended to a customer or the total of credit extended to customers. This would include requiring credit references, limiting the amount of credit available to a customer, increasing the efficiency of collecting debts due to credit extended, etc.

CREDIT MANAGER, that executive responsible for determining a customer's credit worthiness and ability to pay off credit extended.

CREDITOR, a person who advances credit or to whom a debt is owed.

CREDIT OUTSTANDING, the extent of credit allowed to a customer by a company which includes goods on order as well as goods received.

CREDIT RATING, a rating or estimation of how much credit may be extended to a person or firm based upon past performance in paying off debts and present capacity to do so.

CREDIT SALE, a transaction where the seller extends credit to the buyer to purchase goods or services. The buyer agrees to pay off what is owed to the seller in regular installments. In a credit sale the buyer becomes the legal owner of what he purchases at the time of the sale.

CREST, the **crest** is actually the insignia that a knight of old wore on the top of his helmet and frequently also affixed to the top of his horse's bridle. It could be as simple as a tuft of colored feathers or as complex as a representation of a leaping lion carved out of wood. In some coats of arms, in fact, the helmet itself is actually represented as part of the coat of arms. In the Sea Org coat of arms, however, we are not a military sort of group, the helmet is not represented, but simply the cross of the eight dynamics. (FO 3350)

CREW, when we say **crew,** we normally mean all below officer rank. (BO 34, 16 June 67)

CREW MORALE OFFICER, he is the Captain's assistant in matters of **crew** welfare and **morale.** Pride is to be built up by the **Crew Morale Officer.** (ED 240-7 Flag)

CREW STUDENT AND PC LINES, lines handled by routing forms and are similar to but not the same as public lines, as the **crew** are receiving their training and auditing as SO members and are not paying for the service but are expected to do their post and WQSB duties and are assigned to duty aboard even if the assignment is one of full time study. (FSO 137)

CRIMANON, Crimanon has the purpose to ensure that reforms in **criminal** laws and prison systems come about. **Crimanon** is dedicated to the successful rehabilitation of prisoners to make them useful members of society. **Crimanon** is completely reversing the 80% recidivism of **criminals** with fantastic success. (LRH ED 256 INT)

CRIME, 1. the action of the insane or the action of attempting seizure of product without support. Example: robbers who do not support a community seek to rob from it supporting funds. (HCO PL 25 Mar 71) **2.** stems totally and entirely from lack of belonging and understanding that to which one belongs. The **criminal** or juvenile gang is a substitute for society. It is an outlaw pack at the throat of that which forced it not to belong. (HCO PL 16 Sept 70) **3. crime** is directly the result of a lack of hat and training on the hat. (FO 2580) **4.** action without inspection. (SH Spec 90, 6112C07) **5. crime** might be defined as the reduction of the survival level along any one of the eight dynamics. (*SOS*, Bk. 2, p. 33) **6.** there are two types of **crime.** There's the **crime** of commission and the **crimes** of omission and in modern society they pay very little attention to the **crimes** of omission. The penalty is usually awarded to a person really for two reasons: one is for being there and the other for communicating. Now that is the normal penalty in this society. If you want to reduce any **crime** down, it was basically composed of those two elements: being there and communicating. But there are **crimes** of not being there and not communicating, too. The society doesn't pay much attention to these. (SH Spec 73, 6608C02)

Crime (Def. 1)

CRIME REPORT, staff member **report** of any **crime** noted or suspected, but if suspicion only it must be so stated. (HCO PL 1 May 65)

CRIMES, these cover offenses normally considered **criminal. Crimes** are punished by convening Committees of Evidence and may not be handled by direct discipline. **Crimes** may result in suspension of certificates, classifications or awards, reduction of post, or even dismissal or arrest when the **crime** clearly warrants it. But such penalties may not be assigned by direct discipline. Certificates, classifications or awards may not be cancelled for a **crime.** (HCO PL 7 Mar 65 III)

CRIMINAL, 1. the **criminal**, the suppressive person (same thing) is trying to get even with people. That's his common denominator. He does it by covert omissions or overt violence. It all amounts to the same thing. (HCO PL 7 Dec 69 II) **2.** real **criminals** may have bad meters but **crimes** are often so unreal to them that they do not read (meters' needles read only on things within the reality or borderline reality of a person), and the reality level of a **criminal** is too bad for reads to occur in a majority of cases. (HCO PL 15 Nov 70R)

CRIMINAL RECORD, one with the police for the commission and imprisonment for felony. The fact of a **crime** is irrelevant if not seen as a **crime** by law. (HCO PL 13 Mar 69)

CRIMINAL THINK, whether theft or threat or fraud is used, the **criminal think** is to get something without putting out anything. (HCO PL 4 Apr 72)

CRITICAL PATH ANALYSIS, see ANALYSIS, CRITICAL PATH.

CRITICAL THOUGHTS, these are always only indicators that the person being checked has committed an overt against what he or she is **criticizing. Critical thoughts,** comments and attitudes toward something indicate always a prior actual overt. (BPL 3 Feb 62R)

CROSS, the symbol of the **cross** has been widely used in symbolic tradition, and with many interpretations given to it. The many forms of the word **"cross"** itself, however, traditionally are said to derive from (come from) a basic root word meaning "light of the Great Fire." The distinctive **cross** of the Church of Scientology is symbolic because of its eight points, of the eight dynamics. Above the shield of the Sea Org coat of arms, it not only symbolizes the Sea Org member's devotion to the aims of the Church of Scientology, but also his commitment to the greatest good for the greatest number of dynamics. The **cross's** position above the shield also indicates that Sea Org is a religious fraternity within the formalized structure of the Churches of Scientology. (FO 3350)

CROSS DIVISIONS, one person in two different **divisions.** (HCO PL 9 Mar 71 II)

CROSS-HATTING, you're trying to **hat** this person as one thing and somebody has **crossed** your lines and is **hatting** him as something else. That is one of the favorite tricks of a suppressive person: "You really don't want to be here, what you really want to be doing is waffle, waffle, waffle. . . ." (ESTO 10, 7203C05 SO II)

CROSS-ORDERING, **cross-ordering** is where juniors are issuing contrary or confused **orders** into an area where an executive responsible for an area issues an order. Programs cannot exist or be executed. (HCO PL 23 May 68, *WW and SH Recombined (Deadline 15 June '68)*)

CROSS-ORDERING POLICY, **cross-ordering policy** is committed when any action is ordered done that violates a **policy** that should be followed in the situation, or that is ordered out of an illegal **policy** where standard **policy** exists. (FSO 788)

Cross

CROSS ORDERS, 1. a type of dev-t where juniors issue so many orders unknown to a senior and across his lines that a senior's **orders** are obscured or lost. Things get very confused, very active but non-productive. (HCO PL 27 Jan 69) **2.** senior **orders** unattended because of different junior **orders.** (HCO PL 24 Feb 69) **3.** (form of arbitrary) the receipt of a communication is an extremely important part of the sequence of actions that results in a compliance. Common reasons for the non-receipt of a communication is that arbitraries (or arbitrary factors) exist in the area. **Cross-order** means an order received from a local person who is junior to the originator of the **order** or policy that is to be duplicated and complied with, which is contrary to the senior **order** but is not cancelled (as it should be) in favor of the senior **order.** (BPL 10 Nov 73 II)

Cross Orders

CROSS POLICY, operating on **policy** contrary to that of management. (FO 2626)

CROSS TARGETS, a type of dev-t where the senior's **target** system is neglected due to conflicting **targets** being set on lower levels. (HCO PL 27 Jan 69)

CROSS-TRANSFERRING, the whole board can be thrown askew and chaos made in the ship by **cross-transferring.** This is pure destruction. By **cross-transferring** is meant shifting several posts because one is shifted and across divisions, i.e. a Qual personnel is made PRO. A steward is transferred to Qual. An HCO person is **transferred** to steward. Three **transfers** all to fill in one gap. In practice somebody new should be fed into Division 6 and a Division 6 person promoted to PRO. (FO 2127)

C ROUTING, goes up to one's org superior or superiors on channel as per org board only. One's own superiors can send it across if they wish, to their similar post in the other org but it cannot be so routed by the original sender. Do not go up in own org and address across to a superior post than your own in another org. It must only be addressed to superiors in one's own org. Dispatches so routed are clearly marked **C Routing** and have the proper vias for one's own org marked on it by the sender for forwarding inside his own org. (HCO PL 13 Mar 65 II)

CRUSADE, type of article other than straight news usually included in a newspaper. A **crusade** is an attempt by a newspaper to service the public interest. There have been **crusades** as long as there have been newspapers. Often a **crusade** will result from investigatory reporting. A bad spot is turned up, and the paper will work as a team to handle that bad spot. **Crusades** are a traditional part of the newspaper's hat. (BPL 10 Jan 73R)

CRUSH SELL, over-do the hard sell technique and you wind up with **crush sell** (bodily force, duress, threats, etc.) and an ARC broken field. Go to the other extreme called soft sell and you'll wind up with no business, no income and an ARC broken field. (CBO 126)

CRYPTOANALYST, a professional code and cipher breaker usually employed by governments or military units and one who can and does break codes and ciphers without having the original code or cipher. (HCO PL 11 Sept 73)

CRYPTOGRAM, a **cryptogram** (hidden meaning) is something written in code or cipher. (HCO PL 11 Sept 73)

CRYPTOGRAPHER, someone who uses codes and ciphers. (HCO PL 11 Sept 73)

CS, (abbreviation for Case Supervisor). It means one of two things depending on context. (a) that person in a Scientology Organization who directs and oversees the auditing of preclears including the programming of cases (the setting out of a series of auditing actions in correct sequence for each case), the specific written directions for each session, the grading of sessions, and the correction of auditors by sending to cramming when departures from standard tech occur, (b) C/S also means the written instructions of a Case Supervisor, in this context, the abbreviation form only is used. (BPL 4 Dec 71R III)

CS-1, 1. (HCO Aide) from **CS-1** stems the network and know-how of all HCOs in the world in SO and

Scn orgs. (FO 2376) **2.** I expect these things from **CS-1** quite in addition to "regular duties" (a) to see that personnel exists in adequate quantity and that it is being properly trained and apprenticed, (b) to see that senior officers aboard and in outer areas are in-ethics, on post and producing, (c) to note and get handled out-ethics scenes in orgs. (FO 3179) **3.** Communications Aide, responsible for communications, ethics, personnel and transport. It is the opposite number to Division 1 on Ship's Org Board. (FO 1031) **4.** LRH Comm Aide in charge of communications, transport and personnel. (FO 795)

CS-2, 1. (Dissemination Aide) I expect these things from **CS-2,** quite in addition to "regular duties" (a) to see that registration outnesses and unrealities do not occur and that registrars are functional, busy and effective and on policy and that squirrel registration does not occur, (b) to keep books flooding out, (c) to keep central files and addresses up-to-date, properly tabbed and in use, (d) to keep the money flooding in. (FO 3179) **2.** the duties and responsibilities of Division 2 in Scn orgs and Sea Org organizations are now under **CS-2.** All matters concerning Division 2—promotion to CF, CF, org magazines, letter reg functions, reg functions and publications are sent to **CS-2** for handling. (FO 2270) **3.** Training Aide. (BPL 8 May 69R III)

CS-3, 1. Finance Aide (CS-F) is located on the org board in Division VII. Her area of responsibility is that of Finance Offices and FBOs. Treasury Aide (**CS-3**) is located on the org board over Division 3. Her area of responsibility is that of Treasury Division 3s. The Finance Aide will no longer carry the title of **CS-3** but will be posted as CS-Finance. Treasury Aide will assume the title of **CS-3** which is appropriate for her position on the org board. (FDD 18 Treas INT) **2.** I expect of **CS-3** that she will keep the SO viable and reserves mounting. This is in addition to her regular duties. Of Treasury Aide, I expect the following, quite in addition to "regular duties" (a) to keep logistics flowing and crews uniformed, (b) to keep all outstanding money in the world collected up and not back-date which destroys it, (c) to get proper FP known and used in every area. (FO 3179) [The above duties of **CS-3** later became the duties of Finance Aide and the above duties of Treasury Aide became the duties of CS-3 per FDD 18 Treas INT of 16 June 1972, *Clarification of Titles,* which laid out the duties of Finance Aide and merged the posts of Treasury Aide and **CS-3** into one post called **CS-3.**] **3.** financial matters are assigned to **CS-3,** the Commodore's Staff Material Aide (CS Order 71) **4.** Commodore's Staff for Division 3. (FO 1590) **5.** Material Aide, in charge of logistics, finance and stewards. (FO 795)

CS-4, 1. (Training and Services Aide) I expect these things from Training and Services Aide, quite in addition to "regular duties" (a) to spot areas of out tech before they develop seriously and take the actions necessary to handle, (b) to keep tech and admin data flowing to orgs and known and used, (c) to effectively handle by whatever means failures on the part of local and outer terminals to understand and apply tech and admin data. (FO 3179) **2.** the post of **CS-4** will be filled as the opposite number to Tech Div 4 and Ship Div 4. The present duties of **CS-4** and **A/CS-4s** transfer to the Chief of Sea Org Operations at Flag and to the Assistant Chief of SO Operations for ______ (continental area) on every stationship or base. (FO 2474) **3.** is primarily concerned with missions and their successful conduct and completions. (FO 2333) **4.** the hat and responsibilities of the post of **CS-4** are very simple, the basics of which are hereby listed: (1) supervising and operation of CIC, (2) operation of missions, (3) planning and programming of actions of the flotilla, (4) supervising the well functioning of Flag and ship Div 4s, (5) ensuring AO Div 4s are operating well and stats going up, (6) to keep your eye on Div 4s world wide and push on areas with falling stats. (FO 1595) **5.** Operations Aide, in charge of operations, ships, tech and AOs. (FO 795)

CS-5, 1. (Qual Aide) I expect these things from Qual Aide, quite in addition to "regular duties" (a) to get and keep word clearing fully in over the world, (b) to build effective Qual Divisions. (FO 3179) **2.** as Commodore's Staff 4 is primarily concerned with missions and their successful conduct and completions, and as Commodore's Staff Tech is mainly research internally and correction externally then Tech and Qual programs and actions come under **CS-5.** The duties of **CS-5** then consist of internal Flag and ship Tech and Qual actions, including an eye on ship training, on research and tech programs and on Tech and Qual matters in SO and Scn orgs. Keepers of Tech are the responsibility of **CS-5.** (FO 2333) **3.** correction of actions which have gone astray. That is the definition of **CS-5's** post. (6910C30 SO) **4.** will now become Tech and Qual Aide. (FO 995) **5.** Ethics Aide, in charge of petitions, correction and medical. (FO 795)

CS-6, 1. (Distribution Aide) I expect these things from **CS-6,** quite in addition to "regular duties" (a) to keep surveying and PR tech in and in use, (b) to keep up org appearances, (c) to keep floods of new people coming into orgs. (FO 3179) **2.** is now responsible for the Public Divisions and all matters relating. (FO 2270) **3.** Public Aide, in charge of distribution, information, new public and hostess. (FO 795)

CS-7, 1. Flag LRH Comm. (BPL 24 Jul 73R) **2.** I expect these things from **CS-7** quite in addition to "regular duties" (a) to keep SO No. 1 line smartly caught up and on policy in every place it is handled, (b) to keep crews well fed and berthed and COs alert to it, (c) to keep policy known and checksheeted and in full use in orgs, (d) to keep the LRH image and offices bright and in full view. (FO 3179) **3.** makes sure that the LRH Comm Network international is functioning. (CS Order 46) **4.** LRH Communicator Aide, which hat has been worn in conjunction with CS-1 is now separated out. **CS-7** is responsible for my lines, getting compliance and coordination of activities for all other Aides. (FO 1031)

CS-8, Division 8 LRH Aide. (SO ED 72 INT)

CS-9, 1. in charge of LRH Comm Network. (FO 2364) **2. CS-9** is to handle and obtain LRH Comm compliances in SO and other orgs. (CBO 28)

CS BOARD, each **CS** (**Commodore's Staff**) has a **board** with the relevant information of their activities on it. (FO 898)

CS-ES, the post of **Estate-Ship** Aide. It is a full **Commodore's Staff** Aide post and is located on the org board directly under Staff Captain, alongside CS-PA on the org board. Its shortened designation will be **CS-ES.** (FO 3380)

CS-F, the post of **Commodore's Staff-Finance.** (FO 3403)

CS FLUB, consists of gross violations of **case** programming. (HCO PL 8 Sept 70R)

CS-G, Commodore's Staff Guardian is responsible for the **Guardian's** Office over the world and this function is best described as guard and protect Scn. The **CS Guardian** also sees that **Guardian** Office and SO actions are coordinated and complement each other. (FO 1664)

CS-P, 1. Personnel Aide Flag. (CBO 241) [**CS-P** literally abbreviates for **Commodore's Staff-Personnel.**] **2.** the **CS-P** post is abolished. The Staff Aide responsible for personnel and all HCO matters is CS-1. (FO 3313)

CS-PA, see CS-PRAC.

CS-PRAC, Commodore's Staff Aide for **Public Relations Area Control** (now known as CS-PA, Commodore's Staff Aide for Public Affairs). (CBO 262-2)

CS-PrB, the existing post of D/CS-2 Pubs/Books is now moved up and expanded to the post of **Commodore's Staff** Aide for **Promotion** and **Books** (**CS-PrB**). The post has been created to more fully aid LRH with the overall supervision, production, coordination and protection of broad LRH **promotional** lines from Flag to field and to ensure that all LRH products done by the Photo Shoot Org are then actually produced, marketed and correctly used. (FPO 2253)

C/S SERIES, actions of a **case supervisor** are covered in detail in the **C/S Series** HCOBs. (BPL 4 Dec 71R III)

C/S SERIES 53 RI, HCO Bulletin 24 November 1973RA, **C/S Series 53RI,** *Short Hi-Lo TA Assessment C/S.* This is a famous list. It solved the long long problem of high and low TAs and really solved it. Unfortunately it has a name of being done for high and low TAs. In truth it practically handles the whole repair of any difficult **case** today! One assesses it Method 5. One handles the reads from the top down. It can also be reassessed several times until it F/Ns on a whole M5 assessment. (LRH ED 257 INT)

C/S SERIES 54, narrative Dn for drugs and psychosomatic ills. (ED 164 FAO)

CULT, 1. cult is uniformly defined as a system of religious worship or ritual. (LRH ED 28 INT) **2. cult** by the *Merriam-Webster Dictionary* means: (1) a religious practice. (2) a system of beliefs and ritual connected with the worship of a deity, a spirit or a group of deities or spirits. (3a) the rights, ceremonies and practices of a religion, the formal aspect of religious experience; (3b) Roman Catholicism. (LRH ED 28 INT)

CULTURAL LAG, an example is Dr. Semmelweis's discovery of the cause and cure of childbed fever. For over a half a century after that women still died in agony after childbearing. Eventually the **culture** caught up to it and the illness which had accounted for a huge percentage of female deaths ceased to exist. Dr. Semmelweis's discovery of its prevention was "ahead of its time." Pathetically, scoffed and disbelieved, he even died to prove he was right. (HCOB 14 May 69 II)

CULTURE, 1. the amount of technology, knowingness, wisdom in existence in the society. (*Aud 27*

UK) **2.** an accumulated soul which flows over and through a number of individuals and persists after the death of those individuals via other individuals or even other groups. (*DAB* Vol. II, p. 136)

CUMULATIVE INSANITY, the actual point between where a person who is sane goes thereafter **insane** is a very precise point and it's when he begins to stop something. At that moment he is **insane.** Now he is **insane** on that one subject at first and then he can get another idée fixé and become **insane** on another subject and you do get **cumulative insanity** but there is no doubt of his **insanity** on that one subject. (6711C18)

CURRENCY SPECULATOR, a person who exchanges one currency for another in order to profit from fluctuations in exchange rates.

CURRENCY UNIT, we define a **currency unit** as the full cost of one auditing hour at the local per policy cost. (At this time for example this is $50 in the US.) (BPL 10 Sept 65R)

CURRENT ASSETS, see ASSETS, CURRENT.

CURRENT BILLS FILE, every firm or person —even staff members, has a place in our accounts **files** in a separate **file** folder. One firm or person= one folder. All records, **bills,** letters, etc., relating to such are placed in this person or company's file. Any bank or other loan has its own **file.** Cancelled checks and bank statements are kept in their own files by account. But, where possible, a photostat of each back and front is made and **filed** with the firm folder to which it was issued. So are invoice and disbursement copies also **filed** as they apply in these **files.** A summary sheet of **billing** and payments to one firm is kept in the folder of that firm. (HCO PL 27 Jan 60)

CURRENT EVALUATIONS, those **evaluations** that apply to the **evaluated** org or area in present time, and in which the why and handling still apply in full. (FO 3149-2)

CURRENT LIABILITIES, any liability or valid debt which will be paid within a short period of time, usually within a year or before the end of the financial year.

CURRENT PROGRAM, definition of a **current program** used here is a **program** not more than approximately two months old and/or inconsistent with the **current** statistical picture, and/or outmoded by the **current** scene in an org. (ED 520-4 Flag)

CURRENT RATIO, a ratio of an organization's current assets to its current liabilities. This figure is used as an indicator of an organization's working capital and ability to pay off debts. The current ratio can be unreliable due to the quality of assets calculated into it and a cash/bills ratio would be a better indicator to use.

CUSTODIAN OF TECHNOLOGY, the HCO Area Secretary provides the Central Organization with all needful **technology,** bulletins, tapes, records, books (for library) and data so that the Central Org can give the highest quality of service. That HGC auditors use allowed processes well and with the best presentation is a primary concern of HCO. The HCO Area Secretary sees to this personally and consistently. That students are instructed properly and in accordance with standard processes, and that LRH tape or records are played on every course is of primary importance to HCO. The HCO Area Secretary sees to this personally and consistently. **Technology** given in public lectures and performances must be standard and this is of deep concern to HCO when it is not. The HCO Secretary is the **Custodian of Technology** in any Central Organization. (HCO PL 13 Jan 59)

CUSTOMER, a person who buys goods or services from another, especially one who patronizes another regularly.

CUSTOMER COMMUNICATIONS, advertisements, brochures, and promotion that keep a customer or potential customer informed about products or services.

CUSTOMERS, pcs and students. (HCO PL 11 Nov 69)

CUSTOMER SEGMENTATION, the separation of customers in a particular market into distinct categories (age, social status, income bracket, etc.) that can then be addressed more directly through advertising, promotion and marketing techniques.

CUSTOMS BROKERS, are specialists in the paperwork of getting things through **customs** with the minimum of cost and the maximum of speed. When necessary they also apply for government licenses for the import or export of the goods they are handling. However, they never physically touch the goods themselves. (FO 2738)

CUSTOMS DRAWBACK, same as drawback.

CUTATIVE, 1. after 1966 when I left the post of Executive Director WW, a new condition set in.

Checksheets, processes, intensives, grades began to be cut down. This we can dub a **cutative** impulse, to coin a word; shortening things in order to produce a quicker result. (HCO PL 30 May 70, *Important Cutatives*) **2.** an invented word to mean the impulse to shorten or leave out or *the thing* left out. (HCO PL 26 Sept 70 III)

CUTBACK, a reduction in the level of production or activity usually resulting in the laying off of personnel.

CYCLE, anything which has a beginning, a middle and an end. (FO 2528)

Cycle (Def. 1) A. Beginning B. Middle C. End

CYCLE, cycle is a regular series of events that occur over a regular or sometimes irregular period of time. The business cycle consists of: prosperity, decline, depression and recovery. The amount of time a company or nation spends in any portion of the business cycle is attributable directly to management.

CYCLE BILLING, a system of billing whereby a portion or percentage of a firm's debtors are billed with statements each day, week, etc., in a relatively continuous cycle as opposed to trying to bill all debtors at one time such as at the end of each month. This type of billing spreads out the workload and payment of bills.

CYCLE OF ACTION, **1.** the **cycle of action** has at its exact center, conservation. Start, increase, no change, decrease, stop. That really is the **cycle of action.** There is a complete maybe right in the middle of the **cycle of action.** That would be the null between increase and decrease. It would be the null point between growing and decaying. There is a plateau in there where something hits. It's an effort to maintain the state. (PDC 61) **2.** the creation, growth, conservation, decay and death or destruction of energy and matter in a space. **Cycles of action** produce time. (*PXL*, p. 8) **3.** start, change and stop comprise a **cycle of action.** (*POW*, p. 41)

CYCLE OF ACTION OF LIFE, the **cycle of action of life** is creation, survival and destruction. Survival could be said to be any change, whether in size or in age or in position in space. The essence of survival is change. Creation is of course starting, destruction is of course stopping. Thus we have in Scn two very useful **cycles of action,** the first of them being start, change and stop, and the more detailed one being create, survive, destroy. Start, change and stop imply the conditions of a being or an object. Create, survive, destroy imply the intention of life towards objects. (*POW*, p. 42)

CYCLE OF BOOMS AND DEPRESSIONS, there is a phenomenon that takes place and that is the periodic **cycle** which the communists call the **cycle of booms and depressions** without which communism couldn't exist. And the **cycle of a boom and depression** is created by the outflow and answer **cycle** of the department. You don't have any answers coming in so you sit there and outflow very heavily. Then your mail beefs up and you spend your time answering the letters and you don't outflow and after a while business drops off and goes in the trough on the curve and then you get anxious and promptly outflow which brings in lots of business and replies but no outflow. (5812C16)

CYCLE OF CONTROL, see CYCLE OF OBSERVATION.

CYCLE OF DISESTABLISHMENT, it has been long proven that constant transfers of

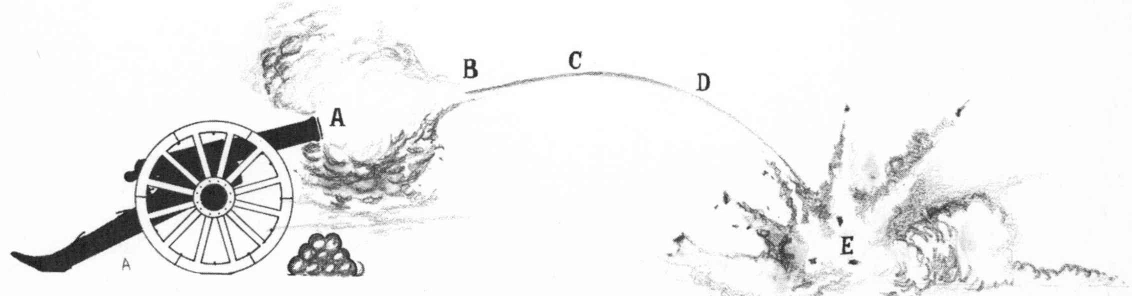

Cycle of Action (Def. 2) A. Creation B. Growth C. Conservation D. Decay E. Destruction

personnel—also known as "musical chairs"—and frequent demotions or dismissals cause a situation of decline in an org, and winds up with staffs: (a) not getting fully hatted and trained on the actions and functions of one post, (b) not gaining the experience they need on the post to learn all the ropes, (c) thus being left with misunderstoods on that post or area, (d) and the same occurring in rapid succession on other posts. In such a situation one winds up finally with confused staff, slow producers due to earlier unhandled misunderstood words, lack of hatting as the Hatting Officer can't keep up, lack of personnel programming as they don't stay long enough on any one post to complete their program for that post. This then leads to unstable terminals, which brings about weak internal lines and reflects on the field by lack of new bodies or if they do show, lack of sign-ups, and finally, lack of a stable, bright, high morale staff which is producing. This is the **cycle of disestablishment.** It doesn't happen overnight. But once started, it disestablishes with increasing momentum. (BPL 9 Aug 71R II)

CYCLE OF HATTING, the **cycle of hatting** is **hat** some and get production, **hat** more and get production, **hat** more and get production. **Hat** to total specialization, get production. **Hat** to more generalized skill and get production. **Hat** an activity until it can do own and everyone else's hat in the activity and get production. You **hat** to get a product. (BPL 3 Apr 73R I)

CYCLE OF OBSERVATION, there are certain conditions necessary for accurate **observation.** First is a means of *perception* whether by remote communication by various comm lines or by direct looking, feeling, experiencing. Second is an *ideal* of how the scene or area should be. Third is *familiarity* with how such scenes are when things are going well or poorly. Fourth is understanding *plus-points* or rightnesses when present. Fifth is knowing *out-points* when they appear. Sixth is rapid ability to *analyze data.* Seventh is the ability to *analyze* the *situation.* Eighth is the willingness to *inspect* more closely the area of outness. Then one has to have the knowledge and imagination necessary to *handle.* One could call the above the **cycle of observation.** If one calls *handle* number 9 it would be the cycle of control. (HCO PL 18 May 70)

CYCLIC CASE, the **cyclic case** (gains and collapses routinely) is connected to a suppressive person. (HCO PL 5 Apr 65)

D

DAAD, *n.* **1.** "Data Addressee." The **DAAD** is a fast but non-tabulated method of gaining data from another station. A **DAAD** leaves no copy in the hands of the ORIGINATOR or the chief communicator and should come back quickly as demanded information means that a maybe has to be resolved in order to resolve other problems. Thus a **DAAD** is traditionally fast, but has the frailty of not leaving tracks. A **DAAD**, returned, is sent to file. (HTLTAE p. 119) **2.** INFADS and **DAADS** are just lonely little pieces of paper which have left no duplicates behind them. They are on their own. **DAADS**, which are very vital, since they represent a need for data to keep the wheels turning from minute to minute, cannot go far astray because the sender is anxiously waiting for an answer. INFADS and **DAADS** are the casual remarks and quick inspirations of the communications system. (*HTLTAE,* pp. 88-89)

DAILY REPORT, 1. usually contains what you have done on post today and what outnesses have been spotted and what outnesses you handled. You can say whatever you wish also. (OODs 19 Apr 72) **2.** (for the Commodore) the **report** should contain: (a) productions and actions taken by you on your post, (b) actions taken by you to correct outnesses you have found in the ship and others, (c) comments. It is an optional line which each person aboard the flagship has with the Commodore to inform him of his **daily** actions. (FSO 127R) **3.** the crew members of a Sea Org installation may write a **daily report** to their Commanding Officer. This should be heartily encouraged by commanding officers, as a **daily report** from each crew member can give the CO excellent data and a general summary of crew activities and morale. The procedure for a crew member writing a **daily report** is (a) productions and actions taken during the **day** on post, (b) actions taken to correct outnesses in the area and in others. (FO 2576) **4. daily reports** to aides, captains, COs, OTL and juniors are not compliance reports but information only. Such **daily reports** contain: (1) the activities of their zone, (2) particularly any important event that is occuring, (3) any data that would be of interest to the senior. (BPL 26 Jan 69RA) **5.** the **report** is a very simple affair. It is headed "To LRH **Daily Report.**" It marks the time of ending work for the **day**, the date, the division and any department and any section numbers, a very brief statement of the **day's** work done by the staff member (for staff auditors the name of any pc audited and instructors the number of students taught that **day** by actual count and any absences or blows), and the signature of the staff member. (HCO PL 14 Apr 65 III) *Abbr.* DR.

DAMAGE CONTROL, 1. this drill is not strictly an all hands operation as the necessary actions of running or using the ship must also go on. Therefore, one trains up a **damage control** and rescue party to care for various accidents which might happen to the ship herself, including getting hulled. This includes getting water out of her bilges fast and rigging pumps. (*Ship's Org Bk.*) **2.** Purpose: to take over an area of disorder before **damage** occurs or to salvage what can be salvaged after **damage** has resulted. (FO 2689) **3. damage control** is the function of the normal precautions taken to guard against fire, flood, general **damage. Damage control** is a function of Div 4 for the handling of the equipment, fire extinguishers, hoses, and the tools and material to control damage. (FO 1611) *Abbr.* D/C. [See Illustration]

DAMAGE REPORT, staff member **report** of any **damage** to anything noted with the name of the person in charge of it or in charge of cleaning it. (HCO PL 1 May 65)

Damage Control (Def. 1)

DANGER CONDITION, 1. a **danger condition** is normally assigned when: (1) an emergency condition has continued too long, (2) a statistic plunges downward very steeply, (3) a senior executive suddenly finds himself or herself wearing the hat of the activity because it is in trouble. (HCO PL 9 Apr 72) 2. a **danger condition** exists where statistics show continuing emergency or a steep, steep fall. If a **danger condition** exists, you handle the situation, bypass anyone at all and then the personnel who ignored it. (HCO PL 15 Jan 66)

DANGER FORMULA, the original **formula** follows: (1) bypass (ignore the junior or juniors normally in charge of the activity and handle it personally), (2) handle the situation and any danger in it, (3) assign the area where it had to be handled a **danger** condition, (4) handle the personnel by ethics investigation and Committee of Evidence, (5) reorganize the activity so that the situation does not repeat, (6) recommend any firm policy that will hereafter detect and/or prevent the condition from recurring. (HCO PL 9 Apr 72)

DANGEROUS, 1. peoples' definition of **dangerous** is something that you don't want to communicate with very much. So you just turn this around and say don't communicate with this very much and they'll believe it's **dangerous**. (SH Spec 200, 6210C09) 2. people consider those things **dangerous** which they are afraid to communicate with. What's the definition of **dangerousness**? Afraid to communicate with. (SH Spec 200, 6210C09)

DANGER RUNDOWN, the Trouble Area Long Form, Trouble Area Short Form or Why handling per HCO PL 9 April 1972, *Ethics—Correct Danger Condition Handling.* (BPL 17 Apr 72)

DANGER RUNDOWN CORRECTION LIST, if any trouble occurs on the application of the **danger rundown** (Trouble Area Long Form, Trouble Area Short Form or Why handling) per HCO PL 9 April 1972, *Ethics—Correct Danger Condition Handling* and the person did not respond favorably to that action, use this **correction list.** The **list** is done by telling the person you are about to ask him some questions on a meter concerning the **Danger Rundown** actions. Further handling would be whatever is found necessary from the assessment and handling in order to get the **Danger Rundown** properly completed with a correct why which leads to a Correct application of the formula. (BPL 17 Apr 72)

DATA, 1. observations leading to investigation. (HCO PL 29 Feb 72 II) 2. when doing an evaluation the **data** you give is not a lot of reports. It is a brief summary of the "strings pulled" on the out-point or plus-point route to finally get the WHY. **Data,** then, is the Sherlock Holming of the trail that gave the why. It at once reflects the command the evaluator has of the **Data** Series. (HCO PL 17 Feb 72) 3. the information one has received that alerts one to the situation. (HCO PL 17 Feb 72) 4. facts, graphs, statements, decisions, actions, descriptions which are supposedly true. (HCO PL 15 May 70) 5. an org owes Flag certain reports—HCO weekly reports, staff lists, ethics orders, personnel orders, OODs, org rudiments, Dissem weekly reports, etc. Other data issued such as debriefs of missions, interrogation of persons from the area or near a FOLO. (FBDL 192R)

DATA AIDE, the **Data Aide** is held accountable for the availability of the **data** and neatness and completeness of the **data** files. (CBO 1 USB)

DATA ANALYSIS, 1. following that chain of out-points which leads you to the idiocy nobody would ever believe. (ESTO 12, 7203C06 SO II) 2. we do this by grading all the **data** for out-points (primary illogics). We now have a long list of out-points. This is **data analysis.** (HCO PL 15 May 70) 3. by studying and isolating the principles that make a situation illogical, one can then see what is necessary to be logical. This gives us a subject that could be called "illogicality testing" or "irrationality location" but which would be better described as **data analysis.** For it subjects **data** and therefore situations to tests which establish any falsity or truth. (HCO PL 12 May 70)

DATA BUREAU, 1. the **Data Bureau** has the cycle of attract **data** from all pertinent areas of all possible types, file it, assemble it, condense it, display it. If you represented it as a receiver of different types of reports from many remote observers, which the **Data Bureau** then got into orderly condition and then condensed them to meaning and displayed them for use by others you would have the operation of the **Data Bureau** and its CIC. Stats provide the clue to meaningful **data.** Very down and very up statistics alike cause the reports of those particular areas in that particular time to be related to those stats and displayed. This flashes all the very successful and the very dangerous areas to display attention and provides the extreme conditions packs vital to understand the why or to permit it to be investigated further. (CBO 7) **2.** it has collection, condensation, evaluation and distribution (of **data**) as its four actions. (FBDL 12) **3.** FOLO **Data Bureau** collects standard reports due from orgs, nudges for standard reports due from orgs, logs **data** on standard **data** checklists, debriefs and gets area observations, keeps a copy of stats, graphs it for Flag Programs Chief, and forwards all **data** and reports via External Comm to Flag. (CBO 192) **4. Data Bureau** contains a Data Receipt Branch, Data Assembly Branch, Data Condensation Branch, and Data Library Branch. (CBO 16R) **5.** the Admin Unit and CIC are now the **Data Bureau.** (OODs 15 Aug 70)

DATA BUREAU FILES I/C, the purpose of **Data Bureau files** is to furnish the reports for any org for any given month in one folder. This requires an exact and kept up filing system. The product of **Data Bureau files I/C** is packages of grouped data complete by org by month ready for evaluation. (FO 3170)

DATA BUREAU STAT REPORT, another set of **data** entirely comes in on telexes. These are the **statistics** of each division of each org in the world. The major **stats** of an org are plotted in big **stat** books. The gross divisional **stats** are plotted in folders. These are gone through carefully each week by an Alert Officer. He is looking for dangerous **stat** situations or extremely good ones. All this information is written up in a published weekly **Data Bureau stat report.** Thus any major situation is spotted by **statistics.** (FBDL 192R)

DATA CHIEF FOLO, the **Data Chief FOLO** is perhaps one of the most vital posts in the **FOLO.** The **Data Chief** is responsible for seeing that **data,** debriefs and stats get to Flag to facilitate swift evaluation in order to increase the viability of our activities. (CBO 222R)

DATA EVALUATION ALERT, a **data evaluation alert** will be used for all **evaluations** done by the **Data Evaluator.** The purpose of an **evaluation alert** is to get all **data** on the subject being **evaluated** to the **Data Evaluator** fast so that all **evaluations** can be done quickly with all **data** to hand. When the **evaluator** is about to start an **eval,** he will distribute **data evaluation alerts** to all terminals who may have **data** on hand which isn't in **data** files which will be pertinent to the **evaluation.** As soon as the person receives the **data evaluation alert,** he searches through all his files, writes down any **data** he knows about the area, attaches it to the **data evaluation alert,** and hand routes it back to the **evaluator.** (CBO 172)

DATA FILES, 1. the purpose of **Data Bureau files** is to furnish the reports for any org for any given month in one folder. This requires an exact and kept up **filing** system. The **data files** are to be broken down by (1) continent (2) org (3) month. All **files** for orgs of a particular continent are to be in cabinets adjoining each other. One **files** the orgs of a continent in alphabetical order. Each **file** drawer is clearly labelled by continent, then org (i.e. Europe: Orebro). A folder exists for each month's reports whether it has sent any or not. It is a folder not unlike a pc folder. It is tabbed "org name, month, year" (i.e. Orebro February 1972). Inside the front cover is the checklist of items in it. (FO 3170) **2.** every org in the world has a **file** for each month in the **data files.** As the **data** pours in from that org—telexes, staff reports, MO reports, finance reports, surveys, personnel records, observations, any and all **data** it goes bang at once into that org's file for the month. All in a folder for that org for that month. And there's that org, not only current, but for each month exactly for years back. As fast as they've been **filed** they are worked. In other words, read and acknowledged. Queries are handled. (FBDL 192R)

DATA FILES RED CARD, when anyone removes a **data** folder from **data files** he has to put a large **red card** in place of the folder showing where it has gone. (CBO 2 USB)

DATA IN SAME CLASSIFICATION, a plus-point. **Data** from two or more different **classes** of material not introduced as the same **class.** (HCO PL 3 Oct 74)

DATA PROVEN FACTUAL, a plus-point. **Data** must be **factual,** which is to say, true and valid. (HCO PL 3 Oct 74)

DATA SERIES, the tool to discover causes. (ESTO 1, 7203C01 SO I) [The **Data Series** is a **series** of policy letters written by L. Ron Hubbard which deal with logic, illogic, proper evaluation of **data** and how to detect and handle the causes of good and bad situations in any organization to the result of increased prosperity.]

DATA SERIES 26, HCO Policy Letter 12 June 1972, *Data Series 26, Esto Series 18 Length of Time to Evaluate.* A list you assess to locate trouble an evaluator might be having. Also for slow evaluators or slow students on a **Data Series** course. (LRH ED 257 INT) See LENGTH OF TIME TO EVALUATE.

DATA SERIES EVALUATORS COURSE, product: a person with demonstrated ability to evaluate competently. Certificate: Hubbard **Evaluator** (provisional), permanent certification is awarded when you have demonstrated the ability to do correct **evaluations** consistently with resulting high statistics. (BPL 6 Jul 73RA) *Abbr.* DSEC

DATA SERIES/EVALUATORS INTEGRITY LIST, this **integrity list** is for use in handling **evaluators** who are consistently slow, backed off or reluctant to **evaluate**, or who have not improved through standard cramming and correction. (CBO 369)

DATA SERIES RUNDOWN, whenever a student cannot grasp or retain the **data** of the **Data Series** Policy Letters, he must be audited on the **Data Series Rundown** (also called the Hubbard Consultant **Rundown**). The reason for this is that he himself has out-points and it is necessary to audit him on this subject. (HCO PL 15 Mar 71 II)

DATA TO AIDES SUMMARY SHEET, as debriefs often contain large volumes of valuable materials and reports, it is the responsibility of the Debriefer to ensure that no material of importance is missed by the individual aide concerned. This is done by means of the **data to aides summary sheet**. This acts as a guide as to what directly concerns their area of control or may be of interest to them. (FO 2267)

DATA TRAIL, the **data trail** of out-points from a highly general situation (that is only an observation like failing stats) will lead one to the situation and *then* a closer look (also by out-points) will lead to the real why and permit fast handling. A **data trail** is a **trail** of out-points. Let us say you see the Machine Division is failing. Now if you simply take masses of **data** about it and just start turning over 10 or 12 sheets at a time looking for out-points only and keep a tally of what they are and to whom they belong, you will wind up with your situation area and probably your situation without reading any significances at all. (HCO PL 18 Jul 74)

DATE COINCIDENCE, a police action called **date coincidence**. It's how you locate geniuses and murderers. Body found in the swamp. Her cousin arrived in town on Tuesday, body found on Wednesday, guy departed on Thursday. That's all the police need. That's called **date coincidence.** That's old time investigatory tech. It's still with us. So when were they gone out of the org and when did they arrive back in the org and what happened during that period of time. (7205C18SO)

DATELINE PAYING, **paying** all the bills behind a certain **date** and none closer to present time than that **date.** (HCO PL 28 Jan 65)

DATUM, a piece of knowledge, something known. *Plural:* **data**. (BTB 4 Mar 65R)

DAY, **Day** Org. (BPL 16 Sept 74RA III)

DAYBOOK, a book that records daily business transactions. It is more commonly called a journal today. The amount of details of a transaction previously written into a daybook are now largely dispensed with due to the increased use of sales slips, invoices and other documents evidencing a transaction.

DAY ORDER, see ORDER, DAY.

DAY ORG, the **Day Org** and the Foundation are two entirely separate orgs. The Foundation is not under the **Day Org. Day Org** executives have no jurisdiction whatsoever over the foundation executives or personnel. **Day Org** hours generally run 9:00 a.m.—6:00 p.m. Monday through Friday. During **Day Org** hours the **Day Org** executives and personnel have full possession and use of the org premises and facilities. **Day Org** and foundation stats are kept and computed separately. The **Day** and Foundation Orgs each have their own staffs. (BPL 11 Aug 72R I)

DAY SHIFT, the work period in a plant which usually covers from 7 a.m. to 3 p.m.

D/CS-1 FLAG ESTABLISHMENT, **D/CS-1** holds the CS-1 functions concerning internal to relieve CS-1 of these in order that he may keep his attention external. **D/CS-1** also assists CS-1 with external matters as required and directed by him. The purpose of the post is to produce an in ethics, efficient, expanding and productive **Flag,** completely aligned to priorities as set by LRH without internal distractions, which actually manages international Scn at the level of effectiveness required to attain our common goals on this planet. (CBO 373)

D/CS-2 FOR LITERATURE, the post of **D/CS-2 for Literature** is created on Flag to take charge of the creation, manufacturing and distribution of **literature** for Scn promotional emanation points. **Literature** in this case means brochures, posters, fliers, sales promo pieces for use by orgs, FSMs, Flag, etc. **Literature** is *not* magazines or ads. The target is high quality, glossy sales literature for orgs and Flag that show very presentably what is being offered. **D/CS-2 for Literature** heads the Flag **Literature** Unit under CS-2. (FO 3557)

DEAD AGENT CAPER, 1. the **dead agent caper** was used to disprove the lies. This consisted of counter-documenting any area where the lies were circulated. The lie "they were . . ." is countered by document showing "they were *not* . . . ." This causes the source of the lie and any other statements from that source to be discarded. (HCO PL 11 May 71 III) **2.** meaning getting documentary proof that what was said was lies. (OODs 22 Jun 70)

DEAD FILE, 1. **dead file** does not mean they stopped communicating with us. It means we stopped communicating with them. (HCO PL 7 Jun 65 *Entheta Letters and the Dead File, Handling of—Definitions*) **2. dead file** does not cover business firms demanding bills, government squawks or dangerous suits or situations. It covers only entheta public letters received on any line including SO 1. (HCO PL 7 Jun 65, *Entheta Letters and the Dead File, Handling of—Definitions*) **3.** Ethics files shall include a **dead file.** This **file** includes all persons who write nasty or choppy letters to an org or its personnel. Rather than go to the trouble of issuing a suppressive person order or even investigating, we assign writers of choppy letters to the **dead file.** When their area is enturbulated and we want to locate a suppressive, we can always consult our **dead file** for possible candidates and then investigate and issue an order. The **dead file** is by sections of the area or the world, and alphabetical in those sections. (HCO PL 7 Jun 65, *Entheta Letters and the Dead File, Handling of—Definitions*) **4. files** which could be junked without any loss of value to the operation. (*HTLTAE*, p. 64)

DEAD POST, the dev-t merchant can't be at cause over the job and will only destroy the post (as witness the way you have to do his work as well as your own—**dead post**). (HCO PL 9 Sept 64 *Putting New Personnel on the Job and taking over when People Quit or are Transferred*)

DEADWOOD, chronic low stats personnel. (HCO PL 15 Feb 67) [The above HCO PL was cancelled by BPL 10 Oct 75 IV.]

DEALER, a person engaged in the trading, buying or selling of something.

DEAN, 1. the post of **Dean** is to assist LRH in achieving the aims of Scn by removing the stops and barriers of individual students and pcs, public and staff, thus ensuring students and pcs are accepted for service, have their services fully delivered to completion and advanced to higher levels of the Classification and Gradation Chart without stops or slows. (HCO PL 16 Sept 72) [The above HCO PL was cancelled by BPL 10 Oct 75 X.] **2.** to individually handle and remove the stops and barriers of students, the post of **Dean** is established. He is LRH's representative in the org to ensure that service is delivered. (HCO PL 16 Sept 72) [The above HCO PL was cancelled by BPL 10 Oct 75 X.]

DEAN OF SCIENTOLOGY, in protest against the abuses and murders carried out under the title of "doctor," I abandon herewith all my rights and legitimate use of this title as the name has been disgraced. Any and all D. Scns may apply for and receive a new certificate and the title **Dean of Scientology.** (HCO PL 14 Feb 66)

DEAN OF TECHNOLOGY, when a Case Supervisor has done the following in addition to the requirements of a Senior C/S, he shall be issued a gold certificate with the title **DEAN OF TECHNOLOGY**: Saint Hill Special Briefing Course, Class VIII Course, case level to the class of his org, has a uniform record of case supervision. His posts and duties are those of a Senior Case Supervisor but extend to all the field of his area including missions, and he has the power to suspend certificates, order retraining or retreading or interneship or re-interneship for all Auditors of his area of whatever class whether staff or not and may only be overruled or personally disciplined by the Guardian Office or a member of the International Board after due hearings and formal ethics. This certificate requires the final authorization by External HCO Bureau, Authorization and Verifications Unit and CS-4 or CS-5. (HCOPL 24 Oct 76 III)

DEATH, 1. could be in part, a cessation of interested production. (HCO PL 6 Jul 70) **2. death** is too much havingness or too darned little. (3ACC-42, 5401C26)

DEATH WISH, 1. succumb postulates. (HCO PL 27 Apr 69) **2.** wants to **die.** (5510C08)

DEBENTURES, 1. promissory notes backed by the credit standing of a company or issuer, and usually not secured by a mortgage or lien. 2. certificate or voucher expressing recognition of a debt.

DEBIT, comes from Latin *debitum* meaning a **debt.** Now in bookkeeping, the word is used to describe any entry made on the left-hand side of an account but the making of a left-hand entry does not always mean the recording of a **debt**. If a left-hand entry is made to an impersonal account of the organization, it means the recording of the receipt of a mest, service or money particle—it is not recording a **debt.** (BPL 14 Nov 70 III)

DEBIT BALANCE, **debit balance** on an account simply means that the sum of the **debit** entries on that account exceeds the sums of the credit entries. (BPL 14 Nov 70 IV)

DEBITED, charged against you. (HCO PL 10 Oct 1970 III)

DEBRIEF, **1.** mission **debriefs** are usually reliable reports of firsthand observations of an area or areas. (FO 3092) **2.** when the Operations Officer is satisfied that he has completed the mission, the mission is complete as far as he can make it complete, it then goes to **debrief** who assembles all reports from all the members of the mission and then the summary report is drawn up by the **debriefing** officer. In other words everybody on the mission is **debriefed.** All the reports written go to the **Debrief** Officer. (6802C28SO) **3.** in **debriefing**, no set questionaire may be employed. No robot sequence of questions will ever apply to all missions. A **debrief** is composed of specifically three things: (1) finding out the purpose of a mission, (2) finding out results of a mission, (3) finding out recommendations of a mission. (FO 674) **4.** on return, a mission is **debriefed** by Division 6. It turns over all its photographs, documents and records to Division 6 and its finance receipts to Division 3. **Debriefing** is done by tape recorder and notes by a Division 6 person at once on mission return. Missions may not recount a mission to others before **debrief**. The **debrief** is by exact questionaire prepared by Division 2. (FO 228)

DEBRIEF OFFICER, **debriefs** mission leader and all the members, then summarizes to get the fullest record. (FO 1243R)

DEBRIEF SUMMARY, **1.** a complete **summary** of all material in the **debrief**, consisting of all the facts; good, bad or odd (plus their "who" and "when", in as concise a form as possible. (FO 2444) **2.** the top item in the **debrief**. It will take the following form: FMO number, name, classification, major target, personnel, date fired, date completed, supervised by ______, brief **summary** of what happened in the mission (events). A statement at the end of what was accomplished, gained, won or produced by the mission (statement of benefit), total cost of the mission, condition assigned. (FO 2170)

DEBRIEF TR, **training drill** to be done in mission school and contained in Public Officer's hat folder. This **TR** will bring about greater reality on **debriefing** and following mission orders. Purpose: to train Sea Org members to **debrief** missions thoroughly and well. (FO 1266)

DEBT, an amount of money, goods, services, etc., owed by one person to another because of a previous agreement or transaction.

DEBTOR, a person or company that owes something (usually money) to another.

DEBUG, 1. *Informal.* to remove or correct the defects or difficulties of. (CBO 208-3R) **2.** the word **bugged** is slang for snarled up or halted. **Debug** is to get the snarls or stops out of it. (HCO PL 29 Feb 72 II)

DEBUG ASSESSMENT, the **assessment** for use by LRH Comms and others when an order or action has **bugged** and must be **debugged.** His purpose is to locate the **bugs** and the real whys. It itself may or may not reveal the whys but if not, it will provide information that if followed up will bring the why into view. The simple fact of non-compliance is reason enough to do the assessment. There is no need to wait until there is a complete mess before doing it. (BPL 12 Apr 72R I)

DECAY, **decay** is everything going the wrong way when it should go the right way. (PDC 61)

DECENTRALIZATION, the delegation of authority, responsibilities, functions, etc., from a central office or point to branch offices or a number of points. Example: a company maintains a central purchasing unit for all offices but decides to decentralize and let each office do its own purchasing.

DECENTRALIZED HIRING, see HIRING, DECENTRALIZED.

DECENTRALIZED MANAGEMENT, see MANAGEMENT, DECENTRALIZED.

DECISION, a resolution to act or behave in a certain way, take a certain course, hold a certain attitude, etc.

DECISIONAL CONFRONT, "**decide** to look at the radar and look at it." "**Decide** to look away from the radar and look away from it." "**Decide** to look at the helm and look at it." "**Decide** to look away from the helm and look away from it." You're moving him straight from effect to cause in the shortest possible route. (ESTO 12, 7203C06 SO II)

DECK DIVISION, **1.** leakless, seaworthy vessels of good appearance that can be utilized and handled and the handlers thereof fairly well covers the **Deck Division** valuable final product. The final test of a **Deck Division** is production. One glance at a ship tells you whether it has a **Deck Division**. Probably the div name itself, forced in though it is by tradition, should be the Shipkeeping Division. And what do you know, that's what it has been called in many times and languages. (FO 2703) **2.** Division IV is responsible for the operational condition and safety of the vessel. Div IV is responsible for lines, mooring, fenders, camels, anchors, winch capstan, heaving lines, 24 hours a day. Div IV is responsible for the hull. This is a basic for a **Deck Division**. This includes seeing that no damage is done to the hull, by any means under Div IV's control. (FO 1662) **3.** Division Four. (6910C17 SO Spec 3)

DECK PROJECT FORCE, **1.** new recruits and those veterans who are not Product Zero or who are tipped for Product One are posted to the **DPF** for Products Zero and One as required. The **DPF**, hitherto used for the retreading of those persons who suffer from robotism or who produce overt products or who need continual supervision and are a liability on lines is now to be permitted and made to be an upstat unit with high standards, high production and high morale unhindered by those who do not belong in such unit but require special handling on their own without distracting others who are doing well. (FO 3434) **2.** An objective of the **DPF** is to keep a recruit or non-producer out of vital FSO and FB lines until he can pull his weight and is valuable. The main objective is to furnish valuable SO members to the SO. (FSO 559) **3.** newly recruited personnel and retread personnel may only be assigned to the **Deck Project Force.** The **DPF** organization in a large org or ship consists of (1) bosun (2) **DPF** Esto (3) **DPF** MAA (4) new recruits (swampers) (5) retreads. It is necessary for **DPF** members to be made available for auditing when called by the D of P. It is vital that 5 hours a day (evening) study be consistent for **DPF** and its members. It is impossible to assign or reassign anyone in the **DPF** to HCO Expeditor or other post until they have completed both auditing and training requirements to be a full fledged SO crew and staff member. It holds in force a one job, one place, one time type of action. It is necessary for the **DPF** to do work of value in maintaining and enhancing the ship or quarters. (FO 3183) *Abbr.* DPF.

DECK PROJECT FORCE MAA, the purpose of the **DPF MAA** post is: to make ethics real to **DPF** members by removing counter-intention and other-intention from the area, and by getting each **DPF** member to crank out products with an honest uptrending statistic. (FO 3126) *Abbr.* DPF MAA.

DECLINE, (or recession) a part of the business cycle characterized by less production, unemployment, job scarcity, tight credit and generally a decrease of business activity.

DEED, 1. a signed and sealed document which constitutes a contract or transfers ownership of something. 2. a written form proving the right of ownership such as a property deed.

DEFALCATION, 1. the misuse or embezzlement of funds or property under one's care. 2. the sum of money misused or embezzled.

DEFENSE BILLING, any and all **defense** or legal expenses expended by WW on behalf of an org or area, **billed** to that area. (LRH ED 10 WW, 1 SH & SH FDN)

DEFENSIVE, (type of legal cycle) any action which handles an incoming threat merely by stopping it—often litigation. (BPL 20 Aug 71)

DEFERRED CHARGES, current expenditures not considered to be current operating costs and carried forward to be written off at a future time such as research expenses incurred now for the sake of future operations.

DEFERRED PAY, earned salary for which payment is postponed until a future date.

DEFERRED SHARES, a special kind of shares which do not receive a dividend until after a stated dividend return has been given to owners of ordinary shares or until a future date or occurrence.

DEFIANCE, the person refuses the correction or refuses to do the action. (HCO PL 27 Feb 71 I)

DEFICIT, the amount by which a sum of money does not meet the required amount as in assets being less than liabilities, profits being less than the amount invested, etc.

DEFICIT FINANCING, borrowing money for the purpose of deficit spending.

DEFICIT SPENDING, 1. the expenditure of borrowed funds. 2. having expenditures greater than income which constitutes insolvency.

DEFLATION, **1.** inflation takes place in the presence of a shortage of goods and a **deflation** takes place in the presence of an abundance of goods. That's really all you need to know about money. If money won't buy things, it inflates and if money will buy too much, it **deflates.** So if people have no facilities to produce or are being disturbed continuously politically you get an inflating state of affairs. (SH Spec 13 6403C24) **2.** when the amount of products in the country exceed the amount of money there is to buy things, that's **deflation.** (ESTO 9, 7203C05 SO I)

DEGRADATION, to **degrade** or vilify or discredit an existing or fancied image. (HCO PL 7 Aug 72)

DEGRADED BEING, **1.** a sick thetan who is all caved in can't direct a postulate *at* anything. When he tries, he lets it wobble around and go elsewhere. The difference between a **degraded being** and an OT is simply that the **DB** can't put out a postulate or intention in a direct line or way and make it hold good. (HCOB 5 Dec 73) **2.** a harsh term but a true one. It means a person who is at effect to such a degree that he or she avoids orders or instructions in any possible covert or overt way because orders of any kind are confused with painful indoctrinations in the past. This person cannot be at cause without attaining OT Level III. Therefore they prevent the org from being at cause as they cannot be at cause themselves and will not let the org or anything else be at cause including executives. (HCO PL 22 Mar 67) *Abbr.* DB.

DEGRADED BEING COMPLEX, an org that goes mad on "process the whole staff" continually regardless of duties has a **degraded being complex** ("us poor equal thetans"). In such an org the **degraded beings** outnumber the big being staff members. Such an org is not at cause over the environment but is a sort of mutual aid society or a self-treating mental ward where the inmates use Scn to treat each other but are but dimly aware of the outer environment. (HCO PL 22 Mar 67)

DEGRADED SCENE, in black PR the **degraded scene** is the way he wants the scene to be condemned by a public. (HCO PL 7 Aug 72)

DELEGATE, *n.* the person to whom authority has been delegated. —*v.* 1. to assign power, responsibility, authority, duty, etc., to someone else usually of lesser rank or junior status. 2. to give someone the power or authority to represent or act on behalf of others.

DELIVER, after promotion obtains response, one must **deliver.** That means good case gains to preclears and students, good reality and useful knowledge and skill to every student. (HCO PL 28 Feb 65, *Deliver*)

DELIVERY ORGS, the front line *orgs*: the AOs, SHs, and outer **orgs—service orgs.** (FO 2426)

DELIVERY SUM, the total monetary value of all paid services **delivered** that week to FCCIs, students plus Flag freeloader payments plus any money earned locally for services delivered that week. This does not include any past delivery or payments for same for or by orgs. (FSO 667RC)

DELUSION, **1.** they can commit overts on things to a point where the thing rematerializes with them all the time as something else and that's **delusion.** So they see something all the time. We're now dealing with spin bin types. (ESTO 5, 7203C03 SO I) **2.** one sees A and believes it to be G. This is a lower band of self-protection. (HCO PL 16 Feb 71 II)

DEMAND, 1. the want of something coupled with the ability to buy it. The want alone without the ability to buy something does not constitute demand for a product. 2. actions to cause a debt to be payable as in the case of a note that must be paid on demand.

DEMAND ANALYSIS, see ANALYSIS, DEMAND.

DEMAND DEPOSIT, a deposit in a bank that may be withdrawn by the depositor at any time without advance notice to the bank.

DEMANDED DIRECTIVE, a senior can simply **demand** an Ad Council pass a **directive** to remedy a situation and let them sort it out. This is only done when one has almost *no* data. In this case the Ad Council passes one, puts it in force and sends a copy to the senior via channels stating "compliance herewith." (HCO PL 17 Nov 66)

DEMAND, ELASTIC, elastic demand is the concept that when the price of a product or service changes, the demand for it changes markedly as opposed to inelastic demand.

DEMAND ELASTICITY, the amount of change in demand or sales of a product or service that folows a change in its price. A product is referred to as being elastic if demand for it changes a lot as a result of a small price change.

DEMAND, EXPANSION, expansion demand is potentiality for or rate at which new customers enter the market for a given product or service.

DEMAND, FINAL, a demand for a product in its final form such as a consumer's demand for a radio. The components within the radio experience an indirect demand, however, since the consumer does not want them directly but does demand them indirectly in the form of a radio.

DEMAND, INDIRECT, a demand for a product as part of or a component of another product. The various components in a camera are indirectly demanded whereas the camera itself experiences a direct or final demand by the consumer.

DEMAND INELASTIC, inelastic demand is the concept that when the price of a product or service changes the demand for it changes only slightly.

DEMAND INFLATION, see INFLATION, DEMAND.

DEMAND NOTE, a note, draft or bill that becomes payable when payment is demanded.

DEMAND, REPEAT, market research term referring to products or services that are in regular, often everyday use, and are in more or less constant demand by consumers.

DEMAND, REPLACEMENT, the demand shown by the frequency with which customers discard and replace consumer durables or capital goods. An example would be how much demand is exerted for appliances that are improved or restyled.

DEMAND, SEASONAL, a demand for a product that varies with seasonal changes such as the demand for winter clothing.

DEMARCATION DISPUTE, industrial dispute in which a demarcation must be made as to which union should have the right to perform a specific task or job.

DEMONSTRATION, getting a student to **demonstrate** things in the bulletin with his hands or bits of things. The reason for this is that in memorizing words or ideas, the student can still hold the position that it has nothing to do with him or her. It is a total circuit action. Therefore, very glib. The moment you say **demonstrate** that word or idea or principle, the student has to have something to do with it. And shatters. Don't get the idea that **demonstration** is a practical section action. Practical gives the drills. These **demonstrations** in theory aren't drills. (HCO PL 4 Oct 64)

DEMO ORG, a kind of floor plan of an org made up of cardboard strips which are laid out on a table. What would you use the **demo org** for? You would use it for working out the lines, routing, actions and activities of an **org** using your **demo** kit as well. (HCO PL 19 Sept 71) [The above HCO PL was cancelled by BPL 10 Oct 75 IX.]

DEMOTION, the reduction of a person in rank, position or status resulting in lesser responsibility, authority, prestige, privilege or salary.

DEPARTMENT, there are five sections plus the **department's** director in a **department**; three **departments** and the secretary, a deputy and a communicator in a division. (HCO PL 28 Feb 66) *Abbr.* Dept.

DEPARTMENT, a portion or section of an organization with its own staff headed by an executive and responsible for the performance of certain functions or production of certain products, i.e., the Purchasing Department, the Printing Department.

DEPARTMENT DIRECTOR, he is the product officer of his **department**. The divisional Esto is senior to him. The **departmental director** is senior to an Esto posted to his specific **department**. (HCO PL 7 Mar 72)

DEPARTMENT 1, **1.** Department of Personnel, HCO Division 1. (HCO PL 18 May 73) **2.** handles personnel PR, personnel hiring, personnel placement, org boards, hat compilations, hat library and hatting hatting hatting. (HCO PL 28 Jul 72) **3.** the actions of that department are effective personnel posted and hatted. (FEBC 12, 7102C03 SO II) **4.** Department of Personnel and Routing. (HCO PL 11 Dec 69, *Appearances in Public Divs*) **5.** HCO Department (Six Department Org). (HCO

PL 21 Oct 66) **6.** Department of Routing, Appearances and Personnel, Division 1. (HCO PL 20 Nov 65) **7.** there are five production departments at Saint Hill. Only these five directly produce income. All other activities are service units to these five. **Department 1** handles production of basic Scn materials, writings and policies. These functions are mainly done by myself. This unit is the basic unit responsible for eventual income. Domestic staff is considered a unit of **Department 1.** (HCO PL 28 May 64)

DEPARTMENT 2, **1.** Department of Routing and Communication, HCO Division 1. (HCO PL 18 May 73) **2.** Dissemination Department (Six Department Org). (HCO PL 21 Oct 66) **3.** Department of Communications, Division 1. (HCO PL 20 Nov 65)

DEPARTMENT 3, **1.** Department of Inspection and Reports, Division 1. (HCO PL 20 Nov 65) **2.** it contains inspection, it contains stats and it contains ethics. (FEBC 12, 7102C03 SO II) **3.** Treasury Department (Six Department Org). (HCO PL 21 Oct 66)

DEPARTMENT 4, **1.** Department of Promotion and Publications. (BPL 25 Jan 76 I) **2.** Department of Promotion, Division 2. (HCO PL 20 Nov 65) **3.** the product of Department 4 (promotion) is effective promotion pieces printed and sent out. (FEBC 12, 7102C03 SO II) **4.** Technical Department (Six Department Org). (HCO PL 21 Oct 66) **5.** (Ship Org Board) Planning Department, Division 2. (FO 976)

DEPARTMENT 4S, (AOSH Org Board) AO Department of Promotion. Its product is effective promotional pieces printed and sent out. (HCO PL 18 Feb 73 VI)

DEPARTMENT 5, **1.** Department of Procurement. (BPL 25 Jan 76 I) **2.** Department of Publications, Division 2. (HCO PL 20 Nov 65) **3.** product of **Department 5** (Publications) is hat and course packs and tapes plus these valuable final products of the org: sold and delivered tapes, sold and delivered meters, sold and delivered insignia. (FEBC 12, 7102C03 SO II) **4.** Qualifications Department (Six Department Org). (HCO PL 21 Oct 66) **5.** (Ship Org Board) Preparation Department, Division 2. (FO 976)

DEPARTMENT 6, **1.** Department of Registration, Division 2. (HCO PL 20 Nov 65) **2.** Distribution Department (Six Department Org). (HCO PL 21 Oct 66) **3.** (Ship Org) Training Department, Division 2. (FO 2615) **4.** (Ship Org Board) Directions Department, Division 2. (FO 1028)

DEPARTMENT 6S, **1.** in the case of a combined AO/SH you will need to add a **Department 6S** devoted solely to registration of advance courses. (LRH ED 159R-1) **2.** AO Department of Registration. (HCO PL 18 Feb 73 VI)

DEPARTMENT 7, **1.** Department of Income, Division 3. (HCO PL 20 Nov 65) **2.** the product of **Department 7** is all funds collected for services and sales. **Department 7** doesn't have anything much to do with viability or anything else. They've just got to collect all the money in sight, that's all. If it's owed, they collect it. (FEBC 12, 7102C03 SO II)

DEPARTMENT 8, **1.** Department of Disbursement, Division 3. (HCO PL 20 Nov 65) **2.** the product of **Department 8** is pleased creditors. (FEBC 12, 7102C03 SO II)

DEPARTMENT 9, **1.** Department of Records, Assets and Materiel, Division 3. (HCO PL 20 Nov 65) **2.** product of **Department 9** is adequate and well cared for materiel. The word **adequate** means it has to get issued and well cared for and so on. (FEBC 12, 7102C03 SO II) **3.** (Ship Org) Stewards Department, Purser's Division 3. (FO 274) **4.** the steward is in **Department 9** in the Supply Division, 3rd Division, on the Ship's Org Board. The awareness level of **Dept 9** is, of course, body. The Chief Cook and any assistant cooks are also in **Dept 9** and the stewards work in coordination with the cooks in smoothly carrying out their duties. (FO 2558)

DEPARTMENT 9A, (Flagship Org) Department of Services, Treasury Division 3. (FSO 776)

DEPARTMENT 10, **1.** Tech Services. The product of **Department 10** is adequately supplied courses; rapid, efficiently scheduled, routed and handled students and pcs. (FEBC 12, 7102C03 SO II) **2.** Dept of Tech Services, Division 4. (HCO PL 20 Nov 65)

DEPARTMENT 10A, Department of Advanced Courses Tech Services, AOLA Division 4A. (BPL 16 Sept 71R II)

DEPARTMENT 11, **1.** Department of Training, Division 4. (HCO PL 20 Nov 65) **2.** the valuable final product of **Department 11** is effectively trained people who can skillfully apply what they have learned and will apply it. (FEBC 12, 7102C03 SO II)

DEPARTMENT 11A, **1.** Department of Advanced Courses Training, AOLA Division IV A. (BPL 16 Sept 71R II) **2.** Hat College Department, Technical Division 4. (HCO PL 16 Jul 71)

DEPARTMENT 12, **1.** Dept of Processing, Division 4. (HCO PL 20 Nov 65) **2.** HGC. The product is the wins of preclears and pre-OTs. (FEBC 12, 7102C03 SO II)

DEPARTMENT 12A, **1.** Department of Solo Auditing, AOLA Division 4A. (BPL 16 Sept 71R II) **2.** the Flag Advanced Org becomes **Dept 12A.** (OODs 12 May 74)

DEPARTMENT 13, **1.** Dept of Validity, Division 5, Correction Division. (HCO PL 14 Aug 71RC II) **2.** the Department of Personnel Enhancement. Its product is effective and well trained org staff members. (FEBC 12, 7102C03 SO II) **3.** Department of Examinations, Division 5. (HCO PL 20 Nov 65)

DEPARTMENT 14, **1.** Department of Personnel Enhancement, Correction Division. (HCO PL 14 Aug 71RC II) **2.** Dept of Review, Division 5. (HCO PL 20 Nov 65)

DEPARTMENT 15, **1.** Department of Correction, Correction Division. (HCO PL 14 Aug 71RC II) **2.** Dept of Certs and Awards, Division 5. (HCO PL 20 Nov 65)

DEPARTMENT 16, **1.** Department of Public Controlling, Distribution Division. (HCO PL 14 Jul 71) **2.** the product of **Department 16** (Public Relations) is effective PR and advertising actions that attract members of the public to become Scientologists. That's your outside advertising. (FEBC 12, 7102C03 SO II) **3.** (Nine Division Org) Department of Ethnics, Division 6. (HCO PL 11 Dec 69) **4.** (Nine Division Org) Department of Public Planning. (HCO PL 26 Oct 67) **5.** Department of Field Activities, Division 6. (HCO PL 20 Nov 65)

DEPARTMENT 17, **1.** Department of Hatting Scientologists, Distribution Division. (HCO PL 14 Jul 71) **2.** Department of Public Servicing, Public Division. (HCO PL 14 Nov 71RA II) **3.** (Nine Division Org) Department of Public Communications. (HCO PL 26 Oct 67) **4.** Dept of Clearing, Division 6. (HCO PL 20 Nov 65)

DEPARTMENT 18, **1.** Department of Clearing, Distribution Division. (HCO PL 14 Jul 71) **2.** (Nine Division Org) Department of Public Reports. (HCO PL 26 Oct 67) **3.** Department of Success, Division 6. (HCO PL 20 Nov 65)

DEPARTMENT 19, **1.** Office of the Executive Director. (HCO PL 18 May 73) **2.** (Nine Division Org) Department of Facilities. (HCO PL 26 Oct 67) **3.** Office of the Org Exec Sec, Division 7. (HCO PL 20 Nov 65)

DEPARTMENT 20, **1.** Office of the Controller, Division 7, Executive Division. (HCO PL 18 May 73) **2.** (Nine Division Org) Department of Activities, Division 7, Public Activities Division. (HCO PL 26 Oct 67) **3.** Office of the HCO Exec Sec, Division 7. (HCO PL 20 Nov 65)

DEPARTMENT 21, **1.** Office of LRH, Division 7. (HCO PL 20 Nov 65) **2.** (Nine Division Org) Department of Clearing. (HCO PL 26 Oct 67)

DEPARTMENT 22, (Nine Division Org) Department of Expansion. (HCO PL 26 Oct 67)

DEPARTMENT 23, (Nine Division Org) Department of Population. (HCO PL 26 Oct 67)

DEPARTMENT 24, (Nine Division Org) Department of Success. (HCO PL 26 Oct 67)

DEPARTMENT 25, Office of Public Executive Secretary. (HCO PL 26 Oct 67)

DEPARTMENT 26, Office of HCO Executive Secretary, Office of Org Executive Secretary. (HCO PL 26 Oct 67)

DEPARTMENT 27, **1.** Office of LRH, Division 9, Executive Division. (HCO PL 26 Oct 67) **2.** Office of the Public Executive Secretary. (HCO PL 29 Nov 69) [The above HCO PL was cancelled by BPL 10 Oct 75 VII.]

DEPARTMENTAL CASH DIFFERENTIAL, the exact **difference** between the **cash** received by or for a production **department** and the **cash** spent by or on behalf of that **department** plus its share of the general cost, so long as the result shows receipts greater than expenses. (HCO PL 26 Jun 64)

DEPARTMENTALIZATION, the grouping together of similar or related functions in order to form departments. Example: all personnel hiring, firing and training being grouped under and done by the Personnel Department.

DEPARTMENTAL LAYOUT, see LAYOUT.

DEPARTMENTAL POLICIES, see POLICIES, DEPARTMENTAL.

DEPARTMENT HEAD, an expert in 1/3 of a division. (FEBC 3, 7101C18 SO II) See DIRECTOR.

DEPARTMENT HEAD, that executive who is in charge of and responsible for the staff and productivity of a department.

DEPARTMENT HEADS COUNCIL, in order to effect financial planning and smooth ship operation a **department heads council** is formed of the following officers and **departments**: Chief Officer, Chairman; Supercargo, Secretary; Purser, Advisor; Deck Dept, 1st Mate; Engine Dept, Chief Engineer; Catering Dept, Chief Steward; Advanced Org Dept, LRH Comm AO. (FO 378)

DEPARTMENT OF ACCOUNTS, 1. (in the Administrative Division) purpose: to keep the business affairs of the organization in good order, to maintain the good business repute of the organization and to see to it that the business activities of Scn are up-to-date in an excellent condition. To make sure that income exceeds outgo. (HCO PL 12 Oct 62) **2.** headed by the Director of Accounts, the **Dept of Accounts** receives, safeguards and expends funds in the organization. No other person can expend money though others can receive it if it is promptly handed to **Accounts**. (HCO PL 20 Dec 62)

DEPARTMENT OF ACTIVITIES, Department 20, Division 7, Public Activities Division. Guides in new body traffic. Makes sure public reception area displays full data making Scn real to the public and includes nothing that would overwhelm or confuse. Sees that the introductory lecture and non-classed courses use no words that will be misunderstood and makes people want to buy training and processing and offers it. Advertises and conducts an extension course. Encourages broad public (lay) memberships. (HCO PL 23 May 69 III) [The above HCO PL was cancelled by BPL 10 Oct 75 VII.]

DEPARTMENT OF ADVANCED COURSES TECH SERVICES, Department 10A, AOLA Division 4A. Valuable final product: rapidly and efficiently scheduled, routed, supplied and handled students and pcs and pre-OTs. (BPL 16 Sept 71R II)

DEPARTMENT OF ADVANCED COURSES TRAINING, Department 11A, AOLA Division 4A. Valuable final product: graduates who know and effectively apply the materials of the courses. (BPL 16 Sept 71R II)

DEPARTMENT OF BUSINESS, that **department** where the finances, bank accounts, and other purely **business** functions of the org were performed. (LRH Def. Notes)

DEPARTMENT OF CERTS AND AWARDS, **1.** Dept. 15, Division 5. It issues credentials that will be seen around—pins that people will wear, **certificates** they will hang up, cards they will show. Never issues anything falsely as it will be hidden or discredited. Heavily promotes auditors outside the org to bring in their pcs for examinations and release declarations. (HCO PL 20 Nov 65) **2.** the **Department of Certifications and Awards**, Department 15, is headed by the Director **of Certifications**. The **Department of Certifications and Awards** has the prime purpose in all its functions to help Ron issue and record valid attestations of skill, state and merit honestly deserved, attained or earned by beings, activities or areas. The validity of issue and decrying any false issue are the concerns of the **department**. (HCO PL 31 Jul 65)

DEPARTMENT OF CLEARING, **1.** Department 17, Division 6. It recruits and handles field staff members to get in pcs and students for the org (and collects past debts). Keeps in touch with franchise holders and keeps them informed. Carries out all FSM and franchise activities and makes them head people toward the org. Trains the FSMs and franchise holders and makes them financially successful. Gets all commissions owed promptly paid to encourage earning more commissions. Advertises and conducts an extension course. Finds and encourages the formation of Scn groups and registers them and offers certificates. Sends out mailings to groups. (HCO PL 20 Nov 65) **2.** Department 18, Distribution Division. Its product is active field Scientologists. (HCO PL 14 Jul 71)

DEPARTMENT OF COMMUNICATIONS, **1.** Dept 2, Division 1. It keeps a complete address file in such shape that mailings are wide and sent to people who will respond. Never lets go of an address or a mailing list and keeps them all properly corrected and up-to-date and in proper categories for ready use. Sees that mailings go out promptly and on schedule. Sees that internal dispatches are swiftly delivered and are in accurate form. Sees that letters and orders arrive safely and are quickly handled and not overlooked. Oversees stationery and typing quality so that communications going outside the org look smart and sound bright. (HCO PL 20 Nov 65) **2.** Department 2, HCO Division. It contains a Mail Section, Dispatch Section, Communication Inspection Unit, Telex and Phone Section, Lost and Found Section, Comm Files Section, Secretarial Executive Director Section and Address Section. (HCO PL 17 Jan 66 II)

DEPARTMENT OF CORRECTION, Dept 15, Correction Division. Its purpose is to help LRH ensure that all Scn and Dn knowledge is freely available, fully used and promptly corrected when misapplied, thus ensuring the technical honesty of the organization. Its ideal scene is an org library full of all Scn and Dn materials and tapes, reference books and dictionaries of all kinds, well tabulated and cross referenced, which is used by the org staff and students. A Cramming finding real whys on a meter for staff, student and auditor flubs and alertly ensuring that materials are known, cleared of misunderstoods and drilled to confident certainty. (BPL 7 Dec 71R I)

DEPARTMENT OF DISBURSEMENT, Dept 8, Division 3. It keeps bills paid in such a way that the org is in excellent credit repute. (Promotes with good credit rating.) Gets salaries accurately and punctually paid to keep staff happy. (HCO PL 20 Nov 65)

DEPARTMENT OF DISBURSEMENTS, **1.** Department 8, Treasury Division. Its product is pleased creditors. (BPL 11 Sept 75) **2.** the purpose and action of a **Dept of Disbursements** is not only to **disburse** monies but to maintain and improve the credit standing and state of solvency of the org or vessel by flawless handling of bills and creditors. (FO 2694)

DEPARTMENT OF ENROLLMENT, **1.** (St. Hill) the purpose of the **Department of Enrollment** is to contact routinely, regularly and intelligently all possible candidates for the Saint Hill Briefing Course. The steps are these: (1) using whatever is to hand, begin contacting, (2) expand what address files are to hand and contact those, (3) eventually have a complete and sound system of filing, addressing and contacting candidates for the course. The purpose is to get people to take the course. To do this one must have very good files and means of address keeping, use and change. To use these one must achieve and maintain a high level of ARC in all letters and releases. (HCO PL 25 Jan 64) **2.** the Department of Promotion and Registration in all Central Organizations will now be termed the **Department of Enrollment.** (HCO PL 21 Feb 64)

DEPARTMENT OF ESTIMATIONS, **1.** (Tech Division) The Book of Letter Scheduling is available to the **Dept of Estimations** if they come over to Prom-Reg to see it. It is not the main **Dept of Estimations'** source of expected students and pcs. There are two other such books in the org—In Person, Phone, and Turn Up, taking care of people who schedule ahead in person (Book of In Person Scheduling) and people who phone in to schedule (Book of Phone Scheduling) and people who just turn up. The **Dept of Estimations** gets the lot and logs the turn up student or pc who simply arrives ready to go in its own records. By sending the **Dept of Estimations** an office printer copy of the next four weeks of pages, and counting the next many months, the **Department of Estimations** can provide the service. (HCO PL 6 Apr 65) **2.** All tech admin is done in the **Department of Estimations.** (HCO PL 11 Jun 65)

DEPARTMENT OF ETHNICS, Department 16, Division 6, Division of Public Planning. It contains an Ethnic Survey Planning Section, Scn Ethnic Survey Planning Section, Ethnics Activity Section, Ethnic Findings Distribution Section and Ethnic Acceptable Appearance Section. (HCO PL 21 Dec 69) [The above HCO PL was cancelled by BPL 10 Oct 75 VII.]

DEPARTMENT OF EXAMINATIONS, **1.** the **Department of Examinations**, Department 13, is headed by the Director **of Examinations**. The prime purpose of the **Department of Examinations** and all its sections and units is to help Ron ensure that the technical results of the organization are excellent and consistent, that students and preclears are without flaw for their skill or state when passed and that any technical deficiency of org personnel is reported and handled so that the technical results of the organization continue to be excellent and consistent. It must be kept in mind that the product of the organization is not Scientologists but conditions changed by Scn. Therefore the ability of the auditor to change conditions in preclears and the ability of the preclear or Clear to change conditions along the dynamics are the only concern of the **Department of Examinations.** The integrity of Scn and its hope for beings in this universe are entrusted to the **Department of Examinations.** (HCO PL 31 Jul 65) **2.** Dept 13, Division 5. It makes sure no untrained student or unsolved case gets past. Finds the real errors in any failures (no student or pc ever gets upset if the actual error is spotted; they only get upset when a wrong error is found). Refuses to get so concentrated on "validating people" that errors are overlooked for this backfires also. Routes those passed quickly to Certs and Awards and those failed quickly to Review and routes any ethics matters discovered promptly to Ethics. (HCO PL 20 Nov 65)

DEPARTMENT OF EXPANSION, Department 23, Division 8, Distribution Division. It contains a Franchise Expansion Section, Franchise Development Section, Franchise Relations Section, Dianetic Counseling Groups Section and Special Programs Section. Note: the franchise sections in this department do not control local franchises. They are to make new franchises and ensure good relations with all local franchises. Franchises are controlled by Franchise Officer WW. (HCO PL 21 Dec 69) [The above HCO PL was cancelled by BPL 10 Oct 75 VII.]

DEPARTMENT OF FACILITIES, SCHEDULES AND PUBLIC EVENTS, Department 19, Division 7, Public Activities Division. Plans and organizes **public events.** Advertises and holds congresses, open evenings, etc. Furnishes lecturers to **public** bodies and groups. Plans and conducts lecture tours and special **events.** (HCO PL 23 May 69 III) [The above HCO PL was cancelled by BPL 10 Oct 75 VII.]

DEPARTMENT OF FACT FINDING AND RESEARCH, Department 16, Division 6, Public Relations Division. Ideal scene: Dept 16 accurately and routinely supplying reliable information, **facts** and evaluation/**research findings** pertaining to PR successful/unsuccessful policies and programs, public trends, local and world events affecting or likely to affect org operations, what is popular/unpopular and acceptable in local Scn, Dn and public circles, the publics we control and don't yet control, the org's PR standing in its environment, org promotional effectiveness, and to what degree the org is being successful in satisfying its customers, to all staff, execs and PR personnel, resulting in heightened awareness of PR and its importance so that contribution to PR and org image is increased. (HCO PL 20 Aug 70 III) [The above HCO PL was cancelled by BPL 10 Oct 75 VIII.]

DEPARTMENT OF FIELD ACTIVITIES, Dept 16, Division 6. It advertises to the broad public, sees that the introductory lecture and non-classed courses use no words that will be misunderstood and makes people want to buy training and processing and offers it, furnishes lectures to groups, gets books placed in book stores, reviewed and in the public view, acquires new mailing lists, sends out excellent information packets, guides in new body traffic, works on the public not on the Scientologists already known to Divisions 1 and 2. (HCO PL 20 Nov 65)

DEPARTMENT OF FIELD RECRUITMENT, ESTABLISHMENT AND RECORDS, Department 22, Division 8, Distribution Division. **Recruits**, appoints and **establishes** FSMs, groups and franchises. Registers franchise center names. Finds and encourages the formation of Scn groups and registers them and offers certificates. **Recruits** field staff members to get pcs and students into the org and collect past debts. Gets all commissions owed promptly paid to encourage earning more commissions. (HCO PL 23 May 69 III) [The above HCO PL was cancelled by BPL 10 Oct 75 VII.]

DEPARTMENT OF FIELD SALES, Department 23, Division 8, Public Sales Division. Ideal scene: an org field filled with many successful Scn and Dn groups and franchises from which a continuous flow of selectees and business is received in a spirit of goodwill, cooperation and teamwork. (HCO PL 20 Aug 70 II) [The above HCO PL was cancelled by BPL 10 Oct 75 VIII.]

DEPARTMENT OF FIELD SERVICES, Department 24, Division 8, Distribution Division. Keeps in touch with the field and keeps them informed and supplies them with advice and data, sends out mailings to the field, gives FSMs and franchise holders and groups things they can use to disseminate and select. (HCO PL 23 May 69 III) [The above HCO PL was cancelled by BPL 10 Oct 75 VII.]

DEPARTMENT OF FIELD TRAINING, Department 23, Division 8, Distribution Division. Trains the FSMs and franchise holders and makes them financially successful, treats the whole departmental activity as salemen are handled by any other business org, carries out all FSM and franchise activities and makes them head people towards the org. (HCO PL 23 May 69 III) [The above HCO PL was cancelled by BPL 10 Oct 75 VII.]

DEPARTMENT OF FSM SALES, Department 22, Division 8, Public Sales Division. Ideal scene: hundreds of FSMs in the org's field have formed a strong sales network, which is successfully active, selecting lots of people for org Scn and

Dn services, getting each selectee to actually enroll, selling Dn and Scn books in volume and responding to support all org sales programs. (HCO PL 20 Aug 70 II) [The above HCO PL was cancelled by BPL 10 Oct 75 VIII.]

DEPARTMENT OF GOVERNMENT AFFAIRS, 1. under this **department** comes the corporation's solicitors, attorneys, chartered accountants and any attorney or accountant hired by the corporation for outside legal or tax or filing purposes. The allotment and issue of shares comes under this department. No contracts, purchases or mortgages may be undertaken without the approval of this **department** and then only by the action of this **department**. (HCO PL 15 Aug 60) **2.** all contracts, filings with the **government**, all tax reports and their preparation, corporation minutes, annual meetings, legal papers, suits against and by the corporation, whether HASI Ltd or HCO Ltd, all contacts with **government** agents, bureaus and departments, all assistance to **governments**, messages to **governments**, handling answers from **governments** or courts shall be cared for by the **department**, whether to advance or protect Scn or its corporations by **government** or legal channels. (HCO PL 15 Aug 60)

DEPARTMENT OF GOVERNMENT RELATIONS, a new **department** for FCDC entitled **Department of Government Relations**. The entire activity of this **department** is to handle matters with IRS, courts, securities commissions, state, city and national **governments** and protect and better the FC position. All persons from these agencies or **governments** must be routed by reception only to **DGR**. The **government** accountant and a part-time attorney and all FC attorneys deal with this department only. The purpose of this **department** is to wall off all **government** and legal affairs from the FC and prohibit them from entering FC lines and disrupting FC activities. (SEC ED 342, 12 Aug 60) *Abbr.* DGR.

DEPARTMENT OF HATTING SCIENTOLOGISTS, Department 17, Distribution Division. It contains a Hatting Courses Establishing Section, Hatting Administrating Section, Scientologists' Hatting Section and Extension Course Section. Its product is **hatted Scientologists**. (HCO PL 14 Jul 71)

DEPARTMENT OF HEM, a glossy new meter is being produced by **Dept of HEM (Hubbard Electrometer)** at Pubs US. They have several Scientologists working and meters are coming off the line rapidly. (AO 528)

DEPARTMENT OF INCOME, **1.** Department 7, Treasury Division. Its product is all funds collected for services and sales. (BPL 11 Sept 75) **2.** the purpose and action of a **Dept of Income** is not only to invoice money but to contribute to the solvency of the org or vessel by actually bringing in the **income** by industry of collection actions. (FO 2694) **3.** Dept 7, Division 3. It persuades payment of cash or increase in purchase whenever possible. Collects outstanding notes by monthly statements. Collects outstanding notes through field staff members via Dept 17. Gets all mail orders invoiced and/or collected so they can be shipped at once. (HCO PL 20 Nov 65)

DEPARTMENT OF INSPECTION AND REPORTS, **1.** Dept 3, Division 1. It sees that the org is there and functioning. Sees that suppressives and enturbulative elements do not block dissemination. Sees that service is accurately given and that no squirrel tech is used. Prevents the phenomenon of no-case-gain by spotting potential trouble sources and handling. Ethics gets case resurgences by finding the right SPs. (HCO PL 20 Nov 65) **2.** the Ethics Section is in **Department** 3. This **department** is called **Inspection and Reports**. In small orgs there is only one person in that **department**. Primarily his duties consist of **inspecting and reporting** to his divisional head and the Executive Council. That is the first section's function. When inspection reveals outness and **reports** (such as graphs or direct information to the Executive Council) do not result in correction, then it is a matter for the second section. The second section of **Department** 3 is Ethics. (HCO PL 7 Dec 69)

DEPARTMENT OF INSPECTIONS, the **Department of Inspections**, Division 4, Department 13, has the actual administration and execution of all justice. HCO's Office of LRH issues all authorities for justice and confirms all findings of justice and publishing results. (HCO PL 31 Mar 65)

DEPARTMENT OF MATERIAL, headed by the Director of Material (Dir Mat), the **Dept of Material** owns every mest object, including pieces of paper, in the entire organization and is responsible for its inventory, existence and good repair and usage. **Material** sets up and clears away rooms, keeps the place clean, maintains everything, orders and supervises construction and even procures new office or auditing space. If it's mest, take it up with **Material**. If it's service or significance or personnel, take it up elsewhere. **Material** does all purchasing for the organization.

(HCO PL 14 Feb 61, *The Pattern of a Central Organization.*)

DEPARTMENT OF MATERIEL, purpose: to hold in readiness and good repair all the communication **materiel**, files, addresses, furniture, equipment, quarters and transport necessary to adequate function of the organization. (HCO PL 12 Oct 62)

DEPARTMENT OF OFFICIAL AFFAIRS, **1.** an extension of the Office of the Continental Association Secretary. Its purpose is the bettering of the public representation, legal position and government acceptance of Scn. We have here in actuality the equivalent of a ministry of propaganda and security, using crude old-time political terms. (HCO PL 13 Mar 61) **2.** anyone now holding post as Dept of Government Relations or as Director of Special Programs should be retitled **Department of Official Affairs**. The field responded only faintly to special programs. Where field activities warrant, a Central Organization may have a **Department of Official Affairs** to combine all former duties and activities performed by the Department of Government Relations and Special Programs. (HCO PL 13 Mar 61 II)

DEPARTMENT OF ORGANIZATION CORRECTION, Dept 14, Division 5, Correction Division. It contains an Organization Situation Recognition Section, Org Correction Section and Org Ideal Scene Attainment Section. (HCO PL 8 Aug 70 III). [The above HCO PL was cancelled by BPL 7 Dec 71R I.]

DEPARTMENT OF PERSONNEL, Department 1, HCO Division 1, hires new **personnel**, posts org board per allowed complement, handles all staff, keeps **personnel** roster, compiles and issues hat folders, hat checks staff. Its product is effective staff posted and hatted. (HCO PL 18 May 73)

DEPARTMENT OF PERSONNEL AND ROUTING, the appearance of the org and staff is transferred out of Department 1 which becomes the **Department of Personnel and Routing** and may still be called RAP but should be changed on the org board. Appearances comes under the Department of Ethnics, Div 6, Dept 16, Ethnic Acceptable Appearances Section. Appearances never worked under Dept 1. (HCO PL 11 Dec 69, *Appearances in Public Divisions*) See DEPARTMENT OF ROUTING, APPEARANCES AND PERSONNEL.

DEPARTMENT OF PERSONNEL ENHANCEMENT, **1.** the **Department of Personnel Enhancement**, Division 5, Qualifications, is held responsible for these things: (1) that *no* misunderstood words exist amongst staff, auditors or in org public; (2) that all training and auditing programs of staff, students, auditors, internes or in-org public are in correct sequence, without skipped gradient and *done*; (3) that all staff cases are progressing satisfactorily with good OCA (APA) gains and that *no* no-case-gain cases are on staff. (HCO PL 16 Feb 72) **2.** Dept 14, Correction Division. It produces a textbook interneship in which auditors become flubless professionals through daily auditing, daily study and practical training. Ensures coordination and execution of staff training progresses optimumly, through expert personnel programming, Staff Training Officer maintaining and controlling training lines and cycles, full use of word clearing, product and purpose clearing and study technology, thus increasing org efficiency and staff ability. Gives Chaplain and Medical Liaison Officer assistance and emergency assist auditing to staff and public as needed, ensuring that all persons handled are properly returned to the right lines. It is individual handling all the way to a win in the **Dept of Personnel Enhancement**. (BPL 7 Dec 71R I) **3.** Dept 13 (**Enhancement**) has been created to permit **personnel** to be **enhanced** or improved. This is done by programming. HCO should make known what it will need in the org in the next year. How many of what kind it now has. Dept 13 must work out what programming is now needed. It posts a board, puts the names on it and sees that part-time study will occur and be followed for the next post. It sees that this will be made. (HCO PL 29 Aug 70 II)

DEPARTMENT OF PR CONTROL, Department 17, Division 6, Public Relations Division. Ideal scene: the **PR Department** is actively creating a popular image for the org and Scn by acceptable interpretation of what Scn is, what our policies are and what the org stands for through bold broad publicity, staged **PR** events, regular day-to-day **PR** actions, achieving excellent **control** and **relations** with all outside org contacts, community contacts, opinion leaders, profession leaders, VIPs and mass media contacts; is constantly expanding this **control** with **PR** programs effectively executed resulting in masses of publics reaching for Dn and Scn in the area. (HCO PL 20 Aug 70 III) [The above HCO PL was cancelled by BPL 10 Oct 75 VIII.]

DEPARTMENT OF PROCESSING, **1.** Dept 12, Technical Division 4. **Department of Proces-**

sing valuable final product is the wins of pcs and pre-OTs. (BPL 4 Jan 73RC) **2.** Dept 12, Division 4. It gets excellent results on all pcs, becomes well-known for standard tech. Spots SPs and PTSes early and routes to Ethics. Routes bogged cases quickly to Review. Takes responsibility for all cases in the whole area where the org is. Gets pcs in such good shape they are walking advertisements for the HGC and Scn. Writes letters to possible pcs (the Director of Processing has had this duty for 15 years). (HCO PL 20 Nov 65) **3.** Co-audits, clinics, processing belong to the **Department of Processing.** (HCO PL 17 May 65 II)

DEPARTMENT OF PROCUREMENT, 1. Department 5, Division 2. Drives tons of business in on the org and Body Registrars by having an up-to-date manned central file and Address, sending out floods of high reality **procurement** letters to all possible candidates for training and processing, ASR packs, selectee mailings and Routing and Gradation Charts by which persons are driven into the org, onto their correct services, signed up, paid in advance and gotten into the org for services. (BPL 25 Jan 76 I) **2.** purpose: to make friends with future Scientologists and to make available to them training and processing and other services and to assist them to receive these. To a degree the **procurement** person is an auditor when writing preclears. (FCPL 15 Nov 58)

DEPARTMENT OF PRODUCT VALIDITY, Dept 15, Division 5, Correction Division. It contains an Examinations Section, Product Correction Section and Certs and Awards Section. (HCO PL 8 Aug 70 III) [The above HCO PL was cancelled by BPL 7 Dec 71R I.]

DEPARTMENT OF PROMOTION, 1. Department 4, Dissemination Division. Its product is effective **promotional** pieces printed and sent out. (BPL 27 Feb 73R) **2.** Department 4, Division 2. It issues magazines on schedule. Properly presents services in ads in org magazines and mailings. Does **promotional** pieces for Publications Dept. Executes planned **promotions** as laid down in SEC EDs. Compiles **promotional** pieces and programs for issue to Scientologists. Sees that the files, addresses and requirements of persons interested in Scn are used to the full. (HCO PL 20 Nov 65)

DEPARTMENT OF PROMOTION AND ADMINISTRATION, administrative personnel, reception, typists, file clerks, come under the **Department of Promotion and Administration.** All typing for all other departments is done by this **department** where they cannot do it themselves. **Administrative** personnel, even when working in other departments, comes under the **department.** (HCO PL 28 May 64)

DEPARTMENT OF PROMOTION AND PUBLICATIONS, Department 4, Division 2. Does hard sell informative **promotion** handouts, brochures and magazines on all services and items the org can or should deliver using survey results and for all departments including Div 6, who provide surveys, dummy and copy. Runs a mail order business and operates a bookstore and sells books through ads in the papers. Ships all orders received within 24 hours and keeps stocks up including course materials and hats for the org and keeps the HCO Book Account fat by promoting and selling the materials. (BPL 25 Jan 76 I)

DEPARTMENT OF PROMOTION AND REGISTRATION, 1. all **registration,** body **registrars** and letter **registrars** and all their functions and actions come under Division 1, HCO, as the **Dept of Prom-Reg,** under the HCO Area Secretary. **Prom-Reg Department** includes the HCO Communicator, who now becomes the Communications Officer. The **department** includes reception, all means of communication, the communication center, org board, central files and address, mail and mailing and any other purely **promotional**-communication function. The **department** is under the Director of **Prom-Reg,** just below HCO Area Secretary. (HCO PL 15 Mar 65 I) **2.** purpose: to procure students and preclears by actual, direct and personal contact using personal letters and assuring an adequate number of students and preclears. (HCO PL 12 Oct 62) **3.** this **department** ensures a flow of bodies into testing and from testing to training and processing. (HCO PL 22 Oct 60) **4.** the **Department of Promotion and Registration** is divided into three distinct categories—present time, past and future. There are three types of **registrars** which handle these three categories. The Immediate **Registrar** is mainly concerned with present time prospects. She answers any questions and handles any problems of those people who want auditing or training in present time. The Assistant **Registrar** is mainly concerned with the past, that is she handles ARC breaks. She is concerned with finding out why people are upset with us and why they have stopped communicating with us. She re-establishes communication with people. The Letter **Registrar** is concerned with future prospects. She writes to all future prospects. Her job is to see to it that we have people to train and audit in the future. (SEC ED 66, 30 Jan 59)

DEPARTMENT OF PUBLICATIONS, 1. Department 5, Dissemination Division. Its product is hat and course packs, tapes, adequate stocks (books, meters, tapes, insignia). (BPL 27 Feb 73R) **2.** Dept 5, Division 2. It sees that good quantities of books are in stock. Sees that books and mimeos look well when completed. Ships swiftly on receipt of orders. Issues the technical and policy materials of the org to get in policy and tech. Gets promotional pieces printed. Gets pins and insignia in stock and ensures broad issue so they will appear in the world and thus disseminate. Sees that book fliers (handbills) are shipped out regularly to Scientologists and book buyers. Sees that tapes are available and that presentation of them is of good tone quality. Sees that any cine material is available and ready for broad use. (HCO PL 20 Nov 65)

DEPARTMENT OF PUBLIC COMMUNICATION, Department 18, Division 6, Public Relations Division. Ideal scene: vast volumes of broad sweepingly effective public promotion going out in a steadily increasing flow to masses and masses of public individuals bringing about floods of response and people into Division 7 reaching for Dn and Scn. (HCO PL 20 Aug 70 III) [The above HCO PL was cancelled by BPL 10 Oct 75 VIII.]

DEPARTMENT OF PUBLIC CONTACT, Department 20, Division 7, Public Services Division. Ideal scene: excellent and professionally presented introductory lectures and **public** testing and evaluations from which a high volume of new people sign up for service with the number increasing weekly. (HCO PL 20 Aug 70 II) [The above HCO PL was cancelled by BPL 10 Oct 75 VIII.]

DEPARTMENT OF PUBLIC CONTROLLING, Department 16, Distribution Division. Its product is effective PR and advertising actions that attract members of the **public** to become Scientologists. (HCO PL 14 Jul 71)

DEPARTMENT OF PUBLIC COURSES, Department 21, Division 7, Public Services Division. Ideal scene: volumes of people in increasing numbers well serviced with basic courses and processing which effectively and rapidly demonstrate Dn and Scn and the results which can be achieved therefrom so that they are well introduced to Dn and Scn and want and are enrolling for training or processing within two weeks of their arrival in Division 7. (HCO PL 20 Aug 70 II) [The above HCO PL was cancelled by BPL 10 Oct 75 VIII.]

DEPARTMENT OF PUBLIC EVENTS, Department 19, Division 7, Public Services Division. Ideal scene: lots of well run **public events** which are attended by volumes of people in increasing numbers, and which create and generate high interest resulting in numerous enrollments for training and processing. (HCO PL 20 Aug 70 II) [The above HCO PL was cancelled by BPL 10 Oct 75 VIII.]

DEPARTMENT OF PUBLIC INFORMATION, Department 16, Division 6, Public Division. Its valuable final product is business driven down on the org. Its stat is number of people driven down on the org. (HCO PL 14 Nov 71RA II)

DEPARTMENT OF PUBLIC PLANNING, Department 17, Division 6, Division of Public Planning. It contains an Analysis Section, Planning Public Events Section, Planning Public Division Promo Section, Public Ad Section and Printer Liaison Section. (HCO PL 21 Dec 69) [The above HCO PL was cancelled by BPL 10 Oct 75 VII.]

DEPARTMENT OF PUBLIC PROMOTION, Department 18, Division 6, Public Planning Division. Advertises to the broad **public** using what is acceptable and valuable (ethnic values). Produces **promotional** material for press releases, TV scripts, book advertising using ethnic values, gets books placed in bookstores reviewed and in public view, acquires new mailing lists, sends out excellent information packs, invites Scientologists to ask that information packets be sent to friends and relatives. (HCO PL 23 May 69 III) [The above HCO PL was cancelled by BPL 10 Oct 75 VII.]

DEPARTMENT OF PUBLIC REGISTRATION, Department 24, Division 8, Public Sales Division. Ideal scene: many people flooding through **public registration** lines, each being rapidly and efficiently helped, 8-C'd and enrolled from service to service resulting in daily mass enrollment of the **public** on to their first major Dn or Scn service. (HCO PL 20 Aug 70 II) [The above HCO PL was cancelled by BPL 10 Oct 75 VIII.)

DEPARTMENT OF PUBLIC REHABILITATION, Department 17, Division 6, Public Planning Division. Sells Scn to governments and broad social stratas, works on the public not on Scientologists already known to Divisions 1 and 2, makes Scn popular and the thing to do, uses the media of press, TV, radio, issues projects of application to advanced Scientologists, particularly those projects involving artists or public figures, appoints committees of Scientologists in various areas and groups to advise on improvements of a civilization. (HCO PL 23 May 69 III) [The above HCO PL was cancelled by BPL 10 Oct 75 VII.]

DEPARTMENT OF PUBLIC RELATIONS, Department 16, Division 6. Product: effective **PR** and advertising actions that attract members of the public to becoming Scientologists. (HCO PL 7 Feb 71 VII) [The above HCO PL was cancelled by HCO PL 14 July 71.]

DEPARTMENT OF PUBLIC RESEARCH AND REPORTS, Department 16, Division 6, Public Planning Division. Discovers the ethnic values of the local area. Sees that ethnic data is correctly evaluated for assimilation and adoption. Makes sure ethnic data is provided for use in rehabilitation and promotion programs. (HCO PL 23 May 69 III) [The above HCO PL was cancelled by BPL 10 Oct 75 VII.]

DEPARTMENT OF PUBLIC SERVICES, Department 17, Division 6. It contains a Public Hat Preparing Section, Public Service Admin Section, Public Hatting Section, Success Section and Wisdom Disseminating Section. Its product is hatted Scientologists. (HCO PL 7 Feb 71 VII) [The above HCO PL was cancelled by HCO PL 14 Jul 71.]

DEPARTMENT OF PUBLIC SERVICING, **1.** Department 17, Division 6, Public Division contains demonstrations/indoctrination, film and tape plays, introductory lectures and events, books and memberships selling. There is a Public Registration Section and the valuable final product is people interested enough to buy something and do. (HCO PL 14 Nov 71RA II) **2. Department** 17, ASHO Foundation, Div 6. Product: SH Foundation **public** brought onto org lines for SH **services** or salvaging. (BPL 24 Mar 74 II)

DEPARTMENT OF PUBLIC SUPERVISION, [This department (**Dept** 20) runs the **public** courses such as HAS Course, HQS Course, Anatomy of the Human Mind Course, etc. It is mentioned in HCO PL 12 Nov 69 II, *PES Account versus HCO Book Account* which has been cancelled by BPL 10 Oct 75 VII.]

DEPARTMENT OF RECORDS, ASSETS AND MATERIEL, **1.** Department 9, Treasury Division. Its products are adequate and well cared for org materiel and a secure financial position for the org. (BPL 11 Sept 75) **2.** Department 9, Division 3. It gets proper quarters to make the org look good, whether for momentary or permanent use for all divisions. Keeps **materiel** of org bright. Acquires reserves to give a reputation of stability to org. Keeps staff clothing issued and in good order (in those orgs providing uniforms). (HCO PL 20 Nov 65)

DEPARTMENT OF REGISTRATION, **1.** Department 6, Division 2. Gets in the gross income that runs the org by having *Big League Sales*-trained **registrars** who close prospects in volume, no-wait reception and resign lines all busily functioning to drive more business down on Tech than it can handle without scheduling or programming cases or making promises org cannot fulfill, but for sure making the GI and from the many. (BPL 25 Jan 76 I) **2.** Department 6, Dissemination Division. Its product is individuals started on a major service. (BPL 27 Feb 73R) **3.** Dept 6, Division 2. Its Letter **Registrar** works to accumulate questionaires and mail from those responding to promotion. Follows exact policy and gets out floods of mail to all possible proper candidates for service. It keeps central files right up and in excellent shape and adds all new names of buyers of books and services. Uses central files to the limit to produce business. Sends out questionnaires with all offers which detect people's plans for training and processing. Accepts advance **registration** and encourages more advance **registration** until months ahead are scheduled full of students and pcs. Does phone **registration** in city areas in addition to other **registration** actions such as Letter **Registrar. Registers** everyone who comes in for services as pleasantly as possible with due regard for the solvency of the org. (HCO PL 20 Nov 65) **4.** the **Department of Registration** is in the Dissemination Division and is **Department** 6 of the organization. This **department** is headed by the Director **of Registration.** It consists of two sections: the Central Files Section and the **Registration** Section. The **Registration** Section has in it the Letter **Registrar**. The prime purpose of the **Department of Registration** is: to help Ron handle individuals who have been contacted so that they can be fully salvaged by org services and increase the size of the organization. (HCO PL 21 Sept 65 VI)

DEPARTMENT OF REGISTRATION AND PROCUREMENT, purpose: to communicate what we have to offer to those who care to be better and to help and to respond effectively when they reply. (HCO London, 9 Jan 58)

DEPARTMENT OF REVIEW, **1.** Dept 14, Division 5. It gives brilliant standard isolation of any errors in students or pcs; discovers them with ease. Repairs thoroughly. Makes a continual effort to get failed cases in the field or ARC broken

Scientologists in for a review. **Review** makes the dissatisfied satisfied with the org by remedying all tech misses. (HCO PL 20 Nov 65) **2.** the **Department of Review, Department** 14, is headed by the Director **of Review**. The prime purpose of the **Department of Review** and all its sections and units is: to help Ron correct any non-optimum result of the organization and also to advise ways and means based on actual experience in the department to safeguard against any continued poor result from any technical personnel or the function of the organization. The **Department of Review** must take over any non-optimum product of the organization, whether a technical project, an activity, a student or a preclear and bring about an attainment of the expected result regardless of obstacles. (HCO PL 31 Jul 65) **3.** the **Department of Review** is in the Qualifications Division. It has a Cramming Section which teaches students what they have missed. It has a Case Cracking Section which audits cases (students or HGC pcs or other pcs in difficulty such as field auditor rejects) to a result. **Review** also has a Staff Training Section. It also has a Staff Co-auditing Section. Any student failing his classification examinations must be ordered to the Review Cramming Section. (HCO PL 24 Apr 65)

DEPARTMENT OF ROUTING AND COMMUNICATION, Department 2, HCO Division 1. Product: **communications** easily accepted and swiftly delivered. (HCO PL 18 May 73)

DEPARTMENT OF ROUTING, APPEARANCES, AND PERSONNEL, **1.** Dept 1, Division 1. It sees that the org has a good clear **appearance**. Sees that **personnel** are properly dressed, well-conducted and give the org a good tone. Requires reception to make known free introductory lectures to all callers. Has books on display at reception. Controls public notice boards of the org and makes sure they also feature org services available. **Routes** people swiftly and accurately to the required services. (HCO PL 20 Nov 65) **2.** the appearance of the org and staff is transferred out of Department 1 which becomes the Department of Personnel and Routing and may still be called RAP but should be changed on the org board. (HCO PL 11 Dec 69, *Appearances in Public Divs*)

DEPARTMENT OF SCHEDULES, HGC Admin (The **Dept of Schedules**, Tech Div) receives folders at the end of the session or the day's auditing and gets them to the Case Supervisor. When the Case supervisor sends them back (before the next session), HGC Admin then sees what should happen in the folders and routes the pc promptly and, as promptly, handles any auditor re-assignment. (HCO PL 4 Jul 65)

DEPARTMENT OF SERVICES, Department 9A Div III Flagship Org. Valuable Final Product: A fully operational galley and berthing unit that provides excellent meals, meal **service**, and berthing **service** to the ship's company and guests at a quality level comparable to a liner with no disturbance to remaining orgs aboard. (FSO 776)

DEPARTMENT OF SOLO AUDITING, Department 12A, AOLA Division 4A. **Dept of Solo Auditing** stats are total (**Solo**) well done auditing hours and total number of case completions. (BPL 16 Sept 71R II)

DEPARTMENT OF SPECIAL CASES, the HCO PL which makes Department 10 a **Department of Special Cases** is cancelled. Dept 10 must remain as the Dept of Tech Services. Drug cases (for whom the **Dept of Special Cases** was primarily established) are audited in the HGC or co-audit on the HSDC course. (HCO PL 2 Feb 72 II) [The above HCO PL was cancelled by BPL 10 Oct 75 X.]

DEPARTMENT OF SUCCESS, Dept 18, Division 6. It collects by letters or verbally **successful** applications of Scn. Issues stories of **successful** application. Handles press. Makes Scn popular or the thing to do. Sells Scn to goverments and broad social stratas. Issues projects of application to advanced Scientologists, particularly those projects involving artists or public figures. Encourages broad public (lay) memberships. Gets spectacular wins posted on the org's public notice boards. Encourages and publicizes various applications of Scn. (HCO PL 20 nov 65)

DEPARTMENT OF TECHNICAL CORRECTION, Dept 15, Division 5, Correction Division. It contains an Examinations Section, Product Correction Section and Certs and Awards Section. (HCO PL 15 Jul 70 II) [The above HCO PL was cancelled by BPL 7 Dec 71R I.]

DEPARTMENT OF TECH SERVICES, **1.** Dept 10, Technical Division 4. **Dept of Tech Services's** valuable final product is rapidly and efficiently scheduled, routed, supplied and handled students and pcs. (BPL 4 Jan 73RC) **2. Department** 10, Division 4. It makes the customers happy and glad to be there. Gives brisk service. Acquires for the org a reputation for swift and excellent handling of people. (HCO PL 20 Nov 65)

DEPARTMENT OF TRAINING, **1.** Dept 11, Technical Division 4. **Dept of Training's** valuable final product is graduates who know and effectively apply the materials of the courses. (BPL 4 Jan 73RC) **2.** Dept 11, Division 4. It gives excellent **training** (the soundest possible promotion quickly mirrored in numbers enrolling). Routes dissidents quickly to Ethics and slows to Review. Briskly and punctually schedules classes. Accomplishes lots of completions. Turns out very competent auditors whose excellence promotes the Academy (or College at SH) and Scn. Writes letters to possible prospective students to get the Academy (or College at SH) full. Makes sure the excellence of **training** that is there is bragged about in magazines, etc. (HCO PL 20 Nov 65)

DEPARTMENT OF VALIDITY, **1.** Division 5, Department 15 is now called the **Department of Validity**. It has a Director **of Validity**, Qualifications Interview and Invoice, the Examiner, and it has Certs and Awards. Now of course there's the Student Examiner, and there is the PC Examiner and anything we once knew as Qual fits there. But there would also be here any review; you know, public review of pcs, a Review auditor would be there, cramming of students would be there. Any Qual that you've known has gone over to 15, and that leaves two other departments open. This is published in HCO PL 14 August 71RC II. (7109C05) **2.** Dept 13, Correction Division. Ensures fast smooth routing of all publics in and out of Qual, expert pc and student examinations, which pass correctly earned gradation and classification and detect and pass for correction all flubbed products. Immediate supply of all earned Certs and Awards, catches any dropped balls, permanently logs all achievements carefully. Provisional certs called in within one week for interneships and inspection and permanent **validation**. All memberships renewed and kept in force. (BPL 7 Dec 71R I)

DEPARTMENT STAFF MEMBER, a **member** of a production **department staff** as posted on the organization board as different from a unit staff member. A unit staff member is not a **member** of a production **department** but appears somewhere else on the organization board. (HCO PL 26 Jun 64)

DEPARTMENT STORE, a store that stocks a large amount of the different goods that customers demand. Such a store is divided into departments like Men's Clothing, Sporting Goods or Hardware Departments, etc.

DEPARTURE FORM, HCO WW **Form Dep**/1. This **form** must be completed by a student before any **departure** from course. (HCO PL 8 Nov 62, *Departure Form*)

DEPOSIT, 1. a sum of money entrusted to a bank for safekeeping. 2. a payment made as a pledge that one will pay more later such as a down payment or initial payment of a purchase price or debt.

DEPOSIT ACCOUNT, same as savings account.

DEPRECIATION, the recognition of the fact that a value has gone down (HCO PL 10 Oct 70 I)

DEPRESSION, too much production without enough money to buy the produce is what causes a **depression**. But that usually follows too much money released without enough produce. (ESTO 11, 7203C06 SO I)

DEPUTY, **1.** the rule is see the Product Officer about past, present and future production. See the Org Officer about internal matters of personnel, supply, hats, etc. The **deputy** is the Org Officer who is always junior to the Product Officer. It's like having (in the Org Officer—the **Deputy**) an HCO right in your own division. The **deputies** are really under the Org Officer of the org. The division heads are under the Product Officer of the org. (OODs 10 Jan 71) **2.** a prefix to a title meaning "in place of." There may be a **deputy** for each executive post in an org in addition to the person with the title, or it means "filling in until an appointment is actually made." (HCO PL 13 Mar 66) **3.** a **deputy** is assigned where the appointment is already filled by another. A **deputy** is a second in command who acts in the absence of the actual appointed person. (HCO PL 18 Nov 65) **4.** if the post is assigned locally by an organization it may only be assigned as a **deputy**. If it is appointed from Saint Hill then that becomes an acting which is the first rank. For awhile the post is held under an acting status and is then held in full status. The acting is simply removed. You'd know then, the difference between a local and a Saint Hill appointment. Your local appointments are all **deputy** where they are executive appointments. If they are Saint Hill appointments, why then they are acting or nothing in front of it. You'd have such a thing as **Deputy** HCO Exec Sec. That doesn't mean any permanency of any kind whatsoever. A small breath of air can come in the window and take that title off the board because it's not anything but an assigned title. It's just somebody filling time until somebody can be put there or they can be confirmed. (SH Spec 61, 6505C18)

DEPUTY CAPTAINS, the **Deputy Captains** are the Chief Officer, Supercargo, 1st Mate, 2nd Mate, 3rd Mate, 4th Mate, Purser and Public Officer in that order. (FSO 1)

DEPUTY COMMANDING OFFICER, **1.** the **CO's** or ED's **deputy** handles the program functions of the **CO** or ED and is the Org's Org Officer. He ranks with the Exec Esto. (HCO PL 7 Mar 72) **2.** actually, the **D/CO** is *not* the **CO's** OO. There could even be a **CO's** (or ED's) OO. It is not a Prod-Org type post (**D/CO,** D/ED). It is the post that establishes and trains on policy the whole org, sees to recruitment, sees that the org form is right and flowing, sees that there are people in training for staff and sees that there are execs I/T for execs, sees that there is a TTC and that it is actually making auditors, etc. He is the guy who puts an actual full org there: the only thing that holds down expansion and increase in Pd Comps and GI is that no one is actively working to put a whole on-policy org there that will do its job. This is the real why of low GI, low delivery and other woes. The **D/** also sees to quarters and their cleanliness and their readiness to do business as an organization. He does not take over posts where these are usually done but copes and gets people on those proper posts to do them. His minimum training is OEC. Orgs prosper when they are there in full org form, fully manned and in good quarters with fully trained staffs. All else is cope. Hence the vital **D/CO** D/ED post. (BO 100)

DEPUTY COMMODORE, FLAG, see DEPUTY COMMODORE FLOTILLA.

DEPUTY COMMODORE FLOTILLA, the title of the 2nd Deputy Commodore operating from Los Angeles is changed to **Deputy Commodore Flotilla.** It is abbreviated **D/Com Flot.** The zone of control is all vessels, bases and orgs of the Sea Org below the level of Flag. There are two Deputy Commodores. Deputy Commodore Flag who operates in the absence of the Commodore. **Deputy Commodore Flotilla** who operates continuously in direct operational control of the Sea Org from a land base. (FO 2123) *Abbr.* D/Com Flot.

DEPUTY COURT OF APPEAL, membership of the **Court of Appeal** consists of a chairman of officer rank, a secretary and from one to three members. There is also a **Deputy Court of Appeal.** This allows for three members to be appointed to cover the post of member, where one or more of the **Court of Appeal** is absent. (BPL 26 Jan 70R I)

DEPUTY EXECUTIVE DIRECTOR, **1.** the program executer, also the hand holder, also the dev-t catcher of the Product Officer (Executive Director). (ESTO 1, 7203C01 SO I) **2.** the CO's or **ED's deputy** handles the program functions of the CO or ED and is the org's Org Officer. He ranks with the Exec Esto. (HCO PL 7 Mar 72)

DEPUTY 4th MATE, handles the ship admin duties of the **4th Mate's** post. (FO 2535)

DEPUTY LRH COMMUNICATOR, where an **LRH Communicator** has a **deputy,** the Product Org Officer System applies. The senior is always a product officer. This makes the **deputy** an Org Officer. The purpose of the **deputy** is to keep a smoothly running **LRH Comm** establishment in existence and to permit the **LRH Comm** to produce. (HCO PL 3 Aug 73)

DEPUTY PORT CAPTAIN, where there is a **Deputy Port Captain** the **deputy** duties would be largely administrative as this is considerable in that division and when dropped behind can wreck all manner of official PR and wonderful ideas for PR takes preparation and execution before it can be effective. The list of admin actions and Division 6 files is extensive. The **deputy** is responsible for the admin actions. When the **Port Captain** is absent the **Deputy Port Captain** acts in his place and must be hatted to do so. The **deputy** handles staff matters, internal ship divisional matters for Div 6, training Div 6 people, the establishment of the division and all its files and programs. (FO 3392)

DEPUTY SECRETARY, the Org Officer in a highly idealized org would have an Organizing Officer in each division of that org as the **Deputy Secretary.** (FEBC 6, 7101C23 SO II)

DEPUTY SYSTEM, training on post is a second stage of any training action. This is essentially a familiarization action. To have a person leave a post and another take it over with no apprenticeship or groove-in can be quite fatal. The **Deputy System** is easily the best system. Every post is **deputied** for a greater or lesser period before the post is turned over and the appointment is made. When the **deputy** is totally familiar he becomes the person on the post. (HCO PL 14 Dec 70)

DEPUTY TECHNICAL SECRETARY, in a large org there is a **Deputy Tech Sec** who is the Tech Org Officer and handles the administrative and programs function of the division. In smaller orgs the hat is worn by the Tech Sec. A **Deputy Tech Sec** is not just another Tech Sec. He is the

Tech Div Programs and Administrative Officer. (BPL 2 Jul 73R)

DERIVED, formed or developed out of something else, which is to say something formed or made from a basic. (HCO PL 9 Nov 68)

DESIGN, 1. the artful format that will interest and lead the viewer to involvement in and finally desire to act (to attain, to fight, to abandon, etc.). (FO 3574) **2.** a plan or scheme intended for subsequent execution; the preliminary conception of an idea that is to be carried into effect by action; the plan of a building or any part of it after which the actual structure is to be completed; a delineation, pattern. (FSO 823)

Design (Def. 1)

DESIGN AND PLANNING COUNCIL, this **Council** is composed of the following: Captain FSO (as D/Chairman), Supercargo FSO (Secretary), Chief Officer FSO, Chief Engineer, First Mate, Purser, LRH Comm FSO. It is understood that the Commodore is the Chairman of this Dept 21 Council and that the Captain takes the chair in his place; the function of the LRH Comm is to keep in policy on the council's proceedings and actions. Any action to change the use or appearance of any space aboard may only occur with the approval of the **Design and Planning Council**. Any proposal to install new machinery must have the **Council's** approval before submission to FP. No mest of the ship may be disposed of without the specific approval of the **Council**, including the method of disposal. (FSO 823)

DESIGN AND PLANNING SECTION, **section** of Dept 21 in the Office of LRH FSO under the administrative care of the LRH Comm FSO. The early org board of the SO had this function in its Div 2 under the supervision of the Supercargo. The purpose of the Flag **Design and Planning Section** is threefold: to coordinate all designing and planning and executions thereof which change or extend Flag's spaces and materiel; to help the Commodore increase and maintain the profitable and viable utilization of Flag's spaces and materiel; to help the Commodore viably enhance and maintain the internal and external appearance of the flagship. (FSO 823)

DESIGN STAGE, (graphic arts) there is a **design stage**. This is how it is going to be folded or prettied up and where what goes and the kind of type, paper, etc. (ED 459-51 Flag)

DESKILLED, a job that has been deskilled is one where automation or specialization have reduced the skills needed for the job to a point where only relatively simple actions remain.

DESK RESEARCH, see RESEARCH, DESK.

DESK TRAINING, see TRAINING, DESK.

DEVALUATION, a reduction of the exchange rate which a country demands for its currency; to lessen in value.

DEVELOP, (increase) as in **develop** traffic. (HCO PL 27 Jan 69)

DEVELOPED TRAFFIC, 1. any executive getting **dev-t** knows at once what posts are not held because **dev-t** is the confusion that should have been handled in that area by someone on post. With that stable terminal not stable, **dev-t** shoots about. (HCO PL 27 Oct 69) **2.** traffic is developed (**developed traffic, dev-t**) by originating or forwarding an off-line or off-policy dispatch to anyone but the sender. (HCO PL 17 Nov 64) **3. developed traffic** is a statement you will begin to see now. It is condemnatory. The symbol **dev-t** means on a dispatch, "This dispatch exists only because its originator has not handled a situation, problem, or an executive order." It also means, "Responsibility for your post very low." Also it means "You should be handling this without further traffic." It also means "You are manufacturing new traffic because you aren't handling old traffic." Also it means "For Gawd's sake!" Every time traffic is developed somebody has flubbed. **Developed traffic** does not mean usual and necessary traffic. It means unusual and unecessary traffic. (HCO PL 2 Jul 59 II) **4.** additionally needless, inhibitive actions are called **dev-t.** Non-compliance, alter-is, no report, false reports, off-origin statements and dispatches, stale dated orders, wrong targets, cross orders, cross targets, are all **dev-t.** They made a great many motions necessary where only the one correct one was needed. (OODs 22 Jan 68) *Abbr.* Dev-t.

Developed Traffic

DEV-T-ITIS, a good way to drive someone nutty is to dev-t them by leaving incomplete cycles in their work area. Suppressive persons must surely have a great time with this type of game! To come into one's working space and to constantly find one's work undone, messes left, things that should be put away left out, and so on. It's enough to make any conscientious person first puzzled, then irritated, then angered, and finally, go into despair. The end product? "Well, no one else cares. Why should I bother?" The sad thing is that most of this **dev-t-itis** doesn't come from suppressive persons but from your "well-meaning" co-worker. Being dispersed by what is obviously too much randomity, they pour a glass of milk and leave the container on the counter to dev-t someone else or to go to waste. Their attention is dispersed by so many incomplete cycles they haven't handled that as soon as the glass is filled, they shift their attention off the container and it's forgotten. So, someone else has to put it away, and also clean up the bit that was spilled. The sloppy job seems to go hand-in-glove with this. (FO 3127)

DEV-T LOG, each staff member keeps a **dev-t log** and writes down the name of anyone he is getting dev-t from. (HCO PL 9 Mar 72 III)

DEV-T MERCHANT, if a new person hasn't gripped it (new post) in a week, is still begging for help from all, he's a **dev-t merchant.** Unload, he won't be any better in ten weeks and the org will be a lot worse. Such a person can't be at cause over the job and will only destroy the post (as witness the way you have to do his work as well as your own—dead post). You have to have three staff members extra for every **dev-t merchant** you have on staff. Why—because the coin has "efficient" on one side and "destructive" on the other—and it never stands on edge. There are no cases on staff—ever. Cases exist only in sessions. (HCO PL 18 Oct 59)

DEV-T REPORT, staff member **report** stating whether off-line, off-policy or off-origin and from whom to whom and subject. (HCO PL 1 May 65)

DEXTERITY, 1. Showing acute skill in the use of the hands, body or a body part. 2. the degree of cleverness exhibited in the execution of some action.

DIALECTIC MATERIALISM, 1. this philosophy is crudely stated in the following statement: It takes two opposing forces to produce an idea. (HCO PL 14 Aug 63) **2.** philosophy that force versus force produces ideas. Actually, ideas versus ideas produce force. (SH Spec 46, 6411C10) **3.** the anatomy of a problem gone mad. A current philosophy. (SH Spec 68, 6510C14)

DIANA, 1. the oldest yacht in the Sea Org. (OODs 28 Feb 69) **2.** *Enchanter's* name is changed to *Diana.* (Ron's Journal 1968)

DIANETIC CASE SUPERVISOR, (Dn C/S) C/S or C/Ses who handle all routine C/Sing of Dn including Drug Rundowns. (HCO PL 25 Sept 74)

DIANETIC CLEAR, 1. there is such a state. Only about 2% go actually Clear on Dn. A **Dianetic Clear** or any other Dn pc now goes on up through the grades of Scn and onto the proper Clearing Course. The **Dianetic Clear** of Book I was clear of somatics. The Book I definition is correct. This is the end phenomenon of Dn as per the Classification Chart and Book I. Two per cent, no more, make **Dianetic Clear** accidentally. They still need expanded lower grades to make Scientology Clear. Becoming a **Dianetic Clear** does not stop them from getting power processing. (LRH ED 101 INT) **2.** a **Dianetic Clear** is just a release, not a real Clear. (LRH ED 104 INT)

DIANETIC COUNSELING GROUP, 1. the **Dianetic Counseling Group** consists of in full action, Hubbard Dianetic Counselors, the administrative few people, even if only part-time, to handle the admin of the unit, and a Hubbard Dianetic Graduate in order to teach Hubbard Dianetic Counselors out in the field, and a Scn auditor to hold down Review. (6905C29) **2.** delivers Dn auditing and a Hubbard Standard Dianetics Course, using a certified HDG from a Scn org as supervisor. Running the Hubbard Standard Dianetics Course is optional, but if conducted, it must be taught by a certified HDG trained at an org. The **DCG** may not undertake to train or graduate HDGs. Only orgs may do this. (BPL 28 Apr 70RA) *Abbr.* DCG.

DIANETIC COUNSELING GROUP PROGRAM, the purpose of the **Dianetic Counseling Group Program** is to boom Dn in the field. It can be delivered in high volume to the masses anywhere and everywhere. The program is designed so that people can operate and run Dn freely. Dianeticists are given a free reign to expand and operate on this planet everywhere. There are no stops or limitations. Dianetic Counseling Groups do not pay 10% to WW or Scn orgs. There are no titles for Dianetic Counseling Groups, its income is its own. A DCG can be set up by either of the following: (1) a Scn org, (2) a mission, (3) an individual. (BPL 28 Apr 70RA)

DIANETIC FOUNDATION, see HUBBARD DIANETIC RESEARCH FOUNDATION.

DIANETIC INFORMATION GROUP, a group formed to provide information on the results of Dn and its applications. The membership is open to doctors, dental surgeons, pharmacists and qualified nurses. (*STCR*, p. 104) *Abbr.* DIG.

DIANETIC INTENSIVE, this is essentially the same as any other old-time intensive, 25 hours. You audit it triple flow. Just standard Dn, triple. (LRH ED 56 INT)

DIANETIC REPAIR INTENSIVE, with all the Dn auditing done in the field, the official org should feature that it repairs Dn. You complete the chains and take, generally, the Scn actions useful to handle the Dn. (LRH ED 57 INT)

DIANETIC RESEARCH FOUNDATION, see HUBBARD DIANETIC RESEARCH FOUNDATION.

DIANETICS, 1. **Dianetics:** *dia* (Greek) through and *nous* (Greek) soul. (BPL 24 Sept 73 V) **2. Dn** is practiced in the Church of Scientology as pastoral counseling, addressing the spirit in relation to his own body and intended to increase well-being and peace of mind. (BPL 24 Sept 73RA XIII) **3. Dn** is a mental therapy addressing the mind, with a basic appeal to materialism. (HCO PL 25 Jan 57) **4. Dn** is a spiritual healing practice supplementing medical treatment. (HCO PL 6 Apr 69) **5. Dn** is really a psychotherapy. You might say, ends track on the subject of psychotherapy. Psychotherapy is an effort to remove neurosis and psychosis from man by immediate address to the individual in the group. (5510C08)

DIANETICS AND SCIENTOLOGY MAILING LIST, this is a list of names and addresses of persons who have bought something from an organization. This in full, is the org mailing list. Every person on this list has a separate file in central files. (BPL 17 May 69R I)

DID-DIDN'T SYSTEM, [Referred to orgs who **did or didn't** make target quotas for a week.]

DIFFERENCES ARE DIFFERENT, a pluspoint. Not made to be identical or similar. (HCO PL 3 Oct 74)

DIFFERENT, two or more facts or things that are totally unlike are **different**. They are not the same fact or same object. (HCO PL 26 Apr 70R)

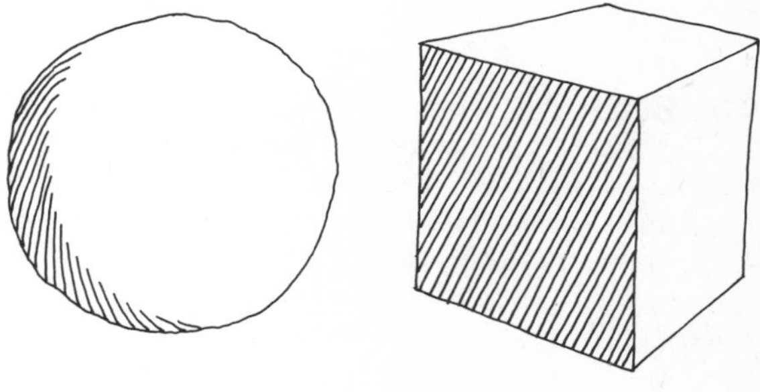

Different

DIGESTION, let us understand this subject of **digestion**. Information is collected, **digested** and disseminated. **Digested** means "can somebody read it?" Now actually it's done by the news services. The radio gives you the events in rapid fire and then gives you the embroidery of the event. The first thing you hear, the captions and so on is in actual fact the digest of the information. Now they might have a 50,000 word news story but it is given in a couple of sentences. (6912C13SO)

DILETTANTE, one who interests himself in an art or science merely as a pastime and without serious study. (HCO PL 16 May 65 II)

DIMINISHING RETURN, (point of diminishing return) the point where increasing the amount of personnel, wages, material, etc., used to obtain a product now yields proportionately less than previous increases. This is often a symptom of the optimum level of productivity for a certain area under certain conditions now being bypassed and thus people are beginning to get in each other's way or some form of inefficiency is setting in.

DIRECT ACTION, taking charge of a matter directly rather than via government bodies or the law.

DIRECT COSTS, see COSTS, DIRECT.

DIRECT HOOK-UP, the telex is a means whereby two stations can be in **direct hook-up** with one another via the keyboard. **Direct hook-up** is used if it is necessary that the information arrive immediately. The information is being received at the same time as it is being transmitted. (HCO PL 9 Aug 66)

DIRECTIONS CHIEF, 1. (Sea Organization) the name of Div 2 Dept 6 is changed to Directions Department headed by the **Directions Chief** and includes Mimeo Section, Mission Plans Section and Navigation Section. (FO 1028) **2.** (Sea Org Org Board) Department 6 under the **Directions Chief** is the Dissemination area, mimeographs, plans and contains the full library section. (FO 1109)

DIRECTIONS DEPARTMENT, the name of Div 2 Dept 6 is changed to **Directions Department** headed by the Directions Chief and includes Mimeo Section, Mission Plans Section and Navigation Section. (FO 1028)

DIRECTIVE, a written communication serving to direct the recipient's attention to a specific matter such as a policy statement or change and often containing orders or instructions to be carried out. Directives are usually numbered for orderly keeping and reference.

DIRECT LABOR, see LABOR, DIRECT.

DIRECT LABOR COSTS, see LABOR, DIRECT.

DIRECT MAIL SELLING, see SELLING, DIRECT MAIL.

DIRECT MAIL SHOT, a simultaneous bulk mailing of direct mail selling promotion to prospective customers.

DIRECT MATERIAL, see MATERIAL, DIRECT.

DIRECT MATERIAL COSTS, see COSTS, DIRECT MATERIAL.

DIRECT NEGATIVE, an amendment proposed at a meeting that is directly opposite to the motion currently before the meeting.

DIRECTOR, 1. there are 18 **directors** in an organization. They head departments. They are appointed by their secretaries with the approval of HCO Personnel and the LRH Communicator. There are three coordinators in an org. They are the same as **directors** but head the three offices (departments) of the Executive Division. (HCO PL 13 Mar 66) **2.** a manager, person in control, a leader. (HCO Admin Ltr 30 Jul 75) *Abbr.* Dir.

DIRECTOR, a member of an executive board or board of **directors** who has been appointed by the stockholders to govern the affairs of a corporation. Also called Company Director.

DIRECTOR OF ACCOUNTS, headed by the **Director of Accounts,** the Dept of Accounts receives, safeguards and expends funds in the organization. No other person can expend money, though others can receive it if it is promptly handed to Accounts. (HCO PL 14 Feb 61)

DIRECTOR OF ADMINISTRATION, 1. the hat of the **Director of Administration** is to expedite, supervise or handle all administrative actions for the organization. (HCO PL 5 Dec 62) **2.** the **Director of Administration**, regardless of the title of the administrative personnel, is directly in charge of all administrative personnel, is responsible for their hiring and firing, their arrival on time and proper performance of their duties, and for the purpose of pay and facilities is in charge of technical personnel. (HCO PL 5 Dec 62) **3.** the **Director of Administration** compares to the head of the administrative corps of a hospital where he runs everything except the doctors and does everything except treat and has charge of all the purposes except trying to make people well. (HCO PL 5 Dec 62) **4.** the terms **Administrator** and **Director of Administration** are interchangeable. (HCO PL 5 Dec 62) **5.** the function of the **Director of Administration** is to see that all policies relating to the Administrative Division as laid down by the Board or the Executive Director but always from the Board via the Executive Director are executed. The post of **Director of Administration** is supposed to make the policies of the Executive Director stick in the Administrative

Division. The post of **Director of Administration** will be backed up fully so long as it devotes its energies, to making the Executive Director's policies work. The task is not to create new policies, but to make existing policies stick. When room space is allocated by the Executive Director, the **Director of Administration** is supposed to make the people and furniture into that allocation plan. When financial policy is laid down, the **Director of Administration** is supposed to see that it alone is the policy used. If such things cannot be done, the post is not being held. (SEC ED 5, 16 Dec 58) **6.** purpose: to ensure good and accurate communication inside the organization, handles business and administrative affairs. To ensure good working quarters and conditions for, and good work from, organizational personnel. (HCO London, 9 Jan 58)

DIRECTOR OF ADVANCED COURSES TECH SERVICES, Director of Department of Advanced Courses Tech Services, Dept 10A, AOLA Division 4A. (BPL 16 Sept 71R II)

DIRECTOR OF ADVANCED COURSES TRAINING, Director of Department of Advanced Courses Training, Dept 11A, AOLA Division 4A. (BPL 16 Sept 71R II)

DIRECTOR OF AUDITORS, the head of the Auditors Division is the **Director of Auditors.** (HCO PL 11 Mar 64, *Departmental Changes Auditors Division)*

DIRECTOR OF BUSINESS, the Dept of Business shall be headed by the **Director of Business.** (FCPL 9 Oct 58)

DIRECTOR OF CERTIFICATIONS, the Department of Certifications and Awards, Department Number 15, is headed by the **Director of Certifications.** (HCO PL 31 Jul 65)

DIRECTOR OF CERTS AND AWARDS, director of Department of Certs and Awards, Qualifications Division. (BPL 2 Nov 67)

DIRECTOR OF CLEARING, Director of Department 18, Department of Clearing. The **Dir of Clearing** hats Scientologists by drilling and mini courses and will use whatever training tool is to hand needed to get a person to produce the four products of a Scientologist (purchased books, disseminated knowledge, environmental control, a cleared planet). (HCO PL 14 Nov 71RA II) *Abbr.* Dir Clear.

DIRECTOR OF COMMUNICATIONS, 1. Director of Department of Communications, Department 2, Division 1. (HCO PL 7 Feb 71 II) **2.** (HCO Div 1, Dept 2) the purpose of the **Director of Communications** is to help LRH handle and speed communications from the public to the org, the org to the public and establish and supervise the internal communications system of the organization and link it with other orgs. (HCO PL 25 Feb 66) **3.** If you think **Dir Comm** is a message clerk, think again. **Dir Comm** sees to it there *is* comm. And that's his hat. Not what dispatch do I route but is there a place to receive dispatches and letters to send dispatches and letters to (comm center baskets, comm stations, address files, incoming mail, outgoing mail). (HCO PL 24 Feb 66) *Abbr.* Dir Comm.

DIRECTOR OF CORRECTION, Director of Department of Correction, Dept 15, Correction Division. (BPL 7 Dec 71R I)

DIRECTOR OF DISBURSEMENTS, Director of Department of Disbursements, Department 8, Treasury Division. (BPL 11 Sept 75) *Abbr.* Dir Disb.

DIRECTOR OF ENROLLMENT, 1. has the full responsibility of filling up the Academy and keeping it full. The Letter Reg Department, including central files and addresso, Body Reg, and Reception are the responsibility of the **Enrollment Director** and all part of the Enrollment Department. (HCO PL 21 Feb 64) **2.** for the sake of simplification and to facilitate a concentration on the training route up through the levels of Scn, the Department of Promotion and Registration in all Central Organizations will now be termed the Department of Enrollment. The Director of P and R is now the **Director of Enrollment.** (HCO PL 21 Feb 64)

DIRECTOR OF EXAMINATIONS, the Department of Examinations, Department Number 13, is headed by the **Director of Examinations.** (HCO PL 31 Jul 65)

DIRECTOR OF INCOME, Director of Department of Income, Dept 7, Treasury Division. (BPL 11 Sept 75) *Abbr.* Dir Inc.

DIRECTOR OF INSPECTION AND REPORTS, Director of Department 3, Department of Inspection and Reports. Handles tech, org and staff inspections, time machine for executive orders, posts weekly stats, weekly OIC reports to WW, issues certs and awards on merit. (HCO PL 18 May 73) *Abbr.* Dir I&R.

DIRECTOR OF INSPECTIONS, requests for an emergency condition should be made to the **Director of Inspections**, Dept 13, Distribution Div 4, who comments and forwards them to the Office of L. Ron Hubbard. Only HCO's Office of LRH may now convene a Committee of Evidence or a Civil Committee of Evidence. The order to convene one is requested of the **Director of Inspections** (Div 4) who forwards it (or originates it) to HCO's Office of L. Ron Hubbard with comments and any statistics. Publication of a Committee of Evidence findings is done by SEC ED of the same number that convened it. Publication is done by the Office of LRH. The **Director of Inspection** takes care of all further actions and the resulting files. The Department of Inspections, Division 4, Department 13, has the actual administration and execution of all justice. (HCO PL 31 Mar 65)

DIRECTOR OF MATERIEL, **1.** purpose: to make certain that the Department of Materiel runs and performs its responsibilities in caring for the material and providing materiel for the Founding Church and to supervise personnel on maintenance and cleaning posts and to see that buildings and storage areas are in good order, and to safeguard materiel and files from damage or theft. (SEC ED 34, 14 Jan 59) **2.** the Dept of Materiel shall be headed by the **Director of Materiel.** (FCPL 9 Oct 58) *Abbr.* Dir Mat.

DIRECTOR OF PERSONNEL, Director of Department of Personnel, Department 1, HCO Division 1. (HCO PL 18 May 73) *Abbr.* Dir Pers.

DIRECTOR OF PERSONNEL ENHANCEMENT, Director of Department of Personnel Enhancement, Dept 14, Correction Division. (BPL 7 Dec 71R I) *Abbr.* DPE.

DIRECTOR OF PROCESSING, **1.** Director of Department of Processing, Dept 12, Technical Division 4. (BPL 4 Jan 73RC) **2.** the **Director of Processing** will interview you on matters concerning your auditing progress and the scheduling of your auditing. You may see the **D of P** at any time regarding your auditing. He is there to see you receive the service and help you. (BPL 29 Jan 72R) **3.** purpose: to do more for people's health and ability than has ever before been possible, and to give the best auditing possible. To help people. To clear people. To run an efficient HGC. (BPL 19 Nov 71R) **4.** the principle duties of the **D of P** are to get auditors putting in auditing time and getting lots of pcs done and interview pcs to check flatness or unflatness or processes. The **D of P** also musters his auditors before the morning session and before the afternoon session and hands out folders at those times with a minimum of session time loss. (HCO PL 1 Feb 66 III) **5.** the **D of P** looks after staff auditors and internes as org personnel and is their immediate superior. The **D of P** is responsible for staff auditor procurement without absolving HCO's personnel officer from it. That auditors are on the job on time and are putting in their session time and their conduct and their actions as staff members are all in the province of the **D of P.** (HCO PL 1 Feb 66 III) **6.** the HGC is headed by the **Director of Processing,** under whom come all individual cases, (public and staff). The **D of P** is the case czar of the organization. The **D of P's** total administration is done by HGC Admin. The **D of P** does not do admin, only technical, but is in charge of admin and all staff auditors and the department. (HCO PL 20 Dec 62) **7.** responsible for auditing rooms, auditors, assignment of pcs to auditors and states of cases. (HCOB 26 Sept 56) *Abbr.* D of P.

DIRECTOR OF PROCUREMENT, **1.** to: **Director of Procurement** D.C., your department's title is changed to Department of Promotion and Registration and your title is changed to Director of Promotion and Registration. The abbreviation for this department is PrR. (SEC ED 4, 16 Dec 58) **2.** the Dept of Procurement shall be headed by the **Director of Procurement** who must not be the Registrar. (FC PL 9 Oct 58) *Abbr.* Dir Procu.

DIRECTOR OF PROMOTION, Director of Department of Promotion, Department 4, Dissemination Division. (BPL 27 Feb 73R) *Abbr.* Dir Prom.

DIRECTOR OF PROMOTION AND ADMINISTRATION, extends his actions into any and all promotion and any and all administration that achieves promotion or otherwise. Under him then comes all other administrative functions including mimeo, filing, typing, reception and all other such personnel except accounts, since these are all in essence promotional activities. All typing for all other departments is done by this department where they cannot do it themselves. Administrative personnel, even when working in other departments comes under the Department of Promotion and Administration. (HCO PL 28 May 64)

DIRECTOR OF PUBLICATIONS, **1.** Director of Department of Publications, Department 5, Dissemination Division. (BPL 27 Feb 73R) **2.** manages all publishing and dissemination activities. Handles all departmental personnel. (HCO PL 18 Dec 74, *Saint Hill Org Board*) *Abbr.* Dir Pubs.

DIRECTOR OF PUBLIC INFORMATION, director of Department of Public Information, Department 16, Public Division. (HCO PL 18 May 73)

DIRECTOR OF PUBLIC SERVICING, director of Department of Public Servicing, Department 17, Public Division. (HCO PL 18 May 73)

DIRECTOR OF RECORDS, ASSETS, AND MATERIEL, Director of Department of Records, Assets and Materiel, Department 9, Treasury Division. (BPL 11 Sept 75) ***Abbr.*** Dir RAM

DIRECTOR OF REGISTRATION, **1.** Director of Department of Registration, Department 6, Dissemination Division. (BPL 27 Feb 73R)**2.** the department head of Dept 6. She is the senior of the Address Officer, C/F Officer, Letter Reg Section Officer, ARC Break Registrar, Chief Body Reg. She patrols the lines of the whole department and gives constant attention to the flow of particles through Dept 6. (HCO PL 8 Jul 73) ***Abbr.*** Dir Reg

DIRECTOR OF REVIEW, the Department of Review, Department Number 14, is headed by the **Director of Review**. (HCO PL 31 Jul 65)

DIRECTOR OF ROUTING AND COMMUNICATION, Director of Department 2, Department of Routing and Communication. Handles org lines and communications swiftly and smoothly, routing forms, signs, badges, mimeo and master files. (HCO PL 18 May 73)

DIRECTOR OF ROUTING, APPEARANCES AND PERSONNEL, Director of Department of Routing, Appearances and Personnel, HCO Division. (BPL 19 Sept 67)

DIRECTOR OF SOLO AUDITING, Director of Department of Solo Auditing, Dept 12A, AOLA Division 4. (BPL 16 Sept 71R II)

DIRECTOR OF SUCCESS, Director of Department of Success, Dept 21, Public Activities Division, Division 7. (HCO PL 29 Jan 69, *Public Division Org Board Revised* (*Corrected*) [The above HCO PL has been cancelled by BPL 10 Oct 75 VII.]

DIRECTOR OF TECHNOLOGY, Mary Sue Hubbard is appointed my personal assistant for the assembly of technical data and new courses under the title of **Director of Technology**. Reg Sharpe is appointed a personal assistant as Director of Compilation including all educational aids, dictionaries and encyclopedias and films. Both appointments are non-organizational and are not part of org comm lines or command lines, being connected with my personal activities in research and being under my direction only. (HCO PL 20 Feb 65)

DIRECTOR OF TECH SERVICES, Director of Department of Tech Services, Dept 10, Technical Division 4. (BPL 4 Jan 73RC) ***Abbr.*** DTS

DIRECTOR OF TRAINING, **1.** Director of Department of Training, Dept 11, Technical Division 4. (BPL 4 Jan 73RC) **2.** the product officer of Dept 11. He gets highly trained and competent auditors, C/Ses and supervisors made in volume. (BPL 25 Feb 73R) ***Abbr.*** D of T

DIRECTOR OF VALIDITY, Director of Department of Validity, Dept 13, Correction Division. (BPL 7 Dec 71RI) ***Abbr.*** Dir Val

DIRECTOR OF ZONING, the **Director of Zoning** is a new post set up to coordinate and bring order to the Special Zone Plan in any area. It is a HASI post, not an HCO post. (HCO PL 20 JUL 60)

DIRECT RESPONSE PROMOTION, see PROMOTION, DIRECT RESPONSE.

DIRECT REVIEW, see REVIEW, DIRECT.

DIRECT SALES, see SALES, DIRECT.

DISAGREEMENT, (form of arbitrary) the receipt of a communication is an extremely important part of the sequence of actions that result in a compliance. The common reason for the non-receipt of a communication is that arbitraries (or arbitrary factors) exist in the area. **Disagreement** means the receipt point has an opinion or subscribes to a local opinion that things are otherwise than as communicated or the handling of them should be different. (BPL 10 Nov 73 II)

DISAGREEMENTS CHECK, you just ask for disagreements on this. They'll give you the disagreements. You don't tell them what they're disagreeing with. (ESTO 12, 7203C06 SO II)

DISASSOCIATION, any things, events, objects, sizes, in a wrong sequence is an out-point. The number series 3, 7, 1, 2, 4, 6, 5 is an altered sequence, or an incorrect sequence. Doing step two of a sequence of actions before doing step one can be counted on to tangle any sequence of actions. The basic outness is no sequence at all. This leads into fixed ideas. It also shows up in what is called **disassociation**, an insanity. Things connected to or similar to each other are not seen as consecutive. Such people also jump about subjectwise without relation to an obvious sequence. **Disassociation** is the extreme case where things that are related are not seen to be and things that have no relation are conceived to have. (HCO PL 19 Sept 70 III)

DISASTER, **1.** could be said to be a totality of out-points in final and sudden culmination. (HCO PL 7 July 70) **2.** is something which has not been predicted or prepared for. (6910C16 SO) **3.** a circumstance or situation that is crippling and may adversely affect a whole or part of an org. (HCO PL 31 Oct 66 I) **4.** big danger condition. (HCO PL 1 Feb 66 IV)

DISBURSEMENT, 1. an expenditure made. 2. money paid out.

DISBURSEMENT A/C, the **Disbursement A/C** is utilized for all the running expenses of the org. (HCO PL 20 Feb 63) [The above HCO PL was cancelled by BPL 10 Oct 75 IV]

DISBURSEMENT CLERK, purpose: break down income into proportions; validate bills; issue checks. (HCO PL 12 Oct 62)

DISBURSEMENT DIVISION, two accounts divisions are created. These are the Income Division and the **Disbursement Division.** The **Disbursement Division** has the responsibility of correctly disbursing the money of HCO WW such as bills, wages, mortgage payments, etc. (HCO PL 6 Jul 61)

DISBURSEMENT FILES, the Disbursement Section is responsible for the payment and recording of all sums owed. Every creditor whether paid in cash or check, whether submitting a bill or not is given a folder in the **disbursement files** and all correspondence of a business nature with that creditor, whether concerned with money or not comes to the **disbursement files.** There must be no separate business files, only the **disbursement files.** (HCO PL 6 May 64)

DISBURSEMENT OFFICER, (Gung-Ho Group) the **Disbursement Officer** pays all bills from Treasury. (HCO PL 2 Dec 68)

DISBURSEMENT SECTION, the **Disbursement Section** is responsible for the payment and recording of all sums owed. (HCO PL 6 May 64)

DISBURSEMENT VOUCHER MACHINE, exactly like an invoice machine except it says, "Disbursement voucher with the Compliments of the Hubbard Communications Office" instead of "Invoice." (HCO PL 24 Aug 59)

DISCHARGE, to permanently dismiss an employee from his work.

DISCOUNT, 1. generally, deduction or subtracted sum from a cost or price. 2. interest deducted from an amount due when payment is made. 3. interest deducted in advance from the total amount of a loan. 4. an allowance given for the payment of a debt at any time before the due date. 5. the difference between the current face value of a security over its original cost. 6. the difference between the estimated future or maturing value of an investment or benefit and its present value. 7. a percentage deducted by a banker or broker for selling securities. 8. a promissory note purchased by a bank for less than its face value and then further discounted with another bank. 9. an allowance on the list price given by a wholesaler to members of his trade.

DISCOUNTED CASH FLOW, accounting method to determine the return on investments of similar risk that have various return cash flows in order to deduct projected future benefits and thus arrive at a current value. *Abbr.* DCF

DISCOUNT HOUSE, 1. retail store that sells its wares for less than list prices. 2. In UK, a business that purchases promissory notes at a reduction, holding them until maturity or reselling them at a profit.

DISCOVERIES, the end product of a sequence of investigatory actions that begin with either a plus-point or an out-point. (HCO PL 19 Sept 70 I)

DISCRETIONARY ACCOUNT, see ACCOUNT, DISCRETIONARY.

Disestablish

DISESTABLISH, **dis** = take apart. **Establish** = put there. **Disestablish** = take apart what is put there. Thus **disestablish** means to take out terminals and tear things up. (HCO PL 7 Jul 71)

DISHONEST, disposed to lie, cheat, defraud or deceive. (HCO PL 3 May 72)

DISHONEST REGISTRATION, the Registrar promised things you didn't deliver or couldn't deliver and did strange things or arranged oddball loans, or told one and all "You can get your money back." (HCO PL 26 Oct 75)

DISHONESTY, the definition of **dishonesty** is whether or not a person is trying to hurt his fellow human beings with malicious talk, hidden actions and injustice or outright crime. (HCO PL 20 Oct 61)

DISINFLATION, a reduction of an inflationary condition to the conditions prevailing prior to inflation and marked by decreasing prices with a resulting increase in purchasing power.

DISINFORMATION, false information. (7007C30)

DISORGANIZATION, consists of each person wearing all hats regardless of assignment. (HCO PL 1 Jul 65 III)

DISPATCH, a memo from another staff member in your organization or in another. (HCO PL 10 Aug 59, *Administration in a Scn Organization*) [The above HCO PL was cancelled by BPL 10 Oct 75 II.]

DISPATCH SECTION, section in Dept 2, Dept of Communications. **Dispatch Section** routes all comms, keeps main comm center, inspects divisional comm centers, provides staff member with a comm station. (HCO PL 17 Jan 66 II)

DISPLAY BOOK, see PRESS BOOK.

DISPUTE, 1. generally, a disagreement or argument as in an employer-employee difference of opinion that threatens an operation. 2. a disagreement between an employer and a union, employees and a union, or a union leader and the government that calls for official arbitration by qualified individuals or government conciliators.

DISSEM AIDE, see CS-2.

DISSEMINATING SCN, getting the materials of Dn and Scn disseminated widely and by efficient presentation. (BPL 15 Mar 60)

DISSEMINATION, **1.** you would have to tell people what you were going to make and all kinds of things of this character, and that would come under the general heading, **dissemination.** (SH Spec 77, 6608C23) **2.** spreading or scattering broadly. The **Dissemination Division** in the org spreads information on Scn broadly, using books, magazines, etc. (HCO Admin Ltr 30 Jul 75)

DISSEMINATION DIVISION, **1.** Division 2. (HCO PL 8 Nov 73RA) **2.** a major function of the **Dissem Division:** to get people into the org for service and those who have paid; to move those into the org for service. And that is an obviously major function. (7201C12 SO) **3.** handles people who have already bought something from the org. An org which is delivering should be getting most of its income from the **Dissem Division.** (LRH ED 167 INT) **4.** Dissem puts out the particles with which the org reaches, and Dissem reges the already buying clientele. (LRH ED 159RA INT) *Abbr.* Dissem Div.

DISSEMINATION DRILL, the **Dissemination Drill** has four exact steps that must be done with a person you are disseminating to. They are (1) contact, (2) handle, (3) salvage, (4) bring to understanding. There is no set patter, nor any set words you say to the person. (HCO PL 23 Oct 65, *Dissemination Drill*)

DISSEMINATION ESTABLISHMENT OFFICER, establishes and maintains the Dissem Division. (HCO PL 7 Mar 72) *Abbr.* DEO.

DISSEMINATION SECRETARY, **1.** Div 2, Dissemination Division is headed by the **Dissemination Secretary.** (BPL 4 Jul 69R VI) **2.** creates the Dissem Div by manning it up and training its personnel in their activities by policy and sees that Dn and Scn materials are widely disseminated and readily available, sees public are procured for service and that records and files of public people, the backbone of procurement, are kept accurate and orderly and are used and that the org thereby makes adequate income. (BPL 25 Jan 76 I) **3.** purpose: to ensure wide dissemination of Dn and Scn by efficient presentation of dissemination materials. (HCO PL 26 Mar 59) *Abbr.* Dissem Sec.

DISSEM PRODUCT OFFICER, the so-called GI Product Officer is hereafter designated the **Dissem Product Officer.** (GI Prod Off was never a legal post.) (LRH ED 234R INT)

DISSEM RECEPTION, a sort of HCO post that receives bodies, work, verifies it as properly AVU okayed and PO'd for and gets the line started. (ED 459-52 Flag)

DISSOCIATIVE GROUPS, see GROUPS, DISSOCIATIVE.

DISTRIBUTE, to spread out so as to cover something. (HCO PL 8 Dec 65)

DISTRIBUTION, **1.** means put it elsewhere so that it will grow there too. (BPL 30 Jan 69R II) **2.** Division 6. (HCO PL 8 Nov 73RA) *Abbr.* Dist, Distrib.

DISTRIBUTION, 1. in marketing, flowing products from producer to ultimate customer. 2. spreading the cost of a capital expenditure to various accounts. 3. payment to stockholders or owners of dividends, property or shares. 4. the disposition by a court of law of property left where there is no legal will.

DISTRIBUTION AIDE, see CS-6.

DISTRIBUTION AIDE FB, Bureau 6 Aide FB over the Distribution Bureau. The Distribution Bureau of the FB has the purpose of: to help LRH distribute Scn by putting Scn orgs in every spot of the globe such that every conceivable geographical area is totally covered. (CBO 351RB) [This post is junior to CS-6]

DISTRIBUTION BUREAU, **1.** (Flag) the purpose of the **Distribution Bureau** (Bureau 6) is to help LRH distribute Scn by putting Scn orgs in every spot of the globe so that every conceivable geographical area is totally covered. The valuable final product of Bureau 6 is new orgs. (FBDL 443) **2.** (FOLO) the **FOLO Distribution Bureau** has the purpose to help LRH distribute Scn by converting its continental population into Scientologists and putting Scn orgs in every spot of the globe such that every conceivable geographical area in the continent is totally covered. (CBO 333R)

DISTRIBUTION CENTER, centers in ANZO that disseminate Scn to new people and select them in volume to orgs. A **distribution center** has the following functions: selling books, pulling in new people, introductory lectures, PE courses and volume selection of new people for org services. Office functions are done such as reception, keeping proper files, performing treasury actions, hiring and hatting personnel. The valuable final product of a **Distribution Center** is public arrived at orgs for service. (BO 9 ANZO, 17 Mar 74)

DISTRIBUTION CENTER INCORPORATED, **1.** the **Distribution Center, Inc.,** has assumed the staff and functions of the Silver Spring Business Service. (HCOB 14 Nov 56) **2. Distribution Center** Silver Spring handles shipping, storing, books, vitamins, manufacturing, storing and shipping tapes; invoices; secretarial to handle customer difficulties. (LRH Directive, 14 Dec 56) **3.** the **Distribution Center** and the HCO are mainly concerned with the continued advertising and handling of Dn materials. (HCO PL 25 Jan 57) *Abbr.* DCI.

DISTRIBUTION DIVISION, **1.** Its product is Scientologists, and these Scientologists of course have products of sold books, contacted people, and sending people in. (FEBC 7, 7101C23 SO III) **2.** (Division 6) handles the people who have never bought anything from an org. Mailing lists of persons who have not bought anything belong to and are used by Division 6. Information packets belong in Division 6, book selling, etc., anything with green public connected with it. Division 6 has press relations, public advertising, field staff members, franchise, etc., all of which is the reach to the broad public. Information packets, new mail lists, book sales, ads even for the Beginning Scientologist Course and even personnel are all Division 6. New unreached bodies = Division 6. People who have no real org business = Division 6. The broad public and unreached areas are reached and owned by Division 6. Without it we never grow. (HCO PL 18 Jun 65 II)

DISTRIBUTION ESTABLISHMENT OFFICER, (PEO for Public Division) establishes and maintains the Distribution Division. (HCO PL 7 Mar 72) *Abbr.* PEO.

DISTRIBUTION SECRETARY, **1.** coordinates and gets done the divisional promotional functions of Division 6 and makes Scn and the org known to the broad public. (HCO PL 20 Nov 65) **2.** Division 8 Secretary, Distribution Division. Purpose: to help LRH make the organization reproduce itself by putting out and expanding points of dissemination which contact and process the public and public bodies and which further make and guide the government of a civilization. (HCO PL 29 Jan 69) [The above HCO PL was cancelled by BPL 10 Oct 75 VII.] *Abbr.* Dist Sec.

DISTRIBUTOR, a **distributor** in the book business is one who provides books to retail sales outlets. While there is nothing wrong with a **distributor** selling a single book to a customer, the bulk of the books are sold to retail outlets, again in quantity. (HCO PL 19 Jul 65, *Discounts Central Orgs Books*)

DISTRIBUTOR, a middleman who is often the exclusive agent for one or more businesses, authorized to buy their products and services and resell them within a specific geographical area.

DISTRIBUTORS DISCOUNT, 50% is a **distributors discount**. To obtain a 50% discount on anything the purchase must consist of an order of quantity. (HCO PL 19 Jul 65, *Discounts Central Orgs Books*)

DISTRICT COMMITTEE OF EVIDENCE, the Convening Authority is the person in charge of a District Office or branch organization or the Association/Organization Secretary of the zone or the HCO Area Secretary. The **District Committee of Evidence** exists for all matters of dispute, repute or discipline in a District Office, its area, or a Scn group. Its powers are the same as any other Committee of Evidence except that of review of lower committees, and that it may not call before it, except as they volunteer, Central Organization or HCO Area personnel or other personnel or executives on higher echelons. The findings of this committee must be reviewed by an HCO Area Committee before the Convening Authority of the **District Committee of Evidence** may put the findings into effect and only those findings passed (after endorsement by the Convening Authority) by the HCO Area Committee of Evidence may be put into effect. A Central Committee of Evidence may not review a **District Committee of Evidence** findings even though convened by an Association Secretary. (HCO PL 7 Sept 63)

DISTRICT OFFICE, 1. a center operating near an org. The **DO** is part of the Central Org and its administrative lines are integrated with those of the org. Its staff are part of the org's staff but are paid according to the income of the **DO.** (HCO PL 20 Mar 64) [The above HCO PL was cancelled by BPL 10 Oct 75 V.] **2.** a **District Office** is regarded as an adjunct of its Area Central Org. The technical standard and proficiency at each **District Office** in the Technical Director's Central Org Control Area are to be under the closest possible supervision of the Area Central Org Technical Director. A **District Office** is intended to run simplified co-audit processes. (HCO PL 4 Apr 63) **3.** a **district office** is a HASI office and is part of the whole team of Scn. The purpose of a **district office** is to introduce Scn in its immediate area and provide, through the means of Clearing Co-audit Units, mass clearing as part of the project World Clear. (HCO PL 4 Jan 63) [The above HCO PL was cancelled by BPL 10 Oct 75 IV.] *Abbr.* DO.

DISTRICT OFFICERS, to enhance management and expansion of the FBO networks, **District Officers** are posted in Continental FBO offices. This is based upon the highly successful Flag Programs Chief system. Each **District Officer** is responsible for a district, which should comprise not more than five orgs, with a single-hatted **District Officer** for Sea Org orgs in any one continent. (This due to collections from Sea Org orgs being the major source of payments to Flag.) Naming of districts follows Programs Chiefs system and the **District Officer's** post title is FBO In-charge (Sea Org) (NWUS) etc. All orgs in that district are included in the **District Officer's** sphere of responsibility whether there is an FBO posted there or not. (CBO 358)

DITTY BOX, the traditional full kit of a sailor consists of (1) a sea bag (2) a "hammock" (3) a waterproof foot locker (sea chest) (4) a ditty box. The **ditty box** is a small wooden box that contains his sewing kit, needle and palm insignia, etc. It is an oblong box about 12 to 15 inches high. (FO 281)

DIVERSIFICATION, 1. in business, to widen one's activities by producing or marketing a greater range of products and services. 2. in finances, to spread out investments among several companies in order to minimize the risk of loss.

DIVIDEND, 1. interest paid on stocks or shares based on retained corporate earnings or earned surplus over a specified time such as quarterly, yearly, etc. 2. a payment made to creditors in a bankruptcy case known as a liquidation dividend. 3. a share of the profits of an insurance company distributed to policy holders.

DIVIDEND COVER, extent to which an organization reinvests earnings in itself rather than paying out in dividends to its stockholders.

DIVISION, a part, section. Example: the research **division** of a company, the engineering division of a university. (HCO Admin Ltr, 30 Jul 75)

DIVISION 1, **1.** HCO—Hubbard Communications Office in Scn orgs has the major functions of: Dept 1—org form, routing, personnel. Dept 2—communications, address, transport. Dept 3—inspection, reports (OIC), ethics. These essentially create the org and hold it there. (HCO PL 7 Feb 70 II) **2.** (Ship Org) HCO is known as the Communications Division and the 3rd Mate is its Divisional Officer. (FO 1109)

DIVISION 2, **1.** Dissemination Division. (HCO PL 7 Feb 70 II) **2.** Dissemination, **Division 2,** handles people who have bought something from an org. (HCO PL 18 Jun 65 II) **3.** the org itself consisting of organization, finance and materiel. **Division 2** has the money and materiel. (HCO PL 31 Mar 65) **4.** Technical (**Division 2**) applies all training for the org and public. (HCO PL 13 Mar 65, *Admin Technology—The Comm Member System*) **5.** training and processing. (HCO PL 5 Mar 65) **6.** (Flagship) the 2nd Mate is in charge of training and HCI (Hubbard College of Improvement)—the **2nd Division.** On the ship all auditing takes place in Div 5. (FO 2674) **7.** (Ship Org) in the **2nd Division,** which is the Preparation and Planning Division, we have the Plans Chief in Department 4, Preparations Chief of Department 5 and Department 6, Directions Chief. **Division 2** assists the Supercargo to plan remunerative activities for the entire ship or flotilla which coordinate activities of the organization. (FO 1109)

DIVISION 3, 1. Treasury. (HCO PL 8 Nov 73RA) **2. Division 3** (Service and Technical) has the technical personnel. (HCO PL 31 Mar 65) **3.** Finance. (HCO PL 13 Mar 65, *Admin Technology—The Comm Member System*) **4.** (Flagship) the Purser is in charge of **Division III** (Supply and Treasury division). (FO 2674) **5.** (Ship Org) Supply Division (FO 1109) **6.** (Ship Org) Purser's Division (FO 274)

DIVISION 4, 1. Technical Division. (HCO PL 8 Nov 73RA) **2.** Distribution Division. (HCO PL 31 Mar 65) **3.** Ship Keeping Division (FSO). (FSO 742) **4.** the Operations Division which cares for the decks, construction and other purely traditionally ship concerns—so the ship can operate as a ship. (FO 2674) **5.** (Ship Org) Deck Division. (SO Spec 3, 6910C17)

DIVISION 4A, 1. Public Clearing Division Celebrity Centre. Its valuable final product is broad public into Scn from celebrity dissemination. (BO 7 PAC, 17 Feb 74) **2.** Flagship Org, Deck Division. (OODs 12 May 74) [Per FSO 776 of 13 May 74 Division 4 is the Technical Division where **Div 4A** is the Deck or Ship Keeping Division.]

DIVISION 5, 1. Qualificatons Division. (HCO PL 31 Jul 65) **2.** Correction Division. (HCO PL 14 Aug 71RC II) **3.** the purpose of **Division 5** is to correct malfunctions in the org. The Product Correction Division. (LRH ED 107 INT)

DIVISION 6, 1. Distribution Division. (HCO PL 18 Jun 65 II) **2.** Div 6 (Public Division) informs and indoctrinates the public to drive them in. The result of course is driven in public pouring into the org. Every function is connected with this. (HCO PL 14 Nov 71RA II) **3. Div 6** reaches into the public. Without that reach the org becomes a withdrawn island out of comm with the world. **Div 6** functioning keeps the org at least a Grade Zero Release. **Div 6** is the org's reach. (LRH ED 159R-1 INT) **4.** a brief description of **Division 6** functions is as follows: Public Relations Area Control, voluminous public contact work, heavy public book sales, attractive convincing introductory demonstrations and miniature courses, active groups and well paid field staff members. (HCO PL 14 Nov 71RA II) **5.** (Nine Division Org) Public Relations Division (HCO PL 24 Jun 70R II) **6.** (Distribution) this division keeps the new people coming in, businesses continuing and expands an organization. (HCO PL 24 Apr 68 II) **7.** (Nine Division Org) Public Planning Division (HCO PL 26 Oct 67) **8.** (Flagship Org) Port Captain's Office (FSO 776) **9.** (Flag Nine Division Org) Flag Promotion Division (FO 2525)

DIVISION 6 BADGE,

(HCO PL 24 Apr 68 II)

DIVISION 7, 1. this division is normally called the Executive Division. (FO 1109) **2.** (Nine Division Org) Public Service Division. (HCO PL 24 Jun 70R II) **3.** (Nine Division Org) Public Activities Division. (HCO PL 26 Oct 67) **4.** (Flag Nine Division Org) Public Contact Division. (FO 2633) **5.** (Flag Nine Division Org) Flag Contact Division. (FO 2525)

DIVISION 7 ESTABLISHMENT OFFICER, Establishment Officer for **Division 7**, the Executive Division. He is not the "Executive Esto." He carries out all the Esto duties for this division. (HCO PL 7 Mar 72)

DIVISION 8, 1. (Nine Division Org) Public Sales Division. (HCO PL 24 Jun 70R II) **2.** (for AOs)

International Executive Division. (FO 1939) **3.** (Nine Division Org) Distribution Division. (HCO PL 26 Jan 69) [The above HCO PL was cancelled by BPL 10 Oct 75 VII.] **4.** (Nine Division Org) Success Division. (HCO PL 26 Oct 67) **5.** (Flag Nine Division Org) Flag Field Division. (FO 2525)

DIVISION 9, **1.** (Flag Nine Division Org) the Office of LRH is in **Division 9** in any Scn Nine Division Organization. The engine room headed by the Chief Engineer, is also in **Div 9** as well as the various Flag Bureaus; such as the Organizing Bureau and Action Bureau. The LRH Communicator is in charge of Flag **Division 9.** (FO 2674) **2.** the Public Divisions are the three former departments of Division 6, each one becoming a division in its own right. The Executive Division now becomes **Division 9** instead of 7. (HCO PL 26 Oct 68)

DIVISIONAL AIDE, aide for their same numbered division. (FO 3064)

DIVISIONAL COMM CENTER, each **divisional communication center** is placed in the divisional working area with a basket for each staff member in that division plus a divisional in-basket and a divisional out-basket. (HCO PL 4 Jan 66 III)

DIVISIONAL CONFERENCES, (Sea Organization) each division has a **Divisional Conference.** It is held by the divisional officer and is attended by all persons in the division, officers, petty officers and hands. Conferences are called to advise and inform and to ask for advice and information. A crew cannot function in the absence of data, plans and intentions. (FO 1021)

DIVISIONAL HEAD, the executive who controls and is responsible for the operation of a division in an organization.

DIVISIONAL OFFICERS COUNCIL, **1.** consists of the LRH Comm and each divisional head of the flagship. The LRH Comm will preside as Chairman of the meetings. A secretary and Master at Arms for the **Council** will be appointed by the members. The **Divisional Officers Council** meeting will be held every Monday at 1300 hours. The sole purposes of the **Divisional Officers Council** are: (1) to coordinate targets amongst divisional heads (2) to propose new policy, and (3) to keep the org informed of the actions of all divisions. (FO 1822) **2.** there will be no separate Production Council and Operation Council. All business of the two Councils are combined into the **DOC.** A council is a group of persons assembled to handle the administrative and legislative functions of an organization. (FSO 138) **3.** they are bodies to approve or modify prepared CSW of members for passing by higher authority. They are not planning bodies which originate. It can approve, reject or modify. Its individual members prepare CSW for the committee before its meeting. Authority senior to the committee is then assisted. The heads of divisions should be the only ones present at a **DOC**, anyone originating must do so only by CSW for the **DOC** beforehand. It then approves, rejects or modifies as a body. This then goes to command for ordering and issue. (FO 2653) ***Abbr.*** DOC.

DIVISIONAL ORDERS, (Issue type) each division has its own order line to its staffs or to its opposite numbered division. The order is followed by the place and org name. The paper is color flashed for the division. (HCO PL 24 Sept 70R)

DIVISIONAL ORGANIZERS, **1.** all those persons now styled or titled Executive Secretary Communicators are changed. World Wide and Continental Executive Divisions (as they expand) are to have on staff and as assistants to the Advisory Council (WW or Continental) executives to be termed **Divisional Organizers** (Division type), (location). The purpose of a **Divisional Organizer** is as follows: to help LRH organize and maintain and supply the division represented (type) in the sphere designated (locales) with all needful data, policy, tech, programs, examinations, plans, courses and activities of every kind needful to the success of that type of division and to organize and raise in efficiency that type of division in the locales for which the **Divisional Organizer** is responsible. (HCO PL 1 Nov 66 I) **2.** there are seven different titles of **Divisional Organizers**: 7 **Divisional Organizer**, Executive. 1 **Divisional Organizer**, HCO. 2 **Divisional Organizer**, Dissem. 3 **Divisional Organizer**, Treasury. 4 **Divisional Organizer**, Tech. 5 **Divisional Organizer**, Qual. 6 **Divisional Organizer**, Distribution. The title is followed by "WW" for Worldwide or the Continental abbreviation for Continental Orgs or, if Area Orgs grow sufficiently large, for area designation. A **Divisional Organizer** is senior to any Secretary in his division but not to an Executive Secretary. He holds the nominal rank of Secretary. It must be at once visible that what a division needs most are its materials, supplies and programs. The **Divisional Organizer** not only assembles and supplies all this or sees it is supplied, he or she makes sure it is properly used or exhibited. (HCO PL 1 Nov 66 I) **3.** (Worldwide) the Ad Council would be composed, on an international basis, of the Continental Representatives from each continental district of which there are five and probably one from Saint Hill since it really isn't part of a Continental District. And then to these are added a bloke called the **Divisional Organizer**. Now this fellow is the representative of every divisional secretary of that type of division in the whole world. For that type of division he is responsible for every piece of its organizational materials and everything that applies to that type of division. So, if some secretary of that type of division in Poughkeepsie or Keokuk hasn't got any policy letters that cover so and so and so and so why they would write to this fellow to find it out. If an org can't get its books it knows who to write to. It writes to the **Divisional Organizer** Dissem Worldwide. And he would catalyse it and go ahead and do that. He would know exactly where an org stands. He is judged by the composite gross divisional statistics of that type of division in the world. He can't give an order unless it's passed by the Ad Council. (SH Spec 81, 6611C01) *Abbr.* DO.

DIVISIONAL PACK, all relevant policies of the division of the staff member. (HCO PL 2 Aug 71 III) [The above HCO PL was cancelled by BPL 10 Oct 75 IX.]

DIVISIONAL SECRETARY, 1. the head of a division is the **Divisional Secretary**. He is the product officer of his division. His boss is the Commanding Officer or Executive Director. He is senior to the divisional Esto or Chief Esto. He is not the divisional Esto's boss. The Exec Esto is. (HCO PL 7 Mar 72) **2.** an expert in one division. (FEBC 3, 7101C18 SO II)

DIVISION 7 SECRETARY, this new post is the secretary who cares for the personnel, communications and administration and quarters of the Executive Division. The **Division 7 Secretary** is called just that as any other title is in conflict with the offices of the division. This Secretary holds an Executive Division Ad Comm. This is junior to the Ad Council and is on a par with other division Ad comms. The rank of this secretary is the same as all other division secretaries and in privilege is just below that of the HCO Area Sec, who is the first secretary of the organization in privilege and precedence. The **Div 7 Sec** never issues orders to other divisions and has no authority to do so. (HCO PL 20 Jan 66 II)

DO, 1. is often defined as "talk" or "refer." But that doesn't get anything done. **Do** is the action which leads to **done**. (OODs 24 Apr 72) **2.** define **do** as **doing** something effective and different than talking. (ED 177 Flag)

DOCS I/C, the post of **Docs I/C** comes under the Ship's Rep. This person sees that all passports are current and available. He gets seaman's papers made up for new crew, he does the filing, he keeps the val docs and legal papers. He looks after contracts, visas, immunization certs, and keeps the ship's stamp in his cabinet. He makes xerox copies of original val docs, makes up crew lists, get declarable items lists, informs Ship's Rep of certificate expirations, etc. (FO 1933)

DOCTOR, 1. through the ages the term **doctor** has meant "a learned man" but in modern times has been strained by its preemption by medical **doctors** and psychiatrists. (HCO PL 14 Feb 66) **2.** the cook is generally addressed as **Doctor**. (FO 87)

DOCTOR OF DIVINITY, religion is basically a philosophic teaching designed to better the civilization into which it is taught. Backed fully by the precedent of all the ages concerning teachings, a Scientologist has a better right to call himself a priest, a minister, a missionary, a **Doctor of Divinity**, a faith healer or a preclear than any other man who bears the insignia of religion of the Western world. I do not see any inconsistency of any kind in the issuance to those well-schooled and well-skilled in Scn the degree of **Doctor of Divinity** as a passport into those areas where they are needed. (PAB 32)

DOCTOR OF SCIENTOLOGY, 1. this is an honorary degree, not granted for scholastic reasons but is purely an award to those who at Class III or IV perform signal service to Scn activities. An HCS or HGA (St. Hill) is understood to qualify. (HCO PL 12 Aug 63) **2. D. Scn** (Commonwealth) or Hubbard Graduate Scientologist (US). (HCO PL 12 Feb 61) **3.** an HGA is senior to HCA and HPA. and the **Doctor of Scientology** degree is senior to HGA. It is an honor award and may be made by nomination or selection; either way it is for those who are consistently producing excellent results in their own fields and to form a grade by which these recruits can be recognized. (PAB 6) See HUBBARD GRADUATE AUDITOR.

DOESN'T KNOW HOW TO PLAY THE PIANO, we say a division head **"Doesn't know how to play the piano"** when he knows so little about org form that he continually violates it by giving his various staff members duties that do not match their hats or posts. (HCO PL 28 Jul 72)

D of P's CHECK TYPE 1, see CHECK TYPE ONE.

DO IT YOURSELF THERAPY, we will call co-audit **Do it yourself therapy**. (HCO PL 23 Jan 61)

DOLLAR EARNINGS, the sum of a worker's take-home pay not including overtime pay or additional pay for working a different shift.

DOMESTIC CORPORATION, see CORPORATION, DOMESTIC.

DOMESTIC EXPORTS, articles produced and exported from the same country.

DOMESTIC STAFF, **domestic staff** is considered a unit of Department 1, under my personal secretary. It includes the butler, cook, housekeepers, nanny, driver, and the outside grounds staff which in turn is headed by the head gardener. (HCO PL 28 May 64)

DOMESTIC UNIT, looks after Saint Hill domestic matters and family. Takes care of the Manor itself and those living in it. (HCO PL 18 Dec 64, *Saint Hill Org Board*)

DORMANT PARTNER, a partner who is not known as a partner to the public or to creditors and who does not participate in the operation of the business but who, nevertheless, is among those liable for its debts.

DOUBLE ASSIGN, assign two or more hats to one person. (HCO PL 17 Nov 64)

DOUBLE CALL, a visit paid to a customer by a senior management person as well as one of his juniors such as a salesman or distributor as in the case of a field inspection.

DOUBLE CONFRONT, two object confront. You make him confront the radar screen and then turn around and confront the helm and then confront the screen and then confront the helm and then confront the screen and then confront the helm. Any hypnotism he has feelings of, of having confronted the screen will start to discharge at a remarkable rate of speed and he'll go into a trance and then he'll come right out of it. Two objects, very simple commands. (ESTO 12, 7203C06 SO II)

DOUBLED UP, means twice as many persons to be posted. (ED 51 Flag)

DOUBLE EMPLOYMENT, see EMPLOYMENT, DOUBLE.

DOUBLE ENTRY, the system of bookkeeping almost universally used today in the Commonwealth and the US is called **double entry** bookkeeping. It is called this because every transaction is recorded twice. (HCO PL 14 Nov 70 IV)

DOUBLE ISSUE, when an item to be mimeo'd is a **double issue** i.e. Flag Order ______ (number) also ED ______ (number) Flag. (FO 3240)

DOUBLE LIABILITY, personal liability that is double the amount of the investment made by a stockholder, a contingency which currently prevails in some states only if a corporation cannot pay its own obligations.

DOUBLE PRICING, see PRICING, DOUBLE.

DOUBLE TAXATION, short term for double taxation of dividends wherein the federal government levies a tax on corporate profits and when remaining profits are disbursed as dividends, stockholders may be taxed again as additional income.

DOUBLE WORK, this is the way you do **double work.** You pick up a dispatch or a piece of work, look it over and then put it aside to do later, then later you pick it up and read again and only then do you do it. This of course doubles your traffic just like that. (HCO PL 29 May 63)

DOUBT, **1.** when one cannot make up one's mind as to an individual, a group, org or project, a condition of **doubt** exists. (HCO PL 6 Oct 67) **2.** a not done job is **doubt**. (ED 62 Flag)

DOUBT FORMULA, the **formula** is: (1) inform oneself honestly of the actual intentions and activities of that group, project or org brushing aside all bias and rumor. (2) examine the statistics of the individual, group, project or org. (3) decide on the basis of "the greatest good for the greatest number of dynamics" whether or not it should be attacked, harmed or suppressed or helped. (4) evaluate oneself or one's own group, project or org as to intentions and objectives. (5) evaluate one's own or one's group, project or org's statistics. (6) join or remain in or befriend the one which progresses toward the greatest good for the greatest number of dynamics and announce the fact publicly to both sides. (7) do everything possible to improve the actions and statistics of the person, group, project or org one has remained in or joined. (8) suffer on up through the conditions in the new group if one has changed sides, or the conditions of the group one has remained in if wavering from it has lowered one's status. (HCO PL 6 Oct 67)

DOWN ON THE LEFT, you use an OCA simply and totally this way; **down on the left** below the center line = wildly screamingly out of valence; down on the right = evil purpose, wildly nuts. (ESTO 3, 7203C02 SO I)

DOWN ON THE RIGHT, see DOWN ON THE LEFT.

DOWNSTAT, **1.** one with low, declining statistics. (HCO PL 31 Jan 69, *Humanitarian Objective and Gung-Ho Groups*) **2. downstats** are defined as ill or enturbulated persons. (SO ED 36 INT)

Downstat (Def. 1)

DOWN STATISTIC, **1.** the purpose of the org is to get the show on the road and keep it going. This means production. Every division is a production unit. It makes or does something that can have a statistic to see if it goes up or down. Example: a typist gets out 500 letters in one week. That's a statistic. If the next week the same typist gets out 600 letters that's an up statistic. If the typist gets out 300 letters that's a **down statistic.** (HCO PL 1 Sept 65 VII) **2.** the current number is less than it was. (HCO PL 16 Dec 65) **3.** that is to say the statistics went down. (SH Spec 62, 6506C25)

DOWN TICK, expression that refers to a stock transaction made at a price lower than the previous transaction, also called a minus-tick.

DRAFT, same as Bill of Exchange.

DRAMATIZATION, see ROLE-PLAYING.

DRAMATIZATION OF WITHHOLDS, I have recently unearthed a widespread aberration that underlies the withhold or obstruction of vital information and wanted to warn you to be on the lookout for it. It is, simply stated, **dramatization of withholds**. This is not just the person with withholds, this is the person who **dramatizes withholds** by preventing the relay, exposure or free distribution of vital information. (HCO PL 19 Oct 74)

DRAMATIZE, to act under the influence of past incidents as dictated by those incidents in the bank. The guy is replaying something now that happened in the past, out of its time and context and out of his control. (HCO PL 19 Oct 74)

DRAWBACK, when goods or products are imported a customs fee is paid. If they are then re-exported after temporary storage or further processing, one receives a refund of the customs fee called a drawback or customs drawback.

DRAWING ACCOUNT, see ACCOUNT, DRAWING.

DRILLING, that action done over and over until it is smooth, competent and professional. (OODs 7 Jun 70)

DRILLS, **1.** just actions the student has to become familiar with before doing processes. The actual process is never used as a **drill**. Because it is left unflat. A **drill** takes the action the auditor will use when doing a process and gets him familiar with it. (HCO PL 17 May 65, *Tech Div, Qual Div, Urgent CCHs*) **2.** the aim and object of **drills** are to make the duties assigned to individual men in preparation for an emergency so well understood and so well known that the duties will be dependably performed under abnormal conditions. Each **drill** has several stations and particular duties. It isn't enough just to know the location of your assigned post. You must know: (1) what your post is; (2) where it is; (3) who's in charge; (4) specifics of what you actually do, operation of equipment, etc. (FO 910) **3.** disciplined, repetitious exercise as a means of teaching and perfecting a skill or procedure. (ED 118 Flag) **4. drills** have several purposes. To groove in a team action is one principal one. To test a system fully. To groove in lines. (OODs 26 Feb 71)

DROP A BALL, a Central Org orders an important number of books or meters. The order gets messed up. The next thing we know we are in a cable rush-to-fill-the-order emergency and up to our ears in phone calls, special letters, etc. Now somebody **dropped a ball** somewhere and routine activities were not carried out. Thus they became emergency activities. (HCO PL 18 Dec 64, *Administrative Traffic Trend*)

DROPPED TIME, time that should be noted and isn't would be an out-point of **dropped time**. It is a special case of an omitted datum. (HCO PL 19 Sept 70 III)

D ROUTING, goes inside one's own org to anyone else in the org up or down. Dispatches forwarded are called **D Routing** with the person to whom addressed clearly marked. **D Routing** is entirely limited to one's own org and is not forwarded across to another org except when demanded or as an enclosure in other dispatches. **D Routing** means "to a specific post in one's own org, superior or junior." (HCO PL 13 Mar 65 II)

DRUCKER, PETER, US management consultant and writer known for advancing corporate planning and the concept of management by objectives.

DRUG PUSHER, definition of **drug pusher**: to urge or promote the use of drugs. To urge the selling of drugs, to actively promote or sell drugs. (FO 2712)

Drug Pusher

DUBLIN TYPE PE COMM COURSE, it will be called the Zero Comm Course. This consists of the same TRs as the real Comm Course but run without the coaching flunking. (HCO PL 22 Apr 65, *Level Zero Comm Course*)

DUMMY, 1. a scrap paper expression of the idea. Includes in the same package the written material (called copy), all surveys used, captions, photos and art work. (FO 3574) **2.** (graphic arts) there is a **dummy**—this is very rough. Usually it has copy and even illustrations, graphs or photos in another separate pack. (ED 459-51 Flag) **3.** a **dummy** in the graphic arts business is a pack of paper folded or stapled to show what goes on what page. It is the first step of design. It gives the general impression. After a **dummy** is done, a layout showing the exact lines, spaces, photo placements and size is done. (ED 459-49 Flag) **4.** in any promotional piece, the first thing submitted. A drawing (rough) of the item showing general layout but with the exact copy (words) to be used in the final product. (ED 62 FAO)

DUMMY DIRECTOR, director of an organization in name only, appointed to meet the number required under law. He holds no company stock and votes as he is instructed by the owner or chairman of the board.

DUMMY RUN, **1.** there's two types of **dummy runs.** There's just plain **dummy runs.** You just go through the organization's public lines one way or the other, and try to get hired or something like this, or try to take advantage of this new free offer, and go into the proper point and just try to get it. You sometimes find yourself in practically a fist fight. The other type of **dummy run** is a bull-bait, and you take a whole bunch of questions which the public would be prone to ask. Your **bull-bait dummy runs** pay off because the **bull-bait dummy runs** test the personnel. The plain **dummy run** just tests the line. Does the line exist? (FEBC 10, 7101C24 SO III) **2.** The **dummy run drill** is designed to test that the org's public lines are there, functioning smoothly, and do not Q and A or get thrown off by originations of the public, but continue to flow, handle and channel the public individual toward service and further service. (BPL 3 Nov 70R I) —*v.* **1.** this means going through the place pretending to be the principal particle. (HCO PL 25 Jul 72) **2.** means start a minor particle down the line so it is cleared at each point. (ED 459-54 Flag)

DUMPING, see UNLOADING.

DUMPING ONE'S MOs FOR THE ORG TO DO, any misionaires who, entering an org to which they have been sent, persuade the org to accomplish their MOs for them, thus escaping any actual work or admin involved are subject to Committee of Evidence. **Dumping one's MOs for the org to do** is the descriptive phrase. (FO 2662)

DUPLISTICKERS, when the Director of Registration receives a copy of a selection slip sent in by a field staff member, selecting someone to the org for training or processing, he types the name and address of the selectee on **duplistickers**. These **duplistickers** are mucilage backed slips of paper that come on a roll. Putting carbon between them gives one an original and copies. These can be torn off their long strip and pasted on envelopes. (HCO PL 12 Jan 66)

DUSTBIN CHECK, see CHECK, DUSTBIN.

DUTCH AUCTION, 1. a public sale in which items are gradiently reduced in price until a buyer is found. **2.** a sale in which the auctioneer takes secret bids with the competitors unaware of each other's identity and relying on the auctioneer's word regarding amounts bid.

DUTY OFFICER, 1. there is a **Duty Officer** appointed by the Flag Executive Office Manager daily to do expediting and comm functions requiring footwork so that all the Flag Executive Office Unit staff will not be pulled off their cycles in progress. Routine requests should be given to him. (FO 2381) [The term **Duty Officer** more generally applies to an officer or person on duty covering specific duties often in rotation with other officers.] **2.** in Condition II the Conning Officer passes his orders as in Condition III to the OOW and calls the Captain on any change. But there is a **Duty Officer** junior to the OOW who keeps the watch in order and attends to the ship internally, such as loose boats or lines, etc. The attention of the OOW in Condition II is outside the ship. (FO 80)

DUTY PR, the purpose of a **Duty PR** is to personally assist LRH in any PR actions, events, activities necessary during the 24 hour period of watch, as well as to keep the crew informed of what the Commodore is doing and needs and wants at any particular time. (COLRHED 168)

DWINDLING SPIRAL OF CONTROL, one must be willing to leave certain parts of the world uncontrolled. If he cannot, he rapidly drops downscale and gets into a situation where he is obsessively attempting to control things which he never will be able to control and thus renders himself unhappy, begins to doubt his ability to control those things which he actually should be able to control and so at length loses his ability to control anything. And this, in essence, is what in Scn we call the **dwindling spiral of control.** (*POW*, p. 64)

DYNAMICS, there could be said to be eight urges (drives, impulses) in life. These we call **dynamics**. These are motives or motivations. We call them the **eight dynamics**. The **first dynamic** is the urge toward existence as one's self. Here we have individuality expressed fully. This can be called the **self dynamic**. The **second dynamic** is the urge toward existence as a sexual or bisexual activity. This **dynamic** actually has two divisions. **Second dynamic** (a) is the sexual act itself and the **second dynamic** (b) is the family unit, including the rearing of children. This can be called the **sex dynamic**. The **third dynamic** is the urge toward existence in groups of individuals. Any group or part of an entire class could be considered to be a part of the **third dynamic**. The school, the society, the town, the nation, are each part of the **third dynamic**, and each one is a **third dynamic**. This can be called the **group dynamic**. The **fourth dynamic** is the urge toward existence as mankind. Whereas the white race would be considered a **third dynamic**, all the races would be considered the **fourth dynamic**. This can be called the **mankind dynamic**. The **fifth dynamic** is the urge toward existence of the animal kingdom. This includes all living things whether vegetable or animal. The fish in the sea, the beasts of the field, or of the forest, grass, trees, flowers or anything directly and intimately motivated by life. This can be called the **animal dynamic**. The **sixth dynamic** is the urge toward existence as the physical universe. The physical universe is composed of matter, energy, space and time. In Scn we take the first letter of each of these words and coin a word, mest. This can be called the **universe dynamic**. The **seventh dynamic** is the urge toward existence as or of spirits. Anything spiritual, with or without identity, would come under the heading of the **seventh dynamic**. This can be called the **spiritual dynamic**. The **eighth dynamic** is the urge toward existence as infinity. This is also identified as the Supreme Being. It is carefully observed here that the science of Scn does not intrude into the **dynamic of the Supreme Being**. This is called the **eighth dynamic** because the symbol of infinity stood upright makes the numeral "8." This can be called the infinity or **God dynamic**. (*FOT*, pp. 36-38)

DYNAMIC SORT OUT ASSESSMENT, HCO Bulletin 2 December 1974, *Dynamic Sort Out Assessment*. This gets those dynamics that are charged and handles them. Increases social personality and even can shift valences. (LRH ED 257 INT)

E

EARNED INCOME, income earned for services rendered; wages, salary.

EARNINGS, 1. the amount of money (wages, bonuses, overtime pay, commissions, etc.) one receives for a job done or services rendered. 2. amount of profits available for dividing up among shareholders after taxes and dividends on preferred shares have been paid.

EARNINGS/DIVIDEND RATIO, the ratio of actual profits to dividends paid.

EARNINGS DRIFT, the increase in wages above national rates due to local conditions including higher local rates, more overtime, local bargaining agreements, payment-by-results plans, etc.

ECHELONS, on any command or communication channel there are always a certain number of points extending from source through relay points down to the final receipt or action point. These may be very numerous. Some may be beyond the authority of any evaluator. But each is capable of having its own situation that will cause an evaluation of the receipt or action point to fail. These can be called **echelons** or step like formations. The receipt or action point that is to comply finally with the program may be the subject of hidden sources of effect in the relay points of any program or order. (HCO PL 25 May 73)

ECONOMETRICS, a branch of economics employing mathematical and statistical techniques to establish economic relationships from economic data.

ECONOMIC GROWTH, the amount of expansion in a country's wealth and survival potential resulting from the management and prudent use of its money, products, resources, etc.

ECONOMICS, **1.** the word originally meant "the science or art of managing a house or household" and that is still its first meaning. From this grew up a study of the whole community as a connected activity. (HCO PL 27 Nov 71) **2.** when one begins to receive and spend money he gets into a field known as **economics.** (HCO PL 27 Nov 71) **3.** in modern language means the social science that studies the production, distribution and consumption (using) of commodities (things). (HCO PL 27 Nov 71)

ECONOMY, 1. the management of the use of the income, products and resources of a country, state, group, etc. 2. the careful management of the use of money, products, resources, etc., so as to prevent wastage, promote efficient utilization and provide for future needs.

ED AREA ESTATES, a new issue is created (**ED Area Estates**). It is for use by all (Flag **area**) **Estates** COs and execs. It should publish evals, programs, personnel, checklists, checksheets and all other materials that apply to all or any estates units in the Flag **area.** It is issued to all **estates** personnel. (ED 1 Area Estates)

ED FB, there shall be a mimeo issue which is for **FB** use and for the communication of orders and information into the **FB,** where the contents of such shall concern only the **FB.** They shall be called **EDs FB.** They are numbered consecutively. **EDs FB** may be originated from within the **FB** and approved by LRH Comm **FB.** The prior approval of the Supercargo or Chief Officer is required on any **ED FB** originated within any of their respective divisions and affecting only the divisions of that officer. **ED's** affecting across the portions of the org require Exec Council approval before issue authority is given. (ED 1 FB)

ED FLAG, an **ED Flag** deals with internal bureaux and divisional type functions, always concerned only with **Flag** itself. An **ED Flag** is distributed broadly aboard to bureaux and crew. They are not distributed to students or pcs. (ED 1 Flag)

EDITORIAL, type of article other than straight news usually included in a newspaper. **Editorials** reflect opinion and viewpoint of the paper. An **editorial** is generally short, varying from a sentence or two to 1000 words or more. It usually has a news peg, that is an introductory statement announcing the subject and tying it to a news development. Forceful and persuasive arguments are marshalled from logical pattern to logical pattern to convince the reader. The **editorial** writer also considers what arguments may be raised in rebuttal and raises them to answer in advance. The **editorial** ends with a firm conclusion, clearly and reasonably stated. The purpose is to have a desired effect on the reader. (BPL 10 Jan 73R)

EDITORIAL DIRECTOR, purpose: to keep material in publications within organizational policy, and to prepare publishable material. (HCO PL 12 Oct 62)

EDITORIAL - IN - CHARGE, (the Publishing Section) supervises or handles all make up, proofs, proofing and final publication of all items published. Sees to it that publishing schedules for magazines and books are met. (HCO PL 18 Dec 64, *Saint Hill Org Board*)

EDUCATION, the process of placing data in the recalls of another. (PAB 110)

EDUCATIONAL AIDS ADVISOR, advises on all **educational aids** materials to be manufactured, tapes, films, TV materials, charts, animated **aids.** (HCO PL 18 Dec 64, *Saint Hill Org Board*)

EDUCATIONAL AIDS IN-CHARGE, supervises or manufactures the arranging, making and stocking of all **educational aids.** (HCO PL 18 Dec 64, *Saint Hill Org Board*)

EDUCATIONAL AIDS SECTION, manufactures and stocks all visual and aural **educational aids** such as tapes, films, records, charts, animated graphs or structures. (HCO PL 18 Dec 64, *Saint Hill Org Board*)

EDUCATION PROGRAM, basically one of collecting together all the vast amount of **educational** material contained in Scn, compiling these into and evolving books and courses on: (a) how to study, (b) how to teach, (c) a workable **education** system, in such a way that the basics of these technologies are enumerated and presented and exporting these so that the technologies go straight into the society, and are taken up and used with tremendous velocity through the English speaking world. (FO 2021)

EFFECTIVENESS, the degree to which one's actions accomplish one's plans or goals.

EFFECTIVE PROMOTION, it would be something that was answered and preferably answered with a body. (FEBC 12, 7102C03 SO II)

EFFICIENCY, the ability to play the game to hand. **Inefficiency** could be defined as an inability to play the game to hand, with a necessity to invent games with things which one should actually be able to control. (*POW*, p. 63)

EFFICIENCY, 1. the level of resourcefulness one displays for achieving what is desired without the wastage of time, personnel, materials, etc. 2. the ability to utilize things (personnel, materials, time, money, energy, etc.) to attain desired purposes and goals.

EFFICIENCY EXPERTS, 1. the word mission may now be used to designate only a Sea Org official mission. It has unlimited ethics powers. Their members are called "missionaires." The word inspection shall be used to designate WW or Continental Org parties sent out. Their members are **efficiency experts.** They have no ethics powers but may recommend action to EC WW or EC Continental on their return. (HCO PL 15 Sept 68)

EFFICIENCY EXPERTS, persons who are familiar enough with an area of operation to spot inefficiencies in the area and make or advise on appropriate corrections.

EFFICIENCY RATING, see RATING, EFFICIENCY.

EIGHT DIVISIONS, there are **eight divisions** at Saint Hill. The difference is that it has two Executive Divisions, one Division 7 for the world, one for the Saint Hill Org. (HCO PL 26 Jan 66)

EIGHTH DYNAMIC, superior life beings is all that is a **dynamic** of. There always are going to be superior life beings around so it is a **dynamic**, a definite **dynamic.** (SH Spec 30, 6407C15)

EIGHT HOUR RULE, staff members must not do more than **eight hours** private auditing in any one week. (HCO PL 21 Jun 62) See JOHANNESBURG RULE.

EIGHTY-TWENTY RULE, the idea that only 20% of things (sales, products, services, outlets, etc.) are very significant and result in 80% of all business activity.

ELASTIC, see DEMAND ELASTICITY.

ELASTIC DEMAND, see DEMAND, ELASTIC.

EL CANAY, there is an old story about the Rough Riders, a regiment in the Spanish-American War. Their most famous exploit was the taking of San Juan Hill (Cuba). The orders of the day were posted and stated explicitly that they were to "jump off" from **El Canay** at five o'clock the following morning and were to take San Juan Hill. The Rough Riders awoke at 4:30 A.M. to discover that one small thing had been omitted from their plans: they had, as yet, to take **El Canay.** (*Scn Jour 14-G*)

ELECTRICAL, **electrical** is another hat under the Chief Engineer, Dept 21. **Electrical** is the supply and conduct of **electricity** in the ship. (FO 212)

ELECTRONIC ATTESTATION, [The concept of **electronic attestation** involves an auditor listening to and fully noting the rhythm, quality and presence of LRH model auditing tapes and doing TRs long and hard to get his auditing to sound like LRH auditing for his class. The auditor makes a tape of his sessions and compares it to LRH tapes till he is satisfied that his own auditing sounds like LRH auditing and that his TR 0, 1 and 2 are comparable to LRH's as are the rhythm, quality, presence and impingement of the auditor's comm cycle. For SHs and AOs the auditor has to have witnessed closed-circuit TV and observed sessions accurately as well as appeared on closed-circuit TV and been passed on by the auditors assembled as to TRs and presence and metering. For Flag there is the requirement that no one could tell the difference between this auditor's auditing presence, impingement and TRs and that of LRH for his class. All the above is **attested** to among other points on a checksheet, subject to a minimum penalty of a condition of liability for false attestation. **Electronic attestation** requirements are more fully covered on BPL 8 Nov 71RB.]

ELECTRONICS, **electronics** is instruments and devices used in communication systems and navigational aids. Electrical is the supply and conduct of electricity in the ship. (FO 212)

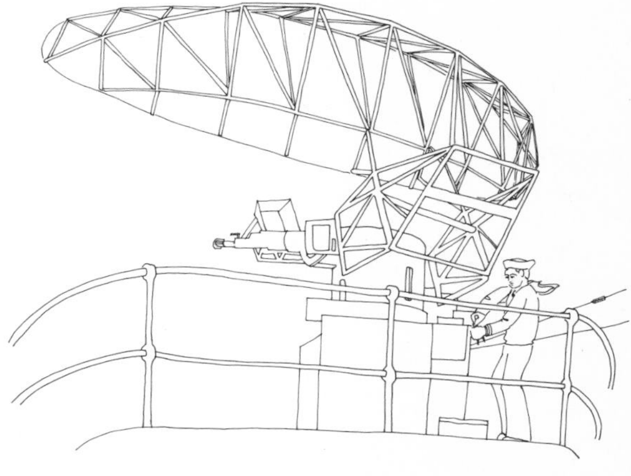

Electronics

ELEMENTARY EMERGENCY FORMULA, the **elementary emergency formula** for a down org is: (1) promote, promote, promote. (2) then change bad spots and reorganize. (3) then economize, cut off all purchase orders except postage, communications and rent. (4) get ready to deliver to the people who will be coming in as result of the promotion and deliver. (HCO PL 1 Sept 65 III)

EMERGENCY, 1. arguments as to what constitutes an **emergency** are settled by the test, "Are they costing or will they cost time or money or loss?" (FO 3195-1) **2.** an unpredictable circumstance which necessitates fast and unplanned handling. (HCO PL 18 Dec 64, *Reissue Series 21 Administrative Traffic Trend*) **3.** they weren't predicted. That's what makes an **emergency.** Did you know that? That's just a failure to predict. (SH Spec 230, 6301C15)

EMERGENCY BOARD, **board** kept by the **Emergency** Officer. On it he posts, with a time-date marked on it, those items requiring handling. These can be a slip of paper with the situation noted or a copy of the actual communication. These remain on the **board** until handled. (FO 3195)

EMERGENCY DRILLS, all **emergency drills** are made up in duplicate for the port and starboard watch. This is so that the full handling of such **emergencies** can be done when half the crew only is aboard or when part of a crew, as in Condition III or II is on watch at sea. Some of the **drills** so arranged are: man overboard **drill**, severe injury **drill**, fire **drill**, sudden leaks **drill**, anchor dragging **drill**, collision **drill**, sea damage **drill**, small boat capsize **drill**, abandon ship **drill.** (BO 28 12 Jun 67)

Emergency Drills

EMERGENCY FOOD STORES, those **food** supplies which are planned to give the ship's company balanced meals for a set period of time in the event of an unplanned for **emergency** (such as breakdown at sea, port epidemics or polluted foods, military blockades, change of destination, slow headway because of storms or ship damage, etc.) and as such are only used by Captain's order. (FO 2002)

EMERGENCY FORMULA, (1) promote, that applies to an organization. To an individual you had better say produce. That's the first action regardless of any other action, regardless of anything else, why that is the first thing you have to put their attention on. The first broad, big action which you take is promote. Exactly what is promotion? Well, look it up in the dictionary. It is making things known; it is getting things out; it is getting one's self known, getting one's products out. (2) change your operating basis. If for instance you went into a condition of emergency and then you didn't change after you had promoted, you didn't make any changes in your operation, well you just head for another condition of **emergency.** So that has to be part of it, you had better change your operating basis, you had better do something to change the operating basis, because that operating basis lead you into an **emergency** so you sure better change it. (3) economize. (4) then prepare to deliver. (5) part of the condition of **emergency** contains this little line—you have got to stiffen discipline or you have got to stiffen ethics. Organizationally when a state of **emergency** is assigned supposing the activity doesn't come out of that emergency, regardless of what caused the **emergency,** supposing the activity just doesn't come out of the **emergency,** in spite of the fact they have been labeled a state of **emergency,** they have been directed to follow the **formula,** they have been told to snap and pop and get that thing straighted out, and they are still found to be goofing, the statistic is going down and continues to go down, what do you do? There is only one thing left to do and that is discipline because life itself is going to discipline the individual. (HCO PL 23 Sept 67)

EMERGENCY HEADQUARTERS, see EMERGENCY LIBRARY.

EMERGENCY LIBRARY, in accordance with HCO Policy Letter of October 24, 1962, of establishing an international headquarters of Scn at Capetown in the event of an atomic war, all Central Orgs are to deposit with Capetown a complete record of all current addresses held at each org every six months, as at 30th June and 31st December. It is incumbent on all HCOs to see that these important records are maintained current. (HCO PL 11 Apr 63, *Important—Emergency Library*)

EMERGENCY OFFICER, 1. in the Org Flag Officer Branch of the Management Bureau there is a section called the **Emergency** Section. In this section are posted **Emergency Officers.** The **Emergency Officer** is on post to ensure org situations get handled. The **Emergency Officer's** primary source of reported situations comes from the Org Flag Officers. The **Emergency Officer** is a vital post in the new Management Bureau and system. It is the stopgap for minor situations in the field turning into major situations. (CBO 203-1) **2.** an **Emergency Officer** exists in the Management Bureau to handle hot and urgent cope actions. (LRH ED 135 INT) **3.** at Flag and in FOLOs there is the post of **Emergency Officer.** The purpose of the post is to note and get handled promptly those things which are **emergencies** or will make **emergencies** if not handled. The **Emergency Officer** if posted in the Operations Bureau just below the Operations Aide or A/Aide and ranks with the Operations Org Officer. He spots and gets handled: (1) **emergencies,** (2) queries, (3) no reports. Note that 2 and 3 turn into **emergencies** if not handled. (FO 3195)

EMERGENCY PORTS, **ports** we could use in case of a bad storm or ship damage which are closest to our course line. (FO 2555)

EMERGENCY PURCHASE ORDER, **emergency purchase orders** may be signed by the Captain in matters of fuel, water, port and credit threats and communications and transport where actual threat to income, credit, the ship, AO, AOSH or base or Sea Org exists. (FO 2057)

EMERGENCY SECTION, in the Org Flag Officer Branch of the Management Bureau there is a **section** called the **Emergency Section.** In this **section** are posted **Emergency** Officers. (CBO 203-1)

EMERGENCY SUM, 5% of the expense sum. (HASI PL 19 Apr 57, *Proportionate Pay Plan*)

EMERGENCY TRAFFIC, all heavy **traffic** and all unexpected loads come under the heading of **emergency.** It is **emergency traffic** that brings about the sudden rushes, the peaks, the overloads and the flaps. (HCO PL 30 Jun 60)

EMPIRICAL FACT, a **fact** observed and proven by observation. (HCO PL 4 Dec 66)

EMPLOYEE, an individual who works for a particular person or organization in return for money or some sort of exchange.

EMPLOYEE HANDBOOK, a booklet or compilation of information from management to the employee that familiarizes the employee with his employer and the employment environment. Such handbooks vary widely in size and make-up from place to place but usually contain a statement of the goals, purposes, policies and products of the employing organization or business. There is often data about conditions of employment, what is expected of the employee (schedule, appearance, manners, etc.) and how employees may establish a relationship with the employer or organization conducive to their continued employment. Depending on the range of products made or services rendered there will be some coverage (general or specific) of how to do the job.

EMPLOYEE, HOURLY, a person who is employed on the basis of being paid a set wage per hour. The number of hours worked forms the basis of such a person's wages.

EMPLOYEE, LOANED, an employee temporarily in the service of an employer other than his own.

EMPLOYEE MANUAL, employee handbook.

EMPLOYEE, MORALE, the collective attitude or feeling of employees toward their employer or organization as shown in their willingness to perform duties and take on responsibility, productivity, efficiency, enthusiasm, etc.

EMPLOYEE RELATIONS, 1. the application of management policies designed to promote a harmonious level of interaction between the management or employer and the employees. 2. pertaining to the nature and quality of the existing relationship between employer and employees.

EMPLOYEE RELATIONS DEPARTMENT, that department which handles employee relations in an organization. Often this function is put in the Personnel Department but it can be as much or more of a public relations function.

EMPLOYEE RELATIONS INDEX, a measurement or estimation of the current state of employee relations by considering such points as amount of labor unrest, grievances brought forth and how handled, personnel turnover, absence from work, amount of accidents and level of concentration on safety.

EMPLOYEE, SALARIED, an employee whose salary is based on a specific amount per week, month or a year in contrast to an employee whose wages are computed by the number of hours he works at a particular hourly rate.

EMPLOYEE SECURITY, the state of an employee feeling secure in his job with no likelihood of a layoff or termination of his employment.

EMPLOYEE SERVICES, services provided by management to employees such as pensions, insurance plans, health care plans, etc. Such services add to employees' security, faith in the company and desire for continued employment there.

EMPLOYEE SKILLS INVENTORY, data or a method of getting data on each employee which lists his skills, abilities, education or training background, previous experience and performance, etc. The data recorded varies from organization to organization but should be sufficient to establish eligibility for promotion, transfer or the value of the employee to the organization.

EMPLOYEES' SHARES PLAN, a plan in which a company sets aside a block of its stock with earnings from these stocks being distributed among employees at certain intervals.

EMPLOYEE TRAINING, see TRAINING, EMPLOYEE.

EMPLOYER, the person or organization for whom a person has agreed to work in exchange for money or some other form of exchange.

EMPLOYERS' ASSOCIATION, an association composed of employers which focuses on matters of personnel, employment, industrial relations, etc., as opposed to matters of products and commercial activities which are the subject of trade associations.

EMPLOYER'S LIABILITY, the degree of legal responsibility that an employer has for employees who suffer on-the-job or on-the-premises injuries.

EMPLOYERS' ORGANIZATION, same as Employers' Association.

EMPLOYMENT, 1. the form of work one is engaged in. 2. the engaging of persons to do specific jobs in return for money or another agreed upon exchange.

EMPLOYMENT AGENCY, an agency which specializes in matching up employees to employers for a fee. Data is collected on each person applying for a type of job and matched up to data from employers needing personnel, in order to choose the person for the job. Often an employment agency will advertise jobs available and may run a service of providing temporary staff to employers needing to fill a job for a few days or weeks only.

EMPLOYMENT COSTS, see COSTS, EMPLOYMENT.

EMPLOYMENT, DOUBLE, one person having two jobs as in moonlighting or a double assignment.

EMPLOYMENT, FULL, 1. the economic condition whereby employment is available to anyone who is capable and willing to work. 2. defined by Lord Beveridge in 1944 as a maximum unemployment level of 3%.

EMPLOYMENT INTERVIEW, see INTERVIEW.

EMPLOYMENT, INVENTORY OF, a list of the number and types of jobs that a firm has or needs.

EMPLOYMENT, SEASONAL, 1. a recurrent type of employment that is associated with or available only at certain seasons due to regional climate conditions, agriculture maturation, etc. 2. a type of industry or activity influenced by seasonal demand such as the fur industry or summer clothing manufacturers, etc.

EMPLOYMENT TEST, a test devised to establish if a job applicant meets the employer's requirements. Such a test could establish a person's skill or knowledge in a given line of work, his general education level, attitude to work or other people, responsibility level, IQ, leadership potential, etc.

ENCHANTER, 1. (Sea Org) sailing vessel. (FO 24) **2.** *Enchanter's* name is changed to *Diana.* (Ron's Journal 1968) [The *Enchanter* was classed as a Bermuda ketch and was approximately 50 ft. long. In 1968, she accompanied the *Royal Scotman* and was used on missions and as a sail training vessel. A picture of her appears on page 29 of the book, *Mission Into Time.*]

ENDING CYCLES, concluding actions. **Ending cycles** doesn't consist of shooting people. It consists of seeing that it stays handled. (HCO PL 4 May 68)

ENDORSEMENT, the Committee of Evidence findings have added to them the **endorsement** by the Convening Authority. The findings have no force until the **endorsement** is added. The Convening Authority makes the **endorsement** on the findings in as brief a fashion as possible. The Convening Authority can (1) accept the findings in full (2) reduce the penalty recommended or (3) suspend or cancel the penalty completely with a pardon. The Convening Authority may make no other **endorsement,** save only to thank the committee and witnesses. The moment the findings are **endorsed** they have the effect of orders as per the **endorsement** and all persons under the authority of the Convening Authority are bound to execute them and abide by them accordingly. (HCO PL 7 Sept 63)

ENDORSEMENT, 1. an act of putting one's signature on the back of a check or on a document. 2. a signature on a legal document the existence of which is taken as an approval, agreement or sanction to the stipulations on the document. 3. an addendum or amendment to a contract which permits a change of the original terms of the contract such as an addition to an insurance policy permitting a change in the coverage previously agreed to.

END PRODUCT, the final product ready for the consumer.

ENEMIES, things, groups, other determinisms that challenged or sought to stop or refused to comply with the basic purpose became **enemies** or opposition. (HCO PL 13 Mar 65, *Division 1, 2, 3 The Structure of Organization What is Policy?*)

ENEMY, 1. when a person is an avowed and knowing **enemy** of an individual, a group, project or org, a condition of **enemy** exists. (HCO PL 6 Oct 67) **2.** an action or inaction resulting in damage or difficulty to another or the organization—**enemy.** (ED 62 Flag)

ENEMY CONNECTED, defined as related to, dependent upon or in communication with or formly employed by anti-Scientology persons or groups. (FO 2772)

ENEMY FORMULA, for **formula** for the condition of **enemy** is just one step: find out who you really are. (HCO PL 23 Oct 67)

ENFORCED OVERT HAVE, means **forcing** upon another a substance, action or thing not wanted or refused by the other. (HCO PL 12 May 72)

ENGINEER, all **engines,** tools and engine space, heating stoves, piping, use of fuel and electricity and generating and wiring systems belong to the **Engineer.** The running and handling of **engines,** generators and heating equipment and stoves is the **Engineer's.** The **Engineer** also has the care of all launch motors and their fuel. Safeguarding the ship against fire is the **Engineer's** responsibility. The **Engineer** must keep the ship free of all odors and must keep the **engine** room spotless. (*Ship's Org Bk.*)

ENGINEERING DEPARTMENT, 1. that department in a business which handles research, design and development of new products or services. 2. the department which handles plant layout and/or maintains and services the machinery, electrical installations, plumbing and heating systems, etc., of a business.

ENGINEERING SECTION, (Estates Section Dept 21) the **Engineering Section** is responsible for all mechanical systems in the org, plumbing, heating, electrical and any others, and for the operational state of all motors and machines of any kind on the premises, including vehicles. (HCO PL 16 Aug 74 IIR)

ENGINEER OF THE WATCH, 1. (**Engine** Room) the **engineer of the watch** is the senior person on the **watch.** (FO 1695) **2.** the engineer of the watch, of course, runs the **engines** and boilers and pumps down in the **engine** room, handy to answer **engine** bells. (FO 80) *Abbr.* EOW.

ENGINEERS LOG, 1. every ship shall keep a full and complete **engineers' log.** Such a **log** is kept by the **engineer** on watch, is entered into each watch, is signed by each watch officer or in his absence the OOD. The readings of gauges, thermometers, r.p.m., bells handled, all **engine** data of each **engine** and installation and pump. All maintenance actions, oil changes, greasing, fuel actions, refueling, consumption, etc., are part of this **log.** The **log** specifically must reflect the behavior and care taken of each and every watch and day installation and every servicing action with regard to same. (FO 820) **2. log** which is to receive all data of interest, the chief's orders and the signature of each watch stander. (FO 29)

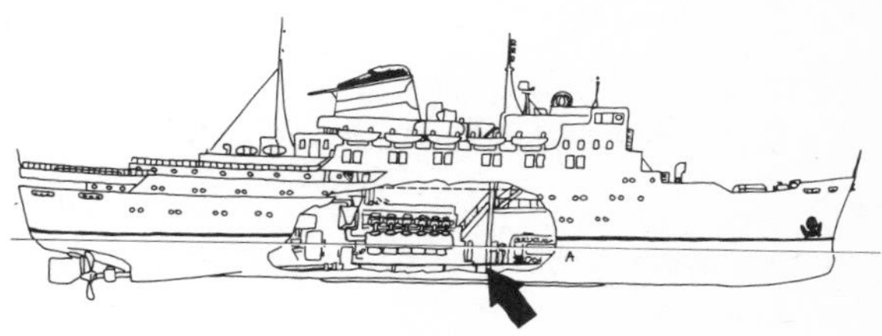

Engine Room

ENGINE ROOM, 1. the theory of the **engine room** operation is that there is a repair section which works consistently on repairs whereas all the rest of the **engine room** works on operation and general maintenance such as oil changes and general upkeep of the **engines.** (FO 1109) **2.** the **engine room's** primary actions are motive power and service to the ship. Clean cold water, clean hot water, economically produced electricity and clean and working drains comprise the basic services. Electronic and other equipment such as winches and pumps and service equipment in good repair are an important part of their product. The definition of operational is able to function without further care or attention. The items of priority are motive power and ship services. (FO 2148) *Abbr.* ER or E/R.

ENGINE ROOM DRILL, lines tracing **drill.** (FO 3053) [This is a **drill** designed aboard Flag for FEBC students. It consisted of having FEBC students trace the pipe systems in the Flag **engine room** to give reality on tracing lines in an org.]

ENGINE ROOM DRILLS, the **engine room** is **drilled** on their stations as a unit by the **engineer** of the watch. Every **engineer** is thoroughly briefed in the duties of every person on the watch. Every **engineer** is thoroughly briefed in the operation of every piece of equipment that (a) he personally operates and (when that is done), (b) every piece of equipment that is operated in the **engine room.** (FO 1020)

ENGINE ROOM I&R, **1.** is responsible for keeping ethics in in the **engine room.** Part of the **I&R's** duty is to spot outnesses, and appropriate conditions must be assigned for these. (FO 1528) **2.** the **I&R** is essentially a communicator. This means looking and making known. The **I&R** is responsible for spotting outnesses before they have a chance to develop. (FO 1517) **3.** does **inspection and reports** in the **I&R** log book of the **engine room,** all important data and happenings which occur in the **engine room** during the watch. (FO 2049)

ENMEST, **1.** property, energy, or space which has been rendered less useful by poor thinking. Time which is wasted. (*HTLTAE,* p. 120) **2.** rotten canvas, broken chairs, things which don't belong in the area, rubbish, etc. (FO 1973)

ENROLLMENT, **1.** an **enrollment** means simply putting a name on a **roll.** (HCO PL 19 Feb 68) **2.** someone who has signed up for a service paying the full fee and who has started the service signed up for. (A sign-up is just a sign-up until he starts the service at which point he is an **enrollment.**) (HCO PL 26 Nov 71 II) [The above HCO PL was revised and reissued as HCO PL 26 Nov 71R II, *Division 6 Public Reg Simplified,* which was cancelled by BPL 1 Dec 72 IV]

ENROLLMENT CHART, (1) general public interested. (2) enrolled in Academies. (3) Academy students kept informed of the Saint Hill Course. (4) Academy students achieving results. (5) eventual **enrollment** at Saint Hill. (6) satisfactory training results at Saint Hill. (7) word of mouth by Saint Hill graduates. (8) continuously expanding Saint Hill Course. If any of the above steps are omitted, it will become a serious matter to the **Enrollment** Department, so the thing to do is be sure that all the steps in the above **chart** are effective. (HCO PL 29 Jan 64)

ENROLLMENT CYCLE, **cycle** starts off at distribution when individuals are reached by broad promotion, buy a book and eventually reach into the org themselves and are replied to by a Letter Registrar, who finds their want, puts them on a channel, and intensifies their reach. She keeps them progressing up the Routing and Gradation Chart until they finally reach for Saint Hill services, at which time they are passed on to the Advance Registration Unit, who schedules them for services. These individuals are written to by the Advance Registration Unit, which has its own Advance Reservations Records I/C who only writes to those people who are booked, encourages them to be here sooner, and in short gives them any and all information to get here in the shortest possible time. Advance Unit carries on with these people until they finally arrive in the org, at which time the Body Registrar takes over, makes them welcome, smooths out any points that aren't clear, completes all registration formalities, and then hands over to Treasury Division. They then go to Tech for auditing and training, Qual for declare, to Success Division stating their successes and on to the Registrar to sign up for their next training or processing. (HCO PL 29 Nov 68)

ENROLLMENT DIVISION, **1.** good files, lists and addresses, good and intelligent communication and a very large increase in **enrollment** are expected from the **Enrollment Division.** The Director of **Enrollment** is under the supervision of the Saint Hill Administrator and the **Enrollment Division** is part of HCO (St. Hill) Ltd. The Director of **Enrollment** has the full responsibility of filling up the course and keeping it full (HCO PL 24 Jan 64, *Enrollment Division*) **2.** transferred from HCO (St. Hill) Ltd., to HCO (WW) Ltd., and renamed Auditors Division. (HCO PL 11 Mar 64, *Departmental Changes Auditors Division*)

ENSURANCE MEMBER, **member** who goes along on separate MOs to see the mission sticks to its MOs and rebriefs the mission I/P. A mission tends to get hit with local requests to handle things and other noise as well as unknown data. The **Ensurance Member** sees the mission rides through it and stays on MOs or Mission Ops adjustments. (OODs 23 Dec 74)

ENSURANCE MISSION, in late '74 the Commodore developed the **ensurance mission.** These **missions** were sent out to accompany another mission and to ensure that the mission did stay on and do its orders. (FO 645R-1, Attachment 3)

ENSURANCE MISSIONAIRE, **1.** **missionaire** whose sole duty is to see that the mission remains on MOs. In many cases the 2nd missionaire can be the **Ensurance** Member. An **Ensurance Missionaire** goes out on separate, pattern orders. (CBO 368) **2.** the **Ensurance Missionaire** is there primarily to keep the mission complying with MOs and telexes, and to make the mission go right. (CBO 368)

ENTERPRISE, (1) any projected task or work; an undertaking. (2) boldness, energy and invention in practical affairs. (BPL 24 Sept 73 I-1)

ENTERPRISE, 1. a business structure formed and operated to make a profit. 2. an undertaking; business venture.

ENTERPRISER, a person who engages in a business venture or undertaking for a profit but at the risk of a loss. One who ventures into new areas of business activity or develops new products for an uncertain market; an entrepreneur.

ENTHETA, **1.** **en**=enturbulated; **theta**=thought or life. (HCO PL 7 Jun 65, *Entheta Letters and the Dead File, Handling Of—Definitions*) **2.** embroidered reports. Data is data. It is not opinion. Data, not **entheta,** brings about action. All **entheta** does is cut the lines. (HCO PL 26 May 58) **3.** irrational or confused or destructive thought, enturbulated thought. (*HTLTAE,* p. 120)

ENTHETA LETTER, a **letter** containing insult, discourtesy, chop or nastiness about an org, its personnel, Scn or the principal figures in Scn. **En**=enturbulated; *theta*=Greek for thought or life. An **entheta letter's** nastiness is aimed at the org, its personnel, Scn or the principal figures of Scn. It is different from an ethics report. (HCO PL 7 June 65, *Entheta Letters and the Dead File, Handling Of—Definitions*)

ENTURBULANCE, commotion and upset (HCO PL 4 Oct 69)

ENVIRONMENTAL CHALLENGE, when sane men and organizations exist in a broad scene that is convulsed with irrationality, it takes very keen observation and a good grip on logic and fast action to stay alive. This is known as **environmental challenge.** It can be overdone! Too much **challenge** can overwhelm. (HCO PL 19 May 70)

EQUAL PAY FOR EQUAL WORK, a job evaluation technique whereby types of work are categorized according to their equality and all types of work within a specific category are assigned equal pay regardless of the race, color, creed, sex, etc., of the worker.

EQUATION FOR BUREAUX PEOPLE, there is an **equation for bureaux people** to know. Lack of know how data=inevitable foul ups=lousy production=lousy team. And its corrollary, good gen=good team. (OODs 20 Dec 70)

EQUILIBRIUM, a balancing point where outflow is equal to inflow such as where a nation's total expenditure equals its total income.

EQUILIBRIUM PRICE, see PRICE, EQUILIBRIUM.

EQUIPMENT, by **equipment** is meant any item costing more than £5 or 10 dollars. (HCO PL 3 Nov 65)

EQUIPMENT, a company's fixed assets or property needed for its operation and the production of its goods and services such as manufacturing and office machinery, furniture, vehicles, etc.

EQUITY, any civil procedure holding citizens responsible to citizens which delivers decisions to persons in accordance with the general expectancy in such cases. (PAB 96)

EQUITY, 1. value of a company's assets arrived at after its liabilities have been subtracted, giving the current net value. 2. ordinary shares that make up the equity capital of a company.

ERGONOMICS, same as Human Engineering.

ERRAND, an **errand** would be a person or group sent by an officer to accomplish a delivery, task or duty and not sent by Operations but by someone else. This would require briefing by the officer sending, preferably taped, or at least with a carbon copy of the orders on which the person or group were briefed. The **errand** ends when the person or group have made a full report to Operations on what they did, accomplished and observed and when the Ops Officer is satisfied that the **errand** has been successfully carried out. The difference between an **errand** and a mission is that missions are sent by an Operations Officer, **errands** are sent by anyone else. When an **errand** involves more than one day it should be handled by Operations not by some other division. It then becomes a mission. (FO 2530R)

ERROR, in the fields of statistics and market research, the difference between a calculated value and the actual value.

ERROR REPORT, staff member **report** of any **error** made. (HCO PL 1 May 65)

Errors

ERRORS, 1. many who begin to use "illogics," who have not drilled on them so they can rattle them off, choose errors instead of out-points." An **error** may show something else. It is nothing in itself. An **error** obscures or alters a datum. It will be found that out-points are really few unless the activity is very irrational. Simple **errors** on the other hand can be found in legions in any scene. That a factory has a few **errors** is no real indicator. A factory has plus-points to the degree it attains its ideal and fulfills its purpose. That some of its machinery needs repair might not even be an out-point. If the general machinery of the place is good for enough years to easily work off its replacement value there is a plus-point. People applying fixed or wrong ideals to a scene are only pointing up **errors** in their own ideals not those of the scene! A reformer who had a strict Dutch mother looks at a primitive Indian settlement and sees children playing in the mud and adults going around unclothed. He forces them to live cleanly and cuts off the sun by putting them in clothes—they lose their immunities required to live and die off. He missed the plus-point that these Indians had survived hundreds of years in this area that would kill a white man in a year! Thus **errors** are usually a comparison to one's personal ideals. Out-points compare to the ideal for that particular scene. (HCO PL 23 May 70) **2.** minor unintentional omissions or mistakes. These are auditing "goofs;" minor alter-is of tech or policy; small instructional mistakes; minor **errors** or omissions in performing duties and admin **errors** not resulting in financial loss or loss of status or repute for a senior. (HCO PL 7 Mar 65 III)

ESCROW, a written agreement not effective, as in the sale or transfer of business and real property, until certain conditions such as a specified sum of money delivered to a third party, are fulfilled by the grantee.

ESCUTCHEON, a word coming from the Latin word, *Scutum,* meaning shield. (FO 3350)

ESPRIT DE CORPS, (**Spirit** of the Group), morale in a military sense applies to the whole group as in **esprit de corps.** (FO 2414)

ESTABLISH, 1. put there. (HCO PL 7 Jul 71) **2.** (to **establish**) meaning training, org boarding, posting, hatting, lines followed and policy and tech known and practiced. (HCO PL 31 Aug 71, *Additional, EC Network*)

Establish (Def. 1)

ESTABLISHING, 1. **establishing** something means that it's been put there so that it is capable and does produce high volume, high quality production with an absence of dev-t. (ESTO 11, 7203C06 SO I) **2.** to have communications you have to have terminals. The org board is the pattern of the terminals and their flows. So you have to have an org board. And the org board must in truth be a representation of what is in the organization. The org board shows where what terminals are located in the org so flows can occur. This action of putting in terminals is called **establishing.** (HCO PL 7 Jul 71)

ESTABLISHING THE ORG, that means to find, hat, train, apprentice persons from outside the **org,** to locate them in the **org** and on the **organizing** board and then route the raw materials (public people in this case) along the line for production, which means changing particles into a final product. (HCO PL 7 Jul 71)

ESTABLISHMENT, 1. the act of improving the general level of all stats. (CBO 50) **2.** consists of quarters, personnel, training, hatting, files, lines, supplies and materiel and all things necessary to **establishment.** (HCO PL 7 Mar 72)

ESTABLISHMENT BUREAU I, formed to enable the Flag Bureaux to have greater control over the establishment of itself and the orgs it manages. The **Bureau** has three branches—Internal HCO/Materials/External HCO. (FO 3591)

ESTABLISHMENT CONFERENCES, Aides Council **Conference** where only **establishment** actions are planned, taken up and gotten in. (FO 3148)

ESTABLISHMENT OFFICER, 1. the purpose of **Establishment Officers** is to establish and maintain the **establishment** of the org and each division therein. The term **Esto** is used for abbreviation. (HCO PL 7 Mar 72) **2.** the **Establishment Officer** is the person who keeps it **established** and makes sure that it produces and that the programs come out straight and that those targets and quotas are met. (ESTO 10, 7203C05 SO II) **3.** an **Esto** is supposed to hat somebody and get him producing what he should be producing on that post. First there's an instant hat and get him producing on the post. Then we mini hat him and get him producing on the post. Then we full hat him and get him producing on the post. (ESTO 10, 7203C05 SO II) **4.** their duties consist of org boarding, training, hatting, apprenticing, pouring in personnel, lines, spaces and materiel and equipment of the Division-Bureau. (OODs 4 Mar 72) **5.** this person operates in a division, not under its secretary but under a senior **Establishment Officer.** He performs the duties of the Departments of HCO for that division. In a small org it requires a trained **Establishment Officer** for Divisions 7, 1 and 2 and another for Divisions 3, 4, 5 and 6. In a larger org there is one in charge of all **Establishment Officers** and an **Establishment Officer** in each division. As the org grows, the larger divisions get Assistant **Establishment Officers** to the divisional one. They do not **establish** and run away. They **establish** and maintain the division staff, personnel hats, posts, lines, materiel and supplies. Their first job is to get staff working at their posts producing something and their next task is to drive dev-t out of existence in that org. (HCO PL 29 Feb 72, *Correct Comm*) **6.** the first **Establishment Officer** Course was developed on Flag in October 1971. This was the Tech **Establishment Officer** Course (**TEO**). There are now **Establishment** Courses for each division of the org. An **Establishment Officer** is a specialist in the operation of a particular division, who also needs to be trained in the skills of **establishing,** which includes: getting production of valuable final products, recruiting staff, posting the org board of the division, getting personnel to study, hatting, training divisional staff, getting volume, quality and viability of production increased, **establishing** the lines of the division. (HCO PL 5 Feb 72 III) **7.** one who **establishes** a division. Junior to the **Establishment Officer** I/C but in the division under its secretary, the **Establishment Officer** puts in the divisional personnel, lines, materiel and trains, hats and maintains and expands the **established** division to the benefit of the org and its staff. (LRH ED 168R INT) **8.** now I've used Establishing and **Establishment Officer** interchangeably. It's a descriptive term. The actual term is **EstablishMENT** Officer. His duties are **establishing.** (ESTO 2, 7203C01 SO II) **9.** a leading **Establishment Officer+**Department is a Departmental **Establishment Officer** who has Section **Estos** under him due to the numerousness of the section. An **Establishment Officer+**Section is an **Establishment Officer** of a section where there is a Departmental and Divisional **Esto.** (HCO PL 7 Mar 72) **10.** an **Esto** is a third dynamic auditor who deaberrates a group by cleanly organizing it so it can produce. (FSO 529) *Abbr.* Esto, ESTO.

ESTABLISHMENT OFFICER CONFERENCE, 1. the **Establishment Officer Conference** is held by the Exec **Esto** (or his deputy). This **conference** handles **Esto** matters, debugs **Esto** targets worked out by the CO-ED or **Esto's** projects, gets in reports of divisions and their personnel, hatting, supply, spaces, quarters etc.

The **Esto Conference** handles financial planning using FP policy in which the **Esto** must be proficient. (FP must be approved by the Treasury Sec, Finance Banking Officer and Assistant Guardian. The org has to be run on FBO/AG allocations and these are the check signers of the org). This **conference** is governed by similar guide rules as a conference to the Product Conference. (HCO PL 7 Mar 72) **2.** the economics of the organization are in the hands of another conference called the **Esto Conference.** An FP is done by the **Establishment Officers.** It's done just according to the rules and therefore they know how much they have to **establish.** (ESTO 1, 7203C01 SO I) **3.** the **Esto Conference** meets daily on **establishment** matters. (OODs 4 Mar 72)

ESTABLISHMENT OFFICER IN-CHARGE, **1.** an **Establishment Officer In-Charge** is an **Esto** who has **Establishment Officers** under him in an activity that has five or less **Estos.** Does duties comparable to an Executive Esto for that activity. (HCO PL 7 Mar 72) **2.** has the duty of maintaining the **Esto** system. (LRH ED 168R INT) *Abbr.* Esto I/C, ESTO I/C.

ESTABLISHMENT OFFICER SERIES 5, see PRODUCT CLEARING SHORT FORM.

ESTABLISHMENT OFFICER SERIES 11, see PRODUCT CLEARING LONG FORM.

ESTABLISHMENT OFFICER SERIES 18, see LENGTH OF TIME TO EVALUATE.

ESTABLISHMENT OFFICER'S ESTABLISHMENT OFFICER, the **Esto's Esto** is the one who trains and hats and checks out ESTOs and establishes the Esto system. He also runs the Esto Course that makes Estos and is the Esto's Course Supervisor. In practice, the hats of Esto Org Officer and **Esto's Establishment Officer** are held as one hat until an org is very large. The person who holds this post has to be a very good course supervisor who uses study tech like a master as his flubs would carry through the whole Esto system. (HCO PL 7 Mar 72) *Abbr.* Esto's Esto, ESTO'S ESTO.

ESTABLISHMENT OFFICER SYSTEM, **1.** the **Establishment Officer system** or "Esto Tech" was developed in the same time period as the Prod-Org system. The **Esto** kept the place established and organized for production and despite heavy production demands. (HCO PL 9 May 74) **2.** the **Establishment Officer system** evolved from the Product-Org system where it was found the HAS alone could not **establish** the org. The **Esto** is an extension of the original HCO system as an **Esto** performs all the functions of HCO for the activity to which he is assigned plus his own tech of being an **Esto.** (HCO PL 7 Mar 72)

ESTATE BUREAU, **1.** the **Estate Bureau** provides quarters and maintains them as clean, attractive and usable. Where the staff is also housed and fed the **Estate Bureau** sees to the proper handling of these functions regardless of what other divisions and persons may also be engaged upon it. (CBO 7) **2.** consists of Household Branch, Quarters Branch, Bureau Representative Branch, and Maintenance Branch. (CBO 19)

ESTATES, as **estates** is a misconception when applied to a ship, it must be realized on Flag that **estates** is actually ship and all its functions. (FO 3576RA)

ESTATE-SHIP AIDE, the post of **Estate-Ship Aide** is established. It is a full Commodore's Staff Aide Post and is located on the org board directly under Staff Captain, alongside CS-PA on the org board. Its shortened designation will be CS-**ES.** (FO 3380) *Abbr.* CS-ES.

ESTATES MANAGER, **1.** the **Estates Manager** is located in Dept 21 and is the head of the **Estates** Section. As such he is responsible for the production of engine room, deck and services products in quantity, quality and viability. (FO 3590) **2.** handles all of **estates** and thus is the Product Officer of the section, and of his juniors, the Chief Engineer, Chief Steward and 1st Mate. (FO 3590) **3.** the **Estates Manager** of local orgs is responsible for seeing the org has proper quarters and that the property is kept up well in its appearance. He is also responsible for the locating of or building of new premises as the org expands or needs new quarters and for seeing that full CSW is presented when such changes are needed. Further he is responsible for the accurate following of all plans or programs of the **Estate** Bureau. (HCO PL 22 Feb 67) **4. Estates Managers** see that the buildings and grounds are kept up well and good in appearance and that they have a building. (HCO PL 22 Feb 67) **5.** the **Estates** Section is in the charge of the **Estates Manager** who in turn is answerable to the LRH Comm. The **Estates Manager** is responsible for locating new premises as the org expands or needs new quarters, for obtaining approval on and securing such premises hence this is the first unit of the **Estates Section.** (HCO PL 16 Aug 74 II)

ESTATES PROJECT FORCE, **1.** under the supervision of the Maintenance Chief, the **Estates**

Project Force handles premises, grounds, cleaning, repair, painting or other maintenance cycles. (FO 3165) **2.** an **Estates Project Force** is established in lieu of a deck project force. Such persons do grounds and buildings maintenance at any of the SO properties under the direction of the Estate Manager and supervised by an **EPF** MAA as assigned by the LRH Comm. (FO 3118R) *Abbr.* EPF.

ESTATES PROJECT FORCE CATEGORY A, people who are just coming into the org could also come in through an **Estates Project Force.** So there's an **Estates Project Force. Category A** are people who are just coming in and getting in their basics before you let them onto a post and then there's Category B; those who have had a chance and they're put back there until they're handled. Do not allow these Category B's back in on your lines before they are handled. (ESTO 4, 7203C02 SO II)

ESTATES PROJECT FORCE CATEGORY B, see ESTATES PROJECT FORCE CATEGORY A.

ESTATES PROJECT FORCE MAA, the most upstat member of the **EPF** is appointed as **EPF MAA.** He musters the group, conducts any exercises, and keeps the schedule in under supervision of the 1st Mate or his deputy. (FO 3434-28) *Abbr.* EPF MAA.

ESTATES SECTION, **1.** the **Estates Section** with all its personnel, functions and equipment reverts to Dept 21, Office of LRH, in all Scientology orgs and in all SO orgs including ships. The **Estates Section** is in the charge of the **Estates** Manager who in turn is answerable to the LRH Comm. Product: adequate, clean, attractive, usable org premises that enhance org promotion, production and asset value. (HCO PL 16 Aug 74 IIR) **2.** an **Estate Section,** Dept 21 (or Dept 27 in a Nine Division Org) is that **section** which keeps up, cleans and maintains the working area of the org. (BO 23, 20 Feb 70)

ESTIMATE ANALYSIS, see ANALYSIS, ESTIMATE.

ESTIMATED PURCHASE ORDER, an **Estimated Purchase Order** is not a purchase order and gives no authority to purchase. An **Estimated Purchase Order** is submitted to Financial Planning in place of an actual and valid Purchase Order when the exact cost of a needed item is not yet known. It serves to hold aside the **estimated** amount needed until an actual purchase order with exact cost can be raised against it. (BPL 4 Nov 70R) *Abbr.* EPO.

ESTO I/T, all persons doing **Esto** work may only use the title **Esto I/T (in training)** until he has successfully and honestly completed: (1) HCOB 21 November 73, *The Cure of Q and A.* (2) the PRD (Primary Rundown). (3) the OEC. (4) the Esto Series. (5) has shown on post the ability to see situations and handle them terminatedly. (6) gets staff members actually producing by increased stats. (HCO PL 22 Nov 73)

ESTOPPEL, a restriction placed upon a person to prevent him from contradicting a previous claim or assertion with a new claim or assertion.

ESTO'S MAA, **1.** the Exec Esto has a Master at Arms who musters the crew, conducts exercises and does Exec Esto investigations. There is an Assistant **Master at Arms.** This is the **Esto's MAA.** He checks up on Estos, handles things for them and acts as liaison with HCO. Student Estos as well as the regular Estos also come under the Asst. **MAA.** (FSO 529) **2.** the Exec **Esto's** Assistant **Master at Arms.** (FSO 534)

ESTO TECH, **Establishment Officer** System. (HCO PL 9 May 74)

ETHICS, **1.** the study of the general nature of morals. The rules or standards governing the conduct of the members of a profession. (HCO PL 3 May 72) **2.** the study of the general nature of morals and the specific moral choices to be made by the individual in his relationship with others. It could also be called "philosophy of morals, and also called moral philosophy." **Ethics** is a first dynamic action. (7204C11 SO) **3.** All **ethics** really does is hold the lines firm so that you can route and audit. All **ethics** is for in actual fact is simply that additional tool necessary to make it possible to get technology in. That's the whole purpose of **ethics**; to get technology in. When you've got technical in, that's as far as you carry an **ethics** action. (SH Spec 61, 6505C18) **4.** the purpose of **ethics** is to remove counter intentions from the environment. And having accomplished that the purpose becomes to remove other intentionedness from the environment. (HCO PL 18 Jun 68) **5.** what we have then, in **ethics,** is a system of removing the counter-effort to the forward push, and that's all an Ethics Officer is supposed to do. (6711C18 SO) **6.** are basically, merely good sense (5904C15) **7.** a study as much as anything else, of the equity of human intercourse. You might say it's how to keep overt-motivator sequences from forming easily. (5904C15) **8.** **ethics** is now refined by experience to a new look. The protection of upstats must be as certain as the handling of downstats. **Ethics** is not the business of just assigning and enforcing conditions. The **ethics** we have has its own tech as contained in HCOBs on suppressives, on meters, on case types. (FO 2245)

ETHICS AIDE, CS-5. (FO 795)

ETHICS AUTHORITY HAT, on review of **Ethics Authority Hat** which has been in the Office of LRH since 1965, CS-7 will handle this function. This consists of the handling and answering of all petitions received. By handling is meant correcting any outnesses found, or gathering together more data so the outness can be corrected. Review of **ethics** orders, issued by WW and SO for correctness and justice. To advise LRH of new **ethics** policies or amendments to **ethics** policy as may appear to be needed from time to time. Cancellation of certificates in the SO. (FO 1066)

ETHICS BAIT, a person in continual heavy **ethics** or who is out-**ethics.** (HCO PL 4 Apr 72)

ETHICS CHIT, report of anything in violation of **ethics** or dev-t Policy Letters. (HCO PL 1 Jul 65)

ETHICS, CORRECT DANGER CONDITION HANDLING, HCO Policy Letter 9 April 1972, *Ethics, Correct Danger Condition Handling.* Locates the trouble area that got him into a **danger condition.** Goes with the famous "3 May P/L," HCO PL 3 May 1972, *Executive Series 12, Ethics and Executives.* (LRH ED 257 INT)

ETHICS E-METER CHECK, in a state of emergency, the Ethics Officer may at any time call in any number of staff members and do an **ethics E-meter check.** This consists of setting the **meter** up, sensitivity 16, and handing the cans to the staff member taking the **check.** No question is asked of the staff member, and the staff member is not informed of readings. The Ethics Officer records the position of the tone arm and the condition of the needle and that is all. The entire **check** takes no more than 5-15 seconds. The staff member's pc folder need not be at hand during the **check.** After the **check** is over, the Ethics Officer examines the pc folder for evidence of NCG (chronic no change of case) or rollercoaster or R/Ses. (HCO PL 26 Aug 65R, *Ethics E-Meter Check*)

ETHICS FILES, **filing** is the real trick of **ethics** work. The **files** do all the work, really. Executive Ethics reports patiently **filed** in folders, one for each member, eventually makes one **file** fat. Whatever report you get, **file** it with a name. Don't **file** by departments or divisions. **File** by names. (HCO PL 11 May 65, *Ethics Officer Hat*)

ETHICS HEARING, an **Ethics Hearing** may be convened by an Ethics Officer to obtain data for further action or inaction. The order is issued as an HCO Ethics Order. The time and place of the **Ethics Hearing** is stated in the order. The purpose of the **Hearing** is stated. Interested Parties are named. An **Ethics Hearing** may name witnesses but not the person's immediate superiors to appear against him in person but may consider a written statement by a superior. An **Ethics Hearing** has no power to discipline but may advise on consequences. If doubt exists in the matter of whether or not a misdemeanor or crime or suppression has occurred, it will be usual to convene an **Ethics Hearing** or Executive **Ethics Hearing** not a Court of Ethics. (HCO PL 26 May 65 III)

ETHICS INTERROGATORY, an **ethics interrogatory** is used as a despatch to carry out an investigation. It is used to collect data to determine the facts of a situation. It is on gold paper with blue ink. (HCO PL 8 May 65 II)

ETHICS OFFICER, **1.** uses **ethics** to protect **ethics** upstats and keep the stats up and to smoke out crimes that push people and stats down. It is a simple function. (HCO PL 7 Dec 69) **2.** when **ethics** isn't in, it's put in. **Ethics Officers** put **ethics** in. An **Ethics Officer** removes counter-intentions from the environment. (FO 918) **2.** the activities of the **Ethics Officer** consist of isolating individuals who are stopping proper flows by pulling withholds with **ethics** technology and by removing as necessary potential trouble sources and suppressive individuals off org comm lines and by generally enforcing **ethics** codes. (HCO PL 11 May 65, *Ethics Officer Hat*) **4.** the purpose of the **Ethics Officer** is to help Ron clear orgs and the public if need be of entheta and enturbulation so that Scn can be done. (HCO PL 11 May 65, *Ethics Officer Hat*) **5.** in Department 3, Department of Inspection and Reports. Handles all **ethics** and security matters, interviews, investigations and orders. (HCO PL 18 May 73) **6.** the title Chief **Ethics Officer** is used when he has three full-time (or in foundations, foundation time) **Ethics Officers.** The title **Ethics Officer** In-Charge is used when one has a Chief **Ethics Officer** over him and at least one other below him. The title **Ethics Officer** is used to denote single occupancy of a section. (HCO PL 20 Jun 68) **7.** the **Ethics Officer** is trying to protect the organization from the consequences of SP's and PTS's and on the other hand he is trying also to bring about justice. (SH Spec 73, 6608C02) **8.** MAA (BPL 25 Jul 70R)

ETHICS OFFICER IN-CHARGE, the title **Ethics Officer In-Charge** is used when one has a Chief Ethics Officer over him and at least one other below him. (HCO PL 20 Jun 68)

ETHICS ORDER, 1. (HCO **Ethics Order**) all **Ethics Orders** will now be on gold paper with blue ink. This includes all local Committee of Evidence issues and other matters. An **Ethics Order** may only be issued by the HCO Executive Secretary or an HCO Area Secretary. Any findings must be passed by the Office of LRH but if so are issued as an **Ethics Order** color flashed gold with blue ink. (HCO PL 8 May 65 II) **2.** *example:* "John Smith in Baltimore, USA, is declared a Suppressive Person. On (date) he discouraged Bill Tucker from taking the Saint Hill Course by writing to him lies about the course, well known by said Smith to be false statements. Evidence: letter from Smith dated _____ to _____ now available in **ethics** files. Charge: suppression of a Scientologist and barring his way to release and Clear. Findings by former evidence of course record and this: Suppressive Person. All certs . . . etc." **Ethics Orders** are supposed to run group engrams out. Always put in what you know, nothing you don't know, and only what you have evidence or witnesses for. **Ethics Orders** are issued on real data, not opinion. (HCO PL 2 Jun 65) *Abbr.* EO.

ETHICS PRESENCE, 1. ethics presence is an "X" quality made up partly of symbology, partly of force, some "now we're supposed to's" and endurance. Endurance asserts the truth of unkillability. We're still here, can't be unmocked. This drives the SP wild. Because of the Sea Org we appear to have unlimited reach and in some mysterious way, unlimited resources. The ability to appear and disappear mysteriously is a part of **ethics presence.** As an executive you get compliance because you have **ethics presence** and persistence and can get mad. The way you continue to have **ethics presence** is to be maximally right in your actions, decisions and dictates. (HCO PL 4 Oct 68) **2.** is basically knowing what you are doing and making sure the junior backs you up and does it. (ED 123 USB)

ETHICS PROGRAM NO. 1, 1. the purpose of this is to pick out and add to persons who should have **ethics** protection because they are producers. The full intentions of **Ethics Program No. 1** are to get **ethics** in in orgs, protect upstats and bring others up to upstat by auditing and training. (LRH ED 78 INT) **2.** the purpose of this **program** is to get ethics protection for actual upstats and prevent oppressive influences on org staff members. (LRH ED 39 INT)

ETHICS REPORT, a **report** to **ethics** (or by error, to the org) concerning the misuse or abuse of technology or the misconduct of a Scientologist. This is routed directly to the **Ethics** Section and becomes a subject for investigation. (HCO PL 7 Jun 65, *Entheta Letters and the Dead File, Handling of—Definitions*)

ETHICS SECTION, 1. is in Department 3. This department is called Inspection and Reports. In small orgs there is only one person in that department. Primarily his duties consist of inspecting and reporting to his divisional head and the Executive Council. (HCO PL 7 Dec 69) **2. Section** in Dept 3, Dept of Inspection and Reports. **Ethics Section** does **ethics** investigations, writes **Ethics** Orders, holds **Ethics** Hearings and suggests Executive **Ethics** Hearings, handles all **ethics** matters, guards and watchmen. (HCO PL 17 Jan 66 II)

ETHICS TYPE CASE, SP, PTS, W/Hs. (HCO PL 17 Jun 65)

ETHICS UPSTATS, an **upstat** rating per **Ethics** Program No. 1. (LRH ED 63 INT)

ETHNIC(S), 1. beliefs, mores, customs, patterns of thought or racial or religious stable data. (HCO PL 12 Nov 69) **2.** it's the mores and customs. It's what do the people believe; it's what is right and what is wrong. It is the solution of good conduct. (6910C21 SO)

Ethnics

ETHNIC SURVEY, 1. you have to find out what is most liked and what is next most liked and what is considered bad and what is considered totally evil. When you have got the list of those things now you know the control buttons of the society. Those are the buttons of control. You do an **ethnic survey** by going out and asking questions, and by looking into books and backgrounds of religions and that sort of thing. (6910C21) **2.** surveys finding out what is needed and wanted in different subjects or areas of interest—i.e. education, health, etc. (FO 2162)

ETHNIC VALUES, 1. publicly admired **values** and publicly detested **values.** (HCO PL 17 Jun 69) **2.** customs. (HCO PL 24 Jan 69)

EVAL SHEET, in the Flag Bureaux and in Continental Liaison Offices and OTLs, aides and assistant aides have definite and specific **evaluation** duties. The **evals** are typed daily on to **eval sheets. Eval sheets** are laid out as follows: (1) heading: **Eval sheet** for __________(date). (2) distribution placed in the top left-hand corner. (3) name of OTL, CLO, or "Flag Bureaux" underneath the main heading. (4) title of originator of the **evals** first to be typed. (5) headings and texts of that aide's or a/aide's evals. (6) pages are numbered consecutively. For the sake of neatness and first **evals** should be CS-1's, then CS-2's etc., across the org board. This may be impractical and should not be adhered to if time is lost thereby. (CBO 163)

EVALUATE, 1. it is an action which is basically an intelligence action. The actual meaning which is supposed to be embraced in the word is "to examine the evidence in order to determine the situation" and then it could have a further—"So as to formulate policy or planning relating thereto." In other words, "What is the enemy going to do?" And therefore the General can say, "Therefore, we should __________." (7201C02 SO) **2.** to examine and judge the significance and condition of. (7201C02 SO) **3.** determine the situation which even more simplified would be, find out the situation. From this body of data, from this indicator we can get a good situation, a bad situation or a no-situation. And that is what one is trying to determine. (7201C02 SO) **4.** tell the pc what it's all about. (HCOB 30 May 70) *Abbr.* Eval.

EVALUATION, 1. the purpose of an **evaluation** is to isolate and handle the cause of a non-optimum situation so as to reverse and improve it toward an ideal scene. An **evaluation** is also done to isolate the cause of a scene which is going well and to reinforce it. (BPL 16 Dec 73) **2.** I found that getting the situation was a common bug. Evidently people don't do a real stat analysis and get an ideal scene, look for its furthest departure and get the situation and then look for data and find the why. There are many ways to go about it but the above is easy, simple and foolproof. It would look like this on a worksheet: gross divisional statistic analysis to find the area and a conditional guess. Ideal scene for that area. Biggest depart from it for the situation. Stats, data, out-point counts, why, ethics why, who, ideal scene, handling, bright idea. If you're very good your gross divisional stat analysis will get confirmed by data. The real why opens the door to handling. And you can handle. This doesn't change **eval** form. It's just a working model. All good **evals** are very consistent—all on same railroad track. Not pies, sea lions, space ships. But pies, apples, flour, sugar, stoves. (HCO PL 19 Sept 73 IR) **3.** by complete **evaluation** we of course mean, situation spotted, analyzed, why, recommended handling, and the agreed upon step. (7201C02 SO) **4. evaluating** tests for public individuals. (HCO PL 15 Feb 61) *Abbr.* Eval.

EVALUATION FORMAT, when doing an **evaluation,** one can become far too fixated on out-points and miss the real reason one is doing an **evaluation** in the first place. To handle this, it is proper **form** to write up an **evaluation** so as to keep in view the reason one is doing one. This is accomplished by using this **form:**

Situation: ____________________
Data: ____________________
Stats: ____________________
Why: ____________________
Ideal Scene: ____________________
Handling: ____________________
(HCO PL 17 Feb 72)

EVALUATION OF PERSONNEL, the **evaluation of personnel** can be done with fair rapidity. It includes the test battery, it includes his ethics record, it includes his personnel record, and it includes any record of statistics the person might have. Now that is very very good to know that you can actually have some index of **evaluation.** You will err more in the direction of failing to believe it than you will err in any other direction. (ESTO 3, 7203C02 SO I)

EVALUATION SCRIPT, script written by Peter Greene on experience with PE Foundation, Johannesburg, based on recent PE Policy Letters. This script is to be used when **evaluating** tests for public individuals. It must be studied and learned by heart by PE **evaluators.** It makes the difference between ample PE Course sign-ups and very few sign-ups. The **evaluation** is given with excellent TR 1, almost tone 40. The idea is to impinge on the person. (HCO PL 15 Feb 61) [See the reference HCO PL for the text of the script.]

EVALUATOR, 1. an **evaluator** is one that **evaluates.** (7201C02SO) 2. PE **evaluators (evaluating** tests for public individuals). (HCO PL 15 Feb 61)

EVENT, 1. meetings, deputations, significant dates, combinings and separations and many other things are **events.** (HCO PL 5 Feb 69 II) 2. **events** are short, evening affairs with the emphasis on personal handling of registration cycles with public. (BPL 4 July 72R)

EVENTS IN CORRECT SEQUENCE, a plus-point. **Events** in actual **sequence.** (HCO PL 3 Oct 74)

EVIDENCE, (Committees of **Evidence**) the spoken word, writings and documents are to be considered as **evidence.** Session withholds may not be used as **evidence** but **evidence** may not be refused because it also has been given in a session. Hearsay **evidence** (saying one heard somebody say that somebody else did) should not be admissible **evidence,** but statements that one heard another make damaging remarks or saw another act or fail to act is admissible. (HCO PL 7 Sept 63)

EVIDENCE, 1. the product derived from investigating and organizing the findings about a business or activity, then interpreting the information in tables, charts and various other statistical forms. 2. in law, any article presented at a court trial serving to test or prove a claim made by the litigants.

EVIL, it might interest you how an SP comes about. He's already got enough overts to deserve more motivators than you can shake a stick at. He has done something to dish one and all in. He's been a bad boy. Now the reason he got to be a bad boy was by switching valences. He had a bad boy over there and he then, in some peculiar way, got into that bad boy's valence. Now he knows what he is—he's a bad boy. Man is basically good but he mocks-up **evil** valences and then gets into them. He says the other fellow is bad. The other fellow was bad. And eventually he got this pasted-up other fellow and one day he becomes the other fellow, see, in a valence shift or personality—whole, complete package of personality. And there he is. So now he is an **evil** fellow. He knows how he is supposed to act. He is supposed to act like the other fellow. That's the switcherroo. That's how **evil** comes into being. The religionists have been having a hard time trying to solve what **evil** was and that is what **evil** is. It is the declaration or postulate that **evil** can exist. In the absence of postulates and declaration of such, man is good. (SH Spec 73, 6608C02)

EVIL PURPOSE, a definite obsessive desire to destroy. (ESTO 3, 7203C02 SO I) *Abbr.* Ev Purp.

EVIL PURPOSE BOY, he's out to destroy the lot. His whole life is monitored by this, and he does it in the most remarkable way. Criminals and that sort of thing are motivated this way. And they are very hard to detect because they very carefully cover it all up while pulling the rug out from underneath anything. (ESTO 3, 7203C02 SO I)

EXACT SCHEDULING, means just that. The course has a daily **schedule,** it is known to each student, and it is adhered to **exactly.** The course commences each day and after each break **exactly** on time, with a brisk, snappy rollcall, it is ended exactly on time by the supervisor. (BPL 8 May 68 R II)

EXAMINATIONS OFFICER, (Gung-Ho Group) the **Examinations Officer** examines anyone trained or being trained and any project or program. (HCO PL 2 Dec 68)

EXAMINER, 1. the **Examiner** is open from 9:00 A.M. to 10:00 P.M. excepting lunch and dinner breaks. (1) the **Examiner** is the terminal for pre-auditing statements and any communications you wish to give to the C/S. (Case Supervisor) (2) the **Examiner** is the terminal to go through to see the Qual Consultant. (**Examiner** will make an appointment for you) (3) the **Examiner** is the terminal to see to give the C/S data regarding any physical body difficulty and any planned visit to or report from a doctor while you are receiving an intensive. (4) the **Examiner** is the terminal you see after each auditing session. (BPL 29 Jan 72R) 2. (Correction Division) the **Examiner examines** all the org's pcs expertly and accurately, catches all flubs by inspecting all folders sent for "Declare?", before calling the pc, ensuring that the process or rundown was run and full end phenomenon attained, and reports all technical deficiencies and ensures these are handled. (BPL 7 Dec 71R I) 3. (**pc examiner**) that person in a Scn organization assigned to the duties of noting pcs' statements, TA position and indicators after session or when pc wishes to volunteer information. (BPL 4 Dec 71R III) 4. the whole duty of the **examiner** is to note the TA needle behavior of the pc. You don't as an **Examiner** care about anything except TA—needle behavior—statement. (HCO PL 13 Oct 68) 5. briefly the **Examiner's** purpose is to ensure standard tech is applied and results are flawless. (FO 1170)

EXAMINER'S 24 HOUR RULE, the **rule** is: any goofed session must be repaired with **24 hours.** (HCO PL 8 Sept 70R)

EXCALIBUR, 1. *Excalibur* was an unpublished book written in the very late 1930s. Only fragments of it remain. (HCO PL 17 Mar 69) **2.** the unpublished work *Excalibur* (most of which has been released in HCOBs, PLs and books). (HCO PL 26 Apr 70R) **3.** the *Excalibur* is the Sea Org training vessel for the Pacific area. (CBO 212) **4.** *Asia* (FSO 559) *Abbr. Excal.* [*Asia* was the former name of the ship, *Excalibur.*]

EXCHANGE, criminal **exchange** is nothing from the criminal for something from another. Whether theft or threat or fraud is used, the criminal think is to get something without putting out anything. That is obvious. A staff member can be coaxed into this kind of thinking by permitting him to receive without his contributing. When you let a person give nothing for something you are factually encouraging crime. It is **exchange** which maintains the inflow and outflow that gives a person space around him and keeps the bank off of him. One has to produce something to **exchange** for money. If he gives nothing in return for what he gets the money does not belong to him. It is interesting that when a person becomes productive his morale improves. Reversely it should be rather plain to you that a person who doesn't produce becomes mentally or physically ill. For his **exchange** factor is out. (HCO PL 4 Apr 72)

Exchange (Def. 1)

EXCHANGE, 1. generally, the barter or trading of money, property or services in return for like rewards of equal or similar value. 2. a business market engaged in handling the trading of a commodity as in a produce or stock exchange. 3. the trading of money of one nation for the currency of another country at a ratio established by the international money market. 4. system of payments wherein negotiable drafts or bills of exchange are used in place of money. 5. the fee or amount charged for handling such a system of payments.

EXCHANGE CONTROL, the jurisdiction by a nation of the ways in which its currency may be traded for other currencies, usually done to influence or enhance the value of its currency on international markets.

EXCHANGE, LOSSES, 1. the net result showing a financial loss in its own national currency taken by companies or individuals in the outcome of transactions dealing in foreign currencies. 2. in financial statements or consolidated accounts the net loss incurred, recorded or unrecorded, in translating rates of foreign accounts to the company's currency.

EXCHANGE RATE, a calculation made of the worth of a currency relative to or in exchange for another currency.

EXCLUSIVE, type of article other than straight news usually included in a newspaper. A feature sent to one newspaper. (BPL 10 Jan 73R)

EXEC ESTO'S ASSISTANT MASTER AT ARMS, the **Esto's MAA.** (FSO 534)

EXEC ESTO'S MAA, the **Executive Esto** has a **Master at Arms** in a large org. The **MAA** musters the crew, conducts any exercises, does ethics investigations as needful especially by the **Exec Esto** and helps hat the Ethics Officers of the org. He does not replace these. He does other duties assigned. (HCO PL 7 Mar 72)

EXECUTING, getting people to get the work done. (HCO PL 30 Oct 62)

EXECUTIONS BRANCH, Programs **Executions Branch.** (FO 3506)

EXECUTIVE, 1. one who obtains **execution** of duties, programs and actions in an organization to further the aims and purposes of that organization. (HCO PL 30 Oct 62) **2.** any person holding an **executive** post (head of department or above) is deemed an **executive.** (HCO PL 3 May 72) **3.** one who holds a position of administrative or managerial responsibility in an organization.

(HCO PL 29 Oct 71 II) **4.** to give one some idea of the power associated with the word, Daniel Webster, in 1826, defined it as: "The Officer, whether King, President, or other Chief Magistrate, who superintends the **execution** of the laws; the person who administers the government, **executive** power or authority in government. Men most desirous of places in the **executive** gift, will not expect to be gratified, except by their support of the **executive.** John Quincy." (HCO PL 29 Oct 71 II) **5.** used in distinction from legislative and judicial. The body that deliberates and enacts laws is legislative; the body that judges or applies the laws to particular cases is judicial; the body or person who carries the laws into effect or superintends the enforcement of them is **executive,** according to its 19th Century governmental meaning according to Webster. (HCO PL 29 Oct 71 II) **6.** the word comes from the Latin *"Ex(s) equī* (past participle *ex(s) ecutus*) execute, follow to the end: *ex-*, completely+*sequī*, to follow." In other words, he follows things to the end and gets something done. (HCO PL 29 Oct 71 II) **7.** an **executive** is in fact a worker who can do all and any of the work in the area he supervises and who can note and work rapidly to repair any outnesses observed in the functioning of those actions in his charge. (HCO PL 28 Jul 71) 8. an **executive** in charge of an org would "single-hand" (handle it all) while getting others to handle their jobs in turn. (HCO PL 28 Jul 71) **9.** essentially an **executive** is a working individual who can competently handle any post or machine or plan under him. (HCO PL 28 Jul 71) **10.** an **executive** handles the whole area while he gets people to help. (HCO PL 28 Jul 71) **11.** an **executive** or foreman is one who can obtain, train and use people, equipment and spaces to economically achieve valuable final products. (HCO PL 14 Dec 70) **12.** anyone in charge of an org, part of an org, a division, a department, a section or a unit. (HCO PL 5 Jan 68) **13.** a general term including any in-charge or above. (HCO PL 13 Mar 66) **14.** those personnel in orgs who are titled as **executives** are: the Board Members, the Commanding Officer or **Executive** Director or head of the org, the HCO **Executive** Secretary, the Org **Executive** Secretary, the Public **Executive** Secretary, the heads of divisions and the heads of departments. In very large orgs the title is extended to heads of large sections. (HCO PL 29 Oct 71 II) **15. executives** are Dept heads, and, anyone who attends the Advisory Council. (HCO PL 27 Nov 59) **16.** the **executives** of the organization are: Organization Secretary, Director of Training, Director of Processing, Director of Materiel, Director of Promotion and Registration, Director of Accounts. (SEC ED 59, 28 Jan 59) *Abbr.* Exec.

EXECUTIVE ABILITY, executive ability is similar to administrative ability in that it requires an ability to formulate and apply policy which will result in the safe, efficient and profitable running of an organization. However, executive ability also implies being able to get others to get the work done and being able to get policy known and used.

EXECUTIVE BOOSTER GROUP, (Flag Only) the basic program for the **Executive Booster Group** is as follows: (1) misunderstood words on earlier materials cleaned up. (2) Ron's new Student Booster Rundown. (3) the full **Exec** hat he was sent for, e.g. ED hat. (4) apprenticeship in the Flag Land Base. (5) Source briefing. (6) fire back to org. The **Executive Booster Group** are seated in the same area while studying and the same area while eating. They are on a very tight schedule with 8 hours sleep and 1 1/2 hours a day for three meals. The rest of the time is spent on study and auditing. They have no free time. They are to return to their orgs within one month, able to hold an **exec** post.(FBDL 596)

EXECUTIVE, CHIEF, 1. a term for the highest level executive in an organization or the Governor of a State. 2. the President of the United States.

EXECUTIVE CONFIDENCE, executives in business and government can fail in three ways and thus bring about a chaos in their department. They can: (1) seem to give endless freedom; (2) seem to give endless barriers; (3) make neither freedom nor barriers certain. **Executive confidence,** therefore, consists of imposing and enforcing an adequate balance between their people's freedom and the unit's barriers and in being precise and consistent about those freedoms and barriers. Such an **executive** adding only in himself initiative and purpose can have a department with initiative and purpose. (PAB 84)

EXECUTIVE CORRECTION LIST, HCO Bulletin 27 March 72, Issue V, *Executive Correction List, Study Correction List 5.* The prepared **list** locates an **executive's** troubles and indicates handling. (LRH ED 257 INT)

EXECUTIVE COUNCIL, 1. the **Exec Council** is composed of the **Exec** Secretaries and their Org Officers and the CO or ED. Their actions are: (a) approval of Ad Council recommended GDS conditions and all Ad Council Planning. **Exec Council** may veto or amend or add to Ad Council planning and is responsible to see that Ad Council performs its duties. In the final analysis, regardless of Ad Council action or inaction, **Exec Council** is responsible for demanding delivery and income and getting it produced. (b) long range promotional planning. (c) the actions of financial planning as given in HCO PL 26 November 1965, *Financial Planning,* designed to maintain outgo below income, balance the budget and keep finance on policy. (d) allocation to divisions of available funds in keeping with divisional planning and stat conditions. **Exec Council** sees to it that production necessities are covered in FP, usually by means of a checklist which lists routine org expenses by division. **Exec Council** adds its allocation to the Ad Council Directive and this then forms the Financial Planning Directive for the week. (HCO PL 23 Jun 75) **2.** puts a functioning Ad Council there and demands income and delivery and handles allocation and solvency matters. (HCO PL 23 Jun 75) **3. Executive Council** would be five—Captain, Supercargo, Super's Org Officer, Chief Officer, Chief's Org Officer. (OODs 12 May 74) **4.** an **Executive Council** has all GDSs available to it every week. The **Executive Council** as a **council,** runs the org by observation of the gross divisional statistics. Conditions are assigned each division by the **Executive Council** each week according to these GDS stats. (HCO PL 5 Feb 70) **5.** consists of the Supercargo, Chief Officer and LRH Comm Ship. (FO 1275) **6.** the **Executive Council** on a vessel consists of the Supercargo and Chief Officer. Any orders must be passed on by the LRH Comm of the vessel as not against Flag Orders and then ratified by the Captain as a Ship's Order before such orders are binding on the whole ship. (FO 1021) **7. Executive Council** will become: Master, Supercargo, Chief Officer. (FO 401) **8.** same as Board of Directors. Board of Directors: this is composed of the HCO **Exec** Sec WW, the Org **Exec** Sec WW, the LRH Comm WW. (HCO PL 6 Sept 67) **9.** the two **Executive** Secretaries (or the HCO Sec and Org Sec of a Six Department Org) constitute an **Executive Council.** This is the highest governing body of an organization. It is assisted by an Advisory Council which meets at a time of week prior to the **Executive Council** meeting. The **Executive Council** has the purpose of conducting a successful organization. (HCO PL 21 Dec 66 II) *Abbr.* EC.

EXECUTIVE COUNCIL ADVANCED ORGANIZATIONS, an **Executive Council AO's** is formed. It acts as the senior body to individual **Advanced Organizations,** and ensures that they continue to expand. It consists of a Commanding Officer **AO,** Supercargo **AO** and Chief Officer **AO** and forms part of the International Exec Div **AO** which is posted as the eighth division of each individual **AO.** The principle that no Exec Division of any kind may exist without being part of an org is held firm and the **ECAO** is attached to AOLA and is housed in the same buildings. The purpose of **ECAO** is to help LRH conduct successful **Advanced Organizations** over the world, provide control over these, and to ensure that **AO's** make OTs and support the Sea Org so that the planet can be brought under control and a safe environment provided in which the planet's 4th dynamic engram can be run out. (FO 1939) *Abbr.* ECAO.

EXECUTIVE COUNCIL EUROPE, ECEU is directly answerable to an SO Commanding Officer and the Continental Captain, Stationship Europe. All **EU** orgs, franchises and groups are directly under **ECEU.** (HCO PL 23 Apr 70) *Abbr.* ECEU.

EXECUTIVE COUNCIL FLAG BUREAUX, is composed of: CO **FB** (Chairman), D/CO **FB,** Supercargo **FB,** Chief Officer **FB,** Supercargo's Org Officer and Chief Officer's Org Officer. The VFP of **Exec Council FB** is: managed and expanding orgs. The function of the **Exec Council FB** is: planning and coordination. (CBO 341)

EXECUTIVE COUNCIL WORLDWIDE, is fully responsible for the running of all Scn (not Sea Org) orgs via its Continental Exec Councils and the org's own Exec Councils. (FO 2220)

EXECUTIVE COURT OF ETHICS, convened in the same way and with the same powers and disciplines as a Court of Ethics. An **Executive Court of Ethics** is convened by the Office of LRH via the HCO Executive Secretary. The presiding person must be at or above the rank of the person summoned. A Court of Ethics may not summons a director, a secretary or an executive secretary. An **Executive Court of Ethics** only may be convened on a director, secretary or executive secretary. The **Executive Ethics Court** is presided over by a secretary or executive secretary as appointed for that one court and one purpose by the Office of LRH via the HCO Executive Secretary. (HCO PL 26 May 65 III)

EXECUTIVE DIRECTIVES, issued by any Executive Council and named for the area it applies to. Thus **ED** WW, meaning issued to Worldwide. They are valid for only one year. They contain various immediate orders, programs, etc. They are blue ink on blue paper. (HCO PL 24 Sept 70R) *Abbr.* EDs.

EXECUTIVE DIRECTIVES ROYAL SCOTMAN, all orders, Captain's orders, conditions orders and organizational orders of the *Royal*

Scotman, published by it, shall hereafter be **Executive Directives RS.** (FO 411) *Abbr.* EDRS.

EXECUTIVE DIRECTOR, 1. the head of the org is the Commanding Officer or **Executive Director.** He is usually also the Product Officer. He is senior to the Exec Esto. (HCO PL 7 Mar 72) **2.** the org is commanded by the Commanding Officer (SO orgs) or the **Executive Director** (non SO orgs). In the triangular system of the Flag Executive Briefing Course (FEBC) (Product—Org Officer system) the CO or **ED** coordinates the work of the Product Officer, Org Officer and Executive Esto. In most orgs the CO or **ED** is also the Product Officer of the org which is a double hat with CO. (HCO PL 7 Mar 72) **3.** the **Executive Director** of an organization is the Product Officer of that organization. He does nothing but think, eat, breathe—product. He knows the valuable final products of the organization, he demands them. When he doesn't get them he investigates by data analysis, finds the why, debugs it, writes a program. (ESTO 1, 7203C01 SO I) **4.** the **Executive Director** has products 1, 2, 3, and 4 (Org Series 10). He is basically when you get it out into a triangular system, the Planning Officer. And he is the fellow that the Product Officer and the Organizing Officer meet with in order to plan up what they're going to do and then the basic team action which occurs, occurs after a planning action of this particular character. Where you have the Product Officer who is also the **Executive Director,** he is also the Planning Officer. He's double hatted. (FEBC 12, 7102C03 SO II) **5.** the CO or **ED** of an org is responsible for managing the org and keeping it going. (LRH ED 153RE INT) **6.** there is only one **Exec Director,** LRH, and he is **Exec Dir** for WW and for each org. There are no assistant or deputy **Executive Directors.** (Orders issued for the **Exec Dir** must be approved by the LRH Communicator as not against policy and by HCO Personnel when personnel is appointed). (HCO PL 13 Mar 66) **7.** the bulk of the job of the **Executive Director** is getting existing policy applied and detecting where it isn't being applied, forecasting slumps, repairing emergencies and keeping orgs on the increase, and all in such a way as to not add further upset to the mess. The **Executive Director** hat does not conflict with the International Org Supervisor hat as the latter is only a portion of the sphere of responsibility of the former. The **Executive Director** deals mainly with Org/Assn Secs, HCO Secs and the Int Org Supervisor reaches much deeper into orgs. (HCO PL 22 Feb 65 III) **8.** oversees all HCO Secretaries, Organization Secretaries and Association Secretaries and all Managers. Appoints all executive personnel in all organizations and these may be removed only by the **Executive Director** or with his concurrence. (HCO PL 18 Dec 64, *Saint Hill Org Board*) **9.** the person in-charge of all Scn organizations including Saint Hill. (HCO PL 26 Jun 64) *Abbr.* ED.

EXECUTIVE DIRECTOR ORG BOARD, an org needs a fully trained **Executive Director** who uses HCO to run the **org.** We have a new **org board** called the **Executive Director Org Board** which is different only in that HCO is used as the senior division to run the **org.** HCO is simply drawn two or three inches higher than the rest of the divisions and the **Executive Director** keeps it manned and doing its job. (LRH ED 129 INT)

EXECUTIVE DIVISION, 1. upon the **Executive Division** depends the management and coordination of the entire org. Without leaders who know and effectively apply LRH policy and technology, the whole org will rapidly diminish to a state of total confusion. The **Executive Division,** under the guidance of LRH sets the direction and pace of the org. The alignment of actions and intentions, coordinated as a whole, brings about the continued prosperity and well-being of the org and its staff. (*OEC* Vol VII, p. 1) **2.** the **Executive Division** becomes **Division** 9 instead of 7. (Nine Division Org). (HCO PL 26 Oct 68) **3.** it is there to get tech in and keep it in, get policy followed and not used to stop growth, keep the group solvent and functioning and the admin and org pattern correct. If it doesn't do these things then it isn't doing its job. (HCO PL 1 Mar 66 II) **4.** the **Executive Division** is **Division** 7. The LRH Communicator is in charge of the **division.** It consists of three departments. The first department is the Office of LRH, Department 21. It is in the charge of the LRH Personal Secretary. The second department is the Office of the HCO Executive Secretary, Department 20. It is in the charge of the HCO Exec Sec Coordinator. The third department is the Office of the Organization Executive Secretary, Department 19. It is in the charge of the Org Exec Sec Coordinator. (HCO PL 2 Aug 65) *Abbr.* Exec Div.

EXECUTIVE ENTURBULENCE, a type of dev-t. An **executive** is seldom hit unless he has had non-compliance on his lines. He is almost never hit if he polices dev-t. When an **executive** is hit by a catastrophe, he should handle it and at once check up on dev-t and handle it. I keep a daily log of dev-t and who and what every time I find my lines heavy or there is a threatened catastrophe. Then I handle the majority offenders. (HCO PL 27 Jan 69)

EXECUTIVE ESTABLISHMENT OFFICER, 1. the one who puts the org there to be run. He does this by having Establishment Officers establishing the divisions, org staff and the materiel of the division. He is like a coach using athletes to win games. He sends them in and they put their divisions there and maintain them. They also put there somebody to work them. (HCO PL 7 Mar 72) 2. the Product Officer of Estos. He produces Esto hours of establishment and an org and ship by using Estos in each division. (OODs 9 Apr 72)

EXECUTIVE ESTABLISHMENT OFFICER ORG OFFICER, (**Esto Org Officer**) the **E-Esto's** deputy and handles his programs and the personal side of Estos. (HCO PL 7 Mar 72)

EXECUTIVE ESTO MAA, 1. the **Executive Esto** has a **Master at Arms** in a large org. The **MAA** musters the crew, conducts any exercises, does ethics investigations as needful especially by the **Exec Esto** and helps hat the Ethics Officers of the org. He does not replace these. He does other duties assigned. (HCO PL 7 Mar 72) 2. is responsible for the schedule and getting to work and exercise and activities of staff members. (HCO PL 6 Apr 72)

EXECUTIVE ETHICS HEARING, no one of the rank of director or above may be summoned for an Ethics Hearing, but only an **Executive Ethics Hearing,** presided over by a person superior in rank. It is convened by the Office of LRH via the HCO Exec Sec. The same rank in a senior org is a senior rank. (HCO PL 26 May 65 III)

EXECUTIVE, JUNIOR, person working under senior executives who is comparatively new to an organization, sometimes in training for higher level work.

EXECUTIVE LETTER UNIT, this **unit** consists of a knowledgeable person who can answer personal **executive** type mail, casual org mail and the public **letters** received by the HCO Exec Sec and Org Exec Sec. This type of mail is then typed and forwarded to the **executive** to whom it was addressed for signature or any change or signature and footnote and is then mailed. (HCO PL 17 Sept 65)

EXECUTIVE, MARKETING, an executive who plans and coordinates the marketing actions to be taken on a particular brand of product or range of products under that brand. He would oversee advertising, distribution, sales, etc.

EXECUTIVE MISBEHAVIOUR POLICY NO. 1, no **executive** who begins or persists in a sexual relationship with a person hostile to or "open minded about" Dn and Scn may be retained on post or in the organization. (HCO PL 9 Feb 71)

EXECUTIVE MISBEHAVIOUR POLICY NO. 2, any **executive** who engages in activities for which he could be blackmailed may not hold any **executive** post. (HCO PL 9 Feb 71)

EXECUTIVE MISBEHAVIOUR POLICY NO. 3, any person who places personal interests and situations above the interests of the group may not hold an **executive** post. (HCO PL 9 Feb 71)

EXECUTIVE OFFICER'S MAST, see CAPTAIN'S MAST.

EXECUTIVE POST, 1. head of department or above. (HCO PL 3 May 72) 2. **Executive posts** are defined as follows: in HASI: Assoc (or Org) Sec, PE Director, Director of Training, Director of Processing, Director of Enrollment, Chief Registrar (body), Letter Registrar, Director of Material, Director of Accounts, in HCO: HCO Continental Secretary, HCO Area Secretary. (HCO PL 16 Jun 64)

EXECUTIVE QUALIFICATION CERTIFICATE, I will qualify and issue a **Qualification Certificate** to any staff personnel who meets **executive** requirements regardless of whether they occupy an **executive** post or not. A person who does not actually hold an **executive** post but who wishes to receive an **Executive Qualification Certificate** must pass all requirements for that **executive** post and must receive as well a high mark on hat check of that post. (HCO PL 26 Feb 61)

EXECUTIVE REPORT, any report prepared for the use of top management.

EXECUTIVE SEARCH CONSULTANT (OR HEAD-HUNTER), an outside professional recruiter or firm offering to clients the service of finding qualified individuals actively engaged in the field who may be open to an offer of new employment, to fill key positions in client organizations.

EXECUTIVE SECRETARY, 1. there are two **Executive Secretaries** at WW, two in Continental Exec Divisions, two in every other Exec Div. They are the HCO **Exec Sec** and the Org **Exec Sec.** They head the 3 HCO and the 4 Org divisions respectively. (HCO PL 13 Mar 66) 2. an expert in three divisions. (FEBC 3, 7101C18 SO II) *Abbr.* Exec Sec.

EXECUTIVE SECRETARY COMMUNICATOR, 1. the title advisory where used as helper to an **Exec Sec** is changed to "(HCO or ORG) **Exec Sec Communicator** for (division represented)." This title has the rank and privileges of a **secretary** in his own org and in a junior org to the one appointed, the privileges of an **executive secretary.** The purpose of the post is to **communicate** for the **Executive Secretary** and help with that official's purpose by **communicating** on matters and/or handling them relating to the type of division represented and to be responsible to the **Executive Secretary** for that type of division and to be responsible to the **Executive Secretary** for that gross divisional statistic. Only in the International Division or in an org having 250 staff members or more would this post be filled. (HCO PL 21 Jan 66) **2.** all those persons now styled or titled **Executive Secretary Communicators** are changed as of date of receipt to Divisional Organizers. (HCO PL 1 Nov 66 I)

EXECUTIVE TRAINING, see TRAINING, EXECUTIVE.

EXECUTOR, 1. generally, a person who performs something or puts it into practice. 2. in law, a person appointed to execute the provisions of a will; also called an Administrator of an Estate.

EXEMPTION, an allowed deduction from one's gross annual income resulting in a lessening of the amount of income one must pay taxes on. In many countries being married and having children as dependents qualifies one to make a specified deduction or exemption.

EXISTING SCENE, 1. the **existing scene** is what is really there. (HCO PL 7 Aug 72) **2.** means the way things are here and now. It takes in the people or personnel, their current state, the lines, the hats, the buildings, equipment, and the state of them, the tech in use and current news. (FO 2779)

EXPANDED DIANETICS, 1. that branch of Dn which uses Dn in special ways for specific purposes. It is not HSDC Dn. Its position on the Grade Chart would be just above Class IV. Its proper number is Class IVA. It uses Dn to change an Oxford Capacity Analysis (or an American Personality Analysis) and is run directly against these analysis graphs and the *Science of Survival Hubbard Chart of Human Evaluation.* **Expanded Dianetics** is not the same as Standard Dn as it requires special training and advanced skills. The main difference between these two branches is that Standard Dn is very general in application. **Expanded Dn** is very specifically adjusted to the pc. Some pcs, particularly heavy drug cases, or who have been given injurious psychiatric treatment or who are physically disabled or who are chronically ill or who have had trouble running engrams (to name a few) require a specially adapted technology. (HCOB 15 Apr 72) **2.** it takes November 1970 discoveries about insanity and puts the handling of the roughest cases and chronic illness into the hands of auditors who do not have to be trained for years. (OODs 15 Sept 72) **3.** research has revealed an upper level strata of Dn. Out of the original Dn project has emerged a new set of skills. These are in fact a sort of OT level handling of Dn for special cases. (ED 149R Flag) *Abbr.* EX DN, XDN, EXP DN.

EXPANDED DIANETICS AUDITOR, certificate is Hubbard Graduate Dianetic Specialist (HGDS). The **Expanded Dn** Course teaches about **Expanded Dn.** Processes taught are **Expanded Dn** basics, **EX DN** set-ups, R3R of intentions and purposes, assessments and R3R to handle the present environment, past auditing, valences, emotional stress, chronic somatics, wants handled, hidden standards, responsibility, metalosis RD, PTS RD, assists and repairs and C/Sing on **EX DN** against the OCA. End result is an ability to **audit** others to **Expanded Dn** case completion. (CG&AC 75)

EXPANDED DIANETICS CASE SUPERVISOR, **(EXDN C/S)** does only **EX Dn.** He can **C/S** the set-up actions for **Ex Dn** if needed, but he is the **EX Dn** specialist. (HCO PL 26 Sept 74)

EXPANDED DIANETICS C/S COURSE, this is a specialist **course** specifically in the **C/Sing** tech of **Expanded Dn. Expanded Dianetics C/S** status is awarded as a provisional status until the SHSBC has been completed at an SH Org. The prerequisite is the **EX Dn** course, Dn and Class IV or VI C/S courses. (BPL 26 Apr 73R I)

EXPANDED DIANETIC SPECIALIST, an HGDS (Hubbard Graduate **Dianetic Specialist**). (HCOB 15 Apr 72)

EXPANDED GF 40 RB, HCO Bulletin 30 June 1971R, *Expanded GF 40RB.* Called GF 40X. This is the "7 resistive type cases" at the end of the **Green Form** expanded out. This is how you get those "earlier practices" and other case stoppers. This done well gives a lot of extensive work in Dn. It's lengthy but really pays off. (LRH ED 257 INT)

EXPANDED LOWER GRADES, the **lower grades** harmonic into the OT levels. They can be run again with full 1950-1960 to 1970 processes as given on the SH Courses all through the 1960s. These are now regrouped and sorted out and are called **Expanded Lower Grades.** Only this route will now be sold. There are no Dn or Scn single—triple or "Quickie Lower Grades" any more. (LRH ED 101 INT)

EXPANDED NON-EXISTENCE FORMULA, the **expanded non-existence formula** is: (1) find and get yourself on every comm line you will need in order to give and obtain information relating to your duties and material. (2) make yourself known, along with your post title and duties, to every terminal you will need for the obtaining of information and the giving of data. (3) discover from your seniors and fellow staff members and any public your duties may require you to contact, what is needed and wanted from each. (4) do, produce and present what each needs and wants that is in conformation with policy. (5) maintain your comm lines that you have and expand them to obtain other information you now find you need on a routine basis. (6) maintain your origination lines to inform others what you are doing exactly, but only those who actually need the information. (7) streamline what you are doing, producing and presenting so that it is more closely what is really needed and wanted. (8) with full information being given and received concerning your products, do, produce and present a greatly improved product routinely on your post. (HCO PL 8 Nov 75)

EXPANSION, 1. an increase in living. To increase living and raise tone and heighten activity one need only apply the **expansion** formula to living. Clean away the barriers, non-compliance and distractions from the basic purpose and reduce opposition and the individual or group or org will seem more alive and indeed will be more alive. (HCO PL 13 Mar 65, *Divisions 1, 2, 3 The Structure of Organization What is Policy?*) **2** product increase. (HCO PL 20 Oct 67, *Admin Know-How—Conditions, How to Assign*) **3. expansion** which when **expanded** can hold its territory without effort is proper and correct **expansion.** (HCO PL 4 Dec 66)

EXPANSION, 1. the circumstance of increasing or extending the dominion of an organization by such things as building new facilities, expanding into new endeavors, capturing new publics, adding personnel, taking over more territory and other similar actions of growth. 2. generally, a time when the trend of business overall is in an upswing.

EXPANSION BUREAU, the Flag Programs Bureau. Officially changed its name to the **Expansion Bureau.** (SO ED 246 INT)

EXPANSION DEMAND, see DEMAND, EXPANSION.

EXPANSION FORMULA, 1. direct a channel toward attainment, put something on it, remove distractions, barriers, non-compliance and opposition. (HCO PL 13 Mar 65, *Divisions 1, 2, 3 The Structure of Organization What is Policy?*) **2.** (a) provide good policy. (b) make it easily knowable. (3) be strenuous in making sure it is followed. This is the most broad possible **formula** for **expansion.** (HCO PL 13 Mar 65, *Divisions 1, 2, 3 The Structure of Organization What is Policy?*)

EXPANSION NEWSLETTER, the **Expansion Newsletter** issued by Flag Dissem Bureau (PR&C) every other week. It can be issued on special occasions as a special edition. The public of the **newsletter** is org staffs. The **newsletter** concerns activities relating directly to staff, orgs, tech and Scn **expansion** and current programs being pushed. (CBO 391R)

EXPECTED TIME PERIOD, a plus-point. Events occurring or done in the **time** one would reasonably expect them to be (HCO PL 3 Oct 74)

EXPEDITE, 1. to free one caught by the feet. To speed up or make easy the progress or action of. Hasten. Facilitate. To do quickly. (CBO 118) **2.** the Registrar may mark a test request slip **expedite** which means the person is to be brought right back. (HCO PL 28 Oct 60)

EXPEDITERS, 1. there should be some people down there in HCO and they're in Department 1 and they're called **expediters.** They're farmed out gradually to get backlogs off the line. You keep a very careful record of them, they don't go on the org board and they don't become members of divisions except HCO Dept 1 **Expediter.** They just handle overloads. Now they're gradually becoming familiar with the ship and they're getting through AB Checksheets. Gradually these guys form a personnel pool. (6912C13 SO) **2.** people assigned to Dept 1 as **expediters** to handle work backlogs in other divisions. They may not be given posts. They are only used to clear backlogs of work seen in comm and area inspections. When given a post it is by Captain's approval or transfer. They are no longer **expediters.** (FO 1008)

EXPEDITERS, persons, often termed troubleshooters, sent in to an area to free up organizational lines, unjam production bottlenecks, ensure the on schedule delivery of finished materials, etc.

EXPEDITER UNIT, HCO Division, Dept. 1. **Expediter Unit** fills in temporarily in spots of overload to **expedite** the backlog and get flows moving. (HCO PL 25 Jan 66)

EXPEDITING, actions used to facilitate the rapid and efficient dispatch of communications, orders, production schedules, etc., a term that implies, additionally, follow-up.

EXPENDITURE, the org buys a truck for £500. After a year, that truck could not be resold for £500 because it has been used and is now second-hand. Say that the org could now resell the truck for £300—this shows that the value of the truck has gone down by £200 because of the passage of time. The amount by which the value of the truck has gone down is an **expenditure** because that amount of value has been used up during the year (HCO PL 10 Oct 70 I)

EXPENDITURE, 1. generally, any cost or outlay of cash charged against a company's revenue. 2. the payment of cash, the acquisition of a liability or the transfer of property brought about by purchasing an asset or service. 3. any cost the realization of which extends beyond the current accounting period.

EXPENDITURES, MANAGED, expenditures which are manageable as opposed to those that fluctuate due to outside factors over which a corporation has no control.

EXPENSE, the financial cost or price involved in some activity.

EXPENSE ACCOUNT, see ACCOUNT, EXPENSE.

EXPENSES, total bills one is committed to. (ED 459-28-1 Flag)

EXPENSE SUM, **1.** this is the cost of all Flag **expenses** on board or elsewhere for FSO, FB and other Flag activities. Refund/Repayment/FSM Commissions are paid off the top of the allocation. (FSO 667 RC) **2.** 25% of the Allocation Sum plus the CBT sum less 12 1/2% of CBT. (HASI PL 19 Apr 57)

EXPERIENCE, **experience** comes from working in similar or parallel situations. (HCO PL 13 Mar 65, *Divisions 1, 2, 3 The Structure of Organization What is Policy?*)

EXPERTISE DRILLS, these drills are numbered as **Expertise Drill**-1 (**ED**-1), **Expertise Drill**-2 (**ED**-2), etc., and run consecutively throughout the series. The odd numbered **drills** are unbullbaited. The even numbered **drills** are bullbaited. Their purpose is to improve the quality of auditing by familiarizing auditors with the exact procedure of each auditing action through the use of **drills.** (BTB 15 Dec 74)

EXPLOSION, order put in too suddenly always discharges disorder too fast. That's an **explosion.** You don't want that. (HCOB 6 Jan 59)

EXPORTS, goods sent out of one country for use or sale in another country.

EXPOSURE, the condition of exposing or presenting to the public a product or service via promotion, special events, television and radio announcements, published articles and the like.

EXTENSION COURSE, an **Extension Course** Section consists of a textbook and a series of lessons done on a glued-top tablet, one sheet per lesson, eight questions or exercises per lesson. The questions concern only vital definitions needed for a knowledge of the subject and examples of the use and meaning. The **Extension Course** should give the taker a passing knowledge of Dn and Scn terminology, phenomena, and parts. This is its goal and purpose. The reasoning or examples in a text are considered secondary, for the purposes of the course, to precision definitions. The **Extension Course** student should finish the course with the feeling he is dealing with a precision science, composed of identifiable parts. (HCOB 16 Dec 58)

EXTERIORIZATION INTENSIVE, many people have gone **exterior** and have been audited past it. This made some uncomfortable. A new technical development makes it possible to continue to audit them. A lower level "Thetan **Exterior**" is not yet Clear unless he has taken the Clearing Course. For the above it is necessary to have an **Exteriorization Intensive** before they can be audited further. Some people audited past **exterior** without an **Exteriorization Intensive** develop somatics. (LRH ED 101 INT)

EXTERNAL COMM BUREAU, **1.** has the traffic out-going, has the missionaire out-going, has all of that out-going and everything that's in-coming, and that's its production. The end product of that is management. (FEBC 1, 7011C17 SO) **2.** FOLO **External Comm Bureau** receives and relays all Flag mail, freight, telexes, bodies and logistics to and from Flag, keeps accurate record of particles relayed, searches for and gathers all data from the entire FOLO that should be going to Flag and sends it to Flag (especially from the FOLO Data and Flag Programs Bureaux), maintains Flag security and sends without fail a copy of FOLO telex masters—no exceptions. (CBO 192)

EXTERNAL COMMUNICATIONS, external communications mean anything which goes on an external line to other HCOs through Continental, through Worldwide. (HCO PL 29 Jan 59)

EXTERNAL HCO BRANCH, 1. (in Establishment Bureau 1) the **External HCO Branch** (3) recruits experienced org personnel for FB and evaluator echelon. It does this through FOLO Bureau 1's. It used FPPO lines to get personnel eligible for and sent to Flag. (FPPO functions do not change) (FO 3591) **2.** Branch 11D, Flag Management Bureau) **Ext HCO** has been made a network. Its purpose is to create on-policy effective HCOs. It also continues to carry out the functions of approving personnel transfers and Comm Evs. (FBDL 488R)

EXTERNAL HCO BUREAUX, 1. the command line from **External HCO** Flag and **External HCO** FOLOs to orgs runs via the Flag Management Bureau. There is no other command channel. The functions of **External HCO** are quite different than those in HCOs of orgs, and serve to augment and back up activities already underway in orgs, as well as to serve in the direction and establishment of the international growth of Scn. **External HCO** Flag has the final say on all HCO matters. **External HCO** duties are: (1) to ensure adequate recruitment and hiring in Sea Org and Scn orgs, and that all newly recruited and hired personnel are properly routed and trained prior to posting as well as after. (2) to ensure that all orgs post their personnel correctly, and that proper org form and complements are used to achieve maximum production, in the orgs. (3) to ensure the administrative upkeep of personnel files in all organizations, and the upkeep of the Central Personnel Office files, where records of every staff member of every org and operation past and present are kept. (4) the training of personnel for future expansion programs, and their placement. (5) to ensure that communications in the form of issues are produced in abundance, so that management can occur and knowledge can be exported and thereby used. (6) to ensure that justice and ethics procedures are followed. Also that the rights of individuals are protected, and that adequate correct justice or ethics is applied for maximum production to occur. (BPL 13 Aug 73R II) **2. External HCO** is established in the Flag Bureaux. It is Bureau 1. It comprises three branches: (1) Personnel Branch, (2) Mimeo Branch, (3) International Justice Branch. The head of the **External HCO Bureau** is the **External HCO** Chief. He has FB Aide status but is called "Chief" so as not to confuse the post with the staff post of CS-1. (FO 3313)

EXTERNAL HCO NETWORK, a new **network** formed with the purpose of putting functioning HCOs into all SO and Scn orgs. This is the **External HCO Network.** The network command line is from CS-1 to CO FB to **External HCO** Aide on Flag, to **External HCO** Chiefs in FOLOs to HASes in orgs. (FBDL 504)

EXTERNAL LINES, there are two types of **lines.** They are internal and **external.** Anything inside a Central Organization is internal. Anything flying about amongst HCO Offices only is **external.** (HCO PL 2 Jan 59)

EXTERNAL ORG, the Flag Bureau is the **external org** taking care of the International and SO orgs over the world and planetary actions. (FSO 562)

EXTERNAL PURCHASE ORDER, all orders from Flag to CLOs for supplies are conveyed on a standard **External Purchase Order** originated by the Logistics I/C on Flag. (FO 2611R)

EXTRA DIVIDEND, a dividend in the form of cash or stock paid in addition to the regular company dividends.

EXTRAORDINARY LOCATIONS, locations which are not served by airmail, telex, or telegraph are considered **extraordinary locations** and stale date occurs only when reasonable expectancy is exceeded. (HCO PL 17 Jul 66)

EXTRAPOLATION, 1. generally, the method of estimating unknown data by extending or projecting known data. 2. in statistics, the process of extending a trend line, based on known information.

EXTREME CONDITIONS, meaning very high upsurges and low falls. (LRH ED 121 INT)

EXTREME CONDITIONS PACK, the Data Bureau must not omit its **extreme conditions** actions. In this, when an org falters—stats go down, an **extreme conditions pack** is assembled from files. This contains stats, dispatches, Thursday reports, LRH Comm reports, anything files for the last 30 to 60 days prior to the decline point. (CBO 2)

EXTREME CONDITIONS REPORT, reports on all **conditions** of affluence and above, danger and below. (FO 3449R)

EXTROVERSION, it means nothing more than being able to look outward. A person who is capable of looking at the world around him and seeing it quite real and quite bright is of course in a state of **extroversion.** He can look out, in other words. He can also work. He can also see situations and handle and control those things which he has to handle and control, and can stand by and watch those things which he does not have to control and be interested in them therefore. (*POW,* p. 92)

EXTROVERTED PERSONALITY, one who is capable of looking around the environment. (*POW,* p. 92)

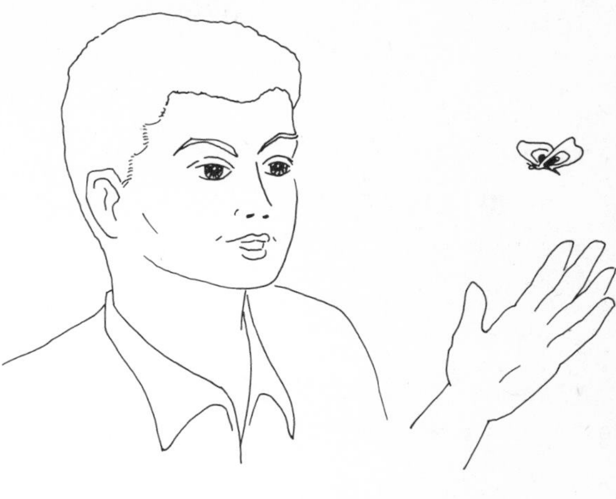

Extroversion

EX URBAN, test form heading to indicate the type the person is: **ex urban** (just in town to be tested). (HCO PL 28 Oct 60, *New Testing Promotion Section—Important*)

F

FACE TO FACE GROUPS, see GROUPS, FACE TO FACE.

FACE VALUE, (or nominal value or par), the value of a stock or share at time of issue as given on the face of the stock certificate, rather than its present market value which may be more, the same or less than par.

FACILITIES, **facilities** normally include: (a) those that unburden lines. (b) those that speed lines. (c) those that gather data. (d) those that compile. (e) those that buy leisure. (f) those that defend. (g) those that extend longevity on the job. One can think of many things that do each of these. The bare minimum are accomplished by giving the executive a communicator. The communicator more or less covers all the categories above. (HCO PL 16 Nov 66)

FACILITY DIFFERENTIAL, when a senior executive has the ability to make money for the organization or greatly raise statistics and when this ability has been demonstrated, that executive should have **facilities.** This ability is often discoverable by the absence of the executive from post for a period or when the executive is pulled off by emergencies. In such a time the income of the org may sink. The degree the income shrinks is the **facility differential** of that executive. It is worth that much to the org in **facilities** to have the executive on post. Example: with that executive on duty—income $8000 per week. With that executive absent—$5000 per week. This is the **facility differential** of that executive. It is, in this example, $3000 per week. This means that the org could afford $3000 per week extreme to provide that executive with facilities for his work to keep him from overload. For it will lose $3000 a week if this executive is distracted or overloaded. (HCO PL 16 Nov 66)

FACILITY VISIT, a term used in Public Relations to describe the technique of arranging for a group of journalists to visit a facility to gather information, take photographs and interview persons for a planned story which will usually result in good publicity.

FACT, something that can be proven to exist by visible evidence. (HCO PL 26 Apr 70R)

FACT, factor analysis chart technique.

FACTOR, an agent who sells goods on behalf of the owner for a commission. A factor usually handles the goods himself and the buyer is usually not aware of the real owner's name. Also known as a Commission Agent.

FACTOR ANALYSIS, see ANALYSIS, FACTOR.

FACTOR ANALYSIS CHART TECHNIQUE, job analysis done by establishing a point system for the main tasks of various management positions within specified salary ranges to determine their relative value to the organization. *Abbr.* FACT.

FACTORING, 1. the buying of accounts receivable, bills, etc., for the purpose of collecting them for oneself. 2. conducting business as a factor.

FACTORY, a building or group of buildings which contain the machinery, tools and equipment necessary for employees to produce specific goods.

FACTORY COSTS, see COSTS, FACTORY.

FACTUAL, true and valid. (HCO PL 3 Oct 74)

FACULTY MEETING, the weekly **meeting** of all instructors, held on Friday, where course reports are made and questions answered. Reviews the general state of the course with an eye to any needed improvements. Sends report to Org Sec. (HCO PL 18 Dec 64, *Saint Hill Org Board*)

FAILED HELP, where an org is having difficulty giving service its **help** buttons are out. It's on a **failed help.** That's why you must train auditors well, so they won't **fail** to **help.** The guy **fails** on enough pcs he stops auditing. (ESTO 12, 7203C06 SO II)

FAILED MISSIONS, **missions** sent in violation of Mission School FOs most often **fail.** Things like only one missionaire, no MOs, no proper briefing, etc. (CBO 25)

FAILURE TO COMPLETE A CYCLE OF ACTION AND REFERRAL, one of your most fruitful sources of dev-t is your own double work. You pick up a despatch or a piece of work, look it over and then put it aside to do later, then later you pick it up and read it again and only then do you do it. This of course doubles your traffic just like that. If you do every piece of work that comes your way when it comes your way and not after awhile, if you always take the initiative and take action, not refer it, you never get any traffic back unless you've got a psycho on the other end. You can keep a comm line in endless ferment by pretending that the easiest way not to work is to not handle things or to **refer** things. Everything you don't handle comes back and bites. Everything you **refer** has to be done when it comes back to you. **Complete** the **action**; do it now. (BPL 30 Jan 69)

FAILURE TO RECORD AN ORDER, **failing to** make an adequate **record** of **an order** given, losing or misplacing the **order** can result in endless dev-t. The original **orders** being lost or not **recorded** at all, wrong items are purchased, incorrect actions are taken, cross orders are given, and a tremendous waste of executive time and money occurs straightening the matter out. (BPL 30 Jan 69)

FAILURE TO TERMINATEDLY HANDLE, REFERRAL, the only tremendous error an organization makes, next to inspection before the fact, is **failing to terminatedly handle** situations rapidly. The fault of an organization's "waffle, waffle, waffle, Joe won't take responsibility for it, it's got to go someplace else," and all that sort of thing, is that it continues a situation. What you should specialize in is terminating the end of a situation, not refer it to someone else. Complete the action now. (BPL 30 Jan 69)

FAILURE TO WEAR YOUR HAT, a person on one post not doing that post but doing every other post creates endless dev-t, all despatches and origins being off-origin and he covering the hole of his own post. The person himself is the dev-t. (BPL 30 Jan 69)

FAIR COPY, (Mimeo files) a **fair copy** is very valuable to files. This means a flawless copy that will respond to electro stencil cutting. Where a stencil gets torn or does not exist one uses the **fair copy.** It is nothing to pull two staples, cut the electro stencils needed and restore the **fair copy** to the folder, stapling it back on. (HCO PL 7 Feb 73 III)

FAIR GAME, by **fair game** is meant, may not be further protected by the codes and disciplines of Scn or the rights of a Scientologist. (HCO PL 23 Dec 65)

FALL ON HIS HEAD, *Slang.* this refers to the fact of a person failing in one area or another. A pc **falls on his head** when he has been improperly audited or attests to grades or actions he has not really attained and then is continued on higher actions or levels of auditing. An administrator **falls on his head** by failing to handle situations and apply correct policy to an area he is responsible for thereby causing the area and himself to fail. A US Western term meaning a person who has erred and fallen from grace such as a horseman who is bucked off a horse. (LRH Def. Notes)

FALSE, contrary to fact or truth; without grounds; incorrect. Without meaning or sincerity; deceiving. Not keeping faith. Treacherous. Resembling and being identified as a similar or related entity. (HCO PL 3 May 72)

FALSE ATTESTATION, **false attestations** are death and dynamite. These come in when an instructor or auditor, D of T or D of P or Board of Review signs a request for class or grade. This request infers and therefore **"attests"** that the student or pc is qualified for the class or grade. If at some later date (barring amnesty intervention) the student or pc is shown to be incompetent in that class or grade, HCO should at once unearth the original class or grade request and call a Committee of Evidence on whoever signed it since it was a **false attestation** of competence for auditors or state of case for pcs. (HCO PL 2 Apr 65, *Urgent Urgent Urgent False Reports*)

FALSE ATTESTATION REPORT, staff member **report** of any **false attestation** noted, but in this case the document is attached to the **report.** (HCO PL 1 May 65)

FALSE COMPLIANCE, **false compliances** come about because a staff member under threat and duress (or not doing his post) seeks to protect himself by false reporting that something has been done when it hasn't. He entirely overlooks the fact that a **false** report will really bring the house down on him. (HCO PL 8 Jan 75)

FALSE DONES, **false** reports that a target has been **done** when it has not been touched or has been half **done** at best. (HCO PL 14 Dec 73)

FALSEHOOD, when you hear two facts that are contrary, one is a **falsehood** or both are. A **false** anything qualifies for this out-point. A **false** being, terminal, act, intention, anything that seeks to be what it isn't is a **falsehood** and an out-point. So the **falsehood** means, "other than it appears," or "other than represented." (HCO PL 19 Sept 70 III)

FALSE PERCEPTION, one sees things that don't exist and reports them as "fact." (HCO PL 24 Feb 69)

FALSE REPORT REPORT, staff member **report** of any **report** received that turned out to be **false.** (HCO PL 1 May 65)

FALSE REPORTS, a type of dev-t where a **report** that is **false** can cause greatly increased useless action including at times Board of Investigation, despatches verifying it, etc. (HCO PL 27 Jan 69)

FALSE TA CHECKLIST, HCO Bulletin 29 February 1972R, *False TA Checklist.* This was a very important discovery about **TAs.** One uses this when another list indicates a **false TA** or one is suspected. (LRH ED 257 INT)

FAMILY DAY, is established as the first Sunday of June each year. The purpose of **Family Day** is to bring young Sea Org members and children of Sea Org parents even closer to their parents (or where their parents are not in the area, their guardians or minor's mates). (FO 3307)

FAMILY GROUPS, see GROUPS, FAMILY.

FAO EDs, (**Flag Admin Org**) **FAO EDs** will be blue ink on blue paper and will be drawn up in the form of plans by the **FAO** Product Officer. **FAO EDs** will be issued to all on the Flagship only. (ED 1 FAO)

FAST FLOW, 1. **fast flow** means the student attests his theory or practical class when he believes he has covered the materials and can do it. There is no examination. (LRH ED 2 INT) 2. built into our org pattern is the principle of **fast flow.** We move slow or troublesome particles off the assembly line and into special slots. We let the main traffic **flow** untroubled by checks designed to restrain the very few. (HCO PL 7 Jun 65)

FAST FLOW REGISTRATION, a **registrar** to apply **fast flow registration** simply signs people up and takes their money regardless of who they are or what they are. That a person might be a troublesome source or whatever, is of no concern to a reg. Such a person would be handled as necessary by Qual or Ethics, but after he's been signed up, invoiced in and routed onto service. (BPL 5 Aug 72)

FAST FLOW SYSTEM OF MANAGEMENT, 1. the **fast flow system of management** is *don't inspect till it goes wrong.* The trouble with every organization since the beginning of time has been that when it was right they inspected it. All they did was hold it up and hold it up. Everytime you get something inspected that hasn't been found wrong you're going to get some kind of a slowdown. When something is found to be wrong swoop down on it from the executive, secretarial and every other level inspect it, cross inspect it, scream, shoot, execute and so forth, after it has been found to be wrong. Then act, don't fail to act at that point. But just let it run up to that point. (SH Spec 77, 6608C23) 2. this is the principle of traffic **flows** we now use. It is called the **fast flow system of management.** A being controlling a traffic or activity **flow** should let the **flow** run until it is to be reinforced or indicates a turbulence will occur and only then inspects the part of the **flow** that is to be reinforced or is becoming enturbulated and inspects and acts on only that one **flow.** (HCO PL 29 Mar 65 II)

FAST STUDENT, the **fast student** is not concerned with necessities to maintain status by asserting how much he or she already knows. The **fast student** is only interested in knowing what he does not know, **studying** it and then knowing that he knows it. (HCO PL 11 Jun 65)

FATIGUE, MENTAL, an introverted condition characterized by lack of motivation or interest in the work, increasing difficulty in mental performance, etc. This is usually the result of continued mental activity such as reading, thinking, evaluation, making critical decisions, etc., without any actions taken to extrovert one's attention such as taking a walk or physical exercise.

FATIGUE, PHYSICAL, a decrease in muscle coordination or motor response due to continued or excessive physical stress without enough in-between rest or rejuvenation to restore one's stamina.

FB BONUS SUM, the **FB bonus sum** each week shall be 10% of income received for management services from orgs which meet the following criteria: (1) cash/bills are not crossed. (2) total amount of advance payments used must be in normal or above by 6 week trend. (3) delivery stats of paid comps, student points and well done auditing hours are all in normal or above by 6 week trends. (4) Public Reg paid starts stat in normal or above by 6 week trend. (FSO 820-1R)

FB ETHICS OFFICER, see CLO ETHICS OFFICER.

FBO BANK RECORDS, the **bank record** is a simple **record** of **bank** transactions, which shows details of deposits, withdrawals and the new balance. Where the **FBO banks** all income and keeps no cash on hand at all, he keeps only a **bank record,** and no reserve journal is needed. The **bank record** shows what went into and out of the FBO's bank account. (FO 1761)

FBO BRANCH, 1. FBO Branch, Management Bureau, Flag, creates, runs and establishes **FBO** Network by recruiting qualified in-ethics personnel, training, apprenticing and posting them into all orgs. Works out means of expanding orgs financially and **FBO** collections. Ensures **FBOs** are keeping accurate records of their accounts and collecting bounced checks. Runs the **FBOs** on evaluated programs and projects, targets, pushes, and gets payments from orgs off the top, keeping in mind to double Scn collections over current SO collections, ensures **FBOs** are collecting from all other possible sources for Flag. (CBO 376) **2.** (Branch 11B Flag Management Bu) It is headed by **FBO** Int I/C. The **FBO** Network is operated from here as before with the only difference being that orders go through the FR Network Coordination and Priorities Setting Section. (FBDL 488R)

FBO BRANCH FOLO, FBO Branch in the Management Bureau at a **FOLO** creates, runs and establishes the **FBO** Network (Cont'l) by recruiting qualified in-ethics personnel, training, apprenticing and posting them with Flag approval in all orgs. Ensures **FBOs** are keeping accurate records of their accounts and collecting bounced checks. Coordinates activities with LRH Comm and FR Networks. Runs **FBOs** on Flag Pgms and projects, ensures and requires the promotional actions of an org are being put in the orgs by every **FBO,** makes **FBOs** force delivery by ensuring monies are wisely allocated to areas that give a return and also by demanding monies allocated get used to produce a result, and debugs **FBOs** as necessary to create income in the org. (CBO 375)

FBO CONTINENTAL EXPENSE, the **FBO Cont'l expense** is paid by the CLO to which it is attached. thus it must make lines flow. It collects for OTC! (HCO PL 9 Mar 72 I)

FBO COURIER LOG, a triplicate invoice book labeled **FBO Courier Log** is kept by every **FBO** junior to Flag. Every amount disbursed to Flag and held for a **courier** is recorded, showing date, voucher number and amount each currency with each entry identified as cash, checks, etc. Two carbons are used so that the total copies is three (3). The white copies have consecutive numbers. (FO 929)

FBO FCCI GI, total monies collected by **FBOs** for Flag services for the week. (BFO 119)

FBO INFO LETTER, the **FBO Info Letter** is issued by the Flag Finance Office twice a month. It can be issued on special occasions as a special edition. The public of the Newsletter is primarily **FBOs,** but org execs and staffs can and do read it. Purpose: to keep **FBOs informed** of the current happenings, successes, and good news of the **FBO** Network which strengthens the image of the network as a team and as being **Flag's Banking Officer.** (ED 32 FB)

FBO LEDGER, 1. a complete record of income handled and only accounts for the disposition of income. (FO 1761) **2.** the **FBO ledger** accounts for all income and where actual disbursements are made from the **ledger.** (FO 1761)

FBO LOCAL EXPENSE, paid by org to which the **FBO** is attached and collects for OTC Ltd. and other management units. (HCO PL 9 Mar 72 I)

FBO NO. 1 ACCOUNT, see FINANCE OFFICE NO. 1 ACCOUNT.

FBO PACIFIC, a central terminal which collects and banks daily the income from the AO, ASHO, OTL and U.S. Operations and who pays out their allocation amounts and prepares a combined financial report monthly for CS-3 which accounts for area income and expense. (FO 2351)

FBO RESERVE JOURNAL, 1. where the **FBO** holds cash or checks for any length of time (not just overnight or until bank opens) he keeps an account of such in the **FBO reserve journal.** The **reserve journal** looks like a bank record showing deposits, withdrawals, all details of each and the new balance each time. If more than one currency is held there is one column for each currency. (FO 1761) **2.** accounts for what went into and out of the **FBO's** cash box. (FO 1761)

FBO U.S., is required to obtain compliance with finance policies and programs, see that the area is a major income source for Flag, and that allocation amounts are adhered to exactly and that funds are never issued above allocation except in payment of Flag bills authorized in advance by CS-3. (FO 2351)

FCCI COLLECTIONS OFFICER FOLO, all FOLOs are to have the post of **FCCI Collections Officer FOLO** on their org board, located in Dept 7. This post exists solely to successfully reg all individuals desiring Flag services anywhere on the continent. (FO 3426)

FCCI ORG OFFICER, the post of **FCCI Org Officer** is in the Office of the Staff Captain. The direct senior of the **FCCI Org Officer** is the FCCI Product Officer. The purpose of the post is to establish and **organize** and thus bring about high, effective, strictly on policy production by all points of the whole cycle of **FCCI** promotion; procurement, arrival, sign-up, delivery, and the earning of income thereby by Flag. (FSO 833-2)

FCCI PRODUCT OFFICER, (Flag) post established in the Office of the Commodore's Staff Captain. The purpose of the post is to coordinate and bring about high, effective, strictly on-policy **production** by all points of the whole cycle of **FCCI** promotion; procurement, arrival, sign-up, delivery and the earning of income thereby by Flag. (FSO 833)

FEAR OF PEOPLE LIST-R, HCO Bulletin 15 November 1973R, *Fear of People List-R.* This is for the handling of timid tech staff who back off from handling rough pcs. (LRH ED 257 INT)

FEATHER BEDDING, an effort as by a labor union to get more men hired by an employer than are needed; an effort to spread work out or create more jobs either unnecessarily or to prevent unemployment.

FEATURE NEWS SHOT, a posed, manipulated picture that tells a story. This is also called a "genre" in the old pictorial school. It is not just a record of an event. It may be but it is also a made event. (HCO PL 21 Nov 68 II)

FEATURE NEWS STORY, 1. the definition given in Webster's New Collegiate Dictionary for **"feature"** is "a distinctive article, story or special department in a newspaper or magazine; something offered to the public or advertized as particularly attractive; a prominent part or characteristic." **News** means "a report of recent events." **Story** means "an account of incidents or events; a **news** article." (BPL 24 Nov 68 I) **2.** type of article other than straight news usually included in a newspaper. Unlike hard news a **feature** is not based on an event. "Astronaut wins award" would be the subject of a regular news story whereas an in-depth story on the subject of space travel or the work and background of a certain astronaut would be a **feature.** (BPL 10 Jan 73R)

FEBC COMPLETIONS SCHEDULING BOARD, a large **FEBC completion scheduling board** is placed in a prominent position in the org (not in the FEBC classroom) where all org terminals can refer to it as required. The **board** reflects the technical individual program (TIP) of each **FEBC,** and shows the progress that the student has made on his TIP. (FO 2994)

FEBC FIRING CHARTS, the registrar keeps a large **chart** on the wall of the office showing the details of the **FEBC** graduates who have **fired,** which include: number of **firing,** name, certificate number, date **fired,** post, org. (FO 2992)

FEBC HATTING DRILLS, these **drills** were originally designed by LRH to handle the inability to overcome confusion and Q and A while **hatting** a junior. Failure to competently **hat** others is a repeated source of executive failure and overload. (FSO 221)

FEBC ORG OFFICER, the function of the **FEBC Org Officer** is to provide the materials, lines, space, routing, and personnel facilities and service necessary in order that all students on the OEC and FEBC can rapidly graduate and thereby aiding the FEBC Product Officer in obtaining the product of graduate **FEBC** students on an airplane going home. (FO 3041)

FEBC PRODUCT OFFICER, 1. the **FEBC Product Officer's** function is to speed all students on the OEC and **FEBC** towards completion, particularly those who can be graduated rapidly and obtain the **product** of graduated **FEBC** students on an airplane going home. (FO 3038) **2.** the purpose of an **FEBC Product Officer** is to get **FEBC** students completed, graduated and departed to their orgs as fast as possible. (FO 3036)

FEE, 1. the sum of money paid or demanded for a professional service such as a doctor's fee or lawyer's fee. 2. any set charge.

FEEDERS, 1. City Offices. (SO ED 327 INT) **2.** all the junior entities on the bridge that are supposed to **feed** people up the bridge to the higher org. (HCO PL 10 Feb 72R III) **3.** any smaller unit in the area of a full Scn organization. (SO ED 326 INT)

FELLOW OF SCIENTOLOGY, 1. Fellow of Scientology is not an auditing degree. It is an honorary award extended by the HASI for spectacular contribution to the science itself. The **F. Scn** award carries with it the specific addition to the science for which the rating was awarded. An **F. Scn** is not necessarily a skilled or degreed auditor. (*Scn Jour* 31-G) **2.** this is an honorary award for signal contributions to Scn technology beyond the scope of a new process. The work must be complete and approved. Usually reserved for a Class IV or V auditor (HCO PL 12 Aug 63) **3.** issued by LRH for some contribution to the knowledge of Scn. (HCO PL 12 Feb 62) *Abbr.* F. Scn.

FIDUCIARY CURRENCY, paper money not redeemable for gold or silver which depends on public trust and confidence for its value.

FIDUCIARY LOAN, a loan granted entirely out of trust or confidence in the person borrowing and requiring no collateral or security.

FIELD ACTIVITIES, getting the **field**—FSM individuals, groups, franchises (all collectively called FSMs)—to sell org books and org services for the org to raw public individuals. Of course groups and especially franchises have their own services to sell but it is a foremost duty to also sell for the org. FSMs are awarded by a commission system on the sales they make for the org. It is operated just like any other groups of professional salesmen. They use big league closing techniques in contacting people, closing sales for the org (selecting), prospecting at every close and in turn developing those prospects. FSM newsletters, Auditors Assn, goodwill assisting, hatting and drilling FSMs, product officering sales are all part of making well-paid FSMs. Setting up and making **active** many, many groups is a key expansion action of Scn and another vital part of **field activities.** (HCO PL 14 Nov 71RA II)

FIELD AUDITOR, 1. a **field auditor** professionally processes preclears up to his classification but not power processing or above. He can run study courses. (HCO PL 21 Oct 66 II) **2.** "A man who is running PE Courses and who is actively active in the **field.**" It doesn't mean "just any auditor." But somebody we know is busy, somebody who is doing things. We give him the label of **field auditor** and that means he's running a little office of his own; therefore we would handle him quite differently than we would handle somebody who just got trained and who went out and is flopping, you see. (HCOB 6 Apr 57)

FIELD AUDITOR CONSULTANT, the post of **Field Auditor Consultant** is created and may be filled by the old Group Secretary where this post has been filled. The **Field Auditor Consultant** will assist all HQS, or above, certificate holders in establishing and maintaining HAS and Class I Courses—this includes helping them with promotion and the handling of their courses, assisting in arranging for HGC assists and ARC Break assessments when they or their groups get in trouble, filling their orders for HAS certificate and Level I classifications, and getting them in to take their examinations for classification. (HCO PL 21 Feb 64)

FIELD DIVISION, Flag Field Officer heads Div VIII (**Field Division**) who has under him the Flag FSM program and the registrar in the Dept of Personal Registration. (FO 2674)

FIELD EXPANSION SECRETARY, where an org has less than five staff appoint this much org board; Org Off, Exec Dir, **Field Expansion Sec.** The **Field Expansion Secretary** works to get new people. He does not work on people who have already bought something unless they are dissatisfied or ARC broken with service and muddying up his **field** at which time he severely gets the Org Off to bring them in and smooth them out and the Exec Dir or a higher org (preferably) to handle them as a tough case. (LRH ED 49 INT) *Abbr.* Field Exp Sec.

FIELD INSPECTION, a tour of the field by a market research manager to inspect operations and performances of Branch offices, distributors and agents as well as personally contact customers to get, firsthand, their opinions of current marketing and sales programs.

FIELD SERVICE, a branch office or chain of branch offices of a firm that provides repair service for the company's products in the areas where their consumers reside.

FIELD STAFF MEMBER, 1. a **Field Staff Member** serves the org of which he is an **FSM,** interests people, patches up cases and operates as a Dissemination, Qualifications function and comes

Fifield Manor

under Distribution for admin purposes. (HCO PL 21 Oct 66 II) **2.** all field auditors of the level of HBA and above are appointed herewith **Field Staff Members** of their nearest Scn organization. Their rank is **Field Staff Member** (Provisional). They come directly under the Department of Clearing, Director of Clearing of their nearest org. The purpose of the **Field Staff Member** is: to help LRH contact, handle, salvage and bring to understanding the individual and thus the peoples of earth. (HCO PL 9 May 65, *Field Auditors Become Staff*) **3. FSMs** get people into Scn by disseminating to bring about an understanding of what Scn can do thus creating a desire for service, and selecting the person for that service. (BPL 15 Jun 73R I) *Abbr.* FSM.

FIELD STAFF MEMBER COMMISSION, **1.** the official Scn organization to which the **Field Staff Member** is attached will pay the **Field Staff Member a** percentage of all training and processing fees received by that organization through its **Field Staff Members.** The **Field Staff Member** selects the person to be trained or processed after direct personal contact with the person and issues to that person a paper stating the contacted person has been selected. This paper bears the hour, date and place of the selection. If the selectee appears at the org, presents the selection paper to the cashier and enrolls for training or processing, and pays or signs the credit papers, the org sends at once a **commission** of 10% for total cash and 6 % for credit+cash payments. The org sends the sum at once. 10% is also paid in memberships bought by the selectee if accompanied by another selection paper marked membership also issued by the **Field Staff Member.** (HCO PL 9 May 65, *Field Auditors Become Staff*) **2. FSM** percentages are corrected and established as follows: 15% will be paid for any selectee routed on for auditor training, 10% will be paid for any selectee routed on the solo line. (HCO PL 5 Jun 68 III)

FIFIELD MANOR, the luxury 7-story French *Normandie Château* located at 5930 Franklin Avenue, Hollywood, California. (BO 23 US, 11 Jul 73) [Located in this building is the USGO and part of AOLA. Primarily the building is used as a hotel for Scientologists from out-of-town who come to AOLA, ASHO and Celebrity Centre for service as outlined in BO 44R U.S., *Fifield Room Rentals*]

FIFO, means first-in, first-out. A term associated with determining the value of inventories meaning the first things purchased or manufactured become the first things sold.

FILE, **1.** you know what a **file** is, down in CF, it's a counterfeit body, and everything pertaining to the person should be either in the CF **files** or in the testing **files.** The CF **file** should have the profile in it, too. (5812C29) **2.** the position in a comstation taken by a communication which is ready to go to the comcenter for **filing.** (*HTLTAE,* p. 120)

File (Def. 1)

FILE, 1. a collection of documents, records, cards or data arranged in an accessible order, usually alphabetically or numerically, such as personnel records, inventories, customer address files, etc. 2. a container, cabinet, shelf, etc., that holds such data. —*v.* the act of putting something into a file so as to retain it.

FILE, COMPANY, a file containing the collection of all company materials relating to its history and events, copies of annual reports, publications, press clippings, etc. Usually kept in categorical order as in a library.

FILE O, see CIRCULAR FILE.

FILE POSTING, see SLIP SYSTEM.

FILING SYSTEM, a system of arranging documents, records, cards, data, etc., so that they are in an accessible and logical order. Such a system may arrange things in alphabetical, alphabetical by subject, numerical, chronological or geographical order or a combination of these such as alphabetical by geographical location, etc.

FILLED FROM THE TOP DOWN, the org board is always **filled from the top down,** that is to say, the most senior post is always **filled** first. If there are only a few people, then they hold the most senior posts and also do the work of each of the posts below them on the org board. A lower post is not **filled** while leaving a higher post vacant. The higher post is **filled** and the lower post or posts held from above. As new people join the group, the lower posts can be turned over to them and **filled.** (BPL 4 Jul 69R V)

FILTER SYSTEM, a **filter system** exists on Flag to ensure that all orders into an org or area are fully coordinated. The personnel who act as **filters** in this system are the Assistant Flag Reps in Branch 12A of the Management Bu. It is their job to **filter** out any uncoordinated, unevaluated or unnecessary programs, projects, orders or advices going to their orgs in their continental areas. They ensure that everything travelling down the single command channel is in harmony and dovetails with org's current Flag program and activities. (CBO 278RA)

FINAL ACCOUNTS, the **final accounts** of an org are financial statements made out at the end of (usually) a year. There are two main statements: (1) income and expenditure account. (2) balance sheet. These **accounts** are used by governments as a basis on which to assess the org's liability to pay tax. (HCO PL 10 Oct 70 V)

FINAL DEMAND, see DEMAND, FINAL.

FINANCE, 1. Finance Office. (FO 2685R) **2.** is a matter of making it and thereafter being clever enough in managing it to get something for your money and stay prosperous as an organization. (BFO 44)

FINANCE, that area of a business concerned with maintaining the inflow of money greater than the outflow and with the management of money.

FINANCE AIDE, Finance Aide (CS-**F**) is located on the org board in Div VII. His area of responsibility is that of **Finance** Officers and FBOs. CS-3 is located on the org board over Div 3. Her area of responsibility is that of Treasury Division 3s. (FDD 18 TREAS INT)

FINANCE BANKING OFFICER, 1. the **Finance Office** is an autonomous **Office** (similar to the Guardian's Office). It has representatives in every Bureaux and every Continental Liaison Office and every org, SO and Scn. It is located on the org board in the Office of LRH. Its representative is called the **Finance Banking Officer** (**FBO**). The **FBO** verifies and collects all income received by the org from the cashier or Income Dept, Div III, Treasury Division. This is done daily. The **FBO** immediately banks this money in a **Finance Office** account or in his safe, making express and useful records of this action. When the org or activity has undertaken its financial planning (FP), the **FBO** on his own discretion then transfers to that org's Main Account the needed funds. This is the allocation. The solvency of the orgs and areas is the responsibility of the **FBO.** The **FBO** statistics consist of cash paid in to management central reserves and the allocation-production ratio of each org and of the area. (HCO PL 29 Jan 71) [BPL 10 Nov 73R reintroduces the term Flag Banking Officer instead of **Finance Banking Officer.**] **2.** an org with an **FBO** makes more money and has a better paid staff and makes it more worthwhile for Flag to manage it than any org ever would without an **FBO.** The purposes of the **FBO** are (1) to make the org make more money. (2) to give the org a well paid staff. (3) to make it very worthwhile for Flag to manage and help it. An **FBO** must know how to make money. An **FBO** must know how an org makes money and keeps its reputation with excellent delivery. An **FBO** must know the policy expertise used in making money (HCO PL 23 Sept 71) **3.** it is a duty of the **FBO** to safeguard incoming monies and to ensure that all income is properly and legibly invoiced by the org and that the exact same amount is collected and receipted and **banked** by himself each day. (BPL 17 Feb 71-1R) *Abbr.* FBO.

FINANCE BUREAU, the **Finance Bureau** inspects, corrects, summates and maintains viability by **Finance** actions. It also traces and polices through all of its points the entrance of **finance** into, through and out of every org. (CBO 7)

FINANCE COLLECTION OFFICER, the post of **Finance Collection Officer** is established in the **Finance Office** at Flag, in the FAO. The post is immediately junior to and answerable to the Flag FBO. The purpose and basic action of this post is increase of income to reserves by reason of effective **collection** activity. Its statistic is total income to central management. (FO 2872)

FINANCE COURSE, this **course** has been devised to enable all Sea Org members to become more familiar with **finance** policy, and to know and apply the subject called "accounts." (FO 2060)

FINANCE DIRECTIVES, **1.** are issued at Flag by Flag **Finance** Office, usually by CS-3 or by authority of CS-3. They contain programs, orders, directions and projects. Where they contain policies they are approved prior to issue by LRH. They are issued in consecutive number series to all **Finance** Office staffs and FBOs and are master filed by them. They are issued blue ink on red or pink paper (same color flash as Gdn Financial Order, HCO PL 18 November, 1968, *Guardians Orders*). They have no other distribution unless designated to Flag Aides for info. Any **Finance Directive** issued locally by FBOs is only after specific approval of CS-3 and is subject to cancellation or alteration by CS-3. **Finance Directives** have continuous validity and do not retire unless specifically cancelled. Flag **Finance** Office is located in Dept 19 of Bureau 7. It is separate and distinct from Treasury Bureau 3. **Finance Directives** do not directly apply to Treasury Divisions unless otherwise stated on the **Directive.** (HCO PL 24 Dec 70) [The above HCO PL was cancelled by HCO PL 16 Mar 72 III.] **2.** no **Finance** Officer personnel may issue any order, **Finance Directive** or advice which in any way establishes policy, alters policy or cancels policy as only a policy letter properly authorized and issued on lines may do such. All such orders and all **Finance Directives** are now cancelled. Only properly issued policy letters are to be followed in **finance** matters and any order, **Finance Directive** or advice given must only re-enforce existing policy. (HCO PL 16 Mar 72 III)

FINANCE FLAG, **Finance Flag** is established in Division 3, Department 8. It is responsible for all legal **financial** matters. It will keep records of all legal **financial** matters pertaining to the Sea Org. It is also responsible for any balance sheets, etc., required or any corporation reports. (FO 640)

FINANCE OFFICE, the **Finance** Network of FBOs and **Finance Offices** operates as a single network in the Flag Bureau Org and in coordination with the other networks established in the Flag Management Bu. (In addition to the GO Network of AGFs). The FBO network is autonomous. By this is meant that it is not subject to local authorities and receives its orders from senior network personnel at Flag. Its actions are **financial** management and the solvency, viability and return to SO reserves from orgs and areas. **Finance** is not the Treasury Bu III network but forms liaison with it to forward the actions of both **Finance** and Treasury at org level and the orders and actions of **Finance** are binding on Div 3s and Bureau IIIs where needful. The org board location of the **Finance Office** for posting purposes is in Div 7, Dept 19 of orgs, FOLOs and at Flag. The direct management office of the FBO Network (FBO Int Branch at Flag) is located in Bureau 4, Branch 11B of the Flag Bureau Org. (FO 2685R) **2.** an autonomous **office** (similar to the Guardian's Office). It has representatives in every bureaux and every Continental Liaison Office and every org, SO and Scn. It is located on the org board in the Office of LRH. Its authority stems from the corporate authority of the company and exists at company director level of the corporation. Its representative is called the **Finance** Banking **Officer.** (HCO PL 29 Jan 71) **3.** an autonomous network situated in Bureau 7, Branch 19 at Flag and in FOLOs, and in Dept 19 in orgs. (CBO 357) *Abbr.* FO.

FINANCE OFFICE NO. 1 ACCOUNT, **1.** all income is banked into the **FO No. 1 Account** and all counter checks and bounced checks are handled by this **account.** A bounced check float is kept in the **FO No. 1 Account** as a cushion against bounced checks. The following amounts are transferred from the **FO No. 1 Account** each week: (1) 5% of the CGI to Main Account for payment to WW by Division 3. (2) 5% of the CGI to (org name) local GO Account. (3) 10% of the CGI to the GO Reserve Account (defense). (4) any support to other orgs such as FOLO or Estates. (5) the payment of the overdue management bills. (6) any set asides for refunds or repayments to GO Reserve Account (defense). (7) the balance which is the org allocation sum goes to the Main Account. (8) the FBO transfers the FSM commission amount over to the Main Account. (9) the FBO transfers the HCO Book Account income to the HCO Book Account. (BPL 6 Jul 75 III) **2.** the FBO never spends any money out of his **No. 1 Account.** Money goes into it and is transferred out of it. Only transfer checks are drawn on it (to management reserves or to Org Main Account). (BPL 17 Feb 71R)

FINANCE OFFICE NO. 2 ACCOUNT, 1. pays for international management expenses incurred locally and is then reimbursed by international management. (BPL 6 Jul 75 III) **2.** the FBO has a second bank **account—FO** (company) **No. 2 Account** to which he transfers money for international management expenses. He transfers money from the first FO (company) No. 1 Account to management (not org) reserves. (BPL 17 Feb 71R)

FINANCIAL ACCOUNTING, the accounting for income, expenses, assets and liabilities of an organization resulting in profit and loss statements and a summary of investments made over a given period for use by management and in reports made to stockholders.

FINANCIAL MANAGEMENT, 1. as in my experience an organization always spends all it makes, **financial management** on an international level consists not of carefully balancing income above outgo in an effort to save a surplus in an organization, but of (a) preventing an org from spending more than it makes and (b) setting aside enough money from its income to care for salvage operations and salvage expenses. (HCO PL 18 Jan 65) **2. financial management** is ordinarily done by the Association Secretary, the Organization Secretary or the Treasurer and possibly, in some cases, the Director of Accounts, but is always under the direct responsibility of the Association Secretary no matter who wears the hat. It is the purpose of the hat to ensure solvency of the organization and its divisions. The basic principle of **financial management** is a simple one. Income must be greater than outgo. (HCO PL 3 Jun 59) **3.** purpose: make certain the organization makes money and continues in good credit. Hat worn by: the Association Secretary and by his deputization, the Director of Administration. Policy comes from Association Secretary. Execution comes from Director of Administration. **Financial management** guarantees solvency. It does not concern itself with accuracy of bills, payments or collection. This is the job of the Treasurer and by deputization, the Disbursement Clerk. The cost of an item must be less than selling price. All pertinent items to cost no matter how remote are part of the cost. Using this rule, **financial management** prices items. He adds to cost all profit that can be made and still make the item sell. He publishes, then, an item's "price." That the price of an item is collected is the business of the Treasurer who issues proper orders concerning it. **Financial management** must now establish cost and price of all items sold. And must adjust, for organization credit, what bills must be paid in concert with how much money there is to pay them. (HCO PL 15 May 70 II, *Financial Management*)

FINANCIAL PLANNING, 1. the **financial planning** hat is worn by the Advisory Council. **Financial planning** means—how to handle the money and assets of an org so as to maintain outgo below income. The actions of **financial planning** are as follows: (1) directing the payment of bills (as designated by the Advisory Council), (2) directing any necessary delay in the payment of certain bills, (3) handling **finances** in accordance with "dateline paying" as covered in an early policy letter, (4) setting limits on the purchase orders that may be signed, (5) preventing divisions or departments in emergency from buying any but essential promotional supplies or postage, (6) adjusting payrolls, (7) setting limits on pay, overtime or bonuses and all authorizations for pay overtime or bonuses, (8) fixing prices, (9) directing any transfer of funds, (10) deciding upon any large purchases, (11) authorizing the sale of any equipment or property, (12) passing upon prices offered for any equipment or property. Any matter affecting the **financial** health of the organization has to be passed upon or **planned** by the Advisory Council. (HCO PL 26 Nov 65R) **2. financial planning** is how one uses the funds one has to keep things running well and make more income. (BPL 19 Mar 71) **3.** is the way you lay out money sensibly within the limits of the money available in order to keep things going well and make more money. (FO 2480) **4.** consists of what to spend money on per division and what bills to pay according to dateline paying. (HCO PL 19 Oct 67 I) **5.** the basic purpose of all **financial planning** is to increase the wealth and assets and value of assets of the company and the general well-being and security of all its members and so contribute to the purposes and activities. (FO 2057) **6.** in essence is the sensible allocation of funds on necessities. (FO 2480) **7. planning** of future expenses. (FSO 771) *Abbr.* FP.

FINANCIAL PLANNING DIRECTIVE OF THE MONTH, the **Financial Planning Directive of the month** is issued promptly after the second Tuesday meeting of the month as an Exec Division Admin Letter with the month and financial planning on it in caps such as FINANCIAL PLANNING FOR MARCH. Long-range **planning** also appears on this **directive,** this long-range **financial planning** is not binding and is often changed in view of current happenings. It is a guide by which other executives can tentatively plan. (HCO PL 26 Nov 65R)

FINANCIAL PLANNING PROGRAM NO. 1, 1. **program** for carefully **planned financial** handling to result in an organization which is not only solvent, but expanding on a sound gradient scale. To do this an organization has to first of all assess the following: (1) how many basic staff members are required to run and handle the organization? (2) how much is required for the basic organizational needs to merely keep the organization there? (3) how much is required for basic promotional actions? (4) how much does it cost weekly to keep in your basic communication lines? After carefully figuring out your weekly costs, you now know exactly how much income you will require weekly in order to exist and to promote. If you do not make this amount of income weekly, you will know at once that you are spending more than you are making, at which point everything must be done to sell more services to your pulblic. (LRH ED 55 INT) **2.** survival of an org depends on solvency. Solvency depends on making more than it spends. This **Financial Planning Program No. 1** ED is a clever one actually written by MSH. She said, "If they will just do this ED they will become solvent." It's true. It is very important to staffs that **financial planning** be done well as if it isn't, it threatens their pay as well as the org's survival. (LRH ED 78 INT)

FINANCIAL REPORTS, the purpose of regular **financial reports** is to (1) summarize original records. (2) provide executives with data for planning. (3) show that all monies issued for disbursement are accounted for. (FO 1510)

FINANCIAL STATEMENT, a presentation of financial data about the current state and operation of a business. Usually it states profits and losses and includes a balance sheet which shows assets, liabilities, and net worth for a certain time period.

FINANCIAL YEAR, the 12 month time period which a company chooses as its accounting year; fiscal year.

FINDINGS, the full report of the committee (Committee of Evidence) accompanied by a tape recording of the evidence given and a full recommendation to the Convening Authority for his action. The **findings** is a document which gives a fast summary of the hearings, their result and a complete recommendation. It must be so written that it may be published without alteration by the Convening Authority. The summary states who appears to be at fault and who does not and why. The recommendation tells the Convening Authority exactly what disciplinary action should be taken and how, including any plea for leniency or insistence upon full penalty. (HCO PL 7 Sept 63)

FINISHED GOODS, these are completely manufactured or produced goods in final form ready for the consumer.

FINK, 1. a professional or habitual strikebreaker; one who works in an area where the workers are striking. 2. an informer; especially one who informs on union activities.

FIRE DRILL, **1.** the best **fire drill** consists of every member of a ship's company learning to handle the whole operation of putting out a major **fire** all by himself anywhere in the ship. (*Ship's Org Bk.*) **2. fire drill** on most ships is usually so bad it is a slang term for a confused mess. (*Ship's Org Bk.*)

FIRM, two or more persons in partnership or forming a company to carry on a business. A firm is not considered to be one legal person as in the case of a corporation.

FIRST DEPUTY CHIEF, (below Chief Engineer of the engine room on Flag) **1st Deputy Chief** is also 1st Engineer and Engineer of the Watch of Watch A, and is in charge of planning all programs, files, plans and finance and stores. 2nd Deputy Chief is 2nd Engineer, is Engineer of the Watch of Watch B, and in charge of all training, checksheets and logs. 3rd Deputy Chief is the 3rd Engineer, is Engineer of the Watch of C and is in charge of inspections, tests and ER personnel procurement. (FO 1958)

FIRST DEPUTY COMMODORE, this is a decision-making post on matters referred and orders origination post on matters not against policy (as attested by the Commodore's Personal Communicator). In matters where there are conflict or question, referral from below can be made to the **First Deputy Commodore** on channels, accompanied by proper CSW or, in extreme urgency, by the contenders. Where inspection or other indicators seem to warrant, or where smoother operation is desirable or where a program apparently beneficial or needful needs to be instigated, the **First Deputy Commodore** may so originate, on channels, via the Personal Communicator who attests that it is not against policy or, should it be, to return it. Any origin so issued is logged by the Personal Communicator as though it were from the Commodore and followed up accordingly on routine lines. In the presence of the Commodore, the post of **First Deputy Commodore** is quiescent as it is normally an additional hat assigned to one with other senior duties. (FO 3342)

FIRST DEPUTY EXECUTIVE DIRECTOR, (Saint Hill Org Board) acts as **Executive Director** in the absence of the **Executive Director.** (HCO PL 18 Dec 64, *Saint Hill Org Board*)

FIRST DEPUTY ORGANIZATION SECRETARY, acts as **Organization Secretary** in the absence of the **Organization Secretary.** (HCO PL 18 Dec 64, *Saint Hill Org Board*)

FIRST DYNAMIC DANGER FORMULA, the **formula** is converted for the **first dynamic** to (1) by-pass habits or normal routines. (2) handle the situation and any danger in it. (3) assign self a danger condition. (4) get in your own *personal ethics* by finding what you are doing that is out-ethics and use self discipline to correct it and get honest and straight. (5) reorganize your life so that the **dangerous** situation is not continually happening to you. (6) formulate and adopt firm policy that will hereafter detect and prevent the same situation from continuing to occur. (HCO PL 9 Apr 72)

FIRST ECHELON ORGS, the **organizations** of Scn now considered **first echelon orgs** (just below Saint Hill) are London, Washington, Los Angeles, New York, Melbourne, Sydney, Perth, New Zealand, Johannesburg, Durban and Capetown. (HCO PL 13 Mar 65, *Admin Technology, The Comm Member System*)

FIRST INDICATOR, the **first indicator** is stats. Your **first** out-point always occurs in stats. (7205C18 SO)

FIRST LEVEL SUPERVISOR, see SUPERVISOR, FIRST LEVEL.

FIRST (1st) MATE, 1. is in charge of Division IV, the Operations Division which cares for the decks, construction and other purely traditional ship concerns—so the ship can operate as a ship. (FO 2674) **2.** the **First Mate** is head of Division 4, the Production Division with the Chief Steward's Department (10), Boatswain (Department 11) and Specialist Chief (Department 12). These are key departments without which missions cannot be run. (*Ship's Org Bk.*) **3.** fourth in command of a ship. (FO 196) **4.** Tech Sec. (FO 1847) **5.** Operations Officer (6802C28 SO)

FIRST POLICY, the **first policy** of a Scn org, laid down on about 8 or 10 March, 1950, is: "Maintain friendly relations with the environment and the public." (HCO PL 2 Sept 70, *First Policy*)

FISCAL MEASURES, a government's financial efforts to regulate inflation or deflation by making tax changes.

FISCAL YEAR, the 12 month period chosen (especially by a government) as the accounting year and representing the period between each annual settlement of financial accounts. The U.S. Government ends its fiscal year on June 30 and Canada and Great Britain end their fiscal year on March 31.

FITNESS BOARD, 1. there are time limits placed on how long it takes to do SS I and SS II. A person who can't make it is routed to Qual where he is off-loaded with advice on how to get more employable. (In the SO it is **Fitness Board**). (HCO PL 23 Jul 72) **2.** a **Fitness Board** is established in every SO activity. Its purpose is to determine the mental and physical **fitness** of personnel and recommend the issuance of probation or denial of a provisional or full **fitness** certificate with the approval of HCO and the Commanding Officer. The **Board** is composed of: Qual Sec, Chairman; Tech Case Supervisor; Review Chief, Secretary; Medical Officer; the Chaplain. (FO 2630R)

FIVE DEPARTMENT ORGANIZATION, there are **five departments** in a Central **Organization** now. There's the **Department** of Accounts. There is the **Department** of Materiel. There is the **Department** of Promotion and Registration. These three **departments** come under Administration: The Administrative Division. Then there are two service units: the Academy and the HGC. (5812C29)

FIVE PRIMARY ILLOGICS, there are **5 primary** ways for a relay of information or a situation to become **illogical**: (1) omit a fact. (2) change sequence of events. (3) drop out time. (4) add a falsehood. (5) alter importance. (HCO PL 11 May 70) [See OUT-POINT for a full list of the illogics or out-points.]

FIVE STAR PROCESS, see STAR.

FIXED ASSETS, see ASSETS, FIXED.

FIXED BUDGET, see BUDGET, FIXED.

FIXED CAPITAL, see CAPITAL, FIXED.

FIXED CONSUMPTION, estimates of the public's **consumption** of product as a limit on production. Any Scn organization (or any organization) which is working in any way upon a **fixed** statistic of **consumption** will eventually fail. Unless one disregards the expectancy and unless one simply furnishes all the service one can, regardless of past statistics, the org will go downhill. (HCO PL 24 Jul 67)

FIXED COSTS, see COSTS, FIXED.

FIXED EXPENSE, same as Fixed Cost.

FIXED IDEAS, **1.** the *"idée fixe"* is the bug in sanity. Whenever an observer himself has **fixed ideas** he tends to look at them not at the information. Prejudiced people are suffering mainly from an *"idée fixe."* A **fixed idea** is something accepted without personal inspection or agreement. It is the perfect "Authority knows best." It is the "reliable source." A **fixed idea** is uninspected. It blocks the existence of any contrary observation. Most reactionaries (people resisting all progress or action) are suffering from **fixed ideas** which they received from "authorities," which no actual experience alters. That British red-coated infantry never took cover was one. It took a score or two of wars and fantastic loss of life to finally break it down. If any single **fixed idea** destroyed the British Empire, this one is a candidate. (HCO PL 19 May 70) **2.** some people have a method of handling a downstat which is a **fixed idea** or a cliché they use to handle all downstat situations in their lives. These people are so at effect they have some idea sitting there "that handles" a down statistic. "Life is always like that." "I always try my best." "People are mean." "It will get better." "It was worse last year." They know it isn't any use trying to do anything about anything and that it is best just to try to get by and not be noticed—a sure route to suicide. Instead of seeking to prevent or raise a declining stat in life such people use some **fixed idea** to explain it. This is a confession of being in apathy. One can always make stats go up. Hard work, foresight, initiative. One can always make stats go up. That's the truth of it, and it needs no explanations. (HCO PL 8 Feb 68)

FIXED INTEREST COVER, the ratio of a company's net earnings to the fixed interest and dividends to be paid to stockholders which comprises the existing cover or protection provided to investors preferred stocks, debentures, etc.

FIXED-PRICE CONTRACT, a contract taken on by a contractor, supplier, etc., to provide specific goods or services for a set price which cannot later be changed for any reason irrespective of increased material or labor costs, inflation, etc.

FIXED SALARIES, a stable wage for staff members. (HCO PL 10 Dec 68)

FIXED TERMINAL POST, a **fixed terminal post** stays in one spot, handles specific duties and receives communications, handles them, and sends them on their way. (HCO PL 22 Jun 64)

FLAG, **1.** the Church of Scientology of California operates a marine mission aboard a chartered vessel. This marine mission is commonly referred to as **Flag.** It is operated under the aegis (protection, support) of the Church of Scientology of California. (BPL 9 Mar 74) **2.** the main vessel of the Sea Org. (HCO PL 9 Mar 72 I) **3.** the center for all international org management. (ED 480 Flag) **4. flagship.** (ED 334-1 Flag) **5. Flag** is the basic research area of Dn and Scn. Over half its crew are Clears today and many are OTs. It is probably the calmest, if one of the busiest areas on the planet! (LRH ED 101 INT) **6. Flag** is currently fully on the Sea Org comm and control lines. The ship is divided into two organizations, the Ship Org which operates the **flagship,** and whose product is the **Flag** Org. The product of the **Flag** Org is "orgs which expand." The **Flag** Org, in order to achieve its purpose—"to create orgs which expand" operates programs. Every program adds up to and forwards the **Flag** Org purpose. (FO 2219) **7.** operates the Sea Org under the guidance of the Commodore. The word **Flag** designates that vessel where the Commodore and Personal Staff are located. The actual **flag** is the blue and white starred **flag** flown on any vessel of the flotilla. When the Commodore is aboard, the **flagship** flies the **flag** daily and has the word **Flag** on its title. (FO 766) **8.** the word **Flag** means the flotilla Commanding Officer and his personal staff and is of timeless usage and is not new. (FO 1) **9. Flag** is viewed primarily as a management organization on a mobile base. (ED 182 Flag) **10.** the purpose of the **flagship** is to enable LRH to carry out his research functions, communicate with orgs, get in and handle ethics and take care of finance, in that order. (FO 263)

FLAG ADMINISTRATION OFFICE, is established in the Office of LRH under CS-7. In charge of the unit is the **Flag Officer** Manager. Only aides, FBO, and currently assigned communicators remain in the other Flag divisions. All other functions and Flag personnel come under the **Office** Manager. The first duty of the **Administration Office** is to get all Flag Org admin up to present time. (FO 2273)

FLAG ADMIN ORG, **1.** the **org** that **administers** to the other two orgs, trains, processes, handles local accounts, etc. The **Flag Admin Org** actually is the basic **org** that forms the other two now. **Flag Admin Org** (all internal **admin** services, comm, training, processing, personnel, hatting, local finance, etc.). (OODs 30 Dec 70) **2.** the service **org** which does the Scn training, processing, financing and **admin** of the three orgs aboard, the Flag Bureaux (which is the International Management Org), the Flag Ship Org (which runs the ship and the **FAO**). The main final valuable products of the **FAO** are income, student completions and preclear or pre-OT completions. **FAO** is a 7 Div Org Board **organization.** (FSO 225) **3.** early in 1971, Flag was divided into 3 orgs: Flag Bureaux, **Flag Admin Org,** and the Flag Ship Org. The **Flag Admin Org (FAO)** is the *service* **org.** It trains, processes and handles finance. It has the pattern of the standard 7 Division Organization. It is the establishing **org.** It establishes through its Div 1 (HCO) itself and the other two orgs. (FO 2856) **4.** a standard 7 Division Org Board **org** named the **Flag Admin Org** for the purpose of providing service to Flag in the fields of income, training and processing and other valuable final products and to provide the HCO functions necessary to the three orgs of Flag. (ED 5 FAO) **5.** the founding org is the FB. But the establishing org is the **FAO.** An architect (Flag Bureau) designs the building. The builders (**Flag Admin Org**) build it, including the architect's office (FB). (OODs 14 Feb 71) *Abbr.* FAO.

FLAG ADVANCED ORG, Flag Advanced Org delivers the upper levels under the highest level of case supervision on the planet. (FO 3426) *Abbr.* FAO.

FLAG AUDITORS, Flag auditors are easily the best in the world. They don't kid around with cases. They know what they can do. Our **Flag auditors** are great for many reasons. Not the least of them is continual brush up and insistence on exact application and achieving the predicted result. They come through reasonableness and all that and emerge as top flight **auditors.** (OODs 18 Mar 71)

FLAG AUXILIARY PERSONNEL TRAINING CORPS, 1. is made up of **personnel** set aside for **Flag** and trained locally on each continent. Each AO, SH, CC, FOLO, Stationship and Scn org that owes **personnel** to **Flag** contributes to the **FAPTC** by sending these persons owed to the **FAPTC.** (FO 3324R-5) **2.** established locally in continental areas as a **Flag personnel** reserve. The **Flag Auxiliary Personnel Training Corps** has been formed up so that we can train in numbers. Valuable final product of the **FAPTC**: fully trained Sea Org members ready and able to take on any job, any place, any time, as demanded by Flag Management. (FBDL 316) **3.** established locally in continental areas as a **Flag personnel** reserve. Members of it are **Flag** crew, and receive training to assist international management expansion, and may be called to **Flag** at anytime, or assigned to orgs to replace veteran staff being called to Flag. (FO 3324R) *Abbr.* FAPTC.

FLAG BANKING OFFICER, 1. the ship will have a **Flag Banking Officer** who receives all income as a **bank** for **Flag** and is answerable to **Flag** and under **Flag** only. This is not a Purser post. The **Flag Banking Officer** allocates receipts to **bank** accounts, etc., and the Purser receives his "income" from the **Flag Banking Officer** and thereafter disburses all disbursements for the ship in accordance with financial planning. In the merchant service the **Flag Banking Officer** is the equivalent of the shore office or company which allocates funds to the ship which are thereafter handled by the Purser in accordance with the heads of depts planning. (FO 401) **2.** receives all money of the Cashier or Dir Income after invoice and records the disposition of it. The **FBO** performs the functions of a **bank** for the org. He is not a Purser and he is not part of the org. (FO 1761) **3.** receives all money of the Purser or ship or cashier after invoice and records its disposition. As we cannot **bank** all money in the flotilla due to different currencies and **bank** problems, we have our *own* **bank.** This is the **FBO.** He or she is not the Purser and is not part of the org. (FO 565). **4.** for Sea Org purposes, the **Flag Banking Officer** fills the role in Scn accounts policy of the **bank.** (FO 412) **5.** the major operating basis of **FBOs** and **FBO** INT is established as a two-way action: (1) **FBOs** and **FBO** INT act to assist the SBO and CS-3 in building **Flag** reserves and to accomplish outgo below income for the Sea Org as a whole, and outgo below income/allocation for each individual Sea Org Unit. (2) act to assist SBO, CS-3 and the ECs of SO orgs and units of their areas to achieve solvency for each unit through good financial management, and to build local reserves while adequately covering needed expenses. These are not long range future actions. They are *now* actions. (FO 2274) *Abbr.* FBO.

FLAG BANKING OFFICER INTERNATIONAL, the post of **Flag Banking Officer International** is established under the Staff Banking Officer, but subject to the orders of the 2nd Deputy Commodore for administrative purposes only. The purpose of this post is to safeguard Sea Org monies by ensuring more is never spent than allocated and substantial reserves are built up. The **FBO Int** receives and evaluates financial data from **FBOs** attached to AOs, AO-SHs, OTL, and the Pursers of any ships and missions in his area. The **FBO Int** in addition to his normal duties has the added responsibility of seeing ships, bases and missions adhere to Sea Org finance policy and handles their financial needs through the **FBOs.**

Responsibility for handling any urgent matters relating to the finance needs of Sea Org missions must be delegated to the local **FBO** in the area. (HCO PL 16 Jun 69) [The above HCO PL was cancelled by BPL 10 Oct 75 VII] *Abbr.* FBO INT.

FLAG BANKING OFFICER INTERNATIONAL IN-CHARGE, 1. the post of **FBO INT I/C** is established in the **Flag** Finance **Office.** The purpose of this action is to increase efficiency and effectiveness in the running of the **FBO** network. Command line: Finance Aide—**FBO INT I/C**—Continental **FBOs**—**FBO** District Heads—Org **FBOs.** (BPL 10 Nov 73R) [The above BPL reintroduces the term **Flag Banking Officer** and is a revised and reissued version cancelling HCO PL 10 Nov 73, *Finance Series 16, FBO Network Organization Location,* which uses the term Finance Banking Officer.] **2.** the **FBO** Branch, Flag Management Bu is headed by the **FBO INT I/C.** The **FBO** network is operated from here. (FBDL 488R) *Abbr.* FBO INT I/C.

FLAG BILL, goods or services ordered by **Flag.** (FO 2278)

FLAG BILLINGS CHART, chart that details the **billings** of **Flag** products exported to the field and services available on **Flag** to all org staff and executives. (SO ED 277RA INT)

FLAG BUREAUX, 1. the **Flag Bureaux** manages orgs. It does not just execute orders of others but initiates orders based on evaluation that directs orgs, handles situations and ensures continued growth. (CBO 435-3R) **2.** the international management body of the SO with additional advisor and management activities. (HCO PL 9 Mar 72 I) **3.** (**FB**) the external org taking care of the international and SO orgs over the world and planetary actions. (OODs 8 May 72) **4.** early in 1971, Flag was divided into 3 orgs: **Flag Bureaux,** Flag Admin Org, and the Flag Ship Org. The **Flag Bureaux**, the International Management Org was the first to be formed fully. It is the Founding Org of the other two. It is doing very well and has stats booming in most areas and is heavily in the mission business. It is mostly involved in establishing the Continental Liaison Offices such as U.S. Liaison Office, UK Liaison Office, etc. These are duplicates of the **Flag Bureaux** for their areas. Its color flash is green. These are the Board of Directors and aides and their staffs. The **Bureaux** Org Board is essentially the 1967 Seven Division original org board with four branches in production: Data No. 10, Action No. 11, External Comm-Transport No. 11A and Org Management Branch No. 12. All under an Operations Aide Bureau IV. Instead of Divs they are **Bureaux.** Instead of depts they are branches. Section is retained. Each of these Division IV Branches is traditionally called a **Bureau**—thus they are referred to as the Data Bureau (collects, condenses, evaluates and distributes data), Action Bureau (plans, briefs and operates missions), the External Comm Bureau and the Management Bureau. (FO 2856) **5.** the "**Flag** Org" or "Aide Divisional Opposite Number System" are combined with the **bureaux** system. All persons in both the "**Flag** Org" and **Bureaux** will be used in the new pattern. **Flag** Org functions just transfer into the 7 Div Org Board. An aide will be in charge of each division and these divisions will adopt the same org board. The name will now be **Flag Bureaux,** thus combining "**Flag** Org" and "SO Central **Bureaux**" into one name, **Flag Bureaux** (FO 2617) **6.** the name of the Central Bureaux on Flag. It now combines the old **Flag** Org with the **Bureaux.** (FBDL 12) **7.** an external management org. Establishes and runs Continental Liaison Offices and orgs. The **Flag Bureaux** are on the 7 Div board with a different product in its "Div" IV and calling a division a **bureau.** (OODs 30 Dec 70) *Abbr.* FB.

FLAG BUREAUX DATA FILES, there must be a **Flag Bureaux data files** as well as a Flag Ship Org data files. The keynote is internal. They are composed of internal traffic and records. These are kept by the month as in the case of any org. The **FB files** include the dispatch files internal of Aides, Action, Pgms Bu, Ext Comm Bu, FB Estos and other personnel on Flag not in the FSO. Internal organizational matters go into these **files.** To know what the **file** should contain one must ask the question: What would I need to have to evaluate the **Flag Bureaux**, revert, or improve its sturcture or activities or trace changes? (CBO 202-1)

FLAG BUREAUX DATA LETTERS, 1. issued by a **Flag** Executive to COs/EDs, FRs and **Flag** execs. Their purpose is to inform executives. May contain news, forewarnings of traffic loads, expansions, PR interest items. Essentially they are newsletters. They are numbered. Printed in black ink on white paper. (Formerly they were blue ink on white paper). (HCO PL 24 Sept 70R) **2. FBDLs** after this date will be used, as originally intended, to give executives data. And Aides Orders will be used for evaluations and will only be distributed on **Flag** for operational use. (FBDL 189) **3.** they may not contain orders or evaluations. They may be written by any Commodore's Staff, Office of LRH or FB executive. (CBO 48R) **4.** issue to advise **bureau** executives on Flag and in continental offices of current area evaluations and planning. (OODs 14 Nov 70) *Abbr.* FBDLs

FLAG CAPTAIN, **1.** each vessel has its own **Captain.** The **Captain** of the **flagship** is known as the **Flag Captain.** (FO 766) **2.** purpose of the **flagship Captain:** to help the Commodore in furthering the purposes of the Sea Org, Scn and Dn by wearing the hat of **Captain** with the intention of producing the ideal scene of a safe, seaworthy, self-supporting, fully operational **flagship** manned with fully trained and processed, competent officers and crew of the Sea Organization. (FO 2613)

FLAG COLLECTION OFFICER, the **Flag Collection Officer** of every FOLO is responsible for the **collection** of all **Flag** credit collections from any source. This covers freeloaders, individuals, missions, orgs and any other debtor owing a debt to **Flag.** (FO 3473-6)

FLAG CONDITIONS ORDER, is the equivalent of a Scn org HCO Div Order such as an Ethics Order. Distributed only to those concerned and Masters at Arms (ethics files). (HCO PL 24 Sept 70R) *Abbr.* FCO.

FLAG CONTACT DIVISION, (DIV VII) this contains all public service and personal **contact** functions of **Flag** relations in the ports and in other zones. It contains the Office of the Chaplain. Parties, entertainments, VIPs, guests, student and pc welcoming and any other personal contact (as different than written or published) required. The safety of the vessel in ports and PRO area control in ports is a primary service of this division. The Office of the Port Captain is the first department of this division. It is headed by the Port Captain. (FO 2525)

FLAG DAY, the first **Flag Days** were held in Aug 1972 at FOLO US and FOLO UK to celebrate the occasion of FOLO staffs becoming **Flag** staff. It consisted of a dinner and speeches and a ceremony inaugurating FOLO members as **Flag** staff. The events were so successful that **Flag Day** became an annual event to celebrate and validate the good work of **Flag** crew who work at FOLOs and to strengthen the communication lines of the FOLO crew with **Flag.** It consists primarily of a dinner and talk by the **Flag** Rep at the FOLO about **Flag.** (CBO 237)

FLAG DISTRIBUTION BUREAU NEWSLETTER, the **Flag Distribution Bureau Newsletter** is published monthly and its public consists of org execs, Distribution Div personnel and all forming orgs, missions, groups and individuals in pioneer areas. The purpose of the **Distribution Bureau Newsletter** is to maintain an ideal scene of expansion throughout the planet and make the purposes, policies and plans of the **Distribution Bu** Flag, **Distribution Bu** FOLOs and org Div 6s better known by the orgs, missions, forming orgs, city offices and individuals in pioneer areas. (ED 36 FB)

FLAG DIVISIONAL DIRECTIVE, **1.** applies to specific **divisions** in Scn and SO orgs alike. Is the SO equivalent of a **divisional** order. Is senior to a WW Divisional Order. Issued by a Flag aide. Printed on **divisional** color flash. (HCO PL 24 Sept 70R) **2.** to provide Flag aides with a personal comm line to their own **divisions.** The **Flag Divisional Directive** has been introduced with the purpose of communicating and pushing command policies, projects and programs. Its distribution is to SO and Scn orgs alike or as designated. It is issued on **divisional** flash colored paper as per HCO PL 4 January 1966, *Scientology Organizations Communications System: Despatches.* They have full force as orders and will be authorized for issue at **Flag.** LRH Comm will log them for compliance if so designated. (BPL 5 Feb 72R II) *Abbr.* FDD.

FLAG ED, see ED FLAG.

FLAG EVALUATION, **Flag evaluation** includes finding the major international successes and outnesses and the big whys or reasons for them. **Flag** puts these into programs and projects and sends them out via Continental Liaison Offices to organizations and sometimes franchises. (HCO PL 22 Jul 71)

FLAG EXECUTIVE BRIEFING COURSE, **1.** the **FEBC** consists of high level administration technology. It is the Class VIII Course for admin. The name, **Flag Executive Briefing Course** reflects the fact that this **course** was initially developed in 1970-71 on **Flag.** The **FEBC** checksheet is built around the Management Series volume plus the **FEBC** tapes which give the Product/Org Officer system. It includes a daily period of training drills through the course time plus some personal Esto actions done on the student such as product clearing and post purpose clearing. (HCO PL 17 May 74R) **2.** the **course** will be conducted on **Flag.** The curriculum will consist of the technology of upper level executive management, using existing materials with a very high concentration on practical drills. The exact intention of the **Flag Executive Briefing Course** is to bring executive action up to the high level of precision now only attained in auditing. (LRH ED 95 INT) **3.** makes the equivalent in management of a Class VIII in auditing. It is the beginning of third dynamic tech. (HCO PL 13 May 70) *Abbr.* FEBC.

FLAG EXECUTIVE MAGAZINE, 1. the purpose of the **magazine** is to unite Scn organizations internationally to clear the planet. The motif of the **magazine** is: 3rd dynamic progress across the globe. Distribution is to include all org staff members in addition to FEBC graduates. (FO 2808) **2.** *The Flag Executive* is a weekly **magazine** sent to students and graduates of the **Flag Executive** Briefing Course. (FO 2761)

FLAG EXECUTIVE OFFICE MANAGER, the "Office" or Admin Unit heretofore placed under CS-7 then CS-9 is now an autonomous unit under the Staff Captain called the **Flag Executive Office** Unit and the person in charge is the **Flag Executive Office Manager.** (FO 2381)

FLAG EXECUTIVE OFFICE UNIT, the "Office" or Admin Unit heretofore placed under CS-7 then CS-9 is now an autonomous unit under the Staff Captain called the **Flag Executive Office Unit** and the person in charge is the **Flag Executive Office** Manager. (FO 2381)

FLAG EXPENSE, the total cost of the Apollo, its crew, the **Flag** Admin Org, the **Flag** Bureaux, **Flag** mission and comm, any **Flag** shore base or **Flag** relay unit, and any repairs on her equipment whether paid on board or on behalf of **Flag** by Continental FBOs. (HCO PL 9 Mar 72 I)

FLAG EXPENSES, total of *all* **Flag** and Bureau and management **expenses,** including bills paid for **Flag** by FBOs but not canteen/bookstore expenses. (HCO PL 9 Mar 72 I)

FLAG FIELD DIVISION, (Div VIII) this **division** is headed by the **Flag Field** Officer. Any sales of offerings by the Flag Promotion Division and any nominated salesmen of Flag offerings such as OTLs or orgs or FSMs, are handled in this regard by the **Flag Field** Officer. (FO 2525)

FLAG FIELD OFFICER, 1. (Div VIII, Flag Field Division) through effective sales campaigns and a high velocity sales force, achieves tons of sales of org services and offerings thus producing huge traffic flows for the org and increasing its size. (FSO 94) **2.** (Nine Division Organization) **Flag Field Officer** who heads Division VIII (**Field** Division) has under him the Flag FSM program and the registrar in the Dept of Personal Registration. (FO 2674)

FLAG FINANCE BACKLOG PROJECT, **project** established in the Office of the Controller to complete the handling of **Flag's finance backlogs** from 1968 to the present while keeping current with the need for present time audits to ensure solvency and prove our financial position where necessary. (FO 3533)

FLAG FLAG REPRESENTATIVE, 1. Programs Aide. Head of Programs Bureau 4B. (CBO 437 Attachment 2) **2.** a **Flag Flag Representative** is in the Management Bureau Flag. He is the terminal for the **Flag Reps** in FOLOs and orgs and looks after them from **Flag**, sees they are on post and performing their duties. All such **Flag Rep** traffic flows through **Flag Flag Rep** and **Flag Rep** Network lines. (BPL 15 Jul 72R I) **3.** the **FR** Network Execution Branch is headed by the **Flag Flag Representative.** (FBDL 488R) *Abbr.* FFR.

FLAG FLOAT, the **Flag float** is used to cover the cost of construction work undertaken on the RSM with the purpose of improving and increasing her value as a ship. Under this heading comes various projects such as tanks, chartroom, qual, welding, radio, lifeboats. These are all classified as **Flag** expenses and are paid by **Flag.** (FO 1400)

FLAG FP, refers mainly to necessary or valuable acquisitions or disposals, regarding the ship and SO property, as an asset and regarding its functioning to be valuable. Fuel, oil and water are included so as not to curtail use of the vessel. (FSO 52)

FLAG GROSS INCOME, 1. money collected from orgs can in no way be considered **Flag GI** today. Flag's real income is FCCI and freeloader. (ED 459-36 Flag) **2.** total amount of money taken in and invoiced that week at **Flag.** (FSO 820)

FLAG HAS COMMITTEE, the **HAS Committee** handles any establishment actions which concern the three orgs aboard. The committee is composed of chairman, HAS FAO, members: HAS FB, and HAS FSO. (FSO 417)

FLAG INCOME, (Flag Admin Org) collections by reason of on-board services, missions, books and manufactured items, plus 10% of CGI of orgs managed (Flag Bu) except where WW has prior claim to the 10%. Does not include canteen or bookstore. (HCO PL 9 Mar 72 I) See FLAG GROSS INCOME.

FLAG LAND BASE, 1. **Flag** has established a new **land base.** It is called the **Flag Land Base,** as it delivers services which formerly were only available on the Flagship of the Sea Organization. (ED 180 USB) **2.** the official name of the base where Flag Service Org activities are continuing is: The **Flag Land Base.** The rest of Flagship activities retain the name Flag as always. (SO ED 498R INT) *Abbr.* FLB.

FLAG LEGAL OFFICER, all correspondence to any lawyer that is about **Flag** business e.g. bills, tax, seamans papers, national licenses, buying or selling of **Flag** Org property or ships, etc., must go via the **Flag Legal Officer.** The purpose of the **Flag Legal Officer** is **Flag**, local SO **legal** matters well handled and up to date. (FO 3252R)

FLAG LEVEL, see CLO LEVEL.

FLAG LITERATURE UNIT, see LITERATURE UNIT.

FLAG LOGISTICS I/C, handles external purchases required by **Flag.** Using a network of **Logistics I/C's** established in CLO Bureau 3s. (CBO 41 R)

FLAG LRH COMM, CS-7. (BPL 24 Jul 73R II) [Per BPL 24 Jul 73R II, *LRH Comm Network Command Chain,* other LRH Comms aboard Flag would be designated LRH Comm FB, LRH Comm FSO or LRH Comm of any Flag bases as established, all junior to **Flag LRH Comm** who is CS-7.]

FLAG MANAGEMENT BUREAU COORDINATION COUNCIL, with the establishment of the **Management Bureau** in the FB, the **Flag Management Bu Coordination Council** is formed. It consists of network branch heads: OFO Aide, LRH Comm Aide, FBO Int I/C, Folo Aide, and FFR, as well as the KOT, A/FRs for execution representatives for each continent and the Emergency Officer I/C from the OFO Branch. It is chaired by the Management Aide, and has a secretary as selected. The purpose of this **council** is coordination. **In it each network head briefs all the** members at the **council** on what are the major actions he is taking on his lines, what evals and programs are being pushed, their progress and results, major bugs (if any) and how they are being handled, the state of the network, any good news, etc. (CBO 378R)

FLAG MISSION ORDER, distributed to those concerned not to others. Usually confidential. Should never be shown around or sent to Bureaux Liaison Offices not concerned with that **mission.** (HCO PL 24 Sept 70R) *Abbr.* FMO.

FLAG NEW NAMES TO CENTRAL FILES, anyone not already in CF who reaches for **Flag** services or anyone who has paid for, started or completed Saint Hill training service, and anyone who has completed Expanded Grades. (ED 608 Flag)

FLAG NEWS, the name of the **Flag** magazine is: *The Flag News.* It is a monthly journal issued by the first of each month. The purposes of *Flag News* are as follows: (1) to unite Scn staff members internationally to clear the planet. (2) to keep in and enhance staff members' ARC with **Flag.** (3) to sell **Flag** products and increase exchange with **Flag** or to promote products and services designated by **Flag** for staff members' consumption. (CBO 280)

FLAG OFFICE MANAGER, a Flag Administration Office is established in the Office of LRH under CS-7. In charge of the unit is the **Flag Office Manager.** (FO 2273)

FLAG OFFICE OF LRH, under the control and administrative command of the LRH Personal Communicator. The **office** contains: CO HU and Household Unit, LRH Pers Sec Flag and LRH Secretariat with Commodore's Messengers, Research, Transcription, Preparations and Compilations. Foundation Collections Officer, liaison with local LRH Comms and with CS-7 and external network. Liaison with CS-Aides, FB and FSO executives, AVU, LRH Pers PRO. (FO 2374R)

FLAG OFFICER, 1. Org **Flag Officer** (CBO 348R) **2.** all **officers** and ratings on the **flagship** are known as **"Flag".** They are senior to comparable ratings on other ships. (FO 766) **3.** a ship on which a **Flag officer** has his office and staff, flies when he is aboard, a blue **flag** from the yardarm which is the **flag** signal that he is aboard. When he leaves or goes or is not aboard, the blue **flag** is lowered. In our case this is called the Commodore's **flag.** We have such a **flag.** Flying this **flag** to denote the presence of the Commodore aboard is probably why the Commodore is called a **Flag officer** since the Captain of the ship is not so designated by flying a **flag** when he is aboard. (FO 1) **4.** one who is above the rank of Captain just as in the Army "Field" rank is major or above. The ranks of Commodore, Rear Admiral, Vice Admiral, Admiral and Admiral of the Fleet are **"Flag"** ranks. Such ranks have staffs. (FO 1)

FLAG OFFICER LEVEL, this **level** operates above several vessels, wherever they may be. It generally handles matters of planning, decision and programs and captains and the heads of organizations are subject to the orders of such a body. (FO 3342)

FLAG OPERATIONS LIAISON OFFICES, 1. Continental Liaison Offices (CLOs) have become **Flag Operations Liaison Offices.** The Programs Bureau in the Continental **FOLO** relays the program to the org and sees that it is executed. (FBDL 191R) **2. FOLOs** have been set up to maintain one single command channel from **Flag** to orgs. They are **Flag's** link to the orgs and are vital to **Flag** management and expansion of orgs. They consist of **Flag** staff members working in the field on making **Flag** planning become an actuality. (BPL 5 Sept 72R) **3. FOLOs** have the duty of getting reports to us and executing **Flag** programs. (OODs 31 May 72) *Abbr.* FOLOs.

FLAG ORDER 38, contains certain points of maritime courtesy whch are observed on ships which should be followed. These are customs and courtesies. The main point is to be thoughtful and helpful to your shipmates (regardless of conduct to others) to make the ship a pleasant place regardless of the dangers of the sea and to form a pattern of agreement for right conduct. (FO 38)

FLAG ORDER INFORMATION LETTERS, within the general classification of **Flag Order**, an **information letter** format is established. Issues in this format are for issue to every Sea Org member attached to each Sea Org unit. They are not for distribution outside the Sea Org. Other formats and lines exist for other networks. **Flag Order Information Letters** are a line from the Commodore to every Sea Org member on duty. Only where specifically designated will they go to SO members on leave. (FO 2460)

FLAG ORDERS, 1. this is the equivalent to a policy letter in the Sea Org. Contains policy and sea technical materials. They are numbered and dated. They do not decay, HCO PLs and **FOs** are both in effect on Sea Org orgs, ships, offices and bases. Black ink on white paper. Distribution to all Sea Org members. It is vital for SO units to have master files and quantity of **FOs** from which hats can be made up for SO personnel and courses. (HCO PL 24 Sept 70R) **2.** hereafter there will be the following types of **Flag Orders:** (1) **Flag Orders**, usually written by LRH or directly approved by the Commodore as heretofore. (2) **Flag** Mission **Orders**, written as always but now always referred to Program and Project orders as below. (3) **Flag** Program **Order**, refers to long range programs which were formerly called "Flag Targets" or were part of "Target Boards." (4) **Flag** Project **Order**, which always refer to a program in (3) above. (5) Base **Orders**, issued on behalf of or by bases or orgs by **Flag** or the Captain. (6) Ships **Orders**, issued on behalf of or by ships by the Captain. **Orders** are given consecutive numbers for the type. **Flag** Program **Orders** are filed by Program for area. All orders applying to that program for that area are then filed with that program. **Flag Orders** as always usually contain the policy of the Sea Org as HCO Policy Letters contain policy for Scn orgs. Orders contained in the OOD signed by the Captain are actually base or ships orders. (FO 2150) [Do not confuse these types of **Flag Orders** with the mimeo issue called a **Flag Order** which is also included here as one of the types of **Flag Orders**] **3.** hereafter all general **orders** affecting the flotilla as a whole or issued by myself shall be termed **Flag Orders.** (FO 1) *Abbr.* FO.

FLAG ORG, 1. contains the Commodore's Aides and performs the management of their divisions in SO and Scn orgs. (OODs 26 Oct 70) **2.** it is involved in coordinating and handling the overall situation of Scn as represented in orgs. (7004C09 SO) **3.** its basic purpose is the external lines of management and the management of all Scn activities on the planet. (7003C15 SO) **4.** is composed of a Staff Captain and other aides. (FO 2389)

FLAG PERSONNEL, the company of the **flagship** in general is known as **Flag personnel.** (FO 467)

FLAG PERSONNEL COMMITTEE, 1. the purpose of the **committee** is to handle **Flag personnel**, recruiting, arrival, departure, utilization, placement and programming, lines, procedures, planning and actions so as to bring about the VFP of "effective **personnel**, posted and hatted" in each org aboard **Flag.** (FSO 301) **2.** the **Flag Personnel Committee** is in Div 7, Dept 21. It is represented by all orgs aboard **Flag.** This **committee** is the control point of allocation of new **personnel** to **Flag** and any inter-org transfers. The chairman: CS-1, representing the Commodore's Staff. Secretary: LRH Pers Sec, representing the Personal Office of LRH. Members: HAS FSO, HAS FB, FPPO Flag. The purpose of the **Flag Personnel Committee** is to ensure that proper allocation of new arrivals is done and to prevent and resolve any inter-org **personnel** disputes. (FO 3513)

FLAG PERSONNEL OFFICE (CONTINENTAL), the posts, org board and space under a Continental I/C, which gets for **Flag** the products of the Central Personnel Office. Continental Offices of the Central Personnel Office (formerly called "FPPO Cont'l") are renamed **Flag Personnel Office (Cont'l).** (CBO 214RA)

FLAG PERSONNEL OFFICER (CONTINENTAL), person in charge of the Continental Personnel Office and all its branches and activities, as directed by Flag. Serves the Central Personnel Office. (CBO 214RA)

FLAG PERSONNEL OFFICER (ORG), **Flag's** liaison terminal in an org on matters of

personnel. Wears all the **Flag Personnel Office** hats in regard to that org. Junior to the **Flag Personnel Officer** Cont'l. (CBO 214RA)

FLAG PERSONNEL ORDER, contains all **personnel** transfers, removals, postings, etc., on **Flag** and ordered by **Flag** in orgs. Issued only by **Flag.** Composed per HCO PL 24 September 1971, *Assignments, Model to be Used.* Distributed to those concerned. (HCO PL 24 Sept 70R) *Abbr.* FPO.

FLAG PERSONNEL PROCUREMENT OFFICE, **1.** the **FPPO** network is autonomous and has total control over its own internal personnel decisions—as does any other org. No one may order any personnel changes, or remove any personnel from the **FPPO** network without OK from the **FPPO** Flag. **FPPOs** are the Commanding Officers of the Cont'l Offices, they have the same status as the Commanding Officer of the FOLO or the Continental Captain. Their job is to supply qualified **personnel** to **Flag.** (FO 3465) **2.** an entirely separate **office** on **Flag.** It is not part of the Central Personnel Office. Its purpose is solely to bring SO veterans and proven Sea Org members to **Flag.** As such, it liaises with the Central Personnel Office as necessary, but is an entirely separate and distinct **office** of its own. (BPL 3 Apr 73R II) **3.** the **FPPO** Network is an autonomous network on Flag with offices in each Continental FOLO. The **FPPO** Network is not situated on the FOLO Org Board, it has its own org board, nor is it situated on the org board of any other org, bureaux or unit. The product of the **FPPO** Network is qualified veterans and recruits to **Flag.** The **FPPO** Network also recruits in volume for the Sea Org. From those it recruits, as with all Sea Org recruits, those most eligible are taken off the top for **Flag**, or those who can most easily be made eligible for **Flag** are put into the Flag Readiness Unit, the rest of the recruits are posted into local Sea Org orgs. (FO 3482) **4.** the purpose of the unit is to assemble and compile data necessary to get veterans reliefs trained and veterans replaced in orgs and to get **personnel** to **Flag** and to keep a continuous flow of highest quality personnel to **Flag** without injury of SO orgs or income. (FSO 44R) *Abbr.* FPPO.

FLAG PERSONNEL PROCUREMENT OFFICE ORDER, an issue for internal use within the **FPPO** Network, similar to a Guardian Order used in the Guardian Network. This issue is to be used for briefing **FPPO** Network crew, for **FPPO** projects, programs, orders or forms and internal **FPPO** Network ethics actions, etc. The color flash of the **FPPO** Network is blue ink on green paper, all **FPPO Orders** are to be printed with this color flash. (FO 3468)

FLAG PERSONNEL PROCUREMENT OFFICER, that post and person on **Flag** who gets recruits and veterans to Flag. (CBO 314RA) *Abbr.* FPPO.

FLAG PERSONNEL PROCUREMENT OFFICER (CONTINENTAL), the direct junior of **FPPO** Flag who locates, informs **FPPO** of, and expedites personnel to **Flag.** (CBO 214RA)

FLAG PLANNING, on **Flag** the basic overall effort is designed and **planned.** The big broad situations are spotted and the whys (reasons for them) found. The **plans,** programs and projects turned out by **Flag** are designed to press on with the major international designs and to spot major falterings or outnesses. The results are policy, tech, programs and projects. Where **Flag planning,** represented by programs or projects, is actually gotten into full action in an org, that org will boom. (HCO PL 22 Jul 71)

FLAG PROGRAM FILES, contain a **file** for every **program** of the Sea Org, with a separate file for each Scn area that **program** applies to. (FO 2156)

FLAG PROGRAM ORDER, issued on **Flag** for internal or external use. Contains long or short range production **programs** which are usually the entirety or major part of the handling of a published evaluation. Distributed as designated. Numbered by area to which they apply. (HCO PL 24 Sept 70R) *Abbr.* FPGMO.

FLAG PROGRAMS BUREAU, **Flag Programs Bureau** in the FOLO nudges for completions of **Flag** assigned org **programs**—including MOs turned over to them from Flag Action, logs compliance of **Flag programs,** maintains two-way comm between orgs and **Flag,** clears all comm out of orgs, ensuring no orders, cross orders and no off-policy originations, helps orgs get what they need to complete **pgms.** (e.g. hats, checksheets, HCO PLs, etc.) Does minor debug evals, and debugs assigned **programs** and gets them progressing, alerts **Flag** to situations spotted, and any non-compliance on **Flag programs,** ensures no deviation from assigned **programs** and reports to **Flag** if any occurs, reports to **Flag** on everything they do, and all data they have on the orgs and makes a full record of all such calls and their content. (CBO 192)

FLAG PROGRAMS CHIEF FOLO, the **Flag Programs Chief** in the Operations Bureau **FOLO,**

assists **Flag** in raising the viability of activities by getting **Flag's programs** in orgs completed precisely but quickly and keeping the ARC of org execs high with **Flag.** (CBO 218RB)

FLAG PROJECT ORDER, issued on **Flag** to execute a target in a program. Like FPGMOs, **FPJOs** are issued on **Flag** for internal or external use. Distributed as designated. Numbered by area to which they apply. (HCO PL 24 Sept 70R) *Abbr.* FPJO.

FLAG PROMOTION DIVISION, (Div VI) this contains all **promotion**, public address, and general public relations functions addressed to the various publics of **Flag.** This is primarily planning, design, mail, flyers and other written or published material. (FO 2525)

FLAG PROMOTION OFFICER, in charge of Division VI (on a Nine Div Org Board). (FO 2674)

FLAG PUBLIC CONTACT DIVISION, the **public** service and **public contact** actions which Div 6 had been handling were moved into Div 7 and this Division became the **Flag Public Contact Division** handling **public** service and personal **contact** matters. (FO 2633)

FLAG RANK, above any organization of ships and men, there is generally an officer of **Flag rank.** This would be a Commodore or a Deputy Commodore. (FO 3342)

FLAG READINESS UNIT, 1. is established under the Flag Personnel Procurement Office in each continental area. Overall responsibility for this **unit** is held by FPPO; **Unit** I/C is FPPO O/O. Some persons are almost eligible for **Flag** and have only a few steps on their GO 824 to complete to fully qualify. The "GO 824 TIP" is the program drawn up by FPPO O/O for that particular person to complete his requirements for **Flag.** The principal doingness of the personnel in the **Flag Readiness Unit** will be: (1) getting the GO 824 TIP done, for each who has one to do. (2) expediting as assigned by FPPO O/O when not working on (1) above or (3) below. (3) completing the initial steps of the routing form to **Flag**, e.g. vaccinations, shots, passport, etc. The goal of the **Flag Readiness Unit** is: expansion of the Sea Org and Scn by providing top management with plenty of good personnel. The purposes of the **Flag Readiness Unit** are: (1) to provide **Flag** with an abundance of qualified recruits fastest to back up LRH's phenomenal international boom. (2) to ensure those recruits and vets who don't qualify for **Flag** but can be made to qualify within a few weeks are expedited fastest and become fully eligible. (FO 3466R) **2.** those who most nearly qualify for **Flag** are channeled into the **Flag Readiness Unit** which has been set up in the Flag Personnel Procurement Office to handle a recruit's out-requirements swiftly for eligibility for **Flag.** (SO ED 274R INT) *Abbr.* FRU.

FLAG REP ADVICE LETTERS, 1. Flag Reps in the CLO and the **Flag Rep** I/C keep each other **advised** of what is happening in their areas daily—by use of an **Advice Letter.** These **letters** are used on **Flag** to keep the Aides informed. (CBO 141) **2.** the format for the **Flag Rep Advice Letter** would be a two or three sheet **letter** with both sides of the pages filled. It would be stapled in upper left hand corner and mailed out to all **Flag Reps** on regular comm lines. It is used to create a strong team of **FRs**, make the network more real, productive, on-Source and in good comm with each other and **Flag.** (ED 35 FB)

FLAG REP ANSWER FORM, see FLAG REP QUERY FORM.

FLAG REP COMPLIANCE LOG, the **Flag Representative** keeps a **Flag Rep Compliance Log.** Each incoming order is entered into this **log** with a copy of the order or program placed or stapled in the **log** so that it can be lifted. The record of actions done on its targets are noted in the **log** with the name of the person who would be nudged to get **compliance** with each target. (HCO PL 7 Aug 73 I)

FLAG REP FOLO FUNCTION CHECKLIST B, a **checklist** of the broad functions of a **FOLO** that should be inspected biweekly by the **FOLO Flag Rep.** The entire **checklist** is thoroughly completed and forwarded to **Flag** by the 1st and 15th of each month. A copy of the report should be given to the CO of the FOLO, for his info. (CBO 155R)

FLAG REP INSPECTION CHECKLISTS, the purpose of these **checklists** is to collect basic data for **Flag**, that will let us know how well each CLO, org, or ship is established and progressing on a week by week basis. The **Flag Rep** should remember to: "Never Accept a conclusion, always look." The inspections are done by actually going into the area and looking, inspecting, interviewing, collecting the data and when complete sending it to **Flag Rep** I/C Flag. (FO 3074)

FLAG REP NETWORK AND EXECUTION BRANCH, 1. Flag Rep Network and Execution Branch, Management Bureau, Flag, creates and runs an operational **FR Network** that receives authorized handlings and programs and gets these complied with through getting the orders sent out, duplicated, **executed,** and debugged for rapid completion that can be verified. Keeps up-to-date program files, target boards and logs required to properly oversee **execution.** Coordinates all orders received for orgs from other parts of the FB and Commodore's Staff. Sets priorities. Ensures orgs are not cross ordered by keeping in a tight filter line. Ensures that **FRs** send in their routine reports and that these are out-point free. Receives, verifies and acknowledges **FR** compliances. Establishes an active, ethical **Flag Rep Network** which upholds **Flag's** image and gets programs rapidly done, to the end result of evaluated situations handled and prospering orgs. (CBO 376) **2.** (Branch 12A, Flag Management Bu) it is headed by the FFR. It continues its functions of establishing and operating the **FR Network,** and has been assigned the additional duties of **execution** of org **Flag** pgms from **Flag** on down and coordination and priority setting of all orders into orgs. It is the filter point which ensures no cross orders into orgs. It sets priorities for all orgs and ensures the FOLOs know and follow these priorities. (FBDL 488R)

FLAG REP ORG FUNCTION CHECKLIST A, the **Flag Rep** has the responsibility of seeing that the org is there, solvent and **functioning** by use of the **Flag Rep** Inspection **checklist.** This **checklist** is thoroughly done once a month by the **FR.** These reports to **Flag** will be used to catch and correct persistent outnesses that the org is not actively correcting as they should be and to get orgs back on their feet where they have been negligent in the past and have not corrected in PT. (HCO PL 28 Jan 72RB) [The above HCO PL was suspended by BPL 23 Jan 75.]

FLAG REP QUERY FORM, **Flag** or FOLO terminals who have items to be: (1) expedited/nudged, (2) unbugged, (3) reported on or inspected fill out a copy of the **Flag Rep Query Form** and route it to the A/FFR for the area, who logs it and sends it on to the Continental **Flag Rep** FOLO who then routes it to the org **Flag Rep.** The org **Flag Rep** then goes into that area and interviews the terminals involved and finds the why and the who. The **Flag Rep** reports all data found on the "Flag Rep Answer Form." (BPL 15 Jul 72 RA I)

FLAG REP REPORT LOG, the **Flag Rep** keeps a **Flag Rep Report Log.** Each report sent to **Flag** is **logged** with its title and date so that it can be identified. Copies of the **report** are filed as well as sent to **Flag.** (HCO PL 7 Aug 73 I)

FLAG REPRESENTATIVE, 1. the **Flag Rep** has the primary duty of safeguarding that those actions necessary to the delivery of Scn by an area or org are implemented and continued and to prevent the destruction of the org by omissions, alter-is or counter-intention and to keep **Flag** abreast of the existing scene so that efficient operation can be directed. (HCO PL 29 Dec 71R) **2.** the **Flag Representative** is the Board Representative's terminal of execution of his orders from Flag. The Board Representative is located at Flag. The **Flag Representative** is located in the org of the board which is represented at Flag by its Board Representative. (BPL 23 Jun 74) **3.** the purpose of the **Flag Representative** is to find and report situations to **Flag** and to obtain compliance on orders from **Flag.** It being understood that such orders result from valid evaluations based on **Flag Rep** reports, routine reports and always with due attention to the actual statistics of the activity. (HCO PL 7 Aug 73 I) **4.** his office shall be in the Office of LRH FOLO or org. His functions shall consist of observing and reporting to **Flag** concerning the FOLO's or org's compliance to **Flag** programs and projects and orders. In FOLOs and orgs the **Flag Representative** is equal to any CO or ED in his area, including any Continental CO (for Continental FRs). (BPL 15 Jul 72R I) **5.** a **Flag Representative** shall be appointed, trained and briefed by **Flag** and sent to each FOLO and org on garrision type orders. He is in fact a Bureaux Liaison Officer from above. His office shall be in the Office of LRH FOLO or org. His functions shall consist of observing and reporting to **Flag** concerning the FOLO's or org's compliance to **Flag** programs and projects and orders. His specialties shall be: (1) recruitment. Observing and reporting that **Flag** Directives regarding the subject are complied with. Observing and reporting that qualifications are on policy, observing and reporting a Recruiting Officer exists in the FOLO or org and does not get musical chaired. Observing and reporting that recruits are sent to Flag on order. (2) Trainees. Observing and reporting that the local service org complies with student promotion and training requirements. Observing and reporting that persons ordered to **Flag** from FOLOs, service orgs or field get to **Flag.** Observing and reporting that **Flag** requirements are met. (3) Logistics. Observing and reporting that the FOLO/CLO has a logistics terminal for itself and **Flag** and that **Flag** requirements and orders are met and shipped. (4) Data. Observing and reporting that **Flag** requirements for data from the **Flag** Data Bureau and the local FOLO are met routinely and regularly. (5) Establishment. Observing and reporting that the FOLO or org is established and operating according to **Flag** Directives and that inspection reports on the FOLO or org regularly go to **Flag.** (HCO PL 15 Jul 72 I) **6.** the importance of the **Flag Rep** is to keep the org there, solvent and functioning, and that's his main thing. (7201C12 SO) **7.** the purpose of the org **Flag Rep** is to see that the legal orders of **Flag** are carried out in that org and that policy is known and followed on the subjects for which the network is responsible. (FO 3078) **8.** the **Flag Rep** is responsible for the program of the org and pushing the paid completions of the org. (LRH ED 153RE INT) *Abbr.* Flag Rep, FR.

FLAG REPRESENTATIVE ADVICE LETTER, a newsletter for **Flag Representatives.** It is issued each week from **Flag** and may be used by **Flag Reps** to keep their orgs' execs and staffs informed, as well as to keep themselves briefed. (SO ED 229 INT)

FLAG REPRESENTATIVE IN-CHARGE, a **Flag Representative in-charge** is in the Programs Bureau Flag. He is the terminal for the **Flag Reps** in FOLOs and orgs and looks after them from **Flag;** sees they are on post and performing their duties. All such **Flag Rep** traffic flows through **Flag Rep I/C** and **Flag Rep** FOLO/CLO lines. (HCO PL 15 Jul 72 I) [The above HCO PL was replaced by BPL 15 Jul 72R I and the term Flag Flag Representative replaces **Flag Representative In-Charge.**]

FLAG REPRESENTATIVE NETWORK, 1. the purpose of this **network** is to safeguard that those actions necessary to the prosperity of an area or org are implemented and continued and to prevent the destruction of the org by omissions, alter-is, or counter-intention and to keep **Flag** abreast of the existing scene so that efficient operations can be directed. The reason for the establishment of this **network** is lack of totally **Flag** oriented **representation** in Continental areas particularly on the subjects of recruits, trainees, logistics, data, establishment and compliances to **Flag** programs, projects and orders. The **network** is brought into being to remedy this lack. (BPL 15 Jul 72 R I) **2.** the **Flag Rep Network** provides **Flag** terminals with a comm line for matters of mystery and urgent actions. Matters on which inspection or nudge are required pass through the A/**FFR** for the area, are routed to the Continental area, are routed to the Continental **Flag Rep** at the FOLO and then to the org **FR** for him to then look further into that specific area and find the bug, the why and/or the who that is slowing command intention. The **Flag Rep** then reports up, with full specifics on what he has found. These reports go direct to data files on **Flag,** where the original terminal requesting the information can review it. (BPL 15 Jul 72RA I)

FLAG RESERVES, any money made by **Flag's** FAO (Flag Admin Org) services and Bureaux management 10%s over and above the total expenses of the ship, the FAO, the Bureaux and the crew. (HCO PL 9 Mar 72 I)

FLAG SAINT HILL, Flag Saint Hill delivers usual **Saint Hill** services plus the renowned L-10, Evaluators Course, and FCCI (Flag Case Completion Intensive). (FO 3426) *Abbr.* FSH.

FLAG SERVICE CONSULTANT, 1. an **FSC** is a Sea Org member specially trained and fully briefed to be the stable terminal in his area as regards **Flag services** which include all Scn and Dn services available elsewhere as well as some exclusive **services** like L-10 processing or the Data Series Evaluators Course. He is **Flag's** terminal in the field to ensure that public get their questions answered concerning **Flag services,** how to get to **Flag,** costs of services, technical estimates, etc., so that there are no stops whatsoever for anyone wishing to take service on the **Flagship** which provides the world's highest quality technical delivery. (FBDL 439R) **2.** the post of **Flag Service Consultant** is relocated to FOLO Div IIIs', Department VIIs. It is external and under the **Flag** Bureau III Treasury Aide with the CO FOLO responsible locally for its production. The FOLO **Flag Service Consultant** will be run in liaison with the CO FOLO by the **Flag Service Consultant** International who is directly under the Treasury Aide (FB). There is to be a **Flag Service Consultant** in each FOLO. The purpose of the post is (1) to line up, reg and collect monies for **Flag services** (FCCI and public courses) and (2) to send to **Flag** for the delivery of services purchased. (FO 3444RA) *Abbr.* FSC.

FLAG SERVICE CONSULTANT I/C, each FOLO now has an **FSC I/C** based in the FOLO at a fixed location and is easily contactable by mail, phone, telex, or in person. Operating as an extension of the **FSC I/C** are his field personnel who are mobile and travel throughout their continent helping those who are preparing to go to **Flag** for **services** with all necessary cycles that make the trip to **Flag** a trouble-free adventure. (FBDL 439R) *Abbr.* FSC I/C.

FLAG SERVICE CONSULTANT INTERNATIONAL, the FOLO **Flag Service Consultant** will be run in liaison with the CO FOLO by the

Flag Service Consultant International who is directly under the Treasury Aide (FB). (FO 3444RA) [Same as **Flag Service Consultant International** I/C]. *Abbr.* FSC INT.

FLAG SERVICE CONSULTANT INTERNATIONAL I/C, the Product Officer over all the Continental **FSC's I/C** is the D/**FSC Int**, in contact with **FSCs** daily expediting public to **Flag** and their funds. Her senior is the **FSC International I/C.** The **FSC Int I/C** puts his network there, sees the D/**FSC Int** gets it producing, writes individual programs for each **FSC** and generally manages his network. He is also the terminal on the Flagship who gets all technical queries answered, prospective FCCI's pc folders checked over by the **Flag** C/S for technical estimates and accounts matters handled in liaison with the respective divisions on **Flag** whose area it concerns. (FBDL 439R) *Abbr.* FSC INT I/C.

FLAG SERVICE CONSULTANT NETWORK, FSCs are now Public Division registrars for Flag. The **FSC Network** is under the **FSC** International which is under the Distribution Secretary Flag in Div 6. Anyone who has bought from other orgs is Flag Div 6 public. At least two **FSCs** should be on post in any FOLO. One more traveling, one more at FOLO. (FO 3666)

FLAGSHIP OPERATION COUNCIL, council that handles matters affecting **ship operation** as a floating, mobile base. (FSO 117)

FLAGSHIP ORDER, never goes off **Flag.** Full distribution to **Flagship's** personnel. (HCO PL 24 Sept 70R) *Abbr.* FSO.

FLAGSHIP ORG, 1. the base **org,** internal (inside the **ship** and **ship** area) functions to care for the Flag Bureaux. (OODs 8 May 72) **2.** early in 1971, Flag was divided into three orgs: Flag Bureaux, Flag Admin Org and the **Flagship Org.** The **Flagship Org (FSO)** is the **ship** itself. It consists of the usual yacht organization functions of command, deck, stewards and galley and engine room. The **ship org** flash color is blue. (FO 2856) **3.** there is a base **org** that puts the **ship** there. This we now call the **Flagship Org. Flagship Org (ship** officers and **ship** crew and domestic services of the **ship**). (OODs 30 Dec 70) **4.** in September/October 1969 the existing org was split and two orgs were formed—Flag Org and **Flagship Org.** The Flag Org divs were to handle the external lines of the Scientology networks and the **Flagship** divs were to "put the Flag Org there." That is, to make and keep the ship a safe, floating, mobile base for the Flag Org. (FO 2633) **5. org** which runs the **ship** and the Flag Admin Org. (FSO 225) *Abbr.* FSO.

FLAGSHIP PRODUCTION COUNCIL, council that handles matters affecting income, promotion, public students and customers, **production,** and service to the public. (FSO 117)

FLAG STEWARD, cares for meals, clothes, quarters of the staff of **Flag.** (FO 1)

Flag Steward

FLAG TECH VFP EXPEDITOR, the **Tech VFP Expeditor** is stationed in Bureau V, **Flag,** directly under the Training and Services Aide who is the immediate senior. A **Tech VFP Expeditor** gets in real courses over the world and real auditing results and real cramming. The product of the post is astronomically increased numbers of **tech** completions. (CBO 118)

FLAG TOURS CHIEF, for management purposes the FOLO should regard the **Tours** Org as any other org on the **Flag**—FOLO—Org system. This makes the FOLO responsible for seeing that the **Tours** Org is on its orders getting them done and that it is sending data and reports to **Flag** regularly. It does not however allow the FOLO to originate management orders into the **Tours** Org as **Tours** Org is handled and run by the **Flag Tours Chief.** (HCO PL 24 Aug 72RA) [The above HCO PL was replaced with BPL 24 Aug 72RC, *Tours Org Series 1RC, Tours Org,* which doesn't use the term **Flag Tours Chief.**]

FLAG TRAINING SPECIALIST COURSE, the purpose of the **FTSC** is to make **Flag** Standard **Training** Experts who apply standard course tech. (FSO 460) *Abbr.* FTSC.

FLAIR, when you're terrifically hot at evaluations it is called **flair.** (7201C02 SO)

FLASH COLORS FOR DIVISIONS, 1. Div 7 blue or white, Div 1 goldenrod, Div 2 light pink or violet, Div 3 deep pink, Div 4 green, Div 5 grey, Div 6 canary yellow. (BPL 5 Feb 72R II) **2.** Div 9 blue or white, Div 1 gold, Div 2 light pink or violet, Div 3 deep pink, Div 4 green, Div 5 grey, Div 6 yellow, Div 7 brown, Div 8 orange. (FO 2521)

FLEETING F/N, the pc **F/Ns** so briefly the auditor misses it and overruns. (HCOB 23 Nov 73R)

FLEXIBLE BUDGET, see BUDGET, FLEXIBLE.

FLEXING, the process of changing a budget to correspond with fluctuations in production, sales or activity levels.

Fliers

FLIERS, fliers are used for stuffing in letters, putting into books or merchandise shipped. Every product an org can deliver rates a **flier.** A **flier** must (a) offer a product, (b) describe it, (c) give a price, (d) say how to get it, (e) picture it, (f) hard sell it. The Letter Reg puts them in letters to describe the particular service she is offering. The Publications Dept has them for books and merchandise and stuffs them into things they are shipping. Stacks of them are made available in cases in reception and for Body Reg and Public Reg use. **Fliers** are not handed out on streets, nor are they "stuffed loose in magazines" which of course is not their purpose at all. Mags carry similar texts in ads. Accounts uses **fliers** for sending out with monthly statements and collection letters and they are so designed to encourage payment by the debtor. (BPL 20 May 72R)

FLIP CHARTS, see CHARTS, FLIP.

FLIP-FLOPS, same as FLIP CHARTS.

FLOAT, 1. petty cash system or cash kept in hand by a business. 2. in finance, a sum of money represented by checks that are outstanding and have not yet cleared. 3. to launch a new business enterprise. —*v.* to release especially a security, for sale.

FLOATING, 1. the action of an employee leaving his work area to socialize with other employees in other work areas of a business; idle wastage of time. 2. designating capital that is available for use because it is not invested permanently or is in circulation. 3. designating a short-term debt that is not funded.

FLOATING ASSETS, see ASSETS, CURRENT.

FLOATING EXCHANGE RATE, not a set or official exchange rate established by a country but one that floats or "finds a natural exchange rate" with other currencies. A floating exchange rate exhibits less responsibility for and causative control over the value of a currency and often leads to a devaluation.

FLOTILLA, 1. those ships and boats which comprise the Sea Org are known as the **flotilla** meaning a group of vessels united under and commanded by one Flag officer such as a Commodore or Admiral. (FO 766) **2.** two or more ships. (BO 34, 16 Jun 67) *Abbr.* Flot.

Flotilla (Def. 2)

FLOTILLA BOARD, **board** showing current location and activity of other ships. (FO 1954)

FLOW CHART, a **chart** showing what particles are received by the post and what changes the post is expected to make in them and to where the post routes them. (HCO PL 22 Sept 70)

Flow Chart

FLOW CONTROL, putting a production line's men, machines and materials in proper balance so that production flows harmoniously.

FLOW DIAGRAM, 1. a flow chart. 2. a diagram of the floor plan of a factory showing the flow lines of work. It is used to plan out efficient placement and use of machines and equipment before purchasing and installation.

FLOWLINE PRODUCTION, see PRODUCTION, FLOWLINE.

FLOW OF WORK, the sequence of actions that occur or should occur to produce a product or accomplish something. Usually the flow of work is depicted on a flow chart that finalizes the most efficient and economical way to produce the product or achieve the desired results.

FLOW PROCESS CHART, see CHART, PROCESS.

FLUB, **1.** *Slang.* an absent, unusable or damaging product. (CBO 63) **2.** an error. (HCOB 21 Aug 70) —*v.* to blunder or make a mess of. (BTB 3 Jul 73 I)

Flub (Def. 1)

FLUB CATCH CIC DISPLAY, as part of each org's **display** board in **CIC** there is a section called **Flub Catch** which is labelled and posted. The information is given to CIC Boards I/C by the Tech Programs Chiefs when they log their **flub catch** reports by means of a fast dispatch and brief details including the date and code designation. (FO 1583R)

FLUB CATCH COLOR CODE, the **code** is a flash **color** system. CIC uses cards of these **colors** or in the absence of **colored** cards uses white cards with broad felt marker **color** slashes in each corner. Blue=minor tech flubs. Green=missing materials or serious tech flubs. Yellow=high refunds and repayments, huge backlogs indicating a refusal to deliver. Orange=gross out tech or verbal tech. Red=squirrel tech. (FO 1583R)

FLUB CATCH SYSTEM, **1.** on Flag, an FES is carefully done so as to detect areas of out tech in the world. This is called the **Flub Catch system.** Auditors and C/Ses so detected are sent to cramming in their areas to smooth out their tech, knowledge, or TRs, all to improve delivery of tech. (HCOB 6 Oct 70) **2.** that **system** which detects, orders and gets corrected out tech. In other words, it **catches** the **flub.** (FO 2442R) **3. flub**=to blunder or make a mess of. **Catch**=to intercept the motion or action of. It is a term coined and used to cover that exact action. **Flub catch**=to notice, intercept and handle after the fact of the motion or action, a blunder or mistake being made. (BTB 3 Jul 73 I)

F/NING STUDENT, what is an **F/Ning student?** Is he chortling and gurgling and slapping his knee? No. He is just calmly going right along. (HCO PL 26 Jun 72)

FOB, free on board.

FOLDER PAGE, nowadays in a very large, busy HGC, a special **folder page** is assigned to the C/S. His sole duties are to collect up and deliver **folders** to the C/S and return to HGC Admin or the **folder**

room, as ordered. This cuts all body traffic into the C/S ivory tower to one person—the **folder page.** (BPL 5 Feb 72)

FOLLOWING POLICY, **following policy** is a matter of grasping situations and knowing **policy** well enough to apply the right **policy** to the right situation—where no **policy** covers, an experienced, quick person can easily extend the idea of general **policy** to cover it knowing it isn't covered. (HCO PL13 Mar 65, *Divisions 1, 2, 3 The Structure of Organization What is Policy?*)

FOLLOW-UP, 1. a regularized or random check to verify that products, contracts, jobs, etc., are being completed on time. 2. a repeat check, action, campaign, etc., following something else and serving to reinforce, elaborate on or expedite the first action such as a follow-up news story, advertising campaign, visit, etc.

FOLO AIDE, the **FOLO** and **FOLO** Network Branch is headed by a **FOLO Aide.** (FBDL 488R)

FOLO AND FOLO NETWORK BRANCH, **1.** (Branch 11C Flag Management Bu) this **branch** is new as a **network** on its own. It is headed by a **FOLO** Aide. It operates and runs the **FOLOs** and is responsible for all **FOLO** functions and within it has the running of other **networks;** A/CS-6, A/CS-2 for Pubs and Books, **FOLO** Tours, and Forming Orgs. (FBDL 488R) **2. FOLO and FOLO Network Branch**, Management Bureau Flag, creates and runs a **network** of effective, active, viable and solvent **FOLOs** which are Flag's operation relay and representation points maintaining safe, speedy comm lines to the field. Ensures **FOLOs** get rapid and real verified compliance to Flag's orders as per priorities set by Flag with the result of productive viable and expanding orgs. Makes the **FOLOs** make money for Flag and themselves by collecting on monies owed to Flag and the **FOLO,** selling Flag and **FOLO** services and running effective Tours units. Creates and runs a network of A/CS-6s at the **FOLOs** that get org Div 6s standard, on policy and driving new people in on the orgs in floods. Ensures via the Forming Orgs Ops Officer at the **FOLOs** that groups are contacted and promoted to become Forming Orgs and gets these and existing Forming Orgs progressing rapidly to complete their requirements to become a full org. Ensures via A/CS-2 for Pubs and Books **FOLO,** continued org expansion through supervising of Pubs Orgs with standard report lines and through getting Pubs plans and programs as set by CS-2 executed and ensures that Pubs Orgs clear what policies they operate on and coordinate their activities with Flag. (CBO 376)

FOLO BRANCH FOLO, **FOLO Branch** in the Management Bureau at a **FOLO** sees that org Div 6s are run standardly on policy and driving new people in on the orgs in floods. Sees that Pubs Orgs are operating per policy and per their plans and programs, with standard report lines to Flag, and that the Pubs Orgs and org's bookselling activities are driving floods of business down on the orgs by widespread booksales. (CBO 375)

FOLO LAST COURT OF APPEAL, membership of the **court** consists of a chairman of officer rank, a secretary and from one to three members. The **court's** duties consist of correcting false reports, false accusations and third party activities which have been detrimental to the repute of the individual or harmful to his well-being. A **Court of Appeal** is not held until the person has taken normal recourse actions available to him in his own org. Persons in the process of a Committee of Evidence, Ethics Hearing, or conditions assignment may not petition a **FOLO** for **Court of Appeal** until the action is concluded. Where Ethics Orders have been issued against a person, the disclosure of one proven incorrect report in the order does not permit all of the findings to be cancelled. Each specific false report must be individually handled and cleared or not cleared. (BPL 26 Jan 70R I)

FOLO MISSIONS, **FOLO missionaires** on Flag Mission Orders run by the Flag Action Bureau. (CBO 218RB)

FOLO TOURS ORG FCCI GI, total monies collected by **FOLO Tours Orgs** for Flag services for the week. (BFO 119)

FOLO U.S., officially renamed **FOLO WUS.** (CBO 238)

FOR, free on rail.

FORECASTING, the action of predicting future business trends and outcomes by studying and correlating current and past trends and data. Statistics provide the primary forecasting tool.

FOREIGN CORPORATION, see CORPORATION, FOREIGN.

FOREMAN, an executive or **foreman** is one who can obtain, train and use people, equipment and spaces to economically achieve valuable final products. (HCO PL 14 Dec 70)

Foreman

FORM, [terms like **Form** 3 or **Form** 6 as mentioned in HCO PL 6 December, 1961, *Saint Hill Training Candidates from Organizations,* will be found under HCO WW Security **Form** 3 or 6.]

FORM 1, I & R **Form 1,** Dept 3, HCO. (7012C04)

FORM 3, Joburg Sec Check. (HCO PL 6 Dec 61) See HCO WW FORM 3.

FORM 5B, "Are you here for any other purpose than what you say/state?" Variations of this question may be used, but this type question designed as a fast check on new students will be referred to henceforth as a **Form 5B.** (HCO PL 8 Aug 63) [The above HCO PL was cancelled by BPL 10 Oct 75 IV.]

FORM 26 June 65, [this is HCO PL 26 June 65, *HGC PC Review Auditing Form.*]

FORMAL CONFERENCE, a conference at which there is an official transcript made of the proceedings as well as an endeavor to reach definite formal recommendations.

FORMAL ORGANIZATION, see ORGANIZATION, FORMAL.

FORMAL TRAINING, see TRAINING, FORMAL.

FORM AO 1, report of session **form** used on Advanced Courses. One of these **forms** is filled out at session end for every session even if two or more in one day. (HCO PL 10 Jan 68) [The above HCO PL was cancelled by BPL 10 Oct 75 IV.]

FORM AO 2, used on Advanced Courses, this **form** advises the Course Supervisor that the student is applying to Qual Advanced Org for award of course completion, and should be accompanied by the student's complete folder. (HCO PL 10 Jan 68) [The above HCO PL was cancelled by BPL 10 Oct 75 IV.]

FORM DEP/1, HCO WW **Form Dep/1. Departure Form.** (HCO PL 8 Nov 62, *Departure Form*)

FORMING ORG, **1.** the minimum number of persons necessary to form a Scn organization is ten. Any **organization** having less than ten persons is classed a City Office or **Forming Org.** (HCO PL 30 Jan 66 II) **2.** a **Forming Org,** unable yet to function fully, is a Class Zero Org. It is only at recognition and gives a Class Zero Course only and uses only Grade Zero processes. When it can give a Level 1 Course and use Grade I processes it is a Class I Org. And so on. (HCO PL 1 May 65 III) **3.** mission or franchise. (BPL 31 Mar 71R)

FORM OF THE ORG, the **form of the org** is made up of such things as flow charts, org board, location plot. In the Sea Org, it's also the Watch Quarter and Station Bill. This includes cleaning stations, one station per one crew member. (OODs 22 Aug 72)

FORMULA EVASION, a type of dev-t where areas or persons fail to follow the conditions **formulas** assigned or actually indicated and pursue the wrong or no **formula.** (HCO PL 27 Jan 69)

FORMULA INVESTING, see INVESTING, FORMULA.

FORMULA OF LIVING, the basic **formula of living** (not life) is: having and following a basic purpose. (HCO PL 13 Mar 65, *Divisions 1, 2 3 The structure of Organization What is Policy?*)

FORMULA OF POLICY, the **formula of policy** consists of: (1) conceiving, recognizing, testing and codifying successful ideas, actions and procedures that forward the basic purpose and retard its opposition, (2) making these **policies** known and in greater or lesser degree understood, and (3) getting these **policies** followed. (HCO PL 13 Mar 65, *Divisions 1, 2, 3 The Structure of Organization What is Policy?*)

FORWARD MARKET, see MARKET, FORWARD.

FOUNDATION, 1. an institution set up with provisions for its future maintenance or survival such as one endowed with a constant flow of funds or income. 2. funds or a fund to ensure the continued existence of some institution, school, college, hospital, art gallery, etc.

FOUNDATION INTENSIVE, the evening period 1900 to 2130 hours Monday to Friday. Amounts to a **foundation intensive.** (ED 140 FAO)

FOUNDATION, THE, 1. an evening, part-time organization. The purpose of the evening organization is to operate as a bridge from the public to the daytime org and to make money in its own right. The evening organization and the weekend is called: **The** Scientology **Foundation.** (HCO PL 11 Jun 65) **2.** the Day Org and **the Foundation** are two entirely separate orgs. **The Foundation** is not under the Day Org. Day Org executives have no jurisdiction whatsoever over **the Foundation** executives or personnel. All orgs Day and **Foundation** are today directly under Flag with communication and control lines through FOLOs. Day Org hours generally run 9:00 A.M. to 6:00 P.M., Monday through Friday, **Foundation** hours 6:00 P.M. to 11:00 P.M., Monday through Friday and 9:00 A.M. to 11:00 P.M. Saturday and Sunday. (BPL 11 Aug 72R I) **3. Foundations** exist to keep an area calm and to prevent a no-auditing situation for many. They also exist to service Day Org staff. (HCO PL 10 Jul 69) *Abbr.* FDN.

FOUNDER, L. Ron Hubbard. In that new boards of directors are being elected for the various corporations and their branches, I am resigning the title of Executive Director and in accordance with a resolution of the general meeting of Charter Members, I am being given the title of **Founder** instead. (BPL 1 Sept 66R)

FOUNDERS' SHARES, special shares or stock issued to the founders, organizers or promoters of a public company or corporation which sometimes allow special voting rights.

FOUNDING CHURCH CONGREGATION, purpose: to communicate to the **congregation** the principles and philosophy of Scn. To ensure for each individual an awareness of their happiness and immortality through good training, processing and fellowship. (HCO PL 12 Oct 62)

FOUNDING CHURCH OF SCIENTOLOGY, purpose: to disseminate Scn. To advance and protect its membership. To hold the lines and data of **Scn** clean and clear. To educate and process people toward the goal of a civilized age on Earth second to none. To survive on all dynamics. (HCO PL 12 Oct 62)

FOUNDING SCIENTOLOGIST, if you were with **Scientology** before 1964 you were an old timer, a **Founding Scientologist.** You were here in the beginning years. You helped. (HCO PL 5 Feb 64)

FOUND REPORT, staff member **report** of anything **found**, sending the article with the dispatch or saying where it is. (HCO PL 1 May 65)

FOUR KEY STATS, the **four key stats** are paid completions, student points, well done auditing hours and gross income of each individual SO and Scn org. (FO 3137)

FOUR PRODUCTS OF A SCIENTOLOGIST, (a) purchased books, (b) disseminated knowledge, (c) environmental control, (d) a cleared planet (or in other words to break it down: new Scientologists or Dianeticists). (HCO PL 28 Nov 71 R II)

FOURTH DEPUTY CHIEF, on a **four** watch system; the **4th Deputy Chief** is **4th** Engineer (is Engineer of the Watch of Watch D) and is in charge of filing, admin, records and graphs and makes ER achievements known to ER personnel. (FO 2080)

FOURTH (4th) MATE, 1. Qual Sec. (FO 3183) **2.** in charge of Division 5. (FO 2535) **3.** seventh in command of a ship. (FO 196) **4.** is the Supercargo's OOW. (FO 123) **5.** is the head of Division 1. (FO 79)

FP COORDINATION COUNCIL, an **FP Coordination Council** is formed. As there are three orgs on board doing their own **FPs**, the **coordination** hat is established and assigned to this **council.** The **council** is composed of the Treasury members for FB (Chairman), FAO and FSO. It meets on the third day of the month and sets preliminary allocation figures for the **FP** bodies on the ship to work against. (FSO 437R)

FPPO EMERGENCY FLOAT, as it has been found vital to a fast flow of personnel to Flag, an **emergency float** is authorized for the **Flag Personnel Procurement Office** in any Continental Area where a Flag Readiness Unit has been established. The **float** is to cover emergency funds needed for birth certificate application, passport application, shots, etc., where the recruit may have arrived without adequate funds to cover these but is a bona fide recruit for Flag and in the FRU. (FO 3466R-6)

FPPO RECRUITERS, these personnel are **recruiters** who work in teams recruiting a volume of qualified personnel for the whole of the Sea Org, their senior is the Unit I/C and they are responsible to him for their production. (FO 3475)

FPPO RECRUITMENT UNIT I/C, the **recruiters** in the **FPPO** Network are broken down into sections with five recruiters in each section plus the **I/C** who is also a **recruiter** but who is responsible for the production of the **recruiters** under him. He is essentially the product officer of his unit and is responsible to the Continental Recruitment Chief. (FO 3475)

FRACTIONAL UNEMPLOYMENT, see UNEMPLOYMENT, FRACTIONAL.

FRANCHISE, 1. a group granted the privilege of delivering elementary Scn and Dn services. Does not have org status or rights. (BTB 12 Apr 72R) **2.** in the U.S., the word **franchise** whose original meaning was "right or privilege" has become associated in common usage with more commercial or business activity. Since the church is not, and never has been concerned with that type of activity, this word will no longer be used to describe its religious field activity. From this date, any legally chartered Scn field activity will be properly designated only as Mission of the Church of Scientology. (BPL 12 Apr 71 II) **3.** a **franchise** is now regarded as a mission of the church run by a minister of the church and bears non-profit status. (HCO PL 10 Nov 69 II) **4.** Forming Org (BPL 31 Mar 71R) **5.** mimeo distribution symbol. A bulletin must also be marked **Franchise** to be sent to **franchises.** When so marked the **Franchise** Secretary receives one copy for his files and one copy for each **franchise** holder he is going to mail it out to. No additional copies or round numbers will be furnished the **Franchise** Secretary. (HCO PL 2 Jul 64)

FRANCHISE, 1. a right or privilege granted by a government or law-making body which gives a person or business authority to do something or operate in a specific manner. 2. the right to sell a product or deliver a service granted to a business by a manufacturer, patent owner, copyright holder, etc., usually in exchange for a percentage of the profits or a flat fee.

FRANCHISE AWARD OF MERIT, see AWARD OF MERIT.

FRANCHISE CENTER, a **Franchise Center** has less than 30 staff members. Its org board simply states who is there and what he does. It is **franchised** by official Scn but is not an "official org" unless it so requests. It trains all levels up to but not including Level Zero. It can run a Dn Course. It processes up to the classification of the auditor auditing but not including or above power processing. It does not have power processing. It concentrates on PE, individual and co-auditing at Dn level. It can do group auditing. It operates day or evening or both. (HCO PL 21 Oct 66 II)

FRANCHISE DEPARTMENT, handles all **franchise** holders and field auditor matters and traffic and supervises their activities. Collects all 10% royalties from **franchise** holders, awards and withdraws **franchises.** Conducts **franchise** programs. Handles all memberships and certifications. (HCO PL 18 Dec 64, *Saint Hill Org Board*)

FRANCHISE DISCOUNT, discount of 40%. (HCO PL 19 Jul 65, *Discounts Central Orgs Books*)

FRANCHISE FILES, franchise holders in good standing may be issued a certain type of list. No list of persons actively in communication with the Central Org may be released and such persons may not be part of any list issued. One simply regards "inactive address plates" as **franchise files.** (HCO PL 30 Oct 64)

FRANCHISE GRANT, a right to use the name approved by **Franchise** WW in a single area by an individual in that area. (HCO PL 10 Nov 69 II)

FRANCHISE HOLDER, a professional auditor, with a classification to Level III or over, who practices Scn full or part-time for remuneration, who conducts processing and training privately or to groups, whose understanding and experience of Scn is sufficiently broad for him to be publicized to others as a stable terminal, who has signed a **franchise** agreement, who receives bulletins, policy letters, advice, advertising, technical information, services and administrative data from HCO WW, and who, in return for same, maintains regularly a weekly report and a weekly payment of ten per cent of his gross income to HCO WW. (HCO PL 2 Jan 65)

FRANCHISE LIAISON OFFICER, a **liaison** point will be set up for the Franchise Officer WW in each CLO. The title would be **Franchise Liaison Office** __________(continent), position would be in Bureau 6 of the CLO posted under the A/Dist Aide

CLO. Each Continental **Franchise Liaison Officer** would be junior and directly responsible to the Franchise Officer WW. A/Dist Aides are posted senior but for administrative purposes. The duties of a Continental **Franchise Liaison Officer** are primarily—getting done whatever the Franchise Officer WW assigns to be done, chasing up incomplete cycles for the Franchise Officer WW, stepping in on any **franchise** emergencies or situations that flare up and handling in liaison with CLO and reporting them to F/O WW, collecting data and accurate observations and sending them to F/O WW, logging, nudging, and seeing that compliances are sent to F/O WW, sees that new **franchises** are set up but only as legally appointed and chartered from F/O WW on application and seeing that **franchises** get hatted and trained. (FBDL 93R) *Abbr.* FLO.

FRANCHISE OFFICER, **franchise** is under the direct supervision of the **Franchise Officer,** the title Franchise Secretary being abolished. (HCO PL 31 May 65)

FRANCHISE OFFICE WW, the **Franchise Office WW** is the enfranchising body. Only **Franchise Officer WW** can approve a **franchise** and issue a mission charter. **Franchise Office WW** receives the weekly reports and tithes from missions and acks, gives advices, issues, mailings and guidance to **franchise** holders. All ethics actions on **franchise** holders—which are only for breach of contract per the **franchise** agreement, are initiated or at least cleared priorly by **Franchise Officer WW.** (CBO 144)

FRANCHISE SECRETARY WW, conducts the **Franchise** Department. (HCO PL 18 Dec 64, *Saint Hill Org Board*)

FRATERNAL, *—adj.* of or characteristic of a brother or brothers, of or like a **fraternal** order. (BPL 9 Mar 74)

FRATERNAL ORDER, a group organized for mutual aid and fellowship. (BPL 9 Mar 74)

FRAUD, the attempt to obtain support without furnishing a product. (HCO PL 25 Mar 71)

FREE ALONGSIDE SHIP, in the case of goods sold and destined to be transported by sea, the term refers to its delivery by the seller to a designated pier at no extra charge to the buyer.

FREE AND OPEN MARKET, see MARKET, FREE AND OPEN.

FREEDOM, **1.** [*Freedom* is Scientology's international newspaper. It is published by Churches of Scientology around the world and appears in many languages. *Freedom* features articles involving human rights and social reform and has a large non-Scn readership. *Freedom* is located in the Public Relations Bureau of the Guardian's Office and is circulated to Guardian Office publics.] **2.** a publication like *Freedom* is a defense action and is for public consumption. It is not distributed to org mailing lists. (LRH ED 59 INT)

FREE ENTERPRISE, an economic system whereby private business is allowed to engage in profitable undertakings of its own choosing under competitive conditions with a minimum amount of government control or restriction.

FREE INTRODUCTORY LECTURE, teaches about elementary points from Dn or Scn data. End result is recognition of Dn and Scn as workable ways to bring about change and improvement. (*CG&AC* 75)

FREELOADER, **1.** any person who has failed to complete a staff contract at a Sea Org or Scn org or mission is a **freeloader.** This includes persons legally dismissed from employment through Scn and Sea Org justice procedures such as Committees of Evidence and Fitness Boards in the Sea Org. It includes persons who blow or desert their post and organization of their own accord. It includes automatically all persons who request a leave of absence from the org or the Sea Organization for one year or longer. (BPL 13 Oct 72R) **2.** a Sea Org mission to orgs in the U.S. uncovered "undermanned" as a reason for low stats. According to this mission many people had joined staffs, signed contracts, gotten free services and then went off staff. This is nice work if one can get it. It leaves the good guys burdened with tech delivery with no proper income. Such contract breakers are to be designated **freeloaders.** They are ineligible for further services at any org until they have corrected their overt. (HCO PL 13 Oct 72)

FREELOADER INCOME, amounts received from **freeloader** collections from Flag blows. Does not include PT crew debts collected, telex and postage collections. (FSO 667RC)

FREELOADER LIST, **list** of **freeloaders.** The **list** is to state name and address of person, when contract was signed, amount of services received in cash including training and processing, the amount of time not served. (LRH ED 44 INT)

FREE MARKET, see MARKET, FREE.

FREE ON BOARD, **free on board** when a price is quoted means that the goods are quoted actually on the vessel that will ship them with all charges paid to that point by the seller. (FO 2738) *Abbr.* FOB.

FREE ON BOARD, indicates that a seller will pay for the cost of transporting goods for a specified destination and on board a ship, truck, freight car, etc., but once on board the buyer assumes transportation or freight charges of the goods to their destination. *Abbr.* FOB.

FREE ON RAIL, indicates that a seller will pay for the cost of transporting goods to the railway for shipment to the buyer but from that point on the buyer assumes transportation costs. *Abbr.* FOR.

FREE PASS, a letter from me for a former release check. The check only is given in Review. The person is not entitled to rehabilitation of the state in Review or to HGC auditing by reason of a **free pass.** If former release is found, the person is routed at once to the Registrar for a sign-up for 5 hours to get the state rehabilitated, the TA down and needle floating. The person may only be declared a former release by Certs and Awards if the rehabilitation work is done. There is no declaration of release on a **free pass** to Review. The **free pass** does not include it. (HCO PL 12 Jul 65)

FREEPORT, 1. a port or zone where goods exported from some country are allowed to be unloaded, stored or processed and shipped again without payment of duties or customs fees provided they are not imported and are for use elsewhere. 2. a port equally open to ships or vessels of any country.

FREE SCIENTOLOGY CENTER, 1. this is not the HGC. It is the student clinic. It is a section in the Dept of Processing. It is open evenings and weekends. It is run by students under org guidance. No fee may be charged. (HCO PL 17 May 65, *Technical Division Distribution Division Free Scientology Center*) **2.** the student auditing in the **Free Scientology Center** (which is just a section of the Department of Processing and the Department of Estimations and is far from the full Foundation which has all services) is standard tech and mostly assists. (HCO PL 12 Jun 65) [The **Free Scientology Center** is cancelled per BPL 10 Oct 75 VIII.]

FREE SERVICE, any **service** whatever in Div IV or Div V that is not invoiced is defined as a **free service.** (OODs 7 Apr 72)

FREE SERVICE=FREE FALL, an auditor or course supervisor delivering a **service** to an individual without having to hand a fully paid invoice for that service and who does not then send the person back to the registrar to be signed up for that **service** is: (a) covertly robbing his fellow staff members of their pay, and (b) in a condition of *doubt* to his org, and is so *assigned.* Similarly, an auditor continuing to audit a person over and above the amount of hours signed and paid for, and who does not send that pc back to the registrar for sign-up and payment of additional hours in order to successfully complete the auditing program, is guilty of (a) and (b) as above. (BPL 22 Dec 71-1)

FREQUENCY DISTRIBUTION, in statistics, an arrangement of data that shows the number of times something occurs in a particular way, as in making a table in order of increasing amounts of the various salary categories within an organization (as between $10,000-$11,000 annually) and noting how many employees fall into each category.

FREUDIAN FOUNDATION OF AMERICA, see HUBBARD DIANETIC RESEARCH FOUNDATION.

FRINGE BENEFIT, a benefit given by an employer additional to required wages or compensation such as paid vacations, pensions, insurance benefits, discounts on merchandise, etc.

FRONT LINES PERSONNEL, Body Reg, FCCI auditors, Interne Supervisor, Cashier, Dept 11, Tech Cramming, Director of Tech Services, HGC Admin, Dissem Sec, Ethics Officer, Tech Sec, Qual Sec. (ED 17 USB)

FRU MAA, the post of **FRU MAA** is established in the FPPO Office, WUS. It replaces the post of PTS and Ethics Handler, in Branch 5 of the FPPO Org Board. The primary purpose of the post is to detect and prevent psychotic cases from being sent to Flag as recruits. (FO61 US)

FRU TIP, an **individual program** is written up for each **FRU** member for handling the requirements for Flag that are out per his GO 824. This program is simply a **TIP** of what he needs to do to become eligible to go to Flag. Each **FRU** member should be able to complete his **TIP** within a month. (FO 3466R-2)

FSC INT GI, total monies collected by the **FSC** Network for the week. (BFO 119)

FSM AWARD PROGRAM, there are basically two types of **FSM Award Programs:** (1) the **FSM**

Award Program which **awards FSMs** of proven selectee success scholarships in courses for required selectee arrivals paid and started on service. This is the regular **Award Program** which encourages **FSM** selection. (2) the Book **Award Program** which awards **FSMs** scholarships in courses for required number of books sold to new public. To qualify for such **awards**, the **FSM** has to route names and addresses of buyers with evidence of sale to the Dir of Clearing and he must have sold them to new people not in Scn and he must have a good record of selections. (BPL 5 Oct 73R)

FSM NIGHT, events at least weekly to exchange successful actions, drill on *Big League Sales* and inform all **FSMs** about AO/SH award programs, services, prices, results with seminars, drills, etc. (LRH ED 159R-1 INT)

FSM OF THE YEAR, at the end of every **year**, each Scn organization sends in the statistics of their best **FSM** to CS-6 Flag. CS-6 then compares all the stats of the most people sent in and picks the best **FSM.** This **FSM** is then the **FSM of the Year** and a special silver cup is sent and presented at the **FSM's** org. Then a full article is prepared on their wins and successes, methods used and photograph. The above is then condensed into an interesting leaflet and sent to all **FSMs.** (BPL 23 Apr 68R I)

FULL ASSIST CHECKLIST FOR INJURY AND ILLNESS, Board Technical Bulletin 28 May 1974R, *Full Assist Checklist for Injury and Illness.* While you don't put the pc on the cans for this one, you mark it as to the state the pc is in and it says what you do for **illness and injury.** (LRH ED 257 INT)

FULL EMPLOYMENT, see EMPLOYMENT, FULL.

FULL FLOW PROGRAM, we have found that whenever one runs **flow** zero self to self on a late action it may then be necessary to run all previous actions—Dn, Grades, etc.—in Quadruple **Flow.** To run in a quad **flow** zero with only singles or triples run earlier can be very upsetting. Thus the rule—no zero **flows** may be run on late actions unless zero **flows** have been put in from the beginning. This action is known as a **Full Flow Program.** (OODs 10 Apr 71)

FULL MEMBER, (Gung-Ho Group) see TRUE GROUP MEMBER.

FULL TIME STAFF MEMBER, one who works a minimum of 40 hours in a week, not including the lunch hour. (HCO PL 26 Jun 64)

FULLY CLEANED UP, see RELEASED.

FULLY HANDLED, anything **fully handled** needs no further care or attention from anyone. (FO 3195)

FULLY HATTED ORG STAFF MEMBERS, (HCO GDS) a **hat** consists of a checksheet and pack fully word cleared and studied and known to a point of full application of the data therein. Instant hats, mini hats do not count on this stat. The **staff member** must be in the **org** and on its staff list. Those on full-time training or in another org for training or processing do not count on this stat. (HCO PL 8 Nov 73RA)

FULLY QUALIFIED, by FULLY QUALIFIED is meant: (1) Not PTS or PTSness fully handled, (2) No drug history or DRD fully completed to an acceptable success story, (3) No R/Ses or all R/Ses fully handled, (4) OCA all above center line, (5) Aptitude acceptable, (6) Leadership scores acceptable, (7) No criminal history or criminal history and tendencies fully handled. (HCOPL 4 Nov 76)

FULLY QUALIFIED AND HATTED, this requires: (a) complete **hat** per A to I of HCO PL 22 September 1970, *Personnel Series 9 Org Series 4 An Urgent Important and Starrate PL, Hats* (b) **hat** examined, passed and attested to at Certs and Awards (c) hat word cleared method 2 and post purpose cleared (d) post competence demonstrated. (FO 3075)

FULLY QUALIFIED AND TRAINED STAFF MEMBER, see FULLY QUALIFIED, see TRAINED.

FULLY TRAINED, means certified by an org and able to bring about the results of his Class or Certificate. (LRH ED 259 INT)

FUNCTIONAL MIDDLEMAN, see MIDDLEMAN, AGENT.

FUNCTION BOARD, 1. there are really three forms of org boards. There is the **functioning** org **board**—the org **board** of **functions**, and then there's the org board of posts and then there's the org board of complements. You can't do one without doing the other. There's what you call a **function board** on which you have listed every **function** known to man and beast that has ever been performed by one of these divisions. That's a **function board** and that's the first form of a **board.** (ESTO 8, 7203C04 SO II) **2.** you write up the **functions** of the org **board** of the division by departments and add the valuable final products. This gives you the **functions** to get out the VFPs expected. These **functions** will or won't get out the VFPs. What **functions** are needed to get them out. By blocking in these you have now a **function** org **board.** (HCO PL 6 Apr 72)

FUNDAMENTAL, means serving as an original or generating force: being the one from which others are derived. (HCO PL 9 Nov 68)

FUNDED DEBT, usually interest-bearing bonds or debentures of a company and possibly long-term bank loans but excluding short-term loans, preferred or common shares.

FUNDS, monies allocated or set aside for a specific purpose.

FUNDS STATEMENT, this is basically a statement that traces the flow of funds through an organization listing the sources of investment capital, breakdown of how it was invested, the use of working capital as in the purchase of materials, payment of wages, etc., etc. Also called a flow statement.

FUTURES, contracts made in present time to sell or buy a specified amount of stocks or securities at a fixed price in the future regardless of what the price is in the future.

G

GAE, 1. there's a thing called a **GAE**, which is a **gross auditing error**, and **GAE** is a slang term for being kicked out of the auditing section. They're returned from the auditing section for heavier work in practical and theory, bang, and that's called being **GAEed**. They've committed a **gross auditing error**. (6209C03) **2. gross auditing error (GAE)** is the action of the auditing supervisor when the pink sheet is not completed by the student or when, in the opinion of the auditing supervisor, the **errors** being made are so **gross** that a preclear is being heavily damaged (such as Auditor's Code breaches). A **GAE** may consist of relegating the auditor to the next lowest class or, if violent and flagrant, and directly against an instructor's instructions, to the lowest unit of the Academy. (HCO PL 21 Oct 62)

GAINFUL OCCUPATION, see OCCUPATION, GAINFUL.

GAINFUL WORKER, see WORKER, GAINFUL.

GAINS CONSULTATION CENTER, consultation center for flubbing solo auditors on AOLA lines. (FBDL 73)

GALLEY PROOFS, a **galley proof** is the material for an issue which has been typeset but not yet placed into pages—it comes in long strips. (BPL 29 Nov 68R)

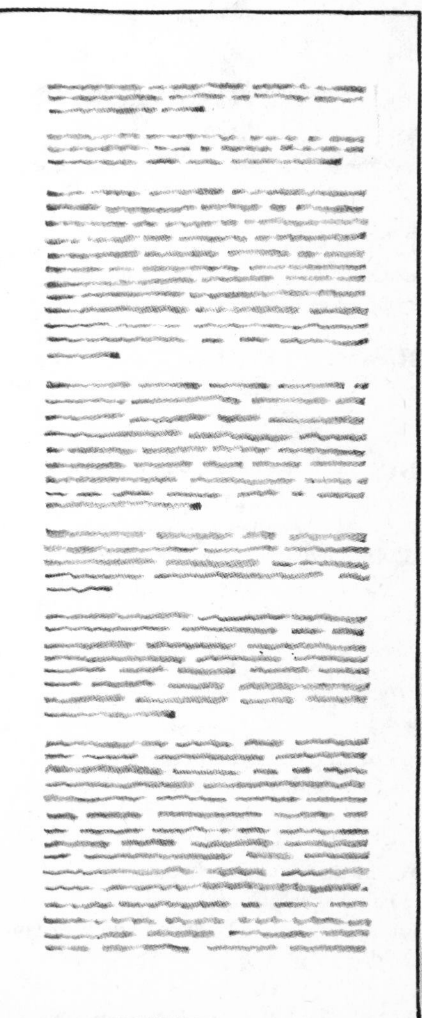

Galley Proofs

GALLEYS, columns of printing. (ED 459-50 Flag)

GALLOPING INFLATION, see INFLATION, GALLOPING.

GAME, a **game** consists of freedom, barriers and purposes. It also consists of control and uncontrol. An opponent in a **game** must be an uncontrolled factor. Otherwise one would know exactly where the **game** was going and how it would end and it would not be a **game** at all. (*POW*, p. 65)

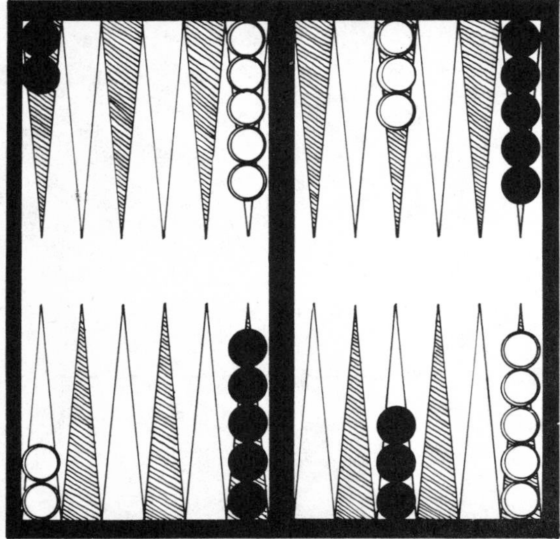

Game

GANG BOSS, a foreman or leader of a group of laborers organized together on one job, such as a railroad gang.

GARRISON MISSION, mission fired from Flag, where the **missionaire** will be in the field for an extended period of time. (FO 3136)

GARRISON MISSION ORDERS, when a person is appointed to a duty post he is given **mission orders**. At first glance these are like other MOs. But they are not. One can mix MO types with disastrous results. A person is sent to duty to continue or improve an activity. His **orders** therefore must not be terminable. Instead each operating target is continuable. They do not end off. **Garrison Mission Orders** are chiefly concerned with policy and the relevant policy letters (and in CLOs or ships or even in SO orgs to some degree, with FOs and CBOs and various manuals). As **garrison missionaires** have different posts, the duties of that post are stressed and on-policy is stressed and what the policy is is stressed. The **mission orders** are essentially, then, duties to be taken up in rotation and handled. If you list the main duties of the post, assemble the relevant policy and list them as ops targets to be done until all are in maintain, the **MOs** are good **MOs**. The **garrison** situation is really a major target of working to stabilize, establish and expand an org so that it is permanent. The key to a **garrison mission** is then continue. (FO 2936)

GEARING, see LEVERAGE.

GEN, British *Slang.* *—n.* inside information, lowdown. *—v.t.* to give inside information to. (*World Book Dictionary*)

GENERAL BONUS, an amount of money paid in excess of salary on a six months or yearly basis. (HCO PL 26 Jun 64)

GENERALIST, a person (executive, teacher, administrator, etc.) who has a general knowledge of several areas as opposed to a detailed knowledge of one or a small number of areas.

GENERALITY, a pet hate of Scn people. Generally its form is "everybody knows." Examples: "They say that George is doing a bad job," or "Nobody liked the last newsletter." The proper rejoinder is "Who is everybody?" You'll find it was one person who had a name. When you have critical data, omit the "everybody" **generality**. Say who, say where. Otherwise, you'll form a bad datum for somebody. When our actions are said to be unpopular the person or persons saying so have names. (HCO PL 22 Oct 62)

GENERAL LETTERS, public **letters** from any source or kind which do not specifically belong to any unit or department. (HCO PL 18 Dec 64, *Saint Hill Org Board*)

GENERAL LIABILITY FUND, the **fund** is to be built up against claims made against organizations or any Scientologist by the public or government for legal costs, libel and slander costs, defense funds, destruction of repute and restraint of trade. Uninsured risks to buildings, lapsed insurance policies, acts of God, war, riot and civil disorder, usurpation of power, restraint of princes, radioactive fallout, atomic destruction, salvage of persons and property, reorganization costs due to departure or demise of Founder. This **fund** is computed by taking the number of Scientologists on the mailing list and the value to each Scientologist is assigned at the Manager's discretion. It is computed every year and added to the **fund**. This **fund** may be kept as a reserve. (HCO PL 3 May 66)

GENERAL NON-REMIMEO, 1. mimeo distribution based on one copy for master files, one copy to LRH Comm, one copy to the Guardian or A/G, one copy each to the FR, ED(CO), HES and OES, one copy to the Qual Library reference files and one copy to the reference files of all bulletins and PLs kept in reception for staff, one copy to the div head(s) and the department head(s) concerned and one copy to the post(s) in the department(s) concerned. (BPL 14 Apr 69R) **2.** key personnel and orgs get copies of it. Limited number of copies. (SH Spec 54, 6503C09) **3.** there are two classes of **non-remimeo**. One is limited **non-remimeo** meaning distribution is: master files, HCO Secretary, and Assn/Org Secretary. The other is **general non-remimeo**, meaning master files, HCO Secretary, Assn/Org Secretary, reception reference files, and department head and post concerned to whom the data applies. (HCO PL 2 Jul 64) **4.** the same as limited non-remimeo but somewhat broader. These usually deal with broader points of admin or tech of interest to one or two production departments as well as the HCO Secretary and Assn/Org Secretary. They are never strewn about or broadly republished as they could be misunderstood. (HCO PL 2 Jul 64)

GENERAL QUESTION, (security checks) the difference between a **general question** and a specific question is a matter of **general** or specific terminal. If the **question** has a **general** terminal such as "anyone," "men," "people," it is harder to clear than a question with a specific terminal such as "your father," "Miss Smith," etc., etc. (HCO PL 9 Oct 61)

GENERAL REGISTRATION, the Letter Registrar is primarily concerned with **general registration.** (a) writing letters to individuals in central files that will bring about a response. (b) handling of central files files and addresses ensuring they are up-to-date, address, the index of CF and address correctly tabulated. (c) getting broad promotion done by Department 4 in the form of the org magazine to arouse and increase the want of individuals. (d) using CF files to find out what people want and then writing to help them get it. (e) letter reg projects—sending Division 2 info packs to specific type publics in CF with the purpose to channel each person to take his next step resulting in the person's arrival at the org to see the registrar and eager to enroll on his next org service. (f) selling and renewing memberships. (HCO PL 28 Nov 71R I)

GENERAL SEMANTICS, **1.** in a subject developed by Korzybski a great deal of stress is given to the niceties of words. In brief a word is not the thing. And an object exactly like another object is different because it occupies a different space and thus "can't be the same object." As Alfred Korzybski studied under psychiatry and amongst the insane (his mentor was William Alanson White at Saint Elizabeth's Insane Asylum in Washington, D.C.) one can regard him mainly as the father of confusion. This work, *General Semantics*, a corruption of **semantics** (meaning really "significance" or the "meaning of words") has just enough truth in it to invite interest and just enough curves to injure one's ability to think or communicate. Korzybski did not know the formula of human communication and university professors teaching **semantics** mainly ended up assuring students (and proving it) that no one can communicate with anyone because nobody really knows what anybody else means. (HCO PL 26 Apr 70R) **2.** an educational "discipline" which trains individuals to evaluate for themselves the meanings of words and symbols. It does not, however, teach them to obtain agreement on meanings. Hence, in **semantics** there can only be confusion because by its basic principles there can be no stable datum in symbols and significance. And thus, since symbols and significance are basic to communication, in **semantics** there can be no real communication. (FBDL 449)

GENERAL SERVICE DEPARTMENT, the department in charge of such duties and cleaning, repairs and general maintenance for an organization.

GENERAL SHARE, the cost of all personnel and activities which are not assigned to production departments. (HCO PL 26 Jun 64)

GENERAL STAFF HAT, there is a **general staff hat.** This **hat** contains: (a) the overall purpose of the org, its aims, goals and products. (b) the privileges or rewards of a **staff** member such as auditing, training on post, general training availability, pay, vacations or leave, etc. (c) the penalties involved in non-production or abuse of post privileges or misuse of the post contracts. (d) the public relations responsibilities of a **staff** member. (e) the interpersonal relations amongst **staff** members including courtesy, cleanliness, attitudes to seniors and juniors, office etiquette, etc. (f) the mest of posts generally, its papers, dispatches, files, equipment. (g) the comm and transport system of the org. (HCO PL 22 Sept 70)

GENERAL STAFF MEMBER, any **staff member** who is not an executive. (HCO PL 13 Mar 66)

GENERAL TRAINING, overall familiarity with all bridge functions at sea. (FSO 413)

GENIUS, **1.** a person having a very great natural power of mind. From the root *gen,* to beget, produce. (ED 383 Flag) **2.** the meaning of **genius,** in

Latin, is "deity of generation and birth, guardian spirit." (CBO 190)

GENNY, a **generator** used in any ship or base to **generate** electrical current for use in lights, appliances, other motors and heating. (FO 1704R)

GENOCIDE, any of the following acts committed with intent to destroy, in whole or in part, a national, ethnical, racial or religious group as such: (a) killing members of the group; (b) causing serious bodily or mental harm to members of the group; (c) deliberately inflicting on the group conditions of life calculated to bring about its physical destruction in whole or in part; (d) imposing measures intended to prevent births within the group; and (e) forcibly transferring children of the group to another group. (LRH ED 28 INT)

GET IN, by **get in** we mean get it applied and effective. (HCO PL 16 Oct 67)

GET IT DONE, the purpose of a mission is to **get it done!** This means to-the-point mission orders that state exactly what is to be accomplished or produced, the mission doing it and the end product of that mission, purpose accomplished fully and proven by stats and production. The Mission Ops and missionaires must be able to do whatever they have to do to get the purpose accomplished. (CBO 337)

GET THE SHOW ON THE ROAD, when we want to get something started, we say, **Get the show on the road!** (HCO PL 28 Jul 72)

GETTING TECH IN, so what is this **getting tech in**? It's just getting a program to **get** it **in** and getting compliance on it. (HCO PL 27 Aug 73)

GI DIVIDED BY NUMBER ON STAFF, (Qual stat) this stat is, of course, a method of computing the individual worth of the **staff**. This stat is counted by adding up all those persons actually working on **staff** for that week. It does not count paying public internes, or staff students off on full-time training in the org or a higher org. It does not count AG Office, FBO or Flag Rep. It does count HCO expeditors and any paid part time staff. It does not count casual volunteers or FSMs doing projects for the org or Auditor's Association personnel. The criterion to the stat is who are the people working on **staff** to get the org stats. (BPL 30 Jun 73R)

GIFT TAX, a tax payable by the donor of a gift or gifts. There may be a certain value of gifts that a person may give annually tax-free such as an annual gift tax exemption of $3,000.

GILT-EDGED, said of a high-grade bond issued by a company with a record of ability to earn a good profit over the years and pay bondholders their interest on a regular basis.

GIMMICK, 1. all successful missions have a **gimmick** that makes them different. The **gimmick** is there for impact mainly. But a **gimmick** can also be to obscure. (FO 2936)

GIMMICK, an attention-getting device or scheme, having often an element of surprise or uniqueness, used in promoting a product or service to motivate consumers to buy.

GI PRODUCT OFFICER, the so-called **GI Product Officer** is hereafter designated the Dissem Product Officer. (**GI Product Officer** was never a legal post.) (LRH ED 234R INT)

GIRL FRIDAY, a competent and dependable female aide or secretary in business.

GLAMOR STOCKS, stocks of special or fashionable appeal to the public such as those sold by electronics, aircraft and avant-garde enterprises.

GLASS, barometer. (OODs 21 Dec 70)

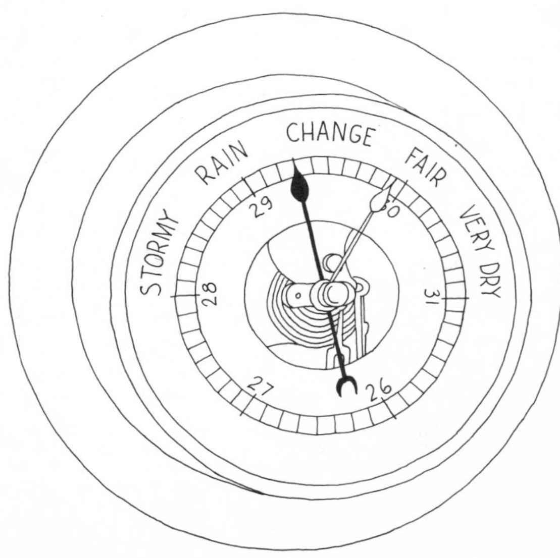

Glass (Barometer)

GLIBNESS, disassociation. They don't associate themselves with the materials; they don't associate the materials with anything; the materials just stand as materials and they're disassociated. (7202C22 SO)

GLIB STUDENT, **1.** the **glib student** can parrot but cannot apply. This is a surface registry without awareness. (HCO PL 16 Feb 71 II) **2.** he reads but can't apply. (7202C22 SO) **3. students** you won't be able to find any fault in who yet won't be able to apply or use the data they are passing. This **student** is discussed as the "bright **student**" in the September 24, 1964, Policy Letter *Instruction and Examination: Raising the Standard of.* (HCO PL 4 Oct 64)

GLUT THE LINE, to permit any and all material to go over it, with no selectivity. Those who are on the receiving end will get so much material to deal with that they will become careless and irresponsible in their handling of the material. (BPL 5 Aug 59)

GO 824, (**Guardian Order**) list of requirements for Flag duty. (FO 3466R)

GO 824 TIP, some persons are almost eligible for Flag and have only a few steps on their **GO 824** to complete to fully qualify. The **GO 824 TIP** is the program drawn up by FPPO O/O for that particular person to complete his requirements for Flag. (FO 3466R)

GOAL, a known objective toward which an action is directed with the purpose of achieving that end.

GOALS PROBLEM MASS, **1.** the **goals problem mass** is made up of past selves or "valences," each one grouped and more or less in a group. Therefore, the characteristic of the part (the valence) is the characteristic of the whole, the collection of valences known as the **goals problem mass.** (HCO PL 17 Jan 62) **2.** what is one of these **GPMs** anyway but a method of limiting the pc's ability to intend? And that is the whole idea behind implanting or anything of that nature. The whole idea is that if he intends positive he gets negative. If he intends negative he gets positive. So therefore he cannot decide. That is his mind kicking back at him which is simply a positive/negative proposition there, of two poles. (SH Spec 5, 6402C06) *Abbr.* GPM.

GODOS, defeated royalist soldiers. (HCO PL 12 Feb 67) [The term **Godos** refers to the "defeated royalist soldiers" in South America during the time Simon Bolivar was the Liberator of South America from the yoke of Spain.]

G.O. FLAG, handles matters pertaining directly to **Flag** and **Flag** environs and operations. (OODs 13 Jun 74)

GO FOR, **1.** this term is derived from the verb "to **go**" and the preposition "**for**." One who **goes** and gets something **for** someone. (FO 3260) **2.** an unskilled to semi-skilled person who works for a terminal who can actually or partially hold a post hat. He **goes for** items required by his senior. (FO 3260)

GOING CONCERN, a business that is flourishing and actively operating to full capacity.

GOING PUBLIC, term noting that a private company is becoming a public company proffering shares for sale to public individuals.

GOLDBRICKING, 1. originally a soldier who shirked duty but now designating any person who avoids work by loafing on the job. 2. a term associated with payment-by-results systems where employees restrict their production in order to prevent the piece-rate from being lowered.

GOLDEN ERA OF TECH, our main objective for 1975 is to get a **Golden Era of Tech** going. That means manned **Tech** Divs, trained C/Ses, trained supervisors, flubless auditors in every org in the world. (OODs 2 Jan 75)

GOLDEN HANDSHAKE, a term for the severance pay handed to a discharged top executive.

GOLDENROD, HCO flash color paper. (HCO PL 20 Nov 65 II)

GOLD STAR, a Class VIII auditor who has completed the Org Exec Course has all the blue and green star ethics protection and also may not have any Comm Ev finalized on him until the Comm Ev held and all evidence forwarded to the Sea Org for review on his request. He is called a **gold star.** None of these ethics protections are valid and none can be claimed unless actually applied for and awarded by blue, green and **gold star** certificates. These can be awarded in any official org and can be applied for also by mail. (HCO PL 13 Feb 69)

GOLD STAR CREDIT RATING, in 1966 we will begin to **gold star** the lifetime members cards, giving them a **gold star credit rating** where they have promptly paid their bills and a **gold star credit** card in Scn will carry a 45% discount. (HCO PL 22 Mar 65, *Current Promotion and Org Program Summary Membership Rundown International Annual Membership*)

GOLD STAR ORG, a project activated wherein any Scn or SO **org** meeting certain requirements will be given a designation as a **gold star org**. The Tech and Qual organizational requirements would make us trust an **org** absolutely to turn out flawless tech in volume. (BTB 17 Jan 75R)

GOOD COMMUNICATION LINE, carries the message quickly, to the right person, not to the wrong people, without altering the message, and in a form that the message can be easily received, understood and answered. A **good communication line** is a certain **communication line.** (FO 2528)

GOOD CONTROL, good control would consist of knowingness and positiveness. (*POW*, p. 43)

GOOD EXECUTION OF THE TECHNOLOGY, this means holding a constant of application without variation in how it is done from person to person or place to place. This outlaws at once all squirreling and individual variations even when they are good for they bring about an inconsistent of execution and this can wipe out technology, leaving one with nothing to promote and a dead end of all spread of technology. Hence, no articles in magazines giving different points of view. Hence, no officially authorized books giving variant methods. Even if they were good, it would halt all promotion and end freedom for the planet. (HCO PL 21 Jan 65)

GOOD EXECUTIVE, he only hands out dispatches and work to the correct hats. (HCO PL 1 Jul 65 III)

GOOD LEADERSHIP, (1) works on not unpopular programs, (2) issues positive orders and (3) obtains or enforces compliance. These facts are as true of a governing body as they are of an individual. (HCO PL 3 Nov 66)

GOOD MANAGER, a **good manager** cares what happens, what's spent, what prosperity can occur, how the work is done, how the place looks, how the staff really fares. He is dedicated to getting the show on the road and he takes out of the line-up obstacles to the org's (and staff's) progress. Caring what goes on and not caring is the basic difference. (HCO PL 10 Nov 66)

GOOD ROADS AND GOOD WEATHER, (letter writing) whatever else you do, keep it a warm **good roads and good weather**. That's the golden rule. Calm, warm, friendly. No "Thank you for yours of the 19th instant." Sounds like we sell shoes. To a letter about a compliment on an org and a win, it's "Dear Bill, yes things are going along okay. Tell me about your next big win. Tell Agnes hello. Best, Ron." (HCO PL 9 Mar 65)

GOODS, 1. generally, the tangible elements we use in everyday life. 2. in economics, the term for commodities and services. 3. in marketing, term for commodities as separate from services. 4. in the clothing industry, the term for fabrics or cloth. 5. in law, the term for property, particularly movable or personal property. 6. in accounting, the term loosely covering inventoriable items which includes supplies and articles in process of production. 7. in the UK especially, a term for freight.

GOOD SERVICE, the public expects **good service**. By this they meam positive scheduling, accurate billing, accurate addressing, **good** technical rendition of training and processing. (HCO PL 28 Apr 73, *Good Service*)

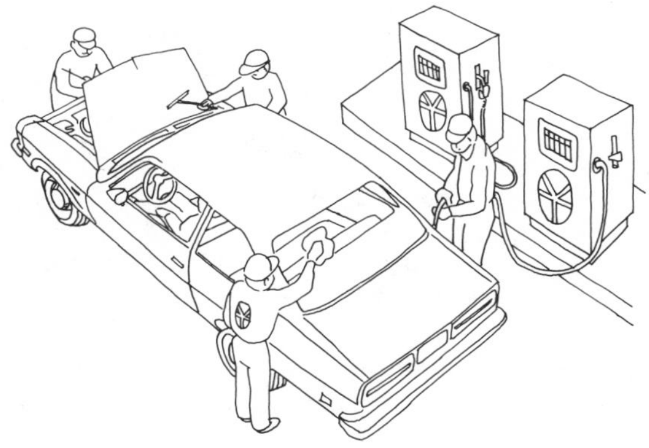

Good Service

GOOD SITUATION, 1. a **good situation** is attaining the ideal scene or exceeding it. (HCO PL 17 Feb 72) **2.** a situation is something that applies to survival and if you evaluate the word "situation" against survival, you've got it. A **good situation** is a high level of survival; a bad situation is a threatened survival; and a no-situation is something that won't affect survival. (7201C02 SO)

GOODWILL, in the sale of an enterprise, those intangibles such as large public patronage, reputation for integrity, quality service, etc., the value of which can be a negotiable matter between seller and buyer and can raise a business' worth above its book value or net worth.

GOODWILL MAILING LIST, just any **mailing list.** (BPL 17 May 69R)

GOODWILL MAILING PIECES, mailing pieces to FSMs and franchises concerning the **willingness** of the org to handle their rougher pcs and more difficult students. (BPL 20 May 72R)

GOOD WORKMAN, one who can positively control his equipment or tools of trade or who can control the communication lines with which he is intimately connected. (*POW*, p. 40)

GOON, a strong-arm person hired by labor or management to create violence during a labor dispute that will serve to pressure the opposite side into an agreement.

GOVERNESS, 1. the post of **Governess** is appointed for children, who are not cadets, above the age of six or as determined by the Captain. The post is under Dept 9. The **Governess** is fully responsible for the acts, conduct and morality of the children. (FO 1630) **2.** cares for the children, their clothing, quarters, serves their meals, washes their dishes. Looks after their dining room and toys and pets and recovers or safeguards toys left outside, playground items and children's vehicles. Looks after the children while swimming. (HCO PL 18 Dec 64, *Saint Hill Org Board*)

GOVERNING ORG, one which manages. (FO 2713)

GOVERNMENT, 1. the basic definition of a **government** is to furnish the protection of an area where you can do business. (6909C01 SO) **2.** a **government** is a **government** so long as it protects the land and citizens against its aggressors. (*AAR*, p. 95) **3.** it could be said that a **government** is the aggregate irresponsibility of a people. They are not taking responsibility for the course of justice or protection of the state from foreign aggression, and they shove all this responsibility over onto a **government.** (*SCP*, p. 12) *Abbr.* Govt.

GRADATION, what does **gradation** mean? Well, there are **grades** to a road and there are **grades** to steps. There are steep steps and shallow steps and so forth, and there are vertical poles. A vertical pole is not a **gradient**. You want a **gradual** grade up. That's what **gradation** means in our particular sense. (SH Spec 66, 6509C09)

GRADE A, the standard we want on *Advance!* cover is known in the trade as **Grade A. Grade A** is correctly defined as color reproduction work that duplicates the color, color balance, clarity and image of the original photograph or artwork. It does not degrade or unfavorably alter the original. (FO 3559-1)

GRADE CASE SUPERVISOR, 1. (Grade C/S) C/S who **C/Ses grade** pcs. (HCO PL 25 Sept 74) **2. (Grades C/S)** does progress and advance programs as needed but mainly **C/Ses** the pcs up the **Grade** Chart. (HCO PL 26 Sept 74)

GRADE CERTIFICATE, certificate furnished to show he has been audited through the level. The **grade certificate** states that the student has received all processes in the level just gone through and is ready for his next grade. It reads, "This will certify that __________ has received all required processes of **Grade** ____ and, having completed **Grade** ____ as a preclear is ready for the processes of the next **grade.**" It is signed by the HCO Board of Review after inspection of the case folder of the student. (HCO PL 27 Feb 65)

GRADE CHECKS, grade checks require no meter test and consist of an inspection of the case folder looking for any TA action left on processes and not flattened. (HCO PL 2 Apr 65, *Meter Checks*)

GRADE CREEP, (or grade drift) term describing the secret regrading the status of employees in order to award them salary increases which otherwise would not be allowed, as in the case of having to abide by government wage regulations.

GRADIENT SCALE, a **gradual** increasing degree of something. A non-gradient scale would be telling someone to enter a skyscraper by a 32nd-story window. (HCO PL 22 Sept 70)

Gradient Scale

GRADUATING TABBING SYSTEM, there is a **graduating system** in address **tabbings**. A person **tabbed** in address as a BB (book buyer) who buys and receives some processing gets **tabbed** under the preclear category. BB is removed as he is no longer in that category. A preclear who buys some academy training and graduates from Level 0 is **tabbed** as a Class 0 Auditor and a preclear. As a person's training level increases, the **tabbing** is changed accordingly. In some cases, a person will be tabbed for two or more categories. Example: pc, Class 0 auditor, HSDC graduate and member.

Or, SHSBC graduate, OT I and member. (BPL 19 May 72R)

GRAMMAR, the study of the classes of words, their inflections, and their functions and relations in the sentence. (BPL 28 Feb 72)

GRANTING OF BEINGNESS, the willingness to have somebody else **be** something. (ESTO 6, 7203C03 SO II)

GRAPEVINE, an unofficial rumor line existing among employees for transmitting from friend to friend, data which has not yet been officially made known.

GRAVEYARD SHIFT, a work shift starting at midnight or thereabouts until morning as from 12:00 a.m. until 8:00 a.m.

GRAVEYARD WATCH, midnight to four a.m. (FO 442)

GREEN, **1.** the flash color of the Flag Bureau. (BPL 15 Jul 72RA I) **2.** the originator's copy of a communication. (*HTLTAE*, p. 120)

GREEN FORM, HCO Policy Letter 7 April 1970RA, *Green Form*. This was the earliest Qual Saint Hill weapon (Form 26 June 1965) for case cracking. It is modernized up to 29 September 1974 in the above issue. (LRH ED 257 INT)

GREEN INVOICE, **1.** these **invoice** copies are distributed to the Department of Records, Assets and Materiel for record purposes. (Invoice routing for all orgs except Saint Hill.) (HCO PL 16 Feb 66) **2.** indicates consecutive series to be kept in the machine until the end of the accounting week. (Saint Hill only) (HCO PL 13 Oct 66) **3.** (Saint Hill invoice routing) the in-series **green invoices** are used for the banking record per HCO Policy Letter 13 January 1966, Issue II, *Records of Bank Deposits*.) (BPL 18 Nov 67R)

GREEN ON WHITE, LRH Policy Letters. (OODs 23 Jan 76)

GREEN ORG, in a **green org** staff members don't know what other staff members do. So they don't know where to send things so they do them themselves. Worse, they don't even know there is an **org** there. It is quite pathetic. Like rookie troops or militia or a mob. Of course the place goes broke. (HCO PL 1 Jul 65 III)

GREENS, **green** invoices. (FO 1346)

GREEN STAR, Scientologists who are Class IV auditors or above and who have graduated from an Org Exec Course may not be assigned arbitrary ethics conditions but may be required by seniors to assign themselves a condition. There is no penalty if they don't. Such may not be given a Court of Ethics. They may be Comm-Eved for high crimes only as per earlier policy letters. These include failure to take responsibility and failure to act with initiative in circumstances which, not handled, bring damage to others or serious overwork. Such a person duly appointed to a post or duty who then, by absence from it, neglect of it or failure to show initiative on it, brings about a decline of the post and damage to it or areas around it or high crimes may be Comm-Eved, but must be Comm-Eved in order to remove him or her from the post. Such a person is called a **green star**. (HCO PL 13 Feb 69)

GREEN TABBED LABEL, (or **green** tape) tape color flash code for commercial copy, for sale to orgs or field or student use in Tech and Qual divisions. (HCO PL 7 Dec 65)

GREENWICH HOUR ANGLE, that **angle** some heavenly body forms when related to **Greenwich** as zero. (HCO PL 18 Sept 67) *Abbr.* GHA.

GREENWICH MEAN TIME, **Greenwich mean** (average) **time.** It is called **mean time** because the sun is not exactly overhead at 1200 noon all the days of the year. (*Ship's Org Bk.*) *Abbr.* GMT.

GREY AREA OCCUPATIONS, see OCCUPATIONS, GREY AREA.

GRID THEORY, management concept under which any type of organization can be divided into the three interacting areas of people, goods or services produced, and management.

GRIEVANCE, 1. a complaint, symptomatic of dissatisfaction, based on an actual or supposed job circumstance which is regarded by either an employee or employer as just cause for protest. 2. discontent with the way in which a contractual agreement reached in collective bargaining is being administered and in which alterations are taking place.

GRIEVANCE COMMITTEE, a group of employees or employee-employer representatives appointed to preside over the airing of grievances in an organization.

GRIEVANCE PROCEDURE, the system, usually written into collective agreements, that has been reached between management and trade unions whereby a worker voices or submits in writing a complaint to a grievance committee regarding his work situation.

GRINNEL, 1. she is 174 ft. long, beam 22, speed 25, sleeps 48 but originally as a steel hulled antisubmarine warfare vessel, slept 105. (OODs 24 Feb 70) **2.** the *US Grinnel* is the *Bolivar* now. (OODs 22 Jun 70) [This vessel mainly known as the *Bolivar* was the Sea Org training vessel and stationship for the Pacific area during 1970.]

GROOVE-IN, a **groove-in** is showing someone how something works so he can then operate or handle it. Usually it is a short action covering the basics of how something works or functions and is thus different from an apprenticeship which is a longer, more detailed action.

GROSS AUDITING ERROR, see GAE.

GROSS BILLS PAID, (Division 3 stat) includes all creditor **bills paid**, staff salaries **paid**, FSM commissions providing that they are **paid** within one week of routing form origination, 5% to WW and any **payments** to Pubs Orgs. Does not include payments to other orgs or against management bills. (BPL 11 Aug 75 III)

GROSS BOOK SALES, 1. the total **sales** of **books**. This statistic no longer includes meter or other bookstore sales other than **book sales**. The term **gross book sales** does not mean gross bookstore sales. Its original and correct definition is exactly what it says, **gross book sales**. (HCO PL 5 Jun 68) **2.** total monies from the sale of books. Does not include meters, tapes, insignia, course packs per HCO Policy Letter 25 May 1968, *GDS Dissem Division*. (BPL 11 Aug 75) *Abbr.* GBS.

GROSS BUSINESS PRODUCT, the portion of the gross national product produced wholly by business.

GROSS DEPARTMENTAL STATISTICS, the gross divisional statistics of a Seven Division Org become the **Gross Departmental Statistics** of a Six **Department** Org. (HCO PL 21 Oct 66)

GROSS DIVISIONAL STATISTIC, 1. each **division** in an org has a **gross divisional statistic**. This is calculated to reflect the production of that **division** by all its **divisional** members. (HCO PL 5 Feb 70) **2.** a **statistic** on which each whole **division** is judged as to condition. While this **gross divisional statistic** does not cover all the statistics of the division, it is the primary **divisional statistic.** (HCO PL 30 Sept 65) *Abbr.* GDS.

GROSS INCOME, 1. gross income of the org is the total amount of valid collections (cash, checks, money orders, bank transfers received, etc.) representing actual money received in the org for the week, either in the mail or over the counter, as collections for past credit, current receipts or advance payments for any amount for any org service or items sold, and invoiced in for the statistic week which ends at 2 p.m. Thursdays. (BPL 11 Aug 75) **2.** how much money an org has made for the statistic week which ends at 2 p.m. on Thursdays. (BPL 28 May 71R) **3. gross income** as reported on OIC is the total of monies collected by the org and is unaffected by bounced checks or bounced check collections. (BPL 17 Feb 71-1R) **4.** total invoiced on **income** lines from all sources. Also called "total receipts." (FO 1828) **5.** the complete **income** for any given week for the HASI less repayment of loans to HASI. (HASI PL 19 Apr 57, *Proportionate Pay Plan*) **6.** is really the valuable final reward for which the VFPs are exchanged. (HCO PL 6 Apr 72) *Abbr.* GI.

GROSS INCOME, the total revenue of an individual or enterprise usually computed on a yearly basis, before deduction of any expenses, allowances or exemptions.

GROSS INVESTMENT, see INVESTMENT, GROSS.

GROSS MARGIN, see PROFIT, GROSS.

GROSS NATIONAL PRODUCT, (or national income) the total market value in terms of money of all a nation's goods and services produced during a given calendar year, including the excess of exports over imports. *Abbr.* GNP.

GROSS PROFIT, see PROFIT, GROSS.

GROSS RECEIPTS, (Flag) this is all money received at Flag from what source. It is not GI. (FSO 667 RC)

GROUNDS UNIT, handles all **grounds** keeping, trees, lawns, paths, roads, gardens, fences, streams and lake at Saint Hill and keeps them safeguarded, clean, policed and of good appearance. (HCO PL 18 Dec 64, *Saint Hill Org Board*)

GROUP, 1. a **group** is not just a number of people, it is a number of people with a shared ideal, ethic and rationale. It is an entity. Individual members of a **group** may come and go, and hundreds of years may pass, but the **group** may still be the "same" **group**. As it has grown older, its component parts have been replaced, like the cells in a body. The memory of a **group** is not equal to the memories of the individuals in the **group**. It may be greater or less than these, depending on whether or not there has been good communication and filing in the **group**. Any **group** which depends wholly upon the memories of individuals and has no common recorded memory has no real memory of its own and is insane as a **group**, though the individuals in it may be quite rational. (*HTLTAE*, p. 120) **2.** a **group** is only a collection of different people, without policy to agree upon. For policies are the points of agreement which make the **group** into a true **group** and an irresistible force. (HCO PL 13 Mar 65 II) **3.** a **group** is composed of individual **group** members. (HCO PL 30 Dec 70) **4.** another type of organization is the **group**. Official **groups** of the HASI and official congregations of the various churches exist in very large numbers in the United States and Great Britain and elsewhere through the world. To charter a **group** one only needs to write the HASI. (PAB 90)

Group (Def. 3)

GROUP BARRIERS, those rules for membership which a group or club maintains as a mark of distinction or to restrict its membership.

GROUP DIANETICS, a science of management should obtain optimum performance potentialities and optimum living conditions for the **group** and its members. Such a science is postulated in **group Dianetics**. It is not an ideology. It is an effort toward rational operation of groups. In **group Dianetics** one is looking at the general form of the government of the world. That government will not extend, as administrator, out from the Dianetic Foundation. But the Foundation will probably train the personnel that governments send to it and will probably be the advisor to all governments. (*An Essay on Management*, 1951)

GROUP IS AT EFFECT, which is to say originates nothing but only defends in the face of threatened disaster. (HCO PL 14 Sept 69)

GROUP LEADER, person made the head of a manufacturing group, who is responsible for the work therein and the degree of competence and speed with which it is accomplished.

GROUP LIAISON OFFICER, (Gung-Ho Group) the **Group Liaison Officer** is in contact with other **groups** to be sure things are going right and patches them up and keeps them going. (Of course, by "other **groups**" we mean civic **groups**, businesses, etc.) (HCO PL 2 Dec 68)

GROUP LOG, when a newly started Gung-Ho Group reports in to the Groups Officer at the nearest org, the Groups Officer must see that it is registered officially as a recognized Scn group as soon as possible. A **group log** is started at the org in which all data is put down by the **Groups** Officer. (BPL 14 Dec 68R I)

GROUP ORGANIZATION, the principle and success of a true **group organization** is each member does his own specialized part. When you have a "group" where everyone in it does all the jobs, you don't have a group, you have chaos. The group won't expand. Thus each **group** member is responsible for his own job as assigned. (HCO PL 3 Dec 68)

GROUP PRESIDENT, in the Dianetic Counseling Group we call the thetan of the **group** the **Group President**. The "thetan" is responsible for the survival of the whole activity and is senior to mind, body and product. (HCO PL 25 Jul 69 VI)

GROUP, PROJECT, a committee chosen expressly to handle a specific situation or problem which usually can be solved in a moderate length of time.

GROUPS, AUTONOMOUS WORK, units which, while they have definite work allocations to meet and operate according to certain policies set by management, are allowed to organize their own work and set production targets without direct supervision.

GROUPS COMMUNICATOR, every org must have a **groups communicator** in the Field Comm Unit of the Field Data and Advice Section of Department 24. The **Groups Communicator** is responsible for the welfare and expansion of all local Dn and Scn groups in the field. (HCO PL 24

Jul 69 III) [The above HCO PL was cancelled by BPL 10 Oct 75 VII.]

GROUPS, DISSOCIATIVE, a group composed of persons from various walks of life brought together to examine a wide range of consumer buying habits or deterrents.

GROUP SECRETARY, **1.** the **Group Secretary** must be: (1) a person interested in **groups**. (2) a person with skill in handling **groups**. (3) a person who can lecture to **groups**. (4) a person who can handle ARC breaks well. The **Group Secretary** handles correspondence, group certificates, programs, lectures, information in general and heals **group** or individual **group** member ARC breaks. All **group** troubles and difficulties are referred to the **Group Secretary** as well as all group promotion. (HASI PL 10 Feb 59) **2.** the **Group Secretary** belongs in the Department of Promotion and Registration. All group troubles and difficulties are referred to him as well as all **group** promotion. He may not have separate **group** files but can have the materials of central files on **groups** for his use. (HCO PL 24 Nov 58)

GROUP SELECTION TECHNIQUES, in personnel selection work, the technique of bringing together for a group interview all the candidates for a vacant position, usually giving them a particular subject to discuss among themselves, while the personnel interviewers observe them.

GROUPS, FACE TO FACE, market research reference unit in which consumers are brought together and encouraged to talk about their preferences, values and motives for buying particular products and services.

GROUPS, FAMILY, a group composed of persons from similar walks of life or who identify with each other because of some strong common trait such as social or economic status. Such a group is used to isolate the buying habits or deterrents of a particular social or economic stratum within a society.

GROUP'S MORALE, the additive result of the **morale** of each individual member. (FO 2414)

GROUPS OFFICER, every org must have a **Groups Officer** who is under the Director of Clearing in Department 18. The **Groups Officer** is responsible for the welfare and expansion of all local Scn groups in the field; to aid and supply them with materials and increase their growth. (BPL 24 Nov 68R II)

GROUP SOLIDARITY, a union of common interests and purposes among members of a group that motivates them to work harmoniously and loyally toward shared goals.

GROWTH STOCK, see STOCK, GROWTH.

GUARANTEE, (or guaranty) 1. an assurance, customarily in writing, that a product or service will serve and operate properly or will be repaired or replaced if necessary, within a specified time period from date of purchase. 2. the assuming by one person of the responsibility for another's debt or default of payment, or failure in the performance of a contract.

GUARANTEED ANNUAL WAGE, see WAGE, GUARANTEED ANNUAL.

GUARANTEED RATE, a specified amount of pay guaranteed to employees particularly where an incentive plan is in use.

GUARANTEED STOCK, see STOCK.

GUARANTOR, an individual who promises to make good if another fails or is unable to pay or meet a contractual obligation.

GUARDIAN, **1.** there is only one **Guardian**, WW for each org. There may be Assistant **Guardians** in larger orgs acting as liaison personnel for the **Guardian**. (HCO PL 1 Mar 66) **2.** the most senior executive of Scn just below the Executive Director. The post is senior to Executive Secretaries. The character of the post is best understood legally as "trustee" or even "proprietor sole" and exercises the powers and carries out duties similar to that of a high church officer entrusted with the funds or survival of his group. The **Guardian** may use the signature "trustee" in business letters or dealing with outside interests such as law firms and may claim and establish the status of proprietor sole when corporate status of Scn funds or interests is in question. The **Guardian** is posted in every executive division by post and name in Division 7. (HCO PL 1 Mar 66) **3.** the purpose of the **Guardian** is: to help LRH enforce and issue policy, to safeguard Scn orgs, Scientologists and Scn and to engage in long term promotion. The keynote of the post of **Guardian** is that it functions without being closely involved with the mechanics of administration or orgs. An Assistant **Guardian** can exist in any org that is big enough. It may not be worn as an additional hat. It is appointed only by the **Guardian**. A **Guardian** is appointed by the Executive Director personally. The first **Guardian**

is Mary Sue Hubbard. (HCO PL 1 Mar 66) *Abbr.* Gdn.

GUARDIAN ACTIVITIES SCIENTOLOGISTS, **1.** FSMs who are recruited or volunteer to help the Office of the **Guardian** are called **GASes** (**Guardian Activities Scientologists**). (BPL 10 Sept 72) **2.** a **GAS** is invited to join by the A/G or a GO terminal in his area, sometimes another **GAS**. He or she is a field Scientologist who has had case gain, knows that Scn works and does not have a history of being a troublesome source. (BPL 10 Sept 72) *Abbr.* GAS.

GUARDIAN FINANCIAL ORDER, the Second Deputy **Guardian** for **Finance** or the **Guardian** or Deputy **Guardian** may write and issue **Guardian Finance Orders**. These are blue ink on red or pink paper. They are initialled at the lower left hand corner by the **Guardian**, Deputy **Guardian** or the Second Deputy **Guardian** for **Finance** or their Communicators. These **orders** normally apply to Assistant **Guardians**. (HCO PL 18 Nov 68)

GUARDIAN OFFICE RESERVE ACCOUNT (DEFENSE), each week's 10% to **defense** is deposited into the **GO reserve account.** Also, all donations and money from the sale of church buildings are transferred from the FO No. 1 Account to the **GO Reserve Account** (**defense**). Monies are also deposited into this account pending approval or not of the Claims Verification Board on a refund or repayment. (BPL 6 Jul 75 III)

GUARDIAN ORDERS, **1.** now blue ink on blue paper. These are issued by the **Guardian's** Office to its staffs. They contain policy, programs, orders, directions. They do not retire. They are usually issued by the Controller or **Guardian** but can be issued by Deputy **Guardians** and Assistant **Guardians** if they so state but no Assistant or Deputy Guardian may issue any order on their own. It must be from the Controller or **Guardian** or in their name and by their authority. They apply to **Guardian** staffs and are filed by **Guardian** Offices. (HCO PL 24 Sept 70R) **2.** these are issued by the **Guardian**, and Deputy **Guardian** to Assistant **Guardians**. To be valid they must be initialed by the **Guardian**, Deputy **Guardian** or their Communicators in the lower left-hand corner. They are issued blue ink on white paper. (HCO PL 18 Nov 68) *Abbr.* GOs.

GUARDIAN ORIGINALS, ship's archives of Dn and Scn materials, tapes and records may only contain copy masters, copies and photostat or extra mimeo files. **Originals** must not be placed in archives. These are kept in separate locked storage not available except by written order and receipt from CS-**G** and for only 24 hours for the purpose of making copies at which time they are restored under lock to which only the CS-**G** Communicator has a key and are designated to **Guardian originals**. The value of **originals** is stated by CS-**G** to be beyond any possible calculation. (FO 1960)

GUARDIAN'S OFFICE, **1.** the **Guardian's Office** will be composed of six bureaux as follows: (1) Service Bureau, (2) Information Bureau, (3) Public Relations Bureau, (4) Legal Bureau, (5) Finance Bureau, (6) Social Coordination Bureau. (BPL 27 May 70RA) **2.** the **Guardian's Office** will be composed of four bureaux as follows: (1) Information Bureau, (2) Public Relations Bureau, (3) Legal Bureau, (4) Finance Bureau. Large continental **Guardian Offices** may also have a Service Bureau as Bureau 0. These changes are made on the basis of the new functions of the LRH Comm Network in relationship to policy and tech. (HCO PL 27 May 70R) [The above HCO PL was cancelled by BPL 27 May 70RA.] **3.** the **Guardian's Office** handles certain publics which are its sole responsibility. These publics are as follows: press relations, government relations, special **Guardian** group relations, opposition group relations, troublesome relations. (BPL 20 May 70 I) **4.** they have the **Guardianship** and the defense of Scn in general. The purpose of that organization is basically protection. (7003C15 SO) **5.** a **Guardian Office** covers PR, tech, personnel, legal and other functions *external* to orgs. Yet they can as easily do internal org work and do splendidly on it. (**Gdn Offices** consist of picked personnel who are well hatted and trained on post by their central **offices**.) (FBDL 10) *Abbr.* GO.

GUEST DRILL, usually the poor Captain is left to struggle with very important persons. This is too hard a lot not to have a **drill**. A ship is usually warned that it is going to have callers by hours or even minutes. Therefore this **drill** includes neating the place up fast, getting the ship snugged up to the dock or the ladder or the gangway squared away, seeing the proper flags are flying, tending the side, helping the **guest** aboard, giving the **guest** a host or hostess without tearing the top brass of the ship to bits, providing the **guest** with a drink or coffee, getting the **guest's** business attended to and the top brass required in and out, getting the **guest** back over the side. This includes providing a boat when at anchor. The stress here is to make a snappy, polite atmosphere and to effectively get **guests** aboard and gone. The same drill is used for dinner **guests** and even for parties given aboard except when they are for ship's company. (*Ship's Org Bk.*)

GUILD-MASTER, same as master.

GUILLOTINE, a way of cutting off debate or discussion of a bill, as is customary in the British Parliament, by predetermining a time for ending or voting on it.

GUK, the word **guk** is taken from the name for rifle cleaning fluid used in the Marine Corps. The tested **guk** formula contained 100 mg B1, 250 mg C, and 7-1/2 grains of calcium lactate, all rapidly assimilable. (LRH Def. Notes)

GULL, Sea Org sail vessel. In sail training the *Gull* is to be used for soloing. (FO 1853) [The *Gull* was a small sailing dinghy approximately 12 feet long.]

GUNG-HO, means "pull together" in Mandarin. (HCO PL 2 Dec 68)

GUNG-HO GROUPS, 1. are composed of local Scientologists in the field, any friends who are interested and general public members. First a captain, secretary, treasurer and public officer must be elected by the group. When the **group** is formed, it must contact the Group Officer of the nearest org and give its address and the names of its officers and members, etc., and apply for a group certificate. **Gung-Ho** means "pull together" in Mandarin. It pulls together other groups in the community to work towards the betterment of society and of the area. The **group's** program works on the motto: a community that pulls together can make a better society for all. (HCO PL 2 Dec 68) **2.** a Franchise Center is different entirely from a **Gung-Ho Group**. One can easily benefit from the other. But the **Gung-Ho Group** is there to speed up and smooth out the society and civic organizations and make a better community atmosphere directly. The **group** is a society entrance point. The Franchise Center is basically a Scn training and processing activity for individuals. The **group** works on other dynamics—notably the third and fourth. (HCO PL 2 Dec 68)

GUTTMAN SCALING, see SCALOGRAM.

HAA (CLEARING) COURSE, purpose: to train HPA students to **clear** and to **clear** HPA students. To make the best auditors in the world. (HCO London, 9 Jan 58)

Halftone

HALFTONE, means having shades of grey as in a photograph. Photographs are printed by photographing them through a screen and reducing them to a pattern of dots. (Dissem Div Advice Ltr 1 Apr 70)

HALO EFFECT, the effect produced when an interviewer concentrates on or favors a good trait of a candidate but does not focus on the less desirable traits of the candidate.

HANDLE, 1. finish off, complete, end cycle on. Service and **handling** are the same thing. When you give service, you **handle.** Part of **handling** cases is **handle** N-O-W! One way or another, one gets the preclear **handled.** (HCOB 15 Jan 70 II) **2.** to control, direct. **Handle** implies directing an acquired skill to the accomplishment of immediate ends. (HCO PL 23 Oct 65)

HANDLE IT, finish **it** off so that is the end of **it.** (HCO PL 4 May 68)

HANDLE THE HELL OUT OF IT, a new policy in December, 1971. It began to overcome the tendency to **handle** weakly and effective **handlings** began to occur. (OODs 15 Sept 72)

HANDLING, the definition of **handling** comes under the policy of "**handle** the hell out of it." Anything fully **handled** needs no further care or attention from anyone. Weak **handling** like half-done targets creates repeating emergencies. (FO 3195)

HAPPINESS, 1. is not itself an emotion. It is a word which states a condition, and the anatomy of that condition is interest. **Happiness,** you could say, is the overcoming of not unknowable obstacles toward a known goal. (8ACC-4, 5410C06) **2.** comes from self-determinism, production and pride.

Happiness is power and power is being able to do what one is doing when one is doing it. (HCO PL 3 Apr 72)

HARD CURRENCIES, **currencies** which are unlikely to suddenly lose their value. (FO 2688)

HARD NEWS (STORY), 1. the press prints **hard news. Hard news** is an event, a meeting, the formation of something, an attack, a campaign. It is not a statement. (HCO PL 3 Feb 69) **2.** a **hard news story** means a staged or actual event as different than a statement by someone. (OODs 8 Jan 71) **3.** a term which is used to denote an *event* as different from a statement or a news release. **Hard news** is normally *made.* In other words it is created. (FO 3451) **4.** an event that has occurred, usually told in past tense. Soft news is anything from speculative story to a feature. (BPL 10 Jan 73R)

HARD SALES PROMOTION, see PROMOTION, HARD SALES.

HARD SELL, 1. means insistence people buy. (HCO PL 4 Mar 65 II) **2.** caring about the person, not being reasonable with stops and barriers and getting him fully paid up and taking the service. (LRH ED 159R-1 INT)

HAS CO-AUDIT SECTION, using precise processes developed for this **section** only, the **HAS Co-Audit** (do it yourself processing) seeks to improve cases and further interest people in Scn so that they will take individual HGC processing and individual training. (HCO PL 20 Dec 62)

HASI ASSN SEC ADMINISTRATIVE ORDER, (dated) green ink on blue paper. By the **Assn** or Org **Sec** of any Central Organization. Distribute and copy as designated. Gives technical or admin data for services or personnel in a Central Organization. May be by the **Assn Sec** or a department head, but if by a department head must be issued for the **Assn Sec** by the department head only on **Assn Sec's** OK. (HCO PL 4 Feb 61)

HASI ASSN SEC TECHNICAL ORDER, (by number) red ink on blue paper. By HCO Continental Secretary for any area. Distribute according to distribution data on letter. Gives admin data, **orders** and information. (HCO PL 4 Feb 61)

HASI INTERNATIONAL ADMINISTRATIVE ACCOUNT, 1. where the 10% of the gross income may not be paid to the international area weekly by reason of local currency regulations, an additional bank **account** must be set up locally to receive them and the 10% must be paid weekly into that **account.** This **account** is to be called the **HASI International Administrative Account.** Only International Board members may be signatories on the **HASI International Administrative Account.** (HCO PL 18 Jan 65) **2.** a bank **account** in the name of the international organization called the **HASI International Administrative Account** opened in the local area of the org or franchise holder. Into this **account** must be deposited weekly 10% of the past week's gross income from Scn. (HCO PL 20 Jan 65)

HASI LIFETIME MEMBERSHIP, see LIFETIME MEMBERSHIPS.

HAT, 1. a **hat** consists of a checksheet and pack fully word cleared and studied and known to a point of full application of the data therein. (HCO PL 8 Nov 73RA) **2.** developed in 1950 for use in Dn orgs as a special technology. The term and idea of a **hat** comes from conductors or locomotive engineers, etc., each of whom wears a distinctive and different type of headgear. A **hat** therefore designates particular status and duties in an organization. (HCO PL 22 Sept 70) **3.** a **hat** designates what terminal in the organization is represented and what the terminal handles and what flows the terminal directs. Every **hat** has a product. (HCO PL 22 Sept 70) **4.** a **hat** is a specialty. It handles or controls certain particles in various actions and receives, changes and routes them. (HCO PL 22 Sept 70) **5.** a term used to describe the write-ups, checksheets and packs that outline the purposes, know-how and duties of a post. It exists in folders and packs and is trained-in on the person on the post. (HCO PL 22 Sept 70) **6.** the duties of a post. It comes from the fact that jobs are often distinguished by a type of **hat** as fireman, policeman, conductor, etc. Hence the term **hat.** A **hat** is really a folder containing the write-ups of past incumbents on a post plus a checksheet of all data relating to the post plus a pack of materials that cover the post. (HCO PL 13 Sept 70) **7.** usually when a person has been on a job a while he knows what it consists of. He then should write up his **hat,** meaning in this case a folder which contains past orders and directions which outline his job plus his own summary of his job. When one is transferred or leaves a post he is supposed to "write up his **hat**" which is to say, modernize this summary of the post. (HCO PL 3 Dec 68) **8.** on a train, a locomotive engineer and a conductor each wears a different kind of **hat.** You will notice that various jobs in the society are designated by different **hats.** From this we get the word **hat** as a slang term meaning one's specialized duties. This is one's **hat.** (HCO PL 3 Dec 68) **9.** a permanent folder, in the possession of a staff member, which describes his duties on that post in full and which contains general organization orders. The folder must be complete and up-to-date. (Organization PL, 10 Jan 58) **10.** every staff department head in every organization should have a folder in his desk in which to place all written material and bulletins which apply to his job. It is his **hat.** This folder should be labelled, for example, "Director of Processing," or "Indoc Instructor" or "HCO Secretary" or any such post. The folder should then receive after study any policy letter or executive order or HCO Bulletin applying in general or in particular to that job. (HCOB 28 Feb 57) **11.** a **hat** is a duty. It outlines the actions necessary to accomplish a production and receive what's needed, change and route it. What defines a **hat** is a product. If you count up the expected products you get the minimum number of **hats.** The steps to get the product is the **hat.** Products are also composed of lesser products, so **hats** can be enlarged. It's what you designate as a product that makes the **hat.** It's the importance of that product to others on the line that makes the **hat's** importance. The completeness and size of the product make the seniority of the **hat.** The overall product of a division determines the **hat** of the divisional officer. The lesser products that when combined make the overall product determine the rest of the division **hats.** Until you can define in one go the overall product of a division you aren't likely to be able to post any real part of its org board for the product of **hats** of that division add up to the divisional product. (OODs 29 Oct 70)

HAT CHECKING, the **check** is done simply by calling the staff members in and asking them one random question taken from some part of the material contained in the bulletin or policy letter. If they fail to correctly answer this one question, they are flunked on a **check**, told to re-study it and come in again for a re-**check.** (HCO PL 9 Jun 61)

HAT COLLEGE DEPARTMENT, Department 11A, technical Division IV. Product: fully hatted Sea Org members. (HCO PL 16 Jul 71)

HAT COMPILATIONS OFFICER, purpose: to make appropriate on-policy checksheets and hat packs for org posts that, when worn by the staff member, will increase production and expansion. (HCO PL 27 Jul 72)

HAT! DON'T HIT, the right motto is **hat! don't hit,** meaning put **hats** on them, don't try to solve it with ethics. (OODs 8 Oct 70)

HAT DRILL, (a) call in a staff member having him bring his **hat,** (b) open the **hat** and read a few lines silently, (c) ask the staff member to directly quote the substance read, (d) should the staff member be unable to quote the substance, return the **hat** with calm advice to study it; or, (e) should the staff member know his **hat,** thank him. (HCO PL 13 Jan 59)

HAT DUMPING, a type of dev-t. This is referring everything to someone else. It greatly increases traffic without producing. (HCO PL 27 Jan 69)

Hat Dumping

HAT FOLDER, there are three classes of folders permanently assigned to each staff member of HCO and the central org. The first of these is a **hat folder.** In it should be included only the **hat** write-up and policies issued which directly relate to the individual post. The second of these is a technical folder into which one places all technical bulletins issued. These must never be put in one's **hat folder.** The third of these is an organizational folder. All bulletins and policy letters relating to one's job but only by reason of being a staff member are included in this folder. (HCO PL 15 Sept 59)

HAT PENAL CODE, ethics actions are now chiefly directed towards cross orders or failures to wear one's hat. The crimes are now: (1) preventing people from wearing their **hats,** (2) preventing people from wearing their **hats** better, (3) taking people's **hats** away from them when they are doing them, (4) making people do things not their **hats,** (5) not wearing one's **hat,** (6) wearing no **hat** at all, (7) pretending to wear a **hat** while preventing its action from occurring, (8) using FOs to stop people wearing their **hats,** (9) wearing a **hat** but not getting done what one with that **hat** is supposed to do, (10) being stupid about one's **hat,** (11) having to be ordered to wear one's **hat,** (12) requiring unnecessary orders to accomplish the purpose of one's **hat,** (13) arguing with a Master at Arms, (14) seniors not making people wear their **hats,** (15) not knowing your **hat,** (16) writing up **hats** for your post you don't really do. (OODs 19 Jun 68, and 20 Jun 68)

HATS, terminals. (HCO PL 10 Jul 65)

HATTED, each org staff member is a specialist in one or more similar functions. These are his specialties. If he is fully trained to do these he is said to be **hatted.** (HCO PL 28 Jul 72)

HATTED SCIENTOLOGIST, a **hatted Scientologist** has been redefined as a **Scientologist** who can produce the four products of a **Scientologist** (purchased books, disseminated knowledge, environmental control, a cleared planet). The Director of Clearing **hats Scientologists** by drilling and mini-courses and will use whatever training tool is to hand needed to get a person able to produce the four products. (HCO PL 14 Nov 71 RA II)

HATTED SCIENTOLOGIST EXPEDITOR, the purpose of the **Hatted Scientologist Expeditor** is to get the field and raw public **hatted** as **Scientologists** in huge volume internationally. Position on the org board is Bureau 6, Branch 17 (CLOs). (CBO 121)

HATTING, see HATTING OFFICER.

HATTING FILES, the purpose of the **hatting files** is to receive, preserve and make available information on the results of personnel **hat** check-outs, orders to **hat** checks, **hatting** completions and progress and other pertinent data this section gathers and **files** on personnel **hatting** actions. (FSO 253)

HATTING OFFICER, **1.** a **hatting officer hats** executives and staff members "on the job." One of the simplest and most effective ways to do this is as follows: the **Hatting Officer** visits the person while he is working on post. He observes what the staff member is doing *right now.* He finds out what product the person is working to produce. He ascertains whether or not the staff member is having any difficulty producing it. We'll say he finds that the staff member is having difficulty. The **Hatting Officer** then goes away and rapidly locates the policy letter that covers how to do that, how to produce that product. He gives this to the staff member and orders him to study it right now, saying he will return in say ten minutes and check him out on it. In ten minutes the **Hatting Officer** returns (with his E-meter), WC M4s the staff member on the policy and gives him a proper starrate checkout, demonstrations and all. He then has the person complete the cycle of action he was engaged in and produce the product using the policy he has just studied. This completes one cycle of action of **hatting.** The **Hatting Officer** goes off then to **hat** another. (BPL 3 Apr 73R I) **2.** a **Hatting Officer** gets people through their basic staff **hats,** sees that they get through Staff Status I and II, gets them trained on their mini **hats** and then their full post **hat,** divisional packs, etc. (BPL 3 Apr 73R I) **3.** seeing that staff get checked out on policy relative to their post and basic org policy is the duty of the **Hats Officer** in the Department of Personnel. (BPL 2 Jan 68R)

HAT WRITE-UP, the **hat write-up** for the post contains the operating procedures of the post. (FSO 31) See WRITE UP HIS HAT.

HAVINGNESS, **1.** the feeling that one owns or possesses. (SH Spec 84, 6612C13) **2.** the concept of being able to reach or not being prevented from reaching. (SH Spec 126, 6203C29)

HAVING TO HAVE BEFORE THEY CAN DO, a type of dev-t. Projects stall "because of financial planning" or "because it would be nice to **have** a . . . ." (HCO PL 27 Jan 69)

HCA/HPA RUNDOWN, [See HCO PL 5 April 1961, *HCA/HPA Rundown or Practical Course Rundown for Academies.*]

HC LIST, **1.** the person has himself an out-point in his routine thinking. This is found and handled by what is called an **HC (Hubbard Consultant) List.** This **list** assessed on a meter detects and handles this. (HCO PL 19 Mar 72 II) **2.** the arbitrary name of the Data Series Correction **List.** (FO 3179)

HCO 1 REPORT, the personal **report** of the **HCO** Secretary on the org. (HCO PL 11 Dec 62, *OIC Reports to HCO WW*) [The above HCO PL was cancelled by BPL 10 Oct 75 IV.]

HCO 3 REPORT, the personal **report** of the Association Sec on the org. (HCO PL 11 Dec 62, *OIC Reports to HCO WW*) [The above HCO PL was cancelled by BPL 10 Oct 75 IV.]

HCO ACCOUNTS, a post will be created in the **HCO Office,** London, called **HCO Accounts.** This post will have as its function the receipt from all HASI Offices the weekly income report sheets, the bank statements for all **accounts,** and a duplicate set of invoices from each **office.** This post will check these reports, add all invoices, check the proportioning of funds and check the bank statements. This post will report to the Director of Accounts, World, the accuracy or inaccuracy of all reports. This post will have as its duty the presentation to the Executive Director of all requests for sums from the building fund of the various organizations. This post will also receive reports from the various organizations of **HCOs** concerning the receipt and expenditure of funds from all **HCO Accounts.** This post will check same. This post will have as its director the Director of **Accounts,** World, Mary Sue Hubbard. (HCO PL 6 Feb 59)

HCO ADMINISTRATOR, the **HCO Administrator** has general charge of **administration** and personnel and is responsible for the general accomplishment of **HCO** functions. The **HCO Administrator** brings order to **HCO** activities. (HCO PL 14 May 59)

HCO ADMIN LETTERS, **1.** (**HCO Administrative Letter**) issued by **HCO** personnel from Flag with AVU okay. Green on salmon. Contain checklist of issues, admin data of an informative nature. Do not contain policy or orders. Distributed as designated. (HCO PL 24 Sept 70R) **2.** (dated) green ink on salmon paper. By members of **HCO** WW. Should be copied or not and distributed according to its distribution designation. Gives **admin** data and requests. (HCO PL 4 Feb 61)

HCO AIDE, see CS-1.

HCO AREA COMMITTEE OF EVIDENCE, the Convening Authority is the HCO Executive or Area Secretary in the sphere of a specific Central Organization or City Office. It handles any matters referred to it by its Convening authority. These may include all matters relating to the suspension or cancellation of certificates, the administrative or technical conduct of any Scn executive or staff member on the basis of personal, administrative or technical conduct prejudicial to good order and discipline, and handles matters relating to the personal and technical misconduct of any Scn executives or staff members. It also handles all disputes with field auditors, students, preclears, and members of the public. It handles especially any dispute between the Central Organization or City Office to which it is attached and non-staff members such as students, preclears, auditing results, refunds, etc. (HCO PL 7 Sept 63)

HCO AREA OFFICE, **1.** an **HCO Area Office** is attached to each Central Organization. It expedites internal and external communications and in particular communications to and from HCO WW and myself. As part of communications supervision it hat checks into existence with staff members HCO Bulletins, HCO Policy Letters and other official releases. It issues and keeps to date the organization hats. **HCO Area** keeps the org board. Fundamentally it is also a library of technical and administrative data consisting of books, mimeos, tapes and general know-how. (HCO PL 20 Dec 62) **2.** the whole activity of an **HCO Area Office** is communication, collection, local book sales, technical level, administrative form, ethics, certificates and awards. To this, through HCO Continental, is added broad promotion and dissemination such as public book sales, the magazine, ads and special events. (HCO PL 20 Dec 62) **3.** an **HCO Area Office** has in its keeping the library of Scn information for the use of the Central Org to which it is attached. It takes care of collections. It makes sure that HCO Bulletins and HCO Policy Letters are read and understood by the Central Org, and its personnel. It keeps the org board. It can security check any Scientologist or Central Org personnel. An **HCO Area Office** does not run the Central Org or hire or fire its personnel, but in case of emergency and in the absence of competent Central Org personnel may find it necessary to take charge temporarily. (HCO PL 31 Jan 61, *Spheres of Influence*) **4.** that **office** that cares for a Central Organization in terms of preserving its form and structure, taking care of its ethics, technology and awards (certificates). It carries on my function of preserving and managing Central Organizations. It is for one Central Organization and makes sure that policies and programs are carried out, that good processing and training are given, that people who are trained get examined and certified. It administers justice. It helps care for special events such as ACCs and congresses given in its area. It sells books only through the local Central Organization. Its personnel consists of an **HCO** Secretary **Area,** an **HCO** Communicator **Area,** an **HCO** Steno **Area** who is also Secretarial Executive (or governing) Director Area, an **HCO** Board of Review part or full-time. It adds clerks and stenos as needful. (HCO PL 2 Jan 59) **5.** an **office** of a duly enfranchised Central Organization manned by an actual **HCO** Secretary and her staff as it may exist. (HCO PL 13 Dec 58)

HCO AREA SECRETARY, **1.** the **HCO Area Secretary** (**HAS**) has the function of establishing the org. (HCO PL 7 Jul 71) **2.** a fully manned, perfect **HCO** is the irreducible minimum of his doing his job. Now if he's got that, he should get on with it, and do his job, which is: put the establishment there. (FEBC 8, 7101C24 SO I) **3.** the **HAS** establishes, forms, puts there, corrects, posts, hats, equips, org boards, stats, corrects the org. All on a long term basis. (FO 2794) **4.** **HCOs** are headed by the **HCO Area Secretary.** (HCO PL 12 Mar 71) **5.** he's basically an auditor to the organization. He audits out all the confusions in the organization. That's how he brings order. Now what are his duties? To put the establishment there. (FEBC 10, 7101C24 SO III) **6.** is responsible for hats and hat folders, org boards, personnel assignments, personnel procurement and readying personnel for posts, routing of bodies through the shop and routing forms for them. She is responsible for internal and external communication and for transport of people and goods as well as vehicles. She is responsible for inspecting the org, comm lines, posts and activities, for compiling the stats and posting them in OIC and for ethics being in in the org and all ethics actions. (HCO PL 7 Feb 70 II) **7.** an **HCO Area Secretary** is supposed to see that technology stays high, that awards are issued properly, that people in Central Orgs know their HCO Bulletins and HCO Policy Letters and that the org board stays straight and that communication first and foremost occurs and that **HCO** remains solvent. (HCO PL 31 Jan 61, *Spheres of Influence*) **8.** the **Area Sec** provides and puts hats on Central Org personnel and is responsible to see that their hats are provided, are put on (repeatedly if necessary), and are changed or turned in when personnel changes. (HCO PL 27 Feb 59) **9.** purpose: to ensure the survival of a Central Organization by assisting it to render sincere, effective service in the fields of policy, ethics, technology and awards; and to assist LRH to wear his hats in this regard. (HCO PL 13 Jan 59) **10.** (Ship Org) Third Mate. (BPL 25 Jul 70R) *Abbr.* HAS, HCO Area Sec, HCO AS.

HCO BOARD OF REVIEW, **1.** purpose: to validate for full results every certificate ever issued in Dn and Scn. To be the final authority on any certificates to be issued. To be the final authority on Clear certification. (HCO PL 27 Nov 59) **2.** the **HCO Board of Review** okays student for certification (or refuses in which case Academy Admin completes folders again and resubmits). (HCO PL 28 Feb 59) **3.** says certificates are okay to sign. Basically, that's an **HCO Board of Review** function. (5812C29) **4.** has the following functions: issue Clear bracelets. Qualifies student for certification. Gives certificate exams. Validation stamp and files. (Administrative Bulletin, 21 Feb 58) **5.** often composed of one or two part-time staff auditors working on off hours for **HCO** and in and under control of **HCO** or one or more full-time expert Scientologists who have served as staff auditors and instructors and who now work full-time for **HCO.** The basis of **HCO Board of Review** authority lies in the basic functions of **HCO.** These are ethics, technology and awards. Ethics and technology are otherwise cared for than by the **HCO Board of Review.** Awards are wholly the function of the **HCO Board of Review.** (HCO PL 25 Nov 58) **6.** purpose: to review and stamp every certificate of any level or task, and every field certificate "Validated for Advanced Processes **HCO Board of Review 1957**" after their passing a proper examination on Five Levels of Indoc and CCH. (HCO London 9 Jan 58)

HCO BOARD OF REVIEW SAINT HILL COURSE, passes on qualifications of **Saint Hill** students before graduation or classification. (HCO PL 18 Dec 64, *Saint Hill Org Board*)

HCO BOOK ACCOUNT, **1.** into this **account** now go **booksales** and E-meter sales. The use of this **account** is solely for books and their shipping and E-meters and their shipping and **book** promotion. (HCO PL 12 Nov 69 II) [The above HCO PL was cancelled by BPL 10 Oct 75 VII.] **2.** in this **account** must be placed all monies obtained from the sale of **books** and tapes. (BPL 3 Sept 59) **3.** the only postage which may be paid from the **account** is **book** or magazine postage. **Book** and tape purchases may be made from the **account.** Magazine printing and postage bills may be paid from the **account,** but no extravagant increases in printing quality or volume may be paid from it, nor may brochures of mailings announcing service be paid from it. Advertising fees may be paid from the **HCO Div Account** but only for **book** ads. (HCO PL 30 Nov 64)

HCO CITY SEC, the title and post of HCO Volunteer Sec is abolished. Such personnel will be known simply as **HCO City Secs.** His/her sole aim and purpose is to act as an **HCO** terminal and relay point for the area, in close cooperation with the Continental HCO of the area, with the purpose of coordinating the dissemination and effectiveness of Scn in the area. (HCO PL 3 Sept 61)

HCO CLERK, **1.** the **HCO Clerk** receives all incoming communications and routes them to the proper hat terminal in the organization. It is the duty of the **HCO Clerk** to determine proper routing of communications received in HCO. (HCOB 4 Oct 56) **2.** all **HCO Clerks** are now to be known as HCO Communicators. (HCO PL 20 Nov 58)

HCO COMMUNICATOR, **1. HCO Communicator** is attached to the Office of L. Ron Hubbard, and this post is charged with the duty (additional to extant duties of **HCO Communicator**) of forwarding **communications** from L. Ron Hubbard and to L. Ron Hubbard. This duty includes the responsibility of seeing that these **communications** are duplicated and understood, and that any confusions on them are queried until the **communication** is duplicated and understood. (HCO PL 1 Apr 65) **2.** the Prom-reg Department includes the **HCO Communicator,** who now becomes the Communications Officer. (HCO PL 15 Mar 65 I) **3. purpose:** to keep the **communication** lines flowing and the files in order in HCO. (HCO PL 27 Nov 59) **4.** is in charge of the HCO comm system in his area and makes sure that a precise, accurate job is done whether the staff is large or small. Therefore, he is no errand boy but in effect the comm line executive of the HCO. (HCO PL 20 Dec 58)

HCO CONFESSIONAL FORM 2, Joburg **Confessional** List. (HCO PL 7 Apr 61RA)

HCO CONTINENTAL, 1. the function of **HCO Continental** is: (1) to be the Central Office of L. Ron Hubbard for the **continent,** (2) to keep communications flowing, (3) to ensure the issue to all orgs of LRH materials and instructions, either personal or through HCO Bulletins, Policy Letters and other issues; similarly, to ensure the issue of other materials sent out by HCO WW, (4) to issue and distribute the **continental** magazine (this function should be delegated to a magazine editor), (5) to issue certificates. (HCO PL 14 May 64) **2.** the duties and activities of **HCO Continental** are generally defined as helping me wear my hat in the **continental** area. To fully understand the duties of **HCO Continental** one has to understand what I do or would do and then see that it is done. First would be the general, mass dissemination of Scn by books, magazines, tapes, etc., and special events such as congresses. Second would be ethics, certificates and awards which would include justice. Third, but not in order of importance, would be technical excellence and results in processing. Fourth would be the good functioning of all HCO Area Offices in a **continental** area, their personnel and finance problems and seeing that they do their job. Fifth would be the preservation and form of Central Organizations and their income and survival. Sixth and throughout would be action as a personal secretary or personal secretarial functions to myself. Seventh would be handling franchise holders and field auditors. Eighth would be legal activities. (HCO PL 17 Feb 61, *HCO Continental*)

HCO CONTINENTAL ADMINISTRATIVE LETTER, (dated) green ink on yellow paper. By **HCO Continental** Secretary for any area. Distribute according to distribution data on letter. Gives **admin** data, orders and information. (HCO PL 4 Feb 61)

HCO CONTINENTAL COMMITTEE OF EVIDENCE, the Convening Authority is the **HCO Continental** Secretary. It handles matters relating to any Scn executives in a whole **continental** zone. It investigates any cases referred to it by the WW Committee of Evidence and reviews any lower HCO Committees of Evidence in its zone when necessary or so requested. (HCO PL 7 Sept 63)

HCO CONTINENTAL LIAISON OFFICER, the Office of the HCO Exec Sec WW contains one Divisional Organizer for Divisions 7, 1 and 2 for each **Continental Office** in the world. The person is called the **HCO Continental Liaison Officer** for (name of **continental office**) at WW. This one person is **liaison** for each and every Division 7, 1 and 2 in that **continental** sphere. (HCO PL 6 Sept 67)

HCO CONTINENTAL OFFICE, 1. an **HCO Continental Office** has these basic functions: to broadly disseminate Scn to masses of people not connected or not yet connected with Scn. This is done by magazines and preparing proper literature. **Continental** legal representative for Scn is an HCO national function. Broadly, the technology and dissemination of Scn and its awards and good name are an **HCO Continental** function. Supervision of all HCO Offices on the **continent** and their activities is an **HCO Continental** activity. An **HCO Continental Office** does not pin down on one Central Organization to the exclusion of broad dissemination and the conduct of other HCO Offices. (HCO PL 31 Jan 61, *Spheres of Influence*) **2.** the Central HCO Office for one or more **continents** or islands. It handles books, tapes, lecture records, a magazine and other functions for a **continent.** Its main order of business is the sale and inventory of books in any given large geographical area and the publishing of a specific magazine for that geographical area and general supervision of it. A **Continental Office** handles the traffic of a **continent** in terms of dissemination and coordinates HCO Area Offices in its zone. It carries on my function of dissemination on a **continental** basis. It also handles ACCs and special events for that **continent.** An **HCO Continental Office** personnel consists of an HCO Executive Secretary Continental, an **HCO** Communicator **Continental,** a Magazine Make-up Personnel **Continental,** a Book Administrator **Continental,** one or more Shipping Clerks **Continental,** one or more File Clerks or Stenos **Continental.** (HCO PL 2 Jan 59)

HCO CONTINENTAL SECRETARY, 1. it's the **HCO Continental Secretary's** task to make more people hear about Scn, to guarantee the quality of presentation, to make sure HCO Area Offices are effective, to conduct special events and, of course, as in the case of all HCO Offices, to make my postulates stick. (HCO PL 31 Jan 61, *Spheres of Influence*) **2.** an **HCO Continental Secretary** is supposed to see that more people hear about Scn on a mass basis—that better handouts and write-ups exist, that Scn stays firm on that continent or part of the world and that HCO Area Offices function well with well-staffed personnel. (HCO PL 31 Jan 61, *Spheres of Influence*) **3.** the Offices of **HCO Continental Sec** and Continental Director exist mainly to increase Scn activity and income in a **continental** area. (HCO PL 14 Jan 64)

HCO CONTINENTAL TECHNICAL LETTER, (dated) red ink on yellow paper. By **HCO Continental** Secretary of any **continent.** Distributed as designated on **letter.** Gives **technical** advices, orders and data. Not a copy of HCO Bulletins through these may be quoted. (HCO PL 4 Feb 61)

HCO COPE OFFICER, **1.** the amount of distraction and orders thrown at a HAS is a why for failures to establish the org. The way to *cope* with all this torrent of distraction and orders is to appoint an **HCO Cope Officer.** The HAS then does orderly expansion. The **HCO Cope Officer** handles the noise and screaming emergencies. In actual fact the **HCO Cope Officer** makes HCO *produce* in some way, any old way. (HCO PL 10 Aug 71) **2.** defends the establishing functions of the HAS by first doing and then getting sections of **HCO** to do all the functions of **HCO.** The **HCO Cope Officer** is actually the product officer of **HCO.** The senior is the HAS because her product is the whole org. (HCO PL 10 Aug 71) **3.** an **HCO Cope Officer** deals with the mad scramble of backlog, must forbid internal transfers and forbid a rip-up of what is already established. (LRH ED 146 INT)

HCO CORPORATIONS, there are five **HCO corporations.** They are: **HCO** (WW) Ltd., **HCO** (St. Hill) Ltd., Scientology Library and Research Ltd., **Hubbard Communications Office** Ltd., and **Hubbard Communications Office.** (HCO PL 30 Sept 64)

HCO DIRECTOR, (org board of a City Office) handles the two "departments" of **HCO** and is a member of the Ad Council, there being no Ad Committees. (HCO PL 21 Oct 66 III)

HCO DISSEMINATION SECRETARY, coordinates and gets done the promotional functions of Division 2 and makes the org and services known to Scientologists. (HCO PL 20 Nov 65)

HCO DISSEMINATION SECRETARY WW, supervises contents of all national magazines and handles international **dissemination.** (HCO PL 18 Dec 64, *Saint Hill Org Board*)

HCO DIV ACCOUNT, the **HCO Div Account** (old Book Account) has very rigid policy on how this money can be spent. The reason for this is that money must be safeguarded to provide for adequate promotion and sale of books. (BPL 6 Oct 66RA)

HCO DIVISIONS, the first two **divisions** of the entire organization are the **HCO divisions.** This is known as the **HCO** portion of the organization. (HCO PL 2 Aug 65)

HCO ELECTRONIC CONSULTANT, advises and renders actual **electronic** engineering service to **HCO** and the Executive Director in matters pertaining to: electrical and electronic communications; tape recording and record production; electrical and electronic special devices related to technical activities; E-meters; and any other similar services requested by the Executive Director. (HCO PL 16 Aug 62)

HCO ESTABLISHMENT OFFICER, establishes and maintains **HCO.** (HCO PL 7 Mar 72) *Abbr.* HCO Esto.

HCO EXEC ESTO, HCO Exec Sec's Org Officer. (HCO PL 9 May 74)

HCO EXEC SEC COORDINATOR, the Executive Division is Division 7. The LRH Communicator is in charge of the division. It consists of three departments. The second department is the Office of the **HCO Executive Secretary,** Department 20. It is in the charge of the **HCO Exec Sec Coordinator.** (HCO PL 2 Aug 65)

HCO EXECUTIVE LETTERS, **1.** blue paper, green ink. Meant for every org. Remimeo or non-remimeo as specified. Purpose: carry advices, how to do things, short term projects, requests for data, information, reports on the states of things in general or some activity in particular or how some extreme condition was caused or how some extreme condition is progressing. (HCO PL 13 Jun 69) [The above HCO PL was cancelled by BPL 10 Oct 75 VII.] **2.** the normal comm line from the **Executive** Director to Assn/Org Secs and HCO Secs or department heads in orgs is the **HCO Executive Letter** of date. This is on legal size blue paper, is mimeographed and is headed to: from: subject: reference: with numbered paragraphs. It is always sent general non-remimeo and goes to all orgs even when addressed only to one org or even to a person in that org. It may also be meant for every org. **HCO Executive** Director uses these rather than individual dispatches in answering requests for instructions from some org officer so that these rundowns are available to everyone rather than just the querying person. The purpose is to save the repeating of similar orders or advices in numerous places by separate dispatches which, received by only one person and having no publishing system thereby lose technology and data. (HCO PL 22 Feb 65 III) **3.** this will now be on white paper with blue ink, using the old Info Letter flash mark to make SEC EDs easier to identify. (HCO PL 8 May 65 II) **4.** from L. Ron Hubbard, usually a direct **executive** order or a request for a report or data or news or merely information. It is not policy but should be answered if any answer is requested. It is blue ink on green paper. (HCO PL 5 Mar 65 II) **5.** an **HCO Executive Letter** is mimeoed at Saint Hill only, blue ink on green paper. By definition it is a **letter** from Ron or the Organization Supervisor addressed personally to a Continental or Area Chief (Continental Director or Assn Secretary) but which is of interest to other organizations. As such communications are often retyped for other orgs, it is easier to mimeo them. They contain interpretations of policy and comments on projects which do not otherwise have a channel of issue. (HCO PL 1 Apr 64, *New Mimeo Line HCO Executive Letter*)

HCO EXECUTIVE SECRETARY, 1. in early days there was an **HCO Sec** in charge of the functions of the first three divisions (Exec, HCO, Dissem) and an Assoc Sec in charge of the functions of the last four divisions. The org board evolved further and the **HCO Exec Sec** became the person in charge of the functions of the first three divisions and the Org Exec Sec, the last four. In the Sea Org these titles became Supercargo and Chief Officer but the functions were similar. (HCO PL 9 May 74) **2. Hubbard Communications Office Executive Secretary**. (HCOB 23 Aug 65) **3.** Supercargo, Product Officer Divisions 7, 1, 2. (HCO PL 9 May 74) **4.** the **HES** was an org officer and the OES was a product officer. In the first two divisions you find the **HES** had hatting, forming and so forth and also had the Executive Division which contained the Estate Section. (FEBC 7, 7101C23 SO III) *Abbr.* HES, HCO Exec Sec.

HCO EXECUTIVE SECRETARY'S COMMUNICATOR, the title Advisory where used as a helper to an **Exec Sec** is changed to (**HCO** or Org) **Exec Sec Communicator** for (Division represented). This title has the rank and privileges of a **secretary** in his own org and in a junior org to the one appointed, the privileges of an **Executive Secretary.** The purpose of the post is: to **communicate** for the **Executive Secretary** and help with that official's purpose by **communicating** on matters and/or handling them relating to the type of division represented and to be responsible to the **Executive Secretary** for that type of division and to be responsible to the **Executive Secretary** for that gross divisional statistic. Only in the International Division or in any org having 250 staff members or more would this post be filled. (HCO PL 21 Jan 66)

HCO EXECUTIVE SECRETARY WW, the primary duties of the **HCO Executive Secretary WW** are: (1) international personnel, (2) international ethics files, (3) all org statistics. (HCO PL 12 Feb 70 II)

HCO EXPEDITERS, a large org or Flag can have some **HCO expediters.** These personnel don't go on the org board except as **HCO expediters** in Division 1. They are used to handle backlogs. You have them work in any area where there is a backlog, when that backlog is handled you put them onto another—you don't transfer them to the post concerned with the backlog, they remain in Division 1. (FO 2314)

HCO HAS CO-AUDIT FRANCHISE, a franchise which permits group processing, the running of an **HAS Co-audit**, the processing of individuals and, eventually, training to professional level. (HCO PL 12 Aug 59)

HCO HATTING SECTION, this unit is responsible for ensuring instant **hatting**, apprenticeship and mini **hatting** occur, that a full **hat** is provided and issued to the staff member and that the full hat is included in the staff member's training program when it is available by the Director of Personnel Enhancement. (FO 2824)

HCO INFORMATION LETTER, 1. an **HCO Information Letter** is now to be issued by me only and is blue ink on white paper. This is not mandatory data. It's just news I'd like to see gotten around. (HCO PL 4 Feb 61) **2.** (dated, do not change date locally) distribution is indicated on it. By LRH, blue ink on white paper. Copying is optional on a Roneo. It is done on one side of paper only so it can be posted on a bulletin board for staff or public. Two copies are sent by HCO WW. One copy must be retained in master **HCO Info Letter** master file. If it's useful for handout, recopy locally, make appropriate copies and issue and file as above. Ordinarily, it would be clip-boarded on a staff board or would be copied in a magazine or mimeoed for general handout. Which is done, is indicated on the copy received. (HCO PL 4 Feb 61)

HCO MASTER FILE, everything pertaining to technology, i.e. books, leaflets, magazines, tapes, technical bulletins and including other bulletins and all policy letters are to be stamped: HCO

MASTER FILE DO NOT REMOVE and **HCO Master Files** are to receive two of each of the above items with the exception of tapes where there is only one master copy. (HCO PL 25 Feb 59)

HCO NEWSLETTER, (dated) blue ink on salmon paper. By any member of HCO WW. Gives data and news, technical, admin or personal of general interest. Usually not copied or mimeoed but clip-boarded on staff bulletin board. (HCO PL 4 Feb 61)

HCO OFFICER, (org board of a City Office) **HCO Officer** is in charge of three units (departments) of the **HCO** Department (Section 1). (HCO PL 21 Oct 66 III)

HCO OFFICES, **1. Hubbard Communications Offices.** The purpose of the **HCO Offices** is to act as stable terminals to an organization in any given area so as to provide immediate administrative assistance to L. Ron Hubbard when in that area and communications from operations to him and from him when he is not. (HCO PL 16 Sept 70 II) **2.** the functions of this center are: (1) the receipt and handling of correspondence addressed to myself, (2) the answering and delivering of telephone communications relating specifically to communications addressed to me or proceeding from me, (3) the typing of manuscripts and investigation material from my Dimaphon records or personal dictation, (4) compilation of investigation and case information submitted to me by auditors, (5) assistance to the Treasurer in receiving bills and expediting their payment, (6) the care of social and governmental matters in which I happen to be concerned, (7) maintaining my comm lines in good order. Casual communication with this **office** inhibits its efficiency and involves it in concerns which inhibit a swift expedition of my work. The **Office** is not concerned with the activities of the central staff beyond acting as a communications relay point from myself to these operations and from these operations to myself. (HCOB 24 Jan 58) **3.** purpose of **HCO Office**: to be the **Office** of LRH. To handle and expedite the comm lines of LRH. To prepare or handle the preparation of all manuscripts and other to-be-published materials of Scn. To keep, use and care for LRH's office equipment. To assist the organization of Scn and their people. To set a good example of efficiency to organizations. (BPL 7 Jan 58) **4.** there are three types of **HCO Offices.** These are (1) Worldwide, (2) Continental and (3) Area. In London all three **office** types exist. In Washington and Melbourne, Continental and Area **Offices** exist together. Where there is no Continental **Office** only an Area **Office** exists. (HCO PL 2 Jan 59) **5.** there are three types of **HCO office.** The first is **HCO** Worldwide, and that actually is **HCO** Limited, a British registered company. Now all copyrights, trademarks, rights of materials and everything else, are assigned over to **HCO** Limited, so they are mine, but are given to **HCO** Limited for use. **HCO** Worldwide is located in London. London is the only organization which has a three-stack office. It has **HCO** Worldwide, **HCO** Continental, **HCO** London. There are three **HCO Offices** working there. There are actually a lot of the personnel just doubling in brass in these **offices.** But nevertheless they have to keep in sight of the fact that there are three **offices.** Worldwide, of course, takes care of the central summary of all organizations which are enfranchised, files their financial reports and gets the final summary on all legal actions that have been taken. It sums it all up, in other words. (5812C29)

HCO ORGANIZATIONAL FRANCHISE, a second and different type of **HCO Franchise** is now available in addition to the HCO HAS Co-audit Franchise. The second is the HCO Processing Franchise where individual processing only would be done. There will be a third type some day but it is not available now. This will be an **HCO Organizational Franchise** where the individual works "outside" Scn organizations to bring order into larger non-Scn activities in which he will be helped by **HCO** as a special activity. (HCOB 12 Aug 59)

HCO PERSONNEL, Divisions 7, 1 and 2. The org personnel are Divisions 3, 4, 5 and 6. (HCO PL 20 Aug 65)

HCO PORTION, the first two divisions of the entire organization are the **HCO** Divisions. This is known as the **HCO portion** of the organization. (HCO PL 2 Aug 65)

HCO PROCESSING FRANCHISE, a second and different type of **HCO Franchise** in addition to the HCO HAS Co-audit Franchise. It permits an individual auditor in practice to receive immediate bulletins, discounts, and tests, and requires that he remit 10% of his income from Dn and Scn to HCO WW. This permits the individual to run an individual practice or a guidance center without running an HAS Co-audit. The **HCO Processing Franchise** is where individual **processing** only would be done. (HCOB 12 Aug 59)

HCO PROJECT ENGINEER, **1.** one who furnishes the line impetus, dedication and guidance necessary to the accomplishment of a special Scn research, administration or diplomatic **project.** (HCO PL 17 Nov 58, *Project Engineering*) **2.** there are three types of **HCO Project Engineers.** First is technical and is assigned to research **projects.** The second is administrative and is assigned to sales and service **projects.** The third is diplomatic and is assigned to areas of special difficulty. (HCO PL 17 Nov 58, *Project Engineers Three Types*)

HCO PROJECT ENGINEERING, a specially designed activity covered by special HCO Bulletins. The time requirements are not great for such projects and they are needed to give specific live interest to unique Scn promotions which heretofore, for lack of watching, have failed. Example of an **HCO Engineering Project** as follows: (1) keeping in stock and alive in ads and the field one book title of Scn, (2) supervision of staff clearing activities, teams and schedules. **HCO Project Engineering** is needed to give life to special Scn dissemination activities and to give staff auditors a share in the broader activities of Scn and to give them a change of pace through the week as well as to give me assistance in carrying out vital actions. (SEC ED 11, 16 Dec 58)

HCO RECEPTION, 1. the purpose of **HCO Reception** is to bring order to the dispatch and body traffic of **HCO**, and reduce the dev-t in **HCO** so that it can get on with its business of forming, stabilizing and expanding the org. The **HCO Receptionist** handles *all* visitors, staff or public, to **HCO** and routes them properly or gets them appointments with HCO staff. (HCO PL 5 Sept 71) **2.** tabbing folders, preparing materials for admin actions, checking logs, keeping and issuing routing forms and other **HCO** forms, routing people and giving information and holding, receiving and handing out mail are all part of the hat of **HCO Reception.** (OODs 4 Feb 71) **3.** an **HCO receptionist** (not the org receptionist) is as deep as staff or public may go into **HCO.** The **HCO Receptionist** handles all routing forms and such traffic. Any central comm basket system is behind or near the receptionist. In a public org the **HCO Receptionist** may call HCO staff out of HCO for interviews for employment or recruitment. **HCO Reception** is in Department 1, Division 1. Again it is not the org receptionist. That is another post in the org reception area. Org reception handles all public customers. (FO 2661)

HCO SECRETARIAL LETTER, very seldom will you get anything that says "Secretarial Executive Director for Washington D.C. Only" because if it's going wrong in one place, it's going wrong someplace else too. But you do get incidental orders to that effect, so they can't be excluded. Instead of that you get an **HCO Secretarial Letter.** Now this **HCO Secretarial Letter** arrives in a central operation and is converted by **Secretarial** Executive Director, after being viewed by the **HCO Secretary.** It is converted. And it says, "**Secretarial** Executive Director, HASI, Johannesburg." She types it all up. They are never mimeographed unless they are for the whole staff or something. She puts a copy on the board, she puts a copy to the persons to, and that's it. She issued it. These things are basically policies. They are hats and so on. They may have particularities, but they definitely have lots of policies connected with them. (5812C29)

HCO SECRETARY, 1. in early days there was an **HCO Secretary** in charge of the functions of the first three divisions (Exec, HCO, Dissem) and an Assoc Sec in charge of the functions of the last four divisions. The org board evolved further and the **HCO** Exec **Sec** became the person in charge of the functions of the first three divisions and the Org Exec Sec, the last four. In the Sea Org these titles became Supercargo and Chief Officer but the functions were similar. (HCO PL 9 May 74) **2.** on the Six Department board the **HCO Secretary** takes the place of the **HCO** Exec **Sec** of a Seven Division Org. (HCO PL 21 Oct 66) **3. HCO Secretary** WW, **HCO Secretary** Continental, or **HCO Secretary** Area. (HCO PL 4 Mar 65 II)

HCO SECRETARY WW, 1. HCO Secretary WW is the **Worldwide** level executive for Division 1 (HCO) and a member of the **Worldwide** Council of three of which the Org Sec WW and the Assistant Treasurer WW are the other two. (HCO PL 4 Mar 65) **2.** is in direct charge of all Continental and Area **HCO Secretaries** around the world. (HCO PL 18 Dec 64, *Saint Hill Org Board*)

HCO SECURITY FORM 19, laudatory withholds, know to mystery processing check. (HCO PL 6 Jan 62)

HCO SPECIAL FUND, see SCIENTOLOGY RESEARCH AND INVESTIGATION FUND.

HCO STANDING ORDER NUMBER 1, correspondence: all mail addressed to me shall be received by me. (HCO PL 18 Dec 61)

HCO STANDING ORDER NUMBER 2, messages: a message box shall be placed in all Scn organizations so that any messages for me may be received by me. (HCO PL 18 Dec 61)

HCO STANDING ORDER NUMBER 3, information on correspondence: all HCO personnel and Scn personnel should not discourage communication to me. I am always willing to help. By my own creed, a being is only as valuable as he can serve others. (HCO PL 18 Dec 61)

HCO STANDING ORDER NUMBER 4, publication of open comm lines: post in permanent fashion on public boards the following excerpts from Standing Orders No. 1 to 3. Communications to Ron: HCO exists to expedite the communications and oversee the policies of L. Ron Hubbard. Excerpts: Standing Order No. 1, "All mail addressed to me shall be received by me." Standing Order No. 2, "A message box shall be placed in all Scn organizations so that any messages for me may be received by me." Standing Order No. 3, "All HCO personnel and Scn personnel should not discourage communication to me." "I am always willing to help. By my own creed, a being is only as valuable as he can serve others." L. Ron Hubbard. This excerpt should be published in magazines frequently in a small box. It should be made into a permanent material (not paper) sign of good aesthetic appearance and placed conspicuously but in good taste in the reception room of all offices. (HCO PL 18 Dec 61)

HCO STANDING ORDER NUMBER 5, all students formally enrolled into any Academy of Scn shall be thoroughly trained. The standard of the lowest professional certificate shall be such as to permit immediate and unashamed use of the student on graduation in any Hubbard Guidance Center. The only lasting overt that can be done with Scn is to fail to disseminate it well and accurately. This includes student training. Students must be trained to expect and achieve spectacular processing results early in training. Students must be oriented during training into caring for the cases of their preclears. In event of a poor or difficult student, it must be demanded by supervisors that the matter be remedied by Review or Ethics. Students must be trained to resolve their problems with Scn. Students must be trained to audit regardless of their own restimulation or cases. When auditing, auditors don't have cases. Students must not be permitted to sag or slack or fall away in attendance and this can be done because all such attitudes result from a student's failure to obtain a reality early in training. We must train new Scientologists so that we can have pride and confidence in them as Scientologists, not from an examination of their record but from the sole fact that they have been academy trained. Students and supervisors alike should fully understand that neither we nor this universe can afford to waste even one potential auditor. (HCO PL 10 Jan 62)

HCO STATION that place where an **HCO** staff member receives, holds and sends his dispatches and work. Appearance: an **HCO** Comm **Station has** three baskets, one above the other. The top is marked with the **station** number or numbers and "in." The middle is marked with "pending." The bottom is marked with "out." These three baskets sit on a corner of a desk or, in case of files, on top of a file case. (HCO PL 20 Dec 58)

HCO STENOGRAPHER, 1. purpose: to assist the HCO Secretary and the HCO Communicator in handling, converting, duplicating and filing the items handled by **HCO** and procurement of supplies thereof. (BPL 7 Jan 58) **2.** the Sec'l ED shall publish all Secretarials to the Exec Dir on blue paper, black ink, marked for local area. The Sec'l to the Exec Dir is also **HCO Steno** and is under the HCO Area Secretary. The Sec'l ED shall act as Secretary to the Board where one exists, to the Ad Comm or Ad Council and at staff meeting, shall type, get signed and distribute the minutes. The Sec'l ED shall put into HCO Secretarial Letters any item she is given originally from LRH intended for all orgs. The Sec'l ED shall convert any HCO Sec'l Letter she receives into a Sec'l ED for the local area. (HCO Secretarial PL, 17 Dec 58) *Abbr.* HCO Steno.

HCO (ST HILL) LTD., 1. this is the corporation that runs the course, handles the internal activities of Saint Hill. All student activities and letters concerning the course, quarters, domestic accounts go under this corporation. Only its letterhead is used for these activities. (HCO PL 30 Sept 64) **2.** has been organized to care for the course, house, grounds, domestic staff, construction, materiel and all personnel (**Saint Hill**). (HCO PL 31 Dec 63)

HCO TECHNICAL ADVICE LETTER, (dated) red ink on pale salmon paper. By any official of HCO WW. Is always **technical** in nature, never administrative. May be copied as mimeo or not according to its distribution designation. Copied or not it is to be conspicuously posted on the staff bulletin board preferably on a clip-board. It is on one side of the paper only. Even if distributed into baskets of staff it would still be posted. (HCO PL 4 Feb 61)

HCO TECHNICAL MATERIAL SECRETARY WW, this post includes Book Administration WW as well as the testing and supply of E-meters, and the administration of all matters pertaining thereto. (HCO PL 15 Feb 62)

HC OUT-POINT PLUS-POINT LISTS RA, HCO Bulletin 28 August 1970RA, *HC Out-point Plus-point Lists RA.* This is a prepared list that locates the out-points in a person's own thinking.

When people can't seem to evaluate (or think brightly) this list will do wonders. Some Data Series Course students make no progress at all until they are assessed on this list and handled. (LRH ED 257 INT)

HCO VOLUNTEER SECRETARY, **1.** the title and post of **HCO Volunteer Sec** is abolished. As from now, such personnel, working in the field, will be known simply as HCO City Secs. The scheme will be entirely disassociated from the franchise scheme. Therefore no person who is currently a franchised auditor will simultaneously be an HCO City Sec, or be appointed to the post. The HCO City Sec is ideally a dedicated person, working for the third dynamic of Scn in the area where he/she operates. He/she has no vested interests, indulges in no personal politics with regard to the other auditors in the area. His/her sole aim and purpose is to act as an **HCO** terminal and relay point for the area, in close cooperation with the Continental **HCO** of the area, with the purpose of coordinating the dissemination and effectiveness of Scn in the area. (HCO PL 3 Sept 61) **2.** purpose: to ensure the survival of enfranchised auditors in the field and future organizational centers. To handle all ethical matters among the auditors by remaining impartial and being loyal to LRH at all times by helping him wear his hats in this regard. To be the direct communication terminal between LRH and the field. (HCO PL 5 Aug 59) [The above HCO PL was cancelled by BPL 10 Oct 75 II.] *Abbr.* HCO Vol Sec.

HCO WORLDWIDE, there are three types of HCO Office. The first is **HCO Worldwide** and that actually is HCO Ltd., a British registered company. Now all copyrights, trademarks, rights of materials and everything else are assigned over to HCO Ltd. So they are mine but are given to, for use, HCO Ltd. Now **HCO Worldwide** is located in London. London is the only organization which has a three-stack office. It has **HCO Worldwide,** HCO Continental, HCO London. **Worldwide** takes care of the central summary of all organizations which are enfranchised, files their financial reports, gets the final summary on all legal actions that have been taken and sums it all up, in other words. **HCO Worldwide** issues a franchise to a Central Organization. That franchise is the thing which gives them the right to materials, the use of trademarks, it gives them the use of copyrights, it gives them several services and rights. Now for that they pay 10% of the gross. Now here's what we have essentially. We have a **Worldwide** organization called **Hubbard Communications Office** which holds all of the copyrights all around the world, all of the trademarks and everything else. Now this organization enfranchises local organizations. It tells them they can operate and if they do not have a franchise in good standing they cannot operate. (5812C29)

HCO (WORLDWIDE) LTD., **1. HCO (Worldwide) Ltd.** with the Organization Supervisor for all Scn organizations around the world and locally will include reception, mimeo, communications, telex, accounts, addresses, central files and franchise. I remain as Executive Director. (HCO PL 31 Dec 63) **2.** this is the corporation that manages international organizations. It has the magazines we publish and handles the international communication lines. All photography and its accounts come under this corporation, also. Use its letterhead for these. (HCO PL 30 Sept 64)

HCO WW FORM 1, Assn Sec (Org Sec) Report. (HCO PL 4 Mar 61) [The above HCO PL was cancelled by BPL 10 Oct 75 III.]

HCO WW FORM 2, department head report—PE Department. (HCO PL 4 Mar 61) [The above HCO PL was cancelled by BPL 10 Oct 75 III.]

HCO WW FORM 3, **1.** Joburg Security Check **HCO WW Form 3.** (HCO PL 4 Jun 61) **2.** department head report—Academy. (HCO PL 4 Mar 61) [The above HCO PL was cancelled by BPL 10 Oct 75 III.]

HCO WW FORM 4, department head report—HGC. (HCO PL 4 Mar 61) [The above HCO PL was cancelled by BPL 10 Oct 75 III.]

HCO WW FORM 5a, department head report—PrR—Letter Reg. (HCO PL 4 Mar 61) [The above HCO PL was cancelled by BPL 10 Oct 75 III.]

HCO WW FORM 5b, department head report—PrR Interview Section. (HCO PL 4 Mar 61) [The above HCO PL was cancelled by BPL 10 Oct 75 III.]

HCO WW FORM 6, department head report—Materiel. (HCO PL 4 Mar 61) [The above HCO PL was cancelled by BPL 10 Oct 75 III.]

HCO WW FORM 7, department head report—Accounts. (HCO PL 4 Mar 61) [The above HCO PL was cancelled by BPL 10 Oct 75 III.]

HCO WW FORM 8, department head report—Government Relations. (HCO PL 4 Mar 61) [The above HCO PL was cancelled by BPL 10 Oct 75 III.]

HCO WW FORM 9, department head form—Special Programs. (HCO PL 4 Mar 61) [The above HCO PL was cancelled by BPL 10 Oct 75 III.]

HCO WW FORM AC 1, AC 1 Form. (HCO PL 19 Sept 62) [The above HCO PL was cancelled by BPL 10 Oct 75 IV.]

HCO WW FORM CT 1, check type one. Pre-intensive interview and pre-goals assessment **check.** Before the preclear is audited in an intensive where SOP Goals may be employed the checksheet is filled out by the D of P and passed by pc before a goals assessment is made. There are eight types of checkouts that the D of P does on a pc. Each one of these is the subject of a technical report form. They are in red ink on white paper. (HCO PL 31 Mar 61)

HCO WW FORM CT 2, 1. D of P form check type one. In view of improved technology and the fact that I've found there aren't enough questions to produce a tone arm shift in D of P's check type one, I have rewritten it. (Pre-intensive interview and pre-goals assessment check.) Before the preclear is audited in an intensive where SOP Goals may be employed the checksheet is filled out by the D of P and passed by pc before a goals assessment is made. (HCO PL 25 Apr 61) **2. check type two** assessment confirmation. **Check** by D of P to confirm case assessment, goals assessment, terminal level and command. Done before any of these are run on pc. Questions are made to pc with pc on the meter. (HCO PL 31 Mar 61)

HCO WW FORM CT 3, check type three. General **checkup** on a session. May be run at any time or when D of P unconvinced of case progress. (HCO PL 31 Mar 61)

HCO WW FORM CT 4, check type four. Rudiments **check.** After eight or ten hours of auditing on processes that were in model session (not CCHs) the D of P **checks** rudiments to make sure that they are cleaned up. (HCO PL 31 Mar 61)

HCO WW FORM CT 5, check type five. Flat **check.** When the staff auditor states that the terminal he has been running is now flat the D of P makes a very careful **check** before he permits a new assessment to be started. The TA does not have to be on clear read for a terminal to be flat. (HCO PL 31 Mar 61)

HCO WW FORM CT 6, check type six. Bog **check.** Done when the auditor reports or D of P thinks case is not progressing well. (This is a "when all else fails" check off.) (HCO PL 31 Mar 61)

HCO WW FORM CT 7, check type seven. A "release" checksheet. Made out on the pc at any time but preferably at a time when the pc is to receive no further intensives at the moment or is leaving the HGC. (HCO PL 31 Mar 61)

HCO WW FORM CT 8, check type eight. Clear **check.** D of P **checks** out this form and then sends it to HCO Area Sec for a second **checkout.** The whole pc file folder with all filed forms, assessments, various sheets and auditor's reports are to hand when this **checkout** is done. **Check** over all goals listed on the goals assessment sheet and any subsequent additions. Look for a fall of the needle on any of them. Any fall disqualifies the pc. **Check** over all terminals listed in all auditor's reports and note any fall on any of them with high sensitivity. Any fall disqualifies pc. We find the needle without reaction and pronounce this person to be Clear. (HCO PL 31 Mar 61)

HCO WW FORM DEP/1, departure form. This **form** must be completed by a student before any **departure** from course. (HCO PL 8 Nov 62, *Departure Form*)

HCO WW FORM G3, R3GA HCOWW Form G3 Fast **Goals** Check. This is a rapid checkout of a **goal** for use by auditors and particularly instructors and auditing supervisors. By an auditor it is done in model session. By an instructor or supervisor it is done as a simple checkout. (HCO PL 24 Jul 62)

HCO WW FORM G3, REVISED, R3M HCO WW Form G3, revised fast **goals** check. This is a rapid checkout of a **goal** for use by auditors and particularly instructors and auditing supervisors. By an auditor it is done in model session. By an instructor or supervisor it is done as a simple checkout. (HCO PL 6 Mar 63)

HCO WW R-3GA FORM 1, Routine 3GA HCO WW R-3GA Form 1, listing prepcheck. Prepcheck completed as a **form** for the pc before and during listing of **goals**, and before beginning to list items for any **goal** from the four lines, and during listing. It must thereafter be done every fifth session. The **form** must be made out for the pc and included in his or her folder. (HCO PL 17 Jul 62)

HCO WW SEC FORM 4, sec check whole track. (HCOB 19 Jun 61)

HCO WW SEC FORM 5, student **security** check. (HCO PL 29 Jun 61)

HCO WW SEC FORM 5a, security form for all HPA/HCA and above students before acceptance on courses. (HCO PL 1 Nov 61)

HCO WW SEC FORM 6, HGC auditor's **sec** check. This check is suitable for anyone who has done a fair amount of auditing, and also for students in professional level courses in the later part of the course. (HCO PL 7 Jul 61 II)

HCO WW SEC FORM 6a, for use by Class II or above auditors only. This is a shortened version of HCO WW Sec Form 6, the valuable processing check for auditors to get off their overts on preclears. (BPL 3 Feb 62R)

HCO WW SEC FORM 8, 1. a processing check for use on children (ages 6-12). (HCOB 21 Sept 61) 2. HGC pre-processing **security** check (for pc's beginning intensives). This check is to be given by HGC Admin on interviewing applicant. It is a pre-processing **security** check. The person giving the check does not have to find out or get off any withhold as this is not a processing check. (HCO PL 23 Oct 61) [These two **HCO WW Sec Form 8s** are completely different forms as defined but have the same number.]

HCO WW SECURITY FORMS 7a AND 7b, these two **security** checks have been devised specifically for employment, i.e., to check applicants for employment, or personnel already employed. (HCOB 28 Sept 61)

HEAD-HUNTER, see EXECUTIVE SEARCH CONSULTANT.

HEAD MIDSHIPMAN, midshipmen are junior officers in training to be good officers, so they have the duty of: (1) thoroughly learning navigation (2) doing the officer's checksheet. A **head midshipman** should be appointed to teach the **midshipmen** the above. (FO 1592)

HEAD OF DEPARTMENT, head of a production **department** and of only that production **department** regardless of other appointments or appearance of name on the organization board. (HCO PL 26 Jun 64)

HEALING, any process labeled **healing**, old or new refers to **healing** by mental and spiritual means and should therefore be looked upon as the relief of difficulties arising from mental and spiritual causes. (HCO PL 7 Apr 65 II)

HEARSAY EVIDENCE, saying one heard somebody say that somebody else did. (HCO PL 7 Sept 63)

HEAVY ETHICS TRIP, this is what a **heavy ethics trip** is made of—the irresponsibility of lower officers for their own people becoming a threat to the survival of the group. The society punishes the high senior for the misconduct or irresponsibility of his juniors. Therefore an officer at whatever level in a chain of command must take responsibility for his juniors and their **ethics.** (FO 3408)

HEAVY HUSSARS, see LRH HEAVY HUSSARS HAT.

HEAVY TRAFFIC WARNING, a **warning** to any department of **heavy traffic** coming. It is to take steps to see that the department is adequately supplied with the materials necessary to handle the coming **traffic.** It's just a case of having a little foresight. (HCO PL 2 Apr 65, *Heed Heavy Traffic Warnings*)

HEDGING, the practice of making counterbalancing investments or decisions as a means of protecting oneself against possible losses from high-risk investments or actions.

HELPER, 1. a person who helps a skilled tradesman on the job and thus learns how to do the job actions. A helper differs from an apprentice or trainee in that he has often had little or no formal trade or technological education and may be lacking in the theory behind the job actions of a trade. 2. a blue-collar term for which assistant is the corresponding white-collar term.

HELP FACTOR, the willing to assist. This also has to do with cause. What can the individual cause? An organization which cannot **help** anybody will have a tendency to fail. (ESTO 12, 7203C06 SO II)

H.E.&R., see HUMAN EMOTION AND REACTION.

HERRING EFFECT, the mobs of people are sufficiently numerous today to cause a **herring effect.** No one **herring** is given any attention by the rest of the **herrings.** Public Relations attempts to break out of this inattention by being a more startling **herring.** But if overdone, the rest of the **herrings** believe one is a shark. (HCO PL 12 Nov 69)

HEY YOU ORGANIZATION, what is sometimes called a **hey you organization** is one that takes orders from anyone=a repeating out-point of wrong source. (HCO PL 30 Sept 73 I)

HGC 1, see HGC 2.

HGC 2, when the well done hours go above 600 a week, a whole new HGC is put in duplicating the first, with its own C/S, D of P, T/S auditing rooms and auditor admin room. It would be **HGC Section Two** or **HGC 2** with the original being HGC 1. (HCOB 5 Mar 71)

HGC ADMINISTRATOR, HGC admin procures and assigns auditors, gives applicants from the registrar their case estimates, keeps the files of cases, oversees proper auditor handling of forms, oversees testing or gets it done for **HGC** pcs when PE testing is closed, finds and assigns rooms for auditing and keeps, in general, the lines moving in the **HGC.** (HCO PL 20 Dec 62)

HIDDEN ASSETS, see ASSETS, HIDDEN.

HIGH CRIME CHECKOUTS, those done starrate by Qual personnel on the auditors, C/Ses, supers, D of T, Cramming Officer or anyone in the org delivering a technical service. The materials **checked out** are the processes of the level and the HCOBs or HCO PLs that directly cover how those processes are done. Not to do these **checkouts** is a **high crime.** (HCO PL 25 Nov 74)

HIGH CRIME REPORT, staff member **report** of any **high crime** noted or suspected but if only suspected must be so stated. (HCO PL 1 May 65)

HIGH CRIMES, 1. these consist of publicly departing Scn or committing suppressive acts. Cancellation of certificates, classifications and awards and becoming fair game are amongst the penalities which can be leveled for this type of offense as well as those recommended by Committees of Evidence. (HCO PL 7 Mar 65 III) **2.** the overt or covert actions or omissions knowingly and willfully undertaken to suppress, reduce, prevent or destroy case gains, and/or the influence of Scn on activities, and/or the continued Scn success and actions on the part of organizations and Scientologists. (BPL 9 Aug 71R I)

HIGHER ORG, an **org** that delivers **higher** services than those of a Class IV Org, i.e., an AO, SH, or AOSH. (HCO PL 10 Feb 72R III)

HIGH HATTING, a term applied to a practice of wearing only one's **highest hat** in a small org using the comm member system and also in receiving an order or advice as a lower comm member and "going upstairs" with one's **hats** to refuse it. In a very small org, it is very wise to write from the **hat** one is talking about to the comm member in a bigger org that wears that **hat,** and then, in receiving the reply, receive it as the **hat** that asked the question or sent the data. (HCO PL 13 Mar 65 II)

HIGH MORALE GROUP, one which by its own competence generates its own wherewithal. (FSO 231)

HIGH WINDS, Sea Organization magazine. The subject of photographs and articles will be: (1) the ships of the Sea Org (2) the Sea Org Captains, officers and crew (3) bridge, boat and deck activities (4) office work where security is not violated (5) training actions: (a) as ethics experts (b) as org experts (c) as top flight auditors (d) as OTs. *High Winds* is printed at WW by the OT Liaison Unit, and distributed by the same on a monthly basis. (FO 579)

HILL 10, 1. slang for a situation that has been worsened by delay or false reports or hat dumps or non-compliance and becomes a mad rush by other persons or a senior to handle. (FO 3407) **2.** our slang for a situation of great complexity requiring rush actions which must be exactly timed. (OODs 2 Nov 73) **3.** a **Hill 10** is where you have to get everything set up with no time whatever to set it up and yet it must go right. In short, it's a battleplan that is frail and exact and in total emergency. (OODs 7 July 72)

Hill 10

HIRE, *n.* 1. a person newly hired by an organization and having no previous record of employment for that organization. 2. payment or the sum of money paid for the use of employment of personnel, equipment, etc. —*v.* 1. to pay money for the services of a person or the use of equipment, property, etc.; the act of employing. 2. to exchange the use of personnel, equipment, etc., for money; to hire out.

HIRE PURCHASE, (British) a type of installment purchase plan whereby an initial down payment is followed by regular installments over a period of time until the merchandise is paid for. It differs from a credit sale in that the merchandise is not legally owned by the buyer until completely paid in full.

HIRING, CENTRALIZED, occurs where all hiring for a company's offices or plants is done through one centralized office.

HIRING, DECENTRALIZED, allowance of hiring for a company's offices or plants to be done at various company locations rather than one centralized location or office.

HIT, to Comm Ev, shoot, fire. (FEBC 1, 7011C17 SO)

HOBBY HORSES, a type of dev-t where a staff member can "ride his favorite **hobby horse**," ordering and complying only in his favorite area, neglecting areas of greater importance. His orders often cross order and distract from important targets and create dev-t, vital actions being neglected. (HCO PL 27 Jan 69)

HOLDING COMPANY, see COMPANY, HOLDING.

HOMEWORK, by **homework** is meant, all relevant facts dug up, the people to be ousted or posted fully looked up and designated, the funding arranged for any purchase, the evaluator's work well completed with all data looked up and noted. (CBO 337)

HONESTY, sanity and **honesty** consist of producing a valuable final product for which one is then recompensed by support and good will, or in reverse flow, supporting and giving good will to the producer of the product. (HCO PL 25 Mar 71)

HONORARY AWARDS, all certificates and **awards** obtained not as a result of courses or examination are termed **honorary**. All **honorary** certificates are marked **honorary** in distinct lettering. An **honorary** certificate may not be substituted for a standard certificate or classification and may not be required as a qualification for anything and does not waive any requirement to have a certificate or classification. **Honorary** certificates and **awards** are only given for achievement in application. They do not however grant any new right to apply. Memorial **awards** are medals or plaques and have the same conditions as **honorary** certificates. (HCO PL 5 Mar 65)

HONORARY SEA ORG MEMBER, celebrities are very special people and have a very distinct line of dissemination. They have comm lines that others do not have and many medias to get their dissemination through. Because of their value as disseminators it is unwise to make them staff members working full time as any other Sea Org member does in an organization, rather they should be allowed to be the celebrity they are, utilizing their talent, to get them more and more into the public eye. If these celebrities want to join the **Sea Org** they may be awarded the status of **Honorary Sea Org Members.** This title is not given to just any celebrity but rather to those who have shown and proved their dedication to the **Sea Org.** This title is awarded to those celebrities, this makes them no less a **Sea Org member** than any other but it does free the celebrity up to disseminte broadly. (FO 3323)

HONORARY STAFF MEMBER, a person who has the same rights and privileges as a permanent **staff member.** (SEC ED 75, 2 Feb 59)

HONORS, any classification may be issued with **honors** providing the candidate has exceeded the checksheet requirements by a notable degree and is also eligible for the upper classification range of that certificate. With **honors** however may not be given without the written recommendation of the candidate's own instructors. (HCO PL 12 Aug 63)

HORIZONTAL COMBINATION, see COMBINATION, HORIZONTAL.

HORIZONTAL FLOW, **1.** a comm line is the line on which particles **flow**, it is **horizontal**. The correct terminals in each department are addressed by terminals outside the department directly and are so answered. This is known as **horizontal flow.** It is a fast flow system. (HCO PL 1 Apr 72) **2.** (**horizontal** fast **flow** communication routing) the normal **flow** lines of an org are **horizontal**. They do not go up, over and down on the organizing board. They pass from one unit to another sideways without going through seniors. Almost all dispatches should travel in this way. It is fast **flow.** None of the comm ever goes to the originator's senior or to the receiver's senior. Only when something goes wrong or there is a conflict do seniors get consulted or dive in on the line. (HCO PL 25 Oct 71 I)

HORIZONTAL INTEGRATION, see INTEGRATION, HORIZONTAL.

HOST, to put the concept of service in fully, the post of **Host** is established in the Office of the LRH

Comm. All persons arriving for services will be checked continually by the host to be sure that service is being delivered without referral or waiting. (FO 2997)

HOSTESS, **1.** post set up to monitor the flow of crew and public through FAO. HCO, Dissem, Tech and Qual functions were to be monitored by the **Hostess** to ensure they were done in such a way to conform to command intention to expedite unfit crew off the ship and ensure fast correct handling of crew and public. (ED 10 Flag) **2.** head of Dept 17, Participation, Ship Div 6. (FO 2334) **3.** this post was the first and basic function of SO Div VI. The post is to see all visitors have a drink and are properly greeted aboard, among, its basic duties. (FO 1717) **4.** the title of **Hostess** is changed to Public Officer. (FO 913) **5.** in command of Div 6. (FO 196)

HOT, **1.** somebody who has originated individually to the organization or has at least taken an HAS course, and this we consider **hot.** (5812C16) **2.** a degree of interest expressed as a reach. (SO ED 122 INT)

HOTEL SERVICES COMMITTEE, (Flag Land Base) the Assistant Manager, Chief Engineer, Food **Service** Manager and Exec Housekeeper form a **Hotel Services Committee.** The Assistant manager is chairman. They meet each Friday outside production hours to attest or give deficiencies or recommend future action regarding: (1) the condition of boilers, utilities, repairs, equipment, buildings, grounds and engineering staff; (2) the condition of dining rooms, kitchens, supplies, food stores, facilities and food service staff; (3) the condition of interiors, laundry, child care and housekeeping staff. (BFO 124)

HOT FILES, **1. hot files** are those that recently expressed a wish to be trained or processed. (HCO PL 8 Apr 65) **2.** any person who has expressed interest (in writing or call) in training or processing of any kind is a **hot file.** (HCO PL 4 Jun 59) **3.** let's take a look at what we mean by a **hot file** or a good prospect as the person would be called, or a **hot** prospect letter. The definition of that is simply somebody who has originated individually to the organization or has taken at least an HAS Course. (5812C16) **4.** a **hot file** is defined as a CF **file** that holds the correspondence and papers of a person who has (1) expressed a desire to be processed, (2) expressed a desire to be trained, (3) completed an HAS course, (4) completed an HCA and is eligible for a B. Scn course, (5) been processed successfully and who might want training. (SEC ED 2, 15 Dec 58)

HOTLINE, the *Hotline* is the official newsletter of the Office of LRH Personal PRO International. The purpose of *Hotline* is to provide Honorary LRH PROs and REPs with information and materials which will help them help others know more about L. Ron Hubbard. (COLRHED 369)

HOT PROSPECT, **1. hot prospect** has been misdefined as "somebody with money." This is so wrong that it costs orgs half their letters-in and loses about 95% of the income. The correct definition is (and was for 20 years) **hot prospect**=someone interested in training or processing. (FBDL 198) **2.** (Class IV Org definition) someone who had expressed an interest in training or processing. (ED 459-37 Flag) **3.** (AO-SH definition) someone who says he is coming. (ED 459-37 Flag) **4.** anyone who has recently expressed a wish to be processed or trained. (HCO PL 21 Sept 65 VI)

HOT PROSPECT LETTER REGISTRAR, **1.** the person appointed should be your most upstat **Letter Registrar** and be posted in the **Letter Registrar** Unit on the org board but should sit at a desk *next* to the ASR and write to *all* those persons advance scheduled in the reservations book. (BPL 18 Feb 73 III) **2.** the **Hot Prospect Letter Reg** is vital. She's your hottest channeller. Her whole interest is to get the person signed up fully paid and on the course on or before the scheduled date. The **Hot Prospect Letter Reg** writes to *all* persons scheduled with the aim of getting them in the org on or before their arrival data. She gives particular attention to those scheduled to arrive in 4-6 months (names are obtained from the ASR). These persons she hits hard as they produce the high income and are the most upstat. (HCO PL 18 Feb 73 IV)

HOT SHOT REG CLUB, **1.** a **club** for **registrars** of any org or franchise with officers, all AOLA **reg** personnel. A sort of honesty **club** to prevent **reges** from different orgs descending upon one person with money and pulling at him from all directions. (FBDL 151) **2.** the most senior org of each area is authorized to conduct such a **club.** The purpose of the **club** is: to help Ron raise the standard of registration through correct application of policy and to use same to resolve registration problems, difficulties and upsets encountered on the sales lines so that public make forward progress on up the bridge to Clear and OT. **Club** membership is open to all sales personnel of orgs, franchises and FOLOs (FSCs included) of that particular continent. (SO ED 306 INT)

HOT SPOT, What is a **hot spot**? Where everything is going to hell? No, not necessarily. It's where attention would save you a great deal of trouble and would make you a great deal of money. (7205C18 SO)

HOURLY EMPLOYEE, see EMPLOYEE, HOURLY.

HOUSE CAPTAIN, each Sea Org **house** has a **House Captain**, who is overall responsible for the condition of the **house**, **household** functions and **household** group activities. In the case where the shore unit has only one **house** for crew quarters, this person is automatically the Estates Officer of the unit. (FO 3176R)

HOUSEHOLD SERVICES CHIEF, chief steward. (FO 3175)

HOUSEHOLD UNIT, **1.** a separate org aboard Flag. It is the highest production **unit** on the planet as the Commodore and CS-G are the production division of the org. It provides the personal service necessary to keep all distraction off of these high speed lines. The kinds of posts available are personal services, cooking, purchasing, external logistics, driving, vehicle maintenance, construction and planning, Esto, D/Captain and more. (BO 88, 1 Oct 73) **2.** the purpose of the Commodore's **Household Unit** is to provide superlative service to the Commodore and his family, spotless quarters and all the comforts of home, aboard ship. (FO 2345) *Abbr.* HU.

HOUSEHOLD UNIT EXPENSES, expenses involved in research and command care and activities as designated by LRH Pers Comm. (FSO 74)

HOUSEHOLD UNIT PURCHASER, the **HU Purchaser purchases** for: the Commodore, CS-G and the Hubbard family. (FSO 711R) [The purchasing lines and procedures for this post are contained in BPL 14 May 1975, LRH Logistics Orders.] *Abbr.* HU Purchaser.

HOUSEKEEPER, looks after the Manor, its supplies and cleanliness. Buys all food and handles domestic accounts. Safeguards supplies and safeguards against damage and breakage. Keeps consumable supplies under lock and issues as needed. (HCO PL 18 Dec 64, *Saint Hill Org Board*)

HOUSE MEETING, the House Captain may at his own discretion call a **house meeting** of all his **house** members. **Meetings** should be held a minimum of once a week, or more often as required. Times for such is determined by the House Captain but must be outside of org working hours. Resolutions may be drawn at the **meeting**, presented to the CO and LRH Comm for approval for issue, and implemented. Such things as house decor, painting, furnishings, etc., may be decided by the group, planned and proposed in the minutes for implementation. (FO 3176R)

HOUSE ORGANIZATION, just as messes have an **organization**, so do Sea Org crew quarters. People are cared and accounted for in their quarters just as they are in their org. They are not set adrift to find their own berths as best they can or to wander around in search of living quarters. These things are provided by a set predictable system that allows planning to occur and the individual crew member to take his attention off personal worries and to allow increased org production and therefore overall bettered conditions. (FO 3176R)

HUBBARD, L. Ron **Hubbard**, Founder and Source of Dn and Scn. (BPL 13 Jul 73R)

HUBBARD ADMINISTRATOR CERTIFICATE, **1.** issued to (1) any staff member, currently on staff, who does not qualify for a Hubbard Executive Certificate; or (2) any person who has previously worked on the staff of a Scn organization no matter how briefly who does not qualify for a Hubbard Executive Certificate. (HCO PL 16 Jun 64) **2. certificate** issued to properly qualified persons who have served two or more years on the staff of an HCO or Scn organization in the **Administrative** Division and who have passed the required examination; or who have successfully completed a course in **administration** given by a Scn organization. (HCO PL 12 Aug 63)

HUBBARD ADVANCED AUDITOR, Class IV **Auditor.** This level teaches about abilities (Service Facsimiles). End result is ability to **audit** others to Grade IV Ability Release. (CG&AC 75) *Abbr.* HAA.

HUBBARD ADVANCED TECHNICAL SPECIALIST, Class IX **Auditor.** This level teaches about advanced developments. Processes taught are advanced procedures and developments since Class VIII. End result is ability to **audit advanced** procedures and **special** rundowns. (CG&AC 75) *Abbr.* HATS.

HUBBARD APPRENTICE SCIENTOLOGIST COURSE, **1.** this level teaches about elementary communication and control. Processes taught are training drills on communication and to put the student at cause over the environment

(TRs 0-4). End result is improved ability in the origination and handling of communication and in handling oneself in life situations and predicting and handling others. (CG&AC 75) **2.** this is another data **course.** It has no auditing connected with it. The "theory" part of the **course** consists of a painstaking coverage of *Dianetics: The Original Thesis* page by page. It is gone over with great thoroughness and no word is left in doubt in the student's mind. The **HAS** has a second stage **course** called the practical **course.** It uses the TRs to teach people to communicate. (HCO PL 31 May 65)

HUBBARD ASSISTANT ADMINISTRATOR, certificate issued to properly qualified persons who have served one year or more in an HCO or Scn organization in the **administrative** division and who have successfully passed the examination of a permanent staff member as issued or amended; or who has successfully completed a course in **administration** given by a Scn organization. (HCO PL 12 Aug 63)

HUBBARD ASSOCIATION OF SCIENTOLOGISTS, an organization. The response to that organization was very good. The purpose of the organization was simply to have a central point of dissemination, where the materials of Dn and Scn could be put out without any great turmoil, turbulence, vias, and to train people in the subject who wanted training, and to give people help and information, who wanted help and information. That is what the **HAS** was formed to do. (5510C08) *Abbr.* HAS.

HUBBARD ASSOCIATION OF SCIENTOLOGISTS INTERNATIONAL, 1. the company which operates all Scn organizations over the world and Saint Hill. (HCO PL 20 Feb 65) **2.** the first organization we ever had in Scn was the Office of L. Ron Hubbard. That was the old Phoenix, Arizona, office that I first put together. It eventually became **HASI.** (SH Spec 57, 6504C06) **3.** the principal Scn organization in the world is the **Hubbard Association of Scientologists International.** The **HASI** in (city) controls all Scn in (country). The **HASI** is (country's) largest mental health organization and has a dozen practitioners for every one in other mental practices. The **association** is not political in nature. It is humanitarian. (HCO Info Ltr 14 Apr 61) **4.** HCO has no interest in the number of personnel employed by **HASI** in tech or admin, this being entirely up to the Central Org officers. If **HASI** thinks it can get along with far less and still render service acceptable to HCO, then it's all up to **HASI.** HCO's primary function today is to do broad dissemination and drive business in on the Central Org by any means within HCO's power. On promotion, driving in people on the Central Org is a primary function. This does not mean individual people. It means masses of people. HCO deals in masses and mobs and **HASI** deals in individuals. HCO is a mass dissemination organization. **HASI** is an individual service organization. HCO is the "Madison Avenue" of Scn, meaning it's the advertising broad public presence unit. But "Madison Avenue" does not run the business it serves. It only makes them look brighter to the potential public. I think this gives us a new look at **HASI**-HCO relationships and their zones of responsibility. (HCO PL 28 Oct 60, *HASI-HCO Relationship Discussed*) **5.** a religious fellowship to which all the people interested in **Scn** or the higher level, higher echelon of life as a science belong. This organization (the **HASI**) was put together by myself first as the HAS and then there was a flaw in its incorporation papers (which flaw is just simply an attorney's foolishness—he didn't state accurately whether it was a profit or non-profit corporation). In order to get over that we organized the **HASI.** In other words changed its name to **Hubbard Association of Scientologists International.** By the addition of that name we got a reincorporation of it merely to clarify its corporation papers. That organization is mainly a professional organization of auditors. It still does publishing, it does handling and more important than that it has a Corporation Service Department and that handles the various business matters for a percentage of these other corporations. The **HASI** is employed by other corporations which have different boards entirely to do its business. Rather than have a big staff for the Foundation (Hubbard Dianetic Research Foundation) which handles the certificates and handles the mailing the Foundation simply hires the **HASI** staff to do this. (5410C04) **6.** the **HASI** is not a successor corporation to the HAS. The **HASI** is a religious fellowship and it is in company with and affiliated with but is not the same corporation as the Church of American Science on the one hand and the Church of Scientology on the other hand. These are three organizations which fit together with the sole and avowed purpose of doing something about the human soul, about life in general. The two churches involved there simply form the public organizations of the **HASI.** With these two corporations we form public congregations and so forth. The public would belong to one of these churches individually. But everybody managing or having anything to do with that church really on an official basis would actually be a member of the **HASI.** The public doesn't belong to the **HASI.** The public belongs to the church. (5410C04) **7.** purpose: to disseminate **Scn.** To advance and protect its membership. To hold the lines and data of **Scn** clean and clear. To educate and process people toward the goal of a civilized age on earth second to none. To survive on all dynamics. (HCO London, 9 Jan 58) *Abbr.* HASI.

HUBBARD ASSOCIATION OF SCIENTOLOGISTS INTERNATIONAL INCORPORATED, 1. (not pertinent to the U.S. offices) unless **HASI Inc.** is in full force the central organizations may not sell memberships as they will be subject to tax and other complications. Scn organizations in England, Australia and South Africa as well as Saint Hill are owned and operated by **HASI Inc.** (HCO PL 6 Nov 64) [See the reference HCO PL for a fuller explanation of **HASI Inc.**, HASI Ltd. and HASI.] **2.** all **HASI Inc.** offices are religious corporations. In the **HASI Inc.** incorporation papers the corporation is clearly designated as a "religious fellowship." (HCO PL 29 Oct 62) *Abbr.* HASI Inc.

HUBBARD ASSOCIATION OF SCIENTOLOGISTS INTERNATIONAL LIMITED, 1. unless HASI Inc. is in full force the Central Organization may not sell memberships as they will be subject to tax and other complications. It is of considerable, even vital interest to all Association Secretaries and HCO Secretaries of the UK and Commonwealth that no transfer or property, funds, business, leases or goodwill from Hubbard Association of Scientologists International, Incorporated in Arizona, has ever been made to any other corporation. No property goodwill or assets was ever transferred to **HASI Ltd.** or to any smaller company anywhere in the world. Scn organizations in England, Australia and South Africa as well as Saint Hill are owned and operated by HASI Inc. Some years ago I sought to organize **HASI Ltd.** as a public corporation to receive these assets but for some reason no non-profit status was granted it by Inland Revenue of the United Kingdom. **HASI Ltd.** is dormant. (HCO PL 6 Nov 64) **2. HASI Ltd.** is a public company, rather than a private company, and as such can advertise shares if the prospectus is okayed by the Registrar of Companies, UK. HASI Inc. does not become **HASI Ltd. HASI Ltd.** is another corporation. It will receive the assets of HASI Inc. at a date to be announced later. This will be the "transfer date." Until this date HASI Inc. continues to run as itself. (HCOB 18 Jul 60) **3.** according to general advices, **HASI Ltd.** is going forward according to schedule and will be a going concern by the 30th July. The opinion of Inland Revenue has been solicited and with some minor changes has been favorable to the corporation's having the status of non-profit. This makes the payment of income taxes in any country by any Central Organization unnecessary. There are however several steps you will have to take in order to complete this transfer from HASI to **HASI Ltd.** These steps consist of a total inventory and evaluation of all equipment, assets and materials held by each Central Organization. Also it is necessary for me to have an exact rundown of the total income from the beginning of each Central Organization to date. I also need an exact rundown of the debts and liabilities of each Central Organization. This is necessary in order to get permission from the Bank of England for the limited company to accept these liabilities. (HCO PL 27 Jun 59) *Abbr.* HASI Ltd.

HUBBARD BASIC SCIENTOLOGY AUDITOR, the graduate of the **Hubbard Basic Scientology Auditor** Course is awarded the certificate of **Hubbard Basic Scientology Auditor.** (BPL 13 Mar 74RA II)

HUBBARD BASIC SCIENTOLOGY AUDITOR COURSE, the **course** produces an **auditor** who has **basic auditing** skills in and can apply the technology of his skills to help others, and can deliver the Second Southern Africa Special Rundown. (BPL 13 Mar 74RA II)

HUBBARD BOOK AUDITOR, 1. this level teaches about application of Dn and/or Scn data in life. Processes taught are application of data in Dn and Scn **books.** End result is ability to help self and others through the application of data contained in **books** of Dn and Scn. (CG&AC 75) **2.** the offer of this certificate may be made in mailings to persons who have bought **books.** The sole requirements are that they have read the **book** and done "some" processing on another successfully. The application is for a certificate as **HBA.** (HCO PL 7 Apr 65) *Abbr.* HBA.

HUBBARD CERTIFIED AUDITOR, 1. Class II **Auditor.** This level teaches about overt acts and withholds. End result is ability to audit others to Grade II Relief Release. (CG&AC 75) **2. HCA** is ranked as the U.S. version of Commonwealth HPA. **HCA**/HPA is the certificate at Level III. (HCO PL 11 Dec 63) **3.** the certificates **Hubbard Certified Auditor** for the U.S. and Hubbard Professional Auditor for the UK and Commonwealth will continue as the professional certificate issued by Central Organizations. It is given for successful completion of an Academy **HCA**/HPA Course. This certificate is requisite for the Saint

Hill Special Briefing Course. (HCO PL 12 Aug 63) **4.** an early course taught in Scn churches only. The certificate of **HCA** (or HPA, the British equivalent) was awarded by examination only. (HCOTB 12 Sept 56) *Abbr.* HCA.

HUBBARD CHART OF HUMAN EVALUATION, **1.** application of the **human evaluation chart** permits the student to estimate with some exactness the behavior and reactions he can expect from the human beings around him and what can happen to him as a result of association with various persons. Additionally, the use of **human evaluation** permits the individual to handle and better live with other human beings. (*SOS*, p. x) **2.** on the many columns of this **chart** we find the majority of the components of the human mind and all those necessary to process an individual. (*SOS*, p. xxxiii)

HUBBARD CLEARING SCIENTOLOGIST, **1.** certificate no longer issued but converted to Hubbard Senior Scientologist. Hubbard Senior Scientologist may be given for HCA/HPA retread. (HCO PL 12 Aug 63) **2.** formerly Level IV certificate. (HCOB 23 Aug 65) *Abbr.* HCS.

HUBBARD CLEARING SCIENTOLOGIST COURSE, **1.** the academy also teaches an upper level **course** once or more a year known as the B. Scn. (**Hubbard Clearing Scientologist**) **Course.** (HCO PL 20 Dec 62) **2.** purpose: to educate auditors in the techniques and skills necessary to **clear** human beings. (HCO PL 27 Nov 59) **3.** the tapes for B. Scn and **HCS courses** are now as follows: 5th London ACC tapes, 21st U.S. supplementary tapes. These are the total data given in these units. (HCO PL 10 Mar 59) **4.** this **course** should sell well. It is an exact duplicate of the 20th ACC and should be instructed by a graduate of the 18th, 19th or 20th ACC. It is released now to bridge in the gap between ACCs. (SEC ED 18, 2 Jan 59)

HUBBARD COLLEGE OF IMPROVEMENT, (Flag) **Hubbard College of Improvement** is under the Department of Training. It supervises the OEC, FEBC, HPCSC, Mini Course Supervisors Course, and Solo. (FSO 388) *Abbr.* HCI.

HUBBARD COMMUNICATIONS OFFICE, **1.** it's in charge of the org boards, in charge of the personnel, it's in charge of hatting, it's in charge of the **communication**, which gives it **communication** lines, because an organization consists of the lines. It's in charge of inspection and it's in charge of ethics. **HCO** builds, holds, maintains, mans and controls the organization and it's the orders issue section. (FEBC 8, 7101C24 SO I) **2.** a stable point to which can be communicated **communications** and difficulties in any area and these **communications** are forwarded to the proper terminal in the organization, or an analysis is made of the difficulty and communicated to another **HCO** terminal for clarification there. In addition to that, LRH may require reports on or about a given area and it is up to the **HCO Office** to supply this information. The **HCO** should consider itself more of a troubleshooting unit than a secretarial **office.** It is true that it is an **office,** and it must be conducted precisely as an **office.** It is true that it is secretarial and it is also true that it does have the function of being an extended pair of eyes for LRH. (HCO PL 16 Sept 70 II) **3.** few people realize that **HCO** is actually a separate company. It is the worldwide comm network of Dn and Scn. As its finances and personnel are meshed in with the rest of the org, its identity does not stay visible. But note it is still called **HCO** and the rest of the divisions are called "the organization" and it is divided off on the org board. (HCO PL 7 Feb 70 II) **4. HCO** was originally organized as the Division I used to operate the org. The **HCO** Area Secretary was looked on as my secretary. (LRH ED 129 INT) **5.** (Ship Org Board) Division 1, **HCO,** is known as the Communications Division and the Third Mate is its divisional officer. (FO 1109) **6. HCO** is the justice agency of Scn and Scientologists in addition to other functions. (HCO PL 17 Mar 65 II, *Rights of a Staff Member; Students and Preclears to Justice*) **7.** this was the original **HCO,** a private unincorporated business which was taken from London when we came to Saint Hill. It became the Hubbard Association of Scientologists Inc. Worldwide Division. This HASI was an American company. HASI Inc. still owns all the property and equipment as it has never been transferred by formal board action. But this company (**HCO**) is dormant and its letterhead should never be used. (HCO PL 30 Sept 64) **8.** purpose: to be the **Office** of LRH. To handle and expedite the **communication** lines of LRH. To prepare or handle the preparation of manuscripts and other to-be-published material of Scn. To keep, use and care for LRH's office equipment. To assist the organizations of Scn and their people. To set a good example of efficiency to organizations. (HCO PL 12 Oct 62) **9. HCO** is (1) a **communications office** and (2) a technical and admin library that gives it something to communicate. (HCO PL 4 Feb 61) **10.** Central Orgs as such have a poor reputation for originating and executing new promotion. **HCO** is responsible for broad new dissemination projects. **HCO's** primary function today is to do broad dissemination and drive business in on the Central Org by any means within **HCO's** power. **HCO** is a mass dissemination organization. HASI is an individual service organization. (HCO PL 28 Oct 60, *HASI-HCO Relationship Discussed*) **11. HCO** is basically a **communications office.** This means fast relay. (HCO PL 14 Oct 59) **12. Hubbard Communications Office** is the enfranchising agency of Dn and Scn and has the say on all copyrights and trademarks, rights of materials and the issuance of publications. **HCO** is the examining and issuing agency of all certificates and awards. (*Abil 95*, 1959) *Abbr.* HCO.

HUBBARD COMMUNICATIONS OFFICE BULLETINS, 1. written by LRH only. These are the technical issue line. They are valid from first issue unless specifically cancelled. All data for auditing and courses is contained in **HCOBs.** An org needs a master file of them (and their stencil file) from which to prepare course packs. These outline the product of the org. They are distributed as indicated, usually to technical staff. They are red ink on white paper, consecutive by date. (HCO PL 24 Sept 70R) **2.** are senior to all other orders in tech. Only **HCOBs** may revise or cancel **HCOBs.** HCO PLs and **HCOBs** require passing by LRH or the full authority of International Board Members as well as the Authority and Verification Unit. (HCO PL 9 Aug 1972) **3.** the material contained in **HCO Bulletins** applies to the first dynamic—self, the individual. In applying **HCOBs** as in auditing a preclear, you see that following a certain procedure results in the remedy of a certain personal situation. Survival is the keynote of the end result. **HCOB** auditing tech increases the survival of the individual as an individual. (HCO PL 11 Apr 70) **4.** technology is covered in **HCO Bulletins. HCO Bulletins** are written by or (more rarely) for L. Ron Hubbard and are issued by **HCO** and **HCO** Secretaries. They do not require sanction by the International Board. No one else may issue or authorize an **HCO Bulletin. HCO Bulletins** are recommended technical data. Certificates are awarded on the data contained in them and violation of it can therefore cause a suspension of the certificate. This is the main power of the **HCO Bulletin.** (HCO PL 5 Mar 65 II) **5.** my priority line here is an **HCO Bulletin.** That means technical. If originated by me only it is on white paper with red ink. It must be copied by an **HCO** office on white paper with red ink. *No* copies of it must be made with any other color scheme. No other type of mimeo is permitted to use this color scheme. (HCO PL 4 Feb 61) *Abbr.* HCOB.

HUBBARD COMMUNICATIONS OFFICE EXECUTIVE SECRETARY, see HCO EXECUTIVE SECRETARY.

HUBBARD COMMUNICATIONS OFFICE LTD., this was a public corporation formed in order to handle the **communications** of another corporation, Hubbard Association of Scientologists Ltd. As the corporation it was formed to serve, HASI Ltd., is inactive, this corporation is dormant. (HCO PL 30 Sept 64) *Abbr.* HCO Ltd. See HCO WORLDWIDE.

HUBBARD COMMUNICATIONS OFFICE POLICY LETTER, 1. written by LRH only. This is a permanently valid issue of all third dynamic, org and administrative technology. These, regardless of date or age, form the know-how in running an org or group or company. The bulk of hat material is made up from **HCO PLs.** They are printed in green ink on white paper. They are filed by consecutive date. More than one issued on the same date are marked Issue I, II, III, etc. Every org must have full master and bulk files of these or it won't be able to make up hats or hat packs for staff or know what it's doing and will fail. Stencil files to replenish supplies of **HCO PLs** are also kept. It took 20 years to find out how to run orgs. It's all in **HCO PLs. HCO PLs** are distributed to all staffs or as indicated or as made up in packs. (HCO PL 24 Sept 70R) **2. HCO Policy Letters** are senior in Admin. HCO Bulletins are senior to all other orders in Tech. Only **policy letters** may revise or cancel **policy letters.** Only HCOBs may revise or cancel HCOBs. **HCO PLs** and HCOBs require passing by LRH or the full authority of International Board Members as well as the Authority and Verification Unit. (HCO PL 9 Aug 72) **3.** the data, material and procedures contained in **Policy Letters** apply to the third dynamic—the dynamic of groups. In applying **HCO Policy Letters,** you see that by following or continuing certain third dynamic procedures you remedy, handle or continue certain situations which relate to groups. Survival is the keynote of the end result. **HCO Policy Letter** third dynamic tech increases the survival of the group. (HCO PL 11 Apr 70) **4.** orders or directions in Scn for **policy:** green ink on white paper, signed by LRH. (HCO PL 13 Mar 66) **5.** a **letter** laying down **policy** continuing until cancelled by a new **policy letter.** (HCO PL 13 Feb 66 II) **6.** one which contains one or more **policies** and their explanation and application. It is issued by the **Hubbard Communications Office,** is written by L. Ron Hubbard or written (more rarely) for him, has the agreement of the International Board and is basic organizational law in organizations. A "**policy letter**" is not Scn org **policy** unless written or authorized by L. Ron Hubbard and passed as a resolution or covered by blanket resolution of the International Board and issued or published by an **HCO.** It is not **policy** if any of those steps are missing. (HCO PL 5 Mar 65 II) **7.** one which contains one or more **policies** and their explanation and application. (HCO PL 5 Mar 65 II) **8. HCO Policy Letters** are now my administrative **policy** line. They are received done in green ink on white paper. They must be copied by local **HCOs** using that exact color scheme. (HCO PL 4 Feb 61) *Abbr.* HCO PL, HCO Pol Ltr.

HUBBARD CONSULTANT, a **Hubbard Consultant** is skilled in testing, two-way comm, **consultation**, programming and interpersonal relations. This is the certificate especially awarded to persons trained to handle personnel, students and staff. These technologies and special training were developed to apply Scn auditing skills to the field of administration especially. An **HC** is not an auditor but a **consultant. HC** is a requisite for course supervisors and student consultants. (HCOB 19 Jun 71 III) *Abbr.* HC.

HUBBARD CONSULTANT RUNDOWNS, whenever a student cannot grasp or retain the data of the Data Series Policy Letters, he must be audited on the Data Series Rundown (also called the **Hubbard Consultant Rundown**). (HCO PL 15 Mar 71 II)

HUBBARD DIANETIC COUNSELOR CERTIFICATE, see HUBBARD STANDARD DIANETICS COURSE.

HUBBARD DIANETIC FOUNDATION, see HUBBARD DIANETIC RESEARCH FOUNDATION.

HUBBARD DIANETIC GRADUATE, Hubbard Dianetic Graduate certificate gives right to supervise HSDC Course. (BPL 4 Jul 69R IV) *Abbr.* HDG.

HUBBARD DIANETIC RESEARCH FOUNDATION, 1. the first organization of Dn in the United States. (5510C08) **2.** the basic organization of Dn is the **Hubbard Dianetic Research Foundation.** This organization was first put together by myself in Elizabeth, New Jersey, and duplicate directorate corporations (same directors in each state) were organized in such states as California, Illinois, Hawaii and so on. These various corporations were all the same corporation. This is the **Hubbard Dianetic Research Foundation.** This organization name was shortened by a successor corporation, the Hubbard Dianetic Foundation of Wichita, Kansas. Now that organization still kept alive this other organization (**Hubbard Dianetic Research Foundation**). Then in a rather misguided effort to push Dianetics and so forth, and because I was hounding them not to use my name, it temporarily dropped the word **Hubbard** and was called the **Dianetic Research Foundation** for the membership corporation and the Dianetic Foundation for the business corporation. These two were both interlocked and interdependent and were essentially and would have been in the eyes of the law the same corporation. That corporation handed over to the HASI an entire quitclaim and deed, a corporation title, and the members of the **Dianetic Research Foundation** recognizing of course themselves as really the **Hubbard Dianetic Research Foundation**, voted and elected me president of the corporation, and it itself became transferred. The corporation which is organized here in Arizona is a fresh set of incorporations but it is all of these corporations to date. That is the original Foundation. It's responsible for all debts, bills and everything else of the original **Foundation.** It also owns all of its materials. Now that's the **Hubbard Dianetic Research Foundation** which is the original **Foundation** and has been put back together now exactly as it was in Elizabeth, New Jersey, with the bugs out of it. The **Hubbard Dianetic Research Foundation** reincorporated in Arizona is not a duplicate directorate of anything of the HASI. The HASI is a religious fellowship. This is slightly different than the **Hubbard Dianetic Research Foundation** which is simply a corporation with a board of directors and a membership which does publishing. The HASI is a religious fellowship to which all the people interested in Scn or the higher level of life as a science belong. (5410C04) **3.** the **HDRF** does training. It trains up to the degree of HDA to Bachelor of Science in Dn and Doctor of Philosophy in Dn. There is a great similarity of training between the HASI for its basic levels of training and the **Hubbard Dianetic Research Foundation.** (5410C04) **4.** there are two corporate groups. Why do we say groups? Because each one of these organizations (**HDRF** and HASI) has certain dependencies; other affiliated organizations. If you see this as two positive groups you'll have a good grip on the entire picture of organization of this. The one group, the oldest group headed by the **Hubbard Dianetic Research Foundation** has two appendant groups. It has been in these two businesses for a long time. It was interested in civil defense and was doing things about civil defense. Those activities have been pooled together in an allied affiliate corporation known as the American Society of Civilian Defense. It knows Dn works and says so loudly. That organization stands 100% behind Dn as the only process it would even vaguely use on hysterical or distressed people. The other is the Freudian Foundation of America organized to be a free offer to any of the people in Russian-held Vienna who wish to take advantage of it. It is the only authorized agency of any kind in the United States authorized to use the name and works of Sigmund Freud. All other Freudian Foundations have no charter or franchise from the old Master. Nobody has. But we have one from the Freudian Institute of Vienna, which makes us the only legal Freudian Foundation. This organization knows that as a sequence to the great work of Sigmund Freud, Dn is the solution to psychoanalysis and it freely says so. So we have the **Hubbard Dianetic Research Foundation** being ably supported by the Freudian Foundation of America and by the American Society of Civilian Defense. (Civilian defense is simply the eight dynamics). People interested in the fields of healing who would listen to such a thing as Freudian analysis will find out they can do it better with Dn. So we have stepping stones up to an organization. The **HDRF** makes a triangle of organizations for its dissemination lines. (5410C04) **5. Hubbard Dianetic Research Foundation**, Elizabeth, New Jersey, USA. The first organization, founded by others in 1950, May. Closed 1951 and I had no control of it and the directors mismanaged it. (LRH Def. Notes) *Abbr.* HDRF.

HUBBARD DIANETIC SUPERVISOR COURSE, the **Hubbard Dianetic Supervisor Course** is taught only in official Scn organizations; it is very tough with lots of drilling. The student graduates as a Hubbard Dianetic Graduate and he, and only he, is authorized to supervise a Hubbard Standard Dianetics Course, a **Hubbard Dianetic Supervisor Course**, or a Hubbard Practicing Dianeticist Course. (BPL 1 Jun 69R II)

HUBBARD EXECUTIVE, certificate issued to properly qualified Hubbard Administrators who have successfully completed the studies required. (HCO PL 12 Aug 63)

HUBBARD EXECUTIVE CERTIFICATE, **certificate** issued to: (1) any staff member currently on staff who can claim to have served on an **executive** post in a Scn organization for a period of at least one year, (2) any person who has previously worked in a Scn org who can claim to have served on an **executive** post for at least one year. (HCO PL 16 Jun 64)

HUBBARD EXPLORATIONAL COMPANY LTD., **1.** the **Hubbard Explorational Company Ltd.** is a **company** formed by me in England with the address of Saint Hill. (FO 42) **2.** the Sea Organization is under the corporate name of the **Hubbard Explorational Company Ltd.** now owned by C of S of California. **HEC Ltd.** is a supported subsidiary of C of S of California. (FO 1) **3. Hubbard Exploration Co. Ltd.** was the owner of the **Apollo.** It was a British Company. The ship was later sold to Operation and Transport Corporation of Panama, a Panama company so the flag and name had to be changed. (OODs 18 Apr 69) *Abbr.* HEC Ltd.

HUBBARD EXTENSION COURSE GRADUATE, the **Hubbard Extension Course** comprises this level. It teaches about the basics of Dn and Scn. Given by mail, the end result is an ability to understand the fundamentals of life and existence and improve your own life. (CG&AC 75)

HUBBARD GRADUATE ASSIST SPECIALIST COURSE, the **course** produces a professional auditor who can and does apply **assist** technology to persons under stress, relieving them and speeding their recovery. (BPL 8 May 74)

HUBBARD GRADUATE AUDITOR, **1.** Class VII **Auditor.** Only available to Sea Org or five-year contracted org staff. This level teaches about power processing and review auditing. Processes taught are Power and Power Plus processes. End result is an ability to audit others to Grade V and VA Power Release. (CG&AC 75) **2.** certificate issued for successful completion of the Saint Hill Special Briefing Course. (HCO PL 12 Aug 63) **3.** the award of **HGA, Hubbard Graduate Auditor,** is intended to designate **auditors** who have considerable experience and whose reputation is well known but who do not necessarily have credits and attendance at the Doctorate Schools. An **HGA** is senior to HCA and HPA and the Doctor of Scn degree is senior to **HGA.** (PAB 6) **4.** this course would be taught as an Advanced Clinical Unit, preferably by LRH only. It would consist of the equivalent of a three week intensive, two weeks of high school indoctrination so as to be able to cope with any kind of case and a week of coaching on processes. This is actually a new type of Advanced Clinical Course only so far as its actual pattern is concerned. It would be instructed by LRH. At the end of course by examination the certificate of **Hubbard Graduate Auditor** or Doctor of Scn abroad would be issued. (HCOTB 12 Sept 56) *Abbr.* HGA.

HUBBARD GRADUATE DIANETIC SPECIALIST, Expanded Dianetics Auditor. This level teaches about Expanded Dianetics. Processes taught are Expanded Dn basics, Ex Dn Set-ups, R3R of intentions and purposes. Assessments and R3R to handle the present environment, past auditing, valences, emotional stress, chronic somatics, wants handled, hidden standards, responsibility, Metalosis Rundown, PTS

Rundown, assists and repairs and C/Sing on Ex Dn, against the OCA. End result is ability to audit others to Expanded Dianetics Case Completion. (CG&AC 75) *Abbr.* HGDS.

HUBBARD GRADUATE SCIENTOLOGIST, D. Scn. (Commonwealth) or **Hubbard Graduate Scientologist** (U.S.). Issued by HCO only on its own behalf after meeting requirements stipulated for any given course. (HCO PL 12 Feb 61) *Abbr.* HGS.

HUBBARD GUIDANCE CENTER, **1.** that department of the Technical Division of a Scn Church which delivers auditing. Department 12, Division 4. (BTB 12 Apr 72R) **2.** the HGC is headed by the Director of Processing, under whom come all individual cases (public and staff). **HGC** quality must be high and stay high. It is the highest technical quality in the continent. The **HGC** was born to show field auditors the results that could be obtained, and lived on to carry the full burden of successful auditing around the world. (HCO PL 20 Dec 62) **3.** purpose: to do more for people's health and ability than has ever before been possible and to give the best auditing possible. To help people. (HCO PL 12 Oct 62) *Abbr.* HGC.

HUBBARD HELP SPECIALIST COURSE, purpose: to get the special help technology that was originally developed by LRH, for Africa, widely known and applied. The graduate of this **course** is awarded the certificate of **Hubbard Help Specialist.** (HCO PL 3 Dec 73)

HUBBARD INTEGRITY PROCESSING SPECIALIST COURSE, purpose: to train the student to the level of an **Integrity Processing Specialist** who knows and can apply the tech flublessly and has the ability to increase a person's personal **integrity** and trust in himself and others by freeing him of past overts, withholds and missed withholds. The graduate of this **course** is awarded the provisional **Hubbard Integrity Processing Specialist** Certificate. (BPL 24 Dec 72R) *Abbr.* HIPSC.

HUBBARD PRACTICAL SCIENTOLOGISTS, the Academy trains **Hubbard Practical Scientologists** and Hubbard Professional (HPA/HCA) Auditors. The **practical** course is the same as the old professional course except that it is for people "who don't want to practice Scn professionally." The professional course is a tougher version with more requirements. (HCO PL 20 Dec 62) *Abbr.* HPS.

HUBBARD PRACTICING DIANETICIST COURSE, **1.** the **Hubbard Practicing Dianeticist Course**, brought into existence by LRH, has as its textbook *Dianetics Today* by L. Ron Hubbard, which contains all the developments of **Dn** since 1950. The **course**, which is three weeks long, full time, has *no* prerequisites and is jam-packed with a lot of doingness. A student upon completion of the **HPDC** can go out into the field or join staff and audit **Dn**, fully qualified to do so. (SO ED 411 INT) **2.** this **course** can be taught in Class IV Orgs, Forming Orgs, Missions, and Dianetic Counseling Groups. It is based on the new LRH book, *Dianetics Today*, and teaches the student to use **Dn** to make people well and happy. There are no prerequisites to the **course.** The graduate of this **course** is awarded the provisional certificate of **Hubbard Practicing Dianeticist** and qualifies for the Dn Internship, Dn C/S Course and any other course for which the HSDC is a pre-requisite. Certificates are awarded by the Qual Division of an official Scn org only. (BPL 1 Jun 69R II) *Abbr.* HPDC.

HUBBARD PROFESSIONAL AUDITOR, **1.** Class III **Auditor.** This level teaches about freedom (ARC and ARC breaks). End result is ability to audit others to Grade III Freedom Release. (CG&AC 75) **2.** HCA is ranked as the U.S. version of Commonwealth **HPA.** HCA/**HPA** is the certificate at Level III. (HCO PL 11 Dec 63) **3.** the certificates Hubbard Certified Auditor for the U.S. and **Hubbard Professional Auditor** for the UK and Commonwealth will continue as the **professional** certificate issued by Central Organizations. It is given for successful completion of an academy HCA/**HPA** Course. This certificate is requisite for the Saint Hill Special Briefing Course. (HCO PL 12 Aug 63) **4.** HCA/**HPA** must cover all types of processing and theory. Clearing a student is not the province of HCA/**HPA.** Teaching how to clear is the emphasis. If they get Clear it's incidental. They're all auditors in HCA/**HPA.** (HCOB 21 Jan 58) *Abbr.* HPA.

HUBBARD PROFESSIONAL COURSE SUPERVISOR, the graduate of the **Hubbard Professional Course Supervisor** Course is awarded the certificate of **Hubbard Professional Course Supervisor.** (BPL 22 Jan 72R-3) *Abbr.* HPCS.

HUBBARD PROFESSIONAL COURSE SUPERVISOR COURSE, **1.** the **course** trains the student to be a real pro in theory and practical **course supervision** and an expert in the use of **course supervisor** tools so that he can produce **course** graduates who efficiently and fully apply what they have studied. (BPL 22 Jan 72R)

2. makes a real pro in theory and practical **supervision.** The graduate is an expert in training auditors, C/Ses, supervisors. (SO ED 376 INT) *Abbr.* HPCSC.

HUBBARD PROFESSIONAL SALESMANSHIP COURSE, the purpose of the **Hubbard Professional Salesmanship Course** is to fully train **sales** personnel of all categories on **sales** technology using Scn study technology and so produce a crackerjack super **salesman** who can sell any service or product. (BPL 5 Jul 74 XVII)

HUBBARD QUALIFIED SCIENTOLOGIST, 1. teaches about co-auditing and how to handle other people with group auditing. Processes taught are TRs 0 to 4 and 6 to 9, co-auditing on CCHs, Op Pro by Dup and Self Analysis Lists. End result is personal case improvement in oneself and ability to handle others with group processing. (CG&AC 75) 2. this course is a basic course in the fundamentals of Scn technology and gives a gradient of application of a few vital principles. This course, particularly its TRs, can be used to get a person off drugs or to help a person who has been on drugs dry out. (BPL 21 Oct 71RA IV) 3. its texts are *Dianetics: Evolution of a Science* and *Dianetics: The Modern Science of Mental Health.* There is no auditing on the theory course and no-co-auditing as we know it on any part of either one, theory or practical. Therefore the auditing part of *Dianetics: The Modern Science of Mental Health* is not covered in the course. These texts are read to the students and clarified. Examples are asked for. The student must learn to think in these principles. The practical course consists of the body steering drill and the body mimcry process. A feature of this course is group processing. (HCO PL 31 May 65) 4. Class I—comm course, upper indoc, assists, 8C, havingness, trio. (HCO PL 23 Sept 64) *Abbr.* HQS.

HUBBARD RECOGNIZED SCIENTOLOGIST, Class Zero Auditor. This level teaches about communication. End result is ability to audit others to Grade Zero Communications Release. (CG&AC 75) *Abbr.* HRS.

HUBBARD SCIENTOLOGY GRADUATE, a certificate issued before the class certificates were worked out and is equivalent to Class VI. (MSH Def. Notes) *Abbr.* HSG.

HUBBARD SCIENTOLOGY RESEARCH FOUNDATION, formed with the purpose of receiving donations, gifts, dues, etc., and then disposing of such accumulated funds as grants, loans or gifts to further Scn research, in accordance with its aims and purposes. Any monies remitted to this proposed foundation pending its formation should be made payable to the "L. Ron Hubbard Trustee Account." (HCO PL 26 Sept 62) [The above HCO PL was cancelled by BPL 10 Oct 75 IV.]

HUBBARD SCIENTOLOGY STUDENT, the *Basic Study Manual* Course comprises this level. It teaches about study. Processes taught are application of Scn **study** technology. End result is an ability to **study.** (CG&AC 75)

HUBBARD SENIOR COURSE SUPERVISOR, the graduate of the **Hubbard Senior Course Supervisor** Course (HSCSC) is awarded the certificate of **Hubbard Senior Course Supervisor.** (BPL 8 Aug 73R) *Abbr.* HSCS.

HUBBARD SENIOR COURSE SUPERVISOR COURSE, 1. a new **course** for Saint Hill Orgs. On the **HSCSC** the highly developed techniques of auditor training (including electronic attest tapes) are incorporated into **supervisor** training, making a **supervisor** who is as competent in his own field as the world's best auditors are in theirs. The **HSCSC** covers the total expertise of the technology of **supervising.** Students on the **HSCSC** learn to handle each student as an individual, to find and handle exactly what that individual student needs to have handled at that time, and ensure rapid and successful progress on course. The **HSCSC** student learns to recognize his product—a student who can really apply the materials he has studied—and to know when he has or doesn't have such a student on course. (FBDL 328) 2. the primary intention of this **course** is to produce at Saint Hills excellent **supervisors** for Class IV Orgs, and thus its major public is contracted staff members of orgs. The **course** however is open to franchise staff members and any other public person wishing to take it. (FO 3362) *Abbr.* HSCSC.

HUBBARD SENIOR EXECUTIVE BRIEFING COURSE, 1. the name for the new admin **course** above the level of FEBC. (COLRHED 714-1) 2. DSEC. (COLRHED 417) 3. suggested material for the new grade above FEBC: investigatory tech, stat management, causative leadership, or retread of these if already done plus apprenticeships, then DSEC and finally an AVU course. (COLRHED 417)

HUBBARD SENIOR EXECUTIVE COURSE, the course material is all policy issued since August 1967 up to the date the checksheet is approved at Flag. The **HSEC** should commence immediately upon completion of the OEC, as this more recent policy modifies data on the OEC. (FO 2112) *Abbr.* HSEC.

HUBBARD SENIOR SCIENTOLOGIST, Class VI auditor. This level teaches about the full practical application of **Scn** grades, repair, set-ups, assists and special cases tech up to Class VI. End result is a superb auditor with full philosophic and technical command of materials to Level VI. (CG&AC 75) *Abbr.* HSS.

HUBBARD SERVICE SPECIALIST, the certificate awarded at the end of the Hubbard Professional Salesmanship Course. (HCO PL 20 Mar 73) [The above HCO PL was cancelled by BPL 10 Oct 75 XI.]

HUBBARD SOLO AUDITOR, successful completion of the **Solo Auditor** Course entitles the graduate to the certificate of **Hubbard Solo Auditor.** (BPL 12 Dec 71RC)

HUBBARD SPECIALIST OF STANDARD TECH, Class VIII Case Supervisor. Class VIII C/S Course teaches about C/Sing of 100% **standard tech** and OT C/Sing. Processes taught are Class VIII procedures, all case set-up actions, all processes and corrective actions, OT processes and reviews. End result is flawless case supervision of all cases. (CG&AC 75) *Abbr.* HSST.

HUBBARD STANDARD DIANETICS CASE SUPERVISOR COURSE, the **Dn C/S Course** is given only in official Scn organizations. The student learns the precise tech of Dn C/Sing. He graduates as a **Hubbard Standard Dianetics Case Supervisor** (provisional). After completion of the Dn C/S Internship, the student is awarded the permanent certificate of **Hubbard Standard Dianetics Case Supervisor.** (BPL 1 Jun 69R II)

HUBBARD STANDARD DIANETICS COURSE, 1. the **course** teaches about the human mind, mental image pictures, the time track, locks, secondaries, engrams. Processes taught are **standard Dn** auditing and **Dn** assists. End result is an ability to restore or bring others to complete health and happiness. Certificate is Hubbard Dianetic Counselor (HDC). (CG&AC 75) **2.** this course produces a **standard Dn** auditor who understands and applies the technology of **Dn** to make people well and happy. (BPL 10 Oct 74R) **3.** the **HSDC** may be taught in any official Scn organization, mission or Dianetic Counseling Group by a qualified person. On this **course**, the student is trained to be a highly competent **standard Dn** auditor. The certificate for this **course** is the Hubbard Dianetic Counselor certificate. The graduate of this **course** is *not* qualified to teach an **HSDC.** (BPL 1 Jun 69R II) *Abbr.* HSDC.

HUBBARD STANDARD TECHNICAL SPECIALIST, Class VIII Auditor. This level teaches about exact handling of all cases to 100% result, **specializes** in OT processes and reviews. Processes taught are Class VIII procedures, all case set-up actions, all processes and corrective actions, OT processes and reviews. End result is ability to handle all cases to 100% result. (CG&AC 75) *Abbr.* HSTS.

HUBBARD TRAINED SCIENTOLOGIST, Class I Auditor. This level teaches about problems. End result is ability to audit others to Grade I Problems Release. (CG&AC 75) *Abbr.* HTS.

HUBBARD VALIDATED AUDITOR, 1. Class V Auditor. This level teaches about chronological development of Scn with full theory and application. Processes taught are all Scn Grades 0 to IV processes, progress programs, assists, advance program processes. End result is ability to **audit** others to all Expanded Lower Grade Releases. (CG&AC 75) **2.** Class V reviews all the classes and retrains where necessary and awards permanent classification for all the lower certificates as well as Class V. (*Aud 8* UK) *Abbr.* HVA.

HUMAN EMOTION AND REACTION, the counter **emotions** and **reactions** which aberrated **human** beings express when they are guided toward survival objectives. They are usually below 2.0 on the Tone Scale. (LRH Def. Notes) *Abbr.* HE & R.

HUMAN ENGINEERING, it's adapting the machinery to fit the person. It's adapting machinery and spatial arrangements and desks and chairs and things like that. You'll find somebody who makes mistakes consistently at typing has a tired back because they're sitting on some kind of weird chair or an old box. So the adjustment of the machinery and spatial arrangements to the people who are operating it is important. You can also adjust the guy to the machinery. You don't necessarily adjust him so that he can run a very uncomfortable set-up. (ESTO 12, 7203C06 SO II)

HUMANITARIAN OBJECTIVE, the **humanitarian objective** is to create a safe environment in which the engram of the fourth dynamic can be audited out. (FO 977)

HUMOR, laughter is rejection, actually. And **humor** you will find usually deals with one or another out-point put in such a way that the reader or audience can reject it. (HCO PL 30 Sept 73 II)

HYGIENE OFFICER, a new post is that of **Hygiene Officer** under MO in Div 5. The MO cares for sick bodies and the **Hygiene Officer** cares for the inspection and correction of any environmental threat to the crew's health including inspection of all food stuffs brought aboard. (FO 2169)

HYMN OF ASIA, an Eastern poem by L. Ron Hubbard. This poem for years has circulated from hand to hand. The poem speaks of Mettaya and how the goals of man (also being the goals of the author) will be achieved. [The *Hymn of Asia* was published in January 1975.] (FBDL 412)

HYPHEN, HCOB lists, Executive Directives, Ethics Orders, Project Orders, Conditions Orders, Flag Conditions Orders, Evaluations, Flag Bureau Data Letters, and all such mimeo issues that carry a number must be so numbered that two or more issues that refer to the same situation carry the same number plus a **hyphen** and number (-1 or -2) so they can be referred back by the reader to the original. Example: a Committee of Evidence, let us say, is No. 1304. The findings of that Comm Ev are not given a new number. The findings are No. 1304-1. If a Review Comm Ev is then done, it is then numbered No. 1304-2. The reader at once knows (with the **hyphen** and 2) that two earlier issues exist (original and -1) and what the number is. (HCO PL 2 May 72)

Hymn of Asia

I

I & R FORM 1, HCO PL 6 October 1970, *Inspection of Low Stats.* It is the duty of Dept 3 **Inspection and Reports** to inspect any area or person in the org who (a) fails to turn in a stat, (b) whose current stat is low or (c) whose stat is down trending. In the case of a divisional stat one of these forms is made for every person in that division or its senior. The intention of this inspection is to "hat don't hit" personnel. (HCO PL 6 Oct 70)

IDEALIZATION, the better side of life or persons or dreams or hopes. (HCO PL 7 Aug 72)

IDEALIZED SCENE, in white PR the **idealized scene** is the way the PR wants the scene to be praised by a public. (HCO PL 7 Aug 72)

IDEAL SCENE, 1. the entire concept of an **ideal scene** for any activity is really a clean statement of its purpose. (HCO PL 5 Jul 70) **2.** the state of affairs envisioned by policy or the improvement of even that. (HCO PL 29 Feb 72 II)

IDÉE FIXE, see FIXED IDEAS.

IDENTICAL, two or more facts or things that have all their characteristics in common with one another. (HCO PL 26 Apr 70R)

IDENTIFICATION, 1. the inability to evaluate difference in time, location, form, composition or importance. (HCOB 24 Jan 59) **2. identification** is a monotone assignment of importance. (HCOB 24 Jan 59)

IDENTITIES ARE IDENTICAL, a plus-point. Not similar or different. (HCO PL 3 Oct 74)

IDIOT METER, the **idiot meter** has been in the works since 1952—an E-**meter** which shows a red light on a read and stays lit until the read is cleared. Maybe we'll have it this year or 1975 or 2000. (HCO PL 17 Sept 62)

IDLE REPORT, staff member **report** of the **idleness** of equipment or personnel which should be in action. (HCO PL 1 May 65)

ILLEGAL, 1. contrary to statistics or policy. (BPL 9 Aug 71R I) **2.** not on-policy or approved program (BPL 9 Aug 71R I) **3.** off-policy, off-program (BPL 9 Aug 71R I)

ILLEGAL EXPENSES, shall be defined as: (a) work and/or goods ordered or bill incurred *prior* to approval by Finance of a Red Purchase Order stating the *exact* cost involved in the cycle; (b) work or goods ordered resulting in a bill in excess of the exact approved amount of the Red Purchase Order covering it; (c) overexpenditure on vital **expenses** imputable to unreal requirements presented at the previous Financial Planning Committee by the person responsible for the overexpenditure. (FO 2694)

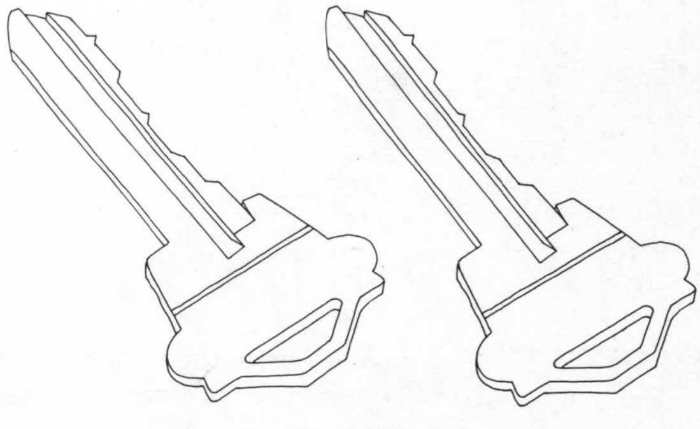

Identical

ILLEGAL ORDER, 1. one contrary to existing issues. (FO 2740) 2. any statement or advice of whatever kind which is not connected with an evaluated program shall be classed as an **illegal order.** (CBO 300RA) 3. **orders** that are off-policy and contrary to existing orders and policy issued by a senior authority, or **orders** issued without a proper passed evaluation. (ED 367-1 Flag)

ILLNESSES, **illnesses** are protests against life. (SH Spec 58, 6109C26)

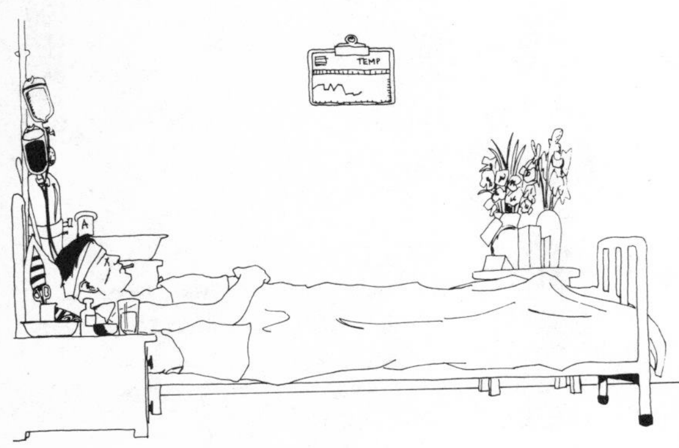

Illness

ILLOGIC, **illogic** occurs when one or more data is misplaced into the wrong body of data for it. An example would be "Los Angeles smog was growing worse so we fined New York." That is pretty obviously a misplace. (HCO PL 23 Jun 70)

IMAGE, representation or reproduction of a person or thing, painted, drawn, photographed, etc.; exact likeness; the concept of a person held by a specific or general public. (BPL 13 Jul 73R)

Image

IMAGE STUDY, an analysis of the image that a company and/or its products presents to consumers from the consumers' viewpoint.

IMAGINE, to be able to think creatively and create **images.** (HCO PL 7 Aug 72)

IMMEDIATE DELIVERY, this means **immediate** no-backlog **delivery** to all fully paid pcs and students. (SO ED 161-2 INT)

IMMEDIATE FAMILY, normally it is taken to mean wife, husband or children of the professional auditor. (HCO PL 29 May 62)

IMMEDIATE REGISTRAR, the Department of Promotion and Registration is divided into three distinct categories—present time, past and future. There are three types of registrars which handle these three categories (the **Immediate Registrar,** the Assistant Registrar, the Letter Registrar). The **Immediate Registrar** is mainly concerned with present time prospects. She answers any questions and handles any problems of those people who want auditing or training in present time. (SEC ED 66, 30 Jan 59)

IMPACT, an advertising term referring to the amount of impingement an advertisement has on the public it is aimed at.

IMPACT TEST, a method of measuring the amount of impingement an advertisement has by discovering the amount of it that people remember.

IMPERSONAL ACCOUNT, see PERSONAL ACCOUNT.

IMPINGEMENT, enough jolt to attract attention. (HCO PL 12 Nov 69)

Impingement

IMPORTER, a merchant who purchases goods from foreign countries and imports them for domestic sale and use.

IMPREST, 1. a loan or advancement of money especially of public or government funds for the purpose of performing a service for the government. 2. a fund or account especially a petty cash fund that contains an initial usually fixed sum of money which is used as needed and is periodically restored to its original balance.

IMPROPER DISPATCH, **1.** by **improper** we don't mean insulting or obscene. We mean: (a) has nothing to do with the person to whom it is sent or forwarded to, or (b) is already covered by policy which should be known to the originator or the forwarding person. (HCO PL 17 Nov 64) **2.** one which hasn't any business on the lines. (HCO PL 17 Nov 64)

IN, **1.** things which should be there and are or things that should be done and are, are said to be **in**, i.e. "We got scheduling **in.**" (HCOB 21 Sept 70) **2.** it is said that its (an organization's) ethics, tech and admin must be **in**, which means they must be properly done, orderly and effective. (LRH Def. Notes)

INACTIVE FILES, (Central Files) **inactive files** are simply those **files** which are not members or prospects. (HCO PL 8 Apr 65)

INADEQUATE PUBLIC RELATIONS, see PERFECT PUBLIC RELATIONS.

IN-AND-OUT, buying and selling the same stock within a very short time in the interest of quick profits rather than dividends or long-term growth.

In-Basket

IN-BASKET, all personnel assigned a desk and a specific stationary working space are to have a stack of three baskets. The top **basket**, labelled **"in,"** should contain those items and dispatches still to be looked at. The middle basket, labelled "pending," is to contain those items which have been looked at, but which cannot be dealt with immediately. The bottom basket, labelled "out," is to contain those items which have been dealt with and are now ready for distribution into the comm lines again, or to files, etc. (HCO PL 30 Mar 66)

INCENTIVE, something that acts to motivate a person toward the performance of some duty or action. The lowest incentive is represented by money and the highest is duty according to the scale of motivation.

IN-CHARGE, **1.** these head units inside sections. (HCO PL 13 Mar 66) **2.** an **in-charge** would be the head of a sub-section or something like that. It's like Address **In-Charge**. That's the first and lowest executive rating. (SH Spec 61, 6505C18) **3.** we will also use another term, **in-charge**, such as "Officer **In-charge** of Film Unit 31" who will, on detached duty, be considered as having the same status as a "Master" or "Commanding Officer." (BO 34, 16 Jun 67)

INCOME, **1.** what is made by the cooperative coordinated efforts of a group in exchange for their delivered goods or services. Often done by the group beating the head in of guys who goof and insisting on quality hat wearing in the group. (OODs, 28 Feb 75) **2.** where a Day Org and a Foundation are operating on the same premises, the definition which is used to determine the **income** of each org is: the org that will deliver the service gets the **income**, regardless of the time of day and night when it is taken in. (BPL 11 Aug 72R II) **3. income** is what it takes to provide fuel, supplies, uniforms, bonuses, allowances, food. (OODs 8 May 72) **4.** money. (BPL 28 May 71R) **5.** the position in a station taken by an arriving communication. (*HTLTAE*, p. 121)

INCOME, 1. the sum total of money that a company or business receives from all sources as a result of business transactions; also called gross income. 2. what one receives such as money or a useful exchange as a result of services rendered, a job done, interest on capital, profit from the buying and selling of something, etc.

INCOME AND EXPENDITURE ACCOUNT, **1.** an **account** covering a particular financial period and which records the following: on the right-hand side or credit side, the value of the mest and service particles outflowed or sold by the organization in the period concerned, i.e. the value earned by the organization in the period. On the left-hand side or debit side, the value of mest and service particles inflowed and used up by the organization for the period concerned. If the value of the outflow exceeds the inflow side, then there is profit; if the value of the inflow is greater, then there is a loss. (BPL 14 Nov 70 III) **2.** the **I&E A/C** shows how much value you received or gave out during a period. The **income** side of the **I&E A/C** is a summary of everything to do with the **Income** Dept. The **expenditure** side of the **I&E A/C** is a summary of everything to do with the Disbursements Dept. The **I&E A/C** shows such things as the amount of depreciation on your assets, and the amount of bad debts written off. These things have not been paid out in money but they are still an **expenditure.** To reflect reality, the **I&E A/C** must show how the values of each item have changed during the period. After allowing for depreciation and writing off bad debts, etc., add up the two sides of the **I&E A/C.** If the **income** side totals more than the **expenditure** side, then you have made a profit—real profit in terms of value not just an apparent money profit. (HCO PL 10 Oct 70 I) *Abbr.* I&E A/C.

INCOME DIVISION, 1. two Accounts Divisions are created. These are the **Income Division** and the Disbursement Division. A folder is made for every organization or person who pays HCO WW money. The **Income Division** sees that statements, pre-addressed by Address on proper envelopes, go out to each foldered person or organization once each month. All invoicing is done by the **Income Division.** Notice of all bank payments paid in go to **Income Division** and all bank statements. The **Income Division** retains and has all invoicing machines but no disbursing machine. (HCO PL 6 Jul 61) **2.** the **Income Div** is a recording, compiling and billing section, and attends to banking and bank records. (HCO PL 16 Oct 61)

INCOME NOTE COLLECTIONS SUMMARY, the **Collections** Section of the Department of Income submits to the Ad Council a form called the **Income Note Collections Summary.** This form carries an amount for cash **collectible** from notes past due and the amount of notes that are apparently uncollectible. The total is added into grand total of credit advanced. It gives the total of payments received during the month past (the 1st to the last day of the month). It gives the number of statements mailed in the month just past. It gives the number of persons with overdue notes who have been handed over to the Director of Clearing and passed on to Field Staff Members. It gives the number of notes to date given to lawyers for **collection** that remain uncollected. This **Income Note Collections Summary** is placed in the hands of the Advisory Council on the second Tuesday of each month. (HCO PL 26 Nov 65R)

INCOME OFFICER, (Gung-Ho Group) the **Income Officer** cashiers and receives and bills for any **income** owed. (HCO PL 2 Dec 68)

INCOME POLICING, to **police** something means, "to control, regulate, keep in order, administer." **Policing income** ensures that the org is collecting the **income** from the services that it delivers, and that all org **income** is channelled into Treasury and into the bank without delays. If you follow a particle of money through the org, you see that it gets into the org, gets exchanged for a service and gets out of the org or into reserves. There is a definite routing for money. If the org fails to collect the money for the service that it delivers the exchange does not occur and there is lost **income.** If the money comes in but does not get to Treasury and for any reason gets side-tracked on the org lines, there is again some lost **income.** Through income **policing** actions, the Treasury Secretary ensures that the correct exchange does occur between the public and the org, and that the org does receive the **income** expected. (BPL 1 Feb 72 I)

INCOME SECTION, the **Income Section** invoices all monies received on the appropriate machines and designates what each amount is for. The **Income Section** also posts all receipts in ledgers, one for each company concerned, furnishes breakdowns of **income** of various types when required, keeps a firm record of every debtor and a file on each debtor and sends out monthly formal statements to each debtor. (HCO PL 6 May 64)

INCOME SHEETS, weekly reports are required from all service departments. They are made on large sheets labelled **Income Sheets.** The **sheets** are compiled by the department heads from the yellow invoice copies which are collected by their departments as proof of payment before delivering a service or item sold. All invoices are simply listed in numerical sequence on the **Income Sheet,** with the date, name of the customer and details of service or item sold. The amount of the invoice is entered in the appropriate column, whether cash payment, debit, credit, or no-charge invoice. The **Income Sheets** are the basic element of an internal income policing system. (BPL 1 Feb 72RA)

INCOME SOURCES SUMMARY, each week your FBO fills in a report called the **Income Sources Summary.** This report shows in what areas geographically you are selling and not selling. It also shows what is being sold. (HCO PL 1 Feb 72R III) [The above HCO PL has been replaced with BPL 1 Feb 72RA.]

INCOMES POLICY, refers to a government being able to intercede in the free negotiation of pay rates by imposing wage freezes to hold down inflation.

INCOME STATEMENT, same as Profit and Loss Statement.

INCOME TAX, a government tax on the earnings of a person, corporation, company or other income making unit. Often a government will allow a certain level of income to remain tax free but once that level is exceeded, income tax is imposed.

IN-COMPANY TRAINING, see TRAINING, IN-COMPANY.

INCOMPETENCE, being competent means the ability to control and operate the things in the environment and the environment itself. When you see things broken down around the mechanic who is responsible for them, he is plainly exhibiting his **incompetence**—which means his inability to control those things in his environment and adjust the environment for which he is responsible—motors. **Incompetence**—lack of know-how, inability to control—makes things go wrong. (HCO PL 30 Dec 70)

INCOMPLETE STAFF WORK, 1. if you are mad at your boss you can always ruin him with **incomplete staff work.** You forward him a fragment of alarming data without collecting the whole picture. This makes him do a full job of information collection. You give him no recommended solution. This makes him have to achieve a solution by remote examination of data; then you make him issue arbitrary and forceful orders that may ARC break (upset) some area and hurt his reputation. (HCO PL 21 Nov 62) **2.** it is **incomplete** because I have to complete it by (1) assembling the data necessary for a solution; (2) dreaming up the solution based on written data only; (3) issuing orders rather than approving orders. (HCO PL 21 Nov 62)

INCORPORATE, to form into a legal **corporation.** (BPL 9 Mar 74)

INCORPORATION, an act of **incorporating** or the state of being **incorporated.** (BPL 9 Mar 74)

INCORRECT CONDITIONS, a type of dev-t where **incorrect conditions** are assigned or assumed with consequent ball up of lines. (HCO PL 27 Jan 69)

INCORRECTLY INCLUDED DATUM, a switch intended for a house put into an airplane electrical system cuts out at 30,000 feet due to the wrong metal to withstand cold and there goes the airplane. A part from one class of parts is included wrongly in another class of parts. So there is an **incorrectly included datum** which is a companion to the omitted datum as an out-point. (HCO PL 23 Jun 70)

Incorrectly Included Datum

INCORRECT ORGANIZATION, a type of dev-t where the comm system or procedures are not **organized** so as to be easily used. They are either not **organized** at all or are made too complex to be useful. (HCO PL 27 Jan 69)

INDEMNIFY, 1. to compensate for the amount of loss, damage or injury to something. 2. to insure or secure something against possible injury, damage, destruction or loss.

INDEMNITY, 1. compensation for the amount of loss, damage or injury to something. 2. insurance or security protecting against possible injury, damage, destruction or loss.

INDENTURE, 1. a contract binding a person to work or serve another for a certain time such as an apprenticeship training agreement. 2. a written agreement or contract which originally was in duplicate with both copies having identically notched or indented edges for easy recognition of authenticity. 3. a contract or agreement between two or more people which lays down reciprocal obligations and privileges such as a lease or rental agreement.

INDENTURED APPRENTICESHIP, see APPRENTICESHIP, INDENTURED.

INDEPENDENT, a business which is not owned, controlled or associated with a larger group or chain of similar businesses such as an independent retail store; one that stands alone and is self-supporting.

INDEX NUMBER, a number that shows changes in magnitude, as of prices, wages, sales, employment, etc., at a given time, relative to the magnitude of a specified standard, usually stated as 100.

INDICATOR, 1. a visible manifestation which tells one a situation analysis should be done. An **indicator** is the little flag sticking out that shows there is a possible situation underneath that needs attention. Some **indicators** about orgs or its sections would be—dirty or not reporting or going insolvent or complaint letters or any non-optimum datum that departs from the ideal. (HCO PL 15 May 70 II) **2.** something that signals an approaching change rather than finding the change is already present and confirmed. (HCO PL 29 Mar 65 II)

Indicator (Def. 1)

INDICATORS, BUSINESS, statistics which may affect business levels. These are grouped under the three basic titles of leaders, coincidents and laggers. Leaders predict future changes, coincidents synchronize with or serve to verify current business activities and laggers apply to relationships or factors which become evident in retrospect.

INDIRECT COSTS, see COSTS, INDIRECT.

INDIRECT DEMAND, see DEMAND, INDIRECT.

INDIRECT EXPENSES, general business expenses such as rent, utilities, taxes, insurance, etc., not charged to one department or operation but apportioned equitably throughout an organization.

INDIRECT LABOR, see LABOR, INDIRECT.

INDIRECT LABOR COSTS, see COSTS, INDIRECT LABOR.

INDIRECT MATERIAL, see MATERIAL, INDIRECT.

INDIRECT MATERIAL COSTS, see COSTS, INDIRECT MATERIAL.

INDIRECT REVIEW, see REVIEW, INDIRECT.

INDIRECT TAX, 1. a tax paid by a consumer in the way of higher prices for taxed goods, especially where a manufacturer or importer passes the burden of his taxes on to the consumer in the way of higher prices. 2. a tax on services or goods such as value added tax, sales tax, purchase tax, customs and import duties, etc.

INDIVIDUAL CONTACT OFFICER, (Gung-Ho Group) the **Individual Contact Officer** is in charge of polls for purposes from individuals in the public. These form up in project planning into specific long-range targets for the area of the group. (HCO PL 2 Dec 68)

INDIVIDUAL HATS, **individual hats** include all post **hats,** including auditor's post "tech" **hats,** third and second class mission school, and any other **hat** which deals with accomplishing a specific purpose or function on an **individual** basis. (FSO 361)

INDIVIDUAL SALES LINE, the usual channel for the sale of books is through orgs, franchises and bookstores. These obtain their books from Pubs Orgs. There is however, another line of book sales from Pubs Orgs to **individuals.** Where an org, through FP troubles or other reasons fails to stock up fully, or fails to push books into the public, its stats falter. **Individuals** in its area cannot get books, tapes or meters from the org. Thus there must be another **line** so **individuals** in an area can order books. All the **individual** book **sales line** consists of is a second **line** to the public from Pubs. (HCO PL 5 Sept 74)

INDOCTRINATION, 1. the act of informing or teaching someone about the doctrines, ways, rules or policies concerning something. 2. any series of training lectures, demonstrations or drills that serve to inform an employee about his job, job environment, company policy or rules, the terms of his employment, etc.

INDUCTION, 1. process of bringing a newly accepted person into a business by going over with him the employment contract, wages, work schedule, overtime, employee benefits, etc. 2. the ceremony of installing a person into office especially one of high stature, rank or position.

INDUSTRIAL DEMOCRACY, a system which allows industry to choose how it will go about producing whatever product or products it decides to produce.

INDUSTRIAL DISPUTE, a dispute between employers and employees over wages, working conditions, company policies or other grievance. Sometimes called a trade dispute in the UK.

INDUSTRIAL ESPIONAGE, the act of spying on or attempting to surreptitiously obtain confidential or classified information from or about a rival business or its products or services. Bribery of rival company employees to obtain data, plans, formulas, designs, etc., hiring on with a rival company to gain data, use of electronic equipment to record or photograph data, etc., are common forms of industrial espionage.

INDUSTRIAL IDEA OF ORGANIZATION, the **industrial idea of organization** is a cog wheel type **organization** with each member of it totally fixed on post, doing only exact duties, with all cog wheels intending to mesh. The **industrial idea** does not differentiate between a *machine* and a human or live **organization.** (HCO PL 2 Nov 70 II)

INDUSTRIAL PROPERTY RIGHTS, the same rights as those granted by a patent.

INDUSTRIAL RELATIONS, the relations and factors influencing the relationship between an employer and employees. The term has been used synonymously with labor relations and to mean collective bargaining from management's point of view.

INDUSTRIAL SOCIOLOGY, a branch of sociology devoted to studying group interactions and the individual's function and relationship to the group in an industrial or business environment.

INDUSTRY, 1. all manufacturing, mining and processing enterprises collectively but not including agricultural and distributive activities. 2. a large business activity or branch of trade, business or manufacturing such as the paper industry, electronics industry, etc.

INEFFICIENCY, an inability to play the game to hand, with a necessity to invent games with things which one should actually be able to control with ease. (*POW,* p. 64)

INELASTIC DEMAND, see DEMAND, INELASTIC.

INERTIA, this is the tendency of a mest object to remain motionless until acted upon by an exterior force, or to continue in a line of motion until acted upon by an exterior force. (HCOB 5 Dec 73)

INFILTRATED, this means people have been put in on your lines. (LRH ED 22 WW)

INFLATION, 1. the amount of money in the country exceeds the amount of thing there is to buy, that's **inflation.** When the amount of products in the country exceed the amount of money there is to buy things, that's deflation. Both of them upset the economic field. (ESTO 9, 7203C05 SO I) **2.** the fact is that you can't take more out of something than is in it. An activity, by its own efforts, has to make money before it can spend it. Governments today are omitting doing that so you have a cheapening of money that is called **inflation.** (ED 459-35 Flag) **3. inflation** takes place in the presence of a shortage of goods and a deflation takes place in the presence of an abundance of goods. That's really all you need to know about money. If money won't buy things it **inflates** and if money will buy too much, it deflates. So if the people have no facilities to produce or are being disturbed continuously politically you get an **inflating** state of affairs. (SH Spec 13, 6403C24) **4.** our answer to **inflation,** which means money buying less, is to do our jobs better and make more money. (OODs 19 Aug 72) **5.** an increase in the volume of money and credit relative to available goods resulting in a substantial and continuing rise in the general price level. In other words if there is too much money and too few goods you will have **inflation.** This is the standard economic definition of the word. In other words, it's quite beyond all these people to solve their current "money crisis" with a simple idea of increasing production in order to handle **inflation.** (OODs 27 Nov 71)

INFLATION, COST-PUSH, a price increase due to an increase in production costs caused by an unstable economic environment. This is different from demand inflation.

INFLATION, DEMAND, inflation resulting when more of a product or service is wanted than is available or is being produced. This increases the value and subsequently the price of the amount of that product or service that is available.

INFLATION, GALLOPING, an inflationary condition moving in upon an economy at a very fast rate.

INFO FAILURE, (**information failure**) a type of dev-t where those in charge **fail** to brief their juniors. These then have no idea of what's going on and develop other traffic in conflict. Reversely, juniors **fail** to **inform** seniors of data they have. (HCO PL 27 Jan 69)

INFORMAL CONFERENCE, a conference, usually of a preliminary nature, at which no official transcript is made and whose purpose is to confer and discuss but not to make any definite recommendations.

INFORMAL ORGANIZATION, see ORGANIZATION, INFORMAL.

INFORMAL TRAINING, see TRAINING, INFORMAL.

INFORMANT, someone that informs on the activities of another or gives information about something; something that serves to inform one.

INFORMATION, 1. knowledge or the communication of facts and ideas derived from study or experience. 2. in law, a complaint or accusation made by a public officer and sworn to before a magistrate, instituting criminal proceedings without a formal indictment. 3. in the electronics field, a signal or message or part of a message in coded form assembled by or used as input to a computer or communications system.

INFORMATION BOARDS, these **boards** are for the posting of **information** relating to the exact job. For example, the Admin **Board** may contain instructions on how to write letters, the Training **Board** may show schedules of classes, etc. These **information boards** may contain personal notes, advertising of cafés, rooms, and other such data. Nothing posted on these **boards** can be considered official for the whole organization and none but the staff to which they apply can be held responsible for not having read them. They are in essence the voices of department heads within their department. (HASI PL 21 Apr 57)

INFORMATION PACKET, 1. an **information packet** is not just one pamphlet all by itself. It is a **packet** containing several pieces. These could be a short punchy article designed to increase the person's interest and cause him to reach more, a book flyer, and a book order form. (HCO PL 15 Aug 66) 2. the idea with **information packs** is to sell the right service to the right public and make people reach for and buy the service/item that is being offered them. An **information pack** no matter what type, must contain several pieces. Example: a letter, flyer and order form and return address envelope, or, questionnaire, short punchy article designed to increase the person's interest on the subject he is being questioned about, order form and return address envelope. As a personal touch, an **information pack** must always give the receiver the name and post of the terminal at the org to contact. The rule with **information packs** is *one* service—*one* **information pack.** Selling too many items could result in confusion for the receiver, who becomes ARC broken and won't buy a thing. (BPL 20 May 72R) **3. packages** made up and mailed by the Letter Registrar for newly interested people whose names have been received. Special **information packages** are made up and mailed by the Letter Registrar to inform various sections of her mailing list on the next service they might be interested in, having already done something. There could be a Book **Info Packet** for a person who has just bought a book, a Test **Info Packet** for a person just tested, a PE **Info Packet** for the person who has just done a PE, etc., etc. In each case it offers the next service. (HCO PL 4 Feb 61) *Abbr.* Info Pack.

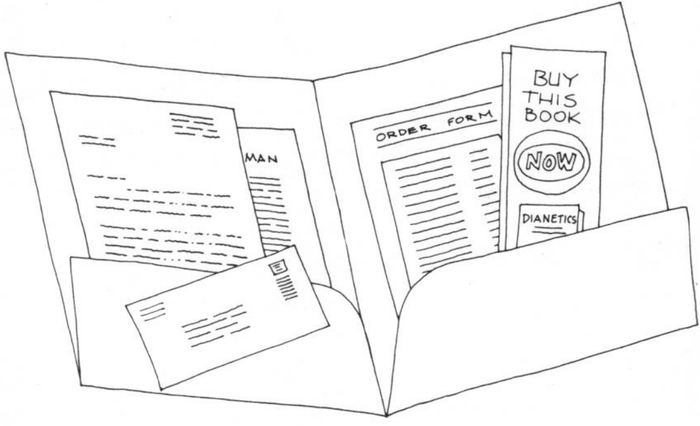

Information Packet (Def. 1)

INFORMATION STORAGE AND RETRIEVAL, the process of storing large amounts of information in various ways as in computerization and being able to retrieve or bring it back into play again as needed.

INFRACTION SHEET, 1. any **infraction** against the Training Course Rules and Regulations will result in the student being required to write a paper of 200 words getting off his overts and withholds against any and all students, instructors and personnel connected with the courses. (HCO PL 22 Nov 61) [The above HCO PL was cancelled by BPL 10 Oct 75 III.] **2. infractions** for breach of auditing regulations may be recommended by instructors but may be given only by the Course Supervisor; the procedure being for the instructor to pass the **Infraction Sheet** to the Course Supervisor for decrease, increase, cancellation or deliv[illegible]y to the student for the student's compliance. Penalties are as follows: (a) failure to comply with instructions which failure might have resulted in slowing or worsening a case: 200 to 500 word **Infraction Sheet.** (b) departure from standard operating procedure SHSBC in any unit: 200 word **Infraction Sheet** to 2 weeks in Unit W. (c) worsening or drawing-out the auditing on a case: 2 weeks in Unit W to Being Sent Down. (d) accumulation of 5,000 words in **Infraction Sheets,** in which 2 weeks re-assignment to Unit W shall constitute 1,500 words: no classifications during current course. (HCO PL 11 Feb 63) **3.** all course **infractions** hence forward will be given solely upon technical matters and results. Example: the student has "passed" an HCOB and does not seem to be able to apply it in a session. The cause of the **infraction** will be because the student is supposed to know it and doesn't and because the student could not make it work. The subject of the **infraction** will be that material required, and various allied matters. (HCO PL 2 Apr 64) **4.** the disciplinary weapon is the **Infraction Sheet.** An auditing supervisor does not give these out for bad auditing, however. He gives these out only for **infractions** of the rules of the Academy, including a refusal to follow his auditing directions. Bad technical is handled by pink sheet and gross auditing errors. (HCO PL 21 Oct 62)

INFRASTRUCTURE, service structures such as housing, schools, roads and air terminals which while they are indicative contributions toward economic growth, do not appear as directly visible and effective as commercial production.

INJUSTICE, 1. a penalty for an unknown crime or a non-existent crime. (SH Spec 51, 6109C07) **2. injustice** is usually a wrong target out-point. Arrest the drug consumer, award the drug company would be an example. (HCO PL 19 Sept 70 III) **3.** failure to administer existing law. (PAB 96) **4.** something that is *not* just, which of course is *not* fair handling and *not* due reward and *not* good treatment. That's **injustice.** (7204C11 SO)

INPUT, the total of what is put or fed in, such as data fed into a computer, electricity into a machine, time resources or manpower into a project or investment, etc.

INPUT-OUTPUT ANALYSIS, see ANALYSIS, INPUT-OUTPUT.

INPUT-OUTPUT CHART, see CHART, INPUT-OUTPUT.

INQUIRIES, persons who **inquire. Inquiries** come from people answering advertisements, by people who have heard of Dn or Scn from other people, and who then **inquire,** and (the weakest classification in **inquiries**) referred names, by which is meant names which are simply referred to the organization as being interested. (HCO PL 7 Jan 64)

INQUIRY, 1. a request sent to a company as in a customer or prospective customer asking for information on their products or services, or requesting a copy of their catalogue. 2. in law, a close examination of a matter in order to discover pertinent information or truth.

INSANE, 1. the **insane** are just one seething mass of overt acts and withholds. And they are very physically sick people. (HCO PL 4 Apr 72) **2.** the most resistence you get toward being cured by anyone is an **insane** person. An **insane** person will resist being cured harder than anybody ever heard of because he knows everybody is Martians and they're all out to get him, he knows there's no help and so on. And that's what makes him **insane.** (FEBC 3, 7101C18 SO II) **3.** having been committed to a public or private institution for the **insane.** (BPL 19 Nov 71R) **4.** having been pronounced **insane** by a psychiatrist or being incapable of any responsibility for social conduct. (FCPL 6 Oct 58)

INSANE ACTS, given some know-how or picking it up by observation, sane people make things go right. The **insane** remain ignorant intentionally or acquire know-how and make things go wrong. **Insane acts** are not unintentional or done out of ignorance. They are intentional, they are not "unknowing dramatizations." So around **insane** people things go wrong. One cannot tell the difference really between the sane and **insane** by behavior. One can tell the difference only by the product. The product of the sane is survival. The product of the **insane** is an overt **act.** As this is often masked by clever explanations it is not given the attention it deserves. The pretended good product of the **insane** turns out to be an overt **act.** (HCO PL 30 Dec 70)

INSANE CASE, the long run look at the **insane case** shows very poor chances. His brain and nerves are damaged by excessive drugs, shock and convulsions which the "psychiatrist" introduces as "treatment." Such a **case** can actually only be handled under institutional conditions and then mostly to give the person rest and security. **Insane cases** are made. We recently tried to recall one **insane case** who had not become so by modern "treatment." We could not find even one **insane case** who had not been in psychiatric hands. So, such **cases** seem to be modernly made. What is called **"insanity"** is actually a pain crazed condition. This would normally pass off. Brutality and injury to "treat" it only confirm it and we get an apparently **"insane"** person. Psychiatric treatment of a person not already in a weakened depressed condition would be bad but would not result in **"insanity."** A pain crazed person then so treated is very hard to fish out of the mess. (LRH ED 67 INT)

INSANITY, 1. (legal definition of) "the inability to tell right from wrong." (OODs 12 Mar 75) **2.** evil purpose is the cause of **insanity** and that's caused by an R/S. The cause of **insanity** is not a "germ" that causes "mental illness" in somebody's brain. That is *not* the cause of **insanity.** It is *not* the second dynamic. It is *not* because someone was interfered with as a little child. It is *not* because one is fixated on panties. **Insanity**—pure, unadulterated **insanity** is an evil purpose. Now anybody's got some nasty purposes but the person who is really **insane,** really is riding that one, boy! They're nutty as fruit cakes and it doesn't matter how competent they are or how incompetent they are. (ESTO 10, 7203C05 SO II) **3.** a refusal to allow others to be, do or have. **Insanities** have as their end product, self or group destruction. (HCO PL 14 Dec 70) **4.** the overt or covert but always complex and continuous determination to harm or destroy. (HCOB 28 Nov 70) **5.** the five primary illogics or out-points as we call them are of course the anatomy of **insanity.** (HCO PL 19 May 70) **6. insanity** isn't an illness. It's an injury. When more injuries called "treatments" are piled on top of it, it becomes very hard to treat just because the person is now desperately injured. He hurts. His nerves as physical structures carry only hurt messages. So he is enturbulated. It's the same thing trying to process a man in agony from a car injury and trying to process an **"insane"** person. You can't really get their attention until they cool down. (LRH ED 67 INT) **7.** what is called **"insanity"** is actually a pain crazed condition. This would normally pass off. Brutality and injury to "treat" it only confirm it and we get an apparently **"insane"** person. Psychiatric treatment of a person not already in a weakened depressed condition would be bad but would not result in **"insanity."** A pain crazed person then so treated is very hard to fish out of the mess. (LRH ED 67 INT) **8.** the actual point between where a person who is sane goes thereafter **insane** is a very precise point, and it's when he begins to *stop* something, and at that moment, he is **insane.** Now he is **insane** on that one subject at first, and then he can get another idée fixé and become **insane** on another subject, and you do get cumulative **insanity,** but there is no doubt of his **insanity** on that one subject. (6711C18 SO) **9.** an **insanity** is just total unreasonability. (6711C18 SO)

INSECURITY, insecurity is unknownness. When one is **insecure,** he simply doesn't know. He is not sure. Men who know are secure. Men who don't know believe in luck. One is made **insecure** by not knowing whether or not he is going to be sacked. Thus he worries. And so it is with all **insecurity. Insecurity** exists in the absence of knowledge. (*POW,* p. 16)

INSIGHT, insight comes from the ability to observe coupled with the courage to see and the wit to realize without any thought of personal importance. (HCO PL 13 Mar 65, *Divisions 1, 2, 3 The Structure of Organization What is Policy?*)

INSOLVENCY, 1. insolvency is only that condition where outgo exceeds income. (HCO PL 6 May 64) **2.** crossed cash-bills. (ED 459-36 Flag)

INSOLVENCY, the financial condition of an individual or a firm in which liabilities exceed assets so that one is unable to pay debts or meet current obligations. In rare instances a business might show more assets than liabilities but still be insolvent if those assets could not be converted into sufficient cash to take care of current financial responsibilities.

INSPECTION, the word mission may now be used to designate only a Sea Org official mission. It has unlimited ethics powers. Their members are called "missionaires." The word **inspection** shall be used to designate WW or Continental Org parties sent out. Their members are "Efficiency Experts." They have no ethics powers but may recommend action to EC WW or EC Continental on their return. (HCO PL 15 Sept 68)

INSPECTION, the act of examining the in-process production of parts or completed components to be certain proper manufacturing standards are being maintained in a plant.

INSPECTION AND REPORTS, 1. Department 3. This department is called **Inspection and Reports.** In small orgs there is only one person in that department. Primarily his duties consist of **inspecting and reporting** to his divisional head and the Executive Council. (HCO PL 7 Dec 69) **2.** section in Dept 3, Dept of **Inspection and Reports. Inspection and Reports** Section **inspects**

projects and orders for completion and **reports** to those executives who issued them. (HCO PL 17 Jan 66 II)

INSPECTION BEFORE THE FACT, that means **inspection before** anything bad has happened. (HCO PL 6 Feb 68)

INSPECTION CHECKLISTS, these are weekly **checklists** which cover in detail all areas of the org premises, grounds, building exteriors and interiors, room by room, including cleanliness and hygiene, state of repair, state of operation, usability and appearance. Engineering **inspection checklists** are included for the **inspection** of all plumbing, electrical, heating, ventilation and other systems and machinery. Each area is **inspected** weekly as to state of repair, state of operation, cleanliness and usability. Items checked are accordingly marked in or out. Maintenance and **inspection checklists** generally parallel one another. (HCO PL 16 Aug 74 IIR)

INSPECTION OFFICER, (HCO Division) the duty of the **Inspection Officer** is to inspect the status of various projects and orders and to report this to the secretary of the division concerned. The **Inspection Officer** does not issue orders or instructions to staff. (HCO PL 4 Sept 65)

INSPECTOR, **1.** an **inspector** is to stop work whenever he spots an out-point in the production and gets this handled before any further work is undertaken. An **inspector** *inspects,* he isn't there to do the job himself. This is so that he can keep an exterior viewpoint and at any time can give a valid report re: work, progress, as well as effecting corrections as needed. (FO 2969) **2.** an **inspector** is an Org Officer with heavy ethics powers. (CBO 125)

INSTANT HATTING, **1.** a sort of an action you do when you slam somebody onto a post and he's got to take the load of it and so forth and you tell him what you want him to do. That's just **instant hatting.** You tell him what his post title is and what he is supposed to be doing on that post. **Instant hatting!** Tell him to get on with it. Then HCO can come along and the first thing they would do is give him a mini hat. (FEBC 6, 7101C23 SO II) **2.** staff at the least are **instant hatted** at once—placed on the org board, work space, supplies, what his title is and what it means, org communication system, what he is supposed to produce on his post. He is gotten producing what he is supposed to produce in some volume at once. (HCO PL 9 Mar 72 III)

INSTITUTIONAL CASE, one who has been in a mental **institution** or asylum or home for any length of time or has been under any psychiatric treatment whether subjected to psychiatric treatments and/or medical electric shock therapies, or not. (BPL 29 Jul 71R II)

INSTITUTIONAL INVESTOR, organizations such as insurance companies, investment companies, banks and pension funds whose principal purpose is to invest their own assets or those held in trust for others.

INSTITUTIONS, 1. established organizations, especially ones dedicated to public service such as professional schools or universities. 2. stock exchange reference to large multi-holdings organizations such as US insurance companies who are important stockholders in various companies and whose trading activities are a major influence on the stock market.

INSTRUCTOR, **1.** the title **Instructor** is changed herewith to Supervisor. **Instructor** is a misnomer in Scn. They don't **instruct** anyone. They actually should only supervise the student to make sure he is **instructed** by HCOBs, tapes and books, and be sure he does his drills. The use of **Instructor** gives a tendency to alter-is tech which alter-is of tech is now the only thing that can prevent case gains. (HCO PL 5 May 65 II) **2.** one who has regular classes and who is assigned to places at specific times. (HCOTB 17 May 57)

INSTRUMENT, a written legal document that gives a person a right or lays down a contract such as a check, deed or stock certificate.

INSURANCE, a contract binding an insurance company to indemnify or protect and compensate the insured party against specified loss or injury, in return for premiums paid.

INSURANCE BROKER, one who acts as an agent for an insurance company in selling coverage and instituting contracts in return for a fee or commission.

INSURANCE OFFICER, **Insurance Officer,** Dept of Records, Assets and Materiel, Org Division. It is the responsibility of the **Insurance Officer** to see that all articles of value are **insured.** (HCO PL 15 Nov 65)

INSURANCE UNDERWRITER, 1. an individual or company engaged in an insurance business whose job it is to assess each transaction for the extent of risk involved in insuring various applicants. 2. one who signs an insurance policy, thereby assuming liability in case of specified loss or injury.

INTANGIBLE ASSETS, see ASSETS, INTANGIBLE.

INT/CONT HANDLINGS, when an **international** or **continental** stat is in difficulty a major evaluation is done for that area at staff level. Likewise an upstat situation can also be evaluated. More infrequently, a major situation may be evaluated that is not directly related to a stat, but nevertheless involves orgs in its implementation. Above categories of evaluations are often loosely terms as **Int/Cont handlings** or broad **handlings.** They exist as written by the Commodore (always priority) or Commodore's staff and are generally issued as Aides Orders, sometimes reissued in another format such as SO EDs. (CBO 274)

INTEGRATION, HORIZONTAL, horizontal merger; an acquiring, merging or reorganizing of one or more businesses which deal with the same area and aspect of a business such as a tool manufacturer merging with another tool manufacturer or a food store chain merging with another food store chain. This is horizontal as opposed to veritical integration.

INTEGRITY, integrity comes from a Latin word meaning untouched, whole, entire. It is now defined as (1) honesty, uprightness; (2) quality or state of being complete, wholeness; (3) undivided or unbroken condition; (4) perfect condition. (BPL 9 Mar 74)

INTELLIGENCE, sanity is the ability to recognize differences, similarities and identities. This is also **intelligence.** (HCO PL 26 Apr 70R)

INTELLIGENCE QUOTIENT, a measurement of intelligence expressed as a ratio of mental age to chronological age, arrived at by use of an IQ test. *Abbr.* IQ.

INTENSIVE, auditing is sold in "numbers of **intensives.**" These are given in chunks exactly scheduled by Tech Services Monday to Friday. Today we would call the 12 1/2 hour **intensive** given in one week **an intensive.** (LRH ED 145R INT)

INTERDEPARTMENTAL CONFERENCE, a conference of two or more departments conducted by an interested higher level executive or by a staff executive who presides but does not adjudicate.

INTERDEPARTMENTAL TRANSFER, see TRANSFER, INTERDEPARTMENTAL.

INTEREST, the amount of money charged or paid for the use of another's money.

INTERESTED PARTY, a person, plaintiff or defendant, called before a Committee of Evidence for whom penalties may be recommended or decisions awarded by the Committee. An **Interested Party** may not be called before another committee or a later convened committee for the same offense or complaint after having been summoned and heard for that offense, or his complaint at one or more meetings of the current committee. (HCO PL 7 Sept 63)

INTERIORIZATION, interiorization means going into it too fixedly, and becoming part of it too fixedly. It doesn't mean just going into your head. (SH Spec 84, 6612C13)

INTERMEDIATE MANAGEMENT, see MANAGEMENT, MIDDLE.

INTERNAL AUDIT, see AUDIT, INTERNAL.

INTERNAL CIC, 1. an **Internal CIC** for Flag is hereby established in the Office of the Staff Captain. It is the **Control Information Center** for the Orgs, units and activities aboard Flag itself. It is called **Internal CIC.** The purpose of **Internal CIC** is to collect data related to management of orgs, units and activities aboard Flag, coordinate it by org, unit, activity and month so that it can be evaluated and on need produce whys for high or low stat situations; to facilitate getting authorized programs aboard Flag done. (FO 3449) [FO 3449 has been replaced with FO 3449R.] **2.** what was formerly called **Internal CIC** is now known as "Staff **CIC.**" (FO 3449R)

INTERNAL CIC OFFICER, what was formerly called **Internal CIC** is now known as "Staff CIC." It is under the charge of the "Staff CIC Officer," formerly known as **Internal CIC Officer.** (FO 3449R)

INTERNAL COMM FLOW SECTION, HCO Div 1, Dept 2, Dept of Comm. Supervises **internal comm;** Consists of distributing mail and dispatches, picking up mail and dispatches and speeding mail and dispatches throughout the org. (HCO PL 25 Feb 66)

INTERNAL COMMUNICATIONS, are anything inside the Central Organization. This means **communications** going from one HCO personnel to another HCO personnel, from HCO personnel to the Central Organization personnel, and from the Central Organization personnel to HCO personnel. (HCO PL 29 Jan 59)

INTERNAL EMERGENCY BOARD, is kept by the Internal Emergency Officer. It is located in Internal CIC. On it he posts, with a time-date marked on it, those items requiring handling. These can be a slip of paper with the situation noted or a copy of the actual comm. These remain on the **board** until handled. (FO 3195-1)

INTERNAL EMERGENCY OFFICER, FLAG, the post of **Internal Emergency Officer, Flag,** is situated in the Office of the Commodore's Staff Captain. The purpose of the post is to note and get handled promptly those things on Flag which are emergencies or will make emergencies if not handled. (FO 3195-1)

INTERNAL HCO BRANCH, (in Establishment Bureau 1) the **Internal HCO Branch** (1) handles **internal** Flag Bureaux HCO functions including personnel control, hatting, inspections, stats, ethics. It has liaison with the External HCO Branch for recruitment. (FO 3591)

INTERNAL LINES, anything inside a Central Organization is **internal.** Anything flying about amongst HCO offices only is external. (HCO PL 2 Jan 59)

INTERNAL REQUISITION FORMS, forms to be filled in whenever supplies are needed. The person who requests the goods, signs his name at the bottom of the **form** and so does his department head. The exact reason why these goods are required should also be included on the **Internal Requisition Form.** (HCO PL 8 Sept 65) *Abbr.* IR.

INTERNAL REVENUE, government income from taxes levied within the country.

INTERNATIONAL ADMIN OFFICER, the post of **Int Admin Officer** is formed. He holds the **admin** pattern of the org in position in every org and makes certain that execs know and follow policy letters as to the form of the org, body flow lines and functions of posts and to org spatial arrangements and sees that all the data taught, on the Org Exec Course, is applied and that Scn executives and staffs are trained in it and use it. He also sees that policy is not used to stop proper flows or halt expansion. He also sees to the correctness and issue of hats in all orgs and does what is needful to make all policy letters available and in useful form. It is under the Dissem Sec WW, Dept 5. (HCO PL 21 Sept 67, *International Oficers at WW Alert Council*)

INTERNATIONAL ADVISORY COUNCIL, the **International Advisory Council** would be made up of representatives of continental parts of the world and executives who represent types of divisions of organizations. It's about a 15 man **Advisory Council.** That **Ad Council** is composed of continental representatives. Now these are representatives which represent the continental area. In other words they represent every organization and all the Scientologists on that continent; in that continental area, they represent the lot. They are specifically a representative and a continental **Ad Council,** but more importantly they represent all of the other orgs, and they represent all of those people too. (SH Spec 81, 6611C01)

INTERNATIONAL ANNUAL MEMBERSHIP, this is the cash discount **membership.** It gives a 50% cash purchase discount across the boards—training, processing, books, meters, tapes, insignia, congress, the lot. If we sell it, an **International Member** gets 50% off. The **membership** must be renewed every year. It expires on the same date the following year at one minute past midnight. It keeps one's certificates in force. No services are ever promised to its holders but a monthly magazine is sent and a copy of the Professional Auditor's Bulletin comes to them from Saint Hill. Anyone can have an **International Annual Membership** providing they are for us and not members of groups seeking to harm mankind. (HCO PL 22 Mar 65, *Current Promotion and Org Program Summary Membership Rundown International Annual Membership*)

INTERNATIONAL BOARD, the **International Board** is composed of three **board** members, L. Ron Hubbard, Chairman, Mary Sue Hubbard, Secretary, and Marilynn Routsong, Treasurer. It is the controlling **board** of Scn. There are no other boards or board members, individual board members, officers or secretaries with the power of issuing policy. (HCO PL 5 Mar 65 II)

INTERNATIONAL BUREAU OF REPRESENTATIVES, the post of Board **Rep** supersedes the Flag Programs Chief post, which is discontinued when replaced by a Board **Rep.** The post is located in the **International Bureau of Representatives** in the Flag Bureaux, which replaces the old Programs Bureau on Flag. The Programs Bureau in the FOLO and the FOLO Programs Officer post remain unchanged. (BPL 22 Jun 74)

INTERNATIONAL CITY, a project having to do with world peace. **International City** Project. Was there anything one could do about destimulating the planet and consolidating the circumstances of war? If all the capitals of the world were located inside one city, they were not likely to bomb each other out. They in effect would be very careful of declaring war. They would be close (cheek by jowl) enough to discuss most of their problems. (SH Spec 13, 6403C24)

INTERNATIONAL COMMITTEE FOR SAFETY OF LIFE AT SEA, the **internationally** accepted standard for ships is that laid down by the **International Committee for Safety of Life at Sea** which is usually abbreviated to "The **Solas** Convention." The publication of the rules of this convention contains detailed requirements for cargo, passenger and tanker ships. (FO 2732R) *Abbr.* SOLAS.

INTERNATIONAL COMMUNICATIONS OFFICER, the post of **International Communications Officer** is formed with the duties of ensuring all Scn **comms** flow within WW and in all orgs and on all lines. It is under the HCO Sec WW in the Dept of Comm. (HCO PL 21 Sept 67, *International Officers at WW Alert Council*)

INTERNATIONAL COUNCIL, International Council of Dianetics and Scientology. The purpose of this **council** shall be: to ensure the smooth running of Dn and Scn throughout the world, to safeguard and increase their money and properties and to provide good administration, excellent service and justice. The first thought of **council** members in event of any untoward event threatening Dn and Scn or their organizations, or in event of my sudden absence, should be to handle the situation and to prevent the breakdown of administrative lines. (HCO PL 9 May 63)

INTERNATIONAL DECLARATIONS OFFICER, the post of **International Declarations Officer** is formed under the Org Exec Sec WW to watch all **declarations** procedures to ensure their correctness and to take action on all incorrect **declares** to correct them and to implement policy relating to examinations of processing results, the only persons amongst Scientologists who have given trouble having been misdeclares. It is under the Qual Sec WW Dept 13. (HCO PL 21 Sept 67, *International Officers at WW Alert Council*)

INTERNATIONAL ETHICS AND JUSTICE OFFICER, this post is in the External HCO Branch on Flag. It parallels the HCO Department 3 and so is responsible for the establishment and functioning of that department. (FBDL 513)

INTERNATIONAL ETHICS OFFICER, the post of **International Ethics Officer** is formed with the duties of maintaining WW personnel files of all org personnel over the world and getting in **ethics** in all orgs and ensuring appointments of only **ethics** free personnel in orgs. His okay is required from an **ethics** standpoint in all post assignments in Scn orgs over the world hereafter. It is under the HCO Sec WW in the Dept of I & R. (HCO PL 21 Sept 67, *International Officers at WW Alert Council*)

INTERNATIONAL EXECUTIVE DIVISION WW, the **International Executive Division WW** is just another Saint Hill division. There are eight divisions at Saint Hill. The difference is that it has two Executive Divisions, one Division 7 for the world, one for the Saint Hill Org. (HCO PL 26 Jan 66)

INTERNATIONAL ISSUE AUTHORITY, International Issue Authority is established in the Office of LRH, Flag. All new books, booklets, magazines, manuals and requests to use Scn and Dn materials for commercial use, such as books by others, use of symbols in medallions, plaques and jewelry, must have prior approval from Office of LRH, Flag **Issue Authority** Section. "New" books, booklets, magazines, etc., are defined as those types of issues being released for the first time. (BPL 2 Mar 73R I) *Abbr.* Int I/A.

INTERNATIONAL MANAGEMENT INCOME, the 10%s collected by Flag Bureaux and Flag for services of **management.** This is 10% of the corrected gross **income** of those orgs or franchises that do not pay 10% to WW. (HCO PL 9 Mar 72 I)

INTERNATIONAL MEMBERSHIP, 1. the cost of £10 sterling per year for **International Membership** or $30. This gives a 10% discount on books, a 30% discount on training and processing. An **International Membership** is **membership** in the main **International** Organization. (HCO PL 23 Dec 64) **2. International Member** receives PAB magazine, Continental Magazine, 10% discount on books, tapes and possibly congress (cash purchases only). (HCO PL 26 Oct 59) See INTERNATIONAL ANNUAL MEMBERSHIP.

INTERNATIONAL ORGANIZATION DEPARTMENT, handles all **international organizations,** increases their efficiency and activity.

Collects their 10% administration and royalty payments. Handles all **organization** traffic. (HCO PL 18 Dec 64, *Saint Hill Org Board*)

INTERNATIONAL ORGANIZATION SUPERVISOR, 1. directs and handles the **International Organization** Department. Receives all cabled reports and keeps close watch on states of organizations. **Supervises** all **Organization** and Association Secretaries and their communications. (HCO PL 18 Dec 64, *Saint Hill Org Board*) 2. he is to do everything possible to increase the efficiency, technical proficiency and income of Central **Organizations** and offices throughout the world and to collect all monies owed by them to Saint Hill and to act to prevent emergencies in them or to handle existing emergencies in them. (HCO PL 28 May 64)

INTERNATIONAL PROMOTION OFFICER, the post of **International Promotion Officer** is formed under the Org Exec Sec WW. It is to push standard **promotion** in all orgs, the sale of books to public, FSM activities, Congresses and general Division 6 actions with the purpose of expanding Scn numbers by pressing on with proven methods of reach and seeing that no org neglects them. It is under the Dissem Sec WW Dept 4. (HCO PL 21 Sept 67, *International Officers at WW Alert Council*)

INTERNATIONAL SECRETARY, all of the **secretarial** hats which the Aides were holding were actually the post of **International Secretary**. They were covering Divisions 1 to 7 as specialized actions **internationally** which actually belong to the Programs Bureau. (7208C02 SO)

INTERNATIONAL SPECIAL PROGRAMS EXECUTION OFFICER, the post of **International Special Programs Execution Officer** is formed under the HCO Exec Sec WW to collect, watch, record, progress and push already originated **special programs** such as junior staff to be trained on Org Exec Course, cash/bills ratio to be improved, Qual Divs to be established, etc. and to propose **programs** of long range improvement. (HCO PL 21 Sept 67, *International Officers at WW Alert Council*)

INTERNATIONAL TECHNICAL OFFICER, the post of **International Technical Officer** is formed with the duties of keeping standard **tech** in and only standard **tech** practiced over the world. It is under the Tech Sec WW Dept 10. (HCO PL 21 Sept 67, *International Officers at WW Alert Council*)

INTERNATIONAL TREASURER WW, the **International Treasurer WW** is under the Guardian WW Dept 21. (HCO PL 21 Sept 67, *International Officers at WW Alert Council*)

INTERNATIONAL UPSTAT CLUB, the **Upstat Club** has long been established aboard the Flagship. It was formed by LRH in 1968 to recognize those Flag crew members who have **up statistics** and who are complying with his orders. This **club** is now extended out into the field as the **International Upstat Club!** All staff are eligible. Requirements are evidence of LRH targets done and the **upstats** to prove it! (FBDL 462)

INTERNE SUPERVISOR, (Correction Division) **Interne Supervisor** helps LRH make real flubless professional auditors through volume auditing, fast correction of flubs and daily precision training. He runs a tight on-policy course which concentrates on a fast route to actual volume auditing, knowing that volume auditing with instant correction is the way to make flubless auditors. (BPL 7 Dec 71R I)

INTERNSHIP, ROTATING, a training method which calls for employees to rotate from one section to various other sections of an organization, with the thought of helping them to become more versatile and assume new responsibilities as needed.

INTERORG BILLS OWING, the total of sums **owed** to Flag, to individual Scientologists, and to other orgs including Pubs and WW. This is *not* additive to the bills owing stat but is its own figure reported and graphed separately. (BPL 1 Jul 72R)

INTERORG COMM, the **comm** lines amongst **orgs.** (LRH ED 83 INT)

INTERORG EXCHANGE, any circumstance or situation which results in a student or pc paying for service in one **org** and receiving that service or other service on the basis of that payment, in another **org.** (BPL 25 Nov 71R)

INTERORG TRANSFER, the **transfer** of funds between **orgs** as a result of **interorg** exchange of students or pcs having occurred. (BPL 25 Nov 71R)

INTERPOLATION, in statistics, an estimate of the value of something between known values or data, such as an estimate of services delivered for a period where records are not available, based on services delivered before and after such a period.

INTERVIEW, a face-to-face meeting between an interviewer and another person such as an employee, job applicant, consumer, etc., during which the interviewer asks the person questions designed to accomplish the purpose of the interview. They may be questions designed to show up a job applicant's suitability, discover a consumer's wants, isolate an employee's attitude toward his job, etc.

INTERVIEWEE, one who is interviewed and who answers questions, gives information, opinions and ideas as requested by the interviewer.

INTERVIEW, EMPLOYMENT, see INTERVIEW.

INTERVIEWER, one who conducts and controls an interview by asking questions and receiving data, information, opinions and ideas.

IN THE ORG LIST, **1.** any person arriving **in the org** for service is logged. When they leave the org after service they are logged out. People arriving give their local address to reception. People departing should depart via reception and give their forwarding address which reception sends on to Address. Reception, from this data, makes up a weekly roster of persons present for service (training or processing or any other service). This is the **in the org list.** (HCO PL 7 Nov 65) **2.** a tally of all those **in the org**; students, pcs, execs, etc. there for any service. (ED 118 FAO)

INTRADEPARTMENTAL TRANSFER, see TRANSFER, INTRADEPARTMENTAL.

INTRAORG COMM SECTION, HCO Div 1, Dept 2, Dept of Comm. The handling of dispatches between **orgs** is the **Intraorg Comm Section.** This has the telex, the packets of pre-addressed envelopes to other **orgs**, etc. (HCO PL 25 Feb 66)

INTRODUCTION AND INDOCTRINATION, consists of testing, **introductory** lectures, film and tape plays, events using demonstrations that effectively **introduce** the public to and demonstrate the workability of Dn and Scn. These activities get the public interested enough to buy something. All these things are public services. They are informative. They **indoctrinate.** The people leaving have been taught something, they feel they know more about Dn and Scn and they want more. (HCO PL 14 Nov 71RA II)

INTRODUCTION TO SCN COURSE, heavy theory pack consisting of: What is Scientology, ARC, Parts of Man, 8 Dynamics, Cycles of Action, Handling Confusion and Exhaustion and Tone Scale. (FPJO 717)

INTRODUCTORY LECTURE, see FREE INTRODUCTORY LECTURE.

INTRO SESSIONS, the **intro session** first came into existence as demonstrations at **introductory** lectures, and events. *The Public Dissemination Manual* often referred to as the "Thomas Package" came out in '71. It gave a simple few minutes pinch-test action on the meter from one specially assigned personnel for five dollars. They were unfortunately called **intro sessions.** This developed into actual **sessions** as the alter-is increased and C/Ses not know what an **Intro Session** was (it not being in any HCOB) started C/Sing ruds flying, etc. and whatever they logically conceived. This service is an illegal service. It is off-policy per HCO PL 28 September 1971, *Selling and Delivering Auditing.* No sale of **intro sessions** at any time by anyone is OK. (FBDL 430)

Introversion

INTROVERSION, looking in too closely. An **introverted** personality is only capable of looking inward at himself. The person who is **introverted** is a person who has probably passed exhaustion some way back. He has had his attention focused closer and closer to him (basically by old injuries which are still capable of exerting their influence upon him) until he is actually looking inward and not outward. He is shying away from solid objects. He does not see a reality in other people and things around him. (*POW*, pp. 92-93)

INTROVERT, the type of person who directs his attention inward to himself.

INTROVERTED, as long as an auditor is **introverted** (looking inside into himself) he will have no real warmth or interest in the pc. (OODs 5 Jun 72)

INTROVERTS, goes inward. (LRH ED 67 INT)

INT RUNDOWN CORRECTION LIST REVISED, HCO Bulletin 29 October 1971R, *Int Rundown Correction List Revised.* As **interiorization**-exteriorization problems (when they exist) have to be handled before any other thing is handled, an auditor sometimes assesses another list and then finds himself doing this **list.** **"Int"** appears on many other lists and when it reads, one does this **list.** One has to go back and complete the original list of course. **"Int"** problems cause high TA, headaches and general upset. (LRH ED 257 INT)

INVENTORY, an itemized list of articles, materials or possessions on the premises or in stock, noting quantity, description, cost or current worth.

INVENTORY AND SPACE ALLOCATION OFFICER, (Flag Land Base) an **Inventory and Space Allocation Officer** is to be appointed by CO Area Estates to serve on his staff and to take monthly **inventories** and reviews of all items and spaces and keep the **inventories** up-to-date and to correct not only the paper work but the people including security guards, room cleaners and MAAs where they have failed to handle or detect. (BFO 43)

INVENTORY OF EMPLOYMENT, see EMPLOYMENT, INVENTORY OF.

INVENTORY MANAGEMENT, see MANAGEMENT, INVENTORY.

INVERTED PYRAMID, the news story has two parts, the lead which quickly tells what has happened, and the body which documents the lead. The oldest form and the most widely used is the **inverted pyramid.** In this form the facts are presented in the top, which takes the head and attracts attention. After that the paragraphs are arranged in diminishing order of news importance. Frequently the story will be chopped off starting at the bottom, according to space and the editor. (BPL 10 Jan 73R)

INVESTIGATION, 1. the careful discovery and sorting of facts. Without good **investigation** we don't have justice, we have random vengeance. **Investigation** must always be aimed at the specific person, the time and the place. Else you'll sink in a morass of generality and get nowhere. (*HCOMOJ*) 2. if an organization is folding up, or becoming less able to make things go, then the effort to stop things is greater than the effort to make them go. This being the case, and because one is dealing with an insanity, any effort to find reasonable explanations will fail. So you're looking for things which are totally unreasonable because an insanity is total unreasonability. Therefore, your **investigation** must proceed along the lines of what you don't understand and you'll arrive with the stopper. That is very condensed but that is it. (6711C18)

INVESTIGATORY REPORTING, this type of **reporting** is the unearthing of wrong doings and their exposé. The results are presented as news with some interpretation. If the paper has comment, it runs on the editorial page. (BPL 10 Jan 73R)

INVESTING, FORMULA, an investment procedure, such as shifting funds from common stock to preferred stock or bonds as the market average climbs above a pre-established point and the return of funds to common stocks as the market average decreases.

INVESTMENT, the act of an individual or company purchasing or putting money into securities, property, other businesses or possessions acquired for future income or benefit.

INVESTMENT APPRAISAL, 1. an evaluation made before engaging in a financial investment, of what the rate of return will be. 2. any evaluation of the relative value of investing one's time, energy, personnel, etc., into some endeavor in comparison to what benefits or results one will receive in exchange.

INVESTMENT BANK, see BANK, INVESTMENT.

INVESTMENT, BLUE CHIP, an investment in a high price stock, called a blue chip stock, from a well established and respected corporation. Blue chip investments are often high priced but are generally considered a very safe and stable investment.

INVESTMENT COUNSEL, one whose occupation is counseling and advising others in matters of investment decisions.

INVESTMENT, GROSS, the amount invested in capital assets such as machinery and plant and in stocks such as raw materials or finished goods.

INVESTMENT, NET, the amount invested in capital assets such as machinery and plant and in stocks such as raw materials or finished goods with a deduction made for the value of depreciation on these things.

INVESTOR, 1. an individual who invests in a business with the idea of making a profit or gaining financially. 2. a person who pays money for stocks or securities in a company in order to profit by the company's ability to use that money to initially or further build and equip itself and operate prosperously; a stockholder, shareholder or bondholder.

INVOICE, **1.** a written document which records the details of an exchange between the org and a public person. An **invoice** is valuable. It represents money and authorizes admission to service. (BPL 1 Feb 72 I) **2. invoices** are the means of crediting someone with monies paid and thus the right to take services on the strength of these, or receive items from the bookstore. **Invoices** are the record, in time sequence, of monies received. (BPL 20 Feb 67R)

WEST INN

INVOICE

DATE ____________

NAME ____________

ADDRESS ____________

	CASH	CHECK NO.	OTHER
AMOUNT RECEIVED			

SIGNATURE

THANK YOU

PQ-10234

DEBIT

CREDIT

CASHIER

Invoice (Def. 1)

INVOICE, a complete list of the merchandise, goods or services sent to a buyer by the seller which also includes quantity, price, shipping charges and any other costs or discounts.

INVOICE ACADEMY, [Post title. Old pre-Tech Services post to do with checking students' **invoices** before letting them on course (to see that they'd paid) and with reporting income for **Academy** for the week.]

INVOICING SECTION, the Income Dept has three sections which must not tangle and cross. These are Area Cashier and Collections Section, **Invoicing Section** and Collections Section. The **Invoicing Section** handles the letter mail and sent in payments. It has its own **invoice** machine and records. It only receives money. Neither Area Cashier and Collections or **Invoice** bank money. Banking is handled by the Dept of Records. (HCO PL 18 Apr 69 II)

INVOICING STATIONS, there are several points on public lines where money can be taken in: bookstore, Qual, Reges in Dept 6 and Dept 17, Cashier. The Treasury Div must control and police all **invoicing stations** so as to channel all monies collected into Treasury at the end of each day. (BPL 1 Feb 72 I)

IRREDUCIBLE MINIMUM, **1.** when an organization or its posts operate only on an **irreducible minimum**, production goes bad and delivery crashes. Take a cook who has his post at an **irreducible minimum.** Food is appearing on the table. If he **reduced** just one bit more the food would no longer be edible at all. He neglects purchasing, menus and preparation. That these occur is invisible to the diners. That food appears on the table is visible to the diners. If the cook operates at any less than he is, no edible food would be visible—hence, **irreducible minimum.** The food served will be bad. But it will be visible. Invisible-to-the-diners actions aren't being done. To improve the food, get the less visible actions done. Get the sequence of actions all done. (HCO PL 14 Dec 70) **2.** the principle of the **irreducible minimum** of a post. A post tends to reduce to only its visible points. In other words, all of the hidden or not too visible actions or which is to say, the preparatory actions that make a good product tend to drop away from a post and tend to drop away from an org. You will wind up with the **irreducible minimum** and that is merely the visible. (FEBC 1, 7011C17 SO)

IRREGULAR SCHEDULE STAFF AUDITOR, audits all **irregularly scheduled** pcs. (HCO PL 24 Mar 61 II)

IRRELEVANT INFORMATION, this form of dev-t can also take the form of forwarding to a senior large quantities of **irrelevant information,** jamming his lines, and reducing his productiveness. The opposite of this of course is failure to inform one's senior of relevant data. (BPL 30 Jan 69)

IS-NESS, something that is persisting on a continuum. That is our basic definition of **is-ness.** (*PXL,* p. 91)

ISSUE, any of an organization's securities, or the act of dispensing securities.

ISSUE AUTHORITY, **1.** prior approval from Office of LRH to **issue** or publish (whether or not previously **issued**), i.e. "new" books, booklets, magazines, all proposed promo pieces, hand-outs, mailings, HCOBs, HCO PLs, EOs, etc. (BPL 2 Mar 73R I) **2.** the LRH Communicator in any org may veto and deny the **issue** of any exec sec or secretary instruction, order or SEC ED that is contrary to policy or technology. The LRH Comm may cancel verbal tech instructions or advices and verbal breaches of policy. An LRH Comm may reject magazines or mailing pieces which do not conform to policy. An LRH Comm may halt the use of unauthorized material or technology. (HCO PL 7 May 66) *Abbr.* I/A.

ISSUE BY TENDER, the inviting to tender bids for the shares of a company and the issue of such to the highest bidder or bidders.

IS THIS OK, executives may not OK anything done or to be done below their level unless their immediate junior has also stated or attested with an initial that it is OK. Unless one can fix responsibility for actions there is no responsibility anywhere and the whole show goes to pot. Never let a junior say **"Is this OK?"**—always make him state or initial "This is OK" on all work, actions or projects. **"Is this OK?"** is dev-t and should be chitted as such. (HCO PL 27 Jan 69)

I WANT TO GO CLEAR CLUB, **1.** the **I Want to go Clear Club** is conducted to obtain new names to CF and put people firmly on the road to **Clear.** (LRH ED 159R-1 INT) **2.** to clarify and increase as a stable datum for **clearing,** to assist the dissemination of the goal of **Clear** as a major stable datum and to recognize and reinforce upstats who **want to go Clear,** the **I Want to go Clear Club** is formed. (FO 3139) *Abbr.* IWGCC

J

JOB, 1. the tasks, duties and responsibilities connected with a type of work that combined distinguish that work from other types of work, i.e. a policeman's job is different from a lawyer's job. 2. a piece of work done such as a finished product or work contract, i.e. it will be four months before the bridge is finished and we have completed the job. —*v.* 1. the action of buying large quantities of goods from manufacturers and selling them in small quantities to retailers. 2. to farm out work to various workers or contractors.

JOB ANALYSIS, see ANALYSIS, JOB.

JOB ANALYST, a person trained in job analysis who can break down the functions, duties and responsibilities of any job in order to make an evaluation of the qualifications, salary and environment or materials appropriate for that job.

JOBBER, a middleman who buys goods in large quantities from manufacturers and sells them in smaller quantities to retailers for a profit; a wholesaler or wholesale merchant.

JOB BREAKDOWN, a breakdown of the purpose, responsibilities, functions, actions, products and statistics of a job. This is one of the functions of job analysis.

JOB CARD, all repair, renovation and construction actions are done against a **job card** system. This goes for engineering repair actions as well as the repair unit. **Job cards** are used for one-time actions concerning repairs, renovations or construction cycles. A **job card** is a small **card** on which is written the date, name of **job** to be done, area of the org involved, a target date for completion and some denotation of priority. (HCO PL 16 Aug 74 IIR)

JOB CLASSIFICATION, the grouping of jobs into classifications such as similarity of functions, salary level, educational prerequisites, etc.

JOB CONDITIONS, the environmental and physical conditions that accompany a particular job such as extreme temperatures, health hazards, excessive noise, fast moving particles, chemical fumes, etc.

JOB CYCLE, that series of actions necessary to completely produce one of the products or subproducts of a job. If it does not result in a product or sub-product the job cycle is not complete.

JOB DESCRIPTION, a write-up of the purpose, level of authority, responsibilities, actions, products and statistics of a job; a write-up of a thorough job analysis.

JOB ENDANGERMENT REPORT, 1. a chit filed on your next highest superior if you are given orders or directions or preventions or denied materials which makes it hard or impossible for you to raise your statistics or do your **job** at all. (HCO PL 31 Oct 66 II) **2.** staff member **report reporting** any order received from a superior that **endangered** one's **job** by demanding one alter or depart from known policy, the orders of a person senior to one's immediate superior altered or countermanded by one's immediate superior, or advice from one's immediate superior not to comply with orders or policy. (HCO PL 1 May 65)

JOB ENTHUSIASM, the amount of enthusiasm or morale a person has for a job. This is seen in the difference between the person who merely arrives at work to put in his time and collect his wages and the person who enjoys maintaining a high level of productivity and actively creates his job out of a sense of duty or self-satisfaction. Inadequate working conditions and monotonous job content can also be factors at work here but the level of productivity a person engages in is the primary basis of morale or job enthusiasm.

JOB FAMILY, a group of jobs which have similar personnel requirements because they require similar experience, skills, training, job actions, etc. Such a group might be policemen, firemen, coast guard and rescue personnel.

JOB HIERARCHIES, a ranking of job families to show a hierarchy of jobs. Salary level is one of the main characteristics used to establish where a job family or job fits in a job hierarchy. Education level, socio-economic status, public opinion, etc., may also be used to establish job hierarchies.

JOB IDENTIFICATION, same as job description.

JOB KNOWLEDGE, knowledge of how to do a specific job.

JOB LOT, a quantity of goods purchased or sold as a unit and often containing a mixture of types of goods such as kitchen appliances, lawn furniture and garden tools.

JOB PRODUCTION, see PRODUCTION, JOB.

JOB RATE, the basic wage rate established for a particular job. This may have come about through collective bargaining, legislation or may have found its own level in competitive industry and become solidified by common agreement.

JOB REQUIREMENTS, the training, skills, attitudes, interests, mental and physical qualifications, etc., that are needed or required of a person prerequisite to either successfully doing a particular job or getting hired for it; job specifications.

JOB ROTATION, a rotating of a person from one job to another to give him familiarity with a group of jobs in order to boost that person up to a supervisory or management level over that group of jobs, to improve individual efficiency and understanding, or to relieve the monotony that so often accompanies assembly line type jobs and increase job interest.

JOB SATISFACTION, same as job enthusiasm.

JOB SECURITY, the amount of assurance a person has that he will have continued employment with a firm. This comes under the subject of conditions of employment which are covered in the contract of employment or collective bargaining agreement. Usually this is a set of rules which govern continued employment so that an employee knows he can hold his job with resulting security providing he adheres to the conditions of employment. For example, he knows he has 10 days sick leave per year during which he cannot be fired or his job taken by another. Where a firm employs on a first in, last out basis, a person's job security grows as his seniority increases.

JOB SHOP, see SHOP, JOB.

JOB SPECIFICATIONS, same as job requirements.

JOB SPOILER, a term applied to a person who produces more than others in a work group thus breaking any restricted output agreement or fiddle; also called a high-flier or rate-buster.

JOB TIME, the time required to complete a sub-product or more commonly the end product of a job; the time required to complete a job cycle.

JOB TRAINING, see TRAINING, JOB.

JO'BURG CONFESSIONAL, this is the **Johannesburg Confessional List.** This is the roughest **confessional** list in Scn. It does not necessarily replace other **confessional** lists but it is probably the most thorough one we have now. (HCO PL 7 Apr 61RA) [This was previously called the **Johannesburg** Security Check or **Jo'burg** Security Check.]

JOHANNESBURG RULE, no auditing for pay may now be undertaken by a staff member on a private basis or, after the staff member leaves the org, on students or pcs within two years after the student or pc leaves the Academy or HGC, on penalty of loss of certificates. Note that this states staff member, not just an HGC auditor. The 8-hour rule is thereby cancelled. If a staff member is given money for this it is to be paid in full into the organization so that all may benefit. The no private pcs for staff members we will call the **Johannesburg Rule.** (HCO PL 16 Oct 62)

JOINT PRODUCTS, those products that are produced as a result of the same manufacturing process such as the variety of petroleum products that result from refining crude oil.

JOINT STOCK COMPANY, see COMPANY, JOINT STOCK.

JOINT VENTURE, a joining of two or more persons and their knowledge and capital in a common business undertaking for profit. Usually its aim is the disposal of a single lot of goods or the completion of a single project. Thus it is a limited relationship and lacks the endurance and continuity of a partnership which usually carries forward in time for a long while; joint adventure.

JOURNAL, in bookkeeping, a book of original entry into which the daily business transactions of a company are first entered noting all transaction details and which account they belong under. These transactions are later posted in a ledger as part of the double-entry bookkeeping system; a day book.

JOURNEYMAN, an experienced reliable workman in any field, (archaic meaning) a tradesman who traveled expanding his skills under different masters. (FO 3260)

JOURNEYMAN, a fully apprenticed person who has achieved excellent technical perfection in his trade but not yet the artistic and creative perfection of a master. A journeyman in Medieval times was competent and confident enough to travel around to work under various masters to obtain artistic and increase technical perfection before becoming a master himself and an employer, taking on apprentices and journeymen in his own right.

JUNIOR COMM MEMBER, a **junior comm member** is one who in relation to Saint Hill holds the duplicate post in any org in the first echelon of eleven orgs just below Saint Hill or in an org in that echelon of eleven junior to the Continental Orgs. (HCO PL 13 Mar 65 II)

JUNIOR EXECUTIVE, see EXECUTIVE, JUNIOR.

JUNIOR PARTNER, a partner who has a comparatively small investment in a partnership and who is not responsible for major decisions nor does he share in the profits or losses to a large degree.

JUSTICE, 1. the action of the group against the individual when he has failed to get his own ethics in. (HCOB 15 Nov 72 II) **2.** (1) moral rightness; equity. (2) honor, fairness. (3) good reason. (4) fair handling: due reward or treatment. (5) the administration and procedure of the law. (HCO PL 3 May 72) **3.** fair and equitable treatment for both the group and individual. (HCO PL 24 Feb 72) **4. justice** safeguards rights, prevents injustice, prevents punishment by whim, and brings order. **Justice** prevents wrongful disgrace, demotion, transfer or dismissal and protects the staff member's reputation and job from being falsely threatened. (HCO PL 17 Mar 65 II) **5.** to us, **justice** is the action necessary to restrain the insane until they are cured. After that it would be only an action of seeing fair play is done. (HCO PL 14 Dec 70) **6.** an effort to bring equity and peace. (HCO PL 14 Dec 70) **7.** the purpose of **justice** is to make a safe environment for the many. (FO 2257) **8. justice** would consist of a refusal to accept any report not substantiated by actual, independent data, seeing that all such reports are investigated and that all investigations include confronting the accused with the accusation and where feasible the accuser, before any disciplinary action is undertaken or any condition assigned. While this may slow the processes of **justice,** the personal security of the individual is totally dependent upon establishing the full truth of any accusation before any action is taken. (HCO PL 24 Feb 69) **9.** an action to deter disorder and secure the public safety. It is a short-term method of bringing order and it is needed for all dynamics. (*HCOMOJ*) **10.** the whole subject of **justice** subdivides for a Scientologist into four phases. These are (1) intelligence activities, (2) investigation of evidence, (3) judgment or punishment, (4) rehabilitation. (*HCOMOJ*) **11. justice** is one of the guards that keeps the channel of progress a channel and not a stopped flow. (HCO PL 17 Mar 65 III) **12.** there can be no personal security without easily accessible, swift and fair **justice** within a group. The jurisprudence employed must be competent, acceptable to the members of the group and effective in accomplishing good order for the group and personal rights and security for its individual members. **Justice** used for revenge, securing advantages for a clique increases disorder. **Justice** should serve as a means of establishing guilt or innocence and awarding damages to the injured. The fact of its use should not pre-establish guilt or award. **Justice** which by its employment alone establishes an atmosphere of guilt or greed is harmful and creates disorder. (HCO PL 7 Sept 63) **13.** could be called the adjudication of the relative rightness or wrongness of a decision or an action. (*AP&A*, p. 10) **14.** the impartial administration of the laws of the land in accordance with the extant level of the severity-mercy ratio of the people. (PAB 96) **15.** don't ordinarily put a head on a pike unless it's the right head. But remember that there *are* times when it's vitally necessary to put some head, any head, on a pike to quell rising disorder. Just remember that **justice** is an action to deter disorder and secure the public safety. But if you *do* put the wrong head on a pike, be sure to put it back on the body again as soon as the need for its being on a pike is over. **Justice** is not always the matter of an individual. It is a short-term method of bringing order and it is needed for all dynamics. (*HCOMOJ*)

JUSTICE BUREAU, 1. sees that orgs, staff, and materiel are secure from legal entanglements, internal infiltration, suppressive ethics and legal attacks. Sees that **justice** reviews and rulings are handled quickly and **justly**. Sees that **justice** trained Ethics Officers are on post in orgs and a high public image of Scn justice exists. (CBO 39) **2. Justice Bureau** consists of Justice Data Branch, Security Branch, Reviews & Rulings Branch and Justice Dissem Branch. (CBO 17)

JUSTICE CODES, ten years ago when the new HCO Ethics Codes were first introduced, they were called **Justice Codes** for a short while. (HCO PL 22 Sept 75 II)

JUSTIFYING A GRAPH, justifying a graph is saying, "Well, **graphs** are always down in December due to Christmas." (HCO PL 6 Nov 66 I)

JUSTIFYING A STATISTIC, the one big God-awful mistake an executive can make in reading and managing by graph is being reasonable about graphs. This is called **justifying a statistic.** This is the single biggest error in graph interpretation by executives and the one thing that will clobber an org. One sees a graph down and says "Oh well, of course, that's . . ." and at that moment you've had it. (HCO PL 6 Nov 66 I)

K

KASTELHOLM, a ship for the Sea Organization in Europe. The *Kastelholm* is very posh and famous in the Scandinavian area. (FBDL 376)

KEEPER OF TECH, 1. the full title of this post is **Keeper of Tech** and Policy Knowledge. The purpose of the **Keeper of Tech** is to help LRH establish **tech** and policy in orgs fully and accurately and in full use and keep it there. (HCO PL 31 Aug 74) **2.** the **Keeper of Tech** is the highest technically trained personnel in the field. He/she is usually located in a very specific area (org), where they can be contacted and communicated with any time. The major duty of any **Keeper of Tech** is to ensure that the standard of Dn and Scn **tech** processing and case supervision is applied and maintained as originated by Source, at its 100% rate, in the area they are **keeping** the **tech** in. (FO 2354) *Abbr.* KOT.

KEEPER OF TECH CONTINENTAL, the org Keeper of Tech or the LRH Comm receives his orders regarding tech and policy from the **Keeper of Tech Continental.** The **Keeper of Tech Continental** is answerable to the LRH Comm Continental. The **K of T Continental** receives his orders from the K of T Flag via LRH Comm Continental. The **K of T Continental** is expected to actively look in on orgs and after inspection, write a targetted program for that org that will establish its Qual, especially cramming and word clearing, its library and to see that on-policy cramming and word clearing *occur.* He then writes a targetted program to establish the org's courses on policy and to see that actual on-policy training is occuring. (HCO PL 31 Aug 74)

KEEPER OF THE SEALS AND SIGNATURES, the LRH Communicator. (HCO PL 21 Jan 66)

KEEP THE LINES MOVING, by this is meant that the people should be routed as fast as possible to the correct destination. (BPL 20 Oct 67R)

KEY INGREDIENTS, when we look at organization in its most simple form, when we seek certain **key** actions or circumstances that make organization work, when we need a very simple, very vital rundown to teach people that will produce results, we find only a few points we need to stress. Thus one gets the points which are the true administrative points: (1) *observation* even down to discovering the users and what is needed and wanted. (2) *planning* which includes imaginative conception and intelligent timing, targeting and drafting of the plans so they can be communicated and assigned. (3) *communicating* which includes receiving and understanding plans and their portion and relaying them to others so that they can be understood. (4) *supervision* which sees that that which is communicated is done in actuality. (5) *production* which does the actions or services which are planned, communicated and supervised. (6) *users* by which the product or service or completed plan is used. (HCO PL 14 Sept 69)

KEY POST, one that has urgent responsibility and great expertise. (HCO PL 19 Mar 71)

KEY QUESTION, a question usually with a set wording, the answer to which will determine or largely determine the interviewer's opinion or evaluation of an employee, applicant, interviewee, etc.; a crucial question.

KEY QUESTION ONE, the **key question** you want answered yes by preclears is **key question**

one, "Would you want someone else to have similar gains to yours?" (HCO PL 7 May 68)

KEY QUESTION TWO, the **key question** for students is **key question two,** "Would you want someone to achieve the knowledge you now have?" (HCO PL 7 May 68)

KEY WORDS, the most important **words** relating to the person's duties or post or the new subject. (HCOB 21 Jun 72 II)

KHA-KHAN, 1. in an ancient army a particularly brave deed was recognized by an award of the title of **Kha-Khan.** It was not a rank. The person remained what he was, but he was entitled to be forgiven the death penalty ten times in case in the future he did anything wrong. That was a **Kha-Khan.** That's what producing high statistic staff members are—**Kha-Khans.** They can get away with murder without a blink from Ethics. (HCO PL 1 Sept 65 VII) **2. Kha-Khan** was like a medal. It ten times forgave a person the death penalty. He could ten times incur the death penalty and not get it. (PDC 26)

KICKBACK, a return of part of one's wages, profits, commissions, fees, etc., to another due to coercion or a confidential agreement. Kickbacks are often associated with unethical activities, i.e. a person in a position to choose which individuals a firm hires, chooses only those persons who will agree to pay him a certain percentage of their wages as a kickback.

KICKED UPSTAIRS, a term used to describe promoting a person to a higher position because his ineffectiveness and inefficiencies are causing too much trouble where he is and will cause less trouble in the higher position. The term was first associated with the promotion of representatives from the House of Commons to the House of Lords in the UK.

KICKOUTS, every day when I do my traffic I get a certain number of items which have to be reworked. I can't do such extensive revisions and still get my traffic out. So I lay them aside, I call them **kickouts.** Such items are incomplete staff work. (OODs 30 May 70)

KITCHEN CABINET, 1. in the US it refers to a group of advisors that the President consults instead of or in addition to his regular cabinet. 2. a group of advisors or aides who serve a very senior executive of a business rather than directly serving the business itself.

KLUDGE, 1. junk, paper, odds and ends, not actual valuables. (ED 240-7 Flag) **2.** any unwanted or unused mest (called **kludge** in the Sea Org). Not anything that is valuable, especially records of any kind. (SO ED 202 INT)

KNOW BEST, a technical and admin term. In tech it refers to an auditor who in misapplying a process on a pc considers he **knows** more than is actually contained in the technical bulletins on the subject and uses this **"know best"** as a basis for altering technical procedure. In admin it refers similarly to a person who considers he has a better way of accomplishing something than is contained in the policy letters covering that subject and messes things up. Management then finds itself left with the task of correcting that person's goofs by applying the correct standard policy to the area. In English, it is a derogatory term meaning the person is pretending to know while actually being stupid. (LRH Def. Notes)

KNOW-HOW, 1. the knowledge and ability to do a particular thing usually implying that a person already has practical experience in that area. 2. the technical knowledge of a subject.

KNOWINGNESS, knowingness would be self-determined knowledge. (5405C20)

KNOWLEDGE REPORT, staff member **report** written on noting some investigation is in progress and having data on it of value to ethics. (HCO PL 1 May 65)

L

L1X HI-LO TA REVISED, HCO Bulletin 1 January 1972RA, *L1X, Hi-Lo TA Revised.* This is the same **list** as *C/S 53 RI.* It has been brought up to date. It gives the whole question for each subject as in *C/S 53RI* and the same handling. It is easier to use on a pc whose attention wanders or who is not very familiar with terms. (LRH ED 257 INT)

L3 EXD RB, HCO Bulletin 2 April 1972 RB II, *Expanded Dianetics Series 3RB, L3 EXD RB Expanded Dianetics Repair List.* This is the prepared **list** for **Expanded Dn.** (LRH ED 257 INT)

L3RD, HCO Bulletin 11 April 1971RA, *L3RD Dianetics and Int RD Repair List.* This is the key **list** of Dn auditing and is the Dn standby in case of trouble. As the Int Rd is also Dn, while doing it, ones uses **L3RD** for trouble. (LRH ED 257 INT)

L4BR, HCO Bulletin 15 December 1968R, *L4BR, For Assessment of all Listing Errors.* An out list (meaning one done by listing and nulling, not a prepared list) can raise more concentrated hell with a pc than any other single auditing error. The amount of misemotion or illness which a wrong list generates has to be seen to be believed. When a pc is ill after a session or up to three days after, always suspect that a listing action done on the pc had an error in it. It must be corrected. This prepared **list L4BR** corrects lists of the listing and nulling variety. It can be run on old lists, current lists, general listing. (LRH ED 257 INT)

L-10, **1. L-10** was based on security checking and was one of the most successful techniques of recent times. (FO 3249) **2.** has mostly consisted of whipsawing overts back and forth. (ESTO 5, 7203C03 SO I) **3.** it came, actually, from the OT grades. It answers the question of why does an OT restrain himself and cease to behave as an OT. It works best in that band, but it also works at the lower end of the band. It turns the insane sane and makes a one life being immortal. (FEBC 3, 7101C18 SO II) **4.** research has disclosed that the reason humans think they have not lived before this life and won't live again is that they are in a condition below existing as beings. Through overts they have become unable to *see* the world around them or things in it. **L-10** runs off all overts and winds up with a thetan exterior who is aware of self. (ED 177 Flag)

L10MX, the new tech breakthrough (**L10MX**) overcomes the slow L10 and PTS problems. Fully grooved in it only takes about 10 hours of auditing. It produces results senior to our already fabulous L-10. (ED 41 FAO)

LABOR, 1. physical work often of a relatively unskilled and manual nature. 2. the quantity of physical work done or required. 3. human resources or manpower collectively. 4. the leaders and representatives who speak for a labor force of a particular industry such as labor union leaders as opposed to management.

LABOR ARBITRATION, see ARBITRATION, LABOR.

LABOR CUTBACK, a reduction in the number of personnel hired or retained for employment usually due to a decrease in the amount of work available.

LABOR DIRECT, workers who are directly processing raw material or directly providing a company's service in contrast to indirect labor such as clerical or plant maintenance workers.

LABOR FORCE, 1. in the U.S. it is the total potentially employable number of persons over 14 years of age. 2. the number of gainful workers employed by a company which collectively represent the company's potential ability to perform a task or tasks.

LABOR, INDIRECT, jobs which are indirectly concerned with production because they act to maintain, repair, or service things that have been produced rather than produce them.

LABOR LAWS, national or state and occasionally municipal legislation pertaining to workers and/or working conditions.

LABOR-MANAGEMENT COMMITTEE, a committee of labor and management representatives concerned with making the best utilization of men and materials.

LABOR MOVEMENT, a uniting of laborers under respected leaders for the purpose of collective action to improve their influence and well being within society. Labor movements concentrate on improved working conditions, better wages, more job security and remedying abuses imposed on labor by management.

LABOR ORGANIZATION, see ORGANIZATION, LABOR.

LABOR PROBLEMS, loosely any conflict between the aims of management and labor but it can also one-sidedly mean management's view of its conflicts with labor.

LABOR RELATIONS, 1. the field of enhancing the relationship between management and labor. 2. a term relating to the quality of the existing relationship management has with labor or the labor union.

LABOR, SWEATED, strenuous exhaustive labor or work done under sub-standard conditions that pays very little and may violate minimum wage statutes and safety or health regulations.

LA CENTRAL MIMEO, (Los Angeles) **LA Central Mimeo** is not an overgrown mimeo unit in Dept 2. It is a special **mimeo** project with the purpose of creating and maintaining a *complete* bulk file of *all* HCO PLs, HCOBs, LRH EDs, FOs, etc. in order to support the current Scn boom by making source material available in quantity for hat and course packs to all orgs under the USLO and Office of the Continental Captain. (LA Central Mimeo Infor Ltr, 10 Aug 71) *Abbr.* LACM.

LACK OF CSW, a type of dev-t where failure to forward an assembled package of information on any given situation, plan or emergency or failure to forward complete information on any dispatch, sufficiently complete to require only an approved or not approved slows down approval and action and develops traffic. It often requires returning for completed staff work, or the senior concerned must take over the person's hat and assemble the missing data using his own time and lines. Thus traffic develops. (HCO PL 27 Jan 69)

LACK OF EXECUTIVE RESPONSIBILITY, (Is this OK?) a type of dev-t. Executives may not OK anything done or to be done below their level unless their immediate junior has also stated or attested with an initial that it is OK. Unless one can fix **responsibility** for actions there is no **responsibility** anywhere and the whole show goes to pot. Never let a junior say "Is this OK?" Always make him state or initial "This is OK" on all work, actions, or projects. (HCO PL 27 Jan 69)

LAISSEZ FAIRE, the *Laissez Faire* is a Sea Org vessel. She has her own Captain per LRH Order. Captain and vessel are located in Dept 19 FSO. It is command intention that she be well maintained, used for training and produce real sailors. (FO 3582) [The *Laissez Faire* is a 25 foot ocean going sail boat.]

LAISSEZ FAIRE, a combination of two French words which together mean "allow it to do as it pleases." *Laissez-faire* is a theoretical economic doctrine which calls for an absence of government control and interference in commercial, industrial and business activities.

LANGUAGE, the cycle of new observations requiring new labels is probably the growth of **language** itself. **Language** is obviously the product of unsung observers who then popularized a word to describe what had been observed. (*DSTD*, p. ix)

LARGE ORGANIZATION, a **large organization** is composed of groups. A small organization is composed of individuals. (SH Spec 77, 6608C23)

LARGE SUM, **large sums** brought to the ship by courier may require special in-transit customs clearance even in countries where currency import and export is unrestricted. A **large sum** is defined as a sum well in excess of what the average traveller might be expected to carry. (FO 2949)

LAST COURT OF APPEAL, see FOLO LAST COURT OF APPEAL.

LAUDABLE WITHHOLD, there's a whole bunch of things called **laudable withholds.** A **laudable withhold** is always something that society expects of you. You have all withholds and all actions divided into laudable actions and **laudable withholds** and the **laudable withhold** goes along with the undesirable action and the laudable action goes along with an undesirable withhold. The U.S. population considers it laudable if you fire a gun at a man in time of war and considers it evil if you refuse to fire a gun at a man at time of war. Now in time of peace the same society considers it **laudable** to **withhold** firing the gun, and evil to fire the gun. (SH Spec 100, 6201C16)

LAUGHTER, **laughter** is rejection, actually. Any humor you will find usually deals with one or another out-point put in such a way that the reader or audience can reject it. (HCO PL 30 Sept 73 II)

LAUNDRESS, washes all domestic **laundry.** Looks after the **laundry** room and its machines. (HCO PL 18 Dec 64, *Saint Hill Org Board*)

Laundress

LAW, a **law** of course is something with which one thinks. It is a thing to which one aligns other junior facts and actions. A **law** lets one *predict* that if *all objects fall* when not supported, then of course cats, books and plates can be predicted in behavior if one lets go of them. (HCO PL 26 Apr 70R)

LAW OF THE OMITTED DATA, where there is no **data** available people will invent it. (HCO PL 21 Nov 72 I)

LAWS, the codified agreements of the people crystalizing their customs and representing their believed in necessities of conduct. (PAB 96)

LAYOFF, 1. a person who is temporarily put out of work due to a slump in production or decreased labor needs. 2. a period of time when business activity is in a slump. —*v.* the act of temporarily dismissing workmen.

LAYOUT, 1. after a dummy is done, a **layout** showing exact lines, spaces, photo placements and size is done. (ED 459-49 Flag) **2.** to plan in detail, arrange, or place all the parts of any material to be reproduced. Also means the finished plan, arrangement or placement of these. (Dissem Advice Ltr 1 Apr 70, *Magazine Layout and Paste up*)

LAYOUT, a plan of how to most efficiently and economically position the personnel and equipment of a department, plant, organization area, etc., so that work and traffic flows in its logical sequence. Variously called departmental layout, plant layout, etc.

LAYOUT DEPARTMENT, that department normally concerned with planning and graphic arts such as the drafting of plans, the design and layout of promotional literature and brochures for advertising, etc.

LEAD, the news story has two parts, the **lead** which quickly tells what has happened, and the body which documents the **lead.** (BPL 10 Jan 73R)

LEAD AUDITOR, 1. the purpose of the **lead auditor** is to help Ron by getting tech applied by his auditor unit with the greatest volume, quality and viability. (BPL 23 Nov 72) **2.** the I/C of a unit of five auditors junior to him. (BPL 23 Nov 72)

LEADER, one who exerts wide primary influence on the affairs of men. (HCO PL 12 Feb 67)

LEADER, a loss leader.

LEADERSHIP, 1. positive, enforced orders, given with no misemotion and toward visible accomplishment are the need of a group if it is to prosper and expand. Many obstacles can exist to that accomplishment but the group will function. We call it **leadership** and other nebulous things, this ability to handle a group, make it prosper and expand. All **leadership** is, in the final analysis, is giving the orders to implement the program and seeing that they are followed. (HCO PL 3 Nov 66) **2. leadership** is one of the most misunderstood subjects in man's dictionary. But it is based almost solely on the ability to give and enforce orders. (HCO PL 3 Nov 66)

Leadership

LEADERSHIP SURVEY, written and devised by L. Ron Hubbard in 1965, this test was developed to help guide personnel appointments to new exec posts during a rapid worldwide expansion. The **survey** measures the current **leadership** level of the testee *and* his potential **leadership** level. (HCO PL 3 Nov 70 II)

LEADING, the amount of space between lines of type. (BPL 29 Nov 68R)

german
dictionary

Leading

LEADING ESTABLISHMENT OFFICER, a **leading Establishment Officer**+Department is a Departmental Establishment Officer who has Section Estos under him due to the numerousness of the section. (HCO PL 7 Mar 72)

LEADING QUESTION, a question worded in such a way as to obtain or suggest the answer one is seeking.

LEAN ORGANIZATION, see ORGANIZATION, LEAN.

LEAP FROG SYSTEM, (Flag only) if there are three pcs in an auditor's line up, he goes 1, 2, 3   1, 2, 3   1, 2, 3   day after day. The pcs assigned to an auditor are consecutively audited and C/Sed. If he has two pcs, he can get in three or even four sessions in the day. This means pcs are always on standby. There is no registrar saying "You will get your sessions at 10:00 a.m. in the morning every Tuesday." Registrars do not schedule. Ever. It means that a pc may expect to get audited as often as possible. If an auditor starts, let us say, at 0830 hours, he can **leap frog** pcs all through the day, auditing each one as far as he can, to a win or to the conclusion of the C/S or lunch or whatever. But the signal to Tech Services to act is that auditor bringing the pc to the examiner. At once, that auditor's next pc must be rounded up by Tech Services, the folder put in the auditor's hands even while the auditor is finishing his admin on the first session. (BFO 46)

LEASE, 1. a contract allowing a person to rent, possess or use something for a specified period of time in exchange for a certain fee. Any conditions of usage or stipulations of liability would also be written into a lease. 2. the length of time that such a contract endures. —*v.* the act of allowing someone to rent or use something for a period of time in exchange for money.

LEAVE OF ABSENCE, an authorized period **of absence** from a course granted in writing by a course supervisor and entered in the student's study folder. (HCOB 21 Sept 70) *Abbr.* LOA.

LEAVE OF ABSENCE, the period of time granted an employee to be temporarily absent from work to handle an urgent matter such as illness, familial tragedy, military duty, etc.

LEDGER, in accounting, the book of final entry, where the chronological record of a business' transactions previously entered in a journal or daybook (book of original entry) are now posted under specific accounts. These accounts are usually in alphabetical order in the ledger and of four main categories: income, expenditures, assets and liabilities.

LEDGER ACCOUNT, see ACCOUNT, LEDGER.

LEFT ARM RATES, administrative personnel without privileges of etiquette and may not order sailors or right arm rates and do not succeed to command of a ship regardless of rank. (FO 196)

LEGAL, 1. handles Committees of Evidence internationally and at Saint Hill. Handles all matters of copyrights and trademark registration in various countries. Handles all book contracts. (HCO PL 18 Dec 64, *Saint Hill Org Board*) **2.** purpose: to make **legal** the actions of the organizations of Dn and Scn and safeguard their public and private interests. (HCO PL 12 Oct 62)

LEGAL BOARD, a **legal board** is formed to handle and arrange the **legal** affairs of the flagship and Sea Org. Its area of operation is strictly the routine matters of contracts, registrations, company laws, etc. The committee will comprise: CS-1, Chairman; CS-1 Comm, Secretary; Ship's Rep and 3rd Mate. (FO 1522)

LEGAL BRANCH, to safeguard the org, let alone affluence, I hereby create a **Legal Branch** in the Office of The Guardian. All other Legal Sections in the org are abolished. (BPL 14 Jan 68)

LEGAL BUREAU, (GO) all relationships with governmental agencies and government officials are handled by the Guardian's Office or are cleared through the Guardian's Office. The **Legal Bureau** receives and then handles or approves all correspondence to and from government officials acting in an official capacity; and whether such are local, county, district (state) or national, all are handled by the **Legal Bureau.** (BPL 20 May 70 I)

LEGAL MATTERS, when we say **legal matters** we mean outside law and law agencies such as attorneys, civil courts, suits, contracts and corporation and copyright matters. (HCO PL 17 Mar 65 II)

LEGAL OFFICER, the purpose of the **Legal Officer** is to help LRH handle every **legal,** government, suit, accounting and tax contact or action for the organization and by himself or employed representative, to protect the organization and its people from harm. (HCO PL 3 Feb 66)

LEGAL ORDERS, **orders** known to and authorized by Flag in writing or as found in policy, FOs, Base Orders, Executive Directives and Flag Division Directives. (FO 2947)

LEGAL SECRETARY, the **Legal Secretary** of the organization is appointed by board resolution. He has full authority to organize, under the Guardian, a full legal branch with necessary clerks, files and facilities, with authority to appoint or dismiss attorneys for any org under the authority of the Guardian. (BPL 14 Jan 68)

LEGAL SECTION, **section** in Dept 3, Dept of Inspection and Reports. **Legal Section** handles all **legal** matters, suits, court appearances, attorney liaison. (HCO PL 17 Jan 66 II)

LENGTH OF TIME TO EVALUATE, HCO Policy Letter 12 June 1972, *Data Series 26, Esto Series 18, Length of Time to Evaluate.* A list you assess to locate trouble an **evaluator** might be having. Also for slow **evaluators** or slow students on a Data Series Course. (LRH ED 257 INT)

LESSEE, the individual who is granted a lease; the user, renter, or possessor of leased property.

LESSOR, the individual granting a lease to another; the person who allows another the use, rent, or possession of something in return for money.

LETTER OF CREDIT, to expedite Flag missions, FBOs may only advance monies to Flag missionaires against a Flag **letter of credit.** A **letter of credit,** as a term, is found in banking practice. A bank issues them and a person holding one can go to another bank somewhere else and draw out money against the **letter of credit.** The **letter of credit** is issued for expenses up to a certain sum. When money is issued, in addition to usual bank procedures, the sum is debited on the back of the **letter of credit** with a signature of the cash issuing bank. We will follow this same practice except that Flag Treasury is the issuer and org FBOs are the banks that give out the funds and debit them on the back. (LRH ED 271 INT)

LETTER OF CREDIT, a letter issued and backed by a bank which allows a specified person to obtain a stated amount of funds from that bank, its branches or an associated bank. A letter of credit allows a person the credible potentiality of funds without the risks of physically transporting money about.

LETTER OUT HAT CHECK UNIT, in Dept 1, Department of Routing, Appearances and Personnel. **Letter Out Hat Check Unit,** keeps all **letter** emanation points **hat checked,** defending HCO's statistic. (HCO PL 17 Jan 66 II)

LETTER REGISTRAR, **1.** the **Letter Registrar** is working to get people moving up the Gradation Chart to a point where their reality is sufficient to effect a want to come to Saint Hill. (HCO PL 29 Nov 68) **2.** the **Letter Registrar** finds individuals who want something and writes that person letters that help him or her to get it. (HCO PL 6 Apr 65) **3.** the **Letter Registrar** is in charge of the **Letter Registration** Section of PrR. The **Letter**

Registrar and assistants keep a steady flow of letters going to applicants to get them to come in for training and processing. (HCO PL 20 Dec 62) **4.** the **Letter Registrar** is responsible for all cases in connection with the organization and on the org mailing lists. It is **Letter Registrar's** job to get these people cleared and trained. (HCO PL 13 Sept 62, *Comments about Letter Registrars*) **5.** the prime purpose of the **Letter Registrar** is: to help LRH guide individuals by **letter** into correct channels to obtain Scn and to increase the size of organizations. (HCO PL 21 Sept 65 VI) **6. Reges** writing to individuals with the CF folder to hand and using the CF folder to find out what individuals want and then helping them get it and guiding them into the org for services. (LRH ED 159RA INT) **7.** the **Letter Registrar** is concerned with future prospects. She writes to all future prospects. Her job is to see to it that we have people to train and audit in the future. (SEC ED 66, 30 Jan 59) *Abbr.* Ltr Reg.

LETTER REGISTRAR SECTION OFFICER, 1. a key person in the **Letter Registrar Section** is the **Letter Registrar Section Officer.** She is the **section** head of the (1) Letter Reg Unit, (2) Typing Unit, (3) Advance Scheduling Reg Unit, (4) Registrar Mail Unit. The **LRSO** has got to be fast on her feet, able to follow policy, know how to handle any post of the section and able to work in Address and CF. (HCO PL 18 Feb 73 IV) **2.** the **Letter Registration Section** is headed by the **Letter Registration Section Officer.** This **officer** designs questionnaires and supervises the **section** and its personnel and letter quality and policy and is responsible for having personnel on the job. This **officer** does not write letters. (HCO PL 29 Nov 68) *Abbr.* LRSO.

LETTER REGISTRAR UNIT, the **Letter Registrar Unit** answers incoming mail and originates via CF folders. Each one, so far as possible answers his or her own mail. The whole action here is getting the individual on a channel, and getting them up it step by step until they finally reach for Saint Hill services, at which time they are forwarded to the Advance Registrations Records Unit for scheduling. (HCO PL 29 Nov 68)

LETTER REGISTRATION SECTION, 1. this **section** has four units. (1) the Letter Registrars Unit. (2) the Registrar Typing Unit. (3) the Advance Registration Records Unit. (4) the Registrar Mail Unit. (HCO PL 29 Nov 68) **2.** handles the writing of **letters**, the packaging of information packets, accumulation of mailing lists, and the handling of all files and addresses. (HCO PL 20 Dec 62)

LETTERS IN AND OUT, letters in and out is defined as personal signed **letters**, not a form letter. This statistic does not include mailing pieces, leaflets or circulars. (HCO PL 5 Feb 71 III) [The above HCO PL was cancelled by BPL 10 Oct 75 IX.]

LETTUCE, a slang term referring to paper money.

LEVEL, level means an Academy course, i.e. **Level** Zero or **Level** 1, etc. (HCO PL 31 May 65)

LEVEL 0, see HUBBARD RECOGNIZED SCIENTOLOGIST.

LEVEL I, see HUBBARD TRAINED SCIENTOLOGIST.

LEVEL II, see HUBBARD CERTIFIED AUDITOR.

LEVEL III, see HUBBARD PROFESSIONAL AUDITOR.

LEVEL IV, see HUBBARD ADVANCED AUDITOR,

LEVEL V, see HUBBARD VALIDATED AUDITOR.

LEVEL VI, see HUBBARD SENIOR SCIENTOLOGIST. [The SHSBC teaches to *Level VI* and results in a Class VI auditor. However Grade VI is a solo-audit grade and is not only done by a Class VI auditor but also by pcs who have attained Grade VA and have completed a special course which teaches them to solo audit.]

LEVEL VII, Level VII contains the materials necessary to totally erase the reactive mind. (SH Spec 71, 6607C26) [The Class VII Course is the course which teaches auditors to audit the power processes. **Level VII** or Clearing Course, as it is more often called, is done by pcs who have successfully solo audited to Grade VI Release, after which they may solo audit to Clear.] See HUBBARD GRADUATE AUDITOR.

LEVELS OF AWARENESS, there are about 52 **levels of awareness** from unexistence up to the state of Clear. By **level of awareness** is meant that of which a being is **aware.** A being who is at a **level** on this scale is **aware** only of that level and the others below it. To get a case gain such a person must become **aware of** the **level** next above him. And so on in orderly sequence, **level** by **level.** (HCO PL 5 May 65)

LEVERAGE, the effect on the per share earnings of common stock of a company when large sums must be paid for bond interest or perferred stock dividends before common stock dividends can be paid. Leverage is favorable for common stock when a company's earnings are up but may work against common stock when earnings decline. Also called gearing.

LIABILITIES, 1. the sum of debts one has to others; the total of claims or potential claims against a person, company, business, etc. 2. the total of claims made or able to be made against a corporation. Such would include claims for payment of accounts, wages, taxes accrued, dividends declared payable, long-term or fixed liabilities like bank loans, debentures, mortgage bonds, etc.

LIABILITY, **1.** below non-existence there is the condition of **liability.** The being has ceased to be simply non-existent as a team member and has taken on the color of an enemy. It is assigned where careless or malicious and knowing damage is caused to projects, orgs or activities. It is adjudicated that it is malicious and knowing because orders have been published against it or because it is contrary to the intentions and actions of the remainder of the team or the purpose of the project or org. It is a **liability** to have such a person unwatched as the person may do or continue to do things to stop or impede the forward progress of the project or org and such a person cannot be trusted. No discipline or the assignment of conditions above it has been of any avail. The person has just kept on messing it up. The condition is usually assigned when several dangers and non-existences have been assigned or when a long unchanged pattern of conduct has been detected. (HCO PL 6 Oct 67) **2.** a half done job is **liability.** (ED 62 Flag) **3.** a **liability** may be defined as something of value owed by the organization at the end of the financial period concerned. (BPL 14 Nov 70 III)

LIABILITY FORMULA, the **formula** of **liability** is: (1) decide who are one's friends. (2) deliver an effective blow to the enemies of the group one has been pretending to be part of despite personal danger. (3) make up the damage one has done by personal contribution far beyond the ordinary demands of a group member. (4) apply for re-entry to the group by asking the permission of each member of it to rejoin and rejoining only by majority permission, and if refused, repeating (2) and (3) and (4) until one is allowed to be a group member again. (HCO PL 6 Oct 67)

LIAISON BUREAU, a duplicate **Bureau** just like one on Flag that is sitting out in a continental area. (7012C04 SO)

LIAISON OFFICE, see CONTINENTAL LIAISON OFFICE AND FLAG OPERATIONS LIAISON OFFICE.

LIBERTY, shore leave. (ED 323 Flag)

LIBRARIAN, see QUAL LIBRARIAN.

LIE, a **lie** of course is a false reality. (HCO PL 13 Aug 70 II)

LIEN, a claim on the property of another which has been pledged or mortgaged to secure the payment of a debt or obligation.

LIE REACTION QUESTIONS, **1.** the **lie reaction questions** were originally used in Scn only to study the needle pattern of the person being checked so that changes in it could then be judged in their true light. Some pcs, for instance, get a slight fall every time *any* question is asked. Some get a fall only when there is heavy charge. Both can be security checked by studying the common pattern of the needle demonstrated in asking the **lie reaction questions.** (HCO PL 25 Mar 61) **2.** nul questions to determine your reaction pattern on a confessional. Example: are you sitting in a chiar? Are you on the moon? Are all cats black? (HCO PL 7 Apr 61RA)

LIFE, **life** is going along a certain course impelled by a purpose and some place to arrive. It consists mostly of removing the barriers in the channel, holding the edges firm, ignoring the distractions, and reinforcing and reimpelling one's progress along the channel. That's **life.** (SH Spec 57, 6504C06)

LIFETIME MEMBERSHIPS, **1.** the **Lifetime Membership** is the credit **membership** of Scn. Its holders can obtain a discount from the list price of courses, intensives, books, meters, tapes, insignia, congresses, etc. They can have one of anything on credit. One course, and one grade worth of intensives. In books, meters, tapes, insignia, congresses, they in actual practice can have a reasonable amount. There is no note, no interest rate, nothing. The **Lifetime** or Credit **Member** is billed monthly on a standard charge account system. However, the Credit **Member** must have paid for his course or his grade worth of intensives or his book bill before he can have another course or grade or beyond a reasonable amount of books. If the bill is not paid in 12 months the **membership** is forfeit. (HCO PL 22 Mar 65, *Current Promotion and Org Program Summary Membership Rundown International Annual Membership*) **2.** receives PAB Magazine as available, Continental Magazine as available, 20% discount on training, processing, books, tapes. (Discount valid on cash purchases only.) (HCO PL 26 Oct 59)

LIFE UPSET INTENSIVE, this is a 5 hour or so **intensive.** It is the ARC break routine mostly. (LRH ED 57 INT)

LIFO, 1. an abbreviation for Last-In, First-Out which is an inventory cost accounting procedure which costs items just sold as if they were just purchased as stock. 2. the basis of laying off or dismissing personnel which assumes that the last one hired is the first one to be dismissed.

LIMITED, chiefly in Britain and Canada where it is attached to a firm's name, Ltd. designates that limit of liability to creditors of each stockholder or limited partner in the business is restricted by law to his actual investment therein. *Abbr.* Ltd.

LIMITED CERTIFICATE, a **certificate,** printed in black and white, on which the words, LIMITED, EXPIRES SIX MONTHS FROM DATE, is printed boldly. (HCO PL 2 Sept 70, *Instruction Protocol Official*)

LIMITED LIABILITY, limited liability means that the amount of liability is limited to a set amount. A corporation is a business structure which offers its owners or shareholders limited liability. If claims are made against a corporation, a shareholder or owner in it is only liable for the amount of money he has invested in the corporation. Claims cannot be made against a shareholder's personal or private holdings outside the corporation unless criminal activity has occurred in connection with the running of the corporation and can be proven. Otherwise his liabilities are limited to the amount of his investment.

LIMITED NON-REMIMEO, 1. non-remimeo means bulletins and policy letters which are intended for use but only by executives and therefore are of **limited** distribution. It means not to be mimeoed again by the receiving org. There are two classes of non-remimeos: general non-remimeo and **limited non-remimeo. Limited non-remimeo** means that copies only go to master files, LRH Comm, the Guardian or A/G, HES, OES, ED (CO) and FR. (BPL 14 Apr 69R) **2.** (mimeo distribution) it is usually important that this does not get wide distribution as it has to do with org know-how, planning, etc., and could be misunderstood. So it is not remimeoed or strewn about. It may be taken up in staff meetings but that is about all. One never republishes a **limited non-remimeo** in a magazine. (HCO PL 2 Jul 64) **3.** there are two classes of non-remimeo. One is **limited non-remimeo,** meaning master files, HCO Sec, and Assn/Org Sec. The other is general non-remimeo, meaning master files, HCO Sec, Assn/Org Sec, reception reference files, and department head and post concerned to whom the data applies. (HCO PL 2 Jul 64)

LIMITED ORDER, see ORDER, LIMITED.

LIMITED PARTNERSHIP, a business partnership in which the liability of the partners is legally limited to the amount of the payment each made into the partnership. A limited partner is entitled to receive a proportionate share of the profits and a return of his investment in the event of dissolution.

LINE, 1. the shortest and most direct distance between two points or terminals. (FSO 137) **2.** in reproduction, any part of the artwork that has no shades of grey—just black and white. (Dissem Advice Ltr 1 Apr 70, *Magazine Layout and Pasteup*)

Line (Def. 2)

LINE, 1. a fixed pattern of terminals who originate and receive or receive and relay orders and information in an organization. A line can be vertical such as a command line where authority and power of position increases the higher up one goes or a line can be horizontal where each terminal on the line shares a similar status. 2. series of interrelated products such as a line of cosmetics which employ one scent and are marketed under one brand name.

LINE AND STAFF ORGANIZATION, see ORGANIZATION, LINE AND STAFF.

LINE AND STAFF RELATIONSHIP, see ORGANIZATION, LINE AND STAFF; LINE RELATIONSHIP; STAFF RELATIONSHIP.

LINEAR RECRUITING, a firm hires a girl to write their letters. After 60 days they find she doesn't do her job. So they get rid of her and hire another. And in 90 days find she can't do her job. So they fire her and hire another . . . that's 150 days of no-correspondence. It's enough to ruin any firm. It's costly. (HCO PL 29 Aug 70 III)

LINE OFFICER, an executive on a command line who receives orders from his seniors and relays these in turn down the line to his juniors. He sends data and compliances up the line to his seniors as required.

LINE ORGANIZATION, see ORGANIZATION, LINE.

LINE PERSON, they keep the **lines** going. They are in motion, they are running particles up and down **lines.** If there is nobody there to chase particles up and down **lines** and separate particles and spread them out and do this and that with them and make sure that the flow continues, then nothing significant really arrives at the fixed positions. (5812C16)

LINE POST, a **line post** has to do with organizational **lines**; seeing that the **lines** run smoothly; ironing out any ridges in the **lines**; keeping particles flowing smoothly from one post to another post. A **line post** is concerned with the flow of **lines,** not necessarily with the fixed terminal posts at the end of the **lines.** An example of this is a communicator. His job is mainly keeping communications flowing smoothly from one terminal to another. Any time there is a stop in the flow of communications, he straightens it out. A fixed terminal post stays in one spot, handles specific duties and receives communications, handles them, and sends them on their way. (HCO PL 22 Jun 64)

LINE RELATIONSHIP, a type of organizational form where orders originating with top management travel vertically down a command line to various lower echelons of executives who in turn issue orders down the line to their subordinates. There is a definite line of command with authority and power of position decreasing from the top down. This is the type of pattern used in military organizations.

LINES, communication **lines.** (OS-9, 5611C08)

LINE STOPS, **stopping** the flow of **lines.** (FSO 384)

LINE SUPERVISOR, see SUPERVISOR, LINE.

LIQUID ASSETS, see ASSETS, LIQUID.

LIQUIDATE, 1. to cause an enterprise to cease to exist as a going concern. 2. to wind up the affairs of a business concern, bankrupt estate, etc., by applying available assets to the discharge of liabilities. 3. to pay off or settle a debt, claim or obligation.

LIQUIDATED DAMAGES, in contractual agreements, the amount stated therein to be paid by a party found to be responsible for breach of contract.

LIQUIDATION, 1. the act of converting stocks or other property into cash. 2. the condition of a company being dissolved by selling its assets to pay its liabilities. Any remaining cash is distributed to its stockholders.

LIQUID CAPITAL, see CAPITAL, LIQUID.

LIQUIDATING DIVIDENDS, a return flow of capital to a company's stockholders.

LIQUIDITY, 1. the extent to which a company has access to cash or can convert assets into cash without appreciable loss in value. 2. the degree to which a company can meet financial obligations in cash or its equivalent. 3. stock market term for the ability of the market, relative to a particular security, to absorb a good amount of buying or selling at reasonable price changes.

LIQUID RATIO, same as Acid Test Ratio.

LIST 1-C, HCO Bulletin 19 March 1971, *List 1-C.* This is the updated version of the earliest *list* ever compiled. It is used during sessions at the auditor's discretion and in other ways. It also prevents some pcs from insisting "It's an ARC break" (which never cleans) when it's really a withhold, a common error. It can also be addressed to life. Usually when a session blows up, an **LIC** is used fast rather than just sit and ack! (LRH ED 257 INT)

LISTED STOCK, see STOCK, LISTED,

LIST PRICE, the published or advertised price of an article or service before any discounts or reduction.

LITERATE, able to read and write. (OODs 14 Apr 72)

LITERATURE UNIT, **1.** **literature** in this case means brochures, posters, fliers, sales promo pieces for use by orgs, FSMs, Flag, etc. What does an FSM have as a leaflet or brochure to hand out to a prospect about org training? What brochures are there that list all Pubs U.S. and DK books and sales items? What actual **literature** could be mailed to prospective FCCIs? This **unit**, the **Literature Unit**, under CS-2, is being formed to handle that. (OODs 26 Apr 75) **2.** the ideal scene of the **Literature Unit** is the conceiving, creating and bringing into being economically, of superlative quality glossy sales **literature** that brings about a high return (money, bodies, recruits, esteem, etc.) for the investment. (FO 3577)

LITTLE CHILDREN, anyone below six is to be called **little children** or babies. (FO 1630)

LIVING, **living** is having and following a purpose. That's the formula of **Life.** (SH Spec 54, 6503C09)

LLOYD'S, world famous insurance firm founded in 1688 at Lloyd's Coffee House in London, specializing originally in marine insurance but now operating extensively in all insurance fields except life insurance. Lloyd's organizational structure is comprised of an association of some 1500 brokers and underwriters throughout the world. As well, they published *Lloyd's Register* giving vital data about many of the seagoing vessels of the world.

LOAN, a sum of money lent or given out at interest.

LOANED EMPLOYEE, see EMPLOYEE, LOANED.

LOAN SHARK, a person or company that lends money at an exorbitant rate of interest.

LOCAL, test form heading to indicate the type the person is: **local** (lives in same city as Central Org). (HCO PL 28 Oct 60, *New Testing Promotion Section Important*)

LOCAL ENVIRONMENT, the surrounding area to the scene being evaluated in the matter or a person would be the general third dynamic or other dynamic in which he or she lives his day to day life and which influence the person and therefore influence his hat or post. Family or distant friends, not visible to an evaluator, or the work **environment** or on the job friends of Joe or Joanna may greatly influence Joe or Joanna. (HCO PL 25 May 73)

LOCAL GO ACCOUNT, the 5% of the CGI for the **local GO** is transferred to the (org name) **local GO account.** This **account** is used to disburse sums for the expenses of the **local GO.** This does not mean that the org **GO** can only operate on this amount, it does mean that where FP is tight the org **GO** can still perform its duties. Responsibility for this account including its admin lies with the AGF (AG in absence of an AGF). (BPL 6 Jul 75 III)

LOCAL ISSUE AUTHORITY, **local I/A** is held by the continental and org LRH Comm who has the **authority** to approve all proposed promo pieces, handouts, mailings, magazines (policy authorized versions only), **local** EDs, EOs, OODs, Bs of I, Courts, Hearings, Comm Evs, etc. Any request to **issue** or publish (whether or not previously **issued**) or requests for copies of HCOBs, HCO PLs, internal routing and report forms of various types must be okayed by **local I/A.** It is the responsibility of **local I/A** to ensure that any written executive instruction, order or directive, any promotional piece, or form for internal or external use, conforms with existing policy and technology. Any **issue** that does not conform with existing policy and technology is vetoed. In case of such veto, the date and paragraph number of the HCOB, policy letter or LRH ED must be stated in the veto. (BPL 2 Mar 73R I)

LOCAL OPTION, the circumstance of a local government or managment having the power to settle or conclude an issue without having to direct the matter to higher officials.

LOCAL RESERVES, the **reserves** built up by an FBO, OTL, CLO, org, ship or activity by reason of booming the org. These may not be built up at the arduous expense or denial of SO reserves. (HCO PL 9 Mar 72 I)

LOCATIONAL, "**Locate** the ________." The auditor has the preclear **locate** the floor, the ceiling, the walls, the furniture in the room and other objects and bodies. (HCOTB 6 Feb 57)

LOCKED IN, an expression for the instance of an investor having a profit on a security but does not sell because his profit would be subject to capital gains tax.

LOCKOUT, industrial action taken by an employer during a time of labor strife in which workers are locked out of the factory or their place of employment, pending settlement of the disagreement. Also called a shutout.

LOG, the word **log** is a verb in sea language as well as a noun. A **log** is a ship's official record. To **log** means to put a person's name in it for an offense. Usually with two weeks loss of pay. (OODs 26 June 72)

Log

LOG BOOK, see LRH COMM LOG.

LOGIC, the subject of reasoning. **Logic** or the ability to reason is vital to an organizer or administrator. If he cannot think clearly he will not be able to reach the conclusions vital to make correct decisions. (HCO PL 11 May 70)

LOGISTIC LINES, **logistic lines** and courier lines are not to be confused. Courier lines carry mail. **Logistic lines** are established to carry **logistic** items and supplies. Couriers travel normally by air. **Logistic** items travel by surface. (FO 2611R)

LOGISTIC MISSIONS, 1. **missions** which deal primarily in the procurement, maintenance and transportation of material, monies and/or personnel would come under the heading of **"logistics."** (FO 2132) **2.** supplies of a certain nature required would be a **logistic mission.** (FO 2505)

LOGISTICS, 1. these are items which have some apparent commercial value such as personal effects, machine parts, food, records and magnetic recording tape, watches and jewelry, raw (unexposed) film, etc. (CBO 387) **2.** the procurement, maintenance and transportation of military material, facilities and personnel. (FO 2132) *Abbr.* Logs.

LONG-RANGE, several months at a time. (ED 135 Flag)

LONG-RANGE POLICY, **policy** is the broad general outline originated by top management. Orders are the instructions issued by the next lower level of management to get things done that result in products. **Long-range policy** already exists in FOs and HCO PLs, CBOs, even HCOBs. Short-range top management programs and plans exist in LRH EDs, SO EDs, programs, even FBDLs. (FBDL 12)

LOOKOUT, 1. the **Lookout** is on **lookout** and watches outside the ship for other ships, objects in the water, hazards, menaces to navigation, cloud changes, sea changes, etc., and reports them to the OOW promptly. (FO 80) **2. Lookouts** are the eyes of the Conning Officer. By careful **looking** and reporting, he keeps the Conning Officer informed of what is happening and the Officer of the Deck informed of navigational aids. (*SWPB*) *Abbr.* L/O.

Lookout

LOSS, the true **loss** of an org is the difference between money it should have made (and didn't) and the money it did make. (ED 459-47 Flag)

LOSS, in business, the condition brought about when an expense or cost incurred is in excess of its revenue, income or selling price.

LOSS LEADER, something sold at a very low price possibly even below cost in order to attract customers who will buy other products too; also called a leader.

LOSS REPORT, staff member **report** of the disappearance of anything that should be there giving anything known about its disappearance such as when it was seen last. (HCO PL 1 May 65)

LOST AND FOUND SECTION, section in Dept 2, Dept of Communications. **Lost and Found Section** cares for all property **found**, looks for all property and dispatches **lost.** (HCO PL 17 Jan 66 II)

LOUSY EXECUTIVE, a lousy executive hands the work to anyone handy, regardless of title. He's in apathy and doesn't know there's an org there. (HCO PL 1 Jul 65 III)

LOWER CONDITIONS, liability, treason, doubt, enemy. (HCO PL 18 Oct 67 IV) [The descending order of these *conditions* was corrected by HCO PL 14 Mar 68 to "Liability, Doubt, Enemy and Treason." The **condition** of "Confusion" was added below Treason by HCO PL 9 Feb 74. HCO PL 18 Oct 67 IV was cancelled by BPL 16 Nov 71RA *Conditions: Awards and Penances.*]

LRH, A DIRECTOR, a director on the Board of **Directors** of several companies. No salary may be paid for this post. (HCO PL 21 Dec 65)

LRH, AN INDIVIDUAL, 1. this is **LRH** a private person. This identity is the one who is entitled to any royalties and leases copyrights and trademarks and technology for use by Scn organizations. This identity paid for and did the research, organized the organizations. This is the identity that loans orgs money or guarantees their bank accounts, etc., and on death is a private trust for my family. (HCO PL 4 Jan 66 VI) **2.** means **L. Ron Hubbard**, a private person as distinct from a trustee, a director or a staff member. **LRH, an individual** often advances goods or sums without reimbursement, has borne the whole cost of research of Scn and used his own money to found organizations. (HCO PL 21 Dec 65)

LRH ARTIST, purpose: to enhance the dissemination of **LRH's** wisdom and understanding through brilliantly designed and well executed visual and graphic ideas of high quality. To promote **LRH** and disseminate Dn and Scn through brilliantly designed **LRH** publications of excellent LRH image. (COLRHED 405)

LRH AUDIO-VISIO BRANCH, the **LRH Audio-Visio Branch** is positioned on the org board in the Personal Office of LRH in the LRH Personal Secretary Office. The purpose of the **LRH A/V Branch** is to bring about LRH's standards as applied to audio and visio, both in the execution of his projects and in the delivery of audio and visio products where his name, voice or image are involved. (FO 3676)

LRH, BOARD MEMBER, this is an unpaid identity on several **boards.** It is entitled only to out-of-pocket expenses and almost never puts in for any. This is a **member** of a **board** of directors. These must be paid no salary in a non-profit corporation, only expenses. "Chairman" comes under this. Also "President." (HCO PL 4 Jan 66 VI)

LRH BOARD OF REVIEW, as it may well be that in the past year there were some injustices or misassignments of conditions by others, I have convened the **LRH Board of Review.** This was once a traditional function of HCO and has not been in use for some time. Anyone on Flag or who has been on Flag for the past year and who may believe that any injustices need correction should contact the Chairman of the **LRH Board of Review** at Flag. (OODs 30 Sept 73)

LRH BRIEFING OFFICER, one who **briefs** others on what **LRH** is doing now in what areas so that his actions can be backed up, followed through and brought to a successful completion of cycle thereby helping him to move off spots that he has handled through observation, development and origination of communications which when duplicated and executed do handle those spots. (BPL 27 Jul 71)

LRH COMM AIDE, 1. Branch 11A, the LRH Comm Branch (Flag Management Bu). This branch consists of all the functions that involve the actual running of the LRH Comm Network. The head of the branch is the **LRH Comm Aide.** (FBDL 488R) [This post is not now CS-7 but a separate post below CS-7.] **2.** CS-7. (FO 1109) **3.** CS-1: **LRH Comm Aide** in charge of communications, transport and personnel. (FO 795)

LRH COMM BRANCH, 1. (Branch 11A Flag Management Bu) this **branch** consists of all the functions that involve the actual running of the **LRH Comm** Network. The head of the branch is the **LRH Comm** Aide. Cont'l **LRH Comms** and org **LRH Comms** will continue to receive their orders from this **branch**, with the only difference being coordination of all orders and priority setting, through the FR Network and Execution Branch. This branch also contains a "Tech and Policy Knowledge Management Section" whence the KOT and PK Network is operated, and as a unit of this section, on Flag a "Tech Quality Control Unit" which handles tech queries and flub catch per policy. (FBDL 488R) **2. LRH Comm Branch,** Management Bureau, Flag, creates and runs an operational **LRH Comm** Network and through this network requires duplication of and gets compliance to LRH orders, policy and tech from all org staff—also gets compliance to CS-7 and Senior **LRH Comm** orders. Operates on programs and CEDS and through effective nudging gets compliances to these. Does debugs where programs not getting done. Keeps track of programs and orders with orderly up-to-date logs and files. Sees that **LRH communications** fly and look well. Safeguards **LRH** admin and ethics procedures. Puts a qualified Keeper of Tech and Policy Knowledge Network there and through it ensures **LRH** tech and policy is safeguarded and adhered to without deviation. Receives and handles technical queries by direct reference to **LRH** tech. Overall enhances **LRH** image and increases orgs and staffs and publics' affinity with him. Takes full responsibility for and handles by evaluation and execution estates and ships for Sea Org and Scn orgs. (CBO 376)

LRH COMM BRANCH FOLO, **LRH Comm Branch** in the Management Bu at a **FOLO** creates and runs an effective fully operational Continental **LRH Comm** Network and through this network requires duplication of and gets compliance to **LRH** orders, policy and tech from all org staff, and to CS-7 and LRH Pers Comm orders. Operates on programs and gets org **LRH Comms** to write CEDS and gets compliance to these, keeps track of programs with up-to-date logs and files and does necessary debug actions per standard **LRH Comm** procedure where programs are not getting done. Sees that **LRH communications** fly and look well and safeguards **LRH** issue authority and ethics procedures. Operates a Continental KOT Network and through it ensures that **LRH** tech and policy knowledge is safeguarded and 100% standard. Receives and handles technical queries by direct reference to **LRH** tech. Handles area and continental estates matters via the Continental Estates Exec and Area Estates Org with proper CSW as needed and ensures that estates programs for orgs, area, or ships are executed. (CBO 375)

LRH COMM BUREAU, the **LRH Comm Bureau** logs, distributes and obtains compliance from all **LRH** issues. It receives and responds to all public response to **LRH.** It maintains **LRH** as image and Source by establishing **LRH** as an image in orgs and with the public. (CBO 7)

LRH COMM LOG, 1. the purpose of the **LRH Comm Log** is to accurately record details of all **LRH communications** received and their acknowledgement and compliance from recipients of those orders. It is further used to detect areas of noncompliance, no reports and false reports (through direct observation or examination of statistics). The basic operating tool of an **LRH Comm** is his **log** book. This is usually a common day ledger divided into separate sections with an index marker. All **LRH** EDs, HCO PLs, HCOBs, telexes and dispatches requiring either acknowledgement or compliance or both are **logged** by the **LRH Comm** immediately after their receipt, prior to mimeo or duplication of issue. The **log** is kept up daily and is never permitted to backlog. (BPL 19 Oct 73) **2.** all SEC EDs, HCO PLs, HCO Exec Letters and dispatches requiring either acknowledgement or compliance or both are **logged** by the **LRH Communicator** in every org. Any common day ledger may be used. The emphasis is on completeness and legibility not on neatness. The thing to watch is to **log** the moment the item or report is received. (HCO PL 17 Mar 66)

LRH COMM MASTER FILES, each **LRH Comm** keeps a **file** for each type of issue from LRH—HCOBs, HCO PLs, EDs, etc., and one marked for indexes containing the monthly lists of mimeo items. (BPL 20 May 70 IV)

LRH COMM NETWORK, the **LRH Comm Network** is one of the oldest established **networks** in Scn organizations. Its major function is to get compliance to **LRH's** orders, policies, projects and programs and to see that these stay in. The **LRH Comm Network** is not a management network. It is a **communication** and compliance **network** for **LRH.** (CBO 116)

LRH COMM PROGRAMS CHIEF, 1. the post heads up its own branch on the Programs Bureau Org Board. The FOLO/CLO **LRH Comm Programs Chief** is the opposite number of the **LRH Comm Programs Chief** Flag and has a direct line to **LRH Comms** of the area orgs for the purpose of getting compliance with **LRH** issues and orders, and **LRH Comm** Network issues and orders, as specified and directed by **LRH Comm Programs Chief** Flag (CBO 252) **2.** the title of **LRH Comm Programs Chief** is hereby abolished. Former **LRH Comm Programs Chiefs** in FOLOs are appointed Deputy LRH Comm—Continental. The title of **LRH Comm Pgms Chief** Flag is hereby changed to that of Deputy LRH Comm Flag. (HCO PL 3 Aug 73-1) [The above HCO PL was cancelled by BPL 10 Oct 75 XI.]

LRH COMM STAFF PROGRAM NO. 1, 1. this is a plan to get all **staff** members up to HDC or HDG and get them through the Org Exec Course. It is done by part-time training, the person carrying on his regular **staff** job. If **staffs** are all trained on the OEC it is very unlikely that the org form and functions will go out. Technical reality on the subject of auditing pcs is highly desirable on the part of admin **staff.** (LRH ED 78 INT) **2.** this **program** is designed to part-time train **staff** up to HDC and HDG and then the Org Exec Course. (SO ED 12 INT)

LRH COMMUNICATOR, 1. the **LRH Comm** is located on the org board in Dept 21, Office of LRH. As part of an autonomous network, the **LRH Comm** does not come under local executive jurisdiction, but is subject to the orders and directions of network seniors. As a personal representative of **LRH**, the **LRH Comm** has full powers to take those actions in accordance with his hat to carry out **LRH's** intention for his org. The prime duty of an **LRH Comm** is getting verification of compliance with existing **LRH** programs or orders intended for that org or area, and new **LRH** issues as released. (BPL 5 Dec 73R II) **2.** the title of that person in a Scn org who is responsible for the **communication** and handling of **LRH** matters with regard to that org. (BTB 12 Apr 72R) **3.** an **LRH Communicator** has a basic duty of getting compliances with **LRH** orders. This remains the basic duty. (HCO PL 27 Feb 71 I) **4.** the department head, Department 21. (FEBC 12, 7102C03 SO II) **5.** is in charge of Flag Division IX. (FO 2674) **6.** as the **LRH Comm** is a split off of the old HCO Area Sec hats, these two combine very easily as HCO Area Secs were **LRH's** first **communicators.** (LRH ED 49 INT) **7.** the **LRH Comm** is responsible for making a functioning HCO and for **LRH** orders to that org and for its ethics condition. These are establishment factors. (LRH ED 153RE INT) **8.** the person in charge of Division 7 is the **LRH Comm** of the ship. This person of course is the divisional officer. This division is normally called the Executive Division. (FO 1109) **9.** the **LRH Comm** has the first and primary duty of "making **Ron's** postulates stick." All his admin and actions have to do with this. The **LRH Communicator** handles the **communications** to and from **LRH** and gets compliance with **LRH** EDs and orders and (in absence of an Asst Guardian) enforces policy letters. (HCO PL 10 May 68) **10.** the primary function of the **LRH Communicator** is getting acknowledgments for SEC EDs issued or getting the Executive Director's orders and policy issued and reporting to **LRH.** (HCO PL 19 Jan 66 II) **11.** the purpose of the **LRH Communicator** is: to forward the **communications** and orders of **LRH** and to make certain that his orders, dispatches, directives, policy letters and secretarials are issued and complied with and that acknowledgment is returned to **LRH** concerning them in due course. (HCO PL 27 Dec 65) *Abbr.* LRH Comm.

LRH COMMUNICATOR PROJECT BOARD, the **LRH Communicator** keeps a **project board.** Every **project** or order or directive or SEC ED issued is noted on this **board**; by routine and regular inspection personally and by dispatch the **LRH Communicator** sees to it that each and every order and **project** is eventually complied with or acknowledged. (HCO PL 27 Dec 65)

LRH COMM WW, he must give first priority to three things: (a) keeping the **LRH Comm** Network manned and operating, as the inter-org network of world communication; (b) ensuring rapid distribution of orders, executive directives, HCOBs, policy letters, materials for HGC and student training; (c) compliance herewith. A forth and important action of **LRH Comm WW** is to see that tapes by **LRH** are played in orgs wherever possible and also with excellent quality. A fifth duty is to see that an actual Office of **LRH** exists in orgs, that busts and photos are displayed and that Source is maintained in orgs. The **LRH Comm WW** should see to it that the **LRH Comm** Network is used, that orders and actions are logged and that all **LRH Comms** are well trained and aware of their duties. (HCO PL 12 Feb 70 II)

LRH COMPILATIONS LIBRARIAN, (**LRH Compilations** Unit) the purpose of the **LRH Compilations Librarian** is: to help **LRH** increase the availability, usage and consumption of **LRH's** Dn and Scn materials through a well organized **library** of these materials. (COLRHED 387)

LRH COMPILATIONS UNIT, on Flag there is an **LRH Compilations Unit** established in the Personal Office of **LRH** which has the sole purpose of aiding and carrying out **Ron's** wishes for new books and articles *he* wants to do. This means an entire, full-time research, artistic and transcription staff that **Ron** can personally call on to **compile** materials for his use or publication. (FBDL 412)

LRH EDs, L. Ron Hubbard Executive Directives, earlier called SEC EDs. These are issued by **LRH** to various areas. They are not valid longer than one year if fully complied with when they are automatically retired. They otherwise remain valid until fully complied with or until amended or cancelled by another **LRH ED.** They carry current line, projects, programs, immediate orders and directions. They are numbered for area and sequence for the area and are sent to staffs or specific posts in orgs. They are blue ink on white paper with a special heading. (HCO PL 24 Sept 70R)

LRH, EXECUTIVE DIRECTOR, this is better understood as "General Manager" as it isn't as a member of the board that it is held but as a manager. This is a paid post in any corporation or association. There are numerous **LRH Exec Dir** titles and identities; for this title repeats in each area and org and in the International Division. It means "highest executive of the organization," "third member of the Advisory Council," "head of the department called the Office of LRH." Therefore there is one of these titles for each org we have and for the International Exec Division as well. Perth for instance has an **LRH Executive Director**, Perth, LA has **LRH Executive Director** LA, etc. Then there is **LRH Executive Director** WW. The identity of the LRH Communicator in the org or activity gives clue to this. *Each* **LRH Executive Director** title has an LRH Communicator. There are two LRH Communicators at Saint Hill, LRH Communicator WW, who attends to each org for **LRH Executive Director** WW via each org's LRH Communicator and LRH Communicator SH who handles the traffic both of **LRH Executive Director** WW as sent to it from the LRH Communicator WW and for **LRH Executive Director** SH. This is only possible as the orgs are all similarly engaged. HCO Area Secs filled this role for years and still do where there is no LRH Communicator. HCO Area Secs *still* have duties for the **Executive Director** regardless of the LRH Communicator as old policy letters show. "SEC ED issue" is one of these. *Proper* routing from an org is through the LRH Comm of that org to **LRH Executive Director** of that org and forwarded on to LRH Comm WW who sees that **LRH Exec Dir** *that org* receives it in absence. **LRH Exec Dir** WW may issue a blanket order concerning it but it is usually answered by **LRH Exec Dir** that org. The Advisory Council of any org operates without its third member, **LRH Exec Dir** of that org but in case of disputes or errors finds **LRH Exec Dir** that org taking it up. (HCO PL 4 Jan 66 VI)

LRH HEAVY HUSSARS HAT, this function is to move in heavily where there is a threat of great importance to an org or Scn. After the usual lines and posts have goofed. The term comes from the old cavalry purpose of **Hussars** who were held in reserve until a battle line was dangerously bowed, at which they were sent in to straighten it out. (HCO PL 1 Mar 66)

LRH MEDIA ORG, the LRH Photoshoot Org was an org that specialized only in photography, assisting LRH. Since that time, it has expanded into other **media** fields such as radio, television ads, billboards and video as well as still doing photography. The name has been changed to a name that encompasses all these products. The new name is: **LRH Media Organization.** (ED 871 Flag) *Abbr.* LMO.

LRH PERSONAL AIDE, 1. per HCO PL 22 February 1967, *Office of LRH, LRH Personal Office Organization,* **LRH Personal Aide** was in the Office of LRH over the **LRH Personal Aide** Branch which includes LRH Audio Visual Aids Section, Processing Unit, Cameras Unit, Tapes Unit, Recorders Unit and Supplies Unit. (HCO PL 22 Feb 67) [The post of **LRH Personal Aide** is abolished per HCO PL 2 Jul 1968 Issue II, *Office of LRH WW Reorganization.*]

LRH PERSONAL COMMUNICATOR, 1. this post coordinates **communications** from all sources to **LRH.** The **LRH Pers Comm** has full control of the Household Unit and LRH Personal Pro and all equipment, vehicles, gear, material and spaces. Thus the hat breaks down into five functions: (1) coordinating and rerouting traffic so it will be handled, (2) logging, nudging and keeping track of LRH projects, (3) library and filing, (4) keeping Household Unit matters up to the mark and the personnel busy and accounted for, (5) setting up schedules and events and getting things coordinated for them. The **LRH Personal Comm** hat is vital to let me produce. (FO 2370) **2.** the Flag Office of LRH is under the control and administrative command of the **LRH Personal Communicator.** In matters of pay, liberty, uniforms, quarters, repairs, etc., the Flag Office of LRH and its personnel operate under the **LRH Personal Communicator.** (FO 2374R) *Abbr.* LRH Pers Comm.

LRH PERSONAL PHOTOGRAPHER, the **LRH Pers Photographer** is in charge of the **LRH Photography** Unit, Technical Arts Section, Production Branch of the Personal Office. All **photographic** equipment is in the care and under the full responsibility of this unit together with their manuals, textbooks, technical papers, ancillary equipment and supplies, and all inventories pertaining to them, all **photogaphs**, slides, negatives are included. It is the duty of **LRH Personal Photographer** to see that the above are in perfect operating condition, in perfect order, and available at a moment's notice. (COLRHED 8)

LRH PERSONAL PRO, the product officer of the **LRH Personal PR** Bureau, and has the purpose to help **LRH** with his **personal** duties in **PRO** and dissemination and provide an image for presentation elsewhere. This is accomplished by controlled good relations with all **LRH** publics. (COLRHED 11)

LRH'S PERSONAL PRO INTERNATIONAL, 1. Ron's Personal PRO International is a new post in the Personal Office of LRH at Flag. The post purpose is to get **LRH's** technologies utilized by the external publics internationally. Ron's external publics are those publics outside of Scn, governments, media, social reform, education, the arts, business, specialist activities are all included in Ron's external publics. **LRH Personal Pro International** creates **international** campaigns that get the technologies developed by **LRH** used throughout the world. (BPL 3 Sept 75 II) **2.** it is located in the Personal Office of LRH directly under LRH's Personal Communicator. The post of **LRH's Personal PRO International** is concerned with external publics. The post is not connected with the present LRH Personal PRO Office. (BPL 3 Sept 75 I) **3. LRH PR International** is solely international and works with GO, governments and **LRH's PR internationally** with her own network. (COLRHED 338)

LRH PERSONAL PRO OFFICE, (Flag) the present **LRH Personal PRO Office** exclusively assists **Ron** with **public relations** activities concerning the internal publics of Dianetics and Scientology. (BPL 3 Sept 75 I) [Note: also called **LRH Personal PRO** Bureaux per COLRHED 11.]

LRH PERSONAL PRO O/O, (**LRH Personal PRO** Bureau) the **LRH Pers PRO O/O** is responsible to see that there is adequate organization for production in the **LRH Pers PRO** Bureau and does so according to the org officer/product officer system. (COLRHED 11)

LRH PERSONAL SECRETARY, the Executive Division is Division 7. The LRH Communicator is in charge of the division. It consists of three departments. The first department is the Office of LRH, Department 21. It is in the charge of the **LRH Personal Secretary.** (HCO PL 2 Aug 65) [This post was created also aboard Flag in 1972. In addition to **personal secretarial** duties to **LRH** she is in charge of the LRH Compilations Unit, SO 1 Unit, LRH Audio-Visio Unit, LRH Artist, LRH Properties Chief and LRH Photographer, which are all engaged in making special products for or assisting **LRH** with his products.] *Abbr.* LRH Pers Sec.

LRH PERSONAL SECRETARY U.S., the post of **LRH Personal Secretary U.S.** is in Dept 21, Personal Office of LRH U.S. within the Office of LRH U.S. the post is an extension of the **LRH Personal Secretary** Office Flag and has as its purpose to predict, service and handle all **LRH secretarial** needs from the U.S., as a counterpart to the **LRH Pers Sec** Office Flag. (FSO 836)

LRH PR FOR PROFESSIONAL SCIENTOLOGISTS, (LRH Personal PRO Bureau) the publics with whom **LRH PR for Professional Scientologists** will be working are those persons in any type of **profession** who are already in **Scn.** The purpose of the post very simply stated is to: hat **Scientologists** in using LRH tech in their **professions** (as well as in their personal life) and thereby expanding the use of **LRH** tech so broadly that all **Scientologists** make **LRH** tech indispensable in every **profession** known to man and acknowledged as such. (COLRHED 359)

LRH PROPERTIES, by definition **property** means furniture, fittings, personal effects and files and papers which are the personal **property** of **LRH**, an individual, or **LRH**, an official of the organization. (HCO PL 27 Dec 65)

LRH SO BRIEFING TAPES, briefings to aides and officers of Flag Org and the Flagship, by the Commodore, which have to do with **SO** operating policies, principles, etc., of incalculable value to Continental Captains, stationships, and all units and their crews. Distribution is limited to **Sea Org** members. (FO 2512)

LRH'S OFFICE, by policy and tradition, the Founder has an **office** of his own in each org. The LRH Comm is responsible for its establishment and upkeep. It is the property of **LRH** personally and the place where his own belongings and material in the org are kept. (BPL 23 Dec 72R)

LRH, STAFF MEMBER, 1. in addition to all other identities and titles there is that of **LRH, Staff Member.** As such I give **staff** lectures in the org where I am, assist where I can, crack cases and train students as "coordinator of research" (meaning application of research), write magazines, take pictures, act as a routing expert, listen to problems, and do a lot of other things. I am chiefly a **staff member** of the org where I am located but am also a **staff member** of each org. (HCO PL 4 Jan 66 VI) **2. LRH,** a **staff member** works on **staffs** as a case consultant, training officer, lecturer, design and planning consultant, promotions adviser, and a department head of the Office of LRH and as such should receive compensation. As a **staff member** his expenses are paid by orgs. The pre-Dn salary level of LRH, an employee, was several times that given by orgs subsequently. (HCO PL 21 Dec 65)

LRH, TRUSTEE, 1. this is **L. Ron Hubbard** in the capacity of a **trustee** as distinct from a director or individual or staff member. **LRH, Trustee,** holds money for corporations or persons or holds property for them. (HCO PL 21 Dec 65) **2.** this identity is a **trustee** who holds in **trust** properties and money for Scn and since 1957 has held UK and Commonwealth corporations in **trust** for the original U.S. company until these assets can be transferred to a UK non-profit corporation. All money sent to LRH an individual is received by **LRH a trustee** or a corporation and is seldom paid to LRH an individual but turned over to companies without being given to LRH, an individual. This is a vital point, often missed even by accountants who then get us involved. "**Trustee**" is an identity and activity almost all movements, churches, and benevolent associations have and in each case the "**trustee**" does just what **LRH** a **trustee** is doing—safeguarding property and assets of an association. It's a very usual role. (HCO PL 4 Jan 66 VI)

LRH, TRUSTEE FOR TRANSFER, for some years the Commonwealth (overseas, not U.S.) interests belonging to the Hubbard Association of Scientologists, International, Incorporated, in Arizona, have been held by **LRH, Trustee for Transfer.** As the overseas interests were worthless to the U.S. corporations in the U.S. (HASI, Arizona) due to currency exchange laws, and was costing it money, the Board of HASI, Arizona, appointed **LRH** a **trustee for transfer** for all Commonwealth corporations property or interests with orders to hand it over to a UK corporation. (HCO PL 21 Dec 65)

L. RON HUBBARD, AS A WRITER, in that new boards of directors are being elected for the various corporations and their branches, I am resigning the title of Executive Director and in accordance with a resolution of the general meeting of charter members, am being given the title of "Founder" instead. I am still available for consultation and for signature. It is called to attention that the signature available is that of **L. Ron Hubbard, as a writer**, and not that of L. Ron Hubbard, an individual. As the two signatures may become somewhat confused, the distinction is emphasized. On specific request, as a writer, I will write books on Scn, its organization, and will write HCOBs and policy letters as requested. This is my **writer** hat. (BPL 1 Sept 66R)

L. RON HUBBARD EXECUTIVE DIRECTIVES, see LRH EDs.

L. RON HUBBARD, FOUNDER, purpose: to develop and disseminate Scn. To support and assist Scientologists. To write better books. To act as a court of appeals in all organizational disputes. To form and to make official policies and orders affecting the Founding Church. (HCO PL 12 Oct 62)

L. RON HUBBARD TRUSTEE ACCOUNT, with regard to past and future ACCs and special events courses, any and all payments received from this date forward from past and future ACCs and special events courses will be paid in full to the **L. Ron Hubbard Trustee Account.** This **account** is a **trust** holding pending the formation of the Hubbard Scientology Research Foundation. (HCO PL 26 Sept 62) [Note: This policy letter has been cancelled per BPL 10 Oct 75 IV.]

LUCK, by **luck** we mean "destiny not personally guided." **Luck** is only necessary amid a strong current of confusing factors. (*POW*, p. 21)

LUNATICS, the characteristics of a **lunatic** is one-way-help-inflow. They don't want to help anyone. They only want to be helped. The moment you insist they help others they either (a) vanish or (b) do so and get well fast. (HCO PL 3 Dec 64)

LUNTEER, in the Sea Org an unpaid server with no regular status. (FO 196)

M

MACHINERY AND EQUIPMENT HATTING OFFICER, this post with the main duty of **hatting** personnel on the proper use of **machinery and equipment** comes directly under the Estates Manager in Dept 21, Div 7. This post, if done well, will save thousands of dollars in **equipment** repair costs and hundreds of production hours, which are lost by having inoperational, broken-down, misused **equipment** and the resulting cope therefrom. The why for these breakdowns is unhatted operators. (FO 3575) *Abbr.* MEHO.

MAGAZINE IMPROVEMENT UNIT, a **unit** established in the Magazine Section of the Promotion and Compilations Branch of the PR and Consumption Bureau. The purpose of this **unit** is to see to the **improvement** of continental and area org **magazines.** (CBO 299)

MAGAZINES, advertising pieces for other items or services. They are not in themselves a primary publications media. By that is meant you do not use a **magazine** as an outlet for the publication of a book in the **magazine** itself, or a poem or an HCOB or policy letter or any other valuable item. **Magazines** review them without giving much content, discuss them, refer to them and direct attention to primary items or services. **Magazines** do not carry the item itself. People do not respect things issued in **magazines.** They respect the same things in books. Newspapers and **magazines** review and discuss and direct attention to things and make them desirable. (HCO PL 4 Nov 73) *Abbr.* Mags.

MAIL AND SHIPPING, envelopes and mails all mail or sees that it is mailed. Handles the franking machine and is responsible to Accounts for the franking record and stamps. Wraps materials to be shipped by other departments than the Books Section. (HCO PL 18 Dec 64, *Saint Hill Org Board*)

MAILING LIST, (DCG) invoice every book sale. Write buyer's full name and address on every invoice. Religiously collect name and address of every book buyer. This collectively is the **mailing list.** A copy of the invoice goes in a CF (central file) made out for the person. (BPL 4 Jul 69R V)

MAILING LIST, a list of the names and addresses of the customers or prospects of a business which is used to send them information, letters and sales promotion.

MAILOGRAM, a **mailogram** is a message that is sent electronically via Western Union Telegraph Company to the post office nearest to the destination address, where the message is printed out on a teletypewriter and put into a specifically marked envelope (looks like a telegram) for delivery by **mail.** (BFO 98)

MAIL ORDER HOUSE, a business that deals in receiving orders for merchandise and shipping the goods so ordered by mail. Usually a mail order house has a catalogue that it sends to customers from which they can find what merchandise is available and how much it costs. The operating costs and overhead of a mail order house are usually less than a business that maintains retail outlets so they often offer discounted prices on merchandise.

MAIL SECTION, **section** in Department 2, Department of Communications. **Mail Section** logs incoming and outgoing **mail,** franks all **mail, mails** all **mail,** bulk **mailings,** package insurance and packaging customs clearances. (HCO PL 17 Jan 66 II)

MAIN ACCOUNT, the **Main Account** receives the full org allocation sum. The usage of the org allocation sum for Class IV Orgs follows: 45% salary, 15% promotion, 30% disbursements, 10% reserves. Set asides are of course retained in the **Main Account** and a set aside ledger is maintained to ensure all sums set aside are only spent on the items they were set aside for. (BPL 6 Jul 75 III)

MAINTENANCE, **1.** the proper lubrication, cooling, adjustment, and preservation of an item, area or installation. (FO 1993) **2.** (engine room) the **maintenance** unit is a separate body which handles **maintenance** of the engines and all repairs necessary. This unit usually works a 12-14 hour day but is on call for 24 hours should anything break down. (FO 1722) **3.** purpose: to **maintain** suitable quarters, clean and in repair, for the organization (HCO London 9 Jan 58)

Maintenance

MAINTENANCE, the repair, upkeep and cleaning of property, buildings, machinery, etc., so as to keep it in good operating order or in attractive condition.

MAINTENANCE ACTIONS, the essence of successful estates operations is to separate out **maintenance** and service **actions** from repair or renovation actions as each of these requires its own unit of time. **Maintenance** are continuing **actions** whereas repairs, renovations and constructions are one time actions. (HCO PL 16 Aug 74 IIR)

MAINTENANCE CHECKLISTS, these are drawn up for use by the **maintenance** and engineering units and must cover the specific actions necessary to **maintain**, service and clean all buildings, grounds, equipment, machinery and mechanical systems. Such **checklists** are for daily or weekly use according to the frequency of the actions they cover. Such **checklists** cover specific physical areas and each has a particular purpose (e.g., servicing an elevator; cleaning and poshing up a room from top to bottom; structural servicing and upkeep of a room or section of the building; **maintenance** of a lawn; **maintenance** of a hot water heating system; etc.). (HCO PL 16 Aug 74 IIR)

MAINTENANCE UNIT, (Estates Section Dept 21) the **Maintenance Unit** is responsible for routine **maintenance** and all cleaning and servicing of org grounds and buildings, excluding those items which come under the Engineering Unit. (HCO PL 16 Aug 74 IIR)

MAJOR ISSUE, **1.** magazines go out **major issue** to members every two months, minor issue to the whole CF list on the in-between months. This means a magazine every month. **Major** and minor alternate, one month a **major**, next month a minor. A **major** is fatter. (LRH ED 59 INT) **2. major issue** of the continental magazine. A **major issue** consists of eight or more pages. It has a separate cover. It can be (but is not necessarily) enveloped. It contains some interesting technical data and results and the various list of items ordinarily advertised in every issue (books, memberships, academy, HGC, extension course, PE, etc.). (HCO PL 23 Sept 64) **3.** Scn magazine Scientologists can read and get busy about things. (HCO PL 2 Jul 59 III)

MAJOR SAINT HILL SERVICES, are defined as Power, SHSBC, Class VII to Class IX, C/S internships for those levels, OEC, FEBC, HPCSC, Ethics and Justice Course, any other specialist course for outer org staff. (BO 42 US, 6 Oct 73)

MAJOR SERVICES, hours of auditing, HSDC, HSDG, Academy training and Qual internships. (LRH ED 112 INT)

MAJOR SUPPLIER, a **major supplier** can mean whoever is **major** in ship use or **major** to the ship. It also means **major suppliers** of quality, volume items especially food stuff. (FO 3386)

MAJOR TARGET, **1.** the broad general ambition, possibly covering a long only approximated period of time. Such as "to attain greater security" or "to get the org up to 50 staff members." (HCO PL 24 Jan 69) **2.** the desirable overall purpose being undertaken. This is highly generalized such as "to become an auditor." (HCO PL 14 Jan 69) *Abbr.* MT.

MANAGED CURRENCY, refers to a situation where a government controls the amount of its currency put in circulation and its buying power usually via a central bank instead of using the gold standard to determine the value of the currency and how much may be put in circulation.

MANAGED EXPENDITURES, see EXPENDITURES, MANAGED.

MANAGEMENT, **1.** the act, manner or practice of **managing**, handling or controlling something. (HCO PL 29 Oct 71 II) **2.** the skill with which goals, purposes, policy, plans, programs, projects, orders, ideal scenes, stats, and valuable final products in any activity are aligned and gotten into action is called **management**. (HCO PL 6 Dec 70) **3. management** consists of getting data, evaluation, planning, programming and really guiding things. It is not an out-point correct activity. (ED 504 Flag) **4. management** consists of ethics, tech and admin as a balanced picture. (6910C30 SO) **5. management** could be said to be the planning of means to attain goals and their assignation for execution to staff and proper coordination of activities within the group to attain maximal efficiency with minimal effort to attain determined goals. (*HTLTAE*, p. 92) **6.** goals for companies or governments are usually a dream dreamed first by one man, then embraced by a few and finally held up as the guidon of the many. **Management** puts such a goal into effect, provides the ways and means, the coordination and the execution of acts leading toward that goal. (*HTLTAE*, p. 93) *Abbr.* Mgmt.

MANAGEMENT, ABSENTEE, this occurs where the top executives managing a business are located remote from the actual area of operations of the business. This is seen in a business with locations around the country but all control and direction stems from the top executives located in one city somewhere else.

MANAGEMENT, ADMINISTRATIVE, means top management.

MANAGEMENT AIDE, **1.** heads Management Bureau 4A, Flag. (CBO 437 Attachment 2) **2.** there is a **Management Aide**, posted as the head of the Management Bureau, Flag. His functions are primarily those of supervision and administration. He has no authority to issue orders into the networks. He does ensure that the different networks work together and coordinate their actions. He is the chairman of coordination conferences between the networks. (FBDL 488R) **3.** coordinates and runs the Management Bureau Flag (OFO Branch, LRH Comm Branch, FBO Branch, FOLO Branch, FR Network and Execution Branch) in coordination with the Network I/Cs and gets the functions of these branches done and their products produced in quantity with quality. (CBO 376)

MANAGEMENT AUDIT, see AUDIT, MANAGEMENT.

MANAGEMENT BUREAU, **1.** the **Management Bureau** 4A is the production bureau of the FB. The **Management Bureau** consists of people in charge of areas and orgs and these people manage those orgs. They are fully responsible for the orgs under their care, their stats and expansion. They evaluate org situations and handle. (CBO 435-3R) **2.** (Flag) the Programs Bureau has been replaced with the **Management Bureau**. This **bureau** consists of the networks, that are in actuality managing the orgs, i.e., the Org Flag Officers, the LRH Comm Network, the FBO Network, the FR Network and the External HCO Network. (FBDL 488R) **3.** the purpose of the **Management Bureau** setup is: to get the actual **management** actions of Flag being done from a coordinated bureau, with no cross orders and the result of rapidly executed LRH and org programs that lead to increasing numbers of viable expanding prosperous orgs. (FBDL 488R) **4.** contains an OFO Branch, LRH Comm Branch, FBO Branch, FOLO Branch, FR Network and Execution Branch. (CBO 376) **5.** the **Management Bureau** at a FOLO contains five branches; these are: LRH Comm Branch FOLO, FBO Branch FOLO, FOLO Branch FOLO, Continental Flag Rep Office, and Management Rep Branch FOLO. (CBO 375) **6.** Program Bureau (ex-**Management Bureau**). (OODs 29 May 72) **7.** the **Management Bureau** coordinates with the CLO all projects and orders so that a single channel of command for orgs exists. (LRH ED 135 INT) **8.** that is the accumulated orders which are in existence at this particular moment being kept track of for every org against which orders are being issued, and that is its primary duty. So the **Management Bureau** is actually involved with the **management** of the individual org or the Continental Captains or the areas and so forth. (7012C04 SO)

MANAGEMENT BUREAU ORG OFFICER, 1. (Flag) assists the Management Aide by **organizing** the **Management Bureau's** functions, lines, terminals, hats and materiel and polices all functions by checklist so that the products of these branches get produced in quantity with quality. (CBO 376) **2.** (Flag) there is a **Management Bureau Org Officer**, who operates from a checklist of functions and so polices the activities of the **Management Bureau**, and prevents any deviations from on-policy and CBO management. (FBDL 488R)

MANAGEMENT, CAESAR, a management system wherein authority is held by one executive who controls the organization's activities and its personnel absolutely.

MANAGEMENT, CENTRALIZED, an organization structure that puts a majority of the decisions and actions of middle management in a single location. Thus decisions about and actions concerning the purchasing, accounting, production, advertising, distribution, sales, etc., of all branch offices would come from one main office.

MANAGEMENT CONSULTANT, a specialist in business organization and management who hires out his services to a business to analyze their present organizational and management setup and make recommendations that will result in greater efficiency and profits.

MANAGEMENT, CORPORATE, type of management operation in which the overall organization is deemed uppermost in its policy, being ruled accordingly by a top executive echelon rather than from a departmental level viewpoint.

MANAGEMENT CYCLE, **1.** (1) recruit—suitable qualifications. (2) HCO expediter—work as expediter. Completes Staff Status I and II. (3) on post as trainee—posted in org. Word clears and starrates mini hat before going on post. Word clears and starrates the divisional summary plus any divisional team member mini checksheet whilst on post. (4) purposes—all purposes of post cleared by two-way comm. (5) full post training—completes full post hat A to I for post, plus any other programmed actions for the post. Then starrates full divisional pack or book. (6) audit—general case advance. Programmed for regular intensives by Staff C/S. (7) on post—fully grooved in and functioning. (BTB 14 Jan 72R I) **2.** the steps by which you get a stable terminal there. (7003C27 SO)

MANAGEMENT CYCLE CHART, the **chart** is for all Sea Org members to follow—exactly as laid out. It is laid out similarly to the Classification and Gradation Chart, reading from bottom up—left to right. It contains the complete training one needs to become fully competent. (FO 2500)

MANAGEMENT, DECENTRALIZED, an organization structure that allows a majority of the decisions and actions of middle management to be distributed to each of the organization's branch offices rather than emanating from one main office. Branch offices would handle most of the decisions about and actions concerning their purchasing, accounting, production, advertising, distribution, sales, etc.

MANAGEMENT EDUCATION, study and instruction in the theory and principles of management. This is textbook education occurring on company premises or at a business college or university. It is distinguished from management training which deals in practical experience, apprenticeships, simulated occurrences and on-the-job training which puts one's management education to use.

MANAGEMENT FUNCTION, those functions performed by management executives. The chief function is to ensure the solvency and continued existence of the company. To this end management's function very basically becomes: setting policy, planning, organizing, issuing relevant orders, ensuring production occurs, staff are happy and the business activity remains profitable.

MANAGEMENT, GOOD, **1.** the essence of **good management** is caring what goes on. (HCO PL 10 Nov 66) **2. good management** carefully isolates every stop on its flow lines and eradicates them to increase speed of flows. (BPL 4 Jul 69R VII)

MANAGEMENT INFORMATION SYSTEMS, systems, sometimes computerized, serving as a source to management of vital information needed on a continuing basis to assist in the making and implementing of decisions and policies. *Abbr.* MIS.

MANAGEMENT, INTERMEDIATE, see MANAGEMENT, MIDDLE.

MANAGEMENT, INVENTORY, synonymous with stock control but sometimes taken to include controlling inventories of factory equipment, plant and items used to help produce goods in addition to control of actual stocks of produced goods.

MANAGEMENT, MANPOWER, by whatever means ensuring that proper personnel selection, training, positioning and utilization occur in a business.

MANAGEMENT, MIDDLE, the level of management below top management and above operating management. This is the level of managers, superintendents and heads of departments, branches, offices, plants, etc. Middle management ensures that the policies, programs, plans, etc., of top management are communicated to the operating management and general employees and are carried out. Also called intermediate management.

MANAGEMENT, MULTIPLE, a system of management or a management program whereby top management allows selected employee representatives from various levels of a company to assist it in the formulation of policy, plans and programs affecting personnel, production and the running of the company. Such a program or system can have the effects of greatly increasing cooperation between all levels of employees, increasing efficiency, production and profits.

MANAGEMENT, OPERATING, the level of management below middle management and directly engaged in overseeing operations. This is the level of supervisors and foremen who deal directly with staff, employees or workers. It is usually the lowest formalized level of management in a business or company.

MANAGEMENT ORG, a service org handles bodies. A **management org** handles messages as the principal flow particle. (HCO PL 27 Jul 72, *Form of the Org and Schedules*)

MANAGEMENT, PERSONNEL, the function of management which is concerned with establishing personnel needs, ensuring competent personnel are procured and trained and then deciding on their placement and best utilization. Following this personnel management consists of maintaining accurate records of personnel performance and service which can be used to decide on promotions, transfers, demotions and dismissals.

MANAGEMENT PREROGATIVE, refers to management's right to assert and maintain the ultimate authority in a business.

MANAGEMENT RATIOS, any of various financial and operating relationships deemed valuable and graphed by management as indicators or forecasts of past, present and future business activity such as cash/bills ratio, direct labor costs to indirect labor costs, etc.

MANAGEMENT REP, the FOLO Programs Chief is now called the **Management Rep.** He carries out the same functions of contacting the org's FR pushing Flag programs, targeting GDSes and getting org programs done. The **Management Rep** receives, checks and forwards compliances of programs to the FR Network and Execution Branch Flag via the Continental FR. The **Management Rep** follows the priorities for each org as set by the FR Network and Execution Branch on Flag. (FBDL 488R)

MANAGEMENT REP BRANCH, the **Management Rep Branch** in the Management Bureau at a FOLO receives from the Continental FR Office and gets executed org programs and orders from Flag in their assigned priorities using direct contact with org FR and any nudging to get specific targets done. Handles the standard phone line regarding delivery to the org Flag Rep. Targets GDSes and the org program targets for completion and with real communication and without entheta on a long distance comm line gets these targets met. Operates in close harmony with priorities set by Flag being careful not to cross order regarding these. Alerts the Emergency Officer on Flag with full specifics regarding any situation in the orgs not handled by existing programs. Refers specifics in writing to the Continental FR Office regarding any flubbing Flag Reps for standard debug. (CBO 375)

MANAGEMENT RESERVES, are used for defenses and potential refunds and management overall cost and viability. (HCO PL 29 Jan 71)

MANAGEMENT, SALES, that function of management concerned with adequate distribution and sales of products. It includes the hiring and training of salesmen, the granting of dealerships or franchises and the establishment of sales quotas and territories. Advertising is usually handled separately but not always.

MANAGEMENT, SCIENTIFIC, type of management that prepares plans for actions beforehand, making an assessment of all factors involved such as resources, budget, manpower, work methods, distribution, pricing, etc., with the decision to establish and/or maintain desired standards and see they are realized according to plan.

MANAGEMENT SPECIALIZATION, the division of management functions among management personnel who are trained in specific fields in order to increase the quality, quantity and viability of production.

MANAGEMENT, STAFF, staff management is part of the line and staff form of organization. Line management is concerned with direct production activities while staff management holds the organizing and backup functions supporting production but not directly engaging in it. Typical staff management functions are accounting, personnel training, maintenance, etc.

MANAGEMENT STYLE, the administrative way management chooses to conduct itself with regard to staff as, for example, following authoritarianism which relies on a rigid employer-employee relationship, or a more relaxed democratic style which relies on employees' initiative to work properly and their active participation in management decisions.

MANAGEMENT SUCCESSION, the planning and providing for future management personnel by assessing current prospects and ensuring that one has access to or has in training future management personnel.

MANAGEMENT, TOP, the highest echelon of management for any business. This is the level of company founders, presidents, vice-presidents and their aides, boards of directors, executive directors, etc. It is the body of management that originates policies and procedures. Top management is ultimately concerned with maintaining the solvency of the business.

MANAGEMENT TRAINING, see MANAGEMENT EDUCATION.

MANAGER, the **manager's** first job is not to "run an organization" but to see that bodies move through the shop and build an organization to care for them and then to keep bodies moving through the shop and increase the body volume. (HCO PL 27 Dec 63)

MANAGER, in a small business it is that person in charge of the business. He may not own the business but he is the top executive on the premises often called the General Manager and assumes overall responsibility for the business. He ensures that staff get the work done, is ultimately responsible for solvency and the accompanying planning and organization that will increase business activity and profits.

MANDATE, 1. a written or spoken order, especially one not likely to change and coming from a person of authority. 2. an order from a higher to a lower court or official. 3. the will of a voting public expressed to their respresentative. Corporately, this is the order of an organization conveyed to its representative on how to vote regarding particular issues at a conference.

MAN FRIDAY, named after Robinson Crusoe's servant whom he called "Friday" or "my man Friday." It signifies a close personal aide or a loyal servant or helper. For a female the term is known as girl Friday.

MAN-HOUR, an approximate unit of work consisting of the work done by one man in one hour. Each industry has a basic idea of how much work a man can do in one hour within a segment of that particular industry. Thus man-hours is useful in calculating how long it will take to complete a contract or fill an order, how much it will cost to produce something or how much wages will be, etc. It is only an approximate unit however.

MANIC-DEPRESSIVE, a type who is up one day and down the next. This is the potential trouble source gone mad. (HCO PL 5 Apr 65)

MAN IN THE STREET, type of interview. This is an individual type of interview that can be anything from a poll to gathering opinions from the "average" person on a particular subject. (BPL 10 Jan 73R)

MANIPULATION, buying or selling a stock in order to create the false impression of active trading or for the purpose of raising or lowering the price to attract purchases or sales by others.

MANNERS, BAD, making an appointment and not keeping it, issuing an invitation too late for it to be accepted, not offering food or a drink, not standing up when a lady or important man enters, treating one's subordinates like lackeys in public, raising one's voice harshly in public, interrupting what someone else is saying to "do something important," not saying thank you or good night—these are all **bad manners**. People who do these or a thousand other discourtesies are mentally rejected by those with whom they come into contact. (HCO PL 30 May 71)

Manners, Bad

MANNERS, GOOD, the original procedure developed by man to oil the machinery of human relationships was good manners. Various other terms that describe this procedure are—politeness, decorum, formality, etiquette, form, courtesy, refinement, polish, culture, civility, courtliness and respect. **Good manners** sum up to (a) granting importance to the other person and (b) using the two way communication cycle. (HCO PL 30 May 71)

Manners, Good

MANPOWER, 1. power supplied by the physical efforts of men. 2. the power represented by the total amount of men potentially available at any time to do work for a company, city, nation, etc. 3. a unit which measures the rate at which one man can do work, and generally agreed as being equal to 1/10 horsepower.

MANPOWER ANALYSIS, see ANALYSIS, MANPOWER.

MANPOWER INVENTORY, a summary record of the current manpower a business has available to it. This might consist of a single card or trait photograph on each employee giving basic data such as name, address, sex, job, education level, previous experience, performance with the company, etc. This is not the same as the personnel files which often occupy several file cabinets. A manpower inventory is only a summary of the data in each employee's personnel file. It occupies one card per employee and may be briefer yet. Usually there is a summary statement giving the total of employees, how many in each department and any summary figures or breakdowns found expedient to management. Also called staff list or manning table.

MANPOWER MANAGEMENT, see MANAGEMENT, MANPOWER.

MANPOWER POLICIES, see POLICIES, MANPOWER.

MANPOWER SURPLUS, this occurs when the available manpower exceeds the available jobs. When the reverse occurs it is called manpower deficit.

Mantling

MANTLING, the **mantling** originally consisted of two strips of material that fell from the top of the helmet on either side of the head and, according to some sources, protected the helmet from the heat and rust. As the designing of coats of arms became more popular during the Middle Ages, the **mantling** was added as part of the design. In the Sea Org coat of arms, it falls to either side of the crest in clothlike or ribbonlike folds. (FO 3350)

MANUAL, a book of instructions on how to do something. Most pieces of machinery have a manual that tells how to operate, maintain and/or repair the machine. Many jobs have manuals that tell a person how to do the job explaining how to handle various job situations. A manual often has labeled diagrams or pictures in it of the things being discussed. *—adj.* relating or having to do with the hands; especially work done by the hands called manual labor.

MANUAL, BUDGET, a manual detailing the company policies and methods for preparing and using the budget.

MANUAL, ORGANIZATION, a manual which shows the structure of a business in terms of offices, departments, units, positions of employment and the relationship of each to the others. There is also a clear delineation of duties, functions, products produced, etc., for each area or position.

MANUAL, POLICY, a manual containing company policies employees need to know to guide them in the performance of their duties or the conduct of company affairs. It is not a procedure manual but company policies may affect certain procedures.

MANUAL, PROCEDURE, a manual which gives the step by step procedures for handling routine operations especially administrative operations. This is not a statement of company policies although company policies may have influenced some of the procedures involved.

MANUAL, SALES, a small reference book or booklet giving the data on a company's sales policies and instructions for its sales personnel on prescribed methods of handling sales work accordingly.

MANUAL WORKER, see WORKER, MANUAL.

MANUFACTURING, literally and historically it means to make by hand. However it has come to mean the using of labor and machines to produce finished goods from raw materials, especially on a large scale as in mass production.

MANUFACTURING PLANT, a factory.

MARGIN, 1. the difference between the cost and the selling price of something, especially stocks or securities. 2. an excess of supplies, money, time, etc., kept or allowed for in case of an emergency or because the amount of what will be needed or used cannot be accurately calculated. 3. the amount a customer pays when he uses his broker's credit to buy commodities, securities, etc. Over the last twenty years Federal Reserve regulations in the US have varied the margin price at anywhere from fifty to a hundred per cent of the purchase price. 4. margin also represents the amount of equity in terms of securities, commodities, etc., a person has in his account if it were to be closed out at current prices.

MARGINAL ACCOUNTS, see ACCOUNTS, MARGINAL.

MARGINAL COSTING, see COSTING, MARGINAL.

MARGIN CALL, a demand made on an investor to put up money or securities with the broker either at the time of purchase or when the investor's equity in a margin account is below standard requirements.

MARGIN, GROSS, see PROFIT, GROSS.

MARGIN, NET, see PROFIT, NET.

MARGIN OF SAFETY, a surplus such as money, products produced, etc., beyond what is necessary in order to cover emergencies.

MARKDOWN, the condition of reducing the price of goods or services rendered for reasons such as being overstocked, making room for new shipments, poor consumer acceptance, slight defects, etc.

MARKET, 1. generally, the field encompassed by buyers and sellers of a specific product or service. 2. in business analysis, a specific group composed of buyers of a particular product or service, who are sometimes further identified by a special range in age, income and residency location or involvement with a type of institution, such as the college market, retired persons, or young professionals markets. 3. in economics, the demand for availability of a product or service. 4. term for an exchange that buys and sells stocks or commodities, as in West Coast market.

MARKET ANALYSIS, see ANALYSIS, MARKET.

MARKET, BEAR, a declining stock market.

MARKET, BULL, a rising stock market.

MARKET DIVERSIFICATION, the widening of a company's market activities by entering new consumer markets, promoting to change consumer habits and tastes, or in some manner to add variety to the product itself to give it appeal to larger numbers.

MARKET ECONOMY, an economy based solely on the production of commodities and services for sale.

MARKET EXPLORATION, an analysis of the existing market potential for a particular product or group of products.

MARKET FACTOR DERIVATION, market and sales forecasting derived from recognizing and evaluating particular factors that in all probability will bring about or increase the demand for a specific commodity or service such as favorable market trends or changes in consumers' tastes.

MARKET FOLLOWER, a product that is newly put on the market in competition with products already being marketed. If three automobile manufacturers had compact cars on the market and a fourth manufacturer was introducing one to compete it would be a market follower.

MARKET, FORWARD, a market that deals in promises to buy or sell stocks, commodities, etc., for a set price but at a future date. This is the market that deals in futures as opposed to a spot market which deals in immediate delivery at present prices.

MARKET, FREE, a *laissez faire* type market, free from government control or regulation where prices are controlled by the law of supply and demand.

MARKET, FREE AND OPEN, a market in which supply and demand are freely indicated in terms of price.

MARKET IDENTIFICATION, could be used interchangeably with market analysis. Basically this is any process that isolates the existing or potential market for a given product, breaks the market down into segments or usable categories and establishes how those segments can best be reached with regard to the specific product.

MARKETING, the conceiving and packaging and the moving of a specific product into public hands. It means to prepare and take to and place on the **market.** (ED 459-56 Flag)

MARKETING AUDIT, see AUDIT, MARKETING.

MARKETING BUREAU, marketing is the conceiving and packaging and the moving of a specific product into public hands. It means to prepare and take to and place on the market. **Marketing Bureau,** Bu 2A FB handles the **marketing** actions of every commodity we sell. (ED 459-56 Flag)

MARKETING CAMPAIGN, a coordinated program undertaken by the advertising and sales departments of an organization to attain successful market performance for its product or service.

MARKETING EXECUTIVE, see EXECUTIVE, MARKETING.

MARKETING FUNCTIONS, those actions taken to ensure products or services go from producer to consumer in an orderly advantageous manner, including financing, costing, selling, promotion, distribution and timing.

MARKETING-ORIENTED COMPANY, see COMPANY, MARKET-ORIENTED.

MARKETING PLAN, a plan done after market analysis that lays out the step-by-step approach to getting a particular product from the manufacturer to the consumer.

MARKETING POLICIES, see POLICIES, MARKETING.

MARKETING, TEST, introducing a new product in a limited area or areas to test consumer acceptance before launching an entire marketing and advertising campaign.

MARKETING INTELLIGENCE, see ANALYSIS, MARKET.

MARKET LEADER, an organization that is at the head of its field for producing and marketing certain products or services.

MARKET, MASS, a large and general consumer market such as the market for dairy products as opposed to a restricted market such as the market for underwater diving equipment.

MARKET ORDER, see ORDER, MARKET.

MARKET PENETRATION, the amount of the total market that has been penetrated by a particular company or product. For example, the percentage of all American automobile owners who own Fords would give you the market penetration of Ford in America.

MARKET POTENTIAL, the volume of sales possible but not yet realized, for a product or service competing in a particular market segment, over a specified time.

MARKET PRICE, see PRICE, MARKET.

MARKET RESEARCH, the comprehensive planned investigation and statistical interpretation service offered by market research agencies to industrial and consumer goods companies whereby current and potential market sizes are found; consumer behavior, buying tastes and influences are assessed; and a corresponding value placed on a product or service, whether existing or in the planning stages, so that it can be appropriately and attractively priced.

MARKET RESEARCH AGENCY, a professional organization serving business clients by instituting market research activities fitted to their special needs, often carrying out various types of surveys to gain socio-economic data, population characteristics, buying habits, etc., from which extensive individualized programs for products or services are written and presented.

MARKET-RIPE, unripe produce which will be ripe by the time it is marketed.

MARKET SATURATION, the percentage of goods on a market compared to what the market will bear.

MARKET SEGMENTATION, isolating the various segments of a market so that advertising can be directed more specifically at the right public. A market breaks down into categories such as socio-economic status, age, race, special interests or needs, etc.

MARKET SEGMENT CAPACITY, the ability of a certain segment of a market to handle a particular quantity of a product or service, determined by the segment's size and absorption powers, without regard to selling price.

MARKET SHARE, a product's or service's sales volume in a particular market segment in proportion to the total sales made by all suppliers in that segment.

MARKET SHARING AGREEMENT, a collective pact made between two or more organizations producing and/or selling similar products or services under which the market is divided among them with each operating and controlling a certain segment or territory rather than openly competing in the market as a whole, which may also include fixing similar prices on their related goods.

MARKET, SPOT, a type of sale on the commodity exchange in which the buyer pays cash to the seller and usually expects immediate delivery of the commodity.

MARKET STABILITY, the factors which serve to keep a product in constant demand on a market. Features that preclude the product becoming obsolete; durability, price, functional and aesthetic design, etc., are all factors of market stability.

MARKET, THIN, a quiet market with comparatively light trading activities, as applied either to a single stock or the entire market.

MARKET VALUE, the amount that a seller may expect to get for products, services or securities at the time he places them on the market for sale.

MARKET VISIT, see FIELD INSPECTION.

MARKUP, 1. the amount added to the cost of a product or service when settling on a selling price which is the difference in price at wholesale and retail levels. 2. a rise in the price of a commodity or service. 3. any of the gradient price rises encountered at various stages as a product or service moves through from originator or producer to distributor to supplier to consumer.

MARRIAGE, marriage would consist of putting together a thetan association without overts and withholds, postulated into existence, continued for the mutual perpetuation and protection of the members and the group. (6001C02)

MASS MARKET, see MARKET, MASS.

MASS NEWS MEDIA, by which is meant newspapers, TV, radio and magazines. (HCO PL 11 May 71 II)

Mass News Media

MASS PRODUCTION, see PRODUCTION, MASS.

MASS SELLING, see SELLING, MASS.

MASS UNEMPLOYMENT, see UNEMPLOYMENT, MASS.

MASTER, **1.** the **Master** of a vessel in port or at sea, is responsible for the safety and activities of the ship, the cargo, the crew, and any passengers, must be in control of these and must assure that the activities of the vessel are remunerative or not too costly and that they do not unnecessarily imperil her before the elements or authorities or forces on the shore. (FO RS 332) **2.** we will call those officers in charge of a ship the **Master** where they are not rated captains and at present will retain Captain as meaning the head of the flotilla. It is common maritime practice to make lieutenants or mates a **master** of another ship in a small flotilla. (BO 34 16 Jun 67) **3.** one who has reached a creative and superlative level of accomplishment in any field. (FO 3260)

MASTER, a highly skilled craftsman in a trade or profession qualified to practice independently and to train others. In Medieval times a Master signified a person who had attained a high level of technical and artistic perfection in a trade. He had his own workshop and was an employer of apprentices and journeymen whom he trained and paid in exchange for their work.

MASTER AT ARMS, **1.** this is a naval term used in the Sea Org and is equivalent (but senior) to the Ethics Officer in a Scientology church. (BTB 12 Apr 72R) **2.** Sea Org Ethics Officer. (FO 2780) **3. Master at Arms**, Dept 3, is inspections and reports, statistics, investigation, ethics, legal, ethics files, brig, assisted by **Master at Arms** mates and contains as well the statistics of the ship or flotilla which are the product of the Communications Division. (FO 1109) **4.** Staff **Master at Arms** has the duties of: (1) inspection: inspecting for compliance of Flag orders and work orders aboard the ships and assigning conditions necessary for false reports and non-compliance. (2) security checking wherever applicable. (3) interrogation of personnel on failed missions. (FO 637) **5.** (Gung-Ho Group) keeps order at meetings and ejects people trying to break the group up. He also inspects things and reports on them to the Communications Executive who in turn informs the President or other group members. (HCO PL 2 Dec 68) *Abbr.* MAA.

MASTER BUDGET, see BUDGET, MASTER.

MASTER CHECKSHEETS, **master checksheets** contain corrections and additions which are specifically designated for a course. They are kept up-to-date. (BPL 11 May 69R)

MASTER COPY, **1.** the **master copy** (of mimeos), received from HCO WW, is stamped as such and DO NOT REMOVE. The **master** is fixed to the inside back of the folder for that issue. Lots of extra copies are then kept in that folder. New copies are issued from that folder. The **master** is never issued. (HCO PL 4 Feb 61) **2.** the message system is based on three copies of every telex. Your third copy is called a **master copy**, it is simply filed chronologically in a **master** file which is kept as a security file by the communicator and is her property. (FO 2528)

MASTER OF THE COMMODORE'S MUSIC, there shall be an office of the **Master of the Commodore's Music** in the Office of LRH UK. The **Master of the Commodore's Music** shall assume the duties of quality checking **music** and giving an **MCM** Seal of Approval, which will be in the form of a certificate signed by him. Official Scn **music** may be recognized in this way. The **Master of the Commodore's Music** is a qualified **musician** in all fields of **music**. He has the ability to compose, orchestrate and arrange any type of **music. Music** sent to the **Master of the Commodore's Music** for approval for **musicians** should include data on public response to it. (LRH ED 239 INT) *Abbr.* MCM.

MASTERS, LRH original tape recordings are called **masters**. **Masters** are used only once to make a production master from which other copies for use can be made. (FO 1655)

MASTER SCHEDULE, a production schedule showing the amount and type of all upcoming production planned by a firm for a certain period of time, such as the total production planned for the next month, quarter or year.

MATE, 1. division heads are called **mates** on the Ship Org Board. (FO 2674) **2.** the **Mate** is responsible for the actual working gear of the ship, its sails, boats and all cleanliness above decks including wheelhouse, but not the salon which is the Purser's Department. The **Mate** is responsible for stowage. Fresh water, stores of all kinds and fuel are also in the Mate's Department who ensures their correctness, purity and proper preservation. Navigation, navigation equipment, charts, pilot books, etc., are the **Mate's**, who must see that they are adequate and properly safeguarded and that charts and pilots are kept up-to-date. The navigating and handling of the ship are the responsibility of the **Mate** under the Captain's supervision. Sail repair equipment, sail repairs and stowage, safety lines and belts and anchors are under the **Mate's** care. (*Ship's Org Bk.*) *Abbr.* M.

MATERIAL AIDE, CS-3. (FO 795)

MATERIAL COSTS, see COSTS, DIRECT MATERIAL; COSTS, INDIRECT MATERIAL.

MATERIAL, DIRECT, sub-products or the separate items that together make up the completed product such as components, paint, etc., as different from indirect material which would include office and cleaning supplies.

MATERIAL, INDIRECT, items used to produce a product which do not become part of the final product such as office supplies, detergents, power, lubricants, fuel, etc.

MATERIALS, "checksheet **material**" means the policy letters, bulletins, tapes, mimeo issues, any reference book or any books mentioned. **Materials** also include clay, furniture, tape players, bulletin boards, routing forms, supplies of pink sheets, roll book, student files, file cabinets and any other items that will be needed. In Scn a course consists of a checksheet with all the actions and **material** listed on it and all the **materials** on the checksheet available in the same order. (HCO PL 16 Mar 71R)

MATERIALS, the items used to make a finished product but not including the tools, machinery or personnel used to do it. In the manufacture of cars, materials would include the metals, glass, paint, etc., which combined together result in a finished car.

MATERIALS BRANCH, the Establishment Bureau 1 (Flag Bureaux) has three branches—Internal HCO, **Materials**, External HCO. The **Materials Branch** has the function of providing hat checksheets and packs for Flag Bureaux and orgs. It also provides admin and tech course checksheets and packs by revising those existing where necessary and supplying those which do not exist. It has close liaison with the Marketing Bureau. These functions restore those of the former "Organizing Bureau," covered in LRH CBO 4, 13 September 1970, *Org Bureau*, with exception of personnel, now part of External HCO. (FO 3591)

MATERIALS FLOW, the flow line of raw materials, components, parts, etc., through a factory or plant until they end up as finished products.

MATERIALS OF SCIENTOLOGY, the **materials of Scn** are not its tools. Its tools are processes—its **materials** are books, tapes, Professional Auditor's Bulletins, journals, letters and experience. (PAB 36)

MATERIALS, RAW, 1. material which has not yet been altered from its natural state through manufacturing or processing. Crude oil and iron ore are examples. 2. anything which can undergo manufacturing or processing in order to become more valuable, usable or saleable; the basic materials, components, parts, etc., which are used to make a product.

MATERIEL, *n.* (French) used as a collective term for the articles, supplies, machinery, etc., used in an army, navy or business, as distinguished from the personnel or body of persons employed. (FSO 823)

MATERIEL ADMINISTRATOR, purpose: to make certain that the Department of **Materiel** runs and performs its responsibilities in caring for the material and providing **materiel** for the HASI and to supervise personnel on maintenance and cleaning posts, and to see that buildings and storage areas are in good order, and to safeguard **materiel** and files from damage or theft. (SEC ED HASI London 1 Dec 58, *Materiel Administrator Hat*)

MATERIEL EXECUTIVE, the office of the HCO Exec Sec WW compiles all needful divisional

materials for every org in the world under a **Materiel Executive**. (HCO PL 6 Sept 67)

MATERIEL OFFICER, (Gung-Ho Group) the **Materiel Officer** keeps up the property and quarters of the group, anything it owns, repairs it, sets up meeting chairs and cleans them away, and inventories things. (HCO PL 2 Dec 68)

MATERIEL SECRETARY, the **Materiel Secretary** post name is changed to Dissem Sec WW. (HCO PL 19 Oct 67)

MATURITY, the time at which a note, bill, bond or debenture is due. Also called maturity date.

MAUNDER, means wander about mentally. (HCO PL 3 Apr 72)

MEANS-ENDS ANALYSIS, see ANALYSIS, MEANS-ENDS.

MECHANIZATION, the process of using or introducing the use of machinery to perform work in an industry, country, etc., rather than having it done by hand.

MEDIA ANALYSIS, see ANALYSIS, MEDIA.

MEDIA RESEARCH, see RESEARCH, MEDIA.

MEDIA TEST, an analysis of the amount of consumer response to a variety of advertisements used in various media.

MEDICAL FLOAT, with this **float**, the **Medical** Officer buys doctor-dentist-**medical**-health specialist visits and treatment, laboratory analysis, X-rays, **medical** equipment essential for a person's health, **medicines** and prescriptions, and transportation. (FO 3082)

MEDICAL LIAISON OFFICER, 1. a **Medical Liaison Officer** in Department 14 of any land based organization is a **Liaison Officer**. He is a terminal in an org to whom a C/S may send public or staff in order to arrange for the necessary **medical** tests or treatment by a properly registered **medical** doctor. A **Medical Liaison Officer** is not permitted to give any **medical** treatment other than first aid or to arrange for a suitable doctor who can administer needed treatment. (BPL 25 Mar 73 II) **2.** (Correction Division) purpose of the **Medical Liaison Officer** is to provide good basic **medical** service, fast handling of any non-optimum physical condition, and bring about the good health of the org staff and its public. (BPL 7 Dec 71R I) *Abbr.* MLO.

MEDICAL LOG, the **Medical** Officer on watch is to ensure that a **log** is kept of all persons visiting the sick bay. The following admin is to be kept for such visits: (1) time in, (2) name, (3) physical condition, (4) ethics condition (the person has currently), (5) time out, (6) date at top of page, right-hand corner. (FO 1125)

MEDICAL OFFICER, 1. the **Medical Officer** makes sure that standard hygiene rules are followed, so that the health of the crew stays high. He handles ill people quickly using isolation methods where necessary to contain any spread of illness through a crew. He alone dispenses **medicine**. The **Medical Officer** must have a basic training in first aid prior to going on post of the **Medical Officer**. He must remain single hatted. He is also a vital terminal on the Fitness Board as he can spot the chronically ill and malingerers who are non producers, also the PTS and those with out tech. (CBO 217) **2.** a post in Qualifications Divisions which has as its main purpose: increasing the number of staff declared in good health. Keeping the environment, health and hygiene standards high. (BPL 3 Oct 70 II) *Abbr.* MO.

MEDICAL OFFICER'S REPORT TO C/S, report to be used by **MO** for any newly reported illness, accident, etc., or as requested by the **Case Supervisor**. States reason pc came to **MO**, what treatment given by **MO**, what further treatment intended, and anything else found to be wrong with pc. (FO 1985)

MEDIUM, 1. an instrument, agent, via, channel, person, etc., used to convey some communication, particle, action, etc., from a point of origin to a point of receipt. 2. a means of communicating or presenting a message to the broad public such as newspapers, magazines, radio, television, mail, billboards, etc., used to advertise, inform, or appeal to the public.

MEDIUM OF EXCHANGE, something considered to have enough value to be trusted as an exchange for goods or services. Currency, checks, gold, silver, etc., are mediums of exchange.

MEDIUM SIZED ORGANIZATION, organization numbering around fifty staff members. (HCO PL 5 Dec 62)

MEETING, a gathering of people or their assigned representatives to discuss and form majority agreements concerning matters of mutual concern.

MEETING, CONTRACT, there are two types of meeting with prospective clients. In the first, called a survey meeting, you must find out what is needed and wanted. The second type of meeting with a prospective client is a **contract meeting.** A full and complete presentation must be prepared to complete the sale. All agreements and **contracts** must be ready for signature. The services that are proposed to provide the solution to his problems must be presented in such a way to completely capture his reality. (BPL 24 Jan 73 I)

MEMBER, (Committees of Evidence) **members** of the committee are specifically named by the Convening Authority. In addition to the Chairman and Secretary, they may not number less than two or more than five. A **member** attends all hearings, may keep his own notes, passes on all findings and votes for or against the findings and their recommendations. (HCO PL 7 Sept 63)

MEMBERSHIP BOOK, the Registrar must be provided with a **membership book.** It is a large, hardcover book, divided into alphabetical sections. The Registrar's duty is merely to write the **member's** name and address, with the date of his or her application, in the correct alphabetical section. (BPL 24 Sept 73R XI)

MEMBERSHIP MONEY, monies received from the sale of international, participating, or associate **memberships** in the HASI. (HCOB 15 Oct 59) [The above HCOB was cancelled by BTB 10 Oct 74 II.)

MEMBERSHIP SECRETARY, handles all matters relating to any and all Scn **memberships** everywhere. (HCO PL 18 Dec 64, *Saint Hill Org Board*)

MEMORANDUM, 1. a short note written as a reminder to oneself or another to do something. 2. a written communication such as an informal letter, report or dispatch showing who it is directed to, who wrote it, the subject matter, date, message and signature. It is primarily for use in communicating to different people, departments, branches or locations of the same organization. In communicating to persons outside of the organization one uses a formal business letter. 3. in commerce, a letter sent by the consigner of a shipment of goods stating the terms of the consignment and authorizing a return of the goods if after a stated period of time they remain unsold.

MEMORIAL AWARDS, see HONORARY AWARDS.

MENTAL DISEASE, there is no evidence of any kind whatsoever that there is anything called a **mental disease.** So therefore the whole of psychiatry is based on a wrong why and the whole of civilization for four and a half hundred years has been tossed into dungeons and tortured and burned at the stake and electric shocked and prefrontal lobotomied and put into ice packs and everything else—wrong why. (ESTO 2, 7203C01 SO II)

MENTAL EFFORT, the amount of attention or concentration required or expended in order to do a particular job.

MENTAL FATIGUE, see FATIGUE, MENTAL.

MENTAL HEALING, to date, people have been subjected, in the name of **mental healing,** to brutalities, even torture and murder. **Mental healing,** apart from Dn, has not been developed in recent centuries and a science or study to relieve man, but rather has been aborted to use as a means of political control. Treatments such as electric shock have killed or permanently crippled millions through the violence of the convulsions it creates. Prefrontal lobotomy makes man into a vegetable. It is true it calms him down but he can never become well again, if he even survives the operation. Drugs can kill through the severity of their effects on the human body. **Mental healing** has become almost totally associated with brutality and control and is used for the most sordid purposes. (BPL 4 Jul 69R II)

MERCANTILE, relating to or concerned with merchants of trade.

MERCHANDISE, products, goods, commodities, etc., that may be bought or sold; consumer goods. —*v.* to buy, sell or exchange goods, services, etc.

MERCHANDISE MANAGER, the manager in a retail store who is in charge of all its buyers and their activities.

MERCHANDISING, buying, promoting and selling merchandise for profit at the various levels of distribution, as from manufacturer to wholesaler, wholesaler to retailer, and retailer to consumer.

MERCHANT, a person who buys and sells goods, commodities, products, etc., for a profit, especially one who does large scale transactions with foreign countries.

MERCHANT MIDDLEMAN, see MIDDLEMAN, MERCHANT.

MERCY, a lessening away from the public's acceptance of discipline necessary to guarantee their mutual security. (PAB 96)

MERE EXPLANATION, a "why" given as the why that does not open the door to any recovery. (HCO PL 13 Oct 70 II)

MERGER, action of one corporation absorbing another or others. The absorbing corporation retains its identity and has claim to all properties, products, brand names, franchises, privileges, etc., of the corporations absorbed. By merger the corporations absorbed terminate their corporate existence. In a consolidation all corporations concerned terminate their corporate existence and a new corporation is formed altogether.

MERIT PAY, additional pay given to an employee because he has qualities or abilities which the employer deems meritorious of extra pay.

MERIT RATING, see RATING, MERIT.

MERIT SYSTEM, the system whereby promotions or appointments are made on the basis of a person's merits or value. In this system a person would be promoted because he has the experience, training, ability or attitude necessary to do the job. He doesn't get promoted because he has friends in positions of power as in a spoils system.

MESS, a nautical term used to designate an organized group which eats together on a ship or shore base or SO org. **Messes** consist of 8 to 20 (optimum is about 10) persons of similar rank or function. (FO 2586)

MESSAGE, 1. every **message** should contain only one subject, except when the **message** is a report on a general situation. A report can contain as many data as it pleases. A **message**, consisting of a forwarding of a datum or a request for a policy or datum, or item, should be highly standardized amongst organizations to minimize the loss of time in communication and to insure a rapid and accurate response to any and all communications received. A **message** consists of one subject and the reason why. It should be written so that enough space remains on the paper to answer the communication. Neatness, clear typing, retyping, are not important as long as the writing is legible. The actual content of the **message** and its placement on a piece of paper large enough to admit of an answer on that piece of paper are of the primary importance. The number of things which must be on the **message** is precise and should be placed in this order: (1) date, (2) the person to whom the **message** is addressed, (3) the person who is sending the **message**, with address, is needful, (4) the actual **message** or datum itself, (5) the reason why it is needed, (6) the initials of the person sending, (7) enough blank space, preferably at least half of the piece of paper, to permit the **message** to be answered on that same sheet of paper. (Communications Plan HASI, 1954 OEC Vol VII p. 254) **2.** (the **message**) the thought or significance which the public relations person is attempting to convey is called the **message**. (HCO PL 7 Aug 72)

MESSAGE CYCLE, in administration of telex and speed **message** lines, we use the **message cycle**. It is a comm **cycle**: (1) query or command (first **message**), (2) reply or compliance (second **message**), (3) acknowledgement (third and final **message** of the **cycle**). (FO 2528)

MESS BOARD, a **mess board** with each person's name on it and divided to represent the spaces for each **mess** is kept by the Chief Steward. He pins the **mess** member's name on it in the spaces assigned, with the member on white paper, the president on green paper, the treasurer on red paper. He keeps the **board** up to date. (FO 2586)

Mess

MESSIAH, the Hebrew definition of **messiah** is one who brings wisdom—a teacher. **Messiah** is from "messenger," but he is somebody with information. (*PXL*, p. 27)

MESS OFFICER, president or treasurer. (FO 2586)

MESS PRESIDENT, each **mess** has its own **President**. The **President presides**, as does a chairman, over the **mess**, supervises elections, settles disputes, keeps order, supervises manners and dress or presentability and presents matters to the members of the **mess** for decision. The **President** represents the **mess** in the matter of food complaints and requests. (FO 2586)

MESS PRESIDENTS COMMITTEE, see COMMITTEE OF MESS PRESIDENTS.

MESS TREASURER, keeps an account notebook for the **mess** and buys or charges the **mess** members for any extras they elect. He divides such small sums pro-rata for the **mess** members and is paid by them on a weekly basis, each **mess** member has an account with him. This is an entirely private arrangement among **mess** members, having nothing to do with the ship's funds. The **Treasurer** safeguards and expends any monies of the **mess**. (FO 2586)

MEST, mathematical symbol for **matter**, **energy**, **space** and **time**. Loosely, property and possessions. (*HTLTAE*, p. 121)

METER CASE ASSESSMENT FORM, [form for use in testing evaluations which appears in HCO PL 15 February 1961, *Evaluation Script*. The five buttons are problems, help, change, responsibility and create. Health, marriage and money were added per HCOB 19 December 1960, *PE Change*.]

METER CHECK, 1. HCO does **meter checks**. When **meter checking** the public or a large group of staff this consists of putting the pc on a **meter** and noting down the TA, state of needle and attitude of pc. When **meter checking** a small number of staff on a specific investigation HCO may also need to ask questions to get data on crimes or whos or specific events. (HCO PL 15 Nov 70R) **2.** the action of **checking** the reaction of a student to subject matter, words or other things, isolating blocks to study, interpersonal relations or life. It is done with an E-**meter**. (HCOB 19 Jun 71 III) **3.** the procedure whereby an ethics officer or trained auditor establishes the state of a person in regard to ethical or technical matters by using the technology of the E-**meter**; an electronic instrument for measuring the mental state or change of state of an individual. (*ISE*, p. 40) **4.** the student is not audited or spoken to during this **check** but is simply put on the **meter** and the **meter** condition noted and written down, which is the end of the **check**. (HCO PL 2 Apr 65, *Meter Checks*)

MICROMOTION, an industrial engineering method of doing motion studies by using high-speed movie cameras to catch all an employee's movements at work, particularly those too small or too fast to otherwise detect, with a view to studying and simplifying his motion patterns or correcting redundancy.

MIDDLE GROUND, common, ordinary dull statement of the is-ness of things. (HCO PL 7 Aug 72)

MIDDLEMAN, an intermediate person or organization that buys from producers and sells to retailers or consumers.

MIDDLE MANAGEMENT, see MANAGEMENT, MIDDLE.

MIDDLEMAN, AGENT, a person or company which functions as an agent in the buying or selling of goods as they go from buyer or seller or vice versa without taking title to the goods as exemplified by a broker or manufacturer's agent. Also called a functional middleman.

MIDDLEMAN, FUNCTIONAL, see MIDDLEMAN, AGENT.

MIDDLEMAN, MERCHANT, a wholesale or retail merchant who owns the goods or commodities he sells or has for sale and commonly handles shipping and delivery of the goods to the buyer.

MID RATZ, **midnight rations.** (ED 19 Area Estates)

MIDSHIPMAN, are junior officers in training to be good officers. **Midshipmen** are future officers of the Sea Organization. (FO 1592) *Abbr.* Msm.

MILITARY ORGANIZATION, see ORGANIZATION, LINE.

MIMEO DISTRIBUTION, materials issued to orgs on **mimeo** lines have on their top left-hand corner the **mimeo distribution** for that item. Unless specifically designated by category such as

"Mission," "FSMs," "BPI," "Magazine Article," these **mimeo** materials are not for public issue and **distribution**, free or for charge. (BPL 10 Feb 71R)

MIMEO FILES, **Mimeo Files** is a separate unit, has its own machine, stencil files and **mimeo files**. Rerun of stencils to re-supply **files** is not done by the routine **mimeo** line. FOs, HCOBs, HCO PLs, LRH EDs are now each one of them separate **files**. Stencil files are separate from main **mimeo files** and stencils are not included in with copies. (CBO 6)

MIMEOGRAPH, handles all **mimeographing**, **mimeograph** equipment and supplies and all **mimeo** routine and master files. (HCO PL 18 Dec 64, *Saint Hill Org Board*)

MIMEOGRAPH OFFICER, is in charge of all **mimeo** activities. (HCO PL 2 Mar 71)

MIMEO I/C, **Mimeo I/C** is responsible for the smooth running, fast coordination and termination of all products out of Mimeo, whilst maintaining a very high standard of workmanship. (FSO 10)

MIMEO MACHINE MAINTENANCE CHIEF, this post is now added to the **Mimeo** org board just below the Mimeo Officer. The post is called **Mimeo Machine Maintenance Chief**, and the duties of the post are (0) that he fully knows each **machine** in his charge and fully understands how to do minor repairs, (1) that he gets fully checked out on each **machine** by Qual, (2) sees to it that each piece of **machinery** in **Mimeo** is operational, (3) sees to it that each **machine** is serviced and full overhauls are done every two months, (4) sees that the simple spares are bought and that those parts needing replacement are done to the benefit of the **machine**, (5) continues to see that the upkeep of the **machines** is done daily by the owner of the **machine** and ensures that any breakdown is handled at once. The product is fully operational **machinery** that enhances all work that is done with that **machine**. (FO 3264-22)

MIMEO SECTION, the **Mimeo Section** has been transferred to HCO Department 2, Communications Department. The **Mimeo Section** is composed of two units—mimeo and mimeo files. The **Mimeograph** Officer is in charge of all **mimeo** activities. **Mimeo** does not belong in promotion as it gets used for promotion which is not a correct use of **mimeo**. (HCO PL 2 Mar 71)

MINI DIVISION 6, the postings of a **Mini Division 6** consist of a Distribution Secretary, Success I/C (also acts as a clerk in Department 16), Tours Officer, Tours Member, Director of Public Servicing, Public Registrar, Public Reg Administrator and a Director of Clearing. This is the **minimum Division 6** you may have. (HCO PL 14 Nov 71RA II)

MINI HAT, those few policies checked out and known, that make the post of the new staff member "do-able" on a broader scale than instant hat with less supervision. A complete **mini hat** checksheet is done in thirty minutes total. (HCO PL 2 Aug 71 III) [The above HCO PL was cancelled by BPL 10 Oct 75 IX.]

MINI HATTING, putting the **hat** on fast and quick until a full hat checksheet and pack can be fully done is a vital action. Until fully studied up one can cope with a **mini hat**. (OODs 16 Jan 71)

MINIMUM STAFF, the **minimum staff** of a Central Organization means the number of posts that must be covered each by one person. The additional hats of the organization are worn by these staff members listed as basic staff. (HCO PL 28 Apr 61 II)

MINISTERIAL BOARD OF REVIEW, established in the HCO Division. It shall be composed of no less than three persons who shall themselves be **ministers** of the church. The **Board of Review** will be headed by the A/Guardian or other Guardian Office personnel assigned by the A/Guardian. The purpose of this **Board of Review** is to help LRH safeguard Scn, Scientology Churches, and Scientologists by ensuring that **ministers** of the Church are and remain of good moral character, continue to uphold the codes of Scn and apply standard technology in their counseling of parishioners. (BPL 24 Sept 73R III)

MINOR ISSUE, **1.** magazines go out major issue to members every two months, **minor issue** to the whole CF list on the in between months. This means a magazine every month. Major and **minor** alternate, one month a major, next month a **minor**. A major is fatter. (LRH ED 59 INT) **2.** Scn magazine anybody can read and be happy he has done so. (HCO PL 2 Jul 59 III)

MINOR'S MATE, all **minors**, i.e., those under 21 (excepting in those countries where the legal age of consent is 18), who are a member of the SO without their legal guardians are to be assigned a **Minor's Mate** who acts in the capacity of guardian. (FO 3303R)

MINUS INVOICE, in invoicing income and in writing disbursement vouchers, all corrections are done on additional invoices or vouchers. This makes it unnecessary to search wildly for the machine copies to correct them. The original invoices or vouchers are often already distributed when a need of correction arises. Instead of correcting the original write a **minus invoice** giving what transaction was being corrected as fully as possible. In case of a refund from cash just received or a correction of amounts just received or in case of a bad check informed from the bank, write a **minus invoice** and clearly mark it so and for how much and to whom and why. In adding the week's income these show up easily. When separating out invoices into classes of income for an audit these **minus invoices** show up clearly and are subtracted from the type of income. Mark the **invoice minus** in big capital letters so nobody can miss it. (HCO PL 30 Jan 66 III)

MINUS VOUCHER, **1.** in invoicing income and in writing disbursement vouchers, all corrections are done on additional invoices or vouchers. This makes it unnecessary to search wildly for the machine copies to correct them. The original invoices or vouchers are often already distributed when a need of correction arises. **Minus** disbursement **vouchers** are made every time a check is voided or when a payment comes back unaccepted or when for any reason something already disbursed is found not to be disbursed after all and must be added back. Mark the **voucher minus** in capital letters so nobody can miss it and give full details. When sorting out classes of disbursement for an audit these **minus vouchers** are dealt into the class of expenditure but when it is totaled they are subtracted. (HCO PL 30 Jan 66 III) **2.** every voided check is accompanied by a **minus voucher** white copy showing a **voucher** has been written to subtract it. This is not the original disbursement voucher but a new one, called a **minus voucher** which clearly has **minus** printed on it in caps. (HCO PL 30 Jan 66 IV)

MINUTES OF THE MEETING, an official record of proceedings at an organizational meeting, conference or convention.

MIRACLE MAKERS, a magazine originating from Division 6 Flag Admin Org on a monthly basis. *Miracle Makers* is designed to reach all Dn auditors (HDCs and HDGs), and all DCGs. (FO 2799)

MISDECLARE, declaring a pc to have made it who has not or failing to declare a pc who has made it. Either one is an incorrect examination. (HCO PL 15 Sept 67 II)

MISDEMEANOR REPORT, staff member **report** of any **misdemeanor** noted. (HCO PL 1 May 65)

MISEMOTION, anything that is unpleasant emotion such as antagonism, anger, fear, grief, apathy or a death feeling. (HCOB 23 Apr 69)

MISMANAGEMENT, **mismanagement** or misgovernment of self, an organization, group or state would consist of failing to forward the basic purpose, not grasping and specifying sub-purposes, and not experiencing and formulating policies to strengthen successful ideas or actions that forward the basic and sub-purposes and impede ideas or actions that retard them and not recognizing actual enemies or oppositions or planning and carrying out successful campaigns to handle them. Failing in any of these actions the individual, group, organization, state, civilization, race or species will falter, fail and die. (HCO PL 13 Mar 65, *Divisions 1, 2, 3, The Structure of Organization What is Policy?*)

MISROUTING, **misrouting** would be **misrouting** indeed if one forwarded an improper dispatch to anyone else and failed to shoot it back to its originator. (HCO PL 17 Nov 64)

MISS, aboard Flag a christening ceremony was held in which the Programs Aide and all the Programs Chiefs were christened—with new names. The Programs Aide became Mrs. Expansion. Programs Org Officer became Mr. Organize Expansion. FOLO Programs=**Miss** FOLO. (FBDL 369)

MISSION, **1.** a group granted the privilege of delivering elementary Scn and Dn services. Does not have church status or rights. (BTB 12 Apr 72R) **2.** (1) a single field or locality covered by **missionary** work; the body of **missionaries** there established; a **missionary** station. (2) a regularly organized church and congregation not having the status of a parish. (BPL 24 Sept 73 I-I) **3.** forming org. (BPL 31 Mar 71R) **4.** the purpose of a **mission** is to get new people in and up the lines to orgs. (CBO 144) **5.** any legally chartered Scn field activity will be properly designated only as **Mission** of the Church of Scientology. A **mission** is a ministry commissioned by a religious organization to propagate its faith or carry on humanitarian work. In Scn, this commission is the right to constitute a **mission** for a certain district or territory and to use the name Applied Philosophy, Scientology, and Dianetics. The powers granted are those to be a group of people, dedicated to a common purpose, acting as a single unit to forward Scn and Dn in a certain area. (BPL 20 Sept 71R I) **6.** standard mimeo distribution symbol. **Missions** receive (for a small fee) technological materials up to their level of classification. The **Mission** Officer WW keeps one copy of an issue for his files and sends one copy to each **Mission** Director. (BPL 14 Apr 69R) **7.** the word **mission** may now be used to designate only a Sea Org official **mission.** It has unlimited ethics powers. Their members are called **"missionaires."** (HCO PL 15 Sept 68) **8.** a **mission** could be defined for our use as a formally authorized individual or group sent to perform a specific task or duty sent by Operations. *That* would require, then, personnel selection, training, briefing, **Mission** Orders, dispatch and full admin. The difference between an errand and a **mission** is that **missions** are sent by an Operations Officer, errands are sent by anyone else. When an "errand" involves more than one day it should be handled by Operations, not by some other division. It then becomes a **mission.** (FO 2530R) **9.** to handle downstat orgs and areas the Sea Org simply gets in ethics. This is done in such a way as to enable that org or area to get in tech, which makes it possible then for them to get in admin. In order to do this we send out **missions.** These have unlimited ethics powers and enough force to accomplish their purpose of getting in ethics. (FO 228) **10.** a **mission** consists of a **missionaire** trained officer and **missionaire** trained personnel. (FO 1802) *Abbr.* Msn.

MISSIONAIRE, **1.** the word **mission** may now be used to designate only a Sea Org official **mission.** It has unlimited ethics powers. Their members are called **missionaires.** (HCO PL 15 Sept 68) **2.** there are five major types of **Mission** Orders. These types are (1) *observation* **mission** orders, (2) *situation handling* **mission** orders, (3) *garrison* **mission** orders, (4) *project* **mission** orders, (5) *courier* **mission** orders. The term **missionaire** is used for the personnel who conduct the first four types and courier is used for the last type. (FO 2936) **3.** the name **missionaire** implies someone going out to handle admin, tech, ethics or PR. He goes off to get an org or ship straightened up. (FO 2494) **4. missionaires** are auditors to orgs. (OODs 6 Jun 74) **5.** someone *in motion* handling a distinct laid out cycle of action. The basic cycle is *go there—do it—come back.* This is very different than the persons in the org who are stable and stay there doing it. When the **missionaire** comes back, he returns to his own post. (FO 2200) *Abbr.* Msnaire.

MISSIONAIRE, APPRENTICE, persons transferred to the Missionaire Unit who have not completed mission school or do not have officer rank are entitled **apprentice missionaires.** The duties performed by the **apprentice** are the same as those of any other missionaire but he may not be an I/C of a mission. If he remains in the unit after completing courses, the **"apprentice"** is removed from his name should he now also be an experienced and competent **missionaire.** (FO 2748)

MISSIONAIRE FIRST CLASS, **1.** the Mission School is Missionaire Third. Mission School plus Org Exec Course and successful missions is a Missionaire Second. All these and Class VIII are **Missionaire First Class.** (FO 1268) **2.** qualifications of a **Missionaire First Class** are (1) Class VIII, (2) AB, (3) SS I, (4) SS II, (5) Sea Org Staff Status, (6) Missionaire Third Class, (7) OEC and Class IV Administrator. (FO 1571) **3.** to qualify as a **First Class Missionaire** the person must have the Second Class Missionaire Certificate (permanent) and the following courses complete: Class VIII, PR Briefing Course, Ops Officer Briefing Course, FEBC. Awarded permanently on the basis of successful experience as a missionaire. Case level: OT III or above. (FO 2526)

MISSIONAIRE OPPORTUNITY CHECK, **missionaires** after briefing are checked in Qual on **opportunity.** The questions asked are: What personal **opportunities** does the **mission** present for you? Are you intending to use the **mission** for some additional purpose not stated? Is there something about this **mission** you haven't disclosed? The three questions are done in Qual out of session. If they read at all they should be handled by an auditor with usual Integrity Processing procedure to find out what it's all about and get the data. (CBO 263)

MISSIONAIRE SECOND CLASS, **1.** the Mission School is Missionaire Third. Mission School plus Org Exec Course and successful missions is a **Missionaire Second.** (FO 1268) **2.** qualifications of **Missionaire Second Class** are (1) Class VI, (2) OEC and Class IV Administrator, (3) Missionaire Third Class. (FO 1571) **3.** completion of **Second Class Missionaire** Checksheet and at least Missionaire Third Class (Provisional). Becomes permanent upon three successfully completed missions. To qualify as I/C of a mission (**Missionaire Second Class** I/C) the OEC and SHSBC must have been completed. Case level: Clear or above. (FO 2526)

MISSIONAIRE THIRD CLASS, **1.** the Mission School is **Missionaire Third.** (FO 1268) **2.** qualifications for **Missionaire Third Class** are (1) **Missionaire Third Class,** (2) SS I, (3) SS II, (4) Sea Org Staff Status, (5) AB. (FO 1571)

MISSIONAIRE UNIT, the purpose of the **Missionaire Unit** is to see in choosing personnel that **missions** are successful and completed without flubs. This means also that **missionaire** personnel must be available from which to choose, both within and without the **unit**. The **Missionaire Unit** may not contain persons unsuitable for **missions**. (FO 1802) *Abbr.* MU.

MISSIONAIRE UNIT ORG OFFICER, **1.** the post of **Missionaire Unit Org Officer** is created as a permanent post. The **MU Org Officer** takes over the drawing up of watch lists, logging in persons transferred to the **unit** and logging them out of it. The **MU Org Officer** takes care of uniforming, personal inspections, general scheduling of the **MU** day to include exercise and study. All admin of the **unit** is done by the **MU Org Officer**. All contact with the unit by orgs is via the **MU Org Officer**. (FO 2725) **2.** is responsible for the discipline and progress of the personnel in the **unit**. (FO 2676R)

MISSION ALERTS, **alerts** which state that "a mission will be firing." This is the Action Bureau's heavy traffic warning. (FO 3264)

MISSIONARY, a person sent to propagate religion or to do educational or charitable work in some place where his church has no self-supporting local organization; hence, one who spreads any new system or doctrine. (BPL 24 Sept 73 I-1)

MISSIONARY SALESMAN, a salesman whose major responsibility is to create and extend good will by helping representatives and dealers promote and sell his company's products to consumers.

MISSION BRIEFING OFFICER, the **Briefing Officer** is overall responsible for seeing that the product of "**missionaires** correctly prepared, **briefed** and launched without out-points" is produced by his section. (FO 3254)

MISSION CHARTER, this **charter** gives official authority to the individual who receives it to conduct a **mission** in the area specified. It does not confer any liability on the Mother Church but it does confer upon the individual a right to practice Dn and Scn in his area. This right is granted by the Mother Church by virtue of authority given it by L. Ron Hubbard, sole owner of the materials and copyrights of Dn and Scn. The right is dependent upon good usage, regular remittance of tithes, and the continued good standing of the grantee. The grantee then has authority to run his **mission**. (BPL 20 Nov 69R)

MISSION CLEAR NAMES, there has been trouble, false reports, and down stats. Therefore we are sending two **missions** to U.S.—one to East U.S., one to West U.S., **Mission Clear Names** to handle false reports in the U.S. and trace back to source of trouble. (FMO 121, 26 Mar 69)

MISSION CYCLE, the **mission cycle** is, (1) a real situation to observe (for lack of data) or to handle (if data is reliable and known). (2) competent and explicit **mission** orders that foresee all eventualities and where the **mission** will return to. (3) the alert of all divisions concerned with data of what's required from each given them with the alert by Division 2. (4) all divisions concerned contributing their share of the action. (5) good selection of competent **mission** personnel. (6) briefing of the **missionaires** (making available all known material) and doing the orders in clay. (7) smooth launch of the **mission**. (8) smooth execution of orders. (9) smooth rapid handling by the Ops Officer. (10) rapid wind-up and return. (11) complete debrief so that all data is made available in the debrief. (12) circulation of the debrief to all who need the data. (13) anything required in debrief handled by the divisions concerned to finalize the action. (14) assignment of a condition to the **mission** and publishing it. (FO 2431)

MISSION ELIGIBLE FILE, **mission eligibility** is based on ethics, training, case and effectiveness. Division One of the Flagship must set up a **mission eligible file**. This will consist of (1) a list of all officers and crew of the Sea Org in alphabetical order giving rank, location, ethics category, case level, case category, auditor level, mission school grading, checksheets completed, missions done, **mission eligible (ME)**, mission ineligible (MI). List names vertically and data across the sheet. (2) a record of personnel currently on missions. (FO 1098)

MISSION FLOAT, the **mission float** includes expenses to cover cost of sending out **missions**, such as transport, living and clothing expenses, tapes for debriefs and maintenance of the tape recorders, clay, etc. (FO 1400)

MISSION HISTORY LOG BOOK, each **mission** member, upon returning to the Flagship, is to turn in a written report containing details and high points of his or her **mission**. This will be turned in to the Flag Hostess, Division 6, for use in keeping an eventful, accurate **mission history log book** that is complete in every detail. (FO 657)

MISSION INTERNATIONAL BOOKS, **1. mission** to go to every org and with a checksheet and fully prepared data, teach the entire staff rigorously how to land **books** in **bookstores**. (FMO 13, 6 Jun 68) **2.** the reason **Mission International Books** failed is that no administrative action was put in to back up their actions. It failed in terms of lack of **book** orders. People were sent out to **bookstores** to place **books** but nobody was arranged to go along to the **bookstores** and act as an agent from the org to collect the money and keep their stands full of **books** and so forth. That's what it takes to sell and place **books** in the **bookstores**. (CS Order 46) *Abbr.* MIB.

MISSION INTO TIME, is a book by L. Ron Hubbard that tells the story of one of the most fascinating adventures undertaken in recent history. It is the story of the famous test of whole track recall mission. *Mission Into Time* also sets out a whole new view of history seen through direct recall, and in the process gives valuable insight into why prosperous ancient civilizations collapsed! (FBDL 365)

MISSION OPERATIONS, the business of **Mission Operations** is not daily stats or stats. It is MO targets fully, swiftly done. Presumably if these targets are done the stats will later rise. (FO 3527) *Abbr.* Msn Ops.

MISSION ORDER BOARD, **board** giving the **MOs** and any reports received from **missions** currently out, plus additional action ordered if any. (FO 1954)

MISSION ORDERS, **1.** there are five major types of **mission orders**. All are written in accordance with Target Series Policy Letters and Flag Orders and Central Bureaux Orders as they apply. These types are (1) *observation* **mission orders**, (2) *situation handling* **mission orders**, (3) *garrison* **mission orders**, (4) *project* **mission orders**, (5) *courier* **mission orders**. The term **mission orders** is used for all five types. The term **"missionaire"** is used for the personnel who conduct the first four types and "courier" is used for the last type. All **MOs** are written with regard to the Data Series Policy Letters which must be very well known to all in Bureau IV. (FO 2936) **2. mission orders** are detailed actions which the **mission** carries out to achieve the purpose of the **mission**. (FO 848) **3. mission orders** are issued by a Flag Operations Liaison Office under authority of its CO. Confidential, no further distribution than those concerned and copy to Flag. (HCO PL 24 Sept 70R) *Abbr.* MOs.

MISSION PACK, the **mission pack** consists of (1) two copies of the **mission** orders for the mission, (2) one copy of each issue mentioned in the mission orders. A **pack** is issued to each **missionaire** on the **mission**. The **mission pack** is quite a time saver for **missionaires**. They need only open their **pack** to refer to the target they are on, or the issue mentioned in the target. (CBO 257)

MISSION PLANNING ALERT, to obtain and correlate the data on the area swiftly, a **mission planning alert** form is used. This form consists of a brightly colored sheet of paper (green, blue, goldenrod, etc.) and has the words **mission planning alert** printed on it in bold red type. It is addressed to someone and has a space for filling in a brief summary of the **mission** plan being worked on. It has a section requesting data, statistics, debriefs into the area being worked on and a request for comments and requirements concerning the **mission** being **planned**. It is printed up on lightweight paper so that carbons can be used in writing up the **mission** outline. (FO 2579)

MISSION PREPS, on the Action Bureau Org Board, **Preps** is in the Briefing Section. A good **mission preps** unloads all actions of material gathering, transport or Ship's Rep liaising, etc., from the Briefing Officer, thus allowing the Briefing Officer to have his full attention on properly briefing the missionaires. (FO 3254)

MISSION PREPS I/C, **Mission Preps I/C** is junior to the Briefing Officer, **Preps I/C** checks the many details of launch time, pack comps, uniform supply, etc., and that the **mission** has everything it needs to accomplish its purpose and major targets, and keeps the Briefing Officer informed of what has been done. (CBO 231)

MISSION SCHOOL, **Mission School** is designed to train a Sea Org member to undertake and execute a **mission**, any **mission**. It provides the know-how and technology to get the job done. (FO 2505)

MISSION SUMMARY REPORTS, a **mission summary report** by the **Mission** I/C is a short concise statement of what was done regarding every **mission** order. (FO 2601)

MISTER, officers normally address other officers of the same rank or officers of lesser rank by the title **Mister** (whether male or female in the Sea Org) while on duty, especially if the duty is on sea watch or while acting officially on post. (FO 38-1)

MISUNDERSTOOD ORDERS, (form of dev-t) **orders misunderstood** by the recipient will not be properly complied with as the **order** was **misunderstood**. The incorrect or no action following will require further traffic to correct. As an executive, originate clear precise instructions and orders. As a junior, duplicate the **order**, and never fail to clarify if you have **misunderstood**. (BPL 30 Jan 69)

MISUSE REPORT, staff member **report** of the **misuse** or abuse of any equipment, materiel or quarters, meaning using it wrongly or for a purpose not intended. (HCO PL 1 May 65)

MIXED COSTS, see COSTS, MIXED.

MIXED LETTER, a **letter** which is an entheta **letter** (couched in nasty terms to the org or its personnel) which also contains a report pretending to be an ethics report. "You awful people have an awful auditor in the field." A **mixed letter** is always routed to dead files. (HCO PL 7 Jun 65 *Entheta Letters and the Dead File, Handling of, Definitions*)

MIXING PRACTICES, **mixing** other **practices** with Scn, e.g. psychotherapy, naturopathy, chiropractic, yogi, etc. Examples: using processing to "help" colonics, using chiropracty to run engrams. (HCO PL 4 Jul 62) [The above HCO PL was cancelled by BPL 10 Oct 75 IV.]

MOBILITY OF LABOR, in business and industry, the movement of labor from organization to organization or to various geographical locations, whether by personal choice, company transfers, employment terminations or relocating where particular skills or people are needed.

MODE, in statistical distribution, the value or item appearing most frequently in a numerical series. Also called norm.

MODEL BALANCE SHEET, balance sheet or accounting report prepared in model form to show the contents ideally placed for easy reference, made possible by clear presentation of items put into proper categories.

MODUS OPERANDI, manner and means by which an individual or an organization operates.

MODUS VIVENDI, 1. way or style of living. 2. a temporary agreement or compromise, in force until a final settlement is reached between contending parties.

MONEY, **1.** the official currency issued by a government that can be exchanged for material objects, services or benefits. (OODs 28 Feb 75) **2. money** is only something that can be exchanged confidently for goods or services. It is a symbol which represents value in terms of goods or services. (HCO PL 27 Nov 71) **3. money** represents *things*. It is a substitute for goods and services. If one performs a valuable service *and* exchanges it for goods he does so through the item of **money.** (HCO PL 27 Nov 71) **4.** simply that which represents delivered production. (HCO PL 27 Nov 71) **5.** a negotiable commodity which can be held in reserves or exchanged with other companies or individuals for goods or services. **Money** is either actual cash received or it is actual cash represented by **money** order, travelers check or bank transfer received or by a check drawn on an account in which there are adequate funds to cover the check at the time it is written and presented to the org. (BPL 28 May 71R) **6. money** is only a substitute for wealth and is not itself wealth. **Money** is only valid to the degree that it can substitute for actual wealth. **Money** is only of any use to the degree that it can purchase things of value. (FEBC 9, 7101C24 SO II) **7.** an idea backed with confidence, or enforced confidence, and is actually a representation. (FEBC 4, 7101C18 SO III) **8. money** is a symbol. It represents success when you have it and defeat when you don't, no matter who is putting out propaganda to the contrary. (HCO PL 30 Jan 66 IV)

Money (Def. 2)

MONEY BROKER, an individual or organization that deals in the international money market, foreign currency, gold and silver as well as in short term securities and loans.

MONEY FOR TRAINING, (stat) this was originally defined as **money** collected **for** certificate **training** courses. This definition still stands. It means that all **money** collected **for** any and all **training** courses, tech or admin, are counted in the statistic. (BPL 30 Jun 73R)

MONEY MANAGER, one who manages and may control financial affairs, including investments, for an organization.

MONKEY ROOM, [this is a **room** in Saint Hill Manor, England, which has painted murals of

monkeys on its walls and is thus called the **monkey room.** It is mentioned in HCO Policy Letter 4 August 1960, *ACC at Saint Hill.*]

MONOPOLY, 1. exclusive control by one group or organization of the means to produce and/or sell a product or service, creating a market situation wherein free competition does not exist and prices may be dictated by the monopolist. 2. in law, a right granted by a government giving exclusive control over a specific business activity or product to a single party.

MONTHLY ACCOUNTS SUMMARY, summary prepared showing the amount in each bank **account**. This too is a mimeographed form showing the names of the bank used, checks outstanding, etc.; it also carries a total sum of monies in the bank. This form also carries a section devoted to loans outstanding that the org must pay. This form, made out, is submitted to the Ad Council on the second Tuesday of each month. (HCO PL 26 Nov 65R)

MONTHLY BILLS SUMMARY, the Disbursement Section has made up a mimeographed form. This is the **monthly bills summary**. This form has the name of each company with which the org does business plus adequate blanks after each alphabet letter for new companies to be added. This form has four columns. The first column is the company owed. The second column is the grand total of money owed that company. The third column is the amount that is past due. The fourth column is the month since when the **bill** has been past due. All bills are filed on arrival. They are not kept out and entered. They are filed in the folders. Then one takes the folders one by one and makes up the **monthly bills summary**. As each folder is taken up the **bills** are examined for correctness, straightened up and entered in the **monthly bills summary**. (HCO PL 26 Nov 65R)

MONTH TIME MACHINE, consists of four baskets on a stalk and each week items on it are moved down one basket and fall off at the end of four weeks. (FSO 119)

MOONLIGHTING, 1. staff members of an org who also have other jobs outside the org are said to be **moonlighting**. (HCO PL 6 Oct 70 II) **2. moonlighting** is the term applied to having two separate jobs and employers. (HCO PL 12 Jun 65)

MORAL, 1. simply, totally and only—of or concerned with the judgment of the goodness or badness of human action and character; pertaining to good and evil. Designed to teach goodness or correctness of character and behavior; instructive of what is good and bad. (7204C11 SO) **2.** (**morals**) the principles of right and wrong conduct and the specific **moral** choices to be made by the individual in his relationship with others. (HCO PL 3 May 72)

MORALE, 1. a sense of common purpose or a degree of dedication to a common task regarded as a characteristic of or dominant in a particular group or organization. Also defined as a confident, resolute, willing, often self-sacrificing and courageous attitude of an individual to the function or tasks demanded or expected of him by a group of which he is a part that is based upon such factors as pride in achievement and aims of the group, faith in its leadership and ultimate success, a sense of fruitful personal participation in its work and a devotion and loyalty to other members of the group. Also a state of well being and buoyancy based upon such factors as physical or mental well-being, a sense of purpose and usefulness and confidence in the future. **Morale** in a military sense applies to the whole group as in *esprit de corps* (spirit of the group). (FO 2414) **2.** the demonstration of competence is the basic factor of **morale**, and production is the evidence of competence. (FEBC 3, 7101C18 SO II) **3. morale** is made up of high purpose and mutual confidence. (HCO PL 14 Dec 70) **4.** moral or mental condition with respect to courage, discipline, confidence, enthusiasm, willingness to endure hardship. (FO 101) **5.** the tone of a group. (HCO PL 1 Nov 70)

MORALE INDEX, term referring to the level of employee morale, as high, low, or at one of the relative positions in between, as discovered through interviews and obvious indicators such as rate of production and eager compliance to orders.

MORE THERE, you could say a competent person was **more there**. But this is really "**more** able to put his attention on what he has his attention on." (HCO PL 3 Apr 72)

MORGUE, clipping files are kept together in **morgues**. They just accumulate everything that any paper has ever said on one subject and that is the **morgue**. (7007C30 SO)

MORTGAGE, a written commitment of real estate property or personal property to secure a promissory note. In each instance the property continues in the possession of the owner while the debt is being paid off.

MORTGAGE BOND, a bond secured by a mortgage on a property.

MORTGAGE DEBENTURES, see DEBENTURES.

MOTION, 1. a formal proposal put to a vote, according to parliamentary procedure rules, at a conference or assembly. 2. in law, an application to a court for a ruling.

MOTION, NEGATIVE, at a conference or meeting, a negative proposal, sometimes contentious, put forward to the chairman for accepting or rejecting.

MOTION, ORIGINAL, the original form or statement of a motion proposed at a meeting or conference regardless of subsequent motions or amendments.

MOTION STUDY, the categorization of all the motions a worker makes on the job such as reaching, selecting, sitting down, standing up, walking, etc., in order to eliminate unnecessary motions and establish the best coordinated, sequential pattern of movements.

MOTIVATION, the provision of incentives or motives to act according to a desired manner. The range of things that motivate a person are on the scale of motivation.

MOTIVATION RESEARCH, see RESEARCH, MOTIVATION.

MOTOR POOL, the **motor pool** is under Estates. It should have a minimum of two full time drivers and one upkeep personnel, who maintains the vehicles, washes them, assigns them, looks after their keys. (ED 10 USB)

MOTTO, the **motto** is generally represented at the base of the coat of arms. It is a sentence, phrase or word adopted by the group as its guiding principle. In the Sea Org coat of arms, the **motto** *Revenimus* (pronounced: re ve nē´moos) is the Latin word for "We come back," the **motto** of the Sea Org. (FO 3350)

Motto

MOTTO FOR ORGANIZATIONS, "standard tech calmly and completely applied." (FO 890)

MOTTO OF AN OTL, "on watch." (FO 745)

MOTTO OF HUBBARD COMMUNICATIONS OFFICE, "bring order." (6101C01)

MOTTO OF THE CENTRAL PERSONNEL OFFICE, "post security for all." (BPL 3 Apr 73R II)

MOTTO OF THE PROJECT FORCE, "one time—one job—one place." (FO 3165)

MOTTO OF THE RPF, "the RPF is what we make it. The RPF is where we make it." (FO 3434)

MOTTO OF THE SEA ORG, "we come back." (FO 234)

Motto of the Sea Org

MOVER, one who moves or initiates a formal motion at a conference or meeting.

MR., aboard Flag a christening ceremony was held in which the Programs Aide and all the Programs Chiefs were christened with new names. The Programs Aide became Mrs. Expansion. Programs Org Officer became **Mr.** Organize Expansion. FOLO Programs=Miss FOLO. (FBDL 369)

MRS., see MR.

MRS. EXPANSION, aboard Flag a christening ceremony was held in which the Programs Aide and all the Programs Chiefs were christened—with new names. The Programs Aide became **Mrs. Expansion.** (FBDL 369)

M-SCOPING, it's the way you locate mines. It's the way you locate most anything. You **M-scope** according to a grid. (6802C28 SO) [This is using a metal detector to locate things buried underground and marking on a paper divided into grid squares where readings occurred so that you end up with a record of an area searched and where readings occurred in that area.]

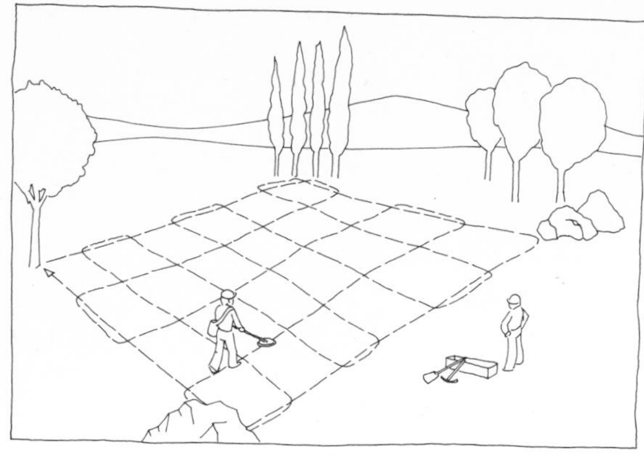

M-Scoping

MUCKRAKER, one who searches for and exposes commercial or political corruption.

MUD BOX BRIGADE, **1.** persons appointed to it clean **mud boxes**, fuel lines, water lines, bilges, etc. It is under the MAA and it reports to whoever needs it. More candidates will be appointed regularly and promptly every time I find a freeloader who is loafing on post and drifting with the wind. (OODs 4 Jan 68) **2.** this group is the most downstat and one gets assigned to it by being a freeloader, invisible on post, loafing and really goofing up on one's job. (FO 1701)

MUD BOXES, those areas in the bilge which collect the **mud** out of the bilge water. Bilges means the inside bottom of the vessel where water collects. (OODs 29 Sept 71)

MULTIPLE BAR CHART, see CHART, MULTIPLE BAR.

MULTIPLE DECLARE, in an effort to raise completions and in confusing particle fast flow with quick auditing, auditors began to use only one process for a grade. Protest of having the pc sent to examiner every ten minutes led to **multiple declare.** The pc declared all lower grades at one time without specifying their abilities. Grades, the very rock basis of results, were then neglected. (LRH ED 104 INT)

MULTIPLE MANAGEMENT, see MANAGEMENT, MULTIPLE.

MULTIPLE OFFER, sales offer in which several or more items are to be sold as a single purchase.

MULTIPLE OPINION, to express a **multiple opinion** (use of "everybody") in vital reports, which could influence assistant board or board decisions. (HCO PL 7 Mar 65 III)

MULTIPLE REPORT, two bad data systems are in current use on data. The first is "reliable source." The other system in use is **multiple report.** If a **report** is heard from several areas or people it is "true." The Russian KGB has a Department D that forges documents and plants them in several parts of the world. They are then "true." Propaganda spokesmen located all over the world say the same thing to the press on every major occasion. This becomes "public opinion" in government circles and so is "true" because it is published and comes from so many areas. Five informants could all have heard the same lie. (HCO PL 17 May 70)

MULTIPLE VIEWPOINT SYSTEM, **1.** something new was added to the world with the **multiple viewpoint system.** What's this new **system**? Well, you see everything from the branch office! You don't see it from headquarters. You have to be as pan-determined as daylight to even conceive of such a **system.** For it's a true OT **system.** Every situation is viewed from the viewpoint of the branch office, or the regiment on the firing line or the squadron in the sky. It takes a pretty humble or pretty OT HQ to say "We don't have a viewpoint. We are not important as a viewpoint. The only viewpoint that's important is that of the man on the firing line, the Squadron Leader in the sky, the Colonel actually engaged in battle." So that's a **multiple viewpoint system!** The key is files. Every org in the world has a file for each month in the data files. As the data pours in from that org—telexes, staff reports, MO reports, finance reports, surveys, personnel records, observations, any and all data it goes bang at once into that org's file for the month. All in a folder for that org for that month. And there's that org, not only current, but for each month exactly for years back. As fast as they've been filed they are worked. In other words read and acknowledged. Queries are handled. (FBDL 192R) **2.** the files are so arranged (one org, one month of data) that one can obtain the **viewpoint** of that org from that org as though one were in that org looking out. All former operations systems on this planet have a single viewpoint system, that of headquarters. As soon as you grasp this fact, that HQ is no viewpoint except of headquarters and that all data puts one's point of view right there in an org, you can file that way. (OODs 1 May 72)

MUNICIPAL BOND, a bond issued by a state, county, city, town or village or by state agencies and authorities.

MUNICIPAL CORPORATION, see CORPORATION, MUNICIPAL.

MUSACK, **1.** must acknowledge. (*HTLTAE*, p. 67) **2.** the position in a comstation which is taken by a communication that originated at another station and must be acknowledged by this station. (*HTLTAE*, p. 121)

MUSCOMP, **1.** must complete. (*HTLTAE*, p. 67) **2.** the position in a comstation taken by a communication originating elsewhere which has been acknowledged by this station but must still be completed by this station. (*HTLTAE*, p. 67)

MUSICAL CHAIRS, **1.** frequent changes of post, using areas of the org as a personnel pool. (HCO PL 28 May 71 II) **2.** constant transfer of personnel. (BPL 9 Aug 71R II) **3.** hectic transfers from working posts. (HCO PL 19 Mar 71) **4.** there is the fact that it takes a while to train someone on a post and get the post in order. So rapid transfers defeat any post training or competence. We call this action **musical chairs**. That is a game in which people rapidly change positions. (HCO PL 29 Aug 70 I) **5.** excessive transfers. (HCO PL 27 Oct 69) **6. musical chairs** in life *is* the mechanism below ARC breaks in Grade III! To unstabilize gives ARC breaks! Whole staff can be put into a sad effect! This is the mechanism governments use. It's the basic tool of the socialist. If he can just unstabilize everyone he can kill them with degrade. It's a basic tool of the insane to maintain their own stability by unstabilizing everyone else. (OODs 20 Aug 71)

MUSICAL FUNCTIONS, now just as there can be musical chairs, so there can be **musical functions**. And you can transfer **functions** from person to person or you can transfer **functions** from department to department until nobody can keep his place in the book. The org can go just as mad changing all of the **functions** amongst the staff members as they can changing staff members. (ESTO 12, 7203C06 SO II)

MUTINY, refusing work or persuading others not to work or refusing duty is a crime called **mutiny** and is criminal and the ship or company may put the person in irons and have him charged and jailed at the first port. (FO 2086)

MUTUAL FUND, an open-end investment company with unfixed capitalization, formed by the acquisition of money from a number of investors for the purpose of reinvesting in a variety of securities, freely buying and selling its own shares and issuing more stock as people demand it.

MYSTIQUE, qualifications or skills that set a person or thing apart and beyond the understanding of an outsider. (HCO PL 29 Oct 71 III)

N

NAMED VOTE, see VOTE, NAMED.

NAME SCREENING, market research method in which by a process of elimination, the most optimum name for a new product or service is selected, conveying correct image, having uniqueness so that it cannot be confused with other product names on the market, and not containing any unfavorable inferences.

Nanny

NANNY, there must be a person on the ship in charge of children eight years and less of age. The rate is ship's **Nanny**, Div 3, Dept 9. There must be a nursery area. The **Nanny** is responsible for the cleanliness and good order of the children and their quarters and possessions. (FO 301)

NARCONON, 1. **Narconon**, meaning **non-narcosis**, is a drug rehabilitation program for the redemption of druggies in or out of prisons. It was organized in Arizona State Prison by an inmate who himself was a hard core addict of thirteen years. He put to use the basic principles of the mind contained in my book *Scientology the Fundamentals of Thought*, and by doing so completely cured himself and helped twenty other inmates do the same. Through **Narconon** no drugs whatever are used for withdrawal and on this program the usual withdrawal effects such as "cold turkey" are most often completely by-passed. (LRH ED 256 INT) **2. Narconon** (drugs—no!). **Narconon** is the *only* successful drug rehabilitation program on the planet. (FBDL 220)

Narconon

NASD, the National Association of Securities Dealers, Inc., an organization of brokers and dealers in over-the-counter securities.

NATIONAL ADVERTISING, see ADVERTISING, NATIONAL.

NATIONAL ASSOCIATION SECRETARIES, manage individual organizations of Scn throughout the world. (HCO PL 18 Dec 64, *Saint Hill Org Board*)

NATIONAL BANK, see BANK, NATIONAL.

NATIONAL COMMISSION ON LAW ENFORCEMENT AND JUSTICE, the **National Commission on Law Enforcement and Justice** formed by Scientologists and non-Scientologists has been assisting individuals who have been victims of false and erroneous records and dossiers collected on them. (LRH ED 256 INT)

NATIONALIZATION, government take-over of the ownership, control and running of private industry, commerce, agriculture and public services.

NATIONAL MAGAZINE, issued monthly under the title for the continent, *Certainty, Ability,* etc., etc., made up by HCO Continental of a continent. Printed and mailed by the largest Central Organization at its expense. Takes articles, material and ads from HCO Information Letter and other sources. Must be okayed by Assn Sec of Central Org and his department heads before being printed to be sure their campaigns are forwarded and offerings brought to public notice. Intelligent use of this minimizes expensive special mailings. Sent to everyone in active CF files, whether members or not. Often used afterwards for literature for the individual public. (HCO PL 4 Feb 61)

NATIONAL ORGANIZATION SECRETARIES, manage individual **organizations** of Scn throughout the world. (HCO PL 18 Dec 64, *Saint Hill Org Board*)

NATIONAL RIOTS, national riots are just the inability of leaders to arrange sequences of action and designate channels for types of particles. (HCO PL 14 Sept 70)

NATIVE ABILITY, there isn't any such thing as **native ability.** There are things that certain guys are very good at but that doesn't mean they can't be good at anything else, and it's the broadening of **ability** that brings one's own **native ability** (so-called) into full view. (ESTO 10, 7203C05 SO II)

NAVAL ENGINE ROOM, 1. one that maintains and repairs itself. A commercial engine room is one repaired by shipyards between trips. (FO 1737) **2.** Sea Org engine rooms are to be **naval engine rooms.** This means that they are set up with enough personnel and enough spare parts to handle all of their own repairs and maintenance. (FO 1722)

NAVIGATION, 1. in actual fact real **navigation** is the science of recognition of positions and objects and estimation of relative distances and angles between them. (HCO PL 18 Sept 67) **2.** man tends to avoid confronting the real and so invents symbols as substitutes. This goes to the extent, in **navigation**, of making fun of direct observation **navigation**, preferring calculation by symbols. Real **navigation** methodology by definition (other planet) is **navigate** by direct observation of visual contact. In the absence of this seek to predict and establish position by a minimum of symbols and vias until visual contact can again occur. (FO 40)

Navigation (Def. 1)

NECESSITIES, products and services considered to be indispensable to a particular standard of living or to an individual with a particular livelihood or who is occupying a particular economic stratum.

NECESSITY, 1. a **necessity** is what it takes to make products and valuable final products. In a cap-in-hand activity food is qualified as "some food, oatmeal maybe." Pay becomes "maybe but no bonuses ever." Uniforms become "none." Recruiting posters YES. Fuel becomes "economical amounts carefully used." Training materials becomes YES. So what's a **necessity?** A **necessity** is what it takes to make the valuable final product, not individual survival but group survival. (HCO PL 13 Feb 71) **2.** materiel needs directly related and **necessary** to the vital functions, promotion, delivery, stats and acceptable image of a division or org or ship. (HCO PL 4 Nov 70 IV [The above HCO PL was revised and reissued as BPL 4 Nov 70R but this definition is not on the new issue.]

NEEDLEBLINDITIS, (disease) the auditor never sees a floating **needle** and plows right on by it. This is detected by high TA right during or after a declare request. The auditor plowed on. The floating **needle** did occur, wasn't seen. (HCO PL 5 Aug 65)

NEEDS, the basic things a person has to have in order to survive, such as food, clothing, shelter. These are distinguished from wants which are the personal desires of an individual. Thus although a person needs shelter to survive and a house may represent that, he may want particular features in that house that his basic survival does not depend upon.

NEGATIVE CASH DIFFERENTIAL, where a department of the organization receives less **cash** than its costs. In this the general share is taken into account as well as direct costs. (HCO PL 26 Jun 64)

NEGATIVE CASH FLOW, the instance of less cash flowing into an activity or business than flowing out of it.

NEGATIVE MOTION, see MOTION, NEGATIVE.

NEGATIVE STATISTICS, some things go up in statistic when they are bad (like car accidents). However we are not using **negative statistics.** We only use things that mean good where they go up or mean bad where they go down. (HCO PL 16 Dec 65)

NEGATIVE STIMULANTS, methods, sometimes of questionable value, to stimulate employees to produce more such as threat of dismissal or transfer or reduction in salary or commissions.

NEGOTIABLE, in investments, stock that can be transferred from one person to another upon delivery.

NEGOTIABLE INSTRUMENT, a legal document regarding an obligation to be met and that upon endorsement, may be transferred from one party to another.

NEGOTIATION, 1. the settling or arranging of a business affair by conferring or discussing it with all parties concerned. 2. the act of transferring title or ownership notes, property or funds to another person in return for value received.

NEPOTISM, the practice of granting unusual favors to relatives such as placing them, sometimes inappropriately, in high business positions.

NEPTUNE, [the *Neptune* was a converted PT boat which served as the stationship for the Pacific area in 1969. It was replaced as stationship by the *Bolivar.* The *Neptune* is mentioned in FO 2199.]

NET, 1. the amount remaining after all necessary deductions or losses have been made, as a company's net profits. 2. term indicating that the amount so designated on an invoice is the final sum that is payable.

NET ASSET VALUE, an investment company term meaning net asset value per share. It is calculated by totaling the market value of all securities owned, deducting liabilities and dividing the balance by the number of shares outstanding.

NET BOOK AMOUNT, as shown on a company's books, the value of a fixed asset after the amount of depreciation has been deducted. Also called net book value.

NET CHANGE, the change in the price of a stock from the closing price on one day and the closing price on the following day if the stock was traded in that period.

NET CURRENT ASSETS, see CAPITAL, WORKING.

NET INCOME, net income is the gross income less all operating costs including salaries; the amount of income over and above expenses; profit. See ALLOCATION SUM.

NET INVESTMENT, see INVESTMENT, NET.

NET LOSS, the amount by which one's income falls short of one's expenditures for a given period of time.

NET MARGIN, see PROFIT, NET.

NET WORTH, 1. a measurement of an individual's or business' worth in terms of earnings determined as the difference between total assets and total liabilities. 2. in corporation accounting, total capital paid in, earned surplus or retained earnings, and accumulated surplus determine net worth.

NEVER PROSPECT, the Scn qualification for a **never prospect** who has not bought anything from the org is someone who does not respond to personal contact, or reach as a result of the Division 6 mailings. A person qualifying as a **never prospect** does not mean the road to total freedom is barred to him forever. Should he reach at a later date such as come into the org for testing or an intro lecture, etc., or his name and address be given again at the close, then he is contacted and followed up. (BPL 1 Dec 72R II)

NEW, **new** books, booklets, magazines, etc., are defined as those types of issues being released for the first time. (BPL 2 Mar 73R I)

NEW BUSINESS, raw public brought into the org and public who have taken or are taking public services but have not yet started a major service. (HCO PL 26 Nov 71 II) [The above HCO PL was revised and reissued as HCO PL 26 Nov 71R II which was cancelled by BPL 1 Dec 72 IV.]

NEW ISSUE, securities or bonds sold by a company for the first time, the proceeds from which may be used to retire outstanding stock of the company or to acquire a new facility, equipment, or additional working capital.

NEW NAMES TO RECRUITMENT APPLICANT PROSPECT FILES, (HCO Department 1 statistic) **new names to recruitment applicant prospect files** shall be defined as: any person who has completed a Sea Org application form or who has expressed a written interest in joining the Sea Org. (BO 86R, 14 Jul 73)

NEW NAME TO CF, 1. only when a person has bought something from the org for the first time is he a **new name to CF**. (BPL 1 Dec 72R II) **2.** anyone who has bought something from the org. (HCO PL 3 Jul 71R) **3.** (for a Saint Hill or AOSH Organization) the **new name** must not already be in the **CF** of the org counting the stat. If it is then it is not valid; it isn't "new." Definition: someone who has completed training (HAS or above) or auditing (one intensive or more) at a lower org or mission for the first time or someone not already in SH **CF** who reaches for SH services or who joins the I Want to Go Clear Club at the AO or who is a Scientologist/Dianeticist buying a book directly from SH for the first time. (HCO PL 10 Feb 72R III) **4.** (for an Advanced Organization) the **new name** must not already be in the **CF** of the org counting the stat. If it is then it is not valid; it isn't **"new."** Definition: a Scientologist or Dianeticist who expresses a desire for AO service for the first time, e.g. joins the I Want to Go Clear Club. Note that the definition says Scientologist or Dianeticist so raw public does not qualify for AO CF. "Expresses a desire" is not defined and may *not* be judged *only* as someone who pays money to the AO. Joining the I Want to Go Clear Club or writing in, a payment of money, or a letter to the AO containing interest in taking an AO service(s) is what qualifies as "expressing a desire." Anything less such as verbal expression is not acceptable. (HCO PL 10 Feb 72R III) **5.** (Public Division statistic) number of **new names to central files:** this is anyone who has bought something from the org for the first time, whether this is a book, HAS Course, HQS Course, or any other service sold—either paid in part or in full, and whose **name** is not already in **central files.** This does not authorize the illegal practice of counting a **new name to CF** as someone who bought an "FSM magazine" or some other small item. The least item bought is a book. A book sold by an org FSM is a **new name to** the org's **CF.** The FSM must, however, send in the name and address of the buyer with evidence of sale to the Dir Clearing. (HCO PL 28 Nov 71R II) *Abbr.* NNCF.

NEW NAME TO PROSPECT CARD FILES, (the gross divisional statistic for Division 6 in a Nine Division Org) someone at the org for the first time who has done either of the following: (a) bought a book, (b) attended an intro lecture, (c) attended a public event, (d) attended a Sunday service, (e) received testing service, (f) bought a public service before graduating HAS or buying a major service from the org. (HCO PL 19 Aug 70) [This stat was cancelled by HCO PL 3 Jul 71R *New Names to CF Change*. Number of people routed to reg was put in as the Division 6 stat.]

NEW PEOPLE BROUGHT INTO THE ORG, (Public Division statistic) number of **new people brought into the org**: these are **new**, raw public coming **into the org** for the first time for testing, events, introductory lectures, to see the Public Registrar or for any reason in the direction of wanting to know about Scn. The statistic is counted whether the person buys a book or service (public service in Div 6 or major service in Divs 4 or 5) or not. The stat is calculated by counting up the number of interviews done by the Public Reg at the end of the week and cross-checking these with the invoices from books sold to raw public. These invoiced can be simply designated RP (raw public) for fast cross-check when bookstore person is invoicing during week. (HCO PL 28 Nov 71R II)

NEW PEOPLE ROUTED TO REG, (Public Division statistic) number of **new people routed to reg**: this stat is self-evident. It is the number of **new people routed to reg.** What matters is that this **new** person is not CF, has come to the org probably for the first time. It doesn't matter what **reg.** It is preferably the Public **Reg** but the stat is still counted if somebody else has to stand in for her. Also, the **new** person has to have arrived at the **reg.** Somebody told that the **reg** is in the first room on the left is not a stat. (HCO PL 28 Nov 71R II)

NEWS, any event, idea or opinion that is timely, that interests or affects a large number of persons in a community, and that is capable of being understood by them. (BPL 10 Jan 73R)

NEW SHIP OR QUARTERS RESERVE, (Flag) all delivery sum monies in excess of $55,000 are allocated to a **new ship** or shore building **reserve** since FCCI and student traffic could soon outstrip existing facilities and crash income. (FSO 667RC)

NEWS INTERVIEW, type of **interview.** This is a meeting between the reporter and the **news** source. Such meetings are not fishing expeditions. In nearly all cases the reporter has some important well-defined questions that he and his newspaper want Source to answer. (BPL 10 Jan 73R)

NEWSLETTER, an informal periodical report, printed in letter format, usually devoted to news for a special interest group or distributed internally in an organization and to its customers and business prospects.

NEWS PEG, that is an introductory statement announcing the subject and tying it to a **news** development. (BPL 10 Jan 73R)

NIBS, L. Ron Hubbard, Jr. (HASI PL 30 Aug 57)

NICKEL AND DIMERS, those who have made a small payment some time ago but nothing since and who haven't communicated to the org. (SO ED 230 INT)

NIGHTMARES, vitamin B1 is the cure for **nightmares.** 100mg a day handles it. A **nightmare** is apparently an effort to locate oneself. (OODs 14 Nov 70)

NIHILISM, nihilism means nothingness. The movement could best be described as wreck everything, make nothing out of everything. (ESTO 11, 7203C06 SO I)

NINE DIVISION ORG, when an **org** gets over 50 staff members, its **divisions** become **9.** It is then called a **Nine Division Org.** At that time the **org** must have three Public Divisions instead of just one division (6) devoted to it. The three new divisions are headed by the Public Executive Secretary. Former Division Six is simply expanded with each department becoming a division with added functions. The division then becomes: Division 9—Executive Div, Division 1—HCO Div, Division 2—Dissem Div, Division 3—Treasury, Division 4—Tech Div, Division 5—Qualifications, Division 6—Public Planning, Division 7—Public Activities, Division 8—Success. (HCO PL 26 Oct 67)

NKAMBI, [the *Nkambi* was a catamaran approximately 20 ft. long used for sail training. It is mentioned in FO 1853.]

NO 1 ACCOUNT, Finance Office **No. 1 Account.** (BPL 17 Feb 71R)

NO. 1 PROJECT, validation of all certificates ever issued. All auditors trained since 1950 are invited in for free special coaching and a validation stamp on their certificates saying "validated for advanced processes 1957 HCO Board of Review." (HCO PL 2 May 57)

NO AUDITING, meaning **no** session of any kind, **no auditor** or pc in the room. (HCO PL 23 May 65 II)

NO CASE FOLDER, an illegible **case folder** is classed as a **no case folder.** (HCO PL 16 Apr 65 II)

NO-CASE-GAIN, **1.** the only reason the insane were hard to understand is that they are handling situations which no longer exist. The situation probably existed at one time. They think they have to hold their own, with overts against a non-existent enemy to solve a non-existent problem. Because their overts are continuous they have withholds. Since such a person has withholds, he or she can't communicate freely to as-is the block on the track that keeps them in some yesterday. Hence, a **no-case-gain.** (HCO PL 5 Apr 65) **2.** if you skip a person on one level several levels up, he or she will experience only an unreality and will not react. This is expressed as **no-case gain.** (HCO PL 5 May 65) **3.** chronic **no** change of **case.** (HCO PL 26 Aug 65R) *Abbr.* NCG.

NO HAVING, the way **not** to **have** is to ignore or combat or withdraw from. These three, ignoring or combatting or withdrawing sum up to **no having.** (HCO PL 17 Jan 62)

NO HOLE NUDGE SYSTEM, the idea of this **system** is for the ASR Unit to ensure that all people advance scheduled get written to regularly, are kept track of with no chance of falling off the lines and so do arrive at the org on or before their scheduled date. It also enables lack of comm from persons scheduled to be located and rapidly handled. A 3" x 5" card file is compiled of all people already in the ASR master card file (names only are written in on the card). This file is called the **nudge** file. The ASR, writes to each person using the proper type of **nudge** letter. (HCO PL 18 Feb 73 II) [See the above issue for a full explanation of the **system.**]

NOISE, **1.** the amount of disturbance and off line actions and chatter and general dev-t in an area. (OODs 7 Nov 70) **2.** a technical term used in the field of public relations to describe the medley of messages hitting a member of a public besides one's own message. (HCO PL 8 May 70)

NOMINAL CAPITAL, see CAPITAL, NOMINAL.

NOMINAL PRICE, see PRICE, NOMINAL.

NOMINAL VALUE, see FACE VALUE.

NON-APPRENTICE, the classification for a person who is not under contract to a company nor covered by an apprenticeship training agreement but who is learning a type of work through a combination of close job supervision and related classroom instruction. He does not become a journeyman when he finishes his studies.

NON-AUTONOMOUS, **non-autonomous** does not mean a unit cannot issue orders. It means it is there to forward the long-range policy originated by a senior body. (FBDL 12)

NON-COMMUNICATION, a **non-communication** consists of barriers. Barriers consist of space, interpositions (such as walls and screens of fast-moving particles), and time. (HCO PL 4 Apr 72 III)

NON-COMPLIANCE REPORT, staff member **report** of **non-compliance** with legal orders. (HCO PL 1 May 65)

NON-COMPLIANCES, a type of dev-t where failure to **comply** with an order can set an emergency flap going which crowds the lines with dispatches. One consequence of **non-compliance** when repeated over a long period is to move a large number of targets into present time in a sort of frantic jam. Catastrophies can occur because of **non-compliance.** (HCO PL 27 Jan 69)

NON CO-OP, we used to have an HCO category known as **non co-op,** meaning **no cooperation** from us. People who demanded 90% of our time comprised only a small per cent of our people. Such we put on a private **non-cooperate** list. We just didn't do anything for them. When they called and demanded action we'd say "uh-huh" and forget it. After a while they'd wander off our lines and we'd be free of them. Dead file is actually only an extension of **non co-op.** It was we who didn't **cooperate.** (HCO PL 7 Jun 65, *Entheta Letters and the Dead File, Handling of, —Definitions*)

NONCUMULATIVE, a type of preferred stock on which unpaid dividends do not accumulate for eventual payment.

NON DELIVERY, the org just didn't **deliver** the service bought. (HCO PL 26 Oct 75)

NON DENOMINATIONAL, Scn is **non denominational.** By that is meant that Scn is open to people of all religions and beliefs and in no way tries to persuade a person from his religion, but assists him to better understand that he is a spiritual being. (BPL 6 Mar 69)

NON DISCLOSURE BOND, all persons offloaded from Flag for any reason (expulsion, Fitness Board or whatever) are required to sign the **non disclosure bond** prior to departure. This **bond** does not require that any actual money be paid over. It does, however, provide that should the person ever reveal the location of Flag, a sum of money will immediately become due and payable. The purpose of this **bond** is to ensure Flag locational security. The **bond** may be used in other circumstances as suggested by the F/MAA and approved by the A/G Flag. (FO 3529)

NON DIVISIONAL AIDES, **aides** and assistant **aides** who do **not** have **divisions.** (CBO 147)

NON ENTURBULATION ORDER, ethics issues a **non enturbulation order.** This states that those named in it (the SPs and PTSes who are students or preclears) are forbidden to **enturbulate** others and if one more report is received of their **enturbulating** anyone, an SP order will be issued forthwith. (HCO PL 1 Jul 65)

NON-EXISTENCE, every new appointee to a post begins in **non-existence.** Whether obtained by new appointment, promotion, or demotion. He is normally under the delusion that now he is "The ________" (new title). He tries to start off in power condition as he is usually very aware of his new status or even a former status. But in actual fact he is the only one aware of it. All others except perhaps the Personnel Officer are utterly unaware of him as having his new status. Therefore he begins in a state of **non-existence.** And if he does not begin with the **non-existence** formula as his guide he will be using the wrong condition and will have all kinds of trouble. (HCO PL 23 Sept 67)

NON-EXISTENCE FORMULA, **formula** is (1) find a comm line, (2) make yourself known, (3) discover what is needed and/or wanted, (4) do produce and/or present it. (HCO PL 22 Sept 67) See EXPANDED NON-EXISTENCE FORMULA.

NON-EXISTENT TARGETTING, a type of dev-t where **targets** are not set, major **targets** are unknown. Actions are then unproductive. (HCO PL 27 Jan 69)

NON-OPERATIONAL, anything that needs constant fiddling or working at to make it run is **non-operational.** It must be repaired fully or replaced. (HCO PL 14 Mar 72 II)

NON-OPERATING COMPANY, see COMPANY, NON-OPERATING.

NON-OPTIMUM, is defined as dirty, broken, damaged, deteriorated or non-operational. (FO 3279-1R)

NON-PRODUCTIVE JOBS, a misnomer for which the preferred term is indirect labor.

NON PROFESSIONAL ROUTE TO CLEAR, the pc **route.** (BPL 6 Aug 72RA)

NONPROFIT CORPORATION, see CORPORATION, NONPROFIT.

NON-REMIMEO, **1. non-remimeo** means HCO Bulletins, policy letters, administrative letters and executive letters which are intended for use but only by executives and therefore of limited distribution. It means **not** to be **mimeoed** again by the receiving org. On **non-remimeo,** a very few copies are sent to main orgs and they in turn distribute to their nearby orgs. (HCO PL 2 Jul 64) **2. non-remimeo** means bulletins and policy letters which are intended for use but only by executives and therefore are of limited distribution. It means **not** to be **mimeoed** again by the receiving org. There are two classes of **non-remimeo:** general **non-remimeo** and limited **non-remimeo.** General **non-remimeo** distribution is based on one copy for master files, one copy to LRH Comm, one copy to the Guardian or A/G, one copy each to the FR, ED(CO), HES and OES, one copy to the Qual library reference files and one copy to the reference files of all bulletins and PLs kept in reception for staff, one copy to the division head(s) and the department head(s) concerned and one copy to the post(s) in the department(s) concerned. General **non-remimeo** issues usually deal with broader points of admin or tech of interest to one or two production departments as well as the LRH Comm, FR, the Guardian or A/G, HES, OES and ED(CO). They are never strewn about or broadly republished as they could be misunderstood. Limited **non-remimeo** means that copies only go to master files, LRH Comm, the Guardian or A/G, HES, OES, ED(CO) and FR. It is usually important that this does not get wide distribution as it has to do with org know-how, planning, etc., and could be misunderstood. So it is **not remimeoed** or strewn about. It may be taken up in staff meetings but that is about all. One *never* republishes a limited **non-remimeo** in a magazine. (BPL 14 Apr 69R) **3.** means that they are cut on a stencil and just run off and a few copies are sent to each org. (SH Spec 57, 6504C06)

NONSTOCK CORPORATION, see CORPORATION, NONSTOCK.

NON-UTILIZED PERSONNEL, people who don't know what they are doing and people who don't but think they do are both **non-utilized personnel.** (HCO PL 22 Sept 70)

NOONDAY REPORT FORM, this is a daily **report form,** compiled from data assembled during the watch by the OOD. When the watch changes over the off-going OOD shows this **report** to the on-coming OOD, together with any other pertinent data. It is then handrouted to the Captain for his attention. (FSO 9RB)

NO REALITY, (form of arbitrary) the receipt of a communication is an extremely important part of the sequence of actions that results in a compliance. Common reasons for the non-receipt of a communication are that arbitraries (or arbitrary factors) exist in the area. **No reality** means an absence of familiarity with the scene effected by the originator's intention which prevents the recipient from connecting the communication with the existing scene, or which precludes in the recipient's mind any possibility of making any change, or the desired change, to the existing scene. It can manifest as an involvement on the part of an individual in a situation in his personal life which occupies all his attention, or as a failure to fully wear a hat on account of one or more of the organizational psychoses. (BPL 10 Nov 73 II)

NO-REPORT, **1.** if one fails to make out a **report** it is a **no-report** situation and may be investigated. (HCO PL 14 Apr 65 III) **2.** an unreadable **report** is classed as a **no-report.** (HCO PL 14 Apr 65 III) **3.** (**no-reports**) a type of dev-t where the scramble to find out if something has been done increases traffic. This includes lack of data forwarded as it should have been. It causes as well anxiety and uncertainty. The scramble to find out if something has been done increases traffic. (HCO PL 27 Jan 69) **4. no-report** means non-compliance. (HCO PL 31 May 68) *Abbr.* NR.

NO-REPORT REPORT, staff member **report** of any failure to receive a **report** or an illegible **report** or folder. (HCO PL 1 May 65)

NO RESPONSIBILITY, the way not to have is to ignore or combat or withdraw from. These three, ignoring or combatting or withdrawing sum up to no having. They also sum up to **no responsibility** for such things. Thus we can define **responsibility** as the concept of being able to care for, to reach or to be. All real difficulty stems from **no responsibility.** (HCO PL 17 Jan 62)

NO RIGHTS, means **no rights.** The normal rights an individual would have, such as eating, sleeping, wearing uniform, having liberty, taking breaks, etc., an individual does not have when he gets himself into a lowered condition. Of course, anyone may have some food and some sleep, this is needed so the body can keep going. But as for dressing nicely, wearing uniforms and doing the same things that you would do in normal operation, the answer is **no.** You got into a low condition because you goofed. Now you are expected to suffer the penalties for the goof you made, apply the condition and as you start coming up, so you start getting your **rights** back. (FO 1421)

NORM, 1. generally, a standard, model or pattern regarded as typical for a specific group. 2. in statistics, a mode or average.

NORMAL OPERATION, a routine or gradual increase. (SH Spec 62, 6505C25)

NORMAL OPERATION FORMULA, (1) the way you maintain an increase is when you are in a state of **normal operation** you don't change anything. (2) ethics are very mild, the justice factor is quite mild, there are no savage actions taken particularly. (3) a statistic betters then look it over carefully and find out what bettered it and then do that without abandoning what you were doing before. (4) every time a statistic worsens slightly, quickly find out why and remedy it. And you just jockey those two factors, the statistic bettering, the statistic worsening, repair the statistic worsening, and you will find out inevitably some change has been made in that area where a statistic worsens. Some change has been made, you had better get that change off the lines in a hurry. (HCO PL 23 Sept 67)

NORMAL OPERATOR, see WORKER, NORMAL.

NORMAL PRICE, see PRICE, NORMAL.

NORMAL WORKER, see WORKER, NORMAL.

NO-SITUATION, a situation is something that applies to survival and if you evaluate the word "situation" against survival, you've got it. A good situation is a high level of survival; a bad situation is a threatened survival and a **no-situation** is something that won't affect survival. (7201C02 SO)

NOT ACTIVE, defined as a person who is off org lines and is **not** progressing up the Routing and Gradation Chart. The person did reach but the reach is withdrawn because of some upset with the org. (HCO PL 30 Sept 71) [The above HCO PL was cancelled by BPL 10 Oct 75 IX.]

NOTE, 1. a piece of paper currency. 2. a promise in writing to pay a debt. 3. a certificate issued by a government or a bank and sometimes negotiable as money. 4. a formal written diplomatic or official communication.

NOT HANDLING, in administration we sometimes find terminals that refer dispatches to others, let them drift, give excuses why not. This adds up to **not handling**. This is the basic reason for dev-t (developed, meaning excessive, traffic). (HCOB 15 Jan 70 II)

NOT SOLVENT, that is to say, our outgo was greater than our income. (7208C02 SO)

NOTICE OF DISHONOR, a notice, given orally or in writing, to makers, endorsers and drawers that a negotiable instrument has not been paid, or honored, when presented at the designated time.

NOTICE OF PROTEST, a statement made before a Notary Public that a check, note or bill of exchange has been refused when presented for payment.

NO TONE ARM ACTION, if you skip a person on one level several levels up, he or she will experience only an unreality and will not react. This is expressed as "no-case-gain." On the E-meter it registers as **no tone arm action** meaning there is **no** meter registry of change on the meter control lever (tone arm). (HCO PL 5 May 65)

NUDGE, **1.** Communication Office query as to the progress of a message. (*HTLTAE,* p. 68) **2.** a slip which asks about the progress of a communication. Comcenter sends a **nudge** to the actad when he fails to acknowledge a message or to complete it in the estimated time. (*HTLTAE,* p. 121)

NUDGE FILE, a 3" x 5" card **file** compiled of all people already in the ASR master card file (names only are written in on the card). This **file** is called the **nudge file.** When the cards are made out they are separated out into fourteen sections depending upon when the person was last contacted, i.e., if a person was just recently written to his 3" x 5" card would be filed in the farthest section from PT, section 14. The **nudge** cards are rotated one section daily, i.e., the **nudge** cards in section one are written to and then moved to the back of the **file** into section fourteen. (HCO PL 18 Feb 73 II)

NULL POINT, see CYCLE OF ACTION.

NUMBER OF FULLY HATTED ORG STAFF MEMBERS, Division 1—HCO GDS. A **hat** consists of a checksheet and pack fully word cleared and studied and known to a point of full application of the data therein. Instant hats, mini hats do not count on this stat. The staff member must be in the org and on its staff list. Those on full-time training or in another org for training or processing do not count on this stat. (HCO PL 8 Nov 73RA)

NUMBER OF RISING GDSES MULTIPLIED BY NUMBER ON STAFF, GDS for Division 1—HCO. Definition of this stat is as follows: **number of rising GDSes** will be **number** of the other divisions' **GDSes** which are up that week. **Number on staff** does not include paying public interns or staff students off on full time training in the org or a higher org. It does not include A/G Office, FBO or Flag Rep, nor does it include casual volunteers or FSMs. It does include HCO expeditors. (HCO PL 8 Nov 73) [This GDS was changed to number of fully hatted org staff members by HCO PL 8 Nov 73RA *The VFPs and GDSs of the Divisions of an Org.*]

NUREMBERG CODE, **code** established effective in all nations after the Nazi war criminal trials and signed by all nations which prohibits all experimental physical treatments. (LRH ED 67 INT)

NURSERY, a **nursery** exists for the care of small children and babies. The in-charge is the Nanny. The **nursery** is located in the Estates Section, Office of LRH. (FO 3167)

O

O AND P FORMS, two additions made to HCOB 18 November 1960, *The Preclear Assessment Sheet.* These are Sections **O and P.** Section **O** lists all the turning points, or changes, in the pc's life. It forms an additional section to the actual preclear assessment, which is unchanged in every other respect. Section **P** is the processing section. Using the data obtained from section **O**, an auditor can run a complete problems intensive, following the procedure outlined in section **P.** The processing section **P** consists of finding what problem existed immediately before the change. Run off the unknowns in the problem. Locate the confusions. Find the persons present in the confusion. Assess the persons for most reaction, take the one with most reaction and run a processing check on that person to get the withholds the pc had from that person. (HCOB 17 Oct 61)

OBJECTIVE, the end one has in sight; what one is striving toward; the goal or purpose one is pushing to achieve.

OBJECTIVE ONE, our first **objective** is: get all persons ever enrolled in an academy audited on and trained to use Routine 2-12, the undercut for all cases. (HCO PL 24 Nov 62)

OBJECTIVE PROCESSES, processes leading to a confront of the universe. (FO 3183)

OBJECTIVE THREE, process selected celebrities. The rehabilitation of celebrities who are just beyond or just approaching their prime. This is **objective three.** (HCO PL 1 Jan 63)

OBJECTIVE TWO, consists of forming district offices wherever there are centers or field offices. (HCO PL 24 Nov 62)

OBNOSIS, this is a coined (invented) word meaning observing the obvious. There is no English or any other language precise equivalent for it. (HCO PL 26 Jun 72)

Observation

OBSERVATION, observation is not a passive thing. It is an active thing and involves the closest possible study of what one is **observing.** One should train himself or herself to react in the following manner: if one is in mystery about something one does not puzzle over it, he or she knows at once that if he is puzzled or in mystery or can't work it out, he or she does not have enough data and the thing to do is get more data. The full thought is, puzzle or mystery or can't figure it out—get more data. (CBO 190)

OBSERVATION DRILL NO. 1, name: **observe** the room. Purpose: to get the student able to **observe** and make simple reports on objects in the room. (FO 2506RA)

OBSERVATION DRILL NO. 2, name: spotting the outness. Purpose: to get the student able to spot and report outnesses seen in an area. (FO 2506RA)

OBSERVATION DRILL NO. 3, name: **observing** people. Purpose: to teach the student to **observe** and identify people. (FO 2506RA)

OBSERVATION DRILL NO. 4, name: shop window. Purpose: to train the student to **observe** and report on many objects in a short space of time. (FO 2506RA)

OBSERVATION MISSION, collection, digestion and dissemination of information. That is actually what an **observation mission** does. (6912C13 SO)

OBSERVER MISSION ORDERS, usually this is a one-man **mission.** The reason for an **observer mission** is very exact: the why of an existing situation is not known sufficiently to be acted upon. A situation exists, out-points have been found that pinpoint an area, but the why cannot be arrived at. The **observer** is sent in to investigate in the area indicated by the out-points already available. The **observation MO** must then consist of situation "as reported," the out-points that direct attention to an area, the why which is so far unknown but must be found. This is the exact extent of **observer MOs.** (FO 2936)

OBSOLESCENCE, the process by which something gradually becomes obsolete, out-of-date or passes out of use because of social, economic or scientific improvements.

OBSOLETE, designating a method, machine, asset, etc., that is no longer useful or profitable compared to or because of recent social, economic or scientific developments; out-of-date.

OCCUPATION, 1. the specific type of job that one does in order to earn a living, such as a lawyer, teacher, carpenter, etc.; trade; employment. 2. a category of jobs which have a lot of the same actions and tasks in common.

OCCUPATIONAL ANALYSIS, see ANALYSIS, OCCUPATIONAL.

OCCUPATION DESCRIPTION, a description of the traits and characteristics of an occupation or those of the various jobs classed as one occupation.

OCCUPATION, GAINFUL, any occupation, job or form of employment for which a person receives money or a profitable exchange.

OCCUPATIONS, GREY AREA, types of work not clearly distinguishable as entirely white or blue collar jobs such as inspection, clerical or supervisory positions closely associated with production lines.

ODD LOT, stocks are usually traded in 100 share units or 10 share units for inactive stocks. Odd lots are groups of 1 to 99 or 1 to 9 shares for inactives, which don't quite add up to the standard trading unit amount.

ODD LOT DEALER, a member firm of a national stock exchange which buys and sells odd lots of securities such as 1 to 9 shares in stocks traded in 10-share units and 1 to 99 for 100-share units.

OFF-BOARD, reference to trading over-the-counter in unlisted securities or to a transaction which was not made on a national securities exchange.

OFFENSES, 1. ideas or procedures that distracted from or balked the basic purpose of an individual, species, organism, organization were called **offenses.** (HCO PL 13 Mar 65, *Divisions 1, 2, 3, The Structure of Organization What is Policy?*) **2.** there are four general classes of crimes and **offenses** in Scn. These are errors, misdemeanors, crimes and high crimes. (HCO PL 7 Mar 65 III)

OFFER, *n.* the price at which an investor is willing to buy or to sell a security. —*v.* to make a proposal; to hold out or extend toward another for acceptance or refusal.

OFFICE, the **Office** or Admin Unit heretofore placed under CS-7 then CS-9 is now an autonomous unit under the Staff Captain called the Flag Executive **Office** Unit and the person in charge is the Flag Executive **Office** Manager. (FO 2381)

OFFICE, the service core of an organization to which all written communications and business records are eventually assigned and from which statistical data often originates or is gathered, daily functions of a general nature are performed and a history of all transactions is maintained.

OFFICE MANAGER, 1. the Deputy LRH Comm FSO, or **Office Manager,** is located on the org board in Department 21, Office of LRH. The purpose of the deputy is to keep a smoothly running LRH Comm establishment in existence and to permit the LRH Comm to produce. She keeps the internal Department 21 activities fully under control and each area being productive. She also gives full back-up of the LRH Comm FSO so the LRH Comm can freely operate in the FSO. The **Office Manager** is the Org Officer to the LRH Comm. The **Office Manager** is responsible for the standard admin of the LRH Comm, i.e., LRH Comm log accurate and in PT, particles correctly filed, nudges and acknowledgments sent out, program folders made and kept up-to-date, extreme conditions reports and other LRH Comm weekly reports submitted up network command line. (FO 3590) **2.** (the post of **Office Manager,** Office of LRH, Department 21) where an **office manager** exists, no admin I/Cs except finance are permitted outside his control and finance if it goes out can come under his control. The point is that where an **office manager** exists he and his "crew" work as needed to get the admin work done and kept in PT and there are no admin personnel other than those under his control. Duty posts such as reception, E/O, tech services, may, however, exist outside his control so long as they are busy and up-to-date in any incidental admin function. The **Office Manager** is responsible under the head of the org for the state of the org's admin. He does not assign his people one for one post, although he may apportion the work to the same people. His action is to get the admin kept up regardless of transfers or failures to perform duties of the post. (FO 2286) **3.** a Flag administration office is established in the Office of LRH under CS-7. In charge of the unit is the Flag **Office Manager.** Only aides, FBO, and currently assigned communicators remain in the other Flag divisions. All other functions and Flag personnel come under the **Office Manager.** (FO 2273) **4.** Flag is to be organized as a Seven Division Org. Each aide is to have a communicator. All other persons in their divisions to be transferred to Division 7, Department 21, **Office Manager.** The **Office Manager** is to have under him all clerks, files, mimeo, addresso, audio-visio, etc., and will use personnel interchangeably to handle on a sort of expeditor basis, except for mimeo which is busy. (FO 2272)

OFFICE MANAGER, the individual in an organization who manages its clerical employees and their work.

OFFICE OF ADVANCE MAG, the **Office of Advance Mag** on Flag is in the PR and Consumption Bureau, located directly under the PR and Consumption Aide. **Advance** is produced by the Editor and Deputy Editor, and other staff as added. The AOs have an **Office of Advance Magazine** in Department 4, Department of Promotion (AOSHs—Department 4s, AO Department of Promotion). It is headed by the Assistant Editor. (FO 3295)

OFFICE OF LRH, 1. Department 21, Division 7. The purpose of the **Office of LRH** is: to direct, authorize and organize Scn and its organizations and to ensure the forward progress of all. The principal sections are the Council Section, LRH Personal Concerns Section, Design and Planning Section, Files Section, Authority to Issue Section, Signature Section, Construction Section and the Household Section. The **office** and these sections are represented in every Scn organization. In this **office** are held the Council Meetings, consisting of LRH, usually by proxy, the HCO Exec Sec and the Org Exec Sec. (HCO PL 2 Aug 65) **2.** this **office** handles the affairs **of LRH** and has the signature and seals of the org. (HCO PL 6 Sept 67) **3.** Department 21. Just speaking organizationally there are three basic hats there; the LRH Comm, who is the Department head, the Bureau Liaison Officer who is the basic communication terminal through which the Bureau communicates to the org and the Finance Banking Office, who is part of the Finance Network. (FEBC 12, 7102C03 SO II)

OFFICE OF LRH WW, the **Office of LRH WW** contains: (a) the Advisory Council WW, (b) the LRH Communicator Advisor WW, (c) Office of LRH production activities and staffs (cine, book writing, magazine articles writing, photography, research, hats, policy writing, etc.), (d) Estate Section, (e) Household Section, (f) Office of LRH Personal Secretary. (HCO PL 16 Dec 65)

OFFICE OF PUBLIC AFFAIRS, as there have been instances of confusion between PRAC (PR Area Control) Bureaux and PR and C (PR and Consumption) Bureau, the PRAC Bureaux aboard Flag are now known as the **Office of Public Affairs.** (FO 3280-6) [The reference FO has been cancelled by FO 3398.]

OFFICE OF THE CAPTAIN, (Sea Org org board) the **Captain** in Department 21 is subject to owner or Board, the highest highest authority aboard in all divisional and departmental matters and subject to the owner's or Board's and their Commodore, but the ship, its cargo, its crew and passengers, and all conduct of operations are subject to the **Captain.** The Chief Engineer's Department is in the **Office of the Captain.** (FO 1109)

OFFICE OF THE CONTROLLER, 1. Department 20, the **Office of the Controller,** which is really the Guardians Office with all Guardian's

Bureaux in it, and is usually manned in an org by an A/G and will often have an A/G Finance. That office is basically external. (FEBC 12, 7102C03 SO II) **2.** MSH's own **office** and oversees the entire Guardian Office network. (OODs 13 Jun 74) **3.** Department 20 is of course the **Office of the Controller** which is really the Guardian's Office with all Guardian's Bureaux in it and it's usually manned in an org by an A/G and will often have an A/G Finance. This has the valuable final product of acceptances of Scn. It would consist of combatting an enemy propaganda action, it would consist of getting in good press, it would consist of quite a few things. But the end of all of that is a product and it is an acceptance. (FEBC 12, 7102C03 SO II)

OFFICE OF THE EXECUTIVE DIRECTOR, **1.** the first one (Department 21) would really be the **Office of the Executive Director** or the General Manager or something of that character. It would be the person who was in charge of it. This could be if the Chairman of the Board or somebody like this were actually the Manager of the Company. Then his **office** would be here. Ideally this would be Source, and this would also be the person who had developed the product. There is normally someone who started the company. In the United States that ought to be the Office of George Washington. (SH Spec 77, 6608C23) **2.** Department 19, Division VII, Executive Division. It handles long-range planning, Exec Council meeting, Org products planning, org programs coordinating, Advisory Council briefing, org products expediting, org establishing and maintaining, staff welfare surveying, line inspecting and correcting, and org programs compliances to Flag. (HCO PL 18 May 73)

OFFICE OF THE HCO EXEC SEC, **1.** Department 20. The primary purpose of the **Office of the HCO Exec Sec** is: to help Ron keep **HCO** and the organization there and make them and the policies, technology and service of Scn well known. In the person **of the HCO Executive Secretary**, this **office** controls the two divisions of **HCO** and controls the routing and handling of dispatches and persons throughout the org and **HCO**, and all personnel of **HCO** and the org. (HCO PL 2 Aug 65) **2.** Department 20, Division 7. It oversees and gets execution on all promotional activities in the **HCO Exec Sec's** two **HCO** Divisions and the Executive Division. (HCO PL 20 Nov 65)

OFFICE OF THE ORG EXEC SEC, **1.** Department 19. The **Office of the Organization Executive Secretary** has as its purpose: to help Ron keep the **organization** solvent and producing and to make Scn well known everywhere. This **office** in the person **of the Org Exec Sec**, directs and controls the four divisions of the **org.** The primary action of the **Org** portion of the entire organization is to handle whatever is routed and so produce results, and in its 6th division Distribution, as well as the other three, to make Scn broadly known and well thought of everywhere by changing personal and social conditions. (HCO PL 2 Aug 65) **2.** Department 19, Division 7. It oversees and gets execution on all promotional actions and functions in the **Org Exec Sec's** four divisions. (HCO PL 20 Nov 65)

OFFICE OF THE PORT CAPTAIN, **1.** Dept 19, Public Contact Division 7 (flagship). Its ideal scene is area control and safety for the ship and company in any port or area we go or wish to go. (FO 2633) **2.** Department 16, Publics Division VI Flagship Organization. It contains an Establishment Section, Briefing Section, Ship Presentation Section and Port Control Section. (FSO 252)

OFFICE OF THE PUBLIC EXECUTIVE SECRETARY, Department 25, Division 9. It contains a Communicator Section, Programs Coordination Section and Area Expansion Section. (HCO PL 21 Dec 69) [The above HCO PL was cancelled by BPL 10 Oct 75 VII.]

OFFICE OF THE TREASURER, the **Office of the Treasurer** is formed at Saint Hill. Its personnel come directly under the **Treasurer** but for staff posting belong in the Org Advisory Section of the Office of the Org Exec Sec International Executive Division. The **Office of the Treasurer** has the following purpose: to help Ron safeguard the funds and assets of the organization and throughout the world and to be responsible for those funds, their proper receipt, accounting and disbursement by all staff persons and to prepare punctually all quarterly and annual accounts for any and all purposes. The **Office of the Treasurer** is formed to make the burden of accounting easier and to regularize the accounting activities of all organizations and improve their position and reputation. (HCO PL 15 Jan 66 II)

OFFICE PERSONNEL, the personnel of a business who work in offices handling, collecting, recording, filing, analyzing, relaying, etc., business information and data. Such functions as stenography, accounting, maintaining and filing records, etc., are done by office personnel.

OFFICER, **1.** by **officer** is meant midshipmen, warrant officers and above. (FO 1040) **2.** these head sections within departments. (HCO PL 13 Mar 66) **3.** he is in charge of a section. You have here the Cramming Section. Well, that would be the Cramming **Officer.** (SH Spec 61, 6505C18)

OFFICER, corporate executives usually appointed by the board of directors but in any case subject to the board of directors and holding official positions of responsibility for the everyday operation and functioning of the corporation.

OFFICER COUNCIL, **Officer Council** is not concerned with org management and operation. It is concerned with the conduct and responsibility of Sea Org officers and members, and maintenance of basic Sea Org traditions. The purpose of the **Officer Council** is: to assist the Commodore by ensuring Sea Org **officers** carry out the responsibilities of their rank and maintain the high traditions of the Sea Organization. (FO 3311) *Abbr.* OC.

OOD (Def. 3)

OFFICER OF THE DECK, **1.** the officer next in command to the Con on a watch. At sea the **Officer of the Deck** has the specialist duty of navigation. (FO 2674) **2.** the **Officer of the Deck** must be proficient in handling emergencies and know how to handle the emergency equipment of the ship and how to man it quickly. The **Officer of the Deck** is responsible for the safety of the ship in port and at sea and must inspect the whole ship once each watch. (FO 424) **3.** navigates the ship underway and handles the radar and charts. He locates the position of the vessel and keeps the vessel on its course. (*SWPB*) **4.** one member of the ship's company has the duty as **Officer of the Deck**, of standing by the ship in daily rotation and may leave it only if all is very secure, but in leaving it the **Officer of the Deck** who has the duty yet remains responsible for the ship if anything happens to her in his absence such as going aground, breaking her warps, dragging her anchor or coming into collision while swinging or with other ships. (*Ship's Org Bk.*) **5.** the **Officer of the Deck** keeps the ship off the ground and keeps her located. (FSO 25) *Abbr.* OOD.

OFFICER OF THE WATCH, **1.** keeps the ship running inside and outside, sees the course is followed and reliefs occur of the wheel, etc. The **Officer of the Watch** is essentially a "change noter." He is there to see the changes in wind, sea, current, land, ships, etc. These he calls to the attention of the Conning Officer (who in turn informs the Captain). The **Officer of the Watch** passes the Conning Officer's (or Captain's) orders to the wheel and engines and gets the steersman's and engine room's replies and the lookouts sightings. (FO 80) **2.** purpose: keep Conning Officer informed of vessels situation and condition in relation with other vessels, land, waves, and weather and be responsible for doing so. Keeps ship on course. Is responsible for internal conditions of the ship and any external changes. (FO RS 32) *Abbr.* OOW.

OFFICE ROUTINE, a set and regular pattern of work functions done in a business office which requires little mental effort.

OFFICERS BOARDS, the following boards are formed: **Officers Board** for the Pacific, **Officers Board** Denmark and **Officers Board** UK. These **boards** meet from time to time as may be decided upon by them for the purpose of recommending an award of rank to those Sea Org members working in the area. The recommendations of these **boards** are forwarded with CSW on each individual to **Officers** Selection **Board** on Flag who will consider the recommendations at their own meeting. (FO 1950)

OFFICER SELECTION BOARD, in addition to promotions, it is also a duty of the **Officers Selection Board** to demote those not worthy of holding a rank. (FO 3352) *Abbr.* OSB.

OFFICERS' LOUNGE, the **Officers' Lounge** is a place for relaxation and social activity for **officers** on liberty or during off duty hours. (FSO 767)

OFFICER'S RESPONSIBILITY COURSE, produces the product of a **responsible** Sea Org officer. The **course** is a hatting action and is specialist training for all **officers.** It is 90% objective with numerous demos, drills, observations, etc. (FO 3355-1)

OFFICES, departments. (HCO PL 13 Mar 66)

OFFICIALDOM, 1. officials or persons of that class spoken of collectively. 2. the authority of office, position, title or level of officials.

OFFICIAL ORG, any **official org** (not a franchise or Gung-Ho Group) can perform and teach any class or grade up to Class IV. This includes standard Dianetics HDC and HDG. Only an **official org** can teach academy courses and qualify students for Scn certificates. The difference between an **official org** and a franchise or a mission is that an **official org** is looked to as a distribution point for Source, runs on policy, is responsible for its area, and looks to its Continental Org and WW for policy. It maintains the quality and standard of tech. It sets a standard for instruction. (HCO PL 15 Dec 69)

OFF-LINE, 1. pieces of paper, sent, that don't belong to one. They are sent back to originator. (HCO PL 27 Feb 72) **2.** a type of dev-t where dispatches or orders are passed in a manner to deny information on record. (HCO PL 27 Jan 69) **3.** a dispatch is **off-line** when it is sent to the wrong person. (HCO PL 17 Nov 64) **4.** communication not cleared through the communication center. (HASI PL 9 Apr 57)

OFF-ORIGIN, 1. things **originated** by a post that aren't the business of that post. (HCO PL 27 Feb 72) **2.** a type of dev-t where a terminal **originates** something not its hat. (HCO PL 27 Jan 69)

OFF-ORIGIN DISPATCH, the **origination** of communication that should have been **originated** by someone else. A staff member occasionally tries to **originate** for another hat than his or her own. (HCO PL 31 Jan 65)

OFF-POLICY, an org run by those ignorant of **policy** has collapsed to the degree it went **off-policy. Off-policy** (not knowing, not applying our procedures) has been the common denominator of every org or continental area collapse. (HCO PL 4 Jun 71)

OFF-POLICY DISPATCHES, 1. by which we mean the staff member doesn't know his **policy** and so does things contrary to it or wants to know if it is **policy.** (HCO PL 17 Nov 64) **2.** a **dispatch** is **off-policy** when originated or forwarded by someone who should know that the matter is already covered by **policy.** (HCO PL 17 Nov 64)

OFF POST, means getting into other people's areas and hair. People who drift about into the areas of other people and waste the time of others are **off post.** A person **off post** during the appointed hours is obviously not only not doing a job but causing others to carry his work and is making somebody else look bad as well. (HCOB 27 Apr 60)

Off-Post

OFF-THE-JOB TRAINING, see TRAINING, OFF-THE-JOB.

OIC CABLE, org information center weekly statistic report sent by telex. (BPL 13 Feb 73R)

OK NEEDED FROM ISSUE AUTHORITY, means an **OK** is **needed** for all things run through the mimeo machine, whether okayed previously to be mimeoed or not. (HCO PL 13 Sept 65 II)

OK TO AUDIT BOARD, the Director of Processing must have an **OK to Audit Board** showing which auditor has an **OK to audit** what and he must not let an **auditor audit** an action for which he has no **OK to audit.** (BPL 19 Nov 71R)

"OK TO BE A ______" SYSTEM, a gradient scale of hatting, programming, checkouts and correction is required to get a staff member fully hatted and functioning competently on post. The **"OK to be a ______" system** parallels the OK to audit system for training auditors. Mini hat completion entitles the staff member to a temporary **OK to be a ______** certificate. The staff member is now serving an apprenticeship or internship on the post. He must continue with his full post hatting cycle part-time during staff study periods. When the full post hat checksheet is completed, the staff member is awarded a provisional OK to do the ______ hat certificate. The staff member is awarded a full permanent post certificate on completion of full hatting, apprenticeship and proven post competence, demonstrated by high statistics. The **"OK to be a ______" system** lays out a more efficient system of getting staff fully hatted. Nearly every post in Qual has a role to play in ensuring that it is put in and maintained. (HCO PL 14 Jan 72 IV) [The above HCO PL was cancelled by BPL 10 Oct 75 X.]

OLIGOPOLY, an economic condition where there are only a few producers or sellers of a particular commodity or service and any one of them can affect its price or exhibit a large amount of control over the market irrespective of the others.

Omitted Data (Def. 1)

OMITTED DATA, **1.** an **omitted** anything is an out-point. This can be an **omitted** person, terminal, object, energy, space, time, form, sequence, or even an **omitted** scene. Anything that can be **omitted** that *should* be there is an out-point. (HCO PL 19 Sept 70 III) **2.** the hardest ones that you will find will always be the **omitted datum.** There aren't any personnel in the division. You don't notice this at first glance. You don't notice the **omitted data** because they're not there. (7012-C04 SO)

ONE b(1b) REPORT, weekly book stocks and sales **report.** (HCO PL 5 Jun 68, *Weekly Book Stock Report Required*)

ONE FLUB SYSTEM, recent experience in operating the Flag Bureaux as a team has demonstrated conclusively that the Commanding Officer, any yeoman and the LRH Comm cannot handle their posts in the face of an aide, a deputy aide, an Assistant Aide or a bureaux member flub. Therefore bureaux personnel hereafter will be handled as auditors are handled on Flag. **One flub**=cramming. Repeat **flub**=retrain. Second repeat **flub**=case, retrain, cramming. The definition of **flub**—is an absent, unusable or damaging product. (CBO 63)

ONE-TIME EXPENSES, these are Title A or B equipment (a new heat exchanger or a new drill press or a new galley mixer) and major work contracts. (FSO 551)

ON LINE, the origin is sent to the right terminal that handles that. (HCO PL 29 Feb 72)

ON ORIGIN, the staff member **originates** things that apply or are the business of his own post. (HCO PL 29 Feb 72)

ON POLICY, knowing and using the procedures with no departures. Knowing and applying our procedures. (HCO PL 4 Jun 71)

ON POST, means activity in the area of one's job during the appointed hours. (HCOB 27 Apr 60)

ON-SOURCE CLUB, a **club** of those who really apply green on white to their posts. (COLRHED 370)

ON THE JOB HATTING, to instant **hat** him and have him produce the product of the post, then **hat** him a little more and have him produce the product of the post and **hat** him a little more and produce the product of the post and **hat** him a little more and produce the product of the post. We're going to do **on the job hatting**, so that you could fully expect to bring in a brand new typist into letter registration and have her immediately getting out some letters. (ESTO 2, 7203CO1 SO II)

ON-THE-JOB TRAINING, see TRAINING, ON-THE-JOB.

OPEN CORPORATION, see CORPORATION, OPEN.

OPEN END, said of investment companies that are not regulated by fixed capitalization and that can issue shares to investors continually or upon request.

OPEN FOR BUSINESS, open for flow. (HCO PL 27 Jul 72, *Form of the Org and Schedules*)

OPEN HOUSE, an occasion where the general public are allowed to observe or inspect operations at a factory, institution or company premises in order to enhance public relations. An open house may include guided tours, receptions, planned events, practical demonstrations, etc.

OPEN MIND, persons who "have an **open mind**" but no personal hopes or desires for auditing or knowingness should be ignored, as they really don't have an **open mind** at all, but a lack of ability to decide about things and are seldom found to be very responsible and waste anyone's efforts "to convince them." (HCO PL 27 Oct 64)

OPEN ORDER, see ORDER, OPEN.

OPEN SHOP, see SHOP, OPEN.

OPERATING EVALUATION, see PRIMARY EVALUATION.

OPERATING MANAGEMENT, see MANAGEMENT, OPERATING.

OPERATING POLICIES, see POLICIES, OPERATING.

OPERATING PROFIT, see PROFIT, OPERATING.

OPERATING RATIOS, the relationship derived from comparisons of items of income and expense.

OPERATING TARGET, 1. an **operating target** would set the direction of advance and qualify it. It normally includes a scheduled time by which it has to be complete so as to fit into other targets. (HCO PL 16 Jan 69) **2.** those which lay out directions and actions and a schedule of events or time table. (HCO PL 24 Jan 69) *Abbr.* OT.

OPERATING THETAN BRACELET, operating thetan is signified by a gold identification **bracelet** with the S and double triangle on it. The gold **operating thetan bracelet** may be purchased when the grade is attained and has to be specially made up. (HCO PL 27 Oct 65)

OPERATING THETAN LIAISON, see OTL.

OPERATIONAL, an item that is **operational** works well without further assistance or attention. This does not say that **operational** means something works. It works well. It works without assistance or patch up or holding on to it. It works without attention. It doesn't have to be continually watched. (HCO PL 12 Oct 67)

OPERATIONAL COMMUNICATION LINE, 1. one on which **communication** cycles can be completed without the sender having to worry about the safe arrival of his messages at the other end. (FO 2528) **2.** a **line**, internal or external, which is in use and on which no failures have occurred for the week, i.e., the telephone would count as one if it is working all week. (FO 1618)

OPERATIONAL COST CONTROL, control of costs through on-the-spot observation and regulation. Operational cost control can often spot material wastage or misuse and poor utilization of personnel and resources. See ACCOUNTING COST CONTROL.

OPERATION AND TRANSPORT CORPORATION LTD., [a ship chartering and management company from which the Church of Scientology has on occasion leased sea-going vessels for use as religious retreat and staff training quarters. Other services have also been rendered. *Abbr.* OTC LTD.]

OPERATION AND TRANSPORT LIAISON OFFICE, see OTL.

OPERATION COUNCIL, see FLAGSHIP OPERATION COUNCIL.

OPERATIONS, 1. the evaluation and the MOs would be at aides level. General observation and getting it executed is the business of **Operations.** In other words **operating** and bringing into effect the planning is the business of **Operations.** (7205C18 SO) **2.** handles briefing and handling of missions. (FO 2461R) **3.** the primary function of **Operations** is to keep the mission on target. To see what they require suddenly on their missions and get it to them. To see that the mission comes off with a successful completion. Mission members are going to disperse. The **Operations** Officer is there to steady the mission member. (FO 890) *Abbr.* Ops.

OPERATIONS AIDE, **1.** the head of Bureau IV Flag is entitled **Operations Aide.** The earlier title of Production Aide is made obsolete by the introduction of the senior post of Product Officer. His opposite number in a CLO is entitled A/**Operations Aide.** To avoid confusion with the title Operations Officer, the **Aide's** title is always written in full, not abbreviated—"**Operations Aide.**" "Ops Aide" is incorrect. To further differentiate, "Ops Officer" now becomes "Mission Ops Officer." (CBO 81) **2.** I expect these things from **Operations Aide**, quite in addition to "regular duties": (a) to keep a fully filed up-to-date data files ready for instant use that give the local viewpoint of any org at any time, (b) to keep comm and logistics flowing and transport well handled, (c) to keep missions on real orders on target and completing, especially that mission orders and actions do not cross order and forward command intention and are effective in handling what they went out to handle so that it stays handled, (d) to keep management functions occurring against the background of stats, evaluation and command intention, which has to be known; to make management at Flag respected. (FO 3179) **3.** CS-4, **Operations Aide**, in charge of **operations**, ships, tech and AOs. (FO 795)

OPERATIONS BUREAU, (FOLO) contains Data Bureau, Action Bureau, External Comm Bureau and Flag Programs Bureau. VFPs of the **Operations Bureau** are (1) an informed Flag enabled to plan and act correctly, enhancing expansion of all Scn, (2) successful completion of assigned Flag programs. (CBO 192)

OPERATIONS CENTER, hold No. 3 RSM has been taken over by staff for an **Operations Center.** Its purpose will be (1) to receive all communication traffic from Division 1 then appreciate and answer the traffic or route the traffic to the party concerned for answering and get it answered, (2) maintain traffic control board, (3) maintain mission board, (4) collect information from each of the CS divisions, (5) maintain an appreciation center for all the data received from each of these divisions, (6) maintain and control briefing of missions. Its overall purpose is to receive, evaluate and act on data. Hold No. 3 is now called Staff CIC. (FO 828)

OPERATIONS DIVISION, **1.** the First Mate is in charge of Division IV, the **Operations Division,** which cares for the decks, construction, and other purely traditional ship concerns—so the ship can operate as a ship. (FO 2674) **2.** (Division 4) that **division** which handles the general **operations** and activities of the ship. (FO 1109)

OPERATIONS ESTABLISHMENT OFFICER, where bureaux are combined with the service org the Divisional Esto also has the duties of the bureau establishment. In such a case there is an **Operations Establishment Officer** in charge of the four **operations** bureaux which combined make up the **operations** bureau. He, as expansion occurs, will shortly become a Chief **Esto** for **Operations** (or Chief **Operations Esto**) with an Esto in each bureau—the Action Leading Esto; the Data Leading Esto; the Management Leading Esto; and the Ext Comm Leading Esto. (HCO PL 7 Mar 72)

OPERATION SHEET, a list of all the operations that must be performed on raw materials or component parts to result in a specific finished product.

OPERATIONS OFFICER, **1.** you as an **Ops Officer** have the duty of keeping a missionaire on his orders and when a mission goes off its orders you get them back on their orders. If you can't get them back on their orders you pull them out. That's very unreasonable, but that's the best definition of an **Ops Officer.** He's unreasonable. If a mission goes off its orders you have lost control of it. If you have lost control of it, it will diddle fiddle around in that area for a long time. If you ran a rigid form on it you will run it faster. (FO 3508) **2.** the head of Bureau IV Flag is entitled Operations Aide. To avoid confusion with the title **Ops Officer**, the Aide's title is always written in full, not abbreviated, "Operations Aide." "Ops Aide" is incorrect. To further differentiate, "**Ops Officer**" now becomes "Mission **Ops Officer.**" (CBO 81) **3.** CS-4. (FO 2399R) **4.** is responsible for successful mission progress and its evidence. (FO 2358) **5.** operates the mission and only ceases to do so when the mission gets sent to debrief. (FO 1243R) **6.** the primary function of **Operations** is to keep the mission on target. To see what they require suddenly on their missions and get it to them. To see that the mission comes off with successful completion. Mission members are going to disperse. The **Ops Officer** is there to steady the mission member. (FO 890) **7.** the function of the **Operations Officer** is to see that a mission stays on target and completes successfully. (FO 769) **8.** First Mate. He conducts the mission. (6802C28 SO)

9. (Gung-Ho Group) the **Operations Officer** actually handles and directs all **operations** programs and projects in progress. (HCO PL 2 Dec 68)

OPERATION - TRANSPORT LIAISON UNIT, the branch office of a CLO managing the area or orgs assigned to it. (HCO PL 9 Mar 72 I) See OTL.

OPERATOR HANDLED, type of telephone call meaning when you dial "O" and get an **operator** to put you through. Her time is charged for on the phone bill. (HCO PL 15 Nov 74)

OPINION, thoughts are infinitely divisible into classes of thought. In other words, in thought there are certain wide differences which are very different indeed. A fact is something that can be proven to exist by visible evidence. An **opinion** is something which may or may not be based on any facts. (HCO PL 26 Apr 70R)

OPINION, an attitude, concept or belief one has towards or about something based upon current knowledge or experience and potentially subject to change with increasing knowledge or experience in that area.

OPINION LEADER, **1.** that being to whom others look for interpretation of publicity or events. Through wisdom, proximity to data sources, personality or other factors including popularity itself, certain members of the group, company, community or nation are looked to by others for evaluation. (HCO PL 11 May 71 II) **2.** "To whom do they listen?" "Whose **opinion** do they accept?" "Whom do they trust?" "On whom do they depend?" are the questions which, answered, identify the **opinion leader** of the group, large or small. (HCO PL 11 May 71 II)

OPINION SURVEY, a set of questions, the responses to which will show a general or select public's current opinions of a particular product, service, institution, symbol, etc.

OPPORTUNITY COSTS, see COSTS, OPPORTUNITY.

OPPOSITION GROUPS, **opposition group** relations are in the sphere of Guardian's Office. These **opposition groups** are those which are acting against Scn or against the goals of Scn. (BPL 20 May 70 I)

OPTIMUM SOLUTION, the greatest good for the greatest number of dynamics. (*HCOMOJ*)

OPTION, 1. the right to choose between more than one course of action in a business deal such as a right to buy or sell something within an agreed time period for a specified price. 2. a right to buy or sell a set amount of a specific stock at a specified price within a limited time period. 3. an insurance policy clause giving the policy holder the right to choose the way that payments will be made to him.

ORAL REPORT, any report given by word of mouth. It could be a verbal report to a group of concerned individuals but based on or read from a written report or notes one has made or received.

ORDER(S), **1.** the verbal or written direction from a lower or designated authority to carry out a program step or apply the general policy. (HCO PL 29 Feb 72 II) **2.** some program steps are so simple that they are themselves an **order** or an **order** can simply be a roughly written project. (HCO PL 29 Feb 72 II) **3.** the program step itself or the verbal or written project to get the program step fully *done.* (HCO PL 29 Feb 72 II) **4.** the direction or command issued by an authorized person to a person or group within the sphere of the authorized person's authority. By implication an **order** goes from a senior to juniors. (HCO PL 25 Nov 70) **5.** policy is the broad general outline originated by top management. **Orders** are the instructions issued by the next lower level of management to get things done that result in *products.* (FBDL 12) **6. orders** are what are issued to get the actions called for in policy done so that a product results. (FBDL 12) **7.** the program is the big solution to a problem. The little problems inside that big solution are solved by projects and inside the projects the littler-littler problems are solved by **orders.** (FO 2192) **8.** chaos is the basic situation in this universe. To handle it you put in **order. Order** goes in by being and making stable terminals arranged to handle types of action and confusion. In organizing units, sections, divisions, departments, orgs or areas of orgs you build by stable terminals. You solve areas by reinforcing stable terminals. Executives who do not grasp this live lives of total harrassment and confusion. (HCO PL 27 Oct 69) **9.** good line and particle control. The difference between **order** and chaos is simply straightforward planned flows and correct particles. (HCO PL 27 Feb 72)

ORDER BOARD, every **order** an executive issues must be in writing. He does this on a clip **board.** There is a sheaf of paper on it of his division's color. It has a sheet of pencil carbon and a ball point slipped through the top of the clip. It can have a hook on the back to slip on a belt for persons walking about. This is the **order board.** (HCO PL 1 May 65 II)

ORDER, DAY, an investor's order to buy or sell a security which if not accomplished by the end of the trading day is automatically cancelled.

ORDER, LIMITED, an order to buy or sell a specified amount of a stock at a fixed price or at a better price, as available after the order is instituted.

ORDERLINESS, 1. the tendency to contain environmental confusion and replace it with predictable actions. 2. the ability to ensure that correct sequences of action take place and that those cycles started get completed. 3. the tendency to designate generally acceptable places for things to be put at certain times and to ensure that they are put there at those times; neatness.

ORDER, MARKET, an order to buy or sell a specified amount of a security at the most beneficial price available after the order is instituted.

ORDER NOT REQUIRING FURTHER EVALUATION, one covered by a verified and approved **evaluation** and contained in the **evaluation** handling and which can be acted on as soon as the **evaluation** is verified and passed, and which is then pushed through to full completion. (FO 3149-2)

ORDER, OPEN, an order to buy or sell that stands until it is either filled or cancelled.

ORDER, PERCENTAGE, a market order to buy or sell a specific amount of a stock after a certain number of shares of that stock have traded.

ORDER, SCALE, an order to buy or sell a security, as the case may be, stating the amount of stock involved and a specified price or price range.

ORDERS OF THE DAY, 1. a type of ship's "newspaper" containing an item from the Commodore, the daily schedule for that **day**, news and notices, as well as **orders** necessary to administration of the ship's business. A copy of the **OODs** is delivered every morning to each in-basket on the ship. It should be read each day carefully so that you keep informed of what is going on around the ship and in the various divisions. (FO 2674) **2. orders of the day**, issued by any Commanding Officer to his own unit **daily** and may contain current activities, ethics **orders**, etc., by others, contains the schedule of the **day**, serves as a crew briefing. **OODs** are also put out to their own orgs by Executive Directors or Executive Councils in Scientology orgs. (HCO PL 24 Sept 70R) **3.** the purpose of the **OODs** is to keep staff informed of executive intention; org expansion and progress, org condition and ethics. The form of the **OODs** is black on white mimeo (or type written and displayed on staff notice board in small orgs). (BPL 30 Sept 69) **4.** it is dated for the **day** for which the schedule applies. It is numbered and given the ship's name. Into it are placed all assignments of conditions, schedules, copies of plans, uniforms, etc. It is posted as soon as it is completed. It is on legal length paper, white. It is on one side of the paper only. Every item is followed by the date such as 14/2/68. (FO 441) *Abbr.* OODs.

ORDERS, QUERY OF, it occasionally happens that an **order** is issued or a policy is enforced or is found to exist which if put into full effect in a certain area would result in loss or destruction. Someone told to man up, for instance, all admin departments, sees that this would upset the tech-admin ratio. Instead of putting the **order** into effect he should **query** the **order** with (a) the name of the issuer and the exact **order**, (b) the reason it would result in loss or destruction if put into effect, (c) a recommendation resolving the problem the **order** sought to solve. (HCO PL 15 Dec 69 II)

ORDER, STOP, an order to buy a security at a price over or sell at a price under the current market.

ORDER, STOP LIMIT, a stop order which when the specified stop price is met becomes a limited order.

ORDER, SWITCH, an order containing two transactions to be made: to purchase (or sell) a particular stock and sell (or purchase) another stock at stipulated prices.

ORDER, TIME, an order that is specified to become effective as a market order on a certain date.

ORDINARY SHARES, (British) common stock.

ORG, 1. short for **organization.** (HCO PL 8 Sept 69) **2. organizing.** (HCO PL 28 Oct 70)

ORG ADMIN CHECKLIST, the LRH Comm Weekly Report revised to become a monthly **admin checklist** for the **org** to be inspected and reported on by the LRH Comm, on the first day of each month. It is a **checklist** that can and should be done quickly; it requires little investigation as most points can be answered by a glance in the area concerned, or by asking one staff member and verifying the answer by checking a few folders, etc., or by cross-checking with another staff member. (HCO PL 23 Feb 70RB) [The **checklist** contains questions for each division that verify if that division is handling its particles and getting its products standardly.]

ORGANIZATION, **1.** an **organization** means the act of **organizing** or the process of being **organized.** The state or manner of being **organized**: "A high degree of **organization.**" Something that has been **organized** or made into an ordered whole. A number of persons or groups having specific responsibilities and united for some purpose or work. Thus an **organization** is an activity or area that is being **organized** or has been **organized** or made into an "ordered whole." (HCO PL 29 Oct 71 II) **2. organization** is composed of terminals and lines and the terminals are there with a common purpose but they are united by lines. (5812C16) **3.** an **organization** is essentially a service delivery unit. The continued expansion of an **organization** depends upon high volume flubless delivery. (HCO PL 29 Aug 71) **4.** an **organization** is composed of trained people, it isn't composed of dead bodies. (FEBC 6, 7101C23 SO II) **5.** a group of people that has more or less constant membership, a body of officers, a purpose and usually a set of regulations. (HCO PL 9 Nov 68) **6.** an interdependent activity coordinated by its leaders. (HCO PL 19 Oct 67 I) **7.** an **organization** is a complex mechanism. It is made up of associated individuals who have an agreed upon goal or intention. They are going along in some direction which they do not too violently disagree with, and it will make progress to the degree that it stays in agreement and holds its form and to the degree that it refines its form to meet new threats to its existence and so it will survive. (SH Spec 77, 6608C23) **8.** evidently an **organization** is a number of terminals and communication lines with a common purpose. The purpose associates and keeps in contact with one another the terminals and the lines. That's all an **organization** is. It isn't a factory, it isn't a house. It isn't a machine, it isn't a product. It's not a command chart. If you look it over in the light of that simplicity you can actually form one and get one to function. (OS-9, 5611C08) **9.** an **organization** optimumly would be composed of communication terminals. If we look it over and find an **organization** is composed of communication terminals then we decide that a communication terminal had better have a communication line. So we find an **organization** consists of communication terminals and communication lines associated with a common purpose or goal. (OS-9, 5611C08) **10.** it's a group of associated comm lines and terminals which is itself a single terminal and it has ingo and outcome lines. (OS-9, 5611C08) **11.** a servo-mechanism to the doingness of people. (OS-10, 5611C15) **12.** an **organization** is something which has its own spirit. It is composed of people or living beings who are governed by certain rules and purposes and who know how to do their jobs. That is an **organization** and when any of those factors are neglected it becomes a "thing" even though it still has a name and legal standing. (PAB 90) **13.** an **organization** is composed of terminals and communication lines related by a common purpose. That's an **organization.** And all the **organizational** pattern does is help separate the types of particles being handled. That, in a nutshell, is an **organization** and what it does. (5812C29) **14.** the word **organization** in Scn policy means an activity **organized** on the seven division system authorized by myself and regular official Scn **organizations** and under Worldwide. (HCO PL 11 Aug 67 II) **15.** the essence of **organization** is **org** boarding, posting with reality and, in keeping with the duties being performed, training and hatting. To this has to be added the actual performance of the duties so that the activity is productive. Another ingredient that goes hand in hand with **organization** and survival is toughness. The ability to stand up to and confront and handle whatever comes the way of the **organization** depends utterly on the ability of the individuals of the **organization** to stand up to, confront and handle what comes the individual's way. The composite whole of this ability makes a tough **organization.** Confidence in one's teammates is another factor in **organization** survival. Confidence in one's self is something that has to be earned. It is respect. This is a compound of demonstrated competence, being on post and being dependable. (OODs 10 Nov 71) **16. organization** is basically foresight and prediction and putting in stable terminals that will handle the flows. What belongs where? (FEBC 1, 7011C17 SO) **17.** consists of a real and functional **org** board, hats consisting of checksheets, packs and manuals and training of this material. (HCO PL 8 Oct 70) **18.** the purpose of **organization** is to make planning become actuality. **Organization** is not just a fancy complex system, done for its own sake. That is bureaucracy at its worst. **Org** boards for the sake of **org** boards, graphs for the sake of graphs, rules for the sake of rules only add up to failures. There is a lot to **organization.** It requires trained administrators who can forward the programs. (HCO PL 14 Sept 69) **19.** the subdivision of actions and duties into specialized functions. (HCO PL 7 Mar 69) **20. organization** consists of certain people doing certain jobs. (HCO PL 1 Jul 65 III) **21.** smooth **organization** consists of having a terminal for each type of activity in which the **organization** is engaged. There can be four or five activities to one terminal so long as three things are obeyed: (1) the terminal itself has to know it; (2) nearby terminals have to know it; (3) distant terminals have to know it. (PAB 78) **22.** the attempt to establish terminals and flows so as to bring about an orderly flow of energy or matter. (5303C25) *Abbr.* Org.

ORGANIZATIONAL CHART, (org board) this board has the force of assignment and is the primary means of assigning personnel in the organization. This board is the publication authority for assignment to post. This is not a communication chart. The org board shows name of post, followed underneath by purpose, followed underneath by person's name. (HCO PL 27 Nov 59)

ORGANIZATIONAL FOLDER, see HAT FOLDER.

ORGANIZATIONAL GENIUS, composed only of arranging sequences of action and designating channels for types of particles. That's all it is. (HCO PL 14 Sept 70)

ORGANIZATIONAL HEALTH CHART, this is an anatomical **chart** of a live organism, the HASI, London. This list of importances tells us what the heart is, the breath and all the rest in order. If anything on this list goes wrong, it and the items above it must be examined in turn. This is diagnosis. Repair consists of setting the function back to order and each in turn after it, since when an organism's highest functions fail, the remainder begin to enter difficulties. This then is a diagnostic **chart** and a **chart** to effect the cure. This list gives each function its proper importance to the rest, not perhaps in social caste, but certainly in **health.** (HCO PL 2 Nov 70) [See the above Policy Letter for the list of nineteen functions making up the **organizational health chart.**]

ORGANIZATIONAL POLICY, that **policy** which makes the **organization** into an **organization** and keeps its flows fast and its design uncomplicated. In absence of these **policies** the design becomes altered and flows cease and the **org** dies. (HCO PL 23 Apr 65)

ORGANIZATIONAL PSYCHOSES, see SANITY SCALE.

ORGANIZATION CASH DIFFERENTIAL, same as the departmental **cash differential** but for the whole **organization.** Departmental **cash differential** is the exact **difference** between the **cash** received by or for a production department and the **cash** spent by or on behalf of that department plus its share of the general cost, so long as the result shows receipt greater than expenses. (HCO PL 26 Jun 64)

ORGANIZATION, CELLULAR, an organizational format of a production plant and machinery in which all the parts and workers needed to produce a completed product are located in one production cell or section of the factory. Cellular organization is in contrast to flow line production wherein parts and workers form a single manufacturing line with work flowing in a single direction through the entire factory as in an assembly line.

ORGANIZATION CHART, see CHART, ORGANIZATION.

ORGANIZATION, COMMITTEE, an organization wherein a joint body of executives is responsible for its management.

ORGANIZATION CONTINENTAL LIAISON OFFICER, the Office of the Org Exec Sec WW contains one Divisional Organizer for Divisions 3, 4, 5, 6 for every Continental Office in the world. This person is called the **Organization Continental Liaison Officer** for (name of Continental Office) at WW. (HCO PL 6 Sept 67)

ORGANIZATION DEPARTMENT, the **Organization Department** is responsible for handling international **organizations** around the world, not Saint Hill, and obtains another near third of the income of Saint Hill by way of organization ten per cents, etc. (HCO PL 28 May 64)

ORGANIZATION DIVISION, we call it Treasury but it's actually the **division** which **organizes** the actual mest of the production activities. It gets together the sand to make the glass for the bottles, the sugar and saccharine for the candy and so forth. It does the assembly of this type of action and it also has the idea of money, assets, what it makes and so forth. You must have your money before you can buy the sand for the glass and so on. (SH Spec 77, 6608C23)

ORGANIZATION EXECUTIVE, in the Dianetic Counseling Group the **Organization Executive** has two divisions under him: Division 3 Treasury Division headed by the Treasurer and

Division 4 Technical Division headed by the Technical Secretary. (BPL 4 Jul 69R VI)

ORGANIZATION EXECUTIVE COURSE, 1. the **Organization Executive Course** is the equivalent in admin of the Saint Hill Special Briefing Course. The **course** packs for the new modern **Organization Executive Course** are the **OEC** Volumes 0 through to 7 in their entirety. (HCO PL 17 May 74R) **2.** this **course** contains the basic laws of **organization.** Primarily intended for Scn **organization executives**, its policy letters are slanted toward a Scn **org** (short for **organization**). However, it covers any **organization** and contains fundamentals vital to any successful or profitable activity. This **course** also applies to the individual. Any individual has his seven (or nine) divisions and his 21 (or 27) departments. Where one or more of these is missing in his conduct of life he will be to that degree an unsuccessful individual. (HCO PL 8 Sept 69) *Abbr.* OEC.

ORGANIZATION EXECUTIVE SECRETARY, **1.** in early days there was an HCO Sec in charge of the functions of the first three divisions (Exec, HCO, Dissem) and an Assoc Sec in charge of the functions of the last four divisions. The Org Board evolved further and the HCO Exec Sec became the person in charge of the functions of the first three divisions and the **Org Exec Sec**, the last four. In the Sea Org these titles became Supercargo and Chief Officer but the functions were similar. (HCO PL 9 May 74) **2.** a product officer of Divisions 3, 4, 5 and 6. (HCO PL 7 Dec 74) **3.** (Sea Org) Chief Officer. (HCO PL 9 May 74) **4.** the HES was an org officer and the **OES** was a product officer. If you look under the **OES** you will find money in Division 3, you will find auditors, and student auditors and the Directors of Training and you will find pcs in the Department of Processing, and then you will find, also, Distribution, you will find the field, and the products which are going out into the field. (FEBC 7, 7101C23 SO III) **5.** where an org has less than five staff the **Org Executive Secretary (OES)** combines Accounts, Tech and Qual functions. Elementary banking and bill paying (with the registrar and PES both able to invoice in, giving the money over to the **OES** with an invoice copy) is done by the **OES.** All auditing and major course supervision is done by the **OES.** The major functions that must be done for the org to be successful are safeguarding funds by recording and banking and paying bills, auditing pcs, teaching students and correcting those cases that fail or students that are slow. (LRH ED 49 INT) *Abbr.* OES, Org Exec Sec.

ORGANIZATION FORM, **1.** each **org** staff member is a specialist in one or more similar functions. These are his specialties. If he is fully trained to do these he is said to be hatted. The combined specialties properly placed and being done add up to the full production of an **org.** The **org form** is then the lines and actions and spaces and flows worked out and controlled by specialists in each individual function. These specialists are grouped in departments which have certain actions in common. The departments having similar functions are grouped into divisions. The divisions combine into the whole **org form.** (HCO PL 28 Jul 72) **2.** an **org form** is that arrangement of specialized terminals which control and change the production and **organization** particles and flow lines of an activity. (HCO PL 25 Jul 72)

ORGANIZATION, FORMAL, an organization with an inflexible organizational structure where employment positions and departments, branches, etc., are clearly delineated as to duties, responsibilities and authorities. In a formal organization there is a great emphasis on maintaining the structure or form of the organization as that is how it is designed to run. A formal organization structure is essential for any organization to operate and expand beyond only a handful of employees.

ORGANIZATION, FORMATION AND REPAIR OFFICER, the full title of the Org Officer is **Organization, Formation and Repair Officer.** He has a hat similar to that of an old-time HCO Area Secretary. He puts an **org** there. (CBO 64)

ORGANIZATION HCO AREA SECRETARIES, handle the communications, technology and awards of single **organizations** around the world. (HCO PL 18 Dec 64, *Saint Hill Org Board*)

ORGANIZATION, INFORMAL, an organization with little or no organizational structure or at best one that is flexible under operating conditions. The distinction between duties, responsibilities and authorities is not clear-cut as there are often no specific employment titles or arrangement into departments. An informal organization usually exists where a few persons are closely associated and each knows every or many aspects of the business which they handle according to who is available or most familiar or as needed, etc. One cannot build a large organization in this manner.

ORGANIZATION INFORMATION CENTER, **1.** this is not a clumsy graph system but a species of mechanical brain that keeps continuous check upon and corrects small bogs of its own accord. It forecasts emergencies. This must have come from the Combat **Information Center** of

World War II, by which swarms of fighter planes, bombers or landing craft could be individually directed with great ease. The board is a smooth finished surface with a number of holders of 8" by 10" (approximate size) graph paper. These papers are not stapled on but drop into a three-sided border, open at the top. New papers every quarter or so are put into the holder in front of the last quarter's sheet so that one can refer back. The board has various signs on it, one for each department. The graphs are in three horizontal lines for one **organization**, with space for two to three charts (in a single line) for each department. It is necessary for quick reading to have the graph sheets in long lines rather than in blocks—hence the board appears to be three long lines of graph, no matter how many graphs there are in how many departments. (HCO PL 11 Aug 60) **2.** in Department 3, Department of Inspection and Reports. **OIC** (Section) designates statistics for Ad Council approval, collects statistics, graphs statistics weekly, posts the **OIC** Board for the org, handles weekly report to **OIC** WW, writes weekly SEC ED of conditions for Ad Council approval and issue by SEC ED. (HCO PL 17 Jan 66 II) *Abbr.* OIC.

ORGANIZATION, LABOR, a group of workers such as a labor union who have the legal power to deal with employers on such issues as wage disputes, better working conditions, grievances, etc., through the process of collective bargaining.

ORGANIZATION, LEAN, an organization which is not overstaffed. It has just enough staff to keep people busy enough to get the job done without staff colliding with each other physically and emotionally. The level of interaction between staff is not high enough to interfere with production and the interaction going on is primarily between a person and his job. "Labor problems" would be less as staff and executives would be too busy to cause them.

ORGANIZATION LIBRARY, a library belonging to a business, accessible to company executives and other employees and ideally containing such books as would be needful to a person handling any aspect of the company's business.

ORGANIZATION, LINE, the military type of organization form whereby there is a definite ascending and descending chain of command. Each executive from the bottom up is responsible to the person directly above him. Thus all persons in a department may be directly responsible to the head of a department who in turn is responsible to an executive who is in charge of, say, six department heads and so on up the line. Orders pass from top management down the line of command and compliances and data pass on up without by-passing the chain of command. Thus responsibility or irresponsibility is easy to pinpoint and functions are clearly defined.

ORGANIZATION, LINE AND STAFF, a combination of line and staff types of organization. Line executives and personnel handle the production factors of the organization utilizing a distinct chain of command and staff executives and personnel handle the organizing and supportive activities such as accounting, training, etc.

ORGANIZATION MANUAL, see MANUAL, ORGANIZATION.

ORGANIZATION, MILITARY, see ORGANIZATION, LINE.

ORGANIZATION PROGRAM NO. 1, **1.** this is an effort to make it easy to reform an **org** whether the **org** is large or small. This gives how to attain your two admin to one tech ratio—which must not be exceeded. If an **org's** tech-admin ratio is greater than two admin to one tech it will only be able to pay poorly and function badly. This ED is to be used to stabilize and establish a workable org form which will produce with good GIs and pay. **Orgs** which have more than two admin to one tech should take from their excess admin their best potential students and full time train them to swell tech ranks and increase student and pc production. **Org** duties and actions are clearly outlined in this program. (LRH ED 78 INT) **2.** an ED International called **Org Program No. 1** which simply describes in very very simple terms the functions of an organization derived from the HCO ES, OES and PES, and just giving a summary of the duties for which they are responsible. (6912C10 SO) **3. program** for well **organized orgs.** (LRH ED 56 INT)

ORGANIZATION, PROJECTIZED, an organization composed of a series of project teams in liaison with staff management, or a group of specialists, who advise and work with managers of the project teams.

ORGANIZATION RUDIMENTS, rudiments of an **org.** (HCO PL 11 Dec 61RA)

ORGANIZATION SECRETARY, **1.** on the Six Department Board the **Organization Secretary** takes the place of the Org Exec Sec. (HCO PL 21 Oct 66) **2.** (Seven Division Org) coordinates and gets done the promotional functions of Division 3. (HCO PL 20 Nov 65) **3. Organization Secretaries** (U.S. and Saint Hill) or Association Secretaries (Commonwealth and South Africa). (HCO PL 5 Mar 65 II) **4.** in full charge of all units, departments and personnel and is fully responsible for carrying out the **organization's** programs and promotion and its solvency. (HCO PL 30 Dec 64) **5.** manages Saint Hill in all its activities. Handles financial management for all accounts of Saint Hill. Hires and dismisses all Saint Hill personnel. Regulates all technology and awards for Saint Hill. Originates or passes upon all promotion for Saint Hill activities. Sees that income is greater than outgo at Saint Hill and in all its departments. (HCO PL 18 Dec 64, *Saint Hill Org Board*) **6.** in general charge of everything that goes on at Saint Hill and all departments, including Department One. This is the equivalent post to a Central Organization's Association or **Organization Secretary.** All departments and personnel are answerable to her for their conduct of duties and the general solvency of their departments. She may hire or dismiss personnel, increase or decrease wages, sign on all accounts and act to improve conditions without further consultation with the board or the Executive Director. (HCO PL 28 May 64) **7.** purpose: to get people to get the work done. To enforce the policies and advise the board. (HCO PL 12 Oct 62) **8.** the Association Secretary or **Organization Secretary** has full authority over his or her organization and personnel. It is his or her task to cope when policy does not exist, to hold the form of the organization, to keep it busy and prosperous and its morale high. (HCO PL 31 Jan 61, *Spheres of Influence*) **9.** the **Organization Secretary** is the person who sees to it that the work gets done. He is Personnel Director for the **organization** but in actuality can only remove department heads and can do this only after receiving permission from the Executive Director. The fundamental job of the **Organization Secretary** is to enforce policy and see that it is carried out. (HCO PL 29 Feb 60) **10.** the **Organization Secretary's** fundamental job is to enforce policy. This is in actuality the full extent of his hat. It is also understood that the **Organization Secretary** will be the foremost promoter of the **organization** and that he will do much reaching the public. The **Organization Secretary** also has the hat of financial management when it has been specifically granted to him. (HCO PL 29 Feb 60) *Abbr.* Org Sec.

ORGANIZATION SECRETARY'S SECRETARY, looks after the dispatches and communication equipment of the **Org Sec.** Transcribes needed transcription. (HCO PL 18 Dec 64, *Saint Hill Org Board*)

ORGANIZATIONS OF AMERICA, a coordinating **organization** in Washington, D.C. (1956) which handled the social reform activities of the member **organizations** which consisted of various Washington D.C. local social groups. Its programs were concluded successfully (including the enfranchisement of the formerly non-voting population of Washington, D.C.) and it was disbanded. (LRH Def. Notes)

ORGANIZATION STRUCTURE, the operating framework of a business or organization. It is established by designating and naming organizational units such as divisions, departments, branches, etc., defining how they interrelate, (relative authority, communication lines, etc.) and establishing the job titles, functions, hierarchy and products of the personnel who will work there.

ORGANIZATION SUPERVISOR, organization supervisor for all Scn organizations around the world and locally will include reception, mimeo, communications, telex, accounts, addresses, central files and franchise. (HCO PL 31 Dec 63)

ORGANIZATION, THE, few people realize that HCO is actually a separate company. It is the worldwide comm network of Dn and Scn. As its finances and personnel are meshed in with the rest of the org, its identity does not stay visible. But note it is still called HCO and the rest of the divisions are called **the organization.** (HCO PL 7 Feb 70 II)

ORGANIZING, 1. in order to **organize** something one has to (1) establish what is the final product, (2) work backwards in sequence to establish the earlier products necessary to make each next product and which all in a row add up to the final product, (3) post it in terms of vertical greater and greater completeness of product to get command channels, (4) adjust it for flows, (5) assign its comm sequence, (6) work out the doing resulting in each product. Write these as functions and actions with all skills included. (7) name these as posts, (8) post it, (9) drill it to get it known, (10) assemble and issue the hats, (11) get these known, (12) get the functions done so that the products occur. This is what is called **organizing.** (HCO PL 28 Oct 70) **2.** the know-how of changing things. (HCO PL 1 Nov 70) **3.** when routing arrangements are made inside the org—from staff member to staff member—we call it **organizing.** (HCO PL 17 Nov 64) **4.** to put order into something. Not **organizing** leads to confusion. This is true of groups and individuals. (BPL 21 Oct 71 III) **5.** the right way to go about it is to have the tech of a job, plan it, get the materials, and then do it. This we call **organizing.** When this sequence is not followed, we have what we call *cope.* Too much cope will eventually break morale. One copes while he **organizes.** If he copes too long without **organizing** he will get a dwindling or no product. If he **organizes** only he will get no product. Coping while **organizing** will bit by bit get the line and action straighter and straighter and with less work you get more product. (OODs 15 May 71) *Abbr.* Org.

ORGANIZING BOARD, (**org board**) a **board** that shows what functions are done in the **org**, the order they are done in, and who is responsible for getting them done. (HCO Admin Ltr 30 Jul 75) **2.** the pattern of the terminals and their flows. You have to have an **org board** and the **org board** must in truth be a representation of what is in the **org.** The **org board** shows where what terminals are located in the **org** so flows can occur. (HCO PL 7 Jul 71) **3. org board** is actually an abbreviation not for an organization (noun) board but an **organiz*ing*** (verb) **board.** The **org board** shows the pattern of **organizing** to obtain a product. A **board** then is a flow chart of consecutive products brought about by terminals in series. We see these terminals as "posts" or positions. Each one of these is a hat. There is a flow along these hats. The result of the whole **board** is a product. The product of each hat on the **board** adds up to the total product. (HCO PL 28 Oct 70) **4.** a proper **org board** is a perpetual combination of flows which do not collide with one another and which do enter and do experience the desired change and which do leave as a product. (HCO PL 13 Sept 70 II) **5.** the **org board** is the general plan, the function indicator, the routing and the personnel situation for the org. (HCO PL 17 Apr 70) **6.** consists of the terminals, actions and flows necessary to achieve an overall purpose and to prevent distractions and stops from the purpose. (6910C20 SO) **7.** that arrangement of persons, lines and actions which classifies types of confusions and gives a stable terminal to each type. It is as effective as its people can conceive of terminals and understand the basic principle of confusions and stable data. (HCO PL 27 Oct 69) **8.** the **org board** consists of a couple sheets of clear blue Formica, 4 feet high by more than 8'9" long. It can be longer than 8'9". That is the minimum. That gives one department only five inches of width. A yellow vertical stripe of cellotape split in half separates departments in a division and divisions are separated by a full width of it. A thin strip of green goes all along the top of the departments. The level word goes above each department and the yellow tape. The command lines are in red cellotape. The names of departments are cut on a Dymo using tape approximating the color flash of the department as feasible. Executive Secretaries and secretary titles and names are in gold Dymo tape. Directors' titles and names are in gold banded brown tape. Other executives' titles and names are in gold banded black tape. Communicators are in this tape. Section names are in the same tape color as the department name. All subsections or units are the same tape color as the department name. All general staff members are in plain green tape. All provisional or temporary staff members are in black tape. The name of a deputy is in green tape but the title, even when preceded by "deputy" is the color code as above. (HCO PL 7 Jun 65, *New Org Board Design*) **9.** the actual diagrammatic pattern of the organization showing the divisions, departments, their personnel, functions and lines of communication. This pattern fully drawn out is known as the **org** (**organizing**) **board.** (BPL 4 Jul 69R VI) **10.** a list of hats with seniorities. The hats are in flow sequence. (OODs 29 Oct 70) **11.** a refined **board** of an old galactic civilization. We applied Scn to it and found why it eventually failed. It lacked a couple of departments and that was enough to mess it all up. They lasted 80 trillion. (SH Spec 57, 6504C06) *Abbr.* Org Bd, Org Board.

ORGANIZING BUREAU, 1. recruits and assigns to a training function or on a low post and training pending programming. It provides the master library of HCO PLs, HCOBs, FOs, Bureau Orders and other data such as books and manuals. It provides the mimeo files of all issues for any and all packs and makes up packs. It also runs off current mimeo and distributes via Comm Bureau. It also handles and runs off the actual printing of promotion as in photo offset work. It also handles publishing actions. Thus its cycle is to provide people and provide the data to make trained people. It also by current mimeo keeps existing people informed by mimeo issue lines and doing the promotion materials. Its keynotes are getting people and data to train people (CBO 7) **2.** the Sea Org **Organizing Bureau** is established in Div 7, Flag. It consists of the SO Personnel Branch, SO Compilations Branch, SO Preparations Branch, and SO Publishing Branch. The general purpose of this bureau is to organize Flag, ships and orgs by procuring, transferring and programming personnel, compiling checksheets and courses, preparing materials and publishing needful orders, instructions and materials needful in establishing or stabilizing ships or orgs throughout the Sea Org. (FO 2473) **3.** the ideal scene toward which the **Org Bureau** is working is fully manned **orgs** and the checksheets and materials necessary to train them for full effectiveness on individual posts and the checksheets and packs needful to service and train the public. The products therefore of the **Org Bureau** are (1) recruited staff members, (2) the materials with which to fully train the staff member on his post, (3) the materials needed to service and train the public. (CBO 4) **4.** the **Org Bureau** is primarily concerned with procuring personnel and setting up hats (checksheets and packs) for that personnel to be trained on. And then the **Org Bureau** is concerned with the checksheets and packs for public courses or services. (CBO 4)

ORGANIZING OFFICER, see ORG OFFICER.

ORG AUDITING, the purpose of the Ethics Officer is to help Ron clear **orgs** and the public if need be of entheta and enturbulation so that Scn can be done. The activities of the Ethics Officer consist of isolating individuals who are stopping proper flows by pulling withholds with ethics technology and by removing as necessary potential trouble sources and suppressive individuals off **org** comm lines and by generally enforcing ethics codes. The trick of this **org auditing** is to find a piece of string sticking out—something one can't understand, and, by interrogatives, pull on it. A small cat shows up. Pull with some more interrogatives. A baby gorilla shows up. Pull some more. A tiger appears. Pull again and wow! You've got a General Sherman tank! (HCO PL 11 May 65, *Ethics Officer Hat*)

ORG BASIC DATA, in light of Flag's extensive attention on all **organizations**, and the need to have a *complete viewpoint* of each **org**, there is additional **data** required from **orgs.** This is the **org's basic data.** The following **data** is therefore required from each **organization.** The Director of Inspections and Reports is to ensure that the following data is sent to the Flag Data Bureau, via the local FOLO, and is kept up to date. (a) the location of the **org** on a local map, (b) a population density map of the city where the **org** is located, (c) a full, complete floor plan of the **organization.** Floor plan must have every space numbered, and each floor has a letter (a copy of the floor plan with these numbers and letters is kept by the **org**). (d) photographs of the **org** that show the mest of the **org,** front entrance of the **org,** and overall appearance of the **org,** (e) copy of the **org** board that the **org** is currently operating on. Any time changes are made in the above, the Director of Inspections and Reports must ensure full **data** on the change must be sent to the Flag Data Bureau. On Flag, the Data Files I/C must ensure that each **org** has a gold file folder with a blue tab labelled **org basic data.** In this folder must go the **org basic data** and a copy of the **org's** current program. This folder is located in the front of the **org's** current **data** file folder. (BPL 4 Jun 73) *Abbr.* OBD.

ORG BOARD BOOK, a ring binder with the **org boards** of political, economical, cultural, financial or religious groups that PRAC deals with. (FO 3279-3)

ORG BOARD DEV-T, 1. a type of **dev-t.** An out-of-date **org board** can cause **dev-t.** A staff that doesn't have a well done **org board** cannot help but make **dev-t.** A staff that doesn't know the **org board** will make **dev-t.** (HCO PL 27 Jan 69) **2.** an out-of-date **org board.** People will misroute continuously—sending their own bits to others and flooding wrong others with dispatches. (HCO PL 31 Jan 65)

ORG BOARD PATTERN, the **org board pattern** (names of divisions, departments and their code words as per any of our org boards) is an analysis system which can be applied to any person or job. (HCO PL 16 Nov 66)

ORG BOARD UNIT, in Department 1, Department of Routing, Appearances and Personnel. **Org Board Unit** keeps main **org board** posted, inspects and causes to be posted all divisional **org boards.** (HCO PL 17 Jan 66 II)

ORG CONDITIONS STAT, the **condition** assigned to the entire **org** will be based on the **statistic:** paid completions accompanied by an acceptable success story. This is the stat of the Executive Director who may have no other **stat.** (HCO PL 29 Aug 71)

ORG CONFERENCE, see ORG OFFICER CONFERENCE.

ORG ESTO, Org Exec Sec's Org Officer. (HCO PL 9 May 74)

ORG EXEC SEC COORDINATOR, the Executive Division is Division 7. The LRH Communicator is in charge of the Division. It consists of three departments. The third department is the Office of the Organization Executive Secretary, Department 19. It is in the charge of the **Org Exec Sec Coordinator.** (HCO PL 2 Aug 65)

ORG EXEC SEC WW, the **OES WW** has definite primary duties which must never be neglected. These are: (a) effective OES and tech execs on post in every org, (b) auditing in high volume in all orgs, (c) training in volume of public students, (d) training in volume of staff students, (e) wide staff auditing, (f) financial high income and solvency in WW and all other Scn orgs with excellent cash-bills and mounting reserves, (g) the effective delivery of high quality auditing and training, (h) the repair of any and all cases incompetently handled, (i) getting new personnel in orgs trained up rapidly. The **OES WW** is responsible for the good performance, training and conduct of every OES in the world and that one is on post in each org. (HCO PL 12 Feb 70 II)

ORG FINANCE BANKING OFFICER, the **FBO** attached to an **org** to help the Continental FBO manage it financially under SO control. (HCO PL 9 Mar 72 I)

ORG FLAG OFFICER, an otherwise posted individual on **Flag** is to represent one **org**, FOLO or unit as a part time duty so that each **org**, FOLO or unit is in full comm with **Flag**. He handles the **org** to which he is assigned. His purpose is to keep in comm with his **org**, answer or acknowledge its reports and dispatches of whatever kind and handle outnesses reported and give guidance for the betterment of the **org**, its stats and expansion and keep its standard reports arriving. (CBO 348R) *Abbr.* OFO.

ORG FLAG OFFICER AIDE, 1. the **Org Flag Officer Aide** is found in the Operations Bu and is overall responsible for **OFOs** doing their job and is the MAA for **OFOs.** (CBO 435-2) **2.** the **Org Flag Officer** Branch, Flag Management Bureau, is headed by an **Org Flag Officer Aide** whose duty it is to ensure that all **Flag Officers** stay in close comm with the **org.** (FBDL 488R) *Abbr.* OFO Aide.

ORG FLAG OFFICER BRANCH, 1. (Branch 10A Flag Management Bureau) this is the **branch** where your **Flag Officer** writes to you. The **branch** is headed by an **Org Flag Officer** Aide whose duty it is to ensure that all **Flag Officers** stay in close comm with the **org.** In addition, this **branch** has an Emergency Officer Section, the purpose of which is to rapidly evaluate and handle any threatening org emergencies so that the orgs can get on with the show. (FBDL 488R) **2.** (Management Bureau Flag) sees that **OFO** data arrives in baskets and is easily available to **OFOs.** Ensures prompt handling of all **org** traffic per policy and CBOs. Sees that **OFOs** are equipped with needed materiel and data, fully briefed and assisted so that they can do their job. Supervises **OFOs** to the result of all **org** comm rapidly handled with a large return flow of high ARC comm and standard **org** reports to Flag. Conducts **OFO** coordination councils. Emergency Section notes and gets handled by rapid program or debug those things which are emergencies or will make emergencies if not handled. Does competent GDS analysis with handlings on critical stat situations. Ensures all emergencies handled or piloted through to complete handling in coordination with the Network Control Branches and FR Execution Branch. (CBO 376)

ORG FORM AND POLICY BUREAU, 1. produces orgs and bureaux that are effectively and causatively managed by operating on a realistic complete org board with correct ideal scenes and stats, by correct hats being available, known and worn, by needed materiel known and provided, and where necessary correction programmed and done realistically so that **org form and policy** are fully utilized to increasingly produce the products of the orgs and bureaux and all its personnel being experts on **organization and policy.** (CBO 34) **2.** consists of a Situations Recognitions Branch, Programming Branch, Research and Correction Branch, and Ideal Scene Achievement Branch. (CBO 37)

ORG INFORMATION OFFICER, see STAFF INFORMATION OFFICER.

ORG INTERNE, 1. anyone serving in an **org** on an unpaid basis to learn an org must be called an **org interne** and must be signed up as such, hatted and trained as such. (FO 785R) **2.** the term **org interne,** not volunteer, should be used to designate personnel signed on for **org** experience. A regular **org** training program must be drawn up with checksheet for such personnel. (BO 48, 22 Aug 70)

ORG LEVEL, see CLO LEVEL.

ORG MAILING LIST, 1. this is a **list** of names and addresses of persons who have bought something from an organization. This in full is the **org mailing list**! Every person on this **list** has a separate file in central files. (BPL 17 May 69R I) **2.** the name and address of every person in central files collectively make up the **org mailing list.** Conversely, every person on the **org mailing list** has a folder in central files. (BPL 17 May 69 I)

ORG MANAGEMENT BUREAU, Branch 12 of the Flag Bureau Org Board. The function of this **bureau** is to handle extant orders and compliance reports between Flag Bureaux and COs, Exec Dirs and missionaires with similar long-range, garrison type orders and act as library for each **org's** relevant current orders. (CBO 60)

ORG MANAGERS, 1. the Management Bureau consists of people in charge of areas and orgs and these people **manage** those **orgs.** They are fully responsible for the **orgs** under their care, their stats and expansion. They evaluate **org** situations and handle. These I/Cs are called **Org Managers,** e.g. AF **Org Manager**, FLEU **Org Manager.** Each person is responsible for a certain area or **org** and he directs that **org** based on evaluation. The **Org Manager** is senior to the COs and EDs of the orgs. He keeps in comm with the execs in his **orgs.** He supervises the OFOs of his **orgs** and makes sure they are wearing their hats according to already existing CBOs. He reviews the stats of each of his **orgs** every week and based on stats **manages** his **orgs** by investigating and handling situations that affect **org** production. He uses the FR and LRH Comm lines to execute programs that will keep the **org** expanding. The product of the **Org Manager** is expanding **orgs.** (CBO 435-3R) **2.** evaluator. (ED 39R FB)

ORG OFFICER, 1. the first thought of an **org officer** was to **organize** things so that the product could get out (prod/**org** system). Now that's not really part of his duties. It's the execution of the program that is his duty (Esto system). (ESTO 9, 7203C05 SO I) **2.** the **Org Officer organizes** production areas for the Product Officer so they produce. (FO 2794) **3.** HCO Exec Sec. (FEBC 11, 7102C03 SO I) **4.** is there to do product 3 which is the correction of the establishment, preferably before the fact and certainly swiftly after the fact. The org's **Org Officer** is there for that purpose, and the **Org Officer** of a division is there for that purpose. He's a product 3 man. (FEBC 5, 7101C23 SO I) **5.** in a fast running organization the total duty of an **Org Officer** is arresting a decline—product three; halting a decline, or a threatened decline. (FEBC 5, 7101C23 SO I) **6.** assists the Product Officer. He gets production lined up, grooves in staff on what they should be getting out and makes sure the Product Officer's plans are executed. (HCO PL 7 Mar 72) **7.** he establishes the establishment and when it goes a little awry he corrects the establishment. So he has products one and three. (FEBC 4, 7101C18 SO III) **8.** the full title of the **Org Officer** is **Organization**, Formation and Repair **Officer.** He has a hat similar to that of an old-time HCO Area Secretary. He puts an org there. The **org officer** has products one and three (Org Series 10). The Product Expeditor has products 2 and 4 (Org Series 10). A CO counts on the **Org Officer** to keep the org recruited, formed, corrected. The **Org Officer** is "**organize**" and the Product Expeditor is "cope." (Org Series 2) (FO 2656) **9.** the rule is see the Product Officer about past, present and future production. See the **Org Officer** about internal matters of personnel, supply, hats, etc. The deputy is the **Org Officer** who is always junior to the Product Officer. It's like having (in the **Org Officer**, the deputy) an HCO right in your own division. The deputies are really under the **Org Officer** of the org. The div heads are under the Product Officer of the org. (OODs 10 Jan 71) **10.** where an org has less than five staff, appoint this much org board: **Org Officer**, Executive Director, Field Expansion Secretary. In such a tiny org the major **Org Officer** duties are as follows: form of org, reception, registration, procurement letters, central files, ethics, personnel, any LRH Comm and Assistant Guardian duties, communications, legal. (LRH ED 49 INT) *Abbr.* OO.

ORG OFFICER CONFERENCE, (org conference) the Product Conference is senior to the **Org Conference.** The Product Conference lays it out. This is what we're going to do and this is how we're going to get the product and so forth. They write up the projects and products and plan everything else of what they're going to do in order to get this thing out and then they make sure that they keep that machine running that way. The **Org Officer** with your **Org Officer Conference**; they've got a certain deadline and they're coming up to the planning of the next fifteen days and so forth of operation. It's the **org** actions which we're going to take because we've got in front of us, the Product Conference. The deputy secretaries would make up the **conference** for **organization,** handling products one and three. (FEBC 4, 7101C18 SO III)

ORG PERSONNEL, personnel in Divisions 3, 4, 5 and 6. (HCO PL 20 Aug 65, *Scientology Org Uniforms Saint Hill*)

ORG PLANNING UNIT, (Office of the Guardian) the **Org Planning Unit** predicts trouble by such things as too much entheta from an area, too much sex going on in an **org** and, working closely with HCO, plans how to reorganize the **org** in that area without destroying it. Such **planning** also handles a public program for an entheta area to weaken anti-Scn propaganda, at the same time stiffening up ethics and quality of service in the area and investigating why ethics and quality of service are down so they can be remedied. (HCO PL 1 Mar 66)

ORG POLICY NUMBER ONE, the first reason and last reason for the existence of a Central Org or City Office is "to hold up the technical standard of an area." That is **policy one** in every Central Org and City Office. (HCO PL 21 Aug 64)

ORG PORTION, the first two divisions of the entire organization are the HCO Divisions. This is known as the HCO portion of the organization. The primary action of the **org portion** of the entire organization is the handle whatever is routed and so produce results, and in its sixth division, Distribution, as well as the other three, to make Scn broadly known and well thought of everywhere by changing personal and social conditions. (HCO PL 2 Aug 65)

ORG PROGRAM NUMBER 1, see ORGANIZATION PROGRAM NO. 1.

ORG QUALS ESTABLISHMENT CHIEF, head of Branch 13A, Enhancement Branch, Correction Bureau VA (CLO). (HCO PL 14 Aug 71 I)

ORG RESERVE ACCOUNT, 1. all monies set aside to untouchable **org reserves**, which is a weekly 10% of the proportionate sum. Any payroll, sales or other payable taxes such as withholding tax in the U.S. and PAYE in the UK pending payment of the taxes. The untouchable **org reserves** (10% of the proportionate sum) may be used in time of emergency only. Such emergencies might be physical damage to the **org's** building for which there's no insurance coverage, or extreme insolvency of an **org.** (BPL 6 Jul 75 III) **2.** the **org reserve account** is built up by astute GO and FBO guardianship of **org** funds and by reason of booming the **org.** It also answers the rule that financial management gathers bit by bit a cushion of cash to fall back on and never falls back on it. However, far more than such **reserves** go to payment of management bills owing and they may not be built up at the arduous expense or denial of management payments. It can also hold Reserved Payment Account type monies. Monthly accounts summaries should show what portion of the **Org Reserve Account** reconciled balance is accumulated **reserves** and what portion is Reserved Payment Account type monies. (BPL 1 Jul 72R)

ORG RESERVES, 1. any **reserves** that may be built up by an FBO by reason of astute guardianship of the org's funds. Far more than such reserves go to SO reserves. (HCO PL 9 Mar 72 I) **2. org reserves** are used for local emergencies or periods of down stats or large acquisitions to increase production. (HCO PL 29 Jan 71)

ORG RUDIMENTS, see RUDIMENTS OF AN ORG.

ORG RUDIMENTS 1-17, see RUDIMENTS 1-17.

ORG RUDIMENT SECTION, HCO Division, Dept 3, **Org Rudiment Section** gets in routinely any **rudiments.** (HCO PL 25 Jan 66)

ORG RUDIMENTS OFFICER, the HCO Division of every org must establish in Department 3, Department of Inspection and Reports, an **org rudiments** section. The section is headed by an **officer.** This person is called the **Org Rudiments Officer.** The **Org Rudiments Officer** ceaselessly gets in the **org rudiments** as issued in the past and revised from time to time. (HCO PL 20 Nov 65 II)

ORGS FUNCTIONING, the end product of missions is **orgs functioning**—which is stable terminals in the **orgs** wearing their hats. (FO 2200)

ORG SO #1, origins by **org** personnel not on official business. (HCO PL 17 Sept 65)

ORIENTATION, getting in the right relation to the things or people around one. (HCO Admin Ltr 30 Jul 75)

ORIENTATION, any training which familiarizes a new employee with his employer, job, the premises, company policy or procedures, etc.

ORIENTATION CHECKSHEET, this **checksheet** is designed to **orient** the new arrival to Flag into his/her new environment, accompanied by his/her buddy or twin. (FSO 65R)

ORIENTATION SHEET, the responsibility of the make-up of the **orientation sheet** is given to the D of T. Included in it are: (1) a copy of the org board of the Tech Div, (2) flow lines that the student in that specific org would travel, expressing the terminals he would be expected to see and in what order, (3) simple floor plans of the org showing where what is and where the student may or may not go. Who's where, etc. Info should be keyed to the student's need with, say, a closet for students' coats well indicated, but relatively little tagging for the CF area. (4) course schedule, (5) other similar info that the D of T may decide is locally needful. (HCO PL 22 Feb 71) [The above HCO PL was cancelled by BPL 10 Oct 75 IX.]

ORIGINAL MOTION, see MOTION, ORIGINAL.

OT ACTIVITY PERSONNEL, persons on the Clearing Course and OT Course, and including all Clears and OTs (Operating Thetans) are eligible for volunteer posts in **OT Activities.** They are called **OT Activity Personnel.** The basic arrangement is that all such persons who volunteer to do so in a continental area or at Worldwide shall be enrolled as volunteers on **OT Activities.** The whole of those in any continental area or Worldwide may elect a committee. This committee is to be called a "Continental Committee" for continental areas and the "Central Committee" for Worldwide. Staff membership in orgs is not a requisite. These committees will handle certain projects, programs and missions. The first and foremost program of **OT activities** is of course the furtherance, support and protection of Scn. (HCO PL 10 Nov 66 II) [The above HCO PL was cancelled by HCO PL 11 Aug 67 III.]

OT BADGE, the cloth **OT badge** for the Sea Org is 7 cm high and 5.5 cm wide, with a bright blue surround, a gold oval O with a cross bar in it above center and a vertical down from the cross bar to the bottom of the O on a white field. The metal badge is the same design but only 1.7 cm in height and 1.25 cm wide, with a safety pin back. (FO 71)

OT CENTRAL COMMITTEE, the **OT Central Committee** is directly under the Executive Council Worldwide and the Divisional Organizer for Distribution WW. The duties of the **OT Central Committee** are: (1) to pass on projects proposed by persons on the Section I and beyond courses or OTs and authorize, expand, replan or reject same, (2) to recruit personnel for OT organizations by keeping lists of enrollees and graduates and informing them routinely of posts available on OT organizations, (3) expedite for OT organizations diverse matters and concerns as these arise, (4) liaison with the Executive Council WW via Divisional Organizer Dist WW for OT organizations or their personnel, (5) regulate all projects and cancel or rearrange those that are not productive or are causing dev-t or trouble or needless expense. The purpose of the **OT Central Committee** is to help LRH organize and channel OT forces, interests and resources for the greatest good for Scn. All other OT committees come under the **OT Central Committee** via their Exec Councils. (HCO PL 11 Aug 67 III)

OT COMMITTEE, these **committees** may be **committees** of 500 or 2,000 for example, or any number of Clears and **OTs.** Only Clears and **OTs** may be members of the **committee.** There are no dues (although the **committee** may raise funds and take up collections). An **OT Committee** membership card is issued to each member. The purpose of the **OT Committee** is to help LRH organize and channel OT forces, interests and resources for the greatest good for Dn and Scn. The **OT Committee** may embark upon and execute projects which further Dn and Scn or improve society. Such projects must be self-supporting and may not use org funds. The first and foremost program of the **OT Committee** is of course the furtherance, support and protection of Dn and Scn. (HCO PL 22 Oct 70)

OT COURSE, the **OT course** is divided into levels. Each level is called a part. Enrollment in each part will be by invitation only. The reason for this is that for the first time in this universe we are making real cleared (not keyed out) OTs. the power of these beings will be unlimited. (HCO PL 12 Aug 66 II)

OT EXPANSION PROGRAM, the sequence of promotion and delivery of OT III and OT III Expanded is (1) OT III. (2) completion of past auditing cycles in the AO HGC and any required case handling actions, such as C/S 53, GF 40X and any other set-up for OT VII, as determined by the C/S. (3) OT VII. (4) OT III Expanded. The surveyed selling name for the section of auditing between OT III and OT VII is **OT Expansion Program.** (FO 3112)

OT FORMULA, cause. (HCO PL 14 Jan 69)

OTHER-INTENTIONEDNESS, (form of arbitrary) the receipt of a communication is an extremely important part of the sequence of actions that results in a compliance. Common reasons for the non-receipt of a communication is that arbitraries (or arbitrary factors) exist in the area. **Other-intentionedness** means a state of mind of wanting to follow a different goal than that known to be the goal of the originator and the goals of the group (either a big or a little goal). (BPL 10 Nov 73 II)

OTHER PRACTICES, do not engage in **other practices** while receiving an auditing intensive. This includes "bathing in light," psychiatry, yoga, hypnotism, meditation, spiritualism, mysticism, extreme dieting, etc. (BPL 29 Jan 72R)

OTL, 1. all **OTLs** have at this point been converted to FOLOs and CLOs. (BPL 3 Oct 72R) **2.** an extension of CLOs for the CLO. (HCO PL 22 Jul 71) **3.** branches of a Continental Liaison Office. (HCO PL 22 Jul 71) **4.** the major purpose of a CLO or **OTL** is to make Flag planning become an actuality in orgs, franchises and thereby the various publics. (HCO PL 22 Jul 71) **5.** the first action and primary duty of an **OTL** is to secure a communication line into its area. Security, speed and effectiveness of comm to and from Flag or senior base is the **OTL's** first concern. This easily extends to include missions as a form of extended comm line. The word **liaison** means "close bond, intercommunication." The second and third immediate concerns of an **OTL** are recruitment of Sea Org members and promotion of customers for AO and SH services. (FO 2461R) **6.** has specific functions such as procurement of personnel for the Sea Org, handling and routing of Advanced Course students, and other duties for the Sea Org. (FO 638) **7.** a mission to facilitate comms, supplies, personnel for SO. (6805C24 SO) **8.** (**OT liaison**) whose function is to act as a Sea Org **Liaison** Office. (FO 1151) **9.** an extension of the Sea Org. Its purpose is to expedite Sea Org business and requirements. It is composed of a commanding officer, a supercargo and a chief officer. It may have other divisions added. (FO 745)

OTL EXPENSE, the same as a CLO. Nearest major org supports it. If any good it will boom that org and others as well. It has to boom others so they will feed to the nearest major org. It is expected to send far more to SO reserves than it consumes. (HCO PL 9 Mar 72 I)

OT LIAISON, a relay point for the Sea Org. (FO 1561) See OTL.

OTL LIAISON UNITS, communication relay points. They are not originating units. They are not interpretation units; **OTLs** do not decide or issue orders on any Flag project. **OTLs** only relay orders exactly without alter-is. (FO 1214) See OTL.

OTL LAST COURT OF APPEALS, see FOLO LAST COURT OF APPEAL.

OTL UK, formerly OTL WW. (FO 1114)

OT PRODUCTION DEPARTMENT, (Ship Org Board) Department 17, Division 6 contains AO Promotion Section and OT Production and Control Section which ensures OT production, picks up inactive OTs, OT programs and SO personnel advertisements. (FO 1109)

OT Symbol

OT SYMBOL, the **symbol** used for **OT** activities is an oval O with a horizontal bar two thirds up from the open bottom of the O and contained within the O and a vertical bar down from its center to the bottom of the O. A person attaining section V OT may have a wreath completely around the outside of the O. (HCO PL 11 Aug 67 III)

OUT, **1.** things which should be there and aren't or should be done and aren't are said to be "**out,**" i.e., "Enrollment books are **out.**" (HCOB 21 Sept 70) **2. out** means "that's the end of traffic, I'm going off the air." Always conclude with an "**out.**" (BO 11, circa 10 Jun 67)

OUT 2-D, **out 2D** is a colloquial expression formed by Scientologists to mean unethical or non-optimum conduct on the **second dynamic.** Most people refer to it as sexual activities which impede or enturbulate a person's, group's, or family's forward progress in life. (FDD 82, Div VII INT)

OUT-BASKET, see IN-BASKET.

OUTER ORG STUDENT DEPOSITS, (Flag) qualifies only as **org** payments and is not part of delivery sum. Only cash personal payments are delivery sum and only when used. (FSO 667 RC)

OUT-ETHICS, **1.** an action or situation in which an individual is involved contrary to the ideals and best interests of his group. An act or situation or relationship contrary to the ethics standards, codes or ideals of the group or other members of the group. An act of omission or commission by an individual that could or has reduced the general effectiveness of a group or its other members. An individual act of omission or commission which impedes the general well-being of a group or impedes it in achieving its goals. (HCO PL 3 May 72) **2.** his own concept of his own ethics is not adequate to his survival—that's what that means. (7204C11 SO)

OUT ETIQUETTE REPORT, in the interest of maintaining Sea Organization tradition, discipline and **etiquette, out etiquette reports** are added to the list of staff member **reports** contained in HCO PL 1 May 1965, *Staff Member Reports.* They are issued and distributed like other ethics chits by officers, petty officers and executives for violations of Flag Orders 38, 87 and other issues on etiquette. As **out etiquette** is a sign of slackening discipline and often indicates possibilities of other out-ethics situations with the individual, an **out etiquette report** will serve to alert the MAA to this fact. (FO 3383)

OUTFLOW AND ANSWER CYCLE, see CYCLE OF BOOMS AND DEPRESSIONS.

OUTFLOW COMM SECTION, Dir Comm must see to it that letters and mail pieces flow outward from the org by seeing to it first that the mail gets signed and sent quickly, that magazines are prepared for with addressed envelopes, that address plates exist for every member of the public in **comm** with us, that any type of person or geographical section can be run off bang by address and seeing to it that letters don't pile up unanswered but forcing them to be answered quickly. This is a section in the Department of Communication, the **Outflow Comm Section.** (HCO PL 25 Feb 66)

OUTGO, the position in a comstation taken by a communication which is **going out** from this station. (*HTLTAE*, p. 122)

OUT HYGIENE CHIT, this may be written on matters of dirty dishes, food, bathrooms, W.C.s, persons serving food in dirty clothes, etc. Persons who consistently do not wash their hands or bathe or wear dirty clothes or who have body odor are also subject to an **out hygiene chit.** (FO 2697)

OUTLAW STRIKE, see STRIKE, OUTLAW.

OUTLET, a market for a product. A wholesale or retail firm which sells goods to customers.

OUT OF COMM, a stacked and unwatched basket in the **comm** center. (HASI PL 9 Apr 57)

OUT OF CONTEXT, something written or done without relation to the principal meaning of a work. (HCO PL 14 Dec 73)

OUT OF VALENCE, a person whose ethics have been **out** over a long period goes **out of valence.** They are "not themselves." (HCO PL 3 May 72)

OUT-POINT, 1. defined more fully in the Data Series, the **out-points** are: (1) omitted, (2) altered sequence, (3) dropped time, (4) falsehood, (5) altered importance, (6) wrong target, (7) wrong source, (8) contrary facts, (9) added time, (10) added inapplicable data, (11) incorrectly included datum. (HCO PL 30 Aug 74 II) **2.** it is a **pointer** toward a situation. (HCO PL 30 Sept 73 II) **3.** when I say **out-points**, there's two classes of **out-points**, the organizational **out-points** and the personal **out-points**. (7205C20 SO) **4.** simply an illogical departure from the ideal scene. By comparing the existing scene with the ideal scene one easily sees the **out-points.** (HCO PL 19 Mar 72 II) **5.** the **out-points** are really a description of idiocy. (ESTO 11, 7203C06 SO I) **6.** aberration is just the basis of **out-points.** (ESTO 4, 7203C02 SO II) **7.** anything that detracts from potential survival in any situation, dangerous or routine, is an **out-point.** (FO 2471) **8.** illogical data. (HCO PL 18 May 70) **9.** primary illogics. (HCO PL 15 May 70, *Data and Situation Analyzing*) **10.** any one datum that is offered as true that is in fact found to be illogical when compared to the five primary **points** of illogic. (HCO PL 15 May 70, *Data and Situation Analyzing*)

OUTPUT, the amount of work accomplished or the quantity of something produced by an employee, machine, plant, company, etc.

OUTPUT POOL, see POOL, OUTPUT.

OUTSIDE AUDITORS, non-staff **auditors.** (HCO PL 21 Aug 64)

OUTSIDE TRAINING, see TRAINING, OUTSIDE.

OUTSTANDING CHECKS, see BANK RECONCILIATION.

OUTWORK, see PUTTING-OUT SYSTEM.

OVER, "**over** to you." (BO 11, circa 10 Jun 67)

OVERALL IMPRESSION METHOD OF SELECTION, see SELECTION, OVERALL IMPRESSION METHOD OF.

OVERBOUGHT, reference for stock market price levels that have reached new highs as the result of a period of strong buying.

OVERBURDEN, a technical term here in management which means "loading so much and so many jobs on a personnel that the personnel can never see any wins in it." (HCO PL 5 Oct 58)

Overburden

OVERCAPITALIZED, 1. the condition of investing too much capital in a business enterprise in relation to probable earnings. 2. to have estimated the value of property too highly. 3. to have placed an extremely or even unlawfully high value on the nominal capital of a business.

OVERDUE, a past due amount or obligation, not paid or met by a specified date.

OVER-EXPANSION, one can **over-expand** by acquiring too much territory too fast without knowing how to handle it. (HCO PL 4 Dec 66)

OVERHEAD, the operating expenses of a business which includes costs of rent, utilities, maintenance taxes but excludes the direct costs of labor and materials. Also called indirect cost.

OVERLOAD, (C/S definition) what is **overload?** When a C/S can't read every worksheet and study and program *every* case he has, due to time, he is **overloaded.** (HCO PL 25 Sept 74)

OVERMANNING, see OVERSTAFFING.

OVER-POST, by which is meant always **post** well above complement. (FSO 96)

OVERPRODUCTION, the condition of a business producing more of its product than can be absorbed at the usual price.

OVERSOLD, reference for stock market price levels be extremely low after a slack selling period.

OVERSTAFFING, the state of providing a business enterprise with more employees than needed to operate properly. Also called overmanning.

OVERT, we have the word "**overt,**" meaning a bad deed. (FO 2610)

OVERT ACTS, **1.** harmful **acts.** (HCO PL 14 Nov 70) **2.** when a product is non-existent or bad it can be classified as an **overt act** against both the org and any customer. (HCO PL 14 Nov 70) **3.** is not just injuring someone or something: an **overt act** is an act of omission or commission which does the least good for the least number of dynamics or the most harm to the greatest number of dynamics. (HCO PL 1 Nov 70 III) **4.** something that harms broadly. (HCO PL 1 Nov 70 III)

OVER THE COUNTER, total monies invoiced as income of whatever type and from whatever source which were received by the cashier on the spot and not by mail or courier. Advance payments received **over the counter** must be marked as such. (FO 1828)

OVER THE COUNTER, stocks bought and sold by securities dealers directly to buyers, often over the telephone as well as over the counter, rather than on the floor of a stock exchange.

OVERTIME, 1. the situation of working hours in addition to those of the regular schedule, and sometimes rewarded at special overtime rates of pay. 2. the payment received for additional work done over and above a regular work schedule.

OVERT PRODUCT, **1.** a bad one that will not be accepted or cannot be traded or exchanged and has more waste and liability connected with it than it has value. (HCOPL 7 Aug 76 II) **2.** these are called so because they are not in actual fact useful **products** but something no one wants and are **overt** acts in themselves—such as inedible biscuits or a "repair" that is just further breakage. (HCOB 10 May 72)

OVERTRADING, trading or acquiring goods or stock beyond the limit of one's capital or beyond what the market demand is. Thus working capital gets tied up.

OVERTURN, see TURNOVER.

OXFORD CAPACITY ANALYSIS, the **OCA** (**Oxford Capacity Analysis**) is the English version of the American Personality Analysis (APA). Either may be used. Their administration, scoring and evaluation are handled in the same way. The **OCA** (or APA) consists of 200 questions. These 200 questions are divided up into series of 20 questions, each of which measures a single personality trait. Thus ten traits are measured in all. The 20 questions that measure each trait are randomly numbered throughout the 200 questions: i.e. the questions that measure trait A are numbered 1, 8, 15, 17, 42, 46, etc. The testee may answer each question either yes, maybe or no. To do this he fills in one of the three small rectangular spaces on the answer sheet which follows each number. (HCO PL 3 Nov 70 II)

P

PAB LIAISON, purpose: to see that **PAB** material is supplied London months in advance. Duties: to edit tape material, transcribed by tape transcription, suitable for **PABS.** (HCO PL 15 Jun 59)

PACE-SETTER, a very productive employee taken as an example of how much of a particular type of work can be done in a certain time so that a rate of pay can be established in a payment-by-results or piece work (piece rate) system.

PACIFIC OPERATIONS, [Usually called **Pac Ops** or US **Ops** as in FO 2351. It was the Continental Management Unit or body located in Los Angeles, California which relayed Flag's orders, got them executed and reported those dones to Flag. It also acted independently to handle situations in the US to do with US Sea Org and Scn orgs and Sea Org vessels and reported its own handlings to Flag. It also ran for Flag any missions Flag sent to US Sea Org or Scn orgs. It was located on land and in 1970 moved to the Sea Org ship *Bolivar*. **Pac Ops** was replaced by USLO in 1970 which was replaced by FOLO West US in 1972.]

PACK, a collection of written materials which match a checksheet. It is variously constituted—such as loose-leaf or a cardboard folder or bulletins in a cover stapled together. A **pack** does not necessarily include a booklet or hardcover book that may be called for as part of a checksheet. (HCOB 19 Jun 71 III)

PACKAGE, several services bought together under a common price. (HCO PL 11 Aug 71 IV) [The above HCO PL was cancelled by BPL 25 Nov 71R, *Inter-Org Exchange of Students and Fees* which does not have this definition on it.]

PACKAGE, 1. a unit consisting of one or more items of value enclosed, contained or protected in a box, bottle, can, crate, container or the like. 2. a bottle, box, can, crate, container or receptacle used to contain or protect something such as goods or products; packaging. 3. a group of related products, services, agreements, laws, etc., treated as a unit and bought, sold, agreed to or rejected as a unit; sometimes called a package deal.

PACKAGING, 1. the material that is used to enclose, contain, wrap or protect a product until the product is bought and used by a consumer. 2. that area of manufacturing dealing with the subject of how to best enclose, contain, wrap or safeguard a product until it is in a consumer's possession. Each product has certain packaging requirements due to its nature and the way in which it is marketed. The area of packaging is essentially a study of what occurs to a product from the time it leaves the manufacturer until it reaches the consumer, is consumed, and the packaging is discarded. Considerations affecting packaging include the cost and availability of materials to protect a product during shipment, protect it against spoilage over a period of time, attractiveness of packaging to entice purchase and ecological considerations affecting the efficient disposal of packaging once discarded, etc.

PACKAGING TEST, market research study for determining the effectiveness of a product's packaging in terms of function, design and color impact, and degree of attraction in comparison with competitor's packaging.

PAC OPS, see PACIFIC OPERATIONS.

PA EXPEDITOR UNIT, an **expeditor unit** is established in **PA** Flag and **PA** orgs. Its function is to carry out emergency actions in the different **PA** areas needed to back up Flag. (FO 3486)

PAGE PROOFS, page proofs are the printed impressions of the **pages** as they will appear in the printed copies. (BPL 29 Nov 68R)

PAID, means money has been received in full. (HCO PL 29 Aug 71)

PAID COMPLETION POINTS, points that may be counted on the **paid completions** stat for pc **completions,** student **completions** and internship **completions.** These **completions** must be **paid** (money received in full), attested or verified by examination (with an F/N VGIs at examiner for pcs) and must be accompanied by an acceptable success story. (BTB 30 Aug 71 RD)

PAID COMPLETIONS, paid completions accompanied by an acceptable success story. **"Completions"** means a finished level or rundown. **"Paid"** means money has been received in full. "Success story" means an originated written statement by the pc. This is the stat of the Executive Director who may have no other stat. The condition assigned to the entire org will be based on the statistic. (HCO PL 29 Aug 71)

PAID COMPLETIONS IS LAGGING GI, means backlogging services instead of delivering to a degree so as to cause refunds and is determined therefore by refund or by slumped **paid completions** below expected level. (FO 3188)

PAID COMPS VERIFICATION FORM, the **paid comps verification form** is an excellent source of data on **paid comps** and from it you can detect falseness of the stat. Of course if the org does not fill it in each week and send it to data files it is highly probable that the stat is false. This **form** can also be used by an evaluator to determine *what* is being delivered in an org, to get the percentage of F/N at the examiner, to determine whether the business is new or old, ratio of processing and training delivery, the ratio of **paid comps** to staff comps, etc. (CBO 363)

PAID-IN CAPITAL, the assets (cash, property, etc.) of a corporation that were paid-in or contributed by stockholders.

PAID START, each service **paid** for and **started** is counted as one **paid start.** If a person signs up and **pays** for a number of services—say Academy Levels 0-IV—he is counted as one **paid start** as each academy level is taken. Similarly, if a person signs up and pays for a number of 12 1/2 hour intensives, as each paid intensive is begun it is counted as one **paid start.** (BPL 11 Aug 75)

PAID START REPORT FORM, this **form** is for persons fully **paid** and enrolled onto service. The purpose of the **paid start report form** is to have a record in the person's CF file of when he enrolled on what service. (HCO PL 12 Oct 72 II) [The above HCO PL was cancelled and replaced by BPL 1 Dec 72 I.]

PAINTING, rendering or executing an idea, through the art of **paint.** It communicates. (LRH Def. Notes)

Painting

Pamphlet

PAMPHLET, a printed booklet with few pages. (FO 3275R)

PANTRY CHECK, see CHECK, PANTRY.

PAPER JOGGER, this is a vibration machine which is used to **"jog"** the **paper,** once collated, into order. This **paper jogger** vibrates the issue and therefore puts the pages into place ready to staple. (FO 3264-17)

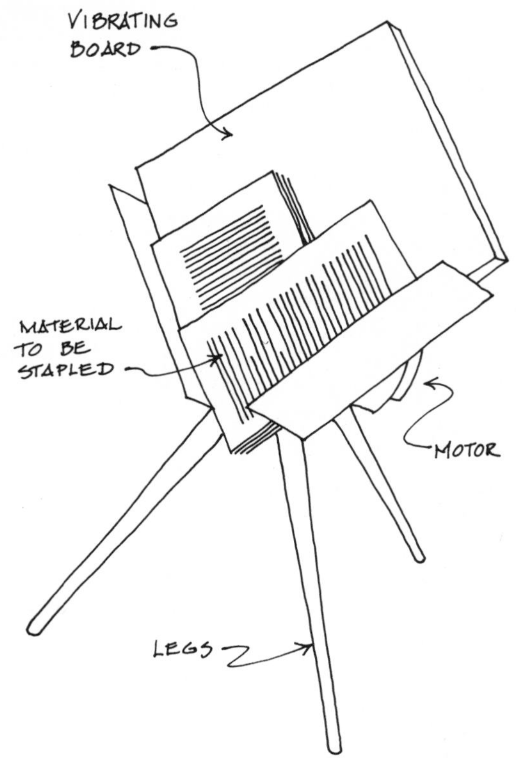

Paper Jogger

PAPER LOSS, a loss due to a decrease in the value of stocks or securities held but which won't be realized by the holder until he sells them at the decreased value.

PAPER PROFIT, see PROFIT, PAPER.

PAPER TRANSLATIONS I/C, the post of **Paper Translations I/C** is nearly the same as that of a standard Mimeo Officer in a mimeo files unit. In a Translations Unit there is a certain amount of paperwork which must accompany each tape course. The paperwork consists of the checksheet, the glossary, charts, auditing lists, picture HCOBs, etc. **Paper Translations I/C** is in charge of mimeoing these manuscript translations and maintaining proper files. (BPL 9 Jan 74 V)

PAR, par, face or nominal value.

PARANOIA, paranoia if anything is attack upon illusion. (7202C22 SO)

PARASITIC, dependent on others outside it, without producing more than it consumes. (HCO PL 19 Dec 69)

PARENT COMPANY, see COMPANY, HOLDING.

PARENT OR GUARDIAN ASSENT FORM, the **form** used when a minor requires *any* service. This **form** is to be filled in by the **parent or guardian** of the minor concerned and is a prerequisite before any Dn or Scn processing, testing or training can be undertaken. (**Parent or guardian assent** to Dn or Scn processing, testing or training.) (BPL 12 Jul 71 I)

PARENTS COMMITTEE, a **committee** formed in each SO org and unit consisting of all SO members with children, small children, babies or cadets under the care of the org or unit. The **Parents Committee** is posted on the org board as an advisory body under the LRH Comm in the Office of LRH. The purpose of the **Parents Committee** is to iron out nursery facilities and ensure the proper care and upbringing of cadets, children, small children and babies of the Sea Org **parents.** (FO 3167)

PARITY, **1.** the equivalent in value of an amount of money expressed in terms of a different currency, at an official rate of exchange. **2.** the equalization of prices of goods or securities in two different markets. 3. a level of farm goods prices, maintained by government support, to ensure farmers the same purchasing power they had during a previous period of time known as the base period.

PARTICIPATING MEMBER, this **membership** is available to anyone, on payment of 3 gns ($10) per annum. It is sold by the Central Org and entitles the person to **participate** in its services and receive the continental magazine. (HCO PL 22 Apr 64) [The above HCO PL was cancelled by BPL 10 Oct 75 V.]

PARTICLE, body, dispatch, raw materials, whatever. (HCO PL 25 Jul 72)

PARTNERSHIP, an agreement between two or more persons to carry on a business with each furnishing a part of the capital and labor in order to share accordingly in the profits (or losses).

PART-TIME AUDITOR, one who works **part** of the working week every week for the organization and always the same **part** of the working week. (HCO PL 23 Sept 64)

PART-TIME STAFF MEMBER, **1. part-time staff** is usually composed of non-practicing Scientologists who audit weekend or evening pcs for the org and are on units every week, rain or shine. (HCO PL 23 Sept 64) **2.** one who works less than forty hours a week. (HCO PL 26 Jun 64) **3.** a person only on post for a few hours a week. This individual can be hired or fired by the department head with the okay of the Organization Secretary. (SEC ED 75, 2 Feb 59) **4.** one who is brought on for a short period and who will be paid in pounds. (HASI PL 19 Apr 57)

PAR VALUE, the value printed on the face of a note, stock, bond, etc. Also called face or nominal value.

PARVENU, a person who has suddenly been elevated above his social and economic class through acquired wealth, modified in business to mean an employee who is promoted beyond his adaptability and the new position shows up his lack of sound qualifications and background.

PASSED DIVIDEND, the passing up of a regular or scheduled dividend.

PASSING THE BUCK, pushing the responsibility for a decision or an action to somebody else. (ESTO 8, 7203C04 SO II)

Paste-up

PASS THE DIVIDEND, phrase for the decision by a board of directors not to pay a regular or scheduled dividend to stockholders for a particular fiscal period.

PASTEUP, to actually **paste** or stick the different parts of the artwork down in finished form. (Dissem Advice Ltr 1 Apr 70, *Magazine Layout and Pasteup*)

PASTORAL COUNSELING, **1.** Dn is practiced in the Church of Scientology as **pastoral counseling,** addressing the spirit in relation to his own body and intended to increase well-being and peace of mind. Auditing is a **pastoral counseling** procedure by which an individual is helped, in stages, to recover his self-determinism, ability and awareness of self, restoring respect for self and others. (BPL 24 Sept 73RA XIII) **2.** auditing. (BPL 24 Sept 73R III)

PATENT, a grant made by the US Federal Government to an inventor, giving him sole right to make, use and sell his invention for a period of 17 years; or by other governments outside the United States, for a specified time according to their individual laws.

PATENT POOL, see POOL, PATENT.

PATENT RELEASE, an agreement signed by an employee stating that he will release or assign to his company any patentable ideas or devices he develops.

PATTERN OF AN ORG, the whole rationale (basic idea) of the **pattern of an org** is a unit of three. These are

Thetan
↓
Mind ⟶ Body ⟶ Product

In Division One the HCO Sec is the thetan, Department One the mind, Department Two the body, and Department Three the product. The same **pattern** holds for every division. It also should hold for every department and lower section and unit. And above these it holds for a portion of an org. (HCO PL 20 Oct 67) See ORGANIZATIONAL PATTERN.

PAUSED STATISTIC, during expansion, one has areas where **statistics** become level. Here **statistics pause** because lines jam. People get overworked and confused. The traffic is just too heavy. A **paused statistic** comes from the jammed lines of the topmost executives and is best remedied by easing them. (HCO PL 1 Feb 66 IV)

PAY-AS-YOU-EARN, the British system of withholding tax. *Abbr.* PAYE.

PAY DIFFERENTIAL, the difference in salary of various kinds of employee.

PAYE, pay-as-you-earn.

PAYEE, a person or business to whom money is paid or in contractual writings, the party in whose favor a promissory note is formulated.

PAYING BY DATELINE, **paying** all the bills behind a certain **date** and none closer to present time than that **date.** (HCO PL 28 Jan 65)

PAY-IN SLIPS, bank deposit **slips.** (HCO PL 10 Oct 70 III)

PAYMENT-BY-RESULTS, a wage system that pays employees according to how much they have produced as opposed to an hourly rate. Piecework is a type of payment-by-results scheme. Performance linked pay is another term for payment-by-results. *Abbr.* PBR.

PAYMENT SYSTEM, the manner in which employees are paid. Basically employees are paid by time or by results. Thus a person may receive a set rate per hour or day as in time-related payment or he may receive a certain rate per completed product as in a payment-by-results scheme.

PAY-OUT PERIOD, the period during which one is still paying for the costs of an operation and/or has not yet reached the break-even point.

PAYROLL, a list of employees receiving wages with the amount due to each as well as the total sum to be paid out for a given period.

PAYROLL A, **1. Payroll A** is base SO allowance for an SO member on duty with a post and stat. (FSO 135R) **2.** basic SO allowance for a Flag SO member on duty with a post and stat. Each SO member is entitled to 3 weeks leave with pay. **Payroll A** includes stewards and snipes (engineers) hazard pay. Auditors and supervisors additional pay, RPF pay. (FSO 359RA) **3.** is the basic allowance for all SO members (FO 3075).

PAYROLL B, **1.** basic bonus related to post dependent upon an acceptable post stat. £10 fine for a false or padded stat. (FSO 135R) **2.** all bonuses of post, rank, class, skills and longevity. In order to receive this bonus one must have acceptable post stats. $25 fine for a false or padded stat. (FSO 359RA) **3.** is the bonus which rewards tech production. (FO 3075)

PAYROLL C, **1.** all bonuses of rank, class, skills, longevity based on gross stats as listed for different activities. (FSO 135R) **2.** one time bonuses payable only once. (FSO 359RA) **3.** is a post production payroll which rewards those who demonstrate good post production by statistics. (FO 3075)

PAYROLL D, **1.** one time bonuses payable only once. (FSO 135R) **2.** tech production bonuses. (FSO 359RA) **3.** is an org production bonus which rewards those staff members who contribute to high overall org production and statistics. (FO 3075)

PAYROLL DEDUCTIONS, deductions made from an employee's gross salary to cover things such as income taxes, old age benefits, pension plan contributions, group insurance premiums, union dues or cost of articles charged during the recent period, as exemplified by a retail store employee with a house account for purchases.

PAYROLL E, tech production bonuses. (FSO 359R) [The above FSO contained the same categories of payroll as those in FSO 135R but added **payroll E.** FSO 359R has since been replaced by FSO 359RA which rearranges the payroll categories to reclassify **payroll E** above as payroll D.]

PAYROLL TAX, a tax levied against a payroll and payable by an employer, employee or both to cover future eventualities such as unemployment compensation, retirement benefits, etc.

PC ADMIN UNIT, **unit** under one in-charge who will regulate all flows and handling of folders and **pcs.** (ED 140 FAO)

PC RESULT, a **pc result** is not an F/N but a remarkable case change. (BPL 10 Oct 74R)

PC ROUTE, **1.** the **pc route** consists of a person being audited up through the grades including power processing and VA and then enrolling on the Solo Audit Course at a Saint Hill, making Grade VI and then enrolling on the Clearing Course. They have little or no academy training in most cases. (HCO PL 11 Dec 69, *Training of Clears*) **2.** there are two routes to Clear and OT:

the training (or professional) route and the processing (or **pc**) **route.** (SO ED 269 INT) **3.** the non-professional **route** to Clear. (BPL 6 Aug 72RA)

PC SCHEDULING BOARD, the **board** has the name of each auditor, intern and FESer posted on it. The name of each is posted with space for his auditor class and each OK to audit noted. This makes it easy to see which auditors are qualified for various actions. Interns are posted in a different color than regular HGC auditors. There is a card posted for every **pc** who has routed into the HGC who has not yet completed his auditing and properly routed out. (BPL 9 Jun 73R II)

PEAK LOAD, the greatest amount of production, energy, strain, etc., that can be handled under the current arrangement or conditions.

PE COURSE SECTION, a five evening **PE course** is given weekly. Its curriculum is precisely laid down. Its total purpose is to explain elementary Scn and prepare and route people into the co-audit. (HCO PL 20 Dec 62)

PEDDLER, a person who travels about selling his wares or a company's wares, usually of the small household variety, going from door-to-door through neighborhoods. Also called a door-to-door salesman.

PE DIRECTOR, takes no classes, makes no lectures, works from two to ten p.m., supervises and interviews and keeps the course and other instructors going. Lack of a **PE Director** without a class leaves the place unsupervised and in a confusion. (HCOB 29 Sept 59)

PE LECTURE COURSE, this is a short **lecture course** covering Scn basics, modeled after the PE Course. (FSO 779)

PENDING BASKET, see IN-BASKET.

PENDING CLEAR CERT, no person may be declared **Clear** who has a bad ethics record which demonstrates suppressiveness. He can be told he is **Clear** but the **Clear cert** must be sent to the Ethics Officer who holds it for six months **pending** any new symptoms of suppressiveness. The person meanwhile may enroll on Advanced Courses but it must be plainly noted he is a **pending Clear cert.** (HCO PL 13 Sept 67)

PENDING MISSIONS, missions not yet in briefing but in the planning stages. (CBO 187)

PENETRATION PRICING, see PRICING, PENETRATION.

PENNY STOCKS, see STOCKS, PENNY.

PENSION, a sum of money paid regularly to a person who has retired from a business, satisfied certain conditions of employment, or has become disabled as through military service or industrial accident.

PEOPLE WHO PRESENT PROBLEMS, a type of dev-t. **Problems presented** by juniors when solved by a senior cause dev-t because the source of the **problem** usually won't use the **presented** solution either. (HCO PL 27 Jan 69)

PEOPLE WRANGLERS, body routers also wear the hat of **people wranglers**—rounding up persons falling off the org lines, putting them back on and taking them to where they should go—namely the Public Registrar. (BPL 1 Dec 72R IV)

PERCENTAGE ORDER, see ORDER, PERCENTAGE.

PE REGISTRAR, registers and handles the Anatomy Course, group processing and **PE** Course procurement and enrollment. (HCO PL 29 Nov 60)

PERFECT, I want every auditor auditing to be **perfect** on a meter. By **perfect** is meant: (1) auditor never tries to clean a clean read; (2) auditor never misses a read that is reacting. (HCO PL 14 Jul 62)

PERFECT ORGANIZATION, 1. organization is composed of terminals and communication lines related by a common purpose. That's an organization. All the organizational pattern does is help separate the types of particles being handled. That, in a nutshell, is an organization and what it does. Now to make a **perfect organization,** evidently all you have to do is find out what particles come in, how they are changed, and how they are gotten rid of. That's all. If there's any friction on the lines, it's got to be smoothed out. (5812C29) **2.** a **perfect organization** is not a machine but a pattern of agreements. (HCO PL 2 Nov 70 II)

PERFECT PUBLIC RELATIONS, these are the three grades of PR: **perfect PR** good works well publicized. Inadequate PR: good works which speak for themselves. Enemy PR: bad works falsely publicized. (BPL 15 Jun 72)

PERFORMANCE, 1. the way an employee or the organization itself functions, usually in comparison to objectives or a set standard. 2. the degree of skill with which something is executed either by an individual or a company.

PERFORMANCE-LINKED PAY, see PAYMENT-BY-RESULTS.

PERFORMANCE TEST, a test designed to measure a person's ability to produce on the job, to solve work-oriented problems, the causativeness of an individual, etc. Such tests often show up the need for future training, potential for promotion, managerial qualities, etc.

PERFUNCTORYITIS, a disease gets amongst auditors called **perfunctoryitis.** They see a floating needle in every blowdown (when, of course, the needle does behave loosely for the moment during the blowdown). As a result such an auditor runs a process to a blowdown and says "floating needle." (HCO PL 5 Aug 65)

PERIODIC REVIEW, any regularized or random check on production, personnel, management policies and decisions, the state of a project, etc., with a view in mind to correct points now found to be unfavorable.

PERMANENT EXECUTIVE, a **permanent executive** uses the full title of and draws the full units of a post. He or she may be transferred to a similar post by the Assn Sec or by the HCO Sec who is handling a state of emergency that applies to that department. He or she may be suspended for no longer than two weeks in any three months from post without pay, to be processed in event of a consistent failure in that department. He or she may be removed from post only by myself after due investigation, and reports are received by me. (HCO PL 17 Feb 61, *Staff Post Qualifications Permanent Executives to be Approved*)

PERMANENT MISSION, a Sea Org **mission** which is located in an area or on a ship or in a flotilla and which does not change but continues its duties there. It is composed of three members who each one covers one of the three points of a **mission**—ethics, tech and admin. (FO 495)

PERMANENT STAFF MEMBER, 1. a **permanent staff member** may not be demoted, transferred or dismissed without a full Committee of Evidence being held. The person may himself request a change of status or another post or may resign without a Committee of Evidence being convened. **Permanent** status is designated on the org board by the numeral "2" after a person's name. To obtain **permanent** status a provisional must obtain his or her basic staff certificate. This has a checksheet for which the HCO Exec Sec is responsible for compiling. (HCO PL 4 Jan 66 V) **2.** a **permanent staff member** is paid in units and will be in the future taken on only at a staff meeting by a majority vote. The status of **permanent staff member** shall be granted only upon majority vote at a staff meeting and is then dismissible only upon majority vote at a staff meeting or by a unanimous vote of the Advisory Committee, both subject to further appeal and approval by the Association Secretary and the Agent for Great Britain. (HASI PL 19 Apr 57) **3.** a person who has passed an examination as per latest qualifications. This individual can only be dismissed by unanimous vote of the Advisory Council or by the Executive Director. In the instance of a **permanent staff member** quitting, he no longer is a **permanent staff member.** (SEC ED 75, 2 Feb 59)

PERMITTING DEV-T, the biggest single goof anyone can make is failing to recognize something as **dev-t** and going on to handle it anyway. One's basket soon overflows. The reason for "overwork" and "heavy traffic" is usually traceable to **permitting dev-t** to exist without understanding it or attempting to put the **dev-t** right. (HCO PL 27 Jan 69)

PERMS, term for permanent employees as distinct from part-time or temporary personnel.

PER PRO, by and for. (HCO PL 31 Mar 65)

PERSONAL ACCOUNT, the **accounts** maintained for outside **persons** are termed **personal accounts** simply because they record the view of the outside **persons.** Thus the **accounts** with Sykes, Biggs and Jones are examples of **personal accounts.** Any **account** that the organization maintains with any outside **person** is termed a **personal account.** By contrast, accounts maintained which show the point of view of the organization are termed impersonal accounts. Thus the examples, motor car account and E-meter sales account are impersonal accounts. Impersonal account means any account recording the organization's viewpoint of a transaction. (BPL 14 Nov 70 III)

PERSONAL AWARENESS AND UNDERSTANDING COURSE, a two-night lecture series using script delivered verbatim by supervisor. Subject matter: ARC triangle, parts of man, locks, secondaries and engrams. By reason of live lectures, this course imposes (a) limited enrollment times, (b) dependency on supervisor, (c) two nights is little time and makes resign-up a scramble, all at once graduates hit reges with greater speed, putting reges at slight disadvantage. (FPJO 717) [This **course** was mentioned in FBDL 516 as replacing the HAS Course and the Introduction to Scn Course. However a new HAS Course laid out in FPJO 717 supersedes the **Personal Awareness and Understanding Course.**]

PERSONAL CONTACT, this by far is the very best method of dissemination. It is better done on individual basis rather than talking to groups since there is the factor in groups of being able to escape by saying "they aren't talking to me." **Personal contact** then means just that. No matter whether it is done to friends and then to other people or secondarily to total strangers there is nothing better than personal contact. (HCOB 15 Sept 59)

PERSONAL EFFICIENCY COURSE, **1.** a five evening **PE Course** is given weekly. Its curriculum is precisely laid down. Its total purpose is to explain elementary Scn and prepare and route people into the co-audit. (HCO PL 14 Feb 61, *The Personal Efficiency Foundation*) **2.** a **PE Course** curriculum should consist of a mixture of drills and lectures. The first evening lecture should talk about definitions in life as found in Scn. The dynamic principle of existence, the eight dynamics, a preview of the next evening's lecture should be given and this lecture should consist of a very rapid survey of Comm Course TRs Zero and One and should sail in the second hour into the ARC triangle, and all data for the rest of the week used in lectures should consist of ARC triangle data taking up the whole subject and one corner at a time. The remainder of the week previews TRs two and three, and says how the TRs are used in life, and how people can't do them. The last lecture's last part sells the HAS Comm Course. (HCOB 29 Sept 59) **3.** what is the goal of a **PE Course?** Internationally the goal is to bring about a superior civilization in which peace can exist on earth. The modus operandi by which this is done is education in the actual, simple facts of existence, the data of which is contained in *Scientology the Fundamentals of Thought.* (5610C18) **4.** use the anatomy of the human mind materials in the **PE** and nothing else. (HCO PL 26 Aug 64) **5.** the data of the **PE course** is contained in *Scientology the Fundamentals of Thought.* (5610C18)

PERSONAL EFFICIENCY FOUNDATION, **1.** a **Personal Efficiency Foundation** has less than ten staff members. It has an org board with its activities and personnel designated. It teaches **PE** Courses and does individual auditing up to classifications held by the auditors concerned but not power processing or above. It copes as it can. (HCO PL 21 Oct 66 II) **2.** the **PE Foundation** is the entrance door of the public into the services of the Central Organization, a knowledge of Scn and a higher level of civilization. (HCO PL 14 Feb 61) **3.** one of the departments of a Central Organization. (6101C01) **4.** purpose: to run an amazingly successful HAS Co-audit course, to keep new people coming in and the co-audit growing, at least five new people per week, and cases cracking and everyone to get training further or cleared fully in the HGC. (HCO PL 27 Nov 59) **5.** a **PE Foundation** is a programmed drill calculated to introduce people to Scn and to bring their cases up to a high level of reality both on Scn and on life. A **PE Foundation** in its attitude goes for broke on the newcomers, builds up their interest with lectures and knocks their cases apart with comm course and upper indoc. (HCOB 29 Sept 59) **6.** the **PE Foundation** is an entrance point to Scn. If it fails to pass people from testing to a **PE** Course, from a **PE** Course to co-audit and from co-audit to the Academy and HGC, then it is failing its functions, the unit will be low and the Central Organization faltering. (HCO PL 14 Feb 61, *The Personal Efficiency Foundation*) **7.** the **PE Foundation** is a separate unit of the HASI with the stature of the Academy or HGC under the Technical Division. (HASI PL 30 Oct 58)

PERSONAL EFFICIENCY FOUNDATION HCO WW, this is an information center on HAS Co-audit. The place of the department is London and all queries about HAS Co-audits or the running of **PE Foundations** should be addressed to it. (HCO PL 28 May 59, *New HCO WW Dept*)

PERSONAL ENHANCEMENT, see PERSONNEL ENHANCEMENT.

PERSONAL GROOMING, **grooming** is defined as the action of taking care of the appearance of; making neat and tidy. By **personal** in this context we mean having to do with the individual; done directly by oneself, not through others; of the body or bodily appearance. **Personal grooming** is defined as the art of making oneself attractive. (FO 3241-1)

PERSONALITY INTERVIEW, type of newspaper **interview.** This procedure is often adopted for lengthy profiles or feature stories about people. In this type of **interview** the reporter conveys as much as possible about the individual. He touches on the subject's philosophy, goals, purposes, likes, dislikes, mannerisms, appearance, etc., and tries to give the reader the "feeling" of being with the person. (BPL 10 Jan 73R)

PERSONALITY PROMOTION, see PROMOTION, PERSONALITY.

PERSONAL OFFICE OF LRH, this is the organization which is Ron's **personal** org and which exists to service him directly, and to assist him in his many activities. The **Personal Office of LRH** is headed by Lt. Commander Ken Urquhart, LRH's Personal Communicator, whose direct senior is, of course, Ron. (SO ED 489 INT)

PERSONAL PROCUREMENT OFFICER, (Flag) the post of **Personal Procurement Officer** falls under Div 6 in the Department of Public Information. It is not a Division 1 function as Div 1 controls personnel assignment, reassignment and admin of persons in the flotilla. By sending out recruitment mailings and pretty posters at AOs, Div 6 procures new personnel. (FO 938)

PERSONAL REGISTRAR, 1. the **Personal Registrars** interview applicants, signs them up on contracts and releases and take their money for individual training and processing. When prospects seem too few, **Personal Registrars** go back over "hot files" and by phone or other means, seek to get people in. (HCO PL 20 Dec 62) 2. body **registrar.** (HCO PL 6 Apr 65)

PERSONAL REGISTRATION SECTION, the **Personal Registration Section** finds and signs up applicants for the Academy and the HGC. The **section** includes one or more **personal registrars,** the receptionist and for admin purposes, various admin personnel in the Technical Division. It is headed by the Chief **Registrar.** (HCO PL 20 Dec 62)

PERSONAL SELLING, see SELLING, PERSONAL.

PERSONAL STAFF OF THE COMMODORE, the purpose of **personal staff of the Commodore** is to handle traffic and relations between **Commodore** and Flag, **Commodore** and WW, **Commodore** and world matters and to care for and handle personal materials, effects and requirements of the **Commodore** and to assist the **Commodore.** (FO 766)

PERSONAL STAFF STEWARD DEPARTMENT, the purpose of the **Personal Staff Steward Department** is to provide the Commodore and **Personal Staff** with service so that they may be free to forward Sea Org targets according to their individual posts. (FO 786)

PERSONNEL, 1. all persons employed by a business firm or a public service organization. 2. the administrative department of an organization concerned with employees and employment matters.

PERSONNEL AUDIT, see AUDIT, PERSONNEL.

PERSONNEL BRANCH, the **Personnel Branch** of the Org Bureau is concerned with recruiting for staff. (CBO 4)

PERSONNEL BUDGET, see BUDGET, PERSONNEL.

PERSONNEL CONTROL, 1. consists of knowing who and where a **personnel** is, what he is doing, how well he is doing it and coordinating his work with other activities. (FO 2410) **2. personnel control**—i.e., basic training, hatting, posting, further training, apprenticing, as well as prediction and planning and the org's tech-admin ratio—is entirely the responsibility of the Department One of each org or unit. (BPL 3 Apr 73R II)

PERSONNEL CONTROL OFFICER, the **Personnel Control Officer** is in actual fact responsible for the effectiveness of staff members, since they influence all statistics and he is blamed for lack of good staff. (HCO PL 13 Feb 66) *Abbr.* PCO.

PERSONNEL COORDINATION BRANCH, (in Flag Bureau 1) the **Personnel Coordination Branch** has been formed to assert and maintain total control of all **personnel** movements and transfers. Its purpose is to help LRH maintain the form of the org in all orgs, vessels, bases, liaison offices and activities through the arrangement of specialized terminals who control and change the production and organization particles and flow lines of an activity. The product of the **branch** is: well posted staff and orgs. (CBO 233)

PERSONNEL COORDINATOR, 1. (Central Personnel Office hat) goals: to create continually growing **personnel** resources in orgs everywhere, by providing an additional external management for their **personnel.** Purposes: to ensure that all **personnel** are well and properly posted and that each one's forward progress as a staff member is uninterrupted. (FO 3332) **2.** the recruit or a new staff member has a terminal of recourse, that he can report to if things don't go right. This is the **Personnel Coordinator** at Flag, who then sees the matter is handled. In the event that a person has been dismissed, or in the Sea Org had a Fitness Board, and dismissed, and the staff member or recruit is requesting recourse, the **Personnel Coordinator** can have a Fitness Board done on Flag, from the file, and determine whether the person should be let on staff. (BPL 12 May 73R II)

PERSONNEL DEPARTMENT, the department of an organization that oversees and executes personnel policies and practices which may cover the enlistment and selection of new employees training programs, salary ranges and reviews, job and performance evaluations, industrial relations, fringe benefits, etc., as well as personnel records and statistics. Sometimes called the Employee Relations Department.

PERSONNEL ENHANCEMENT, 1. you notice this is **personnel enhancement** and not personal **enhancement.** But it actually could be. But if we called it personal **enhancement** it would seem like a public area, which it really isn't. New staff are brought in there and programmed. (7109C05 SO) **2.** there has not been any one person in the org who was concentrating on **personnel enhancement** in the full meaning of those words. **Personnel,** of course, means people who are on staff. It is not "personal" which would mean for the person himself. (HCO PL 22 May 76)

PERSONNEL ENHANCEMENT BUREAU, consists of Personnel Programming Branch, Personnel Phasing Branch, Personnel Progress Branch, and Verifications Branch. (CBO 38)

PERSONNEL FILES, 1. these consist of a **file** by division and department with the **personnel** in separate folders **filed** alphabetically in their department. Nothing is **filed** nebulously by division, department or section only but by a **person's** name in that portion. Example: a report concerning the "Organization Division" is **filed** in the folder of the actual name of the Org Sec. A report concerning the "Department of Tech Services" is **filed** under the actual name of the Director of Tech Services. The **Personnel** Officer puts a separate copy of any SEC ED, Admin Letter or Ethics Order into the folder of every person it mentions. Copies of all contracts, agreements or legal papers connected with the **person** are filed in the org **personnel files.** The originals are kept in Val Docs. The org **personnel file** is used for purposes of promotion and any needful reorganization and so should contain anything that throws light on the efficiency, inefficiency or character of **personnel.** The org **personnel file** is consulted by ethics to determine whether or not a **personnel's** statistics are up or down. (HCO PL 4 Sept 65) **2.** these **files** contain basic data and all relevant information on each individual which is sometimes of a confidential nature as well. (FSO 611) **3.** all conditions assigned by Base and Flag Orders are to be plainly noted on a card in the **person's file.** A commendation wipes out previous condition cards but the **file** is never destroyed. The **file** is divided into three categories, past **personnel,** current **personnel,** future or aspirant **personnel.** These are separate **files.** A **file** folder exists for each name. Into it is also placed appointments, copies of certs and awards as issued by the Sea Org. (FO 160) **4.** there should be two sections in the **personnel files:** (1) present employees, (2) past employees. Keep a **file** folder for each person employed by the org. Folder to contain date employment started, date of birth, permanent address, local address, next of kin, qualifications, name of post or posts held and dates held, date employment ceased and any other pertinent data, plus test copies. (HCOB 27 Jan 58)

PERSONNEL FILES, file folders containing all pertinent data related to specific staff members such as test scores, personnel profile, performance records, previous work experience, etc. Also called a personnel jacket.

PERSONNEL JACKET, see PERSONNEL FILES.

PERSONNEL MANAGEMENT, see MANAGEMENT, PERSONNEL.

PERSONNEL PLACEMENT, the function of placing employees as appropriately and effectively as possible into available positions.

PERSONNEL POINTS STAT, (HCO GDS) the **personnel points stat** consists of: total number of **points** for all org **personnel** from categories, (i.e. Staff Status II = 3 points, Class IV = 10 points, Clear = 20 points) minus, for Class IV Orgs, -5 **points** for each non-contracted staff, for AO/SH Orgs -10 **points** for each non-SO contracted staff. (BPL 5 Apr 73R)

PERSONNEL PROCUREMENT, recruiting and hiring. (BPL 3 Apr 73R II)

PERSONNEL PROCUREMENT OFFICER, **Personnel Procurement Officer** recruits in volume while safeguarding the org from those who have been institutionalized, are insane, or who do not meet the standard requirements of a new staff member. (HCO PL 15 Aug 71) *Abbr.* PPO.

PERSONNEL PROGRAMMER, (Correction Division) **Personnel Programmer** interviews and obtains data from all staff, then **programs** them on the meter, in a gradient of wins, to be fully on post, developing its skills and know-how, and channelling staff into higher achievements through full utilization of all study technology. Quickly corrects programs which are not getting done. (BPL 7 Dec 71R I)

PERSONNEL PROGRAMMING, successful **programming** is shown by the **program** actually getting completed, staff members winning and upstat. The steps of **personnel programming** are: (a) gather data on the **person,** his post and study, (b) evaluate this data, (c) draw up a **program,** (d) interview the staff member on the meter with the **program** and all data to hand, and ensure it is correct. Make any needed changes, to F/N VGIs. (BTB 23 Oct 71RA II)

PERSONNEL PROGRAMMING ADVANCE PROGRAM, the **Personnel Programming Advance Program** is that **program** which lays out the steps necessary to get the **person** fully on post. (HCOB 23 Oct 71 I)

PERSONNEL PROGRAMMING REPAIR PROGRAM, the **Personnel Programming Repair Program** is that which designates **repair** training actions on past posts in order to make the current post occupiable, or short **repair** actions which are interjected into the current post advance **program,** to handle a situation on the **person's** post. (HCOB 23 Oct 71 I)

PERSONNEL REQUISITION, see REQUISITION, PERSONNEL.

PERSONNEL RESEARCH, see RESEARCH, PERSONNEL.

PERSONNEL REVIEW, a regular meeting of a group of seniors to review and evaluate employees' performances, update their knowledge and considerations, and determine anew the status of each employee discussed.

PERSONNEL SECTION, 1. in Department 1, Department of Routing, Appearances and **Personnel. Personnel** interviews all new **personnel,** keeps **personnel** roster, handles staff status matters, routes staff to review, compiles and issues hat folders. (HCO PL 17 Jan 66 II) **2.** purpose: to maintain at all times a complete and accurate record of present and past employees of the organization. (HCOB 27 Jan 58)

PERSONNEL SELECTION, the choosing of the most qualified person available for the position open, the decision being based, usually, on a combination of job history and past performance, degree of current skills, any test results and general attitude shown during interviews.

PERSONNEL TRAINING COORDINATOR, (Central Personnel Office hat) goals: to ensure that all **personnel** are well **trained** before placing, and that all **personnel** are continuously and adequately **trained** able to do any job at any level of management at any time. Purpose: to **coordinate** the **personnel training** activities of all orgs, so that a high standard of **training** takes place in volume. (FO 3332)

PERSONNEL UNIT, it is independent of the Bureaux or Divisions. An I/C and clerk are appointed to it. The title of the I/C is Flag Personnel Procurement Officer. The clerk's title is FPPO Communicator. The purpose of this **unit** is to assemble and compile data necessary to get veterans' reliefs trained and veterans replaced in orgs and to get **personnel** to Flag and to keep a continuous flow of highest quality **personnel** to Flag without injury of SO orgs or income. (FSO 44R)

PERSON TO PERSON, type of call. **Person to person** is when you place a call for a certain **person** through the operator and this is the most expensive of all. (HCO PL 15 Nov 74)

PERT, program evaluation and review techniques.

PERVERT THE LINE, to alter the communications which are going on **the line.** (BPL 5 Aug 59)

PES ACCOUNT, since the beginning of Scn no real special allocation has ever been made to promotion that the Public Division could call their own. The **PES Account** is now created based on the idea that: if the public divisions make it the public divisions get it to make more of it. The **account** is operated as any other account, by Division 3. Every month Division 3 forwards an exact accounting of the **PES Account** expenditures and deposits to the PES of the org. (HCO PL 12 Nov 69 II) [The above HCO PL was cancelled by BPL 10 Oct 75 VII.]

PES WW ACCOUNT, the purpose of this **account** is to enable the Franchise Section WW, through the availability of funds, to expand and improve their services with regard to franchises in the field. Of the total monies received from franchise 10%s at WW each week, 5% of the total amount is automatically deposited to this account. The allocation of monies from this **account** lies at the discretion of the **PES WW**, Distribution Sec WW and Franchise Officer WW with regard to what promotional action will boost stats such as the mailing of an FSM advice letter or FSM material packs. (HCO PL 10 Dec 69 III) [The above HCO PL was cancelled by BPL 10 Oct 75 VII.]

PETITION, 1. it is the oldest form of seeking justice and a redress of wrongs and it may well be that when it vanishes a civilization deteriorates thereby. Any one individual has the right to **petition** in writing any senior or official no matter how high and no matter by what routing. Only one person may **petition** on one matter or the **petition** must be refused. Threat included in a request for justice, a favor or redress deprives it of the status of **petition** and it must be refused. Discourtesy or malice in a request for justice, a favor or redress deprives it of the status of **petition** and it must be refused. If a **petition** contains no request it is not a **petition.** A **petition** is itself and is not a form of recourse and making a **petition** does not use up one's right to recourse. (HCO PL 29 Apr 65 II) **2.** a polite request to have something handled by the Office of LRH or the org. If it is not polite it is not a **petition** and is not covered by the **Petition** Policy Letters. An impolite **petition** is handled as an entheta letter always. (HCO PL 7 Jun 65, *Entheta Letters and the Dead File, Handling of, Definition*)

PETITION, 1. a formal written document to a person or group in authority asking that a right or a privilege be granted to the originator. 2. in law, a formal written application requesting that a special judicial action be taken by a court, such as a petition of appeal.

PETTY OFFICER, 1. the title of **petty officer** is given to a crew member for doing a job or post well, taking responsibility in an area and as a recognition for his applied ability, knowledge and skill in seamanship and Scientology tech and admin. The purpose of a **petty officer** is: to be an experienced able Sea Org member able to command any situation and to be a trusted and valuable terminal for officers and men alike. One usually starts as **Petty Officer** 3rd class (most junior), then by continuing and adding to his good work he can expect to work his way up through the ranks to 2nd, 1st and Chief **Petty Officer.** A **petty officer** is an able being. He's alert to dangers at sea and on his post. He can command a situation where experience and leadership is needed. He's bright, smart, knows what he's doing and is a leader of men. (FO 1978) **2.** head of a section. (FO 196) **3. petty officers** are Third Class (lowest), Second Class and First Class and Chief **Petty Officers.** (FO 922) *Abbr.* PO_3, PO_2, PO_1 and CPO.

PETTY OFFICER COUNCIL, is not concerned with org management and operation. It is concerned with the conduct and responsibility of Sea Org petty officers and members, and maintenance of basic Sea Org traditions. The purpose of the **POC** is: to assist the Commodore by ensuring Sea Org **petty officers** carry out the responsibilities of their rating and maintain the high traditions of the Sea Organization. (FO 3311-1) *Abbr.* POC

PETTY OFFICERS' CONFERENCE, there will be a **Petty Officers' Conference** on the org board under HCO conferences section, Dept 20, Div 7, which will convene once every week. It will be headed by an elected chairman and secretary with two deputies each, one on port and one on starboard. The purpose of this group will be to hold the command line and back up the ship's officers. It shall employ a target board for its projects which is posted in the **petty officers'** mess and facilities must be available for such. (FO 1682)

PHASE I, phase I—beginning a new activity. An executive single-hands while he trains his staff. When he has people producing, functioning well and hatted he then enters the next phase: phase II—running an established activity. (HCO PL 28 July 71)

PHASE II, phase II—running an established activity. An executive gets people to get the work done. (HCO PL 28 Jul 71)

PHILOSOPHY, *n.* derivation: from Latin *philosophia;* Greek *philosophia,* from Greek *philosophos,* from *philos,* (loving), and *sophos,* (wise). Originally, love of wisdom and knowledge. A study of the process governing thought and conduct; theory or investigation of the principles or laws that regulate the physical universe and underlie all knowledge and reality; included in the study are aesthetics, ethics, logic, metaphysics, etc. The general principles or laws of a field of knowledge, activity, etc.; as the **philosophy** of economics. (a) a particular system of principles for the conduct of life; (b) a treatise covering such a system. A study of human morals, character and behavior. The mental balance believed to result from this; calmness; composure. (BPL 6 Mar 69)

PHONE GI, total monies regged over the **phone** and gotten to base (Flag base) for the week. (BFO 119)

PHOTO SHOOT ORG, LRH, 1. Ron has worked throughout this year (1975) on priority programs designed to accelerate the already spectacular expansion of Scn. One of these programs has been the Dissemination Program. Already a master professional photographer, Ron set up the **LRH Photo Shoot Org** to help him in this program. Scripts were written based on surveys, shooting sets, props and models were acquired and set up and soon this program was in high roaring production. (FBDL 585) **2.** an **organization** in the Office of LRH that produces tapes, films, video and artistic dissemination products such as brochures, etc. (BFO 122-6) *Abbr.* PSO.

PHRENOLOGY, reading the bumps on people's skulls to tell their character. That's where psychology came from in the first place and why they eventually went deeper and thought it was the brain. (ESTO 3, 7203C02 SO I)

PHYSICAL EFFORT, the body energy level and endurance required to effectively perform a job or activity.

PHYSICAL FATIGUE, see FATIGUE, PHYSICAL.

PICKETING, the action of a labor union placing persons outside a business where there is a strike to try to prevent customer patronage or other persons from working until the strike is resolved.

PICTURE CONTINUITY, see PICTURE PANEL.

PICTURE PANEL, a comic book or picture continuity, used principally in public relations work, as a novel way to communicate ideas, product information or a service to a specific public.

PIECE-RATE, the rate established by a company at which it will pay employees per completed product component or unit. Also called piece-wage.

PIECE-RATE FORMULA, the formula states that earnings are equal to the number of pieces completed by the employee times the established rate of pay per piece.

PIECE WAGE, see PIECE-RATE.

PIECE-WORK, work that is paid for according to a specified rate per piece completed.

PIE CHART, see CHART, PIE.

PIGGYBACK, 1. a system of transporting loaded truck trailers on railroad flatcars which reduces the amount of loading and unloading of freight. 2. an advertising term for the placement of radio or TV advertisements consecutively such as two 45-second commercials appearing one after the other.

PILFERING, petty thievery in business firms of small items or amounts by employees.

PILOT PRODUCTION, see PRODUCTION, PILOT.

PILOT PROJECTS, in new programs the bugs have not been worked out. It's like a newly designed piece of machinery. The clutch slips or the horse power is sour. New programs are undertaken on a small scale as **pilot projects.** If they work out, good. Spot the bugs, streamline them and prove them. Only then is it all right to give them out as broad orders. (HCO PL 25 Oct 68)

PINCH TEST, for demos, you can do a **pinch test** where you explain to the pc that, to show him how the meter registers mental mass, you will give him a **pinch** as part of the demo. Then get him to think of the **pinch** (while he is holding the cans) showing him the meter reaction and explaining how it registers mental mass. (BTB 8 Jan 71R)

PINK INVOICE, 1. these **invoice** copies are the consecutive series to be kept in the machine until the end of the accounting week. (Invoice routing for all orgs except Saint Hill.) (HCO PL 16 Feb 66) **2. pink invoice** copies are distributed to the department concerned with the service or item purchased. (Saint Hill only.) (HCO PL 13 Oct 66)

PINK SHEETS, pink foolscap size paper. At the top of the **sheet** write the name of the student, student auditor or coach being observed, the date and the name of the observer. Head a wide column on the right hand side of the **sheet** with "observations," a narrow column to the left of center with "theory and practical assignment" and two more narrow columns on the left hand side with "coach" and "supervisor." They are used to improve the student's study, auditing or coaching ability by having him thoroughly learn data and practical skills he is weak in. (BPL 27 Sept 63RA)

PLACEMENT, 1. the act of placing a particular person on a particular job in an organization. 2. referring to a service offered by employment agencies whereby for a fee they find jobs best suited to clients who desire employment.

PLACEMENT DEPARTMENT, a business or company department whose purpose is to place employees in jobs according to individual abilities, skills, temperament and personal interest.

PLAINTEXT, the message in clear without code or cipher. (HCO PL 11 Sept 73)

PLAN(S), 1. short range broad intentions as to the contemplated actions envisaged for the handling of a broad area to remedy it or expand it or to obstruct or impede an opposition to expansion. A **plan** is usually based on observation of potentials (or resources) and expresses a bright idea of how to use them. It *always* proceeds from a real why if it is to be successful. (HCO PL 29 Feb 72 II) **2.** the general bright idea one has to remedy the *why* found and get things up to the ideal scene or improve even that. (HCO PL 29 Feb 72 II) **3. plans** are not targets. All manner of **plans** can be drawn and can be okayed. But this does not authorize their execution. They are just **plans.** When and how they will be done and by whom has not been established, scheduled or authorized. You could **plan** to make a million dollars but if when, how and who were not set as targets of different types, it just wouldn't happen. (HCO PL 18 Jan 69 II) **4.** a **plan,** by which is meant the drawing or scale modeling of some area, project, or thing, is of course a vital necessity in any construction and construction fails without it. A **plan** would be the design of the thing itself. (HCO PL 18 Jan 69 II)

PLANNED ECONOMY, see CONTROLLED ECONOMY.

PLANNING, 1. the overall target system wherein all targets of all types are set. That would be complete **planning.** (HCO PL 18 Jan 69 II) **2. planning** includes imaginative conception and intelligent timing, targeting and drafting of the **plans** so they can be communicated and assigned. (HCO PL 14 Sept 69) **3.** includes writing mission orders or program orders, and includes specifications—material, personnel, etc., which will be required. Includes production targets. This is completed **planning.** (FO 2261)

PLANNING, 1. an activity of business programming to work out beforehand the sequential steps necessary to attain an objective or goal, usually taking into consideration past and present performance as well as future needs. 2. a systematic way of thinking in which ideas are arranged in orderly outline taking an endeavor from present time onward to a given point or conclusion, and which may encompass either short or long range goals.

PLANNING AND COORDINATING OFFICER, see TRIANGULAR SYSTEM.

PLANNING, BUSINESS, any planning that tends to set the future course of a business. This could take the form of a detailed analysis of the company's performance up to now, looking at current market trends and demands to assess the necessity of research and development, an examination of the company's potential to meet future production demands and a realistic look at methods of marketing and distribution. Business planning should culminate in a positive program designed to ethically benefit the company.

PLANNING, CONTINGENCY, specific planning against a possible emergency in the future.

PLANNING, CORPORATE, all-inclusive long-range planning involving the whole company. Corporate planning attempts to project what future economic conditions will be, what products will be in demand then and what changes would have to be made over a period of time to meet future demands and conditions. Often corporate planning will result in a company setting up a pilot or research project or even expanding the scope of such, already existing, in order to stay in touch with future demands and conditions and test new ideas.

PLANNING DEPARTMENT, (Ship Org Board) Dept 4 **Planning Department** will have the functions of writing, research, planning—figuring out what is to be sent out where. Will also contain a CIC Liaison and Ad Council Conference. (FO 976)

PLANNING MEMBER, in a small committee or conference the **planning member** is the chairman. Where there is a **planning member** in the general line-up of posts, **planning** is his hat. (FO 2409)

PLANNING OFFICER, the Executive Director is the fellow that the Product Officer and the Organizing Officer meet with in order to plan up what they're going to do. Then the basic team action which occurs, occurs after a **planning** action of this particular character. Where you have the Product Officer who is also the Executive Director, he is also the **Planning Officer.** He's double hatted. (FEBC 12, 7102C03 SO II)

PLANNING, PRODUCT, planning related to the development, modification, production and sales of products. Product planning utilizes market research, public opinion surveys, sales statistics, etc., to determine what products to introduce or develop, what designs, features or modifications to incorporate in products, what quantity to produce, what price to charge, what markets to develop or utilize, etc. Product planning is a similar term to product strategy but the latter implies a strategy resulting from product planning.

PLANNING, PRODUCTION, any planning that considers how to increase the quality, quantity, viability and sales of a product or service. It includes a knowledge of current productive capacity and planning and scheduling of increased production to meet demands or planning how to increase the market demand first if necessary and how to then increase production to fulfill the created demand.

PLANNING, PROFIT, the establishing of a business operating system that has as its dominant factor the realization of specific profit goals.

PLANNING, SALES, any planning that plots how to maintain and increase sales. It includes setting sales targets for each sales territory, deciding on the scope and timing of advertising campaigns, where to concentrate or how to distribute one's marketing effort and sales force, what sales training to implement in order to increase the efficiency of the sales force, etc.

PLANNING, SALES PROMOTION, planning which results in a program of how much sales promotion one needs to engage in and how it will have to be used in order to meet the sales targets.

PLANNING SECTION, any section that plans out the future activities of some aspect of a company but often it is a section that plans out the work schedules in order to meet a delivery date.

PLANS CHIEF, (Ship Org Board) in the 2nd Division, which is the Preparation and Planning Division, we have the **Plans Chief** in Department 4, who has the development of ideas and **plans** for profitable operation, all ship's **plans,** drawings, key maps, charts, **planning** reference book library, all notes, sketches and copies of **plans,** completeness of detail and requirement, and evaluation activity of them. (FO 1109)

PLANT, the land, buildings, machinery, installation, etc., composing a business. The fixed assets of a business.

PLANT BARGAINING, see BARGAINING, PLANT.

PLANT LAYOUT, see LAYOUT.

PLANT TOUR, usually a guided tour of the general public or a select public around a company plant, factory, etc., to increase public relations or enhance business. It may be part of an open house event.

PLAY THE ORG BOARD, a very good executive knows how to **play the org board** under him. He has to know every function in it. He has to know who to call on to do what or he disorganizes things badly. (HCO PL 28 Jul 71)

PLAY THE PIANO, 1. if a person who could not **play** a **piano** sat down at a **piano** and hit random keys, he would not get any harmony. He would get noise. If the head of a division gave orders to his staff without any regard to their assigned posts or duties, the result would be confusion and noise. That's why we say a division head doesn't know how to **play the piano** when he knows so little about org form that he continually violates it by giving his various staff members duties that do not match their hats or posts. (HCO PL 28 Jul 72) **2.** meaning demand the proper duties of the right posts. (OODs 28 Dec 74) **3.** the Executive Director of an org must **play the piano.** By this is meant he must ensure *all* the parts of the organization are working according to policy. (SO ED 418 INT) **4.** if the fellow cannot **play the piano** (that is to say regulate the division) why he won't get it producing. (ESTO 11, 7203C06 SO I)

PLEDGE, 1. the act of a debtor giving a creditor custody of something qualifying as security or collateral until a loan or debt is paid or an obligation is fulfilled. 2. a written agreement or contract whereby a debtor agrees to turn over such collateral to a creditor including a statement of any conditions agreed between the parties involved.

PLEDGED SECURITIES, securities pledged as collateral to guarantee payment of a debt.

PLURAL-VOTING STOCK, see STOCK, PLURAL-VOTING.

PLUS-POINT, plus-points are very important in evaluation as they show where logic exists and where things are going right or likely to. The following is a list of **plus-points** which are used in evaluation. Related facts known (all relevant facts known). Events in correct sequence (events in actual sequence). Time noted (time is properly noted). Data proven factual (data must be factual, which is to say, true and valid). Correct relative importance (the important and unimportant are correctly sorted out). Expected time period (events occurring or done in the time one would reasonably expect them to be). Adequate data (no sectors of omitted data that would influence the situation). Applicable data (the data presented or available applies to the matter in hand and not something else). Correct source (not wrong source). Correct target (not going in some direction that would be wrong for the situation). Data in same classification (data from two or more different classes of material not introduced as the same class). Identites are identical (not similar or different). Similarities are similar (not identical or different). Differences are different (not made to be identical or similar). In doing evaluations to find why things got better so they can be repeated, it is vital to use the actual **plus-points** by name as above. They can then be counted and handled as in the case of out-points. **Plus-points** are, after all, what makes things go right. (HCO PL 3 Oct 74)

PLUS-POINT EVALUATIONS, a **plus-point evaluation** shows what boomed the place and the targets necessary to reassert the boom. (OODs 23 Jan 76)

POA, power of attorney.

POACHING, unethically procuring trained personnel from other firms instead of setting up one's own facilities to train personnel.

POINT, a unit of measurement of value in the investment field where (a) one point = $1 with reference to shares of stock, (b) one point = $10 with reference to bonds and (c) one point = one point (not equivalent to $1) with reference to market averages such as the Dow-Jones industrial average rising by one point.

POINT OF INFORMATION, a question put to the chairman of a conference requesting clarification of a point currently being discussed or requesting to make a brief statement to clarify such a point.

POINT OF ORDER, a question raised by a member as to whether the agreed upon rules of parliamentary procedures are being followed at a meeting or conference.

POINT OF PERSONAL EXPLANATION, a question put to the chairman of a conference requesting to explain one's personal position related to an issue in order to clear up any points on which he believes he has been or will be misunderstood.

POINTS SYSTEM, see STUDENT POINTS.

POLICE, to control, regulate, keep in order, administer. (BPL 1 Feb 72 I)

POLICIES, COMPANY, a broad term to cover any rules, procedures or methods of operation that the top management of an organization has established as the best means to realize the company's goals and purposes.

POLICIES, COMPANY LABOR, the definite organizational commitments made by management with respect to its labor force, employment terms and conditions.

POLICIES, DEPARTMENTAL, policies which delineate the purpose, position, procedures, responsibilities, authorities and products of each department or similar unit in relation to the whole organization.

POLICIES, MANPOWER, policies with respect to the intentions of management toward its labor force with specific commitments made in order to satisfactorily reach stated management/manpower goals.

POLICIES, MARKETING, principles and applicable data guiding the actions of a company advantageously in dealing with various market conditions.

POLICIES, OPERATING, specific rules or procedures established by an organization in regard to its methods of operation. These would chiefly be policies related to maintaining the overall production, distribution and sales of its products.

POLICIES, WAGE, the established rules, procedures or methods of operation that an organization will follow in setting the amount of wages paid, handling grievances related to wages, or engaging in any programs or practices relating to wages.

POLICY, **1. policy** as a word has many definitions in current dictionaries amongst which only one is partially correct: "a definite course or method of action to guide and determine future decisions." It is also "prudence or wisdom," "a course of action," and a lot of other things according to the dictionary. It even is said to be laid down at the top. Therefore the word has so many other meanings that the language itself has become confused. Yet, regardless of dictionary fog, the word means an exact thing in the specialized field of management and organization. **Policy** means the principle evolved and issued by top management for a specific activity to guide planning and programming and authorize the issuance of projects by executives which in turn permit the issuance and enforcement of orders that direct the activity of personnel in achieving production and viability. **Policy** is therefore a principle by which the conduct of affairs can be guided. (HCO PL 25 Nov 70) **2.** long-range truths or facts which are not subject to change expressed as operational rules or guides. (HCO PL 29 Feb 72 II) **3.** a **policy** is the law on which orders are authorized and originated. (FO 2627RA) **4.** all **policies** actually derive in greater or lesser degree from group experience which more or less adds up to group agreement and **policies** which tend to stay along are actually formed with group agreement and are therefore not outside the perimeter of the group. (7012C04 SO) **5.** the rules of the game, the facts of life, the discovered truths and the invariable procedures. (HCO PL 29 Feb 72 II) **6. policy** is such things as the organizing board, hats. It is how to write letters. It is how to get the show on the road, keep it there and handle the bumps. **Policy** is the broad general outline originated by top management. Orders are the instructions issued by the next lower level of management to get things done that result in products. (FBDL 12) **7. policy** is a growing thing, based on "what has worked." What works *well* today becomes tomorrow's **policy.** (HCO PL 13 Mar 65 II) **8. policy** is derived from successful experience in forwarding the basic purposes, overcoming opposition or enemies, ending distractions and letting the basic purpose flow and expand. (HCO

Police

PL 13 Mar 65, *Divisions 1, 2, 3 The Structure of Organization What is Policy?*) **9. policy** is a guiding thing. It is composed of ideas to make a game, procedures to be followed in eventualities and deterrents to departures. The basic **policy** of an activity must be the defining and recommending of a successful and desirable basic purpose. (HCO PL 13 Mar 65, *Divisions 1, 2, 3 The Structure of Organization What is Policy?*) **10.** a rule or procedure or a guidance which permits the basic purpose to succeed. (HCO PL 13 Mar 65, *Divisions 1, 2, 3 The Structure of Organization What is Policy?*) **11.** political wisdom or cunning; diplomacy; prudence; artfulness. Wise, expedient, or crafty conduct or management. Any governing principle, plan or course of action. The last definition is the one we use. (HCO PL 5 Mar 65 II) **12.** a plan of action; way of management, practical wisdom; prudence. Political skill or shrewdness. Obsolete—the conduct of public affairs; government. (HCO PL 5 Mar 65 II) **13.** the sense in which we use **policy** is the rules and administrative formulas by which we agree on action and conduct our affairs. (HCO PL 5 Mar 65 II) **14.** a method of bringing about agreement and communication along certain matters which lead to a higher level of survival. They lead to a higher level of survival if they are good **policies,** they lead to a lower level of survival if they are poor **policies** and they lead to complete disaster if they are bad **policies.** (SH Spec 39, 6409C15) **15. policy** came from years and years of experience. It's the know-how of handling orgs and groups. (OODs 18 Aug 75) **16.** that is what makes the team. It is simply the extant agreement and if there isn't an extant agreement then you have individualized action. (SH Spec 57, 6504C06) **17. policy** is derived from successful actions and is the agreed upon way that the actions of the group are carried out successfully. These actions are in written form and are followed exactly. (BPL 4 Jul 69R VI)

POLICY KNOWLEDGE BUREAU, the Tech Bureau and **Policy Knowledge Bureau** of the GO have just been phased out. Any personnel posted in the **Policy Knowledge Bureau** in any Guardian Office are transferred to the LRH Comm Office. LRH Comms are now responsible for the correct use and the actual use and application of **policy** in orgs. Therefore any GO personnel or materiel or hats on this subject should be transferred to the Office of the LRH Comm. The main purpose of this transfer came from an evaluation in which it was found that **policy** responsibility was transferred to the Guardian Office and that this is primarily an internal org function. LRH Comms are therefore responsible for the tech quality and the exact application of HCOBs. They are also responsible for **policy knowledge** and use. To the degree that **policy** letters are in active use in the org, the org expands and prospers. (LRH ED 205 INT)

POLICY LETTER, see HUBBARD COMMUNICATIONS OFFICE POLICY LETTER.

POLICY-MAKING, the act of envisioning the already established goals and purposes of a business and formulating workable rules, procedures and methods of operation to attain them now and in the future.

POLICY MANUAL, see MANUAL, POLICY.

POLICY ONE, see ORG POLICY NUMBER ONE.

POLITICIAN, someone who handles people. Even the word means "people." (HCO PL 11 May 71 II)

POLITICS, the study of ideal social organization—not, as is so often supposed, the art of staying in office. It is more the total complex of relations between men in society. This also includes the people taking part—monarchy, aristocracy, democracy, socialism, liberalism, conservatism, etc. (*B&C,* p. 16)

POOL, an agreement to eliminate competition between several companies by agreeing to such things as price control, limited production or setting up different territories for each to sell their products in.

POOL, OUTPUT, an agreement between several companies, usually engaged in manufacturing the same or similar products, to limit the amount of a product manufactured and establish how much each will be allowed to produce.

POOL, PATENT, a compact among several organizations to share the use of patents, sometimes directed to having monopoly of a product and restricting further competition.

POOL, PRICE AND PROFIT, an agreement between several companies to set the prices charged for their products and establish what percentage of the profits each company will receive.

POOL, TERRITORIAL, an agreement between several companies to establish separate and exclusive territories where each will market their goods.

POPULATION SURVEY, a **population survey** is very simple to do. All you are trying to find out is what the public wants and considers valuable. (BPL 25 Jan 72R)

PORT, 1. (a) a town having a harbor for ships (b) the harbor or waterfront district of a city (c) a place of anchorage or shelter. (FO 3396) **2.** the left-hand side of a ship looking forward toward the bow, opposite to starboard. (FO 2674)

PORT CAPTAIN, 1. the **Port Captain** and his division are responsible for the PR area control of **ports** which the ship frequents or which she plans to visit. His is a ship's Division VI activity. (FO 3396) **2.** a division—Division 6—was developed which contains the Ship's Representative and PR terminals external and internal. This division is headed by the **Port Captain.** (FO 3392) **3.** the original reason for the creation of the post of **Port Captain** is to permit the Captain to attend to ship duties and to unburden him from the strain of maintaining as well full **port** relations. When the ship is in **port,** the **Port Captain** is in effect the

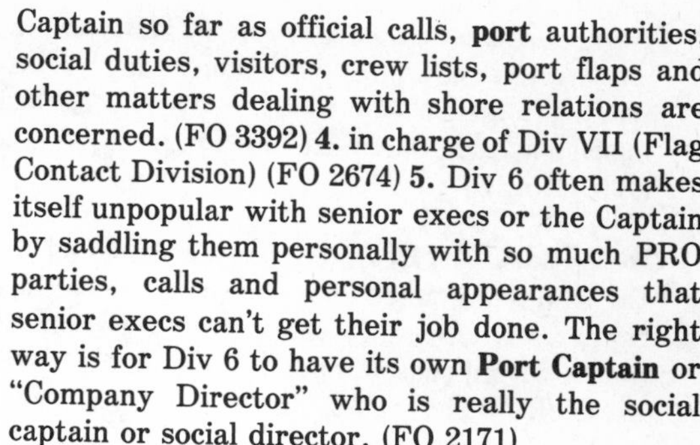

Captain so far as official calls, **port** authorities, social duties, visitors, crew lists, port flaps and other matters dealing with shore relations are concerned. (FO 3392) **4.** in charge of Div VII (Flag Contact Division) (FO 2674) **5.** Div 6 often makes itself unpopular with senior execs or the Captain by saddling them personally with so much PRO parties, calls and personal appearances that senior execs can't get their job done. The right way is for Div 6 to have its own **Port Captain** or "Company Director" who is really the social captain or social director. (FO 2171)

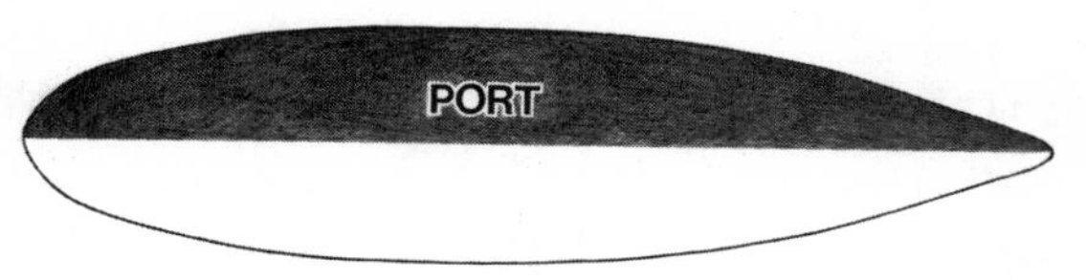

Port (Side) (Def. 2)

PORT CAPTAIN'S OFFICE, 1. Division Six of Flagship Org. (OODs 11 Oct 73) **2. Port Captain** is the **office** concerned with public contacts and public relations, ashore and aboard. (FO 2796-13) **3.** works very hard to keep the shore in ever better condition, with the target of not just safe ports, but of winning countries. (FO 2796-14) **4.** is responsible for safe **ports** for the ship. By standard actions, it protects the ship so that on board business can occur. (FO 3121)

PORTFOLIO, a list of all the stocks, bonds, securities, etc., held by an individual investor, bank, investment organization, etc., the composite holdings themselves.

PORTMANTEAU, 1. portmanteau—originally a stiff leather bag divided into sections. **Portmanteau** word—a word made up from combination of two words of similar form and meaning, e.g. smog—smoke and fog. (FO 2519) **2.** to jam two or

Port (Def. 1)

three missions into one. (7007C15 SO) **3.** it means putting everything in the same bag, **portmanteauing** mission orders, whereby an organizing mission is also made into an operating mission. (7007C15 SO)

PORT READINESS, **port readiness** consists of the ship being made useful in the **port,** her boats, properly equipped, in the water for use and her **ports,** within reason, open and adequate facilities available. (BO 125, 7 Aug 67)

PORT WATCH, see TWO WATCH SYSTEM.

PORT WRITE-UPS, a considerable amount of the expertise which makes a **port** operation a success can be retained for future use of the same and other ships provided the know-how obtained on the first visit is written down. Immediately after a departure from a **port,** the following people particularly are required to make complete **write-ups** on the **port** and forward to Supercargo or Ship's Rep for filing in the **port** folder. They are Supercargo or Ship's Rep, Chief Engineer, Tranport I/C and Communicator, Purser, Dir Supply, Dir Accounts, Chief Steward, 1st Mate, Captain/ Conning Officer, MO, FPO, Hostess, PRO. Anyone else having information on the port should submit a report also. Information contained in these reports should be tabulated and very briefly stated, but should contain every piece of information of note. Examples: price list of chandler, addresses, pilotage dangers, techniques for handling specific terminals. (FO 2068)

POSH OFFICER, **officer** appointed to inspect and enforce a clean ship and E/R. He is located in the Port Captain's Office. He also sets up for events and sees to crew appearance and dress and cleanliness. (ED 240-7 Flag)

Position (Def. 1)

POSITION, **1.** a place or location. It is social standing or status; rank. It is a post of employment; job. (HCO PL 29 Oct 71 II) **2.** a section of a comstation. A slot or box or other receptacle for a communication. There are seven **positions** in every comstation: income, outgo, unack, uncomp, musack, muscomp, and file. (*HTLTAE,* p. 122)

POSITION, in any business it is the name of the particular job one holds which has its own distinguishing duties, responsibilities and products in relation to the other jobs in that business; post title; post; job.

POSITION GUIDE, chiefly a US term for a job description or hat.

POSITIONING, old advertising tech is worn out. So in the '70s they have a new tech called **positioning.** "This means putting a subject (like shaving cream) into a relative **position** with other products. People only remember, they say, by relating one thing to another." "A **position** is where you put a product in somebody's life or mind and in relation to other products." (ED 179 USB)

POSITIVE CASH FLOW, the desirable situation of more money inflowing to a person, business, etc., than is being outflowed. The reverse is called a negative cash flow.

POSITIVE CONTROL, consists entirely of starting, changing and stopping. There are no other factors in **positive control.** If one can start something, change its position in space or existence in time and stop it, all at will, he can be said to **control** it, whatever it may be. (*POW,* p. 43)

POSITIVE POSTULATES, from the viewpoint of **positive postulates** there is no negative aspect. You just skip the whole category of negativism. This has something to do with the granting of beingness. If you can conceive of a **postulate** that doesn't also conceive any negative then you know what I'm talking about when I talk about a **positive postulate.** It's not only that there is no negative given attention to but it does not assume that any negative is possible. It doesn't pay any attention to negatives. It isn't in the **positive**-negative to the degree that there is a dichotomy. It just is itself. Your determination or intention that somebody be a good, effective staff member is of course a **positive postulate.** It will be ineffective to the degree that you doubt it. (ESTO 6, 7203C03 SO II)

POST, **1.** a **post** or terminal is an assigned area of responsibility and action which is supervised in part by an executive. (HCO PL 28 Jul 71) **2.** a position from which a terminal operates in an org, where one knows that somebody is *at*. The one holding it is the stable terminal. (FO 2200) **3.** a **post** in a Scn organization isn't a job. It's a trust and a crusade. (HCOB 21 Sept 58) **4.** a place where there is a communicator running one or more comstations. (*HTLTAE*, p. 122)

POST BOARD, there are really three forms of org boards. There is the functioning org board—the org board of functions, and then there's the org **board** of **posts,** and then there's the org board of complements. Your second form of your **board** is a **post board,** that is to say the **posts** of the org expressed as **posts.** They don't have any name on them. Now that's a **post board** and it may have holes underneath these names to label something into but that is just the **posts.** (ESTO 8, 7203C04 SO II)

POSTED, **posted** does not mean "pinned on a bulletin board." It means "with the persons who hold the **post** named on each **post.**" It goes without saying that the org board is visibly displayed and known. (OODs 28 Oct 70)

POSTED FROM THE TOP DOWN, in 1967 I found that an organization must always be **posted from the top down.** This means it cannot be **posted** with gaps between **the top** or lower levels on the org board. The org, of course, must always have a **top** and there must not be a gap between **the top** and the next lower post or any gaps on the way **down.** Example: an org with a CO or ED, no HAS but only a Master at Arms or Ethics Officer in the HCO Division will not function but disintegrate. (HCO PL 9 May 74)

POSTED ORGANIZING BOARD, the main failure in putting names on an **org board** is that people take the easy way out and try to put a different person's name on each title. This gives you a 100 person division "absolutely vital" while the production is about five man! You take the names you have now in the division and post those to cover all the functions and titles. You post from the top down. You never post from bottom up, and you never leave a gap between persons on lower posts and higher posts. Either of these faults will raise hell in the divisions functioning and are grave faults. Having done this you now have a **posted org board.** (HCO PL 6 Apr 72)

POST HAT, **1. hat** in which the person's **hat** write-up by outgoing persons, policy letters of the **post** and the data about the **post** were kept. (LRH ED 83 INT) **2.** (1) complete write-up of **post** inside cover of **hat,** (2) any bulletins dealing with that **post** arranged chronologically, (3) all Sec'l EDs about that **post** arranged numerically, (4) information about any **posts** that come under that **post.** You may have more than one **post hat.** (SEC ED 58, 27 Jan 59)

POSTING, 1. the transfer of transactional data from the book or original entry to the book of final entry which usually means from a journal to the accounts recorded in a ledger. 2. one's position, job or post in a business.

POSTING NOTICES, each aide is provided with a pack of forms. These are called CIC **posting notices.** While doing his traffic the Aide notes on a form (one datum=one form) the following types of info observed on his lines: (1) good (blue), (2) odd (red), (3) bad (red). Any good bit is written in blue ball point on the **posting notice.** Any odd bit (that he can't dig or doesn't make sense) is written on a **posting notice** in red ball point. Any outness found is written on a **posting notice** in red ball point. All these **posting notices** are routed to CIC **posting.** As they arrive in CIC the Admin Unit (a) staples or pins them on the board of their continental area and (b) puts a pin of matching color in the table map at that geographical location. (FO 2392)

POST ORG BOARD, look over your **post** and you'll see you are running in it, alone, a little **org.** Any **post** has its admin, its preparatory steps, its address and identity files, its plans of procedure, its own tech. There are a lot of these. A **post** is really a small **org** itself. So this is the point we extend the personal org board over into the **post org board.** He can then be budged into the section, the department, the division and the org. (OODs 31 Jan 71)

POST ROUTINE CHECKLIST, each person in the Sea Org is to make a **list** of the actions he/she takes daily on **post** in a **checklist** form. This should help stabilize posts. The **list** does not indicate how the action is taken but simply that it is taken and should be continued. (FO 2043)

POSTULATE, *n.* a self-created truth would be simply the consideration generated by self. Well, we just borrow the word which is in seldom use in the English language, we call that **postulate.** And we mean by **postulate,** self-created truth. He posts something. He puts something up and that's what a **postulate** is. (HPC A6-4, 5608C—) —*v.* in Scn the word **postulate** means to cause a thinkingness or consideration. It is a specially applied word and is defined as causative thinkingness. (*FOT*, p. 71)

POSTULATE CHECKS, 1. the system of promoting a potential customer's **check** against his **"postulate"** that some time in the near future the **check** will be good. And then treating this **postulate check** as real and valid income. It presents a false picture of the actual scene. The **postulate check** system is admitted nowhere in policy as an allowable procedure. Nowhere. You concentrate on real *income;* not on **postulates.** (SO ED 114 INT) **2.** a **check** written against non-existent or inadequate bank balance. A **postulate check** is so named because it is written on the **postulate** that the person will subsequently be able to obtain the money to cover. It amounts to nothing more than a promise to pay. It is not money. A **postulate check** may be in the form of a counter **check** or it may be a regular **check** made on the person's own **check** forms. (CO 1 US, 22 May 71)

POTENTIAL, potential can be ready money or power or even strength. (HCO PL 9 Nov 68)

POTENTIAL EARNINGS, the amount of earnings one has a possibility of making depending on how much work one accomplishes (especially in a payment-by-results or commission system), how much work is available to one, the course of action one takes to secure earnings, etc.

POTENTIAL TROUBLE SOURCE, 1. the **PTS** guy is fairly obvious. He's here, he's way up today and he's way down tomorrow and he gets a beautiful session and then he gets terribly ill. That's the history of his life. If you look into his folder, you will look at a folder summary and you will see that every two or three sessions is a repair. He can't stay on a program. He goes a little distance up the Grade Chart then has to be patched up. It looks like Coney Island—hence rollercoaster. (ESTO 3, 7203C02 SO I) **2.** the main cause of being a **potential trouble source** is being connected with persons (such as marital or familial ties) of known antagonism to Scn. (OODs 4 Jun 71) **3.** those who are connected with the destructively anti-social outside the org. (HCO PL 30 Aug 70) **4.** the mechanism of **PTS** is environmental menace that keeps something continually keyed in. This can be a constant recurring somatic or continual, recurring pressure or a mass. The menace in the environment is not imaginary in such extreme cases. The action can be taken to key it out. But if the environmental menace is actual and persists it will just key in again. This gives recurring pressure unrelieved by usual processing. (HCOB 5 Dec 68) *Abbr.* PTS.

POWER, 1. power is being able to do what one is doing when one is doing it. (HCO PL 3 Apr 72) **2.** a person who is hatted can control his post. If he can control his post he can hold his position in space—in short, his location. And this is **power.** When a person is uncertain, he cannot control his position. He feels weak. He goes slow. (HCO PL 23 Jul 72) **3.** law: the **power** of a thetan stems from his ability to hold a position in space. This is quite true. In *Scientology 8-80* the base of the motor is discussed. It holds two terminals in fixed positions. Because they are so fixed, **power** can be generated. If a thetan can hold a position or location in space he can generate **power.** If he cannot, he cannot generate **power** and will be weak. (HCO PL 29 Jul 71) **4. power** is proportional to the speed of particle flow external and internal in an organization. (FO 747) **5.** the rapidity of particle flow alone determines **power.** (HCO PL 16 Apr 65RA III) **6. power** process(es) (LRH ED 103 INT)

POWER BADGES, all pcs being audited on **power** processes are to wear **power badges** as described below. This **badge** consists of a 3" x 2" white card with the lettering neatly printed on it in black, preferably sheathed in plastic. It is to be issued to the pc and pinned noticeably on a lapel, breast pocket or similar place by pc administrator at the commencement of his **power** processing cycle and collected back when he completes. Text of **badge:** I am on **power** processing. Do not ask me any questions about my case, the processes or my auditing. (BPL 6 Apr 71)

POWER CHANGE, 1. the formula of the **power change** condition is: when taking over a new post **change** nothing until you are thoroughly familiar with your new zone of **power.** (OODs 5 Apr 70) **2.** there are only two circumstances which require replacement, the very successful one or the very unsuccessful one. What a song it is to inherit a successful pair of boots, there is nothing to it, just step in the boots and don't bother to walk. If it was in a normal state of operation, which it normally would have been in for anybody to have been promoted out of it, you just don't change anything. So anybody wants anything signed that your predecessor didn't sign, don't sign it. Keep your eyes open, learn the ropes and depending on how big the organization is, after a certain time, why, see how it is running and run it as normal operating condition if it's not in anything but a normal operating condition. Go through the exact same routine of every day that your predecessor went through, sign nothing that he wouldn't sign, don't change a single order, look through the papers that had been issued at that period of time—these are the orders that are extant, and get as busy as the devil just enforcing those orders and your operation will increase and increase. Now the fellow who walks into the boots of somebody who has left in disgrace had better apply the state of emergency formula to it, which is immediately promote. (HCO PL 23 Sept 67) **3.** a state of **power change** is where you have a company running all right, let us say, but the general manager has been hired by some other company because he has such a successful record, and his job is taken over. (SH Spec 62, 6505C25)

POWER CHANGE VIOLATION FORMULA, to all those who had a **power change,** we must apply the **power change violation formula:** (1) observe, question, and draw up a list of what was previously successful in your area or zone of control. (2) observe and draw up a list of all those things that were unsuccessful in your area in the past. (3) get the successful action *in.* (4) throw the unsuccessful action out. (5) knock off frantically trying to cope or defend. (6) sensibly get back in a working structure. (OODs 4 Apr 70)

POWER FORMULA, (1) the first law of a condition of **Power** is don't disconnect. You can't just deny your connections, what you have got to do is take ownership and responsibility for your connections. (2) the first thing you have got to do is make a record of all of its lines. And that is the only way you will ever be able to disconnect. So on a condition of **Power** the first thing you have to do is write up your whole post. You have made it possible for the next fellow in to assume the state of **power** change. If you don't write up your whole post you are going to be stuck with a piece of that post since time immemorial and a year or so later somebody will still be coming to you asking you about that post which you occupied. (3) the responsibility is write the thing up and get it into the hands of the guy who is going to take care of it. (4) do all you can to make the post occupiable. (HCO PL 23 Sept 67)

POWER OF ATTORNEY, a written document which gives one person the legal right to act on behalf of another. *Abbr.* POA.

POWER OF SOURCE, Ron's new record album, the *Power of Source,* is the first step in reaching the broader public. The pieces on the album, played by the Apollo Stars, are all played in the new sound—Star Sound. (FBDL 420R)

POWER PROCESSES, there are six **power processes.** Use of these **processes** is restricted to Class VIIs. (HCO PL 14 Jun 65)

POWER PROCESS STAFF, mimeo distribution meaning review technical personnel in the Qualifications Division only. (HCO PL 7 May 65)

PRAC BUREAUX, 1. PR Area Control Bureaux. The **PRAC Bureaux** aboard Flag are now known as the Office of Public Affairs. (FO 3280-6) **2.** manages two different activities. (1) **PRAC** shore units. (2) **PRAC** service orgs. The shore units are entirely oriented towards creation of **PR area control.** Service orgs under **PRAC** management do not only create and enhance **PR area control** but also deliver services to publics. (FO 3279-5)

PRAC SERVICE ORGS, see PRAC BUREAUX.

PRAC SHORE UNITS, see PRAC BUREAUX.

PRACTICAL, practical goes through the simple motions. Theory covers why one goes through the motions. (HCO PL 24 Sept 64)

PRACTICAL COACHING, coaching on drills in **practical.** (HCO PL 4 Oct 64)

PRACTICAL EXAMINER, ensures students can apply their theory in a **practical** manner. (HCO PL 15 May 63)

PRACTICAL INSTRUCTOR, assists the **practical** supervisor, handles all **practical** administration and acts as auditing supervisor. (HCO PL 18 Dec 64, *Saint Hill Org Board)*

PRACTICAL SECTION, (training courses) as it has recently been found that theory is more easily confronted than doingness, the **practical section** is created to care for this fact and to make the student confront and do accurate doingness. This **section** may not then become a second theory section where one studies texts. In the **practical section** the student only *does.* Drills and **practical** auditing presence are the whole concentration of this **section.** Any study for it is instantly translated into doingness. (HCO PL 14 May 62)

PRACTICAL SUPERVISOR, 1. the person in charge of the **practical** section is called the **practical supervisor.** This person **supervises** all drills being done by teams of students and gives examinations in another capacity as a **practical** examiner. (HCO PL 14 May 62) **2.** handles all **practical** instruction, acts as auditing **supervisor.** (HCO PL 18 Dec 64, *Saint Hill Org Board)*

PRACTICE MISSION, the **practice mission** orders are written expressly for **mission** school training. They should be done exactly like real **missions** and all standard **mission** briefing and firing actions are to be followed including the use of routing sheets and attestations in Qual. (FO 2508)

PR DUTY OFFICER, ships are by experience visited at all times of the day and night, and since specific PR Department terminals are likely to be asked for, this has the proven result of these terminals either giving up the idea of studying, or of being continually hauled out of study, or of shore terminals being repulsed or left unattended, and none of these results are good. Therefore, the **PR Duty Officer** is established as a Department 4 FSO (or Ship's Div VI) action. The hat of **PR Duty Officer** rotates amongst all Dept 4 personnel, and each person stands one night as **Duty Officer.** The function of **Duty Officer** is to handle anything he can which comes up for the department. (FO 2864)

PRE-AUDITING EXAMINATION, there are two examinations on the Dn Course. The **pre-auditing examination** is done after the student has completed the theory and practical drill sections of the course. The **examination** is standard and has been written up and issued to all Qualifications Divisions in orgs. It must be passed 100% before the student is permitted to audit. (HCO PL 5 May 69 II) [The reference HCO PL was cancelled by HCO PL 29 Jul 72 II, *Fast Flow in Training.*]

PRECLEAR, 1. the church member being audited. (BPL 24 Sept 73RA XIII) **2.** person not yet cleared. (HCO PL 23 May 69) **3. preclears** are persons who have been processed at any organization office or in the field. Anyone who has been processed is therefore classified in the registrar files as **preclear.** (HCO PL 7 Jan 64) **4.** one who is discovering things about himself and who is becoming clearer. (HCO PL 21 Aug 63) *Abbr.* PC.

PRECLEAR ROUTE, the **preclear** progresses up the levels from Grade I to Grade VI or above. He has no formal training, only enough specified education from his auditor to enable him to receive and benefit from the processes of any particular level. (HCO PL 5 May 64)

PRE-CODED QUESTION, a survey question which gives several answers with boxes next to them to check off the correct answer. Surveys employing such questions are easy to tabulate.

PREDICTION, this is the action of weighing all consequences of the projected action; particularly the consequences to other areas of operation; determining the feasibility of the plan for actual execution; final estimation of risks plus costs versus gain. On this basis a recommendation is made or the project is undersigned as-is. (FO 2261)

PREFERRED STOCK, see STOCK, PREFERRED.

PRE-FILE, if you have an ABCD set of stationery boxes and park them on top of the files stuff coming in to be filed, first filed into these ABCD categories and then re-filed into the drawers which are now open will save you a lot of clutter and running back and forth. In other words these ABCD boxes are a **pre-file.** (HCOB 6 Apr 57)

PREMIUM, 1. a sum of money or bonus paid in addition to a regular price, such as a premium paid to a craftsman for excellent work. 2. the amount paid, sometimes in addition to the interest, to obtain a loan. 3. the amount paid, often in installments, for an insurance policy. 4. in merchandising, something offered free or at a greatly reduced price as an inducement to buy something else in the same line at the regular price. 5. the amount paid for an option, contract or franchise. 6. the amount by which a stock or bond may sell above its par or face value. 7. a charge made when a stock is borrowed to make delivery on a short sale.

PRE-OT, by AO PC or **pre-OT** is meant a VA or above. (BPL 12 Sept 72R)

PREPARATION AND PLANNING DIVISION, (Ship Org Board) Division 2. Assists the Supercargo to plan remunerative activities for the entire ship or flotilla which coordinate activities of the organization. (FO 1109)

PREPARATION DEPARTMENT, (Ship Org Board) Div 2 Dept 5. **Preparation Department** is actually the compilation **department,** catalogues, books, etc. It contains the library charts, ship's plans and training functions. (FO 976)

PREPARATIONS BRANCH, (Flag Bureaux Org Board) the Org Bureau is in the business of getting the people and assembling the training materials. To do this it must have a **Preparations Branch** to **prepare** needed materials that may be missing. (CBO 4)

PREPARATIONS CHIEF, Preparations Chief of Department 5 has all specifications, conditions requirements, operational estimates, crew training and drilling, and puts together ideas from Department 4 and trains personnel to carry them out. (FO 1109)

PREPARED LISTS, many years ago I developed a system called **prepared lists.** These isolated the trouble the pc was having in auditing without taxing anyone's imagination and sending the auditor into a figure-figure on the pc. These **prepared lists** were assessed on an E-meter. One took up the biggest read first and then cleaned up all other reads. Time has gone on. The system of **prepared lists** has been expanded to include not only pcs but students and staff. It may have gone overlooked that such lists now include anything that could happen to a pc or student. In other words, **prepared lists** have become very thorough. (LRH ED 257 INT)

PREPARED QUESTION, type of interview. If all else fails, reporters sometimes make up lists of **questions** and send them in writing to news sources with a polite but urgent request for reply. (BPL 10 Jan 73R)

PREPAYMENT, **1.** a **payment** made well in advance of service delivery, whether in the mail or over the counter. **Prepayments** replaces the term "advance payments" for such **payments,** as the former was a misnomer. (HCO PL 15 Sept 71-1 I) **2. prepayments** replaces the term advance payments. (HCO PL 15 Jan 72RA) **3.** payment *well* in advance—not for service to be taken "tomorrow" or "in a few days." (BPL 29 May 70R)

PRE-SCHEDULING BOARD, Tech Services keeps up a **scheduling board** that has on it the name of every pc and student fully paid for a service that has not yet taken that service no matter how far into the future they are advance scheduled. (BPL 9 Jun 73R II)

PRESENCE, the ability to get and hold attention and keep it by continuing to cause an effect. (FO 1851)

PRESENT TIME ORDERS ONLY, a type of dev-t where basic programs or standing **orders** or policy go out by not being enforced. **Present time orders only** are being forwarded or handled. This eventually balls up in a big wad and an organization vanishes. Primary targets go out. (HCO PL 27 Jan 69)

PRESENT VALUE, the value in present time attached to a future incoming cash flow. The present value is calculated as less than the amount of the future incoming cash flow due to money in hand being less risky and more usable.

PRESIDENT, the chief executive of an organization, branch of government, university or board of trustees. In business, the President heads the organization in directing policies originated by a board of directors and is a principal representative for the company in important dealings.

PRE-SORTING, having a series of baskets, one for each letter of the alphabet, into which all particles are **sorted** prior to either filing the particle as in central files (CF) or prior to making an address plate, changing an address plate or tabbing an address plate as in Address. In this fashion all particles can more easily be filed or handled. (HCO PL 5 Feb 71 VI)

PRESS AGENT, an individual who handles particular communication lines of a company regarding publicity or notice for its products, services, personalities, events and operations and who deals directly with the press, answering its questions and holding or arranging press interviews and conferences.

PRESS BOOK, a professional PR who has a "client" always at once constructs a display **book,** and he keeps it added to and up-to-date. The **book** is used to get interviews, bookings, press. Usually it is a loose-leaf big fancy clipping scrapbook. Such a **book** begins with an acceptable story of the group creation which is factual and contains itself PR. There follows **press** cuttings including photos as in the **press.** Such **press** sections go on and on in the **book** as new **press** occurs so other data is sandwiched in between expanses of **press.** Radio and TV appointments or plays are noted or clipped from papers and pasted in. It is of tremendous use and gets bookings and interviews with speed. That it is fat is a big recommendation in itself. No professional PR or booking agent or advance man is ever without a display **book** telling of and selling his client. (HCO PL 18 Mar 74)

PRESS CLIPPINGS, clippings or cut-outs of published material as it appears in newspapers, magazines or other media regarding a company, its products and/or services, special events, personalities, etc.

PRESS CONFERENCE, a meeting between a press agent or other qualified company representative and members of the news media to give them information the company wants them to have and to answer any questions that might arise.

PRESS KIT, a kit containing an assortment of feature stories, photographs, advertising examples and background material on a company, its products and services, prepared for the press' use.

PRESS WORK, this is the actual printing. (FO 3574)

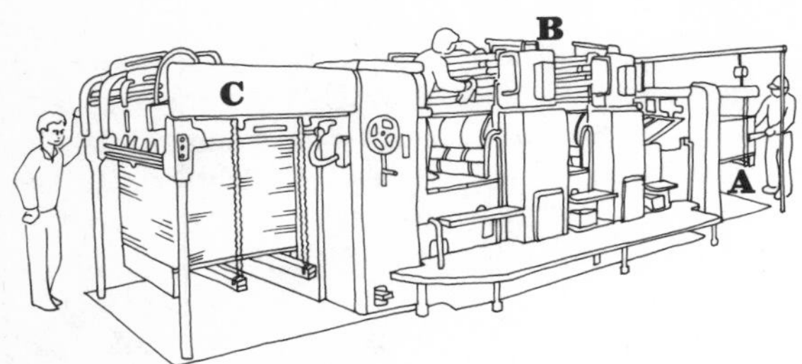

Press Work A. Feeding of Paper B. Printing C. Stacking of Printed Sheets

PRETENSE, 1. a false reason or excuse. A mere show without reality. (HCO PL 3 May 72) **2.** a claim, profession or allegation which is falsely made or assumed or stated. (HCOB 11 May 65)

PREVIOUS QUESTION, in parliamentary procedure, refers to a motion being made that the previous question be put to a vote which, if accepted by the chairman, seconded and carried, causes it to come about immediately.

PRICE, the amount of money that something costs at a specific time in a specific market; the cost to the buyer.

PRICE AND PROFIT POOL, see POOL, PRICE AND PROFIT.

PRICE, CEILING, the maximum price that can be put on something, usually imposed by government regulation in times of war or to ward off severe inflation.

PRICE CONTROLS, the fixing of prices by the government or by private companies, individually or in combination with others, so that market prices change very little or not at all.

PRICE CUTTING, lowering the price of a product or service below what is recognized as normal in order to match competitors' prices or to capture a larger share of the consumers market.

PRICE DISCRETION, the right granted to a salesman to alter the price of a product in order to close a sale.

PRICE-EARNINGS RATIO, the price of a share divided by its earnings for a twelve-month period.

PRICE ELASTICITY, a decrease in sales accompanying a price increase to a product.

PRICE ENGRAM, it's an awful good thing I found *the* **engram** in organizations before we released the new pattern of orgs and began to expand. Had I not found it we would have expanded to insolvency! A few suppressive persons with their "everybody" and "they" have here and there over the years set up a **price engram** ridge between orgs and public. "You charge too much!" "Money." **"Prices** too high!" combined with "everybody thinks" and other generalities have made executives believe that the public won't pay. Not detecting the true reason for this attack, the executive swallowed it whole. The true reason is a suppressive reason—if we don't charge we will vanish. A guilt complex (I won't use a Scn term on anything so low) arose about money. (HCO PL 27 Apr 65 II)

PRICE, EQUILIBRIUM, the selling price of a product which creates enough demand to use up exactly what is produced.

PRICE FIXING, 1. the freezing of prices by a government to control inflation or deflation. 2. the practice of manufacturers who produce the same product setting non-competitive prices. 3. putting a price on something.

PRICE LEADERSHIP, the situation where one company in a group of competing companies leads the way with price increases and the others follow suit.

PRICE LINES, in retailing, the determining of certain prices as unconditional ones at which specific lines of merchandise will be sold.

PRICE LIST, see PRICE SCALE.

PRICE MAKING, see PRICING.

PRICE, MARKET, 1. selling price of a product or service accounted for by total costs involved plus the influence of supply and demand. 2. in investments, it is usually considered to be the last reported price for which the stock or bond sold.

PRICE, NOMINAL, 1. a token price which is not the actual price for which a product or a service is available. 2. a minimal price in comparison to the real value of something.

PRICE, NORMAL, the price that is sufficient to defray all cost plus necessary or accepted profit.

PRICE PLATEAU, the price level for a certain product beyond which the public will not pay.

PRICE, REDEMPTION, 1. the price at which a bond may be turned in before the maturity date, subject to the discretion of the issuing company. 2. price a company must pay to call in particular types of preferred stock.

PRICE RING, a group of manufacturers marketing the same product who agree to charge the same price and not compete on prices.

PRICES AND INCOMES POLICY, the intervention by a government to control the economy by placing restraints on prices and salaries in an effort to curtail inflation.

PRICE SCALE, a standardization of piece rates, usually reached through collective bargaining, accepted for use by companies making similar products. Also called price list.

PRICE SENSITIVE, term applied to a product or service if the consumer demand drops suddenly when its price is raised.

PRICE SYSTEM, 1. an economy which bases the worth of goods and services on monetary values. 2. a comprehensive system of establishing selling price to the trade, especially one which the leaders of an industry advocate.

PRICE WAR, a situation brought about when one seller lowers his price severely so that competitors are forced to match or beat that price.

PRICING, establishing the value in terms of money of a product or service offered for sale. Also called price making.

PRICING, COST PLUS, the practice of establishing the selling price of a product or service by adding a profit sum to costs such as cost plus either a fixed fee or percentage-of-cost fee.

PRICING, DOUBLE, a system of putting two prices on consumer goods and selling the goods at the lower price as an inducement to consumers, thus one often sees goods marked with the regular price and a featured lower price called "our price" referring to the retailer.

PRICING FORMULA, **formula** used in the **pricing** of printed matter from Dissem and Mimeo on Flag. The **formula** is basically "costs times five equal the **price.**" (FSO 780)

PRICING METHODS, there are a number of pricing methods. Most common is to tack on a profit sum to the item's cost before selling it. Other methods include surveying the market to see what consumers will pay or pricing goods according to prices set by rival companies.

PRICING, PENETRATION, the method of introducing a new product at a low selling price to capture quickly as large a part of the market as possible.

PRICING, PRODUCT ANALYSIS, an evaluation made to establish the selling price for a product or service based on realistic production costs, extent of value to the consumer or user and optimum prices to attract the largest possible share of the market.

PRICING, UNIT, establishing and displaying the price of something per unit such as cost per pound or per ounce so that consumers can easily compare the price to that of rival products.

PRIMARY DISTRIBUTION, the original offering or sale of an organization's stock.

PRIMARY EVALUATION, the **evaluation** and the MOs would be at aides level—staff aides. General observation and getting it executed is the business of Operations. In other words operating and bringing into effect the planning is the business of Operations. That is the division of labor. This does not materially change the Ops Bureau but it relieves it from what you might call **primary evaluation.** Now it doesn't relieve it of **evaluation.** You'll suddenly find out that it is very often necessary to **evaluate** something that went on three years ago. What did they do? All right, let's do it. That would be a staff level or a **primary evaluation.** But your secondary evaluation or your operating evaluation (evaluating the org against the MOs that are being executed and missionaire who is in the org) is against the actual conduct of the mission. (7205C18 SO)

PRIMARY RUNDOWN END PHENOMENA, there is an **end phenomena** of an honestly done **Primary Rundown.** A person can read comfortably and instantly translate word data into concepts and so can study accurately and swiftly and can then easily do the actions. (OODs 25 May 72)

PRIMARY TARGET, 1. the organizational, personnel communication type **targets.** These have to be kept *in.* These are the terminals and route and havingness and org board type **targets.** Example: "To put someone in charge of organizing it and have him set remaining **primary targets.**" Or "to re-establish the original communication system which has dropped out." (HCO PL 24 Jan 69) **2.** there is a group of "understood" **targets** which if overlooked, brings about inaction. The first of these is somebody there, then worthwhile purpose, then somebody taking responsibility for the area or action, then form of organization planned well, then form of organization held or re-established, then organization operating. If we have the above "understood" **targets** we can go on but if these drop out or are not substituted for then no matter what **targets** are set thereafter they will go rickety or fail entirely. In the above there may be a continual necessity to reassert one or more of the "understood" **targets** while trying to get further targets going. (HCO PL 16 Jan 69) *Abbr.* PT.

PRIME COSTS, see COSTS, DIRECT.

PRIME RATE, the lowest interest rate charged by banks to commercial enterprises with strong credit ratings.

PRINCIPAL, 1. the amount of money on which one is currently paying or receiving interest. 2. the face value of a note, stock, bond, etc. 3. a person who hires or authorizes an agent to act on his behalf. 4. that person responsible for fulfilling an obligation such as payment of a debt as distinguished from the person who endorses, cosigns, or acts as surety on it.

PRINCIPAL PARTICLE, meaning the most important one for that org. (HCO PL 25 Jul 72)

PRINTER LIAISON, the function of the **Printer Liaison** is found in Dissem Div, Department 5, on the modern org board. When an org uses an outside **printing** firm to **print** a magazine, flyer, etc., the data concerning the function of **Printer Liaison** should be known and used. A good **Printer Liaison,** by comparing prices and being inquisitive, can actually reduce **printing** prices through increasing demand for his work and introducing competitiveness (without third partying) amongst **printers.** (BPL 21 Dec 69) [The reference BPL was cancelled by BPL 29 December 69 Reissued 3 August 75 as BPL cancelled 9 September 1975 *Guide to the Function of Printer Liaison Cancelled.*]

PRINT-THROUGH, the action of one layer of recorded tape, by means of its own magnetic field, **printing** the sound onto the layer of tape below and the layer above. (BPL 16 Sept 71)

PRIORITY MISSIONS, those assigned to accomplish major operational targets or to pilot new operational functions into which the Sea Org can expand. Or are concerning the current targets of Scn as a whole, such as human rights and related areas. (FO 2132)

PRIVATE CORPORATION, see CORPORATION, PRIVATE.

PRIVATE ENTERPRISE, a privately owned business venture or operation not government controlled and usually operating in a free enterprise environment.

PRO AREA CONTROL, 1. PRO (Public Relations Office) Area (port and town and country) **control** (regulate, start change and stop from cause point) is the basic action of the Port Captain's Office (or Div 6 in an org). Customs, immigration, dockmasters, police, officials, town officials, inhabitants, country officials, country inhabitants, and the lines and activities of all these as they affect the ship or org are the subject of **PRO Area Control.** The tech of how this is done is found in the book *Effective Public Relations*, the PR Series Policy Letters, FOs and FSOs. It is a technology. (FO 3094) **2.** keeping the area handled so the org is well thought of no matter how hard this is to do where there is an active enemy or a muddied up field or a hostile press. (LRH ED 49 INT)

PROBATIONARY PERIOD, 1. a trial or test period during which a new employee is allowed to work but is closely monitored to see if he is satisfactory. Usually a person is only a provisional employee during a probationary period and is subject to immediate dismissal if found unsatisfactory or becomes a permanent employee if found satisfactory. 2. any trial or test period during which a new product, process, machine, etc., is tried out often on a limited basis and monitored closely to determine whether to utilize it or discontinue its use.

PROBATIONER STAFF MEMBER, a person who is being employed because we are shorthanded or a person whom we are checking out before putting on as a part-time or temporary **staff member.** This individual can be hired or fired by the department head with the authority of the organization secretary. (SEC ED 75, 2 Feb 59)

PROBLEM, a **problem** is intention counter-intention. It can also be policy counter-policy. (7012C04 SO)

PROCEDURALIZE, the establishment and introduction of procedures or ways of accomplishing something so that a given result or product can be obtained over and over without variation in quality.

PROCEDURE MANUAL, see MANUAL, PROCEDURE.

PROCEEDS, the profits derived from a sale or the money obtained from a fund-raising activity; net profits.

PROCESS, an exact set of steps which when carried out in the order and manner specified will result in some product, subproduct or desired result.

PROCESS CHART, see CHART, PROCESS.

PROCESS ENGINEER, specialist who, using the engineering blueprints furnished him, decides the tool and equipment needs for a job and then prepares notes and instructions for the job planner or person in charge of production operations.

PROCESSING, 1. consists of getting you to look at and break through all the barriers you've erected between yourself and your goals. (HCO Info Ltr 14 Apr 61) **2.** the principle of making an individual look at his own existence, and improve his ability to confront what he is and where he is. (*Aud 23* UK)

PROCESSING ADMINISTRATOR, handles the persons, communications and materials of the HGC to the end of improving and continuing the quality and business of the HGC. (HCO PL 27 Nov 59)

PROCESSING ROUTE, the pc **route** to Clear and OT. (SO ED 269 INT)

PROCUREMENT LETTER, a **procurement** is an originated **letter** by the organization, and that's all it is. It isn't an answer. An answer to it would be "not interested at all," which is a prospect letter; "I am coming in," "I'd sure like to have some training if I could ever afford it, but you know how things are." These are applicant and prospect letters and they are not **procurement letters.** A **procurement letter** is a **letter** originated by the organization in order to interest somebody in training, processing or even memberships. But specifically training and processing. (HCOB 6 Apr 57)

PRODUCE, *v.* to bring into existence, make; to bring about; cause. (HCO PL 7 Mar 72)

PRODUCED GOODS, goods which started out as raw materials, have undergone various processing or manufacturing and have resulted in goods ready for the consumer; consumer goods.

PRODUCER, that individual or group recognized as the source of a particular consumer product and who through agriculture, mining, manufacturing, etc., continues to make it available to the consumer.

PRODUCING, (Public Reg definition) by **producing** is meant contacting the public in volume and using the proper recommended sales techniques to get them to sign-up and route onto service. (BPL 1 Dec 72R IV)

PRODUCT, 1. a completed thing that has exchange value within or outside the activity. (HCO PL 19 Mar 72 II) **2.** someone or something that *has been* brought into existence; the end result of a creation; something or someone who has been brought into existence. (HCO PL 7 Mar 72) **3.** a **product** is a finished high quality service or article, in the hands of the being or group it serves, as an exchange for a valuable. That's a **product.** It's a finished high quality service or article in the hands of the consumer as an exchange for a valuable. In other words it isn't a **product** at all unless it's exchanged. Unless it's exchangeable it's not a **product** at all. Even the individual has to put his service or article in the hands of some other staff member before it could be called a **product. Product** is exchange, exchange is **product.** (ESTO 10, 7203C05 SO II) **4.** is a completed cycle of action which then can be represented as having been done. (FEBC 3, 7101C18 SO II) **5.** the different **products** involved in production are: (1) establishing something that produces (**product** one), (2) operating that which produces in order to obtain a **product** (**product** two), (3) repairing or correcting that which produces (**product** three), (4) repairing or correcting that which is produced (**product** four). (HCO PL 29 Oct 70)

PRODUCT 0, an oriented in-ethics person who knows he is a Sea Org member and able to participate. Prerequisite: contracted SO member. Courses include: Ship Orientation checksheet, Introduction to Scientology Study Tech (Mini Student Hat or *Basic Study Manual*), Welcome to the Sea Org tapes, security check (to be done concurrently with other **Product Zero** actions and completed prior to **Product Zero** graduation).

Confront and Reach and Withdraw drills on the ship, etc., *Introduction to Scientology Ethics,* Introduction to the Sea Org checksheet, DPF and basic ship's drills daily, and Mission School 3rd Class. Maximum time for **Product Zero** from start to completion is two weeks. Must be completed on board as minimum requirement prior to posting to a Service Org. (FO 3155RA) *Abbr.* Prod 0.

PRODUCT 1, **1.** establishing something that produces. The established machine. (HCO PL 29 Oct 70) **2. Product One** is the establishment that produces. (FO 2660) **3.** establishment, establishing the establishment. (FEBC 5, 7101C23 SO I) **4.** well trained effective crew members. Prerequisite: contracted SO member fully and satisfactorily completed Product Zero. Courses include: Basic SO Member Hat Course, Personal Grooming Course, QM of the Gangway checksheet, AB checksheet, *Ship's Org Book,* QM at Anchor checksheet, and apprentice actions aboard. (FO 3155RA) *Abbr.* Prod 1.

Product 1 (Def. 1)

Product 2 (Def. 1)

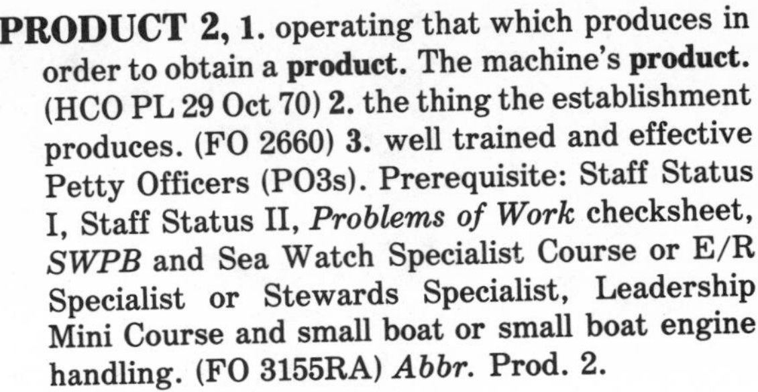

PRODUCT 2, **1.** operating that which produces in order to obtain a **product.** The machine's **product.** (HCO PL 29 Oct 70) **2.** the thing the establishment produces. (FO 2660) **3.** well trained and effective Petty Officers (PO3s). Prerequisite: Staff Status I, Staff Status II, *Problems of Work* checksheet, *SWPB* and Sea Watch Specialist Course or E/R Specialist or Stewards Specialist, Leadership Mini Course and small boat or small boat engine handling. (FO 3155RA) *Abbr.* Prod. 2.

PRODUCT 3, **1.** repairing or correcting that which produces. The corrected machine. (HCO PL 29 Oct 70) **2. Product Three** is the correction of the establishment. (FO 2660) **3.** effective SO missionaires who get MOs done and raise stats. Prerequisite: Products One and Two completed, re-examined and passed. Courses include: Primary Rundown, Investigation and Ethics checksheet, Mission School 2nd Class, Form of an Org Mini Course and Form of a Bureau Mini Course. (FO 3155RA) *Abbr.* Prod 3.

Product 3 (Def. 1)

PRODUCT 4, **1.** repairing or correcting that which is produced. The corrected **product.** (HCO PL 29 Oct 70) **2. Product Four** is the correction of the **product.** (FO 2660) **3.** effective SO Chief Petty Officers that back up command and handle people. Prerequisites: Products One, Two and Three completed, re-examined and passed. Org experience and good stats. Promotion to Petty Officer 2nd and 1st class for merit. Ship experience, case in good condition, well groomed and good appearance. Courses include: QM Course or E/R EOW or Chief Steward. Comm cycles and *Dianetics 55!,* HSDC, Word Clearers checksheet, Esto Drills Course, History of the SO, Organizing Boards (Ship, Org, Bureaux) and how to post them, Watch Quarter and Station Bill and how to post them, piloting or E/R handling or cooks and stewards hat, and apprenticing in-charge of watches as QM, EOW or Stewards Dept. (FO 3155RA) *Abbr.* Prod 4.

Product 4 (Def. 1)

PRODUCT 5, effective and competent Sea Org officers. Prerequisites: OEC and Esto or FEBC at an org. Products One, Two, Three and Four completed, re-examined and passed. Courses include: Officers checksheet, Celestial Navigation, PR Course, OOD checksheet or Repair Chief checksheet, Con checksheet or Chief Engineer checksheet or Treasury Aide—Treasury Sec checksheet, Financial Planning Member checksheet, Investigation checksheet and Ethics checksheet and apprenticing as in-charges of watches or divisions in Treasury. (FO 3155RA) *Abbr.* Prod 5.

PRODUCT 6, Products Six and Seven are Officers Specialist ratings such as division heads, aides and A/Aides, D/Exec Estos, etc. **Six** being officer specialist in own hat and Seven being officers specialist in all hats of a bureaux and similar division. These Products require OEC and SO FO and CBO checklist plus hat for **Six.** They are not done aboard but in an org or bureau. (FO 3155RA) *Abbr.* Prod 6.

PRODUCT 7, see PRODUCT 6.

PRODUCT 8, competent, effective and upstat Commanding Officers. Prerequisites: Products One, Two, Three, Four and Five completed, re-examined and passed. Experienced as a product officer with good stats. Experience as an Esto with good stats. Classed auditor (minimum IV to VIII). Clear or higher grade. Courses include: all hats of an org, done in an org. All hats of a bureau, done in a bureau. FBO hat, done in an FBO office. GO checksheet, done in a Guardian's Office. Apprentice as a Deputy CO. (FO 3155RA) *Abbr.* Prod 8.

PRODUCT ACCEPTANCE, in marketing this signifies the degree to which a product's intended public has accepted it. Sales statistics and opinion surveys would be used to measure product acceptance.

PRODUCT ANALYSIS, see ANALYSIS, PRODUCT.

PRODUCT ANALYSIS PRICING, see PRICING, PRODUCT ANALYSIS.

PRODUCT CLEARING LONG FORM, HCO Policy Letter 23 March 1972, *Establishment Officer Series 11, Full Product Clearing Long Form.* The steps to **clear products.** (LRH ED 257 INT)

PRODUCT CLEARING SHORT FORM, HCO Policy Letter 13 March 1972, *Establishment Officer Series 5, Production and Establishment Orders and Products.* An invaluable text and list for **product clearing.** It's a list of what you do to **clear products.** From it a prepared list can be made. (LRH ED 257 INT)

PRODUCT CONFERENCE, 1. the **Product Conference** is senior to the Org Conference. The **Product Conference** lays it out—this is what we're going to do and this is how we're going to get the **product.** They write up the projects and **products** and plan everything else of what they're going to do in order to get this thing out and then they make sure that they keep that machine running that way. The **product** officers, which are the secretaries, would be handling the **products** which they have to push out. (FEBC 4, 7101C18 SO III) **2.** the Commanding Officer or ED has a conference and that consists of the divisional secretaries. That is the **Product Conference,** and every divisional secretary is himself a **product** officer. That **Product Conference** doesn't even do FP. They eat, think, sleep, do nothing but **products.** (ESTO 1, 7203C01 SO I) **3.** the **Product Conference** is conducted by the CO or ED (or his deputy). It consists of the divisional heads of the org as each of these is a **product** officer. (HCO PL 7 Mar 72) **4.** Aides Council conference where the aides act only as **product** officers. (FO 3148)

PRODUCT DIFFERENTIATION, an advertising and sales technique which attracts customers by pointing out the desirable qualities of the advertised product which competitive products do not possess.

PRODUCT DIVERSIFICATION, the action of a company branching out to produce and market a wider range of products.

PRODUCT EXPEDITOR, the **Product Expeditor** makes certain the org **products** are produced. The Org Officer has products one and three, the **Product Expeditor** has **products** two and four. A CO counts on the **Product Expeditor** to carry out his orders and keep the org producing. The Org Officer is "organize" and the **Product Expeditor** is "cope." (FO 2656)

PRODUCT FEATURES, functional or decorative characteristics of a product which are highlighted in the advertising or promotion of that product. A feature is something worthy of mention because it is a characteristic desired or found attractive by the public, it brings a product up to a level of specification required by a customer or by law, or it increases the performance, status, value, etc., of the product above the level of similar products which do not incorporate that feature.

PRODUCT IDENTIFICATION, the aspect(s) of a product that allow(s) a customer to distinguish it from other products on the market. Such things as trademarks, brand names, distinctive color, design, packaging, fragrance, flavor, etc., are all examples of product identification.

PRODUCTION, 1. the activity of providing a **product** or service. (HCO PL 7 Mar 64) **2. production** means that it's got to deliver. If you do this sensibly the next thing you know you will get expansion. (7205C18 SO) **3. production** is solely the amount of completed cycles that occur. (HCO PL 14 Sept 70) **4. production** is the basis of morale. (HCO PL 29 Feb 72) **5. production** is the evidence of the demonstration of competence. (FEBC 3, 7101C18 SO II) **6. production** as far as staff is concerned is an evaluation which will when operated raise stats right now. **Production** as far as Action is concerned is concluded missions. **Production** as far as the Data Bureau is concerned is a complete set of individual viewpoints, one for each org. As far as Management is concerned, Flag in ARC with the orgs. (7205C18 SO) *Abbr.* Prod.

PRODUCTION AIDE, any communication of any kind whatsoever from an Executive Council has to be cleared through a bureau. This is part of a bureau's functioning and it is done in coordination with and under the supervision of a **production aide** or assistant **production aide.** The exception to this is the Guardian Office communication lines. (FEBC 12, 7102C03 SO II)

PRODUCTION, BATCH, the sporadic manufacture of a product in separate batches as opposed to continuous production of the same product. This could occur where the same plant facilities are being used to make a variety of similar products such as different colors of paint and/or where the market demand will only accept a limited amount of one variety of a product but tends to exert a continuous demand for the product in a variety of forms, colors, styles, etc. The clothing industry uses batch production largely.

PRODUCTION BUREAU, we have a Production Division 4. Division 4 is in a business which consists of: the Data Bureau, the Action Bureau, the Comm Bureau and the Management Bureau. We are being sloppy at this particular time. We're talking about the Action Bureau because it was a bureau previously. I don't know that you would necessarily have to change its name. Really it's an Action Branch of the **Production Bureau** if you want to be very precise. I don't think you need necessarily call them branches. I really can't see somebody writing a letter from the **Production Bureau,** Management Branch and expecting very many people to follow it. But the Management Bureau; somebody might answer that. (7012C04 SO)

PRODUCTION COMMITTEE, a committee operating at any level of management which plans, schedules and resolves matters relating to production. Where top management is not represented directly on the committee, authorization would be required prior to implementing major changes.

PRODUCTION, CONTINUOUS PROCESS, the more or less continuous production of some product because there is a constant demand for that product in that form as opposed to batch production for example.

PRODUCTION CONTROL, planning and supervision of the efficient use of one's personnel, equipment and materials so that one profitably and agreeably satisfies a customer's demands in the allotted time.

PRODUCTION COUNCIL, see FLAGSHIP PRODUCTION COUNCIL.

PRODUCTION DEPARTMENTS, 1. Four of the six departments are **production departments** in a Six Department Org. These are Dissem **Dept,** Tech **Dept,** Qual **Dept** and Dist **Dept.** (HCO PL 21 Oct 66) **2. Production Department** means that subdivision of the organization which directly

produces income. The Course **Department produces** student income. The Publications **Department produces** book, tape and congress income. The International Organization **Department produces** 10% administration and royalty income from all organizations. The Franchise **Department produces** income from franchise 10%s. the whole of Saint Hill income comes from these four sources. Therefore these **departments,** their equipment, supplies and personnel are favored. (HCO PL 18 Dec 64, *Saint Hill Org Board*) **3. departments** that directly **produce** income. The **production departments** are: **Department** 1, the Course **Department,** the Book **Department,** the Organization **Department** and the Franchise **Department.** (HCO PL 28 May 64)

PRODUCTION DIVISION, 1. Technical, in actual fact the right name is **Production. Production Division** is Division 4. (SH Spec 77, 6608C23) **2.** the First Mate is head of Division 4, the **Production Division** with the Chief Steward's Department (10), Boatswain (Department 11) and Specialist Chief (Department 12). These are key departments without which missions cannot be run. (*Ship's Org Bk.*)

PRODUCTION ENGINEER, one who lays out the requirements for a job including necessary materials, methods, production design and organization of men and time factors.

PRODUCTION FLOW, the constant flow of materials in a plant, factory, etc., as they undergo operations that will finally result in finished products ready for the consumer.

PRODUCTION, FLOW LINE, an organized system of production where work flows in a single line through the factory from one person to the next or one section to the next with each person or section performing some operation on the product. A common example is assembly line production. Most mass production relies on a flow line production technique.

PRODUCTION, JOB, a type of production or manufacturing of individual products to individual specifications.

PRODUCTION MANAGER, that person directly overseeing the manufacture of a product or line of products and responsible for their quality, quantity and viability.

PRODUCTION, MASS, the manufacture of commodities in large quantities using standardized designs and parts and often assembly line techniques as exemplified by the manufacture of automobiles.

PRODUCTION MASTER, all LRH *original* (called masters) tape recordings are to be safeguarded and are not to be used or played except to make a **production master** from which other copies for *use* can be made. (FO 1655)

PRODUCTION MISSIONS, missions going out to handle orgs and activities and get them **producing.** (CBO 345)

PRODUCTION-ORIENTED COMPANY, see COMPANY, PRODUCTION-ORIENTED.

PRODUCTION, PILOT, 1. a test of the production of some product in a limited quantity to ensure that the best method is being used and that one will achieve the product desired at the lowest cost. 2. a television program produced as an example of a series being considered by a network.

PRODUCTION PLANNING, see PLANNING, PRODUCTION.

PRODUCTION PROBLEMS, production problems are concerned with the particles which flow on the lines, changed by the hatted personnel, with consumption and general viability. (HCO PL 16 Mar 71 IV)

PRODUCTION RECORDS, statistics or data representative of the amount of production accomplished by a business over a certain period of time.

PRODUCTION, SPECIFIC-ORDER, see PRODUCTION, JOB.

PRODUCTION, SPECULATIVE, production of some product before one has a buyer or has established concretely what markets exist for it.

PRODUCTION TARGETS, 1. those which set quantities like statistics. (HCO PL 24 Jan 69) **2.** setting quotas, usually against time, are **production targets.** (HCO PL 16 Jan 69)

PRODUCTION TRANSFER, see TRANSFER, PRODUCTION.

PRODUCTIVE CAPACITY, the highest amount of production a plant, business, unit, department, person, etc., is capable of maintaining over a certain period of time.

PRODUCTIVITY, basically productivity is a measure of what one puts in to something compared to what one gets out of it. You can usually get it down to a dollar value where if it costs more to employ a person, machine or process than you get out of it there is no productivity.

PRODUCTIVITY DIFFERENTIAL, the difference between the level of productivity existent at two different periods of time.

PRODUCTIVITY INCREASE, an additional amount of pay given to an employee because his productivity has increased.

PRODUCT LAWS, products 1, 2, 3 and 4 as given in the Org Series. (HCO PL 2 Nov 70 II)

PRODUCT LIFE CYCLE, 1. the complete life of a product from inception stage, design, production, ultimate sales, sales decline to taking it off the market. 2. by inference, the life of the product in terms of degree of lasting quality and length of possible usage once in the hands of the consumer.

PRODUCT LINE, the range of products produced by a manufacturer or sold by a wholesale or retail outlet.

PRODUCT MANAGER, an executive responsible for the marketing of a certain product or range of products. Often a product manager is synonymous with a brand manager but a product manager can also be responsible for marketing products that are not sold under a brand name.

PRODUCT OFFICER, 1. controls and operates the org and its staff to get production. (HCO PL 7 Mar 72) **2.** the **Product Officer** gets the **products** of the establishment produced or corrects the **products.** (FO 2794) **3.** Org Exec Sec. (FEBC 11, 7102C03 SO I) **4.** is there to get the final valuable **products.** (FEBC 11, 7102C03 SO I) **5.** a **Product Officer** by definition is a good org officer. (FEBC 3, 7191C18 SO II) **6.** the rule is see the **Product Officer** about past, present and future production. See the Org Officer about internal matters of personnel, supply, hats, etc. The deputy is the Org Officer who is always junior to the **Product Officer.** It's like having (in the Org Officer, the deputy) an HCO right in your own division. The deputies are really under the Org Officer of the org. The Div heads are under the **Product Officer** of the org. (OODs 10 Jan 71) *Abbr.* PO, Prod Off.

PRODUCT OFFICER-ORG OFFICER SYSTEM, within the last four years the **Product Officer-Org Officer system** was developed. The Executive Director or Commanding Officer had (or was) a **product officer.** The **Product Officer** was supported by an **Org Officer** to keep the place organized. (HCO PL 9 May 74)

PRODUCT OFFICER'S CONFERENCE, your **Product Officer's Conference** is your divisional secretaries. (ESTO 2, 7203C01 SO II) See PRODUCT CONFERENCE.

PRODUCT PLANNING, see PLANNING, PRODUCT.

PRODUCT STRATEGY, a plan or strategy of what products to introduce or develop, what designs, features or modifications to incorporate in products, what quantity to produce, what price to charge, what markets to develop or utilize, etc., as a result of product planning.

PROFESSION, an occupation which normally requires a high degree of technical and/or theoretical training usually involving an internship as in theology, medicine, law, teaching or engineering. Professions have duty or personal conviction as their prime motivation rather than personal gain or money. To this end many professions have an established code of ethics or conduct to guide their practitioners. They are distinguished from businesses.

PROFESSIONAL, it isn't magic or luck that makes the **professional.** It's hard won know-how *carefully applied.* A true **professional** may do things pretty easily from all appearances, but he is actually taking care with each little bit that it is just right. (HCO PL 8 Oct 64)

PROFESSIONAL AUDITOR'S BULLETINS, 1. a magazine issued by HCO WW to all International Members from the HCO WW on receipt of the addresses of members on any continent from Central Orgs. Issued monthly. Is mailed directly from HCO WW to members. Copies furnished to HCOs and Central Orgs for their own use. (HCO PL 4 Feb 61) **2.** all PAB material should be taken from the latest and most current tapes of LRH, or from handwritten PABs by LRH. All PABs are technical data. Occasionally LRH will ask that an HCO Bulletin be released as a PAB. The PABs go to all the International Members in good standing. (HCO PL 15 Jun 59)

PROFESSIONAL CO-AUDIT, professional auditors may **co-audit.** The group would then be called a **professional co-audit.** (HCO PL 22 Apr 64) [The above HCO PL was cancelled by BPL 10 Oct 75 V.]

PROFESSIONAL COURSE, HPA/HCA and above. (HCO PL 7 Jun 62)

PROFESSIONAL MEMBERSHIPS, two different memberships for franchised auditors will be available: (1) **professional membership,** (2) consulting membership. The **professional member** will pay an annual subscription of 15 guineas sterling ($45.00) in return for which he receives a certificate, a weekly mailing of bulletins by surface mail, *The Auditor Magazine* monthly, and advice and information personally from the Franchise Secretary at HCO WW. (HCO PL 22 Apr 64) [The above HCO PL was cancelled by BPL 10 Oct 75 V.]

PROFESSIONAL RATES, 1. for the HPA/HCA or above (classed or unclassed). If he or she has an International Annual Membership in good standing (current year and unexpired) intensives cost only 25% of the public list. (HCO PL 22 Mar 65, *Current Promotion and Org Program Summary Membership Rundown International Annual Membership*) **2.** all persons holding a valid, in force, and in hand **professional** certificate in Dn or Scn shall be entitled to a 50% discount on all HGC processing. (HCO PL 27 Oct 61)

PROFESSIONAL ROUTE, 1. there are two routes to Clear and OT: the training (or **professional) route** and the processing (or pc) route. A person on this (**professional) route** co-audits up to Expanded Grade IV Release on his HSDC, Academy levels and SHSBC. He receives power processing at a Saint Hill before beginning solo at an Advanced Org. (SO ED 269 INT) **2.** Preclear progress is as in the preclear route, auditor progress is by training for certificates, and also by training and examination for classification. At Level III and above, **professional** auditors have to proceed through all the levels in turn, but at level III and above they take further training followed by an examination. (HCO PL 5 May 64)

PROFESSOR, the certificate of PROFESSOR shall be issued to any Course Supervisor who has completed or does complete the following: Basic Study Manual, Student Hat, Primary Rundown, Meter Operation, Word Clearer's Course, Full Course Supervisor Checksheet, Obnosis Drills, Staff Status Zero, I and II, PTS Checksheet, his own drug rundown, completes any PTS handling, gets case gain, basic courses leading to an understanding of the basic elements of Scientology. He is thereafter to be referred to as a **Professor** and may display his certificate. (HCOPL 24 Oct 76 II)

PROFILE, personnel profile; a summary of the relevant data concerning an employee, usually all recorded on a single printed form or card. A profile gives data on the name, address, educational background, abilities and skills, previous employment experience, test scores, any conclusions reached by interviewing the person, etc.

PROFIT, 1. the amount by which a business' income exceeds its expenditures and costs. 2. the amount one has gained through a transaction such as selling securities when their value rises above the price initially paid for them.

PROFIT AND LOSS STATEMENT, a statement of net profit or loss which shows the gross income for all goods or services sold, less all costs involved in producing those goods or services for a stated time period. Also called an income statement.

PROFIT, GROSS, the difference between the cost price and the selling price of goods and services. Also called gross margin.

PROFIT MARGIN, the difference between the cost and the selling price of something.

PROFIT MOTIVE, the potential for personal gain or profit in a particular business activity which acts as the motivation for a person to invest or engage in it.

PROFIT, NET, the amount an organization makes above its income that is then paid out to directors or stockholders as a profit. **Net profit** also means taxable **profit.** (HCO PL 26 Jun 64)

PROFIT, NET, the amount of total revenue and income remaining in a business enterprise after the deduction of operating costs, expenses, salaries paid and any losses. Also called net margin.

PROFIT, OPERATING, the profits derived solely from the regular production, sales and operations of a business distinct from profits yielded by investments, holdings or activities outside of the business or its regular operations.

PROFIT, PAPER, a profit due to an increase in the value of stocks or securities held but as yet unrealized to the holder because he has not sold them yet.

PROFIT PLANNING, see PLANNING, PROFIT.

PROFIT SHARING, various plans by which some of a company's profits are distributed to a portion or all its employees in the form of cash or shares, in addition to their regular wages. The distribution of profits may be predetermined by a formula or may be done at the discretion of the board.

PROFITS, STOCK, the increased value or appreciation of stocks compared to the price paid at the time of purchase.

PROFIT TAKING, selling stock which has gone up in value in order to realize cash profits.

PROFIT, UNDIVIDED, the non-contractual part of an organization's income which has not been divided among stockholders or partners.

PROFIT WEDGE, a company incurs certain costs when initially starting up. It incurs debts or expends capital to buy materials to process. It regains this money by marketing its products. After it passes the break-even point, profits begin to increasingly exceed costs ideally. On a graph showing total costs and total sales figures, profits form a wedge shape from the point where sales rise above costs. This is called the profit wedge.

PROGRAM, 1. a series of steps in sequence to carry out a plan. One usually sees a **program** following the discovery of a why. But in actual fact a plan had to exist in the person's mind whether written or not before a **program** could be written. A **program**, thus, carries out the plan conceived to handle a found why. A plan and its **program** require authorization (or OK) from the central or coordinating authority of the general activities of a group before they can be invested in, activated or executed. (HCO PL 29 Feb 72 II) **2.** the sequence of flows and the changes or actions at each point plotted against time are in fact the major sequences and **programs** of a group. (HCO PL 1 Oct 70) **3.** the complete or outline of a complete target series containing all types. (HCO PL 24 Jan 69) **4.** complete planning and **programs** are synonymous at this time and **programs** is the preferred word. (HCO PL 24 Jan 69) **5. programs** are made up of all types of targets coordinated and executed on time. **Programs** extend in time and go overdue to the extent the various types of targets are not set or not pushed home or drop out. **Programs** fail only because the various types of targets are not executed or are not kept in. (HCO PL 16 Jan 69) **6.** a routine activity within an organization, repetitive and continuing. (HCO PL 11 Aug 67 II) **7.** a **program** is the bridge between establishment and production. (ESTO 11, 7203C06 SO I) **8. programs** contain targets that are either straight-forward orders similar to isolated orders, or are more extensive and require that projects be written that when done will accomplish the target. (HCO PL 6 Mar 73) **9.** a **program** has a major target or purpose which describes it. This is stated in a **program** order. It is *implemented* by a series of projects or missions with specific targets to be complied with. (FO 2213) **10.** to make a simpler statement of what is a **program**, the following is offered: (1) the org has a problem relating to its function and survival. (2) unless the problem is solved, the org will not do well and may even go under. (3) the solution is actually an org activity or drill. We call this a **program.** (4) to find and establish a **program** one conceives of a solution and sets it up independent of org lines with its own staff and finance as a special project. (5) when a special project is seen to be effective or, especially, profitable, it is then put into the org lines as worked out in the "special project," bringing its own staff with it. (6) the usual place to carry a special project is under the Office of LRH or the Office of the HCO Exec Sec or Office of the Org Exec Sec. **Programs** go in their appropriate departments and divisions, one to six, not seven. (HCO PL 24 Dec 66 II) *Abbr.* Pgm.

PROGRAM, 1. generally, a schedule of steps and assignments of responsibility in order to bring to realization some aspect of a business activity. 2. in the computer field, the sequence of actions which a computer is instructed, in coded language, to do in order to solve a problem.

PROGRAM CARD INDEX, a **card index** is kept of **programs** by name in alphabetical order of the *major word* in the name. The number and date of the program is also stated. Any project or mission which is part of this program is added to the card with the date and project or mission number. (FO 2156)

PROGRAM CHECKING, HCO Communicator is to have personal charge of an activity called **program checking.** When a **program** comes into the lines, be it by cable, dispatch, or policy letter, the HCO Communicator is to call in the six division secretaries, and carefully **checks** them out on the points in the **program,** and what action is to be taken, in such a way that the open line to Saint Hill and Ron is quite apparent. The drill on this is done in this fashion. (1) first of all, the HCO Communicator checks the Division head on duplication of the communication—that is, questions calculated to assess if the Division Sec has read the comm and knows what it said. (2) Then the Communicator asks the Division Sec questions pertaining to what he is going to do in effecting the comm. (HCO PL 1 Apr 65)

PROGRAM CONFERENCE, Aides Council **conference** where **program** compliances are taken up. (FO 3148)

PROGRAM EVALUATION AND REVIEW TECHNIQUES, a sophisticated computerized management system applied to complex programs such as the development of space vehicles.

Basically it employs advance planning of each component or part of a project and lays out the sequences of action and deadlines to be met for each so that the whole program intermeshes to a completed product without delays due to one part of the program waiting for another to complete. *Abbr.* PERT.

PROGRAM LOG BOOK, every **program** is logged in a thick, hard cover **log book,** *when* a file is made for that **program.** They are **logged** in numerical order, by number, name and date of the **program.** (FO 2156)

PROGRAMMING, 1. making up a sequential schedule to be followed in order to reach a given end or objective, and the delegation of work and responsibilities to persons involved in the undertaking. 2. the action of having data processed in a certain sequence by feeding coded instructions into a computer to obtain a solution to a problem or a sought after result.

PROGRAMMING OF CASES, the setting out of a series of auditing actions in correct sequence for each **case.** (BPL 4 Dec 71R III)

PROGRAM OFFICER, 1. what does the **Program Officer** do—that is, the deputy? The deputy is administrative and lines. He handles the administrative functions of the Product Officer's lines and getting the **program** executed. (ESTO 9, 7203C05 SO I) **2.** Org Officer. (ESTO 9, 7203C05 SO I)

PROGRAMS AIDE, Flag Flag Representative. (FB CO 9-1)

PROGRAMS BUREAU, 1. Bureau 4B is hereby established as the **Programs Bureau.** This **bureau** contains the FFR and A/FFRs for their areas. The **Programs Bureau** executes **programs.** Org **programs,** divisional **programs,** international **programs** are pushed in, debugged as necessary and gotten done from this **bureau.** The **Programs Bureau** coordinates all orders into the field. The **bureau** maintains the function of filtering of orders into the orgs and assigning priorities for **programs.** (CBO 436) **2.** the **Programs Bureau** has been replaced with the Management Bureau. (FBDL 488R) **3.** on Flag there is a **Programs Bureau** headed by the **Programs** Aide. Contained in this **bureau** are many **Programs** Chiefs who have specific orgs under their jurisdiction (usually by continental zones). One of their functions is to evaluate their orgs using the multiple Viewpoint Data System and make **programs** up for the orgs based on the evaluations. (All **programs** and projects come from evaluations. They are the handling part of the evaluation in the **programs** or project.) (CBO 218RB) **4.** the reason we call it **Programs Bureau** is to emphasize **programs,** and so that in FOLOs they will not go autonomous. (7208C02 SO) **5.** the people who manage the respective zones and areas of the planet as our interests apply to them. (7208C02 SO) **6.** the former Management Bureau has become the **Programs Bureau.** (FBDL 191R) *Abbr.* Pgms Bu.

PROGRAMS CHIEF, 1. the usual actions of a **Pgms Chief** consist of keeping tally on targets and doing assemblies of compliances, nudging missing items and generally working from a targetted **pgm** to get it completed; that is to say in full final form each target, target by target so that at the end one has a completed **pgm** with no holes in it of any kind. Advising the status of a target or any bug in it is also a duty. Debugging a target that seems slow is a duty. **Pgms Chiefs** have the additional duties of getting in reports, answering reports and doing evals when aides don't provide **pgms.** (CBO 291) **2.** the **Programs Chief** for an org or area is also responsible for the overall stats of that org, like the ED, but is also responsible for getting **programs** executed. (FO 3364) **3.** the purpose of his post is the prosperity of the continent and orgs to which he is assigned. (CBO 355)

PROGRAMS EXECUTION BRANCH, a **Programs Execution Branch** has now been established in Bureau 4A **Programs** Bureau under the **Programs** Aide. The **branch** is presently separated into three sections: (a) a chief that is I/C of the other two members and covering SO **Programs Execution** Officer, (b) a US **Programs Execution** Officer, (c) a non-US **Programs Execution** Officer. (FO 3506)

PROGRAMS EXECUTION OFFICER, the purpose of the **Programs Execution Officer** is to rapidly **execute** to completion org evaluations and **programs** that expand the org and markedly raise the org to an ideal scene. The statistic of the **Programs Execution Officer** is the number of org **pgms** completed in the field. (FO 3506)

PROGRAMS UNIT, (Flag Div VI) this **unit** is to look into all material of Scn. It is to compile this data into a form which can be presented to the public. There is a tenfold wealth of data on Scn which has not seen the light of day. This unit is to get it out and known. (FO 1717)

PROGRESS BOARD, see STUDENT PROGRESS BOARD.

PROGRESS CHART, see CHART, PROGRESS.

PROGRESSIVE CONSUMER, see CONSUMER, PROGRESSIVE.

PROGRESSIVE TAX, income tax that is scaled to increasingly higher amounts as an individual's or company's income rises.

PROGRESS REPORT, a written or verbal report of how a project or matter is progressing and what has been accomplished over a particular period of time.

PROJECT, **1.** the sequence of steps written to carry out *one* step of a program. **Project** orders often have to be written to execute a program step. These should be written but usually do not require any approval and often are not generally issued but go to the person or persons who will accomplish that step of a program. Under the category of **project** would come orders, work **projects**, etc. These are a series of guiding steps which if followed will result in a full and successful accomplishment of the program target. (HCO PL 29 Feb 72 II) **2.** the program is the big solution to a problem—the big problem is solved by a big solution called a program. The little problems inside that big solution are solved by **projects.** And inside the **projects** the littler-littler problems are solved by orders. (FO 2192) **3.** if something requires more than two weeks to do it is a **project.** (HCO PL 1 May 65 II) *Abbr.* Pjt.

PROJECT 80, a breakthrough on basic auditing which changes organization targets. This technical advance makes many other things possible. We will designate their broad application to Central Org planning and dissemination, **Project 80.** Essentially what has happened is that I have found the minimum essentials of why auditing works, and have selected out the important parts for concentration. These parts are: (1) (in Scientology One and Two) the itsa line; (2) (in Scientology Two) tone arm action; (3) (in Scientology Two) directing the pc's attention to those things which bar him from release and Clear; and (4) (in Scientology Three and Four) directing the pc's attention to handling those things which bar him from OT. (HCO PL 21 Aug 63)

PROJECT BOARD, the LRH Communicator keeps a **project board.** Every **project** or order or directive or SEC ED issued is noted on this **board;** by routine and regular inspection personally and by dispatch the LRH Communicator sees to it that each and every order and **project** is eventually complied with or acknowledged. (HCO PL 27 Dec 65)

PROJECT ENGINEER, see HCO PROJECT ENGINEER.

PROJECT FORCE MAA, the most upstat member of the **project force** is appointed the **Project Force MAA.** The **PF MAA** musters the crew, conducts any exercises, does investigations as needed and is also a terminal for the members of the **project force** and acts upon request as a liaison between other **project force** members and crew in the Estates Section. (FO 3165)

PROJECT FORCES, the purpose of the **project force** is to increase the person's confront of mest and his ability to complete cycles of action—thus creating an able Sea Org member. The motto of the **project force** is: one time—one job—one place. The **project force** works as a team to handle an area that needs handling under an in-charge as appointed by the head of the **project force.** (FO 3165) *Abbr.* PF.

PROJECT GROUP, see GROUP, PROJECT.

PROJECT LEDGER, a record of the planned and actual costs of a project with notations of any departures from the budget.

PROJECTION, 1. in statistics, the process of extending mathematical figures beyond the point where there is observable data. 2. any prediction of occurrences or outcomes based on extending current and past trends into the future.

PROJECTIZED ORGANIZATION, see ORGANIZATION, PROJECTIZED.

PROJECT MISSION OPERATIONS, a new post is created in Action. The title of the post is **Project Mission Operations.** Even when a set of orders are called mission orders, they are really **Project** Orders. These are such orders as a premises **mission,** a logistics **mission,** etc. They are not production missions going out to handle orgs and activities and get them producing. There are also straight Flag Project Orders. These are very dangerous to leave to the operation of an aide or executive as they forget them or are slow on them. Such FPJOs are far better in the hands of Action. On-board missions would also be handled by **Project Mission Operations.** (CBO 345)

PROJECT MISSIONS, a work party or an assembly of materials **project** is commonly sent out under an I/C. The key here is that a job must be done that would overload existing terminals and so a **project** order is written to do it and MOs are then written to take steps to get it done. There are therefore two parts to a **project mission.** To do the work outlined and to do the **mission.** If one had a **project** order one would merely have to write MOs giving the actions necessary to get the **project** actions done. If one doesn't have a **project** one then incorporates the **project** into the MOs as targets. (FO 2936)

PROJECT ORDERS, these are such **orders** as a premises mission, a logistics mission, etc. They are not production missions going out to handle orgs and activities and get them producing. Even when a set of orders are called mission orders, they are really **project orders.** (FO 3485) *Abbr.* PJOs.

PROJECT PLANNING OFFICER, (Gung-Ho Group) the **Project Planning Officer** finds, figures out and draws and writes up all the steps of a **project** or program after it is agreed upon by the Executive Council. (HCO PL 2 Dec 68)

PROJECTS 1-12, see SAINT HILL PROJECT NOs. 1-12.

PROMISSORY NOTE, an unconditional written promise, signed by the maker, to pay a specified amount of money on demand or at a certain date and/or place, either to the bearer or to a designated person.

PROMO ORDERS MANAGER, (Pubs US) it is the job of this post to know what orgs and missions have in stock in way of LRH **promo** and to encourage reorders of same in adequate quantities. (SO ED 16 Pubs US)

PROMO SCHEDULING BOARD, **1.** every Department of Promotion must have and use a **promo scheduling board.** A **promo scheduling board** is used so the cycle of action for all **promo** pieces is visible from start to finish. The **scheduling board** is large and subdivided into the following vertical columns: product, survey, idea, dummy, I/A, assembly, FP, proofs checked and print, I/A (quality check), mail, review results. A card with the product to be promoted and its mailing deadline is posted under the product column. (BPL 1 Nov 71 I) **2.** a **promo scheduling board** is used by Dept 4 so it can be seen at a glance what is happening to each **promo** piece and if any lagging to increase production so ETAs are met. (LRH ED 159R-1 INT)

PROMOTER, a person who undertakes to organize a new company or business venture and who sells the shares or securities that will obtain the capital necessary or otherwise obtains the needed financial backing.

PROMOTION, **1.** means, to make something known and thought well of. In our activities it means to send something out that will cause people to respond either in person or by their written order or reply to the end of applying Scn service to or through the person or selling Scn commodities, all to the benefit of the person and the solvency of the org. (HCO PL 20 Nov 65R) **2. promotion** is making things known. It's getting things out. It's getting one's self known. It's getting one's products out. (SH Spec 62, 6505C25) **3. promotion** consists of getting names and addresses and contacting them and offering service to get them in. The more names, the more contacts, the more people. (HCO PL 15 Mar 65 I) **4.** accumulation of the identities of persons. This is done by getting lists of names, by personal contact, etc., and offering those identities something they will buy, a book or a service. Dissemination and salesmanship are really **promotion.** (HCO PL 21 Jan 65) **5.** when routing arrangements are made or communication invited from org to public and public to org, we call it **promotion.** (HCO PL 17 Nov 64) **6. promotion** is the art of offering what will be responded to. (HCO PL 7 Mar 64) **7. promotion** consists only of what to offer and how to offer it, that will be responded to. That's the extent of it. (HCO PL 7 Mar 64) **8.** by **promotion** in a Scn organization, we mean reach the public. (HCO PL 26 Aug 59) **9.** poor **promotion** gives you a ratio of maybe 98% outflow and 2% inflow, i.e. 98 pieces of mail (of all kinds) mailed and 2 pieces of mail (of all kinds) received. Fair **promotion** would perhaps consist of 90% outflow and 10% inflow, meaning that for 90 pieces of mail (of all kinds) mailed by the org, 10 pieces of mail (of all kinds) were received. Fantastically wonderful **promotion** would consist of 50% outflow, 50% inflow. A miracle would be 10% outflow and 90% inflow. No exact index or chart of this has ever been made. But the above is an educated guestimate. The figures are given to make the following point: the better the **promotion,** the higher the inflow rises in proportion to the outflow. (HCO PL 7 Mar 64)

PROMOTION, 1. the advancement of a person in rank, position or status. A promotion implies giving a person added duties, responsibilities or authorities usually accompanied by an increase in wages. 2. advertising designed to increase a public's knowledge, liking or desire for a product or service.

PROMOTION ACTIVITIES, these two things (how he gets the book and how he is offered further service) are the whole of **promotion activities. Promotion** is never aimed at anything else regardless of how it is done. The ideas used in **promotion** must (a) get books into the hands of people in the public, and (b) offer such persons service, (c) offer such persons already sold lower services, higher services. There is nothing more to it. (HCO PL 7 Apr 65 IV)

PROMOTIONAL ALLOWANCE, same as advertising budget.

PROMOTIONAL ITEMS, those **items** which will produce income for the organization. (FO 1409)

PROMOTION BUREAU, **1.** the **Promotion Bureau** establishes product demand and accomplishment surveys, designs campaigns, issues **promotion** and guides the responses to **promotion** and controls the PR, public service and public sales actions of an org and guides their results into Div 2 actions and purchases. This makes a full spiral from society to public divisions to registration and oversees all such steps. (CBO 7) **2.** its job is to log for compliance, enforce compliance, get data, relay data, inspect, relay inspection data on all **promotional** activities. The **Promotion Bureau** is an extension of Flag comm lines to enforce compliance and get data on all promotional activities. It is very like an LRH Comm Network, only specialized into **promotion.** It does not originate orders but implements orders. Any demanding emergency or situation is handled by implementing existing orders or policy. The **Promotion Bureau** acts solely on the authority of Flag as it is not autonomous. It contains a PR Branch. Promotion Branch, Public Services Branch, and Sales Branch. (CBO 26)

PROMOTION, DIRECT RESPONSE, sales promotion method that calls for a direct response from the reader or recipient as when an order blank, reply card or telephone number is incorporated in the advertising.

PROMOTION, HARD SALES, positive, hard-hitting and aggressive sales techniques that directly, over and over again concentrate on getting the consumer to buy the product; hard sell.

PROMOTION, PERSONALITY, a promotion technique employing a well known celebrity or a celebrity created by the promoters and made well known for the purpose of promoting a certain, usually household, product. Often the created personality has a gimmick costume and may be used to tour neighborhoods or supermarkets where he gives prizes to those consumers who are buying that product or can recite a jingle connected to the product, etc.

PROMOTION PROGRAM NO. 1, **Promotion Program No. 1** is designed to collect all addresses and data for our CF. (HCO PL 25 Jan 64)

PROMOTION, SALES, techniques to improve sales that are additional to direct selling and media advertising. It would include distributing free samples or coupons, store displays, demonstrations, public relations events covered by the media, sales training to increase dealers' ability to sell the product, etc.

PROMOTIONS, CONSUMER, promotion of a product directed at the final user or consumer. This includes free samples, coupons, discounts, store displays and demonstrations, etc.

PROMOTION, SOFT SALES, low-keyed, conservative, subtly persuasive promotion.

PROMOTIONS, TRADE, a type of sales promotion directed at wholesalers, retailers, distributors and sales persons to get them to buy and sell a product. Discounts, dealer education demonstrations, contests, etc., are all part of trade promotions.

PROMPT NOTE, a creditor's note or reminder informing a debtor of the date a loan or sum of money is or was due.

PROPAGANDA, **1.** pushing out statements or ideas. (HCO PL 21 Nov 72 I) **2.** the word **propaganda** means putting out slanted information to populations. (HCO PL 11 May 71 III)

PROPAGANDA, the systematic dissemination of a given doctrine or beliefs that puts forth strong views and often self-interests in such a manner as to proselytize.

PROPAGANDA BY REDEFINITION OF WORDS, a long term **propaganda** technique used by Socialists (Communists and Nazis alike) is of interest to PR practitioners. The trick is—words are **redefined** to mean something else to the advantage of the propagandist. (HCO PL 5 Oct 71)

PROPERTIES CSW ROUTING FORM, this **routing form** is to be used for the purchase, sale, lease or rental of any real **properties** of or for a Scn or senior organization. (BPL 20 Aug 73R)

PROPERTY, a valuable saleable item. (HCO PL 4 Nov 73)

PROPORTIONATE AMOUNT, this is the **proportion** of the CGI that remains after deduction of certain allocations. It is allocated as follows: 45% to salary sum (to include all staff bonuses and commissions and staff taxes), 15% to promotion, 30% to disbursements, 10% to org reserves/back bills. (BPL 4 Dec 72 IIRB)

PROPORTIONATE PAY, the staff of the organization except for "part-time" staff is paid in units under the following system. Staff is paid 50% of the gross income less congress fees, books and tapes, of the organization. A staff member is assigned units of **pay.** The value of the unit varies from week to week. (HASI PL 19 Apr 57, *Proportionate Pay Plan*)

PROPOSITION, 1. a proposal, scheme, plan, offer, etc., put forth for the consideration of another or others; a plan of action. 2. a verbal or written statement made by a buyer or seller suggesting the conditions under which he would be willing to do business or proceed with a transaction; a business or sales proposition.

PROPRIETORSHIP, an unincorporated business owned by a single person; sole proprietorship.

PRO RATA, a sharing or distributing of expenses, profits, dividends, rebates or some item on a proportional basis or in ratio to what is deserved.

PROSPECT, 1. prospects are made up of names and addresses of relatives, family, friends of the person just closed and last but not least, by "**prospecting** at the close." Such names and addresses are valuable as they are a future source of business; another opportunity to close a sale and help that individual onto and up the road to total freedom. (BPL 1 Dec 72R II) **2.** an "applicant" is someone who has applied for staff, personally, or in response to a mailing. A **prospect** is someone who has not applied but is a likely candidate as a staff member. (BPL 28 Apr 73) **3.** any person who has mentioned even vaguely an interest in training or processing and has had neither. It does not matter how long ago such an interest was expressed, just that it was expressed. (HCOB 25 Apr 60) **4.** potential buyer or customer. (SO ED 122 INT)

PROSPECT, a potential customer, client, applicant, candidate, etc.

PROSPECT FILE, 1. a **prospect file** is made up for each **prospect** by the Public Reg Administrator. The color of such a **file** must be of a different color to the CF files and must be bright enough to stand out on its own. The outside of the **prospect files** are stamped, in large, bold letters, **PROSPECT FILE** and are filed in CF by the Public Reg Administrator by alphabet when not in use. The **prospect** data sheets belong inside the **prospect files** and are used by the Public Reg for contacting **prospects.** (BPL 1 Dec 72R II) **2. files** for public bodies set up under the Public Registrar for her use which will eventually contain all attendees at public events, those having tests, book buyers and those only having bought public courses. (LRH ED 112 INT)

PROSPECTING, 1. a term used in marketing to designate the search for new markets, customers or possibilities to do business. 2. when a salesman closes a customer he prospects or asks the customer for the names of other persons who may want to buy the product. 3. the action of searching for obtainable deposits of minerals or natural resources.

PROSPECT LETTER, this is "I am coming in sometime, maybe," "I wish I could" or "I am answering your mail." We have found over a period of years that anybody who corresponds with the organization sooner or later comes in for training or processing. So this **prospect letter** is awfully broad, isn't it? (HCOB 6 Apr 57)

PROSPECTUS, a printed formal summary describing the scope, size and aims of a proposed business venture or company going public, and presented in such a way as to encourage investment. A prospectus offers shares for sale and describes the benefits to investors.

PROSPERITY, that part of the business cycle characterized by a high level of employment, a large amount of production and a high consumer demand and ability to pay.

PROTEST PR, outright **protest PR,** based on facts is a legitimate method of attempting to right wrongs. It has to be kept overt. It has to be true. **Protest PR** can include demonstrations, hard news stories and any **PR** mechanism. (HCO PL 11 May 71 III)

PROVISIONAL, 1. not permanent. (HCO PL 9 May 65, *Field Auditors become Staff*) **2.** is used to designate anyone who has served in orgs less than a year. (HCO PL 18 Nov 65) **3.** a staff member given a **provisional** rating may have recourse to Ethics and have an Ethics hearing if dismissed. He may be transferred to other divisions without a hearing if his division is overmanned. A **provisional** is designated as "1" on the org board after his or her name. (HCO PL 4 Jan 66 V) **4.** (**provisional** status) a Staff Status 1. (SH Spec 61, 6505C18)

PROVISIONAL CERTIFICATION EXAM, this is a written test taken from HCOBs, tapes, policy letters of the theory material the student studies. This test examines the student to ensure the student knows the data. 85% is passing grade. Below 85% is a flunk and the student goes to cramming. (HCO PL 13 Jan 69, *Standard Examinations*) [The above HCO PL was cancelled by HCO PL 29 Jul 72 II, *Fast Flow in Training.*)

PROVISIONAL CLASS VI, the term **Provisional Class VI** means hereafter only has the right to solo audit on **Class VI** materials and may not co-audit on R6 or audit pcs on R6. (HCO PL 13 Nov 64)

PROVISIONAL CLASSIFICATION EXAM, this is a practical **exam.** The test consists of a checkout of TR 0-4, any of the meter drills of the level and the auditing of a doll on that C/S. The student is required to pass this **exam** 100%. The student is flunked for out TRs, out meter drills, out admin, or out tech only. (HCO PL 13 Jan 69, *Standard Examinations*) [The above HCO PL was cancelled by HCO PL 29 Jul 72 II, *Fast Flow in Training.*]

PROVISIONAL OT COURSE STUDENT, a **provisional OT Course student** is one who has not become Clear or checked out Clear after doing the required work of the Clearing Course to the satisfaction of the Clearing Course supervisor. (HCO PL 27 Jan 67)

PROVISIONAL RANK OR RATING, a **rank or rating** for which one has not fully passed the requirements is called **provisional rank or rating** and may be worn if specifically assigned but only on the left arm, shoulder or sleeve and without the star or division symbol. One therefore can be given a **rank** before he has earned it and can then earn it and wear the star or division or department symbol, and in command ranks (leading to command) can wear it as a rank on both sleeves or shoulders or as a rating on the right arm. A **provisional rank** is also permanent in that it cannot be withdrawn except by a court martial. (FO 236)

PROVISIONAL STAFF MEMBER, a **provisional staff member** is a Staff Status 1 and can be shifted about to balance personnel. You do not have to ask his permission to do so. (SH Spec 61, 6505C18)

PROVISIONAL SYSTEM, the **provisional system** requires that the student audit the materials of the level per existing checksheets in order to graduate, requires an internship within one year in order to obtain a permanent certificate but may go onto his next level with a **provisional** certificate. (SO ED 401-1 INT)

PROXY, the written authorization conveyed by a stockholder to another person to represent him and vote on his behalf at a stockholders' meeting.

PROXY FIGHT, the effort between opposing parties seeking control of a corporation to obtain the proxies of other shareholders.

PR PROGRAM DEVELOPMENT ROUTING AND RELEASE FORM, this **form** exists to ensure proper coordination and preparation of **programs** and other **PR** actions. This form is attached to all **PR programs** being developed, targetted and released. (FO 2440)

PSYCHIATRY, psychology and **psychiatry** were developed chiefly by a Russian veterinarian named Ivan Petrovich Pavlov (1849-1936). His basic principle was that men were only animals and could be conditioned and trained much like dancing bears or dogs. This work was only intended to control people and so has found great favor with certain rulers and upper classes. None of the activities of psychology or **psychiatry** were designed to help or cure, only to control the masses. The results of **psychiatry** are physically damaging, consisting of various brutalities and often injure the patient for life or kill him outright. There have never been any cures listed or claimed for **psychiatric** treatment as its interest lies only in control. (HCO PL 23 May 69)

PSYCHIC, spiritual. (BPL 24 Sept 73 V)

PSYCHOLOGICAL NEED, a fancied need based upon a mental concept or attitude one has as distinguished from a basic need which will actually affect or increase one's survival.

PSYCHOLOGY, 1. *Webster's International Dictionary* of the English language *1829* defines "**psychology:** a discourse or treatise on the human soul; the doctrine of the nature and properties of the soul." *Webster's High School Dictionary 1892*, "**psychology:** the powers and function of the soul."

Merriam Webster's 3rd International Dictionary 1961, **"psychology:** the science of mind or mental phenomena or activities; the study of the biological organism (as man) and the physical and social environment." Somewhere along the way, man lost his soul! We pinpoint when and we find Professor Wundt, 1879, being urged by Bismarck at the period of German's greatest militarism, trying to get a philosophy that will get the soldiers to kill men, and we find Hegel, the "great" German philosopher, the idol of super-Socialists, stressing that war is vital to the mental health of people. Out of this we can redefine modern **psychology** as a German military system used to condition men for war and subsidized in American and other universities at the time the government was having trouble with the draft. A reasonable discourse on why "they" had to push **psychology** would of course be a way of redefining an already redefined word, **psychology.** (HCO PL 5 Oct 71) **2.** you're either trying to create or generate, handle, control and so forth, human emotion and reaction. The whole field of public relations, no matter how many little compartments it's got is actually occupying that zone and area, and that is the subject if you've got to have one called **psychology.** (FEBC 2, 7101C18 SO I) **3.** mainly used for testing aptitude or intelligence. It has counseling as part of its activities but is more concerned with and financed for warfare. (HCO PL 23 May 69)

PSYCHOSIS, 1. we know what **psychosis** is these days. It is simply an evil purpose; it means a definite obsessive desire to destroy. Now anybody has a few evil purposes when they suddenly think of this or that, that they don't want to do. They'd say "Boy I'd like to get even with that guy" or something. That's not what we're really talking about. This is the monitoring evil purpose which monitors all of this guy's activities, and that is a real **psycho.** Now there are people who are PTS and who act fairly **psycho** and there are people who are quote "aberrated." They've simply got out-points in their thinking. The psychiatrist never differentiated amongst these people. That's because he thought people had a disease called mental illness. It is not true. There is no such thing as a mental illness. There is no bacteria which produces **psychosis.** (ESTO 3, 7203C02 SO I) **2.** if he's real crazy he can't see anything. He's just got to fight. Well, if you knew what he was fighting you wouldn't feel so sorry for him. He's back there on the track a few trillion years fighting the Ugbugs. He's solving a present time problem which hasn't in actual fact existed for the last many trillenia in most cases, and yet he is taking the actions in present time which solve that problem with the Ugbugs. What the devil is that all about? Well the guy is totally stuck in present time. He's got 99.999999999% of his attention units at some past period of the track. An exact precise period of the track. And in that precise exact instant he is fighting off something and is trying to handle something by some means and those are the means and practices which he is using in present time. He does not have any problem with you. You do not have any problem with him at all. You aren't back there where he is and he isn't up where you are. Now you can assume there are problems, but that isn't the problem he's trying to solve. That is the whole anatomy of **psychosis.** (SH Spec 61, 6505C18) **3.** Dwindling sanity is a dwindling ability to assign time and space. **Psychosis** is a complete inability to assign time and space. (*Scn 8-80,* p. 44)

PSYCHOSOMATIC ILLNESS, physical illness, aches, pains, continual exhaustion, body malfunctions are created or held in an unchanging state by the mind. This is called **psychosomatic (psycho**—spirit, **somatic**—body) **illness.** (HCO PL 23 May 69)

PSYCHOSOMATIC INTENSIVE, standard Dn will let a person recuperate from illness or injury and it will handle beginnings of illness and it will end off chronic illnesses. These add up to recuperation intensives and **psychosomatic intensives** and all this is HCOB 24 July 1969, *Seriously Ill Preclears* and a five-hour intensive. (LRH ED 57 INT)

PSYCHOTICS, people with histories of known breaks, of suicide attempts, of homicidal tendencies. (HCO PL 2 Sept 70, *Instruction Protocol Official*)

PTSNESS, PTSness is actually a PTP (present time problem) and causes roller coaster as it is difficult to audit over a PTP or work either. (LRH ED 241 INT)

PTS PERSONS, those who are connected to suppressive persons or groups and are **potential trouble sources.** (HCO PL 28 May 72)

PTS RD CORRECTION LIST, HCO Bulletin 16 April 1972, *PTS RD Correction List.* It also gives the expected actions of a **PTS Rundown.** Doing **PTS Rundowns** without this prepared **list** handy can be risky. (LRH ED 257 INT)

PTS TYPE ONE, the SP on the case is right in present time actively suppressing the person. **Type One** is normally handled by an Ethics Officer in the course of a hearing. (HCOB 24 Nov 65)

PTS TYPE TWO, **Type Two** is harder to handle than Type One, for the apparent suppressive person in present time is only a restimulator for the actual suppressive. The pc who isn't sure, won't disconnect, or still roller-coasters, or who doesn't brighten up, can't name any SP at all is a **Type Two.** (HCOB 24 Nov 65)

PTS TYPE THREE, the **Type Three PTS** is mostly in institutions or would be. In this case the Type Two's apparent SP is spread all over the world and is often more than all the people there are—for the person sometimes has ghosts about him or demons and they are just more apparent SPs but imaginary as beings as well. (HCOB 24 Nov 65)

PTS TYPE A, persons intimately connected with persons (such as marital or familial ties) of known antagonism to mental or spiritual treatment or Scn. In practice such persons, even when they approach Scn in a friendly fashion, have such pressure continually brought to bear upon them by persons with undue influence over them that they make very poor gains in processing and their interest is solely devoted to proving the antagonistic element wrong. They, by experience, produce a great deal of trouble in the long run as their own condition does not improve adequately under such stresses to effectively combat the antagonism. Their present time problem cannot be reached as it is continuous, and so long as it remains so, they should not be accepted for auditing by an organization or auditor. (HCO PL 27 Oct 64)

PTS TYPE B, criminals with proven criminal records often continue to commit so many undetected harmful acts between sessions that they do not make adequate case gains and therefore should not be accepted for processing by organizations or auditors. (HCO PL 27 Oct 64)

PTS TYPE C, persons who have ever threatened to sue or embarrass or attack or who have publicly attacked Scn or been a party to an attack and all their immediate families should never be accepted for processing by a Central Organization or an auditor. They have a history of only serving other ends than case gain and commonly again turn on the organization or auditor. They have already barred themselves out by their own overts against Scn and are thereafter too difficult to help, since they cannot openly accept help from those they have tried to injure. (HCO PL 27 Oct 64)

PTS TYPE D, responsible-for-condition cases have been traced back to other causes for their condition too often to be acceptable. By responsible-for-condition cases is meant the person who insists a book or some auditor is "wholly responsible for the terrible condition I am in." Such cases demand unusual favors, free auditing, tremendous effort on the part of auditors. Review of these cases show that they were in the same or worse condition long before auditing, that they are using a planned campaign to obtain auditing for nothing, that they are not as bad off as they claim, and that their antagonism extends to anyone who seeks to help them, even their own families. Establish the rights of the matter and decide accordingly. (HCO PL 27 Oct 64)

PTS TYPE E, persons who are not being audited on their own determinism are a liability as they are forced into being processed by some other person and have no personal desire to become better. Quite on the contrary they usually want only to prove the person who wants them audited wrong and so do not get better. Until a personally determined goal to be processed occurs, the person will not benefit. (HCO PL 27 Oct 64)

PTS TYPE F, persons who "want to be processed to see if Scn works" as their only reason for being audited have never been known to make gains as they do not participate. News reporters fall into this category. They should not be audited. (HCO PL 27 Oct 64)

PTS TYPE G, persons who claim that "if you help such and such a case" (at great and your expense) because somebody is rich or influential or the neighbors would be electrified should be ignored. Processing is designed for bettering individuals, not progressing by stunts or giving cases undue importance. Process only at convenience and usual arrangements. Make no extraordinary effort at the expense of other persons who do want processing for normal reasons. Not one of these arrangements has ever come off successfully as it has the unworthy goal of notoriety, not betterment. (HCO PL 27 Oct 64)

PTS TYPE H, persons who "have an open mind" but no personal hopes or desires for auditing or knowingness should be ignored, as they really don't have an open mind at all, but a lack of ability to decide about things and are seldom found to be very responsible and waste anyone's efforts "to convince them." (HCO PL 27 Oct 64)

PTS TYPE I, persons who do not believe anything or anyone can get better. They have a purpose for being audited entirely contrary to the auditor's and so in this conflict, do not benefit. When such persons are trained they use their training to degrade others. Thus they should not be accepted for training or auditing. (HCO PL 27 Oct 64)

PTS TYPE J, persons attempting to sit in judgment on Scn in hearings or attempting to investigate Scn should be given no undue importance. One should not seek to instruct or assist them in any way. This includes judges, boards, newspaper reporters, magazine writers, etc. All efforts to be helpful or instructive have done nothing beneficial as their first idea is a firm "I don't know" and this usually ends with an equally firm "I don't know." If a person can't see for himself or judge from the obvious, then he does not have sufficient powers of observation even to sort out actual evidence. In legal matters, only take the obvious effective steps—carry on no crusades in court. In the matter of reporters, etc., it is not worthwhile to give them any time contrary to popular belief. They are given their story before they leave their editorial rooms and you only strengthen what they have to say by saying anything. They are no public communication line that sways much. Policy is very definite. Ignore. (HCO PL 27 Oct 64)

PUBLIC, 1. the thought or significance which the PR person is attempting to convey is called "the message." The receipt points of the message are called **"publics."** There are many different **publics.** These are types or groups who accept differently from other types or groups. It is the task of the PR person to study and separate out the different **publics** and know what they want or will accept. (HCO PL 7 Aug 72) **2.** there is a specialized definition of the word **"public"** which is not in the dictionary but which is used in the field of **public** relations. **"Public"** is a professional term to **public** relations people. It doesn't mean the mob or the masses. It means "type of audience." (HCO PL 13 Aug 70 III) **3. Publics** is a **public** relation term meaning a type of "users." (HCO PL 22 Jul 71)

PUBLIC, 1. people as a whole. 2. a group of people having a common interest such as the buying public. 3. Followers or admirers of a well-known or important person.

PUBLIC ACTIVITIES DIVISION, **1.** (Nine Div Org) **Division** 7 with Dept 19 Facilities, Dept 20 Activities and Dept 21 Clearing. (HCO PL 26 Oct 67) **2.** (Nine Div Org) **Division** 7 containing Department of Facilities and Schedules and Public Events (Dept 19) Department of Activities (Dept 20) and Department of Success (Dept 21). (HCO PL 29 Jan 69) [The above HCO PL was cancelled by BPL 10 Oct 75 VII.]

PUBLIC ACTIVITIES SECRETARY, Public Activities Division, Division 7 **Secretary.** The purpose of the **Public Activities Secretary** is to help LRH furnish excellent presentation and create maximal demand for Scn on the part of the **public** and public bodies and to route individuals and individual **public** bodies to the Registrar for enrollment for services. (HCO PL 29 Jan 69) [The above HCO PL was cancelled by BPL 10 Oct 75 VII.]

PUBLIC AIDE, CS-6. (FO 795)

PUBLICATIONS DEPARTMENT, handles all publishing activities, book, tape, meter and insignia sales. Composes and edits the PAB, *The Auditor* and *Certainty.* Prepares all manuscripts for printing. Records and copies tapes. Handles all film and TV activities. Has charge of all printing, recording and electronic equipment, materials and supplies. Is fully responsible for achieving a good income for Saint Hill from dissemination materials and widely disseminating Scn. (HCO PL 18 Dec 64, *Saint Hill Org Board)*

PUBLICATIONS ORG, the basic function of a **Publications Org** or department is to advertise and sell books to the public and CF in order to drive business in on the org and to provide tapes, texts and materials to orgs so that they can deliver. (HCO PL 28 May 72)

PUBLIC BOOK SELLING, the large voluminous **selling** of **books** to the **public** on the street and when **public** come into the org. (HCO PL 14 Nov 71RA II)

PUBLIC CLEARING DIVISION, Division 4A Celebrity Centre. Its valuable final product is broad **public** into Scn from celebrity dissemination. It contains Department 10A, Celebrity Planning Department, with a product of planned booked prepared events, Department 11A, Celebrity Dissemination Department with a product of celebrity broad disseminations of Scn and Department 12A, Response Directing Department, with a product of **public** correctly directed into Scn. (BO 7 PAC, 17 Feb 74)

PUBLIC COMMITTEE, a five person **committee** with a chairman and secretary. This **committee,** by actual interviews with Scientologists and **public** is to study and make recommendations on the following: (1) improvement of the Scn image (a) for the public (b) for protection from any government attacks. (2) Listing not contacting local minority groups, social organizations and civic (non-governmental) groups with whom Scn groups may become allied in defense and in revitalizing the society. (3) Listing after due examination what general customs or social actions are most highly revered in the local area. (4) Listing after due examination what general customs or social activities are most thoroughly detested in the local area. The **Public Committee** is not required to recommend or express opinion or criticism of the local Scn organization. The findings and recommendations of the **Public Committee** should be forwarded to the Executive Council WW who will forward xerox copies to me. (LRH ED 7 INT)

PUBLIC COMPANY, see COMPANY, PUBLIC.

PUBLIC CONTACT DIVISION, (Flag Nine Div Org) Flag **Public Contact Division** handles public service and personal contact matters. (FO 2633)

PUBLIC COURSES, see PUBLIC SERVICE.

PUBLIC DISSEMINATION MANUAL, a hat write-up prepared by LRH order (LRH ED 7 US 12 WW, 2 December 1969) containing the promotional know-how, materials and admin actions used by the New York Org in late 1967 through mid-1968. The data in the *Public Dissemination Manual* used by New York produced a rising gross income to over $27,000 in 1968. (HCO PL 2 Apr 71 II) [The above HCO PL was cancelled by BPL 10 Oct 75 IX.]

PUBLIC DIVISION, **1.** the **Public Division** (Div 6) contacts new people who have not before bought anything from the org. This **division** should have its own registrar and should be signing up new people for major or minor services. (LRH ED 167 INT) **2.** the **public divisions** are the three former departments of Division 6, each one becoming a **division** in its own right. Division 6 has the former functions of Dept 16 and Division 7 has the former functions of Dept 17 and Division 8 has the former functions of Dept 18. The Executive Division now becomes Division 9 instead of 7. (HCO PL 26 Oct 68) **3.** the **Public Divisions** have two main purposes with many sub-purposes such as **public** services and **public** sales. (1) getting new names to CF (2) PRO area control. (BO 30, 16 Mar 70) **4.** the Distribution Division or **Public Division** (either name can be used). (HCO PL 14 Jul 71) **5.** prior to September 1969 when there was only the one org aboard the Flagship (and it was a 7 Division Org) the one **public division** (Div 6) was headed by CS-6/**Public** Officer. As well as handling **public** service and **public** contact matters the **division** handled art, promotion, photography, addresso, printer liaison, advertising, history, FSMs, Advanced Orgs, **public** planning, etc. (FO 2633) **6.** the **Public Divisions** are an extremely important area of action on the org board. These **divisions** (6, 7 and 8) keep the new people coming in, businesses continuing and expand an organization. (HCO PL 31 Mar 69 III)

PUBLIC DIVISIONS AO, handles those Scientologists who have not signed up for any **AO** service. This means any Scientologists from Class 0 Academy or Grade IV Release on up, channeling them into the **AO** for sign-up for Clear. The **Public Division's** methods to do this are tours, **AO** public events, the "I want to go Clear Club" and a very strong line FSM program. The **public divisions** are primarily concerned with promoting Clear. (BO 47, 8 Aug 70)

PUBLIC DIVISION SERVICES, the **services** in the **Public Divisions** are of an introductory or demonstrative nature. They give the **public** person a taste of what it is all about and push the final stage—taking a major service in Div 4. The **public services** designed for pulling people in are: book sales, introductory lectures, testing and **public** events. No registration is required for these **services.** The **public services** designed to give more introduction are basically—HAS, HQS (co-audit), Extension Course and group processing. (LRH ED 112 INT)

PUBLIC ESTABLISHMENT OFFICER, the Distribution **Establishment Officer** (**PEO** for **Public** Division) establishes and maintains the Distribution Division. (HCO PL 7 Mar 72) *Abbr.* PEO.

PUBLIC ETHICS OFFICER, field influence on a large org is best handled by having a **public Ethics Officer** (Div 1, Dept 3) to whom the **public** can apply and to whom **Public** Divisions can appeal or to whom **Public** Divisions can direct persons. (HCO PL 21 Apr 70)

PUBLIC EXEC OFFICER, see PUBLIC OFFICER/PORT CAPTAIN.

PUBLIC EXECUTIVE, (Dianetic Counseling Group) the **Public Executive** has two divisions. Div 5, Qualifications Division headed by the Qualifications Secretary. Div 6, **Public** Division headed by the **Public** Secretary. (BPL 4 Jul 69R VI)

PUBLIC EXECUTIVE SECRETARY, **1.** the **Public Executive Secretary** controls the **public** divisions. (HCO PL 26 Oct 68) **2.** the **Public Executive Secretary—Public Exec Sec** works to get new people. (LRH ED 49 INT) **3.** the **PES** and PEO remain mobile to coordinate the actions of the division, production and organizing (**PES**) and establishing (PEO). (FO 3138) *Abbr.* PES.

PUBLIC EXECUTIVE SECRETARY WW, the **PES WW** has certain primary and definite duties which are his primary concern: (1) effective well-trained **PESes** on post in every org. (2) floods of new names being produced by every **PES** in the world. (3) the standard promotion actions of the **Public** Divisions continued in action without dispersal. (4) the appearance of orgs and staffs. (5) the exertion of PRO area control around WW and each org. The **PES WW** is responsible for having an active and effective well-trained **PES** working industriously and productively in each org and is responsible for their production, effectiveness and conduct. All other duties and actions are secondary to the above, which if done, will stabilize and expand orgs. (HCO PL 12 Feb 70 II) *Abbr.* PES WW.

PUBLIC ISSUE BY PROSPECTUS, the circumstance of stock issues being offered for sale to the public by an organization which, since it has not participated in the market before, publishes a prospectus to inform investors of its financial status.

PUBLICITY, any message, notice, event, etc., usually channelled through mass media that brings some person, product or condition to public notice. What it is that is brought to the public's attention and how it is presented determines whether public opinion is going to be favorable or unfavorable toward that which is publicized. Publicity is a synonym to advertising but advertising usually costs more, concentrates harder on the public buying something and usually directs public attention more specifically to the features of a product or service.

PUBLIC LINES, a series of **lines** and terminals which are in place to handle all organizational requirements of a member of the **public** efficiently and in correct sequence. It is a logical arrangement so that out-points do not occur in the handling of the **public** and so that all organizational requirements are met and service is given and verified as having been given correctly. (FSO 137)

PUBLIC OFFICER, 1. the purpose of Div 6, **Public** Division, is to control the **public.** It is headed by the **Public Officer.** (FO 809) **2.** the title of Hostess is changed to **Public Officer.** (FO 913)

PUBLIC OFFICER/PORT CAPTAIN, in September/October 1969, the existing org was split and two orgs were formed—Flag Org and Flagship Org. Thus the two Div 6's had different responsibilities and it was at this point that the Flagship Div 6 began to develop and specialize on the subject of **public** contact. The div head took on the double title of **Public Officer/Port Captain.** (For a short while he was given Executive Council status and became the **Public** Exec **Officer.** This was reverted when the Executive Council was abolished). (FO 2633)

PUBLIC OPINION, public opinion isn't newspapers or magazines or letters. It is attendance, balance sheets, book sales. (*HCOMOJ*)

PUBLIC OPINION, 1. the general attitude, concept or feeling held by the populace of a city, state, nation, etc., about some product, institution, symbol, idea, etc. 2. a percentage breakdown of what a specific or general public's attitude, concept or feeling is about some product, institution, symbol, idea, etc., based upon survey responses.

PUBLIC OPINION RESEARCH, see RESEARCH, PUBLIC OPINION.

PUBLIC ORIGINATION SECTION, HCO Div 1, Dept 2, Dept of Comm, **Public Origination Section,** makes it as easy as possible for a member of the **public** to communicate to the org and the right terminal in an org. Return addresses, getting our address known, self-addressed cards, any system to make it easy and fast for the **public** to comm to the org. (HCO PL 25 Feb 66)

PUBLIC PLANNING DIVISION, 1. (Nine Div Org) Division 6 with Dept 16 Public Planning, Dept 17 Public Communications and Dept 18 Public Reports. (HCO PL 26 Oct 67) **2.** (Nine Div Org Board) Division 6. It contains Dept of Public Research and Reports (Dept 16), Dept of Public Rehabilitation (Dept 17), Dept of Public Promotion (Dept 18). (HCO PL 29 Jan 69) [The above HCO PL was cancelled by BPL 10 Oct 75 VII.]

PUBLIC PLANNING SECRETARY, Division 6 **Secretary, Public Planning** Division. Purpose: to help LRH discover the ethnic values of the **public** and, using these, to contact, rehabilitate the purposes of and control the **public** and **public** bodies to bring about the processing of the **public** and **public** bodies. (HCO PL 29 Jan 69) [The above HCO PL was cancelled by BPL 10 Oct 75 VII.]

PUBLIC PROGRAMS OFFICER, in every org under the Group Officer should be a **Public Programs Officer.** His hat is to organize and coordinate Gung-Ho Groups. He gets them started. His job takes him into the field contacting FSMs, Scientologists and the general **public** (especially those connected to other groups in the community). The **Public Programs Officer** having recruited the group together, has the group do a survey from door to door, etc., to discover the targets and purposes of the community in the area. The **Public Programs Officer** never makes up **programs.** He gets the Gung-Ho Group to put together **programs** (which are composed of short-range targets given to fellow groups to do to achieve the target found in the survey). (HCO PL 30 Dec 68)

PUBLIC PROMOTION, the mock-up of effective **promotion** pieces, that get made up and printed by Dissem, and their distribution to attract floods of new **public** into the org. Every piece has to be based on survey and must address the right **public.** Such items are: information packs, handout tickets, booklets, flyers for Public Reg use, event **promo** mailings, posters, LRH book advertisements placed in news media. LRH books, not other books but LRH books and the introductory services of Dept 17 are promoted heavily in alignment to survey. Heavy volume **public promotion** is a must. FSMs and volunteers are used to distribute **promo** by hand or mail to lists of names. Information packs are mailed to lists of names and they are collected for this. (HCO PL 14 Nov 71RA II)

PUBLIC REGISTRAR, 1. enrolls **public** bodies on **public** lines (testing, intro lectures, **public** events, **public** courses) for their introduction/further introduction to Scn through **public** services (HAS, HQS, co-audits, group processing, Extension Course) but does this only as determined by the gradient wanted by the individual and concentrates upon enrolling these people straight on or as soon as feasible to their first major service in Scn at which point they are a new name to CF. (LRH ED 112 INT) **2.** the **Public Registrar** is the entrance point to Dn and Scn services and thus it is a post of great importance. At least one **Public Reg** must be on post and producing from within the org. By producing is meant contacting the public in volume and using the proper recommended sales techniques to get them to sign-up and route onto service. (BPL 1 Dec 72R IV)

PUBLIC REGISTRAR ADMINISTRATOR, the post of **Public Registrar Administrator** is introduced into the line-up to handle and control the **admin** duties vital to the smooth operation of the **Public Registrar.** (BPL 1 Dec 72R IV)

PUBLIC REGISTRATION, the **Public Registrar** selling HAS Courses, HQS, books, etc., to new people brought in by the **Public** Division from their ads, personal contacts, FSMs. The **Public Reg** also sells higher services to people taking basic courses. (HCO PL 14 Nov 71RA II)

PUBLIC REG PAID STARTS, (**Public** Division statistic) number of **public reg paid starts: Paid** means money received in full for the service. **Start** means **started** the service. These **paid starts** are the **paid starts** the **Public Reg** in Div 6 produced (or Div 6 personnel assisting or deputizing for her). They do not include any **paid starts** Div 2 produced, only the **Public Reg** in Div 6. No **paid start** can be included on both Div 2 and Div 6 **paid start** stats. Whoever got the **paid start** gets the stat and not the other division. **Paid start** for processing = on HGC lines. **Paid start** for training = **started** on course. Each service **paid** for and **started** is counted as one **paid start.** If a person signs up and **pays** for a number of services, say Academy Levels 0-IV, he is counted as one **paid start** as *each* Academy Level is **started.** Similarly, if a person signs up and **pays** for a number of 12 1/2 hour intensives with the **Public Registrar** as each **paid** intensive is begun, it is counted as *one* **paid start.** When a person **pays** and **starts** a public service like HAS or HQS it is counted as one **paid start.** (HCO PL 28 Nov 71R II)

PUBLIC RELATIONS, 1. in the field of **public relations** good works well publicized is one of the definitions which they give in a text book on the subject, that's supposed to be the perfect definition of **PR,** couldn't be further from the truth—effective cause well demonstrated—you see they need a few little refinements. Then you can make forward progress. (FEBC 2, 7101C18 SO I) **2.** the art of making good works well known. (HCO PL 21 Nov 72 I) **3. public relations** is causative. To be effective it must cause something. **PR** is essentially a communications subject and follows the communication formula. The object of **PR** is persuasion to think, either newly or differently or to keep on thinking the same way. (HCO PL 7 Aug 72R) **4.** the social technology of handling and changing human emotion and reaction. (HCO PL 2 Jun 71 II) **5.** the willful broadcast of information. (HCO PL 11 May 71 III) **6.** the duty and purpose of a **public relations** man is: the interpretation of top management policy to the different **publics** of the company—to advise top management so that policy if lacking can be set—to make the company, its actions or products known, accepted and understood by the different **publics**—and to assist the company to exist in a favorable operating climate so that it can expand, prosper and be viable. (HCO PL 18 Nov 70 II) **7.** the technique of communicating an acceptable truth—and which will attain the desirable result. (HCO PL 13 Aug 70 II) **8.** a technique of creating states of mind in different types of audiences or **publics. PR** can be used or abused. (HCO PL 13 Aug 70 I) **9. public relations,** a technique of communication of ideas. (HCO PL 13 Aug 70 I) **10.** the function of **PR** is to interpret the policies of management to the various publics with which management is dealing: interpret, popularize, get them accepted, find facts about the unacceptability of the policies, get campaigns to make them more popular, test **public** opinion with regard to the campaigns. They're molding opinion. (7003C27 SO) **11.** (under HCO) purpose: to maintain and increase good **public relations** for the organizations of Dn and Scn. (HCO PL 12 Oct 62) *Abbr.* PR.

PUBLIC RELATIONS AND CONSUMPTION BUREAU, Flag Dissem Bureau. (CBO 391R) *Abbr.* PR and C Bu.

PUBLIC RELATIONS AREA CONTROL, consists of these duties: (a) classifying and listing the various publics that exist. (b) locating who the opinion leaders are. (c) surveying the various **publics** and opinion leaders for what they want, what is popular. (d) formulating from surveys a tailored message to fit each **public** and for repetitive use. (e) image and appearances of the org, policing same and keeping them acceptable to the **public.** (f) contact and getting opinion leaders on our side giving us favorable mention and assistance. (g) community **PR,** liaison and participation to increase favorable image. (h) campaigns and **PR** programs using surveys, contacts, events, mass media to get across our **PR** message. (i) news stories, press, TV and radio to increase Scn impingement on the public. The use of these must be based on survey. With **PR** you are *informing* in ways that will create favorable opinion and response from **publics.** (HCO PL 14 Nov 71RA II) *Abbr.* PRAC.

PUBLIC RELATIONS BUREAU, (GO) handles visiting government officials, all lobbying actions and carries out all **public relations** programs involved with the government. (BPL 20 May 70 I)

PUBLIC RELATIONS COURSE, the purpose of this **course** is to produce **public relations** officers who know standard policy on **public relations** and can apply the data exactly and produce 100% standard results every time. (FO 1793)

PUBLIC RELATIONS DIVISION, (Nine Div Org) Division 6 with Dept 16 Fact Finding and Research, Dept 17 PR Control and Dept 18 Public Communication. (HCO PL 18 Oct 70) [The above HCO PL was cancelled by BPL 10 Oct 75 VIII.]

PUBLIC RELATIONS OFFICER, 1. the purpose of a **Public Relations Officer** is to formulate, guide and utilize public opinion to the end of enhancing the repute and expansion of his organization or client. To do this the **PRO** provides events to carry forward the message or name he wishes stated. (HCO PL 5 Feb 69 II) **2.** he just changes opinions or molds opinions or gets things well thought of. (7003C27 SO) *Abbr.* PRO.

PUBLIC SALES, (Pubs Org stat) the number of books sold to Scientologists and raw **public.** (BPL 20 Feb 75R)

PUBLIC SALES DIVISION, 1. (Division 8) the **Public Sales Division** of an org trains and organizes its teams of salesmen to sell Scn and Scn products to new **public** and bring these into the org in volume. (SO ED 72 INT) **2.** (Nine Div Org) Division 8 with Dept 22, Dept of FSM Sales, Dept 23 Dept of Field Sales and Dept 24 Dept of Public Registration. (HCO PL 18 Oct 70) [The above HCO PL was cancelled by BPL 10 Oct 75 VIII.]

PUBLIC SECRETARY, Div 6, **Public** Division is headed by the **Public Secretary.** (BPL 4 Jul 69R VI)

PUBLIC SERVICE, any **service** that is given to new **public** by either Division 6 or Division 4. The ones given by Div 6 are book selling, testing, intro lectures, events, demonstrations, Extension Courses. The ones given by Division 4 are introductory auditing sessions, HAS Courses, HQS Courses and are the more advanced services. (HCO PL 26 Nov 71R II) [The above HCO PL was cancelled by BPL 1 Dec 72R IV.]

PUBLIC SERVICES DIVISION, (Nine Div Org) Division 7 with Dept 19 Public Events, Dept 20 Public Contact and Dept 21 Public Courses. (HCO PL 18 Oct 70) [The above HCO PL was cancelled by BPL 10 Oct 75 VIII.]

PUBLIC TOURS OFFICER, the head of **Tours** Org Div 6. His product is raw **public** business driven into orgs. He does group liaison and new group formation functions, FSM liaison, **public** registrar liaison, and **public tours** and events activities—all designed to get brand *new* people onto the bridge to Clear and OT. (BPL 15 Jun 73R I)

PUBLIC UTILITY, a company that supplies water, gas, electricity, transportation, etc., to the public. It is often privately owned operating as a monopoly, but under government regulation and supervision.

PUBLISHING OFFICER, (Gung-Ho Group) the **Publishing Officer** publishes the steps of anything, the literature of anything; if it's **published** he **publishes** it to our outside groups. He also keeps a library and files of programs and any pamphlets issued or sold by the group. He is also the Press Relations Officer until one is appointed to his department. (HCO PL 2 Dec 68)

PUBLISHING SECTION, prepares all manuscripts, and make-ups, and arranges printing of books, magazines, folders, flyers and brochures. (HCO PL 18 Dec 64, *Saint Hill Org Board*)

PUBS CF, the **CF** of **Pubs** is a collection of persons who have individually bought books from **Pubs.** It is accumulated through individual book sales. It is not the whole book buyers list of every org. The **CF** is in two parts (a) organizations and (b) individuals. (HCO PL 5 Sept 74)

PULL A FEW STRINGS, meaning follow down a chain of out-points. (HCO PL 30 Sept 73 II)

PULL A STRING, 1. two facts don't jibe so you try to rationalize these two facts and interrogate on these two facts. You will get another point you don't understand. When you try to get this point understood you will now find another fact that you don't understand and along about that way someplace **pulling** on this **string** you find the General Sherman tank and that is simply somebody who is trying to stop things. (6711C18) **2.** an Ethics Officer's first job is usually cleaning up the org of its potential trouble sources and requesting a Committee of Evidence for the suppressives. That gets things in focus quickly and smooths an org down so it will function. Then one looks for down statistics in the OIC charts. These aren't understandable, of course, so one interrogates by sending interrogatives to the people concerned. In their answers there will be something that doesn't make sense at all to the Ethics Officer. Example: "We can't pay the bills because Josie has been on course." The Ethics Officer is only looking for something he himself can't reconcile. So he sends interrogatives to the person who wrote it and to Josie. Sooner or later some wild withhold or even a crime shows up when one does this. The trick of this "org auditing" is to find a piece of **string** sticking out—something one can't understand, and, by interrogatives, **pull** on it. A small cat shows up. **Pull** with some more interrogatives. A baby gorrilla shows up. **Pull** some more. A tiger appears. **Pull** again and wow! You've got a General Sherman tank! (HCO PL 11 May 65, *Ethics Officer Hat*)

PULL BACK, restrain, retard, give different vectors. (HCO PL 22 Jul 62)

PULSE-TAKING SURVEY, a survey to discover what views, opinions, sentiments, etc., are generally held about a certain subject, product or idea.

PUNCH CARD MACHINE, a machine that punches a card with holes and/or notches that represent information, thus coding data for use in a computer.

PURCHASE, a sale is simply the transfer of the ownership of mest particles by one person to another for an agreed price or else it is the delivery of services by one person to another for an agreed price. A **purchase** is simply the acquisition of mest particles or services by one person from another for an agreed price. These are the basic business transactions—sales and **purchases.** And you can view sales and **purchases** in terms of flows. A sale is an outflow of mest particles or services by one person to another for an agreed price. A **purchase** is an inflow of mest particles or services by one person from another for an agreed price. (BPL 14 Nov 70 II)

PURCHASE ORDER, 1. an actual and valid **purchase order** is on deep pink paper and because of this is called a red **purchase order.** Only an actual (red) **purchase order** exactly priced and signed before purchase authorizes purchase and no purchase or commitment to expense may occur without one. A red **purchase order** has the exact cost of an item and any specifications (size, color, quantity) required to **purchase.** It is not another estimate or an estimated **purchase order** re-copied on a red **purchase order** form. It is exactly costed. (BPL 4 Nov 70R) **2.** this form must give the person or firm from which the **purchase** is to be made. It must give the item, quality, description and actual cost. When bills are presented for payment each and every item on every bill must be covered by a **purchase order.** If it is not then the **purchase** shall be considered unlawful and may have to be paid for by the staff member who placed the order without authority. No check will be signed unless the bill it is paying and all **purchase orders** appertaining thereto accompany the check. (HCO PL 20 Jun 61) *Abbr.* PO

PURCHASE RECORDS, records on file in a purchasing department of the purchase of materials, supplies and other business goods in the form of authorized requisition, purchase contracts, vouchers, invoices and the like.

PURCHASING, that activity concerned with locating, pricing and ordering desired goods or services ensuring intact delivery occurs and payment is made; buying.

PURCHASING, CENTRALIZED, company purchasing done by a central office or purchasing department for all departments, branches, offices, locations, etc., of that company.

PURCHASING, CONTRACT, a method of purchasing where a buyer obtains price advantages by entering into a contract with a seller to buy large amounts of something or to continue buying specified amounts of something over a long period of time.

PURCHASING COORDINATOR, (Flagship) this person makes all calls for the HU purchaser and for the Purchasing Unit in Dept 8. The **Purchasing Coordinator** receives all calls from the shore for **purchasing** and **coordinates** and handles them. (FSO 743)

PURCHASING DEPARTMENT, that department of a company concerned with their procurement and purchasing of goods and/or services.

PURCHASING POWER, 1. the potential one has to buy things represented by the income or funds at one's disposal. 2. the amount of things a particular currency would buy during one period of time as compared to another period of time.

PURCHASING, SCHEDULED, purchasing of several months to a year's worth of materials in order to obtain discounts but having only a certain amount delivered per week or month.

PURCHASING, SPECULATIVE, buying a much larger quantity of materials than one normally would in an attempt to save money due to anticipating that the price of these materials is going to increase.

PURITY OF FORM, a criteria that may be used in calling attention to outnesses in an evaluation. **Purity of form.** (All parts of an evaluation included.) (HCO PL 3 Jul 74R)

PURPLE TAB, (Flag Only) all Medical Officer reports or complaints are to be rushed to the C/S and **purple tabbed** on the folder so they are completely visible. (BFO 46)

PURPOSE, **1.** the lesser goal applying to specific activities or subjects. (HCO PL 6 Dec 70) **2.** the entire concept of an ideal scene for any activity is really a clean statement of its **purpose.** (HCO PL 5 Jul 70)

PURPOSE OF ETHICS, the **purpose of ethics** is to remove counter-intentions from the environment. And having accomplished that the **purpose** becomes to remove other intentionness from the environment. (HCO PL 18 Jun 68)

PURPOSE OFFICER, (Div 6) a **Purpose Officer** should be appointed in Department 15 to ascertain that the **purposes** of all Sea Org hats are being followed, to mock-up any new **purposes** if old ones seem inadequate and mock-up new posts and their **purposes** to help expand the future activities of the Sea Org. (FO 936)

PURSER, **1.** Treasury Sec. (HCO PL 29 Jan 71) **2.** in command of finance and supply (FO 196) **3.** the **Purser** heads the Stewards Department. Inventory: the ship's inventory is kept by the **Purser** who logs all incoming stores and equipment and keeps an inventory thereof, with any known value and all receipts. The ship's cooking, food supplies, beds, bedding, meals and cleaning below decks is in the **Purser's** Department. (*Ship's Org Bk.*)

PURSER'S DIVISION, the 3rd Division handles the money and materials of the ship and provides its meals, accommodations, and services. It handles the inventories, and is responsible for all money and all stores of whatever kind, including balance sheets. It is normally referred to as the Supply Division. (FO 1109)

PUTTING A HEAD ON A PIKE, ethics only exists to hold the fort long enough and settle things down enough to get technology in. We start to hang people and keep right on tying the noose in a workmanlike fashion right up to the instant we can get tech in—which of course makes the noose unnecessary. When things are bad (bad indicators heavily visible) putting a body on the gallows is very salutary. We call it **"putting a head on a pike."** Too many bad indicators and too goofed up a situation and we must **put a head on a pike.** Then things simmer down and we can begin to get tech in. (HCO PL 16 May 65 II)

PUTTING-OUT SYSTEM, work done off company premises especially by people in their private homes such as garment making, envelope stuffing or addressing, etc. This is also termed outwork.

PUTTING THE QUESTION, putting to a vote an issue or motion that has been under consideration at a formal conference, meeting or assembly.

PYRAMIDING, 1. speculating in securities by buying and selling stock on margin and using paper profits to buy and sell more. 2. a situation where a parent company gets control over other companies with the consequent arrangement of having a series of companies leading downward with each having controlling interest in the one below. 3. system of selling in which a company recruits individuals who purchase the right to sell its products to other individuals, who may in turn have the right to sell to more individuals, etc. This creates a pyramid effect with the originator receiving specified varying percentages of all sales made under him.

Q AND A, **Question and Answer**. When the term **Q and A** is used it means one did not get an **answer** to his **question.** It also means not getting compliance with an order but accepting something else. The executive gives an order, the junior says or does something else, the executive does not simply get the original order done, and the result is chaos. Example: executive: do target 21 now. Junior: I don't have any issue files. Executive: What happened to them? Junior: Mimeo goofed. Executive: I'll go see Mimeo. . . . **Q and A** is simply postulate aberration. Aberration is non-straight line by definition. People who can't get things done are simply **Qing and Aing** with people and life. (HCOB 5 Dec 73)

QUACK, **1.** someone who gives service but refuses to refund the fee if the service is unsatisfactory. (6903C27 SO) **2.** the **quack** was a man who purveyed quicksilver (English pronunciation quacksilver) hence **quack**. He appeared at the English county fairs and purveyed bichloride and mercury which often killed people, but it also cured a lot of diseases. Now, a **quack** is anybody the American Medical Association doesn't like. (6804SM—)

QUACKERY, the action of selling service and refusing refund of the fee if the customer isn't satisfied. (FO 1890)

QUAD BONUS SYSTEM, a triple bonus system has three stages of bonus. The bonuses are payrolls B, C and D. Subsequently added was payroll E—tech production bonuses. (FSO 359R)

QUAL AIDE, see CS-5.

QUAL CONSULTANT, in **Qual** there should also be a **consultant** service which uses a meter and two-way communication to find out about cases before patch-up or review. The **Qual Consultant** should also handle students who are slow or dropped out. (LRH ED 92 INT)

QUALIFICATION, that which makes a person fit or competent for a job. The **Qualifications** Division in a Scn Org insures that the right results are obtained from Scn or gets the results corrected if it is necessary. (HCO Admin Ltr 30 Jul 75)

QUALIFICATIONS, the physical, social, experiential or educational requirements a person must meet or possess in order to obtain a particular job, status, promotion, etc.

QUALIFICATIONS CHECK 7A, the **Qualifications Check** is for employment of personnel. Don't hire people who cannot pass this **check**. (HCO PL 6 Dec 68)

QUALIFICATIONS DIVISION, **1.** it could be called the correction division or the adjustment division. But **qualifications** would also serve. (SH Spec 77, 6608C23) **2.** the **Qual Division** monitors not only technical quality and honesty but the administrative quality and honesty of the entire organization. HCO establishes an org but **Qual** makes it run. Therefore, it has to be completely effective in its duties and functions. **Qual** is in the business of finding and restoring lost tech. (BPL 22 Nov 71R) **3.** the **division** (division five (5) of a church) where the student is examined and where he may receive cramming or special assistance and where he is awarded completions and certificates and where his **qualifications** as attained on courses or in auditing are made a permanent record. (HCOB 19 Jun 71 III) **4.** the function of **Qual** in an org is correction of tech. (FO 2476) **5. Qual** was established to correct both the *org form* and the org's products. (FO 2476) **6.** The prime purpose of the **Qualifications Division** is: to ensure the results of Scn, correct them when needful and attest to them when attained. (HCO PL 31 Jul 65) **7.** Division 5 of the organization. This **division** is headed by the **Qualifications** Secretary. It consists of three departments. The Department of Examinations, Dept 13, is headed by the Director of Examinations. The Department of Review, Department 14, is headed by the Director of Review. The Department of Certifications and Awards, Dept 15 is headed by the Director of Certifications. The departments have various sections and units. (HCO PL 31 Jul 65) **8.** the **Qualifications Division** exists to handle flat ball bearings turned out by Tech or old patterns or checksheets or special cases. That keeps the assembly line roaring along. (HCO PL 7 Jun 65, *Entheta Letters and the Dead File, Handling of, Definitions*) **9.** exists to ensure that valid completions do occur and to swiftly spot and correct non-standardness where *it* occurs. (FO 3277) **10.** the custodian of the technology of Dn and Scn in an org and its field. (BPL 30 Jun 73R) *Abbr.* Qual, Qual Div.

QUALIFICATIONS ESTABLISHMENT OFFICER, **establishes** and maintains the **Qual** Division. (HCO PL 7 Mar 72) *Abbr.* QEO.

QUALIFICATIONS FORM AO 3, used on Advanced Courses, this is the attestation of completion of course to **Qual** and application for award of the grade. (HCO PL 10 Jan 68) [The above HCO PL was cancelled by BPL 10 Oct 75 IV.]

QUALIFICATIONS INTERVIEW-INVOICE OFFICER, **1.** the **Qualifications** Division, **Interview-Invoice** Section is handled by the **Qualifications Interview-Invoice Officer**. (BPL 20 Oct 67R) **2.** purpose: to help LRH correctly route all publics into, within and out of **Qual** smoothly and efficiently. (BPL 7 Dec 71R I) **3.** logs in and **invoices** out all paying publics, collects all monies due, reports all non-paying persons as non-handled fast to Dir Validity, logs all staff in and out, **invoicing** contracted staff at no charge and collecting from non-contracted staff. (BPL 7 Dec 71R I)

QUALIFICATIONS INTERVIEW-INVOICE SECTION, this **section** is handled by the **Qualifications Interview-Invoice** Officer. All bodies coming into the **Qualifications** Division are routed through this **section**, and bodies leaving the **Qualifications** Division are routed through this **section**. The **Qualifications Interview-Invoice** Officer **interviews** the student, preclear or staff member in order to decide what routing is necessary. Once the proper routing is ascertained, the student, preclear or staff member is logged in, stating name, date, time and where being routed to, and then is routed to the proper destination. Terminals are logged out and routed out of the Qualifications Division through the **Qualifications Interview-Invoice** Officer. Routing is done in this fashion to insure that the student or preclear is **invoiced** and pays for the services delivered by the **Qualifications** Division and then to route further, if need be, to the Ethics Section of the Department of Inspections and Reports. (BPL 20 Oct 67R) *Abbr.* Qual I and I.

QUALIFICATIONS SECRETARY, Div 5, **Qualifications** Division is headed by the **Qualifications Secretary.** (BPL 4 Jul 69R VI) *Abbr.* Qual Sec.

QUALIFY, 1. to find out if a potential prospect is a bona fide or real prospect by establishing if he is prepared to buy now, later or never. A salesman asks questions designed to discover a potential prospect's purchasing power and attitude or willingness to buy before the salesman invests time in an attempt to sell or close the prospect. 2. to possess the qualifications or meet the requirements stipulated.

QUALITY, **1.** would be the degree of perfection of a product. (HCO PL 29 Oct 70) **2.** value or having a value. (*SPB*, p. 14)

QUALITY CONTROL, (AVU Promotion **Quality Control**) all promotion whether done aboard or in LA for the Commodore or Flag is to be **quality controlled** by AVU. The duty of **Quality Control** is to see that: (1) no sloppily printed promotion or any literature of a downgraded nature gets through; (2) **quality** is of high standard per HCOB 29 July 1973 *Art, More About* on all printing and litho texts; (3) all promotion is top top top quality. Items to which this applies are: books and dust jackets, brochures, magazines, posters, all packs —Reg, ASR, Info, etc., fliers, letterheads, all literature. (FO 3572)

QUALITY CONTROL, constant or periodic inspection at every stage in the manufacture of a product from raw materials to finished product, in order to ensure that the standards of quality set by the manufacturer, by law, or by customer demand, are being met.

QUALITY CONTROL LOG, a **log** for all on board and US printing cycles is to be kept by **Quality Control**. The **log** must contain what the promotion is, who sent to if being printed in the U.S., any corrections ordered by **Quality Control**

for a job and the date of each **Quality Control** pass given the item. (FO 3572)

QUALITY CONTROL OFFICER, as there have been many flagrant degrades of promotion, literature, covers and photographs, and as the general quality of promotion requires, by past experience, vigorous and exact **quality control**, all color photolitho and color printing must be passed upon by duly authorized persons at Flag before any print run may be begun. **Quality control** is vested in the Authorization and Verfication Unit **Quality Control Officer**. Procedure consists of sending the press or other acceptable proof from the color separation company and the original art work or transparency to Flag, fully protected by uncolored cardboards, properly addressed to Flag AVU **Quality Control Officer**. (FO 3570)

QUAL LIBRARIAN, **1.** the **Qual Library** is in Dept 15, Dept of Correction. There is a **Qual Librarian,** whose duties are essentially those of a **librarian,** collecting up the materials, logging and storing them safely, making up cross reference files so that material can be easily located, logging out materials and ensuring that they are returned. (BPL 21 Jan 73R) **2.** they do the standard duties of a **librarian**. They always have a master copy of everything they own and they answer questions. Now that takes an interesting **librarian** because he's the Technical Information Center. (7109C05 SO) **3.** the **librarian** is really the org information officer. (7109C05 SO)

QUAL LIBRARY, see QUAL LIBRARIAN.

QUAL ORG OFFICER/ESTO, **1. establishes** the **Qual** Division. The **QOO/Esto** is in the Office of the **Qual** Sec. The **QOO/Esto establishes** the terminals, lines, spaces and material of the whole Correction Division. The purpose of the post is to more firmly **establish** whatever and whoever already exists in the **Qual** Division and **establish** the division more fully so that it can correct auditors, staff and public effectively, deliver word clearing, program staff, and ensure the technical honesty of the products of the org. (BPL 22 Nov 71R) **2. establishes** the division by producing the terminals, lines, spaces and material for the whole Correction Division, so that it can and does correct auditors, staff, supervisors, C/Ses and students and public effectively, deliver word clearing, program staff and ensure the technical honesty of the org. (BPL 7 Dec 71R I) *Abbr.* QOOE, QOO/Esto.

QUAL REVIEW AUDITOR, **Qual Review auditor** helps LRH minimize upsets to staff and students through fast application of auditing technology. Ensures emergency assists for upsets, loss, injury or illness quickly handled with minimum of upset, then referred to the HGC. Non-optimum TAs for word clearing or word clearing upsets swiftly corrected. Bogged students quickly cleaned up and back to course. (BPL 7 Dec 71R I)

QUANTITY, would be an acceptable, expected or useful volume. (HCO PL 29 Oct 70)

QUARTERMASTER OF THE GANGWAY, **1.** a seaman who guards the security of the ship in port and maintains a written log of events, such as on and off traffic. (FO 2674) **2.** the **QM** at **the gangway** guards the ship. He keeps the log entering every thing. He has charge of the safe mooring of the ship and must adjust mooring lines whenever necessary. (FO 303) **3.** the ship's protector and reception and represents all divisions and his watch when on duty. (FO 304) *Abbr.* QM.

QM of the Gangway

QUARTERMASTER OF THE WATCH, **1.** the **QM of the watch** is a member of the duty watch. The duty watch has a 24 hour officer on the deck. The **QM** must know who is his Officer of the Deck and must call him for any emergency. The **QM of the watch** alongside a dock is responsible for the mooring lines which tighten and loosen with the tide's rise and fall. At anchor the **QM** is responsible for the security of the anchor and must take bearings to make sure the anchor is not dragging and that as tidal currents change, the ship does not swing into other ships anchored near. The **QM** is also responsible for the proper signals at anchor, a black ball by day and anchor light at night and for the raising and lowering of proper flags at 8:00 a.m. or sunset, and flying crews meal pennant and Captains, Commodore's and native or courtesy flag. These flags are also flown alongside the dock. The **QM** at the gangway guards the ship. He keeps the log, entering everything. He has charge of the safe mooring of the ship and must adjust mooring lines whenever necessary. (FO 304) **2.** keeps the **quartermaster's** notebook, notes all changes of course, speed, wind, sea, etc., in it and all occurrences in the ship and signs it at the watch end. He tends to getting the wheel and lookout relieved. When something is to be done within the ship he takes the two stand-bys and does it. He handles the men for the OOW, routes out the next watch, signals any call to emergency stations for the crew, etc. (FO 80) **3.** (Condition III) hat purpose: handles crew and ship's company while watch is in progress. (FO RS 32) **4.** the **QM** is also the Org Officer for the watch and works directly with the cons in training up their watches and correcting goofing watch members. (FSO 546) *Abbr.* QM.

QUARTERMASTER'S LOG, a continuous, minute-by-minute recording of what is happening aboard the ship and upon the sea she travels. All pertinent information is entered (*SWPB*)

QUARTERMASTER'S NOTEBOOK, all noticeable matters are entered in the **Quartermaster's notebook** and all or any comments. The helmsman also notes in the **Quartermaster's notebook** all sightings of ships and landmarks and changes of course and speed, without fail, noting the time accurately, all weather and incidents aboard ship. All gear and persons entering or leaving ship in port, all stores, are entered by the **Quartermaster** of the Watch or Officer of the Deck when the ship is in port, plus all incidents and repairs. (*Ship's Org Bk.*)

QUESTIONABLE RISK LIST, in the case of premeditated fraud we have a person who at the beginning never intended to pay, but intended to defraud. Such persons can usually be spotted by an insistence on courses and processing with no down payment. This is their hallmark. Records should be combed for a **list** of such names and each time a request for totally credit arrangements is made by anyone, that name should be added tentatively to the **list.** This **list** is called the **questionable risk list,** or the **QR** (HCO Secretarial Letter 26 Dec 58) *Abbr.* QR.

QUICK ASSETS, see ASSETS, QUICK.

QUICKIE, means a brush off "lick and a promise" like wiping the windshield on the driver's side when really one would have to work at it to get a whole clean car. (HCO PL 13 Mar 72)

QUICK RATIO, same as Acid Test Ratio.

QUIT, 1. the act of resigning or leaving one's job. 2. the act of ridding oneself of a debt by paying.

QUORUM, a specified number of officers and members of an organization, board or committee, usually constituting a majority, whose presence is required in order to transact business legally.

QUOTA, 1. a production assignment. It would be the number assigned to whatever is produced. As an example, the Director of Training is given the **quota** of 45 letters to produce per day or 225 letters per week as part of his standard promotional actions. Targetting is defined as establishing what action or actions should be undertaken in order to achieve a desired objective. In the case of the Director of Training, it would be as simple as obtaining from central files the necessary 45 folders, writing the required number of letters, returning the folders to central files and determining to remain on post daily until this was accomplished no matter what. Any **quota** can be targetted for increase daily and weekly. For instance, the Director of Training can establish a **quota** of 5 extra letters per day over that of the day before. This would mean he would write 45 letters one day, 50 letters the next day. 55 letters the day after that, and so on. (BPL 8 Feb 72) **2.** a **quota** is a future expectancy. The way one sets a **quota** is quite important. If it is too impossible, a **quota** gets overwhelm not stats. If it is merely "impossible" at first it quite often gets made as it is a challenge. Too low a **quota** is no challenge at all and gets no quota. To set one, one chooses a future date and draws a line from now to it. Where that line crosses each future week is the **quota** for that week. If one makes that weekly **quota** and organizes to make the next week's, one will wind up with the final **quota** made. (LRH ED 228 INT) [The above LRH ED was later cancelled by LRH ED 153RD.]

QUOTATION, the figure quoted on a security at a given time which represents the highest bid to buy and the lowest offer to sell at that time.

R

RABBIT, run away by ending the session. (HCO PL 27 May 65)

RACK-JOBBER, a wholesale distributor who handles items displayed on racks in supermarkets, drug stores, retail stores, etc.

RADIO OFFICE, the **radio office** is responsible for electronics on the ship, is also responsible for caring and ordering parts and spares needed for equipment under him such as Xerox machine and Roneo. (FO 924)

RADIO OPERATOR, operates the **radio** receiver and **radio** transmitter. He listens for any incoming **radio** messages and transmits all outgoing messages. (*SWPB*)

RAIDING, 1. the act of buying up enough stock of a business followed by instituting a proxy fight in order to take over the management of the organization. 2. the effort by speculators to drive stock prices down on a market.

RAKE-OFF, a slang expression for receiving a share of the profits from a business transaction usually underhandedly or illicitly.

RALLY, a notable rise in market prices and trading activity after a decline.

R AND I FORM, [this refers to Recruit **Routing and Information Form** which is FO 3212R-Part 1. It is filled out by all Sea Org new recruits and provides vital personnel data on each person when filled out. It corresponds to BPL 1 Feb 75 II, *New Staff Applicant Information Form* which applies to all SO and Scn Orgs.]

RANDOM MOTION, a confusion in this universe is **random motion.** (*POW*, p. 21)

RANDOM SAMPLING, a sampling or survey of people or things chosen at random such as interviewing every fifth shopper in a store, and taking these results as indicative of that public as a whole.

RANGE, the full extent between the highest and the lowest, as in the range in price for a product or service over a given period.

RANK, the earned title of officers and warrant officers. (FO 236)

RANK AND FILE, all the people in an organization who are not part of management.

RANKING, 1. a market research method of having consumers rank advertisements, products, product features, etc., in order of preference usually by checking off the answer on a sheet of multiple choice questions. 2. any system of putting persons, places or things in an order of preference, value, size, seniority, etc., such as assessing the value of each executive or employee in an organization and placing him on a scale of value relative to the others.

RANKS AND RATINGS CEREMONY, the **ceremony** of becoming a Sea Org officer or Petty Officer. (FO 3345)

RATE CARD, a card which lists the rates charged for different amounts of advertising.

RATE OF EXCHANGE, the rate at which one thing can be exchanged for another such as the rate at which a particular currency may be exchanged for another currency.

RATING, the earned title of Chief Petty Officers, Petty Officers, deckhands, etc. (FO 236)

RATING, ANALYTIC, a rating system of personnel in which an interviewer or person in charge measures an employee's overall performance by making numerous small judgements about the individual so that all the qualities and characteristics that comprise the worth of an employee come into play.

RATING, EFFICIENCY, a rating of the relative ability of a person or machine to utilize a given amount of time, materials, energy, etc., to achieve a maximum amount of productivity of usefulness in comparison to other persons or machines doing the same thing.

RATING, MERIT, a system of evaluating the merits each employee represents to a company by looking at such things as rate of production, attendance at work, punctuality, health, safety record, attitude, etc.

RATING SCALE, procedure of rating a person's characteristics and qualifications during an interview by writing down such judgements as superior, good, fair, etc., on a list of personal and business traits which may be printed on a standard form.

RATING SYSTEM, any system which serves to rate the relative value of persons or things such as the system of rating the merits that each employee represents to a company.

RATIO, the proportion of one thing to another expressed as a percentage or fraction; the number of times one quantity contains another. If you have 4 drivers for 2 trucks the ratio would be 2 to 1 or 2 drivers to each truck.

RATIONALIZATION, employing the use of techniques already proven effective and efficient in the management and administration of a business.

RATIONALIZING A STATISTIC, a derogatory term meaning finding excuses for down **statistics.** (HCO PL 8 Feb 68)

RAW DATA, assembled but otherwise unevaluated **data.** It is "uncooked" and "unflavored" and "untouched" by human hands. It, in short, is uncontaminated or unchanged **data.** It is native and natural and unspoiled. The only data that answers those qualifications is statistical data. "How many or how few and how much or how little in what time." That is the only **data** that a senior official in a group, organization or state ever dare use in selecting and promoting personnel. (HCO PL 13 Mar 65, *Divisions 1, 2, 3 The Structure of Organization What is Policy?*)

RAW MATERIALS, see MATERIALS, RAW.

RAW MATERIALS STOCKS, see STOCKS, RAW MATERIALS.

REACTIONARY, 1. when one is stuck on the time track it may seem pretty difficult to envision a *future.* In politics this is called "**reactionary**" or "conservative". These mean any resistance to change even when it is an improvement. The bad old days seem to be the good old days to such people. Yet the old days will not come again. One has to make the new days good. (HCO PL 11 Aug 74) **2.** (**reactionaries**) people resisting all progress or action. (HCO PL 19 May 70)

REACTIVE, irrational, **reacting** instead of acting. (*HTLTAE,* p. 122)

READINESS, in a state of preparedness for any given purpose or occasion; in suitable condition for use or action. (FSO 654)

READINESS FOR PORT LIST, **lists** which are comprehensive and cover everything you would have to do to make your area **ready for port.** (FSO 327)

READINESS FOR SEA CHECKLISTS, these **checklists** are complete in detail and made up separately for every key post aboard with a general one for supernumerary which would require simply an attestation from the person that his/her own equipment and personal belongings were securely stowed and/or lashed down and ready for the motions of the vessel during a heavy **sea.** (FSO 654)

READINESS FOR THE SEA DRILL, an all hands evolution: the Captain before sailing requires from each of the rest of the ship's company a report on the **readiness** of the area of operation **for** a voyage at **sea** of expressed duration into an expressed climate. These reports are not vague, they are made on a basis of prepared checklists. The crew member must then verify all of his checklists by actual inspection and remedy any defects before reporting his area **ready for the sea**. Every ship requires its own set of checklists. (*Ship's Org Bk.*)

REAL EARNINGS, 1. the purchasing power of money earnings as related to an established standard. Also called real wages, or real income. 2. money earnings which are adjusted when the cost of living index changes sufficiently.

REAL ESTATE, land including anything on or underneath its surface such as water, minerals, trees, buildings, etc.; realty; real property.

REAL INCOME, same as real earnings.

REALITY, **1.** by **reality** we mean the solid objects, the real things of life. (*POW*, p. 72) **2. reality** consists of the is-ness of things. (HCO PL 19 May 70) *Abbr.* R.

REAL PROPERTY, same as real estate.

REAL SOCIETY, one in which the majority are going in some direction toward a desireable goal. But it has to be their goal. This rekindles interest, action and hope. It revitalizes **society**. (HCO PL 31 Jan 69, *Humanitarian Objective and Gung Ho Groups*)

REALTY, same as real estate.

REAL WHY, **1.** the basic **why** is always the major out-point which has all other out-points as a common denominator, and that's the **real why**. That explains everything. But what is this everything? All the other out-points. What is this major out-point that explains all other out-points that I've found in this area? And that could be the definition of a **why**. (ESTO 12, 7203C06 SO II) **2.** a **real why** opens the door to handling. If it does not, then it is a wrong why. When you have a right **why**, handling becomes simple. The more one has to beat his brains for a bright idea to handle, the more likely it is that he has a wrong why. The **why** will be how come the situation is such a departure from the ideal scene and will open the door to handling. (HCO PL 12 Aug 74)

REASONABLENESS, **1.** illogic occurs when one or more data is misplaced into the wrong body of data for it. An example would be "Los Angeles smog is growing worse so we fined New York." "I am sorry, madam, but you cannot travel first class on a third class passport." Humanoid response to such displacements is to be **reasonable**. A new false datum is dreamed up and put into the body of data to explain why that datum is included. (**Reasonableness** is often inserted as explanation of other out-points also.) In the smog one, it could be dreamed up that New York's exports or imports were causing L.A. smog. In the train one, it could be inserted that in that country, passports were used instead of tickets. (HCO PL 23 June 70) **2.** faulty explanations. (HCO PL 30 Aug 70) **3.** a staff member or executive can be **"reasonable"** and accept reasons why something cannot be done, accept incomplete cycles as complete, and fail to follow through and get completions. All of which results in further traffic. (BPL 30 Jan 69) **4.** an objective can always be achieved. Most usually, when it is not being achieved, the person is finding counter-intention in the environment which coincides with his own (this is **reasonableness**), and his attention becomes directed to his own counter-intention rather than to his objective, i.e. he has interiorized into the situation. (FO 2116) **5.** you can safely say that being **reasonable** is a symptom of being unable to recognize out-points for what they are and use them to discover actual situations. (HCO PL 30 Sept 73 II)

REBATE, 1. a return or refund of part of the money paid for goods or services; discount; deduction. 2. a discount on interest payable or a return of interest previously collected if a loan is paid off before its maturity date.

REBUTTAL DAMAGES, if a person who is sued has reason, he can, as defendant, require **damages** in his **rebuttal** and should the suit be fallacious and found against the plaintiff such cases may be awarded. (HCO PL 5 Aug 66 II)

RECAPITALIZATION, any major change in the capital structure of an organization such as a revised or different total amount of the various securities it issues or new securities sold and the money used to retire existing securities.

RECEIPT, a written acknowledgement that something specified has been received. (FO 3251)

RECEIPTS BASKET, **basket** in which to dump all your invoices for summary at end of week. Everything you need for the week's summary goes into **receipts**. You only have to separate out the contents of **receipts** to do an income report. (HCO PL 16 Oct 61)

RECEIVER, a trustee appointed by a court to hold or manage bankrupt property or property under law suit.

RECEIVERSHIP, where a mission places the church or Scn at risk by virtue of uninformed or irresponsible actions, the mission *may* be taken into *receivership* by the church. In such an event the mission comes entirely under the control of the Guardian's Officer. **Receivership** is the state of being in the hands of a person (the receiver) appointed by the church to take into custody, control and management of the property or funds of a mission pending judicial action concerning the mission personnel. (BPL 24 Sept 73 I-1)

RECEIVERSHIP, 1. the office or position of a receiver. 2. the condition of a receiver holding the property of others in trust. An unpaid creditor may resort to legal action to have a court appoint a receiver to hold the property of a debtor in receivership pending litigation or pending use of such property towards the payment of the debt.

RECEIVING DEPARTMENT, that department in a business responsible for receiving raw materials, purchased products or goods, etc., and for notifying the purchasing department of such for payment.

RECEPTION, 1. **Reception** belongs in HCO Division 1, Department 1. **Reception** keeps a log book. In this log book **Reception** notes mail received and outgoing (before it is given to Accounts), persons arriving and departing from the org, supplies received and sent away and all occurrences of note. (HCO PL 7 Nov 65) **2.** handles all body traffic routing, telex, telephone and log book. Keeps a careful record of everything received by or leaving the organization. (HCO PL 18 Dec 64, *Saint Hill Org Board*) **3.** the premises of the **reception** room and the communication center are for the routing of bodies and communications into and out of the organizational communication lines. It is the function of the **receptionist** to see that bodies both of staff and of the public move into and out of the organizational communication lines. This means no bodies are allowed to stack up, gather, or remain on the premises of the **reception** room for any length of time. (SEC ED 25, 8 Jan 59)

RECEPTION CENTER, a place at which people are received and taken care of in some way. (HCO Admin Ltr 30 Jul 75)

RECEPTIONIST, purpose: to create and maintain good communication and service amongst staff, students and the public. The premises of the **reception** room are for the routing of bodies and communications into and out of the organizational communication lines. It is the function of the **receptionist** to see that bodies of staff and the public move into and out of the organizational communication lines. This means that no bodies are allowed to stack up, gather, or remain on the premises of the **reception** room for any length of time. (BPL 31 Oct 63R)

Receptionist

RECEPTION LOG, **Reception** keeps a **log** book. It is usually a cheap, large accounts ledger such as are bought at the dime store. In this **log** book **Reception** notes mail received and outgoing (before it is given to Accounts), persons arriving and departing from the org, supplies received and sent away and all occurrences of note. This **log** book is kept by the day and hour and using day, date, month, year and a 24 hour designation of time. Spaces exist between days and the dates are plainly marked. The **log** is the official registry of activities. It must be legibly kept. It is resorted to when information is required concerning mail, supplies, personnel, students and pc arrivals and departure at the start and end of service. (HCO PL 7 Nov 65)

RECESSION, a decline in economic activity of shorter duration and which is less severe than a depression.

RECOGNITION, the mental process by which a thing once known is perceived to be the same or similar. (FO 3335)

RECOGNITION CERTIFICATE, the free introductory lecture comprises this level. It teaches about elementary points from Dn or Scn data. End result is **recognition** of Dn and Scn as workable ways to bring about change and improvement. (CG&AC 75)

RECOGNITIONS CHIEF, (Sea Org) the head of Department One is the **Recognitions Chief.** His areas of responsibility are: recruitment of personnel, routing, post assignments, watch assignments, boards, transfers, hats and appearances. (FO 1416)

RECONCILE, make agree. (HCO PL 9 May 74)

RECONCILIATION, see BANK RECONCILIATION.

RECORD DATE, the date by which an investor must be registered as a stockholder on the records of a company so that he may receive a declared dividend or vote on company affairs.

RECORDER/FATHOMETER, the **recorder/Fathometer** on bridge watch is responsible for recording in the log all orders being given by the Commodore, Captain or Con, all actions performed on the bridge, and giving depth readings. (FO 2933) *Abbr.* Rec/Fath.

RECORD SHOTS, head-on dull group pictures, or single faces with no spark. Using standard events over and over, always shot from the same angle, always similarly lighted. (HCO PL 21 Nov 68 II)

RECOURSE, means a turning or applying to a person or thing for aid or security. (HCO PL 24 Feb 72)

RECOVERY, 1. a part of the business cycle. That stage where an economy pulls out of a depression characterized by rising production, employment, wages, and general business activity. 2. a regaining of one's investment or costs through sales, production, etc. 3. the final verdict in a court case.

RECRUIT, to **recruit**—reinforce, replenish, renew, restore, to reinvigorate. Latin—*recrescere*, to grow again. (BO 26, 28 Feb 70)

RECRUIT INFORMATION PACKS, recruit information packs are mailed out by Div II (Dissem Div does the layout and printing) and consist of a specific form letter to a correct public, flier to that exact public and reply form, or sign-up form or survey. (BPL 20 May 72R)

RECRUITING OFFICER, 1. defined as the **officer** in the SO Org on the post of SO manning or **recruiting.** (BO 70, 25 Jan 72) 2. (Gung-Ho Group) the **Recruiting Officer** recruits group members and acts as reception and keeps the address files. (HCO PL 2 Dec 68)

RECRUITMENT, HCO has **recruitment** which means it gets people from outside the org to be placed as terminals in the org=posts. (HCO PL 7 Jul 71)

RECRUITMENT, to locate and supply a company with suitable new employees.

RECRUITMENT SUPERVISOR, (Central Personnel Office hat) purpose: to get international **recruitment** in excess done. (FO 3332)

RECUPERATION INTENSIVE, see PSYCHOSOMATIC INTENSIVE.

REDEMPTION PRICE, see PRICE, REDEMPTION.

REDEMPTION PROJECT FORCE, see REHABILITATION PROJECT FORCE.

RED FORM, 1. on the concept that a missionaire on a mission to an org is in fact an auditor to that org, the **red form** and its use is established. The **red form** is in fact an assessment sheet which applies to an org instead of a pc. A long number of items is listed for check off. It is a pre-compiled list of all possible major errors that could be depressing an org's stats or expansion. After each item there is a remedy noted as in the case of a pc's Green Form. (FO 2300) **2.** the **red form** is cancelled. Missionaires do not use **red forms** on an org, or evaluate the situation, and then without any approved plan, handle. (FO 2937)

RED PURCHASE ORDER, see PURCHASE ORDER.

RED TABBED LABEL, (or red marked) tape color flash code for LRH master for music, cine, original tapes of books and tapes LRH wants kept. These belong in the Office of LRH. They are never erased. The designating word "cine" or "book" etc., is added to the label with other descriptive matter, LRH uses also some colored reels. A colored reel (plastic is colored) is always property of LRH. (HCO PL 7 Dec 65)

REFERENCE, 1. a person who can give reliable information about the character, value or ability of another. 2. a letter from someone such as a former employer, giving information about the character or ability of another.

REFERRAL SYSTEM, Body A goes to staff terminal X for some service or other. Terminal X says, "I can't pay you because Financial Planning. . . ." So Body A calls on another staff member who says, "Permission is required from G." So Body A goes to G and is told, "We haven't got a list to hand so. . . ." So Body A goes . . . where's the production? But there's sure a lot of dispatch traffic! The system, in vogue in most bureaucracies, even has a name. It's called "the **referral system.**" No one gives service. No situation is terminatedly handled. (HCO PL 28 May 71 II)

REFERRED NAMES, (the weakest classification in inquiries) **referred names**, by which is meant **names** which are simply **referred** to the organization as being interested. (HCO PL 7 Jan 64)

REFLATION, the instance of inflation after recession, stimulated to restore business conditions to a level where purchasing power, incomes and employment are up.

REFORM CODE, the **Reform Code** of Scn. We sent out mailings and we received back anything that people thought that should be corrected. This resulted in **reform code** in which the sec checks were cancelled and all old folders on this have been burned and disconnection is cancelled as a relief to those suffering family oppression. It's no longer required in SP orders and the person has to handle. The fair game law was cancelled and the prohibition against writing down a recording of professional materials was made and this was actually the extent of the **Reform Code**. (Ron's Journal 1968)

REFUND, a return of money after service. (HCO PL 9 Nov 74)

REFUNDING, (or refinancing) 1. to pay back a debt with a new loan. 2. to take on a new debt through refinancing an old debt. 3. the situation of a company selling new securities and using the money to retire existing securities with the objective of saving interest costs, extending the maturity of the loan, or both.

REFUND/REPAYMENT ROUTING AND REPORT FORM, the purpose of this **form** is to provide a standard, functional line for handling **refunds** and **repayments** to individuals, and to ensure that such situations are handled rapidly, completely and with minimal dev-t. (HCO PL 20 Oct 72) [The above HCO PL was cancelled by BPL 10 Oct 75 X.]

REGGING ADMIN I/C, the Tours Section must have a **Regging Admin I/C** who services both Tours Section and Div 6 Reg. His duties consist of supplying admin supplies, forms, etc., supplying and paging prospect files from CF to be contacted, making up folders of distinguishing color for new CF prospects obtained from events and tours and filing them in CF, collecting all sales records, seeing they are in order and handing them over to Dept 6, keeping tabs of stats and graphing them for tour and event regging and any other clerical assistance to the Div 6 Reg and Tours Section. (LRH ED 159R-1 INT)

REGISTRAR, 1. in a Scn org, the person who signs up people for Scn service. (HCO Admin Ltr 30 Jul 75) **2.** a **registrar** deals in *exchange* between the org and public. She *exchanges* the valuable services of the org in *exchange* for valuables. Valuables in this case being money. (BPL 22 Dec 71R II) **3.** the **registrar** has responsibility for procurement, interview, signing up, legal and finance. The **registrar** is directly responsible for all students and pc procurement and keeping place full. (HCOB 26 Sept 56) **4.** the Department of Promotion and Registration is divided into three distinct categories; present time, past and future. There are three types of **registrars** which handle these three categories. The Immediate **Registrar** is mainly concerned with present time prospects. She answers any questions and handles any problems of those people who want auditing or training in present time. The Assistant **Registrar** is mainly concerned with the past, that is, she handles ARC breaks. She is concerned with finding out why people are upset with us or why they have stopped communicating with us. She re-establishes communication with people. The Letter **Registrar** is concerned with future prospects. She writes to all future prospects. Her job is to see to it that we have people to train and audit in the future. (SEC ED 66, 30 Jan 59) **5.** purpose: to get a great many people processed and trained, and to make certain that the income of the organization is adequate to get the job done. The first duty of the **registrar** is to sign-up persons for something and receive money in hand, passing the next instant to Accounts which takes over all further invoice and paper work and the applicant. The **Registrar** is not supposed to engage in long sales talks or sales letters. She is there to help people sign up and to assist resolution of their problems in signing up. She is not there to sell anything. People want more Scn, not sales talks. She would be brief and efficient and effective. The **Registrar** keeps appointments once made and keeps none waiting. She signs up everybody who comes to see her. (SEC ED 2, 15 Dec 58) *Abbr.* REG.

REGISTRAR, 1. a person, trust company or bank that certifies to the public that stock issues are correctly stated according to the provisions of an organization's charter, and prevents the issuance of more stock than is authorized. 2. An administrative officer of a university or college who is responsible for enrollment records and data on the academic standing of students. 3. a corporation officer in charge of the records of ownership of its securities.

REGISTRAR ASSESSMENT, when a **registrar** has low stats or trouble on post and the why is not easily found this list is assessed on the person by a Scn auditor using a meter. It is assessed Method 5. Handling instructions are given under each item. This **assessment** may be done more than once on any person but should not be repeated on the same person too frequently. (BPL 22 Nov 72R)

REGISTRAR INTERVIEW FORM, this **form** is to be used by Body Registrars when persons interviewed did not immediately enroll onto service. It is not necessary to fill in this **form** when a person signs up, pays in full and routes onto service. The purpose of the **Reg Interview Form** is to provide data on individuals interviewed so that these persons may be kept in contact with and channeled onto service. (HCO PL 12 Oct 72 II) [The above HCO PL was cancelled and replaced by BPL 1 Dec 72 I, *"Big League" Registration Series 2 Sales Data Sheet* and the resulting form called a "Sales Data Sheet."]

REGISTRAR INTERVIEWS, number of persons the **Registrar** has interviewed for the week (includes **reg interviews** by the Public **Reg** and Tours). Interviews over the phone are not included. (BPL 11 Aug 75)

REGISTRAR MAIL UNIT, the **Mail Unit** assembles all letters and mailings, keeps accurate logs of same and sends copies and files to CF and mails the letters. This **unit** also provides supplies and keeps the dictation equipment in working order. (HCO PL 29 Nov 68)

REGISTRAR TYPING UNIT, letters are dictated into the dictating machine by the Letter Registrars. The **Registrar Typing Unit** takes the letters out of the dictation pool and they are **typed**, and envelopes addressed. (HCO PL 29 Nov 68)

REGISTRATION, in the investment field, the act of a company filing a registration statement with the Securities and Exchange Commission giving information on its operation, management, securities and purpose of the new issuance, before a public offering may be made.

REGISTRATION CARD, all introductory lecture attendees or new public coming in for Div 6 service are given these **cards** to fill in at reception. Public Reg ticks off the square of the classification under which the person comes. In the notes section of the **card** the Public Reg can write any details or particulars she needs to remember. The Public Reg after an interview signs the **card** on the signature line provided. When phone regging she also uses the notes section on the **card** to write details. (HCO PL 26 Nov 71R I) [The above HCO PL was cancelled by BPL 1 Dec 72 V.]

REGISTRATION OFFICER, (Gung-Ho Group) the **Registration Officer** registers members, other groups, students, congresses; anything where a membership is concerned is registered by the **Registration Officer** (and any card is issued by Certs and Awards). (HCO PL 2 Dec 68)

REGRESSION ANALYSIS, see ANALYSIS, REGRESSION.

REGULAR STAFF AUDITOR, auditor giving 25 hours per week every week to one pc a week. (HCO PL 24 Mar 61 II)

REGULATION T, the federal regulation controlling the amount of credit that may be extended by brokers and dealers to customers for stock market investments.

REGULATION U, the federal regulation controlling the amount of credit that may be extended by a bank to its customers for stock market investments.

REHABILITATION, what do we mean by **rehabilitation**? Increased awareness of the exact conditions with which the person is surrounded. When he's aware of these actualities, aware of these conditions and he's aware of the real situation he can then act sensibly. (5904C15)

REHABILITATION PROJECT FORCE, 1. brought into being in Div 4 FSO. To it are assigned: (1) R/Sers (2) low OCA non-producers (3) repeated stat crashers (4) overt product makers. The stable datum for the unit and for its individual sections is one job, one place, one time. Its sub-products are completed cycles of action. The 5-hour daily study period for the **RPF** is devoted to tech. In this period, the **RPF** is to learn tech and get themselves handled in co-audit to full clean-up and release. The **RPF** has been created by the Commodore so that redemption can occur. That is basically its only purpose. (FO 3434)

2. Redemption Project Force. (ED 965 Flag) *Abbr.* RPF.

REHABILITATION PROJECT FORCE BOSUN, the **RPF** is under the Area Estates Bosun and is in the charge of the **RPF Bosun.** (FO 3434R)

REHABILITATION PROJECT FORCE MAA, responsible to the RPF Bosun for the ethics of the section leaders to keep ethics in on their sections, and if he has to take ethics action on a section member, that member's leader suffers the same penalty also. He has the section leaders muster their sections before breakfast, after meals and before study, before securing for the day and at any other times required by the Bosun within reason and without distraction from production. (FO 3434) *Abbr.* RPF MAA.

REHABILITATION UNIT, formed in Division Five. It absorbs the old mud box brigade which is cancelled. Those removed or comm eved as ineffective or trouble are sent to the **Rehabilitation Unit** via the Examiner. The Examiner looks them over for outnesses in (1) case (2) ethics (3) training (Scientology and Sea Org ship training) (4) knowledge of policy. He then makes specific recommendations which if followed will rehabilitate the individual as a highly effective and worthwhile Sea Org member. The **unit** is worked hard during the day on a rigorous schedule on jobs assigned by the Review Chief handling corrective areas and jobs needing remedy and repair. The **unit** itself is thus made into an effective ship's review team. It works on a one job, one time, one place formula completing each job before moving into the next. Each individual thus earns the right to the remedial services he or she will receive. (FO 1848)

REIT, Real Estate Investment Trust, an organization which invests mainly in real estate property.

REJECTED MATERIALS REPORT, a report of merchandise that has been rejected by the Receiving Department of an organization which is referred to the Purchasing Department for handling.

RELATED FACTS KNOWN, a plus-point, all relevant **facts known.** (HCO PL 3 Oct 74)

RELAY, (routing used on telex lines). Take and carry further. Example: message from Buffalo to Flag: 010412 Buf CO FOLO **Relay** FFR. . . . On the above, Commanding Officer FOLO will ensure that the telex is **relayed** to the Flag Flag Rep. (BPL 23 Apr 73R)

RELAYING AN ORDER IN A CONFUSING MANNER, (type of dev-t) communicators and messengers can create dev-t and foul up actions by poor **relay** of information. (BPL 30 Jan 69)

RELEASE, **1.** one who knows he can continue to improve by auditing and that he will not now become worse in life. (HCO PL 21 Aug 63) **2.** precisely defined as one who has no psychotic or neurotic tendencies of any kind and has a certainty that he will get no worse. Technically, a **release** is one whose graph has been raised by processing and whose IQ has been improved. (HCO Info Ltr 14 Apr 61)

RELEASE, 1. the act of relinquishing to another, the right, claim or title one holds on something such as releasing one's claim to a piece of property. 2. a legal document stating that one is relinquishing such a right, claim or title.

RELEASE BUTTONS, **release buttons** (an **R** set in the S and double ARC triangle of Scn) may be (and should be) issued to HGC pcs who have attained its requirement by HCO Secs without charge. (HCO PL 12 Aug 63)

RELEASE CHECK, for a **release** (formerly Keyed-Out Clear) **check,** the TA position may be anything from 2.0 to 3.0 with a floating needle. Note that this is the old "Clear Test." It now is classified as a **release.** (HCO PL 2 Apr 65, *Meter Checks*)

RELEASED, the overall statistic of the RPF Tech Unit and its I/C is No. of RPF fully cleaned up and **released.** Fully cleaned up is defined as "in normal operation or above on the first dynamic by actual behavior and able to respond fully to standard grade chart actions." **Released** is defined as "in normal operation or above on the third dynamic by actual production causatively and positively contributing to the Sea Org without requiring undue duress or abnormal supervision to perform Sea Org duties." (FO 3434)

RELEASE FORMS, waivers. (HCO PL 1 Sept 65 IV)

RELEASE LOG BOOK, Certs and Awards **book** for **logging** a **release** in. (HCO PL 23 Aug 65 II)

RELEASE PIN, the standard Scn pin is a plain gold S and double triangle. When a red **"R"** is mounted on the face of this **pin** it signifies a **release,** Grades 0-IV. When the preclear has attained Grades V or VI, the **release pin** is the S and double triangle with the red **"R"** surrounded by a gold disc larger than the **pin** itself. (HCO PL 27 Oct 65)

RELIABLE SOURCE, two bad systems are in current use on data. The first is **"reliable source"**. The other system in use is multiple report. In this system (**reliable source**) a report is considered true or factual only if the **source** is well thought of. This is a sort of authority system. Most professionals working with data collection use this. Who said it? If he is considered **reliable** or an authority, the data is considered true or factual. Sources are graded from A to D. A is highest, D lowest. The frailty of this system is at once apparent. Philby, as a high British intelligence official, was a Russian spy for 30 years. Any data he gave the U.K. or U.S. was "true" because he was a **"reliable source."** He had every Western agent who was being sent into Communist areas "fingered" and shot. Psychiatrists are "authorities" on the mind. Yet insanity and criminality soar. They are the **"reliable sources"** on the mind. (HCO PL 17 May 70)

RELIGION, 1. derivation: from Latin *religio* (*-onis*), (**religion**), (piety), (conscientiousness), (scrupulousness), from *religare*, (to bind back), *re-*, and *ligare*, (to bind), (to bind together). (a) any specific system of belief, worship, conduct, etc., often involving a code of ethics and a philosophy: as the Christian (**religion**), the Buddhist (**religion**), etc. (b) loosely any system of beliefs, practices, ethical values, etc., resembling, suggestive of, or likened to such a system, as, humanism is his (**religion**). (BPL 6 Mar 69) **2.** a **religion** is perforce a method of worship and a civilizing influence having to do with the human spirit. (5510C27)

RELIGIOUS, *adj.* derivation: from Latin *religiosus*, (**religious**), of, concerned with, appropriate to, teaching, or relating to religion; as, a (**religious**) place; (**religious**) subjects. Also careful; scrupulous; conscientiously exact; such as religion requires; as, a (**religious**) observance of vows or promises. (BPL 6 Mar 69)

REMEDY POL-A, when a staff member who is taking a checkout from the Staff Training Officer flunks, regardless of his grade of release or state of case, the following is done: (1) he or she is meter checked out on misunderstood words and these are handled. (2) he or she is checked out for disagreements with **policy** and these are handled. (HCO PL 29 Apr 66)

REMEDY POL-B, when a staff member who has had Remedy Pol-A still has a high flunk rate, he or she is given full meter handling on the subject of earlier admin systems or earlier **policies** and these are handled as to (1) misunderstood words and (2) disagreements with the earlier systems or **policies**. (HCO PL 29 Apr 66)

REMIMEO, 1. (mimeo distribution) this includes main technical or policy materials. Received at a Central Org in stencil form, copies are run off for their staff, and for the staffs of their nearby orgs and for their students as they wish. They keep the stencil on file for additional copies as needed. They file copies in their master and general files in each org including the receiving org. The stencil orgs have considerable discretion in how many they run off, how many they send smaller orgs, whether they issue to students or not. But they must keep the stencil for reuse and file in their own master files with the copy clearly so stamped. (HCO PL 2 Jul 64) **2. remimeo** means mimeo copies to be made by the org. This indicates main technical or policy material. When a fair copy is sent to an org from Flag, copies are run off for their staff, and for the staffs of their nearby orgs and for their students as they wish. They keep the stencil on file for additional copies as needed. They file copies in their master and general files in each org including the receiving org. (BPL 14 Apr 69R) **3.** for internal org use only. It means copies may be made in the org for supply to staff or students on course only. (BPL 10 Feb 71R) **4.** all St. Hill staff. An electronic stencil is made for each org to issue as many copies as needed. (HCO PL 25 Jan 66 III)

REMITTANCE, the act of sending a sum of money to someone or the sum of money sent.

REMOTE REG, any of the various types of **regs** stationed in various areas of the world to **reg** for Flag. (FBOs, FSCs, Flag Tours, FOLO Tours, org **regs**, FSMs). (BFO 122-6)

REMOVING PARTICLES OFF THE LINE, apart from being a serious offense, taking communication **particles off** another's desk or out of their in-basket or **off the** comm **lines** causes dev-t, and lost time in searching for the missing **particles** and can sabotage projects or actions, vital data being missing. (BPL 30 Jan 69)

RENT, the sum of money one has agreed to pay the owner of some property for its use such as a monthly fee for occupying someone else's house.

REORGANIZATION, a thorough alteration of the capital structure and/or the working structure of an organization, especially after a bankruptcy.

REPAIR, to **repair** something is to put it in, or restore it to, a good working condition. That means operational. (FO 2204)

Repair

REPAIR CHIEF, is in charge of all **repairs,** does only **repairs** and has under him electrical, electronics and plumbing as well as motors, machinery, etc. All non-watch electricians and electronics are under the **Repair Chief.** (FO 1958)

REPAIR, CONSTRUCTION AND RENOVATIONS UNIT, (Estates Section Dept 21) the **Repair, Construction and Renovations Unit** is responsible for all buildings and grounds excluding items which come under the Engineering Unit. It handles all **repairs, constructions** of whatever importance and **renovation** cycles including painting, carpentry work, landscaping, any action that will restore or add to asset value or usability of org premises and fixtures. (HCO PL 16 Aug 74 IIR)

REPAIR SECTION, the theory of the engine room operation is that there is a **Repair Section** which works consistently on **repairs** whereas all the rest of the engine room works on operation and general maintenance such as oil changes and general upkeep of the engines. (FO 1109)

REPAYMENT, **1.** a return of money without the service being taken. (HCO PL 9 Nov 74) **2.** return of pre-payments. (BPL 22 Dec 71R II)

REPAYMENT, to reimburse someone with money, goods or services owed.

REPEAT DEMAND, see DEMAND, REPEAT.

REPEATED TRAFFIC, the same **traffic repeated** to the same executive is dev-t. Often takes the form of information or compliance reported by telex and then the same information being sent by dispatch. There are times when a telex is followed by a more lengthy dispatch or report, but this should only occur when extra information is really needed. (BPL 30 Jan 69)

REPEAT MISSIONS, these are **missions** sent out to handle the same matter that a former mission should have handled. (FO 1481)

REPETITIOUS WORK, tedious work which is repeated again and again.

REPLACEMENT COSTS, see COSTS, REPLACEMENT.

REPLACEMENT DEMAND, see DEMAND, REPLACEMENT.

REPLACEMENT TRANSFER, see TRANSFER, REPLACEMENT.

REPORT, **reports** are summaries of areas or people or situations or conditions. (HCO PL 1 Apr 72)

REPORT, a written or verbal statement of what has occurred in the area one is responsible for. Reports are usually sent at regular intervals to those who are senior to the area from which a report comes. They can be on the subject of production, personnel, finances, sales or anything which higher-ups would want to know. Reports contain facts, figures, information, suggestions or recommendations.

REPORT REQUIRED, when an executive letter requests data it is headed under the HCO Executive Letter of Date line, **Report Required.** This is done only when **reports** are **required** from all orgs. A report requested from one org is not so headed. (HCO PL 22 Feb 65 III)

REPS, **"Ron's External Publics Scientologists."** They are valuable volunteers who are carrying out specific actions with **Ron's external publics.** (BPL 3 Sept 75 II)

REPS PROGRAM, a **program** whereby all active FSMs have the opportunity to personally feed power to Ron by assisting his Personal PRO International. The **program** is called the **Reps Program,** and those contributing are called **Ron's External Publics Scientologists.** They are valuable volunteers who are carrying out specific actions with **Ron's external publics.** (BPL 3 Sept 75 II)

REQUIREMENTS CHIEF, FPPO **Requirements Chief,** products: (1) FRU personnel fully completed on their TIPs in good time, fully qualified and fired to Flag. (2) well trained reserve Flag SO members. (FO 3339RA)

REQUISITION, a written request for needed materials or supplies, a requisition form.

REQUISITION FORM, a company form which when filled out specifies materials or supplies needed, who needs them, the reason they are needed, when they are needed by and any other data pertinent. It is sent to the purchasing department which, subject to any prior authorizations, obtains the materials needed.

REQUISITION, PERSONNEL, a written request for personnel to handle the needs of a unit, department, etc.

RES, in law, term for thing, object, property, a trust fund or trust estate.

RESCUE DRILL, another function of the Damage Control and Rescue Party. One uses the same party for a different purpose and hence also calls it the Rescue Party. People and things not of the ship are handled in this drill. Swamped rowboats, exhausted swimmers, sinking ships, etc. The ship's company in general goes on handling the ship and the special actions required are done by the Damage Control and Rescue Party. In a very small ship the Damage Control and Rescue Party may be as few as two hands. But it must be no fewer than two and may not be one person as it can get into trouble, and it must exist. (*Ship's Org Bk.*)

RESEARCH, **research** doesn't consist of a random group of auditors getting some "hot ideas" and rushing them to the field. It consists of L. Ron Hubbard summating and mathematically predicting findings and finding them, then placing very exact codifications in the hands of staff auditors who test them against exact preclear result tests. No work undertaken by man has been more carefully or successfully done. (A 1957 Letter issued by HASI Accounts, London, *What Your Money has Bought*)

RESEARCH, a careful investigation of an area to discover and isolate the basic laws or principles involved plus the formulation and testing of a manner or device which will feasibly and safely allow these principles to be put to use.

RESEARCH, CONSUMER, the area of market research which deals with the marketing of goods to consumers. It includes establishing what markets exist for new and current products, discovering consumer buying habits and analyzing all aspects of getting a product into a customer's hands.

RESEARCH, DESK, expression for the practice of locating, assembling and evaluating data already published or in use as contrasted with raw field work to collect new data.

RESEARCH LIBRARY, the Research Section, Dept 5 of the Sea Org is to be set up as a **research library**. After finding sources of information, which will be a most important part of the **library**, the research section is to obtain reference books, catalogues, magazines, and newspapers with the latest data on political events, historical events, medical and scientific discoveries, aeronautical and oceanographical references and events, etc; anything that may pertain to the present and future plans of the Sea Org. This **library** is to be available for mission planning and **research**. (FO 650)

RESEARCH, MEDIA, an analysis of those who are on the receiving end of any type of mass media such as television viewers, newspaper readers, etc., to probe advertising potential, public opinion, attitudes, types of publics involved, etc.

RESEARCH, MOTIVATION, market research investigation into what the reasons are for consumers buying what they buy or choosing to engage in certain activities in preference to others.

RESEARCH, PERSONNEL, precise, techniques of evaluating personnel for the purposes of employee ratings and establishing incentives as well as setting standards for the selection, placement and training of employees.

RESEARCH, PUBLIC OPINION, any activity that probes a general or specific public to find out their opinions relating to some product, idea, company, etc.

RESEARCH, TECHNICAL, see ANALYSIS, TECHNICAL.

RESEARCH TEN PER CENTS, Central Orgs, City Offices and franchise holders contribute **10%** of their gross weekly income to various expenses and usages at Saint Hill including **research**. But this **10%** shall not include payments recieved for books by anyone. (HCO PL 11 May 65, *HCO Book Account Policy Receipt and Use of Membership Monies*)

RESERVATION LETTER, when a person sends in his/her enrollment forms plus full payment or deposit ($150 or more) send a **Reservation Letter** introducing the person to the

Body Reg. This is in addition to the letter acknowledging the forms and payment. Give the person an R factor in this letter that you are enclosing the **reservation letter** and that he needs to keep it until he actually comes into the org to start his service, at which point he should give it to the Body Reg (who routes it back to you—the ASR). (HCO PL 18 Feb 73 I)

RESERVE, an amount of funds set apart and held back by a bank or organization in order to be able to meet probable or possible demands of despositors, investors or special circumstances.

RESERVE ACCOUNT, the **Reserve Account** has a purpose similar to the General Liability Fund and Building Fund Accounts, and is established for organizations to put aside monies for legal fees, new buildings, mission payments to Sea Org, etc. It is also designed to provide a cushion of cash for organizations to fall back on if ever needed. (HCO PL 10 Dec 68)

RESERVED PAYMENT ACCOUNT, as its name indicates, is money set aside for a certain destination but not yet sent. Purpose of the **Reserved Payment Account**: to prevent a false idea of the financial position of the org from occurring by providing a place where money awaiting disbursement can be placed before it is actually paid out. Thus removing it from the general accounts and estimates of financial position of an org. (HCO PL 4 Mar 65, *Reserved Payment Account*)

RESERVES CHIEF, Staff Banking Officer. (CBO 14)

RESERVE SUM, (Flag) 20% of the delivery sum paid off the top to WW and GO as is usual for all orgs. (FSO 667RC)

RESIDENT BUYER, an agent living in a large or choice merchandising area who, for a fee or commission, is authorized to buy merchandise for retailers and who is usually versed in current and future trends and promotion ideas.

RESIGNATION, a written or verbal statement informing others that one has given up a job or position; a document stating that one is relinquishing or giving up possession of something.

RE-SIGN GI, total collected in the shop for **re-sign**-ups without the person leaving the org, for the week. (BFO 119)

RE-SIGN-UP REGISTRATION, a Body Registrar interviewing pcs and students after completion of a major service, presenting them with their certificate and **re-signing** them up on the spot for further major services and taking their money. (HCO PL 28 Nov 71R I)

RESOLUTION, a motion that has been put before a committee or meeting and passed or accepted.

RESOURCES, **resources** are things like space, furniture, equipment, and the establishment of the factors of the org. (FEBC 7, 7101C23 SO III)

RESPECT, **1.** a broad examination of history shows clearly that men follow those they **respect. Respect** is a recognition of inspiration, purpose and competence. (HCO PL 29 Oct 71 III) **2.** confidence in one's self is something that has to be earned. It is **respect**. This is a compound of demonstrated competence, being on post and being dependable. (OODs 10 Nov 71)

RESPONDENT, 1. a person who responds or informs by giving an answer. 2. in law, a person who is a defendant, as in an equity case.

RESPONSE DIRECTING DEPARTMENT, Celebrity Centre Department 12A, Division 4A, Public Clearing Division. Product: public correctly directed into Scn. (BO 7 PAC, 17 Feb 74)

RESPONSIBILITY, **1.** the state, quality or fact of being **responsible**, and **responsible** means legally or ethically accountable for the care or welfare of another. Involving personal accountability or ability to act without guidance or superior authority. Being the source or cause of something. Capable of making moral or rational decisions on one's own and therefore answerable for one's behavior. Able to be trusted or depended upon; reliable. Based upon or characterized by good judgement or sound thinking. (HCO PL 29 Oct 71 II) **2.** the way not to have is to ignore or combat or withdraw from. These three, ignoring or combatting or withdrawing sum up to no having. They also sum up to no **responsibility** for such things. Thus we can define **responsibility** as the concept of being able to care for or reach or to be. To be **responsible** for something one does not actually have to care for it, or reach it or be it. One only needs to believe or know that he has the ability to care for it, reach it or be it. "Care for it" is a broader concept than but similar to start, change or stop it. It includes guard it, help it, like it, be interested in it, etc. (HCO PL 17 Jan 62)

RESTIMULATE, to key-in. (HCO PL 24 Jan 69 II)

REST PERIOD, a break from work for a period of time to extrovert one's attention, relieve monotony, rest tired body muscles, replenish one's energy, etc.

RESTRAINT OF TRADE, any method employed to limit free competition in business or commerce such as the use of price fixing or creating monopolies.

RESTRICTED LIST, the purpose of this **list** is to help maintain ship security by informing QMs of the gangway about any person who, by reason of being in ethics trouble should be **restricted** to the ship. (FO 3525)

RESUMÉ, a summary of information on a subject, situation or person, the latter containing the individual's experience to date, education, personal and business background, etc., usually submitted when applying for employment.

RETAIL, the sale of goods in small quantities to the final consumer or user.

RETAILER, a merchant who usually owns a store or chain of stores that offer merchandise and products for sale at the consumer level.

RETAINER, no Scn org may pay a **retainer** to a lawyer. By **retainer** is meant the payment of a sum of money *before* he takes on a case. It is merely an advance payment, either for a particular case or for doing legal work generally. (BPL 1 Apr 71)

RETIREMENT, 1. the act of permanently leaving one's employment or occupation, or withdrawing from public life, to live on retirement income, pension or savings. 2. the act of taking out of circulation as the retiring of bonds or currency.

RETRAIN, **1.** the entire course as any green student would take it from beginning to end. (ESTO 4, 7203C02 SO II) **2.** means that the student is sent to cramming to get straight exactly what is missed and then back to course and does the entire course again. (BPL 27 Jul 69R)

RETRAIN, to train again in order to teach a new skill or occupation, or to strengthen something already learned.

RETREAD, **1.** a **retread** is a specific thing. It is just a Method 4, which is just on the meter finding any misunderstood word with regard to a specific piece of material—word clearing. **Retread** simply consists of find the Method 4 of this particular body of materials. They usually give an examination. He doesn't know anything about this specific body of materials so they take that whole body of materials and they make him redo it, and they Method 4 it. Misunderstood word and then misunderstood word and they clear it up and the guy restudies that and polishes up this other thing that he doesn't know much about and so forth. He comes back and he starts auditing again. (ESTO 4, 7203C02 SO II) **2.** picking up the materials the guy was weak on. It's a review course. But it does mean going through the pack and the materials. It's mostly a check of misunderstood words Method 4 on the different sections of materials. (7202C22 SO)

RETROACTIVE PAY, see BACK PAY.

RETROGRESSIVE CONSUMER, see CONSUMER, PROGRESSIVE.

RETURN, same as yield.

RETURNED WORK, see WORK, RETURNED.

RETURN ON CAPITAL, the total of the profits one expects to make from a proposed project over several years, stated as a percentage of the total cost of the project. *Abbr.* ROC

RETURN ON INVESTMENT, a measurement of company performance. The return on investment is the return of profit, expressed as a percentage rate of the amount invested to achieve something. *Abbr.* ROI.

REVALUATION, 1. updating to a higher level the value of an asset to meet present market value. 2. a revision made by a country in its rate at which its currency is exchanged for other currencies.

REVENIMUS, in the Sea Org coat of arms, the motto *revenimus* (pronounced: **re ve nē′moos**) is the Latin word for "We come back," the motto of the Sea Org. (FO 3350)

REVENUE, the total income of an organization or a government derived from all sources, usually calculated for a specified time period.

REVERSE TAKE-OVER BID, a take-over bid that seeks to employ the same management of the company taken over to manage the resultant company.

REVIEW, 1. the Department of **Review** is in the Qualifications Division. The entire purpose of the Department of **Review** is repair and correction of auditing and training difficulties. **Review** is an extension of my own case cracker hat and my own fast instruction hat. (HCO PL 24 Apr 65) **2.** that area where standard tech is corrected back to standard tech. (Class VIII No. 2) **3.** (any Committee of Evidence) findings and convening authority endorsement may be subject to **review** by any upper level committee. **Review** must be applied for by anyone named as an interested party but no other, and only if a penalty was recommended (whether endorsed or not). A Committee of Evidence for **Review** is convened and handled in exactly the same way as an ordinary Committee of Evidence but it cannot call new or even old witnesses or the Interested Parties. All it can do is listen to the tapes of the hearings, examine the evidence given in the original hearings and recommend to its own convening authority one of two things: (1) that a new committee be convened on the site by the Upper Convening Authority to examine points thought to be in question, (2) that the penalty be changed. A Committee of Evidence **Review** can recommend to increase or decrease the penalty. (HCO PL 7 Sept 63)

REVIEW AUDITOR, a **review auditor** looks over the folder and the case, finds out what hasn't been or needs handling and puts the case back together again. The **review auditor** never does major actions. These are done in the HGC. (LRH ED 103 INT)

REVIEW CASE SUPERVISOR, **Review C/S reviews** tech case failures, taking this load off the Senior C/S. (HCO PL 25 Sept 74)

REVIEW, DIRECT, term that refers to the regular checking and inspection of work while being produced to avoid defective or returned work.

REVIEW, INDIRECT, a system of management and quality control that observes the quality, quantity and viability of production indirectly through the number of complaints received about products, lack of sales that can be directly attributed to customer rejection in favor of another brand or returned products that are deemed unsatisfactory. Indirect review alone cannot replace direct observation and supervision of operations.

REVIEW MISSION, 1. a **review mission** is handled by the same officers but is actually operated by the fourth Mate in the Fifth Division because a **review mission** is a correction function. (6802C28 SO) **2.** the second **mission** which went out on the same target is a **review mission** because the first mission failed. (6802C28 SO)

REVOLT, **1. revolt** is only an expression of too long unmended departures from the ideal scene of society. Usually the stitches taken to mend the growing social order are too weak and too hastily improvised to prevent the cultural fabric from being torn to rags. Street battles and angry infantry are the direct opposite of the ideal political scene. (HCO PL 5 Jul 70) **2.** protests against idle status. (HCO PL 7 Jul 70)

REVOLVING LOAN, a type of loan made by a bank or finance company which upon satisfactory repayment, offers the option attached whereby the borrower may again get the same size loan should he require it for a further business affair.

REWARD SYSTEM, ways in which employees are rewarded or encouraged to make progress in an organization such as bonuses, increased responsibilities, special recognition, status symbols, etc.

RE-WORK, 1. to work over again, as in the case of product returned because of defects. 2. to revise or improve, as with a design or manufacturing method. 3. to submit a product, service or system to a new process.

RHYTHM, any kind of movement characterized by the regular recurrence of strong and weak elements. **Rhythm** denotes the regular patterned flow, the ebb and rise of sounds and movements in speech, music, writing, dance, and in other physical activities. (HCOB 25 Apr 74)

Rhythm

RIDE TO THE SOUND OF THE GUNS, that is a cavalrymen's maxim. In other words you keep hitting where it's hot and you gradually will come out of a battle situation. (7205C18 SO)

RIGHT, this would be forwarding a purpose not destructive to the majority of the dynamics. (HCOB 19 Aug 67)

RIGHT ACTION, a **right action** is **right** to the degree that it benefits the greatest number of dynamics. (HCO PL 1 Nov 70 III)

RIGHT ARM INSIGNIA, any officer or petty officer qualified in dock and bridge duties wears **insignia** on the **right** shoulder or collar. Members of the company not so qualified wear insignia on the left shoulder or collar. **Right arm insignia** succeeds to command of any party or activity at sea or shore. Only members of the company with **right arm insignia** succeed to command of parties or ships ashore or at sea in the absence of their senior or when he is disabled for any reason. Only those with **right arm insignia** may take over deck or bridge officer or petty officer duties when a vacancy occurs due to absence, emergency or illness. This is also true of shore portion. (FO 79)

RIGHT ARM RANK/RATING, able to command the ship at sea. (ED 321 Flag)

RIGHT ARM RATES, require privileges of etiquette and can order Sea Org personnel. Means "can succeed to command of ship." Left arm—administrative—personnel without privilege of etiquette and many may not order sailors or **right arm rates** and do not succeed to command of a ship regardless of rank. In wearing shoulder boards on shirts or coats, **right arm** officers wear both boards, left arm officers one board only and that on the left shoulder. (FO 196) *Abbr.* RA.

RIGHT OF RECOURSE, the legal right to recover or demand satisfaction of a debt when the party liable fails to pay.

RIGHT OF REPLY, see MOTION.

RIGHT OF WAY, in real estate, it is an easement which permits a person to travel over land owned by another.

RIGHTS, the franchises of citizenship according to existing codes. (PAB 96)

RIGHTS, (or rights issue) in the case of a company issuing additional securities to raise new capital, a right is the written privilege giving its stockholders, prior to others, the opportunity to buy the new securities within a specified period, in proportion to the number of shares each owns.

RIGHTS ISSUE, see RIGHTS.

RIGHT WHY, now let's go over into auditing tech and we know that if the person doesn't have the **right** problem it won't resolve so they're usually trying to solve the wrong problem. Well that applies to every staff member there is. If he has a problem on his post it is not the problem he has on his post or it would not be a problem. It has to be a false problem for the thing to persist. So the **right why** is another way of saying the correct problem or the correct reason. (ESTO 9, 7203C05 SO I)

RIP OFF, **1.** *Slang.* Scn staff expression meaning "take without exchange." Can be applied to personnel, money, anything. (BPL 11 Aug 72R I) **2.** a new term has emerged in PAC: to denote being removed "wham" from a post. **"Rip off"** and **"ripped off."** (OODs 25 Feb 72)

RISK, 1. generally, the possibility of loss, injury or danger in a business transaction. 2. in insurance, the probability of loss to the insurer or the amount the insurance company stands to lose.

RISK CAPITAL, see CAPITAL, RISK.

ROBERT'S RULES OF ORDER, [A book written by General Henry Martyn **Robert** (U.S. Army). It establishes the rules of Parliamentary procedure and is the accepted standard manual for such in the United States. These rules allow for orderly and just procedure at conferences and meetings.]

ROC, return on capital.

ROCKS AND SHOALS, in most Sea Organizations a list of penalties is called **rocks and shoals** and is read out to the crew at muster. The conditions are our **rocks and shoals.** (FO 87)

ROGER, "I've got it." "Okay" does as well. (BO 11 circa 10 Jun 67)

ROI, return on investment.

ROLE, in organizational terms, it refers to the part taken by a person in a company, usually with reference to an executive, the position and title he holds and the extent of his actual functions on the job.

ROLE-PLAYING, personnel training method in which employees broaden their viewpoints by acting out the roles of managers and foremen who must handle a wide variety of work situations. Also called dramatization.

ROLL BOOK, **1.** every Dn and Scn course has a course **roll book.** The purpose of the **roll book** is to provide a permanent record of all who enrolled on the course and whether or not they graduated.

The **roll book** must be a thick hard cover foolscap size and well bound **book.** (BPL 29 Jul 69R) **2.** a **roll book** has every student's name, address and the course enrolled in and date. (HCO PL 6 Dec 70 II)

ROLL CALL VOTE, see VOTE, ROLL CALL.

ROLLER COASTER CASE, a potential trouble source and just on the other side of him is a suppressive person invalidating his gains. (SH Spec 61, 6505C18)

ROLLERCOASTERING, the pc who goes up and the pc who goes down is **rollercoastering.** During that period of time when the pc was out of sight an SP was either directly contacted or restimulated. The person didn't have to see the SP but only had to see something that reminded him of the SP. He goes PTS so he **rollercoasters.** (SH Spec 73, 6608C02)

RONEOING, running off mimeo issues with the **Roneo** machine. (BPL 7 Feb 73 I) [**Roneo** is the brand name of a mimeograph machine.]

RON'S EXTERNAL PUBLICS SCIENTOLOGISTS, see REPS.

RON'S JOURNAL, a tape recorded lecture by **Ron,** designed for org staffs as an intimate chat with staff members to let them in on what's going on and what we're planning so that staffs could be informative to the Scientology public. (HCO PL 13 Aug 70 III)

RON'S SPECIAL THURSDAY BULLETIN, this is **Ron's special bulletin** to franchise holders which is done on white paper with red ink. (HCO PL 30 Oct 59) [The above HCO PL was cancelled by BPL 10 Oct 75 II.]

RORSCHACH TEST, **Rorschach** is the inkblot **test.** Now the way they make them is they drop some ink on one side of a sheet of paper and then they fold the paper over and then open it up again, and then now they've got ink blots on both sides and that makes an ink blot and then you're supposed to look at the ink blot and see what you see in it. If anybody ever gave you one of these things don't ever bother to answer much and say I don't see anything in it, it absolutely ruins the **test,** or say it's ink and a piece of paper. Actually it was a child's game. Now most of these **tests** and so on were born out of the area of phrenology which is reading the bumps on people's skulls to tell their characters. That's where psychology came from in the first place, and why they eventually went deeper and thought it was the brain. (ESTO 3, 7203C02 SO I)

ROTATING INTERNSHIP, see INTERNSHIP, ROTATING.

ROTATING SHIFT, the act of employees on one shift being periodically relayed to the following shift.

ROUGH LAYOUT, **1.** (graphic arts) first there is a dummy. Then there is a design stage. Then there is **rough layout.** This contains the inches of this or that, the crops indicated. (ED 459-51 Flag) **2.** the precisely measured pages, spaces, type, croppings laid out with great mechanical accuracy so that typesetting can begin and separation negatives or blocks that will fit can be made. (FO 3574)

ROUND TABLE, an informal business discussion with several or more participants.

ROUTE, a **route** is only the agreed upon procedure. The terminals involved make the agreement or the route doesn't work. A **route** along terminals that never agreed is no **route** but a labyrinth. People agree to postulates they can understand and appreciate. Hence a **route** and handling begins with a particle, develops with a theory, comes to life with an agreement and continues to work because of judgement and decision. **Routes** of handling are not orders to handle but directions to go. (HCO PL 22 Oct 62)

ROUTE SHEET, a written form listing the production steps, used in scheduling and sending through work.

ROUTINE MISSIONS, most missions fall into the category of **routine missions.** These would be **missions** which accomplished the **routine** actions of Flag—such as the corporate matters of Flag or AOs, improving AO or org status or conditions, AO or org finance, tech or ethics matters, etc. They may partly include logistics matters, but their major targets do not. They are concerned with the more standard and **routine** actions of Flag, AOs, orgs or the Sea Org itself. Inspection **missions** fall under this category. (FO 2132)

ROUTINE OPERATING COSTS, those are title C mest and **routine** services and **costs.** (Laundry and garbage removal, food, fuel, water, wages, supplies, etc.) (FSO 551)

ROUTING, **1.** this means pointing out the channels on which bodies, materials, products or dispatches and letters flow or making channels on which such things can flow and putting terminals there to handle or change them. (HCO PL 27 Feb 72) **2. routing** consists of forwarding a proper communication to its proper destination or, more pertinent to an executive, indicating how types of dispatches are routed to staff members who route org dispatches. (HCO PL 17 Nov 64)

ROUTING AND INFORMATION CLERK, at FOLO, the **Routing and Information Clerk** in Ext HCO (1) greets the new recruit and logs his name, the date and org that recruited him, in the recruit log book. (2) gives him an R-factor on what tests and **routing** forms he will be required to do. (3) has the new recruit complete his **Routing and Information** Form Part I, in duplicate, if he has not yet done this with the recruiter. (4) gives the new recruit a battery of tests (IQ, Leadership, Aptitude, OCA). (5) body routes the new recruit to the FPPO or FPPO Comm. (FO 3466R-1)

ROUTING FORM, **1.** the **form** that lists the org terminals the pc has to check through in order to arrive in the HGC and in the auditing chair. (BTB 3 Nov 72R) **2.** when particles arrive at the org space proper they must be routed and must continue to be routed from the moment they enter until they leave the org space. Thus there must be a reception for bodies, for mail, for phone, for telexes and for messages in general. There must also be an exit point for all these things and someone to send them on their way *out* of the org space. Once the particle (body, dispatch, raw materials, whatever) is at the door reception must establish the **routing**. This is done usually with each step signed off **Routing Form** that gives the full road map of the particle. (HCO PL 25 Jul 72)

ROUTING PROPERLY, by **routing properly** is meant to see that everyone around them **routes properly**. Forwarding something already improperly routed creates dev-t and fails to handle misrouting where it is occuring. (HCO PL 17 Nov 64)

ROUTING SECTION, **section** in Dept 1, Department of Routing, Appearances and Personnel. **Routing Section** writes and issues Body **Routing** Forms, has reception events log of org, sees that reception is a promotional contact for books and literature, logs phone calls and logs people into and out of org. (HCO PL 17 Jan 66 II)

ROYAL SCOTMAN, **1.** the **Royal Scotman**—the Flagship (6806C01 SO) **2.** now the *Apollo*. (ED 304 Flag) **3.** an organization ship. (FO RS 16) *Abbr.* RSM.

ROYALTY SUM, 12 1/2% of the allocated income plus 12 1/2% of the Congress books and tapes sum or 12 1/2% of the gross income. (HASI PL 19 Apr 57, *Proportionate Pay Plan*)

RPF'S RPF, the following restrictions are applied to members: (1) segregated from other **RPF** members with regard to work, messing, berthing, musters and any other command activity. (2) no pay. (3) no training. (4) no auditing. (5) may only work on mud boxes in the E/R. May not work with **RPF** members. (6) six hours sleep maximum. (7) is under the **RPF** MAA for all matters, including production. The **RPF** MAA may designate another to supervise their production. (8) Standard ethics penalties that apply to them to be triple for each offense they are found guilty of, until they fully join the **RPF** of their own determinism. (9) may communicate only with the **RPF** MAA or his designated assistant. (10) may not join **RPF** fully until acceptable amends made to all **RPF** members. (FCO 2990-2) [The first **RPF's RPF** assignment was made because the person considered their **RPF** assignment amusing, an award and was therefore unable to recognize a need for redemption or any means to effect it. Until such time as the person recognized this need and of their own self-determinism requested to be included in **RPF** redemption actions, the restrictions applied.]

RUDIMENT 1, (organization **rudiment**) *Admin*: be sure organization is properly registered and in proper legal relationship to the International Board of Scn. Be sure key posts are covered even if doubled. Make sure there is an Executive Director on post doing Exec Dir work of running org, a registrar, a Letter Registrar, somebody on public, somebody on accounts, somebody receiving and mailing the mail, somebody answering phone, somebody selling books, and that the persons on these posts are doing these jobs. Do up the org board properly and truly. Get Chinese School done on it daily with all executives and staff. Make sure that quarters exist adequate to need, that bank accounts exist in proper order and that records of income and disbursement are being kept. Be sure the standard unit system is in force without large sums going out on fixed pay or unjust favoritisms. *Tech*: be sure that there is an Academy in the hands of a person who knows his Scn and that there is an HGC in the hands of somebody who can crack cases and that staff auditors exist who can audit. The extent of action of this **rudiment** is to get basic legal, basic posts, basic quarters entirely covered, a condition which may deteriorate at other times than at the org's beginning. So cover all these points by careful review each time this **rudiment** is done. Incidentally, make sure there are no new departments or posts which are contrary to the seven division system. (HCO PL 11 Dec 61RA)

RUDIMENT 2, (organization **rudiment**) *Admin*: get the personnel busy. We don't care at what, but really rip up people who stand around talking and who burn up the staff's units with no production. Get staff meeting reorganized and going. Hold a staff meeting, explain unit system and how nobody can afford idle hands. The way to raise the unit is to get busy. New wild ideas won't work. It's getting busy on the existing ideas that raise the unit. The org makes as much as it can deliver service and no more. Find out who thinks they are overworked and underpaid and find out what they've done on their jobs the past week. Raise a storm and get people busy. *Tech*: get the supervisors training and the auditors auditing. We don't care how at this stage. Just get them busy doing technical actions flat out. We don't care how, but get pcs being audited so they're better and students trained so they can audit. (HCO PL 11 Dec 61RA)

RUDIMENT 3, (organization **rudiment**) *Admin*: get the current policy letter on the seven division system brought to date and then hat checked on everybody including all executive, admin and tech staff and the janitor. Get everyone to pass it from Exec Dir to cat on all departments until every person knows the functions and actions of *all* departments. Then they see what's supposed to be happening. *Tech*: get all trained Scientologists checked over on operating an E-meter until there isn't anybody present who hasn't passed E-meter essentials 100% perfect and can actually run a pc on a meter without goofs of any kind. (HCO PL 11 Dec 61RA)

RUDIMENT 4, (organization **rudiment**) *Admin*: check out the Letter Registrar and all address and mailing personnel on their jobs, making up any non-existent hats from old files and get all the addresses you can that would mean *anything* into action and get them personally getting written to as a steady high volume program. *Tech*: get all Scientologists into line on integrity processing until they never goof a withhold on anyone. (HCO PL 11 Dec 61RA)

RUDIMENT 5, (organization **rudiment**) *Admin*: get the registrar and reception hats made up and checked out and the body lines of students and pcs really straight and working. *Tech*: get Director of Tech and all supervisors hat checked on the latest Academy rundowns and make sure the Academy is running to train students, not to burn time. Get Academy 8C tough and sharp and training pressure up. When the students' tongues are hanging out and their foreheads bead with sweat and they're really learning, this **rud** is in. (HCO PL 11 Dec 61RA)

RUDIMENT 6, (organization **rudiment**) *Admin*: get accounts hats on and collection straightened up and to date. *Tech*: hat check Tech Sec, C/S and D of P on the C/S Series, HCOBs and the Classification and Gradation Chart. (Ref: C/S Series 25) and get them functioning on them. Drill and get the HGC lines in. (HCO PL 11 Dec 61RA)

RUDIMENT 7, (organization **rudiment**) *Admin*: integrity process all personnel, regardless of whether they've been checked before, BTB 24 December 1972R II, *Integrity Processing Form 2 General Staff Integrity List*. *Tech*: integrity process all personnel, regardless of whether they've been checked before, BTB 24 December 1972R II, *Integrity Processing Form 2 General Staff Integrity List* (HCO PL 11 Dec 61RA)

RUDIMENT 7A, (organization **rudiment**) *Admin*: get BPL 1 February 1975 II, *New Staff Applicant Information Form* into full use. Ensure all existing staff have filled one in, have sent it as far as completed to Central Personnel Office Flag (retaining the carbon copy) and are working through it to complete it. Ensure all new personnel receive one when recruited or hired and work through it sending each page to Central Personnel Office Flag as they complete it. *Tech*: hat check Qual Sec, Dir Pers Enhancement and Personnel Programmer on the tech and policy of how to program a staff member, and get them functioning on it. Get all staff personnel properly programmed. (HCO PL 11 Dec 61RA)

RUDIMENT 7B, (organization **rudiment**) *Admin*: hat check the Dir Personnel, Hatting Officers and/or Estos on the tech and policy of how to hat check and get them functioning on it. Get on-the-job hatting going at a high roar. *Tech*: hat check the Qual Sec, Dir Pers Enhancement and Word Clearers on the Word Clearing Series, Bulletins and policy on the subject and get them functioning on them. Get all staff method 6 word cleared on the key words of their post. (HCO PL 11 Dec 61RA)

RUDIMENT 7C, (organization **rudiment**) *Admin*: hat check the Dir I & R and staff Ethics Officer(s) on the tech and policy of PTS detection, interview and handling and get them functioning on it. Get all staff personnel checked for PTS and those who are, handled. Get PTS interview handling done as a rapid, routine action whenever a staff member, student or pc is found to be PTS. *Tech*: hat check the Tech Sec, D of P, C/S and auditors on PTS tech handling and get them using it where applicable. (HCO PL 11 Dec 61RA)

RUDIMENT 7D, (organization **rudiment**) *Admin*: get all posted staff who are not Staff Status II trained on their Staff Status I and II checksheets and awarded their Staff Status II. *Tech*: hat check the Tech Sec, D of T and Staff Hatting College Supervisor(s) on staff hatting college tech and policy and get them functioning on it. Get staff attending regularly. (HCO PL 11 Dec 61RA)

RUDIMENT 7E, (organization **rudiment**) *Admin*: hat check all execs from Dept Heads up on how to write and use admin cramming orders and get them using them. *Tech*: hat check the Dir of Correction and Cramming Officer on cramming tech and policy and get them functioning on it. Get cramming being done including admin cramming. (HCO PL 11 Dec 61RA)

RUDIMENT 7F, (organization **rudiment**) *Admin*: get all staff who have not had it run or co-audited on objective processes, CCHs, 8C, S-C-S, havingness, etc., or (if not advisable immediately for a particular case) get it included at the next suitable point in the person's program. *Tech*: get all staff who have not had it, run or co-audited on objective processes, CCHs, 8C, S-C-S, havingness, etc., or (if not advisable immediately for a particular case) get it included at the next suitable point in the person's program. Get daily tech training of tech personnel including TRs. (HCO PL 11 Dec 61RA)

RUDIMENT 7G, (organization **rudiment**) *Admin*: get into the hands of every executive and staff member a full A-I hat for his post(s) plus a staff hat (Ref: HCO PL 22 September 1970, *Org Series 4 Personnel Series 9, Hats*). Get all execs and staff who are fully hatted working daily on their post hat checksheet using word clearing Methods 6, 7, 9 and 4. *Tech*: hat check Qual Sec, Dir of Pers Enhancement and the STO on staff training officer policy and tech and get them functioning on it. (HCO PL 11 Dec 61RA)

RUDIMENT 8, (organization **rudiment**) *Admin*: get Estates manager hat assembled and checked and get building(s) clean, his personnel straightened out and odd jobs unfinished ended or restarted. Check up on any new quarters or plans and status of buildings regarding mortgages, etc. *Tech*: get staff auditing program in hand and staff staff auditors well hatted and operating and review staff cases with D of P to be sure of progress. Check, by this progress, that no patty cake tacit consent is occuring in view of fact execs choose their own auditors. (HCO PL 11 Dec 61RA)

RUDIMENT 9, (organization **rudiment**) *Admin*: get magazine in hand and outflowing to all available lists, on schedule, straighten up such lists and improve means to acquire more names. Check over comm centers and see that all persons in org have proper comm baskets. Check up on HCO hats and comm system. Get report lines to Flag straightened up. *Tech*: get all staff auditors and supervisors hat checked on all tech bulletins that apply to their jobs. Get all Tech personnel high crime checkouts in PT. (HCO PL 11 Dec 61RA)

RUDIMENT 10, (organization **rudiment**) *Admin*: get Distrib Sec, Dir of Public Servicing and supervisors hat checked on public admin, schedules, advertising, etc. *Tech*: get HAS course and HQS course running on best current rundown and these supervisors hat checked on technical material as it applies to their actions. (HCO PL 11 Dec 61RA)

RUDIMENT 11, (organization **rudiment**) *Admin*: get Exec Dir hat checked on all applicable policy, his comm system, quarters and lines straight, get any personal personnel he has hat checked. Get his OIC board going or up-to-date and gone over with him. Check up on org legal matters and position. Check up org personnel procurement and records. *Tech*: get Extension Course Director hat checked on his or her post, books and answers and his or her technical accuracy of reply to Extension Course students checked. (HCO PL 11 Dec 61RA)

RUDIMENT 12, (organization **rudiment**) *Admin*: get book sales going in reception and through mails, book supplies adjusted and planned out. *Tech*: get all Scientologists on staff checked over on where they stand in classification. Get them working toward or examined for next classification or reviewing developments in their current classification. Go over their needed items on their own classification checklists with them to get them to studying. (HCO PL 11 Dec 61RA)

RUDIMENT 13, (organization **rudiment**) *Admin*: go over CF thoroughly and get it in hand and CF In-charge hat checked. Check over and get straight memberships and certification. Check up on Dept 13, Dept of Validity. *Tech*: go over HGC or public testing or both and hat check all personnel and review their body traffic lines and testing records. (HCO PL 11 Dec 61RA)

RUDIMENT 14, (organization **rudiment**) *Admin*: go over accounts disbursement system and hat check personnel and review policy letters with them and inspect accounts. Check up on HCO Accounts and percentages to WW. *Tech*: step in on HGC admin and interview HGC pcs to establish their attitude toward HGC so any faults can be corrected in technical service. (HCO PL 11 Dec 61RA)

RUDIMENT 15, (organization **rudiment**) *Admin*: arrange open evenings, future events and special courses. Hat check all additional personnel and units not reached in these **rudiments** and get their hats and jobs in order. *Tech*: interview Academy students to see that they are actually learning something worthwhile. Examine two or three at random, talk to many. Try to shorten up their length of time on course and extend their knowledge, reversing any tendency to lengthen time on course and shorten knowledge. (HCO PL 11 Dec 61RA)

RUDIMENT 16, (organization **rudiment**) *Admin*: straighten out Ad Council, read to it the paper creating Ad Councils, get it effective in advising. Straighten out any misconceptions of its position or abuse of its functions. *Tech*: hold several nightly meetings of all Scientologists in org and straighten up any difficulty they may be having with current rundown. Answer their questions by referral to HCOBs or tapes. Set up routine study of materials. (HCO PL 11 Dec 61RA)

RUDIMENT 17, (organization **rudiment**) *Admin*: get HCOBs and policy letter files up-to-date. Be sure tapes are available where needed and tape library well cared for. Examine field auditor relations with org and take up their correspondence with Exec Dir and straighten out any difficulties with them. Check up on any special programs. Check up on ethics problems. *Tech*: look over quality of auditing in field and attempt to get weak spots retreaded at Academy or audited at HGC. Enforce policies on uses of processes. (HCO PL 11 Dec 61RA)

RUDIMENTS OF AN ORG, for some time, I have been advocating that you get one piece of organizational data in before you do another. This has been a very rewarding action. Orgs have become better off at once by doing this. Therefore, let's call it **rudiments of an org**, and have the HCO Area Sec get them in one at a time all the while the Exec Dir is keeping things running. You get in one simple thing. Then you get in another. An org is composed of two factors. These are technical and administration. These must never get out of balance, in either personnel numbers or programs. Therefore when getting in **org rudiments**, you always get one in in Tech and one in in admin at the same time. (HCO PL 11 Dec 61RA)

RUIN, before you can save someone from **ruin**, you must find out what their own personal **ruin** is. This is basically—what is **ruining** them? What is messing them up? It must be a condition that is real to the individual as an unwanted condition, or one that can be made real to him. (HCO PL 23 Oct 65)

RULE 28, [This refers to **Rule 28** of the Training Course Rules and Regulations—"**28.** The above rules and regulations are inflexible, and are to be followed by all students during the course. There will be no exceptions." (HCO PL 22 Nov 61). The above HCO PL was cancelled by BPL 10 Oct 75III.]

RULE OF EXCEPTIONS, the idea of an executive handling the unexpected situations and abnormalities while delegating routine matters to juniors to handle.

RUNNING COSTS, see COSTS, RUNNING.

RUSH, **1.** dispatches marked **rush** are handled by special handling. They go on center of desk like cables and telexes. (HCO PL 31 Jan 61, *Message Placement*) **2.** speed priority. "**Rush**" is our only faster than average label and means personal delivery or swiftest communication such as phone or cable. (HCO PL 12 Sept 58)

Rush (Def. 1)

S

SABOTAGE, a deliberate act to obstruct productivity or normal functioning of an organization, undertaken by a single employee or group of employees, possibly in an effort to force the employer to meet certain demands.

SAFETY PROGRAM, a training program covering all pertinent facets of safety in an organization such as proper utilization and care of equipment to avoid accidents, actions to take in case of fire and other hazards, first aid instructions, etc.

SAILING MASTER, formerly an officer in the Royal Navy responsible to the Captain for the correct navigation of the ship. (ED 313 Flag)

SAILOR, anybody in a ship's company is a **sailor** but deck hands are addressed as **sailor** when not "boots." (FO 87)

SAIL TRAINING SUPERVISOR, sail training is placed under the supervision of the Second Mate. His title will be **Sail Training Supervisor.** (FO 1853)

SAINT HILL, 1. the name of LRH's home in East Grinstead, Sussex, England, and location of the Worldwide headquarters of Scn, and the UK Advanced Organization and **SH** (AOSH UK). LRH taught the original **Saint Hill** Special Briefing Course at **Saint Hill** from 1961 to 1965. The term **SH** now applies to any organization authorized to deliver those upper level Scn services hence we also have the "American **Saint Hill** Organization" (ASHO) and "Advanced Organization and **Saint Hill** in Denmark" (AOSH DK) and "**Saint Hill** Europe" (**SHEU**). (BTB 12 Apr 72R) **2. SHs** are primarily concerned with the production of auditors and C/Ses at the level of **SH**SBC and above and HPCSCs, and in delivering power processing. (SO ED 153R INT) **3.** this spring, with my own money, I bought **Saint Hill,** the former luxury estate of the Maharajah of Jaipur. It is complete with 55 acres of beautiful grounds and gardens, a swimming pool, a ball room, a cinema, uncounted bedrooms, eleven baths, a 2 1/2 acre

Sailor

fishing lake, another fish pond, a huge conservatory, glasshouses, a billiard room and numerous other items. This will be used as a residence abroad and by HCO WW as the communication center of Scn. (HCO PL 26 Jun 59) *Abbr.* SH or STHIL.

SAINT HILL ADDRESSO, a **Saint Hill addresso** includes the names and addresses of those persons who have bought something from **SH** and those persons who are eligible or may come to **Saint Hill.** (BPL 19 May 72R)

SAINT HILL ADMINISTRATOR, **1.** all persons employed at **Saint Hill**, for personnel purposes, except officers of corporations, come under the **Saint Hill Administrator.** This means that acquisitions of new personnel and dismissal of personnel comes under the **Saint Hill Administrator.** Personnel actions by HCO (WW) Ltd. and SLR Ltd. must be referred to the **Saint Hill Administrator.** The **Saint Hill Administrator** may take independent action on any personnel in the interests of efficiency or finance. (HCO PL 1 Apr 64, *Saint Hill Personnel*) **2.** HCO (St. Hill) Ltd., has been organized to care for the course, house, grounds, domestic staff, construction, material and all personnel. **Saint Hill Administrator** is in direct charge of these activities and personnel. (HCO PL 31 Dec 63)

SAINT HILL CERTIFICATE, the definition of a **Saint Hill Certificate** is that it is granted for complete checksheets—not amount of time on course—in theory, practical and on auditing checksheet on others. (HCO PL 9 Apr 65)

SAINT HILL CONSTRUCTION UNIT, handles all **construction**, maintenance and repair at **Saint Hill** except roads and grounds. Receives, safeguards, uses or stores all construction equipment and materials. (HCO PL 18 Dec 64, *Saint Hill Org Board*)

SAINT HILL COURSE, the **Saint Hill** Special Briefing **Course.** (HCO PL 22 Mar 65, *Saint Hill Services, Prices and Discounts*)

SAINT HILLERS, any auditor trained to any level at **Saint Hill.** (HCO PL 9 May 65, *Field Auditors Become Staff*)

Saint Hill (Def. 3)

SAINT HILLERS ASSOCIATION, just as Class IV Orgs have their Auditors Association, a **Saint Hillers Association** is hereby instituted for Saint Hill Orgs. It has the same purpose and format as the Auditors Association but is limited in its memberships to SHSBC graduates. (HCO PL 24 Oct 70) [This HCO PL has been cancelled by BPL 15 Apr 71R, *Auditors Associations and SH Orgs*.]

SAINT HILL ONLY, 1. (mimeo distribution) this is internal management, ideas, events of interest to all **Saint Hill** staff. Sometimes these will also be marked limited or general non-remimeo, at which time only they are also distributed to orgs, it means *all* **Saint Hill** staff. (HCO PL 2 Jul 64) **2. Saint Hill only** means all staff at **Saint Hill**, domestic, typing, grounds, everyone. A mimeo must be marked **Saint Hill only** before it is issued to **Saint Hill** staff and unless also marked "**Saint Hill** students" also may not go to students. (HCO PL 2 Jul 64)

SAINT HILL ORGANIZATION CHART, the **Saint Hill Organization Chart** is exactly the same as the organization chart in every one of the major organizations. The difference is only the numbers on staff. At **Saint Hill** there is the International Council and each major org has its Executive Council. At **Saint Hill** there is an HCO Secretary, an Organization Secretary and a Finance Secretary and in each org there are the same level of officers. At **Saint Hill** there are six departments, the Promotion Department and the Publications Department, both under the HCO Division (1); the Department of Training and the Department of Processing, both under the Technical Division (2); and the Accounts Department and Material Department, both under the Finance Division (3). All posts and functions come under the three divisions and six departments. HCO (Division 1) promotes and registers; Technical (Division 2) applies all training and processing for the org and public; Finance (Division 3) takes care of all money and property. (HCO PL 13 Mar 65, *Admin Technology, The Comm Member System*)

SAINT HILL ORGS, SHUK, SHEU and ASHO. (BPL 19 May 72R)

SAINT HILL PROJECT NO. 1, **1.** at this moment I am holding twelve separate projects at **Saint Hill** in addition to other hats. **Saint Hill Project No. One**: technical. The acquisition and compilation of technical data on Scn from reports, assessments and bulletins. The vetting of all technical papers and letters. (HCO WW PL 22 Aug 59) **2. project** on research and new books. (HCO PL 27 Oct 59)

SAINT HILL PROJECT NO. 2, is to give communication and service to and receive the 10% weekly income from HCO Franchise holders. (HCO WW PL 22 Aug 59)

SAINT HILL PROJECT NO. 3, this is to prepare and sell new books and new tapes to the World in general to be bought directly from HCO. (HCO WW PL 22 Aug 59)

SAINT HILL PROJECT NO. 4, consists of research and commercial activity in the field of plant growth and receives data from the research and income from the commercial activity. (HCO WW PL 22 Aug 59)

SAINT HILL PROJECT NO. 5, consists of the general sale of books, tapes and E-Meters to HCO Offices, Central Organizations, Franchise holders and the general public Worldwide, and the collection and banking of all such sums whether from the sale of books by HCO WW Book Section or by the sale of books by other HCOs. (HCO WW PL 22 Aug 59)

SAINT HILL PROJECT NO. 6, corporate organization, and continuance. This **project** consists of supervision of legalities and sale of shares and transfers, called Hubbard Communications Office Ltd. when formed. (HCO WW PL 22 Aug 59)

SAINT HILL PROJECT NO. 7, magazine preparation, printing and economy of costs, and printing of all leaflets, etc. (HCO WW PL 22 Aug 59)

SAINT HILL PROJECT NO. 8, collection of accounts owed HCO from past transactions. (HCO WW PL 22 Aug 59)

SAINT HILL PROJECT NO. 9, care of all HCO Offices, ensuring that they function properly, that they receive their 5% income from Central Orgs, get out their magazines, provide inspection services, submit proper reports to HCO WW and that all special sums or surpluses are transferred to HCO WW Accounts and to ensure that such offices have adequate personnel. (HCO WW PL 22 Aug 59)

SAINT HILL PROJECT NO. 10, economy **Saint Hill** Manor. To ensure that the services, salaries, purchases and expenses of **Saint Hill** Manor are kept within bounds of income from various sources. To reduce these wherever possible. To see that the budget is balanced. (HCO WW PL 22 Aug 59)

SAINT HILL PROJECT NO. 11, Central Organizations. This is a vitally important project seeing to it that Central Orgs receive proper service, supervision, hats and organization and making sure their 10%'s arrive and are banked to HCO WW weekly. (HCO WW PL 22 Aug 59)

SAINT HILL PROJECT NO. 12, accounting and banking. The invoicing, accounting and banking of all projects separately is to be done in a manner prescribed. Books are separately invoiced on a second machine but all other invoicing is to be done on one other machine. All disbursements shall be done on a disbursement machine plus cheques. All invoices are to be numbered by projects on the invoice and all disbursements shall be so numbered. The assistance of chartered accountants shall be rendered. (HCO WW PL 22 Aug 59)

SAINT HILL SPECIAL BRIEFING COURSE, 1. the **SHSBC** teaches about the full practical application of Scn grades, repair, set ups, assists and special cases tech up to Class VI. Processes taught are Scn set up and repair processes and rundowns for special cases up to Class VI. End result is a superb auditor with full philosophic and technical command of materials to Level VI. (Class VI auditor) (CG&AC 75) **2.** the purpose of the **Saint Hill Special Briefing Course** is to make the auditors and instructors who make the auditors and instructors over the world and to put the final polish on auditing. (HCO PL 22 Mar 65, *Saint Hill Services, Prices and Discounts*) **3.** the **Saint Hill Special Briefing Course** has certain distinct purposes. The **Course** was begun to do two things. (1) to study and resolve training and education. (2) to assist people who wanted to perfect their Scn. The Scientologists studying here are supposed to concentrate on only three things: (a) the acquisition of the ability to achieve a rapid and accurate understanding of data given to them for study and to put that material into effect; (b) to achieve auditing results; (c) to get a reality on the achieving of auditing results by exact duplication of current methodology and not by additives or extraordinary solutions. (HCO PL 9 Jul 62) *Abbr.* SHSBC.

SAINT HILL STUDENTS, (mimeo distribution) nothing goes to **Saint Hill students** unless marked **Saint Hill students**, something could be marked Saint Hill only and also **Saint Hill students** but only then would it go to both. **Saint Hill students** do not automatically get everything mimeoed. In fact they only get after this date what is clearly marked **Saint Hill students**. (HCO PL 2 Jul 64)

SALARIED EMPLOYEE, see EMPLOYEE, SALARIED.

SALARY, a set income paid at regular intervals to executive, clerical or administrative personnel for regular long term employment. A wage is often associated with blue collar work being paid at shorter intervals such as per hour, day, week or per piece of work done.

SALARY INCREMENT, a salary increase plotted to occur at regular intervals such as an increase of $500.00 per year written into an employment contract.

SALARY REVIEW, the restudying of employees' salaries, usually at regular intervals, from the standpoint of individual performances over the past period or possibly in order to compensate for an inflating economy.

SALARY STRUCTURE, the classifying of salary payments by categorizing and evaluating jobs and then establishing salary ranges for each type with sometimes the setting up of a formal ranking structure for an organization. Often intrinsic to salary structure is the policy of regular salary reviews and performance appraisals.

SALARY SUM, 50% of the allocation sum (which is gross income less CBT). This is calculated by first deducting part time staff and then proportioning balance to staff by units. (HASI PL 19 Apr 57 *Proportionate Pay Plan*)

SALE, 1. the exchange of property, products or services for a specified amount of money or its equivalent. 2. in retail business a special reduction of consumer merchandise prices to encourage buying.

SALES AUDIT, see AUDIT, SALES.

SALES CHAIN, the established flow of a product to reach the consumer level, usually from manufacturer to wholesaler to retailer to consumer although some chains may be longer by the introduction of additional middlemen such as a wholesaler's agent, and in the case of direct mail selling, the chain is shortened since the retailer is eliminated.

SALES DATA SHEET, a **sheet** to obtain facts about the individual just sold. (BPL 1 Dec 72 I)

SALES DEPARTMENT, the department of an organization responsible for the direction, performance and accomplishments of its sales activities.

SALES, DIRECT, sales made direct from a company to consumer as exemplified by having one's own sales force on the premises to handle customers as well as having a mail order department.

SALES LEDGER, a book in which is posted the daily record of sales made.

SALES LETTER, a letter that presents a sales offer for a product or service and is designed to gain additional users and customers for an organization.

SALES MANAGEMENT, see MANAGEMENT, SALES.

SALES MANAGER, the person having managerial authority over a company's salesmen and who is responsible for their direction, activities and standard of performance.

SALESMANSHIP, skill or ability in selling products and services.

SALES MANUAL, see MANUAL, SALES.

SALES ORDER PROCESSING, the administration of the clerical elements involved in getting sales finalized on paper and delivered, including verifying customers credit standings, dispatching production or stock notices, invoicing, packing instructions and delivery specifications.

SALES PLANNING, see PLANNING, SALES.

SALES PROMOTION, see PROMOTION, SALES.

SALES PROMOTION PLANNING, see PLANNING, SALES PROMOTION.

SALES REVENUE LINE, the line on a chart or diagram representing the trend or fluctuations of sales earnings in a business usually covering a specific unit of time such as monthly, quarterly or yearly.

SALES TARGET, the amount of sales or money from sales to be made set as a target to be met by a specific time.

SALES TAX, tax levied by a city or state and/or Federal Government that is added to a retail price and collected from the consumer by the retailer.

SALES TEAM, COMMANDO, a special sales team, in addition to regular sales personnel, engaged solely in the promotion and sales of one particular campaign.

SALES TERRITORY, that geographical area assigned to a salesman, sales team, branch office, etc., as solely their territory to develop customers and make sales in.

SALVAGE, to save from ruin. (HCO PL 23 Oct 65, *Dissemination Drill*)

SALVAGE UNIT, is established in Div III, Dept 8 under Supplies Section. The purpose of this **unit** entails collecting up unused and misplaced mest around the ships of the flotilla for restoring and correct issuance of same. (FO 1567)

SAMPLE ISSUE, a rough layout of what the magazine is going to be about. (FO 915)

SAMPLE SURVEY, a market research survey in which a representative part of the total population is chosen and surveyed.

SAMPLING, a random test of a portion of something in order to make decisions or draw conclusions about the whole portion. In surveying every tenth citizen of a town the results would be seen as indicative of that town's population as a whole.

SANDWICH COURSE, a University or College course usually related to industry, in which periods of study are alternated with periods of training and practical experience related to what one is studying.

SANE SCENE, when none of the out-points are present, yet you **do** have reports and the scene is functioning and fulfilling its purpose one would have what he could call a **sane scene.** (HCO PL 19 May 70)

SANITY, 1. is the ability to recognize differences, similarities and identities. (HCO PL 26 Apr 70R) **2. sanity** and honesty then consist of producing a valuable final product for which one is then recompensed by support and good will, or in reverse flow, supporting and giving good will to the producer of the product. (HCO PL 25 Mar 71)

SANITY SCALE, the points of success and failure, the make and break items of an organization are (1) hiring, (2) training, (3) apprenticeships, (4) utilization, (5) production, (6) promotion, (7) sales, (8) delivery, (9) finance, (10) justice, (11) morale. These eleven items must agree with and be in line with the Admin Scale. This then is a **sanity scale** for the third dynamic of a group. The group will exhibit aberrated symptoms where one or more of these points are out. The group will be sane to the degree that these points are in. Internal stresses of magnitude begin to affect every member of the group in greater or lesser degree when one or more of these items are neglected or badly handled. The society at large currently has the majority of these points out. (HCO PL 14 Dec 70)

SAVING, 1. sum of money derived from one's income that is not spent. 2. in law, an exception or reservation.

SAVINGS ACCOUNT, see ACCOUNT, SAVINGS.

SAVINGS BANK, see BANK, SAVINGS.

SCAB, *Slang.* term for a worker who refuses to be a member of a labor union, or who takes a striking worker's job; a strike breaker.

SCALAR PRINCIPLE, the idea that juniors should adhere to the chain of command and when wanting to communicate with higher executives should do so only by going through their intermediate superiors.

SCALE, by **scale** is meant the number of anything per vertical inch of graph. (HCO PL 6 Mar 66 II)

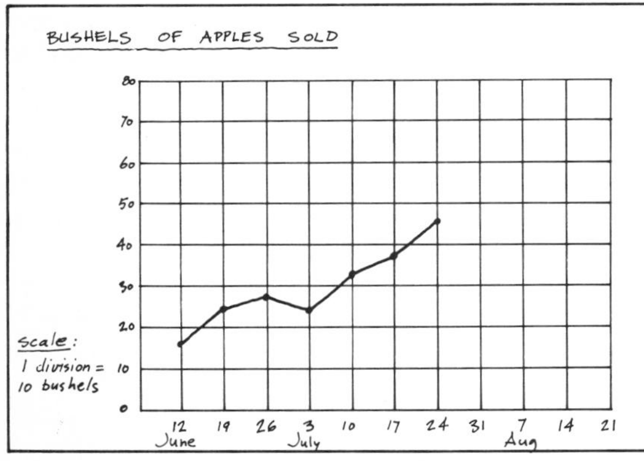

Scale (Def. 1)

SCALE, a series of gradually increasing increments, measurements, values, marks, etc., arranged from lowest to highest and used to measure rate or compare something.

SCALE OF IMPORTANCE, top is a *goal*, next is a *purpose*, next is a *policy*, then you have a *plan* then you have a *program* then you have a *project* and now you have an *order* then you have an *ideal scene* and then you have a *statistic* and then you have a *valuable final product*. That is the **scale of importance**. Now of course anybody can issue an order if there is a project which is derived from a program which is derived from a plan which is directly derived from policy. Policy is no good unless it is derived from a purpose. Skip having any plan at all if it doesn't eventually wind up in a valuable final product. Do you see that there's a band here? It's a band of dwindling authority but it also moves forward down the lines. (7012C04 SO)

SCALE OF MOTIVATION, the **scale of motivation** from the highest to the lowest is: Duty—highest, Personal Conviction, Personal Gain, Money—lowest. (HCO PL 11 Nov 69 II)

SCALE OF PREFERENCE, a definite and positive **scale of preference** for accepting and scheduling preclears (including students sent to Review) for auditing in the HGC and in the Case Cracking Section of the Department of Review. Last on the list is any person who seeks auditing as a favor "to demonstrate to others what it can do" or "because of importance as a person." (HCO PL 9 May 65, *Auditing Fees, Preferential Treatment of Preclears, Scale of Preference*)

SCALE ORDER, see ORDER, SCALE.

SCALOGRAM, market research tool used in evaluating a situation by discovering and extracting hidden or indistinct patterns that exist in a body of data, sufficiently complex to sometimes be relegated to computer processing. Also called Guttman scaling.

SCATTER CHART, see CHART, SCATTER.

SCENE, 1. area. (HCO PL 18 May 70) **2.** it means the way things ought to be or are. (FO 2471)

SCHEDULED PURCHASING, see PURCHASING, SCHEDULED.

SCHEDULING, establishing the time at which some process or action must start, change or stop.

SCHEMA, 1. a system whereby one becomes two, which in turn becomes four, etc. For example, the Dianetics Course also teaches each student to supervise and run the course. (FO 1999) **2.** a mathematical action by which one thing becomes two things, each one of those becomes two more, each one of those becomes two more, etc. (FO 1941)

SCIENCE, expertness or ability to do, resulting from knowledge gained and verified by exact observation and correct thinking. (FO 3335)

SCIENTIFIC MANAGEMENT, see MANAGEMENT, SCIENTIFIC.

SCHIZOPHRENIA, 1. the most prevalent "mental disorder" is supposed to be **schizophrenia**. This means "scissors" or two plus "head." A two-head in other words. And in this case two heads are not better than one (joke). You see this in institutions. A person is changing valences (personalities) click—click—click, one to the next. But the condition is a gradient one that worsens between sanity and the bottom of the scale. Midway, the condition is common but almost never noticed. It is so common today that it passes as normal humanoid. The person is not doing what he is doing. Examples of this are: people who do not like a job with responsibility because they "like to do mechanical things so they can dream of something else before they can _________"; persons who are out of area; persons who continually make dev-t. There is also the person who rams sideways into the work of others with "mistakes", "demands" and prevents them from doing what they are doing while himself not doing what he is doing. One can't say these people are crazy. Not today. But one can say they make problems, which are very difficult unless you know how to unlock the riddle. (HCO PL 3 Apr 72) **2.** a withdrawal from reality. (7202C22 SO) **3. schizophrenia** is the HC list madly out on the point of disassociation. (7202C22 SO)

SCHOOL OF LIFE, the former name (1956) of the lower level Scientology courses which became in later years the Personal Efficiency Foundation and then later, the Hubbard Apprentice Scientologist and Hubbard Qualified Scientologist courses. (LRH Def. Notes)

SCIENTOCRACY, one of the wittier D.Scns invented **Scientocracy** which is "Government of the people, by the thetans." (PAB 25)

SCIENTOLOGIST, 1. someone who can better conditions. A **Scientologist** then, is essentially one who betters the conditions of himself and the conditions of others by using Scn technology. Of course, there are lots of "do-gooders" and people trying to better conditions, but the difference between them and a **Scientologist** is that the **Scientologist** is the one who knows how. He is equipped with far superior know-how. He is in much better shape than the person on the street. (BPL 21 Oct 71I) **2.** an individual interested in Scn. Disseminates and assists **Scientologists**. (HCO PL 21 Oct 66 II, *City Office System*) **3.** the being three feet behind society's head. A trained **Scientologist** is not a doctor. He is someone with special knowledge in the handling of life. (HCOB 10 Jun 60)

SCIENTOLOGISTS HATTED, (Public Division Statistic) number of **Scientologists hatted**: the stat is redefined as any **Scientologist** or Dianeticist who can produce the 4 products of a **Scientologist**. When he can do that he's a **hatted Scientologist**. "Any **Scientologist** or Dianeticist" means any person who has completed any Scn or Dn course or 12 1/2 hour intensive and who is a member of the church. The "produce" means with ease in a reasonable period of time. The 4 products of a **Scientologist** are: (a) purchased books, (b) disseminated knowledge, (c) environmental control, (d) a cleared planet (or in other words to break it down: new Scientologists or Dianeticists). (HCO PL 28 Nov 71R II)

SCIENTOLOGY, 1. the word **Scientology** is one which you might say is anglicized. It comes from the Latin *Scio* and the Greek *Logos*, with *Scio* the most emphatic statement of know we had in the Western world. And ology (from *Logos*) of course means "study of." *Scio* is "knowing in the fullest sense of the word" and the Western world recognizes in it and in the word science something close to a truth. (*PXL*, p. 1) **2.** a religion in the oldest sense of the word, a study of wisdom. **Scn** is a study of man as a spirit in his relationship to life and the physical universe. It is non-denominational. By that is meant that **Scn** is open to people of all religions and beliefs and in no way tries to persuade a person from his religion, but assists him to better understand that he is a spiritual being. (BPL 6 Mar 69) **3.** a religious practice applying to man's spirit and his spiritual freedom (HCO PL 6 Apr 69) **4.** the ability to change condition. The technology of how you change. (SH Spec 57, 6504C06) **5. Scn** as practiced by the Church of **Scientology** is a spiritual and religious guide intended to make persons more aware of themselves as spiritual beings restoring respect for self and others and not treating or diagnosing of human ailments of body or mind nor engaged in the teaching or practicing of the medical arts or sciences. (BPL 24 Sept 73RA XIII) **6.** not the field of the human mind, **Scn** is the overall science which also includes the human mind. (5410C04) **7. Scn** assumes that every man can be more able than he is and then goes ahead with very precise techniques to make him so. (5510C08) **8.** the science of life. It teaches the fundamentals of life, the laws and basics of living. Our technology can be used to handle any condition that you find in life and if applied it will better those conditions. **Scn** is not some esoteric body of knowledge only to be used in the auditing room. It is something one can go out into the world with and use in all walks of life as well. It seems that this is a very broad and an amazing science but this is because **Scn** isolates and aligns the basic truths of life and life is everywhere. (BPL 21 Oct 71 I) *Abbr.* SCN.

SCIENTOLOGY ACCOUNTS SYSTEM, see ACCOUNTS SYSTEM.

SCIENTOLOGY CHURCH REGISTER, a **register** for marriage, recognition and naming, and funeral services kept in every **Church** of **Scientology**. The Chaplain keeps the **register**. It should be in accordance with any local regulations regarding such. (BPL 24 Apr 69R)

SCIENTOLOGY CONSULTANTS, INC., we have now, for the first time, a complete line of books in each of Dn and Scn. These are in actuality separate subjects, and we now have the material and corporations necessary to make them entirely separate. We are going to conduct a very large radio campaign throughout the middle West concerning Dn only. To do this, we will probably revive the Hubbard Dianetic Research Foundation of Arizona, since this is now getting cleared up all past accounts. Scn will be exclusively handled by the Founding Church and the HASI. No letters or literature should cross the words Dn and Scn. They should be maintained separately. It is the basic truth that Dn is a mental therapy which was developed out of the body of knowledge called Scn, as fully discussed in an early *Journal of Scientology* (1952), but the legal position and the actual practice of these two subjects means they must be kept apart. From a management standpoint, these organizations are held separately, in view of the fact that they are to be managed through **Scn Consultants, Inc.,** which is a management corporation. (HCO PL 25 Jan 57) *Abbr.* SCI CON.

SCIENTOLOGY COURSE, running a course with no checksheet is illegal. A **Scn course** is defined as progress through a checksheet. (HCO PL 16 Apr 65 II)

SCIENTOLOGY FOUNDATION, THE, **the** evening week-end **foundation**. Offering all services available in the daytime and delivering them in the evening or week-end. (HCO PL 12 Jun 65) See FOUNDATION, THE.

SCIENTOLOGY GROUPS, **Scn groups** are charted by any official organization. They study texts and have regular group activities and are often headed by book auditors or field auditors and are sometimes addressed by qualified auditors. They have a regular official charter. (HCO PL 21 Oct 66 II)

SCIENTOLOGY LIBRARY AND RESEARCH LTD., **1.** has the purpose of collecting, safeguarding and preserving all Scn materials, and while safeguarding the originals, compiling from such new work and preparing it for direct dissemination as on tapes or designing and printing as in the case of written work. It is a full intention that **SLR** shall provide a flood of new publications and compilations to assist the dissemination of Scn. (HCO PL 24 Jan 64, *Scientology Library and Research Ltd.*) **2.** this is the corporation that sells books, compiles research materials and makes tapes and also cine films. All book letters use this letterhead. (HCO PL 30 Sept 64) *Abbr.* SLR.

SCIENTOLOGY ORGANIZATIONS, there are now two types of **Scn organizations**. One is the large Central Organization. The other is the City Office. (HCO PL 21 Feb 61)

SCIENTOLOGY RESEARCH AND INVESTIGATION FUND, the name of the HCO Special Fund to which the following monies should be transferred: (1) all sterling area HCO 10%s except where needed for office and salary expenses to finish out CBM deficiencies, (2) all HASI and other Central Organization 8%s. This means that all HCO surpluses anywhere above immediate office needs should be now transferred routinely to HCO WW **Research and Investigation Fund** as well as all Central Organizations' 8%s. (HCO PL 9 Jun 59)

Scientology Symbol

SCIENTOLOGY SYMBOL, the **S** and double triangle. There are *two* triangles, over which the **S**

is imposed. The **S** simply stands for **Scn** which is derived from "*Scio*" (knowing in the fullest sense). The lower triangle is the A-R-C triangle—its points being affinity, reality and communication. These are the three elements which combined give understanding. The upper triangle is the K-R-C triangle. The points are K for knowledge, R for responsibility and C for control. (HCO PL 18 Feb 72)

SCIENTOMETRIC TESTING IN CHARGE, gives all and any tests or exams that may be required to any department or organization or personnel and to keep and file results accurately to assist research and presentation, and to have test materials in abundance to hand. (HCO PL 12 Oct 62)

SCREENING, 1. any process of sorting out the good from the bad, the suitable from the unsuitable, the desired from the undesired, etc. Such as interviewing job applicants to determine suitability. 2. statistical quality control method of inspecting 100% of a certain lot or batch of production and removing all defects.

SCRIP, 1. generally, a brief writing such as a note, receipt or short scrip showing a right to something. 2. paper issued for temporary emergency use to be exchanged later for money, merchandise or land. 3. paper which is issued in place of wages, convertible at specific cooperating businesses. 4. a provisional certificate entitling the holder to a fractional or temporary share of stock. 5. certificate of indebtedness, as a promissory note, representing currency issued by a government during a severe depression.

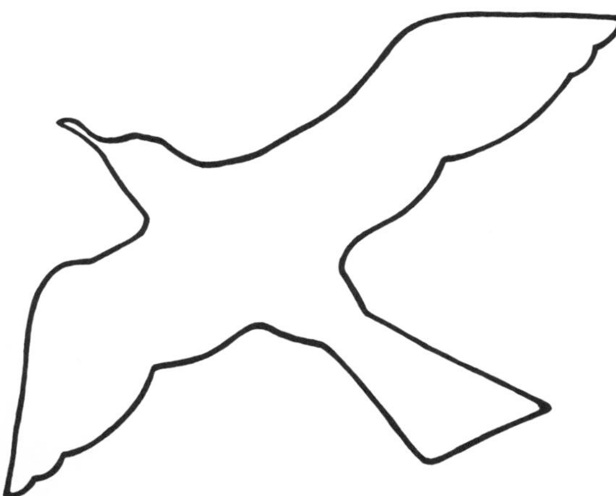

Seagull

SEAGULL, a symbol of the Sea Org going back to its first origin. The **seagull** is associated with the power of the sea. Traditionally, a bird soaring skywards is symbolic of the spirit ascending, or freeing itself, and, generally speaking, birds are symbols of thought, or imagination, and of the swiftness of spiritual processes and relationships. In the Sea Org coat of arms, the bird is used in a group of three. Thusly, it represents such concepts as the third dynamic, the cycle of action, and the Be-Do-Have cycle. A group of three also symbolized spiritual synthesis, and is the formula for the creation of each of the worlds. In our terms, this represents the three universes, one's own, others, and the physical universe. That the **seagull** is white symbolizes the basic purity of the spirit. The red band ascending across the four divisions of the field (the fourth dynamic) represents the bridge which is strengthened by the activity of the Sea Org and the Church of Scientology in line with Ron's purpose. (FO 3350)

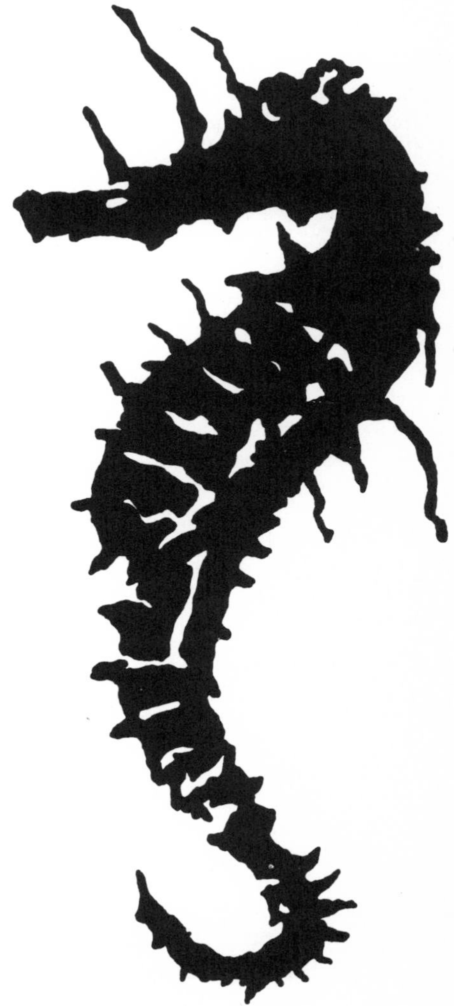

Seahorse

SEAHORSE, the traditional Sea Org symbol for standard technology. Formally adopted in 1968 as the symbol of Class VIII, it is employed on documents of the highest priority as the symbol of the continuous dedication of the Sea Org to the maintenance of standard tech. It expresses our highest aim, in that, by ensuring that standard tech as set down by L. Ron Hubbard is maintained, we protect the bridge for all mankind to attain to a higher spiritual state. (FO 3350)

SEAL OF CORPORATION, a corporate stamp or signet required by law, for impressing. The corporation's seal on its important documents.

SEA ORGANIZATION, 1. that **organization** which functions at a high level of confront and standard. Its purpose is to get ethics in on the planet and eventually the universe. This **organization** operates with a fleet of ships dedicated to this purpose around the world. Being mobile and separate from the pull of land is an absolute necessity to accomplish its plans, missions and purpose: to get ethics in. (FO 508) **2.** the **Sea Organization** is composed of the "aristocracy" of Scientology. These people alone and on their own are all stars in the sky of their areas. It is like one of the old regiments of gentleman where any private would be, in another but common regiment, a colonel. So, the **Sea Organization** is composed of people who alone would excite great admiration but who together, well organized, can actually get the job done. (FO 137) **3.** in 1968 the **Sea Org** became a goodwill activity and an efficient administrative arm of Scientology. The **Sea Org** runs the Advanced Organizations and is the custodian of the Clear and OT processing materials. (Ron's Journal 1968) **4.** the basic purpose of the **Sea Org** is to get in ethics. It also executes other projects, but all these are to assist getting in ethics or to assist the **Sea Org** itself. (FO 228) **5.** a fraternal organization existing within the formalized structure of the Churches of Scientology. It consists of highly dedicated members of the Church. These members take vows of eternal service. The **Sea Organization** life style of community living is traditional to religious orders. (BPL 9 Mar 74) **6.** a disciplined body of persons who have learned to operate in coordination with one another and who are at a higher, much higher level of discipline and purpose than Scientology organizations at large. (6804SM—) **7.** a corporate activity headed by a Board of Directors which owns and controls the ships, orgs and activities of the corporation. (HCO PL 9 Mar 72 I) **8.** our Commodore is L. Ron Hubbard, Source. Our purpose is maintaining the exact degree of ethics, Scn technology and policy on the planet. Our responsibility—the future of mankind. Our business—missions. The **Sea Org** is an organization of expansion. And our prize is a sane planet. (FO 1686) *Abbr.* SO.

SEA ORGANIZATION JUSTICE, see CAPTAIN'S MAST.

SEA ORGANIZATION LETTER TO STAFF, this will be a short ARC **letter** published approximately every 3 weeks by the Public Division of the flagship. Its purpose is to raise ARC and understanding between the **Sea Organization** and the outer Scn organizations, groups and franchises. (FO 2413) *Abbr.* S.O.L.T.S.

SEA ORGANIZATION ORG BOARD, applies at sea and in harbor and ashore. It is the ship's organization and clarified what duties are performed. Each ship has such a **board**. The flotilla has such a **board**. The second column of the Watch Quarter and Station Bill is the sea ship's org post of the person. Every member of a ship's company has a post on the Ship's Org Board. (FO 80)

SEA ORG ARC BREAK PROGRAM, a **Sea Org ARC Break program** introduced with the major purpose of getting worthwhile Sea Org members back on lines. (FO 1836)

SEA ORG CENTRAL BUREAUX, see FLAG BUREAUX.

SEA ORG COAT OF ARMS, it is a very precise symbolic statement of our ideals and beliefs. The principal designs used on it are (1) the 8 dynamic cross of Scientology, (2) the Sea Org wreath and star, (3) ascending seagulls and (4) sea horse. (FO 3351)

SEA ORG DISBURSEMENTS, the amount of money expended in support of **SO** orgs, ships, management, comm, everything including sums paid to management units as expenses and 10%s so paid as all or part of their expenses. (HCO PL 9 Mar 72 I)

SEA ORG ESTATES CAPTAIN, established in the USLO in the Office of LRH under the A/LRH Comm Aide. The purpose of the post is to direct, guide and control the usage of Sea Org properties and Sea Org property expansion in the PAC area, and to supervise the production and establishment of **Sea Org Estates** Sections of all SO orgs and units in the area. (FO 3166)

SEA ORG EXECUTIVE DIRECTIVE, distributed broadly or not to **SO** and/or Scn orgs and binding on both. Usually issued by Flag Management personnel. Contains immediate orders or programs. Blue on blue paper. (HCO PL 24 Sept 70R) *Abbr.* SO ED.

SEA ORG EXTERNAL EXPENSES, expenses that service the whole **SO** or **external** operations. (FSO 52)

SEA ORG FINANCE GRADUATE, a certificate is awarded each person upon completion of the **Finance** Course, as having attained the status of **Sea Org Finance Graduate**. (FO 2060)

SEA ORG INCOME, the amount of money received by the corporation after the allocation to **SO** and Scn orgs and before management expenses are taken out. Includes **SO** orgs, Scn orgs, Pubs and any other activity for which the corporation is advising or managing. It does not include the gross income of Scn orgs or such activities, only the money they pay to the **SO**. (HCO PL 9 Mar 72 I)

Sea Org Coat of Arms

SEA ORG INSIGNIA, the star and crossed branches or wreath and an OT badge. (FO 331)

SEA ORG MANNING CHIEF, the title "Sea Org Personnel Chief," HCO Bureau, Dept One, is abolished. The correct title is **Sea Org Manning Chief,** as the **Sea Org Manning Chief** is responsible for **manning** up each **Sea Org** vessel, stationship, unit, org and Flag. He provides qualified recruits who will back up the most viable and productive activity on this planet. He is the person who provides the man power resources for the expansion of the **Sea Org**. (FO 2826)

SEA ORG MEMBER, 1. the term **Sea Org member** shall mean and be used to designate only those who have their AB certificate and have done a tour of duty on a ship or training base. (FO 2238) **2.** so we define an **SO member** the way you do an OT—at cause over life, thought, matter, energy, space, time and form. (OODs 14 Jan 69)

SEA ORG MEMBER HAT, the basic of this **hat** is the 21 department org board. This org board applies to personal matters. It is the basic **SO member hat**. (FSO 308)

SEA ORG MOTTO, "We come back." Translated into Latin, *revenimus*, (pronounced: re ve nē′ moos). (FO 3351)

SEA ORG ORGS, 1. used to describe churches where a majority of **Sea Org** members are employed or which were first established by **Sea Org** members of the church. (BPL 9 Mar 74) **2.** AO's, AOSH's, and OTL's. (FO 2032) **3.** AO's, SH's, AOSH's, SH Fdn's, CC's. (FO 3124)

SEA ORG PERSONNEL CHIEF, see SEA ORG MANNING CHIEF.

SEA ORG PERSONNEL CONTROL SECTION, SO Personnel Control Section is in HCO Bureau Branch I's. The purpose of the **SO Personnel Control Section** is to: assemble and compile all admin data on **SO personnel** and Scn org trainees (Admin—FEBCs and tech), to oversee the correct programming and training of **SO personnel** and determine their placements for full utilization, and to take all the actions necessary to handle and regulate all **SO personnel** transfers and their readiness, orders, the establishment of pools of trained **personnel** and pressing into higher volume recruitment in all **SO** areas. (CBO 120)

SEA ORG PUBLICITY BRANCH, the **SO Publicity Branch** is in the FPPO network as it is necessary to promote **Sea Org** and Flag in order to get recruits and vets for Flag and FAPTC. This function also assists **SO** orgs with effective, broad promotion to help drive **SO** prospects down on all **SO** units. (FO 3555)

SEA ORG PUBLICITY OFFICER, (Central Personnel Office Hat) goals: to broadly **publicize** the true image of the **Sea Org** and by doing so, drive in applicants for the **Sea Org** onto recruiters so they can channel them in, in volume. (FO 3332)

SEA ORG PURPOSE, 1. to get in ethics. (FO 232) **2.** maintaining the exact degree of ethics, Scn technology and policy on the planet. (FO 1426) **3.** to put ethics in on this planet. (FO 1426) **4.** revised to be: to recruit, train, organize and send out to locations complete org or program units to establish high level functioning Dn and Scn units, activities or courses so that they can attain the best possible results and effectiveness in their areas and to operate AOs. (FO 1992)

SEA ORG RECEIPTS, the combined gross **receipts** of all **SO** orgs, ships and activities, being the total **receipts** of a corporation which is managed by a board. It is *not* the income of "Flag" or "Management" or CLOs or Flag Bureaux or FAO (Flag Admin Org) or ship. (HCO PL 9 Mar 72 I)

SEA ORG RECRUIT, hereafter the term **Sea Org recruit** shall be used to designate anyone on a ship, base or in an org who has not obtained his AB and done a tour on a ship or training base. (FO 2238)

SEA ORG RECRUITER, 1. that person posted in Dept 1 of a **Sea Org** org or ship who is responsible for reaching new people and getting them to join the **Sea Org**. The post is single-hatted and has no personnel control duties ever. (CBO 214RA) **2.** these are the personnel posted in the HCO of each **SO** unit, they are under the Director of Personnel of the orgs for administrative reasons, but their orders and product officering is the concern of the **SO** org Recruitment Chief and the Continental Recruitment Chief. (FO 3475)

SEA ORG RECRUITMENT I/C, this is a full time post in the FPPO network, his function is the product officering of all **Sea Org** org **recruiters** in area **SO** units. (FO 3475)

SEA ORG RESERVES, often miscalled "Flag Reserves" or "Management Reserves" which they are not. **SO reserves** are: the amount of money collected for the corporation over and above expenses that is sent by various units (via FBOs and the Finance network) to the corporation's banks. It is used for purposes assigned by the Board of Directors and for no other purpose. These are normally employed for periods of stress or to handle situations. They are not profit. It is not support money for "Flag" or "Management." It is not operating money. (HCO PL 9 Mar 72 I) *Abbr.* SOR.

Sea Org Symbol

SEA ORG SYMBOL, 1. the **Sea Org symbol** adopted and used as the **symbol** of a Galactic Confederacy far back in the history of this sector, derives much of its power and authority from that association. The laurel wreath represents victory. Used throughout the history of this planet to crown poets, artists, champions and conquerers, it not only represents the physical victory but the series of inner victories achieved by the individual, and the clarification and purification of his inner aims and purposes which lead to the outward victory. It is associated with the head, the traditional abode of the spirit. The star is a symbol of the spirit. The five pointed star most commonly signifies rising up towards the point of origin; thus, it is a potent symbol of alignment to source. The laurel wreath and star, in combination, signify the victory of the spirit which is rising upward towards the point of origin or source. Its proper color is always gold. And note that the star is not trapped in its victory, but is in the open field towards the top of the wreath, allowing free exit, beyond its victory, and that is, in fact, in a field of blue, symbolizing truth. (FO 3350) **2.** the star is the confederation and each one of those leaves is counted, it's the number of stars. (6804SM—)

SEA ORG TRAINING COORDINATOR, a post formed to handle the **coordination** and supervision actions necessary to complete **SO training** completions in liaisons with PCOs. The post is **SO Training Coordinator**. He is in Bureau V, CLOs, under the A/Qual Aide. The purpose of the **SO Training Coordinator** is: to help Ron to create ever increasing numbers of fully **trained Sea Org** members. (FO 3116)

SEA ORG VOICE CONTROL DRILL, TR 8B **voice control**. Purpose: to enable the student to effortlessly talk at the exact point or area where he wants to be heard. To teach good **voice control**. (FO 2585R)

SEA PROJECT, our ships and the **Sea Project** will hereafter be known as the Sea Organization and the word "project" will be dropped having been downgraded by its application to minor volunteer activities. (FO 1)

SEA READINESS, consists of the ability to stand up to unlooked for seas or emergencies or failures. (BO 125, 7 Aug 67)

SEASICKNESS, **1.** motion sickness, means nausea by fear of being unstabilized. (OODs 24 Feb 72) **2. sea,** plane or car **sickness** is all the same thing. It is an effort to hold a position in space and reacts on the body to suppress it. (OODs 2 Sept 71) **3.** first and foremost lack of confidence. It is almost always bad food at sea in times past restimulated. And it is of course motion sickness. But it is fear, and a well drilled crew in a sound ship is confident and unless badly aberrated or very badly knocked about they don't get **seasick**. (FO 80)

SEASONAL DEMAND, see DEMAND, SEASONAL.

SEASONAL EMPLOYMENT, see EMPLOYMENT, SEASONAL.

SEASONAL VARIATION, the variances in business activity that occur on a month-to-month basis in certain businesses due to seasonal demands.

SEAT, the accepted expression for a membership on a stock exchange.

SEA TRAINING, Sea Org members have another training step, which gives them an added strength and versatility, and that is **sea training**. In **sea training** and duties, Sea Org members learn to confront and handle mest and randomity. (BPL 23 Dec 71R)

SEA WATCH DRILLS, sea watch drills are drilled by their Cons. They are drilled on the bridge, with the equipment. Each watch member is taught who the officers are and what they do, what the equipment is and 100% (not brush off) operation of it with practice. Anytime there is a change in the watch line-up, the whole watch is again drilled by their Conning Officer. By this is meant the sea Conning Officer. (FO 1020)

SEA WATCH PICTURE BOOK, 1. book compiled by Mary Sue Hubbard to cover all bridge duties and functions. (FSO 413) **2.** it covers the basic and routing actions of watch members posts on any ship. (FO 2229) *Abbr. SWPB.*

SEC, the Securities and Exchange Commission established by Congress for the benefit and protection of investors.

SEC ED, 1. Secretarial Executive Directive. (HCO PL 7 May 65) **2. Secretarial Executive Director.** (HCO PL 22 Feb 65 III) **3.** LRH EDs were earlier called **SEC EDs.** (HCO PL 24 Sept 70R) **4.** now named "Executive Directives" or EDs. (HCO PL 1 Sept 66R) **5. Secretarily** signed order of the **Executive Director,** expiring one year from date of issue. (HCO PL 13 Feb 66 II) **6.** the meaning of the word **SEC ED** is **Secretarial** to the **Executive Director.** The word "**Secretarial**" applies to the signature meaning it is signed as official by a person other than LRH personally. It is the written initials in the lower left-hand corner that are "**Secretarial.**" The system came into use to accomodate cable orders originally. By being sealed and initialled by an official person like a notary public in the org, the validity of the order was attested as a valid order of LRH. (HCO PL 3 Feb 66 V) **7.** they will be on blue paper with blue ink. The initials **SEC ED** always precede a **SEC ED** number. All personnel orders will now also appear in **SEC ED** form. (HCO PL 8 May 65 II) **8. Secretarial Executive Directives** are explicit temporary urgent orders. It is desirable that a **SEC ED** is broadly distributed to a staff and that **SEC EDs** of broad interest be distributed internationally. (HCO PL 7 May 65) **9. Secretarial Executive Director** orders apply mainly to personnel or local conditions, expire in one year if not stated to expire earlier, may only last one year in any event. Policy letters apply broadly to all orgs and Scientologists without exception. (HCO PL 5 Mar 65 II) **10.** the Executive Director comm lines now include **Secretarial Executive Director** in all orgs including Saint Hill. This consists of a note or cable typed out by the HCO Steno (or Communicator where no HCO Steno exists or by the HCO Area Secretary where no communicator exists). It is sealed with the corporation seal in the lower left-hand corner over the signature of the HCO personnel typing it. It is headed "**Secretarial Executive Director.**" It is on blue paper. The signature of the Executive Director or the Acting Executive Director is typed below the message. Date and subject are included. Each **SEC ED** is numbered by the issuing Executive Director. The exact text of the note or cable is duplicated without additions or deletions. This is never a mimeographed item. The original sealed **SEC ED,** with the note or cable, goes to HCO files. A copy is immediately posted on the staff bulletin board by the HCO personnel who typed it and signed and sealed it. Another copy goes to the org /Assn Sec. Another copy goes to the HCO Area Sec. **SEC EDs** are high speed, urgent communications having the force of policy and require instant emergency compliance. The **SEC ED** is the high velocity comm line used to change personnel, to handle emergencies or to make limited time policies or to handle personnel conflicts or chronic slumps. All **SEC EDs** expire fully one year from date of issue but are kept on record although no longer in force. The subjects of **SEC EDs** are not general in application to all orgs but only to the particular org to which they are addressed. (HCO PL 22 Feb 65 III) **11. Secretarial Executive Director** (numbered), green ink on blue paper. By LRH. Distributed as designated. This is in effect a reissue of Assn Secretary or HCO Continental Orders after review by LRH. Designed to confirm, consolidate or end disputes or differences between HCO Continental or Area Sec and HASI Assn Secs. (HCO PL 4 Feb 61) **12.** a hat is not a hat anymore in a Central Organization unless it's **Secretarial Executive Director** on blue paper, black ink, with a corporation seal on every valid copy. When a **Secretarial Executive Director** is issued, it is published on the bulletin board and given to the persons to whom it applies. Now this means **Secretarial Executive Director** operates as the Secretary to the Advisory Committee or Advisory Council. The **Secretarial Executive Director** operates as Secretary to the board or any other committee action or board action that takes place. This person, who is really the HCO Steno, turns up as the Recording Secretary, prepares the minutes and sends them to their proper places for signature. That's one action. The other action this person takes is to collect old hats. If there's any new hat write-up, the **Secretarial Executive Director** issues it. If there are any changes that take place in the organization by its orders, **Secretarial Executive Director** changes them. So you get, in essence, hat preparation and write-up the issuance of general orders for the local organizations through the **Secretarial Executive**

Director. Now, you get HCO Secretarial Letters. Very seldom will you get anything that says "**Secretarial Executive Director** for Washington D.C. only" because if its going wrong in one place, it's going wrong someplace else too. But you do get incidental orders to that effect, so they can't be excluded. Instead of that you get an HCO Secretarial Letter. Now this HCO Secretarial Letter arrives in a central operation and is converted by **Secretarial Executive Director**, after being viewed by the HCO Secretary. It is converted, and it says: "**Secretarial Executive Director**, HASI, Johannesburg." She types it all up. They are never mimeographed unless they are for the whole staff or something. She puts a copy on the board, she puts a copy to the persons to, and that's it. She's issued it. Now, these are all policies. These things are basically policies. They are hats, and so on. They may have particularities, but they definitely have lots of policies connected with them. (5812C29)

SEC ED (AD COUNCIL), orders or directions in Scn for conditions assigned, personnel appointments and financial planning and directions to secretaries. (Blue paper, blue ink, signed by the **Advisory Council** for LRH Exec Dir, approved by LRH Communicator as not against policy and by HCO for personnel.) (HCO PL 13 Mar 66)

SEC ED (DIVISIONAL AD COMM), for orders to a **division** by its **Advisory Committee**: (Color of paper of the division, blue ink, signed by the **Advisory Committee** of the **division** for LRH Executive Director, approved by the Advisory Council and the LRH Communicator and personnel orders also approved by HCO Personnel Control). (HCO PL 13 Mar 66)

SEC ED (DIVISIONAL SECRETARY), for orders to Directors of the **division** from its **Secretary**: (Color of the paper of the division, blue ink, signed by that **division's Secretary** for LRH Exec Director approved by the Ad Council and LRH Communicator and requiring HCO approval for personnel). (HCO PL 13 Mar 66)

SEC ED (EXECUTIVE SECRETARY), for orders to the divisions under the **Exec Sec**: (Blue paper, blue ink, signed by the HCO **Exec Sec** or Org **Exec Sec** for LRH Executive Director). (HCO PL 13 Mar 66)

SEC ED (GUARDIAN), orders or directions in Scn for transfers of large sums or property, appointments of Exec Secs WW and urgent matters relating to survival actions: (White paper, blue ink, signed by the **Guardian**, MSH for LRH). (HCO PL 13 Mar 66)

SEC ED (SECRETARIAL TO THE EXECUTIVE DIRECTOR) (LRH), for orders, or plans, expires in 1 year. For personnel permanent appointments: (White paper, blue ink, signed personally by the **Executive Director LRH**). (HCO PL 13 Mar 66)

SECONDARY DISTRIBUTION, the instance of a large block of stock being offered for sale again usually well after it was first sold by the issuing company. This could come about as a result of settling an estate or other reasons.

SECONDARY EVALUATION, see PRIMARY EVALUATION.

SECOND DANGER FORMULA, 1. I have worked out the **second danger formula**, meaning the **formula** applied by the person, unit, org or activity which has been assigned a **danger** condition. (a) list the consequences if the situation had remained unhandled. (b) work out any conflicts of orders which prevent compliance and production and get them adjusted. (c) work out any misunderstoods and get them clarified. (d) survey and improve comm outflow and inflow. (e) reorganize mest (matter, energy, space and time) more efficiently. (f) work out means of becoming more secure. (g) present the completed **formula** in writing as above to the one who assigned the condition for permission to upgrade. (HCO PL 7 Feb 70) [The above HCO PL and **formula** have been cancelled by HCO PL 9 Apr 72, *Correct Danger Condition Handling.*] **2.** which we now call a first dynamic **danger formula**. (7204C11 SO)

SECOND DEPUTY CHIEF, see FIRST DEPUTY CHIEF.

SECOND DEPUTY COMMODORE, 1. purpose: to be the inspecting, supervising and training officer of Flag and the flotilla, to be the senior con of Flag and to assist the Commodore and First Deputy in all matters relating to their posts and duties, as requested or ordered and to do such other things as may be necessary to assist these Flag officers to handle their posts and prevent overburden particularly in regard to maritime, ship and crew handling and shore related duties. (FO 3342-2) **2.** whether in the presence or absence of the Commodore, the **Second Deputy Commodore** acts as extension of certain inspection and supervision and social duties of the Commodore's personal office and function. His normal duties are those of an inspection, supervision or social nature and include the training and supervision of very senior officers and conning duties in situations containing danger or harbor or channel ship movement. (FO 3342)

SECOND DEPUTY DIRECTOR, acts as Executive Director in the absence of the Executive Director and 1st Deputy Executive Director. (HCO PL 18 Dec 64, *Saint Hill Org Board*)

SECOND DEPUTY ORGANIZATION SECRETARY, acts as Organization Secretary in the absence of the Organization Secretary and 1st Deputy Organization Secretary. (HCO PL 18 Dec 64, *Saint Hill Org Board*)

SECOND (2nd) MATE, **1.** Tech Sec. (OODs 1 Jun 72) **2.** the **2nd mate** is in charge of training and HCI (Hubbard College of Improvement), the 2nd Division. (FO 2674)

SECOND SOUTHERN AFRICA SPECIAL RUNDOWN, the newest development for the people of **South Africa** by Ron. It is to be run on all pcs who have had the South African Help RD. The **rundown** is quite simple, the processes familiar to some of you. It consists of: (1) ruds at the beginning of each session *stressing W/Hs and MW/Hs*. (2) objective processes each to full EP plus F/N, cog, VGIs. (3) O/W processes, each run thoroughly to EP. (4) havingness after each O/W process and at session end. (5) use of random ruds: MW/H, half-truth, untruth, during each session and as end ruds. (BTB 8 May 74 I)

SECRETARIAL, the meaning of the word **SEC ED** is "**Secretarial** to the Executive Director." The word **Secretarial** applies to the signature meaning it is signed as official by a person other than LRH personally. It is the written initials in the lower left-hand corner that are **secretarial**. The system came into use to accommodate cable orders originally. By being sealed and initialed by an official person like a Notary Public in the org, the validity of the order was attested as a valid order of LRH. (HCO PL 3 Feb 66 V) *Abbr.* SEC, SEC'L.

SECRETARIAL EXECUTIVE DIRECTIVE, see SEC ED.

SECRETARIAL EXECUTIVE DIRECTOR, see SEC ED.

SECRETARIAL EXECUTIVE DIRECTOR SECTION, section in Dept 2, Dept of Communications. Signs and seals **SEC EDs** and certificates, handles all **SEC EDs**, handles all ethics and other HCO Orders. (HCO PL 17 Jan 66 II)

SECRETARIAL TO THE EXECUTIVE DIRECTOR, **1.** the **Sec'l ED** shall publish all **Secretarial to the Executive Director** on blue paper, black ink, marked for local area. One copy to go on staff bulletin board, one copy to each staff person affected. Each copy is separately signed and sealed by the post of **Sec'l ED**. The **Sec'l ED** is also HCO Steno and is under the HCO Area Sec. The **Sec'l ED** shall act as Secretary to the Board, where it exists, to the Advisory Committee or Advisory Council and at staff meeting, shall type and get signed and distribute the minutes. The **Sec'l ED** shall put into HCO Secretarial Letters any item she is given originally from LRH intended for all organizations. The **Sec'l ED** shall convert any HCO Secretarial Letters she receives into a **Secretarial to the Executive Director** for the local area. The **Sec'l ED** shall capture all seals of any organization and shall hold and be the only person to use these. The **Sec'l ED** shall perform any other duties given by the HCO Area Secretary and/or HCO Communicator. The **Sec'l ED** shall capture all random orders from exterior sources which have by-passed the lines of the Executive Director and shall refer them to him for issue or cancellation. All org board changes shall be done by the **Sec'l ED**. All hats and hat changes shall be reviewed and done by **Sec'l ED**. **Sec'l ED** shall keep a copy of all hats and hat material from whatever source and of whatever age. **Sec'l ED** shall act under orders of the Executive Director, the HCO Communicator, and the HCO Area Sec in whatever other capacities are needful, but this shall not be a complete license to HCO to run in all regards an area Central Organization. (SEC ED 36, 14 Jan 59) **2.** purpose: to provide a channel from the organization to the Executive Director. To ensure the arrival of orders from the Executive Director to the organization. To safeguard the hats of the organization. (SEC ED 62, 29 Jan 59) **3.** all new hats and hat changes will appear as **Secretarial to the Executive Director** orders. These are now on blue paper with black ink and every valid copy is sealed with the corporate seal. Org Secs and Assoc Secs desiring to change hats will submit desired changes to the **Secretarial to the Executive Director** for review after which they may or may not be written into **Secretarial to the Executive Director** orders and therefore hats. (SEC ED 12, 16 Dec 58) *Abbr.* SEC ED, SEC'L ED.

SECRETARIAL UNIT, **1.** the purpose of the **Secretarial Unit** is to type answers to letters. (HCO PL 4 Jan 66 III) **2.** purpose: to expedite the communications of the organization. (HCO London, 9 Jan 58)

SECRETARY, 1. there are 7 **secretaries** in each organization. They head divisions. They are the Chairmen of the Divisional Ad Comm. They are appointed by the Ad Council of the org with the approval of HCO Personnel and LRH Comm. (HCO PL 13 Mar 66) **2.** the **Secretary** of a division is the Product Officer. (FEBC 4, 7101C18 SO III) **3.** (Committees of Evidence) the **Secretary** is appointed specifically by the Convening Authority. The **Secretary** is a proper member of the committee and has a vote. The **Secretary** prepares and issues all notices to attend, attends all meetings, keeps all notes, collects all documentary evidence offered in the hearings, procures tapes and a tape recorder, does all the tape recording, and collects all members of the Committee for scheduled hearings. All this is in addition to usual staff duties. The Assoc **Sec's Sec** or the HCO Communicator or HCO Steno would be the ordinary choice, but any others may be chosen for the assignment. (HCO PL 7 Sept 63)

SECRETARY, a person employed to handle correspondence, keep files and perform associated office duties for an individual or company. *Abbr.* Sec.

SECRETARY BOARD OF DIRECTORS OF HASI INC., prepares and keeps all minutes and records of board activities. Gives notice of meetings. Retains originals of all valuable corporate documents and furnishes copies. Signs on all bank accounts worldwide. Has prepared all documents of registration and reports to registrars of companies. Serves as Deputy Chairman in absence of Chairman. (HCO PL 18 Dec 64, *Saint Hill Org Board*)

SECRETARY OF CORPORATION, an officer among whose duties is the keeping of records of Board of Directors' meetings, stock transfers, legal transactions, etc., and safeguarding such records as well as the corporate seal.

SECTION, 1. each one of the departments has 5 **sections**. It shouldn't have more than 5. Those **sections** are divided into subsections. (SH Spec 77, 6608C23) **2.** a City Office has **sections** where higher orgs have departments and divisions. (HCO PL 21 Oct 66 III)

SECTION III BASE, the **Section III Base** shall now be called the Base Organization. It is at the moment without any staff. The staff of the Commodore at the moment are doing a caretake-organizational action on it. Staff must be sent from WW for it. They need have no sea experience or activities and are just like any other org staff. The staff of the Commodore will organize it and get it going but proper staff for **Section III** actions must be supplied by WW in the very near future. Proper base personnel have been demanded from WW for the Base Organization. (FO 1) [**Section III Base** was an idea for a landbase where people could come and safely do Section III OT. A land site was never found and the idea of **Section III Base** became the AO on the *Royal Scotman* which later moved too and was called AO Alicante. This AO eventually moved to Edinburgh, Scotland. The idea of **Section III Base** is briefly mentioned in the tape, Ron's Journal 67.]

SECTION 5, refers to a **section** which started out in HCO before the '67 Org Bd, and before the Guardian Office was established. It was an Investigation **Section** which did investigations. It hired proved private detectives to do this. It was abolished when these functions were taken over by the G.O. (MSH Def. Notes)

SECTION HEAD, an expert in 1/5 of a department. (FEBC 3, 7101C18 SO II)

SECTION HEAD, the person who directs and is responsible for the production of a section, or unit, within a department; also called a unit head.

SECTION MAA, under each RPF Section Leader is to be a specifically appointed **Section MAA** who assists the Section Leader to maintain ethics in the section. (FO 3434-1)

SECTION OFFICER, the **officer** in charge of a **section** is the Product Officer of that **section.** He is junior to all Estos except an Esto posted directly to his specific department. (HCO PL 7 Mar 72)

SECULAR TREND, an economic trend (growth or decline) that continues for a long period of time.

SECURED LIABILITY, a debt or obligation against which specific assets have been pledged, to guarantee the lender repayment in the value of the loan should the borrower default. See COLLATERAL.

SECURE FOR SEA, [to **secure** and lash down any movable objects before sailing and completing preparations for the voyage.] [see illustration]

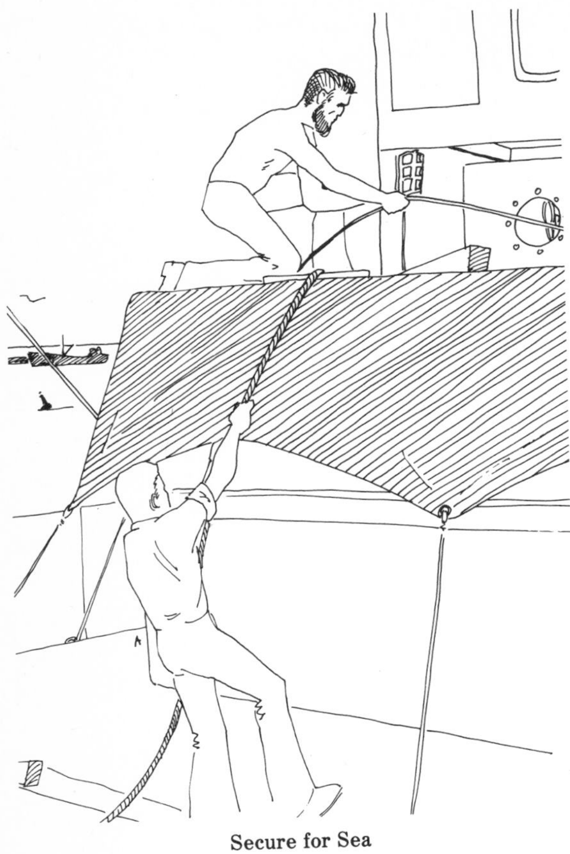

Secure for Sea

SECURING SHIP, in **securing ship** one is seeing to it that for several days the ship can be safely left with only a small guard or watchman. This includes seeing to readiness of boats, shutting off fuel, putting away instruments and valuables under lock, discarding provisions that will spoil, closing ports against rain, etc. When complete the ship can be considered secure from flooding, fire and theft and damage to her gear if left. (*Ship's Org Bk.*)

SECURITIES, written evidence of ownership or creditorship, such as stock certificates or bonds, issued by companies to raise long-term capital.

SECURITY, 1. total **security** would be no open communication, not even couriers. Sensible **security** consists of reducing frequency of action, length of text on open line messages and limiting on open lines the volume of information, and changing in due course previous patterns used. (FO 2396) **2. security** itself is an understanding. Men who know are secure. All **security** derives from knowledge. One knows he will be cared for no matter what happens. That is a **security**. Knowledge of the general underlying rules of life would bring about a **security** of life. Knowledge of the underlying rules of life would also bring about a **security** in a job. (*POW*, p. 16) **3. security** aboard 'Flag' has a *twofold* aspect: outflow—the prevention of anything confidential to those aboard 'Flag' from being passed to unauthorized shore personnel. Inflow—the prevention of activities on the shore from enturbulating 'Flag' or its allies ashore. (FO 3382) **4. security** is not letting others in on your plans, whereabouts and actions. It also includes not giving away data so it can be used to interrupt actions. (FO 1882) **5. security** is mainly a matter of preventing the unwanted passage of particles on or off the ship. (FO 1669) **6.** means not letting the enemy into your camp—as opposed to actual warfare. (FO 1669) **7.** the basic meaning of **security** is "guarding one's self." The dictionary definition is "safety from foreign interference of espionage, safety against attack." (FO 1669) **8.** meaning no unauthorized persons in or items out of the Sea Org files, desks, materials, ship; **secure** from infiltration, theft and loss. (FO 1964) **9.** the ability to go through or around or to bring order to confusion (*POW*, p. 25)

SECURITY, (a) generally, a guarantee or form of assurance given by a borrower, the value of which eliminates any risk taken in making a loan to him. (b) term sometimes used for a stock, share or bond.

SECURITY FORMS 7A AND 7B, see HCO WW SECURITY FORMS 7A AND 7B.

SECURITY PLEDGE, [a printed form one signs before being allowed to see confidential data or work in a confidential area. Usually it requires that one will not divulge the confidential data to unauthorized persons. This term is mentioned in HCO PL 8 Nov 75, *Non-Existence Formula Expanded.*]

SECURITY TR, purpose: to train the student to maintain **security** under scrutiny. (FO 2507)

SELECTEE, the person the Field Staff Member **selects** to be trained or processed after direct personal contact and issues a paper stating he has been selected. This paper bears the hour, date and place of the selection. (HCO PL 26 Mar 65)

SELECTEE FILE, copies of the **selection** paper are kept by the Body Reg in a file alphabetically arranged. This is the **selectee file**. (HCO PL 15 Oct 65)

SELECTEES MAILINGS, this is a series of three **selectee** advice packets sent out by the ASR at intervals of 2 weeks to the person **selected** by an FSM for an org service(s). (BPL 20 May 72R)

SELECTION, choosing the right or desired item from a number of items. Selection usually refers in industry to choosing which applicants to accept as future employees or which items to remove as defective from a batch of production.

SELECTION, ANALYTIC METHOD OF, a method of personnel selection whereby available personnel data on applicants is categorically analyzed considering such things as education, experience, age, etc., in order to make the best choice of personnel.

SELECTION CONSULTANT, a person who specializes in finding and selecting competent executive and management personnel. He usually employs extensive advertising to obtain his applicants and may recruit from the ranks of those already employed much like an Executive Search Consultant.

SELECTION, OVERALL IMPRESSION METHOD OF, a personnel selection procedure where applicants after being read are categorized under titles such as suitable, doubtful and unsuitable according to the overall impression the application gives one about the applicant. This method is particularly useful where a large amount of applications are being considered for only a few openings.

SELECTION PAPER, the Field Staff Member **selects** the person to be trained or processed after direct personal contact with the person and issues to that person a **paper** stating the contacted person has been **selected.** The form must bear the hour, date and place, the block printed name and address of the **selectee** and the block printed name and address and certificate initials and certificate number of the Field Staff Member and what the **selectee** is **selected** for (membership, training or processing) and some approximation of arrival date at the org. (HCO PL 9 May 65, *Field Auditors Become Staff*)

SELECTION ROUTING FORM, FSM **Selection Routing Form** for **routing** documents for FSM commission payments. The Body Registrar initiates a **Selection Routing Form**, which is a document **routing form,** *not* a body routing form. A separate **form** is used for each service signed up. The **form** has spaces to be filled in by the Body Registrar as to person's name, service signed up for, hour and date of sign up, name of FSM who **selected** the person for that service, date service is to start, and initials of the Body Registrar attesting to these data. (BPL 9 Jan 67R)

SELF-DETERMINISM, means the ability to direct himself. (2ACC 30A, 5312CM21)

SELF INVALIDATION, merely the accumulation of **invalidation** of **oneself** by others. (FO 1432)

SELLER, 1. a person who sells or delivers goods, services or property for a price or in exchange for goods or services of like value. 2. in merchandising, an item that sells in a particular way, as a best seller or poor seller.

SELLING, the act of assisting, inducing or being responsible for a person buying a product, service, property or idea.

SELLING AGENT, an individual or company that has the occupation of selling the output of one or more manufacturers for which he receives a commission.

SELLING, BENEFIT METHOD OF, a sales approach which concentrates on the benefits a potential customer can receive by purchasing a specific product.

SELLING COSTS, see COSTS, SELLING.

SELLING, DIRECT, the action of a company using its own sales personnel to sell its goods direct to the consumer rather than using retail outlets. Sales are accomplished by mail order or from the factory.

SELLING, DIRECT MAIL, selling a product or service through the mails by sending promotional literature such as a catalog to a list of established and prospective customers inviting them to place orders directly and providing an order blank to fill in and return.

SELLING, MASS, selling of goods and services on an impressive scale by reaching large segments of the buying public.

SELLING, PERSONAL, marketing term for the act of creating such a strong desire for what you have to sell that it succeeds in overshadowing many other considerations including money.

SELLING PLATFORM, the main idea on which an advertising or marketing campaign is based.

SEMANTICS, **semantics** as we know it is a theory concerned with meanings as expressed in signs, symbols, words and other means of communication. **Semantics** as it deals with words, studies changing forms of meaning and definitions by comparison to other significances and meanings. This can have as many variables as there are words. (FBDL 449)

SEMINAR ASSISTANT, (Congress hat) purpose: to assist **Seminar** Leader in running a smooth, effective **seminar**. (HCOB 13 May 60 [The above HCOB was cancelled by BTB 10 Dec 74 III.]

SEMINAR CAPTAIN, (Congress hat) purpose: to ensure a smooth-running and effective muzzled co-audit for the congress, to run tight, high ARC, 8-C on **Seminar** Leaders and assistants so that individual **seminars** go well. (HCOB 13 May 60) [The above HCOB was cancelled by BTB 10 Dec 74 III.]

SEMINAR LEADER, (Congress hat) purpose: to run a smooth, effective **seminar**. (HCOB 13 May 60) [The above HCOB was cancelled by BTB 10 Dec 74 III.]

SEMI-VARIABLE COSTS, see COSTS, SEMI-VARIABLE.

SEND STUDENT BACK TO TRAINING, means that the student is sent to cramming to get straight exactly what is missed and then back to course and does the entire course again (BPL 27 Jul 69R)

SENIOR ADVANCED ORG, AOLA is nominated as the **senior AO** for final decisions of other **AO's** in case of emergency. This is established not because any emergency is expected, but as a precaution as Flag is not always in comm. (FO 1920)

SENIOR CASE SUPERVISOR, **1.** the **Senior C/S** reviews and **supervises C/Ses**, handles bugged or red tabbed cases, sends C/Ses and auditors to Cramming, handles overloads while getting C/Ses trained, recruits C/Ses, sees that auditors are recruited and trained. (HCO PL 26 Sept 74) **2. Senior C/S** handles bugged cases and very upper level actions and keeps the other C/Ses functioning well. He is the highest classed **C/S** in the org. He is responsible for proper handling and results on all cases. (This is a hat I usually wore in an area.) (HCO PL 25 Sept 74)

SENIOR COMM MEMBER, a **senior comm member** (not senior staff member) is one holding a duplicate post in a **senior** org. (HCO PL 13 Mar 65 II)

SENIOR CONVENING AUTHORITY, the Commodore is the **Senior Convening Authority**. (FSO 131)

SENIOR DATUM OF QUAL, the **senior datum of Qual** is that: **Qual** never never never takes the order or direction of any other division or staff member on what to do technically with a student or pc. (HCO PL 28 Dec 67)

SENIOR EXECUTIVES, 1. such as Div heads or heads of an org. (HCO PL 8 Nov 75) **2.** those posted above Div or Bureau head. (ED 13 FB) **3.** Exec Secs, Secs, LRH Comms, Ethics Officers, and Div 1, Dept 1. (HCO PL 30 Sept 68) [The above HCO PL was cancelled by BPL 10 Oct 75 IV.] **4.** Aides, Captains, Chief Officers, Supercargos, LRH Comms, Division Officers, MAAs, and Div 1, Dept 1. (FO 1422)

SENIOR EXECUTIVE SECRETARY, the **Senior Executive Secretary** at WW is the HCO **Exec Sec.** The HCO **ES** is held fully responsible for any errors or neglect by the other exec secs. The HCO **ES** calls and conducts all meetings of EC WW and establishes their order of business. Anyone addressing "EC WW" is in fact addressing the HCO **ES** WW. Should WW fail in any respect, it is the HCO **ES** who is held responsible. (HCO PL 12 Feb 70 II)

SENIOR INSTRUCTOR, purpose: to create a competent auditor with a good grasp of the theory and practice of Scn. (HCO London, 9 Jan 58)

SENIORITY, the state of a person having rank or precedence over others due to his higher position in an organization and/or the longer length of time he has been with the company.

SENIORITY RIGHTS, special considerations that are given to those who have a long period of service with a company such as promotion, transfer choices or layoff immunity.

SENIOR LRH COMM, LRH Personal Comm, CS-7, **LRH Comm** WW. (BPL 24 Jul 73R)

SENIOR OEC, comprises additional policies from the existing **OEC** Volumes to the end of 1973, as studied by division. (HCO PL 19 Nov 73)

SENIOR ORG, the top **org** heading an echelon of orgs. Saint Hill is the top **org** to eleven other orgs but amongst these there is continental **seniority**. The Continental **Org** is **senior** to the other orgs in that zone but as these all form one echelon to Saint

Hill, Saint Hill is **senior** to the rest. (HCO PL 13 Mar 65 II)

SENIOR PARTNER, a partner who has a comparatively large investment in a partnership and who makes the major decisions and shares in the profits or losses on a larger scale than any other partner.

SENIOR POLICY, the **senior policy** is "deliver what was promised." (LRH ED 131 INT)

SENIOR RATING, a Sea Org officer or petty officer who has completed his AB checksheet and *Sea Watch Picture Book* 3 times. Anyone completing these 3 times will be immediately sent to the Officer Selection Board for a right arm rank. Performance of duty will be considered. (FO 1666) *Abbr.* S/R.

SENIOR WATCH OFFICER, his duties consist of the safe progress of the vessel toward destination and the smart efficient performance of watches. He stands no watch of his own. (OODs 12 Apr 70)

SENSE OF HUMOR, a **sense of humor** is in part an ability to spot out-points that should be rejected from a body of data. In fact a **sense of humor** is based on both rejection and absurd out-points of all types. (HCO PL 23 Jun 70)

SENSITIVITY TRAINING, see TRAINING, SENSITIVITY.

SEPARATION, 1. the discharge of a person as from employment or military service. 2. in law, the court decree separating a husband and wife.

SEPARATION ORDER, there are instances met with by Ethics Officers, especially in relation to husbands and wives, where there may be suppressions on individual people but not suppressive of Scn. In such case a **separation order** for a specific period of time is the best action. For example, Joe S______ and Mary S______ are hereby placed under a **separation order** while Joe is undergoing processing. They are to have no contact with each other during this period from (date) ______ to ______ (in this case to the end of the Power Processing 2nd Stage Release). (HCO PL 19 Jul 65, *Separation Order*)

SEPARATION PAY, see SEVERANCE PAY.

SEQUENCE, means linear (in a line) travel either through space or time or both. (HCO PL 19 Sept 70 III)

SERIAL BOND, a bond that matures in small amounts over a series of intervals.

SERIAL CORRELATION, using past trends, patterns and experiences to forecast future sales and market occurances.

SERVICE, **service** means technical results. (HCO PL 21 Aug 63)

SERVICE BUSINESS, business specializing in providing service, repair or maintenance. A service business usually depends upon the existence of other businesses to provide the primary tangible items to be serviced, repaired or maintained.

SERVICE CONSULTANT, there *are* persons coming into the org who want info, help, advice, guidance and a shoulder to lean on, but they don't always get it. The Body Reg is usually flat out and being pushed for GI and consequently with so much attention on making money not all individuals get the **service** and attention they desire or need. Sometimes it can take hours or even days, maybe weeks, to aid such persons who want and need personalized assistance to terminatedly handle their stops and problems and thus get them on the Gradation Chart. And this is where the **Service Consultant** enters into the picture. Patience and tolerance are two of the virtues needed for effective performance on such a post. He gives persons lots of ARC and attention in order to get them up to the stage of enlightenment where the Body Reg takes over and brings the transaction to a close. The **Service Consultant** frees up the Body Reg so she can *fully* concentrate on the Gross Income—the stat given her by LRH in HCO PL 14 July 1970. *Urgent Registrar Statistic*. (HCO PL 31 Oct 72 I) [The latter HCO PL was cancelled by BPL 10 Oct 75 X.]

Sequence

SERVICE DEPARTMENT, that department which services things by repairing, adjusting, cleaning and maintaining them. This could be servicing of company machinery, property, vehicles, etc., or servicing of the products that consumers have bought from the company.

SERVICE INSIGNIA, rectangular colored bars about 3 cm. long and 1 cm. wide. They consist of a brass backing plate with pins or clip to attach to the uniform, a stiff cardboard backing and a colored tight woven cloth which is attached to the backing and slipped in front of the brass plate which holds it in place. **Service insignia** are worn in a tasteful arrangement (if more than one) on the left breast pocket of the officer's dress uniform starting about one inch down from the top. By a glance officers can be recognized as to their **service** and training and can be more properly afforded the status and etiquette due them. (FO 2327R)

SERVICE MARK, design, symbol or trademark that a company employs and usually has officially registered, to readily identify itself and its products, services or special activities to the public.

SERVICE ORG, 1. a **service org** handles bodies. A management org handles messages as the principal flow particle. (HCO PL 27 Jul 72, *Form of the Org and Schedules*) **2.** a governing org (one which manages) must be attached to a **service org** (one that **serves** it and the public). (FO 2713)

SERVICE RECORD, 1. Department One is to keep its own administrative **service record** for each staff member. These are uniform throughout Scn and are already kept in the Sea Org. They are solely for the purpose of personnel assignment data. The **service record** is kept on light-cardboard weight paper in a two-holed loose-leaf book. The **service records** of staff who have left may be kept in the back of the book or sent on to the org they have gone to. Once the background section has been filled out (which is done in Dept One when the person first comes on staff) there are only 7 things which need to be logged in the **service record**: (1) change of post (include data and whether demoted or promoted). (2) Enemy or Treason declare (date, by whom and reason). (3) completion of training level or staff status (date). (4) attainment of pc grade (date). (5) signed a contract (date, length, org). (6) departure from org staff (date, where to). (7) assignment of power condition (date). (BPL 8 Dec 68R) **2.** the following are the only items which are **recorded** in one's **service record**. *All* of the following must be included in the **service record**. A **service record** is permanent throughout one's Sea Org career and carries on from year to year. (1) checksheet or level completions (including Mission School grade). (2) pc and OT grade completions. (3) change of post (transfer, demotion or promotion). (4) achievement (or demotion) of rank. (5) assignment of Enemy or Treason condition. (6) assignment of Power condition, special award, or LRH commendation. (7) award of upstat status. (8) every mission performed and result of mission. (9) leave of absence. The above are logged daily in the **service record** book from the following sources: (1) Orders of the Day. (2) FOs and FCOs. (3) Mission Orders. (FO 1652)

SERVICES, work or activities that are useful, accommodating or of an advisory nature and needed by the public, such as repair work, travel arrangements or educational counseling.

SERVICES CHIEF, responsible for heat, hot, cold and salt water throughout the ship. If anything goes wrong on this he fixes it himself. (FO 835)

SERVICES LIAISON OFFICER, (LRH Personal PRO Bureau) this post is responsible for providing **services** which help create the desired image. Any kind of **service** may be required. These could be anything from providing a chauffeur or escort to writing a special story. (COLRHED 11)

SERVICES MATE, all fuel and water, heated tanks and evaporator are a section in the Purser's Division 3, Stewards Dept 9. The section is in the charge of a **Services Mate**. (FO 274) See also SERVICES CHIEF.

SERVICE STAR, a red bar with a silver **star** on it. Each time an FSO officer or crew member delivers a high quality service to an FCCI, this **service star** will be awarded to the person who delivers or does the service. (ED 563 Flag)

SERVO-MECHANISM, a **mechanism** which **serves, services** or aids something. (OS-10, 5611C15)

SESSION, a period in which an auditor and preclear are in a quiet place where they will not be disturbed. The auditor gives the preclear certain and exact commands which the preclear can follow. (*FOT*, p. 88)

SESSION CANCELLATION, **session cancellation** as a system is introduced as the only training rebuttal by an instructor in the auditing section for a gross auditing error. When a student auditor commits a gross auditing error in the auditing section, the student's **sessions** as an auditor are **cancelled**; the student is put back through the theory and practical sections on those points involved in the gross auditing error and is then permitted to audit again. All former passes in theory or practical on the subject of the gross auditing error are **cancelled** and the items must be passed again as though they had never been taken before. (HCO PL 24 May 62)

SESSION RESTORED LIST, when the student has redone the theory and practical work required, the Practical Supervisor posts the student on a **session restored list** which advises both the Auditing Supervisor and the student that the student can continue in the auditing section in addition to other work. (HCO PL 24 May 62)

SETTLEMENT, a legal action which one side or other does not wish to fight is **settled.** A **settlement** is an agreement to end the action upon terms, without fighting it out in court. (BPL 27 Jan 70 I)

SEVEN DIVISION ORGANIZATION, the **Seven Division Organization** has more than 75 staff members, has the large 1965 org board complete. It gives services as permitted by Worldwide but not less than Grade IV training, Grade V Power Processing, a full PE and is also served by a Foundation (usually on a Six Dept System). It may have one or more Executive Divisions depending on whether it is Worldwide, continental, zonal, subzonal, or local. (HCO PL 21 Oct 66 II)

SEVEN DIVISION SHIP ORGANIZATION, when we say **Seven Division Ship Organization** we will mean the divisional assignments. All members of the ship's company belong to this too. But it may be that two or more ships (a flotilla) are combined in the organization as they keep company most times at least in port and deputies can serve in their stead when they are separated. So when we say **Seven Division Ships Organization** we really mean flotilla organization. We could say "squadron" but that's military and is also used now for air. "Flotilla" merely means two or more ships. We have two vessels, several launches and pulling boats and may have more, so the word is fitting. Thus we have our Watch Quarter and Station Bill for each ship and we have our flotilla organization chart which is our seven division system. (*Ship's Org Bk.*)

SEVERANCE, the act of termination of employment or separating oneself or being separated from a business firm.

SEVERANCE PAY, extra wages given to employees that are leaving a business or who have been discharged. Also called separation pay.

SEVERITY, an increase in that discipline believed necessary by the people to guarantee their security. (*PAB* 96)

SHARE, a written legal certificate showing the specific extent of ownership the shareholder has in a corporation.

SHAREHOLDER, one who owns shares or stock in a company and who holds written certificates legally documenting the extent of his ownership.

SHARE-THE-WORK PLAN, a plan that maintains a larger number of employees on a payroll than is actually essential to accomplishing a particular company's current production contracts. Employees work shorter hours to distribute the work throughout the entire force.

SHELL COMPANY, see COMPANY, SHELL.

SHIELD, the **shield** or escutcheon forms the basis for the rest of the coat of arms, and

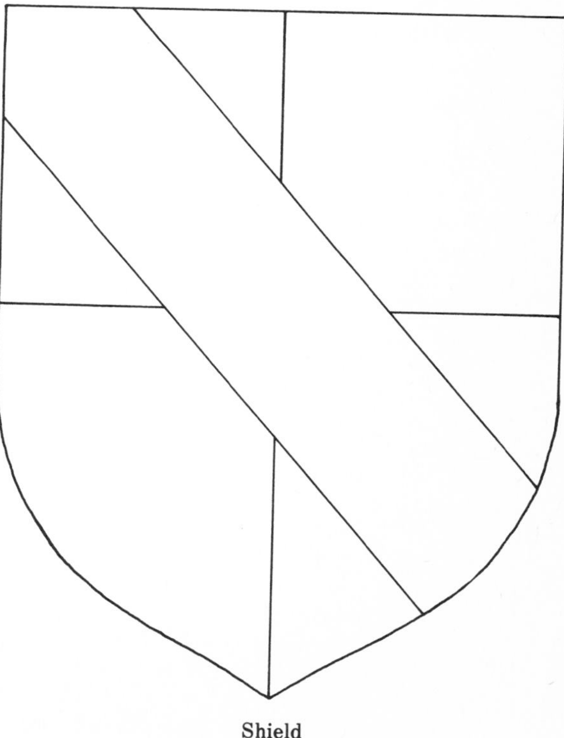

Shield

traditionally contains a major part of the symbology in the choice of design and color used in it. It could be divided in several ways. The Sea Org coat of arms is divided in four divisions as symbolic of the fact that we are operating to handle the fourth dynamic engram. Emblems are then placed on the background in relation to each other. These emblems, according to what was used, gave information to those initiates who had been familiarized with the **shield**. Frequently, they give information on the heritage of the group as well as its goals and aspirations. (FO 3350)

SHIFT, 1. the period of time during which employees work each day such as the 9:00 a.m. to 5:00 p.m. shift or the night shift. 2. all the employees who work during a particular period of time or shift.

SHIP, a definition of a **ship** is something that keeps water out and floats. (OODs 19 Oct 69)

Ship

SHIP ADMIN HAT, under the **ship admin hat** we get the functions within the administrative system of the ship with its papers, records, files and other materials of an admin nature with their upkeep and orderly handling. **Ship admin** and ship handling **hats** are the duties of a ship member relating to his specific hat or post in the ship. (FSO 2)

SHIP COMMITTEE, the First Mate, Chief Engineer, and Chief Steward form a **Ship Committee**. The First Mate is Chairman. They meet daily to attest or give deficiencies or recommend future actions regarding (1) the condition of the hull, boats and ship's gear, deck stores and deck force. (2) the condition of the engines, service to ship, repairs, fuel, water, lub oil and spares and engineer force. (3) the condition of quarters and messes, galleys, supplies, food stores, facilities and steward force. (FO 2037)

SHIP CONSTRUCTION, the real definition of proper **ship construction** (other planet) is "a design capable of withstanding any sea or weather on the planet in complete safety and on schedule." (FO 40)

SHIP DEPT HEADS FINANCIAL PLANNING COMMITTEE, the First Mate for Deck, the Chief Engineer, the Chief Steward and the Hostess. This **committee** apportions the sums granted by Purser accommodation based on the week before last and the needs of their departments. (FO 410)

SHIP FP, refers to the **ship's** company, divisions and their operation and necessities, extended into ports. (FSO 74)

SHIP HANDLING HAT, under the **ship handling hat** we get drill duties, watch functions, how to **handle** or keep up the **ship** as a **ship**. Ship admin and **ship handling hats** are the duties of a ship member relating to his specific hat or post in the ship. (FSO 2)

SHIPKEEPING DIVISION, 1. division 4 Flagship Org Org Board. It contains Dept 10 Ship's Operations Department, Dept 11 Shipkeeping Department, Dept 11A Construction and Repairs Department, and Dept 12 Boats Transport Department. (FSO 742) **2.** probably the div name itself (Deck Division) forced though it is by tradition, should be the **Shipkeeping Division.** And what do you know, that's what it has been called in many times and languages. (FO 2703)

SHIPKEEPING SECTION, the heart of the Shipkeeping Department. It is responsible for arresting the decline that wind, sea and forces exert on the ship. It is also responsible for the shipshape appearance of the ship and her vessels, as well as their ability to float and be utilized at sea, in port or at anchor. (FO 3161)

SHIPMATE, crew members of the same ship refer to each other as **shipmate**. (FO 87)

SHIP ORG, contains the ship divisions and ship's activities. (OODs 26 Oct 70) See FLAG, see FLAGSHIP ORG.

SHIPPING, the action of sending or transporting prepared goods to customers.

SHIPPING AGENTS, **agents** whose major purpose is to service ships calling in their ports, involving the provision of food and fuel, and booking cargo to fill the available capacity of those ships of "their" lines which are calling in the port where they are situated. A single **agent** or a chain of **agents** are contracted to one or more **shipping** lines to provide this service to all of their ships calling at that port. (FO 2738)

SHIPPING CLERK, purpose: to swiftly and competently furnish the public with the materials of Scn. (HCO London, 9 Jan 58)

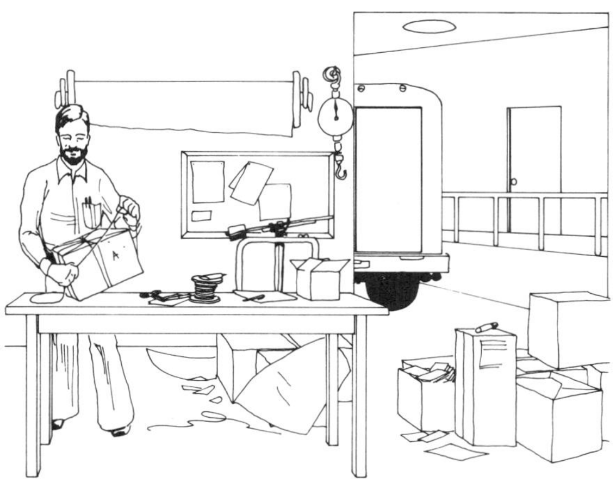

Shipping Clerk

SHIP'S BOAT DRILL, the readying and launching of the **ship's boats** and bringing them aboard again. It includes checking the gear of the boat, setting it up, taking it down, launching the boat, securing it to the ship and bringing it back aboard, checking its gear, fuel, securing it, etc., ready for passage. (*Ship's Org Bk.*)

SHIP'S COMPANY, when one says **ship's company** we mean all officers including the Captain, all petty officers, all engineers, cooks, crew, the lot, everyone aboard including the **ship's** cat (who so long as he is aboard debars salvage total claims even if he is the only one left). That's everyone. (BO 34, 16 Jun 67)

SHIP'S COMPLEMENT, the total number officers and men required to man a ship. (FO 2674)

SHIP'S DIVISION CONFERENCE, **conference** wherein the head of any **division** calls all the persons in that **division** to a **conference**. (FO 2387)

SHIPSHAPE, **1.** it should be right. It should not risk coming to pieces and that's what's known as **shipshape**. (6910C15 SO) **2.** ships are usually very good in terms of care. That's where the word **shipshape** came into the language. (OODs 15 Jul 74)

SHIP'S OFFICER CONFERENCE, there is **Ship's Officer Conference** in Div 4 Dept 11. This is called to advise the **officers** of programs. It is also used to plan targets and missions. It's actions require Captain's approval before they go into effect. Usually they are held by the Captain but can be held by the Chief Officer or the Supercargo. (FO 1021)

SHIP'S OFFICER SCHOOL, as the Sea Org rapidly runs out of **ship's officers** in its expansion, a **Ship's Officer School** is founded on Flag. Its curriculum will be extended to other ships when formed so that time served on any ship with the study program followed will count. In the future, a Captain's School for those who have finished **Ship's Officer School**. (FO 2742)

SHIP'S OPEN HOUSE, the first Sunday after the ship's arrival in any port a **Ship's Open House** may be held during the afternoon. This is a drill which begins with permission of the port authorities, ads in local newspapers, posters placed in ship windows. It ends with streams of public with VGIs leaving the ship and receiving literature and a small souvenir. (FO 2910)

SHIP'S ORG BOOK, our own technology (Scientology) is so far in advance of general engineering, electronic and other current technology that we are always a bit amazed that man's engines and electronic gear don't run without careful nursing, and his ship's don't sail well at all without extreme care. It behooves one to be pretty expert at sea to arrive at all. So in these various articles in this org book, you will find data to fill in the gaps. It is not invented data, it is for the most part painfully traditional. The reason this book exists at all is because man's texts, and his memory, are woefully inadequate. I have given here, amongst various orders, some of the vital technology needed in seafaring which is omitted for the most part from the manuals available. (FO 40)

SHIP'S REPRESENTATIVE, **1.** holds and keeps safe all passports and vaccination cards and is responsible for their validity, and stamping into and out of the country. He is also responsible for shore business relations, and is therefore the person you seek out if you run into any business trouble ashore—such as gross overcharging, customs trouble, etc. (FO 2688)

2. keeps the "in port" legal establishment in. (FO 3121)

SHOOTING BOARD LAYOUT, the exact, final arrangement and execution of each page, its type, art and pictures and page arrangement in signatures, ready for the process camera (or in letter press, the press). (FO 3574)

Shooting Board Layout

SHOP, 1. a small retail store. 2. a specialty department in a large store or factory such as a beauty shop or machine shop. —*v.* to go to stores to buy merchandise.

SHOP, CLOSED, a shop that hires only workers who are union members.

SHOP CONTROL, measures taken directly on the scene to control production. A person touring the factory or shop and merely ensuring employees are doing their jobs would be a form of shop control.

SHOP, JOB, a company specializing in job production which is the manufacturing of products to the customer's design; a company dealing in made-to-order, one of a kind or limited production products to a customer's specifications.

SHOP, OPEN, a shop, factory, business, etc., that employs union as well as non-union workers.

SHOP TALK, talk or conversation relating to one's business or profession.

SHORE BASE, includes FOLO's, Sea Org orgs and any other SO activity **ashore**. (FO 3458)

SHORE FLAP, a non-optimum PR situation (how it was caused being unimportant) or a lowering of PR with a terminal or terminals or a group **ashore**. (FO 3057)

SHORT COVERING, buying stock for the purpose of returning stock previously borrowed to make delivery on a short sale.

SHORT CYCLES, *v.* spending days hatting only one staff member and letting whole departments go is an example of what is meant by "getting stuck in." This is why one "**short cycles**" an area. By that is meant doing a **short** start-change-stop that completes that action. (HCO PL 16 Mar 72 II)

SHORT INTERVAL SCHEDULING, the practice of assigning work to employees in small lots to be completed in specified short periods of time with the idea of improving and better controlling production by close inspection.

SHORT POSITION, the amount of stock an investor has sold short and has not covered as of a particular date.

SHORT SALE, the action of selling stock which one does not own yet but which one anticipates buying at a lower price before delivery is due. Thus if one can sell $500.00 worth of stock and buy the same amount for $400.00 before delivery is due he has made $100.00.

SHOTGUNNING, (promo) the amateur blows *all* his material and themes in one issue. This is known as **shotgunning**. (BPL 18 Sept 72R)

SHUT-DOWN, 1. the temporary closing of a factory which may be brought about by repairs or remodelling, installation of equipment, lack of work contracts or a labor strike. 2. the operational failure or intentional closing down of machinery or equipment.

SHYSTER, *Slang.* a business or professional person who is without scruples in the way he conducts himself and deals with others.

SIAC, Securities Industry Automation Corporation, an organization jointly established by the

New York and American Stock Exchanges to make available automation, data processing, clearing and communications facilities.

SICK LIST, the Medical Officer is to keep a **sick list** of all persons who report to him as **sick**. Any person who is put on the **sick list** remains on the **sick list** until he is well. During the time the person is on the **sick list**, he remains directly under the Medical Officer's care. (FO 1632)

SICK PC'S BOARD, Tech Services is to have a **sick pc's board**. This is posted by Tech Services on information from the MO who ensures its accuracy and that it is up-to-date. On this **board** is entered the person's name, date of first report and sessions given, either Dn or Review, with the date of each. Sessions are given at least daily upon C/S instructions. (FO 2332)

SIDE-CHECKER, a person of comparable post who reviews projects and orders written for publication and execution by an aide or divisional secretary. Instead of a CO or product officer correcting and rejecting (too much impact) the task is done by a **side-checker** before submission. (FO 2964)

SIGHT TRANSLATOR, one equally good in 2 languages who can hear one language and speak the translation into the other language without hesitation. (They are employed in the UN.) Translating Dn, Scn study materials into foreign languages is inexpensively and effectively done by using "**sight**" (instantaneous) **translation** of bulletins, policy letters and tapes onto tapes. (HCOB 20 Nov 71 II)

SIGN-UP AND RESIGN-UP REGISTRATION, this type of **registration** primarily involves **signing up** and closing the transaction of CF persons coming into the org and keeping track of who is in the org taking major services and **resigning up** individuals and receiving the money for further actions. (HCO PL 28 Nov 71R I)

SIGN-UP PACKET, packet so arranged that all the selectee has to do is **sign** his name in order to enroll or be scheduled for processing. (HCO PL 12 Jan 66)

SIGN-UP REGISTRAR, Body Registrar. (HCO PL 21 Sept 65 VI)

SIGN-UPS, total number of people **signed up** as a result of registrar interviews. (HCO PL 11 Dec 62, *OIC Reports to HCO WW*)

SILVER SPRINGS BUSINESS SERVICE, the former name of the "Distribution Center, Inc." which sold books and Scn materials and did mailing for Scn organizations, located at **Silver Springs**, Maryland in the days before the Founding Church of Scientology was established in Washington, D.C. (1955). (LRH Def. Notes)

SIMILAR, two or more facts or things that have something in common with one another. (HCO PL 26 Apr 70R)

Similar

SIMILARITIES ARE SIMILAR, a plus-point. Not identical or different. (HCO PL 3 Oct 74)

SIMULATED TRAINING, see TRAINING, SIMULATED.

SIMULTANEOUS HIRING, in linear recruiting a firm **hires** a girl to write their letters. After 60 days they find she doesn't do her job. So they get rid of her and **hire** another. And in 90 days find she can't do her job. So they fire her and **hire** another. That's 150 days of no-correspondence. It's enough to ruin any firm. It's costly. In **simultaneous hiring** a firm **hires** 3 girls feeling they need 1. At the end of 150 days they have 1 girl. But they had 150 days of correspondence. And a profit. (HCO PL 29 Aug 70 III)

SIN, sin is composed, according to Scn, of lies and hidden actions and is therefore untruth. (HCO PL 29 Oct 62)

SINGLE ENTRY, a type of bookkeeping system in which a business keeps only a single account showing amounts due and amounts owed.

SINGLE-HANDING, **1.** means to handle things by yourself. You can **single-hand** when you are all alone or you can **single-hand** in a large group that is supposed to be working or helping. When only one man, senior or junior, is doing all the controlling and work of an activity he is said to be **single-handing**. The term derives from the sea (like so many English words). **Single** means "one only" and "**hand**" means a sailor. "**Hand***ing*" is the verb of "**single-hand**." (HCO PL 1 Oct 70) **2.** by **single-handing** one means do it himself, being the one responsible for actually handling things. (HCO PL 28 Jul 71) **3.** by **single-hand** means to run it all by himself performing all vital functions. The term comes from a sailor who runs a boat or vessel by himself alone with no other crew. (FO 2111)

Single Handing (Def. 1)

SINGLE HATTED, he wears one **hat**. He has no other duties or functions. (FO 2475)

SINGLE PROPRIETORSHIP, ownership of a business by one person who receives all the profits and who is responsible for all debts of the business.

SINGLE STATUS, designation of staff status to all employees of a company whether blue collar or white collar.

SINGLE VIEWPOINT SYSTEM, operations in any business or air force or navy heretofore has always been a **single viewpoint system.** There was the general manager in Poughkeepsie. There were the branch offices all over the U.S. There on the wall is a map. Pins for each branch office, a big pin is the main office in Poughkeepsie. Ribbons leading from each branch office to the main office. And there's the general manager looking out at these branch offices. He hears something on the phone or the janitor about Torgueville. He sees this situation as it looks from Poughkeepsie. And he issues his snap orders. And the company struggles along somehow. Any general sitting on a hill looking at the strung out battle used that same moth-eaten system. Every major company, every air force uses it. Been traditional since there were main offices or headquarters. And orders can get pretty unreal. (FBDL 192R)

SINKING FUND, a company fund contributed to regularly and set apart for the retirement of a debt, the redemption of stock or to make up depreciation losses on a property investment.

SIPC, Securities Investor Protection Corporation, a non-profit membership organization created by an Act of Congress to provide funds or alleviate losses of investors should a SIPC member firm undergo bankruptcy and liquidation.

SIR, **1.** the term, **Sir**, is normally used when addressing an officer, as in, "Excuse me, **Sir**." "Thank you, **Sir**." Or "**Sir**, May I have your permission . . ." It is also used when answering an officer's question or responding to an order. "Yes, **Sir**." "No, **Sir**." "Aye aye, **Sir**." Or "The report will be on your desk by 1800 hours, **Sir**." (FO 38-1) **2.** only officers are addressed as "**Sir**." And they are so addressed whether male or female. (FO 87)

SIT-DOWN STRIKE, see STRIKE, SIT-DOWN.

SITUATION, **1.** the most major departure from the ideal scene. (HCO PL 11 Aug 74) **2.** departure from or improvement of the ideal scene expressed in policy. (HCO PL 29 Feb 72 II) **3.** a not expected state of affairs. It is either very good or it is very bad. (HCO PL 17 Feb 72) **4.** something that applies to survival. If you evaluate the word **situation** against survival you've got it. A good **situation** is a high level of survival, a bad **situation** is a threatened survival, and a no **situation** is something that won't affect survival. (7201C02 SO) **5.** problem. (HCO PL 16 Mar 71

IV) **6.** a major departure from the ideal scene. This means a wide and significant or dangerous or potentially damaging circumstance or state of affairs which means that the ideal scene has been departed from and doesn't fully exist in that area. (HCO PL 30 Jun 70) **7.** the broad general scene on which a body of current data exists. (HCO PL 15 May 70) *Abbr.* Sit.

Situation (Def. 3)

SITUATION ANALYSIS, in confronting a broad situation to be handled we have of course the problem of finding out what's wrong before we can correct it. This is done by data analysis followed by **situation analysis**. We do this by grading all data for out-points. We now have a long list of out-points. This is data analysis. We sort the out-points we now have into the principal areas of the scene. The majority will appear in one area. This is **situation analysis**. We now know what area to handle. (HCO PL 15 May 70)

SITUATION HANDLING MISSION ORDERS, **mission orders** that send missionaires out to **handle** things have always been referred to simply as "mission orders." A full title is given this type of **situation handling mission orders**. Two or more missionaires are always sent on **situations handling MOs** as such missions fail when attempted by just one missionaire. Such **MOs** cover a **situation**, a calculated why and the **handling** of the **situation** terminatedly. Each target must be terminatable within the time span of the mission. In essence this is a program that can be concluded. (FO 2936)

SIX DEPARTMENT ORGANIZATION, the **Six Department Organization** has up to 75 staff members, an org board similar to the Seven Division Org Board but in **departments**. It delivers up to Grade IV training and Grade V Power Processing as permitted, operates a PE and may or may not have a Foundation attached. If so its Foundation is City Office size. (HCO PL 21 Oct 66 II)

SIX DEPARTMENT SYSTEM, Central Organizations are now running on the **Six Department system**. Each of these **six departments** has its own Director, Deputy Director and function. The **six** are represented either by a Director of a **Department** or a Deputy Director in the Advisory Committee. These **departments** are: Dept of PrR, PE Foundation, Academy, the HGC, Dept of Materiel, and Dept of Accounts. (HCO PL 26 Aug 59)

SIXTEEN-G (16-G), TWENTY-FOUR-G (24-G), [these numbers are mentioned in PAB 36 and refer to specific issue numbers of *Scientology, The Journal of Scientology,* published by the Hubbard Association of Scientologists. Issue **16-G** published around April 1953 has an article by L. Ron Hubbard entitled "This is Scientology" which discusses SOP-8 and other topics. Issue **24-G** published 31 Jan 54 discusses SOP-8C]

SKILL, the level of dexterity and technical and artistic proficiency one can execute in a particular job, craft or profession.

SKILLED WORKER, see WORKER, SKILLED.

SKIMMING, putting a product on the market at a high price to skim off the high profits of immediate sales and then gradually reducing the price and obtaining increasing sales due to lower price which results in greater market penetration.

SKIPPER, the Captain is referred to on his own ship as the **skipper** or "The Captain" and is addressed as "Captain" and not **skipper**. (FO 87)

SKIP TRACING, a debtor who moves without leaving a forwarding address, either intentionally to avoid paying, or unintentionally through neglect, is called a **skip**. The process of **tracing** down such persons is called **skip-tracing**. It is a standard business practice. (SO ED 155 INT)

SLAVE SOCIETIES, **societies** composed only of routes and unthinking terminals. (HCO PL 22 Oct 62)

SLICE SCALE, income tax method in which there are divisions or "slices" of income for which different tax percentages are charged at increasing rates such as the first slice being taxed at 10%, the second slice at 15%, and so forth.

SLIDING SCALE, a scale of prices, wages, taxes, etc., that can be proportionately raised or lowered to meet certain conditions. In a sliding wage scale where salaries range from $5,000.00 to $10,000.00 annually the rising cost of living may cause the scale to slide up to a $6,000.00 to $12,000.00 range with all figures on the scale in between being raised in equal proportions.

SLIP SYSTEM, accounting system, also known as file posting, in which the record consists of original invoices kept in an unpaid file until payment is received.

SLOW COMM LINES, (form of dev-t) despatches held up on **lines** cause other despatches to be originated about the same subject, causing dev-t to both sender and recipient. The power of an organization is directly proportional to its speed of particle flow (letters, despatches, telexes, bodies). (BPL 30 Jan 69)

SLOWDOWN, term referring to production output intentionally diminished by workers in an effort to bring pressure to bear on management to meet a demand or to express dissatisfaction with present work arrangements.

SLOWDOWN STRIKE, see SLOWDOWN.

SLOW EVAL ASSESSMENT, see LENGTH OF TIME TO EVALUATE.

SLUG, every story written for newspaper use must have a name. This is called a **slug**. Generally it is one word, usually the key word that describes the story. Thus, a student riot could be **slugged** "Riot," a heat wave "Heat," an airplane accident "Plane." Where there are several stories, all related, two words are generally needed: "Plane-Accident," "Car Accident." (BPL 10 Jan 73R)

SLUMP, a steep decline in business activity, prices or interest rates.

SLUMP REPORT, **report** of lessened income or traffic. (HCO PL 13 Mar 65 II)

SMALL ORGANIZATION, **1.** 2 to 5 staff not counting Estos. (HCO PL 7 Mar 72) **2.** a large organization is composed of groups. A **small organization** is composed of individuals. (SH Spec 77, 6608C23)

SNIPES, *Slang.* engineers. (FSO 359RA)

Snipes

SO 1 QUARTERLY SUMMARY, thousands of letters are received on the **SO 1** line every month. Of these, the vast majority are pure theta good news (95%). However, a tabulation of complaints, queries and requests (the remaining 5%) shows a very interesting picture of where situations lie that need to be handled. This data is extremely valuable to management for isolating situations well before they blow up and flap. These **summaries** will be issued henceforth on a monthly and **quarterly** basis. (FBDL 439)

SOCIAL COORDINATION BUREAU, frequently PR gets into a situation whereby it creates an entity or group or organization to bring about some change of value within the community or to handle some outstanding social injustice. In many cases the reform or action is brought to a successful conclusion; however, in many instances, the action to be effected is one which will require more time and effort. In expending such time and effort, PR to keep ahead finds itself in the situation of having and running a group or organization within its own bureau; therefore, PR must, when this occurs, realize that it is now in the situation of managing and administrating an established entity which is likely to continue and, therefore, should fully turn over the terminals, lines and organization of same to the **Social Coordination Bureau** which is the Guardian **Bureau** which properly acts as a management unit for such entities, activities, groups and organizations. (BPL 22 Jul 75)

SOCIAL COUNSELLING, under **social counselling** come those areas of tech which enable a person to be a better member of society. (BO 1 MEX, 10 Nov 74)

SOCIAL COUNSELLOR COURSE, (this is the public and sales name) a **course** designed for persons who don't want to be a professional. The graduates are called Social Counsellors. The **course** covers the basic materials of Dn and Scn and teaches the student how to audit. It gives the student the vital knowledge of man, his mind, and his relationship to the world around him necessary to an understanding of and success in life and to handle the behavior and cases of those around them. (SO ED 135 INT)

SOCIAL COUNSELLORS, 1. non-pro auditor **course** graduates. (BPL 15 Jan 73R) **2.** a **social counsellor** is a tech trained person who is posted in Dept 17 under the Public Reg to provide advice to public persons. His purpose is: to help Ron guide public persons toward happiness through properly recommended applications and use of Scn and Dn to become more at cause. The main difference between **Social Counsellor** and Chaplain activities is that the **Social Counsellor** is handling raw public directly, and is a sales person, whereas the Chaplain handles Scientologists and Dianeticists on a higher professional level, as the Chaplain for the entire org field and staff. (HCO PL 2 Dec 72 II) [The above HCO PL was cancelled by BPL 10 Oct 75 X.]

SOCIALISM, an ideology which calls for state or government ownership and control of all the means of production and distribution. There is no private enterprise.

SOCIAL PERSONALITY, the twelve primary characteristics of the **social personality** are as follows: (1) the **social personality** is specific in relating circumstances. "Joe Jones said . . ." "The Star Newspaper reported . . ." And give sources of data where important or possible. (2) the **social personality** is eager to relay good news and reluctant to relay bad. (3) a **social personality** passes communication without much alteration and if deleting anything tends to delete injurious matters. (4) treatment, reform and psychotherapy particularly of a mild nature work very well on the **social personality**. (5) the friends and associates of a **social personality** tend to be well, happy and of good morale. (6) the **social personality** tends to select correct targets for correction. He fixes the tyre that is flat rather than attack the windscreen. In the mechanical arts he can therefore repair things and make them work. (7) cycles of action begun are ordinarily completed by the **social personality**, if possible. (8) the **social personality** is ashamed of his misdeeds and reluctant to confess them. He takes responsibility for his errors. (9) the **social personality** supports constructive groups and tends to protest or resist destructive groups. (10) destructive actions are protested by the **social personality**. He assists constructive or helpful actions. (11) the **social personality** helps others and actively resists acts which harm others. (12) property is property of someone to the **social personality** and its theft or misuse is prevented or frowned upon. (HCOB 27 Sept 66)

SOCIAL SECURITY, measures undertaken by the U.S. Government to provide financial assistance to unemployed, disabled or retired persons. It is financed by taxing employers and employees with a Social Security Tax.

SOCIAL SECURITY ACT, Federal Legislation begun in 1935 by which the U.S. Government provides pensions and other financial assistance to persons who are unemployed, disabled or of retirement age. It is financed by taxing actively engaged employers and employees.

SOFT NEWS, hard news is an event that has occurred, usually told in past tense. **Soft news** is anything from speculative story to a feature. (BPL 10 Jan 73R)

SOFT SALES PROMOTION, see PROMOTION, SOFT SALES.

SOFT SELL, dictating reducing prices or advising "don't be so direct, **soften** up the ads, the public objects . . ." (HCO PL 23 Sept 64)

S.O.L.A.S., the internationally accepted standard for ships is that laid down by the International Committee for Safety of Life at Sea which is usually abbreviated to "The S.O.L.A.S. Convention." The publication of the rules of this convention contains detailed requirements for cargo, passenger and tanker ships. (FO 2732R)

SOLDIERING, see GOLDBRICKING.

SOLICIT, to appeal to a person to buy or contribute to something.

SOLICITED REPLY, a reply or answer that comes in direct response to a solicitation for such a reply.

SOLO AUDITOR, a standard tech **auditor** who is applying standard tech to himself as a pc or pre-OT. (FO 1588)

Solo Auditor

SOLO AUDITOR COURSE, the **Solo Auditor Course** is designed to teach the data and skills of **solo auditing** essential for attaining Grade VI Release, Clear and the OT levels, and to produce a standard **Solo Auditor** who can competently apply the data and auditing skills and can **solo audit**. (BPL 12 Dec 71RC)

SOLO C/S COURSE, it makes a crackerjack **solo C/S**, and covers confidential upper level data nowhere else available. It is taught in AOs only. Its prerequisites are Class VIII, Grade OT III. The checksheet is prerequisite to **solo C/Sing.** (SO ED 377 INT)

SOLO REVIEW CONSULTANT, see ADVANCED COURSE REVIEW CONSULTANT.

SOLVENCY, 1. **solvency** consists only of income greater than outgo and making enough money. (LRH ED 74 INT) 2. meaning outgo less than income and huge reserves building against need. (FO 1664) 3. cash *over* bills ratio. (FO 2389) 4. survival of an org depends on **solvency**. **Solvency** depends on making more than it spends. (LRH ED 78 INT)

SOM-3L, auditing by list—the early research designation. Means **SOM** for "**somatics**" plus **3** for "**third**" and **L** for "prepared **list**." (LRH Def. Notes)

SOUND ORGANIZATION, the only organization that is a **sound organization** is one whose every activity can be tabulated by statistics. (HCO PL 13 Mar 65, *Divisions 1, 2, 3 The Structure of Organization What is Policy?*)

SOURCE, Scientologists recognize and revere the spiritual leadership of L. Ron Hubbard as the Founder, and as the **Source** of the religious philosophy of Scientology. (BPL 24 Sept 73RA XIII)

SOURCE MISSION, 26 top Flag personnel were fired from Flag in 12 separate **mission** teams to take to the orgs of the planet a closer connection with L. Ron Hubbard, their Founder. They began giving the orgs data and details about Ron and his life and actions; about his incredible abilities in the many fields which he has mastered. As this important communication line raised reality on the true brilliance of Ron, planetary affinity for and understanding of **Source** rocketed, and in tremendous surge the Scn orgs of the planet moved more closely on-**Source**! (FBDL 404-1)

SOURCES OF TROUBLE, types of persons who have caused us considerable **trouble**. These persons can be grouped under **sources of trouble**. (HCO PL 7 May 69)

SOUTH, in Scn means worse off. "Amongst the auks and penguins" is a colloquialism that goes along with that. (5904C15) See SOUTH OF THE AUKS in *DSTD*.

SOUTH AFRICA SPECIAL RUNDOWN, this technology has been specially developed for the people of **Africa** by LRH when he was in Africa in 1960-61. The **rundown** is given as follows: (1) any PTS handling per HCOB 10 August 73, *PTS Handling*. (2) ruds at the beginning of each session. (3) havingness is run before each help process. (4) help processing. (5) havingness is again run after each help process. (6) confront is run after help and havingness and then repeats cycle as in steps (3), (4), (5), (6). (BTB 21 Oct 73R)

SPACE BUYING, the buying of advertising space in newspapers or magazines.

SPAN OF CONTROL, the extent of authority of an executive or supervisor as noted by the number of persons or juniors he has under him who report directly to his office.

SPAN SOMEBODY'S ATTENTION, you're actually trying to unfixate his **attention** and free it up. (ESTO 5, 7203C03 SO I)

SPARKS, the radioman is generally addressed as "**Sparks.**" (FO 87)

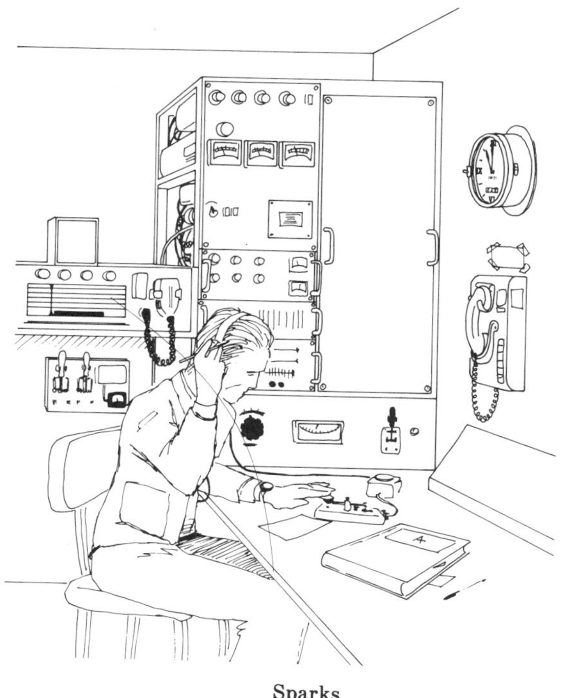

Sparks

SPECIAL, a feature story sent to several newspapers at the same time. (BPL 10 Jan 73R)

SPECIAL AGENT, person or company authorized to act for another in a single matter or a series of matters, whose role is not as broad as a general agent's who has more extensive powers to act on behalf of a principal.

SPECIAL DRUG RUNDOWN, the **special drug rundown** was issued to handle persons currently on **drugs**. Such persons have to be weaned off **drugs** in order to be audited. This is done by having the person do TRs further assisted by vitamins. Those with heavy **drug** histories or recently or currently on **drugs** do not usually run well on engrams until objective processes have been run (CCHs, 8-C, etc.). Thus a person *currently* on **drugs** would require a full TR course as the first step and then objective processing before the standard drug RD per C/S Series 48R could be started. Such a person is therefore enrolled onto the HQS (which includes TRs and co-auditing on objective processes) as their first step. But note that this is for persons currently on **drugs**, not for anyone who has ever taken **drugs**. (BTB 25 Oct 71R II)

SPECIAL EVENT, a carefully prepared promotion offered or sponsored by a business firm such as an open house, fashion show or entertainment program.

SPECIAL EVENTS, under the heading of **special events** comes congresses, ACCs and things such as a film show, for example. (HCO PL 30 Jan 59)

SPECIAL FUND HCO WW, all Assoc Secs should get the immediate opinion of staff and if favorable, should then at once begin the regular, routine weekly transfer of 8% of the proportional income to "**Special Fund HCO WW**, National Provincial Bank Ltd., 6 Fitzroy Sq., London, W.1" and delete the sum from the Building Fund. It should be clearly understood that this money and any funds that can be salvaged from the HCO 10% (which is spent locally in most Central Organizations) will help pay the expenses of the new promotional writing and research center, located at Saint Hill, East Grinstead, Sussex. (HCO PL 28 May 59, *Promotional Writing Fund*)

SPECIAL INFORMATION PACKAGES, **packages** made up and mailed by the Letter Registrar to inform various sections of her mailing list on the next service they might be interested in, having already done something. There could be a book **info packet** for a person who has just bought a book, a test **info packet** for a person just tested, a PE **info packet** for the person who has just done a PE, etc., etc. In each case it offers the *next* service. (HCO PL 4 Feb 61)

SPECIALIST, in the main, Sea Org crews, are **specialist** crews. By **specialist**, one means fully trained on one post per watch or drill. (FO 2469)

SPECIALIST, 1. one who has devoted himself to a special area of study, research and practice related to his occupation or profession. 2. in the investment field, a person who is a member of a stock exchange and who acts as a broker's broker, executing on behalf of a broker, limited orders (clients' orders to buy or sell a specific amount of a stock at a certain price or at a better price if possible). A specialist also buys or sells for his own account when there is a disparity between supply and demand, in the stocks in which he is registered as a specialist.

SPECIALIST BLOCK PURCHASE, the purchase of a large block of stock outside the regular exchange market by a specialist for his own account and subject to special circumstances.

SPECIALIST BLOCK SALE, sale by a specialist from his own account of a large block of stock outside the regular market, allowed only under special circumstances and subject to exact requirements.

SPECIALIST CHIEF'S DEPARTMENT, (Ship Org Board) Department 12, Division 4, the Production Division. He should be all ready to go into action on any of his functions, have the right equipment, keep records, plan ahead and generally I would think be your answer man for problems, like how can I raise that anchor we lost last night? or what can the crew do this afternoon on liberty on this godforsaken rock we've landed on? (*Ship's Org Bk.*)

SPECIALIST RECRUITER, responsible for the **recruitment of specialist** type personnel, that is if auditors are needed for Flag, or engineers or any other specialized field he will concentrate on finding personnel for that area and of that particular skill needed. (FO 3475)

SPECIALIST TRAINED CREW, you have a **specialist trained crew** before you have a generally trained crew. Each person is trained to do his exact duty or his exact part of the drill. (6910C16 SO)

SPECIALIST TRAINING, having a general knowledge of the area but being **trained** fully to total competence on the exact actions and handling of one specific post. (FSO 413)

SPECIAL MAILINGS, issued from time to time to announce **special** events or offers to the public or pro auditors. At the discretion of the Assn Sec. (HCO PL 4 Feb 61)

SPECIAL OFFERING, an offering in which a large block of stock is put up for sale at a fixed price, ordinarily established on the last transaction price, with the seller paying the broker's commission.

SPECIAL PROGRAMS OFFICER, (Flag) the Staff **Special Programs Officer**, under CS-6 to directly coordinate the **Special Programs** Unit via the Public Officer, plus **Special** Projects Worldwide. (FO 1715)

SPECIAL PROGRAMS SECTION, 1. (FB) the **Special Programs Section** is mainly concerned with putting Scn into areas where there is little or no Scn. (CBO 189-1) **2.** pilot project section. Everytime you get one of these wild ideas you put it into **special programs** and it will wind up not wrecking you. All new types of expansions are piloted, they are piloted. Otherwise, you'll go broke, because you're testing consumption. (FEBC 8, 7101C24 SO I)

SPECIAL PROGRAMS UNIT, the Special Projects Unit is transferred under the Public Officer, Div VI (Flag). This unit becomes the **Special Programs Unit**, which will compile data and complete targets as assigned. (FO 1715)

SPECIAL PROJECT, 1. there's a lot of trial and error in developing a program. That's why any new program should be only a "**special project**" for a while, off the org main lines, really, under **special** management. If a "**special project**" starts to show up well in finance (and only in finance), then one should include it "in" with its new staff as an org standard project. (HCO PL 24 Dec 66) **2.** to find and establish a program, one conceives of a solution and sets it up independent of org lines with its own staff and finance as a **special project**. When a **special project** is seen to be effective or, especially, profitable, it is then put into the org lines as worked out in the "**special project**," bringing its own staff with it. (HCO PL 24 Dec 66 II)

SPECIAL PROJECTS UNIT, see SPECIAL PROGRAMS UNIT.

SPECIAL SERVICES UNIT, to accommodate the expansion of AOLA solo and Advanced Courses delivery to the public of the Western Hemisphere and to provide this public with nearby hotel **service**, a **special services unit** is established in the annex adjoining the Fifield Manor. The **Special Services Unit** will be initially manned with: (a) Solo Courses I/C who is I/C of the annex and operates as its Product Officer. Solo Courses I/C holds from above the hats of Solo D of P and Public MAA unit further personnel are provided to fill these posts. (b) Solo C/S. (c) Solo Review Auditor (also audits OT IV and OT VII RDs). (d) Solo and Ad Courses Supervisor. (e) Folder and Pre-OT Admin/Page. (f) Qual/Cramming/Certs and Awards/Success/Examiner. (g) Reception/Registrar/Cashier. (BO 43 U.S., 31 Oct 73)

SPECIAL STATS UNIT, there is obviously a **special stats** post somewhere in the Ops Bureau. The guy is drawing up **stats** for some thing or other. There's somebody always either catching up backlogs of **stats** or drawing up a **special** graph for some evaluation. E.g. "What were the **stats** of Keokuk Org in 1952?" You can call it a **special stats unit.** (7205C18 SO)

SPECIALTY GOODS, goods for which there is a limited market or which are designed for special purposes, demands or needs. A store selling only goods made of Oriental jade or ivory is dealing in specialty goods.

SPECIAL ZONE PLAN, 1. we are masters of IQ and ability. We have know-how. Any of us could select out a **zone** of life in which we are interested and then, entering it, bring order and victory to it. The third and fourth dynamics subdivide. Any third breaks down into many activities and professions, a neighborhood, a business concern, a military group, a city government, etc., etc., etc. The fourth dynamic breaks down just now mainly to races and nations. Now just suppose a Scientologist were to consider himself a professional only for the purposes of treating and repairing or even starting again these third and fourth **zones**? See this: a housewife, already successful employing Scn in her home, trained to professional level, takes over a woman's club as secretary or some key position. She straightens up the club affairs by applying comm practice and making peace and then, incidental to the club's main function, pushes Scn into a **zone** of **special** interest in the club—children, straightening up marriages, whatever comes to hand and even taking fees for it—meanwhile of course going on being a successful and contributing wife. So this is a challenge on the third and fourth. Almost all Scientologists are in a position to begin to help on such a program. (HCOB 23 Jun 60) [See the reference HCOB for a full description of the **Special Zone Plan.**] **2.** To Director of **Zoning**, London: please arrange the following: make a card file out on everybody that comes in; and in particular write down name, address, and the **zone** they're interested in, and the possibility or not that they will do volunteer auditing evenings for some special personality. Keep this list of **special zone** workers and keep it out of CF as such. You can info addressograph that so and so is a **special zone** worker, but for now keep your own card file and build it up. (HCO PL 20 Jul 60)

SPECIFIC ORDER PRODUCTION, see PRODUCTION, JOB.

SPECIFIC QUESTION, the difference between a general and a **specific question** is a matter of general or **specific** terminal. If the question has a general terminal such as "anyone," "men," "people" it is harder to clear than a question with a **specific** terminal such as "your father," "Miss Smith" etc., etc. (HCO PL 9 Oct 61)

SPECIFIC UNEMPLOYMENT, see UNEMPLOYMENT, SPECIFIC.

SPECTATOR, 1. let us look at the definition of OT—cause over thought Life Form Matter Energy Space and Time. As one falls away from that one becomes a **spectator**, then one becomes effect. In the society today **spectatorism** is very common. Magazine writers, reporters write weird pieces that look at how odd things are. The writer doesn't understand them at all. He just watches them. **Spectatorism** is not so low as total effect. The total effect—no cause—person has mainly a case. He doesn't even look. (HCO PL 14 Jan 69) **2. spectatorism** is very great in our modern society. Because some people cannot conceive of causing anything they just watch it. They don't do anything. They are not participants. They are **spectators**. You see this in magazines; a hee, hee, hee article about how odd this is or that is. No understanding of it. It's just odd and one watches it in a detached sort of way. Below this is somebody who doesn't even notice. Such a person has to come up scale just to be a **spectator**. What we need are more participants, more team mates. (OODs 14 Jan 69)

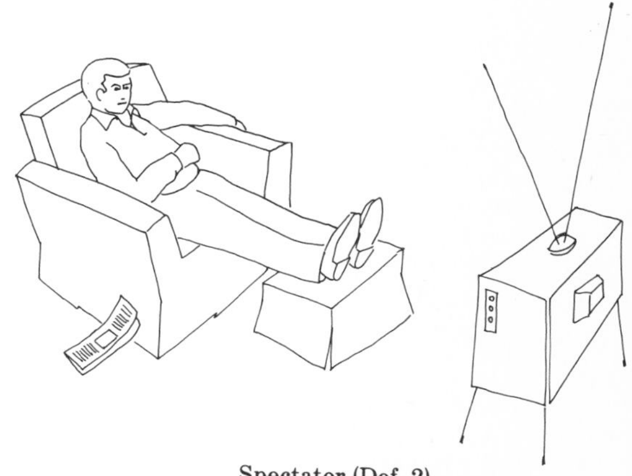

Spectator (Def. 2)

SPECULATIVE MAILING LIST, a **list** of names and addresses of people who *might* be interested. (BPL 17 May 69R I)

SPECULATIVE PRODUCTION, see PRODUCTION, SPECULATIVE.

SPECULATIVE PURCHASING, see PURCHASING, SPECULATIVE.

SPECULATORS, there are "**speculators**" who seek to buy something (like land) cheaply and sell it dear. Or sell it dear, depress the market and buy it back cheaply. In either case they make a profit. It is less well understood that "**speculators**" also operate on the subject of money itself. By manipulating the value of one currency against another they seek to obtain a profit. (HCO PL 3 Dec 71)

SPECULATORS, persons who take large investment risks with the intent of greatly increasing their capital rather than being concerned with dividend income.

SPEED-UP, a state in which workers must increase their production efforts without added reimbursement.

SPLIT-RUN COPY TESTING, advertising practice of running the same advertisement in different media and then comparing results and relative drawing power of the advertisement in those media.

SPLIT SHIFT, a schedule of work hours that is not continuous but is split up into two or more intervals.

SPOILS SYSTEM, a system whereby promotions or appointments are made on the basis of the winning candidate or political party rewarding loyal supporters and friends by appointing them to public office.

SPOT CHECK, in checking out technical materials on students or staff **spot check** the words and materials, do not try to cover it all. This is done the same way a final examination is given in schools: only a part of the material is covered by examination, assuming that if the student has this right the student knows all of it. (HCO PL 4 Oct 64)

SPOT MARKET, see MARKET, SPOT.

SPREAD, 1. in investments, the disparity between the price an investment concern pays for stocks and the selling price for which they are offered to the public. 2. type of advertisement space or an advertisement that runs across two or more pages of a magazine or newspaper.

SP TARGET, some guys are so bad off they set targets like "move the mountain" and give one and all a big failure. Since there's no way to do it and probably no reason to either, that's an **SP target**. So what must be done means just that. What is vital and necessary. Not what is simply a good idea. (HCO PL 14 Jan 69)

SQUARE DEAL, *Slang.* phrase for a business deal that is fair and honest.

SQUIRREL, *n.* what makes a **squirrel**? It is the person on the other side of the **squirrel**. It is a person invalidating him invalidating his goals, invalidating his interest, and kicking the props out from underneath him by covert hostility or overt hostility, but in any way, kicking him apart. He's interested, he's working, but part of another universe. But practically on the same time continuum is an invalidative mechanism about this man not Scn. It isn't kicking Scn around, it's kicking around somebody's stable data and it's creating continuous confusions for him. So he splits off not knowing quite where he stands. Is he in this universe called Scn or is he or she in this universe called husband or wife or something? So here we have this invalidative person who is against it on the other side or our guy and we sometimes can't reach this other person. (5511C03) *—v.* **1.** means go off line. (HCO PL 3 Dec 68) **2.** (going off into weird practices or altering Scn) only comes about from non-comprehension. Usually the non-comprehension is not of Scn but some earlier contact with an off-beat humanoid practice which in its turn was not understood. When people can't get results from what they think is standard practice, they can be counted upon to **squirrel** to some degree. (HCO PL 7 Feb 65) *—adj.* by **squirrel** is meant off-beat technology. (HCO PL 6 Feb 66)

SQUIRREL ADMIN, the departure or alteration of standard admin. The use of the word "**squirrel**" is long standing because **squirrels** in their little cages go 'round and 'round and get nowhere and they are also, a bad pun, "nutty," meaning a bit crazy. The main source of **squirrel admin** is simply ignorance of policy procedure or the neglect of reading and applying it as simply as that. (HCO PL 4 Jun 71)

SQUIRREL ADMINISTRATORS, when a **squirrel** is given a circular wheel he will run it 'round and 'round and 'round. He gets nowhere. When persons in an organization do not know organizing or their org board or hats, they go 'round and 'round and 'round and get nowhere. There is no valuable production. There is no money. When you have an organization that has no valuable production you know that the people there go 'round and 'round and 'round and get nowhere. They are **squirrel administrators**. (HCO PL 25 Jan 71)

SQUIRREL COOKERY, there is also **squirrel cookery**. This normally arises from not having the proper ingredients to hand (supply failure) and not having anyone to wash and slice and peel raw materials so they can be cooked. A standard meal comes from planned menu, correct supply, correct preparation of raw materials and following the exact recipe. (OODs 2 Feb 71)

STABLE DATUM, **1.** we have in Scn a certain doctrine about confusion. It is called the doctrine of the **stable datum**. If you saw a great many pieces of paper whirling about a room they would look confused until you picked out one piece of paper to be the piece of paper by which everything else was in motion. In other words, a confusing motion can be understood by conceiving one thing to be motionless. Until one selects one datum, one factor, one particular in a confusion of particles, the confusion continues. The one thing selected and used becomes the **stable datum** for the remainder. (*POW*, p. 23) **2.** any body of knowledge more particularly and exactly, is built from one datum. That is its **stable datum**. Invalidate it and the entire body of knowledge falls apart. A **stable datum** does not have to be the correct one. It is simply the one that keeps things from being in a confusion and on which others are aligned. (*POW*, p. 24) **3.** a **datum** which keeps things from being in a confusion and around which other data align. (*NSOL*, p. 66)

Stable Datum (Def. 2)

STABLE TERMINAL, **1.** a **stable terminal** pushes the actions that belong to his area on the org board and handles or suppresses the confusions of that area or aligns them with the correct flows. (HCO PL 4 Nov 69) **2.** a post is a position from which a terminal operates in an org, where one knows that somebody is *at*. The one holding it is the **stable terminal**. (FO 2200) **3.** a **stable terminal** is also a terminal to whom programs, projects and orders may be given with the sure knowledge that they will be complied with and executed. (FO 2201)

STABILIZATION INTENSIVE, in cases where a handle or disconnect does not resolve the PTS situation, or in auditing a preclear to maintain **stability** of release levels, the action follows search and discovery technology. This will be called a **stabilization intensive** and may be ordered by ethics in severe cases or may be sold by the registrar. (HCO PL 30 Dec 65)

STAFF, **1.** the personal office of the Flag Officer, consisting of Aides, Yeoman, Stewards, Coxswain, Signalmen, etc. (FO 1) **2.** the beings assigned to the Commodore as personal **staff** are referred to as **Staff** Personnel, or **Staff.** (FO 467) **3. Staff** Aides. (7205C18 SO) **4.** the **Staff** Captain is the leading officer of Commodore's **Staff**. The word **Staff** in this sense means Commodore's **Staff**, not org staffs. **Staff** consists of Commodore's Aides and personnel but not AVU. (FO 3188) **5.** means any **staff** member, crew member or executive or officer who is not directly paying for his or her auditing but is obtaining it as **staff.** (HCO PL 21 Oct 73R)

STAFF, the personnel of an organization who carry out the work planned and directed by those in charge.

STAFF AGENCY, an outside consultancy firm offering management assistance to other companies or clients.

STAFF AIDES, **Staff Aides'** responsibilities are covered in various LRH CBOs. They are responsible for their opposite number divisions in all orgs. They do divisional evals. FB Bureaux Aides run their Bureaux and ensure all their Bureaux functions are carried out which add up to managed orgs. (CBO 435R)

STAFF ASSISTANT, one who is a consultant or specialist and who assists and expedites a manager's or senior's work.

STAFF AUDITING I/C, crew D of P. (BFO 122-5)

STAFF AUDITOR, full time staff members in the Day Org or full time in the Evening and/or Weekend Foundation. No auditor may be "on call" or "part-time" in a Central Org or City Office HGC. An auditor is either a **staff auditor,** working full time on units, or he may not audit for the organization. (HCO PL 21 Aug 64)

STAFF AUDITOR ADDITIONAL TIME, on Monday, time until processing begins and on every day after processing ends, is the definition of **staff auditor additional time**. (SEC ED 11, 16 Dec 58)

STAFF BANKING OFFICER, **1.** the **Staff Banking Officer** (Commodore's **Staff** under CS-3, located at Flag) receives from the FBO Int a monthly costing breakdown and income summary, made up from the combined reports of FBOs and subject to current orders from **SBO** as to content and format. The **SBO** acts as senior to the FBO Int to originate programs related to banking and reserves, and gets finance policy and FOs complied with and to control the AO banking and finance lines in coordination with CS-3. The **SBO** is responsible that the FBO Int performs his duties. (HCO PL 16 Jun 69) [The above HCO PL was cancelled by BPL 10 Oct 75 VII.] **2.** the **Staff Banking Officer** (Commodore's **Staff**) located at Flag, is responsible for receiving from AOs, and AO-SHs, that portion of their income which is paid by them to Flag. All reports formerly forwarded to the **SBO**, will now be received by the FBO Int. The additional duty of the **Staff Banking Officer** with regard to AOs and AO-SHs finance will be to receive monthly figures from the FBO Int and prepare from these a monthly costing analysis and income summary. (HCO PL 20 Apr 69) [The above HCO PL was cancelled by BPL 10 Oct 75 VII.] **3.** Flag Banking Officer post is abolished. In its stead, the post of **Staff Banking Officer** is created which performs the functions previously assigned to that of the Flag Banking Officer. These duties should include the following: (1) receives weekly all income to the Sea Org from all ships of the Flotilla. (2) receives weekly for checking the weekly expenditures of all ships of the Flotilla along with all purchase orders and receipts and a separate breakdown of all unpaid bills. (3) disburses to all vessels of the Flotilla their weekly allowance *less* any average in expenditures the ship may have. (4) receives weekly an attestation from the Purser of each vessel that the bills owing is true and correct and that no further amounts are owing. The **Staff Banking Officer** must report immediately to CS-3 any outnesses found in the accounts of a vessel so that severe ethics action can be immediately undertaken before the outnesses are allowed to multiply. (FO 1102) *Abbr.* SBO.

STAFF CAPTAIN, **1.** the leading officer of Commodore's **Staff**. The word **staff** in this sense means Commodore's **Staff**, not org staffs. **Staff** consists of Commodore's Aides and **Staff** personnel but not AVU. It is the basic duty of the **Staff Captain** to keep **staff**, orgs and personnel working and productive. The post is basically a product officer post. Any situation related to Dn and Scn which I would normally look for and handle is the business of the **Staff Captain**. (CBO 194) **2.** she is handling the Aides area and is the immediate senior of all FB activities. (OODs 4 Feb 76)

STAFF CASE CATEGORY 1, those who have had VGIs, F/Ns at examiner and OK as to case gain. (HCO PL 20 Jul 70)

STAFF CASE CATEGORY 2, those who haven't had VGI, F/Ns at exam recently. (HCO PL 20 Jul 70)

STAFF CASE CATEGORY 3, medically ill in need of thorough assists and medical attention. (HCO PL 20 Jul 70)

STAFF CASE CATEGORY 4, consistent no change, no case gain in their auditing history. (HCO PL 20 Jul 70)

STAFF CASES CASE SUPERVISOR, (**Staff Cases C/S**) **C/S** who **C/Ses** for audited **staff**. (HCO PL 25 Sept 74)

STAFF CIC, what was formerly called "Internal CIC" is now known as **Staff CIC**. It is under the charge of the **Staff CIC** Officer, formerly known as Internal CIC Officer. **Staff CIC** is placed in the Personal Office of LRH under LRH Pers Comm. The purpose of **Staff CIC** is: to help LRH ensure that stats are always consulted, that accurate date coincidences of successful and unsuccessful actions are established for external and internal stats, and that standard stat management occurs especially assignment of conditions and following of their formulas. (FO 3449R)

STAFF CIC OFFICER, what was formerly called Internal CIC is now known as **Staff CIC**. It is under the charge of the **Staff CIC Officer**, formerly known as Internal CIC Officer. (FO 3449R)

STAFF COLLEGE, the **Staff College** is under the Dept of Training of the Flag Admin Org. It is responsible for all crew training. AB, Mission School, SS I, SS II, Checkout Mini Course, SO Member Hat, Staff Hats and full post hats are all in the **Staff College** in the Dept of Training. (FSO 388)

STAFF COLLEGE DEAN, **Staff College Dean** is responsible for the speed and quality of the courses run in the **Staff College**. (FO 2824)

STAFF CONSTRUCTION MANAGER, will handle, arrange and care for the remodelling and construction of any **staff** areas needed. (FO 882)

STAFF FLOAT, includes such expenses as **staff** allowances, **staff** food, **staff** services, **staff** laundry, **staff** uniforms, any of these items of this particular kind. (FO 1400)

STAFF FUNCTION, consultation, advisory and service functions within a company which do not include further involvement in the actual work performances connected to these matters.

STAFF HAT, 1. a folder containing all his duties as a **staff** member, the org itself and its lines and purposes. (HCO PL 13 Sept 70) **2. hat** in which material concerning one's duties as a **staff** member were kept, plus new Executive Directives and Policy Letters. (LRH ED 83 INT)

STAFF HATTING COLLEGE, AB, Mission School, SS I, SS II are courses done in the **hatting college**. Both long full hat checksheets and courses are done in the **Staff Hatting College**. If we called this simply **Staff College** it would serve better. (OODs 21 Mar 71)

STAFF INFORMATION OFFICER, in the Qual Library Section is the **Staff Information Officer**. This post supplies **staff** with exact data they require, on request. This person must develop a great familiarity with library materials so that he can refer **staff** to exact PLs or HCOBs to answer their questions. In a small org, Qual Librarian and **Staff Information Officer** are usually held by the same person. But in a large, busy org, these become full-time, single hatted posts. (BPL 21 Jan 73R) [this post was originally called the Org Information Officer before the above issue was revised to a BPL.]

STAFF LEVEL EVALUATION, see PRIMARY EVALUATION.

STAFF LIBRARIAN, (Correction Division) purpose of the **Staff Librarian** is to help LRH provide a full library of all Scn and Dn knowledge for org **staff** reference and use. To safeguard this knowledge and ensure it never gets lost or removed. (BPL 7 Dec 71R I)

STAFF LRH PERSONAL FINANCE OFFICER, the post of **Staff LRH Personal Finance Officer** established on the Flagship. The duties required of this post are the collecting, accounting and depositing of **LRH** monies and **LRH** monies owed from outer orgs for the following: (a) all **LRH personal finances**, (b) repayment of loans to orgs, (c) **LRH** goodwill repayment monies, collected 10%s to help repay loans LRH made to orgs, (d) all monies loaned by **LRH** to whatever source. Records, notes and collection are included. (e) the relationship of **LRH Personal Finance** to Sea Org, services orgs, etc., and tax matters of **LRH** and MSH. (f) MSH finance matters as related to the above. (g) bank accounts and records for the above. (h) other financial matters as related to **LRH** and MSH as required. (FO 1137)

STAFF MAN, an outside consultant or someone who may be one of a company's own employees who performs research and gives corollary advice but who is not empowered to issue instructions or orders except to his regular subordinates who assist him with his work.

STAFF MANAGEMENT, see MANAGEMENT, STAFF.

STAFF MEETING, staff meetings should convene on the first Tuesday evening of any month at the organization headquarters. The chairman of the **staff meeting** has always been and shall continue to be the Executive Director or his deputy, the Organization Secretary, or the Administrative Assistant to the Organization Secretary. The business of the **staff meeting** shall be: to gather agreement and permit staff origination on matters relating to personnel and duties. To suggest promotional, maintenance and organizational changes to the executives of the organization. (SEC ED 69, 2 Feb 59)

STAFF MEMBER, 1. any full or part-time **member** of the **staff** of any official org and has the title, duties and privileges assigned by policy. (HCO PL 21 Oct 66 II) **2.** any and all persons employed in an org whether an executive or general **staff member**. (HCO PL 13 Mar 66) **3.** one who holds a permanent staff certificate. (HASI PL 22 Sept 58) **4.** now a **staff member** is somebody who handles pcs. Pcs do not easily handle the public. (ESTO 3, 7203C02 SO I)

STAFF MEMBER HATS, 1. a **staff member hat** contains all Secretarial to the Executive Directors which pertain to and affect all **members** of the **staff**. (SEC ED 78, 2 Feb 59) **2.** (a) duties of a **staff member** inside front cover, (b) all bulletins covering **staff members** arranged chronologically, (c) anything that would pertain to *all staff members*. (SEC ED 58, 27 Jan 59) **3.** there is a general **staff hat**. This **hat** contains (a) the overall purpose of the org, its aims, goals and products, (b) the privileges or rewards of a **staff member** such as the auditing, training on post, general training availability, pay, vacations or leave, etc., (c) the penalties involved in non-production or abuse of post privileges or misuse of the post contracts, (d) the public relations responsibilities of a **staff member**, (e) the interpersonal relations amongst **staff members** including courtesy, cleanliness, attitudes to seniors and juniors, office etiquette, etc., (f) the mest of posts generally, its papers, despatches, files, equipment, (g) the comm and transport of the org. (HCO PL 22 Sept 70) **4.** OEC Volume 0. (BPL 3 Feb 72R)

STAFF MEMBER REPORT, a despatch form addressed simply to the Ethics Section. It is dated. It has under the address and in the center of the page the person or portion of the org's name. It then states what kind of a **report** it is. The original goes to ethics by drawing an arrow pointing to "ethics" and the carbon goes to the person or portion of the org being **reported** on by channels. (HCO PL 1 May 65)

STAFF OFFICER, see STAFF MAN.

STAFF OPERATIONS OFFICER, all missions come under the direct supervision of **Staff Operations Officer. Operations** come under the supervision of **Staff Operations Officer**. (FO 644)

STAFF PROGRAM NO. 1, **1.** major target: to consolidate existing organizational structures and so facilitate expansion, better pay, improved facilities and higher organization and **staff** security. Vital targets: (1) all **staffs** fully trained on the OEC. To reduce confusion and overwork by a few by fully educating **staffs** into the functions of every part of an org and their posts in particular. (2) improve service delivery by increasing the technical skill and confidence of every **staff** member and in particular the skill of technically assigned personnel. To vigorously apply the technology of study itself as contained in the HDG pack to this broad educational effort. To expand smoothly and unfalteringly. (LRH ED 27 INT) **2.** the training of org **staffs** on the HDG and OEC. (LRH ED 32 INT)

STAFF R3 CLEARING PROGRAM, a **staff clearing program.** The activity of the **staff** who are auditing each other is as follows: a problems intensive, if necessary; then running on current goals procedures. A Saint Hiller is appointed as **Staff** Supervisor of **staff** cases. He calls them in during the day, checks over cases and progress—can even audit them. Does anything and everything to **clear** them. (HCO PL 17 Jun 63)

STAFF RELATIONSHIP, designating the relationship of staff officers to line officers in a company. A staff relationship is one of providing advisory or consultancy services or performing the organizing functions of accounting, training, transportation, research, etc., as opposed to the actual production line which is handled by line officers.

STAFF REVIEW OFFICER, a staff member is only sent to **Staff Review Officer** for remedies if his flunks have been continual and he is not making progress at all. The Staff Training Officer may not hold any additional post than **Staff Review Officer** and if so checkouts must consistently be at one period of the day and **review** another. If traffic is too heavy not even this additional hat may be worn. If **Staff Review Officer** is singly held the holder may also audit **staff**, and do assists. (HCO PL 20 Jul 66)

STAFF SECTION OFFICER, (Qual Div) purpose: to help Ron make real **staff** members. The person on the post of **Staff Section Officer** has total authority over who will be processed and what they will be processed on, who will be trained and what they will be trained on, and has authority over all persons who are engaged on those duties or at the time they are engaged on those duties. The authority of the **Staff Section Officer** over who will get processed and what he will get processed on is absolute. The authority of the **Staff Section Officer** on who will be trained and what they will be trained on is absolute. In a very small org the **Staff Section Officer** will also hold from above the Staff Training Officer and the Staff D of P. But where this becomes onerous, the other two posts should be filled. The state of in-tech delivery of interns becomes the concern of the **Staff Section Officer** since most of the processing of **staff** is done by interns. (HCO PL 22 May 76) *Abbr.* SSO.

STAFF STAFF AUDITOR, **audits staff** members when called upon to do so by the Org Sec. Handles **auditing** emergency assists on **staff.** (HCO PL 18 Dec 64, *Saint Hill Org Board)*

STAFF STATUS, **1.** a number following the person's name on the org board that shows the state of administrative training of the individual as done in the Staff Training Section. **Status** numbers go from 0 for temporary, 1 for provisional, 2 for qualified general **staff** member on up for the various executive grades. If no number, appears after a name, the person is holding the post without checkout for it. A low ranking **staff** member can have a high **status** number as it is qualified for, not "appointed to." This prevents qualified persons from being by-passed in promotion. (HCO PL 13 Mar 66) **2.** a number giving the value and promotion eligibility of a **staff** member in this organization. The numbers run from zero to ten. They designate the type post to which a person may be promoted or the **status** of the person. (HCO PL 4 Jan 66 V) **3. staff status** is a result like certificate, depending on study, service and examination. It is assigned by number derived from study, service and examination. (HCO PL 18 Nov 65) *Abbr.* SS.

STAFF STATUS, the conditions of employment in a concern such as length of usual work week, overtime arrangements, wage payment method (weekly or hourly basis), holidays, etc., as well as fringe benefits including health insurance, pension plan and bonuses which today generally are extended to all personnel—executives, white collar employees and blue collar workers.

STAFF STATUS 0 (ZERO), 1. a **staff status** is a number giving the value and promotion eligibility of a **staff** member in this organization. The **status** numbers most important to a new **staff** member are **0 (zero)**, 1 and 2. 0=temporary, 1=provisional, 2=permanent. A **staff** member who is newly hired is designated **0 (zero) status** after his or her name on the organization board. (HCO PL 4 Jan 66 V) **2. Staff Status 0** as an exact rundown is added as the initial orientation and hatting step for all new org **staff** members. It precedes **Staff Status** I and II, and is commenced immediately upon joining **staff**. The product is: an oriented, in-ethics person, hatted as a beginning Scientologist and **staff** member, who knows he is a Scn **staff** member and is able to participate. **Staff Status 0** is done per the **Staff Status 0** checksheet. (BPL 27 Apr 73R) *Abbr.* SS 0.

STAFF STATUS I, a **staff** member given a provisional rating may recourse to ethics and have an ethics hearing if dismissed. He may be transferred to other divisions without a hearing if his division is over-manned. A provisional is designated as "**1**" on the org board after his or her name. To obtain permanent **status** a provisional must obtain his or her basic **staff** certificate. This has a checksheet for which the HCO Exec Sec is responsible for compiling. (HCO PL 4 Jan 66 V) *Abbr.* SS I.

STAFF STATUS II, a permanent **staff** member may not be demoted, transferred or dismissed without a full Committee of Evidence being held. Permanent **status** is designated on the org board by the numeral "**2**" after a person's name. (HCO PL 4 Jan 66 V) *Abbr.* SS II.

STAFF STATUS III, 1. Staff Status III is attained by doing the OEC Volume checksheet of one's own division and then passing an examination with a high grade on that OEC Volume. (HCO PL 17 May 74R) **2.** each **staff** member studies and completes OEC Volume 0 and then goes immediately to the OEC Volume checksheet for his own division. When the checksheet for his own division has been completed, the staff member will do a written examination, of which the pass mark is 92%. Additionally, the Examiner will inspect the **staff** member's division for evidence of application of the materials on the checksheet and this examination passed with a high grade on the volume of one's own division will result in the award of **Staff Status III** and is credited on the remaining OEC Course. (HCO PL 19 Nov 73) [The above HCO PL was cancelled by HCO PL 17 May 74R, *The New Staff Status III, OEC and FEBC*] *Abbr.* SS III.

STAFF STATUS IV, Staff Status IV will be awarded when all policy in a **staff** member's portion of the org has been completed, i.e. HCO and the Dissem Division, or Treasury, Tech, Qual and Distribution. (HCO PL 19 Nov 73) [The above HCO PL was cancelled by HCO PL 17 May 74R, *The New Staff Status III, OEC and FEBC*] *Abbr.* SS IV.

STAFF STATUS V, Staff Status V will be awarded when all policy in the remaining portion of the org has been completed. (HCO PL 19 Nov 73) [The above HCO PL was cancelled by HCO PL 17 May 74R *The New Staff Status III, OEC and FEBC.*] *Abbr.* SS V.

STAFF STATUS VI, Staff Status VI will be awarded when the **staff** member has completed all policy on the Executive Division. **Staff** members in the Exec Div will not be awarded **Staff Status VI** until all OEC Volumes (Vols 0-7) have been completed. (HCO PL 19 Nov 73) [The above HCO PL was cancelled by HCO PL 17 May 74R, *The New Staff Status III, OEC and FEBC.*] *Abbr.* SS VI.

STAFF STATUS VII, Staff Status VII will be awarded when the **staff** member has completed the Senior OEC, which comprises additional policies from the existing OEC Vols to the end of 1973, as studied by division. (HCO PL 19 Nov 73) [The above HCO PL was cancelled by HCO PL 17 May 74R *The New Staff Status III, OEC and FEBC.*] *Abbr.* SS VII.

STAFF STATUS VIII, Staff Status VIII will be awarded when the **staff** member has completed the

FEBC. The FEBC is composed of the Management Series plus FEBC tapes. (HCO PL 19 Nov 73) [The above HCO PL was cancelled by HCO PL 17 May 74R, *The New Staff Status III, OEC and FEBC.*] *Abbr.* SS VIII.

STAFF TRAINING OFFICER, **1.** the head of the **Staff Training** Section, Dept 14, Div 5. The purpose of the **STO** is: to help LRH train individual **staff** members and applicants from his own and other orgs in ethics, tech and admin, keeping track of them, guiding them through org courses, giving them checkouts, expediting their **training**, seeing that their personnel records in Dept 1 of their org are factual as to training and assisting them in every way to get training and to be trained rapidly, with the end product that orgs have no untrained **staff** members. (HCO PL 21 Sept 69) **2.** responsible for getting the individual through his program on **training** making full utilization of scheduled and other study time. To do this he uses time machine orders, 2WC, ethics, cramming and any other device needed to get the **staff** member through his course and his program. He is not a supervisor basically. He ensures the **staff** programs are being completed. (FO 2824) *Abbr.* STO.

STAFF TRAINING PROGRAM NO. 2, **program** to improve admin and stats of org, by reviving **staff** status 0, I, II, III on administratively untrained or new **staff.** (LRH ED 121 INT)

STAGE FRIGHT, it is the unwillingness to confront a mass. It is a can't have on the mass. That is all. To prove that, it is only necessary to change one's mind or run a process on having that mass, to cure **stage fright.** It cures just like that. Remedy of havingness. (5611C01)

STAGGER SYSTEM, we will institute the **stagger system** of training up our executives by relieving one or two at a time and returning them to Flag for their training. (FBDL 25)

STALE DATE, the term **stale date** (used previously by banks on cheques) means any despatch or answer that is older than one should reasonably expect when one receives it or any answer that is older in **date** from origin to answer or answer to receipt than one should reasonably expect. (HCO PL 17 Jul 66)

STALEDATED ORDERS AND DISPATCHES, a type of dev-t where **staledating** delays action, often important, and creates anxiety and emergencies. New (developed) traffic results in an attempt to get an answer or compliance. (HCO PL 27 Jan 69)

STALEDATE REPORT, any staff member receiving an internal org despatch that has been enroute more than three days (dated the fourth day earlier than date of receipt) must **report** the matter to the Director of Communications who must thereupon request the Director of Inspection and Reports to investigate and report to Dir Comm and order any resulting ethics action. Anyone sending a **stale date** complaint to the Dir Comm must first answer or handle any despatch he is holding and send it to the Dir Comm with its answer. Dir Comm copies or xeroxes the original and the answer promptly and sends the original onto its next recipient and uses the copy only for investigation. (HCO PL 17 Jul 66)

STANDARD, standard means a definite level or degree of quality that is proper and adequate for a specific purpose. (*Webster's Third New International Dictionary Unabridged.* Standard 3 b, p. 2223).

STANDARD ADMINISTRATION, **1.** to approach the subject of **standard administration** realistically, one first must recognize that a right way to do things can exist. There are an infinity of ways *not* to start a car. There is only one way to start a car. So it is with any **standard** procedure. There is a tech of **admin.** This would be the right ways to do **administrative** actions or organize something. **Standard admin** means the usual "on policy" procedure applied. (HCO PL 4 Jun 71) **2.** solutions that work and are therefore routinely used to handle the situation to which they apply are then called **standard admin.** (HCO PL 25 Jan 71) **3.** we had to have the fundamental or basic laws of organization in order to develop the full structure of organization. **Administration** becomes **standard** when we have the most important points or laws or actions and when we always use these and use them in just the same way. (HCO PL 9 Nov 68) **4.** in **standard admin,** we are acquiring (a) a knowledge of basics, (b) the basics that exist in and around a specific organization, (c) the ability to handle those basics with such speed and certainty that it seems instinct. And when we have this, the organization, will go, go, go with an ease and lack of effort that is astonishing. (HCO PL 9 Nov 68) **5.** there is a thing called **standard admin.** It comes from the policy letters. When we produced the wild, soaring tech stats with the Sea Org Class VIII auditor program it was by putting in the exact processes and grades. By going super **standard** we got 100% case gain. It is the same with policy. If you get an org in with super **standard** policy—promotion, form and admin—the stats soar. (HCO PL 25 Oct 68)

STANDARD ADMINISTRATIVE ACTION, when experienced persons, working from basic theory, have evolved a technique for handling a situation which routinely now handles that situation, we have now a **standard administrative action.** (HCO PL 25 Jan 71)

STANDARD BRIEFING, just as there is standard tech so is there also **standard briefing.** The following lists the actions of a **standard briefing.**

(1) **Briefing** Officer ensures all mission information and orders are available and in writing.

(2) **Briefing** Officer gives each missionaire a copy of the orders to study. Missionaires study the orders.

(3a) **Briefing** Officer has each missionaire do individual clay demos of each target and point of the orders.

(3b) **Briefing** Officer gives starrate checkouts on each demo per HCOB 11 October 67, *Clay Table Training.*

(3c) **Briefing** Officer attests on the missionaire's copy of the Mission Orders that each demo is OK per HCOB 11 October 67, *Clay Table Training.*

(4) **Briefing** Officer checks out starrate each missionaire on his written mission orders (tape recorded per FO 1530)

(5) **Briefing** Officer two way comms and drills the mission on the orders until the missionaires know them and know how to handle any foreseeable stop to the mission (tape recorded per FO 1530)

(6) **Briefing** Officer sends each missionaire to Qual to attest he knows, understands, and will comply with his written mission orders. This is **standard briefing**! (FO 2466)

STANDARD COSTS, see COSTS, STANDARD.

STANDARD DIANETIC AUDITOR, certificate is Hubbard **Dianetic** Counsellor (HDC). The Hubbard **Standard Dianetics** Course teaches about the human mind, mental image pictures, the time track, locks, secondaries, engrams. Processes taught are **Standard Dn auditing** and **Dn** assists. End result is ability to restore or bring others to complete health and happiness. (CG&AC 75)

STANDARD DIANETIC COMPLETION CERTIFICATE, this **certificate** requires a well, happy human being as its end result. Usually this requires at least 25 hours of **Dn** auditing and the auditing of a score or more of items by **Standard Dn** and may also entail in conjunction with auditing, medical treatment for any physical illness or disease. **Standard Dn completion** tends to ensure full gains on Scn grades and the attainment of exteriorization with perception at AO levels. (HCO PL 2 Sept 69 II)

STANDARD DIANETICS, modern **Dn** auditing is called **Standard Dn** and new **Dn.** It is a precision activity. New **Dn** is itself. It produces wonderful results if done exactly. I find it takes a very vigorous course to make a **Standard Dn** auditor. (LRH ED 9 INT)

STANDARD DIANETICS C/S COURSE, the tech of **Dn** is and always has been different from that of Scn processing. **C/Sing** of **Dn** is its own tech. This is a specialist course that teaches and trains one to apply that tech as a **C/S.** Prerequisite is the HSDC (or HPDC). Available at any Scn org. (BPL 26 Apr 73R I)

STANDARD ITEMS, (PR&C) those paper and litho supplies that have been proved through months of experience to be needed in making **standard** products. (FSO 681)

STANDARD OF LIVING, the way of life which a person is willing to accept for himself and those around him. It includes the amount and quality of food, clothing, shelter, entertainment, etc., which he deems necessary for his survival and comfort and for which he is willing to strive to obtain or maintain.

STANDARD PRODUCTS, (PR&C) those **products** which PR&C produce to assist top management achieve their goals. (Includes such things as packs, tapes, promo materials, books, booklets and posters.) (FSO 681)

STANDARDS, the degree of rightness one is trying to establish and maintain. (HCO PL 30 Dec 70)

STANDARD TECH, standard tech isn't a process or a series of processes. It's how to make auditing work. (LRH ED 88 INT)

STANDBY AUDITOR, auditor to do assists or to fill in when a regular Dept 10 auditor or interne is taken off. (ED 140 FAO)

STANDING, continual. (HCO PL 13 Mar 72)

STANDING ORDER NO. 1, all mail addressed to me shall be received by me. (HCO PL 18 Dec 61)

STANDING ORDER NO. 1 LETTERS, letters from Scientologists and the public addressed to LRH. (HCO PL 18 Dec 64, *Saint Hill Org Board*)

STANDING ORDER NO. 1 LINE, 1. the **line** to me is known as the **SO No. 1 line**. This is because the arrangements for it are laid down in **Standing Order Number One.** The actual order, reissued on 18 December 1961, follows: "All mail addressed to me shall be received by me." (LRH ED 223 INT) 2. the **line** used to channel originations to Ron from the public. (LRH ED 36A INT)

STANDING ORDER NO. 2, a message box shall be placed in all Scn organizations so that any messages for me may be received by me. (HCO PL 18 Dec 61)

STANDING ORDER NO. 3, HCO personnel and Scn personnel should not discourage communication to me. I am always willing to help. By my own creed, a being is only as valuable as he can serve others. (HCO PL 18 Dec 61)

STANDING ORDER NO. 4, see HCO STANDING ORDER NUMBER 4.

STANDING ORDER NO. 5, see HCO STANDING ORDER NUMBER 5.

STAR, one of a group of usually four or five conventional stars used to place something in a scale of value (a five-star performance in modern research—J.T. Soby). (*Webster's Third New International Dictionary*) [The terms five star process and ten star process used in this sense appear in *The Creation of Human Ability.*]

STARBOARD, the righthand side of a ship looking forward toward the bow, opposite to port. (FO 2674) *Abbr.* STBD.

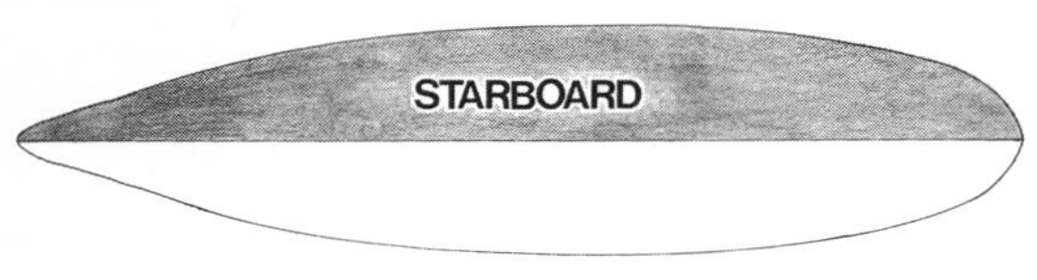

Starboard

STARBOARD AND PORT WATCH, see TWO WATCH SYSTEM.

STAR-RATED BOARD OF REVIEW CHECKOUT, the student may audit on a process of a certain level when he has passed all theory and practical **checkouts** for that process. The **Board of Review** need no longer give provisional classification examinations, but need only ascertain that the student has passed all theory and practical **checkouts** for the next process to be run for a particular level. We will call this a **Star-Rated Board of Review Checkout.** We will have to **starrate**, therefore, each and every HCOB and tape that is required to run an exact process. (HCO PL 2 Apr 65 III)

START CHANGE STOP, the cycle of action of this universe is **start, change** and **stop.** This is also the anatomy of control. Almost the entire subject of control is summed up in the ability to **start, change** and **stop** one's activities, body and one's environment. (*POW*, p. 46)

Start-Change-Stop

START-UP COSTS, see COSTS, START-UP.

STAT BOARD, each course has a **stat board.** It shows each student's daily **stats** as he goes along. (BPL 18 Jul 71R I)

Stat Board

STAT CEILING, for every department the HCO Area Sec could have a **stat**. That **stat** would tell him exactly how many letters could be gotten out, how many this could be done, how many that could be done, how many students could be handled. He could map the whole establishment, the whole establishment **stat ceiling** and that you could call a **stat ceiling**. That **stat ceiling** per department would give you exactly what the potential of the establishment was. (FEBC 10, 7101C24 SO III)

STATE, a **state** is composed of individuals who can work cooperatively. (6910C17 SO)

STATE BANK, see BANK, STATE.

STATEMENT, a summary of an account that shows the amount on hand or due. Usually it includes a summary of the nature and amount of all transactions that occured during a specific time period, usually monthly.

STATEMENT FILES, each debtor of any company we are handling has his own **file**. All invoices and papers relating to such debtors are kept in this **file** folder. A **statement** sheet is also kept. A copy of the contract (photostat) is kept in this **file**. The original is kept in a valuable document file in the safe. This applies to any company, firm or person who sends us money or owes us money. (HCO PL 27 Jan 60)

STATE OF EMERGENCY, 1. the indication of a **state of emergency** can be read beforehand from an Organization Information Center board, being forecast by red lines in three or more graphs, or by three red lines on one graph. If management has tolerated this without action when one red line occurred a **state of emergency** has already begun when it reaches three, since this is patently one or a dozen dropped balls. The organization can be assumed to be out of control. (HCO PL 17 Feb 61 II) **2.** the **state of emergency** is a serious condition. For it takes a series of serious blunders to reduce statistics or bring about local infamy or a public or press smear campaign. The state is not idly assigned and is assigned only after a steadily declining statistic or a series of non-compliances or offences resulting in over work for seniors of the org or near catastrophe. (HCO PL 30 Apr 65) **3.** when an org or portion of an org has consistently down statistics (Organization Information Center) or numerous non-compliances or offences, it is declared to be in a **state of emergency**. This can be assigned to a unit, sub-section, section, department, division or the entire organization. It is not assigned to a person. (HCO PL 30 Apr 65)

STATE OF THE ORGS, a weekly report called **state of the orgs** is submitted by management to the Aides Council and CO FB. This is a mimeo list of all **orgs**. It has a column each for each division, for GI, comps, cash bills, tone and viability. It is marked by the symbols E for excellent, G for good, P for poor, D for dangerous, F for failing. Tone is marked not by symbol but by Tone Scale taken from reports. On the basis of management reports and stats, the **State of the Orgs** is filled in. This also serves as a cross check on aides divisions over the world. Needless to state the **state of the org** list is grouped by continent with the OTL or CLO leading the continental group. The continent as a whole is then added up by division so a line is left for this after each continent. (FO 3113)

STATION, 1. (ship term) the place and action to which a person is fully grooved in, trained and competent and is assigned. (OODs 7 Jun 70) **2.** what his watch duties are. (FO 2674) **3.** the position where a person stands or is placed; the place from which a service is provided or operations directed. (FO 2967)

STATIONSHIP, the **stationship** in each area is the stable terminal for the Commodore and for Flag in that area. The major purpose of **stationships** is: to put in and keep going AOs and SHs and Central Orgs in their areas, and keep the Sea Org solvent. Actions taken by a **stationship** would normally be in the form of missions or projects. Their major observational data of both Scn and SO orgs and units are, of course, statistics. As a general rule, if stats are up, the **stationship** lets the Sea Org COs and Exec Councils under them get on with the job and backs them up. (FO 2199) *Abbr.* SS.

STATIONSHIP ORDER, issued for that **stationship** only by the Captain or Deputy Captain. Goes to all personnel of that ship and a copy to Flag. (HCO PL 24 Sept 70R) *Abbr.* SSO.

STATIONSHIPS' PRODUCT, functioning orgs. (FO 2200)

STATISTIC, 1. the relative rise or fall of a quantity compared to an earlier moment in time. If a section moved ten tons last week and 12 tons this week, the **statistic** is rising. If a section moved ten tons last week and only eight tons this week the **statistic** is falling. (HCO PL 30 Jan 66) **2.** a number or amount compared to an earlier number or amount of the same thing. **Statistics** refer to the quantity of work done or the value of it in money. (HCO PL 16 Dec 65) **3.** a tight reality, a stable point, which is to measure any departure from the ideal scene. (HCO PL 6 Jul 70) **4.** a positive numerical thing that can be accurately counted and graphed on a two dimensional thing. (HCO PL 6 Jul 70) **5.** the **statistic** measures directly the relative survival potential of the organism or its part. (HCO PL 6 Jul 70) **6.** the only sound measure of any production or any job or any activity. (HCO PL 5 Jul 70) **7.** the most direct observation in an org (or a country) is **statistics.** These tell of production. They measure what is done. (HCO PL 5 Feb 70) **8.** a difference between two or more periods in time so is always comparative. (HCO PL 6 Nov 66 I) **9.** the independent continuing survey of production or lack of it. (HCO PL 29 Feb 72 II) **10.** a **stat** actually should consist of volume, quality and viability. (FEBC 12, 7102C03 SO II) *Abbr.* Stat.

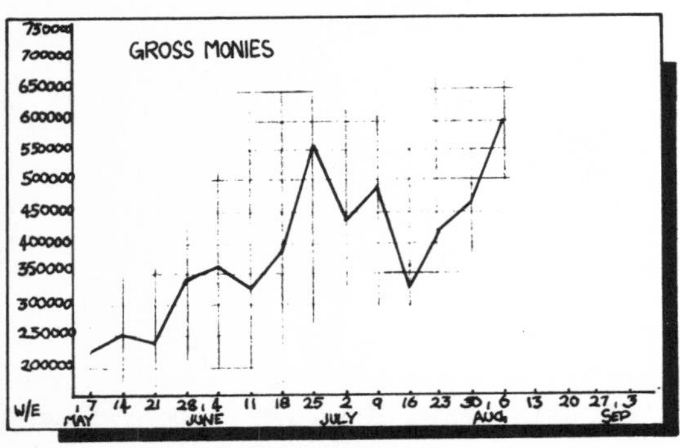

Statistic (Def. 4)

STATISTICS, (Post) purpose: to maintain accurate and continuous visual records of the activities of the HASI for the use of the executives and board of directors in planning future activities and analyzing past and current activity. To help the growth of the HASI along orderly lines by maintaining an historical record of that growth. (HCO London, 23 Apr 58)

STATISTIZED, that means the job he does is a **statistic** that can be verified. (HCO PL 1 May 65 III)

STAT MANAGEMENT CHECKLISTS, **checklists** taken from policy letters on or related to **management** by **statistics** and interpretation of **statistics**. They are *inspection* **checklists**. The items are all taken directly from the PLs and the only change in the wording of any of them consists of making each one a negative. Thus if in using a **checklist** the inspector or observer asks himself, "Does this item on this **checklist** exist here?", and finds that it does exist, then the PL the item belongs to is to that degree, violated, and he knows that he has his hands on an error, an out-point, or a possible why. As the subject is broad and has a lot of materials on it, the **checklists** have been divided into 4 parts. Part A is to do with the indicators and consequences of not having and using stats. Part B concerns the admin and preparation of graphs for inspection and use. Part C has to do with handling **statistics**, reading **statistics**, analyzing **statistics**. Part D concerns inspection of areas with down **stats**, actions to take on **stats**, and what to do about the conclusions arrived at in reading or analyzing the **stats.** (BPL 29 Sept 72R I)

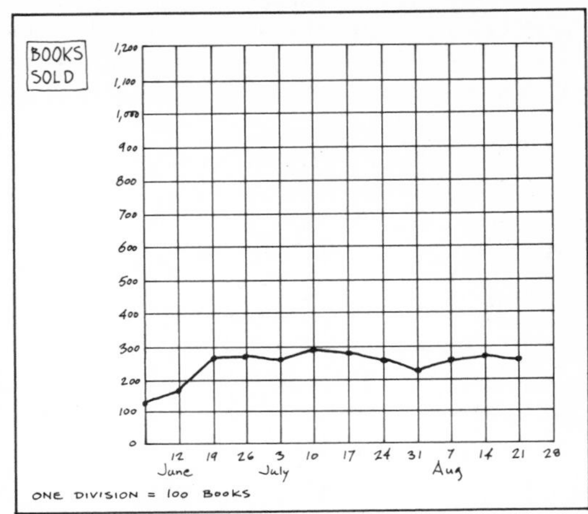

Sticky Graph

STATUS SEEKING, the effort to become more important and have a personal reason for being and for being respected. (HCO PL 14 Sept 69)

STATUS VERIFICATION FORM, form for use on all students entering AOs, all staff coming into employment in any Scn organization, and on any person whose **status** is in question, at the discretion of the 3rd Mate (HCO Area Sec). (FO 1677) [The **form** is done on an E-Meter and is a type of security check.]

STATUTE OF LIMITATIONS, a principle of law which requires that an action, such as a lawsuit, must be instituted within a prescribed period of time to be carried on.

STEAL YOUR HAT, you let somebody do your work for you that you are supposed to do. (HCO PL 1 Jul 65 III)

STEP B (1), the requirement that the SP pay off all debts owed to Scn organizations per HCO PL 23 December 65, *Suppressive Acts, Suppression of Scientology and Scientologists, The Fair Game Law.* (HCO PL 16 Aug 65 II)

STEPPED COSTS, see COSTS, STEPPED.

STEWARD, she looks after the needs of the ship's company with respect to serving food, laying and clearing tables, berthing, linen, laundry and the cleaning of the common domestic areas of the ship. (FO 2558)

STEWARDS PROJECT FORCE, project force under the supervision of the Household Services Chief, handles galley and crew quarters, cleanliness, laundry, stewards assistance and other cycles as directed. (FO 3165) *Abbr.* SPF.

STICKY GRAPH, one that won't rise no matter what one does. Such a **graph** is made. It is not a matter of omission. It is a matter of action. If one is putting heavy effort into pushing a graph up and it won't go up then there must be a hidden counter-effort to keep it down. (HCO PL 6 Nov 66 I)

STOCK, 1. a share issued by a corporation representing fractional ownership in the corporation. 2. a supply of materials, kept for current and future use. 3. total merchandise that a merchant has on hand to sell.

STOCKBROKER, an individual who, for a commission, handles a client's orders to buy and sell stocks, commodities or other property.

STOCK, BUFFER, a surplus stock of goods that a seller maintains as a buffer in order to fill exceptionally large orders or in case of product scarcity.

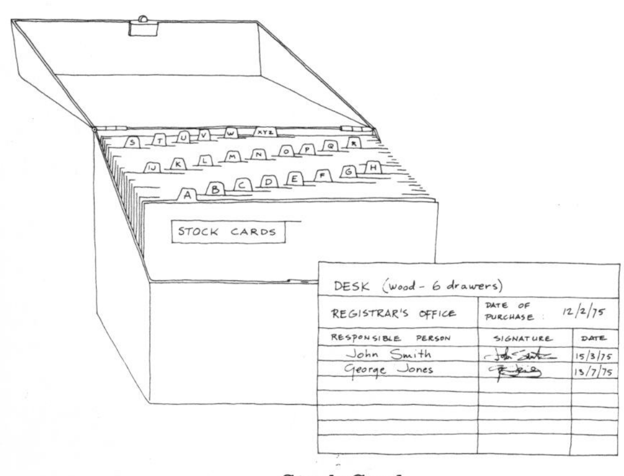

Stock Card

STOCK CARDS, stock cards for all equipment possession or issue in organizations shall be prepared by the administrative head of the organization. The idea of "company property" is both stupid and dangerous. That which is "owned by everyone" is actually owned by no one and falls apart. A car is not issued to "Department of Materiel." It is issued to John John, who happens also to be Director of Materiel. When a person is transferred, his possessions are signed for by the person, as a person, who takes over that position. If it exists somebody owns it and has signed for it. And until a new person signs for it the old owner is liable for it regardless of his whereabouts or new post. Until it is signed for initially it is owned by the administrative head and if anything happens to it or it is lost, the administrative head is liable for it. The **stock cards** should be stiff **cards** of good size kept in a box that fits them. There is only one **card** per piece of equipment. The **card** says where it is and what it is and when bought and has ample area for owning and transferring signatures. (HCO PL 15 Feb 64)

STOCK CONTROL, 1. the maintenance of enough stocks such as raw materials and finished goods, to support the current or expected level of business without losing money due to over or under stocking. Part of stock control is considering the money that can be saved by purchasing raw materials in bulk and weighing this against the current demand for finished goods, costs of storage space and the relative worth of having capital tied up in one's stocks. 2. control or dominating influence held by an individual, group or company having the majority of shares or stock in a particular enterprise.

STOCK COVER, extent of time current stocks will last if sales continue at recent volumes.

STOCK EXCHANGE, 1. a place where stocks, bonds and other securities are bought and sold. 2. an association of stockbrokers who meet to buy and sell securities according to Federal regulations.

STOCK, GROWTH, stock from a company that has shown a rapid rate of growth in earnings.

STOCK, GUARANTEED, in the case of preferred stock, the guarantee by a company other than the issuing company that dividends will be paid.

STOCKHOLDER, an individual owning one or more stock certificates that designate his ownership in a company.

STOCK-IN-TRADE, 1. merchandise kept on hand for sale at a store or shop. 2. materials or supplies kept available to carry on a business, trade, craft or art. 3. any resource or practice that is normally employed by or characterizes a particular individual, group or business.

STOCKJOBBER, in the UK, an individual who is a member of the London Stock Exchange and who deals only with brokers and not the public.

STOCK, LISTED, the stock of a company which is traded on a securities exchange and for which the company must have been approved by the Securities and Exchange Commission as well as the exchange itself.

STOCK, LOSSES, the lessened value of stocks compared to the price paid when they were originally purchased.

STOCK, PLURAL-VOTING, stock, such as founder's shares, granting more than a single vote for each share held. Founder's shares with plural-voting rights allow the founder's or promoters of a company to maintain control over the company they have formed.

STOCK, PREFERRED, a category of stock with a claim on the company's earnings before common stock dividends can be paid, and which is often guaranteed dividends at a specified rate.

STOCK PROFITS, see PROFITS, STOCK.

STOCKS, PENNY, issues that are very low in price, selling at under $1.00 per share.

STOCK SPLIT, the division of the outstanding securities in a corporation into a larger number of securities as exemplified by a 2-for-1 split resulting in each stockholder getting two shares for each one he already holds. This action is usually voted on by the board of directors and has the agreement of the stockholders.

STOCKS, RAW MATERIALS, a supply of materials kept on hand by a manufacturer and used to make particular products.

STOCK TRANSFER, all actions involved in changing the ownership of stock from one person to another which includes the stock certificate transferring from the seller's stockbroker to the buyer's stockbroker, legal change of ownership and a recording of the new owner's name made on the company's books with full up-to-date reports and notices being sent to him.

STOCK, TREASURY, stock issued and later reacquired by a company and held in its treasury, retired or resold to the public. It pays no dividends and has no voting rights during the time the company holds it.

STOCK TURNOVER, 1. the ratio of sales to stock-in-trade. 2. the ratio of sales costs to stock-in-trade. 3. in investments, the volume of trading in a particular security or on the entire stock market.

STOOL PIGEON, 1. slang term for an informer or one who under directions of an employer, joins a union to learn of union plans and activities in order to relay the information back to the employer. 2. a spy or informer for the police.

STOP, as a man all too easily specializes in **stops** he tends to stress what shouldn't be done. While this enters into it, remember that it's a **stop. Stops** all occur because of failed purposes. Behind every **stop** there is a failed purpose. A stuck picture or a motionless org are similar. Each has behind it a failed purpose. (HCO PL 14 Jan 69)

Stop

STOP-A-CHECK, an order to a bank to stop payment on a check one has written but which has not yet cleared.

STOP LIMIT ORDER, see ORDER, STOP LIMIT.

STOP ORDER, see ORDER, STOP.

STOP PAYMENT, see STOP-A-CHECK.

STORE, 1. retail establishment offering merchandise for sale. 2. a stock or reserve supply that a business will use in the future.

STOREMAN, the **storeman** in the engine room knows, keeps, orders all parts to do with the engines. He is totally responsible for obtaining spares and needed equipment for area. (FO 924)

STORES DRILL, loading **stores** is a party action, not an all hands evolution, being done usually at times in port when a lot of crew is otherwise busy or missing ashore. The party is warned by the Purser beforehand. It includes full stowage of all **stores** brought aboard and any restorage of stores shifted because of that or because **stores** need shifting in general. The party usually has two parties, port and starboard watches, and is small. (*Ship's Org Bk.*)

Stores Drill

STORESMAN, the **storesman** and his assistant run the "**store**" for cooks and some items for stewards (bread, milk, soap, coffee, tea, sugar, salt, etc.) He keeps an excellent inventory of his goods. He rotates newer goods through older ones in the Emergency store always putting in before he takes the same item (but older) out. (FSO 270)

STORING, the act of a company keeping merchandise, commodities or supplies in a warehouse until they are needed for purposes of selling, distributing or production functions.

STRIKE, an organized temporary stoppage of work by employees, often with the sanction and leadership of a union, in order to force an employer to meet specific demand such as demands for higher wages, less working hours, etc.

STRIKEBREAKER, 1. an employee who works while others are on strike. 2. a person who takes a job held ordinarily by a worker on strike, and if he was hired specifically for the purpose of strikebreaking, he is known as a fink.

STRIKE, JURISDICTIONAL, a strike wherein a union strives to get an employer to authorize its members to do specific types of work, as yet unassigned, rather than give the work in question to another union and its members.

STRIKE, OUTLAW, a cessation of work ordered by a local union without the agreement and authorization of the National Union Organization.

STRIKE, SIT-DOWN, a strike or work stoppage caused by workers refusing to work or to leave their place of employment pending a strike agreement.

STRIKE, SLOWDOWN, see SLOWDOWN.

STRIKE, SYMPATHY, a strike taken up by a group of workers in sympathy with another group of workers which has already gone on strike against an employer, in an effort to bring additional pressure to bear on that particular employer or in some cases, on the industry involved or on the government.

STRIKE, UNCONSTITUTIONAL, a strike which in its occurrence breaks a previous employer/employee agreement.

STRIKE, WILDCAT, see STRIKE, OUTLAW.

STRUCTURAL UNEMPLOYMENT, see UNEMPLOYMENT, STRUCTURAL.

STUCK IN, an Esto, as well as being mobile, must not get "**stuck in**" on one point of a division or org. Spending days hatting only *one* staff member and letting whole departments go is an example of what is meant by "getting **stuck in**." (HCO PL 16 Mar 72 II)

STUCK ON THE FIRST DYNAMIC, everything is viewed through and only the **first dynamic**. He doesn't see anything that has anything to do with any other dynamic. He doesn't *see*. That doesn't mean mentally conceive of, it is visually with the eyeball. There even is a psychosis of this. It's called narcissism, because the youth Narcissus used to gaze at his reflection in water and sigh longingly. (ESTO 5, 7203C03 SO I)

STUDENT, a **student** is one who **studies.** He is an attentive and systematic observer. A **student** is one who reads in detail in order to learn and then apply. As a **student studies** he knows that his purpose is to understand the materials he is **studying** by reading, observing, and demonstrating so as to apply them to a specific result. He connects what he is **studying** to what he will be doing. (BTB 26 Oct 70 II)

STUDENT AUDITOR, a **student** enrolled on a course **auditing** as stipulated on his checksheet for course requirements. (BPL 4 Dec 71R III)

STUDENT CASE SUPERVISOR, the Academy or **Student C/S** does all the **C/Sing** for **student** auditing in the Academy. He **C/Ses** for **student** co-audits where these exist. (HCO PL 26 Sept 74)

STUDENT COMPLETIONS, number of **student completions** is the departmental statistic of Dept 11. A **student completion** is **completion** of any course delivered in Dept 11 with a Flag checksheet, plus paid major interneship course **completions** (also with a Flag checksheet). The **student** must have paid in full for the **completion** to count. Theory and practical are not counted as separate **completions.** The full course with final pass or attest at Examiner must be completed to count. (BPL 5 Dec 72R)

STUDENT CONSULTANT, **1.** purpose: to help LRH to get the **students** moving to completion of his courses by approaching, taking up and straightening out each **student** individually when he has sporadically attended or discontinued his existing course. (FO 2287) **2.** purpose: to clear the **students** lines of any stop to study which has not been cleared by the Course Supervisor. (FO 2289)

STUDENT CORRECTION LIST, STUDY CORR LIST-1, HCO Bulletin 27 March 1972, Issue I, *Student Correction List, Study Corr List-1.* A **list** for **correcting students** on course. (LRH ED 257 INT)

STUDENT FILE, a folder with the **student's** name on it and which will receive his completed checksheets, exam results, etc. (HCO PL 6 Dec 70 II)

STUDENT FOLDER, each **student** on a Dn or Scn course must have a regular size **folder.** The **folder** contains *all* of the routing forms and attached invoices, all pink sheets issued to the **student,** all essays the **student** has done on the checksheet, all written drills, and the finished checksheet itself. The **folder** is thus a complete record of what the **student** has done in training at the org; the inside front sheet shows you what the **student** has done in all Dn and Scn study. (BPL 18 Jul 71R II)

STUDENT GRAPHS BOARD, a very large cork **board** is placed along one wall of the classroom on which all the **students' graphs** are pinned. Student Admin posts a **graph** for each new **student.** The **graph** has a scale for the **student's** total points for the day and his average points per hour. The **graphs** are pinned on the **board** in alphabetical order, so it is easy to locate any **student's graph.** (FO 3032)

STUDENT IN, the basket marked **student in** is the basket where all communications, bulletins or mail to **students** are placed. (HCO PL 24 May 65)

STUDENT INFORMATION BOARD, this may hold public notices as to living quarters available, ads for sales, class schedules, etc., but this shall not be an official **board.** (HCO PL 9 Apr 57)

STUDENT NOTICE BOARD, a **student notice board** is maintained in the classroom. On the **notice board** are pinned newly issued bulletins, policy letters, and general **notices** to **students.** (FO 3032)

STUDENT POINTS, the purpose and product of a **student** is expressed in the application of knowledge. A statistic must reflect the attainment of that product. Thus, the **points** system has been worked out for use on all Scn and Dn courses. It is designed to measure (1) progress *through* a course and (2) application of the knowledge and skills gained. The written materials of a course per page or column=3 **points.** Clay demos or other checksheet entry requiring the demonstration of some principle (e.g. demo kit, essays, drawings). Per demo=10 **points,** per clay demo=25 **points.** (BPL 17 May 71 RC II)

STUDENT POWER CLUB, (Flag) the **Student's Power Club** purpose is to promote study interest and to recognize and validate upstat **students.** (FO 2205)

STUDENT POWER CLUB SELECTION BOARD, (Flag) this **board** is to consist of (1) Course Supervisor—Chairman of the **Selection Board**, (2) Qual C/S—Secretary of the **Selection Board**, (3) Tech training Officer—member of **Selection Board**. The unanimous vote of the above members is required to elect a **student** to the **Student's Power Club**. (FO 2205)

STUDENT PRODUCT BOARD, a tool for use of Product Officers such as the D of T, Tech Sec, OES. With it, one can see exactly what **student products** there are to be gotten. The **board** is posted and kept up by the D of T and is updated daily. On the **board** is posted the name of every **student** who has routed into the Tech Division for training. Staff on Dept 11 courses are also posted on this **board** on different colored cards. The first column on the left has a card with the **student's** name and date started training. To the right in the next column is a card for the first course with the targetted completion date noted. In the other columns to the right are cards for each paid course on the person's program in the order he will take them, with targetted completion dates for each. When the **student** completes a course, its card is marked off as "Done" with the date. (BPL 30 Jul 69RA)

COMUNICATIONS COURSE

NAME	DATE STARTED	SECTION ONE	SECTION TWO	SECTION THREE	SECTION FOUR	SECTION FIVE	SECTION SIX
FRED ROC	12/3/76	DONE 13/3/76	DONE 14/3/76	DONE 15/3/76			
MAX JONES	12/3/76	DONE 13/3/76	DONE 15/3/76				
JIM HALL	13/3/76	DONE 13/3/76	DONE 14/3/76	DONE 15/3/76			
JOE ROAM	15/3/76	DONE 15/3/76					
SAM BEAL	15/3/76	DONE 15/3/76	DONE 15/3/76				
SUE DALE	16/3/76						

Student Progress Board

STUDENT PROGRESS BOARD, every Dn and Scn course must have a **student progress board**. The purpose of this **board** is to clearly indicate the **progress** of each **student** through his course toward becoming a valuable final product. Each course has its own **board**. The **board** has a column for each section of the course. Each **student's** name is written on a card with the date started and is posted in the left-hand column on the **board**. Additionally, each section has a blank card posted in it horizontally across the **board**. When a **student** completes a section, the appropriate card is marked "Done" with date in bold letters. This is done by the Course Supervisor as he always is aware of the **student's progress**. This is kept up daily. (BPL 30 Jul 69RA)

STUDENT REHABILITATION LIST, HCO Bulletin 15 November 1974, *Student Rehabilitation List*. This is the one that gets a bogged **student** sailing, gets a blown **student** back, gets an auditor back auditing. It even cures the revolutionary **student**! This is the master list for **students**—even **students** in grammar schools and colleges! (LRH ED 257 INT)

STUDENTS RABBLE ROUSE LINE, this is the **line** on which **students** can scream when there is an outness on their course which is not being immediately corrected. (BPL 20 Nov 70R)

STUDY CORRECTION LIST, you go down that **study correction list** and you will find why he can't **study**. It is a very long formidable list and it's an auditing action. (ESTO 3, 7203C02 SO I)

STUDY CORRECTION LIST REVISED, HCO Bulletin 4 February 1972RC, *Study Series 7, Study Correction List Revised*. A real long work out for a person who won't **study** or who is having real trouble on a course. Goes after it in depth. Can be used as a second **list** to student rehab list or by itself. (LRH ED 257 INT)

STUDY TIME, a staff member is entitled to 2 1/2 hours **study** or auditing **time** per day. (HCO PL 2 Aug 71)

STUFFER, an advertisement or promotion piece that is stuffed in with the main particle such as an advertisement of a new product accompanying a charge account statement from a department store.

STUNTS, the employment of innovative advertising devices, actions or tricks to promote a company, product or service.

STUPIDITY, **1.** the essence of **stupidity** can not only be produced by out-points it can be just missing data but that is another thing and that is the guy who isn't trained or hatted but has missed his gradients. He does not know what a potato peeler is, he never checked out on the thing. What it is, is omitted technology. (ESTO 4, 7203C03 SO II) **2.** confusion is the basic cause of **stupidity**. To the **stupid** all things except the very simple ones are confused. (*POW*, p. 22)

STYLE BOOK, each newspaper develops its own **style book.** This is a **book** that lays down the form, grammatical rules, spelling, etc. You find out a newspaper's **style** by reading it and talking with the Managing Editor. He'll tell you the type of stories (party line) and **style** the paper wants. (BPL 10 Jan 73R)

SUBORDINATE, an employee who is subject to the authority or control of another.

SUB-PRODUCTS, those necessary to make up the valuable final **products** of the org. (HCO PL 6 Apr 72)

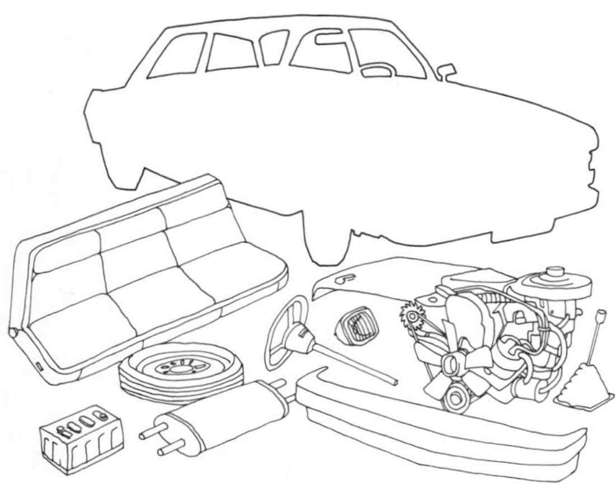

Sub Products

SUB-PURPOSES, the **purposes** of the various sections or parts of the being, organism, group, race or species which forward the basic purpose. They must amplify, qualify and/or describe the action or procedure of the part of the whole in a brief and crisp way so as to hold them in function in their support of the basic purpose. They could also be called, the **purpose** of a part of the whole, or as we use them, the **purpose** of a post, unit, department or an org with a special function. (HCO PL 13 Mar 65, *Division 1, 2, 3 The Structure of Organization What is Policy?*)

SUBSCRIBER, 1. an individual who signs his name at the end of a document as a witness or in attestation, testimony or consent. 2. one who pledges, ordinarily in writing, to buy something such as stock in a company. 3. one who contracts to pay for and to receive a certain number of issues of a newspaper or magazine.

SUB-SECTION, each one of the departments has 5 sections, it shouldn't have more than 5. Those sections are divided into **sub-sections.** (SH Spec 77, 6608C23)

SUBSIDIARY, a company having all or a majority of its stock owned by another company.

SUBSISTENCE, a standard of living which provides only enough income to subsist or keep oneself minimally provided for.

SUBSTITUTION, putting a letter or number or word down to stand for another letter or number or word is called **substitution.** (HCO PL 11 Sept 73)

SELL ALL SHARES AT
3.50 DOLLARS EACH

message

MAKE ALL RUGS AT
3.50 POUNDS EACH

word substitution

Substitution

SUB ZERO PROCESSES, very low level **processes** that get the case moving well before returning to upper grades. (HCO PL 16 Apr 65 II)

SUB-ZONE ORGS, if a Zonal Org gets more than five orgs under it one of these is designated a **sub-zonal org,** taking under it excess orgs. (HCO PL 1 Mar 66 II)

SUCCESS, 1. **Success** handles interviewing all service completions and soliciting **success** stories from same. Putting all completions on the meter to ask key questions to verify satisfactory results. Routing back to Qual for correction and completions that are not happy or satisfied or that do not pass meter questions. Categorizes **success** stories into types of **successes** and results. Distributes and posts **success** stories and makes such available for use in Div 6 and Div 2 promotion pieces and also for Div 2 and Div 6 Regs use. Sees that **success** stories are used. All these duties adds up to ensuring good word of mouth. (HCO PL 14 Nov 71RA II) **2.** could be called a Qual function due to its flub catch aspects or a Div 6 function due to its promotion aspects. Thus question has arisen as to its org board position. Actually the argument is based on sub-products. Senior is the fact that **success** monitors word of mouth and therefore is a vital part of PR area control in Div 6. It is difficult for PR to succeed in the face of poor word of mouth. **Success** is the checkpoint that will ensure good word of mouth and will prevent persons with bad indicators leaving the org which will create bad word of mouth. When **success** functions are really in, good word of mouth results and a PRO can do his job with reality and without stumbling into bad word of mouth. An additional benefit is that **success** provided the vital information line on the results the org is obtaining with its services and this contributes to making PR real. **Success** is a type of PR area control in itself and goes in as an ingredient to make up the whole of PR area control. **Success** monitors word of mouth=part of PR area control=Division 6. This finalizes the position of **success**. (HCO PL 5 Aug 71 II)

SUCCESS DIVISION, (Nine Div Org) Division 8 with Dept 22 Expansion, Dept 23 Population, and Dept 24 Success. (HCO PL 26 Oct 67)

SUCCESSFUL, made statistics rise. (CBO 25)

SUCCESSFUL BUSINESS, one which has its charts on a steady if slight or great increase. (SH Spec 54, 6503C09)

SUCCESS OFFICER, one of the key public line posts in Div 6. He is the last tech police point in the org. It should not be allowed to be unmanned or held from above or, even worse, from the side by Qual. The **Success Officer's** purpose is: to help Ron get volume high communication **success** stories into the hands or notice of the org's publics, enhancing and increasing desire for the Org's services. His immediate day to day function would be to man the **Success Officer** desk on the public flow line, and interview each org completion, do the key questions meter test, to get the person to write up his **success** story in duplicate and to finally read and acknowledge the person for his **success** and congratulate him/her upon this achievement. (BPL 14 Jun 73R II)

SUCCESS STORIES, **1.** the departmental stat of Dept 13. It is defined as the number of creditable **success stories**, less the number of people not passing key questions, less two for any ethics action taken on a student, preclear or staff member for the week. What is creditable? Deserving some credit or praise. The criteria would be: is the **success story** worthy of display or use or positive in its statements? If a **success story** is negative or critical or unhappy, it would not be creditable and would be an indicator of a cert or award which had been improperly given out. (BPL 14 Jun 73R I) **2.** (Qual stat) total number of **success stories** less one for each flunk of key questions less two for any ethics action taken on a student, preclear or staff member for the week. This includes any flunk at **success** per HCOB 24 February 72, *C/S Series 71A, Word Clearing, OCAs.* (BPL 30 Jun 73R)

SUGGESTION BOX, a box or container provided by management for employees' written suggestions regarding any aspect of their company's operation.

SUGGESTIONS CENTER, CIC will contain a desk with pens, paper and message forms openly available so that personnel can sit down and write any **suggestions** they have, incomplete cycles noted, on telex messages. They will place the **suggestion** etc., in the basket which will be on the desk. This area will be called **suggestions center** and should be designated as such. (FO 908)

SUGGESTION SYSTEM, a system in which employees are encouraged by management to offer suggestions regarding improved operating methods, betterment of practices and condition, and freely given constructive ideas for which the individual is rewarded, usually monetarily, upon acceptance of any of his suggestions.

SUMMARY, BUDGET, see BUDGET, SUMMARY.

SUMMARY DEBRIEF, a **summary debrief** was just a few pages. Just a very good little **summary**. (6912C13 SO)

SUPERCARGO, **1.** in early days there was an HCO Sec in charge of the functions of the first three divisions (Exec, HCO Dissem) and an Assoc Sec in charge of the functions of the last four divisions. The org board evolved further and the HCO Exec Sec became the person in charge of the functions of the first three divisions and the Org Exec Sec the last four. In the Sea Org these titles became **Supercargo** and Chief Officer but the functions were similar. (HCO PL 9 May 74) **2.** the **Supercargo**, Dept 20, has general control and authority over Divisions 7, 1 and 2, and Departments 1 to 6, including communications, personnel, inspections, ethics, orders, publications, hand-books, manuals, operators' manuals for equipment, ship plans, crew education, schedules, crew's records, books and papers, shore contacts, entering and clearing vessels. He is responsible for profitable activities. (FO 1109) *Abbr.* S/C.

SUPERCARGO'S CONFERENCE, there is a **Supercargo's** Officer's **Conference** consisting of the heads of Divisions 7, 1 and 2, and the

Supercargo who heads it. It is used by the **Supercargo** to advise or obtain advice from his officers. It is in Div 7, Dept 20. (FO 1021)

SUPERINTENDENT, a person who directs a company department or section and its employees and their work.

SUPERIOR SERVICE IMAGE PROGRAM NO. 1, 1. Instant **Service** Project is part of the **superior** org **image**. An org never backlogs pcs or students. Never makes them wait. Official orgs are really there to **service** groups, franchises and the public. They are supposed to be sources of **superior service**. The **service** must be **superior** to that available from groups, franchises and field auditors and should help them handle their rough pcs and students and assist them to function. An org isn't a competitor to groups, franchises and field auditors. It is the unit to which these feed people and to which those in the field look for help, data and training. An org isn't just another franchise. It must be a snap and pop senior that knows its business and does it. (LRH ED 78 INT) **2. program** to establish and publicize the official org as the source of helpful standard actions. (LRH ED 54 INT)

SUPER-LITERATE, I've coined a word, **super-literate**. This is what a person who really *knows* what he reads is. A real scholar. People are literate. One who knows how to study is **super-literate**. That's what guys doing the study tapes are becoming. Not literate (able to read and write). But **super-literate**, one who really knows. (OODs 14 Apr 72)

SUPERSTAT CLUB, in the FBO network a very successful game was going for ten targets made in a row, with memberships offered in the Upstat Club for two targets in a row and **Superstat Club** for ten in a row. Special certs were made up and issued in addition to awards. This was very popular and very successful. (SO ED 309 INT)

SUPERVISION, 1. means helping people to understand their jobs. **Supervision** means giving them the responsibility and wherewithal to do their jobs. **Supervision** includes the granting of beingness. **Supervision** does not mean doing the job **supervised**. (HCO PL 28 Jul 71) **2.** it serves as a relay point to which plans can be communicated and from which observations as reports can be received; and it serves as the terminal which communicates the plans as orders and sees that they are actually done. (HCO PL 14 Sept 69)

SUPERVISION, the direction, inspection and overseeing of the performance of one's subordinate workers and their production.

SUPERVISION, CONSULTATIVE, type of supervision that emphasizes respect for and attention to the individual employee, his personality and contributing talents by following the policy of personal consultations and the giving of information to employees throughout the organization.

SUPERVISION OF AN ORGANIZATION, consists of keeping the terminals in place and keeping the correct traffic (particles and messages) flowing to the right terminals and planning to adjust the communication flow either from the outside in or from the inside out. (PAB 78)

SUPERVISOR, 1. a course must have a **supervisor**. He may or may not be a graduate and experienced practitioner of the course he is **supervising** but he must be a trained course **supervisor**. He is not expected to *teach*. He is expected to get the students there, rolls called, checkouts properly done, misunderstoods handled by finding what the student doesn't dig and getting the student to dig it. The **supervisor** who tells students answers is a waste of time and a course destroyer as he enters out data into the scene even if trained and actually especially if trained in the subject. The **supervisor** is not an "instructor" that's why he's called a **supervisor**. (HCO PL 16 Mar 71R) **2.** the **supervisor** is there to get the course materials fully understood and applied by the student. (BPL 11 May 69R) **3.** as **supervisor** it is your responsibility to eradicate any barriers or hindrances presented which distract the student from studying. This includes extra curricular activities. (HCO PL 24 Oct 68)

SUPERVISOR, 1. a middle management person who supervises the designated employees under him and their work and who is in an organizational position to be an intermediary between top management and his employees. 2. an elected administrative officer in some U.S. township systems.

SUPERVISOR, FIRST LEVEL, the supervisor in charge of the rank-and-file employees of a company and their type of work.

SUPERVISOR, LINE, a supervisor whose intermediate position and authority serves as a connecting link between the echelons in a line organization of top level management to the rank-and-file.

SUPERVISOR'S CODE, the rules of the game called training. The **Supervisor's Code** has been developed over many years' experience in training. It has been found that any time a supervisor broke one of the rules, to any degree, the course and training activities failed to function properly. (HCO PL 15 Sept 67) [See the reference for the actual **code.**]

SUPPLIER, an individual or company that furnishes commodities or services to other business concerns.

SUPPLY, in economics, the amount of a commodity available for filling a demand or for purchase at a given price.

SUPPLY AND MATERIEL BUREAU, **1.** the **Supply and Materiel Bureau** establishes logistic needs, locates **suppliers**, procures and via the Comm Bureau, ships and distributes. It inventories, safeguards, salvages and disposes of logistic items. (CBO 7) **2.** renamed Accounts and **Materiel Bureau**. (FSO 126)

SUPPLY DIVISION, (Ship Org) the 3rd Division handles the money and materials of the ship and provides its meals, accommodations and services. It handles the inventories, and is responsible for all money and all stores of whatever kind, including balance sheets. It is normally referred to as the **Supply Division.** (FO 1109)

SUPPORT ACTIVITIES, activities of an advisory or specialized nature that support but are not engaged directly in the manufacture of a product or the provision of a service. Typically accounting, maintenance, training, research, etc., are support activities.

SUPPRESS, to squash, to sit on. To make smaller, to refuse to let reach, to make uncertain about his reaching, to render or lessen in any way possible by any means possible, to the harm of the individual and for the fancied protection of a **suppressor**. (SH Spec 84, 6612C13)

SUPPRESSION, a harmful intention or action against which one cannot fight back. Thus when one can do anything about it, it is less **suppressive**. (HCO PL 26 Dec 66)

SUPPRESSION ON LINES, a type of dev-t where **lines** get closed by arbitraries so that vital info does not get through or vital action is not ordered. (HCO PL 27 Jan 69)

SUPPRESSIVE ACTION, by definition a **suppressive action** is to award a down statistic and penalize an upstatistic. (6711C18 SO)

SUPPRESSIVE ACTS, **1. actions** or omissions undertaken to knowingly **suppress**, reduce or impede Scientology or Scientologists. (HCO PL 23 Dec 65) **2.** the overt or covert **actions** or omissions knowingly and willfully undertaken to **suppress**, reduce, prevent or destroy case gains, and/or the influence of Scn on activities, and/or the continued Scn success and actions on the part of organizations and Scientologists. (BPL 9 Aug 71R I)

SUPPRESSIVE GROUPS, those which seek to destroy Scn or which specialize in injuring or killing persons or damaging their cases or which advocate **suppression** of mankind. (HCO PL 29 Jun 68)

SUPPRESSIVE PERSON, **1.** next door to the "theetie-weetie" case is the totally overwhelmed condition we call **SP** (**suppressive person**). When a living being is out of his own valence and in the valence of a thoroughly bad even if imaginary image you get an **SP**. An **SP** is a no-confront case because, not being in his own valence he has no viewpoint from which to erase anything. That is all an **SP** is. (HCO PL 20 Oct 67) **2.** continuous overts, wrong target, non-completions of cycles of actions are primary manifestations. When accompanied by no-case-gain you've got him tagged. (SH Spec 73, 6608C02) **3.** no-case-gain, low OCA, bad ethics record, low production stats. (HCO PL 28 May 72) **4.** now any thetan wants out. Even the **SP** himself, personally wants out. Only he, unfortunately, is sure that you are simply trying to put him in. You see, he knows he belongs in, and he is very described as somebody who is totally surrounded by Martians, regardless of who you are. You see, he is stuck in an incident which has personnel that have nothing to do with present time. Yet, all that personnel is in present time and you are that personnel, so that of course, you have to be held down. Therefore he commits almost continuous crimes in an effort to hold people down. A **suppressive** is in active attack on Scn. He commits overts twenty four hours a day. (SH Spec 73, 6608C02) **5.** it might interest you how an **SP** comes about. He's already got enough overts to deserve more motivators than you can shake a stick at. He has done something to dish one and all in. He's been a bad boy. Now the reason he got to be a bad boy was by switching valences. He had a bad boy over there and he then, in some peculiar way, got into that bad boy valence. Now he knows what he is—he's a bad boy. Man is basically good but he mocks up evil valences and then gets into them. You see, he says the other fellow is bad. The other fellow was bad and eventually he got this pasted-up other fellow and one day he becomes the other fellow, see, in a valence shift or personality—whole, complete package of personality. And there he is. So now he is an evil fellow. He knows how he is supposed to act. He is supposed to act like the other fellow. That's the switcherroo. That's how evil comes into being. (SH Spec 73, 6608C02) *Abbr.* SP.

SUPREME TEST, **1.** the **supreme test** of a thetan is "the ability to make things go right." (HCO PL 30 Dec 70) **2.** the **supreme test** of a thetan is "Can he start at A and go to B?" (7109C05 SO)

SUPREME TEST OF AN EXECUTIVE, the **supreme test of an executive** is to make things go right. (HCO PL 28 Jul 71)

SURCHARGE, 1. generally, an additional amount added to the usual sum or cost. 2. income tax designation for making a percentage addition to a tax amount. 3. in law, the showing of an omission in an account.

SURETY, 1. a formal pledge or guarantee that if loss, damage or default occurs, it will be paid for or paid back. 2. a person who has contracted to be responsible for another, especially his debts or obligations in the event of his defaulting.

SURPLUS, 1. total assets of a business less the sum of all its liabilities. 2. an excess of what is required or demanded such as a surplus of oil.

SURTAX, 1. an additional tax of any kind. 2. a graduated income tax, added to the usual income tax, that becomes effective at the point where a person's net income exceeds a certain amount.

SURVEY, **1.** a careful examination of something as a whole and in detail. The word **survey** as used in Public Relations terminology means to carefully examine public opinion with regard to an idea, a product, an aspect of life, or any other subject. By examining in detail (person to person **surveying**) one can arrive at a whole view of public opinion on a subject by tabulating highest percentage of popular response. (BPL 5 Dec 71) **2.** to find out what people want or will accept or will believe one does **surveys**. In **surveying** you are in actual fact seeking to know what service that you can do will people consider valuable enough to give money or valuables for. (LRH ED 161 INT)

SURVEY MEETING, there are two types of meetings with prospective clients. In the first, called a **survey meeting**, you must find out what is needed and wanted. Your purpose with a **survey meeting** is to find out what is needed and wanted, and to let the prospective client know that you can provide it. You don't tell him how you *will* provide it, you only let him know you will provide it, with a full proposal to be presented to him soon. (BPL 24 Jan 73 I)

SURVEYOR, the **surveyor** contacts the people to be **surveyed**, asks his questions and makes notes of the answers given; he also makes sure he notes the reaction. He should write down the *tone level* of the reaction to each question. He doesn't handle anything—just the question, recording the answer and the reaction. (HCO PL 2 Jun 71 II)

Surveyor

SURVIVAL, **survival** could be said to be any change, whether in size or in age or in position in space. The essence of **survival** is change. (*POW*, p. 42)

SURVIVAL CLUB, **1.** this is an idea. The only thing necessary to bring about a great political reform in a country is simply to raise the intelligence of all the people in the country a few percent. That is the crux of this idea. That is its political connotation. What we have to do is bring people together with the idea of **survival** by mutual activity to the benefit of the person himself **surviving**. There are a number of projects and programs on which such a **club** could act and enter all based on the motive of **survival**. Here then is a **Survival Club** idea. United **Survival Action Clubs**. The reason they're called that is just so you can say

USA Club but the loose term is **Survival Club**. (5712C30) **2.** we are engaging seriously, and not as any test, upon a program of raising the individual capability of every capable person in the United States, and more broadly on the world front, the capability of all capable persons in the vicinity of our International Offices. Toward this end we have organized the **Survival Clubs**. The actual goal of the **club** is to raise the capability of every person who becomes a member of that **club**. This can be done in various ways. It can be done by recreation. It can be done by group participation. It can be done by training courses. It can be done simply by a clarification of ideas. The **USA Clubs** believe that individuals, each made more capable, banded together, can survive a national disaster. (*CERTAINTY* Vol 5, Number 3)

SURVIVORSHIP, the right of an individual who survives a partner or joint owner to the entire ownership of the enterprise that was previously owned jointly.

SUSPENSE ACCOUNT, see ACCOUNT, SUSPENSE.

SWAMPER, 1. the title means cleaner; it does not mean deck hand or some other thing. (ED 240-7 Flag) **2.** is "one who cleans up" and the rank is below deck hand. (FO 201) **3.** persons until they have completed an AB checksheet are **swampers** in rank regardless of post. (FO 517) **4.** new recruits become **swampers** (deck), cleaners (stewards dept), and wipers (engine room). (FO 748)

SWEATED LABOR, see LABOR, SWEATED.

SWING SHIFT, the work shift between the day shift and night shift which usually works from 4 pm. till 12 pm.

SWITCHING, the act of selling one security in order to purchase another.

SWITCH ORDER, see ORDER, SWITCH.

SYMPATHY ACTION, see STRIKE, SYMPATHY.

SYMPATHY STRIKE, see STRIKE, SYMPATHY.

SYNDICALISM, radical movement that advocates bringing industries under the ownership and operation of syndicates or an association of unions by means of a forceful takeover.

SYNDICATE, 1. an association of persons, companies, banks or unions formed to carry out any undertaking or enterprise. 2. an agency or company that sells articles or columns for publication to a number of national or international newspapers or magazines. 3. a group of investment bankers or underwriters who guarantee and distribute either a new issue of stock or a large block of stock.

T

TAKE A WALK, this process is very easy to perform. When one feels tired on finishing his work, no matter if the thought of doing so is almost all that he can tolerate without falling through the floor, he should go out and **walk** around the block until he feels rested. (*POW*, p. 95)

Take a Walk

TAKE-HOME PAY, the net amount of a person's salary remaining after the deduction of withholding taxes, insurance premiums, pension plan contributions, dues and similar charges.

TAKING IN ITS OWN LAUNDRY, an organization can work wholly at **taking in its own laundry**. All the work that gets done is the work generated inside the shop by unreal routes and wierd changes of particles. (HCO PL 22 Oct 62)

TALLY BOARD, each Aide and A/Aide should have a **tally board** which means a **board** giving each evaluation required for each week in a vertical column and date vertical columns which can be checked off when done. (FO 3064)

TANGIBLE ASSETS, see ASSETS, TANGIBLE.

TAPES, these are an issue line of both policy and tech as designated and are recopied at Pubs Org and issued for courses, congresses and other purposes. (HCO PL 24 Sept 70R)

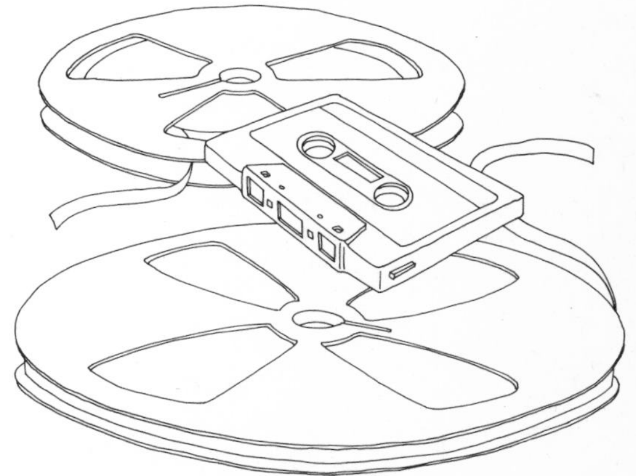

Tapes

TAPE TRANSCRIPTION POST, **tape transcription post** of HCO is to **transcribe** any and all **tapes** given them by LRH—manuscripts, articles, bulletins, letters, or anything else from LRH. (HCOB 4 Oct 56)

TARGET(S), the steps of handling (an evaluation) are in program form. They are numbered 1-2-3 etc. Or A-B-C, etc. They can be in the sequence they will be done but this is mostly important when one person or one team is going to do the whole thing step by step. These steps are called **targets.** Each part of the program (each **target**) is assigned to someone to do or to get done. (HCO PL 17 Feb 72)

TARGET(S), an objective one intends to accomplish within a given period of time.

TARGET APPORTIONMENT OFFICER, (Gung-Ho Group) the **Target Apportionment Officer** apportions short-range **targets** to other groups which when all done make up the completion of long-range **targets** for the whole area. (HCO PL 2 Dec 68)

TARGET LIST, a **target list** is things to accomplish in carrying forward our purpose. (OODs 15 Jun 68)

TARGETTING, establishing what action or actions should be undertaken in order to achieve a desired objective. (BPL 8 Feb 72)

TASK, a piece of work assigned or taken on as part of one's job which may be a one-time duty or a continuing permanent act.

TASK-BASED APPRAISAL, a written appraisal, made by a senior concerning a junior's ability to meet targets, comply with orders on time, terminatedly handle situations, etc.

TASK DESCRIPTION, description of elements and actions involved in the performance of a specific task, including observations, judgments, skills and procedures.

TASK FORCE, a specially trained, self-contained unit assigned to a specific mission or **task**, or any group assigned to a specific project. (FO 3489)

Task Force

TAUT SHIP, most people confuse a **taut ship** with a harshly led ship. Actually, harshness has nothing to do with it. The right word is positiveness. (HCO PL 3 Nov 66)

TAX, 1. a monetary charge levied against the earnings of individuals, groups and businesses of a country to help pay for its local, state, and/or Federal government expenditures. 2. in law, assessments made as for court costs. 3. a fee or dues levied against the staff of an organization or club to meet its expenses.

TAXABLE INCOME, individual or organizational income that is subject to taxation by any governmental agency.

TAX BRACKET, for purposes of taxation income levels are usually divided into ranges or brackets according to amounts. Each bracket gets taxed at a certain percentage. Thus a person in an earning bracket of $8,000.00 to $10,000.00 annually might be taxed 20% of his income. That is the tax bracket he is in.

TAX EVASION, the effort to avoid paying tax or greatly reducing the taxable amount of income by not reporting all monies realized or padding deductible expenses.

TAX YEAR, any fiscal year or 12-month period usually extending from January through December.

Team

TEAM, a **team** has a tendency to know what the other **team** members are doing and thinking and coordinates thereby and therewith. That is a definition of a **team.** It is people who cooperate one with another to push forward a common purpose and they normally get along great. (6910C17 SO)

TEAM HATS, team hats include Intro to SO, SWPB, SS I, SS II, SO SS, Ship's Org Book, AB, MU hat, the Bureaux **team hat,** HCO **team hat,** etc.; and any other training which makes the staff member more a part of, and better able to function in, a **team.** (FSO 361)

TEAM-MATE, 1. someone who assists in the overwhelming of the enemy. (PAB 80) **2.** [fellow members of a group banded together in a common cause, goal, purpose, game or activity.]

Team Mate

TECH, 1. abbreviation for "**technology**" or "**technical,**" depending on context. The **technology** referred to is normally that contained in HCOBs. It also means the **Technical** Division of a Scn org (Division 4, the division of the org that delivers training and processing.) (BTB 12 Apr 72R) **2. tech** consists of a large amount of precision administration and the application exactly of the existing wealth of materials. (HCO PL 27 Aug 73) **3.** there *is* a way to do something right. The right ways to do things are called **technical** procedures or **tech** when it comes to auditing or scientific or mechanical processes. (HCO PL 4 Jun 71)

TECH/ADMIN RATIO, consists of the **ratio** between number of **admin** staff/number of **tech** staff. The **tech/admin ratio** is computed by post function rather than by the **technical** training of a person holding a post. (i.e., a **tech** trained person holding an **admin** post is counted as admin staff.) (BPL 5 Apr 73R)

TECH AND POLICY KNOWLEDGE MANAGEMENT SECTION, Branch 11A the LRH Comm Branch, Flag Management Bureau contains a **Tech and Policy Knowledge Management Section** whence the **KOT** and **PK Network** is operated, and as a unit of this **section,** on Flag, a Tech Quality Control Unit which handles **tech** queries and flub catch per policy. (FBDL 488R)

TECH AND QUAL AIDE, CS-5. (FO 1031)

TECH BUREAU, the **Tech Bureau** and Policy Knowledge Bureau of the GO have just been phased out. It is a vital thing for LRH Comms to get in "on-HCOB" **tech.** This is best done by having a Deputy LRH Comm for **Tech** for that office or org. The duties of the **Tech Bureau** mainly concerned checking refunds, following up out-**tech** on persons, and assuring that celebrities received correct and standard tech. These functions are contained in the GO hats for the **Tech Bureau.** All these functions and hats now apply to LRH Comms. The main purpose of this transfer came from an evaluation in which it was found that policy responsibility was transferred to the Guardian Office and that this is primarily an internal org function. LRH Comms are therefore responsible for the **tech** quality and the exact application of HCOBs. They are also responsible for policy knowledge and use. To the degree that **tech** is exactly and precisely applied, per HCOBs, books and tapes, orgs expand and prosper. (LRH ED 205 INT)

TECH ESTABLISHMENT OFFICER, 1. just as the HAS establishes the whole org (and the Tech Division) the **tech establishment officer establishes tech.** The **TEO** is in the Office of the Tech Sec. There is *no* relationship between the ED, Product Officer and Org Officer of the org and the **TEO.** The **TEO establishes** the terminals, lines, spaces and material of the whole **technical** division. The purpose of the post is to more firmly **establish** whatever and whoever already exists in the **Tech** Division and **establish** the division more fully so that it can deliver training and processing with volume and quality and viability enough to continually expand. (HCO PL 20 Aug 71 II) **2.** the **Tech Establishment Officer** knows exactly how to train supervisors, C/Ses, auditors and to set up the **Tech** Div so it functions flawlessly and turns out high volume very high quality products. (FBDL 103) **3. establishes** and maintains the **Tech** Division. This division amongst all the rest is most likely to have other Estos in the division. (HCO PL 7 Mar 72) *Abbr.* TEO.

TECH ESTIMATE, the **estimated** number of hours of auditing expressed in number of intensives that the D of P and/or C/S consider to be currently required for the pc to attain what he wishes from his current auditing. This is done as part of the registration cycle. (BPL 4 Dec 71 RA II)

TECH HAT, **1.** a **hat** folder for general or **technical** directives issued to all the staff regardless of post. (HCO PL 13 Sept 70) **2. hat** in which the HCOBs relating to the post or newly issued are kept. (LRH ED 83 INT)

TECHNICAL ALTER-IS REPORT, staff member **report** of any ordered **alteration** of **technology** not given in an HCOB, book or LRH tape. (HCO PL 1 May 65)

TECHNICAL ANALYSIS, see ANALYSIS, TECHNICAL.

TECHNICAL CONSULTANT, ARC Break Auditor (called **Technical Consultant** with the public). (SO ED 320RA INT)

TECHNICAL COUNCIL, **1.** purpose: to uphold and increase the **technical** excellence of the organization through supervision, advice and training. Duties: to put in and maintain the **technical** lines and data in the organization. To clarify any **technical** difficulties. The **Technical Council** is headed by the Technical Director and is composed of any staff member who is a Saint Hill Graduate with a classification of III or above. The **council** will meet on order of the Technical Director: as needed to resolve **technical** difficulties as observed by its members; on appeal from a staff member or department head. (HCO PL 4 Oct 63) **2.** the Technical Division shall no longer have a Technical Director but shall be governed by a **Technical Council** which shall consist of the Director of Processing and the Director of Training. (FCPL 9 Oct 58)

TECHNICAL DEGRADES, (1) abbreviating an official course in Dn and Scn so as to lose the full theory, processes and effectiveness of the subjects. (2) adding comments to checksheets or instructions labelling any material "background" or "not used now" or "old" or any similar action which will result in the student not knowing, using and applying the data in which he is being trained. (3) employing after 1 September 1970 any checksheet for any course not authorized by myself and the SO Organizing Bureau Flag. (4) failing to strike from any checksheet remaining in use meanwhile any such comments as "historical," "background," "not used," "old," etc., or verbally stating it to students. (5) permitting a pc to attest to more than one grade at a time on the pc's own determinism without hint or evaluation, (6) running only one process for a grade between 0 to IV. (7) failing to use all processes for a level. (8) boasting as to speed of delivery in a session, such as "I put in Grade Zero in three minutes," etc. (9) shortening time of application of auditing for financial or labor saving considerations. (10) acting in any way calculated to lose the **technology** of Dn and Scn to use or impede its use or shorten its materials or its application. (HCO PL 17 Jun 70)

TECHNICAL DIRECTOR, **1.** purpose: to ensure good training and processing, good service and ARC inside and outside the organization. (HCO PL12 Oct 62) **2.** the function of the **Technical Director** is to take charge of all **technical** activities in the organization. The **Technical Director** is immediately below Association Secretary and immediately above Directors of Technical departments. The **Technical Director** is on a par with the Administrator. The **Technical Director** displaces the Technical Council. The first three objectives of the **Technical Director** are as follows: (1) to make absolutely and personally certain that every HGC preclear achieves positive and real gains in every week's intensive in the HGC. (2) to make absolutely and personally certain that every student in the academy is able to audit on graduation and that graduation is done rapidly. (3) to make absolutely certain that staff morale is kept high, using existing technology. (HCO PL 6 Apr 62) **3.** the **Technical Director** coordinates all training and processing activities. He holds Auditors Conference, checks sessions, assigns preclears, he passes on schedules and subject matter in training. The **Technical Director** is to act as a bridge between service and procurement and should work closely with the registrar and administration. (FCPL 1 Apr 57) **4.** purpose: to ensure good training and processing, good service and ARC inside and outside the organization. (HCO London 9 Jan 58)

TECHNICAL DIVISION, purpose: to ensure good training and processing, good service and ARC inside and outside the organization. (HCO PL 27 Nov 59) **2.** then we get into **technical**, in actual fact the right name is production. Production Division is Division 4. (SH Spec 77, 6608C23) **3.** the Technical Division includes these three departments: the PE Foundation, the Academy of Scn and the Hubbard Guidance Center. These carry out the three basic services of a Central Organization—public training and processing, individual training and individual processing. (HCO PL 20 Dec 62) **4.** an organization is divided into a **Technical Division** and an Administrative Division. The **Technical Division** is composed of those who directly audit or train or directly supervise auditing or training. (HCO PL 5 Dec 62)

TECHNICAL DIVISION ESTABLISHMENT OFFICER, see TECH ESTABLISHMENT OFFICER.

TECHNICAL FOLDER, see HAT FOLDER.

TECHNICAL HATS, this **hat** would contain all HCO Bulletins on **technical** information. These are to be arranged in chronological order. (SEC ED 78, 2 Feb 59)

TECHNICAL INDIVIDUAL PROGRAMS, 1. originated so that personal **programs** for students and pcs coming to Flag may be issued and published, numbered and dated. More than one **program** can be on one issue. They are on green paper on one side of a page so they can be cut up. Distributed only to those concerned. (HCO PL 24 Sept 70R) **2.** to keep check of **programs** on cases and study, a new issue has been created called a **Technical Individual Program** (**TIP**). These will be mimeoed and go to the various interested terminals. They apply to FEBCs, Qual interns and crew. This will keep things sorted out on **individuals** so they and others know what's going. (OODs 21 Jun 71) *Abbr.* TIPS.

TECHNICAL INFORMATION, by which is meant the "how" and "why" of our activities. (HCO PL 31 Dec 64)

TECHNICAL NON-COMPLIANCE REPORT, staff member **report** of any failure to apply the correct **technical** procedure. (HCO PL 1 May 65)

TECHNICAL PROCEDURES, see TECH.

TECHNICAL RESEARCH, see ANALYSIS, TECHNICAL.

TECHNICAL SECRETARY, Division 4, Technical Division is headed by the **Technical Secretary.** (BPL 4 Jul 69R VI) *Abbr.* Tech Sec.

TECHNICIAN, 1. a person skilled in a specific technique or range of technique that form part of a broader field of study such as a dental technician or stock market research technician. 2. one with skill in the arts.

TECHNIQUE, 1. the individual skill possessed by an artist or accomplished person which becomes apparent as soon as you see his work and distinguishes him from others in his field. 2. the exact manner employed to obtain a specific result.

TECHNOLOGICAL UNEMPLOYMENT, see UNEMPLOYMENT, TECHNOLOGICAL.

TECHNOLOGY, 1. the methods of application of an art or science as opposed to mere knowledge of the science or art itself. (HCOB 13 Sept 65) **2.** a body of truths. (Class VIII 4) **3.** the whole body of the science. (5812C29) *Abbr.* Tech.

TECH OF ADMIN, this would be the right ways to do **administrative** actions or organize something. (HCO PL 4 Jun 71)

TECH ORG OFFICER/ESTO, the **Tech Org Officer/Esto establishes** the **Tech** Division. (BPL 22 Nov 71R) *Abbr.* TOOE

TECH PERSON, a **tech person,** by actual definition, does or supervises **tech.** (HCO PL 23 May 68, *WW and SH Recombined (Deadline 15 Jun '68)*)

TECH PROGRAMS CHIEF, the **Tech Programs Chiefs** work with the LRH Comm and Tech Secs and Qual Secs to get **tech** materials and correct practices used. The **Tech Programs Chiefs** for non-English areas push for tape translated **tech** and use the tapes for training in orgs. Each one runs a flub catch system for his continent. (CBO 323)

TECH QUALITY CONTROL UNIT, Branch 11A, the LRH Comm Branch, Flag Management Bureau, contains a Tech and Policy Knowledge Management Section whence the KOT and PK Network is operated, and as a **unit** of this section, on Flag, a **Tech Quality Control Unit** which handles **tech** queries and flub catch per policy. (FBDL 488R)

TECH QUERY LINE, the **tech query line** must be made known to exist and interns are allowed to use it. The **line** is from the Interne Supervisor, Qual Sec, to Flag Tech Quality Control Unit for that continent. Interne confusions can be spotted by these terminals and often can refer to the precise HCOB that handles the **query.** (BPL 22 Feb 72R)

TECH (TECHNICAL) SERVICES, 1. the activity which enrolls, routes, schedules, distributes the mail of and assists the housing of students. (HCOB 21 Sept 70) **2.** the purpose is to get auditors, pcs and materials together and in an auditing room on schedule so that auditing can occur and with minimal loss of the auditor's time and to get students routed and to keep all course materials, folders, records, checksheets, invoices and dispatches handled, filled out and properly filed and so provide service for the org's publics. (SO ED 163 INT) **3.** it is a primary duty of **Tech Services** to get pc and auditor into an auditing room on time on schedule and all auditing delivered by intensive with intensives always delivered within the week without fail and despite ethics, declares or other "reasons" for failure to complete. (BPL 8 Dec 72R) **4. services** the public and ensures **service** is delivered without delays or upsets. (BPL 8 Dec 72R) **5.** Department 10. (FEBC 12, 7102C03 SO II)

TECH SERVICES OFFICER, (Gung-Ho Group) the **Tech Services Officer** sees students are routed and cared for, sees other groups when meeting together are routed and handled. His business is bodies, to what are they assigned, where do they go. (HCO PL 2 Dec 68)

TECH TRAINING CORPS, that body of auditors on full-time **training** or interning who are under their own I/C, and who do their courses in **tech** and internships in Qual; they get transferred to the HGC to audit at that level for which they have been **trained** and interned. When a **TTC** auditor goes to the HGC he ceases to be **TTC.** He can be an interned HSDC, or *any* class, to be transferable to the HGC. He does not have to have the class of the org in order to audit in the HGC. He *must* be fully interned on his class, though. (BFO 141)

TECH VFP EXPEDITOR, see FLAG TECH VFP EXPEDITOR.

TELEPHONE INTERVIEW, type of **interview.** An abbreviated version of the news interview. Because it is conducted by **phone,** the questions must be extremely clear and well defined. It is very important in this type of **interview,** as in all interviews, to apply an understanding of human emotion. The reporter must bear in mind that answers are the product he wants and his only barrier to this is human emotion and reaction. (BPL 10 Jan 73R)

TELESELLING, coined word for selling done on the telephone.

TELEX, **1.** this is a network of machines from city to city, connected like telephones are connected. A message can be typed in on one **telex** and instantly received at a receiving **telex.** It is much cheaper and easier to administer than telephone. It is faster and more direct than telegram and has less vias. **Telex** is a very good method of fast communication. One can own a machine and have it hooked in to the international network of **telex** lines, like a phone. It is like a telephone-typewriter. (FO 2528) **2.** a means whereby two stations can be in direct hookup with one another via the keyboard. The **telex** machine can also be used for telegrams and cables. (HCO PL 9 Aug 66) **3.** that's a teletype like in the telegraph office. (HCOB 12 Aug 59)

TELEX AND PHONE SECTION, **section** in Department 2, Department of Communications. **Telex and Phone Section** handles all **telexes,** handles **phone** comm systems, liaison with GPO. (HCO PL 17 Jan 66 II)

TELEX COMM CYCLE, **telexes** have a definite **comm cycle.** That **comm cycle** is (a) order or question, (b) compliance or answer, and (c) ack. (BPL 12 Jun 73R II)

TELEX LOG BOOK, it is the duty of the **telex** operator to see that enough money is allocated for **telex** bills and to ensure accurate record is kept of all calls made and the time spent on each transmission. A **log book** is to be kept by the **telex** machine and each call out must be **logged.** Each W/E the **telex** operator counts total amount spent in transmission and what the bill will be for that week. (BPL 8 Apr 73 II)

TELEX NUMBER, the only **numbering** system is to be the date system which I use on my **telexes.** The only thing which is different is the symbol on the end of the **numbering,** depending on what is needed. Examples: Mission 4 WW would read 01061WW4. The reply would be 01062WW4. 01=day, 06=month, 2=2nd message sent, WW4 =name of mission. My **telexes** will have R after them, i.e.: 01061R. (FO 824)

TELEX OPERATOR, **1.** the hat of the **telex operator** is to ensure the standardness of the **telex** comm cycle. He nudges **telexes** which have not been answered within 24 hours. He ensures that the origination is clear, concise and clean. In addition, in the case of a reply, he also ensures that it *does* answer the question asked. **Telexes** are returned to the originator or replier for rewriting if in violation of the points above. The **telex** lines are for high velocity, important comm. The **telex operator** as a communicator ensures the integrity of his line by doing the above. (BPL 12 Jun 73R II) **2. telex operator** does not mean "message center." A **telex operator** receives the classified messages in a prepared folder (like OODs) and goes off early, cuts the tape, transmits it quickly, receives the traffic back and cuts the machine off quickly (the longer it runs the more it costs). (FO 1693) *Abbr.* Telex Op.

Telex Operator (Def. 2)

TEMP, a temporary employee usually hired only for a short period of time through an employment agency.

TEMPORARY, 1. a staff member who is newly hired is designated 0 (zero) status after his or her name on the org board. The person is classed as **temporary** until he or she has been to review after a few weeks on post. The **temporary** must obtain a slip from their immediate senior saying they are doing fine on post and present this to Review. Review may require they have a knowledge of the org board and comm lines and their own department before passing them. A **temporary** staff member may be dismissed with or without cause by his immediate superior or by Review or a secretary or anyone senior to a secretary. (HCO PL 4 Jan 66 V) **2.** an impermanent assignment, either for reasons of expediency or under trial. (HCO PL 13 Mar 66)

TEMPORARY EXECUTIVE, a **temporary executive** fills the post on a **temporary** basis, using the word **temporary** in the post title. He or she does not draw the **executive** post's units but draws former units or the units of a leading auditor, whichever is higher. He or she may be removed from post with or without cause by the Assn Sec at any time, or a qualified HCO Sec during the time that HCO Sec is handling a state of emergency. (HCO PL 17 Feb 61, *Staff Post Qualifications, Permanent Executives to be Approved*)

TEMPORARY MAILING LIST, this **list** contains the names and addresses of people who have expressed an interest in Dn or Scn. (BPL 17 May 69R I)

TEMPORARY ORGANIZING BOARD, a **temporary org board** is usually done on a large sheet of paper with the postings in pencil. Corrections can then be made. It is taped up over the old org board for crew display and use, then when corrected in use it is put into Dymo. (OODs 2 Feb 71)

TEMPORARY STAFF MEMBER, 1. a person who is on post but who has not yet been accepted as a permanent staff member; Organization Secretary or LRH can dismiss. (Staff Meeting of the Founding Church, 7 May 57) **2.** a **temporary staff member** is one who is brought on and is going to be or has been here for some time and will be paid in units. He or she would be dismissible by the Association Secretary. (HASI PL 19 Apr 57, *Proportionate Pay Plan*) **3.** a person on post, but not yet accepted as a permanent staff member. This individual can be hired or fired by the department head with the permission of the Organization Secretary. (SEC ED 75, 2 Feb 59)

TENANCY, 1. the possession or occupancy of land or real property by title, under a lease or by payment of rent. 2. the period of time of a tenant's authorized occupancy, possession or use of property. 3. a habitation or dwelling held or occupied by a tenant.

TENANT, 1. one who temporarily holds, occupies or uses land; a dwelling or other property owned by another. 2. in law, one who holds or possesses ownership of land, dwellings or buildings by title.

TENDER, 1. a formal offer of money or services to meet the payment of an obligation. 2. an offer or bid in writing to contract goods or services at a specific price or rate. 3. that which is so offered, particularly money.

TENDER, ISSUE BY, see ISSUE BY TENDER.

TEN PER CENT ROYALTY, LRH, an individual, owns, since he paid for the original research as well as later research and never received a salary for doing it, all copyrights, registered marks and trade marks and rights of Dn and Scn. Orgs send **10%** to Saint Hill and this is used by HASI to administer orgs, paying for communication costs, administration, bulletins, etc., etc. It is invoiced to the Saint Hill Org and has never been given to LRH, an individual, a matter of record. Some U.S. **10%** have been held by LRH, a trustee, and returned in legal in loans and other official matters to orgs in the U.S. Therefore the **10% royalty** owed for use of name, materials and research by orgs has never in fact been paid. The franchise 10% is similarly used up by Saint Hill in giving service. No org or field auditor or franchise holder has ever paid for its use of name, copyrights, material, writing and research. (HCO PL 21 Dec 65)

TERCOM, a terman who is acting as his own communicator. (*HTLTAE,* p. 122)

TERMAN, 1. an individual who is served by a communicator. (*HTLTAE,* p. 74) **2.** an individual who is served by a comstation. The man or woman at the end of a comline. (*HTLTAE,* p. 122)

TERMINAL, 1. something that has mass and meaning which originates, receives, relays and changes particles on a flow line. (HCO PL 25 Jul 72) **2.** a post or **terminal** is an assigned area of responsibility and action which is supervised in part by an executive. (HCO PL 28 Jul 71) **3.** a point that receives, relays and sends communication. When people wear only their own hats then one has **terminals** in the org. (HCO PL 1 Jul 65 III) **4.** the point at the end of a line which performs a specific function with a particle arriving on the line. (FSO 137) **5.** hat. (HCO PL 10 Jul 65) **6.** a group or section which is served by a comstation. Some individuals will not have stations of their own but will be served by the station of their group. **Terminals** can also be remote or roving. (*HTLTAE,* p. 123)

Terminal (Def. 2)

TERMINAL ARBITRATION, see ARBITRATION, TERMINAL.

TERMINAL PEOPLE, organization is composed of **terminals** and lines. The **terminals** are there with a common purpose but they are united by lines. There are really then **terminal people** and line people in the organization. They're two different breeds of cat. It's all right to give a line person a place to sit down but don't let him sit there very long. They are in motion. They are running particles up and down lines. If there is nobody there to chase particles up and down lines and separate particles and spread them out and do this and that with them and make sure that the flow continues then nothing significant really ever arrives at the fixed positions. The fixed positions are necessary to handle traffic to change it, to get it into the organization and get it out of the organization. A person moving line particles would see that a person went to the next **terminal.** That's not a function of the **terminal. Terminals** can't do this. There's a **terminal** and then another **terminal** and there's a line between these two **terminals.** (5812C16)

TERMINATEDLY HANDLE, when I say **terminatedly handle** I mean finishedly **handle.** That it is **handled** and that's all, boy! (HCO PL 4 May 68)

Terminatedly Handle

TERMOTE, 1. a terman who is remote from his comstation and who is in touch with it by telephone, radio, or duplicate, but who does not handle or see the original white. (*HTLTAE,* p. 122) **2.** remote terminal. (*HTLTAE,* p. 122)

TERMS, the exact conditions or stipulations that define the characteristics and limits of an agreement between a seller and a buyer.

TEROV, **1.** roving terman and roving terminal. (*HTLTAE,* p. 76) **2.** similar in function to a remote terman, but moving around. (*HTLTAE,* p. 122)

TERRITORIAL POOL, see POOL, TERRITORIAL.

TESTIMONIAL, 1. a written recommendation or letter on another's worth or character. 2. a written statement recommending a product or service which is used for sales promotion and advertising purposes. 3. something given as a tribute to a person's achievements or long service in an organization such as a testimonial dinner.

TESTING, 1. an examination of the quality and integrity of some product or thing often done by subjecting it to normal or abnormal stress or usage. 2. giving people a series of questions to fill out, the answers to which will determine such things as IQ, leadership potential, aptitude, etc.

TESTING PROCEDURE, the essence of **testing procedure** is (a) to get the person to do a **test** and (b) get him or her to come in to have it evaluated. From this follows his or her buying processing and training as sold to the person by PrR at the same time as the evaluation is done. (HCO PL 28 Oct 60, *New Testing Promotion Section Important*)

TEST MARKETING, see MARKETING, TEST.

TEST SECTION, **1.** by means of advertising mailings and word of mouth, the public is brought in to be **tested** and evaluated. This is done by the **test section** of the PE Foundation. This **section** does everything possible to route new individuals into a PE Course. (HCO PL 20 Dec 62) **2.** contains all **test** files, all **test** supplies, E-meter for case assessment (done by **Test** in-Charge), broad arm type desks (or chairs and tables) and is arranged to **test** a large number of people at once. The door is plainly marked "**Testing Section.**" The walls have signs which mention Scn with positive statements and **test** examples showing what Scn can do (befores and afters). (HCO PL 28 Oct 60, *New Testing Promotion Section Important*)

T-GROUP TRAINING, see TRAINING, T-GROUP.

THEETIE-WEETIE, **1.** a person who is very **theetie weetie** has a tremendous number of significances and has a very high OCA. They're kind of fey, it's all very significant (super-significances), i.e., "Ohhh, I was just wondering if you would come around and see me today because yesterday I sort of had an idea that I saw you looking in my direction and this told me somehow . . . " It's a sort of not quite with it or on it. Such a person with super-significance and a high OCA will fall on the OCA under processing to an extremely low left side and then a very low right side and then will come back up into normal range and be sane. (ESTO 3, 7203C02 SO I) **2.** goodie-goodie. (HCO PL 18 Sept 67)

THEFT REPORT, staff member **report** of the disappearance of anything that should be there giving anything known about its disappearance such as when it was seen last. (HCO PL 1 May 65)

THEME, a recurring pattern, the unifying pattern, the unifying factor of the issue, the basic push, "sell," goal or communications of the issue. (BPL 29 Nov 68R)

THEORY, **theory** covers why one goes through the motions. (HCO PL 24 Sept 64)

THEORY COACHING, there is **theory coaching** as well as practical coaching. **Coaching theory** means getting a student to define all the words, give all the rules, demonstrate things in the bulletin with his hands or bits of things, and also may include doing clay table definitions of Scn terms. That's all **theory coaching.** It compares to coaching on drills in practical. But it is done on bulletins, tapes and policy letters which are to be examined in the future. **Coaching** is not examining. (HCO PL 4 Oct 64)

THEORY EXAMINER, ensures students know their **theory.** (HCO PL 15 May 63)

THEORY INSTRUCTOR, assists the **theory** supervisor, acts as auditing supervisor. Handles all **theory** administration. (HCO PL 18 Dec 64, *Saint Hill Org Board*)

THEORY SECTION, training courses are divided into three, and only three, sections. These are: the **theory section**, the practical section, the auditing section. In the **theory section** is taken up all applicable **theory** in training. The student is given a checksheet on which all **theory** items are named. The student studies HCO Bulletins, tapes and texts as given in his checksheet. These are studied independently by the student, not in a group of students. (HCO PL 14 May 62)

THEORY SUPERVISOR, handles all **theory** instruction of the course and acts as auditing

supervisor. (HCO PL 18 Dec 64, *Saint Hill Org Board*)

THERMOFAX, [brand name of a type of office copier for photostating. However, a *thermographic* copy is not strictly a *photocopy* as it uses the heat of infrared rays, rather than light, for exposure. The term **Thermofax** is used in HCO PL 12 March 1961 Issue III, *Duties of the Assn Sec's Sec in a Central Organization.*]

THETA, AOUK has a new ship, a 14-foot sailor named the *Theta.* (OODs 2 Sept 69)

THETA COMMUNICATION, one which is upscale; above 2.0. (5904C15)

THETA GROUP AGREEMENT, I differentiate between "bank group think" which occurs in the absence of leadership, and **theta group agreement** which is possible and a source of power when leadership exists. (FO 1844)

THETAN, **1.** the living unit we call, in Scn, a **thetan**, that being taken from the Greek letter *theta*, the mathematic symbol used in Scn to indicate the source of life and life itself. (*Abil Mag 1*) **2.** the person himself—not his body or his name, the physical universe, his mind, or anything else; that which is aware of being aware; the identity which is the individual. The **thetan** is most familiar to one and all as you. (*Aud 25* UK)

THETAN-MIND-BODY-PRODUCT, **1.** the principle on which the org board was originally conceived. It is that of **thetan-mind-body-product.** If there is a **thetan**, a **mind** (organization potential not a harmful mass) can be set up, a **mind** which will organize a **body** which will produce a **product.** If any one of these elements (**thetan-mind-body-product**) is missing then an organization will fail. The **mind** must operate to form a **body.** This **body** is the mest (matter energy space and time) and staff or the organization. This **body** must produce a **product.** This in the HGC, for instance, is resolved cases. (HCO PL 4 Dec 66) **2.** the org board used by the Dianetic Counselling Group is philosophically based upon the most workable pattern that exists at present. Man is set up as follows. First there is the **thetan** (spirit, he himself) which is the source point of ideas and purposes. Then there is the **mind**, which can be likened to the data collection center and file. Then the **body**, which moves in the physical universe and creates effects initiated by the thetan, thereby creating a **product.** Thus the **thetan** conceives of an idea, the **mind** is referred to for data and to relate the idea to the environment which the person is operating in, and then the **body** is directed to put the idea into effect and there is a resultant **product** which can be viewed and corrected or not by the **thetan.** Thus we have a pattern.

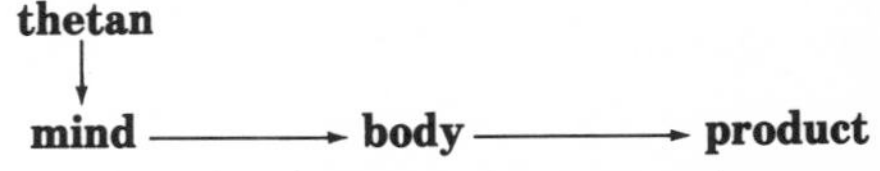

with the **product** matching the original idea of the **thetan.** (BPL 4 Jul 69R VI)

THIN MARKET, see MARKET, THIN.

THIRD DEPUTY CHIEF, see FIRST DEPUTY CHIEF.

THIRD DEPUTY COMMODORE, this is a post by temporary assignment or inheritance of duty in the absence of the Commodore and the First and Second Deputies in order that there will be an official representation of the Commodore when the Commodore and First and Second Deputies are absent. (FO 3342)

THIRD DYNAMIC AUDITING, admin now is on a plane with tech. The administrator is even more skilled as he has to handle numbers of people all at once whereas the auditor handles one at a time. Admin is **third dynamic auditing.** And just like auditing has its standard situations, the tech of admin is a high skill. (OODs 1 Jan 71)

THIRD DYNAMIC DE-ABERRATION, it's a wrong why that causes a group engram, and to de-engramize a group all you have to do is a complete competent evaluation and find the right why and handle it correctly and the group will disemote. In other words data analysis is **third dynamic de-aberration.** (ESTO 2, 7203C01 SO II)

THIRD DYNAMIC (GROUP) DRILLS, an administrator or staff member, even when the group's tech is available and known, must be able to confront and handle the confusions which can occur and which invite a turn away and a squirrel solution. Even this situation of the inabilities to confront and handle can be solved by **third dynamic (group) drills** and drills on the sixth dynamic (physical universe). The **drills** would be practices in achieving general awareness and confronting and handling the noise and confusions which make one oblivious of or which drive one off and away from taking standard actions. (HCO PL 25 Jan 71) See ADMINISTRATIVE TRAINING DRILLS.

THIRD DYNAMIC TRIANGLE, I wonder if there isn't a **third dynamic triangle** like the ARC Triangle that goes:

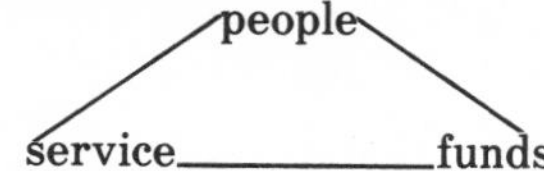

Maybe People are A, Service is R and Funds is C. Sort of a solid ARC triangle. Seems to work that when you drop out people you drop out service you drop out funds. An org that dismisses staff to save money drops service and winds up with a high debt. In an org when I manage one directly, I always push up numbers of staff, push up service and the money rolls in. There is a contrary fact. Governments use tons of people, absorb tons of funds and give no service and are largely out of ARC. So it isn't just numbers of people that made the A. "People" probably needs a special definition. It may be "beings" or "productive individuals" or people in affinity with each other. (OODs 6 Aug 70)

Third Dynamic Triangle (People—Service—Funds)

THIRD (3rd) MATE, **1.** (flagship) the **3rd Mate** is in charge of Division 1 (Personnel Communications and Ethics—similar to a division 1 in a local org). (FO 2674) **2.** Division 1, HCO, is known as the Communications Division and the **3rd Mate** is its divisional officer. (FO 1109) **3.** is in charge of Division 1, the **3rd Mate** is also LRH Comm for the ship. (FO 114)

THIRD PARTY, **1.** one who by false reports creates trouble between two people, a person and a group or a group and another group. (HCO PL 15 Mar 69) **2.** a **third party** adds up to suppression by giving false reports on others. (HCO PL 24 Feb 69)

Third Party (Def. 1)

THIRD PARTY LAW, the **law** would seem to be: a **third party** must be present and unknown in every quarrel for a conflict to exist. Or, for a quarrel to occur, an unknown **third party** must be active in producing it between two potential opponents. Or, while it is commonly believed to take two to make a fight, a **third party** must exist and must develop it for actual conflict to occur. (HCO PL 26 Dec 68)

THOMAS PACKAGE, see PUBLIC DISSEMINATION MANUAL.

THREATENING SOURCES, types of persons who have caused us considerable trouble. (HCO PL 27 Oct 64) See PTS TYPES A TO J.

THREE BASKET SYSTEM, all personnel assigned a desk and a specific stationary working space are to have a stack of **three baskets.** The top **basket**, labelled "in," should contain those items and despatches still to be looked at. The middle **basket**, labelled "pending," is to contain those items which have been looked at, but which cannot be dealt with immediately. The bottom **basket**, labelled "out," is to contain those items which have been dealt with and are now ready for distribution into the comm lines again, or to files, etc. (HCO PL 30 Mar 66)

THREE (3) MAY PL, HCO PL 3 May 1972, *Executive Series 12, Ethics and Executives.* (BPL 4 Oct 72R) [The **3 May PL** lays down the steps an executive must take to get ethics in on a downstat area and lists out the steps of the First Dynamic Danger Formula and how an executive uses it.]

THREE M's, expression standing for "men, money and materials" and which is also written as "3 M's" or "MMM."

THREE R's, reading, writing and arithmetic. (FO 2013)

THREE TECHNOLOGIES, we have **three** invaluable **technologies.** (1) Dn and Scn **tech.** (2) Organizational **tech.** (3) Mission and Missionaire **tech.** (FO 2431)

THREE WAY CO-AUDIT, student A **audits** student B who **audits** student C who **audits** student A. (BPL 26 Jan 72R VIII)

THRESHOLD AGREEMENT, an agreement to raise the salary of employees automatically as soon as the cost of living rises above a set level.

THRIVING, steadily growing membership and Scn activities being carried out regularly. (BO 37 UK, 26 Jan 74)

THROGMAGOG, the Great God **Throgmagog.** He doesn't exist. He's everywhere at once. He's in all drinking water. If we say the Great God **Throgmagog** caused it the condition can never be erased. People get very upset with it because they can never penetrate to the causation. Never being able to penetrate to causation they cannot eradicate the condition so the condition goes on forever. (5611C15)

THROW-AWAY, your promo is going out and gets received amongst thousands of other advertisements for soap, refrigerators, shoes and sealing wax. The public, deluged by this constant flow, tends to briefly glance at the promo and tosses it **away.** They see it and if it's not sharp enough, and if it doesn't push the right button fast enough, they pass on by. Promo that gets this treatment is called **throw-away.** (BPL 13 Jul 72R)

THROW-AWAY TIME, you can actually test the **throw-away time** of your promo with a stop watch. Slip a piece of your promo in a magazine and hand it to someone. **Time** how long they read your promo piece while flicking through the magazine. If they pass right by it, you know there is something wrong. (BPL 13 Jul 72R)

Three R's

THRUSTER, a term designating an individual executive or company which thrusts forward aggressively in its operations and energetically employs opportunities to the greatest possible advantage.

THURSDAY REPORT, the **Thursday Report** should give (a) production personally accomplished since last **Thursday**. (b) org outnesses noted. (c) org outnesses personally corrected. (d) personal progress made in personal training and processing. (LRH ED 128 INT)

TICKER, an instrument for printing the quantity and prices of security transactions within minutes after each trade through the U.S. or Canada.

TIGER, 1. a pretended member (staff member) who has been repeatedly associated with goofed projects and operations and who actually has caused such to occur. He is a person who is a continued out-ethics person. He has failed to get ethics in on himself. (FO 872) **2.** someone who is not about to let the org or staff succeed. (HCO PL 27 Feb 71 I) [This is the derogatory form of this term and when it is used by LRH is not always meant in the above sense.]

TIGER LIST, 1. persons on the **tiger list** may not go on missions or hold major exec posts. It has been found by correlating lists of people in goofed projects that a continual recurrence of several names occurs. So this way we have these people labelled and we will have the trouble sources isolated. (FO 872) **2.** no-change or enturbulative personnel observed over a period of time. (FO 1324)

TIGHT MONEY, a situation where money is hard to come by and the money flow is weak. People are holding on to their money and not spending or investing due to lack of confidence created by unstable conditions such as a depression.

TIME AND A HALF PAY, premium salary rate which is one and one-half times the rate that the employee usually earns, and which is paid to him for overtime work (ordinarily over 40 hours per week) or for work done at an unconventional time such as on a Sunday.

TIME-AND-MOTION STUDY, a study of how long it takes and what motions a person must go through to complete a job. The data is used to get rid of redundant motions or inefficient actions and to set proper work standards throughout a company.

TIME BUDGET, see BUDGET, TIME.

TIME CARD, a standard card form, filled in by an employee or stamped when he inserts it into a time clock, recording his arrival and departure times each day.

TIMEKEEPING DEPARTMENT, the department in charge of handling, auditing and keeping the records of employees' attendance and number of hours at work.

TIME LOAN, a loan that must be paid back by a specific time.

TIME MACHINE, (Department 3) Inspection has a **time machine.** This is a series of baskets advanced one basket every morning. A carbon of an order is placed in today's basket. When the original comes in, the carbon is dug out of the basket (by date and color flash) and original and carbon are clipped together and routed to the issuing executive. Orders not complied with in one week of course fall off the **time machine** by appearing in the basket being emptied today. (It was filed one week ago and advanced once each day.) A copy is made of the order and it is sent to Ethics for filing in the staff member's ethics folder and counts as a report against the staff member. The carbon is returned to issuing executive to show his order has not been complied with, so that he can handle the situation. (HCO PL 1 May 65 II) *Abbr.* TM

TIME NOTE, a promissory note or similar contract specifying a date or series of dates for repayment.

TIME NOTED, a plus-point. **Time** is properly **noted.** (HCO PL 3 Oct 74)

TIME ORDER, see ORDER, TIME.

TIME SPAN OF DISCRETION, the period of time that an executive is able to function on his discretion before he makes an error of commission or omission big enough to have his superiors intervene.

TIME STUDY, a study and recording of how long it takes for someone to do a job so that job standards may be fabricated or so that the results can be compared against already established standards.

TIREDNESS, the more failed purposes a guy has stacked up the **tireder** he will be. The fellow who has a tremendous ambition to be something or other, has got some fire to be it, and he's got some energy, and he's got some action, and he is driving forward toward being that thing. But the guy who wants to be something else which he never will be and he couldn't be in the first place, and you're trying to hat, will just get kind of tired, because you're keying in his failed purpose. But **tiredness** *is* failed purpose. Don't think it's anything else, it isn't. (ESTO 10, 7203C05 SO II)

TITLE, a document that gives one the rights of ownership to a certain piece of tangible property or an intangible such as a patent.

TITLE A, there are three kinds of possessions in organizations. **Title A** are permanent installations, buildings, walls, radiators, anything fixed in place. (HCO PL 15 Feb 64)

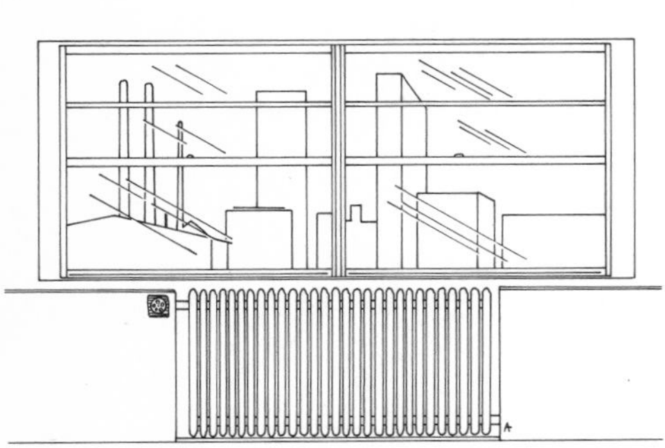

Title "A"

TITLE B, valuable equipment which is not expendable. These are desks, typewriters, mimeo machines, blackboards, chairs, furniture, rugs, decorations, cars, etc. (HCO PL 15 Feb 64)

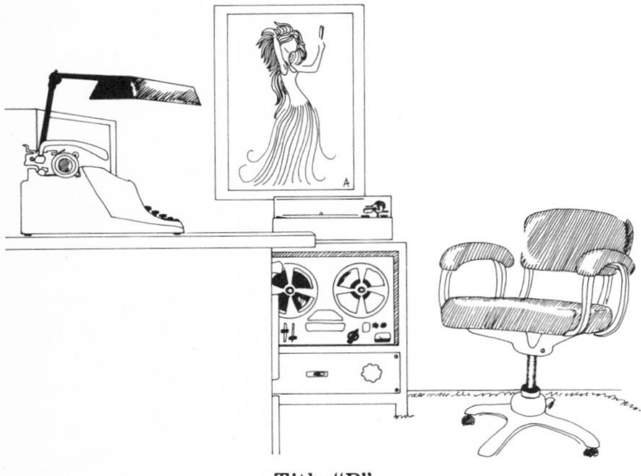

Title "B"

TITLE C, these are expendables. Office supplies, paper, chalk, stencils, dust rags, mops, etc. They are issued on the understanding they will get used up. (HCO PL 15 Feb 64)

TITLES ORG BOARD, you write up the functions of the org board of the division by departments on a separate model and add the valuable final products per HCO Policy Letter 4 March 1972. This gives you the functions to get out the VFPs expected. These functions will or won't get out the VFPs. What functions are needed to get them out? By blocking in these you have now a function org board. From this function org board you can now make up a **titles org board.** Each **title** has some of these functions. The functions must be of the same general type for the **title.** When you have done this (with divisional secretary, divisional org officer and divisional Esto and department heads) you now have **titles org board.** (HCO PL 6 Apr 72)

TOHS, an agent of the spiritual world in primitive cultures. (LRH Def. Notes)

TOLERANCE, an allowable deviation from a certain standard, beyond which the item is classed as substandard.

TONE 40, now of course **tone 40** isn't yelling. It is simply the degree of intention you can put into some of this. It's the amount of intention. Now you radiate that intention if your expectancy is good. You don't have to be loud and haughty or anything of the sort. It's just the normal action but your expectancy on what you say and so on can have a fantastic effect. (ESTO 6, 7203C03 SO II)

Title "C"

TONE SCALE, a person in apathy rises through various **tones.** These **tones** are quite uniform; one follows the next and people always come up through these tones, one after the other. These are the tones of affinity, and the **tone scale** of Dn and

Scn is probably the best possible way of predicting what is going to happen next or what a person actually will do. The **tone scale** starts well below apathy. In other words, a person is feeling no emotion about a subject at all. On many subjects and problems people are actually well below apathy. There the **tone scale** starts, on utter, dead null far below death itself. Going up into improved tones one encounters the level of body death, apathy, grief, fear, anger, antagonism, boredom, enthusiasm and serenity, in that order. There are many stops between these **tones.** A person in grief, when his **tone** improves feels fear. A person in fear, when his **tone** improves feels anger. (*POW*, pp. 77-78)

Tone Scale

TOO LITTLE TOO LATE, the hallmark of bad promotion is **too little too late.** Probably the most aggravating and most suppressive error that can be made by those doing promotion or other PR actions, is to plan or announce an event too close to the date for anyone to come. **Too little** promotion **too late.** (HCO PL 28 May 71)

TOP MANAGEMENT, top management lays down and/or okays policy, programs and plans. Juniors issue the orders to get the plans done. (CBO 51)

TOP-OUT, the point of highest demand or sales in the life of a product.

TOP QUALITY PRINTING, top quality printing doesn't mean top cost. It means having a qualified and competent **printer** and demanding and accepting only **top quality.** (CBO 281)

TORT, in law, a wrongful act by one person causing injury or damage to another or to his property, either intentionally or through negligence as exemplified in assault and battery, defamation or unauthorized entry or use of property.

TOTAL DEPARTMENT 6 INCOME, the **total** collected by **Department 6** for the week, includes re-sign GI, arrival GI, phone GI and Division 2 Travelling Registrar GI. (BFO 119)

TOTAL FLAG EXPENSES, Flag expenses plus canteen/bookstore. (HCO PL 9 Mar 72 I)

TOTAL FLAG RECEIPTS, total Flag (Flag Admin Org) collections, Management Bureau income plus canteen/bookstore. (HCO PL 9 Mar 72 I)

TOTAL INCOME, a person's or company's income left after the deduction of all expenditures from the gross income.

TOTAL RECEIPTS, gross income=total invoiced on income lines by the AO from all sources. Also called **total receipts.** (FO 1828)

TOUR MEMBER, the prime purpose of a **tour member** is: to contact, sign up and collect advance payments from individuals for technical services the org can and will deliver in order that each individual may be fully salvaged by org services and increase the size of the organization. A **tour member** in actual fact is expediting for the Advance Scheduling Registrar. (BPL 15 Sept 71R I)

TOURS, Flag Continental Liaison Offices, with their **tours,** drove people in on the orgs and made the boom in '71. These **tours** drove people in on local org and on Sea Org orgs as well. The original **tours** were clean cut personal contact work. It takes book advertising and book selling and **tour** personal contact work to make booms. These are the two outside the org actions that drive people in on orgs and drive stats up. **Tours** functions should be under a Flag Operations Liaison Office Div 6 and should be coordinated. (HCO PL 28 May 72)

TOURS GI, total monies collected by Div 6 **tours** for the week. (BFO 119)

TOURS ORG, the **Tours Org** is situated within Division 6 of the FOLO. **Tours Orgs** must have expert registrars. The **Tours Orgs** provide additional income assistance to orgs. They drive business in on orgs and push org incomes up into higher ranges than before. The **Tours Org** activities are very successful. They get people into service orgs by contacting them, signing them up and collecting the money from them for org services. This is not only a help to orgs, but an incentive for the org to do more itself. In exchange for this service, the **Tours Org** receives a 10% commission on all monies they collect for an org. (BPL 20 Apr 73 II)

TOURS TARGET AREA, an **area targetted** for promo saturation and a **tour** from Flag. (BFO 122-6) *Abbr.* TTA.

TR 8B VOICE CONTROL, see SEA ORG VOICE CONTROL DRILL.

TRACK RECORD, a term referring to how a person has performed on the job in the past. A person with a history of laudable accomplishments is said to have a good track record.

TRACK SHEET, a write-up of the lines of flow and how materials should be employed throughout the sequence of producing something.

TRADE, 1. an occupation requiring skilled labor, as in a craft. 2. business of buying and selling commodities or stocks. 3. the customers, collectively, of a particular business, store or industry.

TRADEMARK, 1. a legally registered name or design belonging to an individual, group or company and restricted to their use for identifying their products or organization. 2. some distinguishing sign, characteristic or activity associated with a person, product or company by which they are known.

TRADE NAME, 1. name under which a company operates. 2. name, sometimes coined, by which a product, service or process is known.

TRADE PROMOTIONS, see PROMOTIONS, TRADE.

TRADER, 1. a dealer in a trade or commerce who makes a livelihood by buying and selling for profit. 2. one who buys and sells securities for himself only, sometimes for short term profit. 3. a ship engaged in foreign trade.

TRADE UNION, a labor union whose membership is limited to persons engaged in the same trade or industry and whose officials represent the members in matters of terms and conditions of employment, pay rates, holidays and other benefits.

TRADING ON THE EQUITY, borrowing capital at a low rate of interest in order to make an investment wherein anticipated earnings will be higher than the interest charges.

TRADING POST, one of a series of trading areas on the floor of a stock exchange, each of which is assigned certain stocks for buying and selling.

TRADING SYSTEM, see BARTER SYSTEM.

TRAFFIC, 1. the commercial exchange or trading of goods. 2. the flow of persons, vehicles or messages along transportation, commerce or communication lines. 3. the customers, collectively, who patronize a store or business concern.

TRAFFIC CONTROL, the action of reviewing all telex traffic and seeing which cycles have not completed and forcing them to get completed swiftly and correctly. (FO 2528)

TRAFFIC CONTROL BOARD, a large cork board divided up into the different areas to which we communicate. Its purpose is to display message cycles clearly. Messages are displayed for two reasons, to keep people informed and to permit **traffic control. Traffic control** is the action of reviewing all telex traffic and seeing which cycles have not completed and forcing them to get completed swiftly and correctly. The **board** is arranged so that the first telex of a cycle is posted over to the left-hand side of the correct area of the **board.** On a very good **board** a card is posted to the left of the first message stating in one or two words what that message cycle is about, such as the name of the mission or ship it concerns. To the right of the first message is placed the second message of this cycle, when it comes in. To the right of this is placed the third, etc., until the cycle is complete. When the message cycle is complete, it is removed off the **board.** (FO 2528)

TRAFFIC MANAGER, the person in charge of traffic activities in an organization which includes receiving, packing, shipping, warehousing and the scheduling and supervision of company delivery vehicles.

TRAINED, by **TRAINED** is meant: (1) Fully hatted for his post by an approved not mini hat checksheet for that post, (2) **Trained** fully to graduation and Interneship for the Admin or Technical skills ideally acceptable for that post, (3) **Training** validated by acceptable stats for that post. *Note:* Any department head must have done the OEC volume fully in formal study for his division, or any Divisional head must have done the OEC and any CO or ED or Deputy must have done an FEBC. No technical post may be considered fully **trained** unless also fully interned in a competent interneship. (HCOPL 4 Nov 76)

TRAINED SCIENTOLOGIST, a **trained Scientologist** is not a doctor. He is someone with special knowledge in the handling of life. (HCOB 10 Jun 60)

TRAINEE, a person who is actively engaged in training related to some occupation, job or activity.

TRAINEE-APPRENTICE SYSTEM, now if the chief specialist in each specialty is designated and takes each new **trainee**, recruit or crew member, for that action under his wing and really gets him into the groove before declaring him a specialist in that specialty we will really have it made. The scene will continue on a **trainee-apprentice system** which combines theory and practical on the actual post before a new specialist is made. (OODs 6 Jul 70)

Trainee-Apprentice System

TRAINING, **1. training** consists of a **trained training** personnel who *can* **train**, the materials from which to **train** and the use of **training** drills and know-how and two-way comm with students to clean up their studies. (LRH ED 129 INT) **2.** in registration, it is imperative that one pushes **training.** This means Division 4 **training**—HSDC, Scn Academy **training** on levels 0 to IV and Qual internships. (LRH ED 112 INT) **3.** a formal activity imparting the philosophy or technology of Dn and Scn to an individual or group and culminates in the award of a grade or certificate. (*Aud 2* UK) **4.** if **training** is defined as making a person or team into a part of the group then processing is an influencing factor. (HCO PL 14 Dec 70)

TRAINING ADMINISTRATOR, purpose: to keep the materials and comm lines of the Academy in good order. To keep a roll book. To prepare and collect certification materials. (HCO PL 12 Oct 62)

TRAINING AIDE, CS-2. (BPL 8 May 69R III)

TRAINING AND SERVICES AIDE, see CS-4.

TRAINING AND SERVICES BUREAU, 1. that **bureau** on Flag, responsible for **training**, processing and other technical matters. (BTB 12 Apr 72R) **2.** (Bu 5A FB) the **Training and Services Bureau** contains three branches: the Materials Branch, the Qual FB Branch and the Tech Quality Control Branch. In the Materials Branch comes course compilations, under the Qual Branch comes Qual functions for the Flag Bureau, and under the Tech Quality Control Branch comes flub catch, students to Flag from outer orgs for **training**, and TTC and ATC (Admin Training Corps) and establishment and expansion. (SO ED 485 INT) **3.** The Organizing Bureau's keynotes are getting people, and data to train people. The **Training and Service Bureau** joins the data furnished to the people furnished. Its cycle is inspect (by checklist) assess the needful actual demand checksheets and packs (which it files) and **train** the people in its **Training** Unit and when they are slow, process them in its Processing Unit. It says in its Exam-Correct-Cert Branch they have been **trained.** They **train** for orgs and Bureaus and take from orgs to retrain or reprocess and they process bureau personnel. They have the checksheet and pack library as made up and published by the Org Bureau. Their chief cycle is to detect need of and to join with **training** people and data. (CBO 7) **4.** a new complete Bureaux Org Board is posted and displayed on Flag and is being readied for export to CLOs. **Training and Service Bureau** is the fifth division with the present org board of Division 5. A/CS-5 runs the **Training and Service Bureau** and programs, crams (on hat checksheets) the Bureaux people and whoever should be called in and given a workover in the orgs or area on his **training** or case. (FBDL 12)

TRAINING, APPRENTICE, training given to an apprentice by a qualified employer or journeyman. The apprentice assists one already accomplished in the trade and through practical experience and instruction he gradually attains a high level of proficiency. An agreement between the apprentice and employer governs how long the apprentice will work for the employer, at what wages and for how much instruction.

TRAINING, BOOSTER, training received by persons already employed, to improve performance, reacquaint them with the job or bring them up to date on the latest techniques.

TRAINING, CRAFT, the substantial amount of training and apprenticeship needed to make a person a craftsman in his trade.

TRAINING, DESK, office, administrative or commercial training done on the job.

TRAINING, EMPLOYEE, any form of training or education whereby an employee learns how to do a job or whereby employees are improved in their skills or prepared to take on higher or new positions.

TRAINING, EXECUTIVE, any training that develops executive abilities in a person. It would have to teach a person how to get compliance to programs, projects and orders that further the goals or aims of a particular organization.

TRAINING, FORMAL, instruction of employees that uses certain accepted or recognized classroom forms such as courses, textbook study, special criteria, lectures, films, conferences and so forth.

TRAINING, IN-COMPANY, employee training held on the company premises or in its own factory, plant, etc. It may feature outside consultants and lecturers but often the company has its own. Also called in-plant training.

TRAINING, INFORMAL, instruction of employees by demonstration of how to do actual tasks and then observing their performance while giving them additional pointers and advice.

TRAINING, JOB, a very broad term to cover any training that teaches a person how to do or better do a specific job. This can be training to qualify for a job in the future or to better qualify for a job one is already doing. It may be part of a company training program, vocational or trade school training, apprenticeships, in-plant training, in-company training, self-initiated training, etc.

TRAINING, MANAGEMENT, see MANAGEMENT EDUCATION.

TRAINING OFFICER, (Gung-Ho Group) the **Training Officer** handles all **training** of whatever kind, including the **training** of the group, and any school. (HCO PL 2 Dec 68)

TRAINING OFFICER, the executive who has dominant influence and authority over an organization's training systems.

TRAINING, OFF-THE-JOB, training that occurs away from company facilities but which is geared toward meeting company demands. It is training prior to employment or supplementary to on-the-job training and occurs at a university, trade school or any training center.

TRAINING, ON-THE-JOB, training of a person while he is on the job. It would include supervision of his actions and use of machinery and inspection of his products with correction as needed. He may also be engaged in or have completed related textbook study.

TRAINING, OUTSIDE, off-the-job training.

TRAINING ROUTE, there are two routes to Clear and OT: the **training** (or professional) **route** and the processing (or pc) **route.** A person on this **route** (**training**) co-audits up to Expanded Grade IV Release on his HSDC, Academy levels and SHSBC. He receives power processing at a Saint Hill before beginning Solo at an Advanced Org. (SO ED 269 INT)

TRAINING, SENSITIVITY, group training by which each person develops sensitivity, perceptive abilities and proficiency in ascertaining how others see him.

TRAINING, SIMULATED, training given in an environment in which conditions are created that are as alike as possible to actual working conditions.

TRAINING, T-GROUP, human relations training for employees emphasizing the importance and interplay of personal relationships and events, thus heightening an individual's awareness of himself, his actions and his potential within the group.

TRAINING TIME, length of time a trainee takes to become standardly accomplished in a job and thus assume responsibility for his work.

TRAINING, VESTIBULE, employee training given at a location away from the company's work areas but which is equipped to closely approximate actual working conditions.

TRANSCRIPTION, an exact, complete, word-for-word duplication of what LRH said in a taped lecture; it is proofread, but unedited. (BPL 9 Jan 74 IV)

TRANSFER, 1. the moving of an employee from one job to another, from one department to another or from one geographical location to another. 2. to hand over the possession or legal title of something to another.

TRANSFER AGENT, a person who keeps track of the name, address and number of shares owned by each shareholder. He issues new certificates in the name of transferees and cancels certificates sent in for transfer.

TRANSFER, INTERDEPARTMENTAL, a moving of personnel, materials or equipment from one department to another.

TRANSFER, INTRADEPARTMENTAL, the moving of personnel, materials or equipment inside a department.

TRANSFERITIS, people on personnel posts in companies have followed a nineteenth century psychological approach that if a person can't do one post he can be **transferred** to another post to which he is better "adapted." "Talent," "native skill," all sorts of factors are given. But if a person with all things considered in the first place is then found to do badly on that post, the second think of nineteenth century personnel was to transfer him to another post and yet another and another. The third think when again he fails is then to fire him. **Transferring** under these circumstances is usually not only wrong for the person but strews the error all through the org. (HCO PL 10 Sept 70)

TRANSFER, PRODUCTION, the transfer of employees from jobs where production demand has decreased to areas where it has increased. This prevents having to lay off good staff and hire others to man areas of need.

TRANSFER, REPLACEMENT, 1. the transfer of an individual within a company to fill a vacancy brought about by severance of another or a voluntary departure. 2. the transfer that favors a long-service employee, moving him into a position in another department and resulting in the separation of a shorter-service person, done only when a company is deteriorating and management is trying to retain its older employees.

TRANSIT COMPANIES, **transit companies** arrange the collection of goods from one place and delivery to the stevedoring company, including clearing the goods through customs. They may or may not own their own transport with which they do this, and may or may not do their own clearance through customs. (FO 2738)

TRANSLATIONS ADMINISTRATOR, in a Scn **Translation** Unit, there must be someone keeping in the basic admin of the courses being **translated**, such as updating checksheets and packs, obtaining materials, etc.; and handling the **translators'** stats, graphs, routing forms, and so on. The person who holds this post is called the **Translations Administrator.** (BPL 9 Jan 74 III)

TRANSLATIONS AND INTERPRETATION SECTION, the **Translations and Interpretation section** of the Flagship, Division 2, Department 5 now has the duty of training the various languages of this planet to Sea Org members. This **section** is to compile checksheets for French, Spanish, English, German, Greek for a starter. Also all materials (i.e. books, records, tapes, etc.) are to be compiled. (FO 955)

TRANSLATIONS UNIT, (Pubs Org DK) **Translations Unit** produces the valuable final product: the relay of a technology into the understanding of a people. (Includes both **translation** tapes and written **translations.**) (BPL 22 Jan 74 II) *Abbr.* TU.

TRANSPORT OF COMPANY (FLAG) PERSONNEL, this is defined as the cost of **transporting Flag Personnel** to be stationed at **Flag.** These are either (a) recruits, (b) veterans called for **Flag** duty or (c) specialized **personnel** called for **Flag** duty such as translators. This does not include org or Folo or stationship personnel sent to Flag for training, processing or briefing. A telex or written order signed by the Flag Personnel Procurement Officer (FPPO) and Purser Flag authorizes the expense and Flag expense, and the FPPO is the only terminal who may authorize such an order. (BPL 3 Nov 72RA)

TRANSPORT SUPERVISOR, the care and maintenance of vehicles is the responsibility of the **Transport Supervisor. Transport Supervisor** keeps a record of servicing and repairs for each vehicle noting date and mileage. He ensures that servicings are done at the correct intervals. Vehicles may only be used with permission of the **Transport Supervisor** or Chauffeur. **Transport Supervisor** must ensure that vehicles are properly licensed and insured. (BPL 19 Feb 60)

TRANSPORT UNIT, the post of Ship's Boats and Transport I/C and the Boats and **Transport Unit** are in Division 4, Department 12 of the Flagship's org board. It has a 24-hour duty to provide safe, dependable transport service to the orgs aboard Flag. It is manned by an I/C and two deputies who are on a watch system. For convenience it is called the **Transport Unit** and its in-charge, **Transport** I/C. (FO 2677-1)

TRANSPOSITION, (codes and coding) mixing up the sequence of letters, numbers of words is called **transposition.** (HCO PL 11 Sept 73)

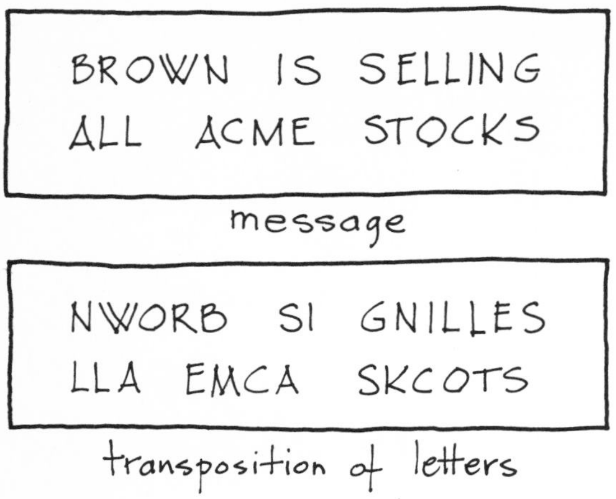

BROWN IS SELLING
ALL ACME STOCKS

message

NWORB SI GNILLES
LLA EMCA SKCOTS

transposition of letters

Transposition

TRAVELLING REG GI, (Division 2 **Travelling Reg GI**) total monies collected by Division 2 **Travelling Registrars** for the week. (BFO 119)

TREASON, 1. when one knowingly takes the pay or favors of a group's or project's enemies while appearing to be a friend of or part of the group or project, the condition is **Treason.** (HCO PL 6 Oct 67) **2.** (below Enemy) is defined as betrayed after trust. Formerly was differently placed and defined as accepting money. (FO 516)

TREASON FORMULA, the **formula** for the condition of **treason** is "find out that you are." (HCO PL 16 Oct 68)

TREASURER, 1. (DCG) Division 3, Treasury Division is headed by the **Treasurer.** (BPL 4 July 69R VI) **2.** purpose: to carry on Scn. To be certain the organization remains solvent. (HCO London, 9 Jan 58)

TREASURER, the financial officer of an organization who has charge of its funds and revenue, authorizes expenditures, maintains records of these and associated transactions, and reports directly to the President and Board of Directors.

TREASURER BOARD OF DIRECTORS OF HASI, INC., oversees all financial records and reports of the company and all branches. Retains the financial, bank account and report files, including tax and non-profit status documents. Enforces financial policy within the company and all branches. (HCO PL 18 Dec 64, *Saint Hill Org Board)*

TREASURY AIDE, 1. Treasury Aide (CS-3) is located on the org board over Division 3. Her area of responsibility is that of **Treasury** Division 3s. (FDD 18 Treas INT) At this time **Treasury Aide** was a full Commodore's Staff **Aide** post not to be confused with the later created, junior post of **Treasury Aide** FB. **2.** I expect these things from **Treasury Aide**, quite in addition to "regular duties," (a) to keep logistics flowing and crews uniformed. (b) to keep all outstanding money in the world collected up and not back-dated which destroys it. (c) to get proper FP known and used in every area. (FO 3179) [At this time **Treasury Aide** and CS-3 were two separate Commodore's Staff **Aide** posts.]

TREASURY AIDE FB, (Bureau head of Flag Bureau 3, **Treasury** Bureau) responsible for the production of **Treasury** Bureau, getting all Bureau 3 products produced in volume, **Treasury** Bureau FP originations, FP No. 1 for the **FB**, seeing that security is maintained with money and data, keeps ethics in in Bureau 3 and **FB** on finance matters, sees that income is far greater than outgo. (BFO 94 Attachment)

TREASURY BUREAU, (Flag) contains Accounts Branch with a VFP of accurate statements that go out on schedule to all orgs and individuals who owe Flag monies, Flag Service Consultant Branch with a VFP of high volume advance payments, Flag Collections Branch with a VFP of high volume credit collections from orgs and individuals, and Income Branch with a VFP of rapidly and accurately invoiced, banked and disbursed income from the field and on-board. (FO 3385-11)

TREASURY DIVISION, 1. Treasury, through its standard actions, creates and maintains and improves those material conditions without which no org could hope to survive or expand. The action is basically one of putting the org there—providing it with the body (mest) and energy (funds) without which production becomes almost impossible. (BPL 26 Feb 72R IV) **2.** the department (or **division**) that has charge of the income and expenses. (HCO Admin Letter 30 Jul 75) **3.** Division 3. (HCO PL 8 Nov 73RA)

TREASURY ESTABLISHMENT OFFICER, the **Treasury Establishment Officer establishes** and maintains the **Treasury** Division. (HCO PL 7 Mar 72) *Abbr.* TREO.

TREASURY FB NEWSLETTER, the **Treasury FB Newsletter** is published monthly and has org execs as its public. The purpose of the **Treasury FB Newsletter** is to keep an ideal scene of prosperity and expansion mocked up and make finance policy better known and accepted by org execs; to create enthusiasm toward getting it applied and keep those who are upstat in regards to solvency highly validated. (ED 33 FB)

TREASURY INSPECTORS, inspectors operate from the **Treasury** Bureau 3 of a Continental Liaison Office. The **inspectors** are a mobile team operating from the CLO, but with only external duties (outside the CLO). The **inspectors** can travel from one org to the next, without being attached to any org in particular, nor subject to any orders from local executives. Their function is to move in heavily to **inspect** and correct, where a Division 3 has failed to be established, manned, supervised and operated successfully by local executives. (CBO 125)

TREASURY SECRETARY, it is the specific duty of the **Treasury Secretary** in an org to pick up and trace the course of every particle of money through the entire organization, from the time it enters through the mail or with a customer, until it exits from the org as a disbursement or a reserve action. That is quite a job, and it is the most important job a **Treasury Secretary** has got. It sums up the purpose of the post. It is called accounts policing. To police something means, "to control, regulate, keep in order, administer." The anatomy of accounts policing is: (1) policing income to ensure that the org is collecting the income from the services that it delivers, and that all org income is channelled into **Treasury** and into the bank without delays. (2) policing disbursements to ensure that financial planning occurs and that only monies which are so designated and authorized are allocated out of the org accounts. (3) policing reserves to ensure that the org never spends more than it makes, and that it builds up substantial reserves through excellent control of its income-outgo flows. (BPL 1 Feb 72 I)

TREASURY STOCK, see STOCK, TREASURY.

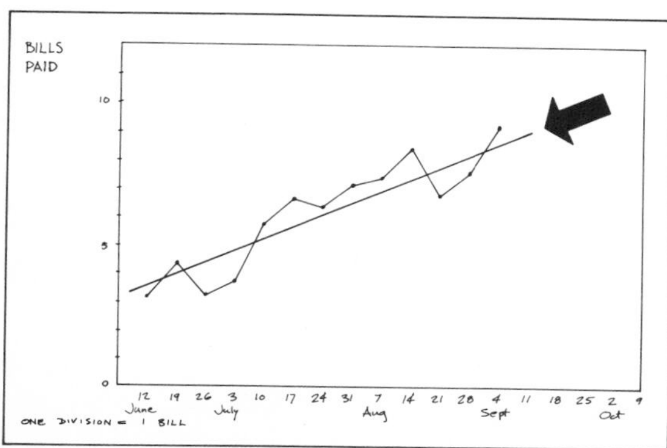

Trend (Def. 1)

TREND, 1. trend means the tendency of statistics to average out up, level or down over several weeks or even months as long as the situation remains. **Trends** can be anything from danger to power, depending on the slant and its steepness. An upward **trend** even if only slightly upward shows people are trying and level or downward shows it is in trouble. **Trend** is the overall measure of expansion or contraction and is the most valuable of statistic messages. (HCO PL 3 Oct 70) **2.** long range drifts up or down. (HCO PL 20 Oct 67)

TREND LINE, one draws a **trend line** by choosing the mid-way point highs and lows and drawing a **line.** (HCO PL 6 Nov 66 I)

TRIAL BALANCE, a check of the debit and credit sides of a double-entry ledger. The sum of the debits should equal the sum of the credits or there is an error.

TRIANGULAR SYSTEM, a **system** by which the Org Officer and the Product Officer are handled by an Executive Director or Commanding Officer. The Commanding Officer, if he were operating with a Product Officer and an Org Officer would be the Planning Officer. He's the Planning and Coordinating Officer. (FEBC 7, 7101C23 SO III)

TRIPLE BONUS SYSTEM, this is called a **triple bonus system** as it has **three** stages of **bonus.** The **bonuses** are payrolls B, C and D. (FSO 135R)

TRIPLE FLOW TRAINING, there are **three** basic **flows** in tech **training**: inflow, outflow,

Triple Flow Training (A) Flow 1

Triple Flow Training (B) Flow 2

Triple Flow Training (C) Flow 3

crossflow. This is the same as in processing where one always runs three flows or "triples." Flow 1 is inflow, or another to self

(1) ←— inflow,

Flow 2 is outflow, or self to another

(2) —→ outflow,

Flow 3 is crossflow, or others to others

(3) ↕ crossflow.

In **training** this becomes: **Flow** 1—learning the data (inflow). **Flow** 2—applying the data (outflow). **Flow** 3—getting others to apply the data (crossflow). One learns the technical data of any level on an Academy or Saint Hill course. One becomes flubless in applying the tech to others by doing a properly supervised internship in the Qualifications Division of a Scn org or Saint Hill. One gets others to apply the data by doing a case supervisor course and apprenticeship for the level in an official Scn org or Saint Hill. Thus we have **triple flow training.** (BPL 26 Apr 73RI)

TROUBLE AREA QUESTIONNAIRE, where a danger condition is assigned to a junior, request that he write up his overts and withholds and any known out-ethics situation and turn them in. Require that each one write up and fully execute the First Dynamic Danger Formula for himself personally and turn it in. If the necessity to by-pass continues or if an area or person did not comply, use a meter and assess the **Trouble Area Questionnaire.** Each **question** that read is given two-way communication until each **question** that read has attained a floating needle. The **questionnaire** can also be used to help find a why (it will not directly find one as the why has to be rephrased for each individual). A why should always be found for individuals in a danger condition. A short form (**Trouble Area** Short Form) can be done on someone who is an "old hand" and knows the tune. (HCO PL 9 Apr 72)

TROUBLE AREA SHORT FORM, see TROUBLE AREA QUESTIONNAIRE.

TROUBLESHOOTER, see EXPEDITERS.

TROUBLESOME RELATIONS, **troublesome relations** is a catch all to include all those **relations** which the organization has not handled with its various publics and which then wind up on Guardian lines. In this category fall business firms which sue the organization, threatening former Scientologists expelled by the Church, non-authorized squirrel groups, hostile members of the immediate community and so on. (BPL 20 May 70I)

TRUE GROUP, could be defined as one which has (a) a theta goal, (b) an active and skilled management working only in the service of the **group** to accomplish the theta goal and (c) participant members who fully contribute to the **group** and its goals and who are contributed to by the **group**; and which has high ARC between goal and management, management and **group**, **group** and goal. (*HTLTAE*, p. 99)

TRUE GROUP MEMBER, (Gung-Ho Group) one must sharply differentiate in giving out "membership" cards between the contributor of money or things and the action member, by always calling the money contributor an "associate" or a "patron" and the time and effort contributor a "full member" or a "**true group member**" or an "active member" on the card. An active member should have a full credentials card with picture, thumb print and description. (HCO PL 3 Dec 68)

TRUNK CALL, toll **call.** (BPL 31 Oct 63R)

TRUST, 1. two or more corporations joined for the purpose of reducing competition and controlling prices throughout an industry. 2. a fund, estate, property, etc., placed in another's nominal ownership to be held, used or disposed of to the advantage of a named beneficiary. 3. the people managing a trust or the assets so held in trust.

TRUSTBUSTER, a government official employed to investigate and dissolve illegal business combinations or trusts.

TRUST COMPANY, see COMPANY, TRUST.

TRUSTEE, 1. an individual or agent, such as a bank, holding legal title to property in order to administer it for a beneficiary. 2. a board member elected or appointed to direct the policies and funds of an institution. 3. in law, a garnishee or debtor against whom a plaintiff has instituted process of garnishment of money or property.

TRUST FUND, an estate, usually money and securities, held or settled in trust.

TRUTH, **truth** is what is **true** for you. (5904C15)

TURNOVER, 1. generally, the amount of business transacted during a given period of time; also called "overturn." 2. in merchandising, the number of times a particular stock of goods is sold and restocked during a given period. 3. in investments, the volume of business in a security or the entire stock market during a given time. 4. in personnel, the number of workers hired by a company to replace those who have left.

TURNOVER COSTS, see COSTS, TURNOVER.

TUTOR, teaches the children or coaches them in their studies. (HCO PL 18 Dec 64, *Saint Hill Org Board*)

Tutor

TWENTY-FOUR HOUR RULE, examiner's **24-hour rule** is: any goofed session must be repaired within **24 hours.** (HCO PL 8 Sept 70R)

TWIN CHECKING, students, being formed into co-audit teams, turnabout, will also do their theory checkouts in pairs. An instructor, in doing a theory checkout will have both students that are listed as co-auditors in the auditing assignment sheet, appear before him when either one requires a checkout and will then check out both students on the same bulletin. The instructor will ask the students alternately his questions and if either student flunks, both flunk the test. This system is called **twin checking.** (HCO PL 28 Feb 65, *Course Checkouts Twin-Checking.*)

TWIN CHECKOUTS, in Scn training we use a system called **twin checkouts.** Each student is assigned a "**twin**" to work with. The student studies his assigned material and is sometimes coached over the rough spots by his **twin.** When the student knows the material, he is then given a **checkout** by his **twin.** If he flunks, he returns to study and when ready gets a new **checkout.** When he passes, the **twin** signs the assignment sheet certifying that he has grasped it. The assignment sheet is turned in to the Course Supervisor at the end of the period. (HCO PL 26 Aug 65)

TWO WATCH SYSTEM, with the **two watch system,** either **watch** can handle a departure or arrival without any changes of system. Example: the starboard **watch** has the **watch,** it is 7 a.m. and we are sailing. The starboard **watch** takes her out and within the starboard **watch** (which is in two parts) stands 3 hour sea **watches,** one part in the bridge. The other part on admin lines. The ship sails along, schools run, actions go on happening. First, the whole ship's company is divided in half. One half is called the starboard **watch.** The other half is called the port **watch.** These refer to sides of the ship. So the starboard **watch** berths and musters on the starboard side. The port **watch** berths and musters on the port side. When one of these has the duty it is of course all over the ship and the other **watch** is "below" (off duty). This is the way they are stood in harbor. When the ship goes to sea, the duty roster and time does not change. But the **watch** that happens to be on duty takes her into or out of harbor and at sea stands the bridge and admin **watches.** This is possible because each of these halves is again divided in half. This gives us starboard **watch** 1st part, starboard **watch** 2nd part, port **watch** 1st part, port **watch** 2nd part. Thus each of these contains 1/4 of the ship's company. (FO 895)

TWO-WAY COMM, (in training) **two-way comm** is not a rote process. That's why it is hard to teach. The trick is to get the person to talk, to keep him looking and talking until he has a cognition and very good indicators—and sometimes an F/N at the end (not vital). If you can listen you have it progressing. If you can get a person to talk about his troubles and listen and ack, you really can run it. (LRH ED 92 INT) *Abbr.* 2WC, TWC.

TYPE S BEING, a **type S being** is so devoted to **stopping** something that he has no time or energy to actually do his job. There is an exact point where a thetan goes mad. It is not a broad gradient. It is an exact point. It is the point when a thetan begins to be devoted to **stopping** something. When such a person is still able to reason, he is suppressive in a degree. The thing he is **stopping** has begun to generalize in quality so he **stops** many things without realizing what he is trying to **stop.** A **type S** S&D is vital. A type W may have to be run first. (FO 1174)

TYPISTS POOL, does any required **typing** for the Communications Unit or organization members who have no other **typing** service. (HCO PL 18 Dec 64, *Saint Hill Org Board*)

U

UNACK, **1.** the position in a comstation taken by a communication which has originated at this station and has not yet been acknowledged by the ACTAD. (*HTLTAE,* p. 123) **2.** unacknowledged. (*HTLTAE,* p. 35)

UNAUTHORIZED ISSUE, means that the material does not have an authority for that purpose and is a misdemeanor. (HCO PL 22 Apr 65, *Office of LRH Design and Planning, All Promotion Functions in an Org, All Mailing Activities in an Org, Booklets, Handouts, Mailing Pieces*)

UNAWARENESS, a sort of blindness where the person looks like he is looking but sees nothing. Degrees of this exist. Mr. A appears to the observer to be noticing, smelling things and hearing whereas he registers no sights, has a blind nose and tunes out all sound. There are even degrees of registry. To **unaware** people, terminals, lines, particles and significances just don't exist. (HCO PL 16 Feb 71 II)

UNCALLED CAPITAL, see CAPITAL, UNCALLED.

UNCERTAINTY, **uncertainty** comes totally from lack of understanding. Understanding is barred out by the misunderstood word. (LRH ED 154 INT)

UNCLASSED ORG, get a small staff trained in technology at the nearest org. Get the legal status of the **org** sound and regular, the proper corporation qualified with the International Board. Get some modest quarters in a population dense area. Distribute books in the area. Run a PE Course. Select persons to the nearest org. Get some Scn groups formed in 'round about areas. Get in org accounting policies as soon as operation starts so that it is easy to begin books—the first gap of poor accounting can cause one trouble. All selectee commissions go to **org. Org** on proportionate pay. Staff works mainly in the evening or weekends, perhaps only one on duty daytimes. Use a rudimentary org board. (HCO PL 6 Feb 66)

UNCLEAR ORDERS, (form of dev-t) an executive giving an **unclear order** puts uncertainty and confusion on the line right at the very beginning of the cycle of command. The safe way on an important program or action is to target it. (BPL 30 Jan 69)

UNCOMP, **1.** an action originated here, which has not yet been completed by ACTAD. (*HTLTAE,* p. 69) **2.** the position in a comstation taken by a communication which was originated at this station and has been acknowledged by the ACTAD but has not yet been completed by the ACTAD. (*HTLTAE,* p. 123)

UNCONSCIOUSNESS, we are talking about **unconsciousness** meaning just **unconsciousness.** You hit a guy on the head and he's **unconscious.** Not Freudian, you know. Hit him in the head, he goes out. Competence on any given subject is what a person is not **unconsciousness** on. We merely mean "knocked in the head" on. And those things he can't see, he is **unconscious** on. (ESTO 10, 7203C05 SO II)

UNCONSTITUTIONAL STRIKE, see STRIKE, UNCONSTITUTIONAL.

UNDERCAPITALIZED, the condition of a company having insufficient capital for it to operate efficiently.

UNDER-EMPLOYMENT, the situation of a business not fully or correctly utilizing personnel by employing them on work that is below their ability, training and experience levels.

UNDERMANNING, the situation of a business having too few employees for it to produce at an optimum level.

UNDERSTANDING, one has to have some affinity for an object, some communication with it, and some concept of its reality, before he can **understand** it. His ability to **understand** any thought or object depends upon his affinity, his communication, and his reality. (*SOS*, p. 43)

UNDERSTANDING INTENSIVE, Word Clearing Method 1 **Understanding Intensive** (the public name for this), produces the most fabulous success stories when done right. High school and college students can actually pass exams they have flunked. People recover whole educations. IQ goes up. Knowledge increases. They feel clearer, brighter, lighter. They speed up. (LRH ED 152 INT)

UNDERSTANDING MAGAZINE, should be issued semi-monthly (fortnightly). Issues shall be used broadly as mailing pieces and are not to go just to the membership and be forgotten. The first *Understanding* of the month shall be an *Understanding* major issue, the second issue of the month shall be an *Understanding* minor issue. *Understanding* major: shall consist of informative technical material, advertisements and programs. *Understanding* minor: shall be dedicated only to programs such as extension course, such as training, such as processing results. *Understanding* major is mainly of interest to the membership and informed Scientologists. *Understanding* minor shall be of interest to the broad public. (HCO PL 24 Oct 58, *Understanding Magazine*)

UNDERSTUDIED, apprenticed. (LRH ED 123 INT)

UNDERSTUDY SYSTEM, the system whereby a person is trained to do the work of another by working directly under an experienced person, studying his performance, acting in his behalf on assigned duties, replacing him during any absence, and eventually succeeding him or taking on the same or a similar job.

UNDERWRITER, 1. one who guarantees the sale of stock. 2. an investment banker who is the middleman between a company issuing new stocks and the public, usually forming a syndicate that buys outright the company's new issue and then sells to individuals and institutions. 3. in insurance, the specialist who assesses the risk involved for the insurance company and accepting certain applications for coverage.

UNDIVIDED PROFIT, see PROFIT, UNDIVIDED.

UNEARNED INCOME, 1. income received from investments or dividend payments as separate from income earned from personal employment. 2. income received but not yet earned, as exemplified by rent received in advance, advance ticket sales, etc.

UNEMPLOYMENT, the condition of being out of remunerative work or jobless.

UNEMPLOYMENT, FRACTIONAL, unemployment of a short term nature which occurs due to seasonal ups and downs, fluctuations in sales or market demand, temporary lack of supplies or resources, etc.

UNEMPLOYMENT, MASS, the condition of large numbers of a nation's population being out of work or jobless and usually stated as a percentage of the total population.

UNEMPLOYMENT, SPECIFIC, unemployment being present in particular kinds of occupations or industries.

UNEMPLOYMENT, STRUCTURAL, unemployment caused by drastic changes in consumer demand for products and/or trade skills.

UNEMPLOYMENT, TECHNOLOGICAL, unemployment due to the installation of new or sophisticated equipment or streamlined methods of production.

UNETHICAL PEOPLE, are those who do not have ethics in on themselves personally. (HCO PL 3 May 72)

UNFAIR DISMISSAL, letting an employee go, for reasons that are biased, unjust or contrary to laws and conventions.

UNHATTED ORGANIZATION, an **unhatted org** is a madhouse to work in as no one knows what he's supposed to handle or what others should do. They don't go idle. They introduce Sahara sand storms of dev-t. An **unhatted org** is also a lazy **org** and refers everything to someone else. Bodies won't channel, correct materials won't arrive, money can't get in or out, production is destructive and the place unpleasantly goes insolvent. (HCO PL 27 Feb 72)

UNIFORM A, **1.** navy blue wool jacket and pants with yachting cap, black shoes or boots with socks and white shirt with black tie. Women may wear a skirt of navy blue and natural colored hose and the remainder as above. (BO 21, 11 Jun 67) **2.** ship officers dress **uniform.** (FO 2577)

UNIFORM B, **1.** denim shirt, slacks, wide leather belt, knife in scabbard, white or blue tennis shoes or boots, with or without blue windbreaker or blue preserver jacket, yachting cap or wool cap. White overalls for engineers, no caps. (BO 21, 11 Jun 67) **2. Uniform B** is for everyday post work other than deck, E/R or other dirty work. (COLRHED 7)

Uniform B (Def. 1)

UNIFORM C, any clothing but white raincoat, white rain hat and black boots when on deck or on watch. (BO 21, 11 Jun 67)

UNIFORM D, white sailor suits and white sailor hats and white tennis shoes and black scarves for crew. Excepting women have white skirts and natural hose all else the same. White choker collar jackets with shoulder boards of rank for officers with officers' caps with white covers, white duck shoes and white socks, with lanyards under shoulder board left shoulder and whistle in left breast pocket. (BO 21, 11 Jun 67)

UNIFORM E, blue wool suits with yachting caps, black scarves, white shirts, black boots or shoes, black socks with women wearing dark blue skirts and natural hose, all else the same. Officers with black braid on sleeves of rank and blue cover officers' caps and lanyard outside. (BO 21, 11 Jun 67)

UNIFORM F, dark blue commando coats, blue wool stocking caps, dark pants, boots or blue or black shoes and socks, clothing under not specified. Officers the same but officers' caps and lanyards outside commando collar and whistle tucked in over button. (BO 21, 11 Jun 67)

UNIFORM G, swimming clothes and sandals of any type or color, crew wearing yachting caps, officers wearing officers' caps and brass chain lanyards around neck. Previous and two-hourly applications of Skol sunburn lotion to exposed parts. (BO 21, 11 Jun 67)

UNIFORM H, movie costumes and uniform A or B as specified. (BO 21, 11 Jun 67)

UNIFORM I, white overalls and peaked white workman's cap. Officers with lanyard. (Specified for idlers particularly and for everyone in crew doing heavy work damaging to denims.) (BO 21, 11 Jun 67)

UNIFORM J, neat and expensive looking business clothes for men and woman. Specified only for personel attached to or detached to base. (BO 21, 11 Jun 67)

UNIFORM K, Purser's personnel. Various serving and cooking **uniforms.** (BO 21, 11 Jun 67)

UNIFORM L, (Special *Enchanter*) consists of white tennis shoes, blue denim slacks, wide leather belt, knife, white polo neck sweater, white sports fisherman cap with broad elastic chin strap. Officers same, but officers' caps, yellow lanyard and whistle. (BO 80, 2 Jul 67)

UNIFORM S, the general category of the **Stewards** Department. The **uniform** is modified for cooks by adding a white apron and a low white cooks' hat. The **uniform** consists of a white waist length short sleeved coat (mess jacket) with white buttons, white trousers, white socks and white shoes, and a white sailor cap with a red bar as per epaulet. The mess jacket is high collared and needs no shirt or ties. It fits down over the top of the trousers and comes into the waist and at the back has a centre point pointing down. A red cord epaulet is on the left shoulder. A Steward 3rd class has one strand of red cord, a steward 2nd class has 2 strands, a steward 1st class has 3 strands. Cooks' ratings are the same but carry a red half moon on the left sleeve. (FO 242)

UNION, a group of workers in the same trade or occupation joined together under accepted leadership to protect and further their interests through collective action. Unions act primarily to obtain increased or uniform wages and improved working conditions and benefits; a trade union or labor union.

UNION DUES, fees charged for membership in a union, due at regular intervals, and used for the operation of the union.

UNION - MANAGEMENT COOPERATION, the state of unions and managements working together toward the common purpose of better conditions, advancements and realizations for all concerned.

UNION MEMBERSHIP, COMPULSORY, the requirement that a person must be or must become a union member in order to work in a particular organization.

UNION ORGANIZER, a staff member at the local, national or international union level who is in charge of organizing new local unions, recruiting members and being an intermediary between the local unions and official union headquarters.

UNION STATION, havingness process current in 1955 and 1956. (Confidential LRH Briefing Notes, 3 Sept 70)

UNIT, 1. we have five members and their in-charge as a **unit**; five **units** and the section executive in a section; five sections plus the department's director in a department. (HCO PL 28 Feb 66) **2.** at the moment they are dividing the sections directly into **units** but one fine day they will have to divide it into subsections, divide it into **units** to subunits in order to make enough space for personnel. (SH Spec 77, 6608C23)

UNIT A, the SHSBC has a checksheet composed of 4 theory sections and a practical section composed of 5 units. The practical units are done part of the day, concurrent with theory study as in the original SHSBC. **Unit A** covers: (a) OT-TR0, TR0-9. (b) TRs/metering (daily). (c) basic auditing drills. (d) processing drills for ARC S/W Expanded. (e) auditing actions: flying ruds and ARC S/W Expanded on a pc. (f) TV demo passed. (g) electronic attest tape of a session passed. (BPL 18 Mar 75 I)

UNIT B, SHSBC **Unit B** covers: (a) OT-TR0, TR0-9. (b) TRs/metering (daily). (c) processing drills for Level 0 Expanded. (d) auditing actions: Level 0 Expanded on a pc. (e) TV demo passed. (f) electronic attest tape of a session passed. (BPL 18 Mar 75 I)

UNIT C, SHSBC **Unit C** covers: (a) OT-TR0, TR0-9. (b) TRs/metering (daily). (c) processing drills for Level I Expanded. (d) auditing actions: Level I Expanded on a pc. (e) TV demo passed. (f) electronic attest tape of a session passed. (BPL 18 Mar 75 I)

UNIT COSTS, see COSTS, UNIT.

UNIT D, SHSBC **Unit D** covers: (a) OT-TR0, TR0-9. (b) TRs/metering (daily). (c) processing drills for Level II Expanded. (d) auditing actions: Level II Expanded on a pc. (e) TV demo passed. (f) electronic attest tape of a session passed. (BPL 18 Mar 75 I)

UNIT E, SHSBC **Unit E** covers: (a) OT-TR0, TR0-9. (b) TRs/metering (daily). (c) processing drills for Level III Expanded. (d) auditing actions: Level III Expanded on a pc. (e) processing drills for Level IV Expanded. (f) auditing actions: Level IV Expanded on a pc. (g) TV demo passed. (h) electronic attest tape of a session passed. (BPL 18 Mar 75 I)

UNITED SURVIVAL ACTION CLUB, the reason they're called that is just so you can say **USA Club** but the loose term is **Survival Club.** (AC-5, 5712C30) See SURVIVAL CLUB.

UNIT E-ONE, the Solo Audit Course Grade VI will be taught in the Technical Division, Department of Training, Saint Hill. It will be called **Unit E-One** and will be handled by the **E-Unit** Course Supervisor who, in case of numbers, may have an **E-One** supervisor under him to handle this course. (HCO PL 25 Oct 65)

UNIT HEAD, see SECTION HEAD.

UNIT PRICING, see PRICING, UNIT.

UNIT RATE, each staff member gets so many **units** according to the post he is holding. The total **units** are totalled for the whole staff and this total of **units** is divided exactly into the salary sum amount, thus you arrive at the **unit rate** for each staff **unit.** (HCO PL 20 Feb 63) [The above HCO PL was cancelled by BPL 10 Oct 75 IV.]

UNITS, **1.** in 1965 the Saint Hill Special Briefing Course was organized as follows. It was divided into four **units, Unit** A covering Level 0. **Unit** B covering levels I and II. **Unit** C covering levels III and IV. **Unit** D covering Level VI. (HCO PL 27 Feb 65) **2.** there are certain classes of auditors, there's Class Ia, Ib, Ic and 2a. These classes each connote certain types of auditing. Class 1a has no auditing; Class Ib has some type of auditing. The administration of the Academy depends upon the auditing requirements more than the classes. You get auditing something on this basis, you have a class of auditor and that requires certain checksheets, and you also have a **unit** and the auditor belongs to that **unit.** So an individual auditor is actually designated by his class, which would be Class Ia, Class Ib, Ic or 2a. That's his classification. What **unit** he appears in is determined by the current auditing he is doing and these **units** are **Unit** W, X, Y and Z. The **unit** in which he finds himself is doing certain auditing actions and you will sometimes GAE somebody down from one auditing activity to another auditing activity, and although he still retains the classes he has he's doing another type of auditing. (HCO PL 17 Sept 62)

UNIT STAFF MEMBER, a **staff member** who is not a member of a production department but appears somewhere else on the organization board. (HCO PL 26 Jun 64)

UNIT SYSTEM, proportionate pay. (HCO PL 10 Dec 68)

UNIT W, (an arrangement of the Academy) what unit he appears in is determined by the current auditing he is doing and these units are **Unit W**, X, Y and Z. The **Ws** are brand new students. They're brand new and they don't do any auditing, nobody'd trust them near an E-meter, and a **W** is involved basically in just studying the fundamentals, just as undoubtedly you have it now. The number of **Ws** you have are divided into A and B, and you get the **WA** then and the **WB** unit. (HCO PL 17 Sept 62)

UNIT X, (an arrangment of the Academy) the **Xs** are the most fundamental and the tiny bit of auditing they do—they do something without any model session or something of this sort. They go through some auditing motions, and they are divided into the **XA** and **XB**, and that gives you your teams—A audits B and B audits A. (HCO PL 17 Sept 62)

UNIT Y, (an arrangement of the Academy) your **Y** is doing something on the order of a model session. They're doing something terribly fundamental like finding a havingness process and doing a model session. This is rather elementary type auditing but nevertheless gives them practice in this line. (HCO PL 17 Sept 62)

UNITY OF COMMAND, the management concept that one person can have only one senior to whom he reports.

UNIT Z, (an arrangement of the Academy) your **Z** is doing the kingpin or the top activity that is done in the Academy, which is in this particular case, as we are dealing with HCA/HPA, a Problems Intensive, and when they can do a Problems Intensive from one end to the other of course that's your Class 2a auditor, but they're auditing in **Unit ZA** and **ZB**. (HCO PL 17 Sept 62)

UNIVERSAL MEDIA PRODUCTIONS, once proficiency was attained in still photography, the Photoshoot Org expanded into other fields of **media**, such as radio, television ads, billboards, cinematography and video as well as continuing still photography. A new name was picked to cover all the activities entered into, and the Photoshoot Org became the **Media** Org. Further expansion and planning has occurred again, and another name was surveyed for that Scn, and as well, non-Scn publics could relate to. The new official name of the Photoshoot **Org/Media** Org is: **Universal Media Productions.** (SOED 570 INT) *Abbr.* Uni-Med.

UNLIMITED CERTIFICATE, at the end of this course, if certifiable by all criteria, the student is granted a limited certificate, printed in black and white, on which the words "Limited, Expires Six Months From Date," is printed boldly. In order to gain an **unlimited certificate**, then, the student must, after graduation, release two persons, one of a mental condition and the other of a serious chronic somatic and must furnish to the Foundation incontrovertible evidence from a medical doctor and psychometrist that this has been accomplished. (HCO PL 2 Sept 70, *Instruction Protocol Official*) [The above excerpts is part of a paper issued at the beginning of Dn, 20 November 1950.]

UNLIMITED LIABILITY, unlimited liability means that a person's assets beyond what he has invested in a business are subject to the legal claims of creditors. Thus in the case of a sole proprietorship the owner is not limited in his liability to his creditors. His personal and private ownings outside of the business are legally subject to the claims of the creditors of his business.

UNLISTED, a stock that is not a stock exchange list.

UNLOADING, the act of disposing of goods, especially by selling in great quantity at a low price; also known as dumping.

UNMOCK, take down or destroy. (HCO PL 13 Jul 74 II)

UNPRODUCTIVE PERSONNEL, a type of dev-t. Keeping a **personnel** on a post who is a flagrant dev-t source. (HCO PL 27 Jan 69)

UNPRODUCTIVE TIME, any amount of time spent in a manufacturing process that does not contribute to the production of the final product.

UNREAL TARGETS, a type of dev-t where **targets** are set and worked on which are not derived from any useful major target. (HCO PL 27 Jan 69)

UNTRAINED STAFF, a type of dev-t where **staff** not grooved in on the lines mainly deal in dev-t and although they even look busy seldom accomplish much. (HCO PL 27 Jan 69)

UNUSUAL FAVORS, using one's org connections to obtain special service or material **favors** for field or friends. (HCO PL 13 Jan 69, *Unusual Favors*)

UNUSUAL SOLUTION, 1. requests for authority to depart from the usual are dangerous when okayed as they then set up areas of difference and cause policy to wander and misfit at the joints. Juniors who propose **unusual solutions** generally don't know the policy or orders anyway. The proper thing to do is order a checkout on the appropriate policy. (BPL 30 Jan 69) **2.** abandonment of standard tech in favor of **unusual solutions.** This is always present when a collapse of tech occurs. An **unusual solution** is one evolved to remedy an abuse of existing technology. (HCO PL 10 Feb 66 II)

UP MAGAZINE, an early Advanced Org mag, in 1968. (FO 2802)

UPPER INDOCTRINATION COURSE, purpose: to attain ability to handle bodies, objects and intentions fully. (HCO PL 27 Nov 59)

UPPER INDOC TRS, the drills that teach the CCHs. The CCHs are then run on pcs. (HCO PL 17 May 65, *Tech Div Qual Div Urgent CCHs*)

Upper Indoc TR's

UPSET, ARC breaks. (BPL 26 Jan 72 VIIRA)

UPSTAT, one who has high **statistics**. (HCOB 8 Aug 71)

UPSTAT CLUB, see INTERNATIONAL UPSTAT CLUB.

UPSTATISTIC, 1. the purpose of the org is to get the show on the road and keep it going. This means production. Every division is a production unit. It makes or does something that can have a **statistic** to see if it goes **up** or down. Example: a typist gets out 500 letters in one week. That's a **statistic.** If the next week the same typist gets out 600 letters that's an **up statistic.** (HCO PL 1 Sept 65 VII) **2.** the current number is more than it was. (HCO PL 16 Dec 65)

UP TICK, expression that refers to a stock transaction made at a price higher than the previous transaction. Also known as a plus-tick.

URGENCY ORDERS, a senior comm member should not give direct orders to his junior comm member on the A routing. Direct orders may be given only with B routing and any direct order not following B routing is off-line except in cases of extreme **urgency** as in the case of books about to be shipped or a spinning pc. Such cases are called **urgency orders.** An **urgency order** given an A routing must be followed at once on slower channels (air mail) by repeating it with B routing through channels. (HCO PL 13 Mar 65 II)

URGENT, a form of cable. **Urgent**=costs twice ORD (ordinary) rate. **Urgent** takes about 15 minutes (travel). (HCO PL 9 Aug 66)

URGENT DIRECTIVE, **1.** a senior executive who discovers a situation which may be disastrous to the org. Issues orders of a remedying or preventive nature instantly by directive, to remain in effect until all data is in. This is called an **Urgent Directive.** (HCO PL 31 Oct 66 I) **2.** if an emergency situation develops, any member of that Ad Council could issue what is called an **Urgent Directive.** It's something that's got to be done right now, right now, it can't wait till tomorrow. His **directive** is only good until a Board of Investigation has investigated it and written a right directive. So these emergency directions then have a tendency to be wiped out. They have to be wiped out. (SH Spec 81, 6611C01)

USED INVOICES, those for which the service bought has been delivered in full. (BPL 3 Jan 72RA I)

USEFUL SPACE, one that promotes the org, may be used by the org, is heated or cooled properly, equipped for its purpose, clean, orderly and serviceable. It may only be scenic but it is still **useful space.** (HCO PL 6 Nov 66 II)

USER, those who will **use** or benefit from the program when it is realized and completed. (HCO PL 14 Sept 69)

USING DEV-T AS AN EXCUSE TO CUT LINES, a type of **dev-t.** An executive must really know what **dev-t** is and really say what the exact **dev-t** was in order to reject or handle **dev-t.** (HCO PL 27 Nov 69)

USING POLICY TO STOP, **1.** they can do that by always applying the wrong **policy** letter. All you have to do is take the **policy** letter that applies to A and instead of following that find another one that doesn't really apply to A. But find something in it that can be construed as to apply to this and they say "Well you see we can't do that." **Policy** was designed to tell people things they could do, and when it tells them not to do something it's trying to put edges on the channel so they won't go off of it. But what channel? The channel of doing something right. Now if a fellow doesn't know the **policy** that gives him the main channel and only knows the **policy** that tells him **to stop** then you will get people **using policy to stop.** (ESTO 11, 7203C06 SO I) **2.** a person not doing his post purpose will pick bits of **policy** out that seem to state the order given cannot be followed. If you track down such a person's post purpose you will find he or she hasn't got it and is **using policy to stop.** (HCO PL 27 Feb 71 I)

U.S. OPS, see PACIFIC OPERATIONS.

UTILIZATION, the actions for which personnel have been trained are the actions being performed. (FSO 113)

V

VALUABLE DOCUMENT FILE, the (**valuable document**) originals shall not leave the safe save only to be photostated and then shall be at once returned with one photostat of it attached to each. The **valuable document file** shall be another **file** than the safe, shall be kept by the Org Sec and shall consist only of photostats in folders which say what the **document** in the folder is so that removing the last copy shall not thus injure the **file.** (FCPL 8 Jun 57)

Valuable Document (Def. 2)

VALUABLE DOCUMENTS, 1. all **valuable documents** are to be stored in a safe under the control of the Treasurer and the Organization Secretary. These include contracts, notes, official papers, awards, etc. The criteria of "**valuable**" is "would their loss financially or publicly embarrass the organization?" (FCPL 8 Jun 57) **2. valuable documents** are registry papers, seaman books, radio and safety certs, minute books of companies, etc. Basically they are any paper which proves one's identity, status or rights. (FO 1669) *Abbr.* Val Docs.

VALUABLE FINAL PRODUCT, 1. something that can be exchanged with other activities in return for support. The support usually adds up to food, clothing, shelter, money, tolerance and cooperation (goodwill). (HCO PL 25 Mar 71) **2.** could as easily be named a **valuable** exchangeable **product.** (HCO PL 25 Mar 71) **3.** one you can exchange with the society for the wherewithal which the society has. By definition it is something for which you can exchange the services and goods of the society. (FEBC 12, 7102C03 SO II) **4.** something that can be translated into the society for the wherewithal to survive. (FEBC 4, 7101C18 SO III) *Abbr.* VFP.

Valuable Final Product (Def. 1)

VALUABLE PRODUCTS OF AN ORG, the basic **valuable products of an org** are auditors, preclears and money. They are the final **valuable products** that are the obvious ones. There are some additional ones. (FEBC 5, 7101C23 SO I) [Note: per HCO PL 6 April 1972, ESTO Series 15, *Product Correction,* "GI is really the Valuable Final REWARD for which the VFPs are exchanged."]

VALUATION, the process of assessing the value of something such as real estate, buildings or personal property according to certain accepted standards.

VALUE, **value** is established by things that are wanted. (FEBC 9, 7101C24 SO II)

VALUE, 1. monetary worth or price of a product or service. 2. worth in terms of usefulness or importance of a product or service to a possessor or client. 3. in mathematics, an assigned numerical quantity.

VARIABLE COSTS, see COSTS, VARIABLE.

VARIABLE WORKING HOURS, working hours that vary and are flexible, not conforming to a regular continuous 8-hour work period.

VENDOR, any person or company engaged in selling something; the one who makes the sale.

VENTS ENGINEER, **engineer** single hatted with the job of clean air, filters, ducts, fans. (ED 240-7 Flag)

VENTURE CAPITAL, see CAPITAL, RISK.

VERBAL SURVEY, the questions are asked **verbally** person to person. Never by written questionnaire. (BPL 25 Jan 72R)

VERBAL TECH, about the most ghastly thing to have around is **verbal tech** which means **tech** without reference to an HCOB and direct handling out of the actual material. (OODs 9 Nov 74)

VERTICAL COMBINATION, see COMBINATION, VERTICAL.

VESSEL, something that floats in water, in this case a ship. (OODs 29 Sept 71)

VESTIBULE SCHOOL, see TRAINING, VESTIBULE.

VESTIBULE TRAINING, see TRAINING, VESTIBULE.

VETERAN, a person who has been in the Sea Org for 2 years or longer. (FO 3454RA)

VIA, (routing used on telex lines) by way of. By a route that passes through. Example: a message going to FBO DC from Flag and is going through FBO U.S. can be routed as: FBO D.C. **via** FBO U.S. (BPL 23 Apr 73R)

VIABILITY, 1. the longevity, usefulness and desirability of the product. (HCO PL 29 Oct 70) **2.** survival value. (HCO PL 20 Jul 70) **3.** "capable of living or growth." It is taken from the Latin *vita* which means life. **Viability** depends, in the main, upon exchange where economics are concerned. A great deal of production can occur, but if it is not exchanged for anything then a group can become nonviable very rapidly. The group does not necessarily live on what it itself produces. A group needs things in addition to those things which it produces thus some of its own production must be *exchanged* with society for the group to survive. (OODs 20 Nov 71)

VIABILITY OF THE ORG, 1. its economic survival including its security from political enemy motivated attack. (HCO PL 23 Sept 70) **2.** how long will it last economically, how will it expand, does income exceed outgo, etc. (HCO PL 29 Oct 70)

VIABLE, 1. capable of supporting itself and thus staying alive. (HCO PL 28 Jul 71) **2.** means capable of living, able to live in a particular climate or atmosphere. (HCO PL 6 Jul 70)

VICE PRESIDENT, an executive ranking next below a president, who usually directs a separate department such as sales, finances, etc., or a separate location, as a branch, and who is sometimes empowered to assume the presidency in case of illness or death of the president.

VICTIM, the basic definition of **victim** must be, unwilling and unknowing effect of life, matter, energy, space and time. (HCOB 3 Sept 59)

VICTIM PROCESS, in any overt act-motivator sequence there is a villain and a **victim.** If the auditor were to choose and run the "villain" then he would be violating the basic definition of operating thetan which is "to be willing and knowing cause over life, matter, energy, space and time," and would be processing the pc at effect point. The basic definition of **victim** must then be, as an HCO staff auditor pointed out, "unwilling and unknowing effect of life, matter, energy, space and time." Therefore, to keep the pc at cause we have no choice but to **process** him in such a way as to face him up to **victim.** A pc should be able to run, easily if lengthly on "From where could you communicate to a **victim?**" (HCOB 3 Sept 59)

VIOLATED PURPOSE, a type of dev-t. A division, department or staff member or materiel used for things it was not organized to do. It disrupts its normal lines. (HCO PL 27 Jan 69)

VIOLENTLY PTS, which is your chronically sick. (7205C11 SO)

VIP/CELEBRITY, any person important in his field or an opinion leader or his entourage, business associates, family or friends, with particular attention to arts, sports and management and government. (BPL 13 Dec 72RB)

VITAL, things we can't operate without. (OODs 22 Jan 68)

VITAL INFORMATION, is **vital** because survival depends on it. Examples include: HCOBs, HCO PLs, books, tapes, course checksheets and packs, hats, OEC volumes, LRH EDs and FOs and other issues, Flag programs and EDs, stats, weekly reports, compliance reports, situation reports, CSWs, evaluations, even dispatches that contain important **information** that must be known. Also, an org requires other **vital** data like accurate CF and addressos, up-to-date files, broad, hardsell promotion and magazines, accurate accounts files and records, monthly statements, tech data that gives pc and student results, word clearing and cramming results, a Qual library, broad public dissemination and promotion to name a few. Data that is **vital** must be relayed, must be made known without alter-is or barriers. You can't survive without it. (HCO PL 19 Oct 74)

VITAL INFORMATION RUNDOWN, I have recently unearthed a widespread aberration that underlies the withhold or obstruction of **vital information.** It is, simply stated, dramatization of withholds. This is not just the person with withholds, this is the person who dramatizes withholds by preventing the relay, exposure or free distribution of **vital information.** The **Vital Information Rundown** is the remedy for the dramatization of withholds. (HCO PL 19 Oct 74)

VITAL TARGET, under this heading comes what we must do to operate at all. This requires an inspection of both the area one is operating into and the factors or materiel or organization with which we are operating. One then finds those points (sometimes while operating) which stop or threaten future successes, and sets the overcoming of the **vital** ones as **targets.** (HCO PL 16 Jan 69) *Abbr.* VT.

VOCATIONAL GUIDANCE/COUNSELING, 1. service offered by a qualified individual or organization that through test results and consultations helps direct a person in the choice of a career or life work. 2. service within a company that helps direct new employees toward types of training and work for which they are best fitted.

VOLUME ZERO, **volume zero** of the OEC, published by Pubs Orgs. It is a basic staff hat. (OODs 7 Jan 71)

VOLUNTARY ARBITRATION, see ARBITRATION, VOLUNTARY.

VOLUNTEER MINISTERS PROGRAM, a **program** that undercuts all current reaches into the public. Ron's new **program** is called the **Volunteer Ministers Program.** It puts basic Dn and Scn tech into view and into use at the raw public level, much as did *Dianetics: The Modern Science of Mental Health* in 1950 which continues to do so today. Surveys have been done in different parts of the world to determine what people really want to handle on a personal level. The basic tech for handling these problems has been compiled into a book fully suitable for raw public. This book will be broadly distributed on Scn and non-Scientology lines, bought by the man on the street. He'll use some of the data, produce some miracles, save a marriage or two, rescue some kid from drugs, help his next door neighbor who's upset because her child's failing in school and couldn't care less, plus brighten up her yawning offspring and teach him to study, and handle Aunt Martha's dizziness with assists. (FBDL 424)

VOLUNTEERS, are looked upon as persons offering help to an activity without recompense. (FO 785R)

VOTE, CASTING, a special vote made by the chairman of a meeting when there is a tie in voting.

VOTE, CARD, an action where a vote is taken at a delegate conference by each delegation leader writing on a card the number of votes he is casting, according to the number of people he represents. When called upon, he holds it up for the count. Also called a block vote.

VOTE, NAMED, in deciding unusually significant issues, a ballot that has the voter's name on it which is kept as part of the voting record.

VOTE, ROLL CALL, a vote taken at a conference or meeting wherein names of those entitled to vote are called out, with each vote being formally recorded.

VOTING RIGHT, the authority of a stock holder to vote on the company's business affairs with the right to give that authority to vote to another person.

VOUCHER SYSTEM, a system of accounting which provides internal control and features the approval of each business transaction by the use of invoices retained and vouchers authorizing each item and disbursement.

V UNIT, 1. in 1962 a Saint Hill Special Briefing Course unit for co-auditing heavily supervised R2-10 or R2-12 directed toward results. There were no checksheets beyond course regulations. (HCO PL 8 Dec 62) **2.** (SHSBC) the **V unit** is a co-audit, one or two weeks long, three hours of auditing given and three received daily, 5 days a week. The purpose of **V unit** is to: (1) get the student into some kind of shape to finish the course. (2) give the student a win as an auditor. (3) establish an auditing reality on Scn. (HCO PL 13 Feb 63)

WAGE(S), payment made on an hourly or piece-rate basis to blue collar workers.

WAGE EARNER, 1. a person who works for wages. 2. a person whose earnings support a family household.

WAGE, GUARANTEED ANNUAL, in collective bargaining, the assurance by an employer that a specific minimum yearly wage or employment or both will be delivered to employees.

WAGE POLICIES, see POLICIES, WAGE.

WAGE-PRICE SPIRAL, the cycle of increased prices resulting in demands for higher wages and vice versa which forms an upward spiral of higher wages and prices.

WAGE RATE, the set amount of money paid per hour, day or piece of work done.

WAGES, APPRENTICE, wage for the term of an apprenticeship which is a minimum of 50 per cent of the prevailing journeyman's wage rate.

WAGES, BOOTLEG, 1. wages that are above standard rates which employers offer to hold or attract new employees when labor is scarce. 2. wages that are below standard rates for the area or industry which a person agrees to in order to have employment.

WAGES DRIFT, see EARNINGS DRIFT.

WAGES, JOURNEYMAN, the established rate of pay for a journeyman who has served his apprenticeship and is skilled in a trade or craft, usually stipulated by the union as a minimum standard set for each trade which may vary somewhat in different locations.

WAGE STRUCTURE, the hierarchy of different wage rates paid to employees holding different types of jobs in a company.

WAGEWORKER, most often a blue collar worker who receives wages rather than a fixed salary.

WAITING LIST BOARD, any pc **waiting list** is posted, with the pc's name on a white card, on another **board** in HGC Admin. It reads from left to right in horizontal lines and the white card is removed to the assignment board. Students who are **waiting** for auditing are also put on the **waiting list board** but their names are on a different (paler) shade of green from that of the auditor's names on the assignment board. (HCO PL 4 Jul 65)

WAIVER, release form. (HCO PL 1 Sept 65 IV)

WAIVER, in contracts or in legal procedure, the act or written signatory of an individual by which he knowingly relinquishes a right, claim or benefit.

WALL OF FIRE, is descriptive and not to be taken literally. It merely means the individual gains a new religious understanding. (HCO PL 20 Dec 69 IX) [There is a further description of this term as it relates to auditing on SHSBC Lecture 271, Tape No. 6305C30 *Programming Cases Part 2.*]

WANT, very simply it is a person's desire to have or attain something. Specifically related to economics a want has been defined as something a person desires but which he hasn't the money or wherewithal to achieve. When he does have the money or capacity to achieve this want it is called a demand.

WAR, **1.** an insanity which is achieved when a bad organization descends to a complete anxiety. (OS-10, 5611C15) **2.** the history of **war** is the history of control. The end goal of **war** is to throw out of its control the population under a government. We are supposed to throw another nation's population out of control so that we can supplant the government or its attitudes and give them their population back in control again. (*AAR*, p. 89) **3.** a means of bringing about a more amenable frame of mind on the part of the enemy. (SH Spec 63, 6506C08) **4.** the antipathies of organization. **War** is chaos. (SH Spec 131, 6204C03) **5.** it used to be **war** was a method of conquering terrain. You see, all it is, is the violence which ensues a diplomatic and political failure. That's what **war** is today. (7003C27 SO)

War (Def. 5)

WAREHOUSE, a place where goods, merchandise or commodities are stored for safekeeping until needed by the individual or organization.

WARRANT, a certified document that a stockholder has the right to buy securities at a stated price within a specified period of time or in some instances, at all times.

WARRANTY, 1. a printed card or certificate accompanying a product which has the manufacturer's assurance that the product will be, function or perform as represented. 2. a statement by the insured that an insurance risk is as stated. A breach of this usually nullifies the policy.

WASTE REPORT, staff member **report** of the **waste** of org materiel. (HCO PL 1 May 65)

WATCH, **1.** a portion of time during which a part of a ship's company is on duty. Also the part of a ship's company required to be on duty during a specific period. (FO 2674) **2.** every member of a ship's company has two general types of activities, one of these is as a member of **watches**, wherein he handles his duties of steering, lookout, engines, etc., including emergency drills. (FO 1109)

WATCH QUARTER AND STATION BILL, **1.** a large board showing what **watch** a member of the ship's company is on, where his berth or cabin (**quarters**) is, what his **watch** duties are (**station**) and also what post he has on the ship's org board. (FO 2674) **2.** a **watch quarter and station bill** is incomplete unless it designates exact duties on **station** as well as what part of the ship. It must also designate where the person is berthed. It includes every person's position and specific duty for every evolution and every drill. The basic **bill** is easier to keep if it is maintained in a standard form for the ship and only names and berthings changed. **Stations**, duties and drills do not change. (FO 1919) **3.** every member of a ship's company has two general types of activities, one of these is as a member of watches, wherein he handles his duties of steering, lookout, engines, etc., including emergency drills. The other is his administrative duty with regard to the vessel. The **watch quarter and station bill** covers his ship duties, the org board covers his administrative duties. (FO 1109) **4.** tells every member of the company where he berths, what his title and duties are as per the ship's org board, what his position and duties are for every evolution and activity and drill of the ship. It is a wide horizontal board with the names of the posts of the ship in the left hand vertical column, the names of the personnel in the second column, the berthing space assigned in the third column. In a small craft the names can be horizontal and the columns of duties vertical to save space. In the next few columns are the Condition I all hands evolutions, such as cleaning **station**, docking, anchoring and entering and leaving harbor and readiness lists for port and readiness lists for sea. Also an entertainment **bill** in which all hands take part. And also a full **bill** converting the ship to a Scn org. In the next columns are the Condition II port and starboard **watch** duties at sea (4 hours on, 4 off) and in port (24 on, 24 off). And any entertainment **bill** doubled so port or starboard watch can give a party. In the next columns are the Condition III (4 on 8 off) duties. In Condition III there are three watches in port and at sea. This includes an entertainment which one third of the ship conducts entirely in each **watch.** The fueling and taking in and lowering boats assignments are next. The next columns are emergency drills of which the first is man overboard, the second fire, etc., with the last an abandon ship. Then comes the landing party assignments for six different types of landing party, day exploratory from harbor and from sea, overnight from harbor and from sea. Then come shore party transport (of goods) which may require, in the main, manual labor. Additional **bills** are added by adding columns as before to the right. The columns are very narrow with only an indication of the place and duty, often abbreviated. (FO 80) *Abbr.* WQSB.

WAYBILL, a list of goods and shipping instructions relative to a shipment that is to be publicly transported. *Abbr.* WB.

WEAR THE HAT, colloquialism for "assume the duties or do the job." (*ISE,* p. 58)

WE COME BACK, the motto of the Sea Org. (FO 234)

WEEDING, the process of eliminating unnecessary, unwanted or unproductive elements in a business whether property, functions, personnel, etc., to increase efficiency.

WEEK END INTENSIVE, a **week end intensive** of 12 1/2 hours. This will consist on Saturday of 0930 to 1200 and 1300 to 1530 and 1700 to 2130. On Sunday it will consist of 0930 to 1200 and 1300 to 1530 with no evening period all on the same pc. (ED 140 FAO)

WEEKLY STAFF BRIEFING, at the end of each **week** a **staff** meeting is convened as a **briefing** of all **staff** on the accomplishment of the org that **week.** The honorary chairman of the meeting is the Executive Director of the org, or in his absence the LRH Comm. The Dir of Public Information (or the Div 6 Sec) takes the role of MC. The purpose of the meeting is to let all **staff** know what actions the org is doing—and what wins and gains were made that week. (BPL 4 Mar 71R)

WELFARE STATE, **1.** the **welfare state** punishes actively every producer. It fines him for producing. He's making money left and right so they take it away from him and give it to somebody who isn't working. In other words neglect the guy who is working and hand it all to the downstat. The cave in of any society begins with the reward of a downstat. (ESTO 9, 7203C05 SO I) **2.** that **state** which rewards non-production at the expense of production. (HCO PL 6 Mar 66) **3.** that **state** in which the member is not permitted to contribute to the state but must take contribution from the **state.** (*DAB* Vol. II, p. 51 1951-52)

WELFARISM, the idea that the people can get something without exchanging anything. (OODs 20 Nov 71)

WELL DONE AUDITING HOURS, Tech Div 4 GDSes are as follows: (1) total number of student points. (2) total number of **well done auditing hours. Well done hours** are defined as those **hours** given a **well done** by the C/S—the session having concluded on F/N VGIs and the pc having F/N VGIs at the examiner immediately after the session, and no gross technical outnesses in the session. Total **well done hours** are to be counted as follows: (a) the number of paid "in the chair" **well done hours** produced by Div 4. (b) for every 10 paid **well done hours,** one staff **auditing well done hour** may be added (10 staff **WDHs** for every 100 paid **WDHs**) provided it was actually delivered to staff by Div 4. (c) plus admin time up to 25% of (a) and (b) above may be added provided it was productive admin time actually done by auditors who did 25 hours "in the chair" auditing. (Admin time by auditors who have not produced 25 hours in the chair may not be included in the GDS.) (BPL 23 Nov 71R) *Abbr.* WDAHs.

WHEELER-DEALER, a person, often of questionable nature, who is crafty and shrewd in business dealings usually accomplishing a rapid number of business turnovers to his advantage in a short time.

WHEN ISSUED, short for "when, as and if issued." Where a security is authorized for issue but has not been issued yet conditional orders may be placed for it that take effect when, as and if issued.

WHISPERING CAMPAIGN, there are random individuals in the society who do not understand very much. This is expressed as a sort of malicious glee about things. Such pass on slanderous rumors very easily. In an illiterate society such people abound. Since they cannot read, the bulk of knowledge is denied to them. Since they do not know very many words much of what is said to them is not understood. This is not isolated to the illiterate only. What they do not understand they substitute for with imaginary things. Thus such persons not only listen to slander but also corrupt and twist even it. Thus a rumor can go through a society that has no basis in truth. When numbers of such rumors exist and are persistent, one suspects a "**whispering campaign.**" This is not because people whisper these things but because like an evil wind it seems to have no source. (HCO PL 21 Nov 72 I)

WHITE, *n.* the completion copy of a communication. The actad's copy. (*HTLTAE,* p. 123)

WHITE COLLAR UNION, a union of persons employed in a white collar occupation such as a union of teachers.

WHITE COLLAR WORKERS, people who hold clerical, professional, executive or management jobs and one paid salaries as opposed to wages. The term was coined after the white shirts associated with businessmen as opposed to the blue or dark colored shirts worn by persons employed in industry and as manual labor.

WHITE FORM, pc assessment or history **form.** It's an assessment on a meter. (LRH ED 67 INT)

WHITE GLOVE INSPECTION, consists of putting on **white gloves** and running them over surfaces, ladders, bulkheads, shelves, etc. If the gloves get dirty the **inspection** is not passed. (FO 88)

White Glove Inspection

WHITE INVOICE, 1. these invoice copies are distributed to the customer. (Invoice routing for all orgs except Saint Hill). (HCO PL 16 Feb 66) **2. white invoice** copies are distributed to the customer (Saint Hill only). (HCO PL 13 Oct 66)

WHITE MUTINY, where a person sees fit only to follow orders and takes no responsibility for his post. (FO 664)

WHITE PAPER, white mimeograph **paper** and red, green and blue ink in combination with white paper in mimeograph work is exclusively the Office of LRH and may not be used casually in mailings or inside other divisions. Any color of ink may be assigned to divisions in combination with colored papers, but never with **white paper.** (HCO PL 8 May 65 II)

WHITE PR, 1. when **PR** is used for the improvement of things, ideals, conditions or any promotion or pro-survival factors, it could be called "**white PR.**" (HCO PL 7 Aug 72) **2. white PR** is engaged in idealization at all times to a greater or lesser degree. The better side of life or persons or dreams or hopes are the subject of **white PR.** (HCO PL 7 Aug 72)

WHOLESALE, the sale of large amounts of goods to retailers who then sell to consumers.

WHOLESALER, a middleman who sells in large quantities to retailers or industrial and commercial users but usually not to domestic consumers.

WHY, 1. the **why** will be how come the situation is such a departure from the ideal scene and will open the door to handling. (HCO PL 12 Aug 74) **2.** any undesirable or desirable situation must have a real **why.** The **why** must permit a closer approach to the ideal scene. The **why** must always improve the existing scene toward a more ideal scene. (CBO 147) **3.** it's always some huge enormous piece of stupidity, an out-point—any one of the various out-points. And it explains all other out-points as a common denominator. Once you find that one all the other ones are dependent on it. It's like finding basic on the chain. The chain goes. (ESTO 12, 7203C06 SO II) **4.** the basic **why** is always the major out-point which has all other out-points as a common denominator and that's the real **why,** that explains everything. What is this everything? All the other out-points! What is this major out-point that explains all other out-points that I have found in this area? That could be the definition of a **why.** (ESTO 12, 7203C06 SO II) **5.** the real reason found by the investigation. (HCO PL 29 Feb 72 II) **6.** we find what caused the situation which we call a **why.** (FEBC 2, 7101C18 SO I) **7.** that basic outness found which will lead to a recovery of stats. (HCO PL 13 Oct 70 II)

WHY IS GOD, THE, when beings operate mainly on illogics, they are unable to conceive of valid reasons for things or to see that effects are directly caused by things they themselves can control. The inability to observe and find an actual usable why is the downfall of beings and activities. This is factually the why of people not finding whys and using them. The prevalence of historical man's use of "fate," "kismet (fatalism)," superstition, fortune telling, astrology and mysticism confirms this. Having forgotten to keep seed grain for the spring, the farmer starves the following year and when asked **why** he is starving says it **is** the **gods**, that he has sinned or that he failed to make sacrifice. In short, unable to think he says "**the why is God.**" (HCO PL 31 Jan 72)

WHY SHEETS, **why's** found by aides are written up by aides on **why sheets** already issued and now being swiftly amended to show the number of the why in that pack, the time of occurrence of the reported situation investigated and a brief description of the state concerned. (CBO 65)

WILDCAT, meaning springing up anywhere. (HCO PL 5 Oct 69)

WILDCAT STRIKE, see STRIKE, OUTLAW.

WILL POWER, self-determinism is entirely and solely the imposition of time and space upon energy flows. Imposing time and space upon objects, people, self, events, and individuals, is causation. The total components of one's self-determinism is the ability to impose time and space. His energy is derived from the discharge of high and low, or different, potentials to which he has assigned time and space. Dwindling sanity is a dwindling ability to assign time and space. Psychosis is a complete inability to assign time and space. This is, as well, **will power.** (*Scn 8-80,* p. 44)

WINDING UP, the action of settling or finishing the last business at hand, such as liquidating assets and apportioning them, before a business enterprise is completely dissolved.

WIPED OUT, informal expression denoting the entire loss of a business, property, finances or possessions.

WIPERS, **1.** new recruits become swampers (deck), cleaners (Stewards Dept), and **wipers** (Engine Room). (FO 748) **2.** in the engine room they are not mechanics or apprentice motormen. They are **wipers.** This means they clean up all spills, drips, puddles, clean and polish the engine room. (FO 3290)

WIRE HOUSE, a company which is a member firm or is associated with a particular stock exchange and which maintains telegraphic communication with that exchange.

WIRE SERVICE, an organization which specializes in gathering national and international news and photographs by telegraph which it relays to associated newspapers, television and radio stations.

WISDOM, **wisdom** is not a fixed idea. It is knowing how to use your wits. (HCO PL 19 Sept 70 II)

WITHHOLD, an unspoken, unannounced transgression against a moral code by which the person was bound. (SH Spec 62, 6110C04)

WITHHOLDING TAX, the deduction by the employer from an individual's salary check of federal and/or state income tax in an amount specified by law that the employer, in turn, must pay to the taxing authority.

WITHHOLD OF NOTHINGNESS, when an F/Ning student is interrupted by the supervisor he can be given a **withhold of nothingness.** The student may say "No, I've just been checked up" and the supervisor goes away. But the student now wonders "Am I trying to hide something?" "Am I really doing all right?" etc. A **withhold of nothingness.** (HCO PL 26 Jun 72)

WITH ORGANIZATION, interested in **org** or post and willing to communicate **with** or about **org.** (HCOB 19 Aug 63)

WITNESS, a **witness** is anyone who is called before the committee (Committee of Evidence) to give evidence who is not an Interested Party. (HCO PL 7 Sept 63)

WORD CLEARING CORRECTION LIST REVISED, HCO Bulletin 21 July 1971RC, *Word Clearing Series 35R, Word Clearing Correction List revised.* Usually written "**WCCL.**" This is the famous **list** that goes with method 1 **word clearing** or with any **word clearing** bog. Also corrects high and low TA when it occurs in a **word clearing** session. This is the **word clearer's** friendly friend. (LRH ED 257 INT) *Abbr.* WCCL.

WORD CLEARING FESTIVAL, the great **word clearing festival!** We are about to begin the greatest efficiency, happiness increasing party of all time. Every man, woman and child on this great ship is about to be **word cleared** method 1 on their education. Method 2 on their hats. Flag has 100 auditors Class III or above, 100! From this stellar assembly will be chosen the most upstat fantastic auditors you have ever seen. For 12 stupendous days these auditors will be assembled in the largest space of the ship performing acts unduplicatable in any other galaxy. Three inch grins will be turned into 10 inch grins. VGIs will turn into VVVVVVVVGIs before your very eyes. The upstat crew is about to move up to the stellar band. (OODs 5 Sept 71)

WORD LISTS, (**word lists** for prepared lists) nearly every prepared list has all its words on a separate sheet, ready for word clearing on the pc. All the **words** on a **list** are cleared on a pc without repeating the same word or asking the list question. Such **lists** are issued for auditor convenience. (LRH ED 257 INT)

WORD OF MOUTH, 1. word of mouth is a public relations comm line superior to press, radio, television or Mr. Big. Radio, press and TV only seek to create "**word of mouth.**" This term means what people say to one another. By standing for what people think is good and opposing what people think is bad greatly speeds **word of mouth.** (HCO PL 17 Jun 69) **2.** there is internal communication amongst the publics and within each public, know as "**word of mouth** advertising" and "goodwill." (HCO PL 22 Jul 71)

WORK, activity with purpose. (*POW,* p. 32)

Work

WORKABLE TECHNOLOGY, something to offer that is desirable and will be received by individuals in the public body. (HCO PL 21 Jan 65)

WORK CARD, (engine room) upon receipt of a reported outness the Section Chief does the following: (1) logs the report in the job log. (2) makes out a **work card** using a standard printed one, filling in: (a) designation—that is the short form of the post title which will handle the job. (b) date—that is the date when he logs the report. (c) information by terminal who sent the comm. (d) running number of job. (e) particulars. (f) if LRH order or any other needing compliance report. The terminal under whose title the **work card** is hung is responsible for the **card** places there as well as the job which he should do that day. (FO 2690)

WORKCARD BOARD, a **board** placed near the Section Chief's desk, at a convenient place, containing each post's name under the Section Chief and providing two hooks for each post. The top one holds the **workcards** to be done and the bottom one the **workcards** which are done. (FO 2690)

WORKER, a person who is gainfully employed or who performs work especially of a manual or mechanical nature.

WORKER, GAINFUL, a person who is normally gainfully employed. This holds true even if the person is not currently employed or seeking employment but excludes the person who is normally unemployed or on welfare.

WORKER, MANUAL, a skilled or unskilled person who habitually uses tools, instruments, or machines in the performance of his job. He usually works under a foreman and is mainly responsible only for his own job. He does not do hiring or firing but may have authority over other workers; a blue collar worker.

WORKER, NEW, person who is a new employee in an organization, particularly denoting one who has never worked for that company before. Also called a new hire.

WORKER, NORMAL, a trained employee who is producing well on his job, using a normal amount of effort to obtain efficiency, with a minimum of mistakes, and consistently high quality work.

WORKER-ORIENTED, the **worker - oriented** fellow cares for the **worker** but not for the organization. So we have a final extinction of the worker by the organization vanishing and no longer able to employ. (HCO PL 10 Nov 66)

WORKER, SKILLED, a person such as a journeyman or craftsman who possesses the skill and experience to do a job which may call for application of a wide range of techniques.

WORK HOURS, the hours when a person is supposed to be on the job such as 9 a.m. to 5 p.m.

WORKING ASSETS, see ASSETS, WORKING.

WORKING CAPITAL, see CAPITAL, WORKING.

WORKING CAPITAL CYCLE, the cycle of spending capital for raw materials and operations which results in saleable products for which income is received that can replenish the original working capital spent.

WORKING CAPITAL RATIO, see CURRENT RATIO.

WORKING CONTROL, although ownership of 51 per cent of a corporation's voting stock is usually considered necessary to have working control, skillful control may also be exercised with a lesser amount of stock owned by a group if it agrees and works with a single purpose.

WORKING EMPLOYER, an employer who works in the business along with his employees.

WORKING FILES, see ACTION FILES.

WORKING INSTALLATION, **1.** something that is operational. (HCO PL 13 Jul 74 II) **2.** a unit, section, department or division operating well. (HCO PL 11 Aug 71 II) **3.** a **working installation** is any group which is delivering an adequate production of that product which they are supposed to deliver and you leave those alone. (FEBC 11, 7102C03 SO II)

WORK IN PROGRESS, work that is not yet finished but is at some partial stage of completion.

WORK LOAD, the amount of work that is assigned or regularly accomplished by an individual employee or department.

WORK MANAGER, a manufacturing executive who is in complete charge of production and responsible for the overall management of employees and the meeting of work targets.

WORK PARTY MISSION, a **work party mission** has come into existence, based on a need to handle a specific area in an org, usually one that is backlogged or badly out of present time. Example: a **work party** is sent to an org to get CF into PT. That is what they do, all day long, every day, until they have completed the **mission**. They are not expected to write letters, act as CF clerk or any other action. (FO 2360)

WORK RESTRICTION, an intentional act by employees to restrict their work output so that it falls below usual or acceptable standards and thus create a noticeable hindrance to a business.

WORK, RETURNED, faulty products that consumers have returned.

WORK SIMPLIFICATION, the streamlining of a work or business operation by reorganization of materials, equipment, methods and environmental characteristics to increase employee morale and raise efficiency, output and product quality.

WORKS STAFF, white collar office employees up to the level of supervisors whose work is connected to the manufacturing operations in a plant.

WORK STOPPAGE, the discontinuance of work by employees in an effort to bring pressure to bear on an employer for a particular benefit such as a pay increase.

WORLDWIDE (WW), **1.** the corporation that owns and controls Scn orgs, currently under the advices of the Sea Organization. (HCO PL 9 Mar 72 I) **2.** to clarify the functions and purposes of Scn organizations, this was the original intention: **Worldwide** was to provide supreme control over Scn and orgs over the world. Continental orgs under the guidance of **WW** took full responsibility for their continental areas, Central Orgs under the guidance of Continental took full responsibility for their zones. Area Orgs took full responsibility for their own areas. **WW** founded new Continental Orgs, Continental Orgs founded Central Orgs. Central Orgs founded Area Orgs. Area Orgs founded Franchise Centers. This was the original pattern of intention. (LRH ED 1 INT) **3.** the Scn **Worldwide** Management Control Center was established at Saint Hill Manor, East Grinstead, Sussex in 1959. It is the organization to which Scn Orgs over the world pay their administrative ten per cents. It is the Commonwealth Center and Board of the Church of Scientology of California. (LRH ED 135 INT) **4. WW's** duty is to keep outer orgs functioning and driving the public into those outer orgs, making sure their tech is good and standard and going on up to SH, which money is then used to again go through this cycle. (6805C24 SO) **5. WW** should be that agency of SH which makes sure that tons of students are driven up to the SH level all the way on standard tech. It's a sort of permanent international mission. (6805C24 SO) **6.** the Central Office of HCO for this planet. There are three types of HCO offices. These are (1) **Worldwide**, (2) Continental and (3) Area. In London all three office types exist. All accounting reports, copyright files, book inventory reports, authority for book printing and shipment, scheduling of ACCs and Congresses, appointment of continental and area personnel, issuance of all policy letters, issuance of book MSS, HCOBs, PABs, magazine materials, tape transcriptions, etc., are done from HCO **WW**. The general management of HCOs is done by me from London even when I am elsewhere than London. The master library of tapes, books, copyrights, MSS, are all in London. All routine reports, finance, requests for books, requests for policy, should be made to London. HCO **WW** has as allowed personnel HCO Executive Sec **World**, HCO Communicator, Magazines and PABs **World**, Tape Transcriptions **W**, Tape Library **W**, HCO Board of Review **W**, Book Administrator **W**, HCO Steno **W**, plus other personnel as needful. (HCO PL 2 Jan 59) *Abbr.* WW.

WORLD WIDE COUNCIL OF THREE, HCO Secretary **WW** is the **Worldwide** level executive for Division One (HCO) and a member of the **World Wide Council of Three** of which the Org Sec **WW** and the Assistant Treasurer **WW** are the other two. (HCO PL 4 Mar 65, *Hat Material, Division 1, HCO Secretary WW*)

WORLDWIDE DIVISION, the **Worldwide Division** at Saint Hill shall hereafter function as a service center to all and shall contain HCO and org representatives for every continental area and for use by every org's Exec Secs in expediting service, students, pcs and material and personnel for their orgs. The **WW** Exec Secs are there to make service to and production for all orgs real and effective. (HCO PL 21 Sept 67, *Worldwide and Saint Hill Functions Redefined*)

WORLDWIDE OPERATING THETAN LIAISON UNIT, in general action it is known as **OT WW Liaison Unit.** It is to consist of a Commanding Officer, a Supercargo and a Chief Officer representing those divisions. It acts as **liaison** with the Sea Org, the Advanced Org, all OT Projects and **Worldwide.** (HCO PL 28 Jan 68)

WRITE-DOWN, the partial write-off or reduction of the posted value of an asset, transferred from an asset account to an expense account.

WRITE-OFF, when an account or asset has lost its value or proves costly it gets treated as an expense and is transferred to an expense account (written off).

WRITE-UP, 1. an overstatement of the true value of one's assets. 2. a review, description or short piece of writing done usually for publication purposes.

WRITE UP HIS HAT, usually when a person has been on a job a while he knows what it consists of. He then should **write up his hat,** meaning in this case a folder which contains past orders and directions which outline his job plus his own summary of his job. When one is transferred or leaves a post he is supposed to "**write up his hat**" which is to say, modernize this summary of the post. (HCO PL 3 Dec 68)

WRITTEN REPORT, any typed or written report but not one given verbally.

WRONG ACTION, 1. a **wrong action** is **wrong** to the degree that it harms the greatest number of dynamics. (HCO PL 1 Nov 70 III) **2. wrong actions** are the result of an error followed by an insistence on having been right. Instead of righting the error (which would involve being **wrong**) one insists the error was a right action and so repeats it. (HCO PL 1 Nov 70 III)

WRONG SOURCE, 1. is the other side of the coin of wrong target. Information taken from **wrong source**, orders taken from the **wrong source**, gifts or materiel taken from **wrong source** all add up to eventual confusion and possible trouble. (HCO PL 26 Nov 70) **2.** this is the opposite direction from wrong target. An example would be a President of the United States in 1973 using the opinions and congratulations of soviet leaders to make his point with American voters. There are many examples of this out-point. (HCO PL 30 Sept 73 I)

WRONG TARGET, 1. mistaken objective wherein one believes he is or should be reaching toward A and finds he is or should be reaching toward B is an out-point. This is commonly mistaken identity. It is also mistaken purposes or goals. (HCO PL 19 Sept 70 III) **2.** this means in effect an incorrect selection of an objective to attempt or attack. (HCO PL 8 Aug 70)

WRONG WHY, 1. a real why opens the door to handling. If you write down a why, ask this question of it: "Does this open the door to handling?" If it does not, then it is a **wrong why.** (HCO PL 12 Aug 74) **2.** the incorrectly identified outness which when applied does not lead to recovery. (HCO PL 13 Oct 70 II)

W UNIT, in 1962 a Saint Hill Special Briefing Course Unit specializing in the theory of the usual beginning course fundamentals, but only GF Model Session, including mid ruds, big mid ruds, and meter, TRs, havingness and CCHs. Practical incuded TRs, meter, GF model session only, CCHs and assists. (HCO PL 8 Dec 62)

WW ADDRESSO COORDINATOR, the post of **WW Addresso Coordinator** is placed under Department 2 WW. He is responsible to see that the lines set up to expedite the routing of new names, flow fast and are not blocked with non-compliances. He sees that the org **addresso** policy is followed to avoid confusion. He makes sure that addresso lists are routed to the right place at the right time. Backlogs are severely treated. (HCO PL 2 Sept 68 II) [The above HCO PL was cancelled by BPL 10 Oct 75 IV.]

WW COMMITTEE OF EVIDENCE, this is the **Worldwide Committee of Evidence,** convened by the Executive Director. It cares for any and all matters arising from committees at lower levels and reviews all cases referred to it. (HCO PL 7 Sept 63)

WW SPEC PROGS EX OFFICER, the WW organization pattern is the same as any other org's. The International Officers are placed in the divisions to which they most closely relate and have only international duties with no org additional duties, i.e., there is a WW Ethics Officer and also an Int Ethics Officer. But there is no **WW Spec Progs Ex Officer** only an Int Spec Officer as it is not an ordinary org post. (HCO PL 19 Oct 67) See INTERNATIONAL SPECIAL PROGRAMS EXECUTION OFFICER.

WW TIME MACHINES, there are two **WW time machines:** one for orders to outer orgs and one for orders to Saint Hill. The outer org **time machine** is a stalk of four baskets. Each basket marks a week of **time.** Your order is placed in the top basket and each week it is moved down a basket. After it has been in the bottom basket a week, it falls off the **time machine** and is returned to you with or without a compliance as the case may be. A month is usually the **time** factor allowed for a compliance to be received back from outer orgs. The **time machine** for the Saint Hill environ consists of five baskets, allowing a week to be given for compliance. (HCO PL 1 Jul 66)

XEROX OFFICER, post in the Department of Communications. Anyone desiring to have anything **xeroxed** must route such to the **Xerox Officer** stating the number of copies required and the purpose of such. (HCO PL 20 Aug 65, *Appointment of the Xerox Officer*)

X UNIT, **1.** in 1962 a Saint Hill Special Briefing Course Unit with theory covering everything relative to R2-12, data on mid ruds, tiger drilling and big tiger. Practical was all R2-12 practical, any drills omitted in W Unit, tiger drilling and big tiger. (HCO PL 8 Dec 62) **2.** rudiments and havingness. That's all they're permitted to audit on the pc. (6209C03)

Y

YELLOW, *n.* The acknowledgment copy of a communication. (*HTLTAE,* p. 123)

YELLOW INVOICE, 1. these **invoice** copies are distributed to the department concerned with the service or item purchased. (**Invoice** routing for all orgs except Saint Hill) (HCO PL 16 Feb 66) **2.** (Saint Hill only) **yellow** debit and credit **invoices** are kept in the Department of Income for collection purposes. **Yellow** not debit or credit **invoices** for students and pcs are routed to Address then to CF via reception, so that reception can check the **invoices** against the in-the-org list. Other not debit or credit are routed from Address straight to CF. (HCO PL 13 Oct 66)

YELLOW LANYARD, officers' **lanyard.** (BO 21, 11 Jun 67)

YELLOW TAB, (Flag only) the examiner is to **yellow tab** (quite apart from red tabbing which is also done) any pc that looks the least bit tired or non-VGIs or withdrawn, and is to rush the **yellow tab** straight to the C/S with the exam report. (BFO 46)

YELLOW TABBED LABEL, (or **yellow**) tape color flash code—for HCO Dissem Master. These are never erased, may not be played or loaned or used. They are for archives only. "Production" is written on the **yellow tab label** of a production master. (HCO PL 7 Dec 65)

YEOMAN, 1. A CO's secretary-receptionist to handle his traffic, shake the dev-t out of it, put in some kind of order, keep his day and tell people about appointments and things of that character. (ESTO 9, 7203C05 SO I) **2.** messenger. (ED 145 Flag) **3.** communicator. (OODs 29 Oct 69) See CAPTAIN'S YEOMAN.

YIELD, the amount an investment brings in return such as dividends or interest paid to holders of stock. A stock currently selling for $30 which paid total annual dividends of $3 has a 10% return or yield.

Y UNIT, in 1962 a Saint Hill Special Briefing Course Unit with theory covering everything relative to finding goals and clearing; 3GAXX, Routine 3-21 and HCOBs on wrong goals. Practical—all Clearing practical, free needle, etc. (HCO PL 8 Dec 62)

Z

ZERO COMM COURSE, all Level 0 courses wherever taught must begin with the Dublin type PE Comm Course. It will be called the **Zero Comm Course.** This consists of the same TRs as the real comm course but run without the coaching flunking. (HCO PL 22 Apr 65, *Level 0 Comm Course*)

ZERO COURSE, Hubbard Recognized Scientologist. The basic point of **Zero** today is Find the Auditor. "Look at me who am I?" "Who would I have to be to audit you?" is the type of process that best defines the level—recognition. (HCO PL 16 May 65 III)

ZERO DEFECTS, a plan to reward employees who can work for a stated length of time producing no defects and wasting no materials.

ZERO-PLUS TICK, term used for a stock transaction made at the exact price as the previous trade but higher than the preceding different price.

ZONAL ORG, if and when a continental (org) has under it more than five orgs, where established by SEC Ed approved by the Guardian, one of these may become a **Zone Org.** A Zone Executive Division is then established with specific orgs under it and the OIC report routing is from area to zone to continental to international at Worldwide. A Zone Exec Division is organized like any other and has a composite statistic made up of the Area Orgs under it. If a **Zonal Org** gets more than five orgs under it one of these is designated a Sub-**Zonal Org**, taking under it excess orgs. (HCO PL 1 Mar 66 II)

ZONE EXECUTIVE DIVISION, see ZONAL ORG.

Z UNIT, in 1962 a Saint Hill Special Briefing Course Unit with theory covering additional clearing data, form of the course and Scn plans. Practical was a review of drills and TRs. (HCO PL 8 Dec 62)

Abbreviations

A, **1.** (affinity) affinity is the ability to occupy the same space. (6910C21SO) **2.** affluence. (FBDL 290) **3.** assistant. (BPL 5 Nov 72RA)

A/, acting. (BPL 5 Nov 72RA)

A/AIDE(S), **1.** Assistant Aides. (FO 2905) **2.** Assistant International Secretary. (HCO PL 7 Mar 72)

AAR, [*All About Radiation.*]

AB, **1.** abandon target. (Target marking and tlx code). (CBO 325) **2.** Aberdeen UK, (HCO PL 2 Mar 59, *HCO Cable and Dispatch Designation System*) **3.** able-bodied seaman. (BPL 5 Nov 72RA)

AB CONFERENCE, Able-Bodied Seaman Conference. (FSO 156)

ABIL, [*Ability Magazine.*]

ABS, (international telex jargon) absent subscriber = absent subscriber, office closed. (BPL 5 Nov 72RA-1)

ABT, about. (BPL 5 Nov 72RA)

ABV, above. (BPL 5 Nov 72RA)

AC, **1.** Ability Congress. (HCOB 29 Sept 66) **2.** Accommodation Counselor. (BFO 45) **3.** account. (BPL 5 Nov 72RA) **4.** Advisory Council. (HCO PL 1 Nov 66 II) **5.** Aides' Council (CBO 173)

AC-1/2, the AC-1 Form or AC-2 Form. (BPL 4 Dec 72 IIRB)

AC 42, financial report. (HCO PL 11 Dec 62, *Change in Report Line.*)

AC 43, HCO Accounts Form AC 43. (HCO PL 16 Apr 63) [The above HCO PL was cancelled by BPL 10 Oct 75 IV.]

ACAD, Academy. (BPL 5 Nov 72RA)

ACAD ADMIN, academy administrator. (HCO PL 28 Feb 59)

ACC, Advanced Clinical Course. (HCO PL 2 Sept 69)

ACCPT, accept. (BPL 5 Nov 72RA)

ACCTNT, accountant. (BPL 5 Nov 72RA)

ACCTS, accounts. (COLRHED 103)

ACE FT, Ace Fighter Team. (BO 37 UK, 26 Jan 74)

ACFB, Ad Council FB. (BPL 11 May 71 II-1)

ACK, acknowledge. (BPL 5 Nov 72RA)

ACK'ED, acknowledged. (*BCR*, p. 23)

ACTN, action. (BPL 5 Nov 72RA)

AD, **1.** Adelaide. (HCO PL 4 Jan 66 II) **2.** advance. (HCO PL 7 Dec 71) **3.** advanced. (HCOB 2 Aug 71)

ADCOM, Advisory Committee. (BPL 5 Nov 72RA)

ADCOMM, Advisory Committee. (HCO PL 12 Aug 65)

AD COUNCIL, Advisory Council. (HCO PL 1 Nov 66 II)

AD CSE, advanced courses. (HCOB 14 Jul 70)

ADD I/C, Addressograph In-Charge. (HCOB 23 Aug 65)

ADDO, addresso. (BPL 5 Nov 72RA)

ADDR, address. (BPL 5 Nov 72RA)

ADDRESSO, **1.** Addresses Section. (HCOB 23 Aug 65) **2.** addressograph. (HCO PL 12 Jan 62)

ADDTN(L), addition(al). (BPL 5 Nov 72RA)

ADD UNK, address unknown. (HCO PL 18 Feb 73 II)

ADMIN, **1.** administration. (HCO PL 4 Jun 71) **2.** administrative. (SEC ED No. 9, 16 Dec 58) **3.** administrator (HCOB 23 Aug 65)

ADMIN TRS, administrative training drills. (BTB 7 Feb 71)

ADV, advanced. (HCO PL 12 Aug 71 IV)

ADV CSES, advanced courses. (FSO 101)

ADV MAG, *Advance Magazine*. (BPL 5 Nov 72RA)

A/E, Area estates. (ED 16 Area Estates)

A/E ESTO, Acting Executive Establishment Officer. (OODS 9 Apr 72)

AF, Africa. (HCO PL 4 Jan 66 II)

AFF, affluence. (BPL 5 Nov 72RA)

A/FFR, Assistant Flag Flag Rep. (BPL 5 Nov 72RA)

A/G, Assistant Guardian. (BPL 6 Jul 75 III)

A/G F, Assistant Guardian for Finance. (BPL 14 Nov 74)

AGL, Assistant Guardian Legal. (BPL 5 Nov 72RA)

AGN, again. (BPL 5 Nov 72RA)

AGRMNT, agreement. (BPL 5 Nov 72RA)

AHMC, [Anatomy of the Human Mind Congress.]

AIHED, American Institute for Human Engineering and Development. (FMO 221, 14 Oct 69)

AK, Auckland. (HCO PL 4 Jan 66 II)

AKH, admin know-how. (BPL 5 Nov 72RA)

ALLOC, allocation. (BPL 5 Nov 72RA)

ALRDY, already. (BPL 5 Nov 72RA)

ALTHO, although. (BPL 5 Nov 72RA)

AM, *ante meridiem* (before noon—morning). (BPL 5 Nov 72RA)

AMA, American Medical Association. (HCO PL 14 Aug 63)

AMER, America(n). (BPL 5 Nov 72RA)

AMS, Amsterdam. (BPL 10 Apr 73R)

AMT, amount. (BPL 5 Nov 72RA)

ANAL, analysis. (BPL 5 Nov 72RA)

ANS (WRD), answer(ed). (BPL 5 Nov 72RA)

ANZACS, Australians and New Zealanders. (FO 3193-1)

ANZO, Australia New Zealand Oceania. (BPL 10 Apr 73R)

AO, **1.** Advanced Org. (FO 331) **2.** aides order. (HCO PL 24 Sept 70R) **3.** the Saint Hill Special Briefing Course student in a Unit is designated for the classes being studied for, as AO = Class Zero Unit A. (HCO PL 14 Oct 65, *Course Pattern*)

AOA, AO Alicante. (ED 68 Flag)

AOG, AO Greece. (FO 1847)

AOL, Advanced Organization Liaison. (FO 986)

AOLA, Advanced Org Los Angeles. (LRH ED 166 Int.)

AOLF, AO liaison for Flag. (FO 1237)

AOL-LA, Advanced Organization Liaison Los Angeles (FO 1364)

AOLS, Advanced Organization Liaison Scotland. (FO 1364)

AOLWW, Advanced Organization World Wide. (FO 1364)

AOSH, **1.** Advanced Org—Saint Hill. (LRH ED 166 Int.) **2.** this is a combination AO and SH. (LRH ED 159R-I Int.)

AOSH DK, AOSH Denmark. (BPL 5 Nov 72RA)

AOSH UK, Advanced Org-Saint Hill United Kingdom. (LRH ED 166 Int.)

AP, advance payment. (HCO PL 26 Nov 65R)

AP&A, [*Advanced Procedure and Axioms.*]

APPRNTC(SHIP), apprentice(ship). (BPL 5 Nov 72RA)

APPROP, appropriate. (BPL 5 Nov 72RA)

APPRV, approve. (BPL 5 Nov 72RA)

APPT, appoint(ment). (BPL 5 Nov 72RA)

APR, **1.** advanced payment received. (FO 2988) **2.** April. (BPL 5 Nov 72RA)

APT, aptitude. (BPL 5 Nov 72RA)

APU, advanced payments used. (BPL 5 Nov 72RA)

AR, *Avon River.* (FO 336)

ARBIT, arbitrary. (BPL 5 Nov 72RA)

ARC BR, ARC break. (ED 473 WW, 842 SH)

ARC X, ARC break. (BPL 5 Nov 72RA)

ARCXC, number of ARC broken individuals contacted. (BPL 5 Nov 72RA)

ARCXF, ARC breaks found. (BPL 5 Nov 72RA)

ARCXH, number of ARC broken individuals handled and signed up for service or returned to service. (BPL 5 Nov 72RA)

ARCXN, ARC broken. (BPL 5 Nov 72RA)

ARND, around. (BPL 5 Nov 72RA)

ARRNG, arrange. (BPL 5 Nov 72RA)

ARRV(L), arrive(al). (BPL 5 Nov 72RA)

AS, administrative staff (number of admin personnel). (BPL 5 Nov 72RA)

A/S, [abbreviation (Danish) meaning aktieselskab which means Limited (Liability) Company.]

ASAP, as soon as possible. (BPL 5 Nov 72RA)

ASHO, American Saint Hill Organization. (BPL 5 Nov 72RA)

ASR, Advance Scheduling Registrar. (BPL 9 Jan 67R)

ASSGN, assign. (BPL 5 Nov 72RA)

ASSN, association. (BPL 5 Nov 72RA)

ASSN SEC, Association Secretary. (HCO PL 19 Oct 64)

ASSN SEC'S SEC, the Association Secretary's secretary. The secretary to the Assn Sec. (HCO PL 12 Mar 61 III)

ASSOC SEC, Association Secretary. (5812C29)

ASST, 1. assist. (BPL 5 Nov 72RA) **2.** assistant. (FSO 529)

ASST/AIDE, Assistant Aide. (FO 2707)

ASST G, Assistant Guardian. (HCO PL 8 Dec 68)

ASST GF, Assistant Guardian for Finance. (HCO PL 8 Dec 68)

AST, Austin. (HCO PL 4 Jan 66 II)

AT, Athens, Greece. (HCO PL 2 Mar 59, *HCO Cable and Dispatch Designation System*)

ATC, Admin Training Corps. (FO 3324R)

ATH, *Athena.* (HCO PL 10 Apr 73) [The above HCO PL was replaced by BPL 10 Apr 73R which deleted the abbreviation of *Athena.*]

ATO, *Apollo* Troupe Org. (OODS 12 May 74)

ATTN, attention. (BPL 5 Nov 72RA)

AU, Australia. (HCO PL 2 Mar 59, *HCO Cable and Dispatch Designation System*)

AUD, [*The Auditor Magazine.*]

AUD(TD)(TNG), audit(ed)(ing). (BPL 5 Nov 72RA)

AUDTR, auditor. (BPL 5 Nov 72RA)

AUG, August. (BPL 5 Nov 72RA)

AUTH, authority. (BPL 5 Nov 72RA)

AUTO-EVALUATION, automatic evaluation. (BPL 28 Apr 61R)

AV, audio-visio. (COLRHED 117)

AVAIL, available. (BPL 5 Nov 72RA)

AVG, average. (BPL 5 Nov 72RA)

AVU, 1. Authority and Verification Unit. (OODs 14 Apr 72) **2.** Authority and Verifications Unit. (HCO PL 15 Aug 73) **3.** Authorizations and Verifications Unit, the unit at Flag that does exactly those functions. HCO PL 28 Jul 73RA) [All three entries here denote the same unit on Flag.]

AWB, airwaybill. (FO 3081)

AWRD, award. (BPL 5 Nov 72RA)

AX, axiom. (BPL 5 Nov 72RA)

B, 1. body. (FO 1109) **2.** books. (FO 2988) **3.** bugged. (Target marking and tlx code). (CBO 325)

BI, the Saint Hill Special Briefing Course student in a Unit is designated for the classes being studied for, as BI = Class I Unit B. (HCO PL 14 Oct 65, *Course Pattern*)

BII, the Saint Hill Special Briefing Course student in a Unit is designated for the classes being studied for, as BII = Class II Unit B. (HCO PL 14 Oct 65, *Course Pattern*)

B/A, see BOOK ADMINISTRATOR.

BA AND D OFFICER, Book Ads and Distribution Officer. (BPL 15 Jun 73R I)

BAL, balance. (BPL 5 Nov 72RA)

B&C, [*Background and Ceremonies of the Church of Scientology of California, World Wide.*]

BB, 1. book buyer. (BPL 4 Apr 73R) **2.** Brisbane. (HCO PL 2 Mar 59, *HCO Cable and Dispatch Designation System)*

BCF, birthday contribution fund. (ED 473 Flag)

BCPC, basic course and processing completion. (BPL 5 Nov 72RA)

BCPT, basic course points. (BPL 5 Nov 72RA)

BCR, [*The Book of Case Remedies.*]

BD, board. (SEC ED 26, 8 Jan 59)

BDCS, The Boards of Directors of the Churches of Scientology. (BPL 1 Sept 66R)

BDN, blowdown. (BPL 5 Nov 72RA)

BE, Berlin. (HCO PL 2 Mar 59, *HCO Cable and Dispatch Designation System*)

BED, Board Executive Directive. (HCO PL 24 Sept 70R)

BEG, beginning. (BPL 5 Nov 72RA)

BER, bad examiner report. (Esto 3, 7203C02 SO I)

BERK, Berkeley. (BPL 5 Nov 72RA)

BFO, Base Flag Order. (BFO 84)

BFR, before. (BPL 5 Nov 72RA)

BGN, begin. (BPL 5 Nov 72RA)

BI, 1. Birmingham UK. (HCO PL 2 Mar 59, *HCO Cable and Dispatch Designation System)* **2.** Board of Issues. (BPL 23 Dec 66R) **3.** bye = goodbye. (BPL 5 Nov 72RA-1)

BIBI, bye bye. (BPL 5 Nov 72RA)

BIs, bad indicators. (Esto 3, 7203C02 SO I)

BK, **1.** book. (BPL 5 Nov 72RA) **2.** (international telex jargon) break = I cut off. (BPL 5 Nov 72RA-1)

BKLOG, backlog. (BPL 5 Nov 72RA)

BKSLS, book sales. (BPL 5 Nov 72RA)

BK/STR, bookstore. (BPL 5 Nov 72RA)

BL, **1.** big league. (BPL 5 Nov 72RA) **2.** Bloemfontein. (HCO PL 2 Mar 59, *HCO Cable and Dispatch Designation System*)

B/L, bill of lading. (FO 3081)

BLDG, building. (BPL 5 Nov 72RA)

BLNCE, balance. (BPL 5 Nov 72RA)

BLRS, see "BIG LEAGUE" REGISTRATION SERIES.

BLS, *Big League Sales.* (BPL 5 Nov 72RA)

BLV, *Bolivar.* (BPL 5 Nov 72RA)

BM, **1.** [Abbreviation for "body motion." Normally used on auditor report forms and on session work sheets. Refer to *Dianetics Today,* p. 685.] **2.** bulk mail. (BPL 5 Nov 72RA)

BMB, the *Books Make Booms* brochure. (FBDL 591)

BMC, business management consultant. (BPL 10 Feb 73 II)

BMO, **1.** bulk mail out. (BPL 5 Nov 72RA) **2.** Business Management Org. (HCO PL 12 Apr 73) [The above HCO PL was cancelled by BPL 10 Oct 75 XI.]

BMTO, Book Marketing Officer. (BPL 5 Nov 72RA)

BNG, being. (BPL 5 Nov 72RA)

BO, Base Order. (HCO PL 24 Sept 70R)

BOD(S), body(ies). (BPL 5 Nov 72RA)

B OF I, Board of Investigation. (BPL 5 Nov 72RA)

BP, bills paid. (BPL 5 Nov 72RA)

BPC, bypassed charge. (BPL 5 Nov 72RA)

BPI, Broad Public Issue. (HCO PL 22 May 59)

BPL, Board Policy Letter. (HCO PL 24 Sept 70R)

BPR, black propaganda (black PR). (BPL 5 Nov 72RA)

BR, body router. (BPL 5 Nov 72RA)

BR DIR, Branch Director. (HCO PL 20 Oct 72) [The above HCO PL was cancelled by BPL 10 Oct 75 X.]

BRE, **1.** bugged requires eval. (Target marking and tlx code) (CBO 325) **2.** [Business Reply envelope.]

B REG, body reg. (BPL 5 Nov 72RA)

BRF, **1.** body routing form. (ED 144 FAO) **2.** brief (BPL 5 Nov 72RA)

BRK, break. (BPL 5 Nov 72RA)

BRKDWN, breakdown. (BPL 5 Nov 72RA)

B RTR, body router. (BPL 5 Nov 72RA)

BS, **1.** Bachelor of Scientology. (HCOB 23 Aug) **2.** Beginning Scientologist. (HCO PL 1 Sept 65 IV) **3.** (gross) book sales. (BPL 5 Nov 72RA)

B'S, bulletins. (HCO PL 24 Sept 70R) [The abbreviation "B's" appears on HCO PL 8 Dec 62. The abbreviation "HCOB's" is more commonly used for "Bulletins" or Hubbard Communications Office Bulletins.]

BSC, basic. (BPL 5 Nov 72RA)

B SCN, Bachelor of Scientology. (HCO PL 20 Dec 62)

BSN, Boston. (BPL 10 Apr 73R)

BTB, Board Technical Bulletin. (HCO POL 24 Sept 70R)

BTR, better. (BPL 5 Nov 72RA)

BTTL PLN, battle plan. (BPL 5 Nov 72RA)

BTWN, between. (BPL 5 Nov 72RA)

BU, **1.** boats unit. (FSO 249) **2.** bureau. (FO 3152RR)

BUF, Buffalo. (BPL 10 Apr 73R)

BUGD, bugged. (BPL 5 Nov 72RA)

BX, bureaux. (FO 3066)

BYO, Bulawayo. (BPL 10 Apr 73R)

C, **1.** Commodore. (ED 459-38 Flag) **2.** communication. (HCO PL 18 Feb 72) **3.** continental. (HCO PL 2 Jan 59) **4.** (mission order target code) cope-C — doing the best one can with it. (FO 2936) **5.** copyright. (FO 3264) **6.** copy tape. (BPL 12 Jan 74 I)

CIII, The Saint Hill Special Briefing Course student in a unit is designated for the classes being studied for, as CIII = Class III Unit C. (HCO PL 14 Oct 65, *Course Pattern*)

CIV, The Saint Hill Special Briefing Course student in a unit is designated for the classes being studied for, as CIV = Class IV Unit C. (HCO PL 14 Oct 65, *Course Pattern*)

CAN, Canada. (BPL 5 Nov 72RA)

CANCE, cancel whole eval. Must be followed by its number. (Target marking and tlx code). (CBO 325)

C AND A, Certs and Awards. (BPL 5 Nov 72RA)

CAPT, Captain. (ED 334-1 Flag)

CAS, Church of American Science. (PAB 74)

CB, Clearwater Building. (BFO 70)

C/B, cash/bills. (BPL 5 Nov 72RA)

CBK, call back = end the transmission and call me back in five minutes. (BPL 5 Nov 72RA-1)

CBL, call back later = call back later please, I am awaiting an important call on this line. (BPL 5 Nov 72RA-1)

CBM, congress, books, memberships. (HCO PL 9 Jun 59)

CBMT ACCOUNT, congress, books, magazines and tape account. (BPL 9 Sept 59)

CBO, Central Bureau Order. (HCO PL 24 Sept 70R)

CBT, congress, book and tapes sum. (HCO London 17 Apr 57)

C BY V, Clearing by valence. (HCOB 4 Jun 58)

CC, **1.** Celebrity Center. (BPL 25 Aug 75) **2.** Clearing Course. (HCO PL 6 Sept 72 II) **3.** Continental Captain. (SO ED 119 INT)

C/C, course change. (FO 3087)

CCH, cut the chatter. (BPL 5 Nov 72RA-1)

CCLA, Celebrity Centre Los Angeles. (BPL 10 Apr 73R)

CCNY, Celebrity Centre New York. (BPL 10 Apr 73R)

CC OFFICER, Case Cracking Section Officer. (HCO PL 4 May 65)

C/E, see CHIEF ENGINEER.

CECS, Committee of Examinations, Certifications and Services. (PAB 39)

CED, Compliance Executive Directive. (HCO PL 24 Sept 70R)

CELEB, celebrity. (BPL 5 Nov 72RA)

CEN-O, Designation on HCO Policy Letters and HCO Bulletins indicates dissemination and restriction as follows: to go to all staff of Central Organizations only plus HCO Area Offices, HCO Cont, HCO WW. (HCO PL 22 May 59)

CEN-O-CON, **1.** Designation on HCO Policy Letters and HCO Bulletins indicates dissemination and restriction as follows; to go to Association Secretaries or Organization Secretaries of Central Organizations only, not to staff; also to HCO Area Sec, HCO Cont, HCO WW. (HCO PL 22 May 59) **2.** HCO Policy Letters which are marked "Cen-O-Con" may be issued to all staff, including HASI personnel. All such HCO Policy Letters carry the same authority as SEC EDs and may be used as hat material if applicable. (BPL 25 Jun 59)

CENT, central. (BPL 5 Nov 72RA)

CF, central files. (HCO PL 19 Aug 59)

CFM, (international telex jargon) confirm = please confirm / I confirm. (BPL 5 Nov 72RA-1)

CG&AC, [The Classification Gradation and Awareness Chart.]

CGI, corrected gross income. (HCO PL 9 Mar 72 I)

CH, **1.** Chicago. (HCO PL 2 Mar 59, *HCO Cable and Dispatch Designation System*) **2.** chief. (BPL 5 Nov 72RA)

CHF(LY), chief(ly). (BPL 5 Nov 72RA)

CHI, Chicago. (BPL 10 Apr 73R)

CHK, check. (BPL 5 Nov 72RA)

CHKLST, checklist. (BPL 5 Nov 72RA)

CHKSHT, checksheet. (BPL 5 Nov 72RA)

CHNG, change. (BPL 5 Nov 72RA)

CHN SCHL, Chinese School. (BPL 5 Nov 72RA)

CH OFF, Chief officer. (ED 14 Area Estates)

CHQ, cheque. (BPL 5 Nov 72RA)

CHRMN, chairman. (BPL 5 Nov 72RA)

CHRT, chart. (BPL 5 Nov 72RA)

CI, counter intention, should be followed by a name for who. (Target marking and tlx code). (CBO 325)

CIC, **1.** Combat Information Center. (*HTLTAE,* P. 65) **2.** Continental Information Center of a CLO. (HCO PL 22 Jul 71) **3.** means Control Information Center. (FO 2392)

CIF, carriage, insurance and freight. (FO 2738)

CITO, city office. (BPL 5 Nov 72RA)

CK, check. (BPL 5 Nov 72RA)

CL, **1.** class. (BPL 5 Nov 72RA) **2.** clearing. (SEC ED 117 Int, 18 Oct 65)

CLARIF, clarify (clarification). (BPL 5 Nov 72RA)

CLASS VIII No.__, [Class VIII tape number __.]

CLD, could. (BPL 5 Nov 72RA)

C LIAISON OFFICER, Consumption Liaison Officer. (FO 3341)

CLN GRNDS, total grounds space in square feet in good appearance and care. [Clean grounds.] (BPL 5 Nov 72RA)

CLN SPCE, total useful space in square feet, building available and clean. [Clean space.] (BPL 5 Nov 72RA)

CLO, 1. Continental Liaison Office. (FO 3152RR) **2.** Continental Liaison Officer. (HCO PL 20 Apr 69 II) [The above HCO PL was cancelled by BPL 10 Oct 75 VII. The term Continental Liaison Officer appears in HCO PL 8 Sept 67 II.]

CLR, clear. (BPL 5 Nov 72RA)

CM, [Copy Master (tape).]

CMD, command. (BPL 5 Nov 72RA)

CMDR, 1. Commander. (FO 38-1) **2.** Commodore. (ED 236 Flag)

CMDRE, Commodore. (BPL 5 Nov 72RA)

CMDR MSNGR, Commodore's Messenger. (ED 319-1 Flag)

CMND, command. (BPL 5 Nov 72RA)

CMO, Commodore's Messenger Org. (FO 3587)

CM ORG, Commodore's Messenger Org. (FO 3385-3)

CMPGN, campaign. (BPL 5 Nov 72RA)

CMPLY, comply. (BPL 5 Nov 72RA)

CMSN, commission. (BPL 5 Nov 72RA)

CN, 1. Capetown. (HCO PL 2 Mar 59, *HCO Cable and Dispatch Designation System*) **2.** correction needed. (FSO 509)

CNCIL, council. (BPL 5 Nov 72RA)

CNCL, cancel. (BPL 5 Nov 72RA)

CNFRNT, confront. (BPL 5 Nov 72RA)

CNTCT, contact. (BPL 5 Nov 72RA)

CNTR CK, counter check. (BPL 5 Nov 72RA)

CNTRCT, contract. (BPL 5 Nov 72RA)

CNTR INTEN, counter intention. (BPL 5 Nov 72RA)

CO, 1. (letter designation on HCOBs) city office. These are issued to all city offices. (HCOB 24 Feb 59) **2.** Commanding Officer. (HCO PL 7 Mar 72) **3.** [Conditions Order.] **4.** Continental Order. (HCO PL 24 Sept 70R)

COF, designation on HCO Policy Letters and HCO Bulletins indicates dissemination and restriction as follows: HCO city offices and all their field auditor HCO franchises, central organizations, HCO Area, Continental and HCO WW. (HCO PL 22 May 59)

C OF, care of. (BPL 5 Nov 72RA)

C OF S, 1. Church of Scientology. (BPL 5 Nov 72RA) **2.** Congress of Scientologists. (HCOB 4 Oct 56)

C OF S OF C, Church of Scientology of California. (BPL 9 Mar 74)

COG, cognition, cognite. (BPL 5 Nov 72RA)

COL, (international telex jargon) collate = collation please/I collate. (BPL 5 Nov 72RA-1)

COLL, collection. (BPL 5 Nov 72RA)

COLLCT, collect. (BPL 5 Nov 72RA)

COLL OFFS, Collections Officers. (FO 3474-1RA)

COLRHED, Central Office of LRH ED. (COLRHED 1R)

COMDR, Commodore. (BPL 5 Nov 72RA)

COMLINE, a communications line. (*HTLTAE*, p. 118)

COMM, committee, communicate, communication, communicator. (BPL 5 Nov 72RA)

COMM BUREAU, see COMMUNICATION BUREAU.

COMM CENTRE, Communication Centre. (HCOB 23 Aug 65)

COMM EV, Committee of Evidence. (HCOB 23 Aug 65)

COMM LAG, communication lag. (BPL 5 Nov 72RA)

COMP, 1. compilations. (HCO PL 31 Jan 66) **2.** complete, completion. (BPL 5 Nov 72RA) **3.** the completed white copy of a message. *–v.* to complete. to stamp "Comp" and initial. (*HTLTAE*, p. 119)

COMP C, total number of completed cases. (BPL 5 Nov 72RA)

COMP C STC, number of completed cases and student comps. (BPL 5 Nov 72RA)

COMPL, compliance. (BPL 5 Nov 72RA)

COMPS, 1. compilations. (BPL 5 Nov 72RA) **2.** [compliances.]

COMSN, commission. (BPL 5 Nov 72RA)

CON, 1. letter designation on HCO Bulletins; city office only. These are issued to city offices only, not reissued. (HCOB 24 Feb 59) **2.** Conning Officer. (FO 1020) **3.** stands for and is short for "control." (FO 2111)

COND, condition. (BPL 5 Nov 72RA)

CONF, conference. (BPL 5 Nov 72RA)

CONFID, confidential. (BPL 5 Nov 72RA)

CONT, continental, continue(d)(ing). (BPL 5 Nov 72RA)

CONT'L, continental. (FO 2544)

CONT'L LO, Continental Liaison Officer. (HCO PL 18 Oct 67 II)

COO, designation on HCO Policy Letters and HCO Bulletins indicates dissemination and restriction as follows; HCO city offices only, not to be shown or given to HCO franchise holders or field auditors; also goes to central organizations, HCO Area, HCO Cont, HCO WW. (HCO PL 22 May 59)

COORD, coordinate, coordination. (BPL 5 Nov 72RA)

COP, Copenhagen, (BPL 10 Apr 73R)

CORP, corporation. (BPL 5 Nov 72RA)

CORR, correction. (OODS, 5 Mar 72)

CORRCT, correct. (BPL 5 Nov 72RA)

COURSE ADMIN, course administrator. (HCO PL 16 Mar 71R)

COURSE SUP, course supervisor. (HCOB 23 Aug 65)

CPA, Certified Public Accountant. (BPL 5 Nov 72RA)

CPL, couple. (BPL 5 Nov 72RA)

CPO, Central Personnel Office(r), Chief Petty Officer. (BPL 5 Nov 72RA)

CR **1.** compliance report. (BPL 19 Oct 73) **2.** correction form. (HCO PL 27 Feb 71 I) **3.** credit. (BPL 5 Nov 72RA)

CRC, credit collected. (BPL 5 Nov 72RA)

CREO, the Committee to Re-Involve Ex-Offenders. (FBDL 522)

CRMMD, crammed. (BPL 5 Nov 72RA)

CRMMNG, cramming. (BPL 5 Nov 72RA)

CRS, course. (BPL 5 Nov 72RA)

CRT, court. (BPL 5 Nov 72RA)

CRV(?), (international telex jargon) can receive = do you receive well?/I receive well. (BPL 5 Nov 72RA-1)

CS, **1.** Case Supervisor. (BPL 4 Dec 71R III) **2.** Commodore's Staff. (FO 795)

CSA, Commodore's Staff Aides. (BPL 1 Sept 66R)

CSC, Clearing Success Congress. (HCOB 29 Sept 66)

CSEO, Comm System Establishment Officer. (FPO 2041)

CS-G, CS-Guardian. (FO 1556)

C/SHEET, also **CH. SHEET** or **✓SHT.** abbreviation for checksheet. (BTB 12 Apr 72R)

CS ORDER, Commodore Staff Order. (FO 795)

CSP, **1.** Clean Ship Program. (ED 240-10 Flag) **2.** crew shore policies. (FO 3057)

CSW, completed staff work. (HCO PL 21 Nov 62)

CSWP, **1.** complete the staff work please. (HCO PL 4 Sept 59) **2.** (CSW please) = "Work out how this problem should be handled and recommend. Don't be dumping problems of your post on my plate" is the real meaning of "CSWP." (HCO PL 27 Feb 72)

CT, **1.** Capetown. (HCO PL 4 Jan 66 II) **2.** clay table. (HCO PL 14 Apr 65) **3.** conditional target. (HCO PL 16 Jan 69)

CT1, check type one. (HCO PL 31 Mar 61)

CTR, **1.** center. (BPL 5 Nov 72RA) **2.** cutter = my tape cutter has jammed. (BPL 5 NOV 72RA-1)

CTRL, central. (CBO 214RA)

CURR, current. (BPL 5 Nov 72RA)

CVB, Claims Verification Board. (BPL 14 Nov 74)

CVR, cover. (BPL 5 Nov 72RA)

D, **1.** danger. (FBDL 290) **2.** dangerous. (CBO 173) **3.** Day and Foundation Orgs add D or F to their designation when separation is necessary. (BPL 10 Apr 73R) **4.** department (5812C16) **5.** deputy. (HCOB 23 Aug 65) **6.** director. (HCOB 25 Oct 58)

DVI, the Saint Hill Special Briefing Course student in a unit is designated for the classes being studied for, as DVI = Class VI Unit D. (HCO PL 14 Oct 65, *Course Pattern*)

DA, dead agent. (BPL 5 Nov 72RA)

DAB VOL II, [*The Dianetic Auditor's Bulletin, Volume II.*]

DA DOC, dead agent documents. (FO 3279-3)

D/A/G, Deputy Assistant Guardian. (HCO PL 20 Oct 72)

D/A/G TECH, Deputy Assistant Guardian for Tech. (HCO PL 20 Oct 72)

DB, **1.** degraded being. (FO 2281) **2.** Durban. HCO PL 2 Mar 59, *HCO Cable and Dispatch Designation System*)

DBL, double. (BPL 5 Nov 72RA)

DBP, done on a by-pass of the senior to whom it was assigned. (Target marking and tlx code). (CBO 325)

DC, **1.** direct current. (FSO 486) **2.** Washington, D.C. (HCO PL 2 Mar 59, *HCO Cable and Dispatch Designation System*)

D/C, 1. damage control. (ED 264 Flag) **2.** make direct contact with person target assigned to, to get this one done. (Target marking and tlx code). (CBO 325)

DCA, Dianetic Co-Auditor. (CG&AC 1 Jan 68)

DCG, Dianetic Counselling Group. (BPL 28 Apr 70RA)

DCI, Distribution Center, Inc. (SEC ED 174, 1 Apr 59)

D/COM FLAG, Deputy Commodore Flag. (FO 2123)

D/COM FLOT, Deputy Commodore Flotilla. (FO 2123)

DD, Doctor of Divinity. (HCOB 23 Aug 65)

DDD, direct distance dialing, type of phone call. (HCO PL 15 Nov 74)

DEBRF, debrief. (BPL 5 Nov 72RA)

DEC, December. (BPL 5 Nov 72RA)

DED-Reckoning, Deduced Reckoning. (FO 41) [Also written Dead Reckoning.]

DELD, Ken Delderfield. (LRH ED 148 INT.)

DEMO, demonstrate, demonstration. (BPL 5 Nov 72RA)

DEO, Dissemination Establishment Officer. (HCO PL 7 Mar 72)

DEP, deputy. (HCO PL 2 Nov 66)

DEP DIR, Deputy Director. (HCOB 23 Aug 65)

DEPT, department. (HCO PL 14 Aug 71RC II)

DER, (international telex jargon) out of order. (BPL 5 Nov 72RA-1)

DER BK, (international telex jargon) out of order, break = out of order, I switch off. (BPL 5 Nov 72RA-1)

DER MOM, (international telex jargon) out of order, wait a moment = bad reception, do not switch off, we check. (BPL 5 Nov 72RA-1)

DESP, despatch. (BPL 5 Nov 72RA)

DET, Detroit. (HCO PL 4 Jan 66 II)

DEV-T, developed traffic. (HCO PL 17 Nov 64)

DF, (international telex jargon) destination found = you are in communication with the called subscriber. (BPL 5 Nov 72RA-1)

DG (or D/G), Deputy Guardian. (BPL 5 Nov 72RA)

D/GF, Deputy Guardian for Finance. (BPL 14 Nov 74)

DGR, Department of Government Relations. (SEC ED 342, 12 Aug 60)

DIFF, difference, different. (BPL 5 Nov 72RA)

DIG, Dianetic Information Group. (*STCR,* p. 104)

DIR, director. (BPL 5 Nov 72RA)

DIR CERTS AND AWARDS, Director of Certificates and Awards. (HCOB 23 Aug 65)

DIR CLEAR, Director of Clearing. (BPL 5 Nov 72RA)

DIR COMM, Director of Communications. (HCOB 23 Aug 65)

DIR COMP, Director of Compilations. (HCOB 23 Aug 65)

DIR DISB, Director of Disbursements. (HCOB 23 Aug 65)

DIR ETH, Director Ethnics. (HCO PL 11 Dec 69, *Appearances in Public Divs*)

DIR EXAMS, Director of Examinations. (HCOB 23 Aug 65)

DIR FA, Director of Field Activities. (HCOB 23 Aug 65)

DIR I & R, Director of Inspections and Reports. (BPL 5 Nov 72RA)

DIR INC, Director of Income. (BPL 5 Nov 72RA)

DIR INSPEC & REP, Director of Inspection and Reports. (HCOB 23 Aug 65)

DIR MAT, Director of Material. (HCO PL 20 Dec 62)

DIR MAT & RECS, Director of Materiel and Records. (HCOB 23 Aug 65)

DIR OF PR, Director of Processing. (HASI PL 8 Feb 58)

DIR OF PROCU, Director of Procurement. (HCOB 25 Oct 58)

DIR PBLS, Director of Publications. (HCOB 23 Aug 65)

DIR PERS, Director of Personnel. (BPL 5 Nov 72RA)

DIR PRO, Director of Processing. (HASI PL 8 Feb 58)

DIR PROM, Director of Promotion. (HCOB 23 Aug 65)

DIR PROMO, Director of Promotion. (BPL 5 Nov 72RA)

DIR PUBS, Director of Publications. (BPL 5 Nov 72RA)

DIR RAM, Director of Records Assets & Materiel. (FO 2570)

DIR RAP, Director of Routing, Appearances and Personnel. (HCO PL 11 Aug 66)

DIR REC, Director of Records. (HCOB 23 Aug 65)

DIR REG, Director of Registration. (HCOB 23 Aug 65)

DIR REV, Director of Review. (HCOB 23 Aug 65)

DIR TECH SERVICES, Director of Technical Services. (HCOB 23 Aug 65)

DIR VAL, Director of Validity. (BPL 5 Nov 72RA)

DISB, disbursements. (HCOB 23 Aug 65)

DISC, discount. (BPL 5 Nov 72RA)

DISP, dispatch. (BPL 5 Nov 72RA)

DISSEM, 1. dissemination. (BPL 5 Nov 72RA) **2.** Division Two, the Dissemination Div. (LRH ED 159R-1 Int)

DISSEM DIV, Dissemination Division. (BPL 5 Nov 72RA)

DISSEM SEC, Dissemination Secretary. (BPL 5 Nov 72RA)

DIST, distribution. (BPL 5 Nov 72RA)

DIST DIV, Distribution Division. (HCOB 23 Aug 65)

DISTOR, distributor. (BPL 5 Nov 72RA)

DISTRIB, distribution. (BPL 2 Aug 71RA I)

DIST SEC, Distribution Secretary. (HCOB 23 Aug 65)

DIV, 1. division. (HCO PL 30 Nov 64) **2.** divisional. (FO 2556)

DIV HDS, division heads. (BPL 5 Nov 72RA)

DIV SEC, Divisional Secretary. (HCO PL 7 Mar 72)

DK, 1. deck. (FSO 507) **2.** Denmark. (BPL 5 Nov 72RA)

DLAY, delay. (BPL 5 Nov 72RA)

DLRS, dollars. (BPL 5 Nov 72RA)

DLVR(Y), deliver(y). (BPL 5 Nov 72RA)

DLY, daily. (BPL 5 Nov 72RA)

DM, direct mail. (ED 128 Flag)

DMDH, Diana Meredith de Wolf Hubbard. (FDD 1 Div 6)

DMSMH, [*Dianetics: The Modern Science of Mental Health.*] (LRH ED 185 Int)

DN, Dianetics, dirty needle. (BPL 5 Nov 72RA)

DN 55!, [*Dianetics 55!*]

DNG, doing. (BPL 5 Nov 72RA)

DNGR, danger. (BPL 5 Nov 72RA)

DO, 1. District Office (HCO PL 4 Jan 63) [The above HCO PL was cancelled by BPL 10 Oct 75 IV.] **2.** Divisional Organizer. (HCO PL 1 Nov 66 I)

DOC, 1. Divisional Officers Conference. (FO 2478) **2.** Divisional Officers Council. (FSO 138) **3.** document (BPL 5 Nov 72RA)

D OF ACC, Department of Accounts. (5812C16)

D OF P, Director of Processing. (HCOB 25 Oct 58)

D OF PrR, Department of Promotion and Registration. (HCO PL 20 Dec 62)

D OF T, Director of Training. (HCO PL 30 Aug 60)

DP, Director of Processing. (HCO PL 13 Mar 65 II)

DPE, Director of Personnel Enhancement. (BPL 5 Nov 72RA)

DPF, Deck Project Force. (FO 3183)

DPI, Director of Public Information. (BPL 5 Nov 72RA)

DPS, Director of Public Servicing. (BPL 5 Nov 72RA)

DR, 1. daily report. (OODs 13 Dec 74) **2.** Dead reckoning. (SWPB)

DRD, drug rundown. (ED 26 USB)

DR OF PRO, Director of Processing. (SEC ED No. 2, 15 Dec 58)

DS, Data Series. (BPL 5 Nov 72RA)

DSC, Data Series Course. (OODs 28 Jun 74)

D/SC, Deputy Staff Captain. (FO 3521)

D. SCN, Doctor of Scientology, honorary award for the application of Scn processes, principles, books or literature. (HCOB 23 Aug 65)

DSEC, Data Series Evaluators Course. (ED 497 Flag)

D/SIT, a down stat situation which needs handling. (FO 3064)

DSM, dissem. (BPL 5 Nov 72RA)

DSTD, [*Dianetics and Scientology Technical Dictionary.*]

D/T, Director of Training. (BPL 25 Feb 73R)

DTS, Director of Tech Services. (BPL 5 Nov 72RA)

DUP, 1. duplicate. (BPL 5 Nov 72RA) **2.** dupli-sticker. (HCO PL 18 May 73)

DUR, Durban. (BPL 10 Apr 73R)

DV, 1. Denver. (HCO PL 2 Mar 59, *HCO Cable and Dispatch Designation System*) **2.** done and verified as done, usually with a date and initial. (Target marking and tlx code). (CBO 325)

D/V, disbursement voucher. (FO 761-1)

DWN, down. (BPL 5 Nov 72RA)

E, **1.** east (BPL 5 Nov 72RA) **2.** emergency. (FBDL 290) **3.** evaluation. (CBO 168) **4.** evaluator. (CBO 168) **5.** excellent. (CBO 173)

EA, each (BPL 5 Nov 72RA)

E/A, ethics authority. (FSO 785)

EAT, ethics action taken. (Target marking and tlx code) (CBO 325)

EC, Executive Council. (HCO PL 31 Aug 71, *The EC Network Disbanded*)

ECAO, Executive Council Advanced Org. (FO 331)

ECC, **1.** Executive Cramming Course. (CBO 110) **2.** External Comm Chief. (BPL 5 Nov 72RA)

ECEU, Exec Council Europe. (HCO PL 24 Apr 68 I)

ECFB, Executive Council Flag Bureaux. (CBO 341)

ECUS, Executive Council US. (HCO PL 31 Aug 71, *The EC Network Disbanded*)

ECWW, Exec. Council World Wide. (HCO PL 24 Apr 68 I)

ED, **1.** editor. (BPL 5 Nov 72RA) **2.** Executive Directive (HCO PL 9 Mar 72 III) **3.** Executive Director. (HCO PL 7 Mar 72)

ED-1, (ED-2, etc.) expertise drill-1. (BTB 15 Dec 74)

ED/CO, Executive Director/Commanding Officer. (BPL 1 Apr 73RA)

ED-F, ED (Executive Directive) Flag. (ED 1 Flag)

EDRS, Executive Directives *Royal Scotman.* (FO 411)

EDUC, education. (BPL 5 Nov 72RA)

EEE, (international telex jargon) error. (BPL 5 Nov 72RA-1)

E-ESTO, Executive Establishment Officer. (HCO PL 7 Mar 72)

EG, East Grinstead. (HCO PL 23 May 68, *WW and SH Recombined*)

ELP, external line personnel. (ED 200-4 Flag)

EMERG, emergency. (FO 3087)

E-MTR, electropsychometer. (BPL 5 Nov 72RA)

ENC, *Enchanter.* (FO 336)

ENH, enhancement. (BPL 5 Nov 72RA)

ENRT, enroute. (BPL 5 Nov 72RA)

ENS, Ensign. (BPL 5 Nov 72RA)

ENSR, ensure. (BPL 5 Nov 72RA)

ENTHUSM, enthusiasm. (BPL 5 Nov 72RA)

ENTURB, enturbulate, enturbulation. (BPL 5 Nov 72RA)

ENUF, enough. (BPL 5 Nov 72RA)

EO, Ethics Officer, Ethics Order. (BPL 5 Nov 72RA)

E/O, Ethics Officer. (HCO PL 7 Dec 69)

EOS, **1.** *Dianetics: Evolution of a Science.* (BPL 5 Nov 72RA) **2.** [Abbreviation for "end of session" normally used on auditor report forms and on session worksheets. Refer to *"Dianetics Today"* pp. 658 & 666]

EOW, Engineer of the Watch. (FO 2542R)

EP, end phenomena. (7205C24SO)

EPF, Estates Project Force. (FO 3118R)

E.P. NUMBER ONE, ethics program number one. (7003C30SO)

EPO, estimated purchase order. (BPL 4 Nov 70R)

ER, engine room. (FO 1109)

E/R, engine room. (FO 1817)

ES, Executive Secretary. (HCO PL 21 Jan 66)

E/S, earlier similar. (BPL 5 Nov 72RA)

ES COMM, Executive Secretary's Communicator. (HCO PL 21 Jan 66)

ES COMM DISSEM, HCO Executive Secretary's Communicator for Dissemination. (HCO PL 21 Jan 66)

ES COMM DIST, Organization Executive Secretary's Communicator for Distribution. (HCO PL 21 Jan 66)

ES COMM HCO, HCO Executive Secretary's Communicator for HCO. (HCO PL 21 Jan 66)

ES COMM ORG, Organization Executive Secretary's Communicator for Organization. (HCO PL 21 Jan 66)

ES COMM QUAL, Organization Executive Secretary's Communicator for Qualifications. (HCO PL 21 Jan 66)

ES COMM TECH, Organization Executive Secretary's Communicator for Technical. (HCO PL 21 Jan 66)

ESK, Eskilstuna. (HCO PL 10 Apr 73) [The above HCO PL was cancelled by BPL 10 Apr 73R which deleted the abbreviation for Eskilstuna Org in Sweden.]

EST, estimate. (BPL 5 Nov 72RA)

ESTAB, establish. (BPL 5 Nov 72RA)

ESTO, Establishment Officer. (FSO 529)

ESTO'S ESTO, Establishment Officer's, Establishment Officer. (HCO PL 7 Mar 72)

ESTS, estates. (BPL 5 Nov 72RA)

ETA, estimated time of arrival. (FO 3087)

ETD, estimated time of departure. (FO 3087)

ETH, ethics. (COLRHED 86)

EU, Europe. (BPL 5 Nov 72RA)

EULO, European Liaison Office. (LRH ED 130 Int)

EUS, East US. (BPL 10 Apr 73R)

EVAL, evaluate, evaluation. (BPL 5 Nov 72RA)

EVID, evidence. (BPL 5 Nov 72RA)

EVNT, event. (BPL 5 Nov 72RA)

EV PURPS, evil purposes. (ED 450 Flag)

EX, ex urban. (HCO PL 28 Oct 60)

EXCAL, *Excalibur.* (BPL 5 Nov 72RA)

EXCH, exchange. (BPL 5 Nov 72RA)

EX DN, Expanded Dianetics. (HCOB 23 Apr 74R)

EXEC, executive. (BPL 5 Nov 72RA)

EXEC DIR, Executive Director. (HCOB 23 Aug 65)

EXEC LTR, Executive Letter. (HCOB 23 Aug 65)

EXEC SEC, Executive Secretary. (HCO PL 2 Aug 65)

EXP, 1. expanded. (ED 149R Flag) **2.** expansion. (LRH ED 231-1R Int)

EXPED, expedite, expeditor. (BPL 5 Nov 72RA)

EXPER, experience. (BPL 5 Nov 72RA)

EXT, 1. extension. (HCO PL 27 Apr 65) **2.** exterior. (HCOB 30 May 70) **3.** exteriorization. (HCOB 30 May 70) **4.** external. (BPL 5 Nov 72RA)

EXT COMM, External Communications Bureau. (BPL 5 Nov 72RA)

EXT HCO, External HCO. (FBDL 504)

F, 1. failing. (CBO 173) **2.** usually the recipient of a comm-member despatch on a C routing just sends it on to files by marking it F with an arrow. (HCO PL 13 Mar 65 II) **3.** finance. (CBO 168) **4.** Flag. (BPL 5 Nov 72RA) **5.** Foundation (when used as an org name). (BPL 5 Nov 72RA) **6.** for ease of recognition, foundation invoices are additionally marked with a large "F" letter. (BPL 11 Aug 72R II)

F/ (OR F), Flag, (BPL 5 Nov 72RA)

FA, 1. field activities. (HCOB 23 Aug 65) **2.** folder admin. (BPL 5 Nov 72RA)

FAO, 1. Flag Admin Org. (FEBC I, 7101C23 SO) **2.** Flag Advanced Organization. (OODs 19 Oct 73)

FAPTC, Flag Auxiliary Personnel Training Corps. (BPL 9 Jun 73R)

FB, Flag Bureaux. (OODs 8 May 72)

FBDL, Flag Bureaux Data Letter. (CBO 48R)

FBL, Flag Bureaux Liaison. (FO 3271)

FBO, 1. Finance Banking Officer. (HCO PL 29 Jan 71) **2.** Flag Banking Officer. (FO 565) **3.** Flag Bureau Org. (FSO 263)

FBO INT, Flag Banking Officer International. (HCO PL 16 Jun 69) [The above HCO PL was cancelled by BPL 10 Oct 75 VII.]

FBO INT I/C, Flag Banking Officer International In-Charge. (BPL 10 Nov 73R)

FC, Founding Church of Scientology. (HCOB 23 Aug 65)

FCCI, Flag Case Completion Intensive. (FO 3426)

FCCI PO, Flag Case Completion Intensive Product Officer. (FO 3663)

FCCSO, Flag Codes and Communication Security Officer. (CBO 289-1)

FCDC, Founding Church of Scientology Washington D.C. (HCOB 23 Aug 65)

FCNY, Founding Church of Scientology New York. (HCOB 23 Aug 65)

FCO, 1. Flag Collection Officer. (FO 3473-6) **2.** Flag Conditions Order. (HCO PL 24 Sept 70R)

FC OF S OF WASH DC, Founding Church of Scientology of Washington D.C. (HCO PL 27 Nov 59)

FCTC, Founding Church of Scientology Twin Cities, Minnesota. (HCOB 23 Aug 65)

F.D., Fellow of Dianetics. (*Scn Jour,* issue 31-G)

FDD, Flag Divisional Directive. (HCO PL 24 Sept 70R)

F/DIV 6, Flag Division 6. (FO 986)

FDN, Foundation. (BPL 5 Nov 72RA)

FEB, February. (BPL 5 Nov 72RA)

FEBC, Flag Executive Briefing Course. (HCO PL 17 May 74R)

FES, folder error summary. (BPL 5 Nov 72RA)

FEU, Flag Extension Unit. (ED 2 FB) [This was a temporary Flag Management Unit set up to manage Scientology in late 1975.]

FEWR, fewer. (BPL 5 Nov 72RA)

FF, fast flow. (BPL 5 Nov 72RA)

FFR, Flag Flag Rep. (BPL 5 Nov 72RA)

FH, 1. fully hatted. (BPL 5 Nov 72RA) **2.** The Fort Harrison. (BFO 70)

FHS, fully hatted staff. (BPL 5 Nov 72RA)

FIELD EXP SEC, Field Expansion Secretary. (LRH ED 49 Int)

FIGS, figures = you are transmitting in figures which should be letters. (BPL 5 Nov 72RA-1)

FILE A, active address files of the Central Organization. (HCO PL 30 Oct 64)

FILE F, franchise file (type of address files). (HCO PL 30 Oct 64)

FIN, 1. finance. (BPL 5 Nov 72RA) **2.** (international telex jargon) finished = I am through with my message. (BPL 5 Nov 72RA-1)

FIN?, (international telex jargon) finished ? = have you finished your message? (BPL 5 Nov 72RA-1)

FL, FOLO (or freeloader if clear in context). (BPL 5 Nov 72RA)

FLAF, FOLO Africa. (BPL 10 Apr 73R)

FLAG REP, Flag Representative. (HCO PL 29 Dec 71R)

FLAG REP I/C, Flag Representative In-Charge. (HCO PL 15 Jul 72 I) [The above HCO PL was replaced by BPL 15 Jul 72R I which uses the term Flag Flag Representative to replace the term Flag Representative In-Charge.]

FLANZO, FOLO ANZO. (BPL 5 Nov 72RA)

FLB, Flag Land Base. (FCO 4414-1)

FLD, field. (BPL 5 Nov 72RA)

FLDR, folder. (BPL 5 Nov 72RA)

FLEU, FOLO Europe. (BPL 5 Nov 72RA)

FLEUS, FOLO East US. (BPL 10 Apr 73R)

FLO, Franchise Liaison Officer. (CBO 144)

FLS, false. (BPL 5 Nov 72RA)

FLUK, FOLO United Kingdom. (BPL 10 Apr 73R)

FLW, follow. (BPL 5 Nov 72RA)

FLWUS, FOLO West US. (BPL 10 Apr 73R)

FM, from. (BPL 5 Nov 72RA)

FMAA, Flag Master at Arms. (BPL 5 Nov 72RA)

FMO, Flag Mission Order. (HCO PL 24 Sept 70R)

F/N, floating needle. (BPL 5 Nov 72RA)

FNCTN, function. (BPL 5 Nov 72RA)

FND, found. (BPL 5 Nov 72RA)

FO, 1. Finance Office. (BPL 8 Jun 71R I) **2.** Flag Order. (HCO PL 24 Sept 70R) **3.** Franchise Officer. (BPL 20 Nov 69R)

FOB, free on board. (FO 2738)

FOC, see FLAGSHIP OPERATION COUNCIL.

FO/CBO, Flag Order/Central Bureaux Order. (FO 3092)

FOLO, Flag Operations Liaison Office. (FBDL 191R)

FO NO. 1, Finance Office No. 1 Account. (BPL 8 Jun 71R I)

FO NO. 2, Finance Office No. 2 Account. (BPL 8 Jun 71R I)

FOT, [*The Fundamentals of Thought.*]

FOWW, Franchise Officer World Wide. (BPL 5 Nov 72RA)

F/O WW, Franchise Officer WW. (CBO 144)

FP, financial planning. (BPL 5 Nov 72RA)

F/P, financial planning. (FO 1256)

FP & MP, Food Purchaser and Menu Planner. (FO 2973)

FPC, Flag Personnel Committee. (FO 3513)

FPGM, Flag Program. (BPL 5 Nov 72RA)

FPGMO, Flag Program Order. (HCO PL 24 Sept 70R)

FPJO, Flag Project Order. (HCO PL 24 Sept 70R)

FPO, 1. Flag Personnel Officer. (BPL 5 Nov 72RA) **2.** Flag Personnel Order. (HCO PL 24 Sept 70R)

FPPO, 1. Flag Personnel Procurement Office. (BPL 23 Mar 74) **2.** Flag Personnel Procurement Officer. (BPL 5 Nov 72RA)

FPTO, Flag Promo Tours Operation. (BFO 122-6)

FPXO, [Flag Programs Execution Officer. See Programs Execution Officer.]

FR, 1. Flag Representative. (BPL 5 Nov 72RA) **2.** France. (HCO PL 2 Mar 59, *HCO Cable and Dispatch Designation System*)

FRANCH(ES), franchise(s). (BPL 5 Nov 72RA)

FRI, Friday. (BPL 5 Nov 72RA)

FRLDR, freeloader. (BPL 5 Nov 72RA)

FR PDI, FR% paid comps increase stat. (BPL 5 Nov 72RA)

FR R/C, combined FR reports/compliances stat. (BPL 5 Nov 72RA)

FRU, Flag Readiness Unit. (BPL 9 Jun 73R)

FS, folder summary. (BPL 5 Nov 72RA)

FSC, Flag Service Consultant. (HCO PL 1 Jan 76)

FSH, Flag Saint Hill Organization. (OODs 19 Oct 73)

FSM, field staff member. (HCO PL 11 Nov 69 II)

FSMC, field staff member commissions. (BPL 5 Nov 72RA)

FSMC PD, value of FSM commissions paid. (BPL 5 Nov 72RA)

FSO, **1.** Flag Service Org. (ED 774R Flag) **2.** Flag Ship Order. (HCO PL 24 Sept 70R) **3.** Flag Ship Org. (FO 3152RR)

F/STORES, food stores. (FO 2002)

FT, full time. (FO 2535)

F TO R, [Abbreviation appearing in HCO PL 27 Sept 63 stands for "Failed to Reveal," which is a prepcheck button on HCOB 22 Sept 63 *Scientology Two Prepcheck Buttons* which was revised in HCOB 14 Aug 64 *Scientology Two Prepcheck Buttons* to be, "didn't reveal."]

FTSC, Flag Training Specialist Course. (FSO 460)

FWD, forward. (BPL 5 Nov 72RA)

FYR, falsely reported done and isn't. (Target marking and tlx code) (CBO 325)

G, **1.** good. (CBO 173) **2.** grand (Americanism for a thousand dollars). (BPL 5 Nov 72RA) **3.** stands for group. (HCO PL 18 Feb 66) **4.** Guardian. (HCO PL 8 Dec 68)

G(?), (international telex jargon) go(?) = you may transmit/may I transmit? (BPL 5 Nov 72RA-1)

G-2, "G-2—military intelligence section of army or marine corps; military intelligence officer." (From *Abbreviations Dictionary, International Edition,* by Ralph de Sola, p. 115). (BPL 11 May 71 II-1)

GA(?), (international telex jargon) go ahead (?) = you may transmit/may I transmit? (BPL 5 Nov 72RA-1)

GAR, garbled = your transmission is garbled. (BPL 5 Nov 72RA-1)

GAS, Guardian Activities Scientologists. (BPL 10 Sept 72)

GB, gross bills (bills owing). (BPL 5 Nov 72RA)

GBOA, Guilty by own admission. (EO 141-1 USB)

GBS, gross book sales. (BPL 5 Nov 72RA)

GC, **1.** [Games Congress.] **2.** gross cash (cash on hand). (BPL 5 Nov 72RA)

GD, good. (BPL 5 Nov 72RA)

GDN, Guardian. (FO 2534)

GDS, gross divisional statistic. (HCO PL 5 Feb 70)

GEE, gross engineering error. (OODs 7 Jul 69)

GEN, general. (HCO PL 7 May 65)

GF, green form. (HCO PL 7 Apr 70RA)

GF 40 X, see EXPANDED GF 40 RB.

GFO, Guardian Finance Order. (GFO 192)

GHA, Greenwich hour angle. (HCO PL 18 Sept 67)

GI, gross income. (BPL 5 Nov 72RA)

GIBY, gross income divided by number on staff. (BPL 5 Nov 72RA)

GI's, good indicators. (BPL 5 Nov 72RA)

GL, Glasgow. (HCO PL 2 Mar 59, *HCO Cable and Dispatch Designation System*)

GM, general manager. (FBDL 192R)

GMT, Greenwich Mean Time. (FO 2020)

GO, Guardian's Office. (OODs 3 Jul 72)

GOT, Göteberg. (BPL 5 Nov 72RA)

GOUS, Guardian Office US. (BPL 10 Apr 73R)

GOVT, government. (HCO PL 15 Aug 60)

GOWW, Guardian Office WW. (BPL 10 Apr 73R)

GP, geographical position. (FO 2020) [mentioned on HCOB 11 June 57, *Training and CCH Processes* and meaning general process.]

GPM, Goals Problem Mass. (BPL 5 Nov 72RA)

GPO, Guardian Personnel Order. (GPO 1114 1 Dec 75 *Appointment*)

GR, **1.** government relations. (HCO PL 22 Aug 60) **2.** grade. (BPL 5 Nov 72RA)

GRAD, graduate. (BPL 5 Nov 72RA)

GRD CHRT, gradation chart. (BPL 5 Nov 72RA)

GRFW, good roads and fair weather. (CBO 245)

GRP, group. (BPL 5 Nov 72RA)

GRT, great. (BPL 5 Nov 72RA)

G/T, Guardian Tech. (HCO PL 20 Oct 72) [The above HCO PL was cancelled by BPL 10 Oct 75 X.]

GWW, Guardian World Wide. (BPL 5 Nov 72RA)

HA, Hubbard Administrator. (HCO PL 12 Aug 63)

HAA, **1.** an alternate name for HAA in 1956 was B Scn or Bachelor of Scientology abroad. (HCOTB 12 Sept 56) **2.** Hubbard Advanced Auditor. (BPL 26 Jan 72 VIIIRA) **3.** Hubbard Assistant Administrator. (HCO PL 12 Aug 63)

HAND, transmit by hand/I am transmitting by hand. (BPL 5 Nov 72RA-1)

HAPI, [This is an abbreviation for "Hubbard Academy of Personal Independence" which is located in Edinburgh, Scotland. This title appears on its letterhead and is the legal corporate name. On BPL 5 Nov 72RA HAPI is written as Hubbard Association for Personal Independence and on BPL 10 Apr 73R it is written Hubbard Academy for Personal Independence.]

HAS, **1.** HCO Area Sec. (FO 2794) **2.** Hubbard Apprentice Scientologist. (BPL 5 Nov 72RA) **3.** Hubbard Association of Scientologists. (5510C08)

HASI, Hubbard Association of Scientologists International. (5410C04)

HASI INC., Hubbard Association of Scientologists International, Incorporated. (HCO PL 6 Nov 64)

HASI LTD., Hubbard Association of Scientologists International Limited. (HCO PL 27 Jun 59, *HASI Ltd.*)

HASUK, Hubbard Association of Scientologists of the United Kingdom. (PAB 75)

HATS, Class IX Hubbard Advanced Technical Specialist. (BPL 2 Nov 71R)

HAW, Hawaii. (HCO PL 4 Jan 66 II)

HBA, Hubbard Book Auditor. (HCO PL 7 Apr 65)

HC, Hubbard Consultant. (HCO PL 19 Mar 72 II)

HCA/HPA, Hubbard Certified Auditor for the US and Hubbard Professional Auditor for the UK and Commonwealth, the professional certificates issued by Central Organizations. It is given for successful completion of an Academy HCA/HPA Course. (HCO PL 12 Aug 63)

HCAP, Hubbard Certified Auditor Course, Phoenix. (HCOB 29 Sept 66)

HCI, Hubbard College of Improvement. (FO 2674)

HCL, Hubbard College Lectures. (HCOB 29 Sept 66)

HCLC, Hubbard Causative Leadership Course. (COLRHED 29)

HCO, Hubbard Communications Office. (HCO PL 7 Jul 71)

HCO AREA SEC, Hubbard Communications Office Area Secretary. (HCOB 23 Aug 65)

HCO AS, HCO Area Sec. (FMO 467)

HCOB, Hubbard Communications Office Bulletin. (HCO PL 24 Sept 70R)

HCO DISSEM SEC, Hubbard Communications Office Dissemination Secretary. (HCOB 23 Aug 65)

HCO ES, HCO Exec Sec. (HCO PL 12 Feb 70 II)

HCO ESTO, HCO Establishment Officer. (HCO PL 7 Mar 72)

HCO LTD., Hubbard Communications Office Ltd. (HCO PL 30 Sept 64)

HCOMOJ, [*Hubbard Communications Office Manual of Justice.*]

HCO PL, Hubbard Communications Office Policy Letter. (HCO PL 24 Sept 70R)

HCO POL LTR, Hubbard Communications Office Policy Letter. (HCOB 23 Aug 65)

HCOTB, [Hubbard Communications Office Technical Bulletin or Hubbard Communications Office Training Bulletin.]

HCO VOL SEC, HCO Volunteer Secretary. (HCO PL 3 Sept 61)

HCO WW, Hubbard Communications Office World Wide. (HCOB 23 Aug 65)

HCS, Hubbard Clearing Scientologist—formerly Level IV certificate. (HCOB 23 Aug 65)

HD, **1.** half done and needs completed, do. (Target marking and tlx code). (CBO 325) **2.** Hollywood. (HCO PL 2 Mar 59, *HCO Cable and Dispatch Designation System*)

HDA, Hubbard Dianetic Auditor. (HCOB 23 Aug 65) [An HDA is a graduate of the Dianetic Auditor's Course, forerunner to the HSDC. A graduate of the HSDC is known as an HDC, which is the current certificate awarded to a Dn auditor.]

HDC, Hubbard Dianetic Counselor. (CG&AC 75)

HDG, Hubbard Dianetic Graduate. One who is trained to teach the Dianetic Course after graduating from the HSDC. (BTB 12 Apr 72R)

HDRF, Hubbard Dianetic Research Foundation. (5410C04)

HE, **1.** highest ever. (OODs 29 Jun 75) **2.** Hubbard Executive. (HCO PL 12 Aug 63)

H, E & R, Human emotion and reaction. (HCO PL 25 Jun 72)

HEC LTD, Hubbard Explorational Company Ltd. (FO 1)

HEI, [Hubbard Executive Institute. This was a staff hatting Academy set up in Los Angeles in 1970 to train org staff on the OEC and their hats. HEI was an extension of USLO.]

HEJSC, Hubbard Ethics/Justice Specialist Course. (SO ED 296 Int)

HEM, Hubbard electrometer. (AO 528)

HES, **1.** HCO Exec Sec. (HCO PL 9 May 74) **2.** HCO Executive Secretary. (BPL 5 Nov 72RA)

HEV, Human Evaluation Course. (HCOB 29 Sept 66)

HFA, held from above. (BPL 5 Nov 72RA)

HGA, Hubbard Graduate Auditor. (BPL 2 Nov 71R)

HGC, **1.** Hubbard Guidance Centre. (HCO PL 13 Apr 63) **2.** test form heading to indicate the type the person is. On academy student testing, all tests are labelled HGC and have the same routing as any other HGC test. (HCO PL 28 Oct 60, *New Testing Promotion Section Important*)

HGDS, Hubbard Graduate Dianetic Specialist. (CG&AC 75)

HGS, see HUBBARD GRADUATE SCIENTOLOGIST.

HI, **1.** high. (BPL 5 Nov 72RA) **2.** Hollywood Inn. (FO 3481R) [The above FO has been replaced by FO 3481RA which doesn't have this abbreviation on it.]

HILY, highly. (BPL 5 Nov 72RA)

HIPS, Hubbard Integrity Processing Specialist. BPL 24 Dec 72R)

HIPSC, Hubbard Integrity Processing Specialist Course. (BPL 24 Dec 72R)

HLD, held, hold. (BPL 5 Nov 72RA)

HMCSC, Hubbard Mini Course Supervisor Course. (BPL 11 Dec 71R I-1)

HNDL, handle. (BPL 5 Nov 72RA)

HNYMOON, honeymoon. (BPL 5 Nov 72RA)

HON, honorary. (SO ED 302 Int)

HOSP, hospitalized. (FO 2498)

HP, **1.** hire purchase. (HCO PL 5 Nov 72) [The above HCO PL has been revised and reissued as BPL 5 Nov 72RA but this abbreviation does not appear on the revised issue.] **2.** hot prospect. (BPL 5 Nov 72RA)

HPA, Hubbard Professional Auditor. (CG&AC 75)

HPC, Hubbard Professional Course. (HCOB 29 Sept 66)

HPCS, Hubbard Professional Course Supervisor. (BPL 22 Jan 72R-3)

HPCSC, Hubbard Professional Course Supervisor Course. (BPL 22 Jan 72R-3)

HPDC, Hubbard Practising Dianeticist Course. (SO ED 411 Int)

HPLR, Hot Prospect Letter Registrar. (BPL 18 Feb 73 III)

HPS, Hubbard Practical Scientologist. (HCO PL 7 Jun 62)

HPTS, Hubbard Precision Technical Specialist, (Class X). (BPL 2 Nov 71R)

HQ, headquarters. (FBDL 192R)

HQS, Hubbard Qualified Scientologist. (CG&AC 75)

HR(S), hour(s). (BPL 5 Nov 72RA)

HRD, hard. (BPL 5 Nov 72RA)

HRS, Hubbard Recognized Scientologist. (CG&AC 75)

HS, number of Scientologists hatted. (BPL 5 Nov 72RA)

HSCS, Hubbard Senior Course Supervisor. (BPL 8 Aug 73R)

HSCSC, Hubbard Senior Course Supervisor Course. The HSCSC covers the total expertise of the technology of supervising. (FBDL 328)

HSDC, Hubbard Standard Dianetics Course. (BPL 1 Jun 69R II)

HSE, Hubbard Senior Executive. (LRH ED 27 Int)

HSEC, Hubbard Senior Executive Course. (FO 2112)

HSG, Hubbard Scientology Graduate. (MSH Def. Note)

H/SIT, a high stat situation which should be reinforced. (FO 3064)

HSO, Hubbard Scientology Organization. (HCO PL 4 Jul 69 IV)

HSS, Class VI Hubbard Senior Scientologist. (BPL 2 Nov 71R)

HSST, **1.** Hubbard Scientist of Standard Tech, Class VIII C/S. (BPL 2 Nov 71R) **2.** Hubbard Specialist of Standard Tech, Class VIII Case Supervisor. (CG & AC 75)

HSTS, Class VIII Hubbard Standard Technical Specialist. (BPL 2 Nov 71R)

HTLTAE, [*How to Live Though an Executive.*]

HTS, Hubbard Trained Scientologist. (CG & AC 75)

HU, **1.** household unit. (FO 3342) **2.** Houston. (HCO PL 2 Mar 59, *HCO Cable and Dispatch Designation System*)

HV, have. (BPL 5 Nov 72RA)

HVA, Hubbard Validated Auditor. (CG&AC 75)

HVLY, heavily. (BPL 5 Nov 72RA)

HVNGNSS, havingness. (BPL 5 Nov 72RA)

HVY, heavy. (BPL 5 Nov 72RA)

I/A, issue authority. (FO 3264-20)

I & E A/C, income and expenditure account. (HCO PL 10 Oct 70 I)

I AND I, interview and invoice. (7109C05SO)

I & R, inspections and reports. (BPL 10 Feb 71R II)

IB, inter-Org bills. (BPL 5 Nov 72RA)

IBSO, the International Board of Scientology Organizations. (HCO PL 19 Feb 73) [The above HCO PL was cancelled by BPL 10 Oct 75 XI.]

I/C, in-charge. (FO 315)

ICDS, International Congress of Dianeticists and Scientologists. (HCOB 29 Sept 66)

IMMED, immediately. (BPL 5 Nov 72RA)

IMO, International Money Order. (BPL 5 Nov 72RA)

IMPRV, improve. (BPL 5 Nov 72RA)

IMPT, important. (BPL 5 Nov 72RA)

INC., **1.** income. (BPL 5 Nov 72RA) **2.** incomcomplete. (FO 3367) **3.** incorporated. (HCO PL 6 Nov 64)

INCL, include(d)(ing). (BPL 5 Nov 72RA)

INCOMP, incomplete. (BPL 5 Nov 72RA)

INCORP, incorporate(d). (BPL 5 Nov 72RA)

INCRSE, increase. (BPL 5 Nov 72RA)

IND, indicate(d)(tion). (BPL 5 Nov 72RA)

INDOC, indoctrination. (BPL 5 Nov 72RA)

INF, (international telex jargon) call information = subscriber temporarily unobtainable, call the information service. (BPL 5 Nov 72RA-1)

INFAD, *n.* the information addressee, also, a communication going to an information addressee. —*v.* to send an Infad to. (*HTLTAE*, p. 121)

IN FLO, inflow. (BPL 5 Nov 72RA)

INFO, **1.** inform, information. (BPL 5 Nov 72RA) **2.** (routing used on telex lines). Supply with knowledge, facts or news. Tell. Info simply means that the person mentioned on the routing to be informed, will get a carbon copy of the message. Example: message from Flag Flag Rep to ED SFO 230412MR ED SFO info CO FOLO WUS, the telex operator in FOLO WUS will relay the message to SFO and give a copy to the CO FOLO West US. (BPL 23 Apr 73R)

INFO LTR, information letter. (HCOB 23 Aug 65)

INFO PACK, information packet. (SO ED 45 Int)

INOP, inoperational. (FSO 354)

INSP, inspection. (HCO PL 17 Jan 66 II)

INSPEC & REP, inspections and reports. (HCOB 23 Aug 65)

INT, **1.** interiorization. (HCOB 30 May 1970) **2.** internal. (CBO 13R) **3.** international (HCO PL 18 Oct 67 II) **4.** interview. (BPL 5 Nov 72RA)

INT/CONT, international continental. (CBO 274)

INTEG, integrity. (BPL 5 Nov 72RA)

INTEL, intelligence. (ED 541 Flag)

INTELL, intelligence. (ED 255 Flag)

INT EXEC DIV, International Executive Division. (HCO PL 26 Jan 66)

INT I/A, International Issue Authority. (BPL 2 Mar 73R I)

INTL, international. (BPL 5 Nov 72RA)

INTN, intention. (BPL 5 Nov 72RA)

INTNSV, intensive. (BPL 5 Nov 72RA)

INT ORG SUPERVISOR, International Org Supervisor. (HCO PL 22 Feb 65 III)

INTRN(SHP), intern(ship). (BPL 5 Nov 72RA)

INTRNL, internal. (BPL 5 Nov 72RA)

INTRO, introduction(ory). (BPL 5 Nov 72RA)

INTRVW, *v.* interview. (BPL 5 Nov 72RA)

INT SPEC OFFICER, see INTERNATIONAL SPECIAL PROGRAMS EXECUTION OFFICER.

INV, invoice. (BPL 5 Nov 72RA)

INVCD, invoiced. (BPL 5 Nov 72RA)

INVST, investigate(ion). (BPL 5 Nov 72RA)

IP, **1.** in progress. (Target marking and tlx code). (CBO 325) **2.** Integrity Processing. (BPL 5 Nov 72RA)

IQ, intelligence quotient. (BPL 5 Nov 72RA)

IR, internal requisition. (HCO PL 30 Oct 73)

IRS, Internal Revenue Service of the US. (FBDL 223)

ISE, [*Introduction to Scientology Ethics.*]

ISS, issue. (BPL 5 Nov 72RA)

I/T, in training. (HCO PL 21 Nov 73)

IWGCC, I Want to Go Clear Club. (BPL 20 May 72R)

JAN, January. (BPL 5 Nov 72RA)

JB, **1.** Joburg (Johannesburg Security Check). (BPL 5 Nov 72RA) **2.** Johannesburg. (HCO PL 4 Jan 66 II)

JBG, Johannesburg. (OODs 5 May 72)

JE, job endangerment. (BPL 5 Nov 72RA)

JFE, (international telex jargon) *jour ferie* (Holiday) = office closed, holiday. (BPL 5 Nov 72RA-1)

JNR, junior. (BPL 5 Nov 72RA)

JOBURG, Johannesburg Security Check. (BPL 5 Nov 72RA)

JUL, July. (BPL 5 Nov 72RA)

JUN, June. (BPL 5 Nov 72RA)

KC/S, kilocycles per second. (FO 317)

KNT, knots. (FO 3087)

KNWN, known. (BPL 5 Nov 72RA)

K OF T, Keeper of Tech. The full title of this post is Keeper of Tech and Policy Knowledge. (HCO PL 31 Aug 74)

KOT, Keeper of Tech. (BPL 20 Nov 70R)

KOT COMPL, KOT compliances. (BPL 5 Nov 72RA)

KRC, knowledge, responsibility, control. (HCO PL 18 Feb 72)

L, **1.** London. (HCO PL 2 Mar 59, *HCO Cable and Dispatch Designation System*) **2.** love (only at telex end). (BPL 5 Nov 72RA)

LA, Los Angeles. (HCO PL 4 Jan 66 II)

LACC, London Advanced Clinical Course. (HCOB 29 Sept 66)

LACM, Los Angeles Central Mimeo. (FPJO 359)

LBAC, LRH Briefing and Conference Policies. (CBO 57)

LC-R, confessional repair list. (LRH ED 176R Int Attachment 2)

LD, land. (FO 3087)

LDN, London. (BPL 10 Apr 73R)

LDR, leader. (BPL 5 Nov 72RA)

LECT(R), lecture(r). (BPL 5 Nov 72RA)

LF, **1.** *Laissez Faire.* (FO 3582) **2.** long fall. (BPL 5 Nov 72RA)

LGL, legal. (BPL 5 Nov 72RA)

LI, letters in. (BPL 5 Nov 72RA)

LIAB, liability. (BPL 5 Nov 72RA)

LIB, **1.** liberty. (BPL 5 Nov 72RA) **2.** librarian. (SO ED 373 Int)

LIBS, liberty. (ED 565 Flag)

LIR, [This stands for List Integrity Repair. Its most recent issue is BTB 8 Dec 72RA, *Integrity Processing and O/Ws Repair List.* The forerunner to this was the LCR or List Confessional Repair. The LIR has often been mistakenly issued as L1R mistaking the letter I for the number 1.]

LK, look. (BPL 5 Nov 72RA)

LKE, like. (BPL 5 Nov 72RA)

LMO, [LRH Media Org.]

LO, letters out. (BPL 5 Nov 72RA)

L/O, lookout. (ED 321 Flag)

LOA, leave of absence. (BPL 5 Nov 72RA)

LOGS, logistics. (BPL 5 Nov 72RA)

LON, London. (BPL 5 Nov 72RA)

LP, Las Palmas. (FMO 82)

LPLS, London Public Lecture Series. (HCOB 29 Sept 66)

LR, Letter Registrar. (BPL 5 Nov 72RA)

LRG, large. (BPL 5 Nov 72RA)

LRH, **1.** definition: LRH; L. Ron Hubbard Founder and Source of Dianetics and Scientology and Commodore of the Sea Organization. (BPL 13 Jul 73R) **2.** designation on HCO Policy Letters and HCO Bulletins indicates dissemination and restriction as follows: only me and my communicator, otherwise confidential. (HCO PL 22 May 59)

LRH ACCTS, LRH accounts. (COLRHED 103)

LRH CC, LRH Comm compliances. (BPL 5 Nov 72RA)

LRH COMM, LRH Communicator. (BPL 5 Nov 72RA)

LRH ED, L. Ron Hubbard Executive Directive. (HCO PL 24 Sept 70R)

LRH PERS COMM, LRH Personal Communicator. (FO 2370)

LRH PERS COMM SEC, [This post acts as Secretary to LRH Personal Communicator.]

LRH PERS PRO, LRH Personal Public Relations Officer. (BPL 5 Nov 72RA)

LRH PERS SEC, LRH Personal Secretary. (COLRHED 291R)

LRH PERS SEC US, LRH Personal Secretary US. (FSO 836)

L/R'S, letter reg's. (ED 384 Flag)

LRSO, Letter Registrar Section Officer. (HCO PL 18 Feb 73 IV)

LS, 1. leadership. (BPL 5 Nov 72RA) **2.** Lower Slobovia (HCO PL 16 Jan 69)

LST, last. (BPL 5 Nov 72RA)

LT, 1. a form of cable, LT = night letter rate. There is a minimum charge for twenty-two words. LT travels overnight. (HCO PL 9 Aug 66) **2.** Lieutenant. (BPL 5 Nov 72RA) **3.** lifetime. (BTB 20 Aug 71R II)

LT COMDR, Lieutenant Commander. (BPL 5 Nov 72RA)

LTD, 1. designation on HCO Policy Letters and HCO Bulletins indicates dissemination and restriction as follows: goes to HCO Area Secs, HCO Cont, HCO WW only but never to Central Organizations or field or public. (HCO PL 22 May 59) **2.** limited. (BPL 5 Nov 72RA)

LTD CONT, designation on HCO Policy Letters and HCO Bulletins indicates dissemination and restriction as follows: goes to HCO Cont only, plus HCO WW. (HCO PL 22 May 59)

LTD WW, designation on HCO Policy Letters and HCO Bulletins indicates dissemination and restriction as follows: goes to HCO WW personnel only. (HCO PL 22 May 59)

LT (JG), Lieutenant Junior Grade. (BPL 5 Nov 72RA)

LTR, letter. (BPL 5 Nov 72RA)

LTR REG, Letter Registrar. (HCO PL 13 Sept 62, *Comments About Letter Registrars.*)

LTRS, letters = you are transmitting in letters which should be figures. (BPL 5 Nov 72RA-1)

LV, Las Vegas. (BPL 10 Apr 73R)

LVE, leave. (BPL 5 Nov 72RA)

LVL, level. (BPL 5 Nov 72RA)

M, 1. maintain, meaning this is organized smooth and functioning. (FO 2936) **2.** mate (eg. 4M), method (eg. M1). (BPL 5 Nov 72RA) **3.** mind. (FO 1109)

MA, 1. designation on HCO Policy Letters and HCO Bulletins indicates dissemination and restriction as follows: magazine article, to go into any and all official magazines. (HCO PL 22 May 59) **2.** Massachusetts. (HCO PL 3 Mar 66 II) **3.** mimeo airmail, airmailings of bulletins. (HCO PL 28 Aug 59, *HCO WW Mail Economy and Methods*)

M/A, Master at Arms. (FO 348)

MAA, Master at Arms. (HCO PL 7 Mar 72)

MAG, magazine. (FSO 360)

MAJR SRV, major services. (BPL 5 Nov 72RA)

MAL, Malmo. (BPL 5 Nov 72RA)

MAN, Manchester. (BPL 5 Nov 72RA)

MAR, March. (BPL 5 Nov 72RA)

MAX, maximum. (BPL 5 Nov 72RA)

MBB, mud box brigade. (FO 1701)

MBP, Management Bureau Policies. (CBO 59)

MBR, member. (BPL 5 Nov 72RA)

MCM, Master of the Commodore's Music. (LRH ED 239 Int)

MCP, Motor Cycle Policy. (FSO 457)

MCSC, Mini Course Supervisor Course. (BPL 5 Nov 72RA)

MD, medical doctor. (HCO PL 24 Jan 61)

ME, 1. Melbourne. (HCO PL 4 Jan 66 II) **2.** "Missions Eligible." (FO 228)

M/E(S), main engine(s). (OODs 15 Jul 74)

MED, medical. (BPL 5 Nov 72RA)

MEHO, Machinery and Equipment Hatting Officer. (FO 3575)

MEL, Melbourne. (BPL 10 Apr 73R)

MER, main engine room. (FO 1002)

MEST, mathematical symbol for matter, energy, space and time. Loosely, property and possessions. (*HTLTAE,* p. 121)

METH, method. (BPL 5 Nov 72RA)

MEX, Mexico. (BPL 10 Apr 73R)

M/F, mimeo files. (FSO 632-1)

MFT, money for training. (BPL 5 Nov 72RA)

MGMT, management. (FO 3113)

MI, 1. mile(s). (BPL 5 Nov 72RA) **2.** "Missions Ineligible." (FO 228)

MIB, Mission International Books. (HCO PL 24 Aug 72) [BPL 24 Aug 72RC is the latest revision of the above but the designation MIB is not on it.]

MIDDIES, Midshipman. (ED 206 Flag)

MIDRATS, midnight rations. (FO 2728R)

MIMEO, mimeograph. (BPL 5 Nov 72RA)

MIN, minimum, minute. (BPL 5 Nov 72RA)

MISC, miscellaneous. (BPL 5 Nov 72RA)

MISDUP, misduplicate(tion). (BPL 5 Nov 72RA)

MISU (OR MIS-U), misunderstood. (BPL 5 Nov 72RA)

MJR(ITY), major(ity). (BPL 5 Nov 72RA)

MJR SRV, major services. (BPL 5 Nov 72RA)

MLO, Medical Liaison Officer. (BPL 25 Mar 73 II)

MM, Miami. (HCO PL 2 Mar 59, *HCO Cable and Dispatch Designation System*)

M'NAIRE, missionaire. (FO 3300)

MNGR, manager. (BPL 5 Nov 72RA)

MNS, (international telex jargon) minutes. (BPL 5 Nov 72RA-1)

MNTH, month. (BPL 5 Nov 72RA)

MNTN, maintain. (BPL 5 Nov 72RA)

MNWHL, meanwhile. (BPL 5 Nov 72RA)

MO, 1. medical officer. (FO 2165) **2.** mission order. (HCO PL 24 Sept 70R)

MOM, (international telex jargon) wait a moment = wait/waiting. (BPL 5 Nov 72RA-1)

MOM PPR, (international telex jargon) wait a moment, paper = wait, I have difficulties with teletype paper. (BPL 5 Nov 72RA-1)

MON, Monday. (BPL 5 Nov 72RA)

MONT, Montreal. (BPL 5 Nov 72RA)

MOS, mail order sales. (BPL 5 Nov 72RA)

MPC, Mess Presidents' Chairman. (ED 295 Flag) [The abbreviation MPC has also been used to mean Mess Presidents' Committee.]

MPR, Management Power Rundown. (FO 2980)

MPT, money paid for training. (BPL 5 Nov 72RA)

MR, 1. Flag. (BPL 10 Apr 73R) **2.** Mediterranean Representative (Flag telex code). (BPL 5 Nov 72RA)

MS, 1. mailslip. (BPL 5 Nov 72RA) **2.** Manuscript. (*World Book Dictionary*)

MSG(S), message(s). (BPL 5 Nov 72RA)

MSGR, messenger. (BPL 5 Nov 72RA)

MSH, Mary Sue Hubbard. (BPL 5 Nov 72RA)

MSM, Midshipman. (BPL 5 Nov 72RA)

MSN, mission. (OODs 18 Apr 75)

MSNAIRE, missionaire. (ED 547 Flag)

MSN OPS, mission operations. (FO 3485)

MSNRE, missionaire. (BPL 5 Nov 72RA)

MSS, manuscripts. (*World Book Dictionary*)

MSTR, master. (BPL 5 Nov 72RA)

MT, major target. (BPL 5 Nov 72RA)

MTG, meeting. (BPL 5 Nov 72RA)

MTL, Montreal. (BPL 10 Apr 73R)

MTR, meter. (BPL 5 Nov 72RA)

M TR, messenger training drill. (FO 2523)

MTRLS, materials. (BPL 5 Nov 72RA)

MU, Missionaire Unit. (FO 2725)

M/U, (or mis/u) abbreviation for misunderstood. (BTB 12 Apr 72RA)

MUN, Munich. (BPL 10 Apr 73R)

MUT, (international telex jargon) mutilated. (BPL 5 Nov 72RA-1)

MVE, move. (BPL 5 Nov 72RA)

MVPT, multiple viewpoint. (FO 3279-3)

MW, Moscow. (HCO PL 2 Mar 59, *HCO Cable and Dispatch Designation System*)

MWH(Y), missed withhold(y). (BPL 5 Nov 72RA)

N, 1. normal. (FBDL 290) **2.** north. (BPL 5 Nov 72RA)

NA, 1. (international telex jargon) not admitted = correspondence to this subscriber is not admitted. (BPL 5 Nov 72RA-1) **2.** not applicable now. (Target marking and tlx code). (CBO 325)

NAS, no auditing since. (FO 2498)

NBR, number. (BPL 5 Nov 72RA)

NC, 1. (international telex jargon) no circuits. (BPL 5 Nov 72RA-1) **2.** not coping, function not touched in any way. (FO 2936)

N/C, no charge. (HCO PL 16 May 69)

NCG, means no-case-gain despite good and sufficient auditing. (HCO PL 12 May 72)

NCH, (international telex jargon) number changed = subscriber's telex number has been changed. (BPL 5 Nov 72RA-1)

NE, 1. New England. (HCO PL 3 Mar 66 II) **2.** (or N/E) non existence. (BPL 5 Nov 72RA)

NEC(ITY), necessary (necessity). (BPL 5 Nov 72RA)

NEG, negative. (BPL 5 Nov 72RA)

NEUS, North East US. (BPL 5 Nov 72RA)

NEW A, new arrivals. (BPL 5 Nov 72RA)

NEW B, new gross book sales statistic. (HCO PL 10 May 73R)

NEW P, (new) number of public reg paid starts stat. (HCO PL 28 Nov 71R II)

NEW PP, (new) personnel points stat. (BPL 5 Apr 73R)

NEW S, (new) number of Scientologists hatted stat. (HCO PL 28 Nov 71R II)

NEW TAR, (new) tech/admin ratio stat. (BPL 5 Apr 73R)

NIA, Niagara. (BPL 5 Nov 72RA)

NITE, night. (BPL 5 Nov 72RA)

NN, new names. (BPL 5 Nov 72RA)

NNCF, new names to CF. (BPL 1 Dec 72R II)

NORM, normal. (BPL 5 Nov 72RA)

N/OTS, new OTs. (BPL 5 Nov 72RA)

NOV, November. (BPL 5 Nov 72RA)

NP, **1.** new people. (BPL 5 Nov 72RA) **2.** (international telex jargon) no party = the called party is not, or is no longer a subscriber. (BPL 5 Nov 72RA-1) **3.** no payment but signed up for service. (HCO PL 26 Nov 71R I) [The above HCO PL was cancelled by BPL 1 Dec 72 V.]

NPI, new people in. (BPL 5 Nov 72RA)

NPRR, number of new people routed to the Registrar. (BPL 5 Nov 72RA)

NR, **1.** any "no reports" should be cabled as "NR." (HCO PL 27 Sept 66) **2.** (international telex jargon) number = indicate your telex number/my telex number is.... (BPL 5 Nov 72RA-1)

NRCRT, number of new recruits. (BPL 5 Nov 72RA)

N/SIT, no situation. (FO 3064)

NVR, never. (BPL 5 Nov 72RA)

NW, network. (FO 3663)

N/WS, networks. (CBO 374R)

NWUS, Northwest US. (BPL 5 Nov 72RA)

NXT, next. (BPL 5 Nov 72RA)

NY, New York. (BPL 10 Apr 73R)

NZ, New Zealand. (HCO PL 4 Jan 66 II)

O, **1.** (international telex jargon) figure 0 (nothing) = stop your transmission. (BPL 5 Nov 72RA-1) **2.** organizing it, meaning that all the parts of it are being grooved in so it can run smoothly. (FO 2936)

OA, Org Assets. (BPL 5 Nov 72RA)

OBD, org basic data. (CBO 334)

OBJ, object(ive). (BPL 5 Nov 72RA)

OBS, observe (observation). (BPL 5 Nov 72RA)

OBSVR, observer. (BPL 5 Nov 72RA)

OC, Officer Council. (FO 3352)

OCA, Oxford Capacity Analysis. (ESTO 3, 7203C02 SO I)

OCC, (international telex jargon) occupied = subscriber or foreign circuit is engaged. (BPL 5 Nov 72RA-1)

O COND, Org condition. (BPL 5 Nov 72RA)

OCT, October. (BPL 5 Nov 72RA)

ODR, order. (FO 3087)

OEC, **1.** Org Exec Course. (HCO PL 8 Sept 69) **2.** Organization Executive Course. (HCO PL 17 May 74R)

OES, **1.** Org Exec Sec. (HCO PL 12 Feb 70 II) **2.** Org Executive Secretary. (LRH ED 49 Int)

OFC, office. (BPL 5 Nov 72RA)

OFF, officer. (BPL 5 Nov 72RA)

OFF A, off allowances and bonuses. (FO 2498)

OFF D, off duty. (FO 2498)

OFF POL, off policy. (HCOB 23 Aug 65)

OFF S, off study. (FO 2498)

OFO, Org Flag Officer. (CBO 348-4)

OIC, Organization Information Center. (HCO PL 5 Feb 70)

OK(?), (international telex jargon) okay(?) = agreed/do you agree? (okay—Cherokee). (BPL 5 Nov 72RA-1)

OM, old man = friend, familiar address. (BPL 5 Nov 72RA-1)

OND, on duty. (FO 2498)

ON MED, on medication. (FO 2498)

OO, Organizing Officer. (BPL 5 Nov 72RA)

OOD, **1.** Officer of the Deck. (FO 1193) **2.** (or OODs) Orders of the Day. (HCO PL 24 Sept 70R) **3.** OOW. (FORS 32)

OOW, Officer of the Watch. (FO 80)

OP, **1.** operation, operator. (BPL 5 Nov 72RA) **2.** operational. (FSO 759)

OP BASIS, operating basis. (BPL 5 Nov 72RA)

OPS, operations. (FO 3195)

OPS OFFICER, Operations Officer. (FO 2358)

ORD, **1.** a form of cable. ORD = full rate and is charged for by the word. (HCO PL 9 Aug 66) **2.** ordinary. (*World Book Dictionary*)

ORDR, order. (BPL 5 Nov 72RA)

ORE, Orebro. (HCO PL 10 Apr 73) [The above HCO PL was cancelled and replaced by BPL 10 Apr 73R but the designation for Orebro Org is not on the new issue.]

ORG, **1.** any organization, not only a Scientology group. (HCO PL 22 Feb 65 III) **2.** short for organization. (HCO PL 8 Sept 69)

ORG BD, "Org Bd" is actually an abbreviation not for an organization *-n.* board, but an organizing *-v.* board. (HCO PL 28 Oct 70)

ORG EXEC COURSE, see ORGANIZATION EXECUTIVE COURSE.

ORG EXEC SEC, Organization Executive Secretary. (HCO PL 2 Aug 65)

ORG OFFICER, organizing officer. (FEBC 6, 7101C23 SO II)

ORG RUD, org rudiment number. (BPL 5 Nov 72RA)

ORG SEC, Organization Secretary. (HCOB 23 Aug 65)

ORG SERIES, Organizing Series. (FEBC 1, 7011C17 SO)

ORIG, **1.** original, originate, origination. (BPL 5 Nov 72RA) **2.** the originator of the message. (*HTLTAE,* p. 35)

OS, Organization Series (tape lecture series). (HCOB 29 Sept 66)

O/S, means outstanding. (HCO PL 10 Oct 70 III)

OSA COND, org self-assigned condition. (BPL 5 Nov 72RA)

OSB, Officer Selection Board. (FO 3352)

OT, **1.** operating target. (SO ED 19 Int) **2.** operating thetan. (BPL 5 Nov 72RA)

OTC, **1.** Operations and Transport Corporation. (BPL 5 Nov 72RA) **2.** OT course. (HCO PL 12 Nov 67)

OT CEN COMM, Operating Thetan Central Committee. (HCO PL 28 Jan 68)

OTC LTD, see OPERATION AND TRANSPORT CORPORATION LTD.

OTL, **1.** Operation and Transport Liaison Offices. (HCO PL 22 Jul 71) **2.** OT Liaison Office. (LRH ED 166 Int)

OT LIAISON, Operating Thetan Liaison. (HCO PL 28 Jan 68)

OTS, operation and transport services. (OODs 3 Feb 68)

OTT, Ottawa. (BPL 5 Nov 72RA)

OTWW LIAISON UNIT, Worldwide Operating Thetan Liaison Unit. (HCO PL 28 Jan 68)

OUTFLO, outflow. (BPL 5 Nov 72RA)

OUTPNT, outpoint. (BPL 5 Nov 72RA)

O/W, overt/withhold. (BPL 5 Nov 72RA)

P, **1.** (international telex jargon) *Parez* (French for stop) = stop your transmission. (BPL 5 Nov 72RA-1) **2.** poor. (CBO 173) **3.** port. (FSO 666) **4.** power. (FBDL 290) **5.** processing. (FO 2988) **6.** product. (FO 1109) **7.** provisional. (FO 236) **8.** public. (CBO 245)

PA, **1.** pioneer areas. (FO 3409) **2.** public address. (BO 59, 23 Jun 67) **3.** public affairs (The PRAC Bureau aboard Flag are now known as the Office of Public Affairs). (CBO 262-2)

PAB, Professional Auditor's Bulletin. (BPL 20 May 72R)

PAC, Pacific. (LRH ED 166 Int)

PAL, (international telex jargon) friend (Hawaiian). (BPL 5 Nov 72RA-1)

P&C, promoting and campaigning. (FO 3138)

P&D, [means printing and distribution as mentioned on CBO 414.]

P AND R, Promotion and Registration. (HCO PL 21 Feb 64)

PAR, Paris. (BPL 10 Apr 73R)

PARTIC(LY), particular(ly). (BPL 5 Nov 72RA)

PAU, Personal Awareness & Understanding Course. (BPL 5 Nov 72RA)

PAYE, (British) pay as you earn government contribution. (BPL 4 Dec 72RA II) [The above BPL was replaced by BPL 4 Dec 72RB II but PAYE is not on the revised issue.]

PBLC(S)(LY), public(s)(ly). (BPL 5 Nov 72RA)

PBLS, publications. (HCO PL 23 Sept 65)

PC, **1.** paid comps. (FBDL 279) **2.** preclear. (BPL 5 Nov 72RA)

PCO, Personnel Control Officer. (HCO PL 24 Sept 71)

PD, **1.** paid. (BPL 5 Nov 72RA) **2.** publications director. (HCO PL 13 Mar 65 II)

P.D., Prayer Day. (COLRHED 325R)

PDC, **1.** paid completions. (BPL 5 Nov 72RA) **2.** [Philadelphia Doctorate Course.]

PDH, PDH stands for Pain Drug Hypnosis. It is known to some psychiatrists as a means of compelling obedience. They sometimes use it on psychotics. (LRH ED 2 US, 2 WW)

PDK, Pubs Denmark. (BPL 10 Apr 73R)

PD REL, paid releases. (BPL 5 Nov 72RA)

PDS, paid starts. (BPL 5 Nov 72RA)

PE, **1.** personal efficiency. (HCOB 23 Sept 59) **2.** Perth. (HCO PL 4 Jan 66 II)

PEL, Port Elizabeth. (HCO PL 4 Jan 66 II)

PEO, **1.** Pac Estates Org. (FO 3481R) **2.** Public Establishment Officer. (HCO PL 7 Mar 72) **3.** Public Ethics Officer. (BPL 5 Nov 72RA)

PERM, permanent. (BPL 5 Nov 72RA)

PERS, **1.** personal. (FO 2370) **2.** personnel. (BPL 5 Nov 72RA)

PERS ENH, personnel enhancement. (HCO PL 14 Jan 72 IV) [The above HCO PL was cancelled by BPL 10 Oct 75 X.]

PES, Public Executive Secretary. (LRH ED 49 Int)

PF, **1.** paid in full. (HCO PL 26 Nov 71R I) [The above HCO PL was cancelled by BPL 1 Dec 72 V.] **2.** project force. (FO 2878R) **3.** prospect files. (HCO PL 14 Nov 71RA II)

PF MAA, project force MAA. (FO 3165)

PG, page. (BPL 5 Nov 72RA)

PGCC, Personal Grooming Course Checksheet. (BFO 93)

PGM, program. (BPL 5 Nov 72RA)

PH, Phoenix. (HCO PL 2 Mar 59, *HCO Cable and Dispatch Designation System*)

PHIL, Philadelphia. (BPL 10 Apr 73R)

PHS, phase. (BPL 5 Nov 72RA)

PI, **1.** Pittsburgh. (HCO PL 2 Mar 59, *HCO Cable and Dispatch Designation System*) **2.** Public Information. (HCO PL 2 Nov 67) [The above HCO PL has been replaced by BPL 2 Nov 67 VI.]

PJO, Project Order. (BPL 5 Nov 72RA)

PJT, project. (BPL 5 Nov 72RA)

PK, **1.** pack. (BPL 5 Nov 72RA) **2.** policy knowledge. (FBDL 488R)

PKG, package. (BPL 5 Nov 72RA)

PL, Philadelphia. (HCO PL 2 Mar 59, *HCO Cable and Dispatch Designation System*)

PL(S), Policy Letter(s). (BPL 5 Nov 72RA)

PLCIES, policies. (BPL 5 Nov 72RA)

P. LIAISON, printer liaison. (HCO PL 21 Dec 69 II) [The above HCO PL was cancelled by BPL 21 Dec 69.]

PLN, plan. (BPL 5 Nov 72RA)

PLOB, Paper Label Org Board. (FBDL 106)

PLS, please. (BPL 5 Nov 72RA-1)

PLY, Plymouth. (BPL 10 Apr 73R)

PM, **1.** *post meridiem* (afternoon), Prime Minister. (BPL 5 Nov 72RA) **2.** production master. (BTB 7 Jan 74)

PMT, payment. (BPL 5 Nov 72RA)

PN, pain, (BPL 5 Nov 72RA)

PNT(S), point(s). (BPL 5 Nov 72RA)

PO, Product Officer (*verb* or *noun*), purchase order, Petty Officer. (BPL 5 Nov 72RA)

POA, [Appears on HCOB 1 Dec 58 *Actions to Start an HCO.* POA abbreviates for Power of Attorney.]

POC, Petty Officer Council. (FO 3311-1)

P.O. EXPRESS, post office express. (HCO PL 28 Aug 59, *HCO WW Mail Economy and Methods*)

POL, policy. (BPL 5 Nov 72RA)

POL LTR, Policy Letter. (HCO PL 11 Apr 70)

POSS(BLTY), possible (ibility). (BPL 5 Nov 72RA)

POW, [*The Problems of Work.*] (BPL 5 Nov 72RA)

POWW, Pubs Org WW. (HCO PL 23 May 68, *Important Purchasing From Pubs Org WW)*

PP, **1.** personnel points. (BPL 5 Nov 72RA) **2.** prepayment. (HCO PL 15 Jan 72RA) **3.** purchasing policy. (FO 2873)

PPBK, paperback. (BPL 5 Nov 72RA)

PPC, post purpose clearing. (HCOB 4 Aug 71R)

PPF, Pursers Project Force. (FO 1889)

PPLE, people. (BPL 5 Nov 72RA)

PPO, **1.** Personnel Procurement Office. (FBDL 161) **2.** Personnel Procurement Officer. (HCO PL 22 May 68 I)

PPP, personnel promotion policies. (FO 2789)

PPR, **1.** (international telex jargon) paper. (BPL 5 Nov 72RA-1) **2.** prepayments received. (BPL 5 Nov 72RA)

PPS, public paid starts. (BPL 5 Nov 72RA)

PPU, prepayments used. (BPL 5 Nov 72RA)

PR, **1.** processing. (HASI PL 8 Feb 58) **2.** *Slang* promotional talk. (HCOB 19 Jun 71 II) **3.** public relations. (HCO PL 7 Aug 72R) **4.** public relations cheery falsehoods. (HCOB 22 Sept 71) **5.** which means public relations to cover up—and in our *Slang* talk "PR" means putting up a lot of false reports to serve as a smoke screen for idleness or bad actions. (HCO PL 4 Apr 72) **6.** Puerto Rico. (HCO PL 2 Mar 59, *HCO Cable and Dispatch Designation System*)

PRA, public relations actions. (BPL 31 Jan 69, *PRO Broadsheets*)

PRAC, Public Relations Area Control. (FO 3279-1R)

PR & C, **1.** change from PR & C to Dissem Bureau. (ED 459-51 Flag) **2.** public relations and consumption. (BPL 5 Nov 72RA)

PrB, promotion and books. (FPO 2253)

PRBLM, problem. (BPL 5 Nov 72RA)

PRC, PR (Public Relations) Chief. (FO 2298)

PRCWW, PR Chief WW. (FO 2284)

PRD, Primary Rundown. (HCO PL 6 Aug 72R)

PRD GLOSS, [*Special Primary Rundown Glossary.*]

PR DRRF, PR Program Development Routing and Release Form. (FO 2440)

PREF, prefer (ence)(ably). (BPL 5 Nov 72RA)

P REG, public reg. (BPL 5 Nov 72RA)

PREPS, preparations. (BPL 13 Feb 73R)

PR'ESE, PR *Slang.* (HCO PL 13 Aug 70 III)

PREV, previous(ly). (BPL 5 Nov 72RA)

PRIM, primary. (BPL 5 Nov 72RA)

PRO, **1.** processing. (HCOB 25 Oct 58) **2.** professional. (BPL 31 Oct 68) **3.** Professional Course. (HCOB 29 Sept 66) **4.** promotion. (SEC ED 27, 8 Jan 59) **5.** public relations office or officer. (HCO PL 11 Nov 69)

PROB, probably. (BPL 5 Nov 72RA)

PROC, **1.** process(es)(ing). (BPL 5 Nov 72RA) **2.** procurement. (BPL 25 Jan 76 I)

PROCU, procurement. (HCOB 25 Oct 58)

PROD, produce, product, production. (BPL 5 Nov 72RA)

PROD OFF, Product Officer (*noun* or *verb*). (BPL 5 Nov 72RA)

PROD OFF SYSTEM, Product Officer—Organizing Officer System. (FEBC 3, 7101C18 SO II)

PROD-ORG SYSTEM, the Product Officer—Org Officer System. (HCO PL 9 May 74)

PROD T, production target. (FO 2919)

PROF, professional. (COLRHED 359)

PROM, promotion. (HCOB 23 Aug 65)

PROMO, promotion. (LRH ED 161 Int)

PROM REG, Department of Promotion and Registration. (6503C09 SH Spec 54)

PROP, proportionate. (HCO PL 2 Jul 59)

PRP, public relations planning. (BPL 31 Jan 69, *PRO Broadsheets*)

PRPS, public reg paid starts. (FBDL 326)

PrR, the abbreviation of the Department of Promotion and Registration is "P," small "r," large "R." (5812C16)

PRR, people routed to reg. (BPL 5 Nov 72RA)

PRSP, public relations security policies. (FO 2680)

PRSPCT, prospect. (BPL 5 Nov 72RA)

PRSSR, pressure. (BPL 5 Nov 72RA)

PRT, **1.** part. (BPL 5 Nov 72RA) **2.** Portland. (HCO PL 4 Jan 66 II)

PS, **1.** paid starts. (BPL 5 Nov 72RA) **2.** Paris. (HCO PL 4 Jan 66 II)

PSE, please. (BPL 5 Nov 72RA-1)

PSH, push. (BPL 5 Nov 72RA)

PSO, Photoshoot Org. (ED 695-1 Flag)

PT, **1.** Port Elizabeth. (HCO PL 2 Mar 59, *HCO Cable and Dispatch Designation System*) **2.** present time. (BPL 5 Nov 72RA) **3.** primary target. (FO 2919)

PTA, Pretoria. (BPL 10 Apr 73R)

PTF, payments to Flag. (BPL 5 Nov 72RA)

PTL, Portland. (BPL 5 Nov 72RA)

PTP, present time problem. (BPL 5 Nov 72RA)

PTS, **1.** points. (ED 31 Flag) **2.** "Potential Trouble Source." It means the person is connected to someone hostile to Scientology. (OODs 5 Apr 72)

PUB, public (LRH ED 159R-1 Int)

PUB DIV, public division. (LRH ED 159R-1 Int)

PUBLIC EXEC SEC, the Public Executive Secretary. (LRH ED 49 Int)

PUBS, publications. (BPL 5 Nov 72RA)

PUBS DK, the Department of Publications AOSH DK. (SOED 142 Int)

PUBS US, Publications Organization, United States. (LRH ED 265 Int)

PURP, purpose. (BPL 5 Nov 72RA)

PWR, power. (BPL 5 Nov 72RA)

PXL, [*The Phoenix Lectures.*]

Q, question. (BPL 5 Nov 72RA)

QBP, Quad Bonus Policy. (FSO 365)

QC, **1.** Qual cramming GDS. (BPL 5 Nov 72RA) **2.** quality control. (ED 769 Flag)

QEO, Qualifications Establishment Officer. (HCO PL 7 Mar 72)

QGA, (international telex jargon) question: may I go ahead = may I transmit? (BPL 5 Nov 72RA-1)

QLTY, quality. (BPL 5 Nov 72RA)

QM, Quartermaster. (HCO PL 5 Feb 69)

QM LOG, Quartermaster Log Book. (FO 316)

QMW, QM of the Watch. (FO 2717R)

QNTY, quantity. (BPL 5 Nov 72RA)

QOK, (international telex jargon) question: okay? = do you agree? (BPL 5 Nov 72RA-1)

QOOE, Qualifications Org Officer/Establishment Officer. (BPL 5 Nov 72RA)

QOO/ESTO, Qual Org Officer/Esto. (BPL 22 Nov 71R)

QR, questionable risk list. (HCO SEC'L LTR 26 Dec 58)

QS, questions. (ED 139 Flag)

QSTNRE, questionnaire. (BPL 5 Nov 72RA)

QUAL, qualifications. (BPL 5 Nov 72RA)

QUAL DIV, Qualifications Division. (BPL 5 Nov 72RA)

QUAL I & I, Qual Interview and Invoice. (7109C05SO)

QUAL SEC, Qualifications Secretary. (BPL 5 Nov 72RA)

R, 1. cable personally originated by myself. The number preceding it is the date sent, e.g. 16R means originated on the 16th day of the month by myself. (HCO PL 4 Jan 66 II) **2.** L. Ron Hubbard. (BPL 10 Apr 73R) **3.** (R, RA, RB, etc.) when an issue is cancelled the number is followed by "R" on the next issue meaning Revised. Example: HCOB List 12 (there is no such list), when revised would be HCOB List 12R, to mean "this is a new issue of list 12 and list 12 is cancelled and we now have List 12 Revised." When a list (List 12R) is further revised it becomes unwieldy to continue to string out Rs (List 12RRRRRR). A Case Supervisor and auditor gets tired of writing Rs! Therefore, after the first R, one adds A, B, C, etc. Thus List 12RRRRRRR would be List 12RF. (HCO PL 2 May 72) **4.** reality. (HCO PL 19 May 70) **5.** (international telex jargon) received. (BPL 5 Nov 72RA-1) **6.** release. (HCO PL 27 Oct 65)

®, in order to protect the words Dianetics and Scientology, all books, magazines, bulletins and policy letters with the word Dianetics or Scientology on them, should bear notice of our trademark registration. The notice looks like this, ® and is placed near the word, thus Dianetics® . (BPL 28 Aug 72 II)

RA, right arm (rank). (BPL 5 Nov 72RA)

RAM, means "records, assets and materiel" and is Dept 9 of Div III of any Org. (FO 3152RR)

R & B, room and board. (ED 118 USB)

R AND I CLERK, Routing and Information Clerk. (FO 3466R-1)

RAP, 1. Department of Routing, Appearances and Personnel. (HCO PL 21 Oct 66 III) **2.** (international telex jargon) *je ropelle* (I call again) = I will call you again. (BPL 5 Nov 72RA-1)

RBN, ribbon = my teletype ribbon has broken. (BPL 5 Nov 72RA-1)

RC, rollercoaster. (BPL 5 Nov 72RA)

RCPT, receipt. (BPL 5 Nov 72RA)

RCRD, record. (BPL 5 Nov 72RA)

RCRT, recruit. (BPL 5 Nov 72RA)

RCT, recut = your tape is badly cut, please recut your tape and call back. (BPL 5 Nov 72RA-1)

RCVD, (international telex jargon) received. (BPL 5 Nov 72RA-1)

RCVR(Y), recover(y). (BPL 5 Nov 72RA)

RD, rundown. (ED 86 FAO)

RDY, ready. (BPL 5 Nov 72RA)

REC, reception. (HCOB 23 Aug 65)

RECD, received. (BPL 5 Nov 72RA)

REC/FATH, recorder/fathometer. (FO 2925)

RECOM, recommend (ation). (BPL 5 Nov 72RA)

RECV(NG), receive (ing). (BPL 5 Nov 72RA)

REF, refer (ence). (BPL 5 Nov 72RA)

REG, register, registrar, registration. (BPL 5 Nov 72RA)

REG INT, registrar interview. (BPL 5 Nov 72RA)

REHAB, rehabilitation. (HCO PL 23 Aug 65 II)

REINF(RCNG), reinforce (ing). (BPL 5 Nov 72RA)

REL, 1. relations. (HCO PL 22 Aug 60) **2.** release. (BPL 5 Nov 72RA)

REP, representative. (BPL 15 Jul 72R I)

REPS, "Ron's external publics Scientologists." (BPL 3 Sept 75 II)

REPT, report. (BPL 5 Nov 72RA)

REQ, requirement. (BPL 5 Nov 72RA)

REQS CHIEF, Requirements Chief. (FO 3466R-5)

RESP, responsible (ility). (BPL 5 Nov 72RA)

RET, reassign target to another. (Target marking and tlx code). (CBO 325)

RET TO, (routing) to be returned to the forwarding staff member. (HCO PL 13 Mar 65 II)

RF, routing form. (ED 34 Flag)

R-FAC, reality factor. (BPL 5 Nov 72RA)

R-FACTOR, reality factor. (FO 2414)

RGDS, regards. (BPL 5 Nov 72RA)

RHIR, RHIP, rank has its responsibilities. Rank has its privileges. RHIR, RHIP as Nelson used to say. (HCO PL 5 Oct 58)

RI, registrar interviews. (BPL 5 Nov 72RA)

RITE, right. (BPL 5 Nov 72RA)

RJ, Ron's Journal. (COLRHED 300)

RLY, relay. (BPL 5 Nov 72RA)

RM, room. (BPL 5 Nov 72RA)

RONY, Flag's Office in NY for handling FCCI's. (CBO 415) [The name means literally Relay Office New York.]

ROY, [Abbreviation for royalties which appears in SOED 510-1 INT.]

RP, raw public. (HCO PL 28 Nov 71R II)

RPF, 1. Redemption Project Force. (ED 965 Flag) **2.** Rehabilitation Project Force (FO 3434)

RPLC, replace. (BPL 5 Nov 72RA)

RPO, registration pack out. (HCO PL 18 Feb 73 I)

RPT, (international telex jargon) repeat = please repeat/I repeat. (BPL 5 Nov 72RA-1)

RPT AA, (international telex jargon) repeat all after = repeat everything from . . . on. (BPL 5 Nov 72RA-1)

RPT AB, (international telex jargon) repeat all before = repeat everything before. . . . (BPL 5 Nov 72RA-1)

RPT ALL, (international telex jargon) repeat all = repeat the complete message. (BPL 5 Nov 72RA-1)

RPT WA, (international telex jargon) repeat the word after. . . . (BPL 5 Nov 72RA-1)

RPT WB, (international telex jargon) repeat the word before. . . . (BPL 5 Nov 72RA-1)

RQR, require. (BPL 5 Nov 72RA)

RQST, request. (BPL 5 Nov 72RA)

RRR, Refund/Repayment Report Form. (HCO PL 20 Oct 72) [The above HCO PL was cancelled by BPL 10 Oct 75 X]

RS, *Royal Scotman.* (FO 411)

R/S, 1. rock slam. (BPL 5 Nov 72RA) **2.** *Royal Scotman.* (FO 496)

RSLT, result. (BPL 5 Nov 72RA)

RSM, *Royal Scotman.* (FO 1483)

RSM AO, the *Royal Scotman* and AO Alicante were more or less the same AO. (ED 68 Flag)

RSN, reason. (BPL 5 Nov 72RA)

RSNABL(NSS), reasonable (ness). (BPL 5 Nov 72RA)

RSRV, reserve. (BPL 5 Nov 72RA)

RSVP, (international telex jargon) *respondez S'il Vous Plaît* (French) = please call back. (BPL 5 Nov 72RA-1)

RT, route. (BPL 5 Nov 72RA)

RTRD, retread. (BPL 5 Nov 72RA)

RTRN, return. (BPL 5 Nov 72RA)

RUDS, rudiments. (BPL 5 Nov 72RA)

RVRT, revert. (BPL 5 Nov 72RA)

RVW, review. (BPL 5 Nov 72RA)

S, 1. south. (BPL 5 Nov 72RA) **2.** staff. (CBO 245) **3.** starboard. (FSO 666)

SA, South Africa. (BPL 5 Nov 72RA)

SAC, Sacramento. (BPL 10 Apr 73R)

S AND D, search and discovery (SH Spec 73 6608C02)

SAPA, SA (South African) Personality Analysis Profile. (HCO PL 15 Nov 60)

SAT, Saturday. (BPL 5 Nov 72RA)

SB('S), shooting board(s). (BPL 5 Nov 72RA)

S.B., station bill. (FO 1684) See WQSB.

SBO, Staff Banking Officer (Commodore's staff under CS-3, located at Flag). (HCO PL 16 Jun 69) [The above HCO PL was cancelled by BPL 10 Oct 75 VII]

SC, 1. Scientology Consultants Inc. (HCO PL 25 Jan 57) **2.** social coordination. (BPL 22 Jul 75) **3.** Supercargo. (BPL 5 Nov 72RA)

SCE, source. (BPL 5 Nov 72RA)

SCHED(LD), schedule (d). (BPL 5 Nov 72RA)

SCICON, Scientology Consultants, Inc. (LRH Directive Washington D.C., 14 Dec 56)

SCN, Scientology. (HCOB 23 Aug 65)

SCN 8-80, [*Scientology 8-80.*]

SCNH, Scientologists hatted. (BPL 5 Nov 72RA)

SCN JOUR 14-G, [*Journal of Scientology Issue 14-G.*]

SCNST, Scientologist. (BPL 5 Nov 72RA)

SCP, [*Scientology Clear Procedure.*]

SCS, Scientology Coordinated Services, start change stop. (BPL 5 Nov 72RA)

SD, 1. San Diego. (HCO PL 2 Mar 59, *HCO Cable and Dispatch Designation System*) **2.** [*Standard Dianetics.*]

SE, Seattle. (HCO PL 4 Jan 66 II)

SEA, Seattle. (BPL 10 Apr 73R)

SEA ORG, Sea Organization. (HCO PL 9 May 68)

SEC, **1.** secretary. (HCOB 23 Aug 65) **2.** security. (BPL 5 Nov 72RA)

SEC CHK, security check. (BPL 5 Nov 72RA)

SEC ED, **1.** Secretarial Executive Directive. (HCO PL 7 May 65) **2.** Secretarial Executive Director. (HCO PL 22 Feb 65 III)

SEC'L ED, Secretarial to the Executive Director. (HCO Secretarial PL 17 Dec 58)

SEC SEC, Secretary's Secretary. (HCO PL 12 Mar 61 III)

SECT, section. (HCO PL 11 Aug 67 III)

SEPT, September. (BPL 5 Nov 72RA)

SER, series. (BPL 5 Nov 72RA)

SER FAC, service facsimile. (BPL 5 Nov 72RA)

SERV, service. (HCO PL 26 Nov 71R I) [The above HCO PL was cancelled by BPL 1 Dec 72 V.]

SESSN(S), session (s). (BPL 5 Nov 72RA)

SEUS, South East US. (BPL 5 Nov 72RA)

SF, San Francisco. (HCO PL 2 Mar 59, *HCO Cable and Dispatch Designation System)*

SFO, San Francisco. (BPL 10 Apr 73R)

SFP, safe point. (BPL 5 Nov 72RA)

SFT, soft. (BPL 5 Nov 72RA)

SG, specialty group. (COLRHED 112R)

SH, Saint Hill, single hatted. (BPL 5 Nov 72RA)

SH AO G, SH AO Greece. (FO 1847)

SHCP, staff hat check points. (BPL 5 Nov 72RA)

SHD, should. (BPL 5 Nov 72RA)

SHF, Saint Hill Foundation. (BPL 10 Apr 73R)

SHG, SH Greece. (FO 1850)

SHIP'S REP, Ship's Representative. (FO 1109)

SHPA, Special Hubbard Professional Auditors Course (London). (HCOB 29 Sept 66)

SHSBC, Saint Hill Special Briefing Course. (BPL 5 Nov 72RA)

SIG, signatory, signature. (BPL 5 Nov 72RA)

SIT, situation. (FO 3064)

SITN, situation. (BPL 5 Nov 72RA)

SLR, Scientology Library and Research Ltd. (HCO PL 30 Sept 64)

SLVG, salvage. (BPL 5 Nov 72RA)

SM, [Substitution Master (tape).]

SMC, State of Man Congress. (HCOB 29 Sept 66)

SND, send. (BPL 5 Nov 72RA)

SNGLHND, single handed. (BPL 5 Nov 72RA)

SINGLHTTD, single hatted. (BPL 5 Nov 72RA)

SNR, senior. (BPL 5 Nov 72RA)

SO, Sea Organization, senior organization. (BPL 5 Nov 72RA)

SO 1, see STANDING ORDER NO. 1.

SO ED, Sea Organization Executive Directive. (HCO PL 24 Sept 70R)

SOL, solution. (BPL 5 Nov 72RA)

S.O.L.T.S., Sea Organization Letter to Staff. (FO 2413)

SO NO. 1, Standing Order Number One. (LRH ED 223 Int)

SOP, standard operating procedure. (FO 2302)

SOR, Sea Org reserves. (ED 512 Flag)

SOS, [Abbreviation for "start of session." Normally used on auditor report forms and on session worksheets. Refer to *Dianetics Today* pp. 658 and 666.]

SOS BK 2, [*Science of Survival,* Book Two.]

SP, suppressive person. (BPL 5 Nov 72RA)

SPB, [*The Basic Scientology Picture Book.*]

SPEC, special. (BPL 5 Nov 72RA)

SPEC PROGS EX OFFICER, see INTERNATIONAL SPECIAL PROGRAMMES EXECUTION OFFICER.

SPF, Stewards Project Force. (FO 3163)

SPR LECT, London Spring Lectures. (HCOB 29 Sept 66)

SQRL, squirrel. (BPL 5 Nov 72RA)

SR, **1.** senior. (SO ED 161-1 Int) **2.** Ship's Rep. (FO 2762) **3.** Ship's Rep Policy. (FO 2762)

S/R, senior rating. (FO 2384)

SRCO, (letter designation on HCOBs) selected release by city office. These are issued to auditors enfranchised by city office. (HCOB 24 Feb 59)

SRI, **1.** sorry. (BPL 5 Nov 72RA) **2.** Student Rescue Intensive. (FO 2980)

SRM, Ship's Rep Major Policy. (FO 2762)

SRU, Student Recovery Unit. (ED 281-2 Flag)

SRVC, service. (BPL 5 Nov 72RA)

SS, **1.** Ship Safety Policy. (FO 2907) **2.** staff status. (HCO PL 17 May 74R) **3.** station ship. (HCO PL 13 Feb 71) **4.** success stories. (BPL 5 Nov 72RA)

SSI, Staff Status One. (BPL 5 Nov 72RA)

SSII, Staff Status Two. (BPL 5 Nov 72RA)

SSBS, Silver Spring Business Service Incorporated. (PAB 74)

SSO, 1. [Staff Section Officer.] **2.** Station Ship Order. (HCO PL 24 Sept 70R)

S.S.S.M., Spotless Shiny Ship Maintenance. (ED 319 Flag)

ST, St. Louis. (HCO PL 2 Mar 59, *HCO Cable and Dispatch Designation System*)

STAT, statistic. (HCO PL 6 Jul 70)

STBD, starboard. (BPL 5 Nov 72RA)

STC, student completions. (BPL 5 Nov 72RA)

STCR, [*Scientology Twentieth Century Religion.*]

STF, staff. (BPL 5 Nov 72RA)

STF C, Staff Captain. (BPL 5 Nov 72RA)

STF NOA, number of staff in normal or above. (BPL 5 Nov 72RA)

STHIL, designation for the distribution of bulletins and HCO Policy Letters for Saint Hill staff only. (BPL 7 Sept 59)

STHIL STUDENTS, a mimeo has to be marked "StHil Students" for the students to receive any at all. (HCO PL 2 Jul 64)

STK, stock, Stockholm. (BPL 5 Nov 72RA)

STL, St. Louis. (BPL 10 Apr 73R)

STM, Stockholm. (BPL 10 Apr 73R)

STN, station. (FSO 263)

STND, standard. (BPL 5 Nov 72RA)

STO, Staff Training Officer. (HCO PL 21 Sept 69)

ST PTS, student points. (BPL 5 Nov 72RA)

STRAT(N), straight (en). (BPL 5 Nov 72RA)

STRRTD, starrated. (BPL 5 Nov 72RA)

STRRTE, starrate. (BPL 5 Nov 72RA)

STRT, start. (BPL 5 Nov 72RA)

STUD, student. (BPL 5 Nov 72RA)

SUCC, success (ful). (BPL 5 Nov 72RA)

SUFF, sufficient. (BPL 5 Nov 72RA)

SUGG, suggest (ion). (BPL 5 Nov 72RA)

SUN, Sunday. (BPL 5 Nov 72RA)

SUP, supervise, supervisor. (BPL 5 Nov 72RA)

SUPER, supervisor. (HCO PL 26 Jun 72)

SUPERLIT, superliterate. (ED 359 Flag)

SURV, survey. (BPL 5 Nov 72RA)

SVF, Status Verification Form. (FO 3568)

SVP, (international telex jargon) *s'il vous plaît* (French = please.) (BPL 5 Nov 72RA-1)

SWAN, Swansea. (BPL 5 Nov 72RA)

SWPB, *Sea Watch Picture Book.* (FSO 413)

SWR, [*Scientology: A World Religion Emerges in the Space Age.*]

SWUS, South West US. (BPL 5 Nov 72RA)

SY, Sydney. (HCO PL 4 Jan 66 II)

SYD, Sydney. (BPL 10 Apr 73R)

SYST, system. (BPL 5 Nov 72RA)

T, 1. reported done by telex. Not verified. Usually with a date. (Target marking and tlx code). (CBO 325) **2.** training (FO 2988)

T/, temporary (when used as post title). (BPL 5 Nov 72RA)

TAB, tabulation. (BPL 5 Nov 72RA)

T & C PLANNING, Town and Country Planning. (HCO PL 3 Feb 66)

T & S, training and services. (BPL 5 Nov 72RA)

TAPE, telex tape = I have run out of telex tape. (BPL 5 Nov 72RA-1)

TAR, tech/admin ratio. (BPL 5 Nov 72RA)

TAX, (international telex jargon) taxe (charge) = what is the charge?/the charge is. . . . (BPL 5 Nov 72RA-1)

TBP, triple bonus policy. (FSO 179R)

TC, Twin Cities. (HCO PL 4 Jan 66 II)

TCH, touch. (BPL 5 Nov 72RA)

TCO, Traffic Control Officer. (FO 815)

TDY, today. (BPL 5 Nov 72RA)

TE, test evaluation. (HCO PL 26 Nov 71R I) [The above HCO PL was cancelled by BPL 1 Dec 72 V.]

TEA, taking ethics action. (Target marking and tlx code). (CBO 325)

TECH, technology. (BPL 5 Nov 72RA)

TECH DIV, Technical Division. (BPL 5 Nov 72RA)

TECH SEC, Technical Secretary. (BPL 5 Nov 72RA)

TEMP, temporary (ily). (BPL 5 Nov 72RA)

TEO, 1. Tech Establishment Officer. (HCO PL 20 Aug 71 II) **2.** Technical Division Establishment Officer. (HCO PL 7 Mar 72)

TERM, terminatedly. (BPL 5 Nov 72RA)

TEST MSG/, (international telex jargon) test message = please send a test message. (BPL 5 Nov 72RA-1)

TEST SVP, (international telex jargon) test *s'il vous plaît* (French) = test and please. (BPL 5 Nov 72RA-1)

TGM, telegram. (BPL 5 Nov 72RA)

TGT, target. (BPL 5 Nov 72RA)

THM, them. (BPL 5 Nov 72RA)

THN, then. (BPL 5 Nov 72RA)

THO, though. (BPL 5 Nov 72RA)

THRU, **1.** through. (BPL 5 Nov 72RA) **2.** (international telex jargon) you are through to a telex position = you are in connection with an international telex position. (BPL 5 Nov 72RA-1)

THURS, Thursday. (BPL 5 Nov 72RA)

T-I-C, test-in-charge. (HCO PL 28 Oct 60, *New Testing Promotion Section Important*)

TIL, until. (BPL 5 Nov 72RA)

TIP, Technical Individual Program. (HCO PL 24 Sept 70R)

TKS, (international telex jargon) thanks. (BPL 5 Nov 72RA-1)

TKT, ticket. (BPL 5 Nov 72RA)

TKU, thank you. (BPL 5 Nov 72RA-1)

TLK, talk. (BPL 5 Nov 72RA)

TLX, (international telex jargon) telex. (BPL 5 Nov 72RA-1)

TM, team, time machine. (BPL 5 Nov 72RA)

TMRO, tomorrow. (BPL 5 Nov 72RA)

TO, **1.** Tours Org. (BPL 5 Nov 72RA) **2.** Training Officer. (BPL 1 Dec 72R VIII) [The above BPL was cancelled by HCO PL 30 Aug 74.]

TONITE, tonight. (BPL 5 Nov 72RA)

TOOE, Technical Org Officer/Establishment Officer. (BPL 5 Nov 72RA)

TOR, Toronto. (BPL 10 Apr 73R)

TOTL, total. (BPL 5 Nov 72RA)

T/P, training/processing. (Admin Directive 6 May 58)

TPR, (international telex jargon) teleprinter. (BPL 5 Nov 72RA-1)

TQC, tech quality control. (FPO 1849R, 21 Jul 75)

TR, training regimen (training drill). (BPL 5 Nov 72RA)

TR & SERV, training and services. (FO 2756)

TRANS, **1.** translations. (BPL 9 Jan 74 III) **2.** transport. (BPL 5 Nov 72RA)

TRB, triple bonus. (FSO 723)

TRBL, trouble. (BPL 5 Nov 72RA)

TRBLSM SCE, troublesome source. (BPL 5 Nov 72RA)

TRC, Tours Reception Center. (OODs 7 Jun 71) [This was a shore base set up as an extension of Flag in one of its areas of operation.]

TREAS, treasury. (BPL 5 Nov 72RA)

TREAS DIV, Treasury Division. (BPL 5 Nov 72RA)

TREAS SEC, Treasury Secretary. (BPL 5 Nov 72RA)

TREO, Treasury Establishment Officer. (HCO PL 7 Mar 72)

TRFC, traffic. (BPL 5 Nov 72RA)

TRMNL, terminal. (BPL 5 Nov 72RA)

TRN(D)(G), train (ed) (ing). (BPL 5 Nov 72RA)

TRNOVR, turnover. (BPL 5 Nov 72RA)

TRNSF, transfer. (BPL 5 Nov 72RA)

TRS, tours. (BPL 5 Nov 72RA)

TRSN, treason. (BPL 5 Nov 72RA)

TS, **1.** tech services. (BFO 46) **2.** tech staff—number of tech personnel. (BPL 5 Nov 72RA)

T/S, tech services. (HCOB 5 Mar 71)

T/S AIDE, Training & Services Aide. (ED 155 Flag)

TSMY, [Twin screw motor yacht, as in TSMY *Apollo.*]

TTA, Tours Target Area. (BFO 122-6)

TTC, Tech Training Corps. (FO 3298 RA)

TTC ST PTS, Tech Training Corps student points. (BPL 5 Nov 72RA)

TU, **1.** Translation Unit. (BPL 5 Nov 72RA) **2.** Tucson. (HCO PL 2 Mar 59, *HCO Cable and Dispatch Designation System*)

TUES, Tuesday. (BPL 5 Nov 72RA)

TWRD, toward. (BPL 5 Nov 72RA)

TX, (international telex jargon) telex. (BPL 5 Nov 72RA-1)

U, you, unit. (BPL 5 Nov 72RA)

UCE, United Churches Extension. (BFO 70)

UK, United Kingdom. (HCO PL 4 Jan 66 II, *HCO Cable Designation System*)

UNI-MED, Universal Media Productions. (SO ED 570 INT)

URG, **1.** urgent. (BPL 5 Nov 72RA) **2.** urgent to get this one done fast. (Target marking and tlx code). (CBO 325)

URGLY, urgently. (BPL 5 Nov 72RA)

US, United States. (HCO PL 4 Jan 66 II)

USA CLUB, United Survival Action Club. (5712C30)

USB, US Base. (Referring to the service org.) (BFO 122-6)

USBCO, US Base Conditions Order. (USB CO 15-1)

USLO, **1.** the duty of USLO is to advise Flag and to handle its area by getting into effect long range policy and programs of the top management of Flag. (FBDL 12) **2.** US Liaison Office. (LRH ED 130 Int)

USSO, [United States Sea Org USSO is ASHO DAY and Foundation, AOLA and Celebrity Centre Los Angeles combined.]

UTILZ(ATN), utilize (ation). (BPL 5 Nov 72RA)

V, very. (BPL 5 Nov 72RA)

VAL, value (able). (BPL 5 Nov 72RA)

VAL DOCS, valuable documents. (SH Spec 54, 6503C09)

VAN, Vancouver. (BPL 10 Apr 73R)

V.A.T., value added tax. (ED 309-1 Flag)

VEP, valuable exchangeable products. (FO 2873)

VERIF, verify (ication). (BPL 5 Nov 72RA)

VFP, valuable final product. (HCO PL 25 Mar 71)

VG, very good. (BPL 5 Nov 72RA)

VGI's, very good indicators. (BPL 5 Nov 72RA)

VIAB, viable (ility). (BPL 5 Nov 72RA)

VIPS, very important people. VIPs to PR are only opinion leaders. (HCO PL 11 May 71 II)

VM, Volunteer Minister. (COLRHED 79RA)

VNA, Vienna. (BPL 10 Apr 73R)

VOL, **1.** volume. (BPL 5 Nov 72RA) **2.** volunteer. (HCO PL 14 Oct 59, *Division of HCO Percentages Revised*)

VSD, value of services delivered. (BFO 46)

V STAFF, voluntary staff. (*Organization Book,* 1954)

VT, **1.** Vermont. (HCO PL 3 Mar 66 II) **2.** vital target. (FO 2919)

VWD, very well done. (BPL 5 Nov 72RA-1)

VWR, very well received. (BPL 5 Nov 72RA)

W, **1.** west, with. (BPL 5 Nov 72RA) **2.** (international telex jargon) words. (BPL 5 Nov 72RA-1) **3.** world. (HCO PL 2 Jan 59) see UNIT W.

WA, Western Australia. (LRH ED 46 Int) see UNIT W.

WASH, Washington. (BPL 5 Nov 72RA)

WATCH QTR AND STN BILL, Watch Quarter and Station Bill. (FO 1919)

WB, see UNIT W.

WC(ER) (D) (NG), word clear (er) (ed) (ing). (BPL 5 Nov 72RA)

WCCL, Word Clearing Correction List. (LRH ED 257 Int)

WCM1, Word Clearing Method 1. (BPL 5 Nov 72RA)

WD, **1.** well done. (FSO 195RR) **2.** word. (ED 121 FAO)

WDAHs, well done auditing hours. (FBDL 279)

WDH, well done hour. (BPL 23 Nov 71R) See WELL DONE AUDITING HOURS.

WE, Wellington. (HCO PL 2 Mar 59, *HCO Cable and Dispatch Designation System*)

W/E, week ending. (BPL 16 Sept 74RA III)

WED, Wednesday. (BPL 5 Nov 72RA)

WFMH, World Federation of Mental Health. (HCO PL 6 Jul 70)

WH(DY), withhold (y). (BPL 5 Nov 72RA)

WHT, what. (BPL 5 Nov 72RA)

WILCO, **1.** this word gets a telex answered fast when the original order will take a while to complete. It means "I will comply." A "wilco" is not a compliance. Its use however serves to let the originator know his order is being done. (BPL 8 Apr 73 I) **2.** wilco means "will comply." (BO 11, Circa 10 Jun 67)

WK, week. (BPL 5 Nov 72RA)

WKLY, weekly. (BPL 5 Nov 72RA)

WKND, weekend. (BPL 5 Nov 72RA)

WLK, would. (BPL 5 Nov 72RA)

WLFR, welfare. (BPL 5 Nov 72RA)

W/O, Warrant Officer. (BPL 5 Nov 72RA)

W OUT, without. (BPL 5 Nov 72RA)

W.Q., watch quarter. (FO 1684)

W/Q AND S/B, watch quarter and station bill. (FO 646)

WQ AND STN BILL, watch quarter and station bill. (FO 2464)

WQSB, watch quarter and station bill. (FSO 812)

WR(?), well received(?) = is the message(s) well received?/the message was well received. (BPL 5 Nov 72RA-1)

W/R, weekly report. (BPL 5 Nov 72RA)

WRK, work. (BPL 5 Nov 72RA)

WRU, (international telex jargon) who are you = who is there? (BPL 5 Nov 72RA-1)

WST, [Washington (D.C.) Staff Talk.]

WT, weight. (BPL 5 Nov 72RA)

WTG, (international telex jargon) waiting = I wait. (BPL 5 Nov 72RA-1)

WUS, Western US (BPL 5 Nov 72RA)

WW, worldwide. (HCO PL 24 Sept 70R)

X, **1.** break, by (measurement e.g. 4 x 8), times. (BPL 5 Nov 72RA) **2.** see UNIT X.

XA, see UNIT X AND UNIT W.

XB, see UNIT X AND UNIT W.

XCPT, except. (BPL 5 Nov 72RA)

XDN, Expanded Dianetics. (HCOB 15 Feb 74)

XLNT, excellent. (BPL 5 Nov 72RA)

XMAS, Christmas. (BPL 5 Nov 72RA)

XPCT, expect. (BPL 5 Nov 72RA)

XTRA, extra. (BPL 5 Nov 72RA)

Y, see UNIT Y.

YA, see UNIT Y AND UNIT W.

YB, see UNIT Y AND UNIT W.

YNR?, (international telex jargon) number? = what is your telex number? (BPL 5 Nov 72RA-1)

YR(S), your(s), you are, year(s). (BPL 5 Nov 72RA)

YRLY, yearly. (BPL 5 Nov 72RA)

YSTDY, yesterday. (BPL 5 Nov 72RA)

YV, you have. (BPL 5 Nov 72RA)

Z, see UNIT Z.

ZA, see UNIT Z AND UNIT W.

ZB, see UNIT Z AND UNIT W.

I II III, [Issue 1, 2 or 3, etc.]

2D, Second Dynamic. (BPL 5 Nov 72RA)

2D COMMODORE, 2nd Deputy Commodore. (FO 1972)

2M, Second Mate. (BPL 5 Nov 72RA)

2WC, two-way communication. (BPL 5 Nov 72RA)

3D, **1.** Third Dynamic. (BPL 5 Nov 72RA) **2.** three dimensional. (BPL 5 Nov 72RA)

3M, Third Mate. (BPL 5 Nov 72RA)

3P, third party. (BPL 5 Nov 72RA)

4M, Fourth Mate. (BPL 5 Nov 72RA)

8C, good and effective control. (BPL 5 Nov 72RA)

*****, [issue not directly prepared or written by L. Ron Hubbard.]

Organizing Boards

This Section shows several diagrams of major Scientology Organizing Boards used between 1961 and 1976. These are basic outlines showing mainly the divisions and/or departments of each organization. In reality each of these org boards would have a lot more post titles on them and the sections, units and functions would also be written in.

A lot of post titles, functions, divisions, departments, bureaux, etc., defined in this dictionary refer to or belong on these org boards.

Thus the purpose of this section is to briefly show the organization form that the definitions refer to. At the right hand corner of each diagram are the references that each board is based on.

It is easy to see that all Scientology Organizing Boards since 1965 have been variations of the Seven Division Org Board of 1965, which is *the* basic Scientology org board from that time forward. Any business activity could be adapted to run more successfully on the Seven Division Org Board of 1965.

Please note that the Org Boards shown in this section are not the most recently authorized Org Boards. New Scientology Org Boards will soon be released.

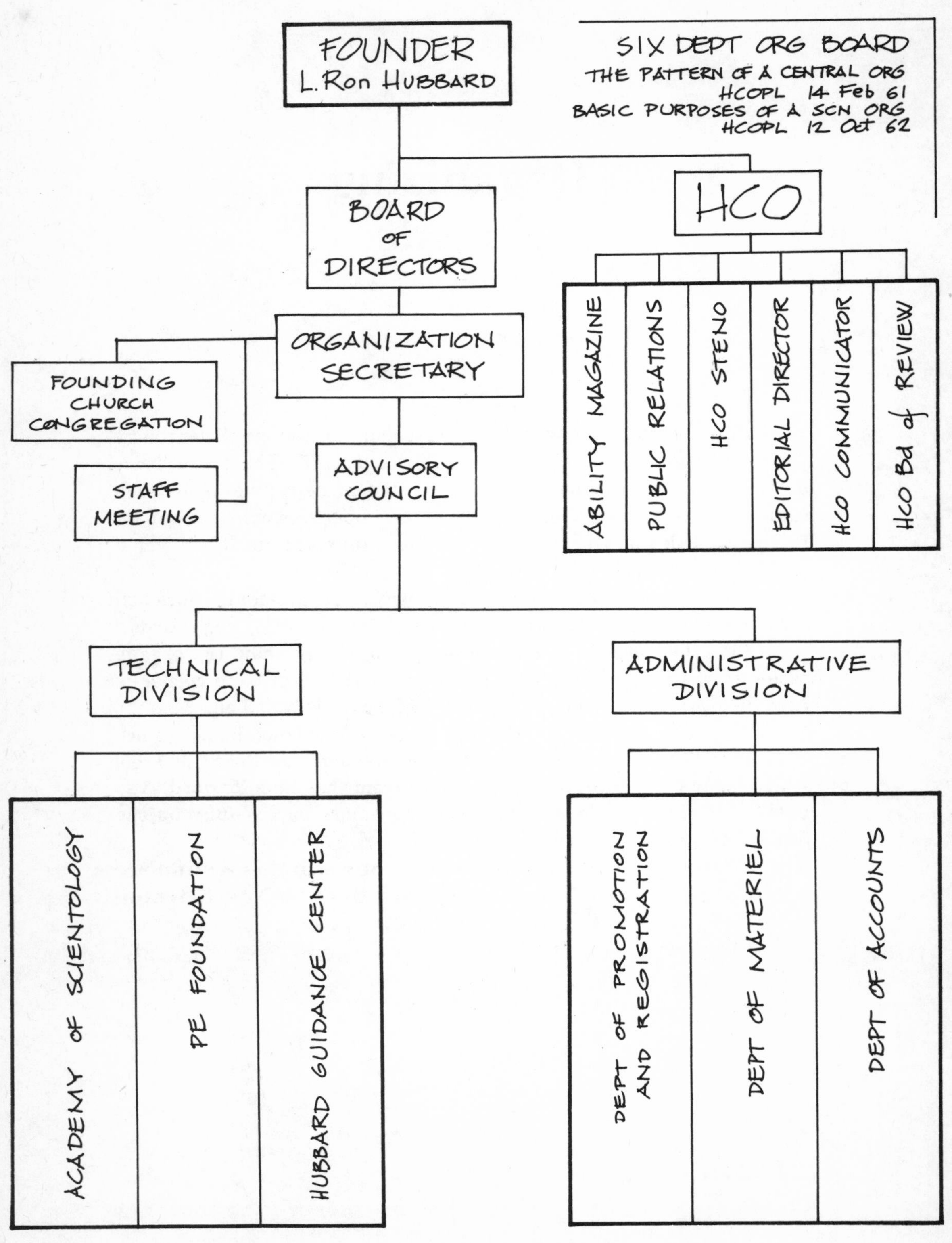
FOUNDER
L. Ron HUBBARD
SIX DEPT ORG BOARD
THE PATTERN OF A CENTRAL ORG
HCOPL 14 Feb 61
BASIC PURPOSES OF A SCN ORG
HCOPL 12 Oct 62
BOARD OF DIRECTORS
HCO
ABILITY MAGAZINE
PUBLIC RELATIONS
HCO STENO
EDITORIAL DIRECTOR
HCO COMMUNICATOR
HCO Bd of REVIEW
ORGANIZATION SECRETARY
FOUNDING CHURCH CONGREGATION
STAFF MEETING
ADVISORY COUNCIL
TECHNICAL DIVISION
ADMINISTRATIVE DIVISION
ACADEMY OF SCIENTOLOGY
PE FOUNDATION
HUBBARD GUIDANCE CENTER
DEPT OF PROMOTION AND REGISTRATION
DEPT OF MATERIEL
DEPT OF ACCOUNTS

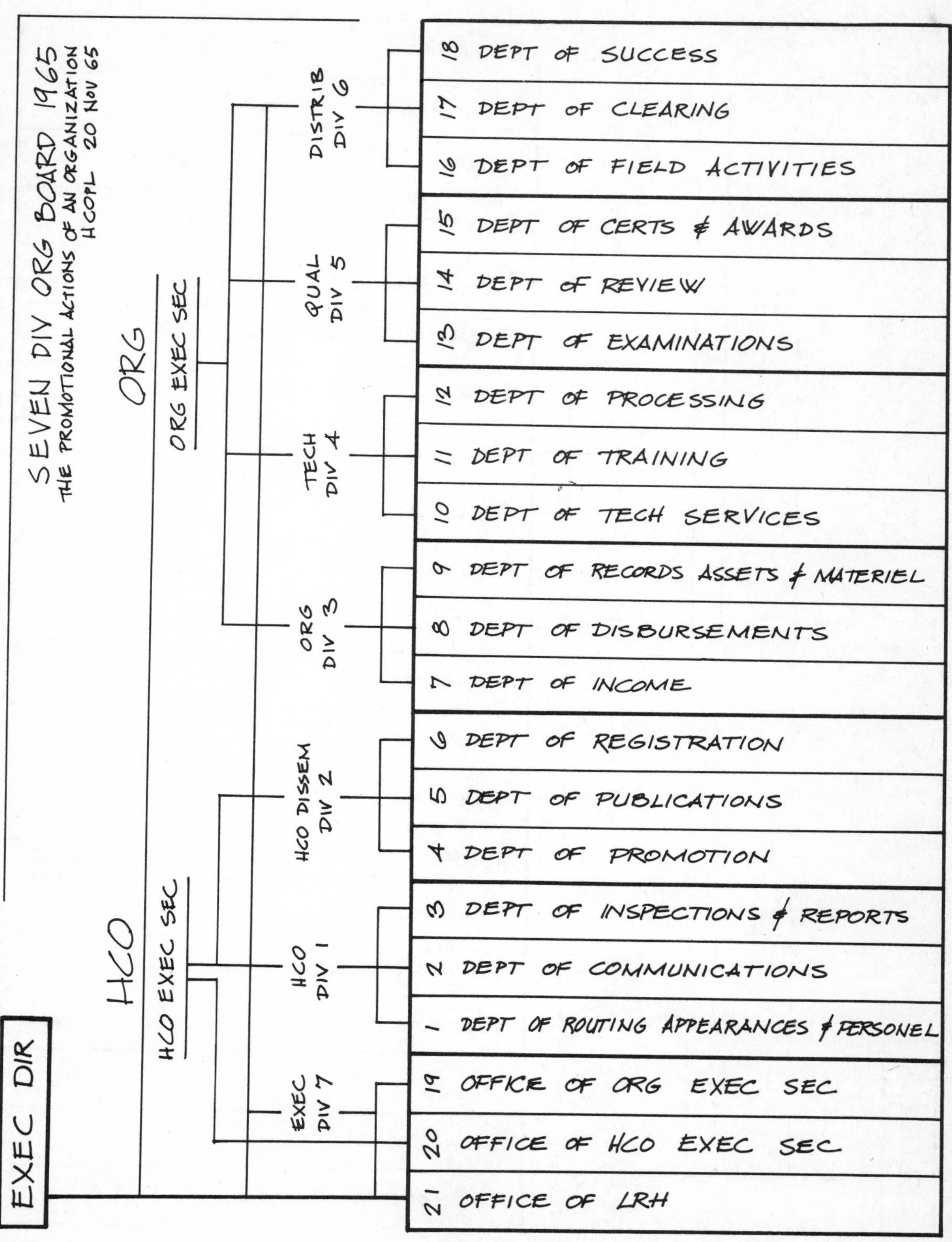
SEVEN DIV ORG BOARD 1965
THE PROMOTIONAL ACTIONS OF AN ORGANIZATION
HCOPL 20 NOV 65
ORG
ORG EXEC SEC
HCO
HCO EXEC SEC
EXEC DIR
DISTRIB DIV 6
QUAL DIV 5
TECH DIV 4
ORG DIV 3
HCO DISSEM DIV 2
HCO DIV 1
EXEC DIV 7
18 DEPT OF SUCCESS
17 DEPT OF CLEARING
16 DEPT OF FIELD ACTIVITIES
15 DEPT OF CERTS & AWARDS
14 DEPT OF REVIEW
13 DEPT OF EXAMINATIONS
12 DEPT OF PROCESSING
11 DEPT OF TRAINING
10 DEPT OF TECH SERVICES
9 DEPT OF RECORDS ASSETS & MATERIEL
8 DEPT OF DISBURSEMENTS
7 DEPT OF INCOME
6 DEPT OF REGISTRATION
5 DEPT OF PUBLICATIONS
4 DEPT OF PROMOTION
3 DEPT OF INSPECTIONS & REPORTS
2 DEPT OF COMMUNICATIONS
1 DEPT OF ROUTING APPEARANCES & PERSONEL
19 OFFICE OF ORG EXEC SEC
20 OFFICE OF HCO EXEC SEC
21 OFFICE OF LRH

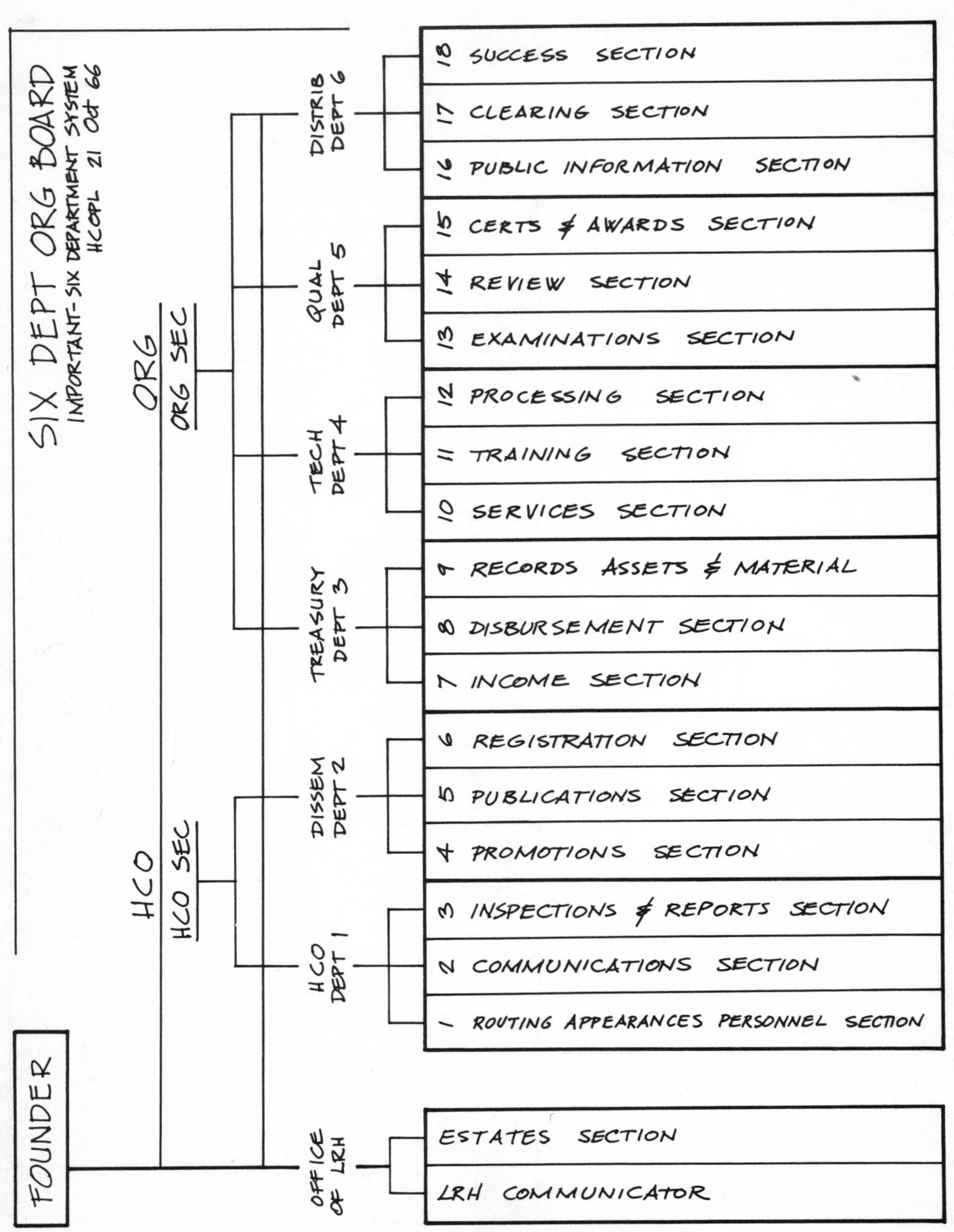

SIX DEPT ORG BOARD
IMPORTANT-SIX DEPARTMENT SYSTEM
HCOPL 21 Oct 66
FOUNDER
HCO
HCO SEC
ORG
ORG SEC
OFFICE OF LRH
ESTATES SECTION
LRH COMMUNICATOR
HCO DEPT 1
1 ROUTING APPEARANCES PERSONNEL SECTION
2 COMMUNICATIONS SECTION
3 INSPECTIONS & REPORTS SECTION
DISSEM DEPT 2
4 PROMOTIONS SECTION
5 PUBLICATIONS SECTION
6 REGISTRATION SECTION
TREASURY DEPT 3
7 INCOME SECTION
8 DISBURSEMENT SECTION
9 RECORDS ASSETS & MATERIAL
TECH DEPT 4
10 SERVICES SECTION
11 TRAINING SECTION
12 PROCESSING SECTION
QUAL DEPT 5
13 EXAMINATIONS SECTION
14 REVIEW SECTION
15 CERTS & AWARDS SECTION
DISTRIB DEPT 6
16 PUBLIC INFORMATION SECTION
17 CLEARING SECTION
18 SUCCESS SECTION

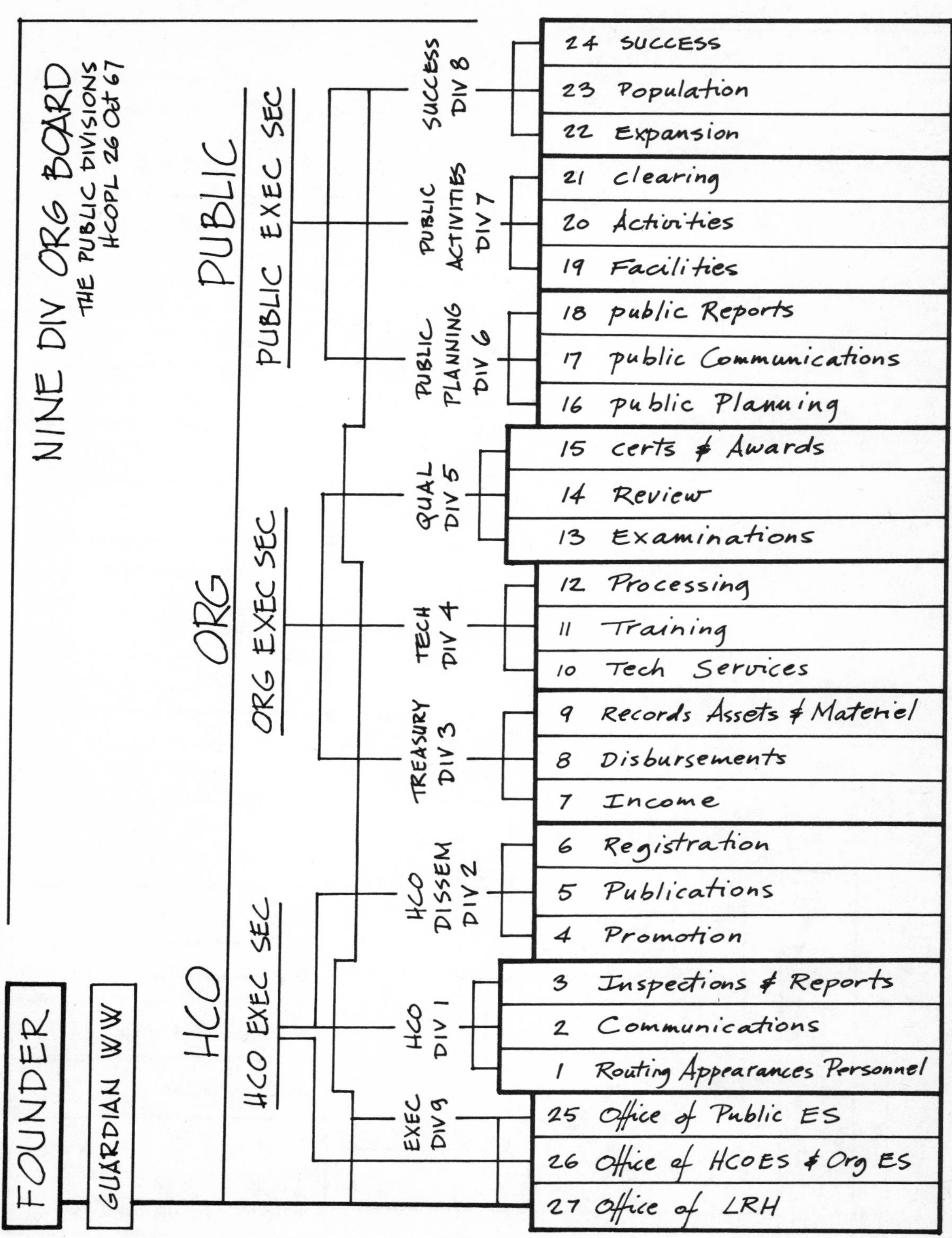
NINE DIV ORG BOARD
THE PUBLIC DIVISIONS
HCOPL 26 Oct 67
FOUNDER
GUARDIAN WW
HCO
HCO EXEC SEC
ORG
ORG EXEC SEC
PUBLIC
PUBLIC EXEC SEC
SUCCESS DIV 8
PUBLIC ACTIVITIES DIV 7
PUBLIC PLANNING DIV 6
QUAL DIV 5
TECH DIV 4
TREASURY DIV 3
HCO DISSEM DIV 2
HCO DIV 1
EXEC DIV 9
24 SUCCESS
23 Population
22 Expansion
21 clearing
20 Activities
19 Facilities
18 public Reports
17 public Communications
16 public Planning
15 certs & Awards
14 Review
13 Examinations
12 Processing
11 Training
10 Tech Services
9 Records Assets & Materiel
8 Disbursements
7 Income
6 Registration
5 Publications
4 Promotion
3 Inspections & Reports
2 Communications
1 Routing Appearances Personnel
25 Office of Public ES
26 Office of HCOES & Org ES
27 Office of LRH

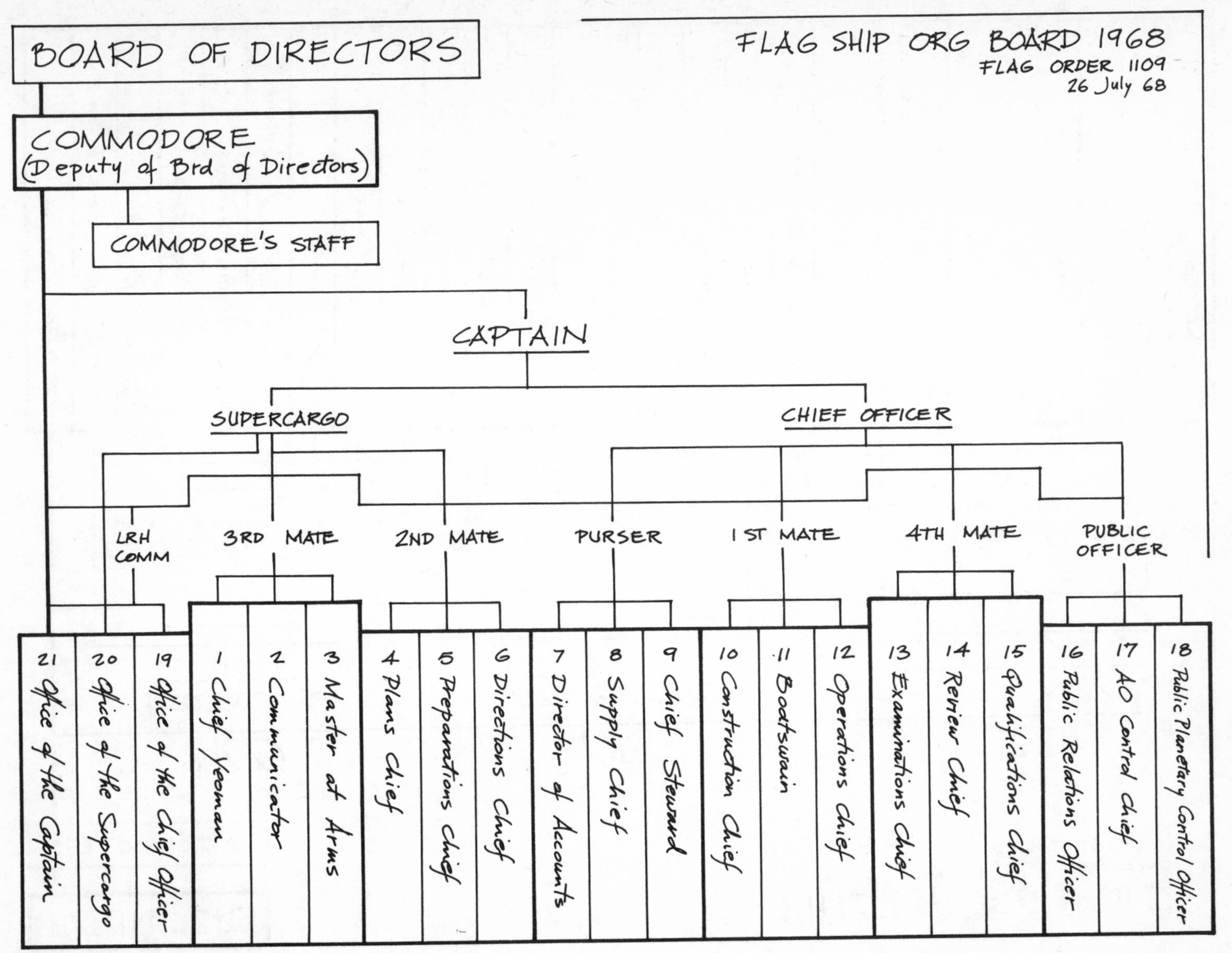

FLAG SHIP ORG BOARD 1968
FLAG ORDER 1109
26 July 68
BOARD OF DIRECTORS
COMMODORE
(Deputy of Brd of Directors)
COMMODORE'S STAFF
CAPTAIN
SUPERCARGO
CHIEF OFFICER
LRH COMM
3RD MATE
2ND MATE
PURSER
1ST MATE
4TH MATE
PUBLIC OFFICER
21 Office of the Captain
20 Office of the Supercargo
19 Office of the Chief Officer
1 Chief Yeoman
2 Communicator
3 Master at Arms
4 Plans Chief
5 Preparations Chief
6 Directions Chief
7 Director of Accounts
8 Supply Chief
9 Chief Steward
10 Construction Chief
11 Boatswain
12 Operations Chief
13 Examinations Chief
14 Review Chief
15 Qualifications Chief
16 Public Relations Officer
17 AO Control Chief
18 Public Planetary Control Officer

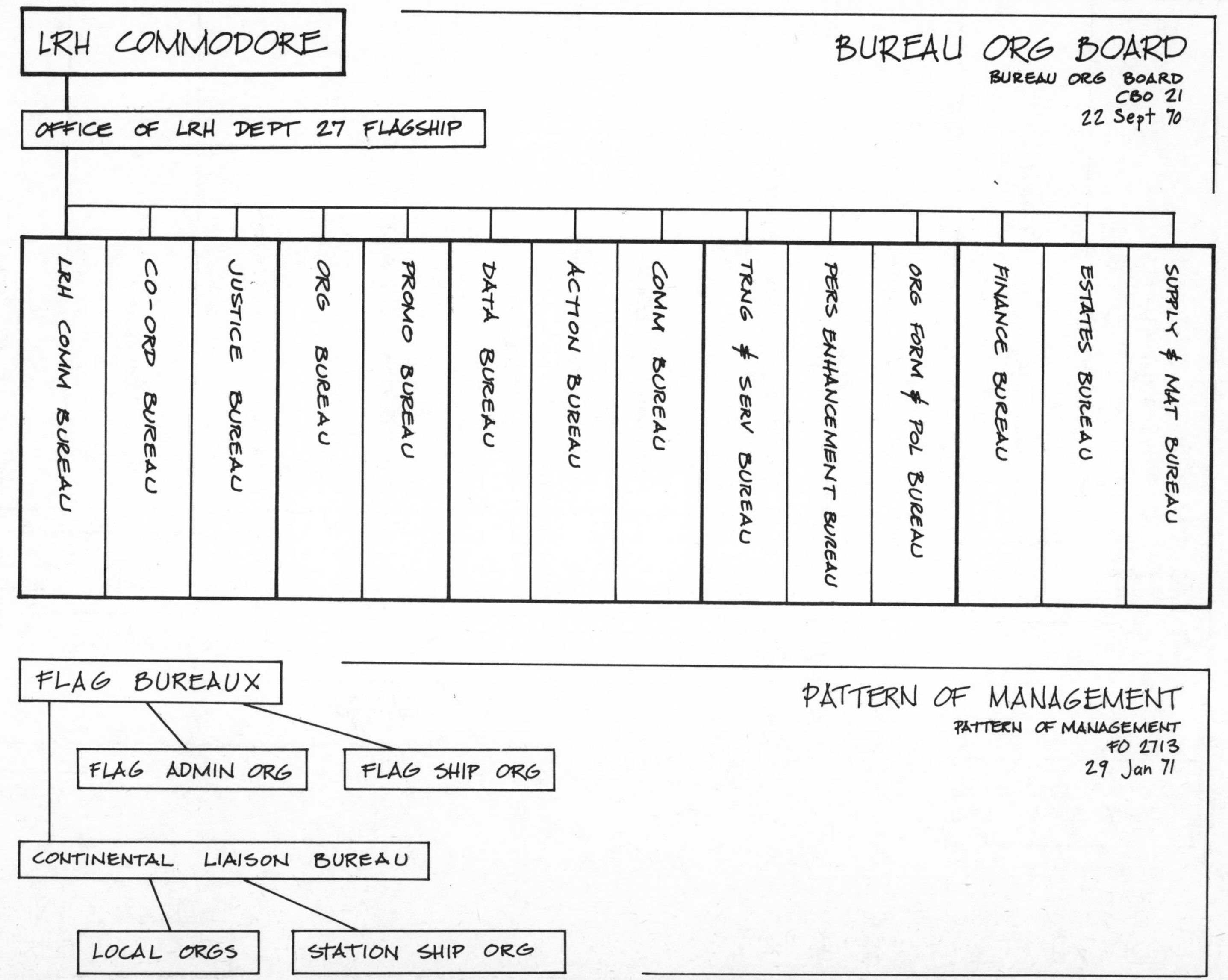
BUREAU ORG BOARD
BUREAU ORG BOARD
CBO 21
22 Sept 70
LRH COMMODORE
OFFICE OF LRH DEPT 27 FLAGSHIP
LRH COMM BUREAU
CO-ORD BUREAU
JUSTICE BUREAU
ORG BUREAU
PROMO BUREAU
DATA BUREAU
ACTION BUREAU
COMM BUREAU
TRNG & SERV BUREAU
PERS ENHANCEMENT BUREAU
ORG FORM & POL BUREAU
FINANCE BUREAU
ESTATES BUREAU
SUPPLY & MAT BUREAU
PATTERN OF MANAGEMENT
PATTERN OF MANAGEMENT
FO 2713
29 Jan 71
FLAG BUREAUX
FLAG ADMIN ORG
FLAG SHIP ORG
CONTINENTAL LIAISON BUREAU
LOCAL ORGS
STATION SHIP ORG

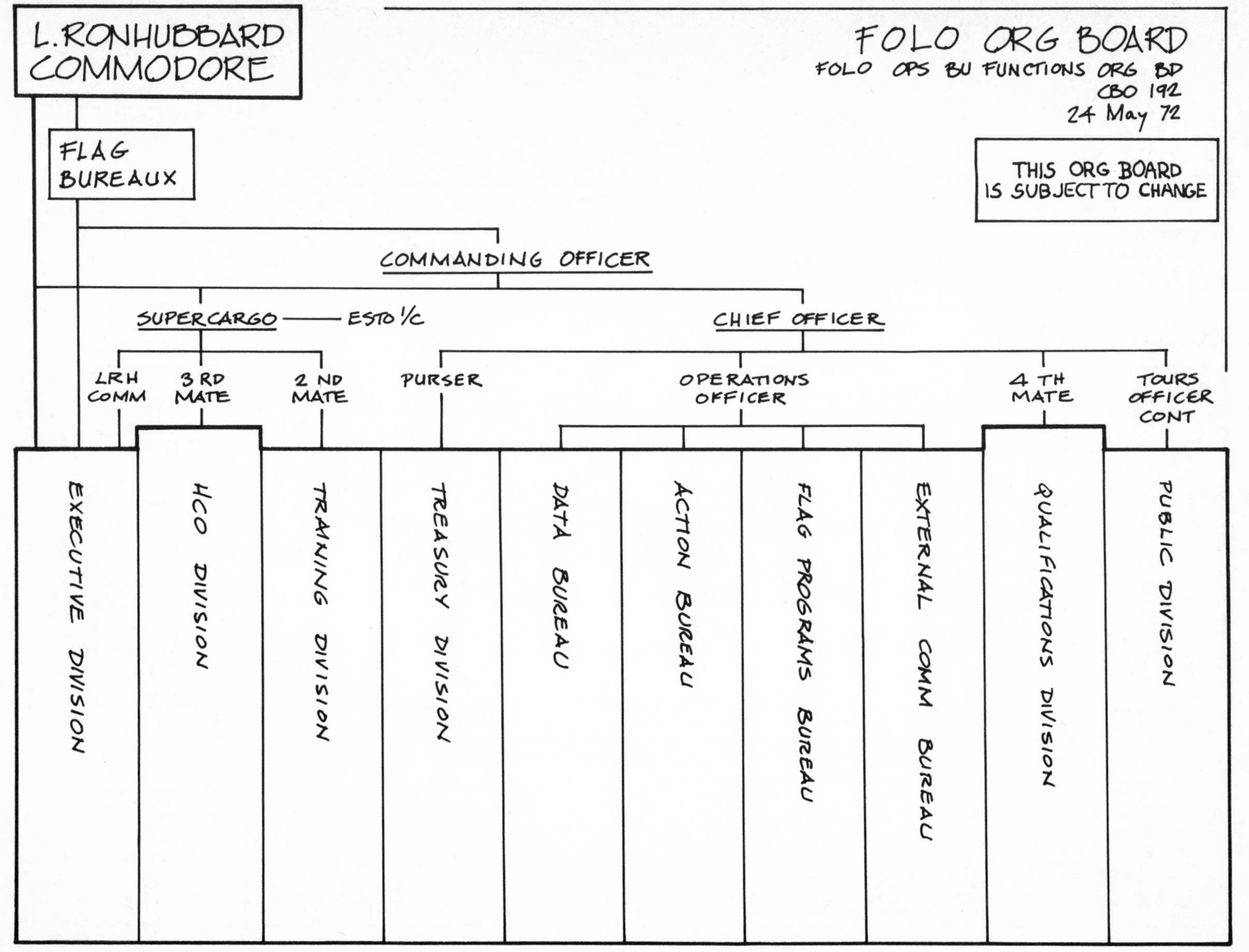

FOLO ORG BOARD
FOLO OPS BU FUNCTIONS ORG BD
CBO 192
24 May 72
THIS ORG BOARD IS SUBJECT TO CHANGE
L. RON HUBBARD COMMODORE
FLAG BUREAUX
COMMANDING OFFICER
SUPERCARGO
ESTO I/C
CHIEF OFFICER
LRH COMM
3 RD MATE
2 ND MATE
PURSER
OPERATIONS OFFICER
4 TH MATE
TOURS OFFICER CONT
EXECUTIVE DIVISION
HCO DIVISION
TRAINING DIVISION
TREASURY DIVISION
DATA BUREAU
ACTION BUREAU
FLAG PROGRAMS BUREAU
EXTERNAL COMM BUREAU
QUALIFICATIONS DIVISION
PUBLIC DIVISION

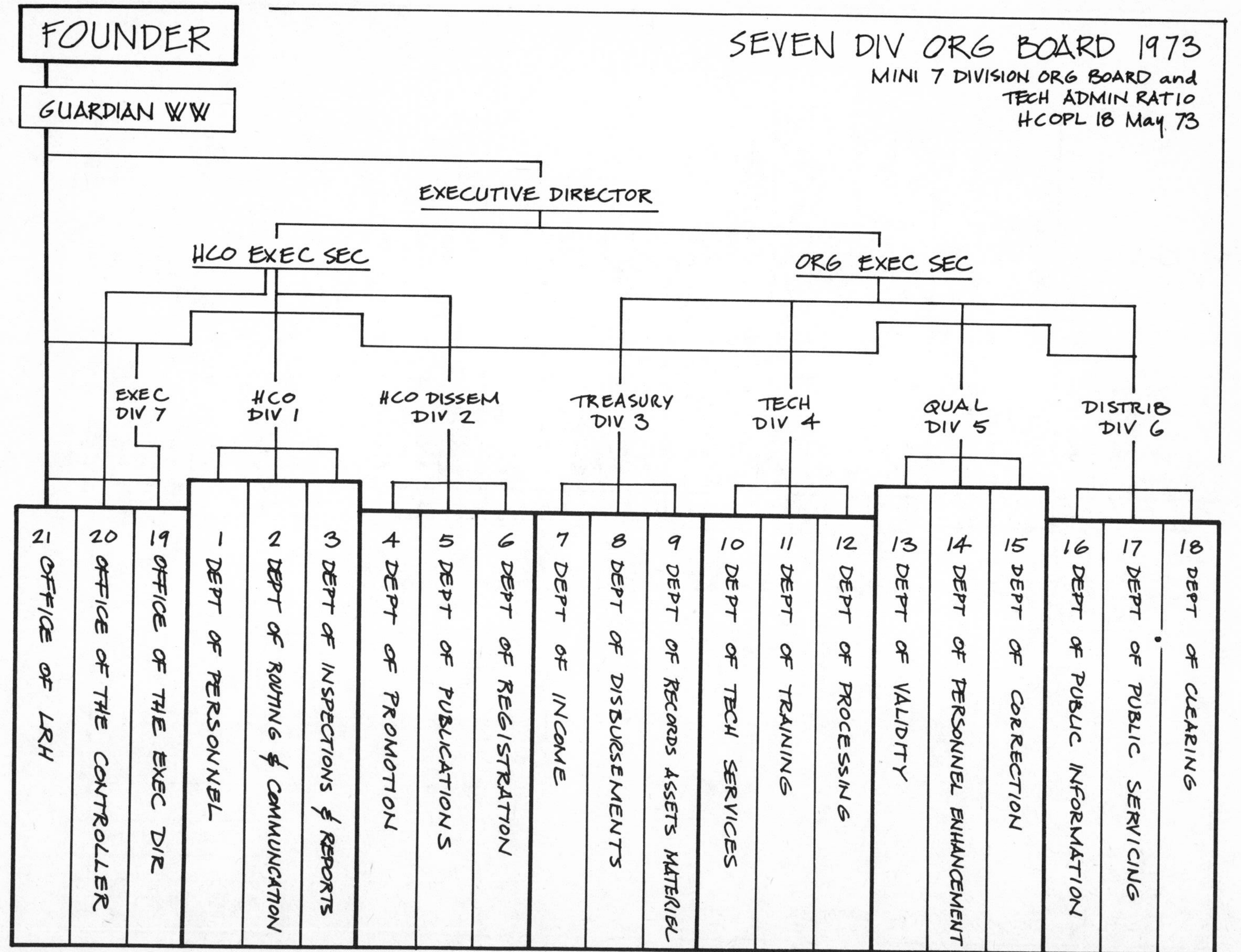

SEVEN DIV ORG BOARD 1973
MINI 7 DIVISION ORG BOARD and TECH ADMIN RATIO HCOPL 18 May 73
FOUNDER
GUARDIAN WW
EXECUTIVE DIRECTOR
HCO EXEC SEC
ORG EXEC SEC
EXEC DIV 7
HCO DIV 1
HCO DISSEM DIV 2
TREASURY DIV 3
TECH DIV 4
QUAL DIV 5
DISTRIB DIV 6
21 OFFICE OF LRH
20 OFFICE OF THE CONTROLLER
19 OFFICE OF THE EXEC DIR
1 DEPT OF PERSONNEL
2 DEPT OF ROUTING & COMMUNCATION
3 DEPT OF INSPECTIONS & REPORTS
4 DEPT OF PROMOTION
5 DEPT OF PUBLICATIONS
6 DEPT OF REGISTRATION
7 DEPT OF INCOME
8 DEPT OF DISBURSEMENTS
9 DEPT OF RECORDS ASSETS MATERIEL
10 DEPT OF TECH SERVICES
11 DEPT OF TRAINING
12 DEPT OF PROCESSING
13 DEPT OF VALIDITY
14 DEPT OF PERSONNEL ENHANCEMENT
15 DEPT OF CORRECTION
16 DEPT OF PUBLIC INFORMATION
17 DEPT OF PUBLIC SERVICING
18 DEPT OF CLEARING

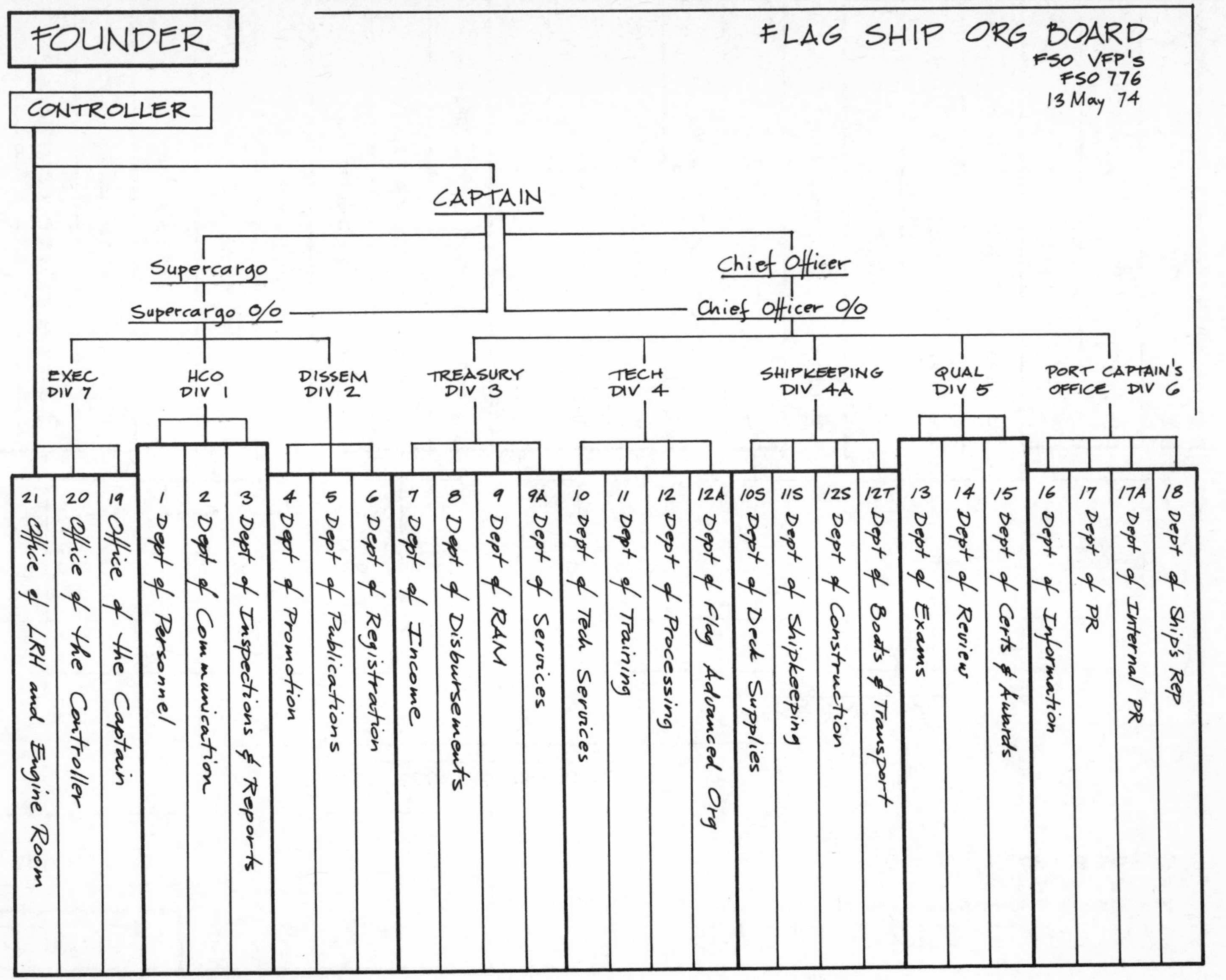

FLAG SHIP ORG BOARD
FSO VFP's
FSO 776
13 May 74
FOUNDER
CONTROLLER
CAPTAIN
Supercargo
Supercargo O/O
Chief Officer
Chief Officer O/O
EXEC DIV 7
HCO DIV 1
DISSEM DIV 2
TREASURY DIV 3
TECH DIV 4
SHIPKEEPING DIV 4A
QUAL DIV 5
PORT CAPTAIN'S OFFICE DIV 6
21 Office of LRH and Engine Room
20 Office of the Controller
19 Office of the Captain
1 Dept of Personnel
2 Dept of Communication
3 Dept of Inspections & Reports
4 Dept of Promotion
5 Dept of Publications
6 Dept of Registration
7 Dept of Income
8 Dept of Disbursements
9 Dept of RAM
9A Dept of Services
10 Dept of Tech Services
11 Dept of Training
12 Dept of Processing
12A Dept of Flag Advanced Org
10S Dept of Deck Supplies
11S Dept of Shipkeeping
12S Dept of Construction
12T Dept of Boats & Transport
13 Dept of Exams
14 Dept of Review
15 Dept of Certs & Awards
16 Dept of Information
17 Dept of PR
17A Dept of Internal PR
18 Dept of Ship's Rep

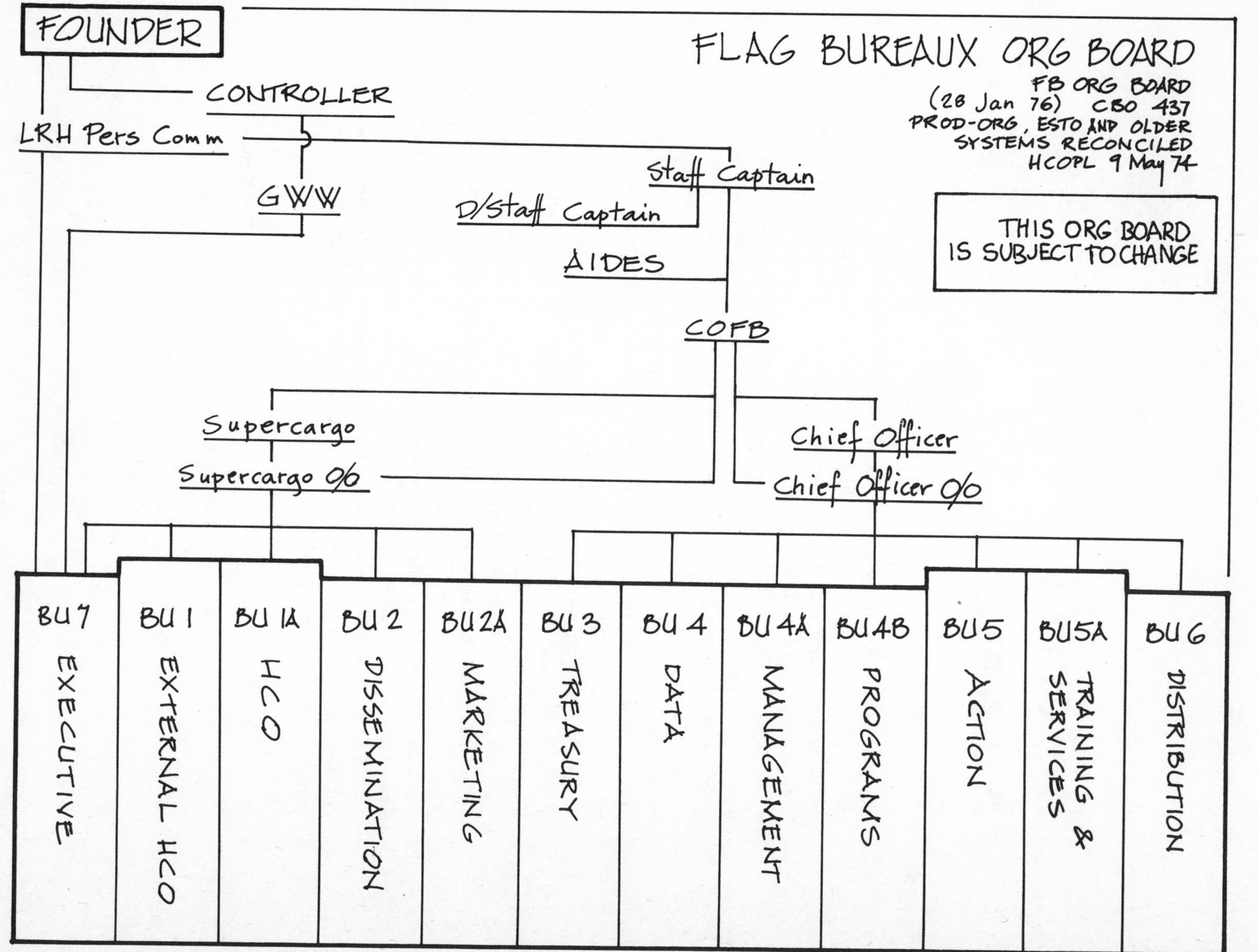
FOUNDER
FLAG BUREAUX ORG BOARD
FB ORG BOARD
(28 Jan 76) CBO 437
PROD-ORG, ESTO AND OLDER
SYSTEMS RECONCILED
HCOPL 9 May 74
THIS ORG BOARD
IS SUBJECT TO CHANGE
CONTROLLER
LRH Pers Comm
GWW
Staff Captain
D/Staff Captain
AIDES
COFB
Supercargo
Supercargo O/O
Chief Officer
Chief Officer O/O
BU 7 EXECUTIVE
BU 1 EXTERNAL HCO
BU 1A HCO
BU 2 DISSEMINATION
BU 2A MARKETING
BU 3 TREASURY
BU 4 DATA
BU 4A MANAGEMENT
BU 4B PROGRAMS
BU 5 ACTION
BU 5A TRAINING & SERVICES
BU 6 DISTRIBUTION

Reference Summary

Following is a summary of all the references mentioned at the end of each definition in this Dictionary. They are written out here in full. You will find these very useful as a means of locating additional information about a given word or subject in Dianetics and Scientology.

The Reference Summary provides another extremely useful service to the student. Data about almost any area of Dianetics or Scientology administration and management can be obtained by merely looking up the word or subject concerned in the Dictionary and consulting those references mentioned. This serves the purpose of a large administration and management cross index which can be of valuable service to executives, administrators, evaluators and students.

The Reference Summary is laid out as follows. Appearing first are explanations about the LRH Definition Notes, MSH Definition Notes, Editor's Notes and Editorial Staff Definitions.

After these are full lists or explanations about the books, charts, DABs, magazines, PABs, Scientology Journals and the various types of issues and tapes that were consulted for definitions.

The asterisk (*) beside a reference indicates that the reference issue was written or prepared by someone other than L. Ron Hubbard.

You are firmly advised to consult the list of abbreviations in looking up any references in the Dictionary or Reference Summary in order to fully understand the abbreviations used.

The Editors

LRH Definition Notes

Many of the LRH Definition Notes have been especially defined by Ron for this dictionary.

Some are LRH Definition Notes that appear in the *Dianetics and Scientology Technical Dictionary* and have been republished for convenience.

MSH Definition Notes

Several definitions appear as MSH Definition Notes. These are definitions written by Mary Sue Hubbard for students on Flag which were then passed on to the Editor and included in the dictionary.

Editor's Notes

The definitions and statements which are editor's notes appear in brackets with no reference at the end. These are usually indications that a reference used in a preceding definition has been cancelled indicating the issue which has superseded the cancelled one.

The editor's notes that represent definitions are based on data given or written by long standing Scientology executives at the Editor's request.

Editorial Staff Definitions

The editorial staff definitions are standard business, finance, administration and management terms used throughout the business world.

These were formulated and included by the editorial staff after extensive research of these subjects.

These entries appear in light face type to differentiate them from the Scientology entry words which appear in bold face type.

Books

Advanced Procedure and Axioms by L. Ron Hubbard. The American Saint Hill Organization, Los Angeles, California, First Hard Cover Edition, 1971.

All About Radiation by L. Ron Hubbard. The Publications Organization World Wide, East Grinstead, Sussex, England, 1967.

Background and Ceremonies of the Church of Scientology of California, World Wide. The Church of Scientology of California, Los Angeles, California, 1972.

Dianetics and Scientology Technical Dictionary by L. Ron Hubbard. Publications Organization United States, The American Saint Hill Organization, First Printing, 1975.

Dianetics 55! by L. Ron Hubbard. The Department of Publications World Wide, Sixth Edition, 1968.

Dianetics Today by L. Ron Hubbard. The Church of Scientology of California, Publications Organization United States, Los Angeles, California, First Printing, 1975.

How to Live Though an Executive by L. Ron Hubbard. The Hubbard College of Scientology, East Grinstead, Sussex, England, Third Edition, 1965, Reprinted 1967.

Introduction to Scientology Ethics by L. Ron Hubbard. The American Saint Hill Organization, Los Angeles, California, Third Edition 1971.

Mission Into Time by L. Ron Hubbard. The American Saint Hill Organization, Los Angeles, California, First Printing 1973.

Organization Executive Course Basic Staff Volume 0 by L. Ron Hubbard. Scientology Publications Organization, Copenhagen, Denmark, First Edition 1970.

Organization Executive Course HCO Division 1 by L. Ron Hubbard. Scientology Publications Organization, Copenhagen, Denmark, First Edition 1970.

Organization Executive Course Dissemination Division 2 by L. Ron Hubbard. Scientology Publications Organization, Copenhagen, Denmark, First Edition 1971.

Organization Executive Course Treasury Division 3 by L. Ron Hubbard. Scientology Publications Organization, Copenhagen, Denmark, First Edition 1971.

Organization Executive Course Technical Division 4 by L. Ron Hubbard. Scientology Publications Organization, Copenhagen, Denmark, Second Printing, 1973.

Organization Executive Course Qualifications Division 5 by L. Ron Hubbard. Scientology Publications Organization, Copenhagen, Denmark, Second Printing 1973.

Organization Executive Course Distribution Division 6 by L. Ron Hubbard. Scientology Publications Organization, Copenhagen, Denmark, First Edition 1972.

Organization Executive Course Division 7 by L. Ron Hubbard. Scientology Publications Organization, Copenhagen, Denmark, First Edition 1974.

Organization Executive Course Management Series 1970 to 1972 by L. Ron Hubbard. Scientology Publications Organization, Copenhagen, Denmark, First Edition 1972.

Science of Survival by L. Ron Hubbard. The Hubbard Communications Office, East Grinstead, Sussex, England, Ninth Printing January 1964.

Scientology: A World Religion Emerges in the Space Age. The Church of Scientology Information Service, Department of Archives, First Printing 1974.

Scientology 8–80 by L. Ron Hubbard. The American Saint Hill Organization, Los Angeles, California, Reprinted 1971.

Scientology Twentieth Century Religion. The Church of Scientology World Wide, 1972.

The Fundamentals of Thought by L. Ron Hubbard. The American Saint Hill Organization, Los Angeles, California, Twelfth Printing 1973.

The Phoenix Lectures by L. Ron Hubbard. The Publications Organization World Wide, Edinburgh, Scotland, First Edition 1968.

The Problems of Work by L. Ron Hubbard. The Publications Department A/S, Copenhagen, Denmark, Eleventh Printing September 1972.

The Scientology Religion, Krisson Printing Ltd., London, England, 1974.

Booklets

Clearing Course Instruction Booklet by L. Ron Hubbard. The Saint Hill Organization, East Grinstead, Sussex, England, 1967.

HCO Manual of Justice by L. Ron Hubbard, Hubbard Communications Office, 37 Fitzroy Street, London W.1, 1959.

Scientology: Clear Procedure Issue One by L. Ron Hubbard. The Department of Publications World Wide, East Grinstead, Sussex, England, 1968.

Sea Watch Picture Book by Mary Sue Hubbard. Hubbard Communications Office, Flagship *Royal Scotman,* 1968.

Ships Organization Book by L. Ron Hubbard. The Office of L. Ron Hubbard Saint Hill, East Grinstead, Sussex, England, 1967.

Special Primary Rundown Glossary, Flag Publications, 1972.

The Basic Scientology Picture Book, Vol. 1, taken from the works of L. Ron Hubbard. The American Saint Hill Organization, Los Angeles, California, Second Printing May 1972.

The Book of Case Remedies by L. Ron Hubbard. The Department of Publications World Wide, East Grinstead, Sussex, England, 1968.

Charts

Classification Gradation and Awareness Chart of Levels and Certificates, the Department of Publications World Wide, Saint Hill Manor, East Grinstead, Sussex, England, 1968.

Classification Gradation and Awareness Chart of Levels and Certificates, the Church of Scientology of California, 1975.

Dianetic Auditor's Bulletins

The Dianetic Auditor's Bulletin was published as an information source on Dianetic development and research by the former Dianetic Research Foundation, Wichita, Kansas, USA.

An Essay on Authoritarianism by L. Ron Hubbard. *The Dianetic Auditor's Bulletin,* Vol. II, pages 132-146, July 1951-June 1952.

Education and the Auditor by L. Ron Hubbard. *The Dianetic Auditor's Bulletin,* Vol. II, pages 3-53, July 1951-June 1952.

Magazines

Ability Magazine is the official publication of Dianetics and Scientology in the Eastern United States. Published by the Hubbard Scientology Organization in Washington, D.C.

Certainty Magazine is the official periodical of Dianetics and Scientology in the British Isles.

The Auditor. This is the monthly journal of Scientology. These are noted in the reference as to whether they are United Kingdom, Publications Organization Denmark or American Saint Hill Organization issues.

Professional Auditor's Bulletins

Professional Auditor's Bulletins by L. Ron Hubbard. The Publications Department, Advanced Organization Saint Hill, Copenhagen, Denmark, 1973, Nos. 1–160, May 1953 to May 1959.

Scientology Journals

Journal of Scientology, articles by L. Ron Hubbard. The Hubbard Association of Scientologists, Phoenix, Arizona, Issues 1G–43G, September 1952 to December 1954.

Aides Orders

*AO 467-1	Clear America Crusade	21 Feb 74
*AO 483-27	Int Training Eval	12 Jun 75
AO 528	E-Meters & Literature	28 Apr 75 Corrected 4 May 75

Base Flag Orders

BFO 1	New Numbered Issues	21 Nov 75
BFO 3R	Crew Registration and Form Handling Revised	18 Jan 76
BFO 43	Space Misuse and Furniture Scrambles	26 Dec 75
BFO 44	POs and PR	23 Dec 75
BFO 45	Confidential	24 Dec 75
BFO 46	Value of Services Delivered, How to Raise	26 Dec 75
BFO 70	Names of Buildings	31 Dec 75
BFO 75	Security Recognition	2 Jan 76
BFO 84	Conferences and Meetings	12 Jan 76
*BFO 93	Staff Good Grooming & Hygiene Checklist, How to Use	24 Jan 76
*BFO 94 Attachment	Treasury and Finance Office Org Boards	12 Jan 76
*BFO 98	Confidential Mailogram Line	22 Jan 76

*BFO 119	Division II Gross Divisional Statistics and Other Income Statistics	20 Feb 76
*BFO 122-5	US Base Div 5 Org Board	14 Feb 76
*BFO 122-6	US Base Div 6 Org Board	10 Feb 76
*BFO 124	Hotel Services Committee	26 Feb 76
BFO 141	Re Auditors	20 Jun 76

Base Orders

BO 14	Yacht *Avon River*	6 Jun 67
BO 11	Radio: Walkie Talkie Procedure	Circa 10 Jun 67
BO 21	Officers Lanyards and Whistles	11 Jun 67
BO 28	Emergency Drills	12 Jun 67
BO 29	Model of OT Ship Organization and Operation Based on 7 Division System	13 Jun 67
BO 34	"When base order 29 . . ."	16 Jun 67
BO 59	*Avon's* Radios	23 Jun 67
BO 80	Add to Uniforms Base Order 21	2 Jul 67
BO 125	Ships Org Book	7 Aug 67
BO 23	Estate Section	20 Feb 70
*BO 26	Recruit and Train	28 Feb 70
*BO 30	Public Relations Checkout	16 Mar 70
*BO 44	Changes List	21 Jun 70
*BO 47	Urgent—"I Want to Go Clear Club," Clear Registrar	8 Aug 70
BO 48	Re: Org Interne	22 Aug 70
BO 70	Recruit Bonus	25 Jan 72
*BO 7 US 1 CC	Celebrity Defined	7 Aug 72
*BO 3 PAC	"The following are . . ."	16 Oct 72
*BO 23 US	Château Elysée	11 Jul 73
*BO 86R (US, UK, EU, AF, ANZO)	New Name to Recruitment Applicant and Prospect Files	14 Jul 73 Revised 21 Jul 73
*BO 88	Introducing the Household Unit, An Opportunity to Work Close to Source	1 Oct 73
*BO 42 US	ASHO Foundation Bonus System	6 Oct 73
*BO 43 US	AOLA—Special Services Unit Operations and Divisional Flow Charts	31 Oct 73
*BO 37 UK	Groups - Battle of Britain	26 Jan 74
*BO 7 PAC	Division IVA - Public Clearing Division	17 Feb 74
*BO 91	Expansion	23 Feb 74
*BO 9 ANZO	Scientology Distribution Centres	17 Mar 74
*BO 61 US	The FRU MAA	12 Aug 74
*BO 1 MEX	Dianetic Org Products	10 Nov 74
BO 100	D/CO Basic Post Functions	1 Sept 76

Board Policy Letters

7 Jan 58	HCO Stenographer Hat
25 Jun 59	"HCO Policy Letters . . ."
5 Aug 59	Stable Data For Communicators
3 Sept 59	HCO Book Account
7 Sept 59	Policy Letter and Bulletin Distribution Code
9 Sept 59	Congress, Books, Magazines and Tape Account
19 Feb 60	Vehicles
15 Mar 60	Disseminating Scientology
28 Apr 61R	Auto Evaluation Slips
3 Feb 62R	Auditor's Processing Check HCO WW Sec Form 6A
27 Sept 63RA	Training Technology Pink Sheets Introduction
31 Oct 63R	Reception Hat
30 Jan 65 Issue II	Public Division Org Board
10 Sept 65R	The Franchise Award of Merit
1 Sept 66R	Founder
6 Oct 66RA	Addition to HCO Div Account Policy of 6 October 1966 Issue II
11 Nov 66R	Postal Economy
23 Dec 66R	Field Staff Member Commissions
9 Jan 67R	FSM System Administration in Organizations
20 Feb 67R	Security of Invoices
19 Sept 67	HCO Division, Department of Routing, Appearances and Personnel
20 Sept 67R	Confidential Data
20 Oct 67R	The Lines of the Qualifications Division—The Interview Invoice Section
2 Nov 67	Qualifications Division, Department of Examinations, Review, and Certifications and Awards
18 Nov 67R	Blue and Green Accounts Invoices
2 Jan 68R	HCO Hat Section Orders to Staff
14 Jan 68	Legal Section
13 Feb 68	Collections Letters
23 Apr 68R Issue I	FSM of the Year
31 Oct 68	Photographers, of Interest to
24 Nov 68 Issue I	Auditor Correspondents
24 Nov 68R Issue II	The Groups Officer
27 Nov 68R	The Standard Auditor Journal
29 Nov 68R	Standard Actions Office of the Auditor Journal The Office of the Auditor
8 Dec 68R	Department One Admin Service Records
14 Dec 68R Issue I	How to Register Groups and Gung-Ho Groups
26 Jan 69RA	Compliance Reports
30 Jan 69	Dev-T Summary List Additions
31 Jan 69	PRO-Broadsheets
6 Mar 69	Scientology Is a Religion
14 Apr 69R	Bulletin and Policy Letter Distribution
24 Apr 69R	A Scientology Church Register
8 May 69R Issue II	How to Teach a Course
8 May 69R Issue III	Enturbulative Students
11 May 69R	Standard Admin for the Course Administrator
17 May 69R Issue I	Mailing Lists, Central Files Addresso Basic Definitions and Policy
1 Jun 69R Issue II	Dianetics Training
4 Jul 69R Issue II	Dianetic Counseling Group Series No. 2R Purpose
4 Jul 69R Issue V	Dianetic Counseling Group Series No. 9 Group Formation
4 Jul 69R Issue VI	Dianetic Counseling Group Series No. 7 The Org Board
4 Jul 69R Issue VII	Dianetic Counseling Group Series No. 10 Communication System
8 Jul 69R Issue IV	Dianetic Counseling Group Series No. 8 Stages of Forming, Increasing and Expanding A Dianetic Counseling Group. Why a Group?
9 Jul 69	"Confessional aids . . ."
27 Jul 69R	What Is a Checksheet
29 Jul 69A	Course Administration Roll Book
30 Jul 69RA	"Student Product Board Student Progress Board" Urgent—All Courses Student Progress Board
30 Sept 69	Orders of the Day

20 Nov 69R	Legal Aspects of Missions
21 Dec 69	Guide to the Function of Printer Liaison
21 Dec 69 Reissued 3 Aug 75 as BPL Cancelled 9 Sept 75	Guide to the Function of Printer Liaison Cancellation
26 Jan 70R Issue I	FOLO Last Court of Appeal
27 Jan 70 Issue I	Legal—Legal Settlements
28 Apr 70RA	Dianetic Counseling Group Series No. 4 The Dianetic Counseling Group Programme
20 May 70 Issue I	Guardian Public Relationships
20 May 70 Issue IV	LRH Comm Master Files
27 May 70RA	The Organization of the Guardian's Office
29 May 70R	Lost Income Credit and Post-Dated Cheques
25 Jul 70R	Security Div I, Security Materials
30 Jul 70R	The Tech and Ethics of Confessionals
3 Oct 70 Issue II	Health Series No. 2 The Role of the Medical Officer
26 Oct 70 Issue II	Definition of a Student
3 Nov 70R Issue I	Public Lines Dummy Run Drill
4 Nov 70R	Estimated Purchase Orders, History
14 Nov 70 Issue II	The Theory of Bookkeeping and Accountancy Part 1—Fundamentals Section 1 Introduction
14 Nov 70 Issue III	The Theory of Bookkeeping and Accountancy Part 2—Fundamentals Section 2 Consolidation
14 Nov 70 Issue IV	The Theory of Bookkeeping and Accountancy Part 3—Preparation of Income and Expenditure Account and Balance Sheet
14 Nov 70 Issue V	The Theory of Bookkeeping and Accountancy Part 4—Final Adjustments
14 Nov 70 Issue VI	The Theory of Bookkeeping and and Accountancy Part 5
20 Nov 70R	The Students Rabble Rouse Line
10 Feb 71R	Sale of Org Material
10 Feb 71R Issue II	Personnel Series No. 18 Adds to Personnel Series No. 8 16 Sept 70, Ethics and Personnel
17 Feb 71R	Finance Series No. 3R Basic FBO Duties
17 Feb 71-1R	Finance Series No. 3-1R Handling of Bounced Checks and Refunds
3 Mar 71R	Starrate Outpoints
4 Mar 71R	Weekly Staff Briefing
19 Mar 71	Finance Series No. 7 Bean Theory Finance as a Commodity
31 Mar 71R	Class IV Org (Central Org) Formation Checksheet
1 Apr 71	Legal: Hiring of Lawyers
6 Apr 71	Power Badges
12 Apr 71 Issue II	Mission Designation
15 Apr 71R	Auditors Association and SH Orgs
25 Apr 71R	Finance Series No. 5R FP Activation
26 Apr 71RA	Finance Series 5RA FP Activation
1 May 71R	Centre Magazine Policy
11 May 71 Issue II-1 Addition to 8 Jul 75	Definition
17 May 71RC Issue II	Study Points
28 May 71R	Gross Income
8 June 71R Issue I	Finance Series No. 8R Finance Office Accounts
12 Jul 71 Issue I	Parent or Guardian Assent Forms
18 Jul 71R Issue I	Stat Board
18 Jul 71R Issue II	The Student Folder
27 Jul 71	LRH Briefing Officer
29 Jul 71R Issue II	Penalties for the Hiring or Recruiting of Institutional or Insane Persons
2 Aug 71RA Issue I	Distribution Secretary Privilege
9 Aug 71R Issue I	Urgent—Operation Staff Stability and Personal Security High Crime Additions
9 Aug 71R Issue II	Urgent—High Crime Policy Operation Staff Stability and Personal Security Personnel Permanent Appointments, Transfers, Demotion and Dismissals
12 Aug 71R Issue I	Additional Policies on Advanced Course Security

20 Aug 71	Legal Statistics
4 Sept 71R	FP and Necessities
15 Sept 71R Issue I	Purpose and Statistics of a Tour Member
16 Sept 71	Quality Mastering Tape
16 Sept 71R Issue II	AOLA Division Four AOLA Division Four A
20 Sept 71R Issue I	Mission, Basic Definition of
21 Oct 71 Issue I	Hatting Scientologists Series No. 1 You as a Scientologist
21 Oct 71 Issue III	Hatting Scientologists Series No. 3 Organizing Board for a Scientologist
21 Oct 71RA Issue IV	HQS Course Checksheet
1 Nov 71 Issue I	Promo Scheduling Board
2 Nov 71R	Names of Upper Tech Courses
8 Nov 71RB	Qual OK to Audit Series No. 5R Internships, Electronic Attestation Form, TRs Training Checklist
16 Nov 71RA	Conditions: Awards and Penances
19 Nov 71R	Director of Processing Hat
22 Nov 71R	Qual Org Officer/Esto
23 Nov 71R	Important—Tech Div Gross Divisional Statistics Clarification
25 Nov 71R	Inter-Org Exchange of Students and Fees
4 Dec 71RA Issue II	Tech Estimates
4 Dec 71R Issue III	Rules for Student Auditors
5 Dec 71	PR Series No. 13 How to Do a PR Survey
7 Dec 71R Issue I	Correction Division—Purposes, Ideal Scenes, Products, Statistics
11 Dec 71R Issue I-1	HMCSC OK to Supervise Interneship
12 Dec 71RC	The Solo Auditor Course
22 Dec 71-1	Free Services—Free Fall
22 Dec 71R Issue II	How and Why a Registrar Prevents Tech Backlogs and Poor Quality of Service
22 Dec 71 Issue III	"After Service" Interviews
23 Dec 71R	Personnel Series No. 23R 1:1 Tech Admin Ratio on New Recruits
3 Jan 72RA Issue I	HGC Admin Invoices
22 Jan 72R	The Hubbard Professional Course Supervisor Course Checksheet
22 Jan 72R-3 Addition of 9 Jul 75	HPCSC OK to Supervise Internship
25 Jan 72R	PR Series No. 15R Population Surveys
26 Jan 72 Issue VIIRA	Scientology Level 3 Standard Academy Checksheet
26 Jan 72R Issue VIII	Scientology Level 4 Standard Academy Checksheet
26 Jan 72 Issue VIIIRA	Scientology Level 4 Standard Academy Checksheet
29 Jan 72R	PC Hat
1 Feb 72 Issue I	Accounts Policing
1 Feb 72RA	Income Report Required
3 Feb 72R	Executive Responsibility for Training Staff Checklist
5 Feb 72	The Saint Hill Tech Page and HCO Courier System
5 Feb 72R Issue II	Flag Divisional Directive
8 Feb 72	Executive Series No. 7 Targetting of Divisional Statistics and Quotas
10 Feb 72R Issue I	LRH Comm Network
22 Feb 72R	Interneship Errors Found
26 Feb 72R Issue IV	Viability or Liability The Quality of the Treasury Division A Treasury Div Checklist for Quality
28 Feb 72	Language Series No. 2 Speed in Learning Languages
12 Apr 72R Issue I	De-Bug Assessment
17 Apr 72	Danger Rundown Correction List
19 May 72R	Important—How to Correctly Tabulate an Addresso
20 May 72R	Types of Promotion
1 Jun 72R	Division II Info Packs, Use of
15 Jun 72	PR Series No. 11 PR Area Control Three Grades of PR
1 Jul 72R	Cash/Bills and Org Reserves
4 Jul 72R	Tours Events Defined
13 Jul 72R	PR Series No. 16R Survey Buttons and Promo
15 Jul 72R Issue I	Flag Representative
15 Jul 72RA Issue I	Flag Rep Query and Answer Forms
5 Aug 72	Fast Flow Registration
6 Aug 72RA	Merchandising of Primary Rundown and Primary Correction Rundown

11 Aug 72R Issue I	Foundation and Day Org Separate
11 Aug 72R Issue II	Foundation Income
24 Aug 72RC	Tours Org Series 1RC Tours Org
28 Aug 72 Issue II	Dianetics and Scientology Trademark Notice
3 Sept 72R	Typos, Query of
5 Sept 72R	FOLO Staff Training and Auditing
10 Sept 72	Guardian Activities, Scientologists
12 Sept 72R	AO Service to Pre-OTs and OTs in Other Orgs and Areas
18 Sept 72R	Accounts Promo
29 Sept 72R Issue I	Stat Management Policy Checklists
3 Oct 72R	Handling Continental Ethics
4 Oct 72R	Establishment Officer Series No. 28R Handling PTS and Out Ethics Personnel
13 Oct 72R	Freeloader Program Administration
25 Oct 72R	Correction Alert Form
2 Nov 72RA	"Big League" Registration Series No. 1 Use of Salesmanship Tech & Skills
3 Nov 72RA	Finance Series No. 14RA Payment of Flag Bills Incurred Locally
5 Nov 72RA	External Communications Series No. 11RA Standard Telex Abbreviations
5 Nov 72RA-1	External Communications Series No. 11RA-1 Standard Telex Jargon
22 Nov 72R	Registrar Assessment
23 Nov 72	The Lead Auditor System
1 Dec 72 Issue I	"Big League" Registration Series No. 2 Sales Data Sheet
1 Dec 72R Issue II	"Big League" Registration Series No. 3R Prospecting at the Close and the Admin Involved
1 Dec 72R Issue IV	"Big League" Registration Series No. 6R The Public Reg Post Simplified and Streamlined
1 Dec 72 Issue V	"Big League" Registration Series No. 7 Registration Cards, Utilization of
1 Dec 72R Issue VIII	"Big League" Registration Series No. 10R Competitive Registration Commission System

4 Dec 72RA Issue II	FBO & Treasury Financial Reports
4 Dec 72 Issue IIRB	Financial Management Standardization Series No. 3 FBO & Treasury Financial Reports
5 Dec 72R	Student Completions Statistic
6 Dec 72	Important—Persons Who Ask Off Mailing Lists
8 Dec 72R	Tech Services Stable Data
13 Dec 72RB	VIPs and Celebrities
23 Dec 72R	LRH's Office in Orgs
24 Dec 72R	Hubbard Integrity Processing Specialist Course Checksheet
4 Jan 73RC	Tech Division Full Org Board
10 Jan 73R	Writing and Placing News Releases
15 Jan 73R	The Hubbard Integrity Processing Specialist Course
21 Jan 73R	Use the Library to Restore Lost Technology
23 Jan 73R	Church Service
24 Jan 73 Issue I	Business Management Tech Series No. 1 Client Meetings and Sales
24 Jan 73 Issue III	Business Management Tech Series No. 3 Programs and Contracts
7 Feb 73 Issue I	Typing/Proofreading and Issuing of LRH Items
10 Feb 73 Issue II	Business Management Tech Series No. 6 Sample Sales Proposal and Contract
13 Feb 73R	Business Management Tech Series No. 8R Essential Business Management Administrative Elements
18 Feb 73 Issue III	Expertise for a Hot Prospect Letter Registrar
20 Feb 73	The Theory of Compliance—1 What Is Compliance? The Parts of Compliance
25 Feb 73R	Director of Training
27 Feb 73R	Dissemination Division, Departments of Promotion, Publications and Registration
2 Mar 73R Issue I	Issue Authority Lines & Procedures
6 Mar 73	The Theory of Compliance—3 How to Comply
8 Mar 73R Issue I	Business Management Tech Series No. 10R All Data Not Being Sent to Data Files
25 Mar 73 Issue II	Medical Liaison Office Functions
1 Apr 73RA	"Battle Plan"

3 Apr 73R Issue I	Personnel Series No. 26R Hatting
3 Apr 73R Issue II	Personnel Management Series No. 1R Flag Central Personnel Office
4 Apr 73R	Book Buyers Your Undeveloped Goldmine
5 Apr 73R	All Orgs—Two Additional HCO GDSes, Tech/Admin Ratio and Personnel Points Stats
8 Apr 73 Issue I	External Communications Series No. 1 How to Write a Telex Telex Altitude
8 Apr 73 Issue II	External Communications Series No. 13 Telex Log Book
9 Apr 73 Issue II	Business Management Tech Series No. 12 Management Evaluation and Handling of Orgs
10 Apr 73R	Org Designation System
20 Apr 73 Issue II	Tours Org Series No. 2 Tours Org Finances
23 Apr 73R	External Communications Series No. 7R Telex Routings
26 Apr 73R Issue I	Triple Flow Training
27 Apr 73R	Staff Status Zero
28 Apr 73	How a Recruiter Builds His Applicant/Prospect Files
12 May 73R Issue II	Personnel Management Series No. 2R Central Personnel Office Files Admin System
4 Jun 73	Org Basic Data
9 Jun 73R	Flag Personnel Exchange
9 Jun 73R Issue II	PC Scheduling Board Pre-Scheduling Board
12 Jun 73R Issue II	External Communications Series No. 9R The Telex Comm Cycle
14 Jun 73R Issue I	The Success Stories Stat
14 Jun 73R Issue II	Success Officer Duties
15 Jun 73R Issue I	Tours Orgs and FSMs
30 Jun 73R	Qual Stats
2 Jul 73R	Tech Sec
6 Jul 73RA	Data Series Evaluators Course
12 Jul 73R Issue II	Auditor's Day
13 Jul 73R	LRH Image in Orgs
24 Jul 73R	New LRH Comm Stat
24 Jul 73R Issue II	LRH Comm Network Command Chain
24 Jul 73R Issue III	Compliance Executive Directives The "CED"
8 Aug 73R	Hubbard Senior Course Supervisor Course (HSCSC)
13 Aug 73R Issue II	External HCO Bureaux and Their Relation to HCOs in Orgs
16 Aug 73	Controller Communicator Network
20 Aug 73R	Properties CSW Routing Form
15 Sept 73	Confidential
24 Sept 73 Issue I-1 Addition of 18 Feb 75	Religion Missions: Relation to the Church
24 Sept 73R Issue III	Religion, All Auditors—Ministers Ministerial Board of Review
24 Sept 73 Issue V	Religion Dianetics: Definition of Word
24 Sept 73R Issue XI	Religion Memberships
24 Sept 73RA Issue XIII Revised 8 May 75	Religion Legal: Registration and Sign-Ups
5 Oct 73R	FSM Award Programs
19 Oct 73	LRH Comm Logging & Nudging Procedures
10 Nov 73R	Finance Series No. 16R FBO Network Organization Location
10 Nov 73 Issue II	The Theory of Compliance—4 Receipt and Duplication
5 Dec 73R Issue II	Position of the LRH Comm
16 Dec 73	Evaluation Targets Ethics Condition
9 Jan 74 Issue III	Duties of the Translations Administrator in a Translations Unit
9 Jan 74 Issue IV	Tape Transcriptions
9 Jan 74 Issue V	Mimeoing Written Translations
12 Jan 74 Issue I	Translation Tape Preamble Format
14 Jan 74R Issue I	New Issues
14 Jan 74 Issue II	Establishment of the Board of Issues
22 Jan 74 Issue II	Translation Unit Flow Chart
23 Jan 74R	Bonuses and Penalities for Staff Statuses

9 Mar 74	Understanding Corporate Integrity
13 Mar 74RA Issue II Revised 20 May 74	Hubbard Basic Scientology Auditor Course
23 Mar 74	FPPO Series No. 1 FPPO Flag—FPPO Network
24 Mar 74 Issue II	ASHO Foundation Div VI
8 May 74	Hubbard Graduate Assist Specialist Course
22 Jun 74	Board Representatives
23 Jun 74	Board Representative Flag Representative Definition of Terms
5 Jul 74 Issue XVII	Hubbard Professional Salesmanship Course Checksheet
12 Aug 74 Issue II	Scientology Who We Help and How
31 Aug 74RA Issue II	LRH Compliances Additional Stat Value
16 Sept 74RA Issue III	All Sea Org Orgs OIC Cable Change
10 Oct 74R Revised 8 Jul 75	Hubbard Standard Dianetics Course Checksheet
14 Nov 74	Refund Payment Claims
23 Jan 75	New Flag Rep Statistic
1 Feb 75 Issue II	New Staff Applicant Information Form
20 Feb 75R Revised 19 Jun 75	Pubs Org New Stat How to Get
18 Mar 75 Issue I	Saint Hill Special Briefing Course
13 Apr 75	Technical Training Corps
14 May 75	LRH Logistics Orders
6 Jul 75 Issue III	Financial Management Standardization Series No. 4 Standardization of Usage of the Church's Bank Accounts
22 Jul 75	PR and Social Coordination Bureau Separation of Functions
11 Aug 75	Dissemination Division Products, Ideal Scenes and Stats of the Div and Its Three Depts
11 Aug 75 Issue III	Division Three Ideal Scenes and Stats
25 Aug 75	Forming Celebrity Center Orgs
3 Sept 75 Issue I	Ron's Personal Public Relations Officer International
3 Sept 75 Issue II	Ron's Personal PRO International and Reps
11 Sept 75 Cancels HCO PL 7 Feb 71 Issue IV FEBC Org Board Div III	Treasury Division Org Board
10 Oct 75 Issue I	Cancellation of Policy Letters 1951-1958
10 Oct 75 Issue II	Cancellation of Policy Letters 1959
10 Oct 75 Issue III	Cancellation of Policy Letters 1960 and 1961
10 Oct 75 Issue IV	Cancellation of Policy Letters 1962 and 1963
10 Oct 75 Issue V	Cancellation of Policy Letters 1964 and 1965
10 Oct 75 Issue VI	Cancellation of Policy Letters 1966-1968
10 Oct 75 Issue VII	Cancellation of Policy Letters 1969
10 Oct 75 Issue VIII	Cancellation of Policy Letters 1970
10 Oct 75 Issue IX	Cancellation of Policy Letters 1971
10 Oct 75 Issue X	Cancellation of Policy Letters 1972
10 Oct 75 Issue XI	Cancellation of Policy Letters 1973-1975
25 Jan 76 Issue I	Division II Function Org Board

Board Technical Bulletins

4 Mar 65R	Level Zero Materials
26 Oct 70 Issue II	Definition of a Student
8 Jan 71R	Auditing CS-1 for Dianetics and Scientology
7 Feb 71	Administrative Training Drills Admin TRs
30 Aug 71RD Issue I	Paid Completion Points—PC Completions, Student Completions and Interneship Completions
30 Sept 71 Issue IV	Auditing
23 Oct 71RA Issue II Revised 2nd Time 31 Jan 75 Personnel Programming Series No. 3RA	How to Write a Personnel Program
25 Oct 71R Issue II	The Special Drug Rundown
24 Nov 71 Issue II	Tape Course Series No. 7 Course Materials
14 Jan 72R Issue I	Personnel Programming Series No. 1R Management Cycle
12 Apr 72R	Further Definitions of Scientology Terms Contained in the Student Hat and Not Elsewhere Defined
2 Nov 72R	Auditor Admin Series No. 1R The Auditor Admin Series for Use by All Auditors
3 Nov 72R	Auditor Admin Series No. 3R The PC Folder and Its Contents
8 Dec 72RA	Integrity Processing and O/Ws Repair List L1RA
3 Jul 73 Issue I	Qual Flub Catch Series No. 1 The Flub Catch Line
21 Oct 73R	A Checklist of Processes for the South Africa Special Rundown
7 Jan 74	Tape Quality Control Checklist for Translation Tapes
8 May 74 Issue I	Checklist of Processes for the Second South Africa Special Rundown
10 Dec 74 Issue II	Cancellation of Bulletins 1959
10 Dec 74 Issue III	Cancellation of Bulletins 1974
15 Dec 74	Auditor Expertise Drills Series No. 2 Basic Session Actions Drills
17 Jan 75R Revised 22 Jan 75	Gold Star Orgs
8 Mar 75 Issue II	Cramming Series No. 3R Types of Cramming Admin Cramming

Central Bureau Orders

CBO 2	Important—Extreme Conditions	28 Aug 70
CBO 4	Org Bureau	13 Sept 70
CBO 6	Mimeo Files	16 Sept 70
CBO 7	Cycle of Action in Bureaus	15 Sept 70
*CBO 13R	Communication Bureau Org Board	10 Oct 70
*CBO 14	Finance Bureau Org Board	19 Sept 70
*CBO 16R	Data Bureau Org Board	22 Sept 70
*CBO 17	Justice Bureau Org Board	22 Sept 70
*CBO 18	Action Bureau Org Board	22 Sept 70
CBO 19	Estate Bureau Org Board	23 Sept 70
*CBO 22	Organizing Bureau Org Board	24 Sept 70
*CBO 23	Coordination Bureau Org Board	23 Sept 70
CBO 25	Mission Writing	29 Sept 70

*CBO 26	Promotion Bureau Org Board	26 Sept 70
CBO 27	Finance Bureau	1 Oct 70
CBO 28	Functions of Activities	1 Oct 70
*CBO 34	Org Form and Policy Bureau	18 Oct 70
*CBO 37	Org Form and Policy Bureau Org Board	18 Oct 70
*CBO 38	Personnel Enhancement Bureau Org Board	18 Oct 70
*CBO 39	Justice Bureau Ideal Scenes & Stats	20 Oct 70
*CBO 41R	Liaison Office Supply Lines	4 Aug 71
CBO 48R	Flag Bureau Data Letters	4 Nov 73
CBO 50	The Ease of Running Bureaux	23 Nov 70
CBO 51	The Bureaux Team	24 Nov 70
CBO 52	The Role of an Aide	24 Nov 70
*CBO 57	Relay of LRH Briefings and Conferences	5 Dec 70
*CBO 57-2	LRH Conferences and Lectures	20 Nov 74
*CBO 59	Management Bureau Policies (Provisional)	9 Dec 70
*CBO 60	Orders to COs and Garrison Terminals	10 Dec 70
CBO 63	One Flub System	15 Dec 70
CBO 64	C/O Assistance	16 Dec 70
CBO 65	Why Sheets	21 Dec 70
*CBO 75	Liaison Office Primary Duty to Flag	26 Jan 71
*CBO 81	BU IV Aide Title	10 Feb 71
*CBO 110	CLO Course Pricings	7 May 71
*CBO 115	Office of the Continental Captain US	6 Jun 71
*CBO 116	The CLO and the LRH Comm Network	5 Jun 71
*CBO 118	Flag Tech VFP Expeditor Hat	17 Jun 71
*CBO 120	SO Personnel Control Section Formation of	18 Jun 71
*CBO 121	Hat Write-Up, Hatted Scientologists, Expeditor	22 June 71
*CBO 125	Treasury Inspector Hat	18 Jul 71
*CBO 126	Hard Sell Checksheet	23 Jul 71
CBO 133	Mission Orders, Types of	31 Aug 71
CBO 134	CLO Finance	30 Aug 71
*CBO 141	Flag Rep Advise Letters	21 Sept 71
*CBO 144	Hat Write-Up, Franchise Liaison Officer Continental	29 Sept 71
CBO 147	Aides and A/Aides Duties	3 Nov 71
*CBO 155R	Flag Rep FOLO Function Checklist B	12 Aug 72
*CBO 163	Evaluations	18 Dec 71
*CBO 166	CLO FBO Financial Report Forms	11 Dec 71
*CBO 168	Evaluation, Numbering of	3 Jan 72
*CBO 172	Data Evaluation Alert	27 Jan 72
CBO 173	Management BU Routing	2 Feb 72
CBO 182	Aides Three Hats	10 Mar 72
*CBO 187	Briefing Progress Board	4 Apr 72
CBO 189	Data Bureau Files Revised	13 Apr 72
*CBO 189-1	Data Bureau Files for Special PGMs Section	14 Sept 72
CBO 190	Aide and A/Aide Responsibility	25 Apr 72

*CBO 192	Flag Operations Liaison Office, Operations Bureau Function Org Board	24 May 72
CBO 194	Staff Captain, Duties of	4 Jun 72
CBO 202-1	FB Data Files	19 Aug 72
*CBO 203-1	Emergency Section OFO Branch, Management BU Flag	18 Feb 75
*CBO 204	Alert Officer Duties	2 Jul 72
*CBO 208-3R	Paid Comps Stat Debug Form	17 Jul 72 Revised 21 Sept 73
*CBO 212	The Role of the *Excalibur*	26 Jul 72
*CBO 214RA	Central Personnel Office Reorganization	12 Sept 72
*CBO 217	Medical Officer, Need of	1 Aug 72
*CBO 218RB	Flag Programmes Chief FOLO	23 Aug 72 Revised 11 Jun 73 Revised 23 Sept 73
*CBO 222R	Data Chief FOLO	27 Aug 72 Revised 22 May 73
*CBO 225	AVU Verification Officer Hat	19 Sept 72
*CBO 230	AVU Authorization Officer Hat	23 Sept 72
*CBO 231	Relation of Mission Briefing Officer to Mission Preps I/C	29 Sept 72 Reissued 29 Dec 72
*CBO 233	Personnel Coordination, Standing Order No. 1	4 Oct 72
*CBO 237	Flag Day	9 Nov 72
*CBO 238	FOLO WUS—FOLO EUS	8 Nov 72
*CBO 241	FPPO Hat	3 Dec 72
*CBO 245	Confidential	17 Jan 73
*CBO 252	LRH Comm Programs Chief	28 Feb 73
*CBO 257	Mission Packs	23 Mar 73
*CBO 260	Briefing Sheets	7 Apr 73
*CBO 262-2	PR Area Control (PRAC) Name Change	7 Jun 73
*CBO 263	Missionaire Opportunity Check	23 Apr 73
*CBO 274	Broad Eval Handlings—How to Incorporate	23 Jun 73
*CBO 278RA	Management BU Filter	12 Jul 73 Revised 10 Mar 75
*CBO 280	Flag's Magazine—A New Era in Flag's Communication	30 Jul 73
*CBO 281	*Advance* Mag Series No. 7 Keeping *Advance!* Standard	24 Jun 73
*CBO 289-1	Confidential	11 Dec 73
*CBO 291	Flag PGMs Chief's Character and Duties	3 Aug 73
*CBO 299	Magazine Improvement Unit	18 Sept 73
*CBO 300RA	Telex and Dispatch Limitation	27 Sept 73 Revised 21 Nov 73 Revised 9 Dec 73 Corrected 11 Dec 73

*CBO 301-2	High Crime, AVU Personnel and Ethics—3	26 Oct 74
CBO 323	Tech PGMs Chiefs	11 Dec 73
CBO 325	Target Marking and TLX Code	15 Dec 73
*CBO 332	Assistant CS-6 Duties	5 Mar 74
*CBO 333R	FOLO BU 6 Org Board	21 Mar 74 Revised 15 Oct 74
*CBO 334	LRH Telexes	13 Mar 74
CBO 337	Mission OPs	6 Jun 74
CBO 340R	AVU Sequence on Evals	23 Jun 74 Revised 2 Oct 74
*CBO 341	Executive Council FB	4 Jul 74
CBO 345	Project Mission Operations	4 Aug 74
CBO 348R	Org Flag Officers	28 Aug 74 Revised 30 Aug 74
*CBO 348-4	Org Flag Officer Duty	4 Dec 74
*CBO 351R	Bureau 6 FB Org Board	3 Oct 74 Revised 12 Jan 75
*CBO 351RB	Bureau 6 FB Org Board	19 Jul 75
CBO 355	Program Chief Purposes	28 Oct 74
*CBO 357	Finance Office Org Board	31 Oct 74
*CBO 358	Duties of District Officers in FBO Network	1 Nov 74
*CBO 363	Push Delivery	24 Nov 74
CBO 368	Mission Tech	8 Jan 75
*CBO 369	Data Series/Evaluators Integrity List	15 Jan 75
*CBO 373	D/CS-1 Flag Establishment	2 Feb 75
*CBO 374R	Management BU and Network Responsibility	6 Feb 75 Revised 12 Mar 75
*CBO 375	FOLO Management Bureau Function Org Board	9 Feb 75
*CBO 376	Management Bureau Function Org Board, Flag	9 Feb 75
*CBO 377	Orders into Orgs, Clearance and Coordination	14 Feb 75
*CBO 378R	Management BU Coordination Councils	15 Feb 75 Revised 2 Mar 75
*CBO 379	Flag Echelon for Org Evaluation	16 Feb 75
*CBO 381	Highly Confidential	5 Mar 75
*CBO 387	Confidential	23 Mar 75
*CBO 391R	Policy and Format of *Expansion Newsletter*	4 Apr 75 Revised 25 Apr 75
*CBO 414	Printing and Distribution Unit FOLO WUS	4 Aug 75
*CBO 415	Security of Rony	10 Aug 75
*CBO 435R	Flag Management	29 Jan 76
*CBO 435-2	FB Operations Bureau	23 Jan 76
*CBO 435-3	Management BU	23 Jan 76
*CBO 435-3R	Management Bureau BU 4A FB	28 Jan 76

*CBO 436	Programs BU	28 Jan 76
*CBO 437 Attachment 2	FB Org Board Sketch	28 Jan 76

Central Bureau Orders US Base

CBO 1 USB	Data Files Change, OFO Important Procedure	19 Dec 75
CBO 2 USB	Data Files Red Card	19 Dec 75

Central Office of LRH Executive Directives

COLRHED 1R	New Series	1 Nov 73 Revised 24 May 75
*COLRHED 7	Immediate Action—Crew Uniforms	11 Nov 73
*COLRHED 8	LRH Personal Photographer	12 Nov 73
*COLRHED 11	LRH Personal PRO Bureau Posts, Intention for	13 Nov 73
*COLRHED 29	Exploitation of HCLC	15 Dec 73
*COLRHED 79RA	The Volunteer Ministers Program Activation	10 Jul 74
COLRHED 86	Photographer Eval	12 Mar 74
COLRHED 103	LRH Accounts Bonus	22 Apr 74
COLRHED 112R	Specialty Group Assignment No. 2	17 May 74
*COLRHED 117	LRH Audio Production Back-Up	15 May 74
*COLRHED 168	Duty PR System: Purpose and Functions	7 Jul 74
*COLRHED 291R	LRH Pers Sec Office Schedule	31 Jul 75
COLRHED 300	Ron's Journal Program	24 Apr 75
*COLRHED 325R	LRH Personal PRO International, Admin Scale P-I-L-O-T	25 Feb 76
*COLRHED 338	LRH PR Bureau Functions Clarified	30 Aug 75
*COLRHED 359	LRH PR for Professional Scientologists Post Operating Program	14 Feb 76
*COLRHED 369	The "Hotline"	10 Mar 76
*COLRHED 370	On-Source Club	17 Mar 76
*COLRHED 387	LRH Compilations Librarian Purpose, Ideal Scene and Stats	4 May 76
*COLRHED 405	LRH Artist—Purpose, VFP & Stats	25 Apr 76
*COLRHED 417	New Admin Course Line-Up	2 Jul 76
*COLRHED 417-1	New Admin Course Name	10 Jul 76

Commodore's Staff Orders

CS Order No. 46	Staff Coordination	27 Oct 68
CS Order 71	Commodore Staff Aide	8 May 69

Continental Orders

*Cont Order 1 US	Counterchecks and Postulate Checks	22 May 71

Ethics Orders, US Base

*EO 141-1 USB	Findings and Recommendations, Committee of Evidence	23 Jun 76

Executive Directives, Area Estates

ED 1 Area Estates	New Issue	5 Feb 76
*ED 14 Area Estates	Office of LRH UCE Estates	4 Mar 76
*ED 16 Area Estates	Domestic Services, Exec Housekeeper's Daily Checklist	7 Mar 76
*ED 18 Area Estates	Re: Handling of SO Children	19 Mar 76
*ED 19 Area Estates	Mid-ratz	18 Mar 76

Executive Directives, Flag

ED 1 Flag	EDs Continued Series	21 Nov 71
ED 8 Flag	FEBCs Quality	25 Nov 71
*ED 10 Flag	Failure to Fire Why	26 Nov 71
*ED 31 Flag	Flag Crew Points System for Study	20 Nov 71
ED 34 Flag	Why No Firings	16 Dec 71
*ED 51 Flag	Posh Up Apollo PGM	2 Jan 72
ED 62 Flag	Current Actions	12 Jan 72
ED 68 Flag	Charter Members of the RSM AO	18 Jan 72
*ED 118 Flag	Physical Fitness and Close Order Drill	20 Feb 72
*ED 128 Flag	Flag Promo Schedule 2	28 Feb 72
*ED 135 Flag	SO Orgs Income Sources Survey	29 Feb 72
ED 139 Flag	Supervisor Resurge PGM	8 Mar 72
*ED 145 Flag	Captain Program	12 Mar 72
ED 149R Flag	Expanded Dianetics	31 Mar 72
*ED 155 Flag	Training PGM—1, Study Tech	23 Mar 72
*ED 177 Flag	General Production	23 Apr 72
*ED 182 Flag	Flag Solvency Plan	22 Apr 72
ED 200-4 Flag	Support International Push	7 Jun 72
ED 206 Flag	Midshipmen	5 Jun 72
*ED 236 Flag	CMDR'S MSGR Appointments	27 Aug 72
ED 240-7 Flag	Clean Ship PGM	3 Dec 72
*ED 240-10 Flag	Clean Ship PGM Debug	20 Jan 73
*ED 255 Flag	Confidential	30 Sept 72
*ED 264 Flag	Damage Control	2 Nov 72

*ED 281-2 Flag	Mission School PJT Wrap Up	7 Apr 73
*ED 295 Flag	Mess Organization System	17 Mar 73
*ED 304 Flag	Visit of Spanish VIP Lawyer	4 Apr 73
*ED 309-1 Flag	Flag UK V.A.T. Survey on Non-Scientologists	21 Apr 73
*ED 313 Flag	WQ & SB Eval	4 May 73
*ED 319 Flag	Spotless Shiny Ship Maintenance	9 May 73
*ED 319-1 Flag	Debug SSSM Hatting	2 Jun 73
*ED 321 Flag	The Why of Specialist Training	13 May 73
*ED 323 Flag	The Why of Condition II	15 May 73
*ED 334-1 Flag	FSO Eval—Top Priority	6 Aug 73
*ED 359 Flag	The Great Superlit Campaign	22 Aug 73
*ED 367-1 Flag	Ethics: Illegal Orders	10 Sept 73
*ED 383 Flag	Basic Operating Policy	27 Sept 73
*ED 384 Flag	Letter Reg Book Buyer Survey	21 Sept 73
*ED 450 Flag	Immediate Tech/Qual Actions to Handle Crew Cases	16 Jan 74
ED 549-28-1 Flag	Flag Bonus Correction	4 Sept 74
ED 459-35 Flag	Bonuses Re-Revised	20 Jan 75
ED 459-36 Flag	Bonus Considerations	19 Feb 75
ED 459-37 Flag	Bonuses = Delivery	18 Apr 75
ED 459-38 Flag	Brochures & Bonuses	16 May 75
ED 459-47 Flag	The Bonus Bulldozer Plows on	26 May 75
ED 459-49 Flag	The Bonus Bulldozer Plows on	31 May 75
ED 459-50 Flag	Bulldozer in Gear	1 Jun 75
ED 459-51 Flag	Bread and Bonuses	4 Jun 75
ED 459-52 Flag	Bulldozing Along	7 Jun 75
ED 459-54 Flag	Bonuses!	14 Jun 75
ED 459-56 Flag	What Makes Bread and Bonuses	1 Jul 75
*ED 472 Flag	Flag Collections	15 Mar 72
ED 473 Flag	Birthday Contributions	16 Mar 74
*ED 480 Flag	Internal Distractions	12 Apr 74
*ED 483 Flag	FSO Eval	18 Apr 74
*ED 497 Flag	Untaught Evaluators, Ref. CBO 340	25 Jun 74
ED 504 Flag	International PGM	6 Jul 74
*ED 512 Flag	Flag FP	11 Jul 74
*ED 520-4 Flag	Neglected Situations, Orgs Not on Current Programs	28 Oct 74
*ED 541 Flag	Confidential	12 Oct 74
*ED 547 Flag	Trained Missionaire Units in Every FOLO	18 Oct 74
*ED 563 Flag	The Service Star	28 Nov 74
*ED 565 Flag	Christmas Liberty Schedule	8 Dec 74
ED 573 Flag	Crew Chow	8 Jan 75
*ED 608 Flag	Urgent Directive—Flag NNCF	24 Mar 75
*ED 695-1 Flag	Confidential	12 Aug 75
*ED 769 Flag	AVU and I/A Functions and Terminals	20 Dec 75
*ED 774R Flag	Distribution of Port Captain's Office	2 Jan 76

ED 871 Flag	LRH Media Org	25 Mar 76
*ED 965 Flag	RPF Reinstated	1 Jul 76

Executive Directives, Flag Admin Org

*ED 1 FAO	FAO Executive Directives	10 Feb 71
ED 5 FAO	Basic Orders	1 Mar 71
ED 41 FAO	FAO Whys	6 Jun 71
*ED 62 FAO	I/A Checklist	5 Jul 71
ED 86 FAO	Class X Training	7 Aug 71
ED 103 FAO	Div III, Depts 7 & 8 Stats	18 Aug 71
*ED 118 FAO	Project: Completed Products Down the Gangway	21 Aug 71
ED 121 FAO	Urgent	3 Sept 71
ED 140 FAO	Project Festival Phase-Over Information	4 Oct 71
*ED 144 FAO	Testing into Div VI	10 Oct 71
ED 164 FAO	Command Team Volunteers	15 Nov 71

Executive Directives, Flag Advanced Org

ED 6 FAO	Flag Advanced Org	12 Feb 74

Executive Directives, Flag Bureau

*ED 1 FB	New Issue Type—EDs FB	4 Jan 76
ED 2 FB	FB Comes Home	3 Jan 76
*ED 13 FB	Lemon Tree	26 Jan 76
*ED 31 FB	LRH Ordered Eval Quotas	28 Feb 76
*ED 32 FB	Policy and Format of FBO Info Letter	27 Feb 76
*ED 33 FB	Purpose, Format and Policy of Treasury FB Newsletter	27 Feb 76
*ED 35 FB	Flag Rep Advice Letter	23 Feb 76
*ED 36 FB	Flag Distribution Bureau Newsletter Purpose, Format and Policy	11 Mar 76
*ED 39R FB	Management BU Bonus System	15 May 76

Executive Directives, U.S. Base

ED 10 USB	Vehicles	18 Oct 75
*ED 17 USB	Expansion	24 Oct 75
*ED 26 USB	TTC Recruits Readiness Unit	24 Oct 75
*ED 118 USB	Project R & B Billing	4 Jan 76
ED 123 USB	Confidential	12 Jan 76

*ED 179 USB	Flag Service Org Positionings	4 Mar 76
*ED 180 USB	Confidential	8 Mar 76

Executive Directives, Worldwide

ED 473 WW 842 SH	WW Emergency Condition	1 Sept 67

Flag Bureau Data Letters

FBDL 3	Personnel	13 Nov 70
FBDL 10	Re US Gdn Office Mission to ASHO	17 Nov 70
FBDL 12	Bureau Liaison Office, Purpose and Organization	19 Nov 70
FBDL 15 UK	Re *Commodore Queen*	23 Nov 70
*FBDL 25	Stagger System for PAC Area	6 Dec 70
*FBDL 73	Bureau V US, Program to Maintain the US Boom	24 Apr 71
*FBDL 93R	Franchise Plan 1	6 Aug 71
FBDL 103	New Product, Tech Establishment Officer C/O FAO Responsible for This PGM	8 Aug 71
*FBDL 106	Paper Label Org Board—Plan 1	14 Aug 71
FBDL 151	General Dissem Info Re: Special Mission to AOLA Dissem—Herbie Parkhouse	24 Mar 72
FBDL 152 Additional FBDL 160 Additional	GO FBO CLO	15 Apr 72
FBDL 161	PRO Units for UK & DK	25 Mar 72
FBDL 189	Change of Line	26 May 72
FBDL 191R	Current Scene	8 Jun 72 Revised 21 Sept 73
FBDL 192R	The Data Files	11 Jun 72 Revised 21 Sept 73
FBDL 198	Stats	8 Jul 72
FBDL 220	Narconon	29 Aug 72
FBDL 223	Publicity	6 Sept 72
*FBDL 279	Weekly Stat Briefing Sheet, W/E 29 Mar 73	30 Mar 73
*FBDL 289	Using ANZO Books to Spark off the Boom	21 Apr 73
*FBDL 290	Weeky Stat Briefing Sheet W/E 19 Apr 73	22 Apr 73
*FBDL 316	FAPTC and E-x-p-a-n-s-i-o-n	12 Jul 73
*FBDL 325	The Five Major Campaigns of Expansion	8 Aug 73
*FBDL 326	Comparison of Div VIs	13 Aug 73
*FBDL 328	A Milestone in Tech Delivery	14 Aug 73
*FBDL 365	*Mission into Time* by L. Ron Hubbard	21 Nov 73
*FBDL 369	Heralding a New Era of Expansion	31 Nov 73
*FBDL 376	1973 Wins from LRH	4 Jan 74
*FBDL 381	The Battle of Britain	28 Jan 74

*FBDL 404-1	A Planet Surges Under the Power of Source	13 Apr 74
*FBDL 412	Announcing New LRH Books	18 Jun 74
*FBDL 420R	The Power of Source	29 Jun 74 Revised 12 Jul 74
*FBDL 422	Ron B-o-o-m-s South Africa	6 Jul 74
*FBDL 424	The Volunteer Ministers Program	11 Jul 74
*FBDL 430	Intro Session Scene	7 Sept 74
*FBDL 439	SO 1 Quarterly Summary	18 Oct 74
*FBDL 439R	Flag Service Consultant Network Reorganized	22 Oct 74 Revised 10 Apr 75
*FBDL 443	Distribution Bureau Newly Established at Flag	24 Oct 74
*FBDL 449	Exposé on the Suppression of Mind, This Century	5 Nov 74
*FBDL 462	Upstats	15 Dec 74
*FBDL 469	Body Routing	5 Jan 75
*FBDL 488R	The New Management Bureau on Flag	15 Feb 75 Revised 12 Mar 75
*FBDL 504	The External HCO Network	14 Apr 75
*FBDL 513	Function of the International Ethics and Justice Officer	27 May 75
*FBDL 516	New Public Course	7 Jun 75
*FBDL 522	Highly Commended	24 Jun 75
*FBDL 523	New Names to CF Campaign	29 Jun 75
*FBDL 585	Current Boom	18 Dec 75
*FBDL 591	Attention—BMB Is Coming	4 Jan 76
*FBDL 596	The Flag Executive Booster Group	13 Jan 76

Flag Conditions Orders

*FCO 2990-2	RPF Assignment	24 Apr 74
*FCO 4414-1	Committee of Evidence	29 Mar 76

Flag Debriefer Forms

*Flag Debriefer Org Area Observation Form	7 Aug 74

Flag Divisional Directives

*FDD 1 Div 6 FEBC Orgs	Division Six—Divisional Summary of Functions	13 Apr 71
*FDD 18 Treas Int	Clarification of Titles	16 Jun 72
*FDD 82 Div VII Int	Common Questions About Ron	24 Jun 75

Flag Mission Orders

*FMO 13	Confidential	6 Jun 68
*FMO 82	Confidential	30 Jan 69
*FMO 121	Confidential	26 Mar 69
*FMO 221	Confidential	14 Oct 69
*FMO 467	Confidential	26 Feb 71

Flag Orders

FO 1	Reorganization	12 Aug 67
FO 4	Security on Post	13 Aug 67
FO 14	Blaming Mest	17 Aug 67
FO RS 16	Comm System	16 Nov 67
FO 20	Operational Orders	17 Nov 67
FO 24	*Enchanter* Handling	18 Aug 67
FO 29	*Avon* Engine Signals	21 Aug 67
FO RS 32	Conning Officer Hat Write-Up	16 Dec 67
FO 38	Etiquette	22 Aug 67
*FO 38-1	Etiquette, Forms of Address	29 Aug 73
FO 40	Study of Seafaring	23 Aug 67
FO 41	The Four Unprofitable Courses	23 Aug 67
FO 42	HEC Company Status	23 Aug 67
FO 71	OT Badges & Pins	29 Aug 67
FO 79	Org Board Change	31 Aug 67
FO 80	Sea Org Org Board	31 Aug 67
FO 87	Titles of Address (Add Etiquette)	2 Sept 67
FO 88	*Avon* White Glove Inspection	2 Sept 67
FO 101	Board of Investigations, Findings Called by Flag Order 82	4 Sept 67
FO 107	Sea Org Training and Processing and Review	5 Sept 67
FO 114	Org Board Change	7 Sept 67
*FO 123	Change to Be Made to FO 80	9 Sept 67
FO 137	"If almost any person . . ."	12 Sept 67
FO 160	Div I Files: Personnel Files	18 Sept 67
FO 196	Ranks and Insignia of the Sea Org Officers	29 Sept 67
FO 201	Ethics Order	30 Sept 67
*FO 210	Addition to Base Order 29	2 Sept 67
*FO 212	Electronics and Electrical	3 Sept 67
*FO 221	Assists	4 Oct 67
FO 228	Purpose of the Sea Org, Character of Missions	9 Oct 67
FO 232	Resignation	10 Oct 67
FO 234	Motto	12 Oct 67

FO 236	Ranks and Ratings	13 Oct 67
FO 242	Uniforms, Stewards	15 Oct 67
FO 253	Sunburn	19 Oct 67
FO 263	The Flagship	24 Oct 67
FO 274	Services Mate	4 Nov 67
FO 281	Delivery Crew Data	10 Nov 67
FO 301	Children—Ships Regulations	16 Nov 67 Reissued 18 Jan 71
FO 303	The Quartermaster of the Watch	18 Nov 67
FO 304	The Quartermaster of the Watch Post	19 Nov 67
*FO 314	Electrical Equipment	14 Dec 67
*FO 315	Cleaning Stations	15 Dec 67
FO 316	Conning Officer Hat Write-Up	16 Dec 67
FO 317	Radio Telephone Use in European & Mediterranean Waters	17 Dec 67
FO 327	Flotilla Assignments	26 Dec 67
FO 331	Organization	27 Dec 67
FO RS 332	The Hat of Master	29 Dec 67
FO 334	Flotilla Reorganization	31 Dec 67
*FO 336	Telex Lines	1 Jan 68
FO 348	Discipline, Officer or Leading Petty Officer	5 Jan 68
FO 378	R.S. Reorganization	15 Jan 68
FO 401	Organization R.S.	21 Jan 68
FO 410	Finance *Royal Scotman*	25 Jan 68
FO 411	*Royal Scotman,* Orders Published by	26 Jan 68
FO 412	Financial Regulations	26 Jan 68
FO 416	Finance, *Royal Scotman*	28 Jan 68
FO 424	OOD	30 Jan 68
FO 441	Orders of the Day	14 Feb 68
FO 442	Rest and Auditing	14 Feb 68
FO 466	Advance Course Security Check	2 Mar 68
FO 467	Commodore's Personal Staff	2 Mar 68
FO 489	"To prevent the . . ."	9 Mar 68
FO 495	Permanent Mission	11 Mar 68
FO 496	Permanent Mission	11 Mar 68
FO 497	"Class VIII Course . . ."	11 Mar 68
*FO 504	International Ethics File	13 Mar 68
*FO 508	Definitions	16 Mar 68
FO 516	"The following is . . ."	14 Mar 68
FO 517	Training	18 Mar 68
FO 558	Contact Unit	25 Mar 68
FO 565	Flag Banking Officer	26 Mar 68
FO 579	Policy on the *High Winds*	30 Mar 68
FO 618	Research Section	22 Apr 68
*FO 637	Confidential	27 Apr 68

*FO 638	Communication Lines	27 Apr 68
FO 640	Legal Flag	20 Apr 68
*FO 644	Staff Operations	28 Apr 68
*FO 645 R-1 Attachment 3 Practice Mission Order 3	Ensurance Practice Mission	circa '75
FO 646	Future Ship Plans	28 Apr 68
*FO 650	Research Library	29 Apr 68
*FO 657	Mission History Log Book	30 Apr 68
FO 664	Non-Enturbulation Order, *Avon River*	2 May 68
*FO 674	How to Do a Debrief	5 May 68
*FO 688RA	*Advance!* Mag Series 1 Policy on *Advance!* Magazine	12 Feb 72 Reissued 5 Aug 74
FO 745	OTL Duties	20 May 68
FO 747	Comm Procedure Over Long Distances	21 May 68 Corrected & Reissued 5 Feb 75
FO 748	Stewards	21 May 68
FO 760	Cadets Children, Designation	25 May 68
*FO 761-1	Division 3—Handling of Missions	11 Jul 73
FO 766	Personal Staff	27 May 68
*FO 769	Operations	27 May 68
FO 785R	Volunteers	11 Oct 70
*FO 786	Personal Staff, Stewart Department	29 May 68
FO 795	Commodore's Staff	30 May 68
FO 800	Scientology Technology	31 May 68
FO 808	Auditors	31 May 68
*FO 809	Public Division (Div VI) Purposes	29 May 68
FO 815	Communication Actions, for Phone, or Telex	2 Jun 68
FO 820	Engineer's Reports	3 Jun 68
*FO 824	"All previous No. system of telex. . . ."	1 Jun 68
*FO 828	Operations	5 Jun 68
FO 835	"The services chief . . ."	5 Jun 68
FO 848	"The purpose of Any Mission . . ."	6 Jun 68
FO 872	A Tiger	12 Jun 68
FO 882	"In addition to his . . ."	13 Jun 68
*FO 890	Operations, Missions, Comm Lines	14 Jun 68
FO 895	Watches, RSM	15 Jun 68
FO 898	CIC	17 Jun 68
FO 908	CIC	18 Jun 68
*FO 910	Aim and Object of Drills	18 Jun 68
*FO 913	"The title of Hostess . . ."	19 Jun 68
*FO 915	"The promotion of AO . . ."	20 Jun 68
*FO 918	Ethics and Application	20 Jun 68

FO 922	Petty Officer Appointments	2 Jun 68
FO 924	Stores	21 Jun 68
*FO 929	Transport of Funds by Courier Rundown	23 Jun 68
*FO 933	Flag Banking Officer	23 Jun 68
*FO 936	Division VI All Sea Orgs	23 Jun 68
FO 938	Personal Procurement Officer	23 Jun 68
*FO 955	"The translations and interpretation section . . ."	26 Jun 68
FO 976	Reorganization, Org Board, Div II	1 Jul 68
FO 977	"WW has taken . . ."	1 Jul 68
*FO 986	AO Liaisons	4 Jul 68
FO 995	"CS-5 will now . . ."	6 Jul 68
*FO 1002	Engine Room — Cleaning Stations	7 Jul 68
FO 1008	Expeditors	7 Jul 68
FO 1020	Sea Watch Drills	10 Jul 68
FO 1021	Conferences	10 Jul 68
FO 1028	Div II and Div VII	11 Jul 68
FO 1031	"CS-5 will now . . ."	11 Jul 68
FO 1040	Officer Discipline	14 Jul 68
FO 1066	Ethics Authority	22 Jul 68
FO 1086	Glee	27 Jul 68
*FO 1098	Mission Eligible Records	27 Jul 68
*FO 1102	F.B.O. Post Abolished	28 Jul 68
FO 1109	"This Flag Order modifies . . ."	26 Jul 68
*FO 1114	Financial Arrangements for OTL UK	28 Jul 68
*FO 1120	Banking Arrangements at AOUK	31 Jul 68
*FO 1125	Medical Log	29 Jul 68
*FO 1137	LRH Personal Finances	2 Aug 68
*FO 1151	Financial Organization of AOs and OTLs	10 Aug 68
*FO 1170	Examinations Are Back	11 Aug 68
FO 1174	Dev-T Data, People Who Don't Do Their Jobs	12 Aug 68
FO 1193	"The officer of the deck . . ."	14 Aug 68
*FO 1194	Standard Tech Program	27 Jul 68
*FO 1214	OTL Do's and Don'ts	17 Aug 68
*FO 1237	"There are three AO liaisons . . ."	20 Aug 68
FO 1243R	Missions	21 Aug 68 Revised 17 Nov 74
FO 1247	"Every condition of liability or doubt is . . ."	22 Aug 68
FO 1256	RSM, F/P	24 Aug 68
*FO 1266	"Debrief TR"	23 Aug 68
FO 1268	Org Missionaires	30 Aug 68
FO 1274	Captains Steward	1 Sept 68
FO 1275	Captain Routing, Flag	1 Sept 68
*FO 1314	"An AO liaison . . ."	9 Sept 68
*FO 1324	Ethics Weekly Report	13 Sept 68

*FO 1330	An Open Letter to Commanding Officers of AO and Those Concerned with AO Promotion	16 Sept 68
*FO 1346	Advanced Money Handling	18 Sept 68
*FO 1364	Addresso Duties	20 Sept 68
FO 1368	Commanding Officer Reports	22 Sept 68
*FO 1400	Floats and Their Uses	29 Sept 68
*FO 1403	Division VI Structure	1 Oct 68
*FO 1409	Financial Planning	1 Oct 68
*FO 1416	"The post of Chief Yeoman . . ."	4 Oct 68
*FO 1421	"It seems . . ."	30 Sept 68
*FO 1422	"The requirements for senior execs . . ."	30 Sept 68
FO 1426	Sea Org Purpose	3 Oct 68
FO 1432	Ethics Presence	4 Oct 68
FO 1450	Class VIII Course	9 Oct 68
*FO 1481	Missions	15 Oct 68
FO 1483	Personnel	17 Oct 68
FO 1490	Flag Divisions	18 Oct 68
*FO 1510	Division III Monthly Summaries	23 Oct 68
*FO 1517	Duties of Engine Room I & R	25 Oct 68
*FO 1522	Legal Board	26 Oct 68
*FO 1528	Engine Room I & R Ethics Duties	28 Oct 68
*FO 1548	Communications to and from Aides	5 Nov 68
FO 1554	Missionaire Organization	7 Nov 68
FO 1556	"The Following is . . ."	8 Nov 68
*FO 1561	Sea Org Personnel	11 Nov 68
*FO 1567	Salvage	12 Nov 68
*FO 1570	How to Handle Communication, Telex Traffic	11 Nov 68
*FO 1571	Missionaire 1st, 2nd & 3rd Class Awards	13 Nov 68
*FO 1583R	Flub Catch CIC Display	15 Nov 68
*FO 1588	Solo Auditing Goofs	16 Nov 68
FO 1590	Appointment	17 Nov 68
*FO 1592	Midshipmen	19 Nov 68
*FO 1593	Form of Telexes from Missionaires to Operations	20 Nov 68
*FO 1595	Hat of CS-4	19 Nov 68
FO 1604	AO's Power	24 Nov 68
*FO 1606	Standard Briefing	24 Nov 68
*FO 1611	Damage Control	26 Nov 68
*FO 1618	"The Statistic of . . ."	29 Nov 68
FO 1630	Governess	3 Dec 68
*FO 1632	Sick List	4 Dec 68
*FO 1652	Service Records	12 Dec 68
*FO 1655	Safeguarding LRH Original Tape Recordings	11 Dec 68
*FO 1662	Division IV Responsibilities	13 Dec 68
FO 1664	Divisional Primary Functions	17 Dec 68
*FO 1666	Senior Ratings	16 Dec 68

*FO 1669	Security	16 Dec 68
*FO 1677	Status Verification Form	23 Dec 68
*FO 1681	AO Allocations—Gross Income	24 Dec 68
*FO 1682	(Addition to FO 1109)	16 Dec 68
*FO 1684	Standard Training WQ & SB	31 Dec 68
*FO 1685	Examinations	31 Dec 68
*FO 1686	This Is the Sea Org	24 Dec 68
FO 1693	Duties of CIC	3 Jan 69
*FO 1695	Engine Room I & R Duties	3 Jan 69
*FO 1701	Mud Box Brigade	5 Jan 69
*FO 1704R	Ship and Base Electrical Generator Checklists	30 Jul 71
*FO 1710	Intelligence	8 Jan 69
*FO 1715	Special Programmes Unit	10 Jan 69
*FO 1717	Division VI	10 Jan 69
*FO 1722	Naval Engine Rooms	9 Jan 69
FO 1737	Shipyards	17 Jan 69
FO 1746	Trained Auditor Programme	20 Jan 69
*FO 1753	Hat of CS-5 Correction	22 Jan 69
*FO 1758	Compliance Reports	26 Jan 69
*FO 1761	Flag Banking Officer	27 Jan 69
*FO 1779	Division VI Organization Board	5 Jan 69
*FO 1793	Public Relations Course	7 Feb 69
FO 1802	Missionaires	18 Feb 69
FO 1817	Overloading E/R	19 Feb 69
*FO 1822	Divisional Officer's Council	16 Feb 69
*FO 1828	Definitions	18 Feb 69
*FO 1836	ARC Break Programme for Sea Org Members	25 Feb 69
*FO 1844	"In response to a letter . . ."	28 Feb 69
*FO 1847	The Org Board Structure of SH and AO Greece	2 Mar 69
*FO 1848	Rehabilitation Unit	3 Mar 69
*FO 1850	SH Greece Premises	4 Mar 69
*FO 1851	Public Relations Course Stage Lighting	4 Mar 69
FO 1853	Sail Training	4 Mar 69
*FO 1872	Crew List	13 Mar 69
FO 1882	Security	21 Mar 69
FO 1889	Reorganization	25 Mar 69
FO 1890	Confidential	26 Mar 69
FO 1919	Watch Quarter and Station Bills	17 Apr 69
*FO 1920	Senior Advanced Org	9 Apr 69
*FO 1933	Hat Ships Rep	12 Apr 69
*FO 1939	International Executive Division for Advanced Organizations Executive Council Advanced Organization	19 Apr 69
*FO 1941	PRO Course	20 Apr 69
*FO 1950	Officers' Board	19 Apr 69
*F0 1954	CIC Revision	19 Apr 69

FO 1958	E/R General Org	26 Apr 69
FO 1960	Archives	27 Apr 69
FO 1972	"CMDR Hana Eltringham . . ."	1 May 69
*FO 1973	Phases of Renovation	2 May 69
*FO 1978	Petty Officers	28 Apr 69
*FO 1980	AO Allocations and Gross Income	3 May 69
*FO 1985	Medical Officers Report to C/S	9 May 69
FO 1992	Confidential	14 May 69
*FO 1993	Proper Maintenance, Keeping the Ship Operational	13 May 69
*FO 1999	Handling a Program	17 May 69
*FO 2002	Emergency Food Stores	18 May 69
FO 2013	Cadet School	5 Jun 69
*FO 2020	Use of H.O. 214 Altitude and Azimuth Tables	10 Jun 69
*FO 2021	The Education Programme	8 Jun 69
FO 2024	Board of Appeal	12 Jun 69
FO 2032	Finance Policies	17 Jun 69
FO 2037	Ship Committee	22 Jun 69
*FO 2043	Post Routine Checklist	29 Jun 69
*FO 2046	Confidential	1 Jul 69
*FO 2049	I & R Engine Room Hat	19 Apr 69
FO 2057	Financial Regulations	12 Jul 69
*FO 2060	Finance Course	18 Jul 69
*FO 2068	Port Write-Ups	28 Jul 69
*FO 2080	E/R Org (Amends FO 1958)	15 Aug 69
FO 2086	Civilian Sailors	20 Aug 69
FO 2111	Conning Officer	10 Sept 69
*FO 2112	Senior Executive Course	11 Sept 69
*FO 2116	Missionaire Success	23 Sept 69
FO 2123	Deputy Commodores	4 Oct 69
FO 2127	Personnel Transfers	6 Oct 69
*FO 2132	Mission Classification and Bonus Awards	7 Oct 69
*FO 2148	Engine Room Primary Actions	25 Oct 69
FO 2150	Order Types	27 Oct 69
FO 2151	Class VIIIs, Duty Time	29 Oct 69
*FO 2152	Photocopier Machines	29 Oct 69
*FO 2156	Flag Programme Files	31 Oct 69
*FO 2162	Survey Form for All Surveys	25 Oct 69
FO 2165	MO Food Inspection	6 Nov 69
*FO 2169	Standard Operating Complement Flagship Crew	7 Nov 69
*FO 2170	Debriefs	4 Nov 69
FO 2171	Port Flaps	7 Nov 69
*FO 2192	Programming Basic Unit Hat	14 Nov 69
*FO 2199	Sea Org Command Lines	17 Nov 69
*FO 2200	Stationship Stable Data	18 Nov 69

*FO 2201	Stable Terminals	18 Nov 69
*FO 2204	Repair Cycles of Handling	14 Nov 69
*FO 2205	Students Power Club	14 Nov 69
*FO 2213	Program Numbering	23 Nov 69
*FO 2219	What Flag Wants on Its Lines	21 Nov 69
*FO 2220	Zones of Authority	24 Nov 69
*FO 2221	Confidential	26 Nov 69
*FO 2229	*Sea Watch Picture Book* Checksheet	2 Dec 69
FO 2238	Recruit and Member Defined	7 Dec 69
FO 2245	Ethics Presence	13 Dec 69
FO 2257	Courts of Appeal	19 Dec 69
*FO 2261	Flag Operating Basis	18 Dec 69
*FO 2267	Data to Aides Summary Sheet	17 Dec 69
*FO 2270	Flag Dissemination and Public Divisions	20 Dec 69
*FO 2272	Flag Org Board No. 3	21 Dec 69
*FO 2273	Flag Administration Office	22 Dec 69
*FO 2274	FBO Statistics and Operating Basis	20 Dec 69
*FO 2278	Allocation Amounts	20 Dec 69
*FO 2281	Confidential	10 Dec 69
*FO 2284	Confidential	10 Dec 69
FO 2286	Admin Actions, Responsibility for	26 Dec 69
*FO 2287	Student Consultant	20 Dec 69
*FO 2289	Student Consultant	22 Dec 69
*FO 2298	Confidential	20 Dec 69
FO 2300	The Red Form	3 Jan 70
*FO 2302	Fresh Water Wash	28 Dec 69
*FO 2310	Celebrity Selections	5 Jan 70
*FO 2314	Personnel Handling	10 Jan 70
*FO 2327R	Service Insignia	16 Jan 74
*FO 2332	Sick PCs—Auditing, Administration	17 Jan 70
FO 2333	Tech and Qual and CS-5	20 Jan 70
*FO 2334	Ship Div VI Org Board *Apollo*	15 Jan 70
*FO 2345	Commodore's Household Unit	17 Jan 70
*FO 2350	Board of Appeal	26 Jan 70
*FO 2351	US FBO Lines	27 Jan 70
*FO 2354	The Keeper of Tech, Duties and Responsibilities	28 Jan 70
FO 2358	Operations, Compliance Reports	18 Feb 70
*FO 2360	Work Parties Are Missions	19 Feb 70
FO 2361	Celebrity Centre	22 Feb 70
*FO 2364	Conditional Org Board and Personnel	28 Feb 70
*FO 2366	RE Confidential Items in the Mail	1 Mar 70
FO 2370	Hat LRH Personal Communicator	5 Mar 70
FO 2374	Flag Office of LRH	7 Mar 70 Revised 10 Apr 73

FO 2376	CS-1 Duties	9 Mar 70
FO 2379	Expeditors Flag Org	12 Mar 70
*FO 2381	Flag Executive Office Unit	16 Mar 70
*FO 2384	Officer Ranks Petty Officer Rates	19 Feb 70
FO 2387	Councils, Meetings and Conferences	21 Mar 70
*FO 2389	Stationship Captain	20 Mar 70
FO 2392	CIC Operation	24 Mar 70
FO 2396	Communication Security Policy	28 Mar 70
*FO 2399R	Mission Condition Assignments	26 May 70
FO 2409	Conference Planning Officer	10 Apr 70
FO 2410	Personnel Control	10 Apr 70
*FO 2413	"S.O.L.T.S."	15 Apr 70
FO 2414	Morale	16 Apr 70
FO 2416	Canteens	21 Apr 70
*FO 2426	Confidential	27 Apr 70
FO 2431	Mission Know-How, Importance of	29 Apr 70
FO 2439	Ship and Aide Organization	6 May 70
FO 2440	PR Program Development Routing and Release Form	7 May 70
*FO 2442R	Flub Catch System Returned	7 May 70 Revised 13 Dec 74
*FO 2444	What a "Debrief Summary" Is and How to Do One	6 May 70
*FO 2451	DK Allocation	20 May 70
*FO 2460	LRH Mimeo Line to All SO Members	31 May 70
*FO 2461R	Stage 1 OTL Pattern	30 May 70
FO 2464	WQ & SB Conditions, Use of	7 Jun 70
*FO 2466	Standard Briefing	30 May 70
FO 2469	Specialist Crews	9 Jun 70
FO 2471	The Drill "Scene"	9 Jun 70
FO 2473	SO Organizing Bureau	14 Jun 70
FO 2474	SO Action Bureau	14 Jun 70
*FO 2475	Operations Officers Are to Be Single Hatted	7 Jun 70
FO 2476	Tech and Qual in AOs	16 Jun 70
FO 2478	Conference Actions	17 Jun 70
FO 2480	Real Planning of Finance	20 Jun 70
*FO 2493	Admin Unit Specialists	23 Jun 70
FO 2494	Courier vs Missionaire	30 Jun 70
FO 2498	Sick List and Designations	2 Jul 70
*FO 2500	Management Cycle	25 Jun 70
*FO 2505	Mission Types of	14 Jul 70
*FO 2506RA	Observation Drills	3 Dec 70 Revised 9 Mar 73
*FO 2507	Security TR	14 Jul 70
*FO 2508	Practice Missions	14 Jul 70
*FO 2512	LRH SO Briefing Tapes	16 Jul 70

*FO 2519	Model Orders for the Establishment of a Shore Base	16 Jul 70
*FO 2521	Flag Divisional Directive	21 Jul 70
*FO 2523	Messenger Training Drills	11 Jul 70
FO 2525	Flagship Public Divisions	27 Jul 70
*FO 2526	Missionaire Classification	20 Oct 70
*FO 2528	Communications Standard Telex Admin Message Discipline	1 Aug 70
FO 2530R	Errands & Missions	18 Oct 70
FO 2532	Confidential	11 Aug 70
FO 2534	Bureau Project Order	14 Aug 70
FO 2535	Health Care	16 Aug 70
FO 2542R	Trim and List	6 Oct 70
FO 2544	Bureau Names and Title Pattern	25 Aug 70
*FO 2555	Voyage Folder Charts	26 Aug 70
FO 2556	Officers (Ships, Orgs and Bases) Duties and Bonuses	14 Sept 70
*FO 2557	Telex Procedure: Confirmation Copies	15 Sept 70
*FO 2558	Basic Hat, Introduction for New Stewards	15 Sept 70
*FO 2570	Director of Records, Assets & Materiel Hat	27 Sept 70
*FO 2576	Daily Report Procedure, From Crew to Commanding Officer	28 Sept 70
*FO 2577	Sea Org Uniforms	29 Sept 70
*FO 2579	Mission Planning & Preparation Alerts	4 Oct 70
FO 2580	Ethics Penalties	6 Oct 70
FO 2584	Admin Cycle Drill	7 Oct 70
*FO 2585R	Sea Org Voice Control Drill	7 Oct 70
FO 2586	Mess Organization	8 Oct 70
*FO 2595	Flag Div VI	2 Oct 70
*FO 2601	Additions to FO 1637 Reports, Returning Missionaires	21 Oct 70
*FO 2608	Scientology Command Lines and Authorities	26 Oct 70
FO 2610	Validation	27 Oct 70
*FO 2611R	Liaison Office Supply Lines	4 Aug 71
*FO 2613	Flag Ship Captain Hat Checksheet	28 Oct 70
*FO 2615	Ship Division II Org Board	6 Nov 70
*FO 2617	New Pattern of Administration	13 Nov 70
FO 2626	Non-Utilization	26 Nov 70
*FO 2627RA	SO Acceptance and Leaving Policies Revised	17 Jul 72
*FO 2630R	Fitness Board	29 Nov 70 Revised 26 Nov 72
*FO 2633	Flagship Division VII Org Board	27 Nov 70
*FO 2645-2	LRH Conferences and Lectures	20 Nov 74
FO 2653	DOC and Aides Conference	13 Dec 70
FO 2656	C/O Assistance	16 Dec 70
FO 2660	Deputy Mates	22 Dec 70
FO 2661	HCO Traffic	23 Dec 70 Reissued 16 Apr 74
FO 2662	Mission Dump	23 Dec 70

*FO 2864	PR Duty Officer	15 Jun 71
*FO 2872	Finance Collection Officer	20 Jun 71
*FO 2873	Purchasing in Other Countries	27 Jun 71
FO 2878R	Recruiting Lines	10 Jul 71 Reissued 9 Mar 72
*FO 2895	Confidential	23 Jul 71
FO 2905	Overwhelmed Aides—Cause and Cure	28 Jul 71
*FO 2907	Ship Safety Policies	28 Jul 71
*FO 2910	Ship Open House Program	2 Aug 71
*FO 2919	Model Target Series for VIP Function	28 Sept 71
*FO 2925	WQ & SB Specialist Checksheet, Recorder/Fathometer	10 Aug 71
*FO 2933	Rec/Fath Hat Write-Up	17 Aug 71
FO 2936	Mission Orders, Types of	31 Aug 71
*FO 2937	Flag Order 2300 Cancellation	30 Aug 71
*FO 2938	Contracts and Bill Paying	28 Aug 71
FO 2945	Aides Responsibility	13 Sept 71
FO 2947	Know Best	15 Sept 71
*FO 2949	Customs Clearance for Couriered Cash	9 Sept 71
*FO 2964	Sidechecking Attestation	23 Sept 71
*FO 2967	Apollo Cleaning Stations List	3 Oct 71
*FO 2969	What an Inspector Should Know	9 Oct 71
*FO 2973	Food Flow Checksheet	11 Oct 71
*FO 2980	Auditing for OEC Students	8 Oct 71
*FO 2982	A Note on TRs and Admin TRs	30 Sept 71
*FO 2988	Invoicing of OECs/FEBCs	14 Sept 71
*FO 2992	Registrar FEBC Firing Charts	18 Sept 71
*FO 2994	FEBC Completions Scheduling Board	22 Sept 71
*FO 2997	Host	29 Sept 71
*FO 2999	Director of Processing, Handling of FEBC Students on L10	18 Sept 71
*FO 3005	OEC/FEBC Exam	25 Sept 71
*FO 3006	OEC/FEBC Pinksheets and Student Classwork	18 Sept 71
*FO 3032	Layout of OEC/FEBC Classroom at Flag	18 Sept 71
*FO 3036	FEBC Product Officer Purpose and How to Achieve	15 Sept 71
*FO 3038	FEBC Product Officer Basic Actions	18 Sept 71
*FO 3041	FEBC Org Officer Basic Actions	18 Sept 71
*FO 3053	Evolution of the FEBC	14 Sept 71
*FO 3057	Shore Flaps	26 Oct 71
FO 3064	Aide's and A/Aides Duties	3 Nov 71
*FO 3066	Franchise Evaluations	5 Nov 71
FO 3067	Ethics and Bureau I	7 Nov 71
*FO 3074	Flag Rep Inspection Checklists	20 Nov 71
*FO 3075	Sea Org Bonus System	18 Nov 71
*FO 3075-1R	Staff Statuses Bonuses and Penalties	26 Nov 73 Revised 23 Jan 74

*FO 3078	Flag Reps in Orgs	25 Nov 71
*FO 3081	Freight Data and Documents to Flag	28 Nov 71
*FO 3082	Medical Finance	15 Nov 71 Reissued 15 Jan 72 Corrected & Reissued 7 Mar 72
*FO 3087	Navigators Log	30 Nov 71
*FO 3092	Evaluations	18 Dec 71
FO 3094	PRO Area Control	16 Dec 71
*FO 3112	OT III Expanded	30 Jan 72
FO 3113	Management Bureau Routing	2 Feb 72
*FO 3116	SO Training Series No. 1 SO Training Coordinator CLOs	30 Jan 72
*FO 3118R	Continental Recruit Training	4 Mar 72
*FO 3121	Confidential	4 Feb 72
*FO 3124	Flag and CLO Mimeo Distribution	7 Feb 72
*FO 3126	Shipkeeping Series No. 1 Duties of the DPF MAA	20 Feb 72
*FO 3127	Galley Series No. 2 "Dev-T-itis"—Incomplete Cycles in the Galley	9 Dec 71
FO 3132	*Athena* as a Cramming Vessel	20 Feb 72
*FO 3136	Missionaires, Case Okay to Fire	21 Feb 72
*FO 3137	Posting of Stats in CLOs and OTLs	24 Feb 72
*FO 3138	AO Division VI Org Board and Posting Guide	17 Feb 72
*FO 3139	I Want to Go Clear Club	19 Feb 72
FO 3148	Aides Three Hats	10 Mar 72
*FO 3149-1	Orders Issuance	5 Sept 73
*FO 3149-2	AVU Submissions Needing Evaluation	7 Apr 74
FO 3152RR	Flag Finance Lines	30 Mar 72
FO 3155RA	The Basic Sea Org Training PGM	12 Mar 72 Revised 30 Apr 73 Revised 1 Dec 74
*FO 3161	Boatkeeping Series No. 2 The Boatswain	6 Apr 72
*FO 3163	Handling of Clinical Assignments to SPF or DPF	6 Apr 72
*FO 3165	Project Forces in Land-Based Units	6 Apr 72
*FO 3166	Sea Org Estates Captain	8 Apr 72
*FO 3167	The Organization of Children in Land-Based Units	6 Apr 72
FO 3170	Data Bureau Files Revised	13 Apr 72
*FO 3175	SO Estates Org Board, Shore Units	21 Apr 72
*FO 3176R	House Organization, Shore Base Units	9 Oct 72
FO 3179	Aide and A/Aide Responsibility	25 Apr 72
FO 3183	High Crime FO	10 May 72
FO 3188	Staff Captain, Duties of	4 Jun 72
FO 3192	Deck Project Forces	16 Jun 72

FO 3193-1	Embassies, Additional	27 Jun 72
*FO 3194RA-2	Basic Complement and Blue-Chip Postings	23 Apr 73
FO 3195	Emergency Officer	3 Jul 72
*FO 3195-1	Internal Emergency Officer, Flag	10 Mar 75
*FO 3196-R	EULO Basic Complement	6 Jul 72
*FO 3212R-Part 1	Recruit Routing and Information Form	25 Jul 72 Revised 31 May 73
FO 3232	WQ & SB Specialist Program Establishment	15 Aug 72
*FO 3240	Mimeo Numbering of "Double Issues"	4 Sept 72
*FO 3241-1	Personal Grooming Series No. 1 Personal Grooming	22 Aug 72
FO 3249	Security	24 Sept 72
*FO 3251	Money Handling	23 Sept 72
*FO 3252R	Sea Org Legal Matters: Local: Flag Only	24 Sept 72
*FO 3254	Relation of Mission Briefing Officer to Mission Preps I/C	28 Sept 72 Reissued 29 Dec 72
*FO 3260	Apprenticeship—Hatting	8 Oct 72
*FO 3264	Flag Mimeo Typist Hat Write-Up	6 Oct 72
*FO 3264-17	How to Collate and Staple Mimeo Issues	6 Feb 73
*FO 3264-20	Handling Issues on "Hold"	6 Feb 73
*FO 3264-22	Mimeo Equipment	12 Dec 73
*FO 3271	AOLA Organizing Board	14 Nov 72
*FO 3275R	Confidential	28 Oct 73
*FO 3276R	FOLO/CLO Confessional Corps	3 Dec 72
*FO 3277	Fast Flow Recruitment, Qual's Vital Role, Product Zero	26 Nov 72
*FO 3279-1R	Public Relations Area, Control Unit GDS's for Shore Bases	30 Jan 73 Revised 9 Mar 73
*FO 3279-3	The PRAC Data Bureau, Its Personnel and Its Files	26 May 73
*FO 3279-5	PRAC Unit OIC, Cable to Flag	9 Jun 73
*FO 3280-6	"Overt Data Collection Filing and Cataloguing"	7 Jun 73
*FO 3281	The Code of a Sea Org Member	7 Jan 73
FO 3287	The Elements of a Post	6 Jan 73
*FO 3290	Priority Posting	26 Jan 73
*FO 3295	*Advance* Mag Series No. 4 *Advance* Mag Production Lines, Terminals and Flows	28 Feb 73
*FO 3298RA	SO Tech Training Corps	20 Mar 73 Revised 19 Aug 74
*FO 3300	Chief M'naire Hat Checksheet	18 Mar 73
*FO 3303R	Minor's Mate Established	29 Mar 73 Revised & Reissued 10 Apr 73
*FO 3307	Family Day	9 Apr 73
*FO 3311	Sea Organization Officer Council	12 Apr 73
*FO 3311-1	Sea Organization Petty Officer Council	4 Aug 73

*FO 3313	External HCO Bureau	17 Apr 73
*FO 3323	Celebrities and the Sea Organization	9 May 73
*FO 3324	Training Corps Establishment and Operation	3 May 73
*FO 3324R	Flag Auxiliary Personnel Training Corps Admin Scale	3 May 73 Revised 27 Jan 75
*FO 3324-3	HCOs TTC/ATC Weekly Report Form to Flag	6 Aug 73
*FO 3324R-5	Flag Auxiliary Personnel Training Corps	30 May 73 Revised 27 Jan 75
*FO 3332	Central Personnel Office Hats Admin Scale	23 May 73
*FO 3335	Basics of Navigation No. 1 The Simplicities of Navigating as a Scientologist	30 May 73
*FO 3339RA	Stats and VFPs of the Continental FPPO Office	20 May 74 Re-Revised 30 Apr 75
*FO 3341	PR and Consumption Liaison Officer Survey Functions	12 Jun 73
FO 3342	Deputy Commodores and Acting Flag Officer	11 Jun 73
FO 3342-2	Second Deputy Commodore Hat	11 Jun 73
*FO 3345	Ranks and Ratings Ceremony	14 May 73
*FO 3348	The Sea Org Change of Command Ceremony	27 Jun 73
*FO 3349	Sea Org Publicity and Promotion Charisma	1 Jul 73
*FO 3350	Confidential	24 Jun 73
*FO 3351	The Sea Org Coat of Arms	20 Jun 73
*FO 3352	Recommended Demotions of Rank	2 Jul 73
*FO 3355-1	Implementation of Officer's Responsibility Course	20 Jul 73
*FO 3362	HSCSC, A New Course for Saint Hill Org	10 Aug 73
FO 3364	Flag Representative, Orders to	15 Aug 73
*FO 3365	Flag Auxiliary Personnel Training Corps Personnel Examination	20 Aug 73
*FO 3367	How to Rotate Staff for SO Product Level Training	22 Aug 73
*FO 3370	Basics of Navigation No. 2 The Recognition of Positions	2 Sept 73
*FO 3373	Mini VII Division Org Board for Pubs US	30 Aug 73
*FO 3380	Estate—Ship Aide	22 Sept 73
*FO 3382	Additional Security Notes for New Arrivals	26 Sept 73
*FO 3383	Out Etiquette Report	26 Sept 73
*FO 3385-3	Superlative Organization Function & Structure of Orgs Aboard Flag	5 Oct 73
*FO 3385-11	Treasury Bureau III, Mini Org Board	17 Jun 74
*FO 3386	"Major Supplier" in Ship Purchasing Defined	8 Oct 73
FO 3392	Hats of Port Captain and His Deputy	21 Oct 73
*FO 3396	Port Captain/Guardian Office Zones of Responsibility	21 Oct 73
*FO 3398	PRAC FOS Cancellation	22 Oct 73
*FO 3403	Post Abolished	6 Nov 73
*FO 3404	Pubs Org Clearance and Coordination with Flag of Policies, Activities and Products	7 Nov 73
FO 3407	"Hill 10" Makers	10 Nov 73

FO 3408	Officer Irresponsibility	12 Nov 73
*FO 3409	Pioneer Areas, Zones of Responsibility	4 Nov 73
*FO 3415-1	Cont'l Finance Office Org Board	21 May 74
*FO 3426	Flag Service Org's Income Flow Chart	24 Nov 73
*FO 3434	The Rehabilitation Project Force	7 Jan 74
*FO 3434-1	Additional on RPF Organization	7 Jan 74
*FO 3434-27	RPF Graduate Enhancement	25 Nov 74
*FO 3434-28	EPF and RPF Organization in Continental Areas	4 Feb 75
*FO 3444RA	Flag Service Consultant	14 Jun 74 Revised 13 Dec 74
FO 3449	CIC for Flag	22 Jan 74
*FO 3449R	Staff CIC	8 May 75
FO 3451	Photographing Hard News	8 Feb 74
*FO 3454RA	Requirements for Personnel to Flag	11 Feb 74 Revised 20 May 74
*FO 3458	Shore Base SO Uniforms	5 Mar 74
*FO 3460R	Mess Voting Criteria	16 May 75
*FO 3465	Flag Personnel Procurement Office Personnel Transfers, Postings	22 Apr 74
*FO 3466R	Flag Readiness Unit	20 May 74
*FO 3466R-1	Selection of New Recruits for the Flag Readiness Unit	19 May 74
*FO 3466R-2	Basic Policies on Operation of the Flag Readiness Unit	20 May 74
*FO 3466R-5	Handling Admin of the Flag Readiness Unit in the FPPO Office	20 May 74
*FO3466R-6	FPPO Emergency Float	20 May 74
*FO 3468	Flag Personnel Procurement Office Order	22 Apr 74
*FO 3473-6	Flag Collections Officer's Duties	3 Apr 75
*FO 3474-1RA	Flag Service Consultant & Flag Collections Officer Stats	27 Jun 74 Revised 13 Dec 74 Revised 1 Jan 75
*FO 3475	Flag Personnel Procurement Office Responsibility for Sea Org Recruitment and Its Relationship with the Central Personnel in External HCO	1 Jul 74
*FO 3481R	PAC Estates Org and Hotel Org	17 Sept 74
*FO 3481RA	PAC Estates Org and Hotel Org	17 Sept 74 Revised 7 Mar 75 Corr. 12 Mar 75
*FO 3482	The Flag Personnel Procurement Office and Financial Planning: Beans for Beans Return	11 Jul 74
FO 3485	Project Mission Operations	4 Aug 74
*FO 3486	PA Expeditor Unit	8 Aug 74
*FO 3489	CF–Addresso Task Forces	20 Aug 74
*FO 3506	Programs Executions Officers	9 Nov 74
*FO 3508	Definition of an Ops Officer	17 Nov 74

*FO 3513	Flag Personnel Committee	30 Nov 74
FO 3521	Deputy Staff Captain's Hat	21 Dec 74
*FO 3525	The "Restricted List," Use of	2 Jan 75
FO 3527	Mission Tech	8 Jan 75
*FO 3529	Non-Disclosure Bond	16 Jan 75
*FO 3531	HU Purchasing & Finance	22 Jan 75
*FO 3533	Finance Foolishness	20 Jan 75
*FO 3555	FPPO Reponsibility for SO Recruitment Cancelled	25 Apr 75
*FO 3557	Flag Literature Unit International Literature Unit Org Boards and Command Lines	30 Apr 75
*FO 3559-1	*Advance!* Series No. 9 Policy on *Advance!* Color Cover Work	26 May 75
*FO 3561	Feasting vs Fasting	13 May 75
*FO 3567R	Confidential	2 Jun 75 Revised 9 Jul 75
*FO 3568	Confidential	2 Jun 75
FO 3570	Color Printing Quality Control	6 Jun 75
*FO 3572	Promotion Quality Control	7 Jun 75
FO 3574	Dummies, Designs, Rough Layout and Shooting Board	9 Jun 75
*FO 3575	Machinery and Equipment Hatting Officer	9 Jun 75
*FO 3576RA	Flagship Estates Command Lines	10 Jun 75 Revised 20 Sept 75
*FO 3577	Tentative—Ideal Scene, Stat, VFP Literature Unit	12 Jun 75
*FO 3582	*Laissez Faire*	10 Jul 75
*FO 3587	Commanding Officer, CMO Hat Checksheet	24 Jul 75
*FO 3590	Office Manager (Deputy LRH Comm FSO)	26 Jul 75
*FO 3591	Establishment Bureau, Bureau I	28 Jul 75
*FO 3663	Flag Service Consultant Network (FSC NW) Expense Account	28 Jan 76
*FO 3666	Flag Service Consultant (FSC) Network Reorganization	28 Jan 76
*FO 3676	LRH Audio-Visio Branch, Purpose and Duties	27 Apr 76

Flag Orders of the Day

Flag OODs	LRH Command Items

Flag Personnel Orders

*FPO 1849R	"No Title"	21 Jul 75 Revised 18 Aug 75
*FPO 2041	Dept Two USB Comm	5 Jan 76
*FPO 2253	Promotion, New Aides Post	17 Mar 76

Flag Project Orders

*FPJO 359	Project Transfer LACM	8 Feb 72
*FPJO 717	New HAS Course	26 Nov 75

Flag Ship Orders

FSO 1	Crew Trainees	22 Oct 69
FSO 2	2nd Mate Training, Duties	23 Oct 69
*FSO 9RB	Noon Day Report Form	4 Feb 70
*FSO 10	Mimeo Statistics and Basic Functions	3 Feb 70
FSO 17	Vehicles	5 Mar 70
*FSO 20	Div III Org Board, Flagship	8 Mar 70
FSO 25	Bridge Watches	26 Mar 70
*FSO 30	Board of Schedules	8 Apr 70
FSO 31	Starrate Policy for Post and Machines	18 Apr 70
*FSO 39	New Recruits—The Buddy System	18 Apr 70
FSO 44R	Personnel Unit	17 May 70
FSO 52	Zones of FP	8 Jun 70
*FSO 65R	New Arrival's Orientation Checksheet	21 Jun 70 Revised 9 Apr 75
*FSO 72	Assignment of Buddies	4 Jul 70
*FSO 74	Zones of FP	6 Jul 70
*FSO 78	Checklists	20 Jul 70
*FSO 94	Div VIII Org Board, Flag Field Division	29 Jul 70
FSO 96	Admin Cycle	1 Aug 70
FSO 101	Ship Co-Audit	13 Aug 70
FSO 111	Ethics Section	3 Sept 70
FSO 113	The Ship as an Org	6 Sept 70
*FSO 117	Ship Org Board	8 Sept 70
*FSO 119	Leaving Post, Inspection & Award	15 Sept 70
FSO 123	Bureaux Reorg.	27 Sept 70
FSO 126	Finance Bureau	1 Oct 70
*FSO 127R	Daily Report Procedure	19 Sept 73
*FSO 131	Convening Authorities Comm Evs	7 Oct 70
FSO 135R	Triple Bonus System	25 Oct 70
*FSO 137	Flagship Public Lines	10 Oct 70 Reissued 20 Nov 73
*FSO 138	DOC Briefings	13 Oct 70
*FSO 156	The AB Conference	26 Oct 70
FSO 179R	Bonus Adjustment	5 Oct 70
*FSO 195RR	Auditing Bonus	8 Apr 71
*FSO 221	FEBC Hatting Drills	27 Jan 71

FSO 225	Flag Admin Org	3 Feb 71
FSO 231	Wherewithal	6 Feb 71
*FSO 249	Boats Unit	27 Feb 71
*FSO 252	Flagship Organization	26 Feb 71
*FSO 253	Hatting Files, Pilot Action	27 Feb 71
*FSO 263	HCO Messenger Comm Runs	6 Mar 71
*FSO 270	Steward WQ SB	9 Mar 71
*FSO 301	Flag Personnel Committee	3 Apr 71
FSO 308	Sea Org Member Hat	9 Apr 71
*FSO 327	Important	22 Apr 71
*FSO 354	Electrician's Weekly Checklist—Motors	18 May 71
*FSO 359R	Quad Bonus System	11 May 71 Revised 21 Feb 75
*FSO 359RA	Flag Bonus System	11 May 71
FSO 360	Dissemination Division FAO, How It Operates	27 May 71
*FSO 361	Staff Hatting College Re-Org	26 May 71
*FSO 365	Quad Bonus Policies	5 Jun 71
FSO 384	Line Stops	12 Jun 71 Revised 4 Apr 75
*FSO 388	Flag Training and Hatting Functions, Tech Div Training	29 Jun 71
*FSO 413	Sea Watch Specialist Training Programme Revival	4 Aug 71
*FSO 417	Flag HAS Committee	5 Aug 71
*FSO 437R	Organization of Flag FP Lines and Allocation	1 Sept 71
*FSO 443	TRC Finances	10 Sept 71
*FSO 457	Regulations Regarding the Use of Motor Cycles or Vehicles Ashore	25 Oct 71
*FSO 460	"Flag Training Specialist" Course (Supervisor Drills Checksheet)	17 Oct 71
FSO 480	Flag's Role	12 Dec 71
*FSO 486	Marine Radars	2 Jan 72
*FSO 507	Fire Safety Checklist	30 Jan 72
*FSO 509	Pinholers Equipment Safety Checklist	30 Jan 72
*FSO 518	Flag Complement	28 Feb 72
FSO 529	Esto Apprentice Training	18 Mar 72
FSO 534	Esto Study	21 Mar 72
*FSO 546	Sea Watch Training Con Responsibility	17 Apr 72
*FSO 551	Zones of FP Redefined	22 Apr 72
FSO 559	Deck Project Force	24 May 72
*FSO 562	Internal Distractions	8 Jun 72
*FSO 611	Central Personnel Office, Personnel Files	7 Oct 72
*FSO 615-1	CIC Clearance	7 Oct 72
*FSO 621-1	The "Credit Account"	31 Oct 72
*FSO 632-1	Mimeo Paper Shredder, Use of	16 Jul 74
*FSO 654	Shiphandling Series No. 1 Ship Readiness Prior to Voyaging	16 Mar 73

*FSO 666	Posh Officer Inspections	3 Apr 73
FSO 667RC	Flag Allocation of Income Defined and Corrected Giving FSO Bonuses	12 Mar 75
*FSO 681	PR & C Paper and Litho Supplies, Basic Stock	3 Jun 73
FSO 711R	HU Purchaser	22 Sept 73 Revision 10 Nov 73
*FSO 723	Vent Eval	23 Oct 73
*FSO 737	Programs Chiefs, Award and Penalties	15 Nov 73
*FSO 742	Ship Keeping, Div IV FSO Org Board	30 Nov 73
*FSO 743	Telephone on Board	27 Nov 73
*FSO 759	Apollo Engine Room Statistic Checklist	7 Jan 74
*FSO 767	Officers' Lounge	26 Feb 74
FSO 771	Financial Planning	7 Apr 74
*FSO 776	FSO VFPs	13 May 74
*FSO 779	The PE Lecture Course	29 Jun 74
*FSO 780	Pricing Formula, Flag Dissem and Mimeo Printed Products	29 Jun 74
*FSO 785	Ethics Actions, Line for	7 Aug 74
*FSO 788	Ethics, Policy and You	23 Aug 74
*FSO 812	Watch Functions, Condition II in Port	7 Dec 74
*FSO 820	FSO Bonuses	23 Feb 75
*FSO 820-1R	FB Bonus	9 Mar 75 Revised 1 May 75
*FSO 823	Flag Design and Planning Section	14 Mar 75
*FSO 833	FCCI Product Officer, Flag	16 May 75
*FSO 833-2	FCCI Org Officer, Flag	4 Oct 75
*FSO 836	LRH Pers Sec US Position, Duties and Functions	27 May 75

Founding Church Policy Letters

1 Apr 57	Technical and Administrative Divisions
8 Jun 57	Valuable Documents, Handling of
6 Oct 58	Who Can Be Processed Who Can Be Trained
9 Oct 58	"Effective October 20 . . ."
15 Nov 58	Confidential

Guardian Finance Orders, Guardian Personnel Orders

*GFO 192	Warning! Reg Bonuses	7 Aug 74
*GPO 1114	Appointment	1 Dec 75

Hubbard Association of Scientologists International, Policy Letters

9 Apr 57	Communication Centre
19 Apr 57	Minutes of Staff Meeting of April 18, 1957
19 Apr 57	Proportionate Pay Plan
21 Apr 57	Information Boards
30 Aug 57	"I have sent . . ."
8 Feb 58	"Since people will . . ."
22 Sept 58	ACC Accounts and Payments
30 Oct 58	Personnel Efficiency Foundation
10 Feb 59	Group Secretary

Hubbard Communications Office Admin Letters

30 Jul 75	Org Orientation Drill Definitions

Hubbard Communications Office Bulletins

3 Aug 56	Mail Line
26 Sept 56	Registrar
4 Oct 56	The Handling of Hubbard Communications Offices
14 Nov 56	Reorganization Washington Operation
28 Feb 57	Hats
6 Apr 57	Central Files and Procurement
11 Jun 57	Training and CCH Processes and Meaning, General Process
21 Jan 58	ACCs HPA/HCA
24 Jan 58	"The following is . . ."
27 Jan 58	Duties of Personnel Post
9 May 58	"The Director of Training . . ."
4 Jun 58	Running Valences
21 Sept 58	Theory of Scientology Organizations
25 Oct 58	Abbreviations
3 Nov 58	For Wide Publication
1 Dec 58	Actions to Start an HCO
16 Dec 58	Extension Course Curriculum
26 Dec 58	B Scn/HCS Course
6 Jan 59	Field Activities
24 Jan 59	Scientology Axiom 58
24 Feb 59	Letter Designations on HCO Bulletins
9 Jul 59	Definition of Scientology
12 Aug 59	A Second Type of Franchise
3 Sept 59	Why "Victim" Works as a Process
12 Sept 59	Programming
15 Sept 59	Dissemination Tips
23 Sept 59	The Perfect Dissemination Program
29 Sept 59	The Organization of a P.E. Foundation
15 Oct 59	Regarding Memberships
31 Dec 59	Blow-Offs
15 Mar 60	Disseminating Scientology
25 Apr 60	PrR Promotion
27 Apr 60	Security of Employment
13 May 60	Congress Seminar Hat
22 May 60	De-Certification How You Should Support It
10 Jun 60	What We Expect of a Scientologist
23 Jun 60	Special Zone Plan
18 Jul 60	Information on HASI Ltd. and HCO Ltd. Status
19 Dec 60	PE Change
5 Jun 61	Processes Allowed
19 Jun 61	Sec Check Whole Track
21 Sept 61	Security Check, Children HCO WW Security Form B
28 Sept 61	HCO WW Security Forms
17 Oct 61	Problems Intensives
7 Nov 62 Issue III	"Roll Your Own" Prehav
19 Aug 63	Scientology Two Starrated HCO Bulletin How to Do an ARC Break Assessment
2 Apr 65	All Scientology, The Road to Clear
11 May 65	Confidential

23 Aug 65	Abbreviations and Symbols of Dianetics and Scientology
30 Aug 65	Art
13 Sept 65	Out Tech and How to Get In
22 Sept 65	Release Gradation New Levels of Release
24 Nov 65	Search and Discovery
27 Sept 66	The Anti-Social Personality, The Anti-Scientologist
29 Sept 66	Library Record of Levels
22 Mar 67	Admin Know-How Alter-is and Degraded Beings
18 Apr 67	Religious Philosophy and Religious Practice
19 Aug 67	The Supreme Test
11 Oct 67	Clay Table Training
5 Dec 68	Unresolving Cases
22 Apr 69	Dianetics vs Scientology
22 Apr 69 Issue II	Somatics and OTs
23 Apr 69	Dianetics, Basic Definitions
14 May 69 Issue II	F/N and Erasure
15 Jan 70 Issue II	Handling with Auditing
30 May 70	Interiorization Intensive Two-Way Comm
14 Jul 70	Solo Cans
21 Aug 70	C/S Series No. 16 Session Grading Well Done, Definition of
28 Aug 70RA	HC Out-Point Plus-Point Lists
21 Sept 70	Study Series No. 1 Study Definitions
6 Oct 70	C/S Series No. 19 Folder Error Summary
28 Nov 70	C/S Series No. 22 Psychosis
28 Feb 71	C/S Series No. 24 Metering Reading Items
5 Mar 71	C/S Series No. 25 The Fantastic New HGC Line
23 May 71R Issue I	The Magic of the Communication Cycle
19 Jun 71 Issue II	C/S Series No. 46 Declares
19 Jun 71 Issue III	Study Definitions for the TR Course
19 Jul 71	C/S Series No. 52 Internes
2 Aug 71	TRs, Solo Course, and Advanced Courses
4 Aug 71R Revised 26 Nov 74	Post Purpose Clearing
8 Aug 71	C/S Series No. 55 The Ivory Tower
23 Aug 71 Revised 24 May 70	C/S Series No. 1 Auditors Rights
25 Aug 71	Auditor Admin Series No. 2 C/S Series No. 56 How to Get Results in an HGC
22 Sept 71	C/S Series No. 61 The Three Golden Rules of the C/S
8 Oct 71 Issue II	Solo C/S Series No. 5 The Scene
23 Oct 71 Issue I	Personnel Programming Series No. 2 Personnel Programming Rules
10 Nov 71 Revised 21 Sept 74	Word Clearing Series No. 25R Tape Course Series No. 6R Tapes, How to Use
20 Nov 71 Issue II	Course Translation to Tape
7 Jan 72	Training and Interning Staff Auditors
15 Apr 72 Revised 31 Mar 72	Expanded Dianetics Series No. 1R
17 Apr 72	C/S Series No. 76 C/Sing a PTS Rundown
20 Apr 72	Expanded Dianetics Series No. 4 Suppressed PCs and PTS Tech
10 May 72	Robotism
21 Jun 72 Issue II	Word Clearing Series No. 39 Method 6
15 Nov 72 Issue II	Students Who Succeed
5 Apr 73 Reissued 19 Sept 74	Axiom 28 Amended
23 Nov 73R Revised 23 Apr 75	Dry and Wet Hands Make False TA
5 Dec 73	The Reason for Q & A
15 Feb 74	Expanded Dianetics Series No. 20 Service Facsimile Theory and Expanded Dianetics
23 Apr 74R	Expanded Dianetics Series No. 22R Expanded Dianetics Requisites
25 Apr 74	Art Series No. 4 Rhythm
20 Dec 75	Confidential

Hubbard Communications Office Information Letters

14 Apr 61 PE Handout

Hubbard Communications Office Policy Letters

25 Jan 57 Concerning the Separateness of Dianetics and Scientology

8 Apr 57 Advisory Committee

9 Apr 57 Bulletin Board

2 May 57 Dissemination

12 Sept 58 Color Flash System

5 Oct 58 Department Heads and Executives —Personnel—How to Fill Jobs

24 Oct 58 *Certainty* Magazine

24 Oct 58 *Understanding* Magazine

24 Oct 58 *Ability* Magazine

17 Nov 58 Project Engineers, Three Types

17 Nov 58 Project Engineering

20 Nov 58 New HCO International Appointments

24 Nov 58 HASI Group Secretary

25 Nov 58 HCO Board of Review Function and Practice

13 Dec 58 Important Information on Policy Letters

20 Dec 58 HCO Communicator Basic Hat and Comm System HCO Offices

2 Jan 59 HCO Office Designations and Personnel

13 Jan 59 HCO Area Secretary Material

29 Jan 59 HCO Communicator Hat

30 Jan 59 HCO Continental Secretary Hat

6 Feb 59 HCO Accounts World Wide

12 Feb 59 Book Administrator

25 Feb 59 HCO Master File

27 Feb 59 Duty of Area Sec Re Personnel

28 Feb 59 HCO Board of Review Duties

2 Mar 59 HCO Cable and Dispatch Designation System

2 Mar 59 Reissued 23 Jun 64 HCO Theory of Communication

10 Mar 59 B.Scn/HCS Course Tapes

26 Mar 59 Dissemination Secretary Hat

12 May 59 Pattern of Organization, Melbourne

14 May 59 HCO Administrator

14 May 59 Hubbard Communications Office

22 May 59 Policy Letter and Distribution Code

26 May 59 What an Executive Wants on His Lines

28 May 59 Promotional Writing Fund

28 May 59 New HCO WW Dept

3 Jun 59 Financial Management

4 Jun 59 Definition of a Hot File

9 Jun 59 HCO Special Fund

15 Jun 59 Hat Write-Up, PAB Liaison

26 Jun 59 Important—HCO WW Changes Quarters and Address

27 Jun 59 H.A.S.I. Ltd.

2 Jul 59 Staff Auditing Requirement

2 Jul 59 Issue II Developed Traffic—The Delirium Tremens of Central Orgs

2 Jul 59 Issue III Scientology Magazines

* 5 Aug 59 HCO Vol. Sec. Material

*10 Aug 59 Administration in a Scientology Organization

12 Aug 59 A Second Type of Franchise

19 Aug 59 Writing of Letters by Staff Auditors

22 Aug 59 HCO WW Projects

24 Aug 59 HCO Financial Arrangements Altered

26 Aug 59 Promotional Functions of Various Depts

28 Aug 59 HCO WW Mail Economy and Methods

4 Sept 59 Completed Staff Work (CSW) How to Get Approval of Actions and Projects

15 Sept 59 Hats and Other Folders

25 Sept 59 Accounting Records and Bills

14 Oct 59 Division of HCO Percentages Revised

14 Oct 59 Comm Speed

20 Oct 59 HCO Area Secretary Material

26 Oct 59	Memberships
27 Oct 59	HCO WW Appointments
30 Oct 59	HCO WW Steno's Hat
27 Nov 59	Key to the Organizational Chart of the Founding Church of Scientology of Washington, D.C.
27 Jan 60	Accounts Policies
*24 Feb 60	ACC Hats
29 Feb 60	Organization Secretary Hat
*15 Mar 60	Hat Co-ordination: Dissemination of Dianetics and Scientology Materials
30 Jun 60	Administrative Traffic Trend
20 Jul 60	Director of Zoning Hat
4 Aug 60	ACC at Saint Hill
11 Aug 60	Organization Information Center
15 Aug 60	Dept. of Govt. Affairs
22 Aug 60	Dept. of Govt. Relations
30 Aug 60	Training Restrictions
*14 Oct 60	Book Department Procedure
22 Oct 60	The Three Service Branches
28 Oct 60	New Testing Promotion Section Important
28 Oct 60	HASI-HCO Relationship Discussed
15 Nov 60	Modern Procurement Letters
29 Nov 60	Testing Programme Change
16 Jan 61	Help Me Put in the New Lines
23 Jan 61	PE Course Abolished
24 Jan 61	A Test Policy on MD Referrals
30 Jan 61	Case Files
31 Jan 61	Academy Meters
31 Jan 61	Message Placement
31 Jan 61	Spheres of Influence
4 Feb 61	Types of Letters Established
12 Feb 61	Certificates and Awards Revised List
14 Feb 61	The Pattern of a Central Organization
14 Feb 61 OEC Volume 6 p. 192	The Personal Efficiency Foundation
15 Feb 61	Evaluation Script
17 Feb 61	HCO Continental
17 Feb 61	Staff Post Qualifications Permanent Executives to be Approved
17 Feb 61 Issue II	State of Emergency
21 Feb 61	Pattern for City Offices
23 Feb 61	Directives from a Board Member
26 Feb 61	Qualification of Executives
2 Mar 61	Automatic Evaluation Packet for P.E. Foundation
* 4 Mar 61	Department Head Report Forms
12 Mar 61 Issue III	Duties of the Assn. Sec.'s Sec. in a Central Organization
13 Mar 61	Department of Official Affairs
13 Mar 61 Issue II	Department of Official Affairs
20 Mar 61 Issue II	Basic Staff Auditor's Hat
24 Mar 61 Issue II	HGC Admin Partial Hat Staff Auditor Assignment
25 Mar 61	Security Rules
31 Mar 61	The Director of Processing's Case Checking
5 Apr 61	HCA/HPA Rundown or Practical Course Rundown for Academies
7 Apr 61RA Revised 30 May 75	Johannesburg Confessional List—Revised
25 Apr 61	D of P Form Check Type One
28 Apr 61 Issue II	Central Organization Minimum Staff
29 May 61	Quality and Admin in Central Orgs
4 Jun 61	Refund of Fee Policy
9 Jun 61	Technical Hat Checking Vital Policy for HCO Area Sec
20 Jun 61	Purchase Order System
29 Jun 61	Student Security Check
6 Jul 61	Accounts
7 Jul 61 Issue II	Processing Security Check
3 Sept 61	HCO Vol. Sec Policy Revised
12 Sept 61	Curriculum for Clearing Courses
29 Sept 61	HGC Allowed Processes
9 Oct 61	Academy Training
16 Oct 61	Income Records
20 Oct 61	Non-Scientology Staff
23 Oct 61	HGC Pre-Processing Security Check
27 Oct 61	Professional Rates Restored
*31 Oct 61	Changes in OIC Data
1 Nov 61	HCO WW Security Form 5A
*22 Nov 61	Training Course Rules and Regulations
23 Nov 61	Accounts

6 Dec 61	Saint Hill Training Candidates from Organizations
11 Dec 61RA Revised 1 Apr 73	Organization Rudiments
18 Dec 61	Standing Orders
6 Jan 62	HCO Security Form 19 Laudatory Withholds
10 Jan 62 Reissued 21 Jun 67	HCO Standing Order No. 5 Students
12 Jan 62	Comments on Letter Reg Department
17 Jan 62 Reissued 7 Jun 67	Responsibility Again
30 Jan 62	Technical Director and Administrator
5 Feb 62	Appointments and Transfers
15 Feb 62	Appointment
27 Feb 62	Clean Hands Clearance Check
6 Apr 62	Technical Director Basic Hat
16 Apr 62	Comments on Letter Registrar Department
14 May 62	Training Sections
14 May 62 Issue II	Training
15 May 62	CCH's Rewritten
21 May 62	Training Classes of Auditors
24 May 62	Training Session Cancellation Auditing Section
29 May 62	Professional Rates
1 Jun 62	Auditing Rudiments Checksheet
7 Jun 62	Professional Training to Be Done in Academy and Saint Hill Only
21 Jun 62	Staff Members Auditing Private PCs
* 4 Jul 62	Mixing Scientology with Various Other Practices
9 Jul 62	Special Briefing Course
14 Jul 62	Urgent—Auditing Allowed
17 Jul 62	Routine 3GA, HCO WW R-3GA Form 1 Listing Prepcheck
22 Jul 62	Routine 3-GA Listing Wording
24 Jul 62	R3-GA, HCO WW Form G3 Fast Goals Check
16 Aug 62	HCO Electronic Consultant Hat
10 Sept 62	Staff Clearing Program
*13 Sept 62	Certificate Application Form
13 Sept 62	Comments About Letter Registrars
17 Sept 62	An Arrangement of the Academy
*19 Sept 62	HCO WW Form AC 1
20 Sept 62	Co-Audit Unit
*26 Sept 62	Hubbard Scientology Research Foundation
12 Oct 62	Reissue Series No. 1 Basic Purposes of a Scientology Organization
16 Oct 62	Auditing Hours Limited
21 Oct 62	Auditing Supervisor and Auditing Instructors, Duties of
22 Oct 62	Reissue Series No. 2 Theory of Scientology Organizations
29 Oct 62	Religion
30 Oct 62	Reissue Series No. 3 Executives of Scientology Organizations
8 Nov 62	Departure Form
21 Nov 62	Reissue Series No. 6 Completed Staff Work (CSW)
24 Nov 62	Urgent—Objective One
5 Dec 62	Administrator's Hat
8 Dec 62	Training—Saint Hill Special Briefing Course—Summary of Subjects by Units
*11 Dec 62	OIC Reports to HCO WW
*11 Dec 62	Change in Report Line
13 Dec 62	Reissue Series No. 7 Scientology Organizations Communications System: Dispatches
20 Dec 62	Reissue Series No. 8 The Pattern of a Central Organization
1 Jan 63	Objective Three—Celebrities
4 Jan 63	Pattern of District Office
11 Feb 63	Auditing Regulations
13 Feb 63	V—Unit
14 Feb 63	The Establishment of Central Orgs Control Areas
*20 Feb 63	The Evolution of a District Office: Two Methods
6 Mar 63	R3M, HCO WW Form G3 Revised Fast Goals Check
4 Apr 63	District Offices Technical Reports to HCO WW
10 Apr 63	Reissue Series No. 12 What an Executive Wants on His Lines
11 Apr 63	Important—Emergency Library
11 Apr 63	Goals Finding and Goal Finders
13 Apr 63	Policy of HGCs

*16 Apr 63	Revision of Congress Payments to HCO WW
9 May 63	International Council
15 May 63	Instructor Hats
29 May 63	Reissue Series No. 14 How to Handle Work
17 Jun 63	Staff Clearing Program
2 Aug 63	Urgent—Public Project One
* 8 Aug 63	"Plants" in Academies— Introduction of "Form" 5B
12 Aug 63	Certificates and Awards
14 Aug 63	Scientology Five Press Policies
21 Aug 63	Change of Organization Targets, Project 80, A Preview
7 Sept 63	Important—Scientology Five, Justice, Committees of Evidence, Scientology Jurisprudence, Administration of
4 Oct 63	Technical Council
26 Nov 63	Certificates and Classification Changes, Everyone Classified
11 Dec 63	Urgent—Classification for Everyone
27 Dec 63 Reissued 21 Apr 70	The "Magic" of Good Management
31 Dec 63	Saint Hill Reorganization
7 Jan 64 Reissued 21 Apr 70	Gradient Scale of Personnel Procurement
14 Jan 64	Future Continental Officer Status
24 Jan 64	HCO (St. Hill) Ltd. Course Staff Transfers
24 Jan 64	Scientology Library and Research Ltd.
25 Jan 64	HCO (StHil) Ltd. Department of Enrollment
26 Jan 64	HCO (WW) Ltd. Central Org Activities
29 Jan 64	HCO (StHil) Ltd. Charts, Routings and Publications— The Enrollment Department
31 Jan 64	Corporation Co-ordinator
5 Feb 64	Founding Scientologist Certificate
9 Feb 64	Comm Baskets
15 Feb 64	The Equipment of Organizations
21 Feb 64	Department of Enrolment
24 Feb 64	Urgent—Org Programming
7 Mar 64	Director of Enrollment The Letter Registrar Administration
11 Mar 64	Auditors Division New HCO WW Organization
11 Mar 64	Departmental Changes Auditor Division
*20 Mar 64	District Office & Org Control Area Policy Revised
31 Mar 64	Scientology Organizations Communications System: Dispatches
1 Apr 64	Saint Hill Personnel
1 Apr 64	New Mimeo Line HCO Executive Letter
2 Apr 64	To the Saint Hill Student: Instruction Targets
*22 Apr 64	Summary of Policies on Classification and Gradation, Certification, Franchise and Memberships, and the Auditors Division
5 May 64	Summary of Classification and Gradation and Certification
6 May 64	Accounts Policies
14 May 64	HCO Continental Change
28 May 64	Reorganization
11 June 64	New Students Data Starrated for New Students
16 Jun 64	Personnel Records Admin Certs.
18 Jun 64	New Posts
22 Jun 64	Reissue Series No. 19 Organization Posts—Two Types
26 Jun 64	Staff Bonuses
2 Jul 64	Bulletin & Policy Letter Distribution
21 Aug 64 Reissued 7 Jun 67	Staff Auditors
26 Aug 64	PE Course
9 Sept 64	Putting New Personnel on the Job and Taking Over When People Quit or Are Transferred
9 Sept 64	Purpose of Adcomm
23 Sept 64	Policies: Dissemination and Programmes
24 Sept 64	Instruction & Examination: Raising the Standard of
30 Sept 64	HCO Corporations
4 Oct 64 Reissued 21 May 67	Theory Checkout Data
8 Oct 64	Artistic Presentation
19 Oct 64	Pricing Formulas
27 Oct 64 Reissued 23 Jun 67	"Policies on Physical Healing, Insanity and Potential Trouble Sources"

30 Oct 64	Mailing Lists for Franchise Holders
31 Oct 64 Issue II	Current Policies, Orgs & Franchise HQS Course Permission
6 Nov 64	Corporate Status
6 Nov 64 Issue II	Urgent—Corporate Structures Western Hemisphere
13 Nov 64	Provisional Class VI Classification
17 Nov 64	Offline and Off Policy Your Full In Basket
30 Nov 64	HCO Book Account
3 Dec 64	Pricing Meetings, Final Policy
11 Dec 64	Full Table of Courses and Classification; Classification Correction
18 Dec 64	Reissue Series No. 21 Administrative Traffic Trend
18 Dec 64	Saint Hill Org Board
23 Dec 64	Field and Public Programming
30 Dec 64	Arrangements During Absence of Exec Dir & Org Sec
31 Dec 64	Use of Dianetics, Scientology, Applied Philosophy
2 Jan 65	Franchise: Who May Have It and How to Maintain It, AD15
18 Jan 65	Financial Management Building Fund Account
20 Jan 65	Finance Currency Regulations and 10%s
21 Jan 65 Revised 5 Apr 65	Vital Data on Promotion
28 Jan 65	Accounts Hats Finance, How to Maintain Credit Standing & Solvency
31 Jan 65	Dev-T
7 Feb 65 Reissued 15 Jun 70	All Levels Keeping Scientology Working
10 Feb 65	Ad and Book Policies
13 Feb 65	Politics
14 Feb 65 Reissued 7 Jun 67	Safeguarding Technology
20 Feb 65	Appointments and Programmes
22 Feb 65 Issue II	HCO Area Secretary, Saint Hill
22 Feb 65 Issue III	Executive Director Comm Lines, Sec EDs
27 Feb 65	Course Pattern
28 Feb 65	Course Checkouts, Twin-Checking
28 Feb 65	Deliver
4 Mar 65	Reserved Payment Account
4 Mar 65	Hat Material, Division I, HCO Secretary WW
4 Mar 65 Issue II	Hat Material, Division I (HCO) Technical and Policy Distribution
5 Mar 65	HCO (Division I) Certificates and Awards New Status of Honorary Awards
5 Mar 65 Issue II	Policy: Source of
6 Mar 65	HCO (Division I) Justice Amnesty Policy
7 Mar 65 Issue III	HCO (Division I) Justices, Offenses and Penalties
9 Mar 65	Purpose of SO No. 1 Line
13 Mar 65	Admin Technology The Comm Member System
13 Mar 65	Divisions, I, II, III The Structure of Organization What Is Policy?
13 Mar 65 Issue II	The Comm-Member System Routing Policies Section
15 Mar 65 Issue I	Registrars, CF and Address
*15 Mar 65 Issue II	Only Accounts Talks Money
17 Mar 65 Issue II	HCO (Division I), Justice Staff Hat Rights of a Staff Member; Students and Preclears to Justice
17 Mar 65 Issue II	HCO (Division I) Justice Fair Game Law, Organizational Suppressive Act, The Source of the Fair Game Law
17 Mar 65 Issue III	HCO (Division I), Justice Hat Administering Justice
22 Mar 65	Saint Hill Services, Prices and Discounts
22 Mar 65	Current Promotion and Org Program Summary Membership Rundown International Annual Membership
26 Mar 65 Revised 30 Mar 65	Field Auditors Become Staff
27 Mar 65	The Justice of Scientology Its Use and Purpose Being a Scientologist
29 Mar 65 Issue II	Administration Flows and Expansion, The Fast Flow System
31 Mar 65	Justice Policy Letters Corrections
1 Apr 65	HCO Communicator has Programme Checking Hat
2 Apr 65	Heed Heavy Traffic Warnings

2 Apr 65	Urgent Urgent Urgent False Reports
2 Apr 65	Meter Checks
2 Apr 65 Issue III	Starrate Checkouts for Process
5 Apr 65	Justice Data Re Academy & HGC Handling the Suppressive Person, The Basis of Insanity
5 Apr 65 Issue II	Academies, Relation to HCO Justice Student Training The No-Gain-Case Student
6 Apr 65	HCO Div II—Dept of Prom-Reg Letter Reg Hat
7 Apr 65	Qualifications Sec HCO Dissem Sec, Book Auditor
7 Apr 65 Issue II	Healing Policy in Field
7 Apr 65 Issue IV	Book Income
8 Apr 65	Cancellation of Mail Lists To Field Auditors
9 Apr 65	Urgent—Correction to Policy Letters on Certification and Awards
10 Apr 65	Dismissals, Transfers and Demotions
14 Apr 65 Issue III	Organization "To LRH Daily Reports"
16 Apr 65	The "Hidden Data Line"
16 Apr 65 Issue II	Drills Allowed
16 Apr 65RA Issue III Second Revision 15 Dec 72	All Divisions The Fundamental
18 Apr 65	Prices Lowered Because of New Organization Streamline
21 Apr 65	Basic Certificate Uncertified Personnel
22 Apr 65	Level Zero Comm Course
22 Apr 65	Office of LRH, Design and Planning, All Promotion Productions in an Org All Mailing Activities in an Org Booklets, Handouts, Mailing Pieces
23 Apr 65	Problems
24 Apr 65	Review
27 Apr 65	Book Promotion Design
27 Apr 65 Issue II	Price Engram
29 Apr 65 Issue II	Petition
29 Apr 65 Issue III	Ethics Review
30 Apr 65	Emergency, State of
1 May 65	Staff Member Reports
1 May 65 Issue II	Order Board and Time Machine
1 May 65 Issue III	Organization The Design of the Organization
4 May 65	Release Award Saint Hill
5 May 65 Reissued 4 Jul 70	Classification, Gradation and Awareness Chart
5 May 65 Issue II	Supervisors
7 May 65	Cancellation Mimeo Distribution Changes
8 May 65 Issue II	Flash Colours and Designations
9 May 65 Revised & Reissued 14 Jan 68	Field Auditors Become Staff
9 May 65	Auditing Fees Preferential Treatment of Preclears Scale of Preference
11 May 65	HCO Book Account Policy Receipt and Use of Membership Monies
11 May 65	Ethics Officer Hat
16 May 65 Issue II	Indicators of Orgs
16 May 65 Issue III	Tech Division Academy Courses General Remarks Zero Courses Hubbard Recognized Scientologist
17 May 65	Tech Div, Qual Div—Urgent CCHs
17 May 65	Technical Division, Distribution Division—Free Scientology Centre
17 May 65 Issue II	Technical Division Academy Processing
23 May 65 Issue II	Rebates
24 May 65	HCO Special Briefing Course Student Guide to Acceptable Behavior
26 May 65 Issue III	Ethics Court of Ethics
27 May 65	Processing
31 May 65	Franchise Summary of Policy
2 Jun 65	Writing of an Ethics Order
7 Jun 65	Entheta Letters and the Dead File, Handling of, Definitions
7 Jun 65	New Org Board Design
11 Jun 65	The Foundation
12 Jun 65	The Foundation
14 Jun 65	"There are six power processes . . ."

17 Jun 65	Staff Auditor Advices
18 Jun 65 Issue II	Areas of Operation
26 Jun 65	HGC Preclear Review Auditing Form
1 Jul 65	Ethics Chits
1 Jul 65 Issue II	Comm Cycle Additives
1 Jul 65 Issue III	Hats, The Reason For
4 Jul 65	PC Routing Review Code
7 Jul 65	Photo News and Statistics For Mags and Auditor
10 Jul 65	Lines and Terminals Routing
12 Jul 65	Release Policies, Starting the PC
16 Jul 65	Continental Magazine to Model After *Certainty*
19 Jul 65	Separation Order
19 Jul 65	Discounts, Central Orgs, Books
31 Jul 65	Purposes of the Qualifications Division
2 Aug 65	Executive Division
2 Aug 65 Issue II	Chaplain
5 Aug 65	Release Checkouts
12 Aug 65	Council and ADcomms
16 Aug 65 Issue II	Collection From SPs and PTSs
20 Aug 65	Appointment of the Xerox Officer
20 Aug 65	Scientology Org Uniforms Saint Hill
23 Aug 65 Issue II	Crediting of Auditor in Release Log Book
26 Aug 65	Scientology Training Twin Checkouts
26 Aug 65R Revised 21 Sept 74	Ethics E-Meter Check
1 Sept 65 Issue III	Mailing List Policies
1 Sept 65 Issue IV	Some Tech Div Policies Legal Aspects of Sign-Ups
1 Sept 65 Issue VII	Ethics Protection
4 Sept 65	Inspection Officer
8 Sept 65	Supply Officer
13 Sept 65 Issue II	Issue Authority Required for Mimeo
17 Sept 65	Executive Letter Unit
21 Sept 65 Issue II	Auditor Estimation Test
21 Sept 65 Issue VI	Purposes of the Department of Registration
23 Sept 65	Keeping Stats Up
30 Sept 65	Statistics for Divisions
12 Oct 65	Advisory Committee
14 Oct 65	College of Scientology
14 Oct 65	Course Pattern
15 Oct 65	Field Staff Member Selection Papers and Commissions
23 Oct 65	Dissemination Drill
25 Oct 65	Saint Hill Solo Audit Course
27 Oct 65	Grade Award Insignia
3 Nov 65	Equipment
7 Nov 65	Reception Log In-The-Org List
10 Nov 65	The Cramming Section
15 Nov 65	Reporting of Theft and Action to Be Taken
18 Nov 65	Appointment of Personnel
20 Nov 65	The Promotional Actions of an Organization
20 Nov 65R Revised & Updated 15 Apr 73	The Promotional Actions of an Organization
20 Nov 65 Issue II	Org Rudiments Section
26 Nov 65R Revised 19 Apr 73	Financial Planning
7 Dec 65	Tape Colour Flash Code
8 Dec 65	Distribute: To Spread Out So As to Cover Something
15 Dec 65	Ethics Chit
16 Dec 65	Organization of the Int Exec Division Statistic of the International Executive Division
21 Dec 65	LRH Financial Relationships to Orgs
23 Dec 65	Suppressive Acts; Suppression of Scientology and Scientologists The Fair Game Law
27 Dec 65	LRH Communicator
30 Dec 65	PTS Auditing and Routing
4 Jan 66 Issue II	HCO Cable Designation System
4 Jan 66 Issue III	Scientology Organizations Communications System: Dispatches
4 Jan 66 Issue V	Personnel Staff Status
4 Jan 66 Issue VI	LRH Relationship to Orgs
11 Jan 66	Adcouncil and Adcomms Orders; Issue of

12 Jan 66	Selectees Mailing
14 Jan 66 Issue II	Hiring Personnel, Line for
15 Jan 66	Hold the Form of the Org; Don't Bring About Danger Conditions
15 Jan 66 Issue II	Office of the Treasurer
16 Jan 66	Danger Condition
17 Jan 66 Issue II	Division I, HCO Division Organization Chart
19 Jan 66 Issue II	LRH Communicator Orders
19 Jan 66 Issue III	Danger Condition Responsibilities of Declaring
20 Jan 66 Issue II	Division VII International Executive Division
21 Jan 66	Executive Division
23 Jan 66	Accounting Policies of Scientology Companies
25 Jan 66	Additions to HCO Policy Letter of 17 Jan 1966; Dept 1, Dept 2, Dept 3 Additions
25 Jan 66 Issue II	Communication Inspector Hat
25 Jan 66 Issue III	Distribution of Mimeo Issues
26 Jan 66	Int Exec Div Relation to Saint Hill Org
30 Jan 66	LRH Communicator Area Reports to WW
30 Jan 66 Issue II	Minimum Personnel of an Org
30 Jan 66 Issue III	Accounts Procedures
30 Jan 66 Issue IV	Accounting: Cheque Signers Cheque Signing Procedure
31 Jan 66	Compilations Section Department 21, Office of LRH
1 Feb 66 Issue III	HGC Cure Interne Training and Staff Auditors
1 Feb 66 Issue IV	Statistics, Actions to Take, Statistic Changes
3 Feb 66	Legal Tax, Accountant and Solicitor Mail and Legal Officer
3 Feb 66 Issue V	Sec EDs Definition and Purpose Cross Divisional Orders
6 Feb 66 Reissued 12 Dec 74	How to Increase and Expand an Organization
10 Feb 66 Issue II	Tech Recovery
13 Feb 66	Personnel Control Officer
13 Feb 66 Issue II	Sec EDs, Sec ED OK (Continued) Policy Letter Changes and Origins
14 Feb 66	Doctor Title Abolished
16 Feb 66	Invoice Routing for All Orgs Except Saint Hill
18 Feb 66	Attacks on Scientology
24 Feb 66	Mail Statistic Dir Comm's Function
25 Feb 66	Communications Functions
28 Feb 66	Danger Condition Data Why Organizations Stay Small
1 Mar 66	The Guardian
1 Mar 66 Issue II	Executive Division Organization and Its Theory and Purpose
3 Mar 66 Issue II	OIC Report Form
6 Mar 66	Rewards and Penalties How to Handle Personnel and Ethics Matters
6 Mar 66 Issue II	Statistic Graphs How to Figure the Scale
8 Mar 66	High Crime
13 Mar 66	Orders, Precedence of Personnel, Titles of
17 Mar 66	LRH Comm Log
30 Mar 66	The Three Basket System
29 Apr 66	Policy Checkouts and E-Meter
3 May 66	Reserve Fund
7 May 66	LRH Communicator, Issue Authority of
4 Jun 66	Board of Investigation
1 Jul 66	Information Concerning the WW Time Machine
17 Jul 66	Despatches, Speed Up Despatches, Stale Date Internal Despatches
20 Jul 66 Amended 19 Mar 68	Staff Status
21 Jul 66	Proportional Pay Plan 1966
5 Aug 66 Issue II	Chaplain's Court, Civil Hearings
8 Aug 66	OT Colour Flash Colour Flash Addition
9 Aug 66	Use of Telex Machine
11 Aug 66	Lamps and Security
12 Aug 66 Issue II	The Operating Thetan Course
15 Aug 66	Information Packets
1 Sept 66R Revised 8 May 73	Founder

27 Sept 66	OIC Report Form
13 Oct 66	Invoice Routing
20 Oct 66 Issue II	Administrative Know-How Executive and Governing Body Errors and Answers
21 Oct 66	Important—Six Department System
21 Oct 66 Issue II	City Office System
21 Oct 66 Issue III	City Office
31 Oct 66 Issue I	Administrative Know-How No. 2 Actions, Executive, for Handling Disastrous Occurrences
31 Oct 66 Issue II Amended & Reissued 5 Mar 68	Administrative Know-How General for All Staff Job Endangerment Chit
31 Oct 66 Issue II	Board of Investigation
1 Nov 66 Issue I	World Wide Organization
1 Nov 66 Issue II	Advisory Council
2 Nov 66	Ad Council Appointments
3 Nov 66	Administrative Know-How Leadership
6 Nov 66 Issue I	Admin Know-How Statistic Interpretative Statistic Analysis
6 Nov 66 Issue II	Statistic Interpretation Estate Statistic
7 Nov 66	Clear Checkouts in Continental Orgs
10 Nov 66	Admin Know-How Good vs Bad Management
10 Nov 66 Issue II	OT Personnel
*11 Nov 66	Staff Responsibility for the Organization as a Whole
16 Nov 66	Admin Know-How Executive Facilities Facility Differential
17 Nov 66	Admin Know-How Intervention
4 Dec 66	Admin Know-How Expansion Theory of Policy
7 Dec 66	Important Magazines Permitted All Orgs
*12 Dec 66	New Org Board Design (2)
16 Dec 66	Clearing Course Regulation
21 Dec 66 Issue I	Advisory Council
21 Dec 66 Issue II	Executive Council
24 Dec 66	Admin Know-How How to Programme an Org Saint Hill Programmes
24 Dec 66 Issue II	Admin Know-How How to Program an Org Corrections and Addition Sequence of Programmes Correction
26 Dec 66	Admin Know-How PTS Sections, Personnel and Execs
27 Jan 67	Clearing and OT Course Reorganization Clearing Course
12 Feb 67	Admin Know-How The Responsibility of Leaders
*15 Feb 67	Allocation of Income
22 Feb 67	Office of LRH LRH Personal Office Organization
22 Feb 67	LRH Property, Building and Plans Branch
22 Mar 67	Urgent and Important Personnel Requirement
25 Jun 67	Scientology Orgs Tax and Balance Sheets
24 Jul 67	Fixed Public Consumption of Product
11 Aug 67 Issue II	Organization, Definition of
11 Aug 67 Issue III	OT Central Committee
6 Sept 67	WW Division Reorganization
8 Sept 67 Issue II	Continental Liaison Officers at WW
13 Sept 67	Clear Checkouts
15 Sept 67	The Supervisor's Code
15 Sept 67 Issue II	Examiner Bonuses
18 Sept 67	Study Complexity and Confronting
21 Sept 67	World Wide and Saint Hill Functions Redefined
21 Sept 67 Amended & Reissued 23 Oct 67 Amended & Reissued 5 Jun 69	International Officers at WW Alert Council
22 Sept 67	Non Existence Formula
23 Sept 67	New Post Formula The Conditions Formulas
26 Sept 67	Urgent—Guardian and LRH Comm Division of Duties
6 Oct 67	Condition of Liability
12 Oct 67	Operational, Definition of
16 Oct 67	Admin Know-How No. 16 Suppressives and the Administrator

	How to Detect SPs as an Administrator
18 Oct 67 Issue II	WW—How to Comm to WW Continental Liaison Officers
18 Oct 67 Issue IV	Penalties for Lower Conditions
18 Oct 67 Issue V	Conditions on Orgs or Divisions or Depts, Clarification
19 Oct 67	WW 7 Divisions
19 Oct 67 Issue I	Urgent and Important No. 2 in Exec Sec Hats Folders HCO Exec Sec Duties Org Exec Sec Duties
20 Oct 67	Admin Know-How Conditions, How to Assign
23 Oct 67	Enemy Formula
26 Oct 67	The Public Divisions
* 2 Nov 67	HCO Division, Department of Communications
* 2 Nov 67	Qualifications Division, Departments of Examinations, Review and Certifications and Awards
* 2 Nov 67	Distribution Division, Departments of Public Information, Clearing and Success
*12 Nov 67	Clearing and OT Course Regulations
28 Dec 67	Qual Senior Datum
5 Jan 68	Ethics, Dev-T, Policy Letter No. 2 in Every Hat Conditions Orders, Executive Ethics
*10 Jan 68	Clearing Course and OT Course Materials
16 Jan 68	Starting of Preclears
28 Jan 68	OT WW Liaison Unit OT Cen Comm
6 Feb 68	Organization—The Flaw
8 Feb 68	Admin Know-How No. 18 Statistic Rationalization
19 Feb 68	Stats Dissem
22 Feb 68	Ethics and Admin Slow Admin
14 Mar 68	"The following is the corrected table of Conditions. . . ."
24 Apr 68 Issue I	"Exec Council World Wide must . . ."
*24 Apr 68 Issue II	Division VI, Distribution
4 May 68	Handling Situations
7 May 68	Urgent—The Key Question
9 May 68	Sea Organization Personnel
10 May 68	LRH Comms Functions
22 May 68 Issue I	Hiring Personnel, Line for
23 May 68	Important Purchasing from Pubs Org WW
23 May 68	WW and SH Recombined (Deadline 15 June '68)
*31 May 68	LRH Comm Log
5 Jun 68	Stats Dissem
5 Jun 68	Weekly Book Stock Report Required
5 Jun 68 Issue III	FSM Commissions
18 Jun 68	Ethics
20 Jun 68	Ethics Officers
29 Jun 68	Enrollment in Suppresive Groups
2 Jul 68 Issue II	Office of LRH WW Reorganization
2 Sept 68	Chaplain
* 2 Sept 68 Issue II	World Addresso Co-ordination
15 Sept 68	Sea Org
*30 Sept 68	Executives Training and Case Level
4 Oct 68	Ethics Presence
13 Oct 68	Examiner
16 Oct 68	"The formula . . ."
24 Oct 68	Supervisor Know-How Running the Class
25 Oct 68	Important, Admin Know-How
26 Oct 68	Executive Council
9 Nov 68	Important—Standard Admin
18 Nov 68	Guardian's Orders
21 Nov 68 Issue II	Photo Policy for Magazines
25 Nov 68	Saint Hill Income Peaks Reinforcement of Auditor Promotion
*27 Nov 68	The Standard Auditor Journal
*29 Nov 68	Enrollment Cycle
2 Dec 68	Gung-Ho Groups
3 Dec 68	Gung-Ho Groups Policy Letter No. 2
6 Dec 68	Qualifications Check 7A
8 Dec 68	Assistant Guardian for Finance
10 Dec 68	Percentage Adjustments and Fixed Salaries
26 Dec 68	The Third Party Law
30 Dec 68	The Public Programmes Officer
13 Jan 69	Unusual Favours
*13 Jan 69	Standard Examinations
14 Jan 69	OT Orgs

16 Jan 69	Targets, Types of
18 Jan 69 Issue II	Planning and Targets
21 Jan 69	Controller
23 Jan 69	OT Orgs Correction
24 Jan 69	Target Types
24 Jan 69 Issue II	Purpose & Targets
*26 Jan 69	Compliance Reports
27 Jan 69	Dev-T Summary List
*29 Jan 69	Public Division Org Board Revised (Corrected)
*30 Jan 69	Public Divisions Org Board
*31 Jan 69	PRO Broadsheets
31 Jan 69	Humanitarian Objective and Gung-Ho Groups
3 Feb 69	Public Image
5 Feb 69	Double Hats
5 Feb 69 Issue II	PRO Actions
13 Feb 69	Ethics Protection, Conditions, Blue Star, Green Star, Gold Star
24 Feb 69	An Ethics Policy Letter—Justice
* 6 Mar 69	Scientology Is a Religion
7 Mar 69	Organization
13 Mar 69	Addition to HCO Policy Letter of 23 June 1967 "Policies on Physical Healing, Insanity and Potential Trouble Sources," Potential Trouble Sources (B)
15 Mar 69	Third Party, How to Fine One
17 Mar 69	Politics
*31 Mar 69 Issue III	Public Divisions Staff Qualifications
6 Apr 69	Dianetics
*14 Apr 69	Bulletin and Policy Letter Distribution
18 Apr 69 Issue II	Org Division Income Dept
*20 Apr 69	AO-SH Financial Control
*20 Apr 69 Issue I	Board of Review
*20 Apr 69 Issue II	CLO Council WW
27 Apr 69	Death Wish
* 5 May 69 Issue II	Dianetic Course Examinations
7 May 69	Policies on "Sources of Trouble"
16 May 69	Course Administration
*17 May 69 Issue I	Mailing Lists, Central Files, Addresso Basic Definitions and Policy
*20 May 69	Hubbard Standard Dianetics Course Course Materials, Papers and Files
23 May 69	Dianetic Contract
*23 May 69 Issue III	Public Divisions Promotional Actions
*23 May 69 Issue IV	Public Divisions Flash Colours
12 Jun 69	Dianetic Registration
*13 Jun 69	Summary of Policy on Executive Directives, Admin and Advice Letters and Executive Letters
*16 Jun 69 Amends 20 Apr 69	AO-SH Finance Control
17 Jun 69	The Org Image
* 4 Jul 69 Issue IV	Dianetic Counseling Groups No. 4 Why a Group?
* 4 Jul 69 Issue V	Dianetic Counseling Groups No. 5 Group Formation
10 Jul 69	Org Personnel Recruitment
*11 Jul 69 Issue II	Areas of Operation
*24 Jul 69 Issue II	Public Divisions Book Distribution Unit
*24 Jul 69 Issue III	The Groups Communicator
*25 Jul 69 Issue VI	Dianetic Counseling Groups No. 6 The Org Board
2 Sept 69 Issue II	Triple Grades
8 Sept 69	The Org Exec Course Introduction
14 Sept 69	Admin Know-How No. 22 The Key Ingredients
21 Sept 69	Staff Training Officer
4 Oct 69	Organizational Enturbulence
5 Oct 69 Revised & Reissued 10 Dec 69	Dianetic Courses, Wildcat
27 Oct 69 Corrected & Reissued 27 Oct 73	Admin Know-How No. 23 Dev-T
4 Nov 69	Dev-T Graphed
10 Nov 69 Issue II	Franchise Grants or Charters
11 Nov 69	Accounts & PRO
11 Nov 69 Issue II	Promotion and Motivation
12 Nov 69	Appearance and PRO

*12 Nov 69 Issue II	PES Account Versus HCO Book Account
18 Nov 69 Issue I	Central Files, Value of, The Gross Income of the Org and Why
*29 Nov 69	New Public Divisions Org Board
7 Dec 69	Ethics, The Design of
7 Dec 69 Issue II	The Ethics Officer, His Character
*10 Dec 69 Issue III	PES WW Account
11 Dec 69	Training of Clears
11 Dec 69	Appearances in Public Divs
15 Dec 69	Class of Orgs
15 Dec 69 Issue II	Urgent—Orders, Query of
19 Dec 69	Executive Duties
*20 Dec 69 Issue VIII	Confidential
*20 Dec 69 Issue IX	Confidential
*21 Dec 69	Revised New Public Divisions Org Board
*21 Dec 69 Issue II	Guide to Function of Printer Liaison
5 Feb 70	Statistics, Management by
7 Feb 70 Adds to 23 Sept 67	Danger Condition, 2nd Formula
7 Feb 70 Issue II	HCO Makes the Org
12 Feb 70 Issue II	Urgent and Important to WW ECWW, Primary Duties of
*23 Feb 70RB Revised 8 Aug 72 Revised 8 Jun 73	Org Admin Checklist
28 Mar 70	R6EW and Clear
7 Apr 70RA	Green Form
11 Apr 70	Third Dynamic Tech
17 Apr 70	Vital—Department One
21 Apr 70	Field Ethics
23 Apr 70	SH-UK-ANZO-EU Relationships
26 Apr 70R Revised 15 Mar 75	Data Series No. 1R The Anatomy of Thought
8 May 70	Admin Know-How No. 24 Distraction and Noise
11 May 70	Data Series No. 2 Logic
12 May 70	Data Series No. 3 Breakthroughs
13 May 70	Training Requirements Eased
14 May 70	Hat Checkout Sequence
15 May 70	Data Series No. 4 Data and Situation Analyzing
15 May 70 Issue II	Data Series No. 5 Information Collection
15 May 70 Issue II	Financial Management
17 May 70	Data Series No. 6 Data Systems
18 May 70	Data Series No. 7 Familiarity
19 May 70	Data Series No. 8 Sanity
23 May 70	Data Series No. 9 Errors
*27 May 70R Revised 25 Sept 73	The Organization of the Guardian's Office
*29 May 70	Lost Income & Credit
30 May 70	Important—Cutatives
17 Jun 70	Technical Degrades
23 Jun 70	Data Series No. 10 The Missing Scene
24 Jun 70R Issue II Revised 30 Apr 75	Personnel Pools
30 Jun 70	Data Series No. 11 The Situation
5 Jul 70	Data Series No. 12 How to Find and Establish an Ideal Scene
6 Jul 70	Data Series No. 13 Irrationality
7 Jul 70	Data Series No. 14 Working and Managing
*15 Jul 70 Issue II	Reorganization of the Correction Division
20 Jul 70	Cases and Morale of Staff
*30 Jul 70	Important—Registration Breakthrough
8 Aug 70	Data Series No. 15 Wrong Target
* 8 Aug 70 Issue III	Reorganization of the Correction Division
13 Aug 70 Issue I	PR Series No. 1 Liabilities of PR
13 Aug 70 Issue II	PR Series No. 2 The Missing Ingredient

13 Aug 70 Issue III	PR Series No. 3 Wrong Publics
*19 Aug 70	Division VI, Division VIII GDS
*20 Aug 70 Issue II	Division VIII The Public Sales Division
*20 Aug 70 Issue III	Division VI The Public Relations Division
29 Aug 70 Issue I	Personnel Series No. 1 Personnel Transfers Can Destroy an Org
29 Aug 70 Issue II	Personnel Programming
29 Aug 70 Issue III	Personnel Series No. 3 Recruit in Excess
30 Aug 70	Personnel Series No. 4 Recruiting Actions
2 Sept 70	First Policy
2 Sept 70	Instruction Protocol Official
8 Sept 70R Revised 18 Nov 73	Examiner's 24 Hour Rule
10 Sept 70	Personnel Series No. 5 Transferitis
13 Sept 70	Personnel Series No. 7 Hats—Vital Data
13 Sept 70 Issue II	Org Series No. 1 Basic Organization
14 Sept 70	Org Series No. 2 Cope and Organize
16 Sept 70	Personnel Series No. 8 Ethics and Personnel
16 Sept 70 Issue II Reissue of HCOB 30 Jul 58	The Handling of Hubbard Communications Offices
19 Sept 70 Issue I	Data Series No. 16 Investigatory Procedure
19 Sept 70 Issue II	Data Series No. 17 Narrowing the Target
19 Sept 70 Issue III	Data Series No. 18 Summary of Out-Points
22 Sept 70	Personnel Series No. 9 Org Series No. 4 Hats
23 Sept 70	Quarters, Policy Regarding Historical
24 Sept 70R Revised 23 Jun 75	Issues, Types of
26 Sept 70 Issue III	Org Series No. 5 Org Board Cutatives
1 Oct 70	Org Series No. 7 Hats and Counter Effort
3 Oct 70	Stat Interpretation
6 Oct 70	Inspection of Low Stats
6 Oct 70 Issue II	Personnel Series No. 10 "Moonlighting"
8 Oct 70	Organizing and Product
*10 Oct 70 Issue I	Accounts Audit Series No. 1 Introduction to an Accounts Audit
*10 Oct 70 Issue III	Accounts Audit Series No. 3 How to Do an Accounts Audit—Breakdown Function
*10 Oct 70 Issue IV	Accounts Audit Series No. 4 How to Do an Accounts Audit—Summarizing Function
*10 Oct 70 Issue V	Accounts Audit Series No. 5 How to Do Final Accounts
13 Oct 70 Issue II	Data Series No. 19 The Real Why
*14 Oct 70	Division IV Org Board, Ideal Scenes and Stats
*18 Oct 70	Public Divisions Org Board
*22 Oct 70	OT Service and OT Committee and AO's Public
*24 Oct 70	Saint Hillers Association
28 Oct 70	Org Series No. 9 Organiz*ing* and Hats
29 Oct 70	Org Series No. 10 The Analysis of the Organization by Product
1 Nov 70	Org Series No. 11 Organization & Morale
1 Nov 70 Issue III	You Can Be Right
2 Nov 70	Organizational Health Chart
2 Nov 70 Issue II	Org Series No. 13 The Theory of Scientology Organizations
3 Nov 70 Issue II	Confidential
4 Nov 70	HCO Bulletin August 27, 1958 Executives of Scientology Organizations
* 4 Nov 70 Issue IV	Estimated Purchase Orders
14 Nov 70	Org Series No. 14 The Product as an Overt Act
*14 Nov 70 Issue IV	The Theory of Bookkeeping and Accountancy Part I Fundamentals Section I
15 Nov 70R Revised 21 Sept 74	HCO and Confessionals
18 Nov 70 Issue II	PR Series No. 5 PR Definition

25 Nov 70	Org Series No. 16 Policy & Orders
26 Nov 70	Data Series No. 20 More Outpoints
6 Dec 70	Personnel Series No. 13 Org Series No. 18 Third Dynamic De-Aberration
6 Dec 70 Issue II	Teaching a Tape Course
14 Dec 70	Personnel Series No. 14 Org Series No. 19 Group Sanity
*24 Dec 70	Finance Directives
30 Dec 70	Personnel Series No. 15 Org Series No. 20 Environmental Control
25 Jan 71	Org Series No. 22 Squirrel Admin
29 Jan 71	Finance Banking Officers
* 5 Feb 71 Issue III	FEBC Executive Director Org GDSes
5 Feb 71 Issue VI	CF and Address Pre-Sorting
* 7 Feb 71 Issue II	FEBC Org Board Division I
* 7 Feb 71 Issue VI	FEBC Org Board Division V
* 7 Feb 71 Issue VII	FEBC Org Board Division VI
9 Feb 71	Executive Misbehavior
13 Feb 71	Financial Planning Tips
16 Feb 71 Issue II	Org Series No. 23 Lines and Terminals
*22 Feb 71	Use of the Student Hat
27 Feb 71 Issue I	LRH Comm New Basic Duties
2 Mar 71	Mimeo Section
4 Mar 71 Issue II	How to Do Theory Checkouts and Examinations
* 5 Mar 71 Revised 6 Sept 71 & Reissued 31 Aug 74	Checkout Mini Course
9 Mar 71 Issue II	Posting an Org Board
*10 Mar 71	Finance Series No. 6 FBO Hat
12 Mar 71	Putting an HCO There
*12 Mar 71 Issue II	Treasury Divisions GDSes All Orgs
15 Mar 71 Issue II Corrected	Data Series No. 21 Data Series Auditing
16 Mar 71R Revised 29 Jan 75	What Is a Course?
16 Mar 71 Issue III	HAS/Hatting Routing Forms Amendment
16 Mar 71 Issue IV	Org Series No. 25 Personnel Series No. 19 Lines and Hats
19 Mar 71	Personnel Series No. 20 Personnel Prediction
25 Mar 71	Org Series No. 26 Valuable Final Products
* 2 Apr 71 Issue II	Public Dissemination Manual
*13 Apr 71	Hubbard Qualified Scientologist Course Checksheet
*15 Apr 71R Revised 30 Mar 73	Hubbard Apprentice Scientologist Course
11 May 71 Issue II	PR Series No. 6 Opinion Leaders
11 May 71 Issue III	PR Series No. 7 Black PR
27 May 71	Service
28 May 71	PR Series No. 8 Too Little Too Late
28 May 71 Issue II	Service and Workload
30 May 71	PR Series No. 9 Manners
2 Jun 71 Issue II	PR Series No. 10 PR and Production Tone Scale Surveys The Laws of PR
4 Jun 71	Standard Admin Series No. 1 Standard Admin
* 3 Jul 71R Revised & Reissued 13 Jun 73	New Names to CF Change
7 Jul 71	Org Series No. 27 HCO Establishment Functions
*14 Jul 71 Cancels 7 Feb 71 FEBC Org Board Div VI	FEBC Org Board Division VI Expanded
*16 Jul 71	Hat Checksheet for Dean of the Hatting College
21 Jul 71 Issue II	Vital HAS Apprenticing Action

22 Jul 71	Admin Know-How No. 25 CLOs, OTLs and Flag
28 Jul 71	Admin Know-How No. 26
29 Jul 71	Org Series No. 28 Personnel Series No. 27 Why Hatting
2 Aug 71	Study Time
* 2 Aug 71 Issue III	Hatting Points, GDS Change
* 4 Aug 71	Post Protection Assistant Qual Aides and Correction Div Secretaries
* 5 Aug 71 Issue II	FEBC Div VI Org Board Amendment
* 6 Aug 71 Issue XII Addition to 4 Feb 70	PC Application Form for any Major Auditing Action
10 Aug 71	HCO Cope Officer
11 Aug 71 Issue I	Basic Hat Pack
11 Aug 71 Issue II	Personnel Series No. 22 Don't Unmock a Working Inst
*11 Aug 71 Issue IV	Inter Org Exchange of Students
11 Aug 71 Issue V	Security of Data
12 Aug 71 Issue IV	OT Courses
14 Aug 71 Issue I Revised 5 Sept 71	Bureau VA
14 Aug 71 Issue II	Div V, Qual Org Board
14 Aug 71RC Issue II Revised 17 Feb 75	Div V, Mini Qual Org Board
*15 Aug 71	Personnel Procurement Officer Hat Checksheet
*18 Aug 71	Important Merchandising Expertise
20 Aug 71 Issue II	Tech Establishment Officer
24 Aug 71	Interne Checksheets Okays to Audit
29 Aug 71 Corrected & Reissued 14 Oct 71	Urgent—Org Conditions— Stat Change—Important
31 Aug 71	The EC Network Disbanded
31 Aug 71	Additional EC Network
5 Sept 71	HCO Reception
*15 Sept 71 Issue I	Statistic of the Advance Scheduling Registrar
*15 Sept 71-1 Issue I Addition of 20 Nov 73	Stat Change— Prepayments Received
*16 Sept 71	Quality Mastering Tape
*16 Sept 71 Issue II	AOLA Division IV
*16 Sept 71 Issue III	Urgent—High Crime Policy Letter Operation Staff Stability and Personal Security Personnel Permanent Appointments, Transfers, Demotions and Dismissals
*19 Sept 71	The Demo Org, Instructions for
23 Sept 71	Important Finance Series No. 9 Finance Banking Officers Purposes
24 Sept 71	Assignment, Model to Be Used
*30 Sept 71	The Role of ARC Break Registrar
5 Oct 71	PR Series No. 12 Propaganda by Redefinition of Words
25 Oct 71 Issue I	Comm Routing—How to Tie Up a Whole Org and Produce Nothing
26 Oct 71	Tech Downgrades
29 Oct 71 Issue II	Executive Series No. 1 The Executive
29 Oct 71 Issue III	Executive Series No. 2 Leadership
* 4 Nov 71 Issue II	Important— Academy Pre-Requisite
*14 Nov 71RA Issue II Revised & Reissued 4 Dec 72	"Big League" Registration Series No. 12 Mini Public Division Org Board
*19 Nov 71	Director of Processing Hat
*22 Nov 71R Issue II	Division VII Mini Org Board
*26 Nov 71R Issue I Revised & Reissued 29 Oct 72	Public Reg Interview Admin
*26 Nov 71 Issue II	Division VI Public Reg Reinstated
*26 Nov 71R Issue II Revised & Reissued 30 Oct 72	Div VI Public Reg Simplified
27 Nov 71	Executive Series No. 3 Money

*28 Nov 71R Issue I Revised 28 Oct 72	The Types of Div VI Registration
*28 Nov 71R Issue II Revised 28 Oct 72	Public Division Statistics
3 Dec 71	Exec Series No. 4 Exchange
7 Dec 71	Advance Course Violations
29 Dec 71R Revised 7 Dec 74	Flag Representative, Duties of
*14 Jan 72 Issue IV	Personnel Series No. 24 Personnel Programming Series No. 11 The "OK to be a . . ." System
*15 Jan 72RA	Important—Riches or Poverty, The Quality of the Dissem Division A Dissem Div Checklist for Quality
26 Jan 72 Issue I	Admin Know-How No. 29 Executive Series No. 5 Not Dones, Half Dones & Backlogs
*26 Jan 72R	Scientology Level 4 Standard Academy Checksheet
*28 Jan 72RB Revised 26 Aug 73	Flag Rep Org Function Checklist
31 Jan 72	Data Series No. 22 The Why Is God
* 1 Feb 72R Issue III	Income Report Required
* 2 Feb 72 Issue II Cancelled 26 Aug 72	Division IV—Stage Two Org Board Cancelled
* 5 Feb 72 Issue III	Establishment Officer Course Establishment Officer Basic Course Checksheet
* 7 Feb 72 Issue I Corrected & Reissued 4 Mar 72	Division VII Establishment Officer Course Checksheet, Part 2
* 7 Feb 72 Issue III Revises & Cancels 6 Dec 71	Dissem Establishment Officer Course, Part 2
* 7 Feb 72 Issue VII	Public Establishment Officer Course Checksheet, Part 2
*10 Feb 72R Issue III Modifies 3 Jul 71 "Registration Change" Cancels 18 Sept 71 "AOLA Division VI Defined"	Higher Org New Name to CF Definitions
16 Feb 72	The Purpose of the Department of Personnel Enhancement
17 Feb 72 Reissued 26 Feb 72	Data Series No. 23 Proper Format and Correct Action
18 Feb 72	Executive Series No. 8 The Top Triangle
24 Feb 72	Injustice
27 Feb 72	Executive Series No. 9 Routing
29 Feb 72	Executive Series No. 10 Correct Comm
29 Feb 72 Issue II	Data Series No. 24 Handling Policy, Plans, Programs, Projects and Orders Defined
7 Mar 72 Revised 13 Apr 72	Establishment Officer Series No. 1R The Establishment Officer
9 Mar 72 Issue I	Finance Series No. 11 Income Flows and Pools Principles of Money Management
9 Mar 72 Issue III	Establishment Officer Series No. 3 Dev-T and Unhattedness
13 Mar 72	Establishment Officer Series No. 5 Production and Establishment Orders and Products
14 Mar 72 Issue I	Establishment Officer Series No. 6 Sequence of Hatting
14 Mar 72 Issue II	Establishment Officer Series No. 7 Follow Policy and Lines
16 Mar 72 Issue II	Establishment Officer Series No. 9 Stuck in
16 Mar 72 Issue III	Finance Directives Cancelled
19 Mar 72 Issue II	Data Series No. 25 Learning to Use Data Analysis
1 Apr 72	Establishment Officer Series No. 12 Executive Series No. 11 Making an Executive, Flow Lines
3 Apr 72	Establishment Officer Series No. 13 Doing Work
4 Apr 72	Establishment Officer Series No. 14 Ethics
4 Apr 72 Issue III Revised 7 Apr 72	Ethics and Study Tech
6 Apr 72	Establishment Officer Series No. 15 Product Correction
9 Apr 72	Ethics—Correct Danger Condition

24 Apr 72	Establishment Officer Series No. 16 Hatting the Product Officer of the Division
2 May 72	HCO—Numbering of Mimeo Issues
3 May 72	Executive Series No. 12 Ethics and Executives
12 May 72	Ethics Executive Series No. 13 Finance Series No. 12 Personnel Series No. 25 PTS Personnel and Finance
13 May 72	Study Series No. 4 Establishment Officer Series No. 17 Language Series No. 4 Chinese School
28 May 72	Boom Data, Publications Basic Functions
25 Jun 72	Recovering Students and PCs
26 Jun 72	Establishment Officer Series No. 20 Supervisor Tech
* 5 Jul 72	Definition of a Hot Prospect
* 6 Jul 72	Mini SH Foundation Public Division Org Board
*15 Jul 72 Issue I	Flag Representative
23 Jul 72	Establishment Officer Series No. 23 Executive Series No. 15 Org Series No. 31 The Vital Necessity of Hatting
25 Jul 72	Establishment Officer Series No. 24 The Form of the Org
*27 Jul 72	Hat—Compilations Hat Checksheet
27 Jul 72	Establishment Officer Series No. 25 Form of the Org and Schedules
28 Jul 72	Establishment Officer Series No. 26 Executive Series No. 16 Org Series No. 32 Establishing, Holding the Form of the Org
*29 Jul 72 Issue II	Fast Flow in Training
* 1 Aug 72	Qual Handling of Students and Internes on the Fast Flow System
* 6 Aug 72R Revised 10 Oct 72	Merchandising of Primary RD
7 Aug 72 Revised 9 Aug 72	PR Series No. 17R PR and Causation
9 Aug 72	Seniority of Orders
15 Aug 72 Issue II	Saint Hill Special Briefing Course Structure Revert
*24 Aug 72	FOLO UK Pilot—Tours Org Mini Org Board
*24 Aug 72RA Revised 3 May 73	Tours Org Series No. 1 Tours Org
* 6 Sept 72 Issue II	Confidential
*16 Sept 72	The Post of Dean
*24 Sept 72 Issue I	The Duties of the Deputy Qual Sec
*12 Oct 72 Issue II	Registrar Interview Form
13 Oct 72	Freeloaders
*20 Oct 72	Refund/Repayment Routing and Report Form
*31 Oct 72 Issue I	The Service Consultant
* 5 Nov 72	Standard Abbreviations
13 Nov 72	Affluence Attainment
21 Nov 72 Issue I	PR Series No. 18 How to Handle Black Propaganda
* 1 Dec 72 Issue IX	"Big League" Registration Series No. 4
* 2 Dec 72 Issue II	The Div VI Social Counselor
4 Dec 72 Issue II	FBO & Treasury Financial Reports
7 Feb 73 Issue III	Mimeo, Files Folders and Files
*18 Feb 73 Issue I	The Advance Scheduling Registrar Hat
*18 Feb 73 Issue II	No Hole Nudge System
*18 Feb 73 Issue IV Amends & Enlarges Upon 29 Nov 68 of Same Title	Enrollment Cycle
*18 Feb 73 Issue VI	AOSH UK Organizing Board for the Dissemination Division
*19 Feb 73	Cancellation
*27 Feb 73	Dissemination Division Full Organizing Board
* 1 Mar 73 Issue II	Stage One Mini Public Division Org Board
* 6 Mar 73	The Theory of Compliance—3 How to Comply
*20 Mar 73	Two New Salesmanship Courses
* 1 Apr 73RA Issue III	Solo D/P Weekly Report
* 9 Apr 73 Issue II	Business Management Tech Series No. 12

	Management Evaluation and Handling of Orgs
*10 Apr 73	Org Designation System
*12 Apr 73	Business Management Tech Series No. 13 Management Organization Rudiments
*19 Apr 73	OIC Cable Addition
28 Apr 73	Good Service
*28 Apr 73	How a Recruiter Builds His Applicant/Prospect Files
*29 Apr 73 Issue I	CF Information Slip
* 2 May 73	Org Orientation Drill Definitions
*10 May 73R Revised 22 Sept 73	Gross Book Sales GDS How to Count
*18 May 73	Mini VII Division Org Board and Tech Admin Ratio
25 May 73	Data Series No. 27 Supplementary Evaluation
24 Jun 73	Establishment Officer Series No. 29 Personnel Series No. 27 "The concept of . . ."
* 2 Jul 73	Tech Sec
* 8 Jul 73	Enrollment Cycle
28 Jul 73RA Revised 25 Apr 75	Cancellation of AVU Fast Flow
3 Aug 73	LRH Comm Secondary Stats
* 3 Aug 73-1 Addition 23 Aug 73	Deputy LRH Comms
7 Aug 73 Issue I	Flag Representative Purpose, Duties and Statistic
15 Aug 73	Flag Representative, Orders to
*16 Aug 73	Controller Communicator Network
27 Aug 73	Tech and LRH Comms
11 Sept 73	Codes and Coding, Correct Practice
19 Sept 73 Issue IR Revised 22 Jun 75	Data Series No. 28R Checking Evals
30 Sept 73 Issue I	Data Series No. 29 Outpoints, More
30 Sept 73 Issue II	Data Series No. 30 Situation Finding
* 1 Oct 73	Office of LRH—Org Board
15 Oct 73	Admin Know-How Series No. 31 Administrative Skill
21 Oct 73R Updated 28 Jan 75	Case Supervisor Statistic
*30 Oct 73	Organization Executive Course Checksheet, Volume Zero Basic Staff Volume
4 Nov 73	Publishing Policy Books and Magazines
8 Nov 73	The VFPs and GDSs of the Divisions of an Org
8 Nov 73RA Revised 9 Mar 74	The VFPs and GDSs of the Divisions of an Org
*10 Nov 73	Compliance Series No. 4 Receipt and Duplication
19 Nov 73	New Organization Executive Course Checksheets
21 Nov 73	LRH Comm Drills
22 Nov 73	Establishment Officer Series No. 30
* 3 Dec 73	The Hubbard Help Specialist Course
14 Dec 73	Data Series No. 32 Target Troubles Targets Junior to Policy
9 Feb 74	Ethics, Condition Below Treason
27 Feb 74	PR Series No. 21 Wasted Planning
18 Mar 74	PR Series No. 23 The Press Book
9 May 74	Prod-Org, Esto and Older Systems Reconciled
17 May 74R Revised 27 Aug 74	The New Staff Status III, OEC and FEBC
3 Jul 74R Revised 17 Sept 74	Data Series No. 33R Evaluation, Criticism of
13 Jul 74 Issue II	Org Series No. 34 Working Installations
18 Jul 74	Data Series No. 34 Situation Correction
11 Aug 74	Data Series No. 36 Envisioning the Ideal Scene
12 Aug 74	Data Series No. 37 Whys Open the Door
16 Aug 74 Issue II	Estates Section Back to Dept 21
*16 Aug 74 IIR	Estates Section Back to Dept 21
30 Aug 74	"Big League" Registration Series No. 10RA Registration Commission System
30 Aug 74 Issue II	Qual Stat Change
31 Aug 74	Keeper of Tech, Office of LRH
31 Aug 74 Issue II	Fast Flow Training Reinstated

5 Sept 74	Book Sales to Individuals from Pubs
25 Sept 74	Reduction of Refunds C/Ses and Overload
26 Sept 74	Important New Case Supervisor Postings
3 Oct 74	Data Series No. 38 Pluspoint List
19 Oct 74	The Dramatization of Withholds on Vital Information Lines
27 Oct 74	PR Series No. 25 Safe Ground
9 Nov 74	Important Urgent Refunds and Repayments
15 Nov 74	Phone Tips
19 Nov 74 Corrected & Reissued 10 Dec 74	Finance Stress in an Org
25 Nov 74	Urgent—Fast Flow and Qual
7 Dec 74 HCO PL 9 May 74 Re-Established Cancellation of HCO PL 12 Nov 74 "Prod-Org Reinstated"	Prod-Org, Esto and Other Systems Reconciled Reinstated
8 Jan 75	Compliance, How to Get One
23 Jun 75	Ad Council Income Planning
22 Sept 75 Issue II	The HCO Ethics Codes
26 Oct 75	Gross Income/Corrected Gross Income Ratio, Failed Cases and Failed Students
8 Nov 75	Non Existence Formula Expanded
1 Jan 76	FSMs—Folos Commissions
22 May 76	Staff Section Officer Hat
23 May 76	Celebrities
7 Aug 76 Issue II	Admin Know-How 34 Esto Series 32 Product/Org Officer System Want Your Product
24 Oct 76 Issue II	Supervisors Can Become Professors
24 Oct 76 Issue III	Senior Case Supervisor Requirements
4 Nov 76	Statistic Change, Gross Divisional Statistics, HCOs and Quals OIC Telex Change

Hubbard Communications Office Technical Bulletins

12 Sept 56	Executives in Washington and London

Hubbard Communications Office Training Bulletins

6 Feb 57	"The following procedure is not for general release to the field . . ."
17 May 57	Definitions

LRH Executive Directives

LRH ED 67 Int	Electric Shock Cases	15 Dec 68
LRH ED 2 Int	Attestation Reinstated	20 Jan 69
LRH ED 1 Int	Organizational Intention	9 Feb 69
LRH ED 2 US & 2 WW	PDH	9 Mar 69
LRH ED 7 Int	Public Committees	4 Apr 69
LRH ED 9 Int	Urgent—Dianetics	11 May 69
LRH ED 28 Int	Scientology: A Religion The Legal Proofs of Scientology as a Religion	25 Aug 69
LRH ED 27 Int	Important—Staff, LRH Comm; Staff Programme No. 1	21 Oct 69
LRH ED 32 Int	Income of Staff Program No. 1	22 Oct 69
LRH ED 34 Int	The Role of the Central Org	18 Nov 69

*LRH ED 36A Int	Originations to LRH	19 Nov 69
LRH ED 39 Int	Ethics Program No. 1	23 Nov 69
LRH ED 10 WW 1 SH & SH FDN	Solvency of WW and SH and SH FDN	29 Nov 69
LRH ED 44 Int	Freeloaders	2 Dec 69
LRH ED 46 Int	Western Australia Ban Invalidated	7 Dec 69
LRH ED 49 Int	Organization Program No. 1	9 Dec 69
LRH ED 53 Int	Orders to ECs	10 Dec 69
LRH ED 54 Int	Superior Service, Image Program No. 1	10 Dec 69
LRH ED 55 Int	Financial Planning Programme No. 1	10 Dec 69
LRH ED 56 Int	Intentions	12 Dec 69
LRH ED 57 Int	What to Sell	14 Dec 69
LRH ED 59 Int	Magazines	14 Dec 69
LRH ED 63 Int	Ethics Upstats	16 Dec 69
LRH ED 74 Int	Solvency	14 Jan 70
LRH ED 78 Int	Subject: Summary of Int No. 1 Programs	28 Jan 70
LRH ED 22 WW	Ethics in Orgs, WW Actions	12 Feb 70
LRH ED 83 Int	Stat Recovery—An Analysis of Board Outnesses	17 Feb 70
LRH ED 88 Int	Standard Tech and Invalidation	26 Feb 70
LRH ED 92 Int	Tech Volume and 2-Way Comm	25 Mar 70
LRH ED 95 Int	Flag Executive Briefing Course	8 Apr 70
LRH ED 103 Int	Fast Flow Grades Cancelled	21 May 70
LRH ED 104 Int	Auditing Sales and Delivery, Program No. 1	2 Jun 70
LRH ED 107 Int	Orders to Divisions for Immediate Compliance	3 Jun 70
LRH ED 101 Int	Popular Names of Developments	21 Jun 70
LRH ED 112 Int	Urgent and Important—Registration: Breakthrough	25 Jul 70
LRH ED 121 Int	Staff Training Program No. 2	29 Aug 70
LRH ED 123 Int	Org Management Program No. 2	4 Sept 70
LRH ED 128 Int	Thursday Reports	27 Sept 70
LRH ED 129 Int	Org Aberration Results	4 Nov 70
LRH ED 130 Int	New Command Channels	19 Nov 70
LRH ED 131 Int	Life Repair Block	8 Dec 70
LRH ED 135 Int	Status of Worldwide Org	15 Jan 71
LRH ED 143 Int	The World Begins With TR 0	22 May 71
LRH ED 145 Int	Why Something New	4 Jul 71
LRH ED 146 Int	The Beginning and Maintaining of a Boom	20 Jul 71
LRH ED 148 Int	"26071R Rly Pubs DK . . ."	12 Aug 71
LRH ED 152 Int	Fast TRs and High Stat Program	26 Aug 71
LRH ED 145R Int	Bonus Completion Points	6 Oct 71
LRH ED 154 Int	Tech Certainty and High Stats	7 Oct 71
*LRH ED 159RA Int	Registration Program No. 1R	28 Nov 71 Revised 23 Sept 73
LRH ED 161 Int	Surveys Are the Key to Stats	18 Dec 71
LRH ED 166 Int	Plans for 1972	1 Jan 72
LRH ED 167 Int	Your Dissem Division	16 Jan 72

LRH ED 168R Int	Establishment Officers—An Answer to HCOs; Special Offer	8 Feb 72
*LRH ED 176R Int	Auditor Recovery, Attachment 2	24 Apr 72 Revised 10 Nov 72
*LRH ED 159R-1 Int	Registration Program, SO Special No. 1	18 Feb 73
LRH ED 185 Int	The 23rd Anniversary of DMSMH	2 May 73
LRH ED 205 Int	Transfer of Guardian Functions in Tech and Policy to LRH Comms	28 Sept 73
LRH ED 223 Int	Letters to Ron	19 Feb 74
LRH ED 228 Int	Org Programs	24 Apr 74
LRH ED 239 Int	Charter for the Cultivation of a Scientology Music Culture	8 Jul 74
LRH ED 241 Int	Potential Trouble Sources	22 Jul 74
LRH ED 231-1R Int	Expansion Targets Date Modified and Re-Programmed for 153RC	31 Jul 74
LRH ED 234R Int	Registration	22 Aug 74
LRH ED 153 RD	10X 27 December 1973 by 13 March 1975	25 Oct 74
LRH ED 256 Int	The Role of Community Leadership	28 Nov 74
LRH ED 257 Int	Delivery Repair Lists	1 Dec 74
LRH ED 153RE Int	Org Conditions Stat	7 Dec 74
LRH ED 259 Int	A Call for 100,000 Auditors, C/Ses and Supervisors and 10,000 OTs by 13 March 1976	16 Mar 75 Corrected 17 Mar 75
LRH ED 265 Int	Pubs US	17 Sept 75
LRH ED 271 Int	Mission Expenses, Letter of Credit	2 Jan 76

Miscellaneous References

Administrative Bulletin	To be in Effect—Monday, February 24, 1958	21 Feb 58
Administrative Directive	Modified Procedure for Signing Up Prospective Students & PCs	6 May 58 OEC Volume 2 p. 314
Communications Plan HASI, 1954	"No Title"	OEC Volume 7 p. 254
Directive	Certifications, Board Duties and Responsibilities	12 Dec 50 OEC Volume 5 p. 115
*Dissemination Advice Letter	Magazine Layout and Paste-Up	1 Apr 70 OEC Volume 2 p. 145
An Essay on Management 1951	"No Title"	OEC Volume 7 p. 251
*FB CO 9-1	FB Staff and Bureaux, Conditions W/E 19 Feb 76	22 Feb 76
Founding Church of Scientology, Wash., DC	Staff Meeting of the Founding Church	7 May 57
The Hubbard Association of Scientologists	Organization Book	Circa 54
HCO London	Proportionate Disbursement Plan Computation	17 Apr 57
HCO London	H.A.S.I. "Purposes" as per Organizational Board	9 Jan 58 OEC Volume 7 p. 122

HCO London	Later Additions to List of Purposes on Organization Board	23 Apr 58 OEC Volume 7 p. 123
HCO Secretarial Letter	Collection of Accounts	26 Dec 58 OEC Volume 3 p. 277
HCO Secretarial Policy Letter	Duties of Sec'l Ed	17 Dec 58 OEC Volume 1 p. 232
*LA Central Mimeo Info Letter	"No Title"	10 Aug 71
A 1957 Letter Issued by HASI Accounts, London	"What Your Money Has Bought"	OEC Volume 3 p. 275
LRH Briefing Notes	Confidential	3 Sept 70
LRH Directive Washington, DC	Conversion of Administration from Several Organizations to SciCon	14 Dec 56
Minutes of Staff Meeting	"No Title"	18 Apr 57 OEC Volume 3 p. 296
Organization Policy Letter	Inspection of Hat Folders	10 Jan 58
*SO ED 16 Pubs US	Sales and Shipment of LRH Promo	2 Mar 76

Sea Organization Executive Directives

*SOED 12 Int	LRH Comm, Staff Program No. 1, In the Nick of Time	5 Feb 70
*SO ED 19 Int	Clear Mimeo Backlog Project	14 Feb 70
*SO ED 36 Int	Answers to LRH ED 77 Int, "Auditing Mystery"	9 Apr 70
*SO ED 41 Int	The Scn Auditor's Image	29 Apr 70
*SO ED 43 Int	Dissemination Division GDS	10 May 70
*SO ED 45 Int	Org Promotion	18 May 70
*SO ED 53 Int	The Organization of the Guardian's Office	27 May 70
*SO ED 72 Int	What Is the Existing Scene in Div VIII?	8 Jul 70
*SO ED 96 Int	Central Authority New Command and Communication Lines	17 Dec 70
*SO ED 114 Int	Postulate Checks, Off Policy Actions	27 Jun 71
*SO ED 119 Int	Office of the Continental Captain US	19 Jul 71
*SO ED 122 Int	Definition of a Hot Prospect	21 Aug 71
*SO ED 135 Int	The Social Counselor Course	18 Jan 72
*SO ED 142 Int	Study Tape Word List Booklets, Info and References—Urgent	30 May 72
*SO ED 145R Int	Fast Flow in Training	25 Jul 72 Revised 9 Aug 72
*SO ED 153R Int	Paid Completion Points Revised	16 Nov 72
*SO ED 155 Int	Freeloader Program, How to Raise Your Credit Collections	12 Oct 72
*SO ED 161-1 Int	C/S Series No. 57 Success	12 Dec 72

*SO ED 161-2 Int	Tech Personnel, Recruit Training and Post Stability	5 Feb 73
*SO ED 163 Int	Tech Services—The Vital Link	16 Dec 72
*SO ED 191 Int	Student Points	11 May 73
*SO ED 202 Int	Establishment Mini Program No. 1	29 Jun 73
*SO ED 205 Int	Tech Div Stable Terminal and Expansion Pgm	9 Jul 73
*SO ED 214 Int	Let's Make Some ABs—and Some Potential Sea Org Officers!	10 Aug 73
*SO ED 229 Int	Flag Rep Newsletter	25 Nov 73
*SO ED 230 Int	Prepayments Received—How the ASR Gets Her New Stat	11 Nov 73
*SO ED 246 Int	The Expansion Bureau	6 Feb 74
*SO ED 269 Int	The Two Routes to Clear and OT	18 May 74
*SO ED 274R Int	New SO Recruits, Case Data and PC Folders	20 May 74 Revised 22 Jun 74
*SO ED 277RA Int	Flag Billings Chart	9 Jul 74 Amended 14 Oct 74
*SO ED 296 Int	Correct Application of Ethics	1 Sept 74
*SO ED 302 Int	Awards & Penalties for Honorary LRH PROs	21 Sept 74
*SO ED 306 Int	Hot Shot Reg Club	15 Oct 74
*SO ED 309 Int	Targetting Tech as Evolved in the FBO Network	31 Oct 74
*SO ED 320RA Int	Maximum Effort, Delivery	11 Nov 74 Revised 19 Nov 74 Revised 6 Jan 75
*SO ED 326 Int	Central Org Feeders	30 Nov 74
*SO ED 327 Int	Forming Orgs as Feeders	30 Nov 74
*SO ED 362-1 Int	Relief Staff Rules	10 Apr 75
*SO ED 373 Int	Routing of Requests to LRH Personal Staff at WW	19 May 75
*SO ED 376 Int	Train Your Course Supervisors	28 May 75
*SO ED 377 Int	The Solo C/S Course	27 May 75
*SO ED 401-1 Int	Graduation Requirements Ease, Further Clarification	12 Aug 75
*SO ED 411 Int	Facts About the HPDC	16 Aug 75
*SO ED 418 Int	FOLO's Responsibility for Ensuring COs/EDs Play the Piano of the Org Board	6 Sept 75
*SO ED 485 Int	The New Training and Services Bureau, Bureau 5A of the Flag Bureau	12 Feb 76
*SO ED 489 Int	LRH's Personal PRO International	18 Feb 76
*SO ED 498R Int	Flag Land Base	28 Feb 76 Revised 10 Mar 76
*SO ED 510-1 Int	New Targets of Payments to Flag	25 Mar 76
*SO ED 570 Int	Universal Media Productions	19 May 76

Secretarial Executive Directives

SEC ED (HASI London)	Materiel Administrator Hat	1 Dec 58
SEC ED 1	To: CF/Promotion Liaison	15 Dec 58
SEC ED 2	Registrar Hat	15 Dec 58
SEC ED 4	To: Director of Procurement DC	16 Dec 58
SEC ED 5	Director of Administration Hat	16 Dec 58
SEC ED (FC Wash. No. 9)	"The following appointments . . ."	16 Dec 58
SEC ED 11	Additional Duties of Staff Auditors	16 Dec 58
SEC ED 12	Hats and Hat Changes	16 Dec 58
SEC ED 18	Cost of HCS Course	2 Jan 59
SEC ED 25	To: Reception Hat	8 Jan 59
SEC ED 26	Qualifications of HGC Staff Auditors	8 Jan 59
SEC ED 27	"This supersedes . . ."	8 Jan 59
SEC ED 34	Director of Materiel Hat	14 Jan 59
SEC ED 36	Duties of the Secretarial to the Executive Director	14 Jan 59
SEC ED 37	Training Department	15 Jan 59
SEC ED 41	Organization Policy	15 Jan 59
SEC ED 58	Hat Folder Arrangement	27 Jan 59
SEC ED 59	Scheduling Policy	28 Jan 59
SEC ED 62	Secretarial to the Executive Director Hat	29 Jan 59
SEC ED 66	Department of Promotion and Registration	30 Jan 59
SEC ED 69	Staff Meeting	2 Feb 59
SEC ED 75	Policy—Personnel	2 Feb 59
SEC ED 78	Policy—Hats	2 Feb 59
SEC ED 117	Field Staff Member Program	18 Oct 65
SEC ED 150	Director of Processing Hat	9 Mar 59
SEC ED 174	Founding Church Board Minutes re: DCI Shares	1 Apr 59
SEC ED 342	Department of Government Relations	12 Aug 60

US Base Conditions Orders

*USB CO 15-1	Base Affluence Attainment	9 Nov 75

LRH Tape Recorded Lectures

1952

5203C03A	HCL-1	Introduction to Scientology: Milestone One
5212C09	PDC-26	Flows: Characteristics of
5212C18	PDC-61	How to Talk to Friends About Scientology

1953

5303C25	SPR LECT-5	The Elements, with Stress on How to Run Matched Terminals
5304C07	SPR LECT-13	Data on Case Level 5, Step for Case 5
5310C03	ICDS-11	Uses and Future of Scientology
5312CM21	2ACC-30A	Ability to Accept Direction
5312C22	2ACC-31B	Postulates
1954		
5401C26	3ACC-22	Exteriorization, Knowingness, Reality
5405C20	6ACC-17	Definitions, ARC
5410C04	8ACC-1	Introduction: Organization of Scientology
5410C06	8ACC-4	Two-Way Communication
1955		
5510C08	LPLS-1	Goals of Dianetics and Scientology
5510C13	4LACC-18	Affinity, Reality and Communication
5510C27	4LACC-37	The Role of a Scientologist
5511C03	4LACC-48	Attitude and Conduct of Scientologists
1956		
5608C--	HPC A6-4	Axioms 1-5
5609C01	GC-5	Third Dynamic Application of Games Principles
5610C18	OS-2	How to Create and Instruct a PE Course, Part 2
5611C01	OS-6	How to Handle Audiences
5611C08	OS-9	The Definition of Organization, Part 1
5611C15	OS-10	The Definition of Organization, Part 2
5612C06	OS-15	Money
1957		
5712C30	AC-5	Creating a Third Dynamic
1958		
5812C16	WST-1 Pr&R-1	Promotion and Registration
5812C29	LECT	HCO Area Sec Hat
1959		
5904C15	SHPA-11	Code of a Scientologist
1960		
6001C02	SMC-5	Marriage
1961		
6101C01	AHMC-6	Scientology Organizations

Saint Hill Special Briefing Course Tape Lectures

6109C07	SH Spec 51	Reality in Auditing
6109C26	SH Spec 58	Teaching the Field—Sec Checks
6110C04	SH Spec 62	Moral Codes: What Is a Withhold?
6112C07	SH Spec 90	Expectancy of 3-D
1962		
6201C16	SH Spec 100	Nature of Withholds

6203C29	SH Spec 126	CCHs
6204C03	SH Spec 131	The Overt-Motivator Sequence
6209C03	CSC-9	Scientology Orgs and What They Do for You
6210C09	SH Spec 200	Future Org Trends
1963		
6301C15	SH Spec 230	R2-12, Dead Horses
6305C30	SH Spec 271	Programming Cases, Part 2
1964		
6402C06	SH Spec 5	Comm Cycle in Auditing
6403C24	SH Spec 13	International City
6407C15	SH Spec 30	Organizational Operation
6409C15	SH Spec 39	Scientology and Tradition
6411C10	SH Spec 46	PTP's, Overts and ARC Breaks
1965		
6503C09	SH Spec 54	The New Organization Structure
6504C06	SH Spec 57	Org Board and Livingness
6505C18	SH Spec 61	Organization and Ethics
6505C25	SH Spec 62	The Five Conditions
6506C08	SH Spec 63	Handling the PTS
6509C09	SH Spec 66	Classification and Gradation
6509C21	SH Spec 67	Out Tech
6510C14	SH Spec 68	Briefing to Review Auditors
1966		
6607C26	SH Spec 71	The Classification Chart and Auditing
6608C02	SH Spec 73	Suppressives & GAEs
6608C23	SH Spec 77	Organization
6608C25	SH Spec 78	The Antisocial Personality
6611C01	SH Spec 81	Government and Organization
6611C29	SH Spec 82	OT and Clear Defined
6612C13	SH Spec 84	Scientology Definitions III
1967		
6711C18	SO	A Talk to Saint Hill and Worldwide Ethics Officers
1968		
6802C28	SO	"Ship Missions" (Given at Carthage)
6804SM		Ron's Talk to Pubs Org WW
6805C24	SO	"Officers Conference"
6806C01	SO	Transition of Operation Back to Staff
Ron's Journal '68		
6809C25SO	CL VIII-2	What Standard Tech Does
6809C27SO	CL VIII-4	Stanaard Tech Defined
1969		
6903C27	SO LECT	Current Planning Operations and Actions
6905C29	SD Spec 1	The Dianetic Program
6909C01	SO LECT	"Flag Central Command Area—Its Security & Activities"
6910C15	SO Series	Lecture No. 1, Welcome to the Sea Org

6910C16	SO Series	Lecture No. 2 Welcome to the Sea Org
6910C17	SO Series	Lecture No. 3 Welcome to the Sea Org
6910C20	SO Series	Lecture No. 4 Welcome to the Sea Org
6910C21	SO Series	Lecture No. 5 Welcome to the Sea Org
6910C30	SO LECT	New Flag Management System
6912C10	SO LECT	Actions on UK
6912C13	SO LECT	Programmes
1970		
7003C15	SO LECT	Talk on Leadership
7003C27	SO LECT	Confidential
7003C30	SO LECT	Talk to Aides in CIC
7004C09	SO LECT	History of Missions, Bottlenecks & Arbitraries
7007C15	SO LECT	Missions & Orders Portmanteau
7007C30	SO LECT	Succinct View of PR
7011C17 SO	FEBC 1	Welcome to the FEBC
7012C04	SO LECT	LRH Talk to Flag Bureau
1971		
7101C18 SO I	FEBC 2	PR Becomes a Subject
7101C18 SO II	FEBC 3	The Org Officer/Product Officer System, Part 1
7101C18 SO III	FEBC 4	The Org Officer/Product Officer System, Part 2
7101C23 SO I	FEBC 5	How to Post an Org
7101C23 SO II	FEBC 6	The Org Officer and His Resources, Part 1
7101C23 SO III	FEBC 7	The Org Officer and His Resources, Part 2
7101C24 SO I	FEBC 8	Viability and the Role of the HAS
7101C24 SO II	FEBC 9	Prediction and the Resources of the HAS
7101C24 SO III	FEBC 10	The HAS and the "Coins" of Organization
7102C03 SO I	FEBC 11	As You Return to Your Org
7102C03 SO II	FEBC 12	The FEBC Org Board and Its VFP
7109C05	SO LECT	A Talk on Basic Qual
7112TC17	SO LECT	An Aides Briefing
1972		
7201C02	SO LECT	Evaluations
7201C12	SO LECT	LRH—Talk on Flag Reps
7202C22	SO LECT	On Flag Internship
7203C01 SO I	ESTO 1	Establishment Officers Instant Hat
7203C01 SO II	ESTO 2	Establishment Officers Instant Hat
7203C02 SO I	ESTO 3	Evaluation and Handling of Personnel
7203C02 SO II	ESTO 4	Evaluation and Handling of Personnel
7203C03 SO I	ESTO 5	Handling Personnel
7203C03 SO II	ESTO 6	Handling Personnel
7203C04 SO I	ESTO 7	Hold the Form of the Org
7203C04 SO II	ESTO 8	Hold the Form of the Org

7203C05 SO I	ESTO 9	Revision of Prod/Org System
7203C05 SO II	ESTO 10	Revision of Prod/Org System
7203C06 SO I	ESTO 11	F/Ning Staff Members
7203C06 SO II	ESTO 12	F/Ning Staff Members
7204C11	SO LECT	Re: Policy Letter "Justice"
7205C11	SO LECT	LRH Talk with Action Aide—"Ops Briefing"
7205C18	SO LECT	Current and Future Ops Actions
7205C20	SO LECT	LA MO's, How to Write
7208C02	SO LECT	The Purpose and Actions of the Programs Bureau

About the Author

L. Ron Hubbard was born on the 13th of March, 1911, in Tilden, Nebraska, USA, to Commander Harry Ross Hubbard of the US Navy and Dora May Hubbard (née Waterbury de Wolfe).

He grew up in Montana with old frontiersmen and cowboys, and had an Indian medicine man as one of his best friends. Here in Montana, L. Ron Hubbard had his first encounter with another culture, the Blackfoot (Pikuni) Indians. He became a blood brother of the Pikuni and was later to write about them in his first published novel, *Buckskin Brigades.*

By the time he was twelve years old, he had read a good number of the world's greatest classics and began to take interest in the fields of religion and philosophy. During this time, while living in Washington, D.C., he became a close friend of President Calvin Coolidge's son, Calvin Jr., whose early death accelerated L. Ron Hubbard's interest in the mind and spirit of Man.

From 1925 to 1929, his father's career took the family to the Far East where L. Ron Hubbard journeyed throughout Asia, exploring out-of-the-way places, and saw many new peoples and customs.

In 1929 with the death of his grandfather, the Hubbard family returned to the United States and there L. Ron Hubbard continued his formal education. He attended Swavely Prep School in Manassas, Virginia, and went to high school at Woodward School for Boys in Washington, D.C.

In 1930, he graduated from Woodward with honors, and enrolled at George Washington University Engineering School in the fall. He became the associate editor of the university newspaper and was a member of many of the university's clubs and societies, including the Twentieth Marine Corps Reserve and the George Washington College Company.

While at George Washington University, he learned to fly and discovered a particular aptitude as a glider pilot. Here, also, he was enrolled in one of the first nuclear physics courses ever taught in an American university.

As a student, barely twenty years old, he supported himself by writing, and within a very few years he had established himself as an essayist in the literary world.

Even though he was very busy during these college years, L. Ron Hubbard still found time for his exploring. In 1931, at the age of twenty, he led the Caribbean Motion Picture Expedition as a director, and underwater films made on that journey provided Hydrographic Office and the University of Michigan with invaluable data for the furtherance of their research. And again in 1932, at twenty-one years of age, L. Ron Hubbard led another expedition conducting the West Indies Mineralogical Survey and made the first complete mineralogical survey of Puerto Rico.

Although very active now in several areas, L. Ron Hubbard continued his writing. Under about twenty different pen names millions of words poured from his pen and into print, including both fact and fiction, travel articles, stories of exploration and adventure, essays and anecdotes, science fiction, and western stories appearing in over ninety magazines and journals.

In 1935, L. Ron Hubbard went to Hollywood and worked under motion picture contracts as a scriptwriter. He is still very active in Hollywood's movie production.

While in Hollywood he continued his study of "What makes men tick," and in his own statement, L. Ron Hubbard dates the discovery of the primary law of life, summarily expressed by the command "Survive!" at 1938.

In 1940, as a duly elected member of the Explorers Club of New York, L. Ron Hubbard conducted the Alaskan Radio Experimental Expedition. He was awarded the Explorers Club flag for conducting this expedition. Also, in 1940, he earned his "License to Master of Steam and Motor Vessels," and within four and a half months obtained a second certificate attesting to his marine skill: "License to Master of Sail Vessels" ("Any Ocean").

Between the years of 1923 and 1928, he received an extensive education in the field of the human mind from Commander Thompson of the Medical Corps of the US Navy, a friend of his father and a personal student of Sigmund Freud. Some of his early research was spent determining whether the mind regulated the body or the body regulated the mind. If the mind was capable of putting restraint upon the physical body, then obviously the fact that was commonly held to be true, that the body regulated the mind, was false. He went about proving this.

And so, L. Ron Hubbard continued studying, researching, and synthesizing this knowledge with what he had learned of Eastern philosophy, his understanding of nuclear physics, and his experiences among men, to form some of the basic tenets of Dianetics and Scientology.

The study, work, writing and research continued at a rapid pace. And then in 1948, he wrote *Dianetics: The Original Thesis*, his first formal report of the mysteries of the mind and life, which was a thirty-thousand word revelation.

The interest in Dianetics spread like wildfire. Letters asking for clarifications and advice and more data poured in, and just answering them was becoming a full-time occupation.

So the work continued, work, on an extensive popular text on the subject of Dianetics that would answer all questions. In May of 1950, *Dianetics: The Modern Science of Mental Health* exploded onto the booklists, leapt to the top of the *New York Times* Best-Seller List and stayed there. It is still a best seller today.

L. Ron Hubbard then founded in 1950 the Hubbard Dianetic Foundation in Elizabeth, New Jersey to facilitate auditing and training the public in Dianetics.

During the next twenty-six years many, many churches and missions were established all over the planet to professionally deliver L. Ron Hubbard's technology standardly to the peoples of the world.

The Founder of Dianetics and Scientology, L. Ron Hubbard, lives with his wife, Mary Sue, and their children: Quentin, twenty-two; Suzette, twenty-one; and Arthur, seventeen. Their eldest daughter, Diana, twenty-three, is happily married.

Today, L. Ron Hubbard continues his life's work unabated, writing, researching and exploring new avenues and hitherto unexplored realms of life and the human spirit.

FREE SIX-MONTH MEMBERSHIP

You are eligible for a free six-month membership as an International Member of Scientology. You can receive a 10% discount on all books, tape recorded lectures, and other items priced over $1.25. You also receive free magazines with vital data, world Dianetic and Scientology news and modern technical information. New members are eligible for all International Membership privileges (including 10% discounts) as of the date of your application.

Write to: MEMBERSHIP OFFICER, your nearest Church of Scientology.

Church and Mission List

Contact Your Nearest Church or Mission

UNITED STATES

ADVANCED ORGANIZATION

Church of Scientology of California
Advanced Organization of Los Angeles
5930 Franklin Avenue
Los Angeles, California 90028

SAINT HILL ORGANIZATION

Church of Scientology of California
American Saint Hill Organization
2723 West Temple Street
Los Angeles, California 90026

PUBLICATIONS ORGANIZATION

Church of Scientology of California
Publications Organization
2723 West Temple Street
Los Angeles, California 90026

LOCAL CHURCHES

AUSTIN

Church of Scientology
2804 Rio Grande
Austin, Texas 78705

BOSTON

Church of Scientology
448 Beacon Street
Boston, Massachusetts 02215

BUFFALO

Church of Scientology
1116 Elmwood Avenue
Buffalo, New York 14222

CHICAGO

Church of Scientology
1555 Maple Street
Evanston, Illinois 60201

DENVER

Church of Scientology
1640 Welton
Denver, Colorado 80202

DETROIT

Church of Scientology
3905 Rochester Road
Royal Oak, Michigan 48075

HAWAII

Church of Scientology
143 Nenue Street
Honolulu, Hawaii 96821

LAS VEGAS

Church of Scientology
2108 Industrial Road
Las Vegas, Nevada 89102

LOS ANGELES

Church of Scientology of California
2005 West 9th Street
Los Angeles, California 90006

Church of Scientology
Celebrity Centre Los Angeles
1551 North La Brea Avenue
Hollywood, California 90028

MIAMI

Church of Scientology
1235 Brickell Avenue
Miami, Florida 33131

NEW YORK

Church of Scientology
28-30 West 74th Street
New York, New York 10023

PHILADELPHIA

Church of Scientology
8 West Lancaster Avenue
Ardmore, Pennsylvania 19003

PORTLAND

Church of Scientology
333 South West Park Avenue
Portland, Oregon 97205

SACRAMENTO

Church of Scientology
819 19th Street
Sacramento, California 95814

SAN DIEGO

Church of Scientology
926 "C" Street
San Diego, California 92101

SAN FRANCISCO

Church of Scientology
414 Mason Street, Rm. 400
San Francisco, California 94102

SEATTLE

Church of Scientology
1531 4th Avenue
Seattle, Washington 98101

ST. LOUIS

Church of Scientology
3730 Lindell Boulevard
St. Louis, Missouri 63108

TWIN CITIES

Church of Scientology
730 Hennepin Avenue
Minneapolis, Minnesota 55403

WASHINGTON, D.C.

Founding Church of Scientology
2125 "S" Street N.W.
Washington, D.C. 20008

CANADA

LOCAL CHURCHES

MONTREAL

Church of Scientology
15 Notre Dame Quest
Montreal, Quebec H2Y 1B5

OTTAWA

Church of Scientology
292 Somerset Street West
Ottawa, Ontario K2P 9Z9

TORONTO

Church of Scientology
124 Avenue Road
Toronto, Ontario M5R 2H5

VANCOUVER

Church of Scientology
4857 Main Street
Vancouver 10, British Columbia

UNITED KINGDOM

ADVANCED ORGANIZATION/ SAINT HILL

Hubbard College of Scientology
Advanced Organization Saint Hill
Saint Hill Manor
East Grinstead, Sussex RH19 4JY
England

LOCAL CHURCHES

EAST GRINSTEAD

Saint Hill Foundation
Saint Hill Manor East Grinstead
Sussex RH19 4JY
England

LONDON

Hubbard Scientology Organization
68 Tottenham Court Road
London W.1.
England

MANCHESTER

Hubbard Scientology Organization
48 Faulkner Street
Manchester M1 4FH
England

PLYMOUTH

Hubbard Scientology Organization
39 Portland Square
Sherwell
Plymouth
Devon
England PL4 6DJ

EDINBURGH

Hubbard Academy of Personal
Independence
Fleet House
20 South Bridge
Edinburgh
Scotland EH1 1LL

EUROPE

ADVANCED ORGANIZATION

Church of Scientology
Advanced Organization Denmark
Jernbanegade 6
1608 Copenhagen V
Denmark

SAINT HILL ORGANIZATION

Church of Scientology
Saint Hill Denmark
Jernbanegade 6
1608 Copenhagen V
Denmark

PUBLICATIONS ORGANIZATION

Scientology Publications Organization
Demark
Jernbanegade 6
1608 Copenhagen V
Denmark

LOCAL CHURCHES

AMSTERDAM

Church of Scientology
Singel 289-293
Amsterdam C,
Netherlands

COPENHAGEN

Church of Scientology
Hovedvagtsgade 6
1103 Copenhagen K
Denmark

Church of Scientology of Copenhagen
Frederiksborgvej 5
2400 Copenhagen V
Denmark

GOTEBORG

Church of Scientology
Magasinsgatan 12
S-411 18 Goteborg
Sweden

MALMO

Church of Scientology
Skomakaregatan 12
S-211 34 Malmo
Sweden

MUNICH

Church of Scientology
8000 Munchen 2
Lindwurmstrasse 29
Munich
West Germany

PARIS

Church of Scientology
12 Rue de la Montagne
Ste Genevieve 75005
Paris
France

STOCKHOLM

Church of Scientology
Kammakaregatan 46
S-111 60 Stockholm
Sweden

AFRICA

LOCAL CHURCHES

BULAWAYO

Church of Scientology
508 Kirrie Bldgs.
Cnr Abercorn & 9th Avenue
Bulawayo
Rhodesia

CAPETOWN

Church of Scientology
3rd Floor Garmour House
127 Plein Street
Capetown
South Africa 8001

DURBAN

Church of Scientology
57 College Lane
Durban
South Africa 4001

JOHANNESBURG

Church of Scientology
99 Polly Street
Johannesburg
South Africa 2001

PORT ELIZABETH

Church of Scientology
2 St. Christopher's
27 West Bourne Road
Port Elizabeth
South Africa 6001

PRETORIA

Church of Scientology
224 Central House
Cnr Central & Pretorius Streets
Pretoria
South Africa 0002

AUSTRALIA/NEW ZEALAND

LOCAL CHURCHES

ADELAIDE

Church of the New Faith
57 Pulteney Street
Fullarton
Adelaide 5000
South Australia

MELBOURNE

Church of the New Faith
724 Inkerman Road
North Caulfield 3161
Melbourne
Victoria
Australia

PERTH

Church of the New Faith
Pastoral House
156 St. George's Terrace
Perth 6000
Western Australia

SYDNEY

Church of the New Faith
1 Lee Street
Sydney 2000
New South Wales
Australia

AUCKLAND

Church of Scientology
New Imperial Buildings
44 Queen Street
Auckland 1,
New Zealand

CELEBRITY CENTERS

UNITED STATES

Church of Scientology
Celebrity Centre Los Angeles
1551 North La Brea Avenue
Hollywood, California 90028

Celebrity Center Baton Rouge
7939 Jefferson Hwy
Baton Rouge, Louisiana 70809

Celebrity Center Boulder
Marine Street No. 1
Boulder, Colorado 80302

Celebrity Center
1912 E. Yandell
El Paso, Texas 79903

Celebrity Center Las Vegas
2004 Western Avenue
Las Vegas, Nevada 89102

Celebrity Center Lewisburg (Greensbriar)
Laird House, Underwood Estates
Lewisburg, West Virginia 24901

Celebrity Centre Maine
Boot Cove
Lubec, Maine 04652

Celebrity Center Mountainview
2483 Old Middlefield Way
Mountain View, California 94040

Celebrity Center New York
65 East 82nd Street
New York, New York 10021

Celebrity Center San Antonio
2120 San Pedro Avenue
San Antonio, Texas 78212

Celebrity Centre San Francisco
2456 Clay St.
San Francisco, California 94115

Celebrity Center Santa Fe
330 Montezuma
Santa Fe, New Mexico 87501

Celebrity Center Steamboat Springs
P.O. Box 1987
Steamboat Springs, Colorado 80477

Celebrity Center Washington, D.C.
3411 Massachusetts Avenue N.W.
Washington, D.C. 20007

CANADA

Celebrity Center Toronto
67 Pembroke Street
Toronto, Ontario

AUSTRALIA

Celebrity Center Melbourne
46 Clingin
E. Rosewain
Melbourne, Victoria
Australia 3073

MEXICO

Celebrity Centre Mexico
Centro Cultural Latino Americano
Plaza Rio de Janeiro 52
Col. Roma, Mexico 7DF
Mexico

SWEDEN

Celebrity Centre Sweden
Malmvagen 4C, 9TR
191 61 Sollentuna, Sweden

MISSION LIST

UNITED STATES

ALASKA

Scientology Mission of Anchorage
155 E. Potter Street
Anchorage, Alaska 99502

ARIZONA

Scientology Mission of Flagstaff
4469 Mountain Meadow Drive
Flagstaff, Arizona 86001

Scientology Mission of Phoenix
331 North 1st Avenue
Phoenix, Arizona 85003

Scientology Mission of Phoenix
1722 East Indian School Road
Phoenix, Arizona 85016

Scientology Mission of Tucson
2100 East Speedway
Tucson, Arizona 85719

CALIFORNIA

Scientology Mission of Adams Avenue
6911 El Cajon
San Diego, California 92115

Scientology Mission of Berkeley
1918 Bonita
Berkeley, California 94704

Scientology Mission of Burbank
124 N. Golden Mall
Burbank, California 91502

Scientology Mission of Castro Valley
20730 Lake Chabot Road
Castro Valley, California 94546

Scientology Mission of Chula Vista
192 Landis Street
Chula Vista, California 92010

Scientology Mission of Davis
1046 Olive Drive
Davis, California 95616

Scientology Mission of East Bay
411 15th Street
Oakland, California 94612

Scientology Mission of Fresno
1350 "O" Street, Room 200
Fresno, California 93721

Scientology Mission of Goldengate
1807 Union Street, No. 2
San Francisco, California 94128

Scientology Mission of Lake Tahoe
P.O.Box 1540
South Lake Tahoe, California 95705

Scientology Mission of Long Beach
1261 Long Beach Boulevard
Long Beach, California 90813

Scientology Mission of Los Angeles
(Los Feliz)
1570 N. Edgemont, No. 107
Los Angeles, California 90027

Scientology Mission of Los Gatos
10 Jackson Street, No. 111
Los Gatos, California 95030

Scientology Mission of Orange County
1451 Irvine Boulevard, No. 30
Tustin, California 92680

Scientology Mission of Palo Alto
600 Middlefield Road
Palo Alto, California 94301

Scientology Mission of Pasadena
634 East Colorado Boulevard
Pasadena, California 91101

Scientology Mission of Riverside
3485 University Street
Riverside, California 92501

Scientology Mission of Sacramento
1725 23rd Street
Sacramento, California 95816

Scientology Mission of Sacramento
5136 Arden Way
Carmichael, California 95608

Scientology Mission of Santa Barbara
20 W. Della Guerra Street
Santa Barbara, California 93101

Scientology Mission of Santa Clara
4340 Stevens Creek, No. 180
San Jose, California 95129

Scientology Mission of Santa Monica
(Coast Line)
309 Santa Monica
Santa Monica, California 90401

Scientology Mission of Santa Rosa
806 Sonaoma Avenue
Santa Rosa, California 95402

Scientology Mission SCS
3802 Riverside Drive
Burbank, California 91505

Scientology Mission of South Bay
607 South Pacific Coast Highway
Redondo Beach, California 90277

Scientology Mission of Stockton
47 West Acadia
Stockton, California 95202

Scientology Mission of Sunset Strip
8863 Sunset Boulevard
Hollywood, California 90069

Scientology Mission of Valley
13561 Ventura Boulevard
Sherman Oaks, California 91403

Scientology Mission of Vista
1027 East Vista Way
Vista, California 92083

Scientology Mission of Walnut Creek
2363 Boulevard Circle, No. 5
Walnut Creek, California 94595

Scientology Mission of Westwood/Wilshire
10930 Santa Monica Boulevard
Los Angeles, California 90025

COLORADO

Scientology Mission of Boulder
2049 Broadway, P.O. Box 995
Boulder, Colorado 80302

Scientology Mission of Colorado Springs
Suite 207, 228 North Cascade
Colorado Springs, Colorado 80903

CONNECTICUT

Scientology Mission of Berlin
1240A Farmington Avenue
Berlin, Connecticut 06037

Scientology Mission of New Haven
109 Church Street, No. 505
New Haven, Connecticut 06520

Scientology Mission of New London
183 Williams Street
New London, Connecticut 06320

Scientology Mission of Waterbury
42 Bank Street
Waterbury, Connecticut 06702

FLORIDA

Scientology Mission of Coral Gables
4615 Ponce de Leon Boulevard
Coral Gables, Florida 33134

Scientology Mission of Fort Lauderdale
423 North Andrews Avenue
Fort Lauderdale, Florida 33301

Scientology Mission of Orlando
P.O. Box 14045
Orlando, Florida 32807

Scientology Mission of Tampa
12205 Dale Malory, Suite B
Tampa, Florida 33609

GEORGIA

Scientology Mission of Atlanta
2979 Grandview Avenue
Atlanta, Georgia 30305

HAWAII

Scientology Mission of Hawaii
1282 Kapiolani Boulevard
Honolulu, Hawaii 96814

ILLINOIS

Scientology Mission of Carbondale
417 South Illinois Avenue
Carbondale, Illinois 62901

Scientology Mission of Chicago
108 East Oak Street
Villa Park, Illinois 60181

Scientology Mission of Lakeview
1928 West Montrose
Chicago, Illinois 60613

NEVADA

Scientology Mission of the Meadows
1326 Las Vegas Boulevard
Las Vegas, Nevada 89101

Scientology Mission of Washoe Valley
319 East 6th Street
Reno, Nevada 89501

NEW JERSEY

Scientology Mission of Delaware Valley
1 Cherryhill Mall, Suite 924
Cherryhill, New Jersey 08034

Scientology Mission of Flemington
27 Church Street
Flemington, New Jersey 08822

NEW MEXICO

Scientology Mission of Albuquerque
613 San Mateo Boulevard, N.E.
Albuquerque, New Mexico 87108

NEW YORK

Scientology Mission of Albany
141 Brunswick Road
Troy, New York 12180

Scientology Mission of Bayshore
(Long Island)
7 Smith Avenue
Bayshore, New York 11706

Scientology Mission of East Manhattan
17 East 79th Street
New York, New York 10021

Scientology Mission of Elmira
111 North Main Street
Elmira, New York 14902

Scientology Mission of Fifth Avenue
434 6th Avenue, 2nd Floor
New York, New York 10011

Scientology Mission of New York
500 West End Avenue
New York, New York 10024

Scientology Mission of North Manhattan
Apt. 2A, 251 West 98th Street
New York, New York 10025

Scientology Mission of Putnam Valley
Dunderberg Road
Putnam Valley, New York 10579

NORTH CAROLINA

Scientology Mission of Charlotte
1000 Dilworth Road
Charlotte, North Carolina 28209

Scientology Mission of Peoria
920 West Main Street
Peoria, Illinois 61606

Scientology Mission of Urbana
1004 South Fourth Street
Champaign, Illinois 61820

INDIANA

Scientology Mission of Anderson
1111 Meredian Plaza, P.O. Box 664
Anderson, Indiana 46016

Scientology Mission of Indianapolis
6728 Everglades Court
Indianapolis, Indiana 46217

MARYLAND

Scientology Mission of Bethesda
4823 Fairmont at Woodmont
Bethesda, Maryland 20014

MASSACHUSETTS

Scientology Mission of Cambridge
8 Essex Street
Cambridge, Massachusetts 02139

Scientology Mission of Marshfield
34 Flames Road
Marshfield, Massachusetts 02050

Scientology Mission of Worchester
16 Front Street
Worchester, Massachusetts 01608

MICHIGAN

Scientology Mission of Huron Valley
203 East Ann Street
Ann Arbor, Michigan 48108

MINNESOTA

Scientology Mission of Excelsior
21 Water Street
Excelsior, Minnesota 55331

MISSOURI

Scientology Mission of Kansas City
4528 Main Street
Kansas City, Missouri 64111

Scientology Mission of St. Charles
138A North Main Street
St. Charles, Missouri 63301

NEBRASKA

Scientology Mission of Omaha
5061 California Street
Omaha, Nebraska 68132

OHIO

Scientology Mission of Central Ohio
3894 North High Street
Columbus, Ohio 43214

Scientology Mission of Cincinnati
3352 Jefferson Avenue
Cincinnati, Ohio 45220

Scientology Mission of Cleveland
2055 Lee Road
Cleveland Heights, Ohio 44118

Scientology Mission of Columbus
1074 East Broad Street
Columbus, Ohio 43205

Scientology Mission of Toledo
3257 West Bancroft
Toledo, Ohio 43606

OREGON

Scientology Mission of Portland
709 South West Salmon Street
Portland, Oregon 97205

Scientology Mission of Sheridan
Route 2, Box 195
Sheridan, Oregon 97378

PENNSYLVANIA

Scientology Mission of Chaddsford
Box 171, Brintion Bridge Road
Chaddsford, Pennsylvania 19317

Scientology Mission of Erie
528 West 18th Street
Erie, Pennsylvania 16502

PUERTO RICO

Scientology Mission of Puerto Rico
P.O. Box 211
Old San Juan Post Office
San Juan, Puerto Rico 00902

RHODE ISLAND

Scientology Mission of Rhode Island
264 Wey Bosset
Providence, Rhode Island 02903

TENNESSEE

Scientology Mission of Norris
P.O. Box 66
Norris, Tennessee 37828

TEXAS

Scientology Mission of Amarillo
2046 South Hayden
Amarillo, Texas 79109

Scientology Mission of Houston
4034 Westheimer
Houston, Texas 77027

Scientology Mission of Richardson
114 North McKinley
Richardson, Texas 75080

Scientology Mission of San Antonio
Colony North Mall
3723 Colony Drive
San Antonio, Texas 78230

Scientology Mission of South West
P.O. Box 8386
Dallas, Texas, 75205

UTAH

Scientology Mission of Salt Lake City
253 East 2nd Street
Salt Lake City, Utah, 84111

VERMONT

Scientology Mission of Putney
Wabena Stables
Putney, Vermont 05346

VIRGINIA

Scientology Mission of Arlington
818 North Taylor Street
Arlington, Virginia 22203

CANADA

Scientology Mission of Calgary
335 11th Avenue SW.
Calgary, Alberta T2R 0C7

Scientology Mission of Edmonton
9610 82nd Avenue
Edmonton, Alberta

Scientology Mission of Halifax
2514 Robie Street
Halifax, Nova Scotia

Scientology Mission of Hamilton
28½ John Street North
Hamilton, Ontario L8R 1G9

Scientology Mission of Kitchener
Apt. 14 241 King Street
Kitchener, Ontario N2G 1B3

Scientology Mission of North Vancouver
146 West 15th Avenue 15N
Vancouver, British Columbia

Scientology Mission of Quebec
224½ St. Joseph Est.
Quebec, P.Q. G1K 349

Scientology Mission of Regina
2023 St. John Street
Regina, Saskatchewan

Scientology Mission of St. Catharines
455 St. Pauls Street
St. Catharines, Ontario

Scientology Mission of St. John
15 Charlotte Street
St. John, New Brunswick

Scientology Mission of Vancouver
1562 West 6th Avenue
Vancouver, British Columbia V6J 1R2

Scientology Mission of Windsor
437 Ouelette Avenue
Windsor, Ontario N9A 4J2

Scientology Mission of Winnipeg
410 Spence Street
Winnipeg, Manitoba R3B 2R6

UNITED KINGDOM

Scientology Mission of Birmingham
3 Saint Mary's Road
Moseley
Birmingham, 13
England

Mission of Botley (Southampton)
16 Rectorey Court
Holmesland, Garden Est.
Botley, England

Scientology Mission of Bournemouth
43 Markham Rd.
Winton Bornemouth,
Dorset, England

Scientology Mission of Charnwood Forest
109 Meeting Street
Quorn, Loughborough
Leicestershire
England

Scientology Mission of Helensborough
121 West King Street
Helensborough
Dunbartonshire G84 8DQ
Scotland

Scientology Mission of Hove
Flat 1, 56 Wilbury Road
Hove, Sussex
England

Scientology Mission of Kirkwood
"Kirkwood House"
Biggar
Lanarkshire
Scotland

Scientology Mission of Leeds
27 Manor Drive
Leeds
Yorkshire LS6 IDE
England

Scientology Mission of Reading
"St. Michael's" Shinfield Road
Reading
Berkshire RG2 9B4
England

Scientology Mission of Swansea
1 High Pool Close
Newton
Mumbles
Swansea
Wales

EUROPE

AUSTRIA

Scientology Mission of Vienna
Museumstrasse 5/18
1070 Vienna
Austria

BELGIUM

Centre de Scientology du Brabant
Rue Du Pacifique 4
B-1180 Bruxelles
Belgium

Eglise de Scientology
45A Rue de l'Ecuyer
B-1000 Bruxelles
Belgium

DENMARK

Scientology Mission of Virum
Kaplevej 301
DK 2830
Virum, Denmark

FRANCE

Scientology Mission of Angers
43 Rue Proust
49000 Angers
France

Scientology Mission of Paris
147 Rue St. Charles
Paris
F-75015, Paris
France

Scientology Mission of Versailles
29 Bis Rue Des Noailles
F-78000 Versailles
France

SWEDEN

Scientology Mission of Helsingborg
Sodergaten 4
S-252/25 Helsingborg
Sweden

SWITZERLAND

College fur Angewandte Philosophie
Haldenstrasse 37
6006 Luzern
Switzerland

Scientology Mission of Basel
Gerberleinstrasse 25
CH-4051 Basel
Switzerland

Scientology Bern
2 Sudbanhofstrasse
CH-3007 Bern
Switzerland

Scientology Zentrum Bern
Hotelgasse 3
CH-3011 Bern
Switzerland

Scientology Mission of Geneva
8 Rue Masbov
1205 Geneva
Switzerland

Scientology Mission of Luzern
Grossweidstrasse 1
CH-6010 Kriens
Switzerland

Scientology Mission of Zurich
Mulibachstrasse 423/6
CH-8185 Winkelruti
Zurich
Switzerland

Scientology Mission of Zurich
Lowenstrasse 69
CH-8001
Zurich
Switzerland

WEST GERMANY

College fur Angewandte Philosophie
Kennedy Allee 33
D-6000 Frankfurt Am Main
West Germany

College fur Angewandte Philosophie
Fleinerstrasse 37
D-71 Heilbronn
West Germany

College fur Angewandte Philosophie
Widenmayer 28
8 Munchen 28
West Germany

College fur Angewandte Philosophie
Kidlerstr. 10
8 Munchen 70
West Germany

Dianetic College
Stegstrasse 37
D-6000 Frankfurt 70
West Germany

Dianetic Stuttgart
Hauptsatterstr. 126A
D-7000 Stuttgart 1
West Germany

Scientology Center Hamburg
Gerhofstrasse 18
D-2 Hamburg 36
West Germany

Scientology Kirche Stuttgart
Neue Brucke 3
D-7000 Stuttgart 1
West Germany

Scientology Mission of Berlin
Giesebrechtstr. 10
D-1000 Berlin 12
West Germany

AFRICA

Scientology & Dianetics Center
11 First Avenue
Highlands North
Johannesburg 2001
South Africa

AUSTRALIA/NEW ZEALAND

The New Faith Mission of Melville
15 Birdwood Road
Melville
West Australia 6156

Scientology Mission of Christchurch
35 Rapaki Road
Christchurch 2
New Zealand

Scientology Mission of Ellerslie
1 Ranier Street
Ellerslie
Auckland
New Zealand

OTHER ORGANIZATIONS OF DIANETICS & SCIENTOLOGY

MEXICO

Academia de Dianetica
Ave. Revolucion 591-B1
Mexico 18DF, Mexico

Associación de Dianetica
Matamoros No. 5
A.P. 21875
Mexico 21DF, Mexico

Centro de Dianetica A.C.
Campos Eliseos 205
Mexico 5DF
Mexico

Instituto de Dianetica en Guadalajara A.C.
Mexicaltzingo No. 1985
Sector Juarez
Guadalajara, Jalisco
Mexico

Organización de Dianetica A.C.
Provencia No. 1000
Col. de Valle
Mexico 12DF
Mexico

Scientology Centre Empalme
AP 181 Guaymas
Empalme
Sonora
Mexico

Scientology Organization Mexico A.C.
Avenida Nuevo Leon 159 1°
Piso, Mexico 11DF
Mexico

ISRAEL

Scientology Centre of Negev
P.O. Box 2098
Beer Sheva
Israel

Scientology Center of Tel Aviv
7 Fichman Street
Tel Aviv, Israel

PHILIPPINES

Scientology Centre of Philippines
P.O. Box 1182
Makati
Rizal
Philippines

BRAZIL

Scientology Centre of Rio De Janeiro
Praia de Botafogo 472, Apt. 913
Rio de Janeiro, GB
Brazil

NEW! SUCCESSFUL!
TECHNIQUES IN MANAGEMENT

Communication is the major tool in working with a group. Business communications can be made remarkably simple.

Everyone knows communication is important in business. Yet so many otherwise very bright people make communication mistakes every day that keep them strangers to success—*without ever knowing what is stopping them from advancing!*

For example, have you:

1. Ever put reports ahead of answering letters from customers?
2. Ever picked up a letter or memo, read it, put it back on your desk to pick up again and handle later?
3. Ever found yourself getting wrapped up doing work that is actually someone else's job?
4. Assigned more than 5 immediate juniors to one person?
5. Ever referred traffic to someone else which you could have handled yourself?
6. Tried to handle an employee far away that you were displeased with by direct letter?
7. Permitted letters in your office to go unanswered for more than 24 hours?
8. Ever acted on a generality in a report you received?

Some of these are commonly known errors; but you may never have heard others of them are even dangerous. How is one to know what is right and what is wrong in business communications?

At last here is a set of books which tell you CLEARLY and SIMPLY *how* to improve your communicative skills in business or administrative situations. In these volumes you will find proven techniques that WORK.

These books show what communications are essential in every part of your organization. What is more, you will learn HOW and WHY.

THE ORGANIZATION EXECUTIVE COURSE VOLUMES

These eight volumes contain policies originally developed by L. Ron Hubbard to cope with the rapid expansion of Scientology organizations. But they apply to *any* group.

Here is how the volumes could be applied to business situations:

Volume 0: The Basic Staff Volume. What you must know to survive in an organization. 371 pages.

Volume 1: How to handle personnel, communication channels, ethics. 592 pages.

Volume 2: How to promote and sell your products to existing customers or clients. 402 pages.

Volume 3: How to keep solvent. The secret to good credit. How to keep equipment and assets well cared for. 368 pages.

Volume 4: How to run the division that makes and delivers the product. 606 pages.

Volume 5: How to correct products. How to correct the people who produce them. 368 pages.

Volume 6: How to get new customers. 464 pages.

Volume 7: How to succeed as an executive in running the show. 711 pages.

THE MANAGEMENT SERIES, 1970-1974

This is the simple basic handbook for management. With it you can look down into any part of your organization and quickly spot and handle any problem area. Contains the Data Series, Public Relations Series, Personnel Series, Organizing Series, Finance Series, Executive Series, and Establishment Series.

Gets to the heart of any management problem FAST. 532 pages.

THE POLICY SUBJECT INDEX

Your key to the right policy right now. *All* policies by L. Ron Hubbard in either the OEC Volumes or Management Series by title, by date. 355 pages.

RESULTS

What does this mean to you in dollars and cents? Better communication with your customers and customers-to-be means more income. Better communication inside your organization means less cost. It also means more sanity for everyone concerned!

$200/week to $500/week

Read this letter from a construction engineer who purchased only *The Management Series:*

> *"By just applying a few pages of The Management Series I have increased my income in construction from $200 a week to $500 in 3 months. I can see quite a career ahead of me in construction management and I've only started the volume!" Alan James*

And read this one from an Iowa businessman who purchased the whole set:

> *"For ten years, my business affairs ranged from fair to lousy. I couldn't seem to figure out what I was doing wrong. With each new endeavor I'd wonder how I'd fail this time.*
>
> *Then I bought the Organization Executive Course Volumes and Management Series.*
>
> *Two months later I was making twice what I normally did and to date, five months later, I actually make what I want and need.*

From one man business to large corporations, there are many more stories of people who, like you, wanted to know more about communication in business. The OEC Volumes gave them the knowledge they were looking for.

LASTING VALUE

The data in these books is the result of nearly a quarter century of testing by L. Ron Hubbard in the real world—the best testing ground there is. Time after time, it has been proven these principles *work.*

And now these materials are bound in a tough, emerald green encyclopedia binding that will stand *your* test of time as well. Use them every day for years and years—you'll never worry about wearing them out. Should you find *any* defect in the binding of these books SIMPLY SEND THEM BACK AND WE WILL REPLACE THEM AT NO CHARGE.

Beautifully embossed with gold titles. You will treasure these books above all others on your library shelf.

EASY TO USE

The material in these books is light years ahead of what you could learn in business school. Yet it is so down to earth and easy to apply you don't need a wall of degrees—or any degree at all—to understand it.

YOU CAN BE SURE

You *can* be sure about communication in business. You *can* get far better results than even you now expect. Thousands have and *you will too* when you get your own set of these priceless books by L. Ron Hubbard!

Write the Letter Registrar for up-to-date prices at:

The Church of Scientology of California
PUBLICATIONS ORGANIZATION,
Dept. MMTD-1
2723 West Temple Street
Los Angeles, California 90026

A DIANETICS PUBLICATION—Copyright © 1973, 1976 by L. Ron Hubbard. ALL RIGHTS RESERVED. THE CHURCH OF SCIENTOLOGY OF CALIFORNIA—a non-profit organization. Scientology is an applied religious philosophy. Dianetics from DIA (Greek) "through" and NOUS (Greek) "soul". Dianetics is the trademark of L. Ron Hubbard in respect of his published works. Dianetics® and Scientology® are registered names.

New Answers to Human Life, Behavior and Man

The TECHNICAL BULLETINS of Dianetics® and Scientology®

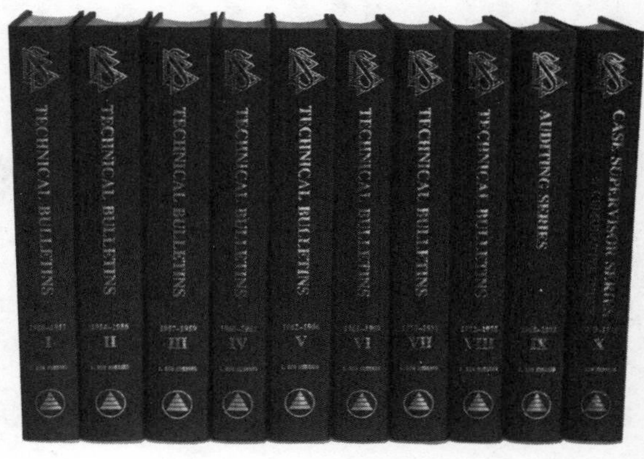

As you climb the management ladder you become increasingly aware of the problems of others.

Sometimes the old answers don't work. And you need new answers to the basic problems of human life and human behavior that give you more understanding of people.

Answers to those questions and more are for the first time available—real workable answers—in a set of magnificent volumes. The TECHNICAL BULLETINS of Dianetics and Scientology by L. Ron Hubbard.

The volumes are the complete collection of L. Ron Hubbard's research and developments in understanding the problems of others and better relations with people.

If you really want to know how to handle interpersonal (or personnel) relationships in your business or organization the information is here.

If you have a worker or associate who runs into a difficult problem in his life you will find that with the knowledge in these books you can help him to handle it.

Individual problems and troubles are no longer mysterious things. There is technology for their resolution. Scientology works—it is *precise* and *exact* with tried, tested and proven techniques and literally thousands of case histories and fully documented materials that show its effectiveness.

This knowledge is important to the continued viability of any organization or business.

Order your set, and use the data in these volumes.

For prices (and a complete list of other books by L. Ron Hubbard) write:

The Letter Registrar
The Church of Scientology of California
PUBLICATIONS ORGANIZATION, Dept. MMTD-1
2723 West Temple Street
Los Angeles, California 90026

A DIANETICS PUBLICATION—Copyright © 1973, 1976 by L. Ron Hubbard. ALL RIGHTS RESERVED. THE CHURCH OF SCIENTOLOGY OF CALIFORNIA—a non-profit organization. Scientology is an applied religious philosophy. Dianetics from DIA (Greek) "through" and NOUS (Greek) "soul". Dianetics is the trademark of L. Ron Hubbard in respect of his published works. Dianetics® and Scientology® are registered names.

The Dianetics® and Scientology® TECHNICAL DICTIONARY by L. Ron Hubbard

You'll need and want this fantastic volume for a more complete study of the Technology of L. Ron Hubbard.

It's over 3000 words defined! Most will be new to you but, there are also many familiar words freshly defined.

Read what L. Ron Hubbard himself has to say about this special dictionary.

"In the early sixties the research which I did on study and study materials brought to view the necessity of an accurate and modernized dictionary of Dianetics and Scientology.

Almost all the words used in Dianetics and Scientology are defined in the early bulletins in which they first appeared. However, a complete dictionary is a vital necessity and use of it can mean the difference between understanding and not understanding.

In the search which brought about Dianetics and Scientology many new phenomena were encountered which resulted, for the first time, in a workable, predictable science of the humanities. The introduction of a few words of new meaning to make this possible seems to be a small price to pay.

I hope this dictionary will be of use. Not only in clarifying some of the phenomena of existence, but also speeding greatly your study of Dianetics and Scientology and the results you will be able to attain thereby."

L. Ron Hubbard
(From the Introduction to
The Dianetics and Scientology Technical Dictionary)

Order your copy.

For prices (and a complete list of other books by L. Ron Hubbard) write:

The Letter Registrar
The Church of Scientology of California
Publications Organization, Dept. MMTD-1
2723 West Temple Street
Los Angeles, California 90026

A DIANETICS PUBLICATION—Copyright © 1973, 1975, 1976 by L. Ron Hubbard. ALL RIGHTS RESERVED. THE CHURCH OF SCIENTOLOGY OF CALIFORNIA—a non-profit organization. Scientology is an applied religious philosophy. Dianetics from DIA (Greek) "through" and NOUS (Greek) "soul". Dianetics is the trademark of L. Ron Hubbard in respect of his published works. Dianetics® and Scientology® are registered names.